LIQUIDITY RATIOS

Current ratio	$$\frac{\text{Current Assets}}{\text{Current Liabilities}}$$	Measures short-term debt-paying ability	Chapter 5, LO5
Quick ratio	$$\frac{\text{Cash + Marketable Securities + Receivables}}{\text{Current Liabilities}}$$	Measures short-term debt-paying ability	Chapter 17, LO3
Receivable turnover	$$\frac{\text{Net Sales}}{\text{Average Accounts Receivable}}$$	Average number of times receivables are turned into cash during an accounting period	Chapter 8, LO1
Days' sales uncollected	$$\frac{\text{Days in Year}}{\text{Receivable Turnover}}$$	Average number of days a company must wait to receive payment for credit sales or to collect accounts receivable	Chapter 8, LO 1
Inventory turnover	$$\frac{\text{Costs of Goods Sold}}{\text{Average Inventory}}$$	Number of times a company's average inventory is sold during an accounting period	Chapter 7, LO1
Days' inventory on hand	$$\frac{\text{Days in Year}}{\text{Inventory Turnovers}}$$	Average number of days taken to sell inventory on hand	Chapter 7, LO1
Payables turnover	$$\frac{\text{Costs of Goods Sold +/−Change in Inventory}}{\text{Average Accounts Payable}}$$	Average number of times a company pays its accounts payable in an accounting period	Chapter 9, LO1
Days' payable	$$\frac{\text{Days in Year}}{\text{Payables Turnover}}$$	Average number of days a company takes to pay accounts payable	Chapter 9, LO1

PROFITABILITY RATIOS

Profit margin	$$\frac{\text{Net Income}}{\text{Net Sales}}$$	Percentage of each sales dollar that contributes to net income	Chapter 5, LO5
Asset turnover	$$\frac{\text{Net Sales}}{\text{Average Total Assets}}$$	How efficiently assets are used to produce sales	Chapter 5, LO5
Return on assets	$$\frac{\text{Net Income}}{\text{Average Total Assets}}$$	How efficiently a company uses its assets to produce income, or the amount earned on each dollar of assets invested	Chapter 5, LO5
Return on equity	$$\frac{\text{Net Income}}{\text{Average Owner's Equity}}$$	Relates the amount earned by a business to the owner's investment in the business	Chapter 5, LO5

LONG-TERM SOLVENCY RATIOS

Debt to equity ratio	$$\frac{\text{Total Liabilities}}{\text{Owner's Equity}}$$	Proportion of a company's assets financed by creditors and the proportion financed by the owner	Chapter 5, LO5
Interest coverage ratio	$$\frac{\text{Income Before Income Taxes + Interest Expense}}{\text{Interest Expense}}$$	Degree of protection a company has from default on interest payments	Chapter 13, LO1

CASH FLOW ADEQUACY RATIOS

Cash flow yield	$$\frac{\text{Net Cash Flows from Operating Activities}}{\text{Net Income}}$$	Measures a company's ability to generate operating cash flows in relation to net income	Chapter 15, LO2
Cash flows to sales	$$\frac{\text{Net Cash Flows from Operating Activities}}{\text{Net Sales}}$$	Ratio of net cash flows from operating activities to sales	Chapter 15, LO2
Cash flows to assets	$$\frac{\text{Net Cash Flows from Operating Activities}}{\text{Average Total Assets}}$$	Measures the ability of assets to generate operating cash flows	Chapter 15, LO2
Free cash flow	Net Cash Flows from Operating Activities − Dividends − Net Capital Expenditures	Measures the amount of cash that remains after deducting the funds a company must commit to continue operating at its planned level	Chapter 11, LO1

MARKET STRENGTH RATIOS

Price/earnings ratio	$$\frac{\text{Market Price per Share}}{\text{Earnings per Share}}$$	Measures investors' confidence in a company's future; a means of comparing stock values	Chapter 12, LO1
Dividends yield	$$\frac{\text{Dividends per Share}}{\text{Market Price per Share}}$$	Measures a stock's current return to an investor or stockholder	Chapter 12, LO1

Principles of
Accounting

Tenth Edition

Belverd E. Needles, Jr., Ph.D., C.P.A., C.M.A.
DePaul University

Marian Powers, Ph.D.
Northwestern University

Susan V. Crosson, M.S. Accounting, C.P.A.
Santa Fe Community College, Florida

Houghton Mifflin Company   Boston   New York

To Jennifer, Jeffrey, Annabelle, and Abigail
To my family—Bruce, Brent, and Courtney Crosson—and
in loving memory of my parents Helen and Bryce Van Valkenburgh

Executive Publisher: George Hoffman
Senior Sponsoring Editor: Ann West
Senior Marketing Manager: Mike Schenk
Marketing Coordinator: Erin Lane
Senior Development Editor: Chere Bemelmans
Editorial Assistant: Diane Akerman
Project Editor: Margaret M. Kearney
Art and Design Manager: Gary Crespo
Cover Design Manager: Anne S. Katzeff
Senior Photo Editor: Jennifer Meyer Dare
Composition Buyer: Chuck Dutton

Cover photo © Don Smetzer/Stone/Getty Images

CVS Annual Report reprinted with permission of CVS
Portions of Southwest Airlines Annual Report courtesy of Southwest Airlines

COMPANY LOGO CREDITS: p. 7, Reprinted with permission of CVS; p. 53, Logo provided by The Boeing Company, Copyright 2006, All Rights Reserved; p. 104, ©2006 Yahoo! Inc. Yahoo! and the Yahoo! logo are the trademarks of Yahoo! Inc.; p. 152, Reprinted with permission of Best Buy; p. 293, Reprinted with permission of Costco Wholesale; (*Continued on p.* 1312)

PHOTO CREDITS: p. 3, Getty Images; p. 9, AP Images; p. 17, © Jim West/The Image Works; p. 26, © Frank Trapper/Corbis; p. 51, Boeing Image Licensing; p. 56, © Reuters/Corbis; p. 72, Getty Images; p. 103, © Yahoo! Inc. Yahoo! and the Yahoo! logo are the trademarks of Yahoo! Inc.; p. 111, AP Images; p. 118, © Norbert von der Groeben/The Image Works; (*Continued on page* 1312)

Printed in the U.S.A.

Library of Congress Control Number: 2006936632

Instructor's examination copy
  ISBN-10: 0-618-83349-8
  ISBN-13: 978-0-618-83349-8
For orders, use student text ISBNs
  ISBN-10: 0-618-73661-1
  ISBN-13: 978-0-618-73661-4

2 3 4 5 6 7 8 9-VH-11 10 09 08 07

Brief Contents

Contents

CHAPTER 9 Current Liabilities and the Time Value of Money   410

CHAPTER 10 Internal Control   456

CHAPTER 11 Long-Term Assets   490

CHAPTER 12 Contributed Capital   **540**

CHAPTER 13 Long-Term Liabilities   **584**

CHAPTER 14 The Corporate Income Statement and the Statement of Stockholders' Equity   **638**

CHAPTER **15**   **The Statement of Cash Flows**   **684**

CHAPTER **16**   **Investments**   **732**

CHAPTER 20 Costing Systems: Job Order and Process Costing — **934**

CHAPTER 21 Activity-Based Systems: ABM and JIT — **986**

Preface

This revision of *Principles of Accounting* is the most significant in the book's long history. The substantial changes we have made meet the needs of today's students, who not only face a business world increasingly complicated by ethical issues, globalization, and technology, but who also have more demands on their time. To help them meet these challenges, we place a heavy emphasis on developing their decision-making and critical-thinking skills and on providing information that is easy to understand and process.

We invite you to read the User's Guide that follows this preface to get a sense of how this book was written to help students master accounting. Here, we elaborate on exactly what we set out to achieve in this tenth edition.

Streamlined Coverage and Redesign of the Text

While maintaining a solid foundation in double-entry accounting, we reduced complexity by eliminating approximately 30 percent of in-text journal entries and all nonessential procedural coverage and by condensing learning objectives. We also reduced excessive detail, shortened headings, simplified explanations, and increased readability. In addition, we made the text more accessible to students by using small, diverse companies to illustrate concepts and techniques and well-known public companies to relate the concepts and techniques to the real world.

To make the text more readable, visually appealing, and pedagogically useful, we broke it into "user friendly" portions with bulleted and numbered lists and new art, photographs, end-of-section review material, and Focus on Business boxes.

▶ New line art clarifies concepts and appeals to students who are visual learners.

▶ Photographs, with captions that underscore concepts in the text, increase visual interest.

▶ A new feature called "Stop, Review, and Apply" presents review questions; the answers to the questions are available on the student website (Online Study Center). Many of these new sections also include short exercises and solutions.

▶ To reduce distractions, the margins of the text include only Study Notes, which alert students to common misunderstandings of concepts and techniques; key ratio and cash flow icons, which highlight discussions of profitability and liquidity; and accounting equations. Icons and equations appear in the financial chapters (Chapters 1-17).

Emphasis on Accounting Information and Successful Decision Making

Throughout the text, we increased our emphasis on how businesses use accounting information to make decisions, thus providing a uniform framework for developing decision-making skills.

▶ Each chapter opening includes a new Decision Point that shows how a well-known company—one that students will immediately recognize—

uses accounting information to make decisions. The Decision Point poses questions that challenge students to think about the relationship between this information and the decisions management makes. The company discussed in the Decision Point is highlighted in the chapter and is revisited in "A Look Back At," a feature that shows how the questions introduced in the Decision Point can now be answered.

▶ To relate accounting information to real-world decision making, we refer to more than 200 actual companies and use some of those companies' recent financial statements as illustrations.

▶ We use the latest available data in tables, figures, and exhibits and incorporate the most recent FASB pronouncements in the text. We illustrate current practices in financial reporting by referring to data from *Accounting Trends and Techniques* (AICPA) and integrate international topics wherever appropriate.

Financial Accounting Coverage: Using Financial Statements for Decision Making

In the financial chapters, our emphasis is on teaching students how to tell a company's "story" through its financial statements.

▶ To emphasize how important financial statements are in decision making, the first page of each financial chapter includes a graphic model of the income statement, balance sheet, and statement of cash flows and a brief description of how these statements relate to the chapter's topic.

▶ We emphasize how ratios are used in evaluating a company's profitability and liquidity and highlight those discussions with key ratio and cash flow icons.

▶ The assignment material in every financial chapter includes a case that compares CVS with Southwest Airlines or Walgreens and refers to both companies' financial statements. Among other things, the comparison cases require students to compute ratios, make assumptions, report on the effect of seasonal sales, and describe each company's inventory management system. CVS's complete annual report and Southwest Airlines' financial statements and Note 1 to the statements appear in the Supplement to Chapter 5.

Management Accounting Coverage: Applying Accounting Concepts to Real Businesses

Today, management's use of information goes far beyond computing the cost of products and services. In the managerial chapters (Chapters 18-26), we explore the full range of innovative managerial systems in a value-centered economy in which managers must make critical decisions about product quality, customer service, and long-term relationships.

▶ Rather than focusing on the technical details of cost accounting, we emphasize the management process critical to operating a successful business. A figure entitled "The Management Process: To-Dos for Managers," which appears in the first section of each chapter, highlights managerial activities important at each stage of the management process.

▶ We emphasize the approaches learned from the most progressive companies, such as how to manage supply chains, analyze value chains, operate in a just-in-time environment, utilize activity-based management, apply the theory of constraints, and improve quality.

▶ We discuss the latest in management models and technology and emphasize that performance measurement and evaluation are essential to a manager's success in today's competitive environment.

▶ Service businesses, in which many students will ultimately work, receive expanded emphasis in the text discussion and the chapter assignments.

Ethical Financial Reporting

We believe students need to know more about what constitutes ethical financial reporting and good corporate governance. We revised the text to address this need.

▶ The previews at the start of many chapters point out ethical and governance issues related to the chapter topic that are discussed in the chapter.

▶ We cover the provisions of the Sarbanes-Oxley Act of 2002 and stress its importance in Chapter I and at appropriate points throughout the text.

▶ In the end-of-chapter material, we continue to provide short cases, based on real companies, that require students to address an ethical dilemma directly related to the chapter content.

Reorganized Assignment Material

This text has always provided a rich assortment of assignments that address instructors' needs. While keeping the range and depth of assignments from previous editions, we have simplified their organization for easier use.

▶ The end-of-chapter assignments are organized into two main sections: Building Your Basic Knowledge and Skills—which consists of Short Exercises, Exercises, Problems, and Alternate Problems—and Enhancing Your Knowledge, Skills, and Critical Thinking—which consists of cases.

▶ The first exercises in many chapters present questions useful in generating class discussion about the decision-making aspects of the chapter topics.

▶ Problems have been carefully scrutinized to reduce the number of transactions involved and the time it takes to work them. Many of the problems have a requirement labeled "User Insight" or "Manager Insight." These requirements challenge students to think about the numbers and how they are used in business decision making.

▶ Cases are grouped by skill: Conceptual Understanding; Interpreting Financial or Management Reports; Decision Analysis Using Excel; Ethical Dilemma; Internet; Group Activity; and Business Communication. Each financial chapter also has an Annual Report Case that focuses on CVS's annual report and, as noted earlier, a Comparison Case.

New Instructional Technologies for Today's Business Environment

New technologies are today a driving force behind business growth and accounting education. For this tenth edition of *Principles of Accounting*, we developed an integrated text and technology program to help instructors take advantage of the opportunities created by new instructional technologies.

Whether an instructor takes a user or procedural approach to teaching, wants to incorporate new instructional strategies, wants to develop students' core skills and competencies, or desires to integrate technology into the classroom, this edition provides a total solution. (See the inside back cover of the book for a complete listing of supplements.)

Course Management

We know that homework and practice are integral parts of accounting courses, and grading homework and tests can present a challenge to instructors. The **Eduspace®** online learning tool pairs the widely recognized resources of Blackboard with quality, text-specific content from Houghton Mifflin. Auto-graded homework comprising end-of-chapter short exercises, exercises, and problems; algorithmic practice exercises; SMARTHINKING online tutoring; multimedia ebook with links to tutorials; demonstration videos; and other text-supporting content come ready to use. Premium Blackboard course cartridges and WebCT ePacks are also available.

Included in Eduspace and new to this edition of *Principles of Accounting* is **HM Assess**, an online diagnostic assessment and study tool. Working in HM Assess, students take Chapter Assessments and receive Individual Study Paths, with links to tutorials, video, algorithmic practice questions, and online text content. Reporting and tracking are also available.

HMTesting

HMTesting—now powered by *Diploma®*—contains the computerized version of the Test Bank. HMTesting provides instructors with the tools they need to create, customize, and deliver multiple types of tests. Instructors can select, edit, and add questions—some with algorithms—or generate randomly selected questions to produce a test master for easy duplication. All test questions are now tagged with AACSB learning outcomes, learning objectives, and key concepts. Online Testing and Gradebook functions allow instructors to administer tests via their local area network or the Internet, set up classes, record grades from tests or assignments, analyze grades, and compile class and individual statistics. HMTesting can be used on both PCs and Macintosh computers.

The Test Bank is also available in print. The printed Test Bank provides the same questions found in HMTesting—more than 4,000 true-false, multiple choice, short essay, and critical-thinking questions, as well as exercises and problems, all of which test students' ability to recall, comprehend, apply, and analyze information. Two achievement tests are provided for each chapter.

Instructor and Student Websites

The Online Teaching and Online Study Centers provide instructors and students with text-specific resources that reinforce key concepts in the *Principles of Accounting* program. For instructors, the Online Teaching Center includes password-protected course materials, such as completely revised PowerPoint slides with video and original content; Classroom Response System content; sample syllabi; the *Accounting Instructor's Report*, which explores a wide range of contemporary teaching issues; and Electronic Solutions, which are fully functioning Excel spreadsheets for all exercises, problems, and cases in the text.

For students, the Online Study Center offers open access to helpful supplementary materials, such as ACE practice tests, answers to Stop, Review, and Apply questions, weblinks to companies discussed in the text, chapter outlines and summaries, glossaries (chapter-based and complete), and much more. In addition, all new texts are packaged with a passkey providing access to a set of "Your Guide to an 'A'" premium resources, which focus on helping students succeed in their course. "Your Guide to an 'A'" material includes additional (ACE+)

self-test quizzes, Flashcards, crossword puzzles, *Study Guide* content, Demonstration Videos, HMAccounting Tutor, and audio chapter reviews (MP3 chapter summaries and quizzes). Both the student and instructor websites can be accessed at college.hmco.com/info/needles. See the User's Guide and endpapers of the text for a complete listing of all the student supplements available.

The Bottom Line

Although we have done more in this revision than in any previous one to make accounting concepts accessible to students, there is one thing we have not changed: we still teach students how to use financial statements and the accounting systems that provide the data needed to make business decisions and that tell a company's story. For investors and creditors, financial information reveals a company's financial health, prosperity, and future. For management, both financial information and nonfinancial information are a means of guiding a company's progress and profitability. Our goal is to improve students' understanding of the "story" revealed in a company's financial and nonfinancial data, and never has that goal been as critical as in current times, with business events underscoring this fact: accounting really matters.

To follow the "story," students have to learn how to think. *Principles of Accounting* teaches students to think about what they are reading, how they might make financial decisions, and what roles they might play as future users of accounting information. Students also have to learn how to analyze and interpret data—where did the numbers come from? What is the meaning behind the numbers? What do the numbers say about a company's financial health? Today, accounting students need to learn more than how to prepare financial statements; they also must learn how to analyze meaningful information in them and in the supporting data. *Principles of Accounting*, Tenth Edition, focuses on teaching students to do just that.

Acknowledgments

A successful textbook is a collaborative effort. We are grateful to the many professors, other professional colleagues, and students who have taught and studied from our book, and we thank all of them for their constructive comments. In the space available, we cannot possibly mention everyone who has been helpful, but we do want to recognize those who made special contributions to our efforts in preparing the tenth edition of *Principles of Accounting*.

We wish to express our deep appreciation to colleagues at DePaul University, who have been extremely supportive and encouraging.

The thoughtful and meticulous work of Edward H. Julius (California Lutheran University) is reflected not only in the Study Guide, but in our Test Bank and Eduspace course as well. Eric Blazer (Millersville University) wrote the managerial chapters of the study guide, and Judy R. Colwell (Northern Oklahoma College) wrote the managerial chapters of the test bank. We also thank Jeri Condit for creating the PowerPoint slides, Linda Burkell for HMAccounting Tutor and GLS, and Cathy Larson for her accuracy review of the text and solutions. Sarah Evans deserves special recognition for her thoroughness and clarity in editing portions of the text and laying out the tenth edition.

Also very important to the quality of this book is the supportive collaboration of our senior sponsoring editor, Ann West; senior development editor, Chere Bemelmans; editorial assistant, Diane Akerman; and project editor, Margaret Kearney—to whom we give special thanks.

Others who have had a major impact on this book through their reviews, suggestions, and participation in surveys, interviews, and focus groups are listed below. We cannot begin to say how grateful we are for the feedback from the many instructors who have generously shared their responses and teaching experiences with us.

Daneen Adams, *Santa Fe Community College*
Gregory D. Barnes, *Clarion University*
Mohamed E. Bayou, *The University of Michigan—Dearborn*
Charles M. Betts, *Delaware Technical and Community College*
Michael C. Blue, *Bloomsburg University*
Gary R. Bower, *Community College of Rhode Island*
Lee Cannell, *El Paso Community College*
Gerald Carnes, *Edinboro College*
John D. Cunha, *University of California—Berkeley*
Julie Dailey, *Central Virginia Community College*
Mark W. Dawson, *Duquesne University*
Patricia A. Doherty, *Boston University*
Lizabeth England, *American Language Academy*
David Fetyko, *Kent State University*
Albert Fisher, *Community College of Southern Nevada*
Robert Flemming, *Northern Michigan University*
Sue Garr, *Wayne State University*
Roxanne Gooch, *Cameron University*
Christine Uber Grosse, *The American Graduate School of International Management*
Dennis A. Gutting, *Orange County Community College*
John Hancock, *University of California—Davis Graduate School of Management*
Yvonne Hatami, *Borough of Manhattan Community College*
Robert Holtfreter, *Centra, Washington University*
Harry Hooper, *Santa Fe Community College*

Mark Henry, *Victoria College*
Margaret Hoskins, *Henderson State Univ.*
Marianne James, *California State University, Los Angeles*
Sharon Johnson, *Kansas City Kansas Community College*
Edward H. Julius, *California Lutheran University*
Howard A. Kanter, *DePaul University*
Ann Kelley, *Providence College*
Debbie Luna, *El Paso Community College*
Kevin McClure, *ESL Language Center*
George McGowan
Gail A. Mestas
Jenine Moscove
Beth Brooks Patel, *University of California—Berkeley*
LaVonda Ramey, *Schoolcraft College*
Roberta Rettner, *American Ways*
Gayle Richardson, *Bakersfield College*
James B. Rosa, *Queensborough Community College*
Donald Shannon, *DePaul Univeristy*
S. Murray Simons, *Northeastern University*
Marion Taube, *University of Pittsburgh*
Kathleen Villani, *Queensborough Community College*
Vicki Vorell, *Cuyahoga Community College*
John Weber, *DeVry Institute*
Brenda Werts, *Park University*
Kay Westerfield, *University of Oregon*
Andy Williams, *Edmunds Community College*

Finally, we want to thank the facilitators for the last five years of COAE (Conference on Accounting Education):

2006 COAE Facilitators
Salvador Aceves, *University of San Francisco*
Rita Grant, *Grand Valley State University*
Emmanuel Onifade, *Morehouse College*
Janet Papiernik, *Indiana University—Purdue University*
Andy Williams, *Edmonds Community College*

2005 COAE Facilitators
Peter Aghimien, *Indiana University, South Bend*
Charles Bunn, *Wake Technical College*
James Dougher, *DeVry University*
Frank Lordi, *Widener University*
Elizabeeth Murphy, *DePaul University*
Karen Novey, *Robert Morris College*
Wendy Tietz, *Kent State University*

2004 COAE Facilitators
Star Brown, *Western Piedmont Community College*
Rosie Bukics, *Lafayette College*
Stanley Chu, *Borough of Manhattan Community College*
Michael Cottrill, *Northeastern University*
Mark Mitschow, *SUNY—Genesee*
Elizabeth Murphy, *DePaul University*

2003 COAE Facilitators
Charlene Abendroth, *California State University*
Daneen Adams, *Santa Fe Community College*

Richard Fern, *Eastern Kentucky University*
Terry Grant, *Mississippi College*
Yvonne Hatami, *Borough of Manhattan Community College*
Rodger Holland, *Columbus State University*

2002 COAE Facilitators
Sharon Bell, *University of North Carolina—Pembroke*
Mark Henry, *Victoria College*
Harry Hooper, *Santa Fe Community College*
Richard Irvine, *Pensacola Junior College*
Nancy Kelly, *Middlesex Community College*
Paul Mihalek, *University of Hartford*
Paul Weitzel, *Eastern Shore Community College*

2001 COAE Facilitators
Salvador Aceves, *University of San Francisco*
Betty Habershon, *Prince George's Community College*
Jim Mazza, *Heald College*
Roselyn Morris, *Southwest Texas State University*
Ginger Parker, *Creighton University*
David Rogers, *Mesa State College*
Jeanne Yamamura, *University of Nevada—Reno*

—B.N., M.P., and S.C.

User's Guide to *Principles of Accounting*

We have designed *Principles of Accounting* with you—the student—in mind. Becoming familiar with this textbook will help you succeed in this course: you will study more effectively and improve your grades on tests and assignments. The following User's Guide will introduce you to your *Principles of Accounting* textbook.

Preview the Chapter

Use these features to preview the chapter. First, become familiar with the **Learning Objectives** (they appear throughout the chapter), and then read how a leading business uses accounting information. Review **Making a Statement** in Chapters 1–17; this feature tells you which financial statements are important in the chapter.

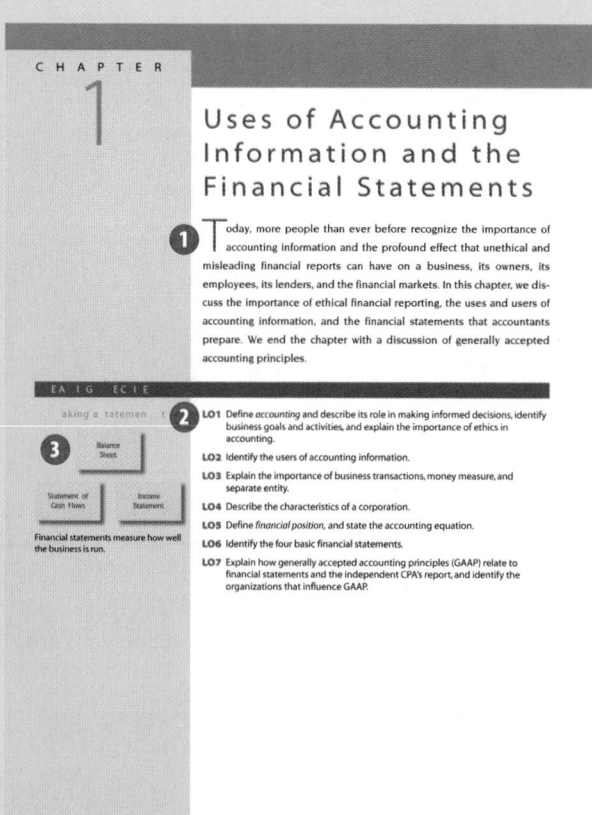

1 Each **Chapter Preview** focuses on management issues; many also present ethical issues. As you read this section, consider the following: Why are the concepts in this chapter important to managers? What are the ethical issues?

2 The **Learning Objectives (LOs)** help guide you toward mastery of the material. These brief statements summarize what you should know after reading the chapter. You will see many references to **LOs** throughout each chapter.

3 **Making a Statement** (Chapters 1–17) reinforces the connection between the financial statements and the chapter's topics. It indicates which financial statements are important in each chapter.

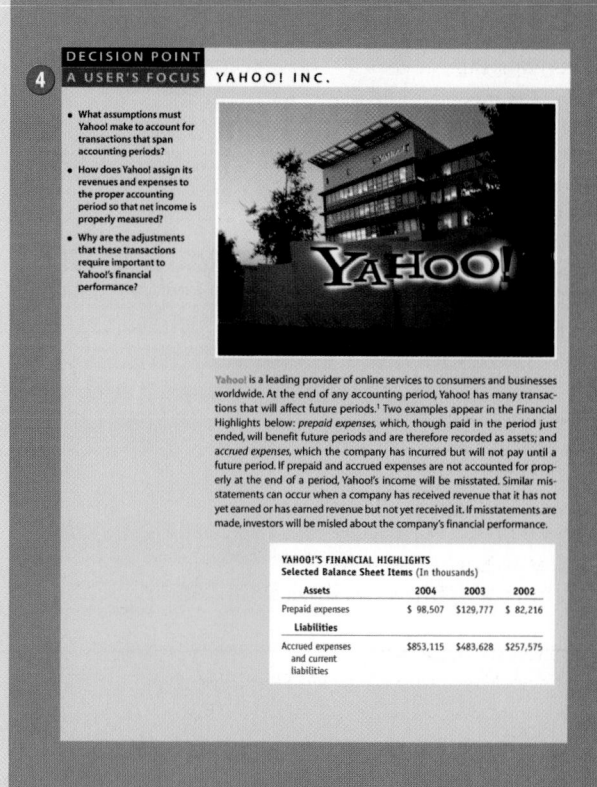

4 Use the **Decision Point** feature to see how real companies depend on accounting information in decision making. Look for references to the **Decision Point** company throughout the chapter. Many of the companies profiled are among the most successful in the world.

Reinforce What You Read

As you read each chapter, use the features described below to reinforce the concepts. Look for the LO before each main section, and note boldface words: they are terms and definitions you should know. Use the *Stop, Review, and Apply* questions at the end of each main section to assess your understanding of the material.

5 *Learning Objectives* introduce the key points of each section and are integrated throughout the text.

6 **Boldface** terms call out important concepts and their definitions. These words also appear in a glossary at the end of the chapter.

7 *Study Notes* highlight important information and provide useful tips on ways to avoid common mistakes.

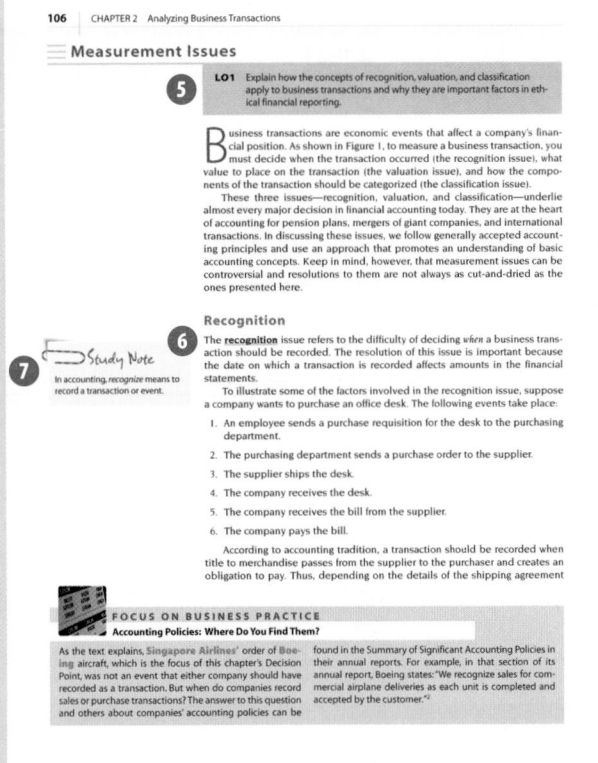

106 CHAPTER 2 Analyzing Business Transactions

Measurement Issues

5 **LO1** Explain how the concepts of recognition, valuation, and classification apply to business transactions and why they are important factors in ethical financial reporting.

Business transactions are economic events that affect a company's financial position. As shown in Figure 1, to measure a business transaction, you must decide when the transaction occurred (the recognition issue), what value to place on the transaction (the valuation issue), and how the components of the transaction should be categorized (the classification issue).

These three issues—recognition, valuation, and classification—underlie almost every major decision in financial accounting today. They are at the heart of accounting for pension plans, mergers of giant companies, and international transactions. In discussing these issues, we follow generally accepted accounting principles and use an approach that promotes an understanding of basic accounting concepts. Keep in mind, however, that measurement issues can be controversial and resolutions to them are not always as cut-and-dried as the ones presented here.

Recognition

6 The **recognition** issue refers to the difficulty of deciding *when* a business transaction should be recorded. The resolution of this issue is important because the date on which a transaction is recorded affects amounts in the financial statements.

7 *Study Note*

In accounting, *recognize* means to record a transaction or event.

To illustrate some of the factors involved in the recognition issue, suppose a company wants to purchase an office desk. The following events take place:

1. An employee sends a purchase requisition for the desk to the purchasing department.
2. The purchasing department sends a purchase order to the supplier.
3. The supplier ships the desk.
4. The company receives the desk.
5. The company receives the bill from the supplier.
6. The company pays the bill.

According to accounting tradition, a transaction should be recorded when title to merchandise passes from the supplier to the purchaser and creates an obligation to pay. Thus, depending on the details of the shipping agreement

FOCUS ON BUSINESS PRACTICE
Accounting Policies: Where Do You Find Them?

As the text explains, Singapore Airlines' order of Boeing aircraft, which is the focus of this chapter's Decision Point, was not an event that either company should have recorded as a transaction. But when do companies record sales or purchase transactions? The answer to this question and others about companies' accounting policies can be found in the Summary of Significant Accounting Policies in their annual reports. For example, in that section of its annual report, Boeing states:"We recognize sales for commercial airplane deliveries as each unit is completed and accepted by the customer."²

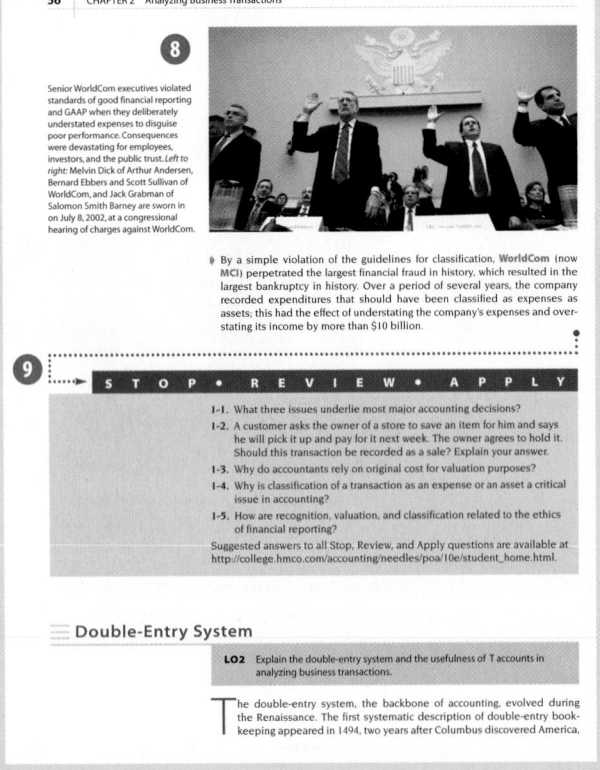

56 CHAPTER 2 Analyzing Business Transactions

8 Senior WorldCom executives violated standards of good financial reporting and GAAP when they deliberately understated expenses to disguise poor performance. Consequences were devastating for employees, investors, and the public trust. *Left to right*: Melvin Dick of Arthur Andersen, Bernard Ebbers and Scott Sullivan of WorldCom, and Jack Grabman of Salomon Smith Barney are sworn in on July 8, 2002, at a congressional hearing of charges against WorldCom.

By a simple violation of the guidelines for classification, WorldCom (now MCI) perpetrated the largest financial fraud in history, which resulted in the largest bankruptcy in history. Over a period of several years, the company recorded expenditures that should have been classified as expenses as assets; this had the effect of understating the company's expenses and overstating its income by more than $10 billion.

9

STOP • REVIEW • APPLY

1-1. What three issues underlie most major accounting decisions?
1-2. A customer asks the owner of a store to save an item for him and says he will pick it up and pay for it next week. The owner agrees to hold it. Should this transaction be recorded as a sale? Explain your answer.
1-3. Why do accountants rely on original cost for valuation purposes?
1-4. Why is classification of a transaction as an expense or an asset a critical issue in accounting?
1-5. How are recognition, valuation, and classification related to the ethics of financial reporting?

Suggested answers to all Stop, Review, and Apply questions are available at http://college.hmco.com/accounting/needles/poa/10e/student_home.html.

Double-Entry System

LO2 Explain the double-entry system and the usefulness of T accounts in analyzing business transactions.

The double-entry system, the backbone of accounting, evolved during the Renaissance. The first systematic description of double-entry bookkeeping appeared in 1494, two years after Columbus discovered America,

8 **Photographs** with detailed captions reinforce concepts in the textbook and show how accounting is used in the business world.

9 *Stop, Review, and Apply* features at the end of every section help you review important concepts in the section. These questions can also be used for discussion in class.

10 **Accounting equations** next to important journal entries reinforce the impact of the transaction on the financial statements.

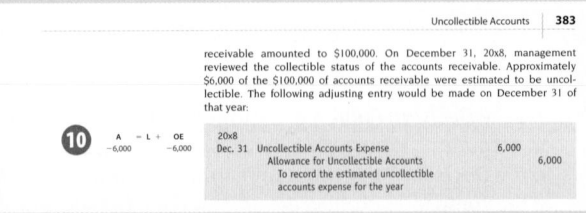

Uncollectible Accounts **383**

receivable amounted to $100,000. On December 31, 20x8, management reviewed the collectible status of the accounts receivable. Approximately $6,000 of the $100,000 of accounts receivable were estimated to be uncollectible. The following adjusting entry would be made on December 31 of that year:

10

A	= L +	OE
−6,000		−6,000

20x8			
Dec. 31	Uncollectible Accounts Expense	6,000	
	Allowance for Uncollectible Accounts		6,000
	To record the estimated uncollectible accounts expense for the year		

Reinforce Concepts Visually

These features visually reinforce the concepts in your textbook. Line art helps explain concepts, exhibits show financial statements and other information, and tables include material to support topics covered in the chapter. Also look for icons throughout the text; they are visual guides to key features.

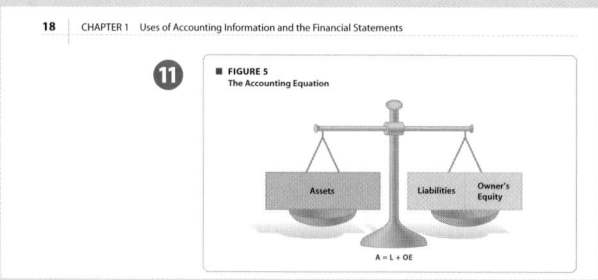

(11) An abundance of **line art** illustrates the relationships between concepts and processes.

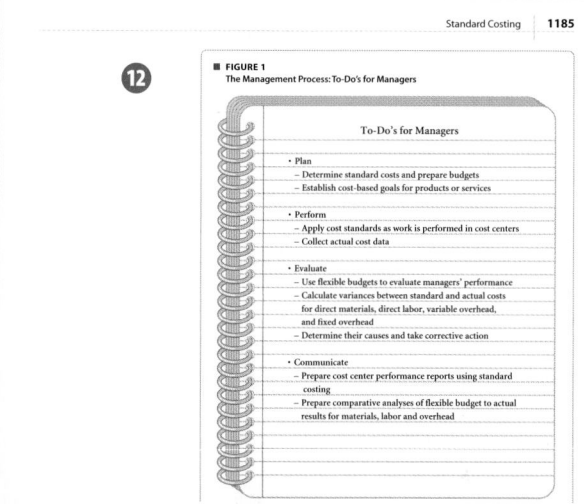

(12) Each managerial chapter (Chapters 18–26) includes a graphic: To-Do's for Managers. These figures highlight managerial activities important to each stage of the management process.

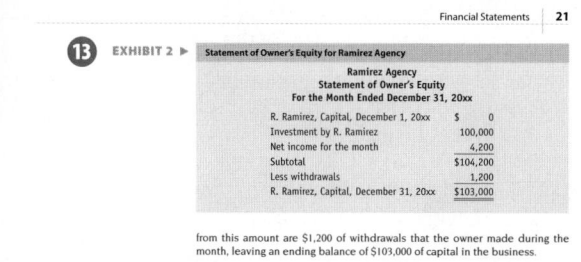

(13) **Exhibits** throughout the text show financial information.

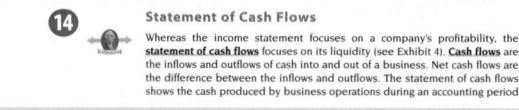

(14) The **cash flow icon** highlights discussion of cash as a measure of liquidity. Measurement of cash flows serves as an indicator of a company's success; hence the emphasis on cash flows in this book.

(15) **Tables** present factual information referred to in the text.

Learn Why Accounting Is Relevant

These features demonstrate how and why accounting is relevant. *Focus on Business Practice* boxes introduce you to real companies and real issues. The Supplement to Chapter 5 helps you learn how to read—and understand—real financial statements and interpret what management says about them.

16 *Focus on Business Practice* boxes highlight the relevance of accounting to business today.

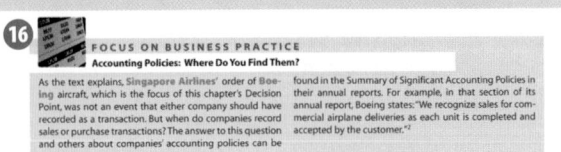

17 The textbook refers to over 200 public, private, and not-for-profit companies. The **Needles Online Study Center** website (**http://college.hmco.com/info/needles**) provides a direct link to the websites of these companies. The book also has a company name index.

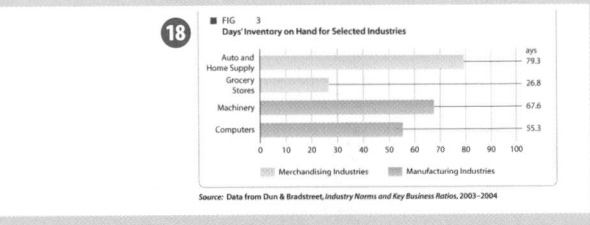

18 **Graphs** and **tables** illustrate how actual business practices relate to chapter topics. Data for these illustrations come from *Accounting Trends & Techniques* and from Dun & Bradstreet, key sources of business information.

19 **Ratios** are used to measure a company's performance. The key ratio icon appears in the margin to highlight discussions of important ratios.

> Current Ratio   The current ratio is closely related to working capital. Many bankers and other creditors believe it is a good indicator of a company's ability to pay its debts on time. The **current ratio** is the ratio of current assets to current liabilities. For Ling Auto Supply Company, it is computed like this:
>
> $$\text{Current Ratio} = \frac{\text{Current Assets}}{\text{Current Liabilities}} = \frac{\$248,712}{\$85,366} = 2.9$$
>
> Thus, Ling Auto Supply has $2.90 of current assets for each $1.00 of current liabilities. Is that good or bad? The answer requires a comparison of this year's current ratio with ratios for earlier years and with similar measures for companies in the same industry.

20 The complete **annual report** for CVS and the **financial statements** of Southwest Airlines are in the Supplement to Chapter 5. CVS's financial statements with annotations also appear in the Supplement to Chapter 5.

Summarize and Review

The end-of-chapter features provide summary, review, and assignments for practice. *A Look Back At* relates the chapter's concepts to the company you read about in the *Decision Point* at the beginning of the chapter. Review sections include a *Review of Learning Objectives* and a *Review of Concepts and Terminology*.

21 *A Look Back At* shows how the concepts learned in the chapter can be used to evaluate a company's performance.

22 The *Chapter Review* restates each learning objective and its main ideas.

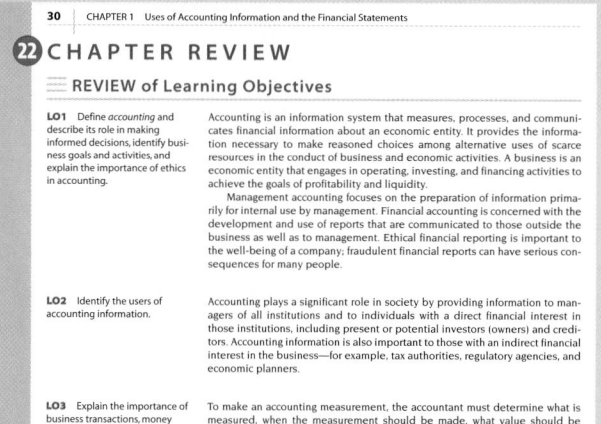

30 CHAPTER 1   Uses of Accounting Information and the Financial Statements

22 CHAPTER REVIEW

REVIEW of Learning Objectives

LO1 Define *accounting* and describe its role in making informed decisions, identify business goals and activities, and explain the importance of ethics in accounting.	Accounting is an information system that measures, processes, and communicates financial information about an economic entity. It provides the information necessary to make reasoned choices among alternative uses of scarce resources in the conduct of business and economic activities. A business is an economic entity that engages in operating, investing, and financing activities to achieve the goals of profitability and liquidity. Management accounting focuses on the preparation of information primarily for internal use by management. Financial accounting is concerned with the development and use of reports that are communicated to those outside the business as well as to management. Ethical financial reporting is important to the well-being of a company; fraudulent financial reports can have serious consequences for many people.
LO2 Identify the users of accounting information.	Accounting plays a significant role in society by providing information to managers of all institutions and to individuals with a direct financial interest in those institutions, including present or potential investors (owners) and creditors. Accounting information is also important to those with an indirect financial interest in the business—for example, tax authorities, regulatory agencies, and economic planners.
LO3 Explain the importance of business transactions, money measure, and separate entity.	To make an accounting measurement, the accountant must determine what is measured, when the measurement should be made, what value should be placed on what is measured, and how to classify what is measured. The objects of accounting measurement are business transactions. Financial accounting uses money measure to gauge the impact of these transactions on a separate business entity.
LO4 Identify the three basic forms of business organization.	The three basic forms of business organization are the sole proprietorship, the partnership, and the corporation. Accountants recognize each form as an economic unit separate from its owners, although legally only the corporation is separate from its owners. A sole proprietorship is a business owned by one person. A partnership is like a sole proprietorship in most ways, but it has two or more owners. A corporation, on the other hand, is a business unit chartered by the state and legally separate from its owners (the *stockholders*).
LO5 Define *financial position*, and state the accounting equation.	*Financial position* refers to a company's economic resources and the claims against those resources at a particular time. The accounting equation shows financial position as Assets = Liabilities + Owner's Equity. Business transactions affect financial position by decreasing or increasing assets, liabilities, and owner's equity in such a way that the accounting equation is always in balance.
LO6 Identify the four basic financial statements.	The four basic financial statements are the income statement, the statement of owner's equity, the balance sheet, and the statement of cash flows. They are the primary means by which accountants communicate the financial condition and activities of a business to those who have an interest in the business.

23 Each chapter includes a glossary of the key concepts and terms defined in the chapter. The *LO* next to each term indicates the section in which it is discussed.

Want more study aids and review exercises? The *Study Guide* for this book provides a thorough review of each learning objective, a detailed outline, true/false and multiple-choice questions, and exercises. Answers are included. Access the Study Guide with "Your Guide to an A" passkey.

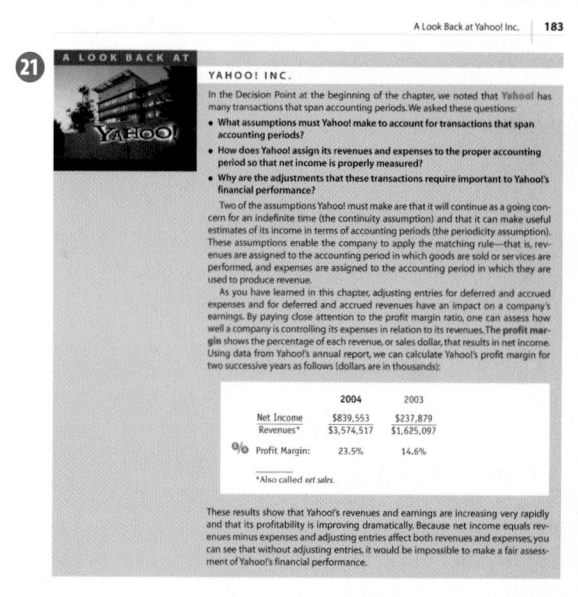

A Look Back at Yahoo! Inc.   **183**

21 A LOOK BACK AT

YAHOO! INC.

In the Decision Point at the beginning of the chapter, we noted that Yahoo! has many transactions that span accounting periods. We asked these questions:

- What assumptions must Yahoo! make to account for transactions that span accounting periods?
- How does Yahoo! assign its revenues and expenses to the proper accounting period so that net income is properly measured?
- Why are the adjustments that these transactions require important to Yahoo!'s financial performance?

Two of the assumptions Yahoo! must make are that it will continue as a going concern for an indefinite time (the continuity assumption) and that it can make useful estimates of its income in terms of accounting periods (the periodicity assumption). These assumptions enable the company to apply the matching rule—that is, revenues are assigned to the accounting period in which goods are sold or services are performed, and expenses are assigned to the accounting period in which they are used to produce revenue.

As you have learned in this chapter, adjusting entries for deferred and accrued expenses and for deferred and accrued revenues have an impact on a company's earnings. By paying close attention to the profit margin ratio, one can assess how well a company is controlling its expenses in relation to its revenues. The profit margin shows the percentage of each revenue, or sales dollar, that results in net income. Using data from Yahoo!'s annual report, we can calculate Yahoo!'s profit margin for two successive years as follows (dollars are in thousands):

		2004	2003
	Net Income	$839,553	$237,879
	Revenues*	$3,574,517	$1,625,097
%	**Profit Margin:**	23.5%	14.6%

*Also called *net sales*.

These results show that Yahoo!'s revenues and earnings are increasing very rapidly and that its profitability is improving dramatically. Because net income equals revenues minus expenses and adjusting entries affect both revenues and expenses, you can see that without adjusting entries, it would be impossible to make a fair assessment of Yahoo!'s financial performance.

Chapter Review   **31**

LO7 Explain how generally accepted accounting principles (GAAP) relate to financial statements and the independent CPA's report, and identify the organizations that influence GAAP.	Acceptable accounting practice consists of the conventions, rules, and procedures that make up generally accepted accounting principles at a particular time. GAAP are essential to the preparation and interpretation of financial statements and the independent CPA's report.
	  Among the organizations that influence the formulation of GAAP are the Public Company Accounting Oversight Board, the Financial Accounting Standards Board, the American Institute of Certified Public Accountants, the Securities and Exchange Commission, and the Internal Revenue Service.
	  All accountants are required to follow a code of professional ethics, the foundation of which is responsibility to the public. Accountants must act with integrity, objectivity, and independence, and they must exercise due care in all their activities.
	  The board of directors is responsible for determining corporate policies and appointing corporate officers. It is also responsible for corporate governance, the oversight of a corporation's management and ethics. The audit committee, which is appointed by the board and made up of independent directors, is an important factor in corporate governance.

23 REVIEW of Concepts and Terminology

The following concepts and terms were introduced in this chapter:

Accounting: An information system that measures, processes, and communicates financial information about an economic entity. **(LO1)**

Accounting equation: Assets = Liabilities + Owner's Equity. **(LO5)**

American Institute of Certified Public Accountants (AICPA): The professional association of certified public accountants. **(LO7)**

Assets: The economic resources of a company that are expected to benefit future operations. **(LO5)**

Audit: An examination of a company's financial statements in order to render an independent professional opinion about whether they have been presented fairly, in all material respects, in conformity with GAAP. **(LO7)**

Audit committee: A subgroup of a corporation's board of directors that is charged with ensuring that the board will be objective in reviewing management's performance; it engages the company's independent auditors and reviews their work. **(LO7)**

Balance sheet: The financial statement that shows a business's assets, liabilities, and owner's equity as of a specific date. Also called the *statement of financial position*. **(LO6)**

Bookkeeping: The process of recording financial transactions and keeping financial records. **(LO1)**

Business: An economic unit that aims to sell goods and services to customers at prices that will provide an adequate return to its owners. **(LO1)**

Business transactions: Economic events that affect a business's financial position. **(LO3)**

Cash flows: The inflows and outflows of cash into and out of a business. **(LO6)**

Certified public accountant (CPA): A public accountant who has met stringent state licensing requirements. **(LO7)**

Corporate governance: The oversight of a corporation's management and ethics by the board of directors. **(LO7)**

Corporation: A business unit granted a state charter recognizing it as a separate legal entity having its own rights, privileges, and liabilities distinct from those of its owners. **(LO4)**

Due care: Competence and diligence in carrying out professional responsibilities. **(LO7)**

Ethics: A code of conduct that addresses whether actions are right or wrong. **(LO1)**

Exchange rate: The value of one currency in terms of another. **(LO3)**

Expenses: Decreases in owner's equity that result from operating a business. **(LO5)**

Financial accounting: The process of generating and communicating accounting information in the form of financial statements to those outside the organization. **(LO1)**

Financial Accounting Standards Board (FASB): The most important body for developing rules on accounting practice; it issues *Statements of Financial Accounting Standards*. **(LO7)**

Review and Practice

Continue your review of the chapter with the *Review Problem*, which reflects computations or analyses covered in the chapter. For practice at different levels of difficulty, *Chapter Assignments*—from *Short Exercises* to *Cases*—let you develop skills learned in the chapter. All assignments are identified by *Learning Objective* so you can easily review the concepts presented in the text.

24 Not sure if you understand the techniques and calculations? Want to find out if you're ready for a test? The *Review Problem* models main computations or analyses presented in the chapter and end-of-chapter assignments. The answer, often shown in Excel, is provided for immediate feedback.

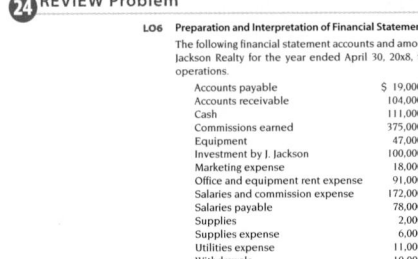

24 REVIEW Problem

LO6 Preparation and Interpretation of Financial Statements

The following financial statement accounts and amounts are from the records of Jackson Realty for the year ended April 30, 20x8, the company's first year of operations.

Accounts payable	$ 19,000
Accounts receivable	104,000
Cash	111,000
Commissions earned	375,000
Equipment	47,000
Investment by J. Jackson	100,000
Marketing expense	18,000
Office and equipment rent expense	91,000
Salaries and commission expense	172,000
Salaries payable	78,000
Supplies	2,000
Supplies expense	6,000
Utilities expense	11,000
Withdrawals	10,000

25 **Short exercises** provide additional practice. Learning Objectives appear in the margin next to all assignments so you can refer to the text for help.

25

CHAPTER ASSIGNMENTS

≡ BUILDING Your Basic Knowledge and Skills

Short Exercises

LO1 Objectives and Qualitative Characteristics

SE 1. Identify each of the following statements as either an objective (O) of financial information or as a qualitative (Q) characteristic of accounting information:

1. Information about business resources, claims to those resources, and changes in them should be provided.
2. Decision makers must be able to interpret accounting information.
3. Information that is useful in making investment and credit decisions should be furnished.
4. Accounting information must be relevant and reliable.
5. Information useful in assessing cash flow prospects should be provided.

LO2 Accounting Conventions

SE 2. State which of the accounting conventions—comparability and consistency, materiality, conservatism, full disclosure, or cost-benefit—is being followed in each of the cases listed below.

1. Management provides detailed information about the company's long-term debt in the notes to the financial statements.
2. A company does not account separately for discounts received for prompt payment of accounts payable because few of these transactions occur and the total amount of the discounts is small.

26 **Single-topic exercises** stress the application of the chapter's concepts.

26

Exercises

LO1, LO2, LO3 Discussion Questions

E 1. Develop a brief answer to each of the following questions:

1. How do the four basic financial statements meet the third objective of financial reporting?
2. What are some areas that require estimates to record transactions under the matching rule?
3. How can financial information be consistent but not comparable?
4. When might an amount be material to management but not to the CPA auditing the financial statements?

LO4, LO5 Discussion Questions

E 2. Develop a brief answer to each of the following questions:

1. Why is it that land held for future use and equipment not currently used in the business are classified as investments rather than as property, plant, and equipment?
2. Which is the better measure of a company's performance—income from operations or net income?
3. Why is it important to compare a company's financial performance with industry standards?
4. Is the statement "Return on assets is a better measure of profitability than profit margin" true or false and why?

LO1, LO2 Financial Accounting Concepts

E 3. The lettered items below represent a classification scheme for the concepts of financial accounting. Match each numbered term in the list that follows with the letter of the category in which it belongs.

a. Decision makers (users of accounting information)
b. Business activities or entities relevant to accounting measurement

Develop Important Skills

Use these end-of-chapter features to develop important skills. Five problems and three alternate problems per chapter allow extensive application of chapter topics, often covering more than one *Learning Objective*. *Cases* provide opportunities for group assignments, Internet research, analysis with Excel, and critical thinking.

27 Most problems include at least one *User Insight* or *Manager Insight* question. These questions challenge you to think about how financial information is used for business decision making.

28 Problems with this icon can be solved by using **General Ledger Software**, which is available on your student CD. Problems often contain financial data and cover more than one *Learning Objective*.

29 *Cases* at the end of each chapter have been organized to highlight important skills, such as conceptual understanding, interpretation of financial statements or management reports, Excel analysis, decision making, Internet research, and business communication.

27 User Insight: For each of these cases, identify the accounting convention that applies, state whether or not the treatment is in accord with the convention and GAAP, and briefly explain why.

LO4 Forms of the Income Statement

28 **P 2.** Ramos Nursery Corporation's single-step income statements for 20x7 and 20x6 follow.

Ramos Nursery Corporation
Income Statements
For the Years Ended April 30, 20x7 and 20x6

	20x7	20x6
Revenues		
Net sales	$525,932	$475,264
Interest income	800	700
Total revenues	$526,732	$475,964
Costs and expenses		
Cost of goods sold	$234,948	$171,850
Selling expenses	161,692	150,700
General and administrative expenses	62,866	42,086
Interest expense	3,600	850
Total costs and expenses	$463,106	$365,486
Income before income taxes	$ 63,626	$110,478
Income taxes	15,000	27,600
Net income	$ 48,626	$ 82,878
Earnings per share	$ 2.43	$ 4.14

Ramos Nursery Corporation had 20,000 shares of common stock outstanding during both 20x7 and 20x6.

ENHANCING Your Knowledge, Skills, and Critical Thinking

Conceptual Understanding Cases

29 **LO2** Consistency and Full Disclosure

C 1. Cuyahoga Parking, which operates a seven-story parking building in downtown Cleveland, has a calendar year end. It serves daily and hourly parkers, as well as monthly parkers who pay a fixed monthly rate in advance. The company traditionally has recorded all cash receipts as revenues when received. Most monthly parkers pay in full during the month prior to that in which they have the right to park. The company's auditors have said that beginning in 20x6, the company should consider recording the cash receipts from monthly parking on an accrual basis, crediting Unearned Revenues. Total cash receipts for 20x6 were $1,250,000, and the cash receipts received in 20x6 and applicable to January 20x7 were $62,500. Discuss the relevance of the accounting conventions of consistency and full disclosure to the decision to record the monthly parking revenues on an accrual basis.

Decision Analysis Using Excel

LO5 Financial Analysis for Loan Decision

C 5. Esteban Almada was recently promoted to loan officer at First Federal Bank. He has authority to issue loans up to $75,000 without approval from a higher bank official. This week two small companies, Dubrovnik Supplies, Inc., and Shimano Fashions, Inc., have each submitted a proposal for a six-month, $75,000 loan. To prepare financial analyses of the two companies, Almada has obtained the information summarized below.

Dubrovnik Supplies, Inc., is a local lumber and home improvement company. Because sales have increased so much during the past two years, Dubrovnik Supplies has had to raise additional working capital, especially as represented by receivables and inventory. The $75,000 loan is needed to assure the company of enough working capital for the next year. Dubrovnik Supplies began the year with total assets of $1,110,000 and stockholders' equity of $390,000. During the past year, the company had a net income of $60,000 on net sales of $1,140,000. Dubrovnik Supplies' unclassified balance sheet as of the current date appears as follows:

Annual Report Case: CVS Corporation

LO3, LO4, LO5 Classified Balance Sheet and Multistep Income Statement

C 6. Refer to CVS Corporation's annual report in the Supplement to Chapter 1 to answer the following questions. (Note that 2004 refers to the year ended January 1, 2005, and 2003 refers to the year ended January 3, 2004.)

1. Consolidated balance sheets: (a) Did the amount of working capital increase or decrease from 2003 to 2004? By how much? (b) Did the current ratio improve from 2003 to 2004? (c) Does the company have long-term investments or intangible assets? (d) Did the debt to equity ratio of CVS change from 2003 to 2004? (e) What is the contributed ratio for 2004? How does contributed capital compare with retained earnings?
2. Consolidated statements of operations: (a) Does CVS use a multistep or single-step income statement? (b) Is it a comparative statement? (c) What is the trend of net earnings? (d) How significant are income taxes for CVS?

Interpreting Management Reports

LO3, LO4 ABC and Selling and Administrative Expenses

C 4. Sandy Star, the owner of Star Bakery, wants to know the profitability of each of her bakery's customer groups. She is especially interested in the State Institutions customer group, which is one of the company's largest customer groups. Currently, the bakery is selling doughnuts and snack foods to ten state institutions in three states. The controller has prepared the following income statement for the State Institutions customer group:

Star Bakery
Income Statement for State Institutions Customer Group
For the Year Ended December 31, 20x8

Sales ($5 per case × 50,000 cases)	$250,000
Cost of goods sold ($3.50 per case × 50,000 cases)	175,000
Gross margin	$ 75,000
Less: Selling and administrative activity costs	94,750
Operating income (loss) contributed by State Institutions customer group	($19,750)

Activity	Activity Cost Rate	Actual Cost Driver Level	Activity Cost
Make sales calls	$60 per sales call	60 sales calls	$ 3,600
Prepare sales orders	$10 per sales order	900 sales orders	9,000
Handle inquiries	$5 per minute	1,000 minutes	5,000
Ship products	$1 per case sold	50,000 cases	50,000
Process invoices	$20 per invoice	950 invoices	19,000
Process credits	$20 per notice	40 notices	800
Process billings and collections	$7 per billing	1,050 billings	7,350
Total selling and administrative activity costs			94,750

Student Resources and Study Aids

Principles of Accounting offers a variety of print and multimedia tools to complement the way you learn. From study guides to downloadable MP3 audio review files, the Needles *Principles of Accounting* program keeps you engaged and on track for success. The following student resources may come packaged with your new copy of *Principles of Accounting*, or can be purchased separately at your local college bookstore or directly from Houghton Mifflin's virtual bookstore at **http://college.hmco.com/students**.

The **Online Study Center** contains a variety of resources, including ACE practice tests, chapter outlines and reviews, links to companies mentioned in the text, glossaries, and additional appendixes. Content to help you improve your grade is available with the **"Your Guide to an A"** passkey and includes Flashcards, Crossword Puzzles, MP3 audio summaries and quizzes, Demonstration Videos, and the complete Study Guide.

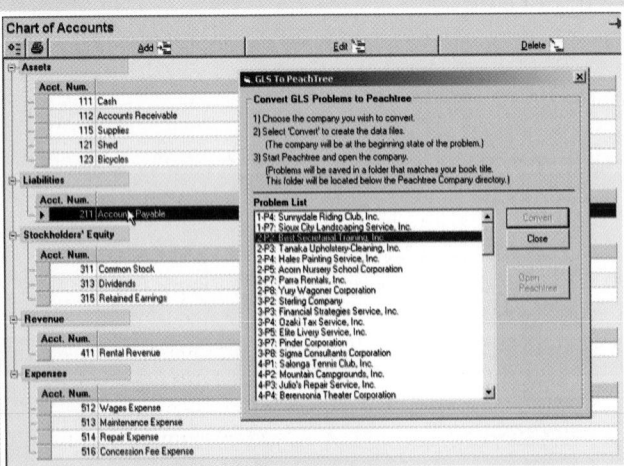

Nearly all the problems in Chapters 1 to 17 can be worked using Houghton Mifflin's **General Ledger Software (GLS).** These problems are clearly identified with an icon. Our updated GLS includes *Export to Peachtree* functionality.

The *Principles of Accounting* **Electronic Working Papers CD** (0-618-73649-2) is an alternative to printed working papers. These Excel-based files contain templates that allow you to work the exercises, problems, and cases in the text; a new interface makes it easy to navigate among assignments. With the Electronic Working Papers CD, you master both accounting concepts and the basic skills required for spreadsheet applications.

Also available are print **Working Papers** (Vol. 1: 0-618-73643-3; Vol. 2: 0-618-73644-1), which provide the appropriate accounting forms for solving the exercises, problems, and cases from the text.

The **SMARTHINKING**™ online tutoring center provides real-time access to experienced "e-structors" (online tutors). In addition to live, one-on-one interaction, you can submit questions, assignments, and spreadsheets and receive personalized feedback—usually within 24 hours.

The *Principles of Accounting* **Study Guide** is designed to help you improve your performance in the course. This resource consists of five parts: "Reviewing the Chapter," "Self-Test," "Testing Students' Knowledge," "Applying Your Knowledge," and "Answers." The Study Guide is available with the "Your Guide to an A" passkey.

To help you become familiar with computerized accounting systems used in practice, the **Peachtree Accounting CD** (0-618-62683-2) features the educational version of this leading software program. The experience you gain from working with actual software makes you more desirable as a potential employee.

The Houghton Mifflin Accounting **Bridge Tutorial CD** (0-618-31876-3) emphasizes accounting transactions, presents a review of the debit/credit mechanism, and provides a foundation for the preparation of financial statements. This CD features pre- and post-test activities on accounting concepts, designed to test your basic understanding of the accounting cycle. Key concept tutorials provide reinforcement and practice. Interactive Review and Reinforce questions with rejoinders provide feedback on right and wrong answers. Tutorials also include demonstration problems with voice-over narrations and a built-in glossary with pop-up definitions.

Check Figures

Chapter 1
P 1. No check figure
P 2. Total assets, Set C: $380; Total liabilities and owner's equity, Set A: $4,600; Total liabilities and owner's equity, Set B: $31,000
P 3. Total assets: $151,500
P 4. Total assets: $20,900
P 5. No check figure
P 6. Total assets, Set A: $2,700; Total liabilities and owner's equity, Set B: $18,000; Total liabilities and owner's equity, Set C: $1,900
P 7. Total assets: $156,700
P 8. Total assets: $27,300

Chapter 2
P 1. Total assets: $28,540
P 2. No check figure
P 3. Trial balance: $16,200
P 4. Trial balance: $14,800
P 5. Trial balance: $23,805
P 6. Total assets: $67,790
P 7. Trial balance: $10,540
P 8. Trial balance: $30,710

Chapter 3
P 1. No check figure
P 2. No check figure
P 3. Adjusted trial balance: $121,792
P 4. Adjusted trial balance: $29,778
P 5. Adjusted trial balance: $642,209
P 6. No check figure
P 7. No check figure
P 8. Adjusted trial balance: $106,167

Chapter 4
P 1. Income Summary transfer to E. Graff, Capital: $11,425
P 2. Adjusted trial balance, May 31: $10,288; Adjusted trial balance, June 30: $10,858
P 3. Net income: $98,622
P 4. Income Summary transfer to S. Perez, Capital: $7,978
P 5. Net income: $62,392

Chapter 5
P 1. No check figure
P 2. Income from operations: 20x8: $66,426; 20x7: $110,628
P 3. Total assets: $595,600
P 4. No check figure
P 5. Net income: $86,260; Total assets: $1,083,800
P 6. No check figure
P 7. No check figure
P 8. Income from operations: 20x9: $34,320; 20x8: $84,748

Chapter 6
P 1. Net income: $15,435
P 2. No check figure
P 3. Net income: $23,941
P 4. No check figure
P 5. Net income: $10,522
P 6. No check figure
P 7. Net income: $3,435
P 8. No check figure

Chapter 7
P 1. 1. Cost of goods available for sale: $157,980
P 2. 2. Cost of goods sold: March, $4,500; April, $10,540
P 3. 1. Cost of goods sold: March, $4,579; April, $10,518
P 4. Estimated inventory shortage: At cost, $6,052; At retail, $8,900
P 5. Estimated loss of inventory in fire: $653,027
P 6. Cost of goods available for sale: $10,560,000
P 7. 1. Cost of goods sold: April, $9,660; May, $22,119
P 8. 2. Cost of goods sold: April, $9,500; May, $21,880

Chapter 8
P 1. Adjusted book balance: $149,473.28
P 2. Uncollectible accounts expense, percentage of net sales method: $17,952; Uncollectible accounts expense, accounts receivable aging method: $15,700
P 3. Amount of uncollectible accounts expense: $9,109
P 4. Total accrued interest on June 30: $1,928.22
P 5. Adjusted book balance: $54,485.60
P 6. Uncollectible accounts expense, percentage of net sales method: $24,965; Uncollectible accounts expense, accounts receivable aging method: $27,100
P 7. Amount of uncollectible accounts expense: $73,413

Chapter 9
P 1. No check figure
P 2. June 30. Interest Expense: $552.33
P 3. 1. b. Estimated Product Warranty Liability: $10,800
P 4. Total current liabilities: $36,988.20
P 5. Fund Balance: $58,300; Initial Deposit: $110,250; Purchase Price: $399,300; Annual Payments: $136,355.89
P 6. December 31. Interest expense: $426.08
P 7. 1. b. Estimated Product Warranty Liability: $20,160
P 8. Fund Balance: $3,310,000; Annual Payment: $327,600; Cost of Buyout: $317,000; Fund Balance: $798,600

Chapter 10
P 1. No check figure
P 2. No check figure

P 3. No check figure
P 4. Cash Short or Over, $20.00
P 5. No check figure
P 6. No check figure
P 7. Cash Short or Over, $13.50

Chapter 11
P 1. No check figure.
P 2. Totals: Land: $426,212; Land Improvements: $166,560; Building: $833,940; Machinery: $1,262,640; Expense: $18,120
P 3. 1. Depreciation, Year 3: a. $5,000; b. $8000; c. $2,813
P 4. 1. Depreciation, Year 3: a. $54,250; b. $81,375; c. $53,407
P 5. 2. Depletion expense: $288,000
P 6. Totals: Land: $723,900; Land Improvements: $142,000; Building: $1,383,600; Equipment: $210,800
P 7. 1. Depreciation, Year 3: a. $165,000; b. $132,000; c. $90,000
P 8. 2. Depletion expense: $243,000

Chapter 12
P 1. 2. Total stockholders' equity: $1,342,000
P 2. 1. 20x9 Total dividends: Preferred, $280,000; Common, $820,000
P 3. No check figure
P 4. 2. Total stockholders' equity: $1,765,900
P 5. 1. Ending balance, Treasury Stock, Common: 0
P 6. 2. Total stockholders' equity: $302,400
P 7. 1. 20x9 Total dividends: Preferred, $80,000; Common, $180,000
P 8. 2. Total stockholders' equity: $473,040

Chapter 13
P 1. No check figure
P 2. 1. d. Interest expense: $510,000; 2. d. Interest Expense: $540,000
P 3. 1. Aug. 31. Bond Interest Expense: $377,200; 2. Aug. 31. Bond Interest Expense: $382,200
P 4. June 30. Bond Interest Expense: $289,332; Sept. 1. Bond Interest Expense: $186,580
P 5. 2. Loss on early retirement: $2,261,504
P 6. 1. d. Interest expense: $374,400; 2. d. Interest Expense: $385,600
P 7. 1. Nov. 30. Bond Interest Expense: $1,040,300; 2. Nov. 30. Bond Interest Expense: $1,057,300
P 8. June 30. Bond Interest Expense: $93,195; Sept. 30. Bond Interest Expense: $191,900

Chapter 14
P 1. 2. Difference in net income: $97,600
P 2. 1. Income before extraordinary items: $216,000
P 3. 1. Income from continuing operations, December 31, 20x9: $157,500
P 4. 2. Total stockholders' equity, December 31, 20x8: $2,964,000

P 5. 2. Retained earnings: $250,000; Total stockholders' equity: $2,350,000
P 6. 2. Retained earnings: $148,800; Total stockholders' equity: $2,802,800
P 7. 1. Income before extraordinary items: $410,000
P 8. 2. Retained earnings: $211,600; Total stockholders' equity: $524,500

Chapter 15
P 1. No check figure
P 2. 1. Net cash flows from: operating activities, $46,800; investing activities, ($14,400); financing activities, $102,000
P 3. 1. Net cash flows from: operating activities, ($106,000); investing activities, $34,000; financing activities, $24,000
P 4. 1. Net cash flows from: operating activities, $548,000; investing activities, $6,000; financing activities, ($260,000)
P 5. No check figure
P 6. 1. Net cash flows from: operating activities, $63,300; investing activities, ($12,900); financing activities, $7,000

Chapter 16
P 1. No check figure
P 2. Investment in Waters Corporation, Ending Balance: $734,000
P 3. Total Assets, Consolidated Balance Sheet: $1,280,000
P 4. Total Assets, Consolidated Balance Sheet: $4,488,000
P 5. No check figure
P 6. No check figure
P 7. Total Assets, Consolidated Balance Sheet: $4,790,000

Chapter 17
P 1. No check figure
P 2. Increase: a, b, e, f, l, m
P 3. 1.c. Receivable turnover, 20x8: 14.1 times; 20x7: 14.4 times; 1.e. Inventory turnover, 20x8: 3.6 times; 20x7: 3.5 times
P 4. 1.b. Quick ratio, Lewis: 1.5 times; Ramsey: 1.2 times; 2.d. Return on equity, Lewis: 8.8%; Ramsey: 4.9%
P 5. Increase: d, h, i
P 6. 1.a. Current ratio, 20x8: 1.5 times; 20x7: 1.5 times; 2.c. Return on assets, 20x8: 5.0%; 20x7: 10.7%

Chapter 18
P 1. No check figure
P 2. Projected Cost per Unit: $22.25
P 3. No check figure
P 4. 2. Molding, Week 4, Second shift: −23.53%
P 5. Total traffic flow goal, 24,182
P 6. No check figure

P 7. 2. Decrease in number of rejects: 202
P 8. Average output, week eight: 92,899

Chapter 19
P 1. Cost of goods manufactured: $10,163,200
P 2. 2a. Gross Margin: $191,800; 2d. Cost of Goods Manufactured: $312,100
P 3. 2. Total unit cost: $13.72
P 4. 2. Overhead applied to Job 2214: $29,717
P 5. 2. Total costs assigned to the Grater order, activity-based costing method: $69,280.40
P 6. 1. Predetermined overhead rate for 20x9: $5.014 per machine hour
P 7. 2. Total costs assigned to the Kent order, activity-based costing method: $41,805.60
P 8   1c. Rigger II: $11,665; BioScout: $14,940

Chapter 20
P 1. b. $66,500; i. $57,800
P 2. 1. Overhead applied, January 15: $108,000
P 3. 3. Costs of units sold: $182,857
P 4. 1. Cost per equivalent unit: $6.05; Ending inventory: $7,225
P 5. 1. Cost per equivalent unit: $2.00; Ending inventory: $5,372
P 6. 2. Cost of units sold: $89,647
P 7. 1. Contract revenue, Job Order No. P-12: $28,990
P 8. 1. Cost per equivalent unit: $7.00; Ending inventory: $37,200

Chapter 21
P 1. No check figure
P 2. 1. Product unit cost: $270.00; 4. Product unit cost: $280.47
P 3. 1a. Total materials handling cost rate: 30% per dollar of direct materials
P 4. 3. Total direct cost, toy car work cell: $17,000
P 5. 3. Cost of goods sold: $564,400
P 6. 1. Product unit cost: $878.25
P 7. 3. Product unit cost: $10.43
P 8. 3. Cost of goods sold: $391,520

Chapter 22
P 1. 4. Cost per Job: $81.56
P 2. 1. 7,500 Billable Hours
P 3. 1.a. 3,500 Units
P 4. 2. 190,000 Units
P 5. 3. $805.23 per Job (rounded)
P 6. 1. 740 Systems
P 7. 1.a. 7,900 Units
P 8. 2. 418 Loans

Chapter 23
P 1. 1. Total manufacturing costs budgeted, November: $1,157,000
P 2. 8. Income from operations: $3,086
P 3. 1. Ending cash balance, February: $6,000
P 4. Ending cash balance, February: $17,660
P 5. 1. Net income: $101,812
P 6. 7. Manufactured cost per unit: $0.34
P 7. 1. Ending cash balance, February: $19,555
P 8. 1. Net income: $52,404

Chapter 24
P 1. 1. Flexible Budget, Total Cost: $7,248,000
P 2. 2. Operating Income: $194,782
P 3. 1. Flexible Budget, Contribution margin: $88,200
P 4. 3. Economic value added for 20x8: $21,850
P 5. 1. Residual income: ($2,500)
P 6. 2. Operating Income: $418,555
P 7. 3a. Actual Return on Investment: 6.30%
P 8. 3. Economic value added: $126,000

Chapter 25
P 1. Total standard unit cost of front entrance: $8,510
P 2. 2. Flexible budget formula: Total Budgeted Costs = ($.35 x Units Produced) + $10,500
P 3. 1. Direct materials price variance-Metal: $832 (F); 2. Direct labor rate variance-Molding: $510 (F)
P 4. 1.b. Direct materials quantity variance: $3,720 (U); 1.h. Fixed overhead volume variance: $320 (F)
P 5. a. Actual variable overhead: $42,500
P 6. 1. Total standard direct materials cost per unit: $167.52
P 7. 1. Direct materials price variance-Liquid Plastic: $386 (F); 2. Direct labor rate variance-Trimming/Packing: $56 (U)
P 8. 1.a. Direct materials price variance-Chemicals: $12,200 (F); 1.e. Variable overhead spending variance: $100 (U)

Chapter 26
P 1. 3. Operating income from further processing, bagel sandwiches: $.50
P 2. 1. Segment margin for Book X: $223,560
P 3. 2. $68.20
P 4. 1. Net present value: $99,672
P 5. 1. HTZ Machine: 13.4 %; 2. XJS Machine: 5.5 years
P 6. 1. Total cost to buy: $1,293,750
P 7. 1. Contribution margin per hour for phone calls: $130
P 8. 1.a. Net present value: ($26,895)

About the Authors

Central to the success of any accounting text is the expertise of its author team. This team brings to the text a wealth of classroom teaching experience, relevant business insight, and pedagogical expertise, as well as first-hand knowledge of today's students.

Belverd E. Needles, Jr., Ph.D., C.P.A., C.M.A.
DePaul University

During his more than 30 years of teaching beginning accounting students, Belverd Needles has been an acknowledged innovator in accounting education. He has won teaching and education awards from DePaul University, the American Accounting Association, the Illinois CPA Society, the American Institute of CPAs, and the national honorary society, Beta Alpha Psi. The Conference on Accounting Education, started by Dr. Needles and sponsored by Houghton Mifflin, has been in existence for over 20 years and has helped more than 2,000 accounting instructors improve their teaching. Dr. Needles is editor of the *Accounting Instructors' Report*, a newsletter that thousands of accounting teachers rely on for new ideas in accounting education.

Marian Powers, Ph.D.
Northwestern University

In the course of more than 25 years, Marian Powers has taught beginning accounting at every level, from large lecture halls of 250 students to small classes of graduate students. She is a dynamic teacher who incorporates a variety of instructional strategies designed to broaden students' skills and experiences in critical thinking, group interaction, and communication. Dr. Powers consistently receives the highest rating from students. She brings practical experience to her students, including examples of how managers in all levels of business use and evaluate financial information. In recent years, Dr. Powers has concentrated on executive education. She has taught thousands of executives from leading companies around the world how to read and analyze the financial statements of their own companies and those of their competitors.

Susan V. Crosson, M.S., C.P.A.
Santa Fe Community College, (Florida)

With more than 25 years of teaching experience at the college and university level, Susan Crosson is recognized for her pedagogical expertise in teaching managerial accounting. She has a reputation for being able to engage university students in very large course sections and for encouraging community college students to master accounting. She believes in integrating technology into accounting education and actively uses the Internet to teach online, on-campus, and blended courses. Professor Crosson continues to promote the improvement of accounting education by serving the American Accounting Association and the Florida Institute of CPAs on a variety of committees, task forces, and sections. She is a past recipient of an IMA Faculty Development Grant to blend technology into the classroom, the Florida Association of Community Colleges Professor of the Year Award for Instructional Excellence, and the University of Oklahoma's Halliburton Education Award for Excellence.

Principles of
Accounting

Uses of Accounting Information and the Financial Statements

Today, more people than ever before recognize the importance of accounting information and the profound effect that unethical and misleading financial reports can have on a business, its owners, its employees, its lenders, and the financial markets. In this chapter, we discuss the importance of ethical financial reporting, the uses and users of accounting information, and the financial statements that accountants prepare. We end the chapter with a discussion of generally accepted accounting principles.

LEARNING OBJECTIVES

Making a Statement

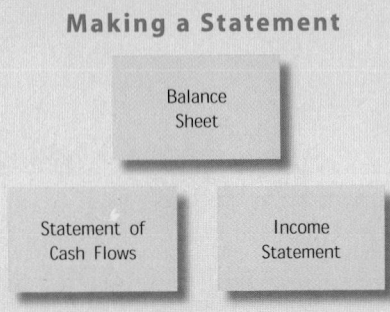

Financial statements measure how well the business is run.

LO1 Define *accounting* and describe its role in making informed decisions, identify business goals and activities, and explain the importance of ethics in accounting.

LO2 Identify the users of accounting information.

LO3 Explain the importance of business transactions, money measure, and separate entity.

LO4 Identify the three basic forms of business organization.

LO5 Define *financial position,* and state the accounting equation.

LO6 Identify the four basic financial statements.

LO7 Explain how generally accepted accounting principles (GAAP) relate to financial statements and the independent CPA's report, and identify the organizations that influence GAAP.

CVS CORPORATION

- Is CVS meeting its goal of profitability?

- As a manager at CVS, what financial knowledge would you need to measure progress toward the company's goals?

- As a potential investor or creditor, what financial knowledge would you need to evaluate CVS's financial performance?

CVS operates a nationwide chain of more than 5,000 drugstores. Having opened more than 1,300 new stores in the last five years, the company has increased sales and profits by more than 50 percent. This performance places it among the fastest-growing retail companies.

Why is CVS considered successful? Customers give the company high marks because of the quality of the products that it sells and the large selection and good service that its stores offer. Investment firms and others with a stake in CVS evaluate the company's success in financial terms.

Whether a company is large or small, the same financial measures are used to evaluate its management and to compare it with other companies. In this chapter, as you learn more about accounting and the business environment, you will become familiar with these financial measures.

Accounting as an Information System

LO1 Define *accounting* and describe its role in making informed decisions, identify business goals and activities, and explain the importance of ethics in accounting.

A**ccounting** is an information system that measures, processes, and communicates financial information about an economic entity.[1] An economic entity is a unit that exists independently, such as a business, a hospital, or a governmental body. Although the central focus of this book is on business entities, we include other economic units at appropriate points in the text and end-of-chapter assignments.

Accountants focus on the needs of decision makers who use financial information, whether those decision makers are inside or outside a business or other economic entity. Accountants provide a vital service by supplying the information decision makers need to make "reasoned choices among alternative uses of scarce resources in the conduct of business and economic activities."[2] As shown in Figure 1, accounting is a link between business activities and decision makers.

1. Accounting measures business activities by recording data about them for future use.

2. The data are stored until needed and then processed to become useful information.

3. The information is communicated through reports to decision makers.

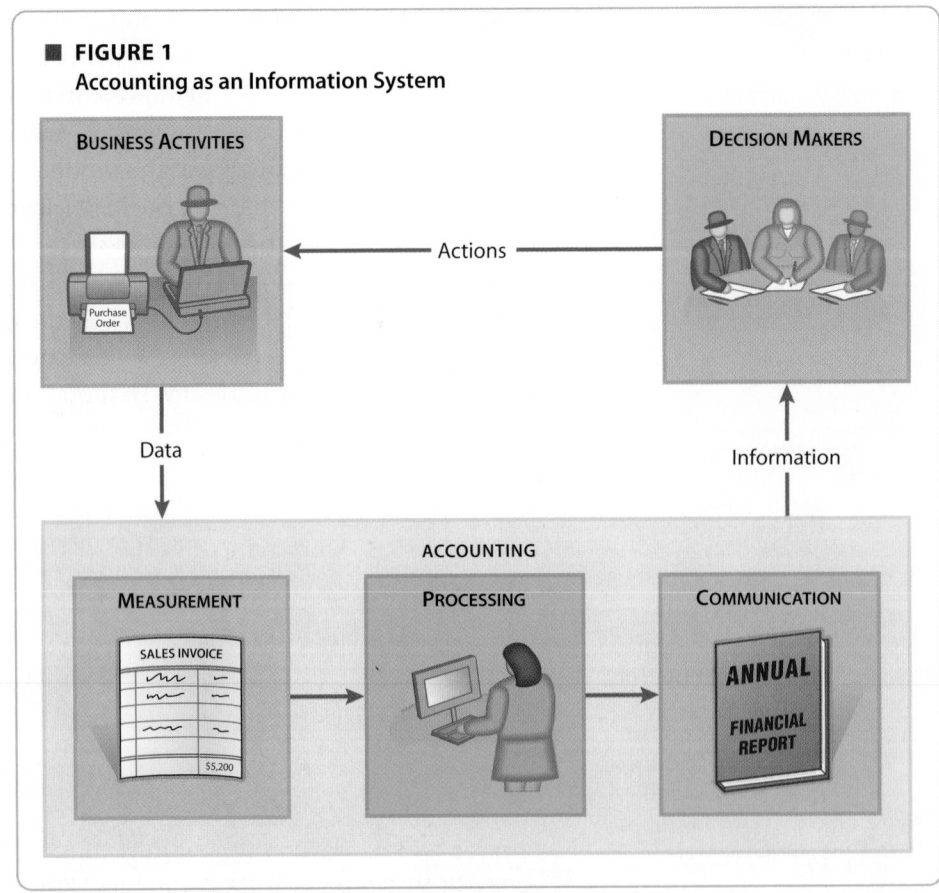

■ **FIGURE 1**
Accounting as an Information System

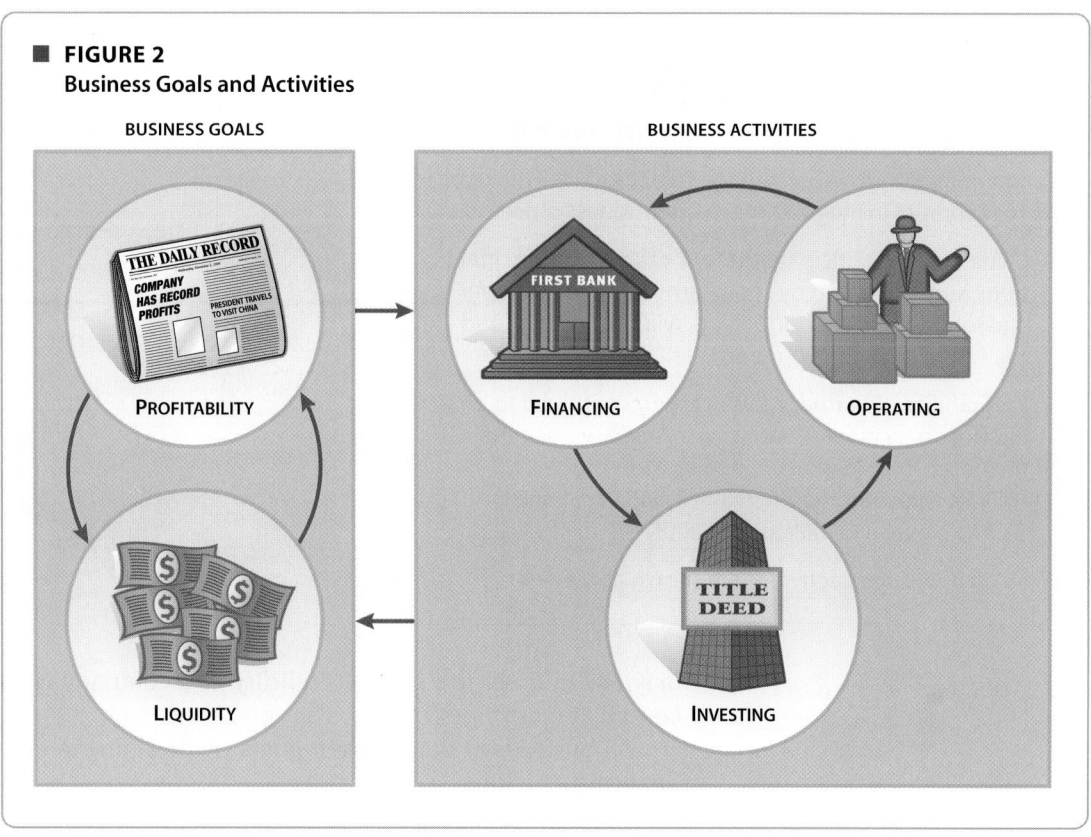

■ FIGURE 2
Business Goals and Activities

In other words, data about business activities are the input to the accounting system, and useful information for decision makers is the output.

Business Goals, Activities, and Performance Measures

A **business** is an economic unit that aims to sell goods and services to customers at prices that will provide an adequate return to its owners. The list that follows contains the names of some well-known businesses and the principal goods or services that they sell.

Wal-Mart Corp.	Comprehensive discount store
Reebok International Ltd.	Athletic footwear and clothing
Best Buy Co.	Consumer electronics, personal computers
Wendy's International Inc.	Food service
Starbucks Corp.	Coffee
Southwest Airlines Co.	Passenger airline

Despite their differences, these businesses have similar goals and engage in similar activities, as shown in Figure 2.

The two major goals of all businesses are profitability and liquidity.

✓ ▶ **Profitability** is the ability to earn enough income to attract and hold investment capital.

✓ ▶ **Liquidity** is the ability to have enough cash to pay debts when they are due.

For example, **Toyota** may meet the goal of profitability by selling many cars at a price that earns a profit, but if its customers do not pay for their cars quickly enough to enable Toyota to pay its suppliers and employees, the company

Study Note

Multiple financial goals, namely profitability and liquidity, signal that more than one measure of performance is of interest to users of accounting information. For example, lenders are concerned primarily with cash flow, and owners are concerned with earnings and withdrawals.

What Does CVS Have to Say About Itself?

In its annual report, CVS's management describes the company's progress in meeting the major business objectives:

Liquidity: "We anticipate that our cash flow from operations, supplemented by short-term commercial paper and long-term debt borrowings, will continue to fund the future growth of our business."

Profitability: "Pharmacy sales growth continued to benefit from new market expansions, increased penetration in existing markets,…and favorable industry trends.…Net earnings increased $305.9 million or 33.3% to over $1.2 billion…in 2005."[3]

CVS's main business activities are shown at the right.

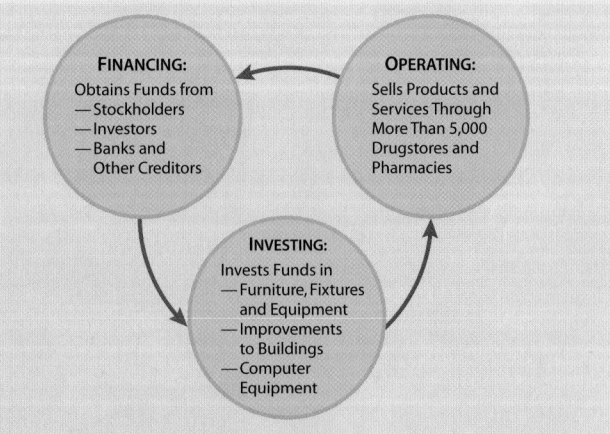

may fail to meet the goal of liquidity. If a company is to survive and be successful, it must meet both goals.

All businesses pursue their goals by engaging in operating, investing, and financing activities.

 ▶ **Operating activities** include selling goods and services to customers, employing managers and workers, buying and producing goods and services, and paying taxes.

 ▶ **Investing activities** involve spending the capital a company receives in productive ways that will help it achieve its objectives. These activities include buying land, buildings, equipment, and other resources that are needed to operate the business and selling them when they are no longer needed.

 ▶ **Financing activities** involve obtaining adequate funds, or capital, to begin operations and to continue operating. These activities include obtaining capital from creditors, such as banks and suppliers, and from owners. They also include repaying creditors and paying a return to the owners.

An important function of accounting is to provide **performance measures**, which indicate whether managers are achieving their business goals and whether the business activities are well managed. These performance measures must align with the goals of the business. For example, **CVS**, like all other companies, considers earned income to be a measure of profitability and cash flow to be a measure of liquidity.

Ratios of accounting measures are also used as performance measures. For instance, a performance measure for operating activities might be the ratio of

Cash Bonuses Depend on Accounting Numbers!

Nearly all businesses use the amounts reported in their financial statements as a basis for rewarding management. Because managers act to achieve these accounting measures, selecting measures that are not easily manipulated is important. Equally important is maintaining a balance of measures that reflect the goals of profitability and liquidity.[4]

expenses to the revenue of the business. A performance measure for financing activities might be the ratio of money owed by the company to the total resources that it controls. Because managers are usually evaluated on whether targeted levels of specific performance measures are achieved, they must have a knowledge of accounting to understand how they are evaluated and how they can improve their performance. In addition, because managers will act to achieve targeted performance measures, these measures must be crafted in a way that motivates them to act in the best interests of the owners of the business.

Financial and Management Accounting

Accounting's role of assisting decision makers by measuring, processing, and communicating financial information is usually divided into the categories of management accounting and financial accounting. Although the functions of management accounting and financial accounting overlap, the two can be distinguished by the principal users of the information they provide.

Management accounting provides *internal* decision makers who are charged with achieving the goals of profitability and liquidity with information about operating, investing, and financing activities. Managers and employees who conduct the activities of the business need information that tells them how they have done in the past and what they can expect in the future. For example, **The Gap**, a retail clothing business, needs an operating report on each outlet that tells how much was sold at that outlet and what costs were incurred, and it needs a budget for each outlet that projects the sales and costs for the next year.

Financial accounting generates reports and communicates them to *external* decision makers so they can evaluate how well the business has achieved its goals. These reports are called **financial statements**. **CVS**, whose stock is traded on the New York Stock Exchange, sends its financial statements to its owners (called *stockholders*), its banks and other creditors, and government regulators. Financial statements report directly on the goals of profitability and liquidity and are used extensively both inside and outside a business to evaluate the business's success. It is important for every person involved with a business to understand financial statements. They are a central feature of accounting and a primary focus of this book.

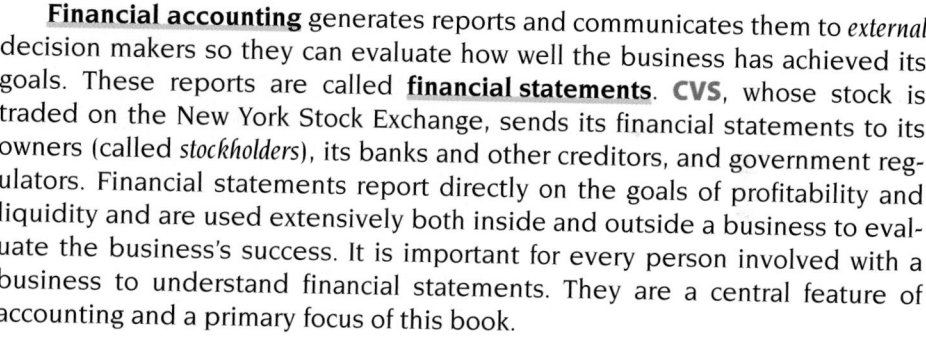

Processing Accounting Information

It is important to distinguish accounting from the ways in which accounting information is processed by bookkeeping, computers, and management information systems.

Accounting includes the design of an information system that meets users' needs, and its major goals are the analysis, interpretation, and use of information. **Bookkeeping**, on the other hand, is mechanical and repetitive; it is the process of recording financial transactions and keeping financial records. It is a small—but important—part of accounting.

Today, computers collect, organize, and communicate vast amounts of information with great speed. Computers can perform both routine bookkeeping chores and complex calculations. Accountants were among the earliest and most enthusiastic users of computers, and today they use computers in all aspects of their work.

FOCUS ON BUSINESS PRACTICE
How Did Accounting Develop?

Accounting is a very old discipline. Forms of it have been essential to commerce for more than five thousand years. Accounting, in a version close to what we know today, gained widespread use in the 1400s, especially in Italy, where it was instrumental in the development of shipping, trade, construction, and other forms of commerce. This system of double-entry bookkeeping was documented by the famous Italian mathematician, scholar, and philosopher Fra Luca Pacioli. In 1494, Pacioli published his most important work, *Summa de Arithmetica, Geometrica, Proportioni et Proportionalita*, which contained a detailed description of accounting as practiced in that age. This book became the most widely read book on mathematics in Italy and firmly established Pacioli as the "Father of Accounting."

Study Note

Computerized accounting information is only as reliable and useful as the data that go into the system. The accountant must have a thorough understanding of the concepts that underlie accounting to ensure the data's reliability and usefulness.

Computers make it possible to create a management information system to organize a business's many information needs. A **management information system (MIS)** consists of the interconnected subsystems that provide the information needed to run a business. The accounting information system is the most important subsystem because it plays the key role of managing the flow of economic data to all parts of a business and to interested parties outside the business.

Ethical Financial Reporting

Ethics is a code of conduct that applies to everyday life. It addresses the question of whether actions are right or wrong. Actions—whether ethical or unethical, right or wrong—are the product of individual decisions. Thus, when an organization acts unethically by using false advertising, cheating customers, polluting the environment, or treating employees unfairly, it is not the organization that is responsible—it is the members of management and other employees who have made a conscious decision to act in this manner.

Ethics is especially important in preparing financial reports because users of these reports must depend on the good faith of the people involved in their preparation. Users have no other assurance that the reports are accurate and fully disclose all relevant facts.

The intentional preparation of misleading financial statements is called **fraudulent financial reporting**.[5] It can result from the distortion of records (e.g., the manipulation of inventory records), falsified transactions (e.g., fictitious sales), or the misapplication of various accounting principles. There are a number of motives for fraudulent reporting—for instance, to cover up financial weakness to obtain a higher price when a company is sold, to meet the expectations of investors, owners, and financial analysts, or to obtain a loan. The incentive can also be personal gain, such as additional compensation, promotion, or avoidance of penalties for poor performance.

Whatever the motive for fraudulent financial reporting, it can have dire consequences, as the accounting scandals that erupted at **Enron Corporation** and **WorldCom** in 2001 and 2002 attest. Unethical financial reporting and accounting practices at those two major corporations caused thousands of people to lose their jobs, their investment incomes, and their pensions. They also resulted in prison sentences and fines for the corporate executives who were involved.

In 2002, Congress passed the **Sarbanes-Oxley Act** to regulate financial reporting and the accounting profession among other things. This legislation

In the wake of one of the largest accounting scandals in history, current and former members of Enron's board of directors John Duncan (*left*), Herbert Winokur (*center*), and Norman Blake listen to opening remarks at a hearing of the Senate Permanent Subcommittee on Investigations, May 7, 2002. Unethical accounting practices at Enron led to the collapse of the company and the loss of thousands of jobs and pensions.

ordered the Securities and Exchange Commission (SEC) to draw up rules requiring the chief executives and chief financial officers of all publicly traded U.S. companies to swear that, based on their knowledge, the quarterly statements and annual reports that their companies file with the SEC are accurate and complete. Violation can result in criminal penalties.

A company's management expresses its duty to ensure that financial reports are not false or misleading in the management report that appears in the company's annual report. For example, **CVS's** management report contains the following statement:

> We are responsible for establishing and maintaining effective internal control over financial reporting. . . .Based on our evaluation, we conclude our Company's internal control . . . provides reasonable assurance that assets are safeguarded and that the financial records are reliable for preparing financial statements.[6]

However, it is accountants, not management, who physically prepare and audit financial reports. To meet the high ethical standards of the accounting profession, they must apply accounting concepts in such a way as to present a fair view of a company's operations and financial position and to avoid misleading readers of their reports. Like the conduct of a company, the ethical conduct of a profession is a collection of individual actions. As a member of a profession, each accountant has a responsibility—not only to the profession, but also to employers, clients, and society as a whole—to ensure that any report he or she prepares or audits provides accurate, reliable information.

The high regard that the public has historically had for the accounting profession is evidence that an overwhelming number of accountants have upheld the ethics of the profession. Even as the Enron and WorldCom scandals were making headlines, a Gallup Poll showed an increase of 14 percent in the accounting profession's reputation between 2001 and 2002—larger than the increase for any other profession and one that placed it among the most highly rated.[7]

Accountants and top managers are, of course, not the only people responsible for ethical financial reporting. Managers and employees at all levels must be conscious of their responsibility for providing accurate financial information to the people who rely on it.

S T O P • R E V I E W • A P P L Y

1-1. Why is accounting considered an information system?

1-2. What is the role of accounting in the decision-making process, and what broad business goals and activities does it help management achieve and manage?

1-3. Distinguish between management accounting and financial accounting.

1-4. Distinguish among these terms: *accounting, bookkeeping,* and *management information systems.*

1-5. What is the difference between misstated financial statements and fraudulent financial reporting?

Suggested answers to all Stop, Review, and Apply questions are available at http://college.hmco.com/accounting/needles/poa/10e/student_home.html.

Decision Makers: The Users of Accounting Information

LO2 Identify the users of accounting information.

As shown in Figure 3, the people who use accounting information to make decisions fall into three categories:

1. Those who manage a business

2. Those outside a business enterprise who have a direct financial interest in the business

3. Those who have an indirect financial interest in a business

These categories apply to governmental and not-for-profit organizations as well as to profit-oriented ventures.

Management

Management refers to the people who are responsible for operating a business and meeting its goals of profitability and liquidity. In a small business, management may consist solely of the owners. In a large business, management usually consists of people who have been hired to do the job. Managers must decide what to do, how to do it, and whether the results match their original plans. Successful managers consistently make the right decisions based on timely and valid information. To make good decisions, managers at **CVS** and other companies need answers to such questions as:

▶ What were the company's earnings during the past quarter?

▶ Is the rate of return to the owners adequate?

▶ Does the company have enough cash?

▶ Which products or services are most profitable?

▶ What is the cost of manufacturing each product or providing each service?

Study Note

Managers are internal users of accounting information.

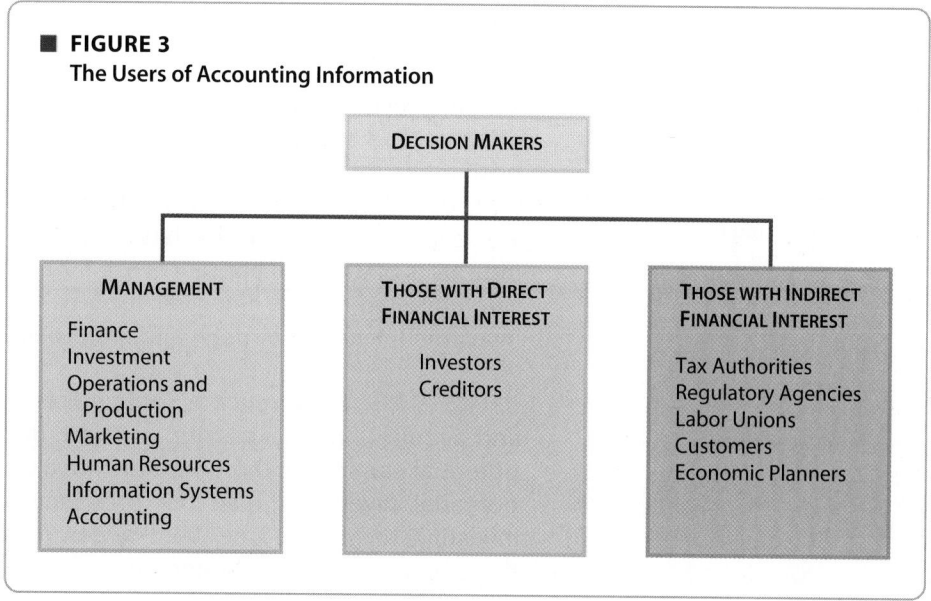

■ FIGURE 3
The Users of Accounting Information

Because so many key decisions are based on accounting data, management is one of the most important users of accounting information.

In its decision-making process, management performs functions that are essential to the operation of a business. Although large businesses have more elaborate operations than small ones, the same basic functions must be performed, and each requires accounting information on which to base decisions. The basic management functions are:

Financing the business—obtaining funds so that a company can begin and continue operating

Investing resources—investing assets in productive ways that support a company's goals

Producing goods and services—managing the production of goods and services

Marketing goods and services—overseeing how goods or services are advertised, sold, and distributed

Managing employees—overseeing the hiring, evaluation, and compensation of employees

Providing information to decision makers—gathering data about all aspects of a company's operations, organizing the data into usable information, and providing reports to managers and appropriate outside parties. Accounting plays a key role in this function.

FOCUS ON BUSINESS PRACTICE
What Do CFOs Do?

According to a recent survey, the chief financial officer (CFO) is the "new business partner of the chief executive officer" (CEO). CFOs are increasingly required to take on responsibilities for strategic planning, mergers and acquisitions, and tasks involving international operations, and many of them are becoming CEOs of their companies. Those who do become CEOs are finding that "a financial background is invaluable when they're saddled with the responsibility of making big calls."[8]

Users with a Direct Financial Interest

Another group of decision makers who need accounting information are those with a direct financial interest in a business. They depend on accounting to measure and report information about how a business has performed. Most businesses periodically publish a set of general-purpose financial statements that report their success in meeting the goals of profitability and liquidity. These statements show what has happened in the past, and they are important indicators of what will happen in the future. Many people outside the company carefully study these financial reports. The two most important groups are investors (including owners) and creditors.

Investors   Those, such as **CVS's** stockholders, who may invest in a business and acquire a part ownership in it are interested in its past success and its potential earnings. A thorough study of a company's financial statements helps potential investors judge the prospects for a profitable investment. After investing, they must continually review their commitment, again by examining the company's financial statements.

Creditors   Most companies, including **CVS**, borrow money for both long- and short-term operating needs. Creditors, those who lend money or deliver goods and services before being paid, are interested mainly in whether a company will have the cash to pay interest charges and to repay the debt at the appropriate time. They study a company's liquidity and cash flow as well as its profitability. Banks, finance companies, mortgage companies, securities firms, insurance firms, suppliers, and other lenders must analyze a company's financial position before they make a loan.

Users with an Indirect Financial Interest

In recent years, society as a whole, through governmental and public groups, has become one of the largest and most important users of accounting information. Users who need accounting information to make decisions on public issues include tax authorities, regulatory agencies, and various other groups.

Tax Authorities   Government at every level is financed through the collection of taxes. Companies and individuals pay many kinds of taxes, including federal, state, and city income taxes; social security and other payroll taxes; excise taxes; and sales taxes. Each tax requires special tax returns and often a complex set of records as well. Proper reporting is generally a matter of law and can be very complicated. The Internal Revenue Code, for instance, contains thousands of rules governing the preparation of the accounting information used in computing federal income taxes.

Regulatory Agencies   Most companies must report periodically to one or more regulatory agencies at the federal, state, and local levels. For example, all publicly traded corporations must report periodically to the **Securities and Exchange Commission (SEC)**. This body, set up by Congress to protect the public, regulates the issuing, buying, and selling of stocks in the United States. Companies listed on a stock exchange also must meet the special reporting requirements of their exchange.

Other Groups   Labor unions study the financial statements of corporations as part of preparing for contract negotiations; a company's income and costs often play an important role in these negotiations. Those who advise investors and creditors—financial analysts, brokers, underwriters, lawyers, economists, and the financial press—also have an indirect interest in the financial performance and prospects of a business. Consumer groups, customers, and the general public have become more concerned about the financing and earnings of corporations as well as the effects that corporations have on inflation, the environment, social issues, and the quality of life. And economic planners, among them the President's Council of Economic Advisers and the Federal Reserve Board, use aggregated accounting information to set and evaluate economic policies and programs.

Governmental and Not-for-Profit Organizations

More than 30 percent of the U.S. economy is generated by governmental and not-for-profit organizations (hospitals, universities, professional organizations, and charities). The managers of these diverse entities perform the same functions as managers of businesses, and they therefore have the same need for accounting information and a knowledge of how to use it. Their functions include raising funds from investors (including owners), creditors, taxpayers, and donors, and deploying scarce resources. They must also plan how to pay for operations and to repay creditors on a timely basis. In addition, they have an obligation to report their financial performance to legislators, boards, and donors, as well as to deal with tax authorities, regulators, and labor unions. Although most of the examples in this text focus on business enterprises, the same basic principles apply to governmental and not-for-profit organizations.

STOP • REVIEW • APPLY

2-1. Who are the decision makers that use accounting information?

2-2. A business is an economic unit whose goal is to sell goods or services at prices that will provide an adequate return to its owners. What functions must management perform to achieve this goal?

2-3. Why are investors (and owners) and creditors interested in reviewing a company's financial statements?

2-4. Among the users of accounting information are people and organizations with an indirect interest in business entities. Briefly identify these people and organizations.

2-5. Why has society as a whole become one of the largest users of accounting information?

Accounting Measurement

LO3 Explain the importance of business transactions, money measure, and separate entity.

In this section, we begin the study of the measurement aspects of accounting—that is, what accounting actually measures. To make an accounting measurement, the accountant must answer four basic questions:

1. What is measured?

2. When should the measurement be made?

3. What value should be placed on what is measured?

4. How should what is measured be classified?

Accountants in industry, professional associations, public accounting, government, and academic circles debate the answers to these questions constantly, and the answers change as new knowledge and practice require. But the basis of today's accounting practice rests on a number of widely accepted concepts and conventions, which are described in this book. We begin by focusing on the first question: What is measured? We discuss the other three questions (recognition, valuation, and classification) in the next chapter.

Every system must define what it measures, and accounting is no exception. Basically, financial accounting uses money to gauge the impact of business transactions on separate business entities.

Business Transactions

Business transactions are economic events that affect a business's financial position. Businesses can have hundreds or even thousands of transactions every day. These transactions are the raw material of accounting reports.

A transaction can be an exchange of value (a purchase, sale, payment, collection, or loan) between two or more parties. A transaction also can be an economic event that has the same effect as an exchange transaction but that does not involve an exchange. Some examples of "nonexchange" transactions are losses from fire, flood, explosion, and theft; physical wear and tear on machinery and equipment; and the day-by-day accumulation of interest.

To be recorded, a transaction must relate directly to a business entity. Suppose a customer buys toothpaste from **CVS** but has to buy shampoo from a competing store because CVS is out of shampoo. The transaction in which the toothpaste was sold is entered in CVS's records. However, the purchase of the shampoo from the competitor is not entered in CVS's records because even though it indirectly affects CVS economically, it does not involve a direct exchange of value between CVS and the customer.

Money Measure

All business transactions are recorded in terms of money. This concept is called **money measure**. Of course, nonfinancial information may also be recorded, but it is through the recording of monetary amounts that a business's transactions and activities are measured. Money is the only factor common to all business transactions, and thus it is the only unit of measure capable of producing financial data that can be compared.

The monetary unit a business uses depends on the country in which the business resides. For example, in the United States, the basic unit of money is the dollar. In Japan, it is the yen; in Europe, the euro; and in the United Kingdom, the pound. In international transactions, exchange rates must be used to translate from one currency to another. An **exchange rate** is the value of one currency in terms of another. For example, a British person purchasing goods from a U.S. company like **CVS** and paying in U.S. dollars must exchange British pounds for U.S. dollars before making payment. In effect, currencies are goods that can be bought and sold.

Table 1 illustrates the exchange rates for several currencies in dollars. It shows the exchange rate for British pounds as $1.75 per pound on a particular

Study Note

The common unit of measurement used in the United States for financial reporting purposes is the dollar.

TABLE 1. Examples of Foreign Exchange Rates

Country	Price in $ U.S.	Country	Price in $U.S.
Australia (dollar)	0.73	Hong Kong (dollar)	0.13
Brazil (real)	0.47	Japan (yen)	0.008
Britain (pound)	1.75	Mexico (peso)	0.09
Canada (dollar)	0.87	Russia (ruble)	0.036
Europe (euro)	1.21	Singapore (dollar)	0.62

Source: The Wall Street Journal, April 17, 2006.

date. Like the prices of many goods, currency prices change daily according to supply and demand. For example, a year earlier, the exchange rate for British pounds was $1.88. Although our discussion in this book focuses on dollars, some examples and assignments involve foreign currencies.

Separate Entity

For accounting purposes, a business is a **separate entity**, distinct not only from its creditors and customers but also from its owners. It should have its own set of financial records, and its records and reports should refer only to its own affairs.

For example, Just Because Flowers Company should have a bank account separate from the account of Holly Sapp, the owner. Holly Sapp may own a home, a car, and other property, and she may have personal debts, but these are not the resources or debts of Just Because Flowers. Holly Sapp may own another business, say a stationery shop. If she does, she should have a completely separate set of records for each business.

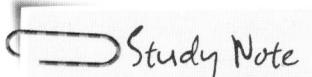
Study Note

For accounting purposes, a business is *always* separate and distinct from its owners, creditors, and customers. Note, however, that there is a difference between separate economic entity and separate legal entity.

S T O P • R E V I E W • A P P L Y

3-1. Use the terms *business transactions*, *money measure*, and *separate entity* in a single sentence that demonstrates their relevance to financial accounting.

3-2. Suppose you buy a disposable camera from **CVS**. From CVS's perspective, how would the terms *business transactions*, *money measure*, and *separate entity* relate to your purchase?

The Forms of Business Organization

LO4 Identify the three basic forms of business organization.

The three basic forms of business organization are the sole proprietorship, the partnership, and the corporation. Accountants recognize each form as an economic unit separate from its owners. Legally, however, only the corporation is separate from its owners. Here, we point out the most important features of each form of business.

■ FIGURE 4
Number and Receipts of U.S. Proprietorships, Partnerships, and Corporations, 2004

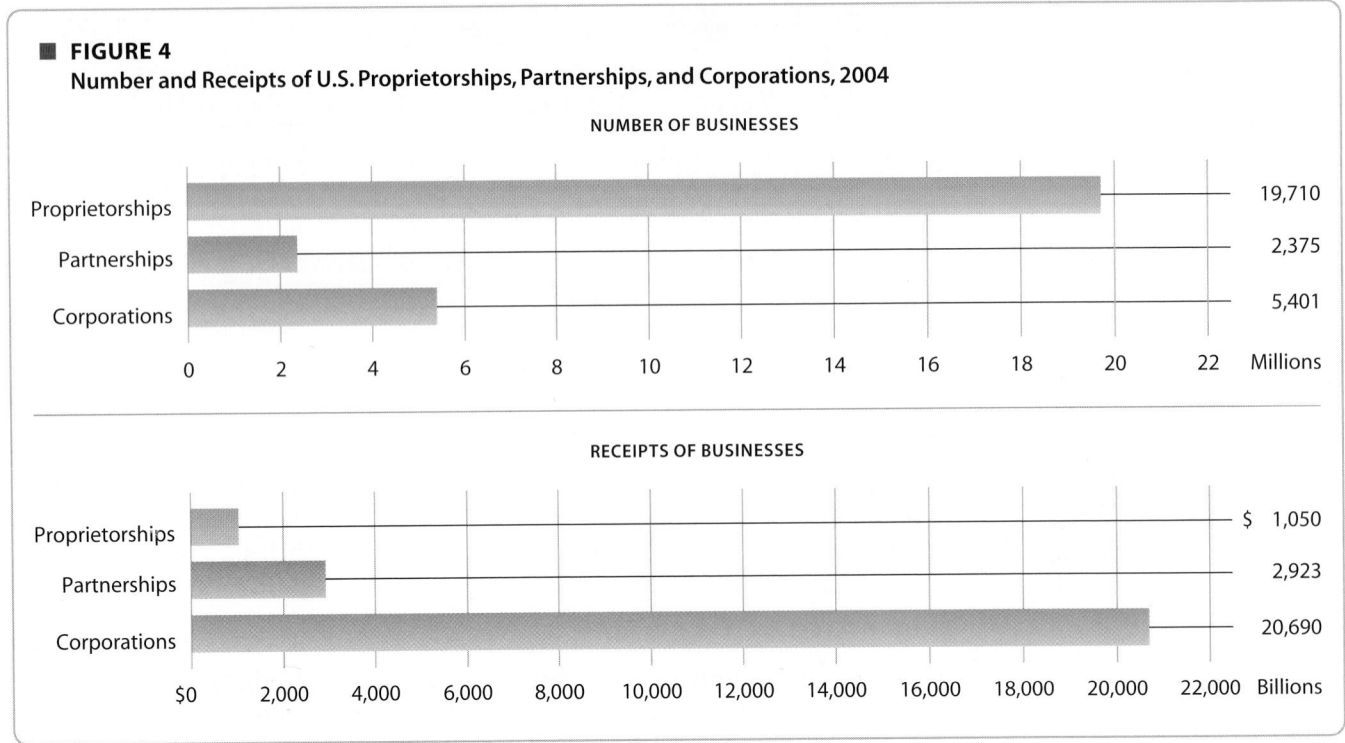

Source: U.S. Treasury Department, Internal Revenue Service, *Statistics of Income Bulletin,* Winter 2006.

A **sole proprietorship** is a business owned by one person.* The owner takes all the profits or losses of the business and is liable for all its obligations. As Figure 4 shows, sole proprietorships represent the largest number of businesses in the United States, but typically they are the smallest in terms of receipts.

A **partnership** is like a sole proprietorship in most ways, but it has two or more owners. The partners share the profits and losses of the business according to a prearranged formula. Generally, any partner can obligate the business to another party, and the personal resources of each partner can be called on to pay the obligations. A partnership must be dissolved if the ownership changes, as when a partner leaves or dies. If the business is to continue as a partnership after this occurs, a new partnership must be formed.

Both the sole proprietorship and the partnership are convenient ways of separating the owners' commercial activities from their personal activities. Legally, however, there is no economic separation between the owners and the businesses. A **corporation**, on the other hand, is a business unit chartered by the state and legally separate from its owners (the stockholders). The stockholders, whose ownership is represented by shares of stock, do not directly control the corporation's operations. Instead, they elect a board of directors to run the corporation for their benefit. In exchange for their limited involvement in the corporation's operations, stockholders enjoy limited liability; that is, their risk of loss is limited to the amount they paid for their shares. Thus, stockholders are often willing to invest in risky, but potentially profitable activities. Also, because stockholders can sell their shares without dissolving the corpo-

> ⌐◯ Study Note
>
> A key disadvantage of a partnership is the unlimited liability of its owners. Unlimited liability can be avoided by organizing the business as a corporation or, in some states, by forming what is known as a limited liability partnership (LLP).

---

*Accounting for a sole proprietorship is simpler than accounting for a partnership or corporation. For that reason, we focus on the sole proprietorship in the early part of this book. At critical points, however, we call attention to the essential differences between accounting for a sole proprietorship and accounting for a partnership or corporation.

Avalon International Breads in Detroit is a partnership owned by Jackie Victor and Ann Perrault. Because it is a partnership, the owners share the profits and losses of the business, and their personal resources can be called on to pay the obligations of the business.

ration, the life of a corporation is unlimited and not subject to the whims or health of a proprietor or a partner.

S T O P • R E V I E W • A P P L Y

4-1. How do sole proprietorships, partnerships, and corporations differ?

4-2. How is the owner of a sole proprietorship similar to an investor in a corporation? How do the two differ?

4-3. What are the principal characteristics of a partnership?

Financial Position and the Accounting Equation

LO5 Define *financial position*, and state the accounting equation.

inancial position refers to a company's economic resources, such as cash, inventory, and buildings, and the claims against those resources at a particular time. Another term for claims is *equities*.

Every company has two types of equities: creditors' equities, such as bank loans, and owner's equity. The sum of these equities equals a company's resources:

$$\text{Economic Resources} = \text{Creditors' Equities} + \text{Owner's Equity}$$

FOCUS ON BUSINESS PRACTICE

Are Most Corporations Big or Small Businesses?

Most people think of corporations as large national or global companies whose shares of stock are held by thousands of people and institutions. Indeed, corporations can be huge and have many stockholders. However, of the approximately 4 million corporations in the United States, only about 15,000 have stock that is publicly bought and sold. The vast majority of corporations are small businesses privately held by a few stockholders. Illinois alone has more than 250,000 corporations. Thus, the study of corporations is just as relevant to small businesses as it is to large ones.

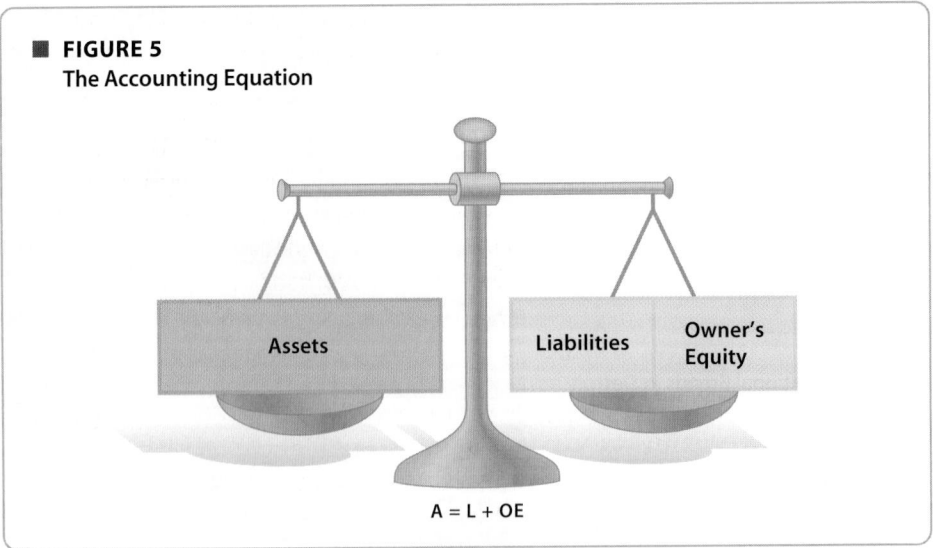

■ **FIGURE 5**
The Accounting Equation

A = L + OE

In accounting terminology, economic resources are called *assets* and creditors' equities are called *liabilities*. So the equation can be written like this:

Assets = Liabilities + Owner's Equity

This equation is known as the **accounting equation**. The two sides of the equation must always be equal, or "in balance," as shown in Figure 5. To evaluate the financial effects of business activities, it is important to understand their effects on this equation.

Assets

Assets are the economic resources of a company that are expected to benefit the company's future operations. Certain kinds of assets—for example, cash and money that customers owe to the company (called *accounts receivable*)—are monetary items. Other assets—inventories (goods held for sale), land, buildings, and equipment—are nonmonetary, physical items. Still other assets—the rights granted by patents, trademarks, and copyrights—are nonphysical.

Liabilities

Liabilities are a business's present obligations to pay cash, transfer assets, or provide services to other entities in the future. Among these obligations are amounts owed to suppliers for goods or services bought on credit (called *accounts payable*), borrowed money (e.g., money owed on bank loans), salaries and wages owed to employees, taxes owed to the government, and services to be performed.

As debts, liabilities are claims recognized by law. That is, the law gives creditors the right to force the sale of a company's assets if the company fails to pay its debts. Creditors have rights over owners and must be paid in full before the owners receive anything, even if payment of the debt uses up all the assets of the business.

Owner's Equity

Owner's equity represents the claims by the owner of a business to the assets of the business. Theoretically, owner's equity is what would be left if all liabilities were paid, and it is sometimes said to equal **net assets**. By rearranging the accounting equation, we can define owner's equity this way:

$$\text{Owner's Equity} = \text{Assets} - \text{Liabilities}$$

Owner's equity is affected by the owner's investments in and withdrawals from the business and by the business's revenues and expenses.

Owner's investments are assets that the owner puts into the business (e.g., by transferring cash from a personal bank account to the business's bank account). In this case, the assets (cash) of the business increase, and the owner's equity in those assets also increases. Owner's withdrawals are assets that the owner takes out of the business (e.g., by transferring cash from the business's bank account to a personal bank account). In this case, the assets of the business decrease, as does the owner's equity in the business.

Simply stated, **revenues** and **expenses** are the increases and decreases in owner's equity that result from operating a business. For example, the amount a customer pays (or agrees to pay in the future) to **CVS** for a product or service is a revenue for CVS. CVS's assets (cash or accounts receivable) increase, as does its stockholders' (owner's) equity in those assets. On the other hand, the amount CVS must pay out (or agree to pay out) so that it can provide a product or service is an expense. In this case, the assets (cash) decrease or the liabilities (accounts payable) increase, and the owner's equity decreases.

Generally, a company is successful if its revenues exceed its expenses. When revenues exceed expenses, the difference is called **net income**. When expenses exceed revenues, the difference is called **net loss**. It is important not to confuse expenses and withdrawals, both of which reduce owner's equity. In summary, owner's equity is the accumulated net income (revenues − expenses) less withdrawals over the life of the business.

STOP • REVIEW • APPLY

5-1. What are assets?

5-2. How are liabilities and owner's equity similar, and how do they differ?

5-3. What three elements affect owner's equity? What is the effect of each?

The Accounting Equation and Net Income Johnson Company had assets of $140,000 and liabilities of $60,000 at the beginning of the year, and assets of $200,000 and liabilities of $70,000 at the end of the year. During the year, $20,000 was invested in the business, and withdrawals of $24,000 were made. What amount of net income did the company earn during the year?

Beginning of the year

Assets	=	Liabilities	+	Owner's Equity
$140,000	=	$60,000	+	**$80,000**

During year

		Investment	+	$20,000
		Withdrawals	−	24,000
		Net income		?

End of year

$200,000	=	$70,000	+	**$130,000**

SOLUTION

Net income = $54,000

Start by finding the owner's equity at the beginning of the year. (Check: $140,000 − $60,000 = $80,000)

Then find the owner's equity at the end of the year. (Check: $200,000 − $70,000 = $130,000)

Then determine net income by calculating how the transactions during the year led to the owner's equity amount at the end of the year. (Check: $80,000 + $20,000 − $24,000 + $54,000 = $130,000)

Financial Statements

Study Note

Businesses use four basic financial statements to communicate financial information to decision makers.

Financial statements are the primary means of communicating important accounting information about a business to those who have an interest in the business. These statements are models of the business enterprise in that they show the business in financial terms. As is true of all models, however, financial statements are not perfect pictures of the real thing. Rather, they are the accountant's best effort to represent what is real. Four major financial statements are used to communicate accounting information about a business: the income statement, the statement of owner's equity, the balance sheet, and the statement of cash flows.

Income Statement

The **income statement** summarizes the revenues earned and expenses incurred by a business over an accounting period (see Exhibit 1). Many people consider it the most important financial report because it shows whether a business achieved its profitability goal—that is, whether it earned an acceptable income. Exhibit 1 shows that Ramirez Agency had revenues in the form of commissions earned of $7,000. From this amount, total expenses of $2,800 were deducted (equipment rental expense of $1,400, wages expense of $800, and utilities expense of $600) to arrive at net income of $4,200. To show the period to which the statement applies, it is dated "For the Month Ended December 31, 20xx."

Statement of Owner's Equity

The **statement of owner's equity** shows the changes in owner's equity over an accounting period. In Exhibit 2, beginning owner's equity is zero because Ramirez Agency began operations in this accounting period. During the month, the owner, Rosa Ramirez, invested $100,000 in the business, and the company earned an income (as shown on the income statement) of $4,200. Deducted

EXHIBIT 1 ▶   Income Statement for Ramirez Agency

Ramirez Agency
Income Statement
For the Month Ended December 31, 20xx

Revenues

Commissions earned		$7,000
Expenses		
Equipment rental expense	$1,400	
Wages expense	800	
Utilities expense	600	
Total expenses		2,800
Net income		$4,200

EXHIBIT 2 ▶ | **Statement of Owner's Equity for Ramirez Agency**

Ramirez Agency
Statement of Owner's Equity
For the Month Ended December 31, 20xx

R. Ramirez, Capital, December 1, 20xx	$ 0
Investment by R. Ramirez	100,000
Net income for the month	4,200
Subtotal	$104,200
Less withdrawals	1,200
R. Ramirez, Capital, December 31, 20xx	$103,000

from this amount are $1,200 of withdrawals that the owner made during the month, leaving an ending balance of $103,000 of capital in the business.

The Balance Sheet

The purpose of a **balance sheet** is to show the financial position of a business on a certain date, usually the end of the month or year (see Exhibit 3). For this reason, it often is called the *statement of financial position* and is dated as of a specific date. The balance sheet presents a view of the business as the holder of resources, or assets, that are equal to the claims against those assets. The claims consist of the company's liabilities and the owner's equity in the company. Exhibit 3 shows that Ramirez Agency has several categories of assets, which total $104,200. These assets equal the total liabilities of $1,200 (accounts payable) plus the ending balance of owner's equity of $103,000. Notice that the amount of the owner's Capital account on the balance sheet comes from the ending balance on the statement of owner's equity.

Statement of Cash Flows

Whereas the income statement focuses on a company's profitability, the **statement of cash flows** focuses on its liquidity (see Exhibit 4). **Cash flows** are the inflows and outflows of cash into and out of a business. Net cash flows are the difference between the inflows and outflows. The statement of cash flows shows the cash produced by business operations during an accounting period

▼ EXHIBIT 3

Balance Sheet for Ramirez Agency

Ramirez Agency
Balance Sheet
December 31, 20xx

Assets		Liabilities	
Cash	$ 31,200	Accounts payable	$ 1,200
Accounts receivable	2,000	Total liabilities	$ 1,200
Supplies	1,000		
Land	20,000	**Owner's Equity**	
Buildings	50,000	R. Ramirez, Capital	103,000
Total assets	$104,200	Total liabilities and owner's equity	$104,200

▼ **EXHIBIT 4**

Statement of Cash Flows for Ramirez Agency

Ramirez Agency
Statement of Cash Flows
For the Month Ended December 31, 20xx

Cash flows from operating activities

Net income		$ 4,200
Adjustments to reconcile net income to net cash flows from operating activities		
Increase in accounts receivable	($ 2,000)	
Increase in supplies	(1,000)	
Increase in accounts payable	1,200	(1,800)
Net cash flows from operating activities		$ 2,400

Cash flows from investing activities

Purchase of land	($ 20,000)	
Purchase of building	(50,000)	
Net cash flows from investing activities		(70,000)

Cash flows from financing activities

Investments by owner	$100,000	
Withdrawals	(1,200)	
Net cash flows from financing activities		98,800
Net increase (decrease) in cash		$31,200
Cash at beginning of month		0
Cash at end of month		$31,200

Note: Parentheses indicate a negative amount.

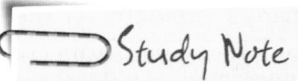 Study Note

The purpose of the statement of cash flows is to explain the change in cash in terms of operating, investing, and financing activities over an accounting period. It provides valuable information that cannot be determined in an examination of the other financial statements.

as well as important investing and financing transactions that took place during the period. Notice that the statement of cash flows in Exhibit 4 explains how Ramirez Agency's cash balance changed during the period. Cash increased by $31,200. Operating activities produced net cash flows of $2,400, and financing activities produced net cash flows of $98,800. Investing activities used cash flows of $70,000.

The statement of cash flows is related directly to the other three financial statements. Notice that net income comes from the income statement and that withdrawals come from the statement of owner's equity. The other items in the statement represent changes in the balance sheet accounts: accounts receivable, supplies, accounts payable, land, and buildings. Here we focus on the importance and overall structure of the statement. Its construction and use are discussed in a later chapter.

Relationships Among the Financial Statements

Exhibit 5 illustrates the relationships among the four financial statements by showing how they would appear for Ramirez Agency. The period covered is the month of December 20xx. Notice the similarity of the headings at the top of each statement. Each identifies the company and the kind of statement. The income statement, the statement of owner's equity, and the statement of cash

▼ **EXHIBIT 5**

Income Statement, Statement of Owner's Equity, Balance Sheet, and Statement of Cash Flows for Ramirez Agency

Ramirez Agency
Income Statement
For the Month Ended December 31, 20xx

Revenues

Commissions earned		$7,000

Expenses

Equipment rental expense	$1,400	
Wages expense	800	
Utilities expense	600	
Total expenses		2,800
Net income		$4,200

Ramirez Agency
Statement of Cash Flows
For the Month Ended December 31, 20xx

Cash flows from operating activities

Net income		$4,200
Adjustments to reconcile net income to net cash flows from operating activities		
Increase in accounts receivable	($ 2,000)	
Increase in supplies	(1,000)	
Increase in accounts payable	1,200	(1,800)
Net cash flows from operating activities		$2,400

Cash flows from investing activities

Purchase of land	($20,000)	
Purchase of building	(50,000)	
Net cash flows from investing activities		(70,000)

Cash flows from financing activities

Investments by owner	$100,000	
Withdrawals	(1,200)	
Net cash flows from financing activities		98,800
Net increase (decrease) in cash		$31,200
Cash at beginning of month		0
Cash at end of month		$31,200

Ramirez Agency
Statement of Owner's Equity
For the Month Ended December 31, 20xx

R. Ramirez, Capital, December 1, 20xx	$ 0
Investment by R. Ramirez	100,000
Net income for the month	4,200
Subtotal	$104,200
Less withdrawals	1,200
R. Ramirez, Capital, December 31, 20xx	$103,000

Ramirez Agency
Balance Sheet
December 31, 20xx

Assets		Liabilities	
Cash	$ 31,200	Accounts payable	$ 1,200
Accounts receivable	2,000	Total liabilities	$ 1,200
Supplies	1,000		
Land	20,000	**Owner's Equity**	
Buildings	50,000	R. Ramirez, Capital	103,000
		Total liabilities and owner's equity	
Total assets	$104,200		$104,200

Study Note

Notice the sequence in which these financial statements must be prepared. The statement of owner's equity is a link between the income statement and the balance sheet, and the statement of cash flows is prepared last.

flows indicate the period to which they apply; the balance sheet gives the specific date to which it applies. Much of this book deals with developing, using, and interpreting more complete versions of these statements.

STOP • REVIEW • APPLY

6-1. What is the purpose of the statement of owner's equity?

6-2. Why is the balance sheet sometimes called the *statement of financial position*?

6-3. Contrast the purposes of the balance sheet and the income statement.

6-4. A statement for an accounting period that ends in June can be headed "June 30, 20xx" or "For the month ended June 30, 20xx." Which heading is appropriate for (a) a balance sheet and (b) an income statement?

6-5. How do the income statement and the statement of cash flows differ?

Interrelationship of the Financial Statements   Complete the following financial statements by determining the amounts that correspond to the letters. (Assume no new investments by owners.)

Income Statement	
Revenues	$2,775
Expenses	2,025 (a)
Net income	$750 (b)

Statement of Owner's Equity	
Beginning balance	$7,250
Net income	750 (c)
Less withdrawals	500
Ending balance	$7,500

Balance Sheet	
Total assets	$ (d)
Liabilities	$4,000
Owner's equity	
L. Buckman, Capital	7,500 (e)
Total liabilities and owner's equity	$11,500 (f)

SOLUTION

Net income links the income statement and the statement of owner's equity. The ending balance of owner's equity links the statement of owner's equity and the balance sheet.

Thus, start with (c), which must equal $750 (check: $7,250 + $750 − $500 = $7,500). Then, (b) equals (c), or $750. Thus, (a) must equal $2,025 (check: $2,775 − $2,025 = $750). Because (e) equals $7,500 (ending balance from the statement of owner's equity), (f) must equal $11,500 (check: $4,000 + $7,500 = $11,500). Now, (d) equals (f), or $11,500.

Generally Accepted Accounting Principles

LO7 Explain how generally accepted accounting principles (GAAP) relate to financial statements and the independent CPA's report, and identify the organizations that influence GAAP.

To ensure that financial statements are understandable to their users, a set of practices, called **generally accepted accounting principles (GAAP)**, has been developed to provide guidelines for financial accounting. Although the term has several meanings in the literature of accounting, perhaps this is the best definition: "Generally accepted accounting principles

TABLE 2.   Large International Certified Public Accounting Firms

Firm	Home Office	Some Major Clients
Deloitte & Touche	New York	General Motors, Procter & Gamble
Ernst & Young	New York	Coca-Cola, McDonald's
KPMG	New York	General Electric, Xerox
PricewaterhouseCoopers	New York	ExxonMobil, IBM, Ford

encompass the conventions, rules, and procedures necessary to define accepted accounting practice at a particular time."[9] In other words, GAAP arise from wide agreement on the theory and practice of accounting at a particular time. These "principles" are not like the unchangeable laws of nature in chemistry or physics. They evolve to meet the needs of decision makers, and they change as circumstances change or as better methods are developed.

In this book, we present accounting practice, or GAAP, as it is today,* and we try to explain the reasons or theory on which the practice is based. Both theory and practice are important to the study of accounting. However, accounting is a discipline that is always growing, changing, and improving. Just as years of research are necessary before a new surgical method or lifesaving drug can be introduced, it may take years for new accounting discoveries to be implemented. As a result, you may encounter practices that seem contradictory. In some cases, we point out new directions in accounting. Your instructor also may mention certain weaknesses in current theory or practice.

GAAP and the Independent CPA's Report

Because financial statements are prepared by management and could be falsified for personal gain, all companies that sell shares of their stock to the public and many companies that apply for sizable loans have their financial statements audited by an independent **certified public accountant (CPA)**. *Independent* means that the CPA is not an employee of the company being audited and has no financial or other compromising ties with it. CPAs are licensed by all states for the same reason that lawyers and doctors are—to protect the public by ensuring the quality of professional service. The firms listed in Table 2 employ about 25 percent of all CPAs.

An **audit** is an examination of a company's financial statements and the accounting systems, controls, and records that produced them. The purpose of the audit is to ascertain that the financial statements have been prepared in accordance with generally accepted accounting principles. If the independent CPA is satisfied that this standard has been met, his or her report contains the following language:

> In our opinion, the financial statements . . . present fairly, in all material
> respects . . . in conformity with generally accepted accounting principles . . .

This wording emphasizes that accounting and auditing are not exact sciences. Because the framework of GAAP provides room for interpretation and the application of GAAP necessitates the making of estimates, the auditor can render

⌐‾‾‾ *Study Note*

The purpose of an audit is to lend credibility to a set of financial statements. The auditor does *not* attest to the absolute accuracy of the published information or to the value of the company as an investment. All he or she renders is an opinion, based on appropriate testing, about the fairness of the presentation of the financial information.

---

*In May 2005, the AICPA passed a resolution to start working with the FASB to develop GAAP for privately held, for-profit companies, which would result in recognition, measurement, and disclosure differences, where appropriate, from current GAAP for public companies. If and when this resolution is acted upon, two sets of GAAP will exist: one for private companies and one for public companies.

Accountants from Ernst & Young arrive at the 55th Annual Emmy Awards at the Shrine Auditorium in Los Angeles. The independent accounting firm receives and tallies the votes. *Independent* means that the firm has no financial or other compromising ties with the Academy of Television Arts & Sciences, the organization that presents the Emmy Awards.

only an opinion about whether the financial statements *present fairly* or conform *in all material respects* to GAAP. The auditor's report does not preclude minor or immaterial errors in the financial statements. However, a favorable report from the auditor does imply that, on the whole, investors (owners) and creditors can rely on the financial statements.

Historically, auditors have enjoyed a strong reputation for competence and independence. As a result, banks, investors (owners), and creditors are willing to rely on an auditor's opinion when deciding to invest in a company or to make loans to it. The independent audit has been an important factor in the worldwide growth of financial markets.

Organizations That Influence GAAP

Many organizations directly or indirectly influence GAAP and so influence much of what is in this book.

The **Public Company Accounting Oversight Board (PCAOB)**, a governmental body created by the Sarbanes-Oxley Act, regulates the accounting profession and has wide powers to determine the standards that auditors must follow and to discipline them if they do not.

The **Financial Accounting Standards Board (FASB)** is the most important body for developing rules on accounting practice. This independent body has been designated by the Securities and Exchange Commission (SEC) to issue the *Statements of Financial Accounting Standards*.

The **American Institute of Certified Public Accountants (AICPA)**, the professional association of certified public accountants, influences accounting practice through the activities of its senior technical committees.

The **Securities and Exchange Commission (SEC)** is an agency of the federal government that has the legal power to set and enforce accounting practices for companies whose securities are offered for sale to the general public. As such, it has enormous influence on accounting practice.

The **Governmental Accounting Standards Board (GASB)**, which was established in 1984 under the same governing body as the FASB, is responsible for issuing accounting standards for state and local governments.

With the growth of financial markets throughout the world, global cooperation in the development of accounting principles has become a priority. The

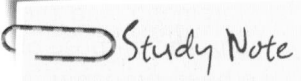

The FASB is the primary source of GAAP.

The AICPA is the primary professional organization of certified public accountants.

International Accounting Standards Board (IASB) has approved international standards, which are used in many countries including those in the European Union. These standards are in some cases different from those in the United States. The FASB and the IASB are working to bring the standards of the two bodies into closer agreement.

U.S. tax laws that govern the assessment and collection of revenue for operating the federal government also influence accounting practice. Because a major source of the government's revenue is the income tax, the tax laws specify the rules for determining taxable income. The **Internal Revenue Service (IRS)** interprets and enforces these rules. In some cases, the rules conflict with good accounting practice, but they are nonetheless an important influence on practice. Cases in which the tax laws affect accounting practice are noted throughout this book.

Professional Ethics

Professional ethics are key to the accountant's reputation for independence and competence. The code of professional ethics of the American Institute of Certified Public Accountants (and adopted, with variations, by each state) governs the conduct of CPAs. Fundamental to this code is responsibility to clients, creditors, investors (owners), and anyone else who relies on the work of a CPA. The code requires CPAs to act with integrity, objectivity, and independence.

⬦ **Integrity** means the accountant is honest and candid and subordinates personal gain to service and the public trust.

⬦ **Objectivity** means the accountant is impartial and intellectually honest.

⬦ **Independence** means the accountant avoids all relationships that impair or even appear to impair his or her objectivity.

The accountant must also exercise **due care** in all activities, carrying out professional responsibilities with competence and diligence. For example, an accountant must not accept a job for which he or she is not qualified, even at the risk of losing a client to another firm, and careless work is unacceptable. These broad principles are supported by more specific rules that public accountants must follow; for instance, with certain exceptions, client information must be kept strictly confidential. Accountants who violate the rules can be disciplined or even suspended from practice.

The **Institute of Management Accountants (IMA)** also has a code of professional conduct. It emphasizes that management accountants have a responsibility to be competent in their jobs, to keep information confidential except when authorized or legally required to disclose it, to maintain integrity and avoid conflicts of interest, and to communicate information objectively and without bias.[10]

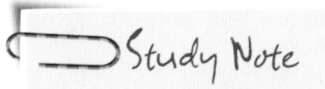 Study Note

The IMA is the primary professional association of management accountants.

Corporate Governance

The financial scandals at **Enron, WorldCom**, and other companies highlighted the importance of **corporate governance**, which is the oversight of a corporation's management and ethics by its board of directors. Corporate governance is growing and is clearly in the best interests of a business. A recent survey of 124 corporations in 22 countries found that 78 percent of boards of directors had established ethical standards, a fourfold increase over a 10-year period. In addition, research has shown that, over time, companies with codes of ethics tend to have higher stock prices than those that have not adopted such codes.[11]

To strengthen corporate governance, a provision of the Sarbanes-Oxley Act requires boards of directors to establish an **audit committee** made up of independent directors who have financial expertise. This provision is aimed at ensuring that boards of directors are objective in evaluating management's performance. The audit committee is also responsible for engaging the corporation's independent auditors and reviewing their work. Another of the committee's functions is to ensure that adequate systems exist to safeguard the corporation's resources and that accounting records are reliable. In short, the audit committee is the front line of defense against fraudulent financial reporting.

S T O P • R E V I E W • A P P L Y

7-1. What are GAAP? Why are they important to readers of financial statements?

7-2. As used in an auditor's report, what does *in all material respects* mean?

7-3. What organization has the most influence on GAAP?

7-4. What is the PCAOB, and why is it important?

7-5. Why are codes of ethics important in the accounting profession?

7-6. What is the role of an audit committee?

A LOOK BACK AT

CVS CORPORATION

The Decision Point at the beginning of this chapter focused on **CVS**, a successful nationwide chain of more than 5,000 drugstores. It posed these questions:

● Is CVS meeting its goal of profitability?

● As a manager at CVS, what financial knowledge would you need to measure progress toward the company's goals?

● As a potential investor or creditor, what financial knowledge would you need to evaluate CVS's financial performance?

As you've learned in this chapter, managers and others with an interest in a business measure its profitability in financial terms, such as net sales, net income, total assets, and owner's (stockholders') equity. Managers report on the progress they have made toward their financial goals in their company's financial statements.

As you can see in the following highlights from CVS's financial statements, the company's net sales, net earnings, net income, total assets, and stockholders' equity have increased over the years:[12]

CVS'S FINANCIAL HIGHLIGHTS
(In millions)

	2005	2004	2003
Sales	$37,006.2	$30,594.3	$26,588.0
Net earnings	1,224.7	918.8	847.3
Total assets	15,283.4	14,546.8	10,543.1
Stockholders' equity	8,331.2	6,987.2	6,021.8

How do we use these data to determine if CVS is meeting its goal of profitability? As mentioned earlier in the chapter, one way to measure financial performance is through ratios. Ratios are used to compare a company's financial performance from one year to the next and to make comparisons among companies. The ratio that tells us if CVS is meeting its goal of profitability is the **return on assets** ratio. This ratio shows how efficiently a company is using its assets to produce income.

We use two values to calculate return on assets: net income, which is what is left over after expenses are subtracted from revenues (see the income statement in Exhibit 1), and average total assets. Average total assets are the total of this year's assets plus last year's assets divided by two (see the balance sheet in Exhibit 3).

The return on assets ratio for CVS is calculated as follows (amounts are in millions):

	2005	2004
$\dfrac{\text{Net Income}}{\text{Average Total Assets}}$	$\dfrac{\$1,224.7}{(\$15,283.4 + \$14,546.8) \div 2}$	$\dfrac{\$918.8}{(\$14,546.8 + \$10,543.1) \div 2}$
$/_®	$\dfrac{\$1,224.7}{\$14,915.1}$	$\dfrac{\$918.8}{\$12,545.0}$
Return on Assets:	$.082 \times 100 = 8.2\%$	$.073 \times 100 = 7.3\%$

We can draw several conclusions from this ratio. First, CVS earned 7.3 to 8.2 cents on each dollar it invested in assets. Second, from 2004 to 2005, its profitability increased from 7.3 to 8.2 percent. Third, CVS is a growing company as demonstrated by the increases in its net sales, net earnings, total assets, and stockholders' equity in every year of the three-year period. These amounts indicate that CVS is a profitable and successful company but faces challenges in maintaining its profitability. You will learn much more about ratios in the chapters that follow.

If you aspire to be a manager of a business, an accountant, an investor, a business owner, or just a good employee, you will need to be familiar with measures like the return on assets ratio. You will also need to master other accounting concepts and terminology and know how financial information is produced, interpreted, and analyzed. The purpose of this book is to help you acquire that knowledge.

CHAPTER REVIEW

REVIEW of Learning Objectives

LO1 Define *accounting* and describe its role in making informed decisions, identify business goals and activities, and explain the importance of ethics in accounting.

Accounting is an information system that measures, processes, and communicates financial information about an economic entity. It provides the information necessary to make reasoned choices among alternative uses of scarce resources in the conduct of business and economic activities. A business is an economic entity that engages in operating, investing, and financing activities to achieve the goals of profitability and liquidity.

Management accounting focuses on the preparation of information primarily for internal use by management. Financial accounting is concerned with the development and use of reports that are communicated to those outside the business as well as to management. Ethical financial reporting is important to the well-being of a company; fraudulent financial reports can have serious consequences for many people.

LO2 Identify the users of accounting information.

Accounting plays a significant role in society by providing information to managers of all institutions and to individuals with a direct financial interest in those institutions, including present or potential investors (owners) and creditors. Accounting information is also important to those with an indirect financial interest in the business—for example, tax authorities, regulatory agencies, and economic planners.

LO3 Explain the importance of business transactions, money measure, and separate entity.

To make an accounting measurement, the accountant must determine what is measured, when the measurement should be made, what value should be placed on what is measured, and how to classify what is measured. The objects of accounting measurement are business transactions. Financial accounting uses money measure to gauge the impact of these transactions on a separate business entity.

LO4 Identify the three basic forms of business organization.

The three basic forms of business organization are the sole proprietorship, the partnership, and the corporation. Accountants recognize each form as an economic unit separate from its owners, although legally only the corporation is separate from its owners. A sole proprietorship is a business owned by one person. A partnership is like a sole proprietorship in most ways, but it has two or more owners. A corporation, on the other hand, is a business unit chartered by the state and legally separate from its owners (the *stockholders*).

LO5 Define *financial position*, and state the accounting equation.

Financial position refers to a company's economic resources and the claims against those resources at a particular time. The accounting equation shows financial position as Assets = Liabilities + Owner's Equity. Business transactions affect financial position by decreasing or increasing assets, liabilities, and owner's equity in such a way that the accounting equation is always in balance.

LO6 Identify the four basic financial statements.

The four basic financial statements are the income statement, the statement of owner's equity, the balance sheet, and the statement of cash flows. They are the primary means by which accountants communicate the financial condition and activities of a business to those who have an interest in the business.

LO7 Explain how generally accepted accounting principles (GAAP) relate to financial statements and the independent CPA's report, and identify the organizations that influence GAAP.

Acceptable accounting practice consists of the conventions, rules, and procedures that make up generally accepted accounting principles at a particular time. GAAP are essential to the preparation and interpretation of financial statements and the independent CPA's report.

Among the organizations that influence the formulation of GAAP are the Public Company Accounting Oversight Board, the Financial Accounting Standards Board, the American Institute of Certified Public Accountants, the Securities and Exchange Commission, and the Internal Revenue Service.

All accountants are required to follow a code of professional ethics, the foundation of which is responsibility to the public. Accountants must act with integrity, objectivity, and independence, and they must exercise due care in all their activities.

The board of directors is responsible for determining corporate policies and appointing corporate officers. It is also responsible for corporate governance, the oversight of a corporation's management and ethics. The audit committee, which is appointed by the board and made up of independent directors, is an important factor in corporate governance.

REVIEW of Concepts and Terminology

The following concepts and terms were introduced in this chapter:

Accounting: An information system that measures, processes, and communicates financial information about an economic entity. **(LO1)**

Accounting equation: Assets = Liabilities + Owner's Equity. **(LO5)**

American Institute of Certified Public Accountants (AICPA): The professional association of certified public accountants. **(LO7)**

Assets: The economic resources of a company that are expected to benefit future operations. **(LO5)**

Audit: An examination of a company's financial statements in order to render an independent professional opinion about whether they have been presented fairly, in all material respects, in conformity with GAAP. **(LO7)**

Audit committee: A subgroup of a corporation's board of directors that is charged with ensuring that the board will be objective in reviewing management's performance; it engages the company's independent auditors and reviews their work. **(LO7)**

Balance sheet: The financial statement that shows a business's assets, liabilities, and owner's equity as of a specific date. Also called the *statement of financial position*. **(LO6)**

Bookkeeping: The process of recording financial transactions and keeping financial records. **(LO1)**

Business: An economic unit that aims to sell goods and services to customers at prices that will provide an adequate return to its owners. **(LO1)**

Business transactions: Economic events that affect a business's financial position. **(LO3)**

Cash flows: The inflows and outflows of cash into and out of a business. **(LO6)**

Certified public accountant (CPA): A public accountant who has met stringent state licensing requirements. **(LO7)**

Corporate governance: The oversight of a corporation's management and ethics by the board of directors. **(LO7)**

Corporation: A business unit granted a state charter recognizing it as a separate legal entity having its own rights, privileges, and liabilities distinct from those of its owners. **(LO4)**

Due care: Competence and diligence in carrying out professional responsibilities. **(LO7)**

Ethics: A code of conduct that addresses whether actions are right or wrong. **(LO1)**

Exchange rate: The value of one currency in terms of another. **(LO3)**

Expenses: Decreases in owner's equity that result from operating a business. **(LO5)**

Financial accounting: The process of generating and communicating accounting information in the form of financial statements to those outside the organization. **(LO1)**

Financial Accounting Standards Board (FASB): The most important body for developing rules on accounting practice; it issues *Statements of Financial Accounting Standards*. **(LO7)**

Financial position: The economic resources that belong to a company and the claims (equities) against those resources at a particular time. **(LO5)**

Financial statements: The primary means of communicating important accounting information to users. They include the income statement, statement of owner's equity, balance sheet, and statement of cash flows. **(LO1)**

Financing activities: Activities undertaken by management to obtain adequate funds to begin and to continue operating a business. **(LO1)**

Fraudulent financial reporting: The intentional preparation of misleading financial statements. **(LO1)**

Generally accepted accounting principles (GAAP): The conventions, rules, and procedures that define accepted accounting practice at a particular time. **(LO7)**

Governmental Accounting Standards Board (GASB): The board responsible for issuing accounting standards for state and local governments. **(LO7)**

Income statement: A financial statement that summarizes the revenues earned and expenses incurred by a business over an accounting period. **(LO6)**

Independence: The avoidance of all relationships that impair or appear to impair an accountant's objectivity. **(LO7)**

Institute of Management Accountants (IMA): A professional organization made up primarily of management accountants. **(LO7)**

Integrity: Honesty, candidness, and the subordination of personal gain to service and the public trust. **(LO7)**

Internal Revenue Service (IRS): The agency that interprets and enforces the tax laws governing the assessment and collection of revenue for operating the federal government. **(LO7)**

International Accounting Standards Board (IASB): An organization that encourages worldwide cooperation in the development of accounting principles. **(LO7)**

Investing activities: Activities undertaken by management to spend capital in productive ways that will help a business achieve its objectives. **(LO1)**

Liabilities: A business's present obligations to pay cash, transfer assets, or provide services to other entities in the future. **(LO5)**

Liquidity: Having enough cash available to pay debts when they are due. **(LO1)**

Management: The people who have overall responsibility for operating a business and meeting its goals. **(LO2)**

Management accounting: The process of producing accounting information for internal use by managers. **(LO1)**

Management information system (MIS): The interconnected subsystems that provide the information needed to run a business. **(LO1)**

Money measure: The recording of all business transactions in terms of money. **(LO3)**

Net assets: Assets minus liabilities; owner's equity. **(LO5)**

Net income: The difference between revenues and expenses when revenues exceed expenses. **(LO5)**

Net loss: The difference between expenses and revenues when expenses exceed revenues. **(LO5)**

Objectivity: Impartiality and intellectual honesty. **(LO7)**

Operating activities: Activities undertaken by management in the course of running a business. **(LO1)**

Owner's equity: The claims of the owner of a company to the assets of the business. **(LO5)**

Partnership: A business that is owned by two or more people and that is not incorporated. **(LO4)**

Performance measures: Indicators of whether managers are achieving business goals and whether business activities are well managed. **(LO1)**

Professional ethics: A code of conduct that applies to the practice of a profession. **(LO7)**

Profitability: The ability to earn enough income to attract and hold investment capital. **(LO1)**

Public Company Accounting Oversight Board (PCAOB): A governmental body created by the Sarbanes-Oxley Act to regulate the accounting profession. **(LO7)**

Revenues: Increases in owner's equity that result from operating a business. **(LO5)**

Sarbanes-Oxley Act: An act of Congress that regulates financial reporting in public corporations. **(LO1)**

Securities and Exchange Commission (SEC): A governmental agency that regulates the issuing, buying, and selling of stocks. It has the legal power to set and enforce accounting practices for firms whose securities are sold to the general public. **(LO2)**

Separate entity: A business that is treated as distinct from its creditors, customers, and owners. **(LO3)**

Sole proprietorship: A business that is owned by one person and that is not incorporated. **(LO4)**

Statement of cash flows: A financial statement that shows the inflows and outflows of cash from operating activities, investing activities, and financing activities over an accounting period. **(LO6)**

Statement of owner's equity: A financial statement that shows the changes in owner's equity over an accounting period. **(LO6)**

Key Ratio

Return on assets: A ratio that shows how efficiently a company is using its assets to produce income; Net Income ÷ Average Total Assets.

REVIEW Problem

LO6 Preparation and Interpretation of Financial Statements

The following financial statement accounts and amounts are from the records of Jackson Realty for the year ended April 30, 20x8, the company's first year of operations.

Accounts payable	$ 19,000
Accounts receivable	104,000
Cash	111,000
Commissions earned	375,000
Equipment	47,000
Investment by J. Jackson	100,000
Marketing expense	18,000
Office and equipment rent expense	91,000
Salaries and commission expense	172,000
Salaries payable	78,000
Supplies	2,000
Supplies expense	6,000
Utilities expense	11,000
Withdrawals	10,000

Required

1. Prepare an income statement, statement of owner's equity, balance sheet, and statement of cash flows for Jackson Realty. For examples, refer to Exhibit 5.
2. From the statement of cash flows, does it appear that Jackson Realty will need to borrow money to continue operations? Why or why not?

Answer to Review Problem

1.

	A	B	C	D	E
1			Jackson Realty		
2			Income Statement		
3			For the Year Ended April 30, 20x8		
4	Revenues:				
5		Commissions earned			$375,000
6					
7	Expenses:				
8		Marketing expense		$ 18,000	
9		Office and equipment rent expense		91,000	
10		Salaries and commission expense		172,000	
11		Supplies expense		6,000	
12		Utilities expense		11,000	
13	Total expenses				298,000
14	Net income				$ 77,000
15					

Jackson Realty
Statement of Owner's Equity
For the Year Ended April 30, 20x8

J. Jackson, Capital, April 30, 20x7	$ —
Investment by J. Jackson	100,000
Net income for the year	77,000
	$177,000
Less withdrawals	10,000
J. Jackson, Capital, April 30, 20x8	$167,000

Jackson Realty
Balance Sheet
April 30, 20x8

Assets		Liabilities		
Cash	$111,000	Accounts payable	$19,000	
Accounts receivable	104,000	Salaries payable	78,000	
Supplies	2,000	Total liabilities		$ 97,000
Equipment	47,000			
		Owner's Equity		
	—	J. Jackson, Capital		167,000
Total assets	$264,000	Total liabilities and owner's equity		$264,000

Jackson Realty
Statement of Cash Flows
For the Year Ended April 30, 20x8

Cash flows from operating activities:			
Net income			$ 77,000
Adjustments to reconcile net income to net cash flows			
from operating activities:			
Increase in accounts receivable		($104,000)	
Increase in supplies		(2,000)	
Increase in accounts payable		19,000	
Increase in salaries payable		78,000	(9,000)
Net cash flows from operating activities			$ 68,000
Cash flows from investing activities:			
Purchase of equipment		($ 47,000)	
Net cash flows from investing activities			(47,000)
Cash flows from financing activities:			
Investment by owner		$100,000	
Withdrawals		(10,000)	
Net cash flows from financing activities			90,000
Net increase (decrease) in cash			$111,000
Cash at beginning of year			—
Cash at end of year			$111,000

2. It does not appear that Jackson Realty will need to borrow money to continue in business next year. Total cash increased $111,000. In the current year, cash flows from operating activities are sufficient to cover 100 percent of the investing activities.

CHAPTER ASSIGNMENTS

BUILDING Your Basic Knowledge and Skills

Short Exercises

LO1   **Accounting and Business Enterprises**

SE 1. Match the terms on the left with the definitions on the right:

____ 1. Accounting	a. The process of producing accounting information for the internal use of a company's management
____ 2. Profitability	
____ 3. Liquidity	b. Having enough cash available to pay debts when they are due
____ 4. Financing activities	
____ 5. Investing activities	c. Activities management engages in to obtain adequate funds for beginning and continuing to operate a business
____ 6. Operating activities	d. The process of generating and communicating accounting information in the form of financial statements to decision makers outside the organization
____ 7. Financial accounting	
____ 8. Management accounting	e. Activities management engages in to spend capital in ways that are productive and will help a business achieve its objectives
____ 9. Sole proprietorship	f. The ability to earn enough income to attract and hold investment capital
____ 10. Fraudulent financial reporting	g. An information system that measures, processes, and communicates financial information about an identifiable economic entity
	h. The intentional preparation of misleading financial statements
	i. Activities management engages in to operate the business
	j. A business one person owns that is not incorporated

LO3   **Accounting Concepts**

SE 2. Indicate whether each of the following words or phrases relates most closely to (a) a business transaction, (b) a separate entity, or (c) a money measure:

1. Partnership
2. U.S. dollar
3. Payment of an expense
4. Sole proprietorship
5. Sale of an asset

LO4   **Forms of Business Organization**

SE 3. Match the descriptions in the column on the left that follows with the forms of business organization on the right.

_____ 1. Most numerous   a. Sole proprietorship
_____ 2. Commands most revenues   b. Partnership
__B__ 3. Two or more co-owners   c. Corporation
__C__ 4. Has stockholders
__A__ 5. Owned by only one person
_____ 6. Has a board of directors

LO5 The Accounting Equation

SE 4. Determine the amount missing from each accounting equation below.

	Assets	=	Liabilities	+	Owner's Equity
1.	?		$50,000		$ 70,000
2.	$156,000		$84,000		?
3.	$292,000		?		$192,000

LO5 The Accounting Equation

SE 5. Use the accounting equation to answer each question below.

1. The assets of Tiller Company are $240,000, and the liabilities are $180,000. What is the amount of the owner's equity?
2. The liabilities of Cochran Company equal one-fifth of the total assets. The owner's equity is $40,000. What is the amount of the liabilities?

LO5 The Accounting Equation

SE 6. Use the accounting equation to answer each question below.

1. At the beginning of the year, Salinas Company's assets were $90,000, and its owner's equity was $50,000. During the year, assets increased by $30,000 and liabilities increased by $5,000. What was the owner's equity at the end of the year?
2. At the beginning of the year, Alejandro Company had liabilities of $100,000 and owner's equity of $96,000. If assets increased by $40,000 and liabilities decreased by $30,000, what was the owner's equity at the end of the year?

LO5 The Accounting Equation and Net Income

SE 7. Carlton Company had assets of $280,000 and liabilities of $120,000 at the beginning of the year, and assets of $400,000 and liabilities of $140,000 at the end of the year. During the year, the owner invested an additional $40,000 in the business, and the company made withdrawals of $48,000. What amount of net income did the company earn during the year?

LO6 Preparation and Completion of a Balance Sheet

SE 8. Use the following accounts and balances to prepare a balance sheet with the accounts in proper order for Anatole Company at June 30, 20x7, using Exhibit 3 as a model:

Accounts Receivable	$ 1,600
Wages Payable	500
D. Anatole, Capital	27,500
Buildings	20,000
Cash	?

LO6 Preparation of Financial Statements

SE 9. Tarech Company engaged in activities during the first year of its operations that resulted in the following: service revenue, $4,800; expenses, $2,450; and withdrawals, $410. In addition, the year-end balances of selected accounts were as follows: Cash, $1,890; Other Assets, $1,000; and Accounts Payable, $450. In proper format, prepare the income statement,

statement of owner's equity, and balance sheet for Tarech Company (assume the year ends on December 31, 20x7). (**Hint:** You must solve for the amount of investment to the W. Tarech, Capital account during 20x7.)

Return on Assets

 SE 10. Jason Company had net income of $15,000 in 20x8. Total assets were $100,000 at the beginning of the year and $140,000 at the end of the year. Calculate return on assets.

Exercises

LO1, LO2, LO3, LO4   Discussion Questions

E 1. Develop a brief answer to each of the following questions.

1. What makes accounting a valuable discipline?
2. Why do managers in governmental and not-for-profit organizations need to understand financial information as much as managers in profit-seeking businesses?
3. Are all economic events business transactions?
4. Sole proprietorships, partnerships, and corporations differ legally; how and why does accounting treat them alike?

LO5, LO6, LO7   Discussion Questions

E 2. Develop a brief answer to each of the following questions.

1. How are expenses and withdrawals similar, and how are they different?
2. In what ways are **CVS** and **Southwest Airlines** comparable? In what ways are they not comparable?
3. How do generally accepted accounting principles (GAAP) differ from the laws of science?
4. What are some unethical ways in which a business might do its accounting or prepare its financial statements?

LO1, LO2, LO7   The Nature of Accounting

E 3. Match the terms below with the descriptions that follow.

＿＿ 1. Bookkeeping	＿＿ 7. Communication
＿＿ 2. Creditors	＿＿ 8. Securities and Exchange
＿＿ 3. Money measure	Commission (SEC)
＿＿ 4. Financial Accounting	_A_ 9. Investors (owners)
Standards Board (FASB)	＿＿ 10. Sarbanes-Oxley Act
_k_ 5. Business transactions	＿＿ 11. Management
＿＿ 6. Financial statements	＿＿ 12. Management information system

a. The recording of all business transactions in terms of money
b. A process by which information is exchanged between individuals through a common system of symbols, signs, or behavior
c. The process of identifying and assigning values to business transactions
d. Legislation ordering CEOs and CFOs to swear that any reports they file with the SEC are accurate and complete
e. Shows how well a company is meeting the goals of profitability and liquidity
f. Collectively, the people who have overall responsibility for operating a business and meeting its goals
g. People who commit money to earn a financial return
h. The interconnected subsystems that provide the information needed to run a business

    i. The most important body for developing and issuing rules on accounting practice, called *Statements of Financial Accounting Standards*

    j. An agency set up by Congress to protect the public by regulating the issuing, buying, and selling of stocks

    k. Economic events that affect a business's financial position

    l. People to whom money is due

LO2, LO4   **Users of Accounting Information and Forms of Business Enterprise**

E 4. Siglo Pharmaceuticals has recently been formed to develop a new type of drug treatment for cancer. Previously a partnership, Siglo has now become a corporation. Describe the various groups that will have an interest in the financial statements of Siglo. What is the difference between a partnership and a corporation? What advantages does the corporate form have over the partnership form of business organization?

LO3   **Business Transactions**

E 5. Max owns and operates a minimart. Which of Max's actions described below are business transactions? Explain why any other actions are not considered transactions.

1. Max reduces the price of a gallon of milk in order to match the price offered by a competitor.
2. Max pays a high school student cash for cleaning up the driveway behind the market.
3. Max fills his son's car with gasoline in payment for his son's restocking the vending machines and the snack food shelves.
4. Max pays interest to himself on a loan he made to the business three years ago.

LO3, LO4   **Accounting Concepts**

E 6. Financial accounting uses money measures to gauge the impact of business transactions on a separate business entity. Tell whether each of the following words or phrases relates most closely to (a) a business transaction, (b) a separate entity, or (c) a money measure:

1. Corporation	6. U.S. dollar
2. Euro	7. Partnership
3. Sales of products	8. Owner's investment
4. Receipt of cash	9. Japanese yen
5. Sole proprietorship	10. Purchase of supplies

LO3   **Money Measure**

E 7. You have been asked to compare the sales and assets of four companies that make computer chips to determine which company is the largest in each category. You have gathered the following data, but they cannot be used for direct comparison because each company's sales and assets are in its own currency:

Company (Currency)	Sales	Assets
DigiChip (U.S. dollar)	2,000,000	1,300,000
Nanhai (Hong Kong dollar)	5,000,000	2,400,000
Tosa (Japanese yen)	350,000,000	250,000,000
Holstein (Euro)	3,000,000	3,900,000

Assuming that the exchange rates in Table 1 are current and appropriate, convert all the figures to U.S. dollars and determine which company is the largest in sales and which is the largest in assets.

LO5 **The Accounting Equation**

E 8. Use the accounting equation to answer each question that follows. Show any calculations you make.

1. The assets of Dusan Company are $400,000, and the owner's equity is $155,000. What is the amount of the liabilities?
2. The liabilities and owner's equity of Highbeam Company are $72,000 and $79,500, respectively. What is the amount of the assets?
3. The liabilities of Acosta Company equal one-third of the total assets, and owner's equity is $160,000. What is the amount of the liabilities?
4. At the beginning of the year, Leary Company's assets were $275,000, and its owner's equity was $150,000. During the year, assets increased $75,000 and liabilities decreased $22,500. What is the owner's equity at year end?

LO5, LO6 **Identification of Accounts**

E 9. 1. Indicate whether each of the following accounts is an asset (A), a liability (L), or a part of owner's equity (OE):

   a. Cash
   b. Salaries Payable
   c. Accounts Receivable
   d. Owner's Capital
   e. Land
   f. Accounts Payable
   g. Supplies

2. Indicate whether each account below would be shown on the income statement (IS), the statement of owner's equity (OE), or the balance sheet (BS).

   a. Repair Revenue
   b. Automobile
   c. Fuel Expense
   d. Cash
   e. Rent Expense
   f. Accounts Payable
   g. Withdrawals

LO6 **Preparation of a Balance Sheet**

E 10. Listed in random order are some of the account balances for the Rojas Company as of December 31, 20xx.

Accounts Payable	$ 50,000	Accounts Receivable	$62,500
Buildings	112,500	Cash	25,000
J. Rojas, Capital	212,500	Equipment	50,000
Supplies	12,500		

Place the balances in proper order and prepare a balance sheet similar to the one in Exhibit 3.

LO6 **Preparation and Integration of Financial Statements**

E 11. Kaisha Company engaged in the following activities during the year: Service Revenue, $13,200; Rent Expense, $1,200; Wages Expense, $8,340; Advertising Expense, $1,350; Utilities Expense, $900; and Withdrawals, $700. In addition, the year-end balances of selected accounts were as follows: Cash, $1,550; Accounts Receivable, $750; Supplies, $100; Land, $1,000; Accounts Payable, $450. Y. Kaisha, Capital, had a beginning balance of $1,000.

In proper format, prepare the income statement, statement of owner's equity, and balance sheet for Kaisha Company (assume the year ends on December 31, 20x7). (**Hint:** You must solve for the amount of investments to the Y. Kaisha, Capital account during 20x7.)

LO5 **Owner's Equity and the Accounting Equation**

E 12. The total assets and liabilities at the beginning and end of the year for Luther Company follow.

	Assets	Liabilities
Beginning of the year	$175,000	$ 68,750
End of the year	275,000	162,500

Determine Luther Company's net income or loss for the year under each of the following alternatives:

1. The owner made no investments in or withdrawals from the business during the year.
2. The owner made no investments in the business but withdrew $27,500 during the year.
3. The owner invested $16,250 in the business but made no withdrawals during the year.
4. The owner invested $12,500 in the business and withdrew $27,500 during the year.

LO6 **Statement of Cash Flows**

E 13. Primorsk Company began the year 20x7 with cash of $55,900. In addition to earning a net income of $32,500 and making cash withdrawals of $19,500, Primorsk borrowed $78,000 from the bank and purchased equipment with $117,000 of cash. Also, Accounts Receivable increased by $7,800, and Accounts Payable increased by $11,700. Determine the amount of cash on hand at December 31, 20x7, by preparing a statement of cash flows similar to the one in Exhibit 4.

LO4, LO5, LO6 **Statement of Owner's Equity**

E 14. Below is information from the statement of owner's equity of Mrs. Bell's Cookies for a recent year.

Withdrawals	0
Net income	?
W. Bell, Capital, January 31, 20x7	$159,490
W. Bell, Capital, January 31, 20x6	$102,403

Prepare the statement of owner's equity for Mrs. Bell's Cookies in good form. You will need to solve for the amount of net income. What is owner's equity? Why might the owner decide not to make any withdrawals from the company?

LO7 **Accounting Abbreviations**

E 15. Identify the accounting meaning of each of the following abbreviations: AICPA, SEC, PCAOB, GAAP, FASB, IRS, GASB, IASB, IMA, and CPA.

Return on Assets

E 16. Saxon Company wants to know if its profitability performance has increased from 20x7 to 20x8. The company had net income of $24,000 in 20x7 and $25,000 in 20x8. Total assets were $200,000 at the end of 20x6, $240,000 at the end of 20x7, and $280,000 at the end of 20x8. Calculate return on assets for 20x7 and 20x8 and comment on the results.

Problems

LO6 **Preparation and Interpretation of the Financial Statements**

P 1. The following is a list of financial statement items:

____ Utilities expense	____ Net income
____ Buildings	____ Land
____ J. Katz, Capital	____ Equipment

___ Revenues   ___ Fees earned
___ Accounts receivable   ___ Cash
___ Accounts payable   ___ Supplies
___ Rent expense   ___ Wages expense
___ Withdrawals

Required

1. Indicate whether each item is found on the income statement (IS), statement of owner's equity (OE), and/or balance sheet (BS).
2. **User Insight:** Which statement is most closely associated with the goal of profitability?

LO6   **Integration of Financial Statements**

P 2. Below are three independent sets of financial statements with several amounts missing.

Income Statement	Set A	Set B	Set C
Revenues	$1,100	$ g	$240
Expenses	a	5,200	m
Net income	$ b	$ h	$ 80
Statement of Owner's Equity			
Beginning balance	$2,900	$24,400	$340
Net income	c	1,600	n
Less withdrawals	200	i	o
Ending balance	$3,000	$ j	$ p
Balance Sheet			
Total assets	$ d	$31,000	$ q
Liabilities	$1,600	$ 5,000	$ r
Owner's equity			
Owner's capital	e	k	380
Total liabilities and owner's equity	$ f	$ l	$380

Required

1. Complete each set of financial statements by determining the amounts that correspond to the letters.
2. **User Insight:** In what order is it necessary to prepare the financial statements and why?

LO1, LO6   **Preparation and Interpretation of Financial Statements**

P 3. Below are the financial accounts of Landscape Design. The company has just completed its third year of operations ended November 30, 20x8.

Accounts Receivable	$ 9,100
Accounts Payable	7,400
Cash	141,600
Design Service Revenue	248,000
J. Hope, Capital, November 30, 20x7	70,400
Marketing Expense	19,700
Office Rent Expense	18,200
Salaries Expense	96,000
Salaries Payable	2,700
Supplies	800
Supplies Expense	3,100
Withdrawals	40,000

Required

1. Prepare the income statement, statement of owner's equity, and balance sheet for Landscape Design. There were no investments by the owner during the year.
2. **User Insight:** Evaluate the company's ability to meet its bills when they come due.

LO4, LO6 **Preparation and Interpretation of Financial Statements**

P 4. Below are the accounts of Collegiate Painters. The company has just completed its first year of operations ended September 30, 20x7.

Accounts Payable	$10,500
Accounts Receivable	13,200
Cash	2,600
Equipment	4,700
Equipment Rental Expense	1,300
Marketing Expense	1,500
Painting Service Revenue	78,800
Salaries Expense	56,000
Salaries Payable	700
Supplies	400
Supplies Expense	4,100
T. Brush, Capital	2,000*
Truck Rent Expense	7,200
Withdrawals	1,000

*Represents the initial investment by the owner.

Required

1. Prepare the income statement, statement of owner's equity, and balance sheet for Collegiate Painters.
2. **User Insight:** Assume T. Brush has an opportunity to bring in a friend to form a partnership. What would be an advantage of doing this? What are some disadvantages of the partnership form of business over the sole proprietorship?

LO1, LO6, LO7 **Use and Interpretation of Financial Statements**

P 5. The financial statements for the Wichita Riding Club follow.

Wichita Riding Club Income Statement For the Month Ended November 30, 20xx		
Revenues		
Riding lesson revenue	$4,650	
Locker rental revenue	1,275	
Total revenues		$5,925
Expenses		
Salaries expense	$1,125	
Feed expense	750	
Utilities expense	450	
Total expenses		2,325
Net income		$3,600

Wichita Riding Club
Statement of Owner's Equity
For the Month Ended November 30, 20xx

A. Cooper, Capital, October 31, 20xx	$34,975
Investments by A. Cooper	5,000
Net income for the month	3,600
Subtotal	$43,575
Less withdrawals	2,400
A. Cooper, Capital, November 30, 20xx	$41,175

Wichita Riding Club
Balance Sheet
November 30, 20xx

Assets		Liabilities	
Cash	$ 7,125	Accounts payable	$13,350
Accounts receivable	900		
Supplies	750	**Owner's Equity**	
Land	15,750	A. Cooper, Capital	41,175
Buildings	22,500		
Horses	7,500	Total liabilities and	
Total assets	$54,525	owner's equity	$54,525

Wichita Riding Club
Statement of Cash Flows
For the Month Ended November 30, 20xx

Cash flows from operating activities		
Net income		$3,600
Adjustments to reconcile net income to net cash flows from operating activities		
Increase in accounts receivable	($400)	
Increase in supplies	(550)	
Increase in accounts payable	400	(550)
Net cash flows from operating activities		$3,050
Cash flows from investing activities		
Purchase of horses	$2,000	
Sale of horses	(1,000)	
Net cash flows from investing activities		1,000
Cash flows from financing activities		
Investment by owner	$5,000	
Withdrawals	(2,400)	
Net cash flows from financing activities		2,600
Net increase (decrease) in cash		$6,650
Cash at beginning of month		475
Cash at end of month		$7,125

Required

1. **User Insight:** Explain how the four statements for Wichita Riding Club are related to each other.
2. **User Insight:** Which statements are most closely associated with the goals of liquidity and profitability? Why?
3. **User Insight:** If you were the owner of this business, how would you evaluate the company's performance? Give specific examples.
4. **User Insight:** If you were a banker considering Wichita Riding Club for a loan, why might you want the company to get an audit by an independent CPA? What would the audit tell you?

Alternate Problems

LO6 **Integration of Financial Statements**

P 6. The following three independent sets of financial statements have several amounts missing:

Income Statement	Set A	Set B	Set C
Revenues	$5,320	$ 9,000	$ m
Expenses	a	g	1,900
Net income	$ 490	$ h	$ n
Statement of Owner's Equity			
Beginning balance	$1,800	$15,400	$ 200
Net income	b	i	450
Less withdrawals	c	1,000	o
Ending balance	$ d	$16,000	$ p
Balance Sheet			
Total assets	$ e	$ j	$1,900
Liabilities	$ f	$ 2,000	$1,300
Owner's equity			
Owner's capital	2,100	k	q
Total liabilities and owner's equity	$2,700	$ l	$ r

Required

1. Complete each set of financial statements by determining the amounts that correspond to the letters.
2. **User Insight:** Why is it necessary to prepare the income statement prior to the balance sheet?

LO1, LO6 **Preparation and Interpretation of Financial Statements**

P 7. Below are the financial accounts of Dodge Realty. The company has just completed its 10th year of operations ended December 31, 20x8.

Accounts Payable	$ 3,600
Accounts Receivable	4,500
Cash	91,600
Commissions Expense	225,000
Commissions Payable	22,700
Commission Sales Revenue	450,000
Equipment	59,900
Marketing Expense	29,200
Office Rent Expense	36,000
Supplies	700
Supplies Expense	2,600
T. Dodge, Capital, December 31, 20x7	50,300

Telephone and Computer Expenses	$ 5,100
Wages Expense	32,000
Withdrawals	40,000

Required

1. Prepare the income statement, statement of owner's equity, and balance sheet for Dodge Realty. There were no investments by the owner during the year.

2. **User Insight:** The owner is considering expansion. What other statement would be useful to the owner in assessing whether the company's operations are generating sufficient funds to support the expenses? Why would it be useful?

LO4, LO6 **Preparation and Interpretation of Financial Statements**

P 8. The following are the accounts of Creative Advertising, an agency owned by Art Francis that develops marketing materials for print, radio, and television. The agency's first year of operations ended on January 31, 20x7.

Accounts Payable	$ 19,400
Accounts Receivable	24,600
Advertising Service Revenue	159,200
A. Francis, Capital	5,000
Cash	1,800
Equipment Rental Expense	37,200
Marketing Expense	4,500
Office Rent Expense	10,800
Salaries Expense	86,000
Salaries Payable	1,300
Supplies	900
Supplies Expense	19,100
Withdrawals	0

Required

1. Prepare the income statement, statement of owner's equity, and balance sheet for Creative Advertising.

2. **User Insight:** Review the financial statements and comment on the financial challenges Creative Advertising faces.

ENHANCING Your Knowledge, Skills, and Critical Thinking

Conceptual Understanding Cases

LO1, LO2 **Business Activities and Management Functions**

C 1. Costco Wholesale Corporation is America's largest membership retail company. According to its letter to stockholders:

> Our mission is to bring quality goods and services to our members at the lowest possible price in every market where we do business...A hallmark of Costco warehouses has been the extraordinary sales volume we achieve.[13]

To achieve its strategy, Costco must organize its management by functions that relate to the principal activities of a business. Discuss the three basic activities Costco will engage in to achieve its goals, and suggest some examples of each. What is the role of Costco's management? What functions must its management perform to carry out these activities?

LO3 **Concept of an Asset**

C 2. **Southwest Airlines Co.** is one of the most successful airlines in the United States. Its annual report contains this statement: "We are a company of People, not Planes. That is what distinguishes us from other airlines and other companies. At Southwest Airlines, People are our most important asset."[14] Are employees considered assets in the financial statements? Why or why not? Discuss in what sense Southwest considers its employees to be assets.

LO7 **Generally Accepted Accounting Principles**

C 3. **Fidelity Investments Company** is a well-known mutual fund investment company. It makes investments worth billions of dollars in companies listed on the New York Stock Exchange and other stock markets. Generally accepted accounting principles (GAAP) are very important for Fidelity's investment analysts. What are generally accepted accounting principles? Why are financial statements that have been prepared in accordance with GAAP and audited by an independent CPA useful for Fidelity's investment analysts? What organizations influence GAAP? Explain how they do so.

Interpreting Financial Reports

LO6 **Nature of Cash, Assets, and Net Income**

C 4. **H&R Block, Inc.** is a well-known income tax services firm. Information for 2005 and 2004 from the company's annual report is presented below.[15] (All numbers are in thousands.) Three students who were looking at H&R Block's annual report were overheard to make the following comments:

> *Student* A: What a great year H&R Block had in 2005! The company earned income of $306,551,000 because total assets increased from $5,232,732,000 to $5,539,283,000.

> *Student* B: But it didn't do that well because the change in total assets isn't the same as net income! Its net income was only $27,468,000 because its cash increased from $1,072,745,000 to $1,100,213,000.

> *Student* C: I see from the annual report that H&R Block paid $142,988,000 in the form of dividends to its owners in 2005. Don't you have to consider that when analyzing a company's performance?

H&R Block, Inc.
Condensed Balance Sheets
April 30, 2005 and 2004
(In thousands)

	2005	2004
Assets		
Cash	$1,100,213	$1,072,745
Other assets	4,439,070	4,159,987
Total assets	$5,539,283	$5,232,732
Liabilities		
Total liabilities	$3,562,912	$3,412,917
Owners' Equity		
H&R Block, Capital	1,976,371	1,819,815
Total liabilities and owners' equity	$5,539,283	$5,232,732

1. Comment on the interpretations of Students A and B, and then answer Student C's question.
2. Calculate H&R Block's net income for 2005. (**Hint:** Reconstruct the statement of owner's equity using H&R Block, Capital.)

Decision Analysis Using Excel

LO5, LO6 **Effect of Transactions on the Balance Sheet**

C 5. The summer after finishing her junior year in college, Judy Miller started a painting business in her neighborhood. On June 1, she deposited $2,700 in a new bank account in the name of her company. The $2,700 consisted of a $1,000 loan from her father and $1,700 of her own money.

Using the money in this checking account, Miller rented equipment, purchased supplies, and hired local high school students to do painting jobs for neighbors who had agreed to pay her for the service. At the end of each month, she mailed bills to her customers.

On August 31, Miller was ready to dissolve her business and go back to school for the fall term. Because she had been so busy, she had not kept any records other than her checkbook and a list of amounts owed by customers.

Her checkbook had a balance of $3,520, and her customers owed her $875. She expected these customers to pay her during September. She planned to return unused supplies to the hardware store for a full credit of $50. When she brought back the rented equipment, the hardware store would also return a deposit of $200 she had made in June. She owed the hardware store $525 for equipment rentals and supplies. In addition, she owed the students who had worked for her $100, and she still owed her father $700. Although Miller thinks she did quite well, she is not sure just how successful she was. You have agreed to help her find out.

1. Prepare one balance sheet dated June 1 and another dated August 31 for Miller Painting Company.
2. Using information that can be inferred from comparing the balance sheets, write a memorandum to Miller commenting on her company's performance in achieving profitability and liquidity. (Assume that she used none of the company's assets for personal purposes.) Also, mention the other two financial statements that would be helpful to her in evaluating these business goals.

Annual Report Case: CVS Corporation

LO6 **Analysis of Four Basic Financial Statements**

C 6. Refer to the **CVS** annual report in the Supplement to Chapter 5 to answer the questions below. Keep in mind that every company, while following basic principles, adapts financial statements and terminology to its own special needs. Therefore, the complexity of CVS's financial statements and the terminology in them will differ somewhat from the financial statements in the text.

1. What names does CVS give to its four basic financial statements? (Note that the word *consolidated* in the names of the financial statements means that these statements combine those of several companies owned by CVS.)
2. Prove that the accounting equation works for CVS on December 31, 2005, by finding the amounts for the following equation: Assets = Liabilities + Shareholders' (Owner's) Equity.

3. What were the total revenues of CVS for the year ended December 31, 2005?
4. Was CVS profitable in the year ended December 31, 2005? How much was net income (loss) in that year, and did it increase or decrease from the year ended January 1, 2005?
5. Did the company's cash and cash equivalents increase from January 1, 2005, to December 31, 2005? If so, by how much? In what two places in the statements can this number be found or computed?
6. Did cash flows from operating activities, cash flows from investing activities, and cash flows from financing activities increase or decrease from 2004 to 2005?
7. Who is the auditor for the company? Why is the auditor's report that accompanies the financial statements important?

Comparison Case: CVS Versus Southwest

LO1, LO5, LO7   **Performance Measures and Financial Statements**

C 7. Refer to the **CVS** annual report and the financial statements of **Southwest Airlines Co.** in the Supplement to Chapter 5 to answer these questions:

1. Which company is larger in terms of assets and in terms of revenues? What do you think is the best way to measure the size of a company?
2. Which company is more profitable in terms of net income? What is the trend of profitability over the past three years for both companies?
3. Compute the return on assets for each company for 2005. By this measure, which company is more profitable? Is this a better measure than simply comparing the net income of the two companies? Explain your answer.
4. Which company has more cash? Which increased its cash the most in the last year? Which has more liquidity as measured by cash flows from operating activities?

Ethical Dilemma Case

LO7   **Professional Ethics**

C 8. Discuss the ethical choices in the situations below. In each instance, describe the ethical dilemma, determine the alternative courses of action, and tell what you would do.

1. You are the payroll accountant for a small business. A friend asks you how much another employee is paid per hour.
2. As an accountant for the branch office of a wholesale supplier, you discover that several of the receipts the branch manager has submitted for reimbursement as selling expenses actually stem from nights out with his spouse.
3. You are an accountant in the purchasing department of a construction company. When you arrive home from work on December 22, you find a large ham in a box marked "Happy Holidays—It's a pleasure to work with you." The gift is from a supplier who has bid on a contract your employer plans to award next week.
4. As an auditor with one year's experience at a local CPA firm, you are expected to complete a certain part of an audit in 20 hours. Because of your lack of experience, you know you cannot finish the job within that time. Rather than admit this, you are thinking about working late to finish the job and not telling anyone.

5. You are a tax accountant at a local CPA firm. You help your neighbor fill out her tax return, and she pays you $200 in cash. Because there is no record of this transaction, you are considering not reporting it on your tax return.

6. The accounting firm for which you work as a CPA has just won a new client, a firm in which you own 200 shares of stock that you received as an inheritance from your grandmother. Because it is only a small number of shares and you think the company will be very successful, you are considering not disclosing the investment.

Internet Case

LO1, LO5   **Financial Performance Comparison of Two High-Tech Companies**

C 9. **Microsoft** and **Intel** are two very successful high-tech corporations. Access their websites, find each company's annual report, and locate their consolidated balance sheets and consolidated statements of income. Find the amount of total assets, revenues, and net income for the most recent year shown. Then compute net income to revenues and net income to total assets for both companies. Which company is larger? Which is more profitable?

Group Activity Case

LO2, LO7   **Users of Accounting Information**

C 10. Public companies report quarterly and annually on their success or failure in making a net income. The following item about **Coca-Cola Co.** appeared in *The Wall Street Journal*: "Coke shares have fallen 20% since [the new chief executive officer took] the helm, with many investors skeptical that he can restore the company to consistent growth. Revenue grew 6% last year to $23.1 billion, but the company's profit was essentially flat at $4.87 billion in 2005." [16]

Your instructor will divide the class into groups representing the following users. Discuss why the user your group is representing needs accounting information.

1. The management of Coca-Cola
2. The stockholders of Coca-Cola
3. The creditors of Coca-Cola
4. Potential stockholders of Coca-Cola
5. The Internal Revenue Service
6. The Securities and Exchange Commission
7. The Teamsters' union
8. A consumers' group called Public Cause
9. An economic adviser to the president of the United States

Business Communication Case

LO1, LO6   **Business Goals, Financial Performance, Financial Statements**

C 11. Assume you are working part-time for a small business that does not make any use of financial statements. Based on your knowledge after studying Chapter 1, write the owner a brief business memo in good form that identifies the two major goals of a business. In the memo, explain how financial statements can help the owner achieve these goals. Be sure to tell which statements relate to each of the goals.

2

Analyzing Business Transactions

Most accounting frauds and mistakes violate basic accounting concepts. They may involve recording a transaction at the wrong time, placing the wrong value on it, or calling it by the wrong name. What you learn in this chapter will help you avoid making such mistakes. It will also help you recognize correct accounting practices.

LEARNING OBJECTIVES

LO1 Explain how the concepts of recognition, valuation, and classification apply to business transactions and why they are important factors in ethical financial reporting.

LO2 Explain the double-entry system and the usefulness of T accounts in analyzing business transactions.

LO3 Demonstrate how the double-entry system is applied to common business transactions.

LO4 Prepare a trial balance, and describe its value and limitations.

LO5 Show how the timing of transactions affects cash flows and liquidity.

SUPPLEMENTAL OBJECTIVE

SO6 Define the *chart of accounts,* record transactions in the general journal, and post transactions to the ledger.

Making a Statement

Balance Sheet

Statement of Cash Flows

Income Statement

Business transactions can affect all the financial statements.

- An order for airplanes is obviously an important economic event for both the buyer and the seller. Is there a difference between an economic event and a business transaction that should be recorded in the accounting records?

- Should Boeing record the order in its accounting records?

- How important are liquidity and cash flows to Boeing?

In April 2006, the Chinese government announced that it had ordered 80 Boeing commercial jet liners, thus fulfilling a commitment it had made to purchase 150 planes from Boeing. Valued at about $4.6 billion, the order for the 80 planes was one of many activities that brought about Boeing's resurgence in the stock market. After Boeing received this order, as well as orders from other customers, its stock began trading at an all-time high.

Typically, it takes Boeing almost two years to manufacture a plane. In this case, the aircraft delivery cycle was expected to peak in 2009.[1]

Measurement Issues

LO1 Explain how the concepts of recognition, valuation, and classification apply to business transactions and why they are important factors in ethical financial reporting.

Business transactions are economic events that affect a company's financial position. As shown in Figure 1, to measure a business transaction, you must decide when the transaction occurred (the recognition issue), what value to place on the transaction (the valuation issue), and how the components of the transaction should be categorized (the classification issue).

These three issues—recognition, valuation, and classification—underlie almost every major decision in financial accounting today. They are at the heart of accounting for pension plans, mergers of giant companies, and international transactions. In discussing these issues, we follow generally accepted accounting principles and use an approach that promotes an understanding of basic accounting concepts. Keep in mind, however, that measurement issues can be controversial and resolutions to them are not always as cut-and-dried as the ones presented here.

Recognition

The **recognition** issue refers to the difficulty of deciding *when* a business transaction should be recorded. The resolution of this issue is important because the date on which a transaction is recorded affects amounts in the financial statements.

To illustrate some of the factors involved in the recognition issue, suppose a company wants to purchase an office desk. The following events take place:

1. An employee sends a purchase requisition for the desk to the purchasing department.

2. The purchasing department sends a purchase order to the supplier.

3. The supplier ships the desk.

4. The company receives the desk.

5. The company receives the bill from the supplier.

6. The company pays the bill.

According to accounting tradition, a transaction should be recorded when title to merchandise passes from the supplier to the purchaser and creates an obligation to pay. Thus, depending on the details of the shipping agreement

Study Note

In accounting, *recognize* means to record a transaction or event.

FOCUS ON BUSINESS PRACTICE

Accounting Policies: Where Do You Find Them?

As the text explains, the order of 80 **Boeing** jet liners by the Chinese government, which is the focus of this chapter's Decision Point, was not an event that either the buyer or the seller should have recorded as a transaction. But when do companies record sales or purchase transactions? The answer to this question and others about companies' accounting policies can be found in the Summary of Significant Accounting Policies in their annual reports. For example, in that section of its annual report, Boeing states: "We recognize sales for commercial airplane deliveries as each unit is completed and accepted by the customer."[2]

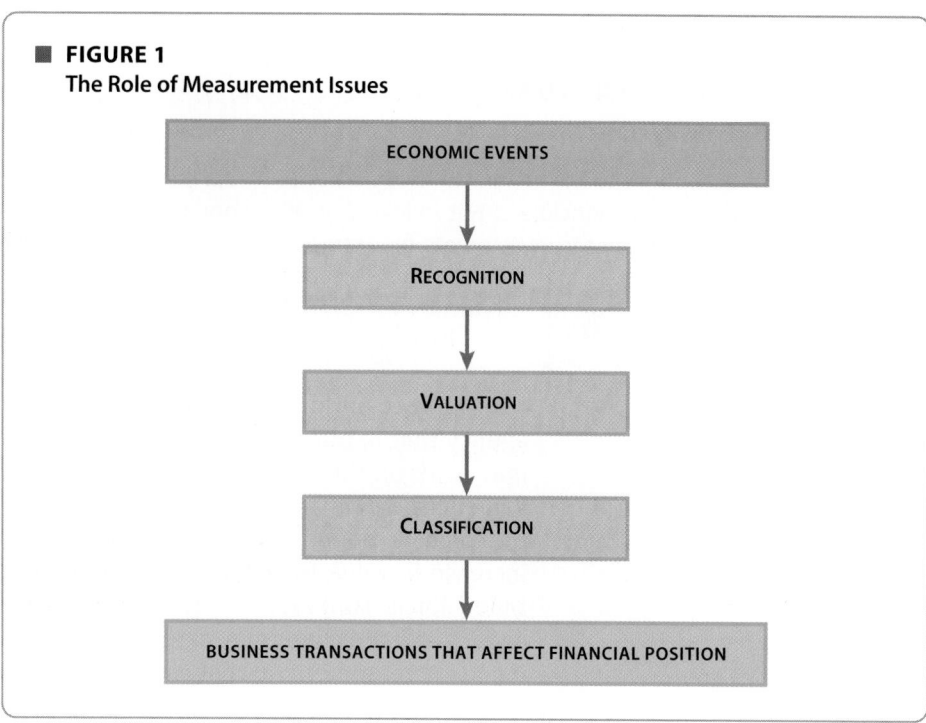

■ **FIGURE 1**
The Role of Measurement Issues

ECONOMIC EVENTS

↓

RECOGNITION

↓

VALUATION

↓

CLASSIFICATION

↓

BUSINESS TRANSACTIONS THAT AFFECT FINANCIAL POSITION

A purchase should usually not be recognized (recorded) before title is transferred because until that point, the vendor has not fulfilled its contractual obligation and the buyer has no liability.

for the desk, the transaction should be recognized (recorded) at the time of either event **3** or **4**. This is the guideline we generally use in this book. However, many small businesses that have simple accounting systems do not record a transaction until they receive a bill (event **5**) or pay it (event **6**) because these are the implied points of title transfer. The predetermined time at which a transaction should be recorded is the **recognition point**.

Although purchase requisitions and purchase orders (events **1** and **2**) are economic events, they do not affect a company's financial position, and they are not recognized in the accounting records. Even the most important economic events may not be recognized in the accounting records. For example, the order of 80 commercial jet liners described in the Decision Point was a very important economic event for both the Chinese government and **Boeing**. Once Boeing reaches final, definitive agreements with customers, it receives deposits from them for the airplanes they have ordered. When the airplanes are delivered, Boeing receives the rest of the payments that are due. The deposits do have a financial impact on revenue in the year in which the orders are booked, but the recognition point for the transaction—for both the buyer and the seller—will not occur until the planes are delivered and title to them transfers from Boeing to the Chinese government.

Here are some more examples of economic events that should and should not be recorded as business transactions:

Events That Are Not Recorded as Transactions	Events That Are Recorded as Transactions
A customer inquires about the availability of a service.	A customer buys a service.
A company hires a new employee.	A company pays an employee for work performed.
A company signs a contract to provide a service in the future.	A company performs a service.

There are some exceptions to the general rules of accounting. For instance, the cost principle is not followed in all parts of the financial statements. Investments, for example, are often accounted for at fair, or market, value. Because these investments are available for sale, the fair value is the best measure of the potential benefit to the company. In its annual report, **Intel Corporation** states: "Investments designated as available-for-sale on the balance sheet date are reported at fair value."[3]

The recognition issue can be difficult to resolve. Consider an advertising agency that is planning a major advertising campaign for a client. Employees may work on the plan several hours a day for a number of weeks. They add value to the plan as they develop it. Should this added value be recognized as the plan is being developed or at the time it is completed? Usually, the increase in value is recorded at the time the plan is finished and the client is billed for it. However, if a plan is going to take a long time to develop, the agency and the client may agree that the client will be billed at key points during its development. In that case, a transaction is recorded at each billing.

Valuation

Valuation is perhaps the most controversial issue in accounting. The **valuation** issue focuses on assigning a monetary value to a business transaction. Generally accepted accounting principles state that the original cost (often called *historical cost*) is the appropriate value to assign to all business transactions—and therefore to all assets, liabilities, and components of owner's equity, including revenues and expenses. **Cost** is defined as the *exchange price* associated with a business transaction at the time the transaction is recorded.

According to GAAP, the purpose of valuation is not to account for value in terms of worth, which can change after a transaction occurs, but to account for value in terms of cost at the time of the transaction. Thus, the cost of an asset is recorded when the asset is acquired. The value is held at that level until the asset is sold, expires, or is consumed. In this context, *value* means the cost at the time of the transaction. The practice of recording transactions at cost is called the **cost principle**.

The cost principle is used because the cost, or exchange price, is verifiable. The **exchange price** results from an agreement between the buyer and

Determining the value of a sale or purchase transaction isn't difficult when the value equals the amount of cash that changes hands. However, barter transactions, in which exchanges are made but no cash changes hands, can make valuation more complicated. Barter transactions are quite common in business today. Here are some examples:

- A consulting company provides its services to an auto dealer in exchange for the loan of a car for a year.

- An office supply company provides a year's supply of computer paper to a local weekly newspaper in exchange for an advertisement in 52 issues of the newspaper.

- Two Internet companies each provide an advertisement and link to the other's website on their own websites.

Determining the value of these transactions is a matter of determining the fair value of the items being traded.

seller that can be verified by evidence created at the time of the transaction. It is this price at which the transaction is recorded. For example, when the order referred to in the Decision Point is finally complete and **Boeing** delivers the jet liners to the Chinese government, both the buyer and the seller will record the transaction at the price they have agreed on.

To illustrate further, suppose a person offers a building for sale at $120,000. It may be valued for real estate taxes at $75,000, and it may be insured for $90,000. One prospective buyer may offer $100,000 for the building, and another may offer $105,000. At this point, several different, unverifiable opinions of value have been expressed. Finally, suppose the seller and a buyer settle on a price and complete the sale for $110,000. All these figures are values of one kind or another, but only the last is sufficiently reliable to be used in the accounting records. The market value of the building may vary over the years, but the building will remain on the new buyer's records at $110,000 until it is sold again. At that point, the accountant will record the new transaction at the new exchange price, and a profit or loss will be recognized.

Classification

The **classification** issue has to do with assigning all the transactions in which a business engages to appropriate categories, or accounts. Classification of debts can affect a company's ability to borrow money, and classification of purchases can affect its income. For example, purchases of tools may be considered repair expenses (a component of owner's equity) or equipment (asset).

As indicated in the Decision Point, it will take **Boeing** some years to manufacture and deliver the 80 jet liners that the Chinese government ordered. During that time, many classification issues will arise. One of the most important is how to classify the numerous costs that Boeing will incur in building the planes. As you will see, generally accepted accounting principles require that these costs be classified as assets until the sale is recorded at the time the planes are delivered. At that time, they will be reclassified as expenses. In this way, the costs will offset the revenues from the sale. It will then be possible to tell whether Boeing made a profit or loss on the transaction.

As we explain later in the chapter, proper classification depends not only on correctly analyzing the effect of each transaction on a business, but also on maintaining a system of accounts that reflects that effect.

Ethics and Measurement Issues

Recognition, valuation, and classification are important factors in ethical financial reporting, and generally accepted accounting principles provide direction about their treatment. These guidelines are intended to help managers meet their obligation to their company's owners and to the public. Many of the worst financial reporting frauds over the past several years have resulted from violations of these guidelines.

▸ **Xerox Corporation** violated the guidelines for recognition when it overstated its revenues by recording revenue from lease agreements at the time the leases were signed rather than over the lease term.

▸ Among its many other transgressions, **Enron Corporation** violated the guidelines for valuation when it valued assets that it transferred to related companies at far more than their actual value.

Senior WorldCom executives violated standards of good financial reporting and GAAP when they deliberately understated expenses to disguise poor performance. Consequences were devastating for employees, investors, and the public trust. *Left to right:* Melvin Dick of Arthur Andersen, Bernard Ebbers and Scott Sullivan of WorldCom, and Jack Grabman of Salomon Smith Barney are sworn in on July 8, 2002, at a congressional hearing of charges against WorldCom.

➧ By a simple violation of the guidelines for classification, **WorldCom** (now **MCI**) perpetrated the largest financial fraud in history, which resulted in the largest bankruptcy in history. Over a period of several years, the company recorded expenditures that should have been classified as expenses as assets; this had the effect of understating the company's expenses and overstating its income by more than $10 billion.

S T O P • R E V I E W • A P P L Y

1-1. What three issues underlie most major accounting decisions?

1-2. A customer asks the owner of a store to save an item for him and says he will pick it up and pay for it next week. The owner agrees to hold it. Should this transaction be recorded as a sale? Explain your answer.

1-3. Why do accountants rely on original cost for valuation purposes?

1-4. Why is classification of a transaction as an expense or an asset a critical issue in accounting?

1-5. How are recognition, valuation, and classification related to the ethics of financial reporting?

Suggested answers to all Stop, Review, and Apply questions are available at http://college.hmco.com/accounting/needles/poa/10e/student_home.html.

Double-Entry System

LO2 Explain the double-entry system and the usefulness of T accounts in analyzing business transactions.

The double-entry system, the backbone of accounting, evolved during the Renaissance. The first systematic description of double-entry book-keeping appeared in 1494, two years after Columbus discovered America, in a mathematics book by Fra Luca Pacioli. Goethe, the famous German poet and dramatist, referred to double-entry bookkeeping as "one of the finest discoveries of the human intellect." Werner Sombart, an eminent economist-sociologist, believed that "double-entry bookkeeping is born of the same spirit as the system of Galileo and Newton."

What is the significance of the double-entry system? The system is based on the *principle of duality*, which means that every economic event has two aspects—effort and reward, sacrifice and benefit, source and use—that offset, or balance, each other. In the **double-entry system**, each transaction must be recorded with at least one debit and one credit, and the total amount of the debits must equal the total amount of the credits. Because of the way it is designed, the whole system is always in balance. All accounting systems, no matter how sophisticated, are based on the principle of duality.

Study Note

Each transaction must include at least one debit and one credit, and the debit totals must equal the credit totals.

Accounts

Accounts are the basic storage units for accounting data and are used to accumulate amounts from similar transactions. An accounting system has a separate account for each asset, each liability, and each component of owner's equity, including revenues and expenses. Whether a company keeps records by hand or by computer, managers must be able to refer to accounts so that they can study their company's financial history and plan for the future. A very small company may need only a few dozen accounts; a multinational corporation may need thousands.

An account title should describe what is recorded in the account. However, account titles can be rather confusing. For example, *Fixed Assets*, *Plant and Equipment*, *Capital Assets*, and *Long-Lived Assets* are all titles for long-term assets. Moreover, many account titles change over time as preferences and practices change.

When you come across an account title that you don't recognize, examine the context of the name—whether it is classified in the financial statements as an asset, liability, or component of owner's equity—and look for the kind of transaction that gave rise to the account.

The T Account

The **T account** is a good place to begin the study of the double-entry system. Such an account has three parts: a title, which identifies the asset, liability, or owner's equity account; a left side, which is called the **debit** side; and a right side, which is called the **credit** side. The T account, so called because it resembles the letter T, is used to analyze transactions. It looks like this:

Study Note

Many students have preconceived ideas about what *debit* and *credit* mean. They think *debit* means "decrease" (or implies something bad) and *credit* means "increase" (or implies something good). It is important to realize that *debit* simply means "left side" and *credit* simply means "right side."

TITLE OF ACCOUNT	
Debit	Credit
(left) side	(right) side

Any entry made on the left side of the account is a debit, and any entry made on the right side is a credit. The terms *debit* (abbreviated Dr., from the Latin *debere*) and *credit* (abbreviated Cr., from the Latin *credere*) are simply the accountant's words for "left" and "right" (*not* for "increase" or "decrease"). We present a more formal version of the T account, the ledger account form, later in this chapter.

The T Account Illustrated

Suppose a company had several transactions during the month that involved the receipt or payment of cash. These transactions can be summarized in the Cash account by recording receipts on the left (debit) side of a T account and payments on the right (credit) side.

CASH	
100,000	70,000
3,000	400
	1,200
103,000	**71,600**
Bal. **31,400**	

The cash receipts on the left total $103,000. (The total is written in bold figures so that it cannot be confused with an actual debit entry.) The cash payments on the right side total $71,600. These totals are simply working totals, or **footings**. Footings, which are calculated at the end of each month, are an easy way to determine cash on hand. The difference in dollars between the total debit footing and the total credit footing is called the **balance**, or *account balance*. If the balance is a debit, it is written on the left side. If it is a credit, it is written on the right side. Notice that the Cash account has a debit balance of $31,400 ($103,000 − $71,600). This is the amount of cash the business has on hand at the end of the month.

Rules of Double-Entry Accounting

The two rules of the double-entry system are that every transaction affects at least two accounts and that total debits must equal total credits. In other words, for every transaction, one or more accounts must be debited, or entered on the left side of the T account, and one or more accounts must be credited, or entered on the right side of the T account, and the total dollar amount of the debits must equal the total dollar amount of the credits.

Look again at the accounting equation:

$$\text{Assets} = \text{Liabilities} + \text{Owner's Equity}$$

You can see that if a debit increases assets, then a credit must be used to increase liabilities or owner's equity because they are on opposite sides of the equal sign. Likewise, if a credit decreases assets, then a debit must be used to decrease liabilities or owner's equity. These rules can be shown as follows:

ASSETS		=	LIABILITIES		+	OWNER'S EQUITY	
Debit	Credit		Debit	Credit		Debit	Credit
for	for		for	for		for	for
increases	decreases		decreases	increases		decreases	increases
(+)	(−)		(−)	(+)		(−)	(+)

1. Debit increases in assets to asset accounts. Credit decreases in assets to asset accounts.

2. Credit increases in liabilities and owner's equity to liability and owner's equity accounts. Debit decreases in liabilities and owner's equity to liability and owner's equity accounts.

One of the more difficult points to understand is the application of double-entry rules to the components of owner's equity. The key is to remember that withdrawals and expenses are deductions from owner's equity. Thus, transactions that *increase* withdrawals or expenses *decrease* owner's equity. Consider this expanded version of the accounting equation:

$$\text{Assets} = \text{Liabilities} + \underbrace{\text{Owner's Capital} - \text{Withdrawals} + \text{Revenues} - \text{Expenses}}_{\text{Owner's Equity}}$$

ASSETS		LIABILITIES		OWNER'S CAPITAL		WITHDRAWALS		REVENUES		EXPENSES	
+	−	−	+	−	+	+	−	−	+	+	−
(Dr.)	(Cr.)	(Dr.)	(Cr.)	(Dr.)	(Cr.)	(Dr.)	(Cr.)	(Dr.)	(Cr.)	(Dr.)	(Cr.)

Normal Balance

The **normal balance** of an account is its usual balance and is the side (debit or credit) that increases the account. Table 1 summarizes the normal account balances of the major account categories. If you have difficulty remembering the normal balances and the rules of debit and credit, try using the acronym AWE: Asset accounts, Withdrawals, and Expenses are always increased by debits. All other normal accounts are increased by credits.

TABLE 1.   Normal Account Balances of Major Account Categories

Account Category	Increases Recorded by		Normal Balance	
	Debit	Credit	Debit	Credit
Assets	x		x	
Liabilities		x		x
Owner's equity:				
Owner's Capital		x		x
Withdrawals	x		x	
Revenues		x		x
Expenses	x		x	

Owner's Equity Accounts

Figure 2 illustrates how owner's equity accounts relate to each other and to the financial statements. The distinctions among these accounts are important for both legal purposes and financial reporting.

Study Note

Although withdrawals are a component of owner's equity, they normally appear only in the statement of owner's equity. They do not appear in the owner's equity section of the balance sheet or as an expense on the income statement.

Study Note

Although revenues and expenses are components of owner's equity, they appear on the income statement, not in the owner's equity section of the balance sheet. Figure 2 illustrates this point.

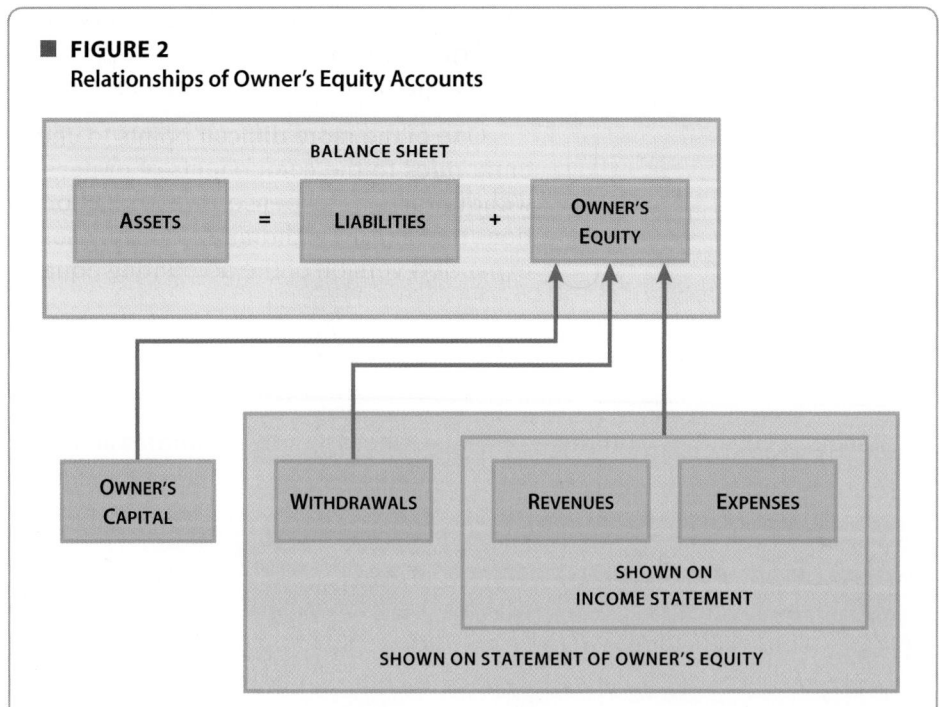

■ **FIGURE 2**
Relationships of Owner's Equity Accounts

S T O P • R E V I E W • A P P L Y

2-1. Why is the system of recording entries called the double-entry system? What is significant about this system?

2-2. Is the statement "Debits are bad; credits are good" true? Explain your answer.

2-3. What is an account, and what is its normal balance?

2-4. What are T accounts, and why are they useful?

2-5. What are the rules of double entry for (a) assets, (b) liabilities, and (c) owner's equity?

T Accounts, Normal Balance, and the Accounting Equation   You are given the following list of accounts with dollar amounts:

J. Morgan, Withdrawals	$ 75
Accounts Payable	200
Wages Expense	150
Cash	625
J. Morgan, Capital	400
Fees Revenue	250

Insert the account title at the top of the corresponding T account that follows and enter the dollar amount as a normal balance in the account. Then show that the accounting equation is in balance.

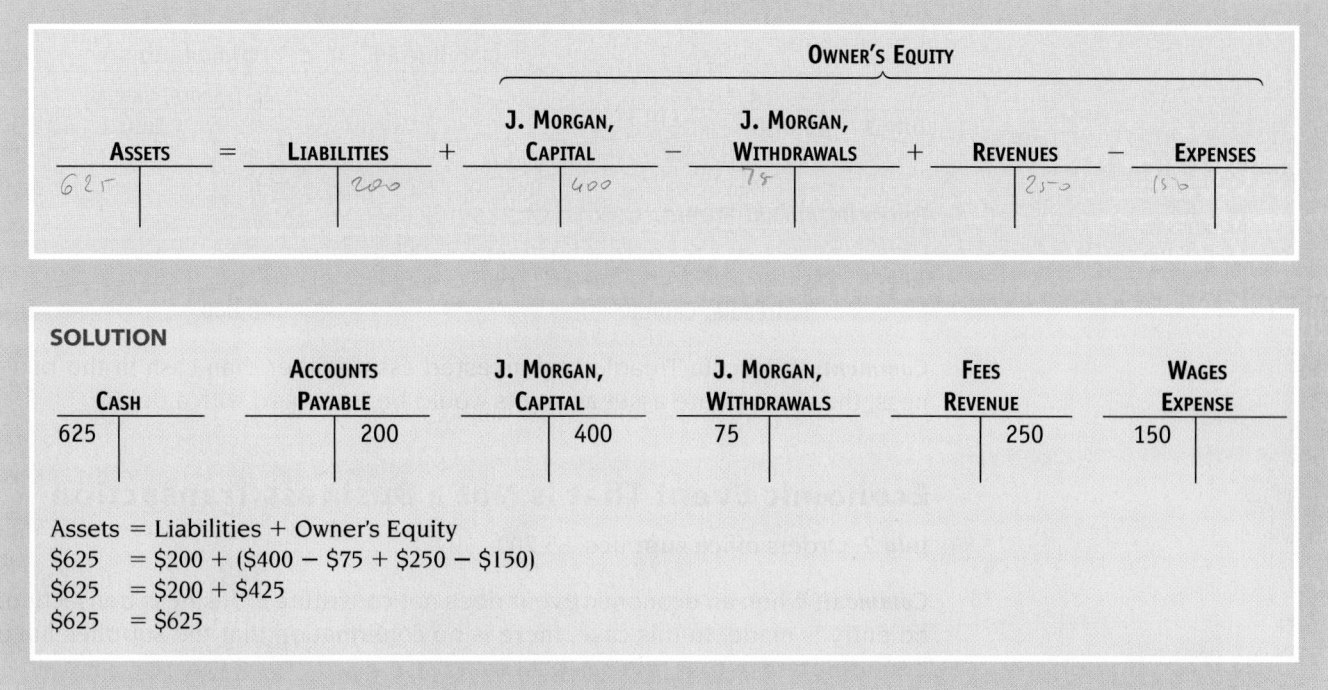

	ASSETS	=	LIABILITIES	+	J. MORGAN, CAPITAL	−	J. MORGAN, WITHDRAWALS	+	REVENUES	−	EXPENSES
handwritten	625		200		400		75		250		150

SOLUTION

CASH	ACCOUNTS PAYABLE	J. MORGAN, CAPITAL	J. MORGAN, WITHDRAWALS	FEES REVENUE	WAGES EXPENSE
625	200	400	75	250	150

Assets = Liabilities + Owner's Equity
$625   = $200 + ($400 − $75 + $250 − $150)
$625   = $200 + $425
$625   = $625

Business Transaction Analysis

LO3 Demonstrate how the double-entry system is applied to common business transactions.

In the pages that follow, we show how to apply the double-entry system to some common business transactions. **Source documents**—invoices, receipts, checks, or contracts—usually support the details of a transaction. We focus on the transactions of a small firm, Treadle Website Design. For each transaction, we follow these steps:

1. State the transaction.

2. Analyze the transaction to determine which accounts are affected.

3. Apply the rules of double-entry accounting by using T accounts to show how the transaction affects the accounting equation.

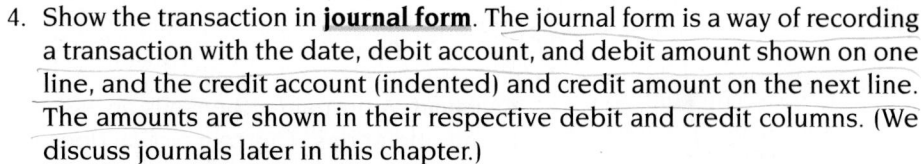

4. Show the transaction in **journal form**. The journal form is a way of recording a transaction with the date, debit account, and debit amount shown on one line, and the credit account (indented) and credit amount on the next line. The amounts are shown in their respective debit and credit columns. (We discuss journals later in this chapter.)

5. Provide a comment that will help you apply the rules of double entry.

Owner's Investment to Form the Business

July 1: Priscilla Treadle invests $40,000 in cash to form Treadle Website Design.

Analysis: An owner's investment in the business *increases* the asset account *Cash* with a debit and *increases* the owner's equity account *P. Treadle, Capital* with a credit.

Application of Double Entry:

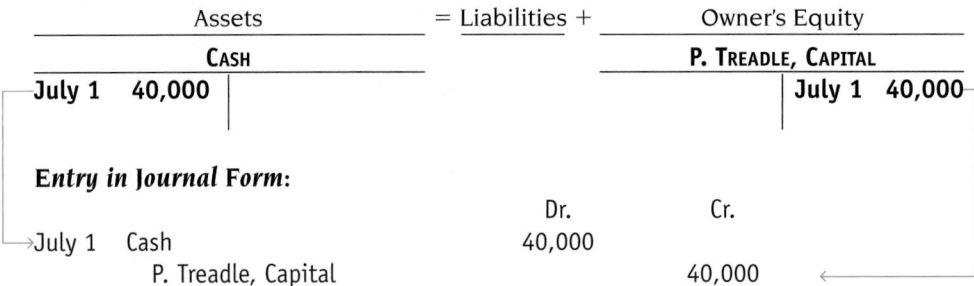

Assets	= Liabilities +	Owner's Equity
CASH		**P. TREADLE, CAPITAL**
July 1 40,000		July 1 40,000

Entry in Journal Form:

		Dr.	Cr.
July 1	Cash	40,000	
	P. Treadle, Capital		40,000

Comment: If Priscilla Treadle had invested assets other than cash in the business, the appropriate asset accounts would be increased with a debit.

Economic Event That Is Not a Business Transaction

July 2: Orders office supplies, $5,200.

Comment: When an economic event does not constitute a business transaction, no entry is made. In this case, there is no confirmation that the supplies have been shipped or that title has passed.

Prepayment of Expenses in Cash

July 3: Rents an office; pays two months rent in advance, $3,200.

Analysis: The prepayment of office rent in cash *increases* the asset account *Prepaid Rent* with a debit and *decreases* the asset account *Cash* with a credit.

Application of Double Entry:

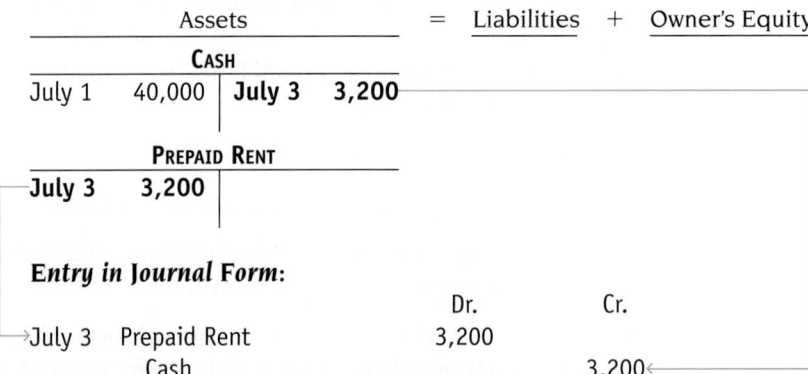

Assets	= Liabilities + Owner's Equity
CASH	
July 1 40,000 | July 3 3,200	
PREPAID RENT	
July 3 3,200	

Entry in Journal Form:

		Dr.	Cr.
July 3	Prepaid Rent	3,200	
	Cash		3,200

Comment: A prepaid expense is an asset because the expenditure will benefit future operations. This transaction does not affect the totals of assets or liabilities and owner's equity because it simply trades one asset for another asset. If the company had paid only July's rent, the owner's equity account *Rent Expense* would be debited because the total benefit of the expenditure would be used up in the current month.

Purchase of an Asset on Credit

July 5: Receives office supplies ordered on July 2 and an invoice for $5,200.

Analysis: The purchase of office supplies on credit *increases* the asset account *Office Supplies* with a debit and *increases* the liability account *Accounts Payable* with a credit.

Application of Double Entry:

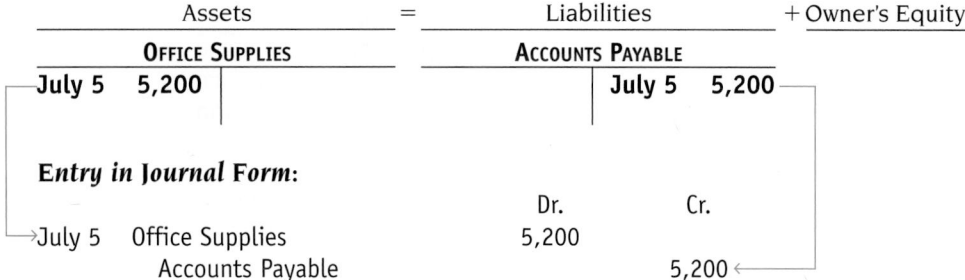

Comment: Office supplies are considered an asset (prepaid expense) because they will not be used up in the current month and thus will benefit future periods. Accounts Payable is used when there is a delay between the time of the purchase and the time of payment.

Purchase of an Asset Partly in Cash and Partly on Credit

July 6: Purchases office equipment, $16,320; pays $13,320 in cash and agrees to pay the rest next month.

Analysis: The purchase of office equipment in cash and on credit *increases* the asset account *Office Equipment* with a debit, *decreases* the asset account *Cash* with a credit, and *increases* the liability account *Accounts Payable* with a credit.

Application of Double Entry:

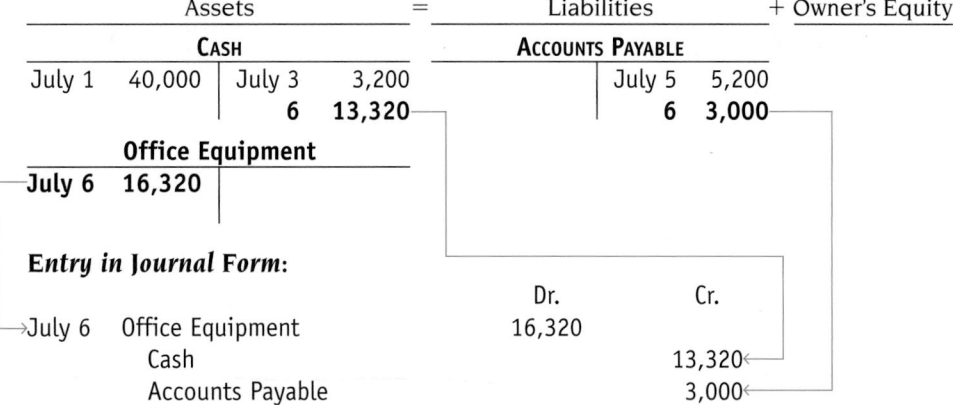

Comment: As this transaction illustrates, assets may be paid for partly in cash and partly on credit. When more than two accounts are involved in a journal entry, as they are in this one, it is called a **compound entry**.

Payment of a Liability

July 9: Makes a partial payment of the amount owed for the office supplies received on July 5, $2,600.

Analysis: A payment of a liability *decreases* the liability account *Accounts Payable* with a debit and *decreases* the asset account *Cash* with a credit.

Application of Double Entry:

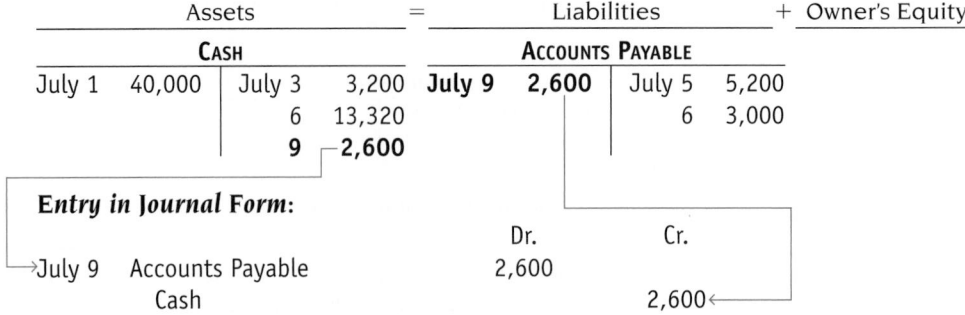

Comment: Note that the office supplies were recorded when they were purchased on July 5.

Revenue in Cash

July 10: Performs a service for an automobile dealer by designing a website and collects a fee in cash, $2,800.

Analysis: Revenue received in cash *increases* the asset account *Cash* with a debit and *increases* the owner's equity account *Design Revenue* with a credit.

Application of Double Entry:

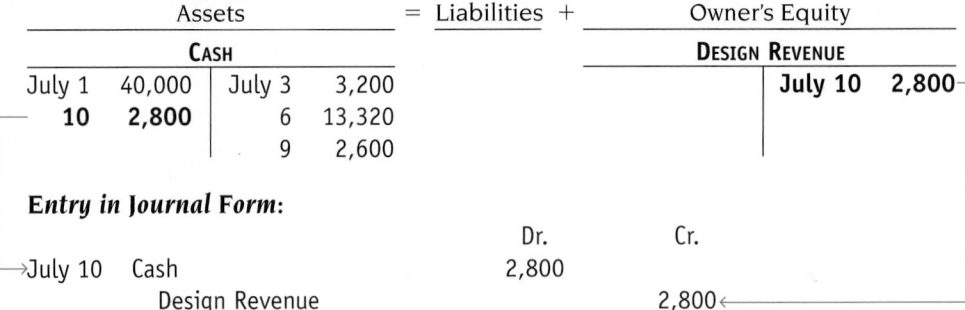

Comment: For this transaction, revenue is recognized when the service is provided and the cash is received.

Revenue on Credit

July 15: Performs a service for a department store by designing a website; bills for the fee now but will collect the fee later, $9,600.

Analysis: A revenue billed to a customer *increases* the asset account *Accounts Receivable* with a debit and *increases* the owner's equity account *Design Revenue* with a credit. Accounts Receivable is used to indicate the company's right to collect the money in the future.

Application of Double Entry:

Assets	= Liabilities +	Owner's Equity
ACCOUNTS RECEIVABLE		DESIGN REVENUE

July 15 9,600		July 10	2,800
		15	9,600

Entry in Journal Form:

	Dr.	Cr.
July 15 Accounts Receivable	9,600	
Design Revenue		9,600

Comment: In this case, there is a delay between the time revenue is earned and the time the cash is received. Revenues are recorded at the time they are earned and billed regardless of when cash is received.

Revenue Collected in Advance

July 19: Accepts an advance fee as a deposit on a website to be designed, $1,400.

Analysis: Revenue received in advance *increases* the asset account *Cash* with a debit and *increases* the liability account *Unearned Design Revenue* with a credit.

Application of Double Entry:

Assets		=	Liabilities	+ Owner's Equity
CASH			UNEARNED DESIGN REVENUE	

July 1	40,000	July 3	3,200	July 19 1,400	
10	2,800	6	13,320		
19	1,400	9	2,600		

Entry in Journal Form:

	Dr.	Cr.
July 19 Cash	1,400	
Unearned Design Revenue		1,400

Comment: In this case, cash is received before the fees are earned. Unearned Design Revenue is a liability because the firm must provide the service or return the deposit.

Collection on Account

July 22: Receives cash from customer previously billed on July 15, $5,000.

Analysis: Collection of an account receivable from a customer previously billed *increases* the asset account *Cash* with a debit and *decreases* the asset account *Accounts Receivable* with a credit.

Application of Double Entry:

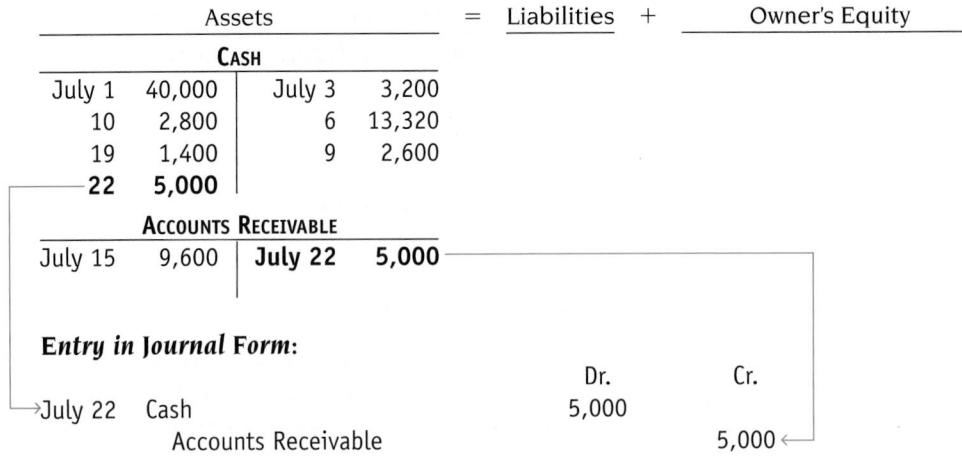

Comment: Note that the revenue related to this transaction was recorded on July 15. Thus, no revenue is recorded at this time.

Expense Paid in Cash

July 26: Pays employees four weeks' wages, $4,800.

Analysis: This cash expense *increases* the owner's equity account *Wages Expense* with a debit and *decreases* the asset account *Cash* with a credit.

Application of Double Entry:

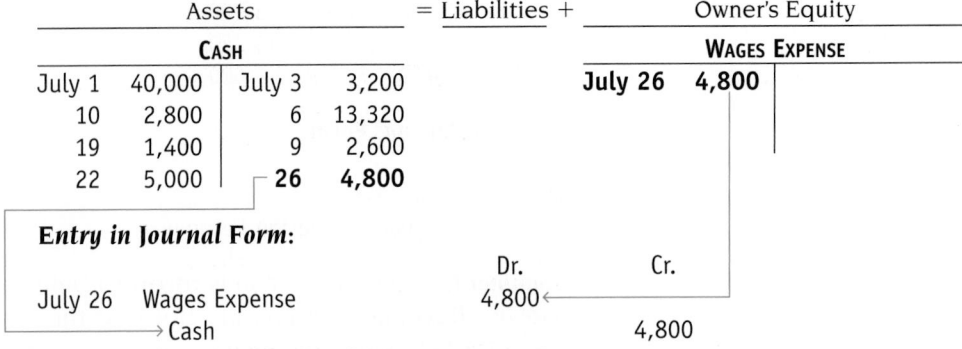

Comment: Note that the increase in Wages Expense will *decrease* owner's equity.

Expense to Be Paid Later

July 30: Receives, but does not pay, the utility bill that is due next month, $680.

Analysis: This cash expense *increases* the owner's equity account *Utilities Expense* with a debit and *increases* the liability account *Accounts Payable* with a credit.

Application of **Double Entry**:

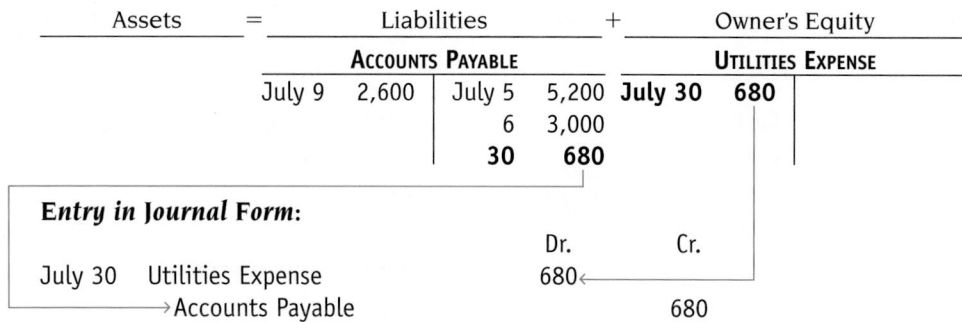

Entry in Journal Form:

		Dr.	Cr.
July 30	Utilities Expense	680	
	→Accounts Payable		680

Comment: The expense is recorded if the benefit has been received and the amount is owed, even if the cash is not to be paid until later. Note that the increase in Utilities Expense will *decrease* owner's equity.

Withdrawals

July 31: Withdraws $2,800 in cash.

Analysis: A cash withdrawal *increases* the owner's equity account *Withdrawals* with a debit and *decreases* the asset account *Cash* with a credit.

Application of **Double Entry**:

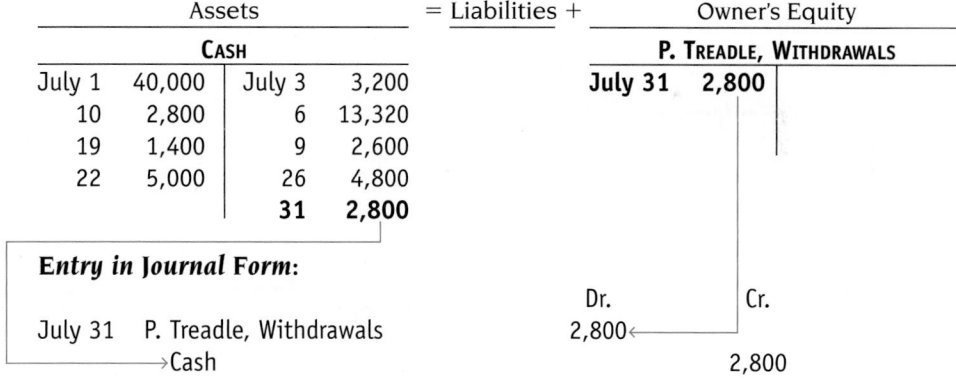

Entry in Journal Form:

		Dr.	Cr.
July 31	P. Treadle, Withdrawals	2,800	
	→Cash		2,800

Comment: Note that the increase in Withdrawals will *decrease* owner's equity.

Summary of Transactions

Exhibit 1 uses the accounting equation to summarize the transactions of Treadle Website Design. Note that the income statement accounts appear under owner's equity and that the transactions in the Cash account will be reflected on the statement of cash flows.

▼ EXHIBIT 1

Summary of Transactions of Treadle Website Design

Assets	=	Liabilities	+	Owner's Equity

Cash

July	1	40,000	July	3	3,200
	10	2,800		6	13,320
	19	1,400		9	2,600
	22	5,000		26	4,800
				31	2,800
		49,200			26,720
Bal.		22,480			

→ This account links to the statement of cash flows.

Accounts Payable

July 9	2,600	July	5	5,200
			6	3,000
			30	680
	2,600			8,880
		Bal.		6,280

P. Treadle, Capital

		July 1	40,000

P. Treadle, Withdrawals

July 31	2,800	

Accounts Receivable

July 15	9,600	July 22	5,000
Bal.	4,600		

Unearned Design Revenue

	July 19	1,400

Design Revenue

	July 10	2,800
	15	9,600
Bal.		12,400

Office Supplies

July 5	5,200	

Wages Expense

July 26	4,800	

Prepaid Rent

July 3	3,200	

Utilities Expense

July 30	680	

These accounts link to the income statement. ←

Office Equipment

July 6	16,320	

Assets	=	Liabilities	+	Owner's Equity
$51,800	=	$7,680	+	$44,120
	=		+	

STOP • REVIEW • APPLY

3-1. Explain the meaning of this statement: "The Cash account has a debit balance of $500."

3-2. Explain why debits, which decrease owner's equity, increase expenses, which are a component of owner's equity.

3-3. What steps are followed in analyzing a business transaction?

3-4. What is the normal balance of Accounts Payable? Under what conditions could Accounts Payable have a debit balance?

The Trial Balance

For every amount debited, an equal amount must be credited. This means that the total of debits and credits in the T accounts must be equal. To test this, the accountant periodically prepares a **trial balance**. Exhibit 2 shows a trial balance for Treadle Website Design. It was prepared from the accounts in Exhibit 1.

Preparation and Use of a Trial Balance

Although a trial balance may be prepared at any time, it is usually prepared on the last day of the accounting period. The preparation involves these steps:

> **Study Note**
>
> The trial balance is usually prepared at the end of an accounting period. It is an initial check that the accounts are in balance.

1. List each account that has a balance, with debit balances in the left column and credit balances in the right column. Accounts are listed in the order in which they appear in the financial statements.

2. Add each column.

3. Compare the totals of the columns.

Once in a while, a transaction leaves an account with a balance that isn't "normal." For example, when a company overdraws its bank account, its Cash account (an asset) will show a credit balance instead of a debit balance. The "abnormal" balance should be copied into the trial balance columns as it stands, as a debit or a credit.

The trial balance proves whether the ledger is in balance. *In balance* means that the total of all debits recorded equals the total of all credits recorded. But the trial balance does not prove that the transactions were analyzed correctly or recorded in the proper accounts. For example, there is no way of determining from the trial balance that a debit should have been made in the Office

EXHIBIT 2 ▶

Trial Balance		
Treadle Website Design		
Trial Balance		
July 31, 20xx		
Cash	$22,480	
Accounts Receivable	4,600	
Office Supplies	5,200	
Prepaid Rent	3,200	
Office Equipment	16,320	
Accounts Payable		$ 6,280
Unearned Design Revenue		1,400
P. Treadle, Capital		40,000
P. Treadle, Withdrawals	2,800	
Design Revenue		12,400
Wages Expense	4,800	
Utilities Expense	680	
	$60,080	$60,080

Supplies account rather than in the Office Equipment account. And the trial balance does not detect whether transactions have been omitted, because equal debits and credits will have been omitted. Also, if an error of the same amount is made in both a debit and a credit, it will not be evident in the trial balance. The trial balance proves only that the debits and credits in the accounts are in balance.

Finding Trial Balance Errors

If the debit and credit balances in a trial balance are not equal, look for one or more of the following errors:

1. A debit was entered in an account as a credit, or vice versa.
2. The balance of an account was computed incorrectly.
3. An error was made in carrying the account balance to the trial balance.
4. The trial balance was summed incorrectly.

Other than simply adding the columns incorrectly, the two most common mistakes in preparing a trial balance are

1. Recording an account as a credit when it usually carries a debit balance, or vice versa. This mistake causes the trial balance to be out of balance by an amount divisible by 2.
2. Transposing two digits when transferring an amount to the trial balance (for example, entering $23,459 as $23,549). This error causes the trial balance to be out of balance by an amount divisible by 9.

So, if a trial balance is out of balance and the addition of the columns is correct, determine the amount by which the trial balance is out of balance and divide it first by 2 and then by 9. If the amount is divisible by 2, look in the trial balance for an amount that is equal to the quotient. If you find such an amount, chances are it's in the wrong column. If the amount is divisible by 9, trace each amount back to the T account balance, checking carefully for a transposition error. If neither of these techniques is successful in identifying the error, first recompute the balance of each T account. Then, if you still have not found the error, retrace each posting from the journal to the T account.

STOP • REVIEW • APPLY

4-1. What is a trial balance, and why is it useful?

4-2. Is it possible for errors to be present in a trial balance whose debit and credit balances are equal? Explain your answer.

FOCUS ON BUSINESS PRACTICE

Should Earnings Be Aligned with Cash Flows?

Electronic Data Systems Corporation (EDS), the large computer services company, recently announced that it was reducing past earnings by $2.24 billion to implement a new accounting rule that would more closely align its earnings with cash flows. Analysts had been critical of EDS for recording revenue from its long-term contracts when the contracts were signed rather than when the cash was received. In fact, about 40 percent of EDS's revenue had been recognized well before the cash was to be received. Analysts' response to the change in EDS's accounting was very positive. "Finally, maybe, we'll see cash flows moving in line with earnings," said one.[4] Although there are natural and unavoidable differences between earnings and cash flows, it is best if accounting rules are not used to exaggerate these differences.

Cash Flows and the Timing of Transactions

LO5   Show how the timing of transactions affects cash flows and liquidity.

To avoid financial distress, a company must be able to pay its bills on time. Because the timing of cash flows is critical to maintaining adequate liquidity to pay bills, managers and other users of financial information must understand the difference between transactions that generate immediate cash and those that do not. Consider the transactions of Treadle Website Design shown in Figure 3. Most of them involve either an inflow or outflow of cash.

As you can see in Figure 3, Treadle's Cash account has more transactions than any of its other accounts. Look at the transactions of July 10, 15, and 22. On July 10, Treadle received cash of $2,800. On July 15, the firm billed a customer $9,600 for a service it had already performed. On July 22, it received cash of $5,000 from the customer, but it had not received the remaining $4,600 by the end of the month. Because Treadle incurred expenses in providing this service, it must pay careful attention to its cash flows and liquidity.

One way Treadle can manage its expenditures is to rely on its creditors to give it time to pay. Compare the transactions of July 3, 5, and 9 in Figure 3. On July 3, Treadle prepaid rent of $3,200. That immediate cash outlay may have caused a strain on the business. On July 5, the company received an invoice for office supplies in the amount of $5,200. In this case, it took advantage of the

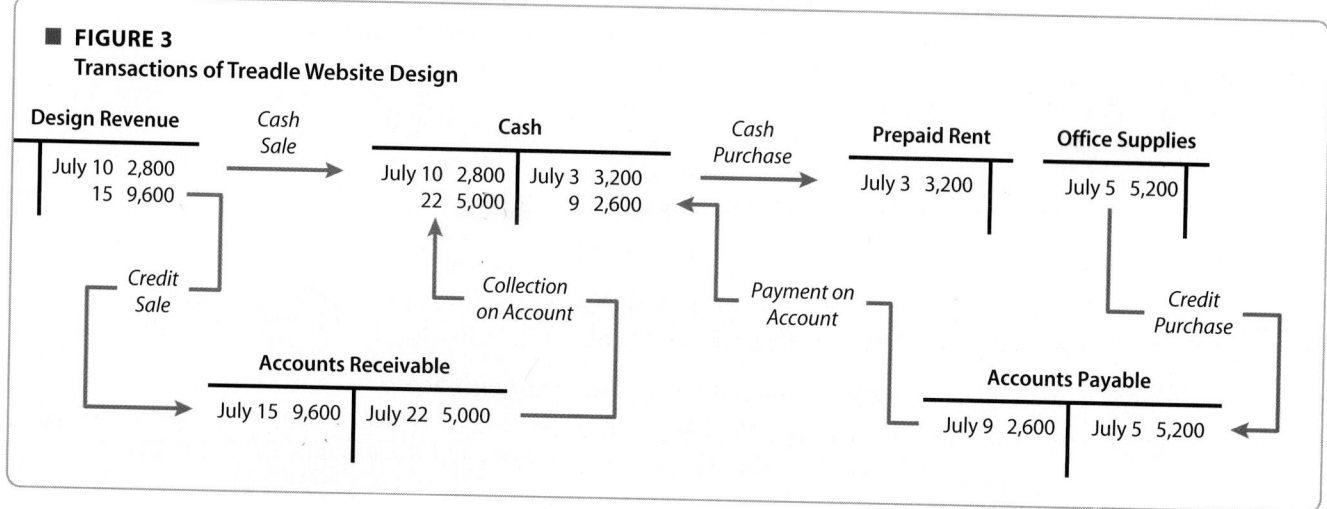

■ **FIGURE 3**
Transactions of Treadle Website Design

Because Boeing takes years to plan and make the airplanes that customers have ordered, its management must carefully plan the company's needs for cash. The timing of cash flows is critical to maintaining adequate liquidity.

Study Note

Recording revenues and expenses when they occur will provide a clearer picture of a company's profitability on the income statement. The change in cash flows will provide a clearer picture of a company's liquidity on the statement of cash flows.

opportunity to defer payment. It paid $2,600 on July 9, but it had not paid the remaining $2,600 by the end of the month.

Of course, Treadle expects to receive the rest of the cash from the customer that it billed on July 15, and it must eventually pay the rest of what it owes on the office supplies. In the meantime, it must perform a delicate balancing act with its cash flows to ensure that it achieves the goal of liquidity.

Large companies face the same challenge, but often on a much greater scale. For example, it can take **Boeing** a number of years to plan, develop, and manufacture the planes that its customers order. At the end of 2005, Boeing had orders for 7,377 planes, totaling $124 billion, or about $16.8 million per plane.[5] Think of the cash outlays Boeing must make before it delivers the planes and collects payment for them. To maintain liquidity so that Boeing can eventually reap the rewards of delivering the planes, Boeing's management must carefully plan the company's needs for cash.

STOP • REVIEW • APPLY

5-1. Why is the timing of cash flows important?

5-2. Under what circumstance is there a delay between the time a sale is made and the time cash is collected?

Cash Flow Analysis A company engaged in the following transactions:

Oct. 1 Performed services for cash, $750.
2 Paid expenses in cash, $550.
3 Incurred expenses on credit, $650.
4 Performed services on credit, $900.
5 Made payment on account, $350.
6 Collected cash on account, $600.

Enter the correct titles in the following T accounts, and enter the above transactions in the accounts. Determine the cash balance after these transactions, the amount still to be received, and the amount still to be paid.

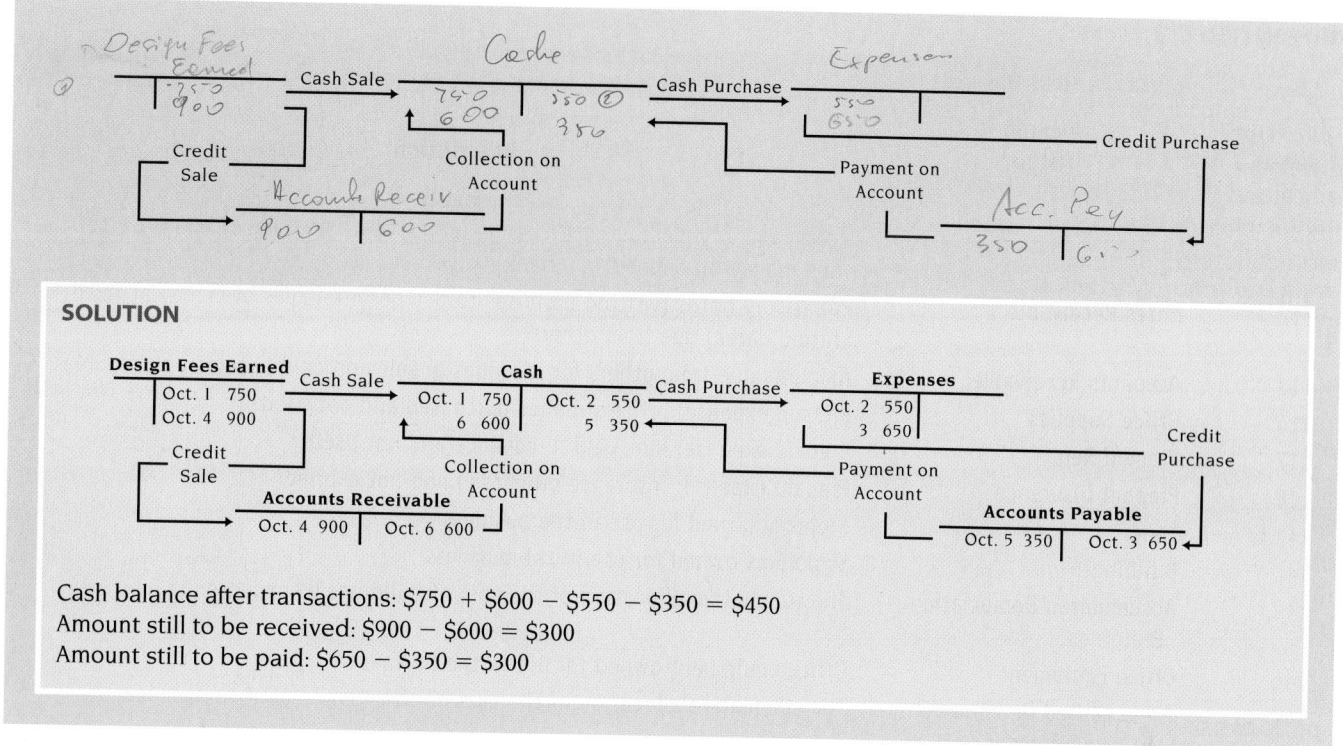

SOLUTION

Cash balance after transactions: $750 + $600 − $550 − $350 = $450

Amount still to be received: $900 − $600 = $300

Amount still to be paid: $650 − $350 = $300

Recording and Posting Transactions

SO6 Define the *chart of accounts,* record transactions in the general journal, and post transactions to the ledger.

Earlier in the chapter, we described how transactions are analyzed according to the rules of double entry and how a trial balance is prepared. As Figure 4 shows, transaction analysis and preparation of a trial balance are the first and last steps in a four-step process. The two intermediate steps are recording the entry in the general journal and posting the entry to the ledger. In this section, we demonstrate how these steps are accomplished in a manual accounting system.

■ **FIGURE 4**

Analyzing and Processing Transactions

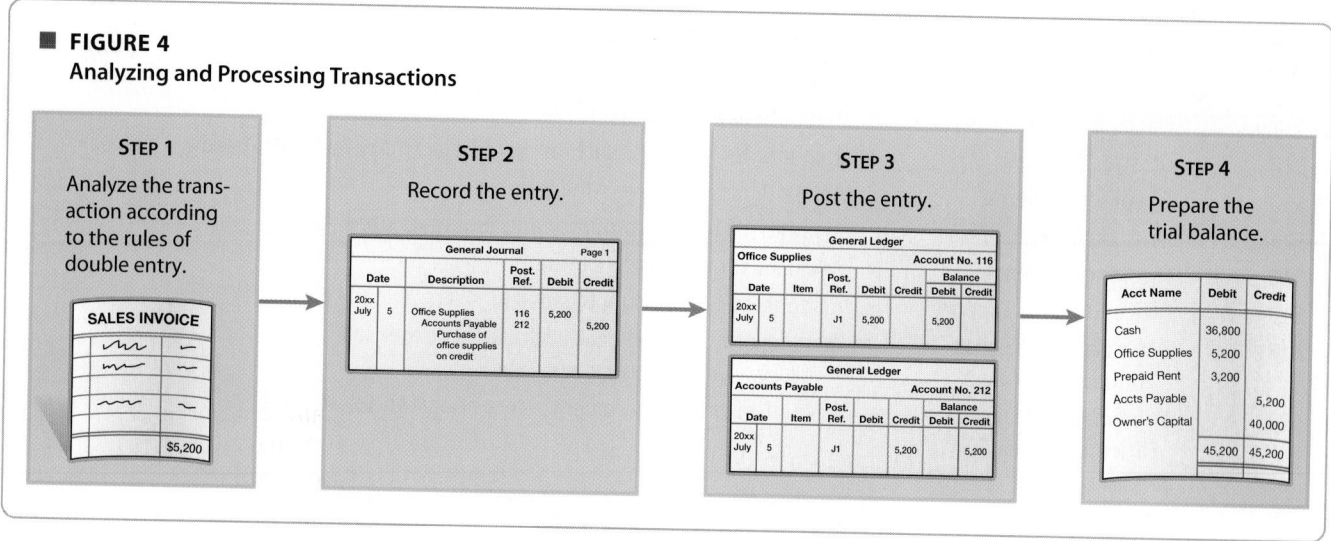

▼ **EXHIBIT 3**

Chart of Accounts for a Small Business

Account Number	Account Name	Description
		Assets
111	Cash	Money and any medium of exchange (coins, currency, checks, money orders, and money on deposit in a bank)
112	Notes Receivable	Promissory notes (written promises to pay definite sums of money at fixed future dates) due from others
113	Accounts Receivable	Amounts due from others for revenues or sales on credit (sales on account)
116	Office Supplies	Prepaid expense; office supplies purchased and not used
117	Prepaid Rent	Prepaid expense; rent paid in advance and not used
118	Prepaid Insurance	Prepaid expense; insurance purchased and not expired
141	Land	Property owned for use in the business
142	Buildings	Structures owned for use in the business
143	Accumulated Depreciation, Buildings	The cumulative allocation of the cost of buildings to expense
146	Office Equipment	Office equipment owned for use in the business
147	Accumulated Depreciation, Office Equipment	The cumulative allocation of the cost of office equipment to expense
		Liabilities
211	Notes Payable	Promissory notes due to others
212	Accounts Payable	Amounts due to others for purchases on credit
213	Unearned Design Revenue	Unearned revenue; advance deposits for website design to be provided in the future
214	Wages Payable	Amounts due to employees for wages earned and not paid
		Owner's Equity
311	Owner's Capital	Owner's investments in a company and claims against company assets derived from profitable operations
313	Withdrawals	Distributions of assets (usually cash) that reduce owner's capital
314	Income Summary	Temporary account used at the end of the accounting period to summarize the revenues and expenses for the period
		Revenues
411	Design Revenue	Revenues derived from website design services
		Expenses
511	Wages Expense	Amounts earned by employees
512	Utilities Expense	Amounts for utilities, such as water, electricity, and gas, used
513	Telephone Expense	Amounts of telephone services used
514	Rent Expense	Amounts of rent on property and buildings used
515	Insurance Expense	Amounts for insurance expired
517	Office Supplies Expense	Amounts for office supplies used
518	Depreciation Expense– Buildings	Amount of buildings' cost allocated to expense
520	Depreciation Expense– Office Equipment	Amount of office equipment's cost allocated to expense

Chart of Accounts

In a manual accounting system, each account is kept on a separate page or card. These pages or cards are placed together in a book or file called the **general ledger**. In the computerized systems that most companies have today, accounts are maintained electronically. However, as a matter of convenience, accountants still refer to the group of company accounts as the *general ledger*, or simply the *ledger*.

To help identify accounts in the ledger and make them easy to find, the accountant often numbers them. A list of these numbers with the corresponding account titles is called a **chart of accounts**. A very simple chart of accounts appears in Exhibit 3. The first digit in the account number identifies the major financial statement classification—that is, an account number that begins with the digit 1 means that the account is an asset account, an account number that begins with a 2 means that the account is a liability account, and so forth. The second and third digits identify individual accounts. The gaps in the sequence of numbers allow the accountant to expand the number of accounts.

General Journal

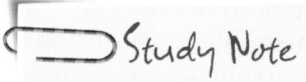

Although transactions can be entered directly into the ledger accounts, this method makes identifying individual transactions or finding errors very difficult because the debit is recorded in one account and the credit in another. The solution is to record all transactions chronologically in a **journal**. The journal is sometimes called the *book of original entry* because it is where transactions first enter the accounting records. Later, the debit and credit portions of each transaction are transferred to the appropriate accounts in the ledger. A separate **journal entry** is used to record each transaction; the process of recording transactions is called **journalizing**.

Most businesses have more than one kind of journal. The simplest and most flexible kind is the **general journal**, the one we focus on here. Businesses will also have several special-purpose journals, each for recording a common transaction, such as credit sales, credit purchases, cash receipts, and cash disbursements. At this point we cover only the general journal. Exhibit 4, which displays two of the transactions of Treadle Website Design that we discussed earlier, shows the format for recording entries in a general journal.

EXHIBIT 4 ▶ **The General Journal**

	General Journal				Page 1
Date	Description	Post. Ref.	Debit	Credit
20xx				
July 3	Prepaid Rent		3,200	
	Cash			3,200
	Pays two months' rent in advance			
5	Office Supplies		5,200	
	Accounts Payable			5,200
	Purchases office supplies on credit			

A = L + OE
+ 3,200
− 3,200

A = L + OE
+ 5,200 + 5,200

As you can see in Exhibit 4, the entries in a general journal include the following information about each transaction:

1. The date. The year appears on the first line of the first column, the month on the next line of the first column, and the day in the second column opposite the month. For subsequent entries on the same page for the same month and year, the month and year can be omitted.

2. The names of the accounts debited and credited, which appear in the Description column. The names of the accounts that are debited are placed next to the left margin opposite the dates; on the line below, the names of the accounts credited are indented.

3. The debit amounts, which appear in the Debit column opposite the accounts that are debited, and the credit amounts, which appear in the Credit column opposite the accounts credited.

4. An explanation of each transaction, which appears in the Description column below the account names. An explanation should be brief but sufficient to explain and identify the transaction.

5. The account numbers in the Post. Ref. column, if they apply.

At the time the transactions are recorded, nothing is placed in the Post. Ref. (posting reference) column. (This column is sometimes called LP or *Folio*.) Later, if the company uses account numbers to identify accounts in the ledger, the account numbers are filled in. They provide a convenient cross-reference from the general journal to the ledger and indicate that the entry has been posted to the ledger. If the accounts are not numbered, the accountant uses a checkmark (✓) to signify that the entry has been posted.

General Ledger

The general journal is used to record the details of each transaction. The general ledger is used to update each account.

The Ledger Account Form   The T account is a simple, direct means of recording transactions. In practice, a somewhat more complicated form of the account is needed to record more information. The **ledger account form**, which contains four columns for dollar amounts, is illustrated in Exhibit 5.

The account title and number appear at the top of the account form. As in the journal, the transaction date appears in the first two columns. The Item col-

> **Study Note**
>
> A T account is a means of quickly analyzing a set of transactions. It is simply an abbreviated version of a ledger account. Ledger accounts, which provide more information, are used in the accounting records.

EXHIBIT 5 ▶

Accounts Payable in the General Ledger

General Ledger

Accounts Payable   Account No. 212

Date		Item	Post. Ref.	Debit	Credit	Balance Debit	Balance Credit
20xx							
July	5		J1		5,200		5,200
	6		J1		3,000		8,200
	9		J1	2,600			5,600
	30		J2		680		6,280

EXHIBIT 6 ▶ | **Posting from the General Journal to the Ledger**

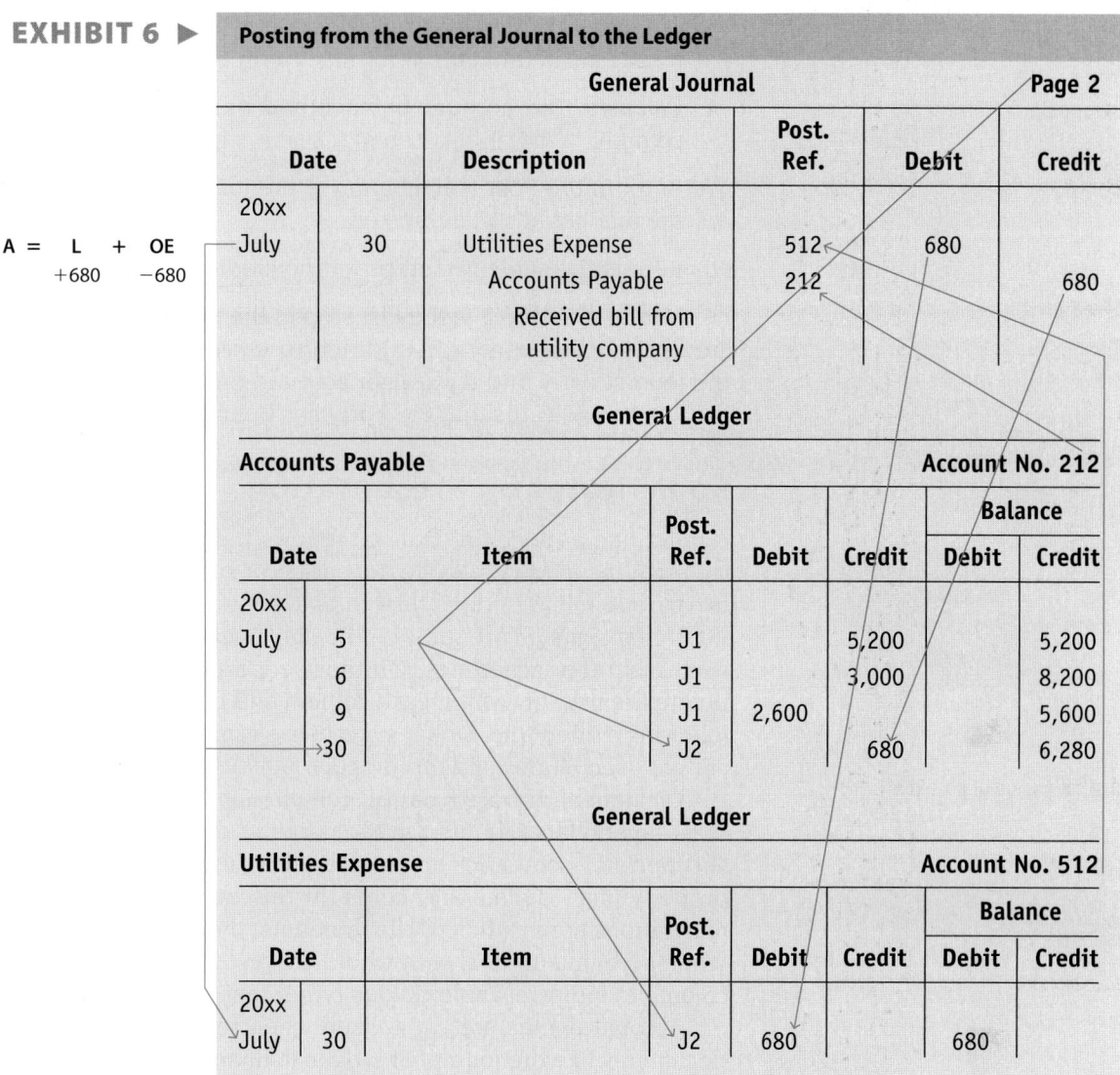

A = L + OE
+680 −680

umn is rarely used to identify transactions because explanations already appear in the journal. The Post. Ref. column is used to note the journal page on which the original entry for the transaction can be found. The dollar amount is entered in the appropriate Debit or Credit column, and a new account balance is computed in the last two columns opposite each entry. The advantage of this account form over the T account is that the current balance of the account is readily available.

Posting   After transactions have been entered in the journal, they must be transferred to the ledger. The process of transferring journal entry information from the journal to the ledger is called **posting**. Posting is usually done after several entries have been made—for example, at the end of each day or less frequently, depending on the number of transactions. As Exhibit 6 shows, in posting, each amount in the Debit column of the journal is transferred to the Debit column of the appropriate account in the ledger, and each amount in the Credit column of the journal is transferred to the Credit column of the appropriate account in the ledger. The steps in the posting process are as follows:

1. In the ledger, locate the debit account named in the journal entry.

2. Enter the date of the transaction in the ledger and, in the Post. Ref. column, the journal page number from which the entry comes.

3. In the Debit column of the ledger account, enter the amount of the debit as it appears in the journal.

4. Calculate the account balance and enter it in the appropriate Balance column.

5. Enter in the Post. Ref. column of the journal the account number to which the amount has been posted.

6. Repeat the same five steps for the credit side of the journal entry.

Notice that step **5** is the last step in the posting process for each debit and credit. As noted earlier, in addition to serving as an easy reference between the journal entry and the ledger account, this entry in the Post. Ref. column of the journal indicates that the entry has been posted to the ledger.

Some Notes on Presentation

A ruled line appears in financial reports before each subtotal or total to indicate that the amounts above are added or subtracted. It is common practice to use a double line under a final total to show that it has been verified.

Dollar signs ($) are required in all financial statements and on the trial balance and other schedules. On these reports, a dollar sign should be placed before the first amount in each column and before the first amount in a column following a ruled line. Dollar signs in the same column are aligned. Dollar signs are not used in journals and ledgers.

On normal, unruled paper, commas and decimal points are used when recording dollar amounts. On the paper used in journals and ledgers, commas and decimal points are unnecessary because ruled columns are provided to properly align dollars and cents. In this book, because most problems and illustrations are in whole dollar amounts, the cents column usually is omitted. When accountants deal with whole dollars, they often use a dash in the cents column to indicate whole dollars rather than taking the time to write zeros.

Account names are capitalized when referenced in text or listed in work documents like the journal or ledger. In financial statements, however, only the first word of an account name is capitalized.

STOP • REVIEW • APPLY

6-1. List the following events in the order in which they occur in an accounting system:

   a. Analysis of the transaction

   b. Posting of debits and credits from the journal to the ledger

   c. Occurrence of the transaction

   d. Recording of an entry in the journal

   e. Preparation of the trial balance

6-2. In recording entries in a journal, which is written first, the debit or the credit? How is indentation used in the journal?

6-3. What is the relationship between the journal and the ledger?

6-4. Indicate whether each of the following is more closely related to the journal, the ledger, or both:

a. Chart of accounts   d. Journalizing

b. Book of original entry   e. Posting

c. Post. Ref. column   f. Footings

A LOOK BACK AT

THE BOEING COMPANY

The Decision Point at the beginning of the chapter described the order for 80 jet liners that the Chinese government placed with **Boeing**. It posed the following questions:

- **An order for airplanes is obviously an important economic event for both the buyer and the seller. Is there a difference between an economic event and a business transaction that should be recorded in the accounting records?**

- **Should Boeing record the order in its accounting records?**

- **How important are liquidity and cash flows to Boeing?**

Despite its importance, the order did not constitute a business transaction, and neither the buyer nor the seller should have recognized it in its accounting records. At the time the Chinese government placed the order, Boeing had not yet built the planes. Until it delivers them and title to them shifts to the Chinese government, Boeing cannot record any revenue.

Even for "firm" orders like this one, Boeing cautions that "an economic downturn could result in airline equipment requirements less than currently anticipated resulting in requests to negotiate the rescheduling or possible cancellation of firm orders."[6] In fact, in the period following the 9/11 attacks on the World Trade Center and the war in Iraq, many airlines cancelled or renegotiated orders they had placed with Boeing.

Because it takes almost two years to manufacture an airplane, Boeing must pay close attention to its liquidity and cash flows. One measure of liquidity is the **cash return on assets** ratio, which shows how productive assets are in generating cash flows from operations. In other words, it shows how much cash is generated by each dollar of assets invested in operations. This ratio is different from the return on assets ratio, a profitability measure that we discussed in Chapter 1. Using amounts (in millions) from Boeing's balance sheet and statement of cash flows in its annual report, we can calculate the company's cash return on assets as follows:[7]

		2005	**2004**
$\dfrac{\text{Cash Return}}{\text{on Assets}} = \dfrac{\text{Net Cash Flows from Operating Activities}}{\text{Average Total Assets}}$		$\dfrac{\$7,000}{(\$60,058 + \$56,224) \div 2}$	$\dfrac{\$3,504}{(\$56,224 + \$55,171) \div 2}$
		$\dfrac{\$7,000}{\$58,141}$	$\dfrac{\$3,504}{\$55,697.5}$
		.120 (12.0%)	.063 (6.3%)

What do these results tell us? First, in 2005, each dollar of assets that Boeing invested in operations generated about 12.0¢, which was better than the 6.3¢ generated a year earlier. Second, cash flows from operations increased from $3,504 million to $7,000 million, while average total assets increased slightly. This trend is favorable. It indicates that Boeing had a stronger cash-generating ability and that it may have improved operations after the effects of 9/11 and subsequent events.

CHAPTER REVIEW

REVIEW of Learning Objectives

LO1 Explain how the concepts of recognition, valuation, and classification apply to business transactions and why they are important factors in ethical financial reporting.

To measure a business transaction, you must determine when the transaction occurred (the recognition issue), what value to place on the transaction (the valuation issue), and how the components of the transaction should be categorized (the classification issue). In general, recognition occurs when title passes, and a transaction is valued at the exchange price—the cost at the time the transaction is recognized. Classification refers to assigning transactions to the appropriate accounts. GAAP provide guidance about the treatment of these three basic measurement issues. Failure to follow these guidelines is a major reason some companies issue unethical financial statements.

LO2 Explain the double-entry system and the usefulness of T accounts in analyzing business transactions.

In the double-entry system, each transaction must be recorded with at least one debit and one credit, and the total amount of the debits must equal the total amount of the credits. Each asset, liability, and component of owner's equity, including revenues and expenses, has a separate account, which is a device for storing transaction data. The T account is a useful tool for quickly analyzing the effects of transactions. It shows how increases and decreases in assets, liabilities, and owner's equity are debited and credited to the appropriate accounts.

LO3 Demonstrate how the double-entry system is applied to common business transactions.

The double-entry system is applied by analyzing transactions to determine which accounts are affected and by using T accounts to show how the transactions affect the accounting equation. The transactions may be recorded in journal form with the date, debit account, and debit amount shown on one line, and the credit account (indented) and credit amount on the next line. The amounts are shown in their respective debit and credit columns.

LO4 Prepare a trial balance, and describe its value and limitations.

A trial balance is used to check that the debit and credit balances are equal. It is prepared by listing each account balance in the appropriate Debit or Credit column. The two columns are then added, and the totals are compared. The major limitation of a trial balance is that even when it shows that debit and credit balances are equal, it does not guarantee that the transactions were analyzed correctly or recorded in the proper accounts.

LO5 Show how the timing of transactions affects cash flows and liquidity.

Some transactions generate immediate cash. For those that do not, there is a holding period in either Accounts Receivable or Accounts Payable before the cash is received or paid. The timing of cash flows is critical to a company's ability to maintain adequate liquidity so that it can pay its bills on time.

Supplemental Objective

SO6 Define the *chart of accounts,* record transactions in the general journal, and post transactions to the ledger.

The chart of accounts is a list of account numbers and titles; it serves as a table of contents for the ledger. The general journal is a chronological record of all transactions; it contains the date of each transaction, the titles of the accounts involved, the amounts debited and credited, and an explanation of each entry. After transactions have been entered in the general journal, they are posted to the ledger. Posting is done by transferring the amounts in the Debit and Credit columns of the general journal to the Debit and Credit columns of the corresponding account in the ledger. After each entry is posted, a new balance is entered in the appropriate Balance column.

REVIEW of Concepts and Terminology

The following concepts and terms were introduced in this chapter:

Accounts: Basic units for accumulating and storing accounting data from similar transactions. **(LO2)**

Balance: The difference in dollars between the total debit footing and the total credit footing of an account. Also called *account balance*. **(LO2)**

Chart of accounts: A list of account numbers and titles that facilitates finding accounts in the ledger. **(SO6)**

Classification: The process of assigning transactions to the appropriate accounts. **(LO1)**

Compound entry: An entry that has more than one debit or credit entry. **(LO3)**

Cost: The exchange price associated with a business transaction at the point of recognition. **(LO1)**

Cost principle: The practice of recording transactions at cost. **(LO1)**

Credit: The right side of an account. **(LO2)**

Debit: The left side of an account. **(LO2)**

Double-entry system: The accounting system in which each transaction is recorded with at least one debit and one credit, so that the total amount of debits equals the total amount of credits. **(LO2)**

Exchange price: The price resulting from an agreement between the buyer and seller that can be verified by evidence created at the time of the transaction; the price at which a transaction is recorded. **(LO1)**

Footings: Working totals of columns of numbers. To *foot* means to total a column of numbers. **(LO2)**

General journal: The simplest and most flexible type of journal. **(SO6)**

General ledger: A book or file that contains all of a company's accounts arranged in the order of the chart of accounts. Also called the *ledger*. **(SO6)**

Journal: A chronological record of all transactions; the place where transactions first enter the accounting records. Also called *book of original entry*. **(SO6)**

Journal entry: A journal notation that records a single transaction. **(SO6)**

Journal form: A way of recording a transaction in which the date, debit account, and debit amount appear on one line and the credit account and credit amount appear on the next line. **(LO3)**

Journalizing: The process of recording transactions in a journal. **(SO6)**

Ledger account form: An account form that has four dollar amount columns: one column for debit entries, one column for credit entries, and two columns (debit and credit) for showing the balance of the account. **(SO6)**

Normal balance: The usual balance of an account; the side (debit or credit) that increases the account. **(LO2)**

Posting: The process of transferring journal entry information from the journal to the ledger. **(SO6)**

Recognition: The determination of when a business transaction should be recorded. **(LO1)**

Recognition point: The predetermined time at which a transaction should be recorded; usually, the point at which title passes to the buyer. **(LO1)**

Source documents: Invoices, checks, receipts, or other documents that support a transaction. **(LO3)**

T account: The simplest form of account, which is used to analyze transactions. **(LO2)**

Trial balance: A comparison of the total of debit and credit balances in the accounts to check that they are equal. **(LO4)**

Valuation: The process of assigning a monetary value to a business transaction. **(LO1)**

Key Ratio

Cash return on assets: A ratio that shows how much cash is generated by each dollar of assets; Net Cash Flows from Operating Activities ÷ Average Total Assets.

REVIEW Problem

Transaction Analysis, T Accounts, Journalizing, and the Trial Balance

LO1, LO3, LO4, SO6 After graduating from veterinary school, Laura Cox started a private practice. The transactions of her company in May follow.

20xx

May 1   Laura Cox invested $2,000 in cash to form Pet Clinic.

     3   Paid $300 in advance for two months' rent of an office.

     9   Purchased medical supplies for $200 in cash.

    12   Purchased $400 of equipment on credit; made a 25 percent down payment.

    15   Delivered a calf for a fee of $35 on credit.

    18   Made a payment of $50 on the equipment purchased on May 12.

    27   Paid a utility bill of $40.

Required

1. Record the company's transactions in journal form.
2. Post the transactions to the following T accounts: Cash, Accounts Receivable, Medical Supplies, Prepaid Rent, Equipment, Accounts Payable, L. Cox, Capital; Veterinary Fees Earned, and Utilities Expense.
3. Prepare a trial balance for the month of May.
4. How does the transaction of May 15 relate to recognition and cash flows? How do the transactions of May 9 and May 27 relate to classification?

Answer to Review Problem

1. Transactions recorded in journal form:

	A	B	C	D	E	F	G	H
1	May	1				Cash	2,000	
2						Common Stock		2,000
3						Issued 2,000 shares of $1 par		
4						value common stock		
5		3				Prepaid Rent	300	
6						Cash		300
7						Paid two months' rent in advance		
8						for an office		
9		9				Medical Supplies	200	
10						Cash		200
11						Purchased medical supplies for cash		
12		12				Equipment	400	
13						Accounts Payable		300
14						Cash		100
15						Purchased equipment on credit,		
16						paying 25 percent down		
17		15				Accounts Receivable	35	
18						Veterinary Fees Earned		35
19						Fee on credit for delivery of a calf		
20		18				Accounts Payable	50	
21						Cash		50
22						Partial payment for equipment		
23						purchsed May 12		
24		27				Utilities Expense	40	
25						Cash		40
26						Paid utility bill		
27								

2. Transactions posted to T accounts:

	A	B	C	D	E	F	G	H	I	J	K	L	M
1			Cash							Accounts Payable			
2	May	1	2,000	May	3	300		May	18	50	May	12	300
3					9	200					Bal.		250
4					12	100							
5					18	50				L. Cox, Capital			
6					27	40					May	1	2,000
7			2,000			690							
8	Bal.		1,310							Veterinary Fees Earned			
9											May	15	35
10			Accounts Receivable										
11	May	15	35							Utilities Expense			
12								May	27	40			
13			Medical Supplies										
14	May	9	200										
15													
16			Prepaid Rent										
17	May	3	300										
18													
19			Equipment										
20	May	12	400										
21													

3. Trial balance:

	A	B	C	D	E
1			Pet Clinic		
2			Trial Balance		
3			May 31, 20xx		
4					
5	Cash			$1,310	
6	Accounts Receivable			35	
7	Medical Supplies			200	
8	Prepaid Rent			300	
9	Equipment			400	
10	Accounts Payable				$ 250
11	L. Cox Capital				2,000
12	Veterinary Fees Earned				35
13	Utilities Expense			40	
14				$2,285	$2,285
15					

4. The transaction of May 15 is recorded, or recognized, on that date even though the company received no cash. The company earned the revenue by providing the service, and the customer accepted the service and now has an obligation to pay for it. The transaction is recorded as an account receivable because the company allowed the customer to pay for the service later. The transaction of May 9 is classified as an asset, Medical Supplies, because these supplies will benefit the company in the future. The

transaction of May 27 is classified as an expense, Utilities Expense, because the utilities have already been used and will not benefit the company in the future.

CHAPTER ASSIGNMENTS

BUILDING Your Basic Knowledge and Skills

Short Exercises

LO1 **Recognition**

SE 1. Which of the following events would be recognized and entered in the accounting records of Tanaka Company? Why?

Jan. 10 Tanaka Company places an order for office supplies.
Feb. 15 Tanaka Company receives the office supplies and a bill for them.
Mar. 1 Tanaka Company pays for the office supplies.

LO1, LO3 **Recognition, Valuation, and Classification**

SE 2. Tell how the concepts of recognition, valuation, and classification apply to this transaction:

CASH		SUPPLIES	
	June 1 500	June 1 500	

LO1 **Classification of Accounts**

SE 3. Tell whether each of the following accounts is an asset, a liability, a revenue, an expense, or none of these:

a. Accounts Payable
b. Supplies
c. Withdrawals
d. Fees Earned
e. Supplies Expense
f. Accounts Receivable
g. Unearned Revenue
h. Equipment

LO2 **Normal Balances**

SE 4. Tell whether the normal balance of each account in **SE 3** is a debit or a credit.

LO3 **Transaction Analysis**

SE 5. Leon Stoker started a computer programming business, Stoker's Programming Service. For each transaction that follows, indicate which account is debited and which account is credited.

May 2 Leon Stoker invested $10,000 in cash to start the business.
5 Purchased a computer for $5,000 in cash.
7 Purchased supplies on credit for $600.
19 Received cash for programming services performed, $1,000.
22 Received cash for programming services to be performed, $1,200.
25 Paid the rent for May, $1,300.
31 Billed a customer for programming services performed, $500.

LO3 **Recording Transactions in T Accounts**

SE 6. Set up T accounts and record each transaction in **SE 5**. Determine the balance of each account.

LO4 **Preparing a Trial Balance**

SE 7. From the T accounts created in **SE 6**, prepare a trial balance dated May 31, 20x8.

LO5 **Timing and Cash Flows**

SE 8. Use the T account for Cash below to record the portion of each of the following transactions that affect cash. How do these transactions affect the company's liquidity?

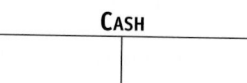

CASH

Jan. 2	Provided services for cash, $1,200
4	Paid expenses in cash, $700
8	Provided services on credit, $1,100
9	Incurred expenses on credit, $800

SO6 **Recording Transactions in the General Journal**

SE 9. Prepare a general journal form like the one in Exhibit 4 and label it Page 4. Record the following transactions in the journal:

| Sept. | 6 | Billed a customer for services performed, $3,800. |
| | 16 | Received cash from the customer billed on Sept. 6, $1,800. |

SO6 **Posting to the Ledger Accounts**

SE 10. Prepare ledger account forms like the ones in Exhibit 5 for the following accounts: Cash (111), Accounts Receivable (113), and Service Revenue (411). Post the transactions that are recorded in **SE 9** to the ledger accounts, at the same time making the proper posting references.

Cash Return on Assets

SE 11. Calculate cash return on assets for 20x8 using the following data: A company has net cash flows from operating activities of $3,000 in 20x8, beginning total assets of $26,000, and ending total assets of $28,000.

Exercises

LO1, LO2, LO3 **Discussion Questions**

E 1. Develop a brief answer to each of the following questions.

1. Which is the most important issue in recording a transaction: recognition, valuation, or classification?
2. What is an example of how a company could make false financial statements through a violation of the recognition concept?
3. How are assets and expenses related, and why are the debit and credit effects for assets and expenses the same?
4. In what way are unearned revenues the opposite of prepaid expenses?

LO4, LO5, SO6 **Discussion Questions**

E 2. Develop a brief answer to each of the following questions.

1. Which account would be most likely to have an account balance that is not normal?

2. A company incurs a cost for a part that is needed to repair a piece of equipment. Is the cost an asset or an expense? Explain.

3. If a company's cash flows for expenses temporarily exceed its cash flows from revenues, how might it make up the difference so that it can maintain liquidity?

4. How would the asset accounts in the chart of accounts for Treadle Website Design differ if it were a retail company that sold advertising products instead of being a service company?

LO1 Recognition

E 3. Which of the following events would be recognized and recorded in the accounting records of Villa Company on the date indicated?

Jan. 15 Villa Company offers to purchase a tract of land for $140,000. There is a high likelihood that the offer will be accepted.

Feb. 2 Villa Company receives notice that its rent will increase from $500 to $600 per month effective March 1.

Mar. 29 Villa Company receives its utility bill for the month of March. The bill is not due until April 9.

June 10 Villa Company places an order for new office equipment costing $21,000.

July 6 The office equipment Villa Company ordered on June 10 arrives. Payment is not due until August 1.

LO1 Application of Recognition Point

E 4. Davis Parts Shop uses a large amount of supplies in its business. The following table summarizes selected transaction data for supplies that Davis Parts Shop purchased:

Order	Date Shipped	Date Received	Amount
a	June 26	July 5	$300
b	July 10	15	750
c	16	22	400
d	23	30	600
e	27	Aug. 1	750
f	Aug. 3	7	500

Determine the total purchases of supplies for July alone under each of the following assumptions:

1. Davis Parts Shop recognizes purchases when orders are shipped.
2. Davis Parts Shop recognizes purchases when orders are received.

LO2 T Accounts, Normal Balance, and the Accounting Equation

E 5. You are given the following list of accounts with dollar amounts:

Rent Expense	$ 450
Cash	1,725
Service Revenue	750
M. Powell, Withdrawals	375
Accounts Payable	600
M. Powell, Capital	1,200

Insert the account names at the top of the corresponding T accounts that follow and enter the dollar amount as a normal balance in the account. Then show that the accounting equation is in balance.

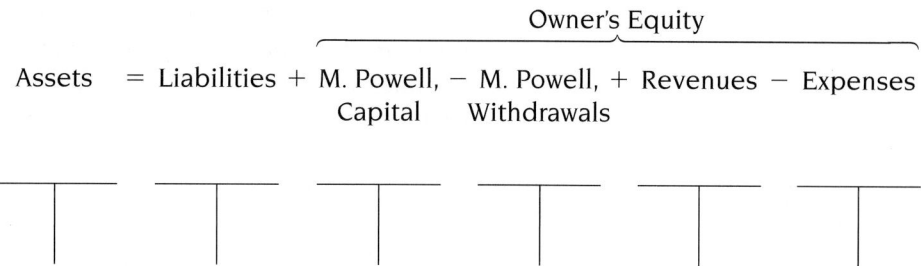

Owner's Equity

Assets = Liabilities + M. Powell, − M. Powell, + Revenues − Expenses
Capital Withdrawals

LO2 Classification of Accounts

E 6. The following ledger accounts are for the Tuner Service Company:

a. Cash
b. Wages Expense
c. Accounts Receivable
d. R. Shuckman, Capital
e. Service Revenue
f. Prepaid Rent
g. Accounts Payable
h. Investments in Securities
i. Land
j. Supplies Expense
k. Prepaid Insurance
l. Utilities Expense
m. Fees Earned
n. R. Shuckman, Withdrawals
o. Wages Payable
p. Unearned Revenue
q. Office Equipment
r. Rent Payable
s. Notes Receivable
t. Interest Expense
u. Notes Payable
v. Supplies
w. Interest Receivable
x. Rent Expense

Complete the following table, using X's to indicate each account's classification and normal balance (whether a debit or a credit increases the account).

| | | | Type of Account | | | | Normal Balance (increases balance) | |
| | | | Owner's Equity | | | | | |
Item	Asset	Liability	R. Shuckman, Capital	R. Shuckman, Withdrawals	Revenue	Expense	Debit	Credit
a.	X						X	

LO3 Transaction Analysis

E 7. Analyze transactions **a–g**, following the example below.

a. Sarah Linton invested $2,400 in cash to establish Kitty-Kat Beauty Parlor.
b. Paid two months' rent in advance, $1,680.
c. Purchased supplies on credit, $120.
d. Received cash for beauty services, $600.
e. Paid for supplies purchased in **c**.
f. Paid utility bill, $72.
g. Withdrew $100 in cash.

Example:

a. The asset account Cash was increased. Increases in assets are recorded by debits. Debit Cash $2,400. A component of owner's equity, S. Linton, Capital, was increased. Increases in owner's capital are recorded by credits. Credit S. Linton, Capital, $2,400.

LO3 Transaction Analysis

E 8. The accounts that follow are from Dale's Lawn Service, a company that maintains condominium grounds.

1. Cash	5. Accounts Payable
2. Accounts Receivable	6. Lawn Services Revenue
3. Supplies	7. Wages Expense
4. Equipment	8. Rent Expense

Dale's Lawn Service completed the following transactions:

		Debit	Credit
a.	Paid for supplies purchased on credit last month.	5	1
b.	Received cash from customers billed last month.	___	___
c.	Made a payment on accounts payable.	___	___
d.	Purchased supplies on credit.	___	___
e.	Billed a client for lawn services.	___	___
f.	Made a rent payment for the current month.	___	___
g.	Received cash from customers for lawn services.	___	___
h.	Paid employee wages.	___	___
i.	Ordered equipment.	___	___
j.	Received and paid for the equipment ordered in **i**.	___	___

Analyze each transaction and show the accounts affected by entering the corresponding numbers in the appropriate debit or credit columns as shown in transaction **a**. Indicate no entry, if appropriate.

LO3   Recording Transactions in T Accounts

E 9. Open the following T accounts: Cash; Repair Supplies; Repair Equipment; Accounts Payable; M. Change, Capital; M. Change, Withdrawals; Repair Fees Earned; Salaries Expense; and Rent Expense. Record the following transactions for the month of June directly in the T accounts; use the letters to identify the transactions in your T accounts. Determine the balance in each account.

a. Michael Change opened Ceramics Repair Service by investing $8,600 in cash and $3,200 in repair equipment.
b. Paid $800 for the current month's rent.
c. Purchased repair supplies on credit, $1,000.
d. Purchased additional repair equipment for cash, $600.
e. Paid salary to a helper, $900.
f. Paid $400 of amount purchased on credit in **c**.
g. Accepted cash for repairs completed, $3,720.
h. Withdrew $1,200 in cash.

LO4   Trial Balance

E 10. After recording the transactions in **E 9**, prepare a trial balance in proper sequence for Ceramics Repair Service as of June 30, 20xx.

LO3   Analysis of Transactions

E 11. Explain each transaction (**a–h**) entered in the following T accounts:

CASH				ACCOUNTS RECEIVABLE				EQUIPMENT			
a.	30,000	b.	7,500	c.	3,000	g.	750	b.	7,500	h.	450
g.	750	e.	1,500					d.	4,500		
h.	450	f.	2,250								

ACCOUNTS PAYABLE				B. CALDWELL, CAPITAL				SERVICE REVENUE			
f.	2,250	d.	4,500			a.	30,000			c.	3,000

WAGES EXPENSE		
e.	1,500	

LO4 **Preparing a Trial Balance**

E 12. The list that follows presents the accounts (in alphabetical order) of the Chapala Metal Company as of March 31, 20xx. The list does not include the amount of Accounts Payable.

Accounts Payable	?
Accounts Receivable	$ 1,800
Building	20,400
Cash	5,400
Equipment	7,200
G. Chapala, Capital	18,870
Land	3,120
Notes Payable	12,000
Prepaid Insurance	660

Prepare a trial balance with the proper heading (see Exhibit 2) and with the accounts listed in the chart of accounts sequence (see Exhibit 3). Compute the balance of Accounts Payable.

LO4 **Effects of Errors on a Trial Balance**

E 13. Which of the following errors would cause a trial balance to have unequal totals? Explain your answers.

a. A payment to a creditor was recorded as a debit to Accounts Payable for $129 and as a credit to Cash for $102.
b. A payment of $150 to a creditor for an account payable was debited to Accounts Receivable and credited to Cash.
c. A purchase of office supplies of $420 in cash was recorded as a debit to Office Supplies for $42 and as a credit to Cash for $42.
d. A purchase of equipment for $450 in cash was recorded as a debit to Supplies for $450 and as a credit to Cash for $450.

LO4 **Correcting Errors in a Trial Balance**

E 14. The trial balance for Kilda Services at the end of July is as follows:

Kilda Services
Trial Balance
July 31, 20xx

Cash	$ 3,840	
Accounts Receivable	5,660	
Supplies	120	
Prepaid Insurance	180	
Equipment	8,400	
Accounts Payable		$ 4,540
J. Kilda, Capital		11,560
J. Kilda, Withdrawals		700
Revenues		5,920
Salaries Expense	2,600	
Rent Expense	600	
Advertising Expense	340	
Utilities Expense	26	
	$21,766	$22,720

The trial balance does not balance because of a number of errors. Kilda's accountant compared the amounts in the trial balance with the ledger, recomputed the account balances, and compared the postings. He found the following errors:

a. The balance of Cash was understated by $400.
b. A cash payment of $420 was credited to Cash for $240.
c. A debit of $120 to Accounts Receivable was not posted.
d. Supplies purchased for $60 were posted as a credit to Supplies.
e. A debit of $180 to Prepaid Insurance was not posted.
f. The Accounts Payable account had debits of $5,320 and credits of $9,180.
g. The Notes Payable account, with a credit balance of $2,400, was not included on the trial balance.
h. The debit balance of J. Kilda, Withdrawals was listed in the trial balance as a credit.
i. A $200 debit to J. Kilda, Withdrawals was posted as a credit.
j. The actual balance of Utilities Expense, $260, was listed as $26 in the trial balance.

Prepare a corrected trial balance.

LO5 **Cash Flow Analysis**

E 15. A company engaged in the following transactions:

Dec. 1 Performed services for cash, $1,500
    1 Paid expenses in cash, $1,100
    2 Performed services on credit, $1,800
    3 Collected cash on account, $1,200
    4 Incurred expenses on credit, $1,300
    5 Made payment on account, $700

Enter the correct titles on the following T accounts and enter the above transactions in the accounts. Determine the cash balance after these transactions, the amount still to be received, and the amount still to be paid.

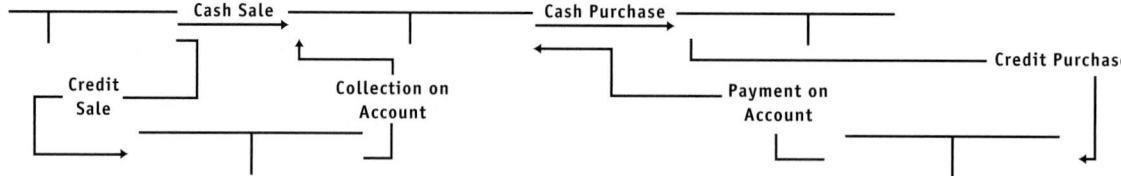

LO3, SO6 **Analysis of Unfamiliar Transactions**

E 16. Managers and accountants often encounter transactions with which they are unfamiliar. Use your analytical skills to analyze and record in journal form the following transactions, which have not yet been discussed in the text.

May 1 Purchased merchandise inventory on account, $1,200.
    2 Purchased marketable securities for cash, $2,800.
    3 Returned part of merchandise inventory purchased for full credit, $250.
    4 Sold merchandise inventory on account, $800 (record sale only).

May 5 Purchased land and a building for $300,000. Payment is $60,000 cash, and there is a 30-year mortgage for the remainder. The purchase price is allocated as follows: $100,000 to the land and $200,000 to the building.

  6 Received an order for $12,000 in services to be provided. With the order was a deposit of $4,000.

SO6 **Recording Transactions in the General Journal and Posting to the Ledger Accounts**

E 17. Open a general journal form like the one in Exhibit 4, and label it Page 10. After opening the form, record the following transactions in the journal:

Dec. 14 Purchased equipment for $12,000, paying $4,000 as a cash down payment.

  28 Paid $6,000 of the amount owed on the equipment.

Prepare three ledger account forms like the one shown in Exhibit 5. Use the following account numbers: Cash, 111; Equipment, 144; and Accounts Payable, 212. Then post the two transactions from the general journal to the ledger accounts, being sure to make proper posting references. Assume that the Cash account has a debit balance of $16,000 on the day prior to the first transaction.

Cash Return on Assets

E 18. Julio Company wants to know if its liquidity performance has improved. Calculate the company's cash return on assets for 20x8 and 20x7 using the following data:

Net cash flows from operating activities, 20x7	$ 4,300
Net cash flows from operating activities, 20x8	5,000
Total assets, 20x6	36,000
Total assets, 20x7	40,000
Total assets, 20x8	46,000

By this measure has liquidity improved? Why is it important to use average total assets in the calculation?

Problems

LO2 **T Accounts, Normal Balance, and the Accounting Equation**

P 1. The Anderson Construction Company builds foundations for buildings and parking lots. The following alphabetical list shows Anderson Construction's account balances as of April 30, 20xx:

Accounts Payable	$ 1,950
Accounts Receivable	5,060
Cash	?
Equipment	13,350
M. Anderson, Capital	20,000
M. Anderson, Withdrawals	3,900
Notes Payable	10,000
Revenue Earned	8,700
Supplies	3,250
Supplies Expense	3,600
Utilities Expense	210
Wages Expense	4,400

Required

Insert the account at the top of its corresponding T account and enter the dollar amount as a normal balance in the account. Determine the balance of cash and then show that the accounting equation is in balance.

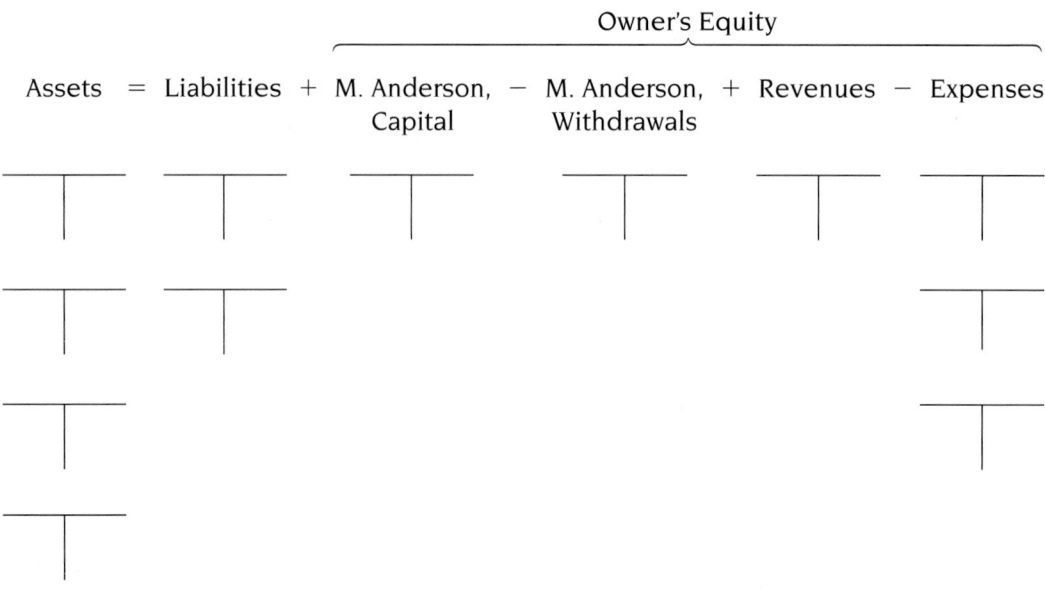

Assets = Liabilities + M. Anderson, Capital − M. Anderson, Withdrawals + Revenues − Expenses

LO3 Transaction Analysis

P 2. The following accounts are applicable to Walter's Chimney Sweeps:

1. Cash
2. Accounts Receivable
3. Supplies
4. Prepaid Insurance
5. Equipment
6. Notes Payable
7. Accounts Payable
8. W. Norman, Capital
9. W. Norman, Withdrawals
10. Service Revenue
11. Rent Expense
12. Repair Expense

Walter's Chimney Sweeps completed the following transactions:

		Debit	Credit
a.	Paid for supplies purchased on credit last month.	7	1
b.	Billed customers for services performed.	—	—
c.	Paid the current month's rent.	—	—
d.	Purchased supplies on credit.	—	—
e.	Received cash from customers for services performed but not yet billed.	—	—
f.	Purchased equipment on account.	—	—
g.	Received a bill for repairs.	—	—
h.	Returned part of the equipment purchased in **f** for a credit.	—	—
i.	Received cash from customers previously billed.	—	—
j.	Paid the bill received in **g**.	—	—
k.	Received an order for services to be performed.	—	—
l.	Paid for repairs with cash.	—	—
m.	Made a payment to reduce the principal of the note payable.	—	—
n.	Made a cash withdrawal.	—	—

Required

Analyze each transaction and show the accounts affected by entering the corresponding numbers in the appropriate debit or credit column as shown in transaction **a**. Indicate no entry, if appropriate.

LO3, LO4, LO5

Transaction Analysis, T Accounts, and Trial Balance

P 3. Bob Lutz opened a secretarial school called Best Secretarial Training and engaged in the following transactions:

a. Contributed the following assets to start the business:

Cash	$5,700
Computers	4,300
Office Equipment	3,600

b. Paid the first month's rent, $260.
c. Paid for an advertisement announcing the opening of the school, $190.
d. Received applications from three students for a four-week secretarial program and two students for a ten-day keyboarding course. The students will be billed a total of $1,300.
e. Purchased supplies on credit, $330.
f. Billed the enrolled students, $1,740.
g. Purchased a second-hand computer, $480, and office equipment, $380, on credit.
h. Paid for the supplies purchased on credit in **e**, $330.
i. Paid cash to repair a broken computer, $40.
j. Received partial payment from students previously billed, $1,080.
k. Paid the utility bill for the current month, $90.
l. Paid an assistant one week's salary, $440.
m. Made a cash withdrawal of $300.

Required

1. Set up the following T accounts: Cash; Accounts Receivable; Supplies; Computers; Office Equipment; Accounts Payable; B. Lutz, Capital; B. Lutz, Withdrawals; Tuition Revenue; Salaries Expense; Utilities Expense; Rent Expense; Repair Expense; and Advertising Expense.
2. Record the transactions directly in the T accounts, using the transaction letter to identify each debit and credit.
3. Prepare a trial balance using today's date.
4. **User Insight:** Examine transactions **f** and **j**. What were the revenues and how much cash was received from the revenues? What business issues might you see arising from the differences in these numbers?

LO1, LO3, LO4

Transaction Analysis, T Accounts, and Trial Balance

P 4. Hiroshi Mori began an upholstery cleaning business on October 1 and engaged in the following transactions during the month:

Oct. 1 Began the business by depositing $12,000 in a bank account in the name of the company.
2 Ordered cleaning supplies, $1,000.
3 Purchased cleaning equipment for cash, $2,800.
4 Made two months' van lease payment in advance, $1,200.
7 Received the cleaning supplies ordered on October 2 and agreed to pay half the amount in 10 days and the rest in 30 days.

Oct.   9   Paid for repairs on the van with cash, $80.
       12   Received cash for cleaning upholstery, $960.
       17   Paid half the amount owed on supplies purchased on October 7, $500.
       21   Billed customers for cleaning upholstery, $1,340.
       24   Paid cash for additional repairs on the van, $80.
       27   Received $600 from the customers billed on October 21.
       31   Made a cash withdrawal of $700.

Required

1. Set up the following T accounts: Cash; Accounts Receivable; Cleaning Supplies; Prepaid Lease; Cleaning Equipment; Accounts Payable; H. Mori, Capital; H. Mori, Withdrawals; Cleaning Revenue; and Repair Expense.
2. Record transactions directly in the T accounts. Identify each entry by date.
3. Prepare a trial balance for Mori Upholstery Cleaning as of October 31, 20xx.
4. **User Insight:** Compare and contrast how the issues of recognition, valuation, and classification are settled in the transactions of October 7 and 9.

LO3, LO4, LO5, SO6

Transaction Analysis, General Journal, Ledger Accounts, and Trial Balance

P 5. The Acorn Nursery School Company provides baby-sitting and child-care programs. On January 31, 20xx, the company had the following trial balance:

Acorn Nursery School Company
Trial Balance
January 31, 20xx

Cash (111)	$ 1,870	
Accounts Receivable (113)	1,700	
Equipment (141)	1,040	
Buses (143)	17,400	
Notes Payable (211)		$15,000
Accounts Payable (212)		1,640
J. Wells, Capital (311)		5,370
	$22,010	$22,010

During the month of February, the company completed the following transactions:

Feb.   2   Paid this month's rent, $270.
       3   Received fees for this month's services, $650.
       4   Purchased supplies on account, $85.
       5   Reimbursed the bus driver for gas expenses, $40.
       6   Ordered playground equipment, $1,000.
       8   Made a payment on account, $170.
       9   Received cash from customers on account, $1,200.
       10   Billed customers who had not yet paid for this month's services, $700.
       11   Paid for the supplies purchased on February 4.
       13   Received and purchased playground equipment ordered on February 6 for cash, $1,000.
       17   Purchased equipment on account, $290.
       19   Paid this month's utility bill, $145.

Feb. 22 Received cash for one month's services from customers previously billed, $500.

26 Paid part-time assistants for services, $460.

27 Purchased gas and oil for the bus on account, $325.

28 Made a cash withdrawal of $110.

Required

1. Open accounts in the ledger for the accounts in the trial balance plus the following ones: Supplies (115); J. Wells, Withdrawals (313); Service Revenue (411); Rent Expense (511); Gas and Oil Expense (512); Wages Expense (513); and Utilities Expense (514).

2. Enter the January 31, 20xx, account balances from the trial balance.

3. Enter the above transactions in the general journal (Pages 17 and 18).

4. Post the entries to the ledger accounts. Be sure to make the appropriate posting references in the journal and ledger as you post.

5. Prepare a trial balance as of February 28, 20xx.

6. **User Insight:** Examine the transactions for February 3, 9, 10, and 22. What were the revenues and how much cash was received from the revenues? What business issue might you see arising from the differences in these numbers?

Alternate Problems

LO2 **T Accounts, Normal Balance, and The Accounting Equation**

 P 6. The Buy-It Design Company creates radio and television advertising for local businesses in the twin cities. The following alphabetical list shows Buy-It Design's account balances as of January 31, 20xx:

Accounts Payable	$ 3,210	E. Fox, Withdrawals	$18,000
Accounts Receivable	36,000	Loans Payable	5,000
Cash	7,200	Rent Expense	5,940
Design Revenue	105,000	Telephone Expense	480
Equipment	?	Unearned Revenue	9,000
E. Fox, Capital	32,000	Wages Expense	62,000

Required

Insert the account title at the top of its corresponding T account and enter the dollar amount as a normal balance in the account. Determine the balance of Equipment and then show that the accounting equation is in balance.

Owner's Equity

Assets = Liabilities + E. Fox, − E. Fox, + Revenues − Expenses
Capital   Withdrawals

LO1, LO3, LO4   Transaction Analysis, Journal Form, T Accounts, and Trial Balance

P 7. Nomar Parra bid for and won a concession to rent bicycles in the local park during the summer. During the month of June, Parra completed the following transactions for his bicycle rental business:

June   2   Began the business by placing $7,200 in a checking account in the name of the company.

       3   Purchased supplies on account for $150.

       4   Purchased 10 bicycles for $2,500, paying $1,200 down and agreeing to pay the rest in 30 days.

       5   Paid $2,900 in cash for a small shed to store the bicycles and to use for other operations.

       8   Paid $400 in cash for shipping and installation costs (considered an addition to the cost of the shed) to place the shed at the park entrance.

       9   Hired a part-time assistant to help out on weekends at $7 per hour.

    10   Paid a maintenance person $75 to clean the grounds.

    13   Received $970 in cash for rentals.

    17   Paid $150 for the supplies purchased on June 3.

    18   Paid a $55 repair bill on bicycles.

    23   Billed a company $110 for bicycle rentals for an employee outing.

    25   Paid the $100 fee for June to the Park District for the right to operate the bicycle concession.

    27   Received $960 in cash for rentals.

    29   Paid wages of the assistant, $240.

    30   Made a cash withdrawal of $500.

Required

1. Prepare entries to record these transactions in journal form.
2. Set up the following T accounts and post all the journal entries: Cash; Accounts Receivable; Supplies; Shed; Bicycles; Accounts Payable; N. Parra, Capital; N. Para, Withdrawals; Rental Revenue; Wages Expense; Maintenance Expense; Repair Expense; and Concession Fee Expense.
3. Prepare a trial balance for Parra Rentals as of June 30, 20xx.
4. **User Insight:** Compare and contrast how the issues of recognition, valuation, and classification are settled in the transactions of June 3 and 10.

LO3, LO4, LO5, SO6   Transaction Analysis, General Journal, Ledger Accounts, and Trial Balance

P 8. Yury Wagoner Company is a marketing firm. The company's trial balance on July 31, 20xx, appears below.

Yury Wagoner Company
Trial Balance
July 31, 20xx

Cash (111)	$10,200	
Accounts Receivable (113)	5,500	
Supplies (115)	610	
Office Equipment (141)	4,200	
Accounts Payable (212)		$ 2,600
Y. Wagoner, Capital (311)		17,910
	$20,510	$20,510

During August, the company completed the following transactions:

Aug. 2 Paid rent for August, $650.
   3 Received cash from customers on account, $2,300.
   7 Ordered supplies, $380.
   10 Billed customers for services provided, $2,800.
   12 Made a payment on accounts payable, $1,100.
   14 Received the supplies ordered on August 7 and agreed to pay for them in 30 days, $380.
   17 Discovered some of the supplies were not as ordered and returned them for full credit, $80.
   19 Received cash from a customer for services provided, $4,800.
   24 Paid the utility bill for August, $280.
   26 Received a bill, to be paid in September, for advertisements placed in the local newspaper during the month of August to promote Yury Wagoner Company, $700.
   29 Billed a customer for services provided, $2,700.
   30 Paid salaries for August, $3,800.
   31 Made a cash withdrawal of $1,200.

Required

1. Open accounts in the ledger for the accounts in the trial balance plus the following accounts: Y. Wagoner, Withdrawals (313); Marketing Fees (411); Salaries Expense (511); Rent Expense (512); Utilities Expense (513); and Advertising Expense (515).
2. Enter the July 31, 20xx, account balances from the trial balance.
3. Enter the above transactions in the general journal (Pages 22 and 23).
4. Post the journal entries to the ledger accounts. Be sure to make the appropriate posting references in the journal and ledger as you post.
5. Prepare a trial balance as of August 31, 20xx.
6. User Insight: Examine the transactions for August 3, 10, 19, and 29. How much were revenues and how much cash was received from the revenues? What business issues might you see arising from the differences in these numbers?

ENHANCING Your Knowledge, Skills, and Critical Thinking

Conceptual Understanding Cases

LO1 Valuation Issue

C 1. Nike, Inc. manufactures athletic shoes and related products. In one of its annual reports, Nike made this statement: "Property, plant, and equipment are recorded at cost."[8] Given that the property, plant, and equipment undoubtedly were purchased over several years and that the current value of those assets is likely to be very different from their original cost, what authoritative basis is there for carrying the assets at cost? Does accounting generally recognize changes in value after the purchase of property, plant, and equipment? Assume you are an accountant for Nike. Write a memo to management explaining the rationale underlying Nike's approach.

LO3 Recording of Rebates

C 2. Is it revenue or a reduction of an expense? That is the question companies that receive manufacturer's rebates for purchasing a large quantity of product must answer. Food companies like **Sara Lee, Kraft Foods,** and **Nestlé** give supermarkets special manufacturer's rebates of up to 45 percent, depending on the quantities that are purchased. Some supermarkets were recording these rebates as revenue, whereas others were recording them as a reduction of the cost until the SEC said that only one way is correct. What, then, is the correct way for supermarkets to record these rebates? Would your answer change net income?

Interpreting Financial Reports

LO2, LO3 **Interpreting a Bank's Financial Statements**

C 3. **Mellon Bank** is a large bank holding company. Selected accounts from the company's 2005 annual report are as follows (in millions):[9]

Cash and Due from Banks	$ 2,373
Loans to Customers	6,573
Securities Available for Sale	17,245
Deposits by Customers	26,074

1. Indicate whether each of the accounts just listed is an asset, a liability, or a component of stockholders' equity (owner's equity) on Mellon Bank's balance sheet.
2. Assume that you are in a position to do business with this large company. Show how Mellon Bank's accountants would prepare the entry in T account form to record each of the following transactions:
   a. You sell securities in the amount of $2,000 to the bank.
   b. You deposit in the bank the $2,000 received from selling the securities.
   c. You borrow $5,000 from the bank.

LO5 **Cash Flows**

C 4. You have been promoted recently and now have access to the firm's monthly financial statements. Business is good. Revenues are increasing rapidly, and income is at an all-time high. The balance sheet shows growth in receivables, and accounts payable have declined. However, the chief financial officer is concerned about the firm's cash flows from operating activities because they are decreasing. What are some reasons why a company with a positive net income may fall short of cash from its operating activities? What could be done to improve this situation?

Decision Analysis Using Excel

LO2, LO3, LO4 **Transaction Analysis and Evaluation of a Trial Balance**

C 5. Demetrius Carver hired an attorney to help him start Carver Repair Service Company. On March 1, Carver deposited $14,375 in a bank account in the name of the company. When the company paid the attorney's bill of $875, the attorney advised the company to hire an accountant to keep its records. Carver was so busy that it was March 31 before he hired you to straighten out his records. Your first task is to develop a trial balance based on the March transactions, which are described in the next two paragraphs.

After the business began and the company had paid the attorney's bill, the company borrowed $6,250 from the bank. It later paid $325, including interest of $75, on this loan. It also purchased a used pickup truck in the company's name, paying $3,125 down and financing $9,250. The first payment on the truck is due April 15. The company then rented an office and paid three months' rent, $1,125, in advance. Credit purchases of office equipment of $1,000 and repair tools of $625 must be paid by April 10.

In March, Carver Repair Service completed repairs of $1,625, of which $500 were cash transactions. Of the credit transactions, $375 were collected during March, and $750 remained to be collected at the end of March. The company paid wages of $562 to its employees. On March 31, the company received a $93 bill for the March utilities expense and a $62 check from a customer for work to be completed in April. A customer requested a repair on March 31 to be done the following week and agreed to pay $250 for it. The company is considering recording this agreement as revenue in March to make the business look better.

1. Record all of the transactions for March in journal form. Label each of the entries alphabetically.
2. Set up T accounts. Then post the entries to the T accounts. Identify each posting with the letter corresponding to the transaction.
3. Determine the balance of each account.
4. Prepare a trial balance for Carver Repair Service Company as of March 31.
5. Demetrius Carver is unsure how to evaluate the trial balance. The Cash account balance is $15,550, which exceeds the original investment of $14,375 by $1,175. Did the company make a profit of $1,175? Explain why the Cash account is not an indicator of business earnings. Cite specific examples to show why it is difficult to determine net income by looking solely at figures in the trial balance.
6. What are the ethical implications of recording the repair order received on March 31 as revenue in March?

Annual Report Case: CVS Corporation

LO1 **Recognition, Valuation, and Classification**

C 6. Refer to the Summary of Significant Accounting Policies in the notes to the financial statements in the **CVS Corporation** annual report at the end of Chapter 5 to answer these questions:

1. How does the concept of recognition apply to advertising costs?
2. How does the concept of valuation apply to inventories?
3. How does the concept of classification apply to cash and cash equivalents?

Comparison Case: CVS Versus Southwest

Cash Return on Assets

C 7. Refer to the financial statements of **CVS** and **Southwest Airlines Co.** in the Supplement to Chapter 5. Compute cash return on assets for the past two years for both companies and comment on the results. Total assets in fiscal 2003 were $10,543.1 million for CVS and $9,878 million for Southwest.

Ethical Dilemma Case

LO1 **Recognition Point and Ethical Considerations**

C 8. Jerry Hasbrow, a sales representative for Penn Office Supplies Company, is compensated on a commission basis and received a substantial bonus for meeting his annual sales goal. The company's recognition point for sales is the day of shipment. On December 31, Hasbrow realizes he needs sales of $2,000 to reach his sales goal and receive the bonus. He calls a purchaser for a local insurance company, whom he knows well, and asks him to buy $2,000 worth of copier paper today. The purchaser says, "But Jerry, that's more than a year's supply for us." Hasbrow says, "Buy it today. If you decide it's too much, you can return however much you want for full credit next month." The purchaser says, "Okay, ship it." The paper is shipped on December 31 and recorded as a sale. On January 15, the purchaser returns $1,750 worth of paper for full credit (approved by Hasbrow) against the bill. Should the shipment on December 31 be recorded as a sale? Discuss the ethics of Hasbrow's action.

Internet Case

LO1 **Financial Misstatements**

C 9. **WorldCom** changed its name to **MCI.** Go to www.CFO.com and enter the words "extreme makeover" into the search box. From a review of the article, identify the major steps the new CFO carried out to fix WorldCom's financial statements. Also, find out what eventually happened to MCI. Be prepared to discuss your findings in class.

Group Activity Case

LO1, LO3 **Valuation and Classification Issues for Dot-Coms**

C 10. The dot-com business has raised many issues about accounting practices, some of which are of great concern to both the SEC and the FASB. Important ones relate to the valuation and classification of revenue transactions. Many dot-com companies seek to report as much revenue as possible because revenue growth is seen as a key performance measure for these companies. **Amazon.com** is a good example. Consider the following situations:

a. An Amazon.com customer orders and pays $28 for an electronic Gameboy on the Internet. Amazon sends an email to the company that makes the product, which sends the Gameboy to the customer. Amazon collects $28 from the customer and pays $24 to the other company. Amazon never owns the Gameboy.
b. Amazon agrees to place a banner advertisement on its website for another dot-com company. Instead of paying cash for the advertisement, the other company agrees to let Amazon advertise on its website.
c. Assume the same facts as in situation **b** except that Amazon agrees to accept the other company's common stock in this barter transaction. Over the next six months, the price of that stock declines.

Your instructor will divide the class into three groups and will assign each group one of the above situations. Each group should discuss the valuation and classification issues that arise in the assigned situation, including how Amazon should account for each transaction.

Business Communication Case

LO1, LO3 **Valuation and Classification of Business Transactions**

C 11. Hibbard Garden Center has purchased two pre-owned trucks for delivery of plants and flowers to its customers. The trucks were purchased at a cash-only auction for 15 percent below current market value. The owners have asked you to record these trucks in the financial records at current market value. You don't think that is correct. In response to the owners, write a brief business memorandum in good form based on your knowledge of Chapter 2. Explain how the purchase of the pre-owned trucks will affect the balance sheet, include the entry to record the transaction, and explain why the amount must be at the price paid for the trucks.

3

Measuring Business Income

Income, or earnings, is the most important measure of a company's success or failure. Thus, the incentive to manage, or misstate, earnings by manipulating the numbers can be powerful, and because earnings are based on estimates, manipulation can be easy. For these reasons, ethical behavior is extremely important when measuring business income.

LEARNING OBJECTIVES

Making a Statement

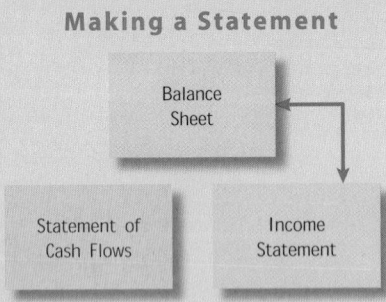

Adjusting entries affect the balance sheet and income statement but not the statement of cash flows.

LO1 Define *net income,* and explain the assumptions underlying income measurement and their ethical application.

LO2 Define *accrual accounting,* and explain how it is accomplished.

LO3 Identify four situations that require adjusting entries, and illustrate typical adjusting entries.

LO4 Prepare financial statements from an adjusted trial balance.

LO5 Use accrual-based information to analyze cash flows.

- What assumptions must Yahoo! make to account for transactions that span accounting periods?

- How does Yahoo! assign its revenues and expenses to the proper accounting period so that net income is properly measured?

- Why are the adjustments that these transactions require important to Yahoo!'s financial performance?

Yahoo! is a leading provider of online services to consumers and businesses worldwide. At the end of any accounting period, Yahoo! has many transactions that will affect future periods. Two examples appear in the Financial Highlights below: *prepaid expenses*, which, though paid in the period just ended, will benefit future periods and are therefore recorded as assets; and a*ccrued expenses*, which the company has incurred but will not pay until a future period.[1] If prepaid and accrued expenses are not accounted for properly at the end of a period, Yahoo!'s income will be misstated. Similar misstatements can occur when a company has received revenue that it has not yet earned or has earned revenue but not yet received it. If misstatements are made, investors will be misled about the company's financial performance.

YAHOO!'S FINANCIAL HIGHLIGHTS
Selected Balance Sheet Items (In thousands)

Assets	2005	2004	2003
Prepaid expenses	$166,976	$ 98,507	$129,777
Liabilities			
Accrued expenses and current liabilities	$827,589	$853,115	$483,628

Profitability Measurement: Issues and Ethics

> **LO1** Define *net income,* and explain the assumptions underlying income measurement and their ethical application.

As you know, profitability and liquidity are the two major goals of a business. For a business to succeed, or even to survive, it must earn a profit. **Profit**, however, means different things to different people. Accountants prefer to use the term **net income** because it can be precisely defined from an accounting point of view as the *net increase in owner's equity that results from a company's operations.*

Net income is reported on the income statement, and management, owners, and others use it to measure a company's progress in meeting the goal of profitability. Readers of income statements need to understand what net income means and be aware of its strengths and weaknesses as a measure of a company's performance.

Net Income

Net income is accumulated in the owner's Capital account. In its simplest form, it is measured as the difference between revenues and expenses when revenues exceed expenses:

$$\text{Net Income} = \text{Revenues} - \text{Expenses}$$

When expenses exceed revenues, a **net loss** occurs.

Revenues are increases in owner's equity resulting from selling goods, rendering services, or performing other business activities. When a business delivers a product or provides a service to a customer, it usually receives cash or is promised that it will receive cash in the near future. The amount of cash promised is recorded in either Accounts Receivable or Notes Receivable. The total of these accounts and the total cash received from customers in an accounting period are the company's revenues for that period.

Expenses are decreases in owner's equity resulting from the cost of selling goods or rendering services and the cost of the activities necessary to carry on a business, such as attracting and serving customers. In other words, expenses are the cost of the goods and services used in the course of earning revenues. Examples include salaries expense, rent expense, advertising expense, utilities expense, and depreciation (allocation of cost) of a building or office equipment. These expenses are often called the *cost of doing business* or *expired costs.*

Not all increases in owner's equity arise from revenues, nor do all decreases in owner's equity arise from expenses. Owner's investments increase owner's equity but are not revenues, and withdrawals decrease owner's equity but are not expenses.

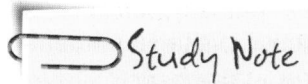
Study Note

The essence of revenue is that something has been *earned* through the sale of goods or services. That is why cash received through a loan does not constitute revenue.

Study Note

The primary purpose of an expense is to generate revenue.

Income Measurement Assumptions

Users of financial reports should be aware that assumptions play a major role in the measurement of net income and other key indicators of performance. **Yahoo!**'s management acknowledges this in its annual report, as follows:

> The preparation of . . . financial statements requires us to make estimates, judgments, and assumptions that affect the reported amounts of assets, liabilities, revenue, and expense.[2]

The major assumptions made in measuring business income have to do with continuity, periodicity, and matching.

Continuity

Measuring business income requires that certain expense and revenue transactions be allocated over several accounting periods. Choosing the number of accounting periods raises the issue of **continuity**. What is the expected life of the business? Many businesses last less than five years, and in any given year, thousands of businesses go bankrupt. The majority of companies present annual financial statements on the assumption that the business will continue to operate indefinitely—that is, that the company is a **going concern**. The continuity assumption is as follows:

> Unless there is evidence to the contrary, the accountant assumes that the business will continue to operate indefinitely.

Justification for all the techniques of income measurement rests on the assumption of continuity. Consider, for example, the value of assets on the balance sheet. The continuity assumption allows the cost of certain assets to be held on the balance sheet until a future accounting period, when the cost will become an expense on the income statement.

When a firm is facing bankruptcy, the accountant may set aside the assumption of continuity and prepare financial statements based on the assumption that the firm will go out of business and sell all of its assets at liquidation value—that is, for what they will bring in cash.

Periodicity

Measuring business income requires assigning revenues and expenses to a specific accounting period. However, not all transactions can be easily assigned to specific periods. For example, when a company purchases a building, it must estimate the number of years the building will be in use. The portion of the cost of the building that is assigned to each period depends on this estimate and requires an assumption about **periodicity**. The assumption is as follows:

> Although the lifetime of a business is uncertain, it is nonetheless useful to estimate the business's net income in terms of accounting periods.

Financial statements may be prepared for any time period, but generally, to make comparisons easier, the periods are of equal length. A 12-month accounting period is called a **fiscal year**; accounting periods of less than a year are called **interim periods**. The fiscal year of many organizations is the calendar

Study Note

Accounting periods are of equal length so that one period can be compared with the next.

FOCUS ON BUSINESS PRACTICE

Fiscal Years Vary.

The fiscal years of many schools and governmental agencies end on June 30 or September 30. The table at the right shows the last month of the fiscal year of some well-known companies:

Company	Last Month of Fiscal Year
Caesars World	July
The Walt Disney Company	September
Fleetwood Enterprises	April
H.J. Heinz	March
Kelly Services	December
MGM-UA Communications	August
Toys "R" Us	January

year, January 1 to December 31. However, retailers often end their fiscal years during a slack season, and in this case, the fiscal year corresponds to the yearly cycle of business activity.

Matching The **cash basis of accounting** is the practice of accounting for revenues in the period in which cash is received and for expenses in the period in which cash is paid. Some individuals and businesses use this method to account for income taxes. With this method, taxable income is calculated as the difference between cash receipts from revenues and cash payments for expenses.

Although the cash basis of accounting works well for some small businesses and many individuals, it does not meet the needs of most businesses. To measure net income adequately, revenues and expenses must be assigned to the accounting period in which they occur, regardless of when cash is received or paid. This is an application of the **matching rule**:

> Revenues must be assigned to the accounting period in which the goods
> are sold or the services performed, and expenses must be assigned to
> the accounting period in which they are used to produce revenue.

In other words, expenses should be recognized in the same accounting period as the revenues to which they are related. However, a direct cause-and-effect relationship between expenses and revenues is often difficult to identify. When there is no direct means of connecting expenses and revenues, costs are allocated in a systematic way among the accounting periods that benefit from the costs. For example, a building's cost is expensed over the building's expected useful life.

Ethics and the Matching Rule

As shown in Figure 1, applying the matching rule involves making assumptions. It also involves exercising judgment. Consider the assumptions and judgment involved in estimating the useful life of a building. The estimate should be

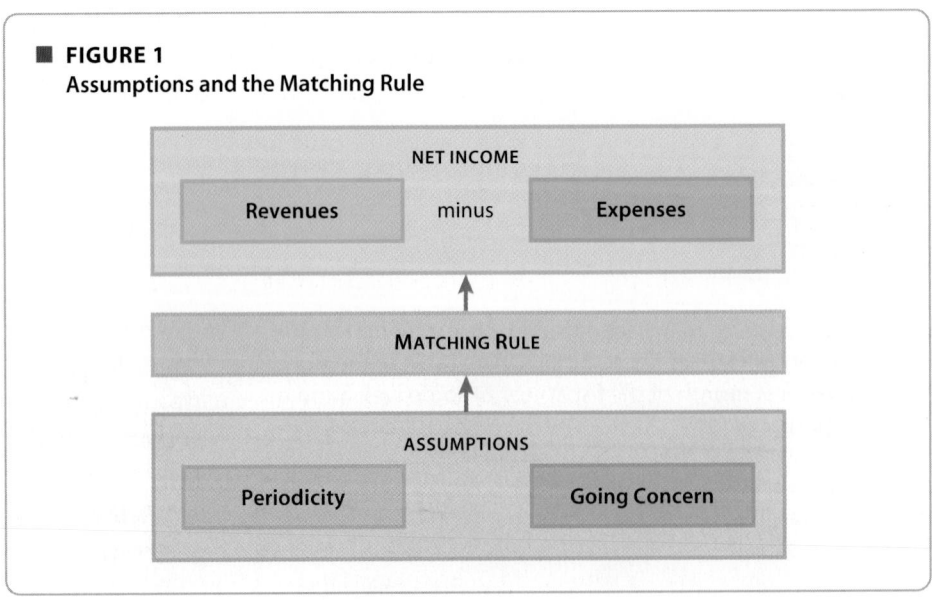

■ **FIGURE 1**
Assumptions and the Matching Rule

FOCUS ON BUSINESS PRACTICE

Are Misstatements of Earnings Always Overstatements?

Not all misstatements of earnings are overstatements. For instance, privately held companies, which do not have to be concerned about the effect of their earnings announcements on owners or investors, may understate income to reduce or avoid income taxes. In an unusual case involving a public company, the SEC cited and fined **Microsoft** for understating its income. Microsoft, a very successful company, accomplished this by overstating its unearned revenue on the balance sheet. The company's motive in trying to appear less successful than it actually was may have been that it was facing government charges of being a monopoly.[3]

based on realistic assumptions, but management has latitude in making that estimate, and its judgment will affect the final net income that is reported.

The manipulation of revenues and expenses to achieve a specific outcome is called **earnings management**. Research has shown that companies that manage their earnings are much more likely to exceed projected earnings targets by a little than to fall short by a little. Why would management want to manage earnings to keep them from falling short? It may want to

◗ Meet a previously announced goal and thus meet the expectations of the market.

◗ Keep the company's stock price from dropping.

◗ Meet a goal that will enable it to earn bonuses.

◗ Avoid embarrassment.

Earnings management, though not the best practice, is not illegal. However, when the estimates involved in earnings management begin moving outside a reasonable range, the financial statements become misleading. For instance, net income is misleading when revenue is overstated or expenses are understated by significant amounts. As noted earlier in the text, the preparation of financial statements that are intentionally misleading constitutes fraudulent financial reporting.

Most of the enforcement actions that the Securities and Exchange Commission has brought against companies in recent years involve misapplications of the matching rule resulting from improper accrual accounting. In the rest of this chapter, we focus on accrual accounting and its proper application. ●

S T O P • R E V I E W • A P P L Y

1-1. Why do accountants refer to *profit* as *net income*?

1-2. How does the need to assign revenues and expenses to a specific accounting period create problems?

1-3. What is the significance of the continuity assumption?

1-4. "The matching rule is the most significant concept in accounting." Do you agree with this statement? Explain your answer.

Suggested answers to all Stop, Review, and Apply questions are available at http://college.hmco.com/accounting/needles/poa/10e/student_home.html.

Accrual Accounting

> **LO2** Define *accrual accounting,* and explain how it is accomplished.

Accrual accounting encompasses all the techniques accountants use to apply the matching rule. In accrual accounting, revenues and expenses are recorded in the periods in which they occur rather than in the periods in which they are received or paid.

Accrual accounting is accomplished in the following ways:

1. Recording revenues when they are earned.

2. Recording expenses when they are incurred.

3. Adjusting the accounts.

Recognizing Revenues

As you may recall, the process of determining when revenue should be recorded is called **revenue recognition**. The Securities and Exchange Commission requires that all the following conditions be met before revenue is recognized:[4]

▶ Persuasive evidence of an arrangement exists.

▶ A product or service has been delivered.

▶ The seller's price to the buyer is fixed or determinable.

▶ Collectibility is reasonably assured.

For example, suppose Treadle Website Design has created a website for a customer and that the transaction meets the SEC's four criteria: Treadle and the customer agree that the customer owes for the service, the service has been rendered, both parties understand the price, and there is a reasonable expectation that the customer will pay the bill. When Treadle bills the customer, it records the transaction as revenue by debiting Accounts Receivable and crediting Design Revenue. Note that revenue can be recorded even though cash has not been collected; all that is required is a reasonable expectation that cash will be received.

Recognizing Expenses

Expenses are recorded when there is an agreement to purchase goods or services, the goods have been delivered or the services rendered, a price has been established or can be determined, and the goods or services have been used to produce revenue. For example, when Treadle Website Design receives its utility bill, it recognizes the expense as having been incurred and as having helped produce revenue. Treadle records this transaction by debiting Utilities Expense and crediting Accounts Payable. Until the bill is paid, Accounts Payable serves as a holding account. Note that recognition of the expense does not depend on the payment of cash.

Adjusting the Accounts

Accrual accounting also involves adjusting the accounts. Adjustments are necessary because the accounting period, by definition, ends on a particular day. The balance sheet must list all assets and liabilities as of the end of that day,

Study Note

The accountant waits until the end of an accounting period to update certain revenues and expenses even though the revenues and expenses theoretically change during the period. There usually is no need to adjust them until the end of the period, when the financial statements are prepared.

EXHIBIT 1 ▶ | **Trial Balance**

Treadle Website Design
Trial Balance
July 31, 20xx

Cash	$22,480	
Accounts Receivable	4,600	
Office Supplies	5,200	
Prepaid Rent	3,200	
Office Equipment	16,320	
Accounts Payable		$ 6,280
Unearned Design Revenue		1,400
P. Treadle, Capital		40,000
P. Treadle, Withdrawals	2,800	
Design Revenue		12,400
Wages Expense	4,800	
Utilities Expense	680	
	$60,080	$60,080

and the income statement must contain all revenues and expenses applicable to the period ending on that day. Although operating a business is a continuous process, there must be a cutoff point for the periodic reports. Some transactions invariably span the cutoff point, and some accounts therefore need adjustment.

As you can see in Exhibit 1, some of the accounts in Treadle Website Design's trial balance as of July 31 do not show the correct balances for preparing the financial statements. The trial balance lists prepaid rent of $3,200. At $1,600 per month, this represents rent for the months of July and August. So, on July 31, one-half of the $3,200 represents rent expense for July, and the remaining $1,600 represents an asset that will be used in August. An adjustment is needed to reflect the $1,600 balance in the Prepaid Rent account on the balance sheet and the $1,600 rent expense on the income statement.

As you will see, several other accounts in Treadle Website Design's trial balance do not reflect their correct balances. Like the Prepaid Rent account, they need to be adjusted.

Adjustments and Ethics

Accrual accounting can be difficult to understand. The account adjustments take time to calculate and enter in the records. Also, adjusting entries do not affect cash flows in the current period because they never involve the Cash account. You might ask, "Why go to all the trouble of making them? Why worry about them?" For one thing, the SEC has identified issues related to accrual accounting and adjustments as an area of utmost importance because of the potential for abuse and misrepresentation.

All adjustments are important because of their effect on performance measures of profitability and liquidity. Adjusting entries affect net income on the income statement, and they affect profitability comparisons from one accounting period to the next. They also affect assets and liabilities on the balance sheet and thus provide information about a company's *future* cash inflows and outflows. This information is needed to assess management's performance in achieving sufficient liquidity to meet the need for cash to pay ongoing obligations. The potential for abuse arises because considerable judgment underlies the application of adjusting entries. When this judgment is misused, performance measures can be misleading.

S T O P • R E V I E W • A P P L Y

2-1. What are the conditions for recognizing revenue?

2-2. What is the difference between the cash basis and the accrual basis of accounting?

2-3. In what three ways is accrual accounting accomplished?

2-4. Why are adjusting entries necessary?

2-5. "Why worry about adjustments? Doesn't it all come out in the wash?" Describe how you would answer these questions.

The Adjustment Process

LO3 Identify four situations that require adjusting entries, and illustrate typical adjusting entries.

When transactions span more than one accounting period, accrual accounting requires the use of **adjusting entries**. Figure 2 shows the four situations in which adjusting entries must be made. Each adjusting entry affects one balance sheet account and one income statement account. As we have already noted, adjusting entries never affect the Cash account.

The four types of adjusting entries are as follows:

Type 1. Allocating recorded costs between two or more accounting periods.
Examples of these costs are prepayments of rent, insurance, and sup-

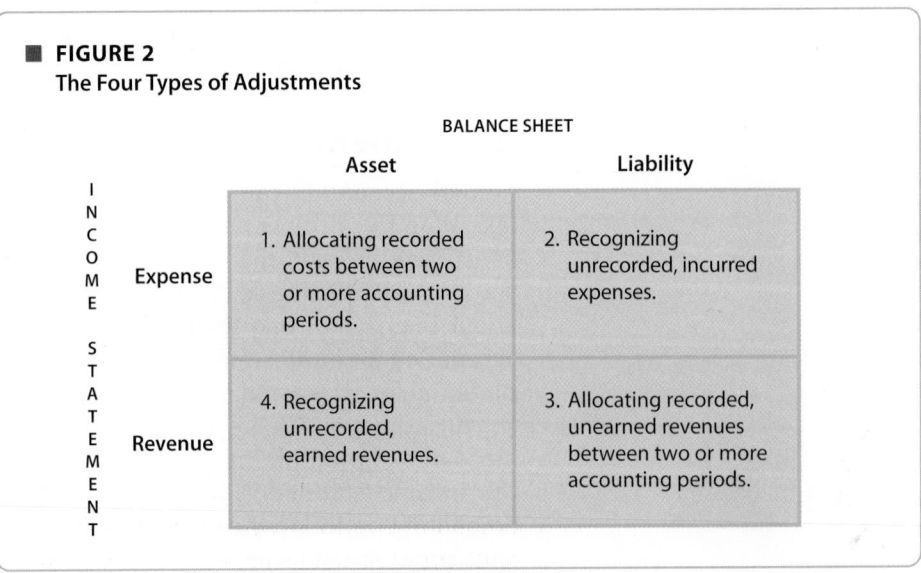

■ **FIGURE 2**
The Four Types of Adjustments

		BALANCE SHEET	
		Asset	Liability
INCOME STATEMENT	Expense	1. Allocating recorded costs between two or more accounting periods.	2. Recognizing unrecorded, incurred expenses.
	Revenue	4. Recognizing unrecorded, earned revenues.	3. Allocating recorded, unearned revenues between two or more accounting periods.

When transactions span more than one accounting period, an adjusting entry is necessary. Depreciation of plant and equipment, such as that found in this book warehouse area of Amazon.com's shipping and receiving facility in Fernley, Nevada, is a type of transaction that requires an adjusting entry. In this case, the adjusting entry involves an asset account and an expense account.

plies, and the depreciation of plant and equipment. The adjusting entry in this case involves an asset account and an expense account.

Type 2. Recognizing unrecorded, incurred expenses. Examples of these expenses are wages and interest that accrue but are not recorded during an accounting period. The adjusting entry involves an expense account and a liability account.

Type 3. Allocating recorded, unearned revenues between two or more accounting periods. Examples include cash received in advance and deposits made on goods or services. The adjusting entry involves a liability account and a revenue account.

Type 4. Recognizing unrecorded, earned revenues. An example is revenue that a company has earned for providing a service but for which it has not billed or collected a fee by the end of the accounting period. The adjusting entry involves an asset account and a revenue account.

Adjusting entries are either deferrals or accruals.

- A **deferral** is the postponement of the recognition of an expense already paid (Type 1 adjustment) or of revenue received in advance (Type 3 adjustment). The cash payment or receipt is recorded before the adjusting entry is made.

- An **accrual** is the recognition of a revenue (Type 4 adjustment) or expense (Type 2 adjustment) that has arisen but not been recorded during the accounting period. The cash receipt or payment occurs in a future accounting period, after the adjusting entry has been made.

Type 1 Adjustment: Allocating Recorded Costs (Deferred Expenses)

Companies often make expenditures that benefit more than one period. These costs are debited to an asset account. At the end of an accounting period, the

■ **FIGURE 3**
Adjustment for Prepaid (Deferred) Expenses

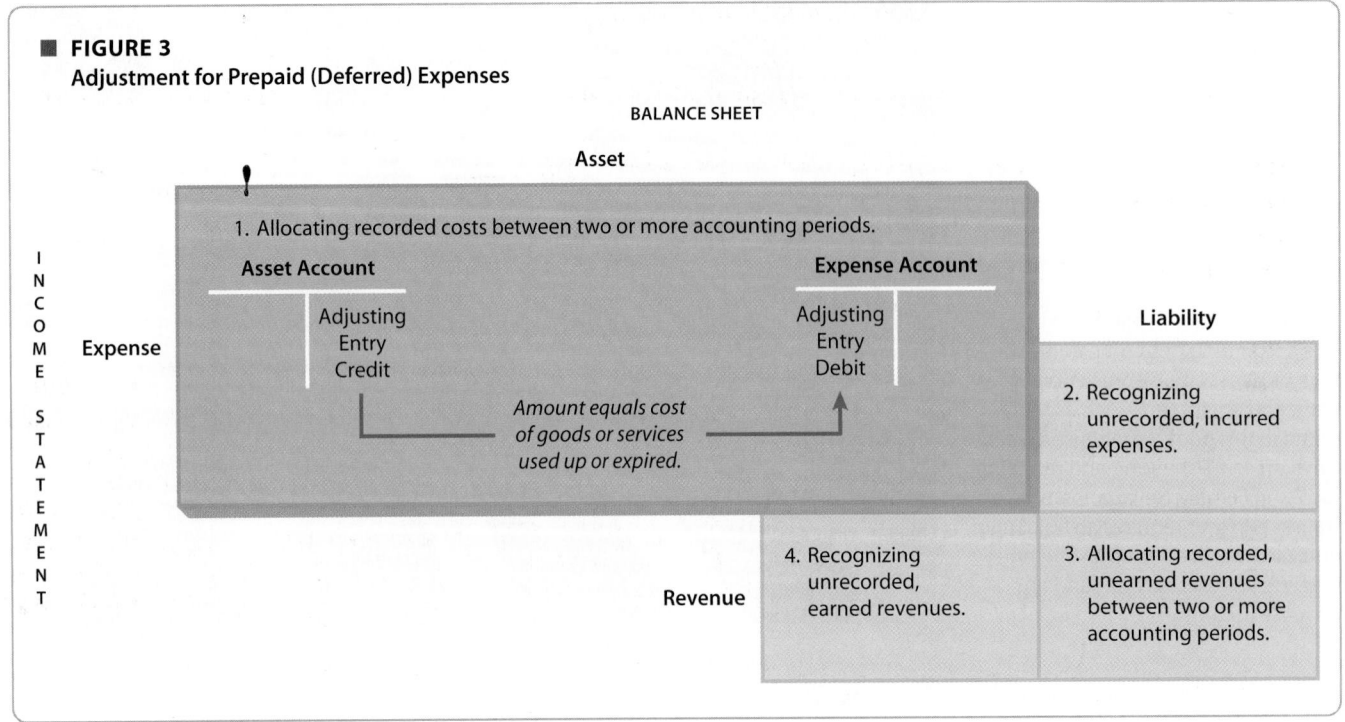

---

amount of the asset that has been used is transferred from the asset account to an expense account. Two important adjustments of this type are for prepaid expenses and the depreciation of plant and equipment.

Prepaid Expenses   Companies customarily pay some expenses, including those for rent, supplies, and insurance, in advance. These costs are called **prepaid expenses**. By the end of an accounting period, a portion or all of prepaid services or goods will have been used or have expired. The required adjusting entry reduces the asset and increases the expense, as shown in Figure 3. The amount of the adjustment equals the cost of the goods or services used or expired.

If adjusting entries for prepaid expenses are not made at the end of an accounting period, both the balance sheet and the income statement will present incorrect information. The company's assets will be overstated, and its expenses will be understated. Thus, owner's equity on the balance sheet and net income on the income statement will be overstated.

To illustrate this type of adjusting entry and the others discussed below, we refer again to the transactions of Treadle Website Design.

At the beginning of July, Treadle Website Design paid two months' rent in advance. The advance payment resulted in an asset consisting of the right to occupy the office for two months. As each day in the month passed, part of the asset's cost expired and became an expense. By July 31, one-half of the asset's cost had expired and had to be treated as an expense. The adjustment is as follows:

Adjustment for Prepaid Rent
July 31: Expiration of one month's rent, $1,600

Analysis: Expiration of prepaid rent *decreases* the asset account Prepaid Rent with a credit and *increases* the owner's equity account Rent Expense with a debit.

⌐◯Study Note

The expired portion of a prepayment is converted to an expense; the unexpired portion remains an asset.

Application of Double Entry:

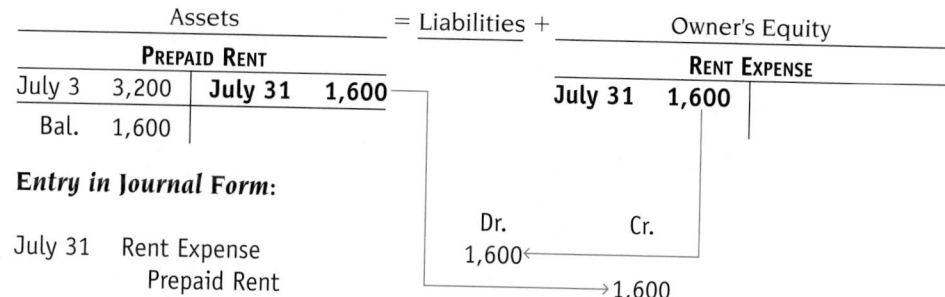

Entry in Journal Form:

July 31   Rent Expense
              Prepaid Rent

Comment: The Prepaid Rent account now has a balance of $1,600, which represents one month's rent that will be expensed during August. The logic in this analysis applies to all prepaid expenses.

Treadle purchased $5,200 of office supplies in early July. A careful inventory of the supplies is made at the end of the month. It records the number and cost of supplies that have not yet been consumed and are thus still assets of the company. Suppose the inventory shows that office supplies costing $3,660 are still on hand. This means that of the $5,200 of supplies originally purchased, $1,540 worth were used (became an expense) in July. The adjustment is as follows:

Adjustment for Supplies
July 31: Consumption of supplies, $1,540

Analysis: Consumption of office supplies *decreases* the asset account *Office Supplies* with a credit and *increases* the expense account *Office Supplies Expense* with a debit.

Application of Double Entry:

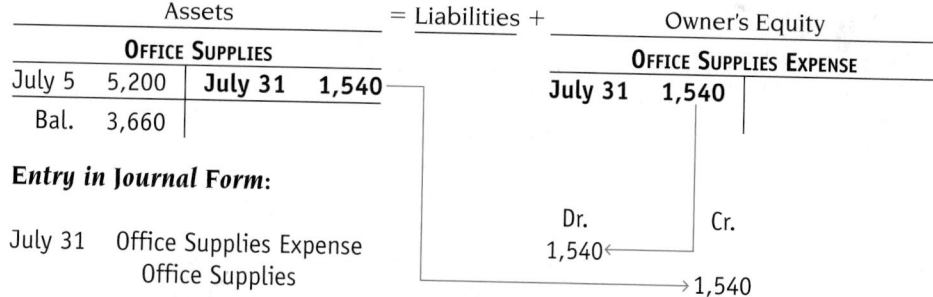

Entry in Journal Form:

July 31   Office Supplies Expense
              Office Supplies

Comment: The asset account Office Supplies now reflects the correct balance of $3,660 of supplies yet to be consumed. The logic in this example applies to all kinds of supplies.

Depreciation of Plant and Equipment

When a company buys a long-term asset—such as a building, truck, computer, or store fixture—it is, in effect, prepaying for the usefulness of that asset for as long as it benefits the company. Because a long-term asset is a deferral of an expense, the accountant must allocate the cost of the asset over its estimated useful life. The amount allocated to any one accounting period is called **depreciation**, or *depreciation expense*. Depreciation, like other expenses, is incurred during an accounting period to produce revenue.

It is often impossible to tell exactly how long an asset will last or how much of the asset has been used in any one period. For this reason, depreciation

Study Note

The difficulty in estimating an asset's useful life is further evidence that the net income figure is, at best, an estimate.

must be estimated. Accountants have developed a number of methods for estimating depreciation and for dealing with the related complex problems. (In the discussion that follows, we assume that the amount of depreciation has been established.)

Because depreciation is an estimate, a separate account —the **Accumulated Depreciation account**—is used to accumulate the depreciation on specific long-term assets. This account, which is deducted from its related asset account on the balance sheet, is called a *contra account*. A **contra account** is a separate account that is paired with a related account—in this case, an asset account. The balance of a contra account is shown on a financial statement as a deduction from its related account. The net amount is called the **carrying value**, or *book value*, of the asset. As the months pass, the amount of the accumulated depreciation grows, and the carrying value of the asset declines.

Adjustment for Plant and Equipment

July 31: Depreciation of office equipment, $300

Analysis: Depreciation *decreases* the asset account *Office Equipment* by *increasing* the contra account *Accumulated Depreciation–Office Equipment* with a credit and *increasing* the owner's equity account *Depreciation Expense–Office Equipment* with a debit, as shown below.

Application of Double Entry:

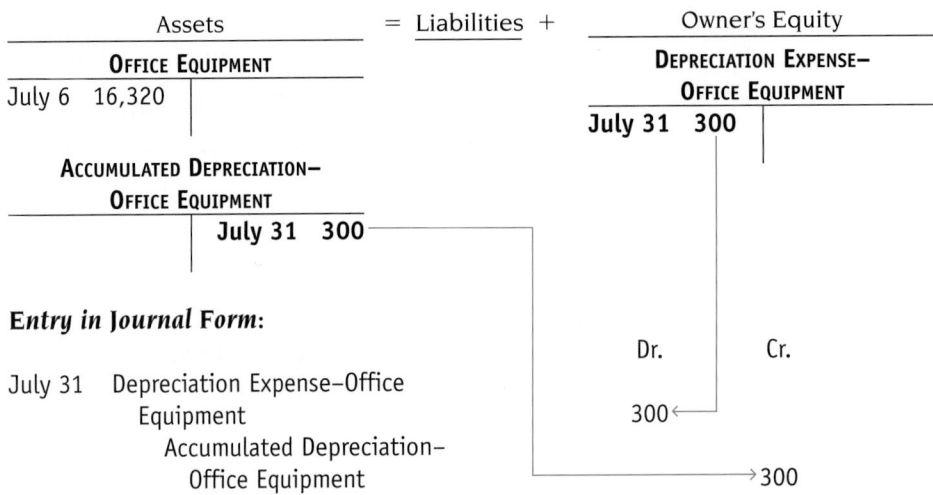

Entry in Journal Form:

July 31   Depreciation Expense–Office
              Equipment
                 Accumulated Depreciation–
                    Office Equipment

Comment: The carrying value of Office Equipment is $16,020 ($16,320 − $300) and is presented on the balance sheet as follows:

Property, Plant, and Equipment:

Office equipment	$16,320	
Less accumulated depreciation	300	$16,020

Application to Yahoo! Inc.

Yahoo! has prepaid expenses and property and equipment similar to those in the examples we have presented. Among Yahoo!'s prepaid expenses are fixed payments that it makes to other Internet companies in an effort to increase the number of visitors to its site. These fixed payments are debited to prepaid expense when the payments are made and are expensed through adjusting entries "proratably over the term the fixed payment covers."[5]

■ **FIGURE 4**
Adjustment for Unrecorded (Accrued) Expenses

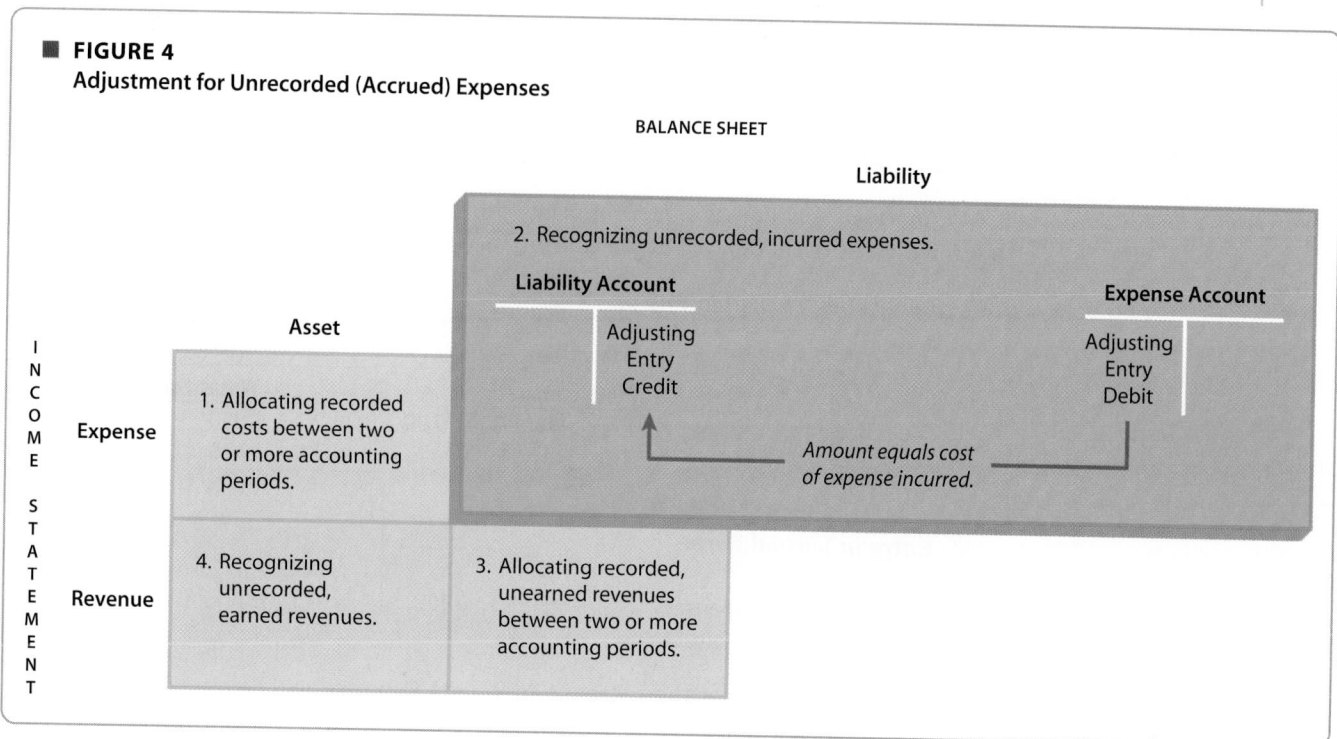

Type 2 Adjustment: Recognizing Unrecorded, Incurred Expenses (Accrued Expenses)

Study Note

Remember that in accrual accounting, an expense must be recorded in the period in which it is incurred regardless of when payment is made.

Usually, at the end of an accounting period, some expenses incurred during the period have not been recorded in the accounts. These expenses require adjusting entries. One such expense is interest on borrowed money. Each day, interest accumulates on the debt. As shown in Figure 4, at the end of the accounting period, an adjusting entry is made to record the accumulated interest, which is an expense of the period, and the corresponding liability to pay the interest. Other common unrecorded expenses are wages, and utilities. As the expense and the corresponding liability accumulate, they are said to *accrue*—hence, the term **accrued expenses**.

To illustrate how adjustments are made for unrecorded, incurred wages, suppose Treadle Website Design has two pay periods a month rather than one. In July, its pay periods end on the 12th and the 26th, as indicated in this calendar:

July

Sun	M	T	W	Th	F	Sat
	1	2	3	4	5	6
7	8	9	10	11	12	13
14	15	16	17	18	19	20
21	22	23	24	25	26	27
28	29	30	31			

By the end of business on July 31, Treadle's assistant will have worked three days (Monday, Tuesday, and Wednesday) beyond the last pay period. The employee has earned the wages for those days but will not be paid until the first payday in August. The wages for these three days are rightfully an expense for July, and the liabilities should reflect that the company owes the assistant for those days. Because the assistant's wage rate is $2,400 every two weeks, or $240 per day ($2,400 ÷ 10 working days), the expense is $720 ($240 × 3 days).

Adjustment for Unrecorded Wages

July 31: Accrual of unrecorded wages, $720

Analysis: Accrual of wages *increases* the owner's equity account *Wages Expense* with a debit and *increases* the liability account *Wages Payable* with a credit.

Application of Double Entry:

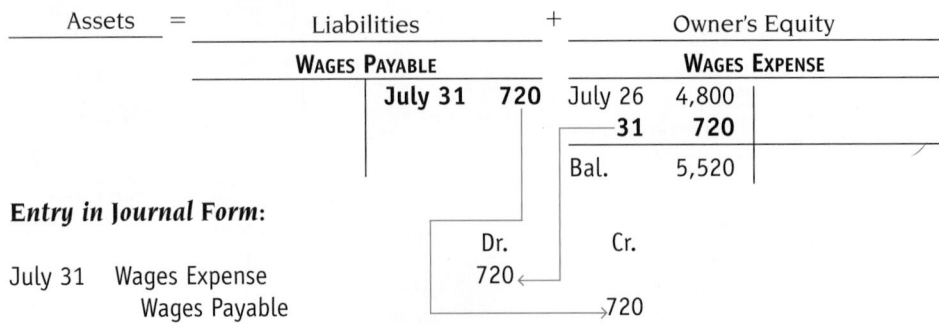

Comment: Note that the increase in Wages Expense will *decrease* owner's equity and that total wages for the month are $5,520, of which $720 will be paid next month.

Application to Yahoo! Inc. In 2005, **Yahoo!** had accrued expenses and current liabilities of $827,589 million.[6] If the expenses were not accrued, Yahoo!'s liabilities would be significantly understated, as would the corresponding expenses on its income statement. The result would be an overstatement of the company's earnings.

Type 3 Adjustment: Allocating Recorded, Unearned Revenues (Deferred Revenues)

Study Note

Unearned revenue is a liability because there is an obligation to deliver goods or perform a service, or to return the cash. Once the goods have been delivered or the service performed, the liability is converted to revenue.

Just as expenses can be paid before they are used, revenues can be received before they are earned. When a company receives revenues in advance, it has an obligation to deliver goods or perform services. **Unearned revenues** are therefore shown in a liability account.

For example, publishing companies usually receive cash in advance for magazine subscriptions. These receipts are recorded in a liability account, Unearned Subscriptions. If the company fails to deliver the magazines, subscribers are entitled to their money back. As the company delivers each issue of the magazine, it earns a part of the advance receipts. This earned portion must be transferred from the Unearned Subscriptions account to the Subscription Revenue account, as shown in Figure 5.

During July, Treadle Website Design received $1,400 from another firm as advance payment for a website design. By the end of the month, it had completed $800 of work on the design, and the other firm had accepted the work.

Adjustment for Unearned Revenue

July 31: Performance of services for which cash was received in advance, $800

Analysis: Performing the services for which cash was received in advance *increases* the owner's equity account *Design Revenue* with a credit and *decreases* the liability account *Unearned Design Revenue* with a debit.

■ **FIGURE 5**
Adjustment for Unearned (Deferred) Revenues

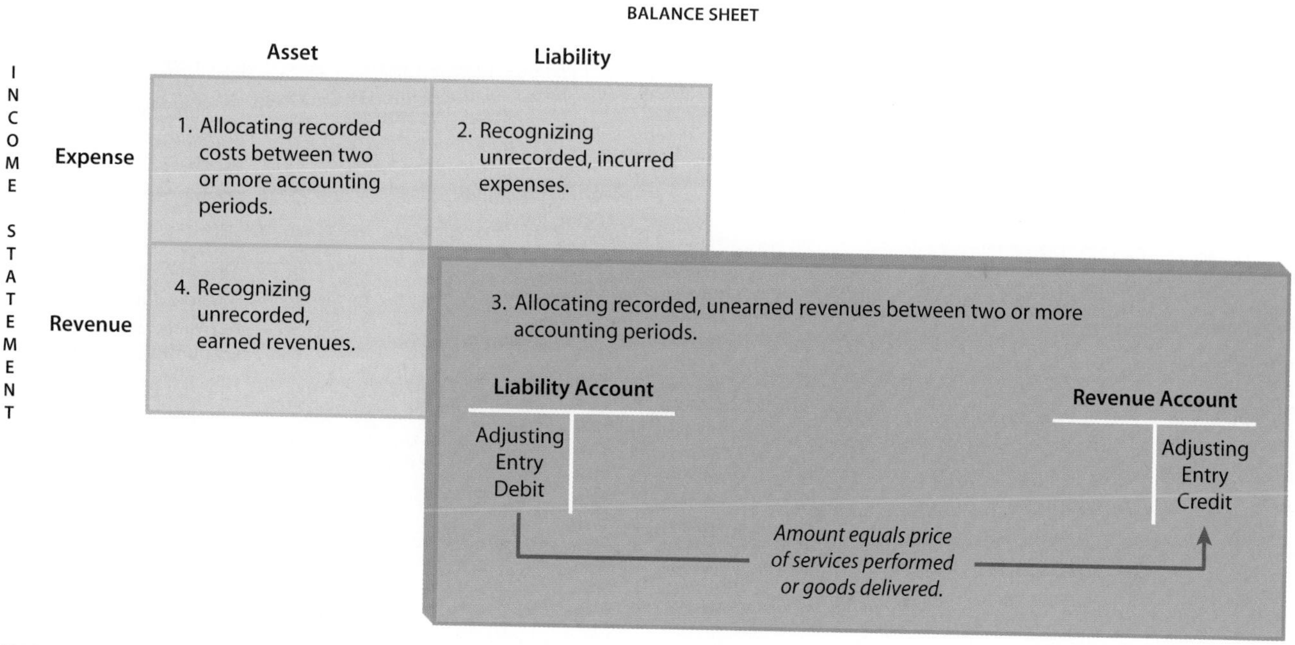

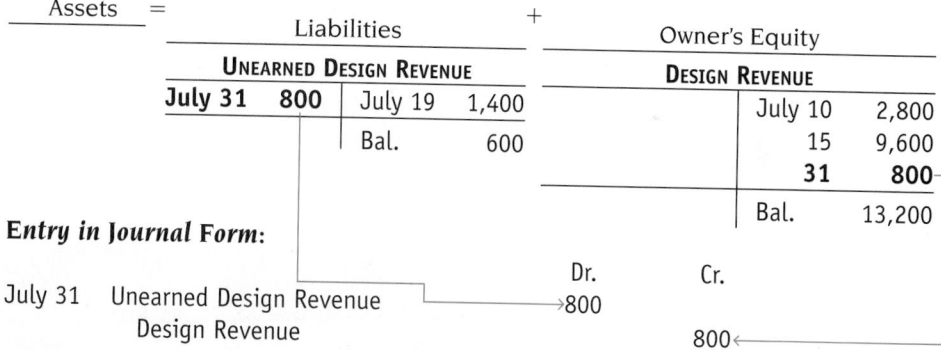

Application of Double Entry:

Assets	=			+		
		_____Liabilities_____			____Owner's Equity____	
		UNEARNED DESIGN REVENUE			**DESIGN REVENUE**	
		July 31 800	July 19 1,400		July 10	2,800
			Bal. 600		15	9,600
					31	**800**
					Bal.	13,200

Entry in Journal Form:

			Dr.	Cr.
July 31	Unearned Design Revenue		800	
	Design Revenue			800

Comment: Unearned Design Revenue now reflects the amount of work still to be performed, $600.

Application to Yahoo! Inc.

Yahoo! has a current liability account called Deferred Revenue. It represents revenues for advertisements for which Yahoo! has billed but that it has not yet earned. These advertisements appear as "banners" when users access Yahoo!'s site. As they appear, the revenue is transferred from Deferred Revenue to Yahoo!'s Earned Revenue account.

Type 4 Adjustment: Recognizing Unrecorded, Earned Revenues (Accrued Revenues)

Accrued revenues are revenues that a company has earned by performing a service or delivering goods but for which no entry has been made in the accounting records. Any revenues earned but not recorded during an accounting period require an adjusting entry that debits an asset account and credits a

■ **FIGURE 6**
Adjustment for Unrecorded (Accrued) Revenues

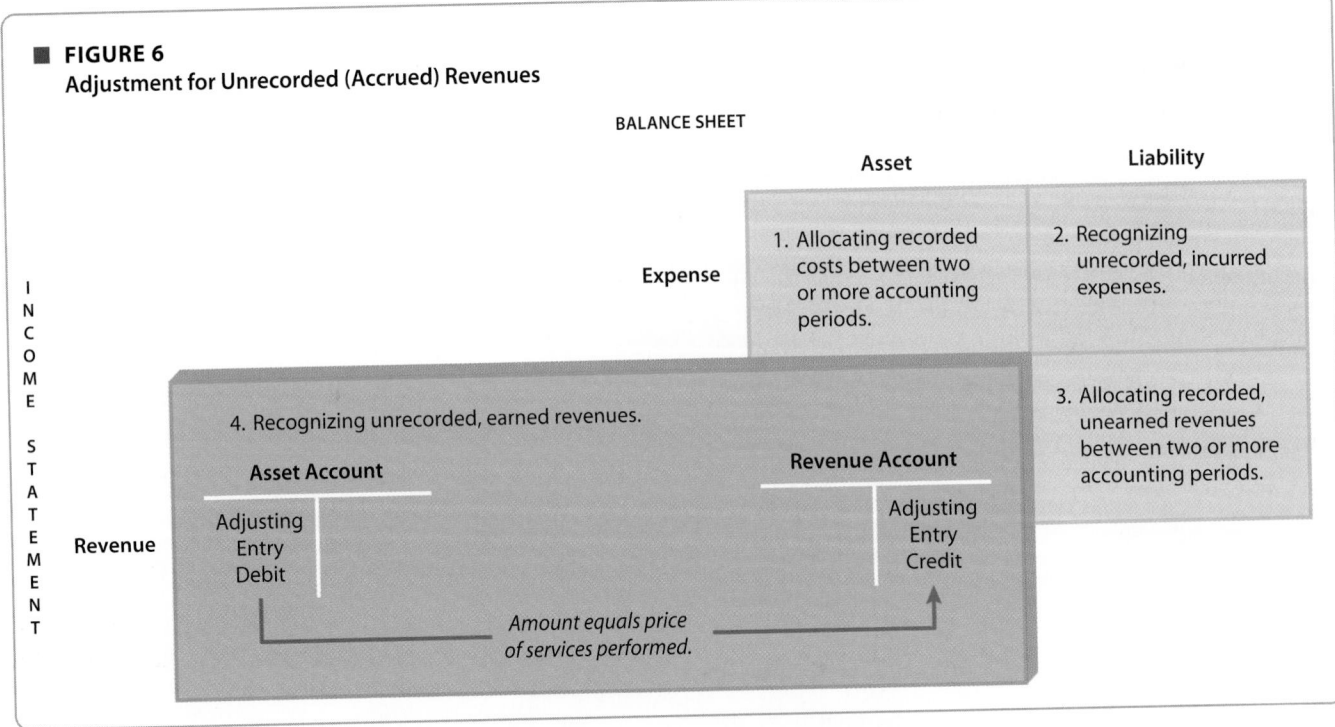

BALANCE SHEET

	Asset	Liability
Expense	1. Allocating recorded costs between two or more accounting periods.	2. Recognizing unrecorded, incurred expenses.
Revenue	4. Recognizing unrecorded, earned revenues.	3. Allocating recorded, unearned revenues between two or more accounting periods.

I N C O M E S T A T E M E N T

4. Recognizing unrecorded, earned revenues.

Asset Account

Adjusting
Entry
Debit

Revenue Account

Adjusting
Entry
Credit

*Amount equals price
of services performed.*

revenue account, as shown in Figure 6. For example, the interest on a note receivable is earned day by day but may not be received until another accounting period. The Interest Receivable account should be debited and the Interest Income account should be credited for the interest accrued at the end of the current period.

During July, Treadle Website Design agreed to design a website for Marsh Tire Company. It also agreed to have the first section of the site operational by July 31. By the end of the month, Treadle had earned $400 for completing the first section but had not billed Marsh Tire Company or recorded the fee.

When a company earns revenue by performing a service—such as designing a website or developing marketing plans—but will not receive the revenue for the service until a future accounting period, it must make an adjusting entry. This type of adjusting entry involves an asset account and a revenue account.

Adjustment for Design Revenue
July 31: Accrual of unrecorded revenue, $400

Analysis: Accrual of unrecorded revenue *increases* the owner's equity account *Design Revenue* with a credit and *increases* the asset account *Accounts Receivable* with a debit.

Application of Double Entry:

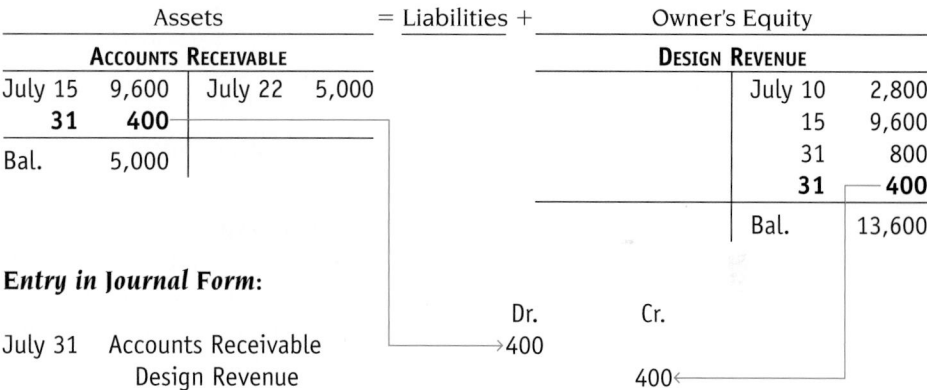

Assets			= Liabilities +		Owner's Equity	
ACCOUNTS RECEIVABLE					**DESIGN REVENUE**	
July 15	9,600	July 22 5,000			July 10	2,800
31	400				15	9,600
Bal.	5,000				31	800
					31	400
					Bal.	13,600

Entry in Journal Form:

		Dr.	Cr.
July 31	Accounts Receivable	400	
	Design Revenue		400

Comment: Design Revenue now reflects the total revenue earned during July, $13,600.

Application to Yahoo! Inc.   **Yahoo!** recognizes revenue from text-link and hypertext link advertisements, including pay-for-performance advertisements of search results, in the period in which "click-throughs" occur. "Click-throughs" are the number of times users click on an advertisement or search result. They are the performance measure that enables Yahoo! to accrue revenue and establish a receivable.

A Note About Journal Entries

Thus far, we have presented a full analysis of each journal entry. The analyses showed you the thought process behind each entry. By now, you should be fully aware of the effects of transactions on the accounting equation and the rules of debit and credit. For this reason, in the rest of the book, we present journal entries without full analysis.

S T O P • R E V I E W • A P P L Y

3-1. What are the four situations that require adjusting entries? Give an example of each.

3-2. "Some assets are expenses that have not expired." Explain this statement.

3-3. What do plant and equipment, office supplies, and prepaid insurance have in common?

3-4. How do accumulated depreciation and depreciation expense differ?

3-5. What is a contra account? Give an example.

3-6. Why are contra accounts used to record depreciation?

3-7. How does unearned revenue arise? Give an example.

3-8. Where does unearned revenue appear in the financial statements?

3-9. Under what circumstances does a company have accrued revenues? Give an example. What asset arises when an adjustment for accrued revenues is made?

3-10. What is an accrued expense? Give two examples.

Identification of Adjusting Entries   The four types of adjusting entries are as follows:

Type 1. Allocating recorded costs between two or more accounting periods

Type 2. Recognizing unrecorded, incurred expenses

Type 3. Allocating recorded, unearned revenues between two or more accounting periods

Type 4. Recognizing unrecorded, earned revenues

For each of the following items, identify the type of adjusting entry required:

_____ a. Revenues earned but not yet collected or billed to customers

_____ b. Interest incurred but not yet recorded

_____ c. Unused supplies

_____ d. Costs of plant and equipment

SOLUTION
a. Type 4
b. Type 2
c. Type 1
d. Type 1

Using the Adjusted Trial Balance to Prepare Financial Statements

LO4 Prepare financial statements from an adjusted trial balance.

 **Study Note**

The adjusted trial balance is a second check that the ledger is still in balance. Because it reflects updated information from the adjusting entries, it is used in preparing the formal financial statements.

After adjusting entries have been recorded and posted, an **adjusted trial balance** is prepared by listing all accounts and their balances. If the adjusting entries have been posted to the accounts correctly, the adjusted trial balance will have equal debit and credit totals. The adjusted trial balance for Treadle Website Design is shown in Exhibit 2.

Some accounts in Exhibit 2, such as Cash and Accounts Payable, have the same balances as in the trial balance in Exhibit 1 because no adjusting entries affected them. The balances of other accounts, such as Office Supplies and Prepaid Rent, differ from those in the trial balance because adjusting entries did affect them. The adjusted trial balance also has some new accounts, such as depreciation accounts and Wages Payable, that are not in the trial balance.

The adjusted trial balance facilitates the preparation of the financial statements. As shown in Exhibit 2, the revenue and expense accounts are used to prepare the income statement. Then, as shown in Exhibit 3, the statement of owner's equity and the balance sheet are prepared. Notice that the net income from the income statement is combined with the Withdrawals account on the statement of owner's equity to give the net change in the P. Treadle, Capital

▼ EXHIBIT 2

Relationship of the Adjusted Trial Balance to the Income Statement

Treadle Website Design
Adjusted Trial Balance
July 31, 20xx

Cash	$ 22,480	
Accounts Receivable	5,000	
Office Supplies	3,660	
Prepaid Rent	1,600	
Office Equipment	16,320	
Accumulated Depreciation–		
Office Equipment		$ 300
Accounts Payable		6,280
Unearned Design Revenue		600
Wages Payable		720
P. Treadle, Capital		40,000
P. Treadle, Withdrawals	2,800	
Design Revenue		13,600
Wages Expense	5,520	
Utilities Expense	680	
Rent Expense	1,600	
Office Supplies Expense	1,540	
Depreciation Expense–		
Office Equipment	300	
	$61,500	$61,500

Treadle Website Design
Income Statement
For the Month Ended July 31, 20xx

Revenues		
Design revenue		$13,600
Expenses		
Wages expense	$5,520	
Utilities expense	680	
Rent expense	1,600	
Office supplies expense	1,540	
Depreciation expense–		
office equipment	300	
Total expenses		9,640
Net income		$ 3,960

 **Study Note**

The net income figure from the income statement is needed to prepare the statement of owner's equity, and the bottom-line figure of that statement is needed to prepare the balance sheet. This dictates the order in which the statements are prepared.

▼ **EXHIBIT 3**

Relationship of the Adjusted Trial Balance to the Balance Sheet and Statement of Owner's Equity

Treadle Website Design
Adjusted Trial Balance
July 31, 20xx

Cash	$22,480	
Accounts Receivable	5,000	
Office Supplies	3,660	
Prepaid Rent	1,600	
Office Equipment	16,320	
Accumulated Depreciation– Office Equipment		$ 300
Accounts Payable		6,280
Unearned Design Revenue		600
Wages Payable		720
P. Treadle, Capital		40,000
P. Treadle, Withdrawals	2,800	
Design Revenue		13,600
Wages Expense	5,520	
Utilities Expense	680	
Rent Expense	1,600	
Office Supplies Expense	1,540	
Depreciation Expense–Office Equipment	300	
	$61,500	$61,500

Treadle Website Design
Balance Sheet
July 31, 20xx

Assets

Cash		$22,480
Accounts receivable		5,000
Office supplies		3,660
Prepaid rent		1,600
Office equipment	$16,320	
Less accumulated depreciation	300	16,020
Total assets		$48,760

Liabilities

Accounts payable		$ 6,280
Unearned design revenue		600
Wages payable		720
Total liabilities		$ 7,600

Owner's Equity

P. Treadle, Capital		41,160
Total liabilities and owner's equity		$48,760

Treadle Website Design
Statement of Owner's Equity
For the Month Ended July 31, 20xx

P. Treadle, Capital, July 1, 20xx		$ 0
Investment by P. Treadle		40,000
Net income		3,960
Subtotal		$43,960
Less withdrawals		2,800
P. Treadle, Capital, July 31, 20xx		$41,160

account. The resulting balance of P. Treadle, Capital at July 31 is used in preparing the balance sheet, as are the asset and liability account balances in the adjusted trial balance.

S T O P • R E V I E W • A P P L Y

4-1. Why is the income statement usually the first statement prepared from the adjusted trial balance?

4-2. Why does the ending balance for owner's capital not appear on the adjusted trial balance?

Cash Flows from Accrual-Based Information

> **LO5** Use accrual-based information to analyze cash flows.

Management has the short-range goal of ensuring that its company has sufficient cash to pay ongoing obligations—in other words, management must ensure the company's liquidity. To plan payments to creditors and assess the need for short-term borrowing, managers must know how to use accrual-based information to analyze cash flows.

Almost every revenue or expense account on the income statement has one or more related accounts on the balance sheet. For instance, Office Supplies Expense is related to Office Supplies, Wages Expense is related to Wages Payable, and Design Revenue is related to Unearned Design Revenue. As we have shown, these accounts are related by making adjusting entries, the purpose of which is to apply the matching rule to the measurement of net income.

The cash inflows that a company's operations generate and the cash outflows that they require can also be determined by analyzing these relationships. For example, suppose that after receiving the financial statements in Exhibits 2 and 3, management wants to know how much cash was expended for office supplies. On the income statement, Office Supplies Expense is $1,540, and on the balance sheet, Office Supplies is $3,660. Because July was the company's first month of operation, there was no prior balance of office supplies, so the amount of cash expended for office supplies during the month was $5,200 ($1,540 + $3,660 = $5,200).

Thus, the cash flow used in purchasing office supplies—$5,200—was much greater than the amount expensed in determining income—$1,540. In planning for August, management can anticipate that the cash needed may be less than the amount expensed because, given the large inventory of office supplies, the company will probably not have to buy office supplies in the coming month. Understanding these cash flow effects enables management to better predict the business's need for cash in August.

The general rule for determining the cash flow received from any revenue or paid for any expense (except depreciation, which is a special case not covered here) is to determine the potential cash payments or cash receipts and deduct the amount not paid or not received. As shown below, the application of the general rule varies with the type of asset or liability account:

Type of Account	Potential Payment or Receipt Not Paid or Received				Result
Prepaid Expense	Ending Balance	+ Expense for the Period	− Beginning Balance	=	Cash Payments for Expenses
Unearned Revenue	Ending Balance	+ Revenue for the Period	− Beginning Balance	=	Cash Receipts from Revenues
Accrued Expense	Beginning Balance	+ Expense for the Period	− Ending Balance	=	Cash Payments for Expenses
Accrued Revenue	Beginning Balance	+ Revenue for the Period	− Ending Balance	=	Cash Receipts from Revenues

For instance, suppose that on May 31, a company had a balance of $480 in Prepaid Insurance and that on June 30, the balance was $670. If the insurance expense during June was $120, the amount of cash expended on insurance during June can be computed as follows:

Prepaid Insurance at June 30	$670
Insurance Expense during June	120
Potential cash payments for insurance	$790
Less Prepaid Insurance at May 31	480
Cash payments for insurance during June	$310

The beginning balance is deducted because it was paid in a prior accounting period. Note that the cash payments equal the expense plus the increase in the balance of the Prepaid Insurance account [$120 + ($670 − $480) = $310]. In this case, the cash paid was almost three times the amount of insurance expense. In future months, cash payments are likely to be less than the expense.

S T O P • R E V I E W • A P P L Y

5-1. Explain the effects that adjusting entries have on a company's cash flows.

5-2. Why does the cash paid for expenses in an accounting period often differ from the amount of expenses on the income statement?

5-3. Why does the cash received for services in an accounting period often differ from the amount of revenue on the income statement?

A LOOK BACK AT

YAHOO! INC.

In the Decision Point at the beginning of the chapter, we noted that **Yahoo!** has many transactions that span accounting periods. We asked these questions:

- **What assumptions must Yahoo! make to account for transactions that span accounting periods?**
- **How does Yahoo! assign its revenues and expenses to the proper accounting period so that net income is properly measured?**
- **Why are the adjustments that these transactions require important to Yahoo!'s financial performance?**

Two of the assumptions Yahoo! must make are that it will continue as a going concern for an indefinite time (the continuity assumption) and that it can make useful estimates of its income in terms of accounting periods (the periodicity assumption). These assumptions enable the company to apply the matching rule—that is, revenues are assigned to the accounting period in which goods are sold or services are performed, and expenses are assigned to the accounting period in which they are used to produce revenue.

As you have learned in this chapter, adjusting entries for deferred and accrued expenses and for deferred and accrued revenues have an impact on a company's earnings. By paying close attention to the profit margin ratio, one can assess how well a company is controlling its expenses in relation to its revenues. The **profit margin** shows the percentage of each revenue, or sales dollar, that results in net income. Using data from Yahoo!'s annual report, we can calculate Yahoo!'s profit margin for two successive years as follows (dollars are in thousands):

	2005	2004
Net Income	$1,896,230	$839,553
Net Revenues*	$5,257,668	$3,574,517
K/R Profit Margin:	36.1%	23.5%

*Also called *net sales*.

These results show that Yahoo!'s revenues and earnings are increasing very rapidly and that its profitability is improving dramatically. Because net income equals revenues minus expenses and adjusting entries affect both revenues and expenses, you can see that without adjusting entries, it would be impossible to make a fair assessment of Yahoo!'s financial performance.

CHAPTER REVIEW

REVIEW of Learning Objectives

LO1 Define *net income,* and explain the assumptions underlying income measurement and their ethical application.

Net income is the net increase in owner's equity that results from a company's operations. Net income equals revenues minus expenses; when expenses exceed revenues, a net loss results. Revenues equal the price of goods sold or services rendered during a specific period. Expenses are the costs of goods and services used in the process of producing revenues.

The continuity assumption recognizes that even though businesses face an uncertain future, without evidence to the contrary, accountants must assume that a business will continue to operate indefinitely. The periodicity assumption recognizes that although the lifetime of a business is uncertain, it is nonetheless useful to estimate the business's net income in terms of accounting periods. The matching rule holds that revenues must be assigned to the accounting period in which the goods are sold or the services performed, and expenses must be assigned to the accounting period in which they are used to produce revenue.

Because applying the matching rule involves making assumptions and exercising judgment, it can lead to earnings management, which is the manipulation of revenues and expenses to achieve a specific outcome. When the estimates involved in earnings management move outside a reasonable range, financial statements become misleading. Financial statements that are intentionally misleading constitute fraudulent financial reporting.

LO2 Define *accrual accounting,* and explain how it is accomplished.

Accrual accounting consists of all the techniques accountants use to apply the matching rule. It is accomplished by recognizing revenues when they are earned, by recognizing expenses when they are incurred, and by adjusting the accounts.

LO3 Identify four situations that require adjusting entries, and illustrate typical adjusting entries.

Adjusting entries are required when (1) recorded costs must be allocated between two or more accounting periods, (2) unrecorded expenses exist, (3) recorded, unearned revenues must be allocated between two or more accounting periods, and (4) unrecorded, earned revenues exist. The preparation of adjusting entries is summarized as follows:

Type of Adjusting Entry	Debited	Credited	Examples of Balance Sheet Accounts
1. Allocating recorded costs (previously paid, expired)	Expense	Asset (or contra-asset)	Prepaid rent Prepaid insurance Office supplies Accumulated depreciation–office equipment
2. Accrued expenses (incurred, not paid)	Expense	Liability	Interest payable Wages payable
3. Allocating recorded, unearned revenues (previously received, earned)	Liability	Revenue	Unearned design revenue
4. Accrued revenues (earned, not received)	Asset	Revenue	Accounts receivable Interest receivable

Type of Account

LO4 Prepare financial statements from an adjusted trial balance.

An adjusted trial balance is prepared after adjusting entries have been posted to the accounts. Its purpose is to test whether the adjusting entries have been posted correctly before the financial statements are prepared. The balances in the revenue and expense accounts in the adjusted trial balance are used to prepare the income statement. The balances in the asset and liability accounts in the adjusted trial balance and in the statement of owner's equity are used to prepare the balance sheet.

LO5 Use accrual-based information to analyze cash flows.

To ensure a company's liquidity, managers must know how to use accrual-based information to analyze cash flows. The general rule for determining the cash flow received from any revenue or paid for any expense (except depreciation) is to determine the potential cash receipts or cash payments and deduct the amount not received or not paid.

REVIEW of Concepts and Terminology

The following concepts and terms were introduced in this chapter:

Accrual: The recognition of an expense or revenue that has arisen but has not yet been recorded. **(LO3)**

Accrual accounting: Recording transactions in the periods in which they occur, rather than in the periods in which cash is received or paid; all the techniques that accountants use to apply the matching rule. **(LO2)**

Accrued expenses: Expenses incurred but not recognized in the accounts; unrecorded expenses. **(LO3)**

Accrued revenues: Revenues for which a service has been performed or goods delivered but for which no entry has been made; unrecorded revenues. **(LO3)**

Accumulated Depreciation account: A contra-asset account used to accumulate depreciation on specific long-term assets. **(LO3)**

Adjusted trial balance: A trial balance prepared after all adjusting entries have been recorded and posted to the accounts. **(LO4)**

Adjusting entries: Entries made to apply accrual accounting to transactions that span accounting periods. **(LO3)**

Carrying value: The unexpired portion of the cost of an asset. Also called *book value*. **(LO3)**

Cash basis of accounting: Accounting for revenues and expenses on a cash-received and cash-paid basis. **(LO1)**

Continuity: The difficulty associated with not knowing how long a business will survive. **(LO1)**

Contra account: An account whose balance is subtracted from an associated account in the financial statements. **(LO3)**

Deferral: The postponement of the recognition of an expense already paid or of revenue received in advance. **(LO3)**

Depreciation: The portion of the cost of a long-term asset allocated to any one accounting period. Also called *depreciation expense*. **(LO3)**

Earnings management: The manipulation of revenues and expenses to achieve a specific outcome. **(LO1)**

Expenses: Decreases in owner's equity resulting from the costs of goods and services used in the course of earning revenues. Also called *cost of doing business* or *expired costs*. **(LO1)**

Fiscal year: Any 12-month accounting period. **(LO1)**

Going concern: The assumption that unless there is evidence to the contrary, a business will continue to operate indefinitely. **(LO1)**

Interim periods: Accounting periods of less than one year. **(LO1)**

Matching rule: The principle that revenues must be assigned to the accounting period in which the goods are sold or the services performed, and expenses must be assigned to the accounting period in which they are used to produce revenue. **(LO1)**

Net income: The net increase in owner's equity that results from business operations and is accumulated in the owner's Capital account; revenues less expenses when revenues exceed expenses. **(LO1)**

Net loss: The net decrease in owner's equity when expenses exceed revenues. **(LO1)**

Periodicity: The assumption that although the lifetime of a business is uncertain, it is still useful to estimate its net income in terms of accounting periods. **(LO1)**

Prepaid expenses: Expenses paid in advance that have not yet expired; an asset account. **(LO3)**

Profit: The increase in owner's equity that results from business operations. **(LO1)**

Revenue recognition: The process of determining when revenue is earned. **(LO2)**

Revenues: Increases in owner's equity resulting from selling goods, rendering services, or performing other business activities. **(LO1)**

Unearned revenues: Revenues received in advance for which the goods have not yet been delivered or the services performed; a liability account. **(LO3)**

Key Ratio

Profit margin: A ratio that shows the percentage of each sales dollar that results in net income; Net Income ÷ Net Revenues.

Review Problem

LO3, LO4 **Posting to T Accounts, Determining Adjusting Entries, and Using an Adjusted Trial Balance to Prepare Financial Statements**

The following is the unadjusted trial balance for Certified Answering Service on December 31, 20x8:

	A	B	C	D	E
1			Certified Answering Service		
2			Trial Balance		
3			December 31, 20x8		
4					
5	Cash			$2,160	
6	Accounts Receivable			1,250	
7	Office Supplies			180	
8	Prepaid Insurance			240	
9	Office Equipment			3,400	
10	Accumulated Depreciation--Office Equipment				$ 600
11	Accounts Payable				700
12	Unearned Revenue				460
13	S. Goldstein, Capital				4,870
14	S. Goldstein, Withdrawals			400	
15	Answering Service Revenue				2,900
16	Wages Expense			1,500	
17	Rent Expense			400	
18				$9,530	$9,530
19					

The following information is also available:

a. Insurance that expired during December amounted to $40.

b. Office supplies on hand on December 31 totaled $75.

c. Depreciation for December totaled $100.

d. Accrued wages on December 31 totaled $120.

e. Revenues earned for services performed in December but not billed by the end of the month totaled $300.

f. Revenues received in December in advance of services yet to be performed totaled $160.

Required

1. Prepare T accounts for the accounts in the trial balance, and enter the balances.
2. Determine the required adjusting entries, and record them directly in the T accounts. Open new T accounts as needed.
3. Prepare an adjusted trial balance.
4. Prepare an income statement, a statement of owner's equity, and a balance sheet for the month ended December 31, 20x8.

Answer to Review Problem

1. T accounts set up and amounts from trial balance entered
2. Adjusting entries recorded

	A	B	C	D	E	F	G	H	I	J	K	L	M	N
1		**Cash**					**Accounts Receivable**					**Office Supplies**		
2	Bal.	2,160				Bal.	1,250				Bal.	180	(b)	105
3						(e)	300				*Bal.*	*75*		
4						*Bal.*	*1,550*							
5												**Accumulated Depreciation--**		
6		**Prepaid Insurance**					**Office Equipment**					**Office Equipment**		
7	Bal.	240	(a)	40		Bal.	3,400						Bal.	600
8	*Bal.*	*200*											(c)	100
9													*Bal.*	*700*
10														
11		**Accounts Payable**					**Unearned Revenue**					**Wages Payable**		
12			Bal.	700		(f)	160	Bal.	460				(d)	120
13								*Bal.*	*300*					
14												**Answering**		
15		**S. Goldstein, Capital**					**S. Goldstein, Withdrawals**					**Service Revenue**		
16			Bal.	4,870		Bal.	400						Bal.	2,900
17													(e)	300
18													(f)	160
19													*Bal.*	*3,360*
20														
21		**Wages Expense**					**Rent Expense**					**Insurance Expense**		
22	Bal.	1,500				Bal.	400				Bal.	40		
23	(d)	120												
24	*Bal.*	*1,620*												
25							**Depreciation Expense--**							
26		**Office Supplies Expense**					**Office Equipment**							
27	(b)	105				(c)	100							
28														

3. Adjusted trial balance prepared

		C	D	E
		Certified Answering Service		
		Adjusted Trial Balance		
		December 31, 20x8		
5	Cash		$ 2,160	
6	Accounts Receivable		1,550	
7	Office Supplies		75	
8	Prepaid Insurance		200	
9	Office Equipment		3,400	
10	Accumulated Depreciation--Office Equipment			$ 700
11	Accounts Payable			700
12	Unearned Revenue			300
13	Wage Payable			120
14	S. Goldstein, Capital			4,870
15	S. Goldstein, Withdrawals		400	
16	Answering Service Revenue			3,360
17	Wages Expense		1,620	
18	Rent Expense		400	
19	Insurance Expense		40	
20	Office Supplies Expense		105	
21	Depreciation Expense--Office Equipment		100	
22			$10,050	$10,050

4. Financial statements prepared

		C	D	E
		Certified Answering Service		
		Income Statement		
		For the Month Ended December 31, 20x8		
5	**Revenues**			
6	Answering service revenue			$3,360
8	**Expenses**			
9	Wages expense		$1,620	
10	Rent expense		400	
11	Insurance Expense		40	
12	Office Supplies Expense		105	
13	Depreciation Expense--Office Equipment		100	
14	Total expenses			2,265
15	**Net income**			$1,095

	A	B	C	D
1			**Certified Answering Service**	
2			**Statement of Owner's Equity**	
3			**For the Month Ended December 31, 20x8**	
4				
5	S. Goldstein, Capital, November 30, 20x8			$4,870
6	Net income			1,095
7	Subtotal			$5,965
8	Less S. Goldstein, Withdrawals			400
9	S. Goldstein, Capital, December 31, 20x8			$5,565
10				

	A	B	C	D	E
1			**Certified Answering Service**		
2			**Balance Sheet**		
3			**December 31, 20x8**		
4					
5			**Assets**		
6	Cash				$2,160
7	Accounts receivable				1,550
8	Office supplies				75
9	Prepaid insurance				200
10	Office equipment			$3,400	
11		Less accumulated depreciation		700	2,700
12	Total assets				$6,685
13					
14			**Liabilities**		
15	Accounts Payable				$ 700
16	Unearned Revenue				300
17	Wage Payable				120
18	Total liabilities				$1,120
19					
20			**Owner's Equity**		
21	S. Goldstein, Capital, November 30, 20x8			$5,565	
22	Total owner's equity				5,565
23	Total liabilities and owner's capital				$6,685
24					

CHAPTER ASSIGNMENTS

≡ BUILDING Your Basic Knowledge and Skills

Short Exercises

LO1, LO2   Accrual Accounting Concepts

SE 1. Match the concepts of accrual accounting on the right with the assumptions or actions on the left:

____ 1. Assumes expenses should be assigned to the accounting period in which they are used to produce revenues	a. Periodicity
	b. Going concern
	c. Matching rule
____ 2. Assumes a business will last indefinitely	d. Revenue recognition
____ 3. Assumes revenues are earned at a point in time	
____ 4. Assumes net income that is measured for a short period of time, such as one quarter, is a useful measure	

LO3   Adjustment for Prepaid Insurance

SE 2. The Prepaid Insurance account began the year with a balance of $460. During the year, insurance in the amount of $1,040 was purchased. At the end of the year (December 31), the amount of insurance still unexpired was $700. Prepare the year-end entry in journal form to record the adjustment for insurance expense for the year.

LO3   Adjustment for Supplies

SE 3. The Supplies account began the year with a balance of $380. During the year, supplies in the amount of $980 were purchased. At the end of the year (December 31), the inventory of supplies on hand was $440. Prepare the year-end entry in journal form to record the adjustment for supplies expense for the year.

LO3   Adjustment for Depreciation

SE 4. The depreciation expense on office equipment for the month of March is $100. This is the third month that the office equipment, which cost $1,900, has been owned. Prepare the adjusting entry in journal form to record depreciation for March and show the balance sheet presentation for office equipment and related accounts after the March 31 adjustment.

LO3   Adjustment for Accrued Wages

SE 5. Wages are paid each Saturday for a six-day workweek. Wages are currently running $1,380 per week. Prepare the adjusting entry required on June 30, assuming July 1 falls on a Tuesday.

LO3   Adjustment for Unearned Revenue

SE 6. During the month of August, deposits in the amount of $1,100 were received for services to be performed. By the end of the month, services in the amount of $760 had been performed. Prepare the necessary adjustment for Service Revenue at the end of the month.

LO4   Preparation of an Income Statement and Statement of Owner's Equity from an Adjusted Trial Balance

SE 7. The adjusted trial balance for Shimura Company on December 31, 20x7, contains the following accounts and balances: J. Shimura, Capital, $4,300;

J. Shimura, Withdrawals, $175; Service Revenue, $1,300; Rent Expense, $200; Wages Expense, $450; Utilities Expense, $100; and Telephone Expense, $25. Prepare an income statement and statement of owner's equity in proper form for the month of December.

LO5 **Determination of Cash Flows**

SE 8. Unearned Revenue had a balance of $650 at the end of November and $450 at the end of December. Service Revenue was $2,550 for the month of December. How much cash was received for services provided during December?

Profit Margin

SE 9. Calculate profit margin for 20x8 using the following data: A company has net income of $7,000 and net sales of $82,000 in 20x8.

Exercises

LO1, LO2, LO3 **Discussion Questions**

E 1. Develop a brief answer to each of the following questions.

1. When a company has net income, what happens to its assets and/or to its liabilities?
2. Is accrual accounting more closely related to a company's goal of profitability or liquidity?
3. Will the carrying value of a long-term asset normally equal its market value?

LO4 **Discussion Questions**

E 2. Develop a brief answer to each of the following questions.

1. If, at the end of the accounting period, you were looking at the T account for a prepaid expense like supplies, would you look for the amounts expended in cash on the debit or credit side? On which side would you find the amount expensed during the period?
2. Would you expect profit margin to be a good measure of a company's liquidity? Why or why not?

LO1, LO2, LO3 **Applications of Accounting Concepts Related to Accrual Accounting**

E 3. The accountant for Villegas Company makes the assumptions or performs the activities listed below. Tell which of the following concepts of accrual accounting most directly relates to each assumption or action: (a) periodicity, (b) going concern, (c) matching rule, (d) revenue recognition, (e) deferral, and (f) accrual.

1. In estimating the life of a building, assumes that the business will last indefinitely
2. Records a sale when the customer is billed
3. Postpones the recognition of a one-year insurance policy as an expense by initially recording the expenditure as an asset
4. Recognizes the usefulness of financial statements prepared on a monthly basis even though they are based on estimates
5. Recognizes, by making an adjusting entry, wages expense that has been incurred but not yet recorded
6. Prepares an income statement that shows the revenues earned and the expenses incurred during the accounting period

LO2   Application of Conditions for Revenue Recognition

E 4. Four conditions must be met before revenue should be recognized. In each of the following cases, tell which condition has *not* been met.

a. Company A accepts a contract to perform services in the future for $2,000.
b. Company B ships products worth $3,000 to another company without an order from the other company but tells the company it can return the products if it does not sell them.
c. Company C performs $10,000 of services for a firm with financial problems.
d. Company D agrees to work out a price later for services that it performs for another company.

LO3   Adjusting Entry for Unearned Revenue

E 5. City-Alive Company of Fargo, North Dakota, publishes a monthly magazine featuring local restaurant reviews and upcoming social, cultural, and sporting events. Subscribers pay for subscriptions either one year or two years in advance. Cash received from subscribers is credited to an account called Magazine Subscriptions Received in Advance. On December 31, 20x7, the end of the company's fiscal year, the balance of this account is $750,000. Expiration of subscriptions revenue is as follows:

During 20x7 $150,000
During 20x8   375,000
During 20x9   225,000

Prepare the adjusting entry in journal form for December 31, 20x7.

LO3   Adjusting Entries for Prepaid Insurance

E 6. An examination of the Prepaid Insurance account shows a balance of $10,280 at the end of an accounting period, before adjustment. Prepare entries in journal form to record the insurance expense for the period under the following independent assumptions:

1. An examination of the insurance policies shows unexpired insurance that cost $4,935 at the end of the period.
2. An examination of the insurance policies shows insurance that cost $1,735 has expired during the period.

LO3   Adjusting Entries for Supplies: Missing Data

E 7. Each of the following columns represents a Supplies account:

	a	b	c	d
Supplies on hand at July 1	$264	$217	$196	$?
Supplies purchased during the month	52	?	174	1,928
Supplies consumed during the month	194	972	?	1,632
Supplies on hand at July 31	?	436	56	1,118

1. Determine the amounts indicated by the question marks.
2. Make the adjusting entry for column **a**, assuming supplies purchased are debited to an asset account.

LO3   Adjusting Entry for Accrued Salaries

E 8. Basil Company has a five-day workweek and pays salaries of $70,000 each Friday.

1. Prepare the adjusting entry required on May 31, assuming that June 1 falls on a Wednesday.
2. Prepare the entry to pay the salaries on June 3, including the amount of salaries payable from requirement 1.

LO3 Revenue and Expense Recognition

E 9. Schuss Company produces computer software that Dushan Company sells. Schuss receives a royalty of 15 percent of sales. Dushan Company pays royalties to Schuss Company semiannually—on May 1 for sales made in July through December of the previous year and on November 1 for sales made in January through June of the current year. Royalty expense for Dushan Company and royalty income for Schuss Company in the amount of $6,000 were accrued on December 31, 20x7. Cash in the amounts of $6,000 and $10,000 was paid and received on May 1 and November 1, 20x8, respectively. Software sales during the July to December 20x8 period totaled $150,000.

1. Calculate the amount of royalty expense for Dushan Company and royalty income for Schuss during 20x8.
2. Record the adjusting entry that each company made on December 31, 20x8.

LO4 Preparation of Financial Statements

E 10. Prepare the monthly income statement, monthly statement of owner's equity, and the balance sheet at August 31, 20xx, for Fish Bowl Cleaning Company from the data provided in the adjusted trial balance below. The owner made no investments during the period.

Fish Bowl Cleaning Company
Adjusted Trial Balance
August 31, 20xx

Cash	$ 4,590	
Accounts Receivable	2,592	
Prepaid Insurance	380	
Prepaid Rent	200	
Cleaning Supplies	152	
Cleaning Equipment	3,200	
Accumulated Depreciation–Cleaning Equipment		$ 320
Truck	7,200	
Accumulated Depreciation–Truck		720
Accounts Payable		420
Wages Payable		80
Unearned Janitorial Revenue		920
S. Rogers, Capital		15,034
S. Rogers, Withdrawals	2,000	
Janitorial Revenue		14,620
Wages Expense	5,680	
Rent Expense	1,200	
Gas, Oil, and Other Truck Expenses	580	
Insurance Expense	380	
Supplies Expense	2,920	
Depreciation Expense–Cleaning Equipment	320	
Depreciation Expense–Truck	720	
	$32,114	$32,114

LO3 **Adjusting Entries**

E 11. Prepare year-end adjusting entries for each of the following:

1. Office Supplies has a balance of $168 on January 1. Purchases debited to Office Supplies during the year amount to $830. A year-end inventory reveals supplies of $570 on hand.
2. Depreciation of office equipment is estimated to be $4,260 for the year.
3. Property taxes for six months, estimated at $1,750, have accrued but have not been recorded.
4. Unrecorded interest income on U.S. government bonds is $1,700.
5. Unearned Revenue has a balance of $1,800. Services for $600 received in advance have now been performed.
6. Services totaling $400 have been performed; the customer has not yet been billed.

LO3 **Accounting for Revenue Received in Advanced**

E 12. Waldemar Gott, a lawyer, received $72,000 on October 1 to represent a client in real estate negotiations over the next 12 months.

1. Record the entries required in Gott's records on October 1 and at the end of the fiscal year, December 31.
2. How would this transaction be reflected on the income statement and balance sheet on December 31?

LO5 **Determination of Cash Flows**

E 13. After adjusting entries had been made, the balance sheets of Matuska Company showed the following asset and liability amounts at the end of 20x7 and 20x8:

	20x8	20x7
Prepaid insurance	$1,200	$1,450
Wages payable	600	1,100
Unearned fees	2,100	950

The following amounts were taken from the 20x8 income statement:

Insurance expense	$1,900
Wages expense	9,750
Fees earned	4,450

Calculate the amount of cash paid for insurance and wages and the amount of cash received for fees during 20x8.

LO5 **Relationship of Expenses to Cash Paid**

E 14. The income statement for Leon Company included the following expenses for 20xx:

Rent expense	$ 78,000
Interest expense	11,700
Salaries expense	124,500

Listed below are the related balance sheet account balances at year end for last year and this year.

	Last Year	This Year
Prepaid rent	—	$ 1,350
Interest payable	$1,800	—
Salaries payable	7,500	114,000

1. Compute the cash paid for rent during the year.

2. Compute the cash paid for interest during the year.
3. Compute the cash paid for salaries during the year.

Profit Margin

E 15. Julio Company wants to know if its profitability has improved. Calculate its profit margin for 20x7 and 20x8 using the following data:

Net Income, 20x7	$ 4,300
Net Income, 20x8	5,000
Net Sales, 20x7	80,000
Net Sales, 20x8	96,000

By this measure has profitability improved?

Problems

LO3 Determining Adjustments

P 1. At the end of its fiscal year, the trial balance for Roosevelt Cleaners appears as follows:

Roosevelt Cleaners
Trial Balance
September 30, 20x7

Cash	$ 11,788	
Accounts Receivable	26,494	
Prepaid Insurance	3,400	
Cleaning Supplies	7,374	
Land	18,000	
Building	185,000	
Accumulated Depreciation–Building		$ 45,600
Accounts Payable		20,400
Unearned Cleaning Revenue		1,600
Mortgage Payable		110,000
T. Roosevelt, Capital		56,560
T. Roosevelt, Withdrawals	10,000	
Cleaning Revenue		157,634
Wages Expense	101,330	
Cleaning Equipment Rental Expense	6,000	
Delivery Truck Expense	4,374	
Interest Expense	11,000	
Other Expenses	7,034	
	$391,794	$391,794

The following information is also available:

a. A study of the company's insurance policies shows that $680 is unexpired at the end of the year.
b. An inventory of cleaning supplies shows $1,244 on hand.
c. Estimated depreciation on the building for the year is $12,800.
d. Accrued interest on the mortgage payable is $1,000.
e. On September 1, the company signed a contract, effective immediately, with Kings County Hospital to dry clean, for a fixed monthly charge of $400,

the uniforms used by doctors in surgery. The hospital paid for four months' service in advance.

f. Sales and delivery wages are paid on Saturday. The weekly payroll is $2,520. September 30 falls on a Thursday and the company has a six-day pay week.

Required

All adjustments affect one balance sheet account and one income statement account. For each of the above situations, show the accounts affected, the amount of the adjustment (using a + or − to indicate an increase or decrease), and the balance of the account after the adjustment in the following format:

Balance Sheet Account	Amount of Adjustment (+ or −)	Balance after Adjustment	Income Statement Account	Amount of Adjustment (+ or −)	Balance after Adjustment

LO2, LO3 **Preparing Adjusting Entries**

P 2. On June 30, the end of the current fiscal year, the following information is available to Sterling Company's accountants for making adjusting entries:

a. Among the liabilities of the company is a mortgage payable in the amount of $240,000. On June 30, the accrued interest on this mortgage amounted to $12,000.

b. On Friday, July 2, the company, which is on a five-day workweek and pays employees weekly, will pay its regular salaried employees $19,200.

c. On June 29, the company completed negotiations and signed a contract to provide services to a new client at an annual rate of $3,600.

d. The Supplies account shows a beginning balance of $1,615 and purchases during the year of $3,766. The end-of-year inventory reveals supplies on hand of $1,186.

e. The Prepaid Insurance account shows the following entries on June 30:

Beginning Balance $1,530
January 1   2,900
May 1   3,366

The beginning balance represents the unexpired portion of a one-year policy purchased in April of the previous year. The January 1 entry represents a new one-year policy, and the May 1 entry represents the additional coverage of a three-year policy.

f. The following table contains the cost and annual depreciation for buildings and equipment, all of which were purchased before the current year:

Account	Cost	Annual Depreciation
Buildings	$185,000	$ 7,300
Equipment	218,000	21,800

g. On June 1, the company completed negotiations with another client and accepted an advance of $21,000 for services to be performed in the next year. The $21,000 was credited to Unearned Service Revenue.

h. The company calculates that as of June 30 it had earned $3,500 on a $7,500 contract that will be completed and billed in August.

Required

1. Prepare adjusting entries for each item listed above.
2. **User Insight:** Explain how the conditions for revenue recognition are applied to transactions **c** and **h**.

LO3 Determining Adjusting Entries, Posting to T Accounts, and Preparing an Adjusted Trial Balance

P 3. The trial balance for Financial Strategies Service on December 31, 20xx, is as follows:

Financial Strategies Service
Trial Balance
December 31, 20xx

Cash	$ 16,500	
Accounts Receivable	8,250	
Office Supplies	2,662	
Prepaid Rent	1,320	
Office Equipment	9,240	
Accumulated Depreciation–Office Equipment		$ 1,540
Accounts Payable		5,940
Notes Payable		11,000
Unearned Service Revenue		2,970
L. Gang, Capital		24,002
L. Gang, Withdrawals	22,000	
Service Revenue		72,600
Salaries Expense	49,400	
Rent Expense	4,400	
Utilities Expense	4,280	
	$118,052	$118,052

The following information is also available:

a. Ending inventory of office supplies, $264.
b. Prepaid rent expired, $440.
c. Depreciation of office equipment for the period, $660.
d. Accrued interest expense at the end of the period, $550.
e. Accrued salaries at the end of the period, $330.
f. Service revenue still unearned at the end of the period, $1,166.
g. Service revenue earned but unrecorded, $2,200.

Required

1. Open T accounts for the accounts in the trial balance plus the following: Interest Payable; Salaries Payable; Office Supplies Expense; Depreciation Expense–Office Equipment; and Interest Expense. Enter the balances shown on the trial balance.
2. Determine the adjusting entries and post them directly to the T accounts.
3. Prepare an adjusted trial balance.
4. **User Insight:** Which financial statements do each of the above adjustments affect? Which financial statement is *not* affected by the adjustments?

LO3, LO4 Determining Adjusting Entries and Tracing Their Effects to Financial Statements

P 4. Joyce Ozaki opened a small tax-preparation service. At the end of its second year of operation, Ozaki Tax Service had the trial balance that appears on the next page.

Ozaki Tax Service
Trial Balance
December 31, 20x8

Cash	$ 2,268	
Accounts Receivable	1,031	
Prepaid Insurance	240	
Office Supplies	782	
Office Equipment	7,100	
Accumulated Depreciation–Office Equipment		$ 770
Accounts Payable		635
Unearned Tax Fees		219
J. Ozaki, Capital		5,439
J. Ozaki, Withdrawals	6,000	
Tax Fees Revenue		21,926
Office Salaries Expense	8,300	
Advertising Expense	650	
Rent Expense	2,400	
Telephone Expense	218	
	$28,989	$28,989

The following information is also available:

a. Office supplies on hand, December 31, 20x8, $227.
b. Insurance still unexpired, $120.
c. Estimated depreciation of office equipment, $770.
d. Telephone expense for December, $19; the bill was received but not recorded.
e. The services for all unearned tax fees had been performed by the end of the year.

Required

1. Open T accounts for the accounts in the trial balance plus the following: Office Supplies Expense; Insurance Expense; and Depreciation Expense–Office Equipment. Record the balances shown in the trial balance.
2. Determine the adjusting entries and post them directly to the T accounts.
3. Prepare an adjusted trial balance, an income statement, a statement of owner's equity, and a balance sheet. The owner made no investments during the period.
4. **User Insight:** Why is it not necessary to show the effects of the above transactions on the statement of cash flows?

LO3, LO4   **Determining Adjusting Entries and Tracing Their Effects to Financial Statements**

P 5. Elite Livery Service was organized to provide limousine service between the airport and various suburban locations. It has just completed its second year of business. Its trial balance is on the opposite page. The following information is also available:

a. To obtain space at the airport, Elite paid two years' rent in advance when it began the business.
b. An examination of insurance policies reveals that $2,800 expired during the year.

Elite Livery Service
Trial Balance
June 30, 20x8

Cash (111)	$ 9,812	
Accounts Receivable (112)	14,227	
Prepaid Rent (117)	12,000	
Prepaid Insurance (118)	4,900	
Prepaid Maintenance (119)	12,000	
Spare Parts (141)	11,310	
Limousines (142)	200,000	
Accumulated Depreciation–Limousines (143)		$ 25,000
Notes Payable (211)		45,000
Unearned Passenger Service Revenue (212)		30,000
J. Pieter, Capital (312)		78,211
J. Pieter, Withdrawals (313)	20,000	
Passenger Service Revenue (411)		428,498
Gas and Oil Expense (511)	89,300	
Salaries Expense (512)	206,360	
Advertising Expense (513)	26,800	
	$606,709	$606,709

c. To provide regular maintenance for the vehicles, Elite deposited $12,000 with a local garage. An examination of maintenance invoices reveals charges of $10,944 against the deposit.

d. An inventory of spare parts shows $1,902 on hand.

e. Elite depreciates all of its limousines at the rate of 12.5 percent per year. No limousines were purchased during the year.

f. A payment of $10,500 for one full year's interest on notes payable is now due.

g. Unearned Passenger Service Revenue on June 30 includes $17,815 for tickets that employers purchased for use by their executives but which have not yet been redeemed.

Required

1. Determine the adjusting entries and enter them in the general journal (Page 14).

2. Open ledger accounts for the accounts in the trial balance plus the following: Interest Payable (213); Rent Expense (514); Insurance Expense (515); Spare Parts Expense (516); Depreciation Expense–Limousines (517); Maintenance Expense (518); and Interest Expense (519). Record the balances shown in the trial balance.

3. Post the adjusting entries from the general journal to the ledger accounts, showing proper references.

4. Prepare an adjusted trial balance, an income statement, a statement of owner's equity, and a balance sheet. The owner made no investments during the period.

5. **User Insight:** Do adjustments affect the profit margin? After the adjustments, is the profit margin for the year more or less than it would have been if the adjustments had not been made?

Alternate Problems

LO3 ### Determining Adjustments

P 6. At the end of the first three months of operation, the trial balance of Metropolitan Answering Service appears as shown below. Oscar Rienzo, the owner of Metropolitan, has hired an accountant to prepare financial statements to determine how well the company is doing after three months. Upon examining the accounting records, the accountant finds the following items of interest:

a. An inventory of office supplies reveals supplies on hand of $133.
b. The Prepaid Rent account includes the rent for the first three months plus a deposit for April's rent.
c. Depreciation on the equipment for the first three months is $208.
d. The balance of the Unearned Answering Service Revenue account represents a 12-month service contract paid in advance on February 1.
e. On March 31, accrued wages total $80.

Metropolitan Answering Service
Trial Balance
March 31, 20x8

Cash	$ 3,482	
Accounts Receivable	4,236	
Office Supplies	903	
Prepaid Rent	800	
Equipment	4,700	
Accounts Payable		$ 2,673
Unearned Answering Service Revenue		888
O. Rienzo, Capital		5,933
O. Rienzo, Withdrawals	2,130	
Answering Service Revenue		9,002
Wages Expense	1,900	
Office Cleaning Expense	345	
	$18,496	$18,496

Required

All adjustments affect one balance sheet account and one income statement account. For each of the above situations, show the accounts affected, the amount of the adjustment (using a + or – to indicate an increase or decrease), and the balance of the account after the adjustment in the following format:

Balance Sheet Account	Amount of Adjustment (+ or −)	Balance after Adjustment	Income Statement Account	Amount of Adjustment (+ or −)	Balance after Adjustment

LO2, LO3 ### Preparing Adjusting Entries

P 7. On November 30, the end of the current fiscal year, the following information is available to assist Pinder Company's accountants in making adjusting entries:

a. Pinder Company's Supplies account shows a beginning balance of $2,174. Purchases during the year were $4,526. The end-of-year inventory reveals supplies on hand of $1,397.

b. The Prepaid Insurance account shows the following on November 30:

Beginning balance	$3,580
July 1	4,200
October 1	7,272

The beginning balance represents the unexpired portion of a one-year policy purchased in September of the previous year. The July 1 entry represents a new one-year policy, and the October 1 entry represents additional coverage in the form of a three-year policy.

c. The following table contains the cost and annual depreciation for buildings and equipment, all of which Pinder Company purchased before the current year:

Account	Cost	Annual Depreciation
Buildings	$286,000	$14,500
Equipment	374,000	35,400

d. On September 1, the company completed negotiations with a client and accepted an advance of $16,800 for services to be performed in the next year. The $16,800 was credited to Unearned Services Revenue.

e. The company calculated that as of November 30, it had earned $4,000 on an $11,000 contract that would be completed and billed in January.

f. Among the liabilities of the company is a note payable in the amount of $300,000. On November 30, the accrued interest on this note amounted to $15,000.

g. On Saturday, December 2, the company, which is on a six-day workweek, will pay its regular salaried employees $12,300.

h. On November 29, the company completed negotiations and signed a contract to provide services to a new client at an annual rate of $17,500.

Required

1. Prepare adjusting entries for each item listed above.
2. **User Insight:** Explain how the conditions for revenue recognition are applied to transactions **e** and **h**.

LO3, LO4   **Determining Adjusting Entries, Posting to T Accounts, and Preparing an Adjusted Trial Balance**

P 8. The trial balance for Sigma Consultants Company on December 31, 20x8, appears on the next page. The following information is also available:

a. Ending inventory of office supplies, $86.
b. Prepaid rent expired, $700.
c. Depreciation of office equipment for the period, $600.
d. Interest accrued on the note payable, $600.
e. Salaries accrued at the end of the period, $200.
f. Service revenue still unearned at the end of the period, $1,410.
g. Service revenue earned but not billed, $600.

Required

1. Open T accounts for the accounts in the trial balance plus the following: Interest Payable; Salaries Payable; Office Supplies Expense; Depreciation Expense–Office Equipment; and Interest Expense. Enter the account balances.
2. Determine the adjusting entries and post them directly to the T accounts.
3. Prepare an adjusted trial balance.
4. **User Insight:** Which financial statements do each of the above adjustments affect? What financial statement is *not* affected by the adjustments?

Sigma Consultants Company
Trial Balance
December 31, 20x8

Cash	$ 12,786	
Accounts Receivable	24,840	
Office Supplies	991	
Prepaid Rent	1,400	
Office Equipment	6,700	
Accumulated Depreciation–Office Equipment		$ 1,600
Accounts Payable		1,820
Notes Payable		10,000
Unearned Service Revenue		2,860
L. Schwartz, Capital		29,387
L. Schwartz, Withdrawals	15,000	
Service Revenue		58,500
Salaries Expense	33,000	
Utilities Expense	1,750	
Rent Expense	7,700	
	$104,167	$104,167

ENHANCING Your Knowledge, Skills, and Critical Thinking

Conceptual Understanding Cases

LO1, LO2, LO3   **Importance of Adjustments**

C 1. Never Flake Company, which operated in the northeastern part of the United States, provided a rust-prevention coating for the underside of new automobiles. The company advertised widely and offered its services through new car dealers. When a dealer sold a new car, the salesperson attempted to sell the rust-prevention coating as an option. The protective coating was supposed to make cars last longer in the severe northeastern winters. A key selling point was Never Flake's warranty, which stated that it would repair any damage due to rust at no charge for as long as the buyer owned the car.

For several years, Never Flake had been very successful in generating enough cash to continue operations. But in 20x7, the company suddenly declared bankruptcy. Company officials said that the firm had only $5.5 million in assets against liabilities of $32.9 million. Most of the liabilities represented potential claims under the company's lifetime warranty. It seemed that owners were keeping their cars longer now than previously. Therefore, more damage was being attributed to rust. Discuss what accounting decisions could have helped Never Flake survive under these circumstances.

LO1   **Earnings Management and Fraudulent Financial Reporting**

C 2. In recent years, the Securities and Exchange Commission (SEC) has been waging a public campaign against corporate accounting practices that manage or manipulate earnings to meet the expectations of Wall Street analysts. Corporations engage in such practices in the hope of avoiding shortfalls that might cause serious declines in their stock price. For each of the following cases that the SEC challenged, tell why each is a violation of the matching rule and how it should be accounted for:

a. **Lucent Technologies** sold telecommunications equipment to companies from which there was no reasonable expectation of payment because of the companies' poor financial condition.

b. **America Online (AOL)** recorded advertising as an asset rather than as an expense.

c. **Eclipsys** recorded software contracts as revenue even though it had not yet rendered the services.

d. **KnowledgeWare** recorded revenue from sales of software even though it told customers they did not have to pay until they had the software.

Interpreting Financial Reports

LO2, LO3 **Application of Accrual Accounting**

C 3. The **Lyric Opera of Chicago** is one of the largest and best-managed opera companies in the United States. Managing opera productions requires advance planning, including the development of scenery, costumes, and stage properties and the sale of tickets. To measure how well the company is operating in any given year, management must apply accrual accounting to these and other transactions. At year end, April 30, 2004, Lyric Opera's balance sheet showed deferred production costs of $2,289,573 and deferred ticket revenue of $18,984,555.[7] Be prepared to discuss what accounting policies and adjusting entries are applicable to these accounts. Why are they important to Lyric Opera's management?

LO2, LO3 **Analysis of an Asset Account**

C 4. **The Walt Disney Company** is engaged in the financing, production, and distribution of motion pictures and television programming. In Disney's 2005 annual report, the balance sheet contains an asset called "film and television costs." Film and television costs, which consist of the costs associated with producing films and television programs less the amount expensed, were $5,427,000,000. The notes reveal that the amount of film and television costs expensed (amortized) during the year was $3,243,000,000. The amount spent for new film productions was $2,631,000,000.[8]

1. What are film and television costs, and why would they be classified as an asset?

2. Prepare an entry in T account form to record the amount the company spent on new film and television productions during the year (assume all expenditures are paid for in cash).

3. Prepare an adjusting entry in T account form to record the expense for film and television productions.

4. Suggest a method by which The Walt Disney Company might have determined the amount of the expense in **3** in accordance with the matching rule.

Decision Analysis Using Excel

LO1, LO3 **Adjusting Entries and Withdrawal Policy**

C 5. Maurice Turner, the owner of a newsletter for managers of hotels and restaurants, has compiled the data that follow from his company's financial statements for 20x7.

Revenues	$432,500
Expenses	352,500
Net income	$ 80,000
Total assets	$215,000
Liabilities	$ 60,000
Owner's equity	155,000
Total liabilities and owner's equity	$215,000

Given these figures, Turner is planning a cash withdrawal of $62,500. However, Turner's accountant has found that the following items were overlooked:

a. Although the balance of the Printing Supplies account is $40,000, only $17,500 in supplies is on hand at the end of the year.

b. Depreciation of $25,000 on equipment has not been recorded.

c. Wages of $11,750 have been earned by Turner's employees but not recognized in the accounts.

d. A liability account called Unearned Subscriptions has a balance of $20,250, although it has been determined that one-third of these subscriptions have been mailed to subscribers.

1. Prepare the necessary adjusting entries.

2. Recast the condensed financial statement figures after you have made the necessary adjustments.

3. Discuss the performance of Turner's business after the adjustments have been made. (**Hint:** Compare net income to revenues and total assets before and after the adjustments.) Do you think Turner should make the withdrawal? Why or why not?

LO3 Annual Report Case: CVS Corporation

Analysis of Balance Sheet and Adjusting Entries

C 6. In **CVS Corporation's** annual report in the Supplement to Chapter 5, refer to the balance sheet and the Summary of Significant Accounting Policies in the notes to the financial statements.

1. Examine the accounts in the current assets, property and equipment, and current liabilities sections of CVS's balance sheet. Which are most likely to have had year-end adjusting entries? Describe the nature of the adjusting entries. For more information about the property and equipment section, refer to the notes to the financial statements.

2. Where is depreciation (and amortization) expense disclosed in CVS's financial statements?

3. CVS has a statement on the "Use of Estimates" in its Summary of Significant Accounting Policies. Read this statement and tell how important estimates are to the determination of depreciation expense. What assumptions do accountants make that allow these estimates to be made?

Comparison Case: CVS Versus Southwest

Profit Margin

C 7. The profit margin is an important measure of profitability. Use data from **CVS's** income statement and the financial statements of **Southwest Airlines Co.** in the Supplement to Chapter 5 to calculate the profit margin for the past two years. By these measures, which company is more profitable?

Ethical Dilemma Case

LO1, LO2, LO3 **Importance of Adjustments**

C 8. Central Appliance Service Co. has achieved fast growth in the St. Louis area by selling service contracts on large appliances, such as washers, dryers, and refrigerators. For a fee, Central Appliance agrees to provide all parts and labor on an appliance after the regular warranty runs out. For example, by paying a fee of $200, a person who buys a dishwasher can add two years (years 2 and 3) to the regular one-year (year 1) warranty on the appliance. In 2007, the company sold service contracts in the amount of $1.8 million, all of which applied to future years. Management wanted all the sales recorded as revenues in 2007, contending that the amount of the contracts could be determined and the cash had been received. Discuss whether you agree with this logic. How would you record the cash receipts? What assumptions do you think Central Appliance should make? Would you consider it unethical to follow management's recommendation? Who might be hurt or helped by this action?

Internet Case

LO3 **Comparison of Accrued Expenses**

C 9. How important are accrued expenses? Randomly choose four different companies. Go to each company's website and find their annual reports. For each company, find the section of the balance sheet labeled "Current Liabilities" and identify the current liabilities that are accrued expenses (sometimes called accrued liabilities). More than one account may be involved. On a pad, write the information you find in four columns: name of company, total current liabilities, total accrued liabilities, and total accrued liabilities as a percentage of total current liabilities. Write a brief statement listing the companies you chose, telling how you obtained their reports, reporting the data you have gathered in the form of a table, and stating a conclusion, with reasons, as to the importance of accrued expenses to the companies you studied.

Group Activity Case

LO3 **Types of Adjusting Entries**

C 10. In this chapter, we discussed adjusting entries for deferred revenue, deferred expense, accrued revenue, and accrued expense. In informal groups in class, discuss how each type of adjusting entry applies to **Yahoo!.** Be prepared to present your group's findings to the class.

Business Communication Case

LO3 **Real-World Observation of Business Activities**

C 11. Visit a company with which you are familiar and observe its operations. (The company can be where you work, where you eat, or where you buy things.) Identify at least two sources of revenue for the company and six types of expenses. For each type of revenue and each type of expense, determine whether it is probable that an adjusting entry is required at the end of the accounting period. Then specify the adjusting entry as a deferred revenue, deferred expense, accrued revenue, or accrued expense. Design a table with columns and rows that summarize your results in an easy-to-understand format.

4

Completing the Accounting Cycle

All companies prepare financial statements annually, and whether required by law or not, preparing them every quarter, or even every month, is a good idea because these interim reports give management an ongoing view of a company's financial performance. The preparation of financial statements requires not only adjusting entries, which we described in the last chapter, but also closing entries, which we explain in this chapter.

LEARNING OBJECTIVES

Making a Statement

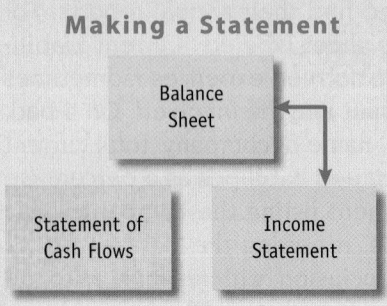

Closing entries set the accounts on the income statement to zero and transfer the resulting balance of net income or loss to the owner's capital account on the balance sheet.

LO1 Describe the accounting cycle and the role of closing entries in the preparation of financial statements.

LO2 Prepare closing entries.

LO3 Prepare reversing entries.

LO4 Prepare and use a work sheet.

- How does seasonality affect the company's revenues and operating income?

- Have the company's revenues and operating income continued to grow?

Best Buy™ is a leading retailer of consumer electronics, home-office products, entertainment software, appliances, and related services. As a company whose shares are publicly traded, Best Buy must file annual and quarterly financial statements with the Securities and Exchange Commission. Selected quarterly results for the company appear below.[1]

Financial statements prepared at quarterly intervals give management a more timely view of ongoing operations. They also enable external users to judge how a company performs at different times of the year. They reveal the natural patterns, or seasonality, of a company's business, which is useful in understanding fluctuations in earnings and cash flows.

Each time a company prepares financial statements, it must make adjusting and closing entries. Doing so takes time and effort, but the results benefit both management and external users of the company's financial statements by providing important information about revenues and operating income.

SELECTED QUARTERLY RESULTS FOR BEST BUY (In millions)

	2005				
Quarter	1st	2nd	3rd	4th	Year
Revenue	$5,479	$6,080	$6,647	$9,227	$27,433
Operating income	184	242	233	783	1,442
	2004				
Quarter	1st	2nd	3rd	4th	Year
Revenue	$4,669	$5,398	$6,032	$8,449	$24,548
Operating income	114	229	202	759	1,304

From Transactions to Financial Statements

LO1 Describe the accounting cycle and the role of closing entries in the preparation of financial statements.

To interpret and analyze a company's performance requires an understanding of how transactions are recognized and eventually end up in financial statements. Two concepts that foster this understanding are the accounting cycle and closing entries.

The Accounting Cycle

As Figure 1 shows, the **accounting cycle** is a series of steps whose ultimate purpose is to provide useful information to decision makers. These steps are as follows:

1. *Analyze* business transactions from source documents.

2. *Record* the transactions by entering them in the general journal.

3. *Post* the journal entries to the ledger, and prepare a trial balance.

4. *Adjust* the accounts, and prepare an adjusted trial balance.

5. *Prepare* financial statements.

6. *Close* the accounts, and prepare a post-closing trial balance.

You are already familiar with steps 1 through 5 from previous chapters. In the next section, we describe step 6, which may be performed before or after step 5.

Closing Entries

Balance sheet accounts, such as Cash and Accounts Payable, are considered **permanent accounts**, or *real accounts*, because they carry their end-of-period balances into the next accounting period. In contrast, revenue and expense accounts, such as Revenues Earned and Wages Expense, are considered **temporary accounts**, or *nominal accounts*, because they begin each accounting period with a zero balance, accumulate a balance during the period, and are then cleared by means of closing entries.

Closing entries are journal entries made at the end of an accounting period. They have two purposes:

1. They set the stage for the next accounting period by clearing revenue and expense accounts and the Withdrawals account of their balances.

2. They summarize a period's revenues and expenses by transferring the balances of revenue and expense accounts to the Income Summary account. The **Income Summary account** is a temporary account that summarizes all revenues and expenses for the period. It is used only in the closing process—never in the financial statements. Its balance equals the net income or loss reported on the income statement. The net income or loss is then transferred to the owner's Capital account.

Figure 2 shows an overview of the closing process. The net income or loss is transferred from the Income Summary account to the owner's Capital account because even though revenues and expenses are recorded in individual accounts, they represent increases and decreases in owner's Capital. Closing entries transfer the net effect of increases (revenues) and decreases

■ **FIGURE 1**
Overview of the Accounting Cycle

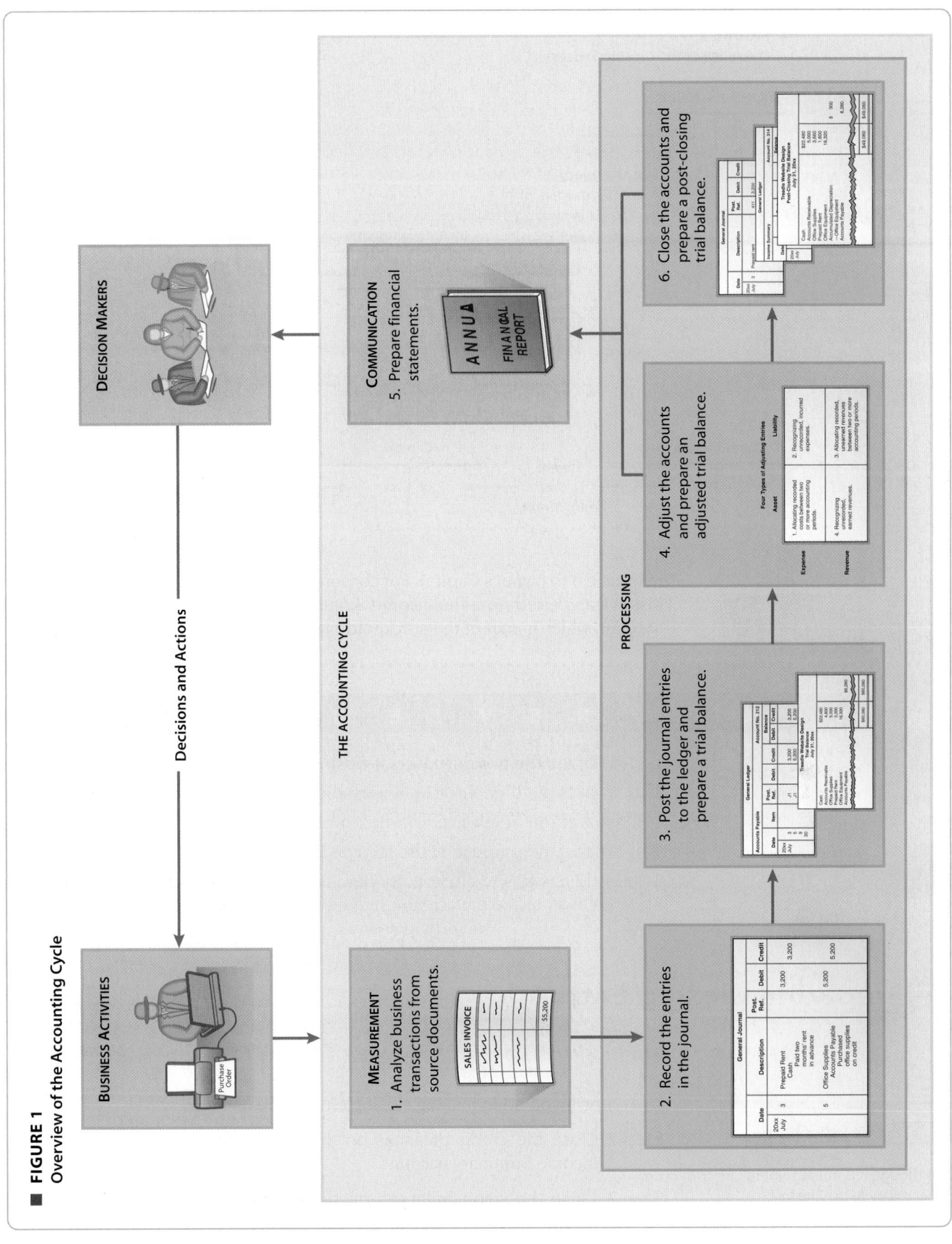

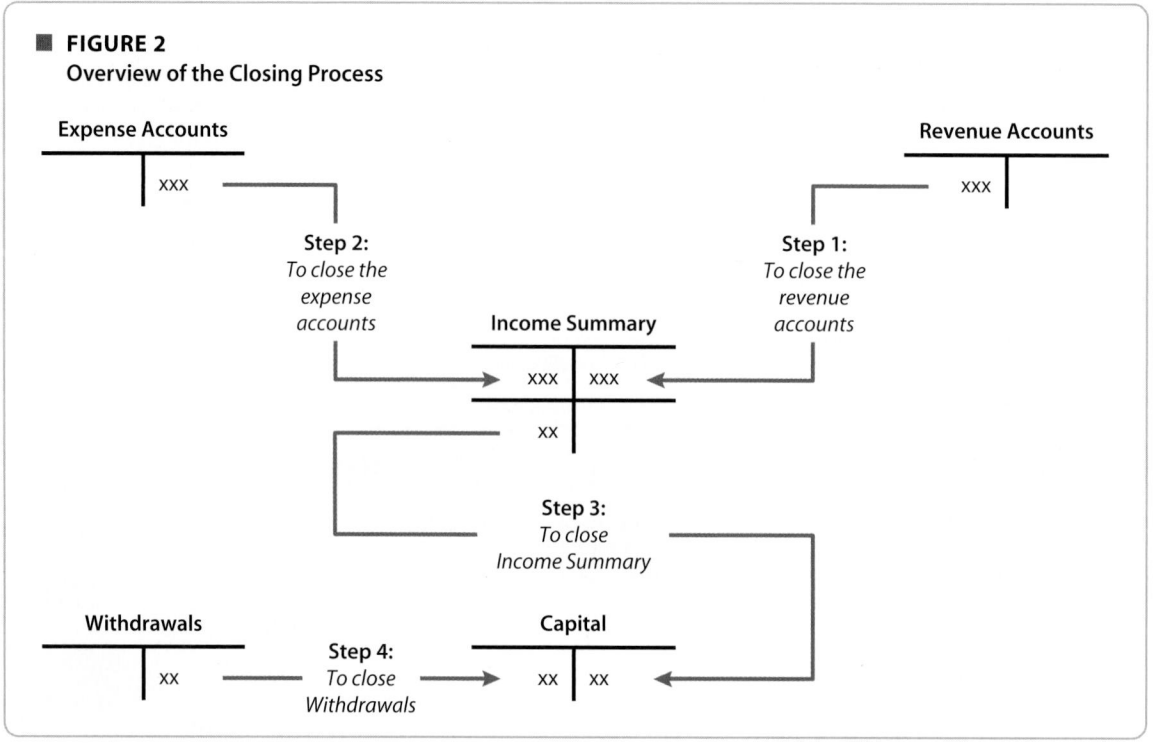

■ **FIGURE 2**
Overview of the Closing Process

 (expenses) to owner's Capital. For corporations like **Best Buy**, the net income or loss is transferred from the Income Summary account to the Retained Earnings account, which is part of the stockholders' (owner's) equity of a corporation.

S T O P • R E V I E W • A P P L Y

1-1. What are the two purposes of closing entries?

1-2. What is the difference between adjusting entries and closing entries?

1-3. What is the difference between permanent and temporary accounts?

1-4. What is the purpose of the Income Summary account?

Suggested answers to all Stop, Review, and Apply questions are available at http://college.hmco.com/accounting/needles/poa/10e/student_home.html.

Preparing Closing Entries

LO2 Prepare closing entries.

Study Note

Although it is not absolutely necessary to use the Income Summary account when preparing closing entries, doing so simplifies the procedure.

The steps involved in making closing entries are as follows:

Step 1. Close the credit balances on the income statement accounts to the Income Summary account.

Step 2. Close the debit balances on the income statement accounts to the Income Summary account.

Step 3. Close the Income Summary account balance to the owner's Capital account.

▼ **EXHIBIT 1**

Preparing Closing Entries from the Adjusted Trial Balance

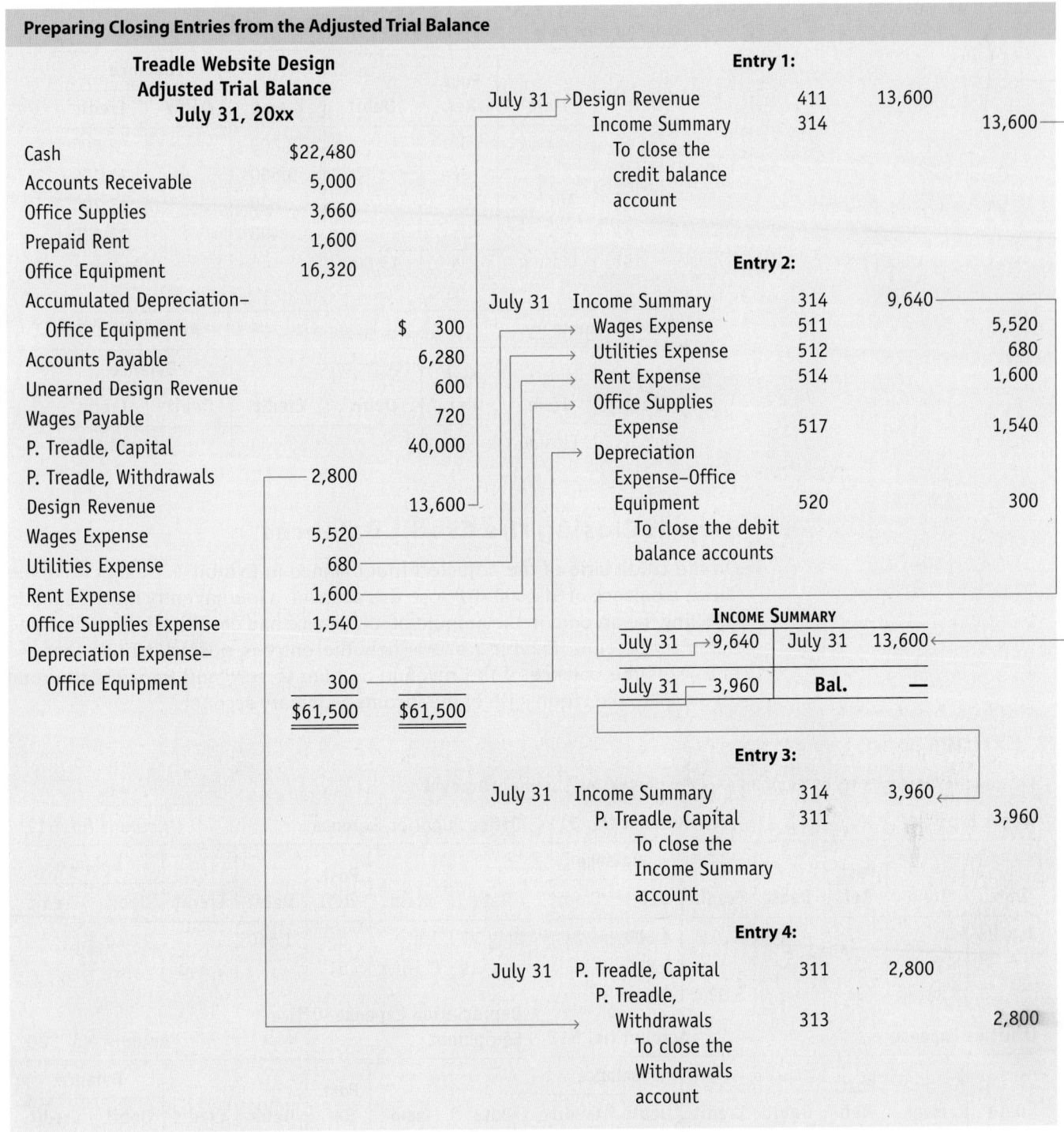

Treadle Website Design
Adjusted Trial Balance
July 31, 20xx

Cash	$22,480	
Accounts Receivable	5,000	
Office Supplies	3,660	
Prepaid Rent	1,600	
Office Equipment	16,320	
Accumulated Depreciation– Office Equipment		$ 300
Accounts Payable		6,280
Unearned Design Revenue		600
Wages Payable		720
P. Treadle, Capital		40,000
P. Treadle, Withdrawals	2,800	
Design Revenue		13,600
Wages Expense	5,520	
Utilities Expense	680	
Rent Expense	1,600	
Office Supplies Expense	1,540	
Depreciation Expense– Office Equipment	300	
	$61,500	$61,500

Entry 1:

July 31	Design Revenue	411	13,600	
	Income Summary	314		13,600
	To close the credit balance account			

Entry 2:

July 31	Income Summary	314	9,640	
	Wages Expense	511		5,520
	Utilities Expense	512		680
	Rent Expense	514		1,600
	Office Supplies Expense	517		1,540
	Depreciation Expense–Office Equipment	520		300
	To close the debit balance accounts			

INCOME SUMMARY

July 31	9,640		July 31	13,600
July 31	3,960		Bal.	—

Entry 3:

July 31	Income Summary	314	3,960	
	P. Treadle, Capital	311		3,960
	To close the Income Summary account			

Entry 4:

July 31	P. Treadle, Capital	311	2,800	
	P. Treadle, Withdrawals	313		2,800
	To close the Withdrawals account			

Step 4. Close the Withdrawals account balance to the owner's Capital account.

As you will learn in later chapters, not all revenue accounts have credit balances, and not all expense accounts have debit balances. For that reason, when referring to closing entries, we often use the term *credit balances* instead of *revenue accounts* and the term *debit balances* instead of *expense accounts*.

An adjusted trial balance provides all the data needed to record the closing entries. Exhibit I shows the relationships of the four kinds of closing entries to Treadle Website Design's adjusted trial balance.

EXHIBIT 2 ▶ **Posting the Closing Entry of a Credit Balance to the Income Summary Account**

Design Revenue   **Account No. 411**

Date	Item	Post. Ref.	Debit	Credit	Balance Debit	Balance Credit
July 10		J2		2,800		2,800
15		J2		9,600		12,400
31	Adj.	J3		800		13,200
31	Adj.	J3		400		13,600
31	Closing	J4	13,600			—

Income Summary   **Account No. 314**

Date	Item	Post. Ref.	Debit	Credit	Balance Debit	Balance Credit
July 31	Closing	J4		13,600		13,600

Step 1: Closing the Credit Balances

On the credit side of the adjusted trial balance in Exhibit 1, Design Revenue shows a balance of $13,600. To close this account, a journal entry must be made debiting the account in the amount of its balance and crediting it to the Income Summary account. Exhibit 2 shows how the entry is posted. Notice that the entry sets the balance of the revenue account to zero and transfers the total revenues to the credit side of the Income Summary account.

▼ EXHIBIT 3

Posting the Closing Entry of Debit Balances to the Income Summary Account

Wages Expense   **Account No. 511**

Date	Item	Post. Ref.	Debit	Credit	Balance Debit	Balance Credit
July 26		J2	4,800		4,800	
31	Adj.	J3	720		5,520	
31	Closing	J4		5,520	—	

Office Supplies Expense   **Account No. 517**

Date	Item	Post. Ref.	Debit	Credit	Balance Debit	Balance Credit
July 31	Adj.	J3	1,540		1,540	
31	Closing	J4		1,540	—	

Utilities Expense   **Account No. 512**

Date	Item	Post. Ref.	Debit	Credit	Balance Debit	Balance Credit
July 30		J2	680		680	
31	Closing	J4		680	—	

Depreciation Expense–Office Equipment   **Account No. 520**

Date	Item	Post. Ref.	Debit	Credit	Balance Debit	Balance Credit
July 31	Adj.	J3	300		300	
31	Closing	J4		300	—	

Rent Expense   **Account No. 514**

Date	Item	Post. Ref.	Debit	Credit	Balance Debit	Balance Credit
July 31	Adj.	J3	1,600		1,600	
31	Closing	J4		1,600	—	

Income Summary   **Account No. 314**

Date	Item	Post. Ref.	Debit	Credit	Balance Debit	Balance Credit
July 31	Closing	J4		13,600		13,600
31	Closing	J4	9,640			3,960

▼ EXHIBIT 4

Posting the Closing Entry of the Income Summary Account Balance to the Owner's Capital Account

Income Summary						Account No. 314	P. Treadle, Capital						Account No. 311
		Post.			**Balance**				Post.			**Balance**	
Date	Item	Ref.	Debit	Credit	Debit	Credit	Date	Item	Ref.	Debit	Credit	Debit	Credit
July 31	Closing	J4		13,600		13,600	July 1		J1		40,000		40,000
31	Closing	J4	9,640			3,960	31	Closing	J4		3,960		43,960
31	Closing	J4	3,960			—							

Step 2: Closing the Debit Balances

Several expense accounts show balances on the debit side of the adjusted trial balance in Exhibit 1. A compound entry is needed to credit each of these expense accounts for its balance and to debit the Income Summary account for the total. Exhibit 3 shows the effect of posting the closing entry. Notice how the entry reduces the expense account balances to zero and transfers the total of the account balances to the debit side of the Income Summary account.

Step 3: Closing the Income Summary Account Balance

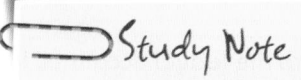Study Note

At this point, the credit balance of the Income Summary account ($3,960) represents net income—the key measure of performance. When a net loss occurs, you debit the owner's Capital account (to reduce it) and credit the Income Summary account (to close it).

Study Note

Note that the Withdrawals account is closed to the owner's Capital account, not to the Income Summary account.

After the entries closing the revenue and expense accounts have been posted, the balance of the Income Summary account equals the net income or loss for the period. A credit balance in the Income Summary account represents a net income (i.e., revenues exceed expenses), and a debit balance represents a net loss (i.e., expenses exceed revenues).

At this point, the balance of the Income Summary account, whatever its nature, is closed to the owner's Capital account, as shown in Exhibit 1. Exhibit 4 shows how the closing entry is posted when a company has a net income. Notice the dual effect of closing the Income Summary account and transferring the balance to owner's Capital.

Step 4: Closing the Withdrawals Account Balance

The Withdrawals account shows the amount by which owner's Capital decreased during an accounting period. The debit balance of the Withdrawals account is closed to the owner's Capital account, as illustrated in Exhibit 1. Exhibit 5 shows the posting of the closing entry and the transfer of the balance of the Withdrawals account to the owner's Capital account. In a corporation like

▼ EXHIBIT 5

Posting the Closing Entry of the Withdrawals Account Balance to the Owner's Capital Account

P. Treadle, Withdrawals						Account No. 313	P. Treadle, Capital						Account No. 311
		Post.			**Balance**				Post.			**Balance**	
Date	Item	Ref.	Debit	Credit	Debit	Credit	Date	Item	Ref.	Debit	Credit	Debit	Credit
July 31		J2	2,800		2,800		July 1		J1		40,000		40,000
31	Closing	J4		2,800	—		31	Closing	J4		3,960		43,960
							31	Closing	J4	2,800			41,160

EXHIBIT 6 ▶

Post-Closing Trial Balance

Treadle Website Design
Post-Closing Trial Balance
July 31, 20xx

Cash	$22,480	
Accounts Receivable	5,000	
Office Supplies	3,660	
Prepaid Rent	1,600	
Office Equipment	16,320	
Accumulated Depreciation–Office Equipment		$ 300
Accounts Payable		6,280
Unearned Design Revenue		600
Wages Payable		720
P. Treadle, Capital		41,160
	$49,060	$49,060

Best Buy, payments to owners are called *dividends*, and they are closed to the Retained Earnings account.

The Accounts After Posting

After all the steps in the closing process have been completed and all closing entries have been posted, everything is ready for the next accounting period. The revenue, expense, and Withdrawals accounts (temporary accounts) have zero balances. The owner's Capital account has been increased or decreased to reflect net income or net loss (net income in our example) and has been decreased for withdrawals. The balance sheet accounts (permanent accounts) show the correct balances, which are carried into the next period.

The Post-Closing Trial Balance

Because errors can be made in posting closing entries to the ledger accounts, it is necessary to prepare a **post-closing trial balance**. As you can see in Exhibit 6, a post-closing trial balance contains only balance sheet accounts because the income statement accounts and the Withdrawals account have been closed and now have zero balances. It is a final check that total debits equal total credits.

S T O P • R E V I E W • A P P L Y

2-1. What does the balance of the Income Summary account represent before it is closed to the owner's Capital account?

2-2. What is the one account on the balance sheet that closing entries affect?

2-3. Which of the following accounts do not show a balance after the closing entries are prepared and posted?

a. Insurance Expense
b. Accounts Receivable
c. Commission Revenue
d. Prepaid Insurance

e. Withdrawals
f. Supplies
g. Supplies Expense
h. Owner's Capital

2-4. Which financial statement is closely related to the post-closing trial balance, and why is it useful to prepare a post-closing trial balance?

Preparation of Closing Entries   Prepare the necessary clossing entries from the following partial adjusted trial balance for Pines Recreational Park, and compute the ending balance of the owner's Capital account. (Except for E. Howes, Capital, balance sheet accounts have been omitted.)

Pines Recreational Park
Partial Adjusted Trial Balance
June 30, 20x7

E. Howes, Capital		$93,070
E. Howes, Withdrawals	$36,000	
Campsite Rentals		88,200
Wages Expense	23,850	
Insurance Expense	3,784	
Utilities Expense	1,800	
Supplies Expense	1,320	
Depreciation Expense–Building	6,000	

SOLUTION
Closing entries prepared:

June 30	Campsite Rentals	88,200	
	Income Summary		88,200
	To close the credit balance account		
30	Income Summary	36,754	
	Wages Expense		23,850
	Insurance Expense		3,784
	Utilities Expense		1,800
	Supplies Expense		1,320
	Depreciation Expense–Building		6,000
	To close the debit balance accounts		
30	Income Summary	51,446	
	E. Howes, Capital		51,446
	To close the Income Summary account		
	$88,200 − $36,754 = $51,446		
30	E. Howes, Capital	36,000	
	E. Howes, Withdrawals		36,000
	To close the Withdrawals account		

Ending balance of the E. Howes, Capital account computed:

E. HOWES, CAPITAL

June 30	36,000	Beg. Bal.	93,070
		June 30	51,446
		End. Bal.	108,516

Reversing Entries: An Optional First Step

Study Note

Reversing entries are the opposite of adjusting entries and are dated the first day of the new period. They apply only to certain adjusting entries and are never required.

A reversing entry is an optional journal entry made on the first day of an accounting period. It has the opposite effect of an adjusting entry made at the end of the previous period—that is, it debits the credits and credits the debits of an earlier adjusting entry. The sole purpose of reversing entries is to simplify routine bookkeeping procedures, and they apply only to certain adjusting entries. Deferrals should not be reversed because doing so would not simplify bookkeeping in future accounting periods. As used in this text, reversing entries apply only to accruals (accrued revenues and expenses).

To see how reversing entries can be helpful, consider this adjusting entry made in the records of Treadle Website Design to accrue wages expense:

July 31	Wages Expense	720	
	Wages Payable		720
	Accrued unrecorded wages		

When the company pays its assistant on the next regular payday, its accountant would make this entry:

Aug. 23	Wages Payable	720	
	Wages Expense	4,080	
	Cash		4,800
	Paid four weeks wages to assistant, $720 of which accrued in the previous period		

If no reversing entry is made at the time of payment, the accountant would have to look in the records to find out how much of the $4,800 applies to the current accounting period and how much applies to the previous period. That may seem easy in our example, but think how difficult and time-consuming it would be if a company had hundreds of employees working on different schedules. A reversing entry helps solve the problem of applying revenues and expenses to the correct accounting period.

For example, consider the following sequence of entries and their effects on the Wages Expense account:

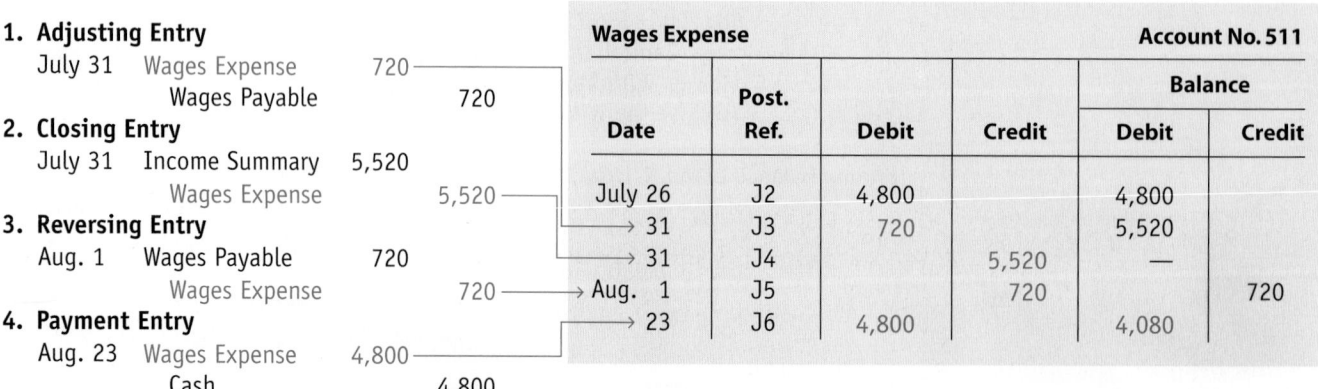

1. **Adjusting Entry**
   July 31   Wages Expense   720
             Wages Payable   720
2. **Closing Entry**
   July 31   Income Summary   5,520
             Wages Expense   5,520
3. **Reversing Entry**
   Aug. 1   Wages Payable   720
            Wages Expense   720
4. **Payment Entry**
   Aug. 23   Wages Expense   4,800
             Cash   4,800

| **Wages Expense** | | | | **Account No. 511** | |
Date	Post. Ref.	Debit	Credit	**Balance** Debit	Credit
July 26	J2	4,800		4,800	
31	J3	720		5,520	
31	J4		5,520	—	
Aug. 1	J5		720		720
23	J6	4,800		4,080	

If this employee at a Swedish advertising agency works any days at the end of the month for which she will be not be paid until the next month, a reversing entry for the Wages Expense account will ensure that revenues and expenses are applied to the correct accounting period.

Entry **1** adjusted Wages Expense to accrue $720 in the July accounting period.

Entry **2** closed the $5,520 in Wages Expense for July to Income Summary, leaving a zero balance.

Entry **3**, the reversing entry, set up a credit balance of $720 on August 1 in Wages Expense, which is the expense recognized through the adjusting entry in July (and also reduced the liability account Wages Payable to a zero balance). The reversing entry always sets up an abnormal balance in the income statement account and produces a zero balance in the balance sheet account.

Entry **4** recorded the $4,800 payment of wages as a debit to Wages Expense, automatically leaving a balance of $4,080, which represents the correct wages expense to date in August. The reversing entry simplified the process of making the payment entry on August 23.

Reversing entries apply to any accrued expenses or revenues. Treadle Website Design's only accrued expense was wages expense. An adjusting entry for the company's accrued revenue (Design Revenue) would require the following reversing entry:

Aug. 1	Design Revenue	400	
	Accounts Receivable		400
	Reversed the adjusting entry		
	for accrued revenue earned		

S T O P   •   R E V I E W   •   A P P L Y

3-1. What are reversing entries, and why are they useful?

3-2. Do reversing entries apply to both accruals and deferrals?

3-3. Which of the following would most likely require a reversing entry: supplies expense or wages expense?

The Work Sheet: An Accountant's Tool

LO4   Prepare and use a work sheet.

To organize data and avoid omitting important information that might affect the financial statements, accountants use **working papers**. Because working papers provide evidence of past work, they enable accountants to retrace their steps when they need to verify information in the financial statements.

A **work sheet** is a special kind of working paper. The work sheet is extremely useful when a company prepares financial statements on both an annual and seasonal basis, as **Best Buy** does, and when an accountant must make numerous adjustments. It is often used as a preliminary step in preparing financial statements. Using a work sheet lessens the possibility of omitting an adjustment and helps the accountant check the arithmetical accuracy of the accounts. The work sheet is never published and is rarely seen by management. It is a tool for the accountant. Because preparing a work sheet is a mechanical process, many accountants use a computer for this purpose.

Preparing the Work Sheet

A work sheet often has one column for account names and multiple columns with headings like the ones shown in Exhibit 7. A heading that includes the name of the company and the period of time covered (as on the income statement) identifies the work sheet. As Exhibit 7 shows, preparation of a work sheet involves five steps.

Best Buy's business is very seasonal. About one-third of its annual sales and over half of its annual operating income come in the fourth quarter, which includes the holiday season. Companies that prepare financial statements both annually and seasonally, as Best Buy does, find the work sheet very useful.

▼ **EXHIBIT 7**

The Work Sheet

Treadle Website Design
Work Sheet
For the Month Ended July 31, 20xx

Account Name	Trial Balance Debit	Trial Balance Credit	Adjustments Debit	Adjustments Credit	Adjusted Trial Balance Debit	Adjusted Trial Balance Credit	Income Statement Debit	Income Statement Credit	Balance Sheet Debit	Balance Sheet Credit
Cash	22,480				22,480				22,480	
Accounts Receivable	4,600		(f) 400		5,000				5,000	
Office Supplies	5,200			(b) 1,540	3,660				3,660	
Prepaid Rent	3,200			(a) 1,600	1,600				1,600	
Office Equipment	16,320				16,320				16,320	
Accumulated Depreciation–Office Equipment				(c) 300		300				300
Accounts Payable		6,280				6,280				6,280
Unearned Design Revenue		1,400	(e) 800			600				600
P. Treadle, Capital		40,000				40,000				40,000
P. Treadle, Withdrawals	2,800				2,800				2,800	
Design Revenue		12,400		(e) 800 (f) 400		13,600		13,600		
Wages Expense	4,800		(d) 720		5,520		5,520			
Utilities Expense	680				680		680			
	60,080	60,080								
Rent Expense			(a) 1,600		1,600		1,600			
Office Supplies Expense			(b) 1,540		1,540		1,540			
Depreciation Expense–Office Equipment			(c) 300		300		300			
Wages Payable				(d) 720		720				720
			5,360	5,360	61,500	61,500	9,640	13,600	51,860	47,900
Net Income							3,960			3,960
							13,600	13,600	51,860	51,860

Note: The columns of the work sheet are prepared in the following order: (1) Trial Balance, (2) Adjustments, (3) Adjusted Trial Balance, and (4) Income Statement and Balance Sheet columns. In the fifth step, the Income Statement and Balance Sheet columns are totaled.

⊂▭⊃ Study Note

The Trial Balance columns of a work sheet take the place of a trial balance.

Step 1. Enter and total the account balances in the Trial Balance columns. The debit and credit balances of the accounts on the last day of an accounting period are copied directly from the ledger into the Trial Balance columns (the green columns in Exhibit 7). When accountants use a work sheet, they do not have to prepare a separate trial balance.

Step 2. Enter and total the adjustments in the Adjustments columns.

The required adjustments are entered in the Adjustments columns of the work sheet (the purple columns in Exhibit 7). As each adjustment is entered, a letter is used to identify its debit and credit parts. For example, in Exhibit 7, the letter **a** identifies the adjustment made for the rent that Treadle Website Design prepaid on July 3, which results in a debit to Rent Expense and a credit to Prepaid Rent. These identifying letters may be used to reference supporting computations or documentation for the related adjusting entries and can simplify the recording of adjusting entries in the general journal.

A trial balance includes only accounts that have balances. If an adjustment involves an account that does not appear in the trial balance, the new account is added below the accounts listed on the work sheet. For example, Rent Expense has been added to Exhibit 7. Accumulated depreciation accounts, which have a zero balance only in the initial period of operation, are the sole exception to this rule. They are listed immediately after their associated asset accounts. For example, in Exhibit 7, the Accumulated Depreciation–Office Equipment account is listed immediately after Office Equipment.

When all the adjustments have been made, the two Adjustments columns must be totaled. This procedure proves that the debits and credits of the adjustments are equal, and it generally reduces errors in the work sheet.

Step 3. Enter and total the adjusted account balances in the Adjusted Trial Balance columns.

The adjusted trial balance in the work sheet is prepared by combining the amount of each account in the Trial Balance columns with the corresponding amount in the Adjustments columns and entering each result in the Adjusted Trial Balance columns (the yellow columns in Exhibit 7).

Exhibit 7 contains examples of **crossfooting**, or adding and subtracting a group of numbers horizontally. The first line shows Cash with a debit balance of $22,480. Because there are no adjustments to the Cash account, $22,480 is entered in the debit column of the Adjusted Trial Balance columns. On the second line, Accounts Receivable shows a debit of $4,600 in the Trial Balance columns. Because there is a debit of $400 from adjustment **f** in the Adjustments columns, it is added to the $4,600 and carried over to the debit column of the Adjusted Trial Balance columns at $5,000. On the next line, Office Supplies shows a debit of $5,200 in the Trial Balance columns and a credit of $1,540 from adjustment **b** in the Adjustments columns. Subtracting $1,540 from $5,200 results in a $3,660 debit balance in the Adjusted Trial Balance columns. This process is followed for all the accounts, including those added below the trial balance totals. The Adjusted Trial Balance columns are then *footed* (totaled) to check the accuracy of the crossfooting.

Step 4. Extend the account balances from the Adjusted Trial Balance columns to the Income Statement or Balance Sheet columns.

Every account in the adjusted trial balance is an income statement account or a balance sheet account. Each account is extended to its proper place as a debit or credit in either the Income Statement columns or the Balance Sheet columns (the blue columns in Exhibit 7). As shown in Exhibit 7, revenue and expense accounts are extended to the Income Statement columns, and asset, liability, Capital, and Withdrawals accounts are extended to the Balance Sheet columns.

To avoid overlooking an account, the accounts are extended line by line, beginning with the first line (Cash) and not omitting any subsequent lines. For instance, the Cash debit balance of $22,480 is extended to the debit column of the Balance Sheet columns; then, the Accounts Receivable debit balance of $5,000 is extended to the debit column of the Balance Sheet columns; and so forth.

Step 5. Total the Income Statement columns and the Balance Sheet columns. Enter the net income or net loss in both pairs of columns as a balancing figure, and recompute the column totals.

This fifth and last step, shown in the brown columns of Exhibit 7, is necessary to compute net income or net loss and to prove the arithmetical accuracy of the work sheet.

Net income (or net loss) is equal to the difference between the total debits and credits of the Income Statement columns. It is also equal to the difference between the total debits and credits of the Balance Sheet columns.

Revenues (Income Statement credit column total)	$13,600
Expenses (Income Statement debit column total)	(9,640)
Net Income	$ 3,960

In this case, revenues (credit column) exceed expenses (debit column). Thus, Treadle Website Design has a net income of $3,960. The same difference occurs between the total debits and credits of the Balance Sheet columns.

The $3,960 is entered in the debit side of the Income Statement columns and in the credit side of the Balance Sheet columns to balance the columns. Remember that the excess of revenues over expenses (net income) increases owner's equity, and that increases in owner's equity are recorded by credits.

When a net loss occurs, the opposite rule applies. The excess of expenses over revenues—net loss—is placed in the credit side of the Income Statement columns as a balancing figure. It is then placed in the debit side of the Balance Sheet columns because a net loss decreases owner's equity, and decreases in owner's equity are recorded by debits.

As a final check, the four columns are totaled again. If the Income Statement columns and the Balance Sheet columns do not balance, an account may have been extended or sorted to the wrong column, or an error may have been made in adding the columns. Of course, equal totals in the two pairs of columns are not absolute proof of accuracy. If an asset has been carried to the Income Statement debit column (or an expense has been carried to the Balance Sheet debit column) or a similar error with revenues or liabilities has been made, the work sheet will balance, but the net income figure will be wrong.

EXHIBIT 8 ▶

Adjustments from the Work Sheet Entered in the General Journal

		General Journal			Page 3
Date		Description	Post. Ref.	Debit	Credit
20xx					
(a) July 31		Rent Expense	514	1,600	
		Prepaid Rent	117		1,600
		To recognize expiration of one month's rent			
(b)	31	Office Supplies Expense	517	1,540	
		Office Supplies	116		1,540
		To recognize office supplies used during the month			
(c)	31	Depreciation Expense–Office Equipment	520	300	
		Accumulated Depreciation–Office Equipment	147		300
		To record depreciation of office equipment for a month			
(d)	31	Wages Expense	511	720	
		Wages Payable	214		720
		To accrue unrecorded wages			
(e)	31	Unearned Design Revenue	213	800	
		Design Revenue	411		800
		To recognize performance of services for which payment was received in advance			
(f)	31	Accounts Receivable	113	400	
		Design Revenue	411		400
		To accrue website design fees earned but unrecorded			

Using the Work Sheet

Accountants use the completed work sheet in performing three principal tasks. These tasks are as follows:

1. **Recording the adjusting entries in the general journal.** Because the information needed to record the adjusting entries can be copied from the work sheet, entering the adjustments in the journal is an easy step, as shown in Exhibit 8. The adjusting entries are then posted to the general ledger.

2. **Recording the closing entries in the general journal.** The Income Statement columns of the work sheet show all the accounts that need to be closed, except for the Withdrawals account. Exhibits 1 through 5 show how the closing entries are entered in the journal and posted to the ledger.

3. **Preparing the financial statements.** Once the work sheet has been completed, preparing the financial statements is simple because the account balances have been sorted into the Income Statement and Balance Sheet columns.

> ⌐◯ **Study Note**
>
> Theoretically, adjusting entries can be recorded in the accounting records before the financial statements are prepared or even before the work sheet is completed. However, they always precede the preparation of closing entries.

S T O P • R E V I E W • A P P L Y

4-1. Why are work sheets, which are never published and rarely seen by management, important to accountants?

4-2. Why should the Adjusted Trial Balance columns of a work sheet be totaled before the adjusted amounts are carried to the Income Statement and Balance Sheet columns?

4-3. What sequence should be followed in extending the amounts in the Adjusted Trial Balance columns to the Income Statement and Balance Sheet columns? What is the reason for this sequence?

4-4. Do the Income Statement and Balance Sheet columns of a work sheet balance after the amounts from the Adjusted Trial Balance columns are extended? Why or why not?

4-5. Do the totals of the Balance Sheet columns of the work sheet agree with the totals on the balance sheet? Explain your answer.

A LOOK BACK AT

BEST BUY ENTERPRISE SERVICES, INC.

Best Buy's preparation of quarterly financial statements requires more effort than the preparation of a single set of financial statements for the entire year. To prepare financial statements, a company must make adjusting entries and prepare the ledger accounts for the next accounting period, and, as we indicated in this chapter's Decision Point, these procedures are time-consuming and costly. However, the advantages of interim financial statements usually outweigh the costs. Interim reports give management timely information for making decisions that will improve operations, and they provide external users with answers to the following questions:

- **How does seasonality affect the company's revenues and operating income?**

- **Have the company's revenues and operating income continued to grow?**

For instance, an examination of Best Buy's quarterly data for 2004 and 2005 shows that the company's business is very seasonal. About one-third of its annual sales and over half its annual operating income come in the fourth quarter, which includes the holiday season. The first quarter is lowest in terms of sales and operating income.

We can also assess Best Buy's performance by computing the percentage change in its revenue and operating income from 2004 to 2005. To do this, we divide the differences in the two years by the 2004 amounts. The results are as follows:

Quarter	First	Second	Third	Fourth	Year
Revenue	17.3%	12.6%	10.2%	9.2%	11.8%
Operating income	61.4	5.7	15.3	3.2	10.6

These quarterly figures give both management and investors a better understanding of Best Buy's performance. Compared with the annual increases in revenue and operating income—11.8 percent and 10.6 percent, respectively—quarterly results show much more variation. For example, Best Buy substantially improved its performance in the first quarter, in which a 17.3 percent increase in revenue resulted in a 61.4 percent increase in operating income.

CHAPTER REVIEW

REVIEW of Learning Objectives

LO1 Describe the accounting cycle and the role of closing entries in the preparation of financial statements.

The steps in the accounting cycle are as follows: (1) analyze business transactions from source documents; (2) record the transactions by entering them in the general journal, (3) post the entries to the ledger, and prepare a trial balance; (4) adjust the accounts, and prepare an adjusted trial balance; (5) prepare financial statements; and (6) close the accounts, and prepare a post-closing trial balance. (Step 6 may occur before or after step 5.)

Closing entries have two purposes: (1) they clear the balances of all temporary accounts (revenue, expense, and Withdrawals accounts) so that they have zero balances at the beginning of the next accounting period, and (2) they summarize a period's revenues and expenses in the Income Summary account so that the net income or loss for the period can be transferred as a total to owner's Capital.

LO2 Prepare closing entries.

The first two steps in preparing closing entries are to transfer the balances of the revenue and expense accounts to the Income Summary account. The balance of the Income Summary account is then transferred to the owner's Capital account. Finally, the balance of the Withdrawals account is transferred to owner's Capital. After the closing entries have been posted to the ledger accounts, a post-closing trial balance is prepared as a final check on the balance of the ledger and to ensure that all temporary (nominal) accounts have been closed.

LO3 Prepare reversing entries.

Reversing entries are optional journal entries made on the first day of an accounting period. Reversing entries have the opposite effect of adjusting entries made at the end of the previous period—that is, a reversing entry debits the credits and credits the debits of an earlier adjusting entry. The sole purpose of reversing entries is to simplify routine bookkeeping procedures, and they apply only to certain adjusting entries. As used in this text, reversing entries apply only to accruals.

LO4 Prepare and use a work sheet.

The five steps in preparing a work sheet are (1) enter and total the account balances in the Trial Balance columns; (2) enter and total the adjustments in the Adjustments columns; (3) enter and total the adjusted account balances in the Adjusted Trial Balance columns; (4) extend the account balances from the Adjusted Trial Balance columns to the Income Statement or Balance Sheet columns; and (5) total the Income Statement and Balance Sheet columns, enter the net income or net loss in both pairs of columns as a balancing figure, and recompute the column totals.

A work sheet is useful in recording both adjusting and closing entries and in preparing the financial statements. The income statement and balance sheet can be prepared directly from the Income Statement and Balance Sheet columns of the completed work sheet. The statement of owner's equity is prepared using owner's Withdrawals, net income, additional investments, and the beginning balance of the owner's Capital account.

REVIEW of Concepts and Terminology

The following concepts and terms were introduced in this chapter:

Accounting cycle: The series of steps followed in measuring business transactions and transforming them into financial statements. **(LO1)**

Closing entries: Entries made at the end of an accounting period that set the stage for the next period by clearing temporary accounts of their balances and transferring them to the owner's Capital account; they summarize a period's revenues and expenses. **(LO1)**

Crossfooting: Adding and subtracting numbers across a row. **(LO4)**

Income Summary account: A temporary account used in the closing process that holds a summary of all revenues and expenses before the net income or loss is transferred to the owner's Capital account. **(LO1)**

Permanent accounts: Balance sheet accounts that carry their balances into the next accounting period. Also called *real accounts.* **(LO1)**

Post-closing trial balance: A trial balance prepared after all adjusting and closing entries have been posted to ensure that all temporary accounts have zero balances and that total debits equal total credits. **(LO2)**

Reversing entry: An optional journal entry made on the first day of an accounting period that is the exact opposite of an adjusting entry made at the end of the previous period. **(LO3)**

Temporary accounts: Revenue and expense accounts whose balances are transferred to owner's Capital at the end of an accounting period. Also called *nominal accounts.* **(LO1)**

Working papers: Documents that accountants use to organize their work and that support the information in the financial statements. **(LO4)**

Work sheet: A type of working paper used as a preliminary step in recording adjusting and closing entries and that is used in preparing the financial statements. **(LO4)**

REVIEW Problem

LO2 Preparation of Closing Entries

Prepare the necessary closing entries from the following partial adjusted trial balance for Westwood Movers. (Except for the owner's Capital account, all balance sheet accounts have been omitted.) In addition, compute the ending balance of the owner's Capital account.

	A	B	C	D	E
1			Westwood Movers		
2			Partial Adjusted Trial Balance		
3			June 30, 20xx		
4					
5		J. Thomas, Capital			$ 24,740
6		J. Thomas, Withdrawals		$ 18,000	
7		Moving Services Revenue			185,400
8		Driver Wages Expense		88,900	
9		Fuel Expense		19,000	
10		Wages Expense		14,400	
11		Packing Supplies Expense		6,200	
12		Office Equipment Rental Expense		3,000	
13		Utilities Expense		4,450	
14		Insurance Expense		4,200	
15		Interest Expense		5,100	
16		Depreciation Expense		10,040	
17					

Answer to Review Problem

Closing entries prepared:

	A	B	C	D	E	F	G	H	I	J	K	L
1	June	30				Moving Services Revenue					185,400	
2						Income Summary						185,400
3						To close the credit balance account						
4		30			Income Summary						155,290	
5						Driver Wages Expense						88,900
6						Fuel Expense						19,000
7						Wages Expense						14,400
8						Packing Supplies Expense						6,200
9						Office Equipment Rental Expense						3,000
10						Utilities Expense						4,450
11						Insurance Expense						4,200
12						Interest Expense						5,100
13						Depreciation Expense						10,040
14						To close the debit balance accounts						
15		30			Income Summary						30,110	
16						J. Thomas, Capital						30,110
17						To close the Income Summary account						
18						$185,400 – $155,290 = $30,110						
19		30		J. Thomas, Capital							18,000	
20						J. Thomas, Withdrawals						18,000
21						To close the Withdrawals account						
22												

Ending balance of the J. Thomas, Capital account computed:

	A	B	C	D	E	F
1			**J. Thomas, Capital**			
2	June	30	18,000	Beg. Bal.		24,740
3				June	30	30,110
4				End. Bal.		36,850
5						

CHAPTER ASSIGNMENTS

BUILDING Your Basic Knowledge and Skills

Short Exercises

LO1   **Accounting Cycle**

SE 1. Resequence the following activities to indicate the usual order of the accounting cycle:

a. Close the accounts.
b. Analyze the transactions.
c. Post the entries to the ledger.
d. Prepare the financial statements.

e. Adjust the accounts.
f. Record the transactions in the journal.
g. Prepare the post-closing trial balance.
h. Prepare the initial trial balance.
i. Prepare the adjusted trial balance.

LO2 **Closing Revenue Accounts**

SE 2. Assume that at the end of the accounting period there are credit balances of $3,400 in Patient Services Revenues and $1,800 in Laboratory Fees Revenues. Prepare the required closing entry in journal form. The accounting period ends December 31.

LO2 **Closing Expense Accounts**

SE 3. Assume that debit balances at the end of the accounting period are $1,400 in Rent Expense, $1,100 in Wages Expense, and $500 in Other Expenses. Prepare the required closing entry in journal form. The accounting period ends December 31.

LO2 **Closing the Income Summary Account**

SE 4. Assuming that total revenues were $5,200 and total expenses were $3,000, prepare the entry in journal form to close the Income Summary account to the H. Blake, Capital account. The accounting period ends December 31.

LO2 **Closing the Withdrawals Account**

SE 5. Assuming that withdrawals during the accounting period were $800, prepare the entry in journal form to close the H. Blake, Withdrawals account to the H. Blake, Capital account. The accounting period ends December 31.

LO2 **Posting Closing Entries**

SE 6. Show the effects of the transactions in **SE 2, SE 3, SE 4,** and **SE 5** by entering beginning balances in appropriate T accounts and recording the transactions. Assume that the H. Blake, Capital account had a beginning balance of $1,300.

LO3 **Preparation of Reversing Entries**

SE 7. Below, indicated by letters, are the adjusting entries at the end of March.

Account Name	Debit	Credit
Prepaid Insurance		(a) 180
Accumulated Depreciation–Office Equipment		(b) 1,050
Salaries Expense	(c) 360	
Insurance Expense	(a) 180	
Depreciation Expense–Office Equipment	(b) 1,050	
Salaries Payable		(c) 360
	1,590	1,590

Prepare the required reversing entry in journal form.

Effects of Reversing Entries

LO3 **SE 8.** Assume that prior to the adjustments in **SE 7**, Salaries Expense had a debit balance of $1,800 and Salaries Payable had a zero balance. Prepare a T account for each of these accounts. Enter the beginning balance; post the adjustment for accrued salaries, the appropriate closing entry, and the reversing entry; and enter the transaction in the T accounts for a payment of $480 for salaries on April 3.

LO2, LO4 **Preparation of Closing Entries from a Work Sheet**

SE 9. Prepare the required closing entries in journal form for the year ended December 31, using the following items from the Income Statement columns of a work sheet and assuming that withdrawals by the owner, M. Dye, were $6,000:

Account Name	Debit	Credit
Repair Revenue		32,860
Wages Expense	12,260	
Rent Expense	1,800	
Supplies Expense	6,390	
Insurance Expense	1,370	
Depreciation Expense–Repair Equipment	2,020	
	23,840	32,860
Net Income	9,020	
	32,860	32,860

Exercises

LO1, LO2 **Discussion Questions**

E 1. Develop brief answers to each of the following questions:

1. Why is the accounting cycle called a "cycle"?
2. Could closing entries be made without using the Income Summary account?
3. Why does the post-closing trial balance contain only balance sheet accounts?

LO3, LO4 **Discussion Questions**

E 2. Develop brief answers to each of the following questions:

1. Why are reversing entries helpful?
2. Under what circumstances would the Income Statement and Balance Sheet columns on a work sheet balance when they are initially totaled?

LO2 **Preparation of Closing Entries**

E 3. The income statement accounts for the Beede Realty Company at the end of its fiscal year are shown below. Prepare the required closing entries in journal form. John Beede is the owner.

Commission Revenue		$25,620
Wages Expense	$8,110	
Rent Expense	1,200	
Supplies Expense	4,260	
Insurance Expense	915	
Depreciation Expense–Office Equipment	1,345	
Total Expenses		15,830
Net Income		$ 9,790

LO3 **Reversing Entries**

E 4. Selected September T accounts for Quintera Company are presented below.

SUPPLIES			
9/1 Bal.	860	9/30 Adj.	1,280
Sept. purchases	940		
Bal.	520		

SUPPLIES EXPENSE			
9/30 Adj.	1,280	9/30 Closing	1,280
Bal.	—		

WAGES PAYABLE			
		9/30 Adj.	640
		Bal.	640

WAGES EXPENSE			
Sept. wages	3,940	9/30 Closing	4,580
9/30 Adj.	640		
Bal.	—		

1. In which of the accounts would a reversing entry be helpful? Why?
2. Prepare the appropriate reversing entry.
3. Prepare the entry to record a payment on October 25 for wages totaling $3,140. How much of this amount represents wages expense for October?

LO4 **Preparation of a Trial Balance**

E 5. The following alphabetical list presents the accounts and balances for Abby's Cleaners on June 30, 20x8. All the accounts have normal balances.

Accounts Payable	$15,420
Accounts Receivable	7,650
Accumulated Depreciation–Office Equipment	1,350
Advertising Expense	1,800
A. Turner, Capital	30,630
A. Turner, Withdrawals	27,000
Cash	7,635
Office Equipment	15,510
Prepaid Insurance	1,680
Rent Expense	7,200
Revenue from Commissions	57,900
Supplies	825
Wages Expense	36,000

Prepare the trial balance by listing the accounts in the correct order, with the balances in the appropriate debit or credit column.

LO4 **Completion of a Work Sheet**

E 6. The following is a highly simplified alphabetical list of trial balance accounts and their normal balances for the month ended March 31, 20xx:

Accounts Payable	$ 4
Accounts Receivable	7
Accumulated Depreciation–Office Equipment	1
Cash	4
Office Equipment	8
Prepaid Insurance	2
Service Revenue	23
Supplies	4
T. Julius, Capital	12
T. Julius, Withdrawals	6
Unearned Revenues	3
Utilities Expense	2
Wages Expense	10

1. Prepare a work sheet, entering the trial balance accounts in the order in which they would normally appear and entering the balances in the correct debit or credit column.
2. Complete the work sheet using the following information: expired insurance, $1; estimated depreciation on office equipment, $1; accrued wages, $1; and unused supplies on hand, $1. In addition, $2 of the unearned revenues balance had been earned by the end of the month.

LO4 **Preparation of Statement of Owner's Equity**

E 7. The Capital, Withdrawals, and Income Summary accounts for Axel's Hair Salon are shown in T account form below. The closing entries have been recorded for the year ended December 31, 20x7.

A. TYLER, CAPITAL

12/31/x7	4,500	12/31/x6	13,000
		12/31/x7	9,500
		Bal.	18,000

INCOME SUMMARY

12/31/x7	21,500	12/31/x7	31,000
12/31/x7	9,500		
Bal.	—		

A. TYLER, WITHDRAWALS

4/1/x7	1,500	12/31/x7	4,500
7/1/x7	1,500		
10/1/x7	1,500		
Bal.	—		

Prepare a statement of owner's equity for Axel's Hair Salon.

LO3, LO4 **Preparation of Adjusting and Reversing Entries from Work Sheet Columns**

E 8. The items that appear below are from the Adjustments columns of a work sheet dated June 30, 20xx.

	Adjustments	
Account Name	**Debit**	**Credit**
Prepaid Insurance		(a) 240
Office Supplies		(b) 630
Accumulated Depreciation–Office Equipment		(c) 1,400
Accumulated Depreciation–Store Equipment		(d) 2,200
Office Salaries Expense	(e) 240	
Store Salaries Expense	(e) 480	
Insurance Expense	(a) 240	
Office Supplies Expense	(b) 630	
Depreciation Expense–Office Equipment	(c) 1,400	
Depreciation Expense–Store Equipment	(d) 2,200	
Salaries Payable		(e) 720
	5,190	5,190

1. Prepare the adjusting entries in journal form.
2. Where required, prepare appropriate reversing entries in journal form.

LO2, LO4 **Preparation of Closing Entries from the Work Sheet**

E 9. The items that follow are from the Income Statement columns of the work sheet for O'Malley Repair Shop for the year ended December 31, 20xx. Prepare entries in journal form to close the revenue, expense, Income Summary, and Withdrawals accounts. Martin O'Malley withdrew $5,000 during the year.

	Income Statement	
Account Name	Debit	Credit
Repair Revenue		25,620
Wages Expense	8,110	
Rent Expense	1,200	
Supplies Expense	4,260	
Insurance Expense	915	
Depreciation Expense–Repair Equipment	1,345	
	15,830	25,620
Net Income	9,790	
	25,620	25,620

LO4 **Adjusting Entries and Preparation of a Balance Sheet**

E 10. In the partial work sheet for T. Lang Company that follows, the Trial Balance and Income Statement columns have been completed. All amounts are in dollars.

	Trial Balance		Income Statement	
Account Name	Debit	Credit	Debit	Credit
Cash	14			
Accounts Receivable	24			
Supplies	22			
Prepaid Insurance	16			
Building	50			
Accumulated Depreciation–Building		16		
Accounts Payable		8		
Unearned Revenues		4		
T. Lang, Capital		64		
Revenues		88		92
Wages Expense	54		60	
	180	180		
Insurance Expense			8	
Supplies Expense			16	
Depreciation Expense–Building			4	
Wages Payable				
			88	92
Net Income			4	
			92	92

1. Show the adjustments that have been made in journal form without giving an explanation.
2. Prepare a balance sheet.

Problems

LO2 **Preparation of Closing Entries**

P 1. The adjusted trial balance for Phoenix Consultant Company at the end of its fiscal year is shown below.

Phoenix Consultant Company Adjusted Trial Balance December 31, 20xx		
Cash	$ 7,275	
Accounts Receivable	2,325	
Prepaid Insurance	585	
Office Supplies	440	
Office Equipment	6,300	
Accumulated Depreciation–Office Equipment		$ 765
Automobile	6,750	
Accumulated Depreciation–Automobile		750
Accounts Payable		1,700
Unearned Consulting Fees		1,500
E. Graff, Capital		14,535
E. Graff, Withdrawals	7,000	
Consulting Fees Earned		31,700
Office Salaries Expense	13,500	
Advertising Expense	2,525	
Rent Expense	2,650	
Telephone Expense	1,600	
	$50,950	$50,950

Required

1. Prepare the required closing entries.
2. **User Insight:** Explain why closing entries are necessary at the end of the accounting period.

LO1, LO2 **The Complete Accounting Cycle Without a Work Sheet: Two Months**

(second month optional)

P 2. On May 1, 20xx, Javier Munoz opened Javier's Repair Service. During the month, he completed the following transactions for the company:

May 1 Began business by depositing $5,000 in a bank account in the name of the company.
  1 Paid the rent for the store for current month, $425.
  1 Paid the premium on a one-year insurance policy, $480.
  2 Purchased repair equipment from Motley Company, $4,200. Terms were $600 down and $300 per month for one year. First payment is due June 1.

May 5 Purchased repair supplies from AWD Company on credit, $468.
8 Paid cash for an advertisement in a local newspaper, $60.
15 Received cash repair revenue for the first half of the month, $400.
21 Paid AWD Company on account, $225.
31 Received cash repair revenue for the last half of May, $975.
31 Recorded a withdrawal by owner, $300.

Required for May

1. Prepare journal entries to record the May transactions.
2. Open the following accounts: Cash (111); Prepaid Insurance (117); Repair Supplies (119); Repair Equipment (144); Accumulated Depreciation–Repair Equipment (145); Accounts Payable (212); J. Munoz, Capital (311); J. Munoz, Withdrawals (313); Income Summary (314); Repair Revenue (411); Store Rent Expense (511); Advertising Expense (512); Insurance Expense (513); Repair Supplies Expense (514); and Depreciation Expense–Repair Equipment (515). Post the May journal entries to the ledger accounts.
3. Using the following information, record adjusting entries in the general journal and post to the ledger accounts:
   a. One month's insurance has expired.
   b. The remaining inventory of unused repair supplies is $169.
   c. The estimated depreciation on repair equipment is $70.
4. From the accounts in the ledger, prepare an adjusted trial balance. (**Note:** Normally, a trial balance is prepared before adjustments but is omitted here to save time.)
5. From the adjusted trial balance, prepare an income statement, a statement of owner's equity, and a balance sheet for May.
6. Prepare and post closing entries.
7. Prepare a post-closing trial balance.

(Optional)

During June, Javier Munoz completed these transactions for Javier's Repair Service:

June 1 Paid the monthly rent, $425.
1 Made the monthly payment to Motley Company, $300.
6 Purchased additional repair supplies on credit from AWD Company, $863.
15 Received cash repair revenue for the first half of the month, $914.
20 Paid cash for an advertisement in the local newspaper, $60.
23 Paid AWD Company on account, $600.
30 Received cash repair revenue for the last half of the month, $817.
30 Recorded a withdrawal by owner, $300.

8. Prepare and post journal entries to record the June transactions.
9. Using the following information, record adjusting entries in the general journal and post to the ledger accounts:
   a. One month's insurance has expired.
   b. The inventory of unused repair supplies is $413.
   c. The estimated depreciation on repair equipment is $70.
10. From the accounts in the ledger, prepare an adjusted trial balance.
11. From the adjusted trial balance, prepare the June income statement, statement of owner's equity, and balance sheet.
12. Prepare and post closing entries.
13. Prepare a post-closing trial balance.

LO2, LO4 **Preparation of a Work Sheet, Financial Statements, and Adjusting and Closing Entries**

 P 3. Beauchamp Theater Company's trial balance at the end of its current fiscal year is as follows:

Beauchamp Theater Company
Trial Balance
June 30, 20x7

Cash	$ 31,800	
Accounts Receivable	18,544	
Prepaid Insurance	19,600	
Office Supplies	780	
Cleaning Supplies	3,590	
Land	20,000	
Building	400,000	
Accumulated Depreciation–Building		$ 39,400
Theater Furnishings	370,000	
Accumulated Depreciation–Theater Furnishings		65,000
Office Equipment	31,600	
Accumulated Depreciation–Office Equipment		15,560
Accounts Payable		45,506
Gift Books Liability		41,900
Mortgage Payable		300,000
D. Beauchamp, Capital		312,648
D. Beauchamp, Withdrawals	60,000	
Ticket Sales Revenue		411,400
Theater Rental Revenue		45,200
Usher Wages Expense	157,000	
Office Wages Expense	24,000	
Utilities Expense	112,700	
Interest Expense	27,000	
	$1,276,614	$1,276,614

Required

1. Enter Beauchamp Theater Company's trial balance amounts in the Trial Balance columns of a work sheet and complete the work sheet using the following information:
   a. Expired insurance, $17,400.
   b. Inventory of unused office supplies, $244.
   c. Inventory of unused cleaning supplies, $468. calculate
   d. Estimated depreciation on the building, $14,000.
   e. Estimated depreciation on the theater furnishings, $36,000.
   f. Estimated depreciation on the office equipment, $3,160.
   g. The company credits all gift books sold during the year to the Gift Books Liability account. A gift book is a booklet of ticket coupons that is purchased in advance as a gift. The recipient redeems the coupons at some point in the future. On June 30 it was estimated that $37,800 worth of the gift books had been redeemed.

    h. Accrued but unpaid usher wages at the end of the accounting period, $860.

2. Prepare an income statement, a statement of owner's equity, and a balance sheet. Assume no additional investments by Dan Beauchamp.
3. Prepare adjusting and closing entries from the work sheet.
4. **User Insight:** Can the work sheet be used as a substitute for the financial statements? Explain your answer.

Alternate Problems

LO2 **Preparation of Closing Entries**

P 4. Do-It-Yourself Trailer Rental rents small trailers by the day for local moving jobs. This is its adjusted trial balance at the end of the current fiscal year:

Do-It-Yourself Trailer Rental Adjusted Trial Balance June 30, 20x8		
Cash	$ 692	
Accounts Receivable	972	
Supplies	119	
Prepaid Insurance	360	
Trailers	12,000	
Accumulated Depreciation–Trailers		$ 7,200
Accounts Payable		271
Wages Payable		200
S. Perez, Capital		5,694
S. Perez, Withdrawals	7,200	
Trailer Rentals Revenue		45,546
Wages Expense	23,400	
Insurance Expense	720	
Supplies Expense	266	
Depreciation Expense–Trailers	2,400	
Other Expenses	10,782	
	$58,911	$58,911

Required

1. From the information given, record closing entries in journal form.
2. **User Insight:** If closing entries were not prepared at the end of the accounting period, what problems would result in the next accounting period?

LO2, LO3, LO4 **Preparation of a Work Sheet, Financial Statements, and Adjusting, Closing, and Reversing Entries**

P 5. At the end of the current fiscal year, the trial balance of Natchez Delivery Service appeared as shown on the next page.

Required

1. Enter the trial balance amounts in the Trial Balance columns of a work sheet and complete the work sheet using the information that follows.

Natchez Delivery Service
Trial Balance
August 31, 20x7

Cash	$ 10,072	
Accounts Receivable	29,314	
Prepaid Insurance	5,340	
Delivery Supplies	14,700	
Office Supplies	2,460	
Land	15,000	
Building	196,000	
Accumulated Depreciation–Building		$ 53,400
Trucks	103,800	
Accumulated Depreciation–Trucks		30,900
Office Equipment	15,900	
Accumulated Depreciation–Office Equipment		10,800
Accounts Payable		9,396
Unearned Lockbox Fees		8,340
Mortgage Payable		72,000
H. Natchez, Capital		128,730
H. Natchez, Withdrawals	30,000	
Delivery Service Revenue		283,470
Lockbox Fees Earned		28,800
Truck Drivers' Wages Expense	120,600	
Office Salaries Expense	44,400	
Gas, Oil, and Truck Repairs Expense	31,050	
Interest Expense	7,200	
	$625,836	$625,836

a. Expired insurance, $3,060.
b. Inventory of unused delivery supplies, $1,430.
c. Inventory of unused office supplies, $186.
d. Estimated depreciation, building, $14,400.
e. Estimated depreciation, trucks, $15,450.
f. Estimated depreciation, office equipment, $2,700.
g. The company credits the lockbox fees of customers who pay in advance to the Unearned Lockbox Fees account. Of the amount credited to this account during the year, $5,630 had been earned by August 31.
h. Lockbox fees earned but unrecorded and uncollected at the end of the accounting period, $816.
i. Accrued but unpaid truck drivers' wages at the end of the year, $1,920.

2. Prepare an income statement, a statement of owner's equity, and a balance sheet. Assume no additional investments by Honore Natchez.
3. Prepare adjusting, closing, and, when necessary, reversing entries from the work sheet.
4. **User Insight:** Can the work sheet be used as a substitute for the financial statements? Explain your answer.

ENHANCING Your Knowledge, Skills, and Critical Thinking

Conceptual Understanding Cases

LO1 **Interim Financial Statements**

C 1. Offshore Drilling Company provides services for drilling operations off the coast of Louisiana. The company has a significant amount of debt to Southern National Bank in Baton Rouge. The bank requires the company to provide it with quarterly financial statements. Explain what is involved in preparing financial statements every quarter.

LO1 **Purpose of Closing Entries**

C 2. Maury Jacobs, owner of Jacobs Furniture Company, notices the amount of time it takes the company's accountant to prepare closing entries. He suggests that the company could save time and money by not doing closing entries. He argues that only adjusting entries are needed to determine the company's earnings. Explain the purposes of closing entries and why they are worth doing.

Interpreting Financial Reports

LO2 **Closing Entries**

C 3. Robert Half International, Inc. is a global specialized staffing firm. Adapted information from the statement of earnings (in thousands, without earnings per share information) in its annual report for the year ended December 31, 2005, follows.[2] The firm reported distributing cash (dividends) in the amount of $47,781,000 to the owners in 2005.

Revenues	
Service revenues	$3,338,439
Interest income	10,948
Total revenues	$3,349,387
Expenses	
Employee compensation and benefits	$1,965,390
Selling, general, and administrative expenses	991,823
Income taxes	154,304
Total expenses	$3,111,517
Net income	$ 237,870

1. Prepare in journal form the closing entries Robert Half would have made on December 31, 2005. Treat income taxes as an expense and cash distributions to owners as withdrawals.
2. Based on your handling of step 1 and the effect of expenses and cash distributions on owner's capital, what theoretical reason can you give for not including expenses and cash distributions in the same closing entry?

Decision Analysis Using Excel

LO1, LO2 **Conversion from Accrual to Cash Statement**

C 4. Claudine, owner of Claudine's Internet Service, is puzzled by the income statement on the next page. She knows she withdrew $15,600 in cash from the company for personal expenses; yet the cash balance in the company's bank account increased from $460 to $3,100 from last June 30 to this June 30. She wants to know how her net income could be less than the cash she took out of the business if there is an increase in the cash balance. Her accountant has completed the closing entries and shows her the balance sheets for June 30, 20x8, and June 30, 20x7. He explains that besides the change in the cash balance, Accounts Receivable decreased by $1,480 and Accounts Payable increased by $380 (supplies are the only items Claudine buys on credit). The only other asset or liability account that changed during the year was Accumulated Depreciation–Office Equipment, which increased by $2,200.

Claudine's Internet Service		
Income Statement		
For the Year Ended June 30, 20x8		
Revenue		
Word processing services		$20,980
Expenses		
Rent Expense	$2,400	
Depreciation expense–office equipment	2,200	
Supplies expense	960	
Other expenses	1,240	
Total expenses		6,800
Net income		$14,180

Verify the cash balance increase by preparing a statement that lists the receipts of cash and the expenditures of cash during the year. Explain your treatment of word processing services, supplies expense, withdrawals, and depreciation.

Annual Report Case: CVS Corporation

LO1 **Fiscal Year, Closing Process, and Interim Reports**

C 5. Refer to the notes to the financial statements in the **CVS** annual report in the Supplement to Chapter 5. When does CVS end its fiscal year? For what reasons might it have chosen this date? From the standpoint of completing the accounting cycle, what advantage does this date have? Does CVS prepare interim financial statements? What are the implications of interim financial statements for the accounting cycle?

Comparison Case: CVS Versus Southwest

LO1 **Interim Financial Reporting and Seasonality**

C 6. Both **CVS** and **Southwest Airlines** provide quarterly financial information in their financial statements. Quarterly financial reports provide important information about the "seasonality" of a company's operations. *Seasonality* refers to how dependent a company is on sales during one season of the year, such as the Christmas season, and how it affects a company's need to plan for cash flows and inventory. From the quarterly financial information for CVS in the Supplement to Chapter 5, determine the effects of seasons on CVS's sales and income by calculating for the most recent year the percentage of quarterly net sales and net earnings to annual net sales and net earnings. Discuss the results. How do you think the effect of seasons might differ for Southwest's sales and income?

Ethical Dilemma Case

LO1 **Ethics and Time Pressure**

C 7. Thomas Logos, an accountant for Manner Company, has made adjusting entries and is preparing the adjusted trial balance for the first six months of the year. Financial statements must be delivered to the bank by 5 P.M. to support a critical loan agreement. By noon, Logos has been unable to balance the adjusted trial balance. The figures are off by $1,320, so he increases the balance of the owner's Capital account by $1,320. He closes the accounts, prepares the statements, and sends them to the bank on time. Logos hopes that no one will notice the problem and believes that he can find the error and correct it by the end of next month. Are Logos' actions ethical? Why or why not? Did he have other alternatives?

Internet Case

LO1 **Interim Financial Statements**

C 8. Go to **Best Buy's** website and find the latest quarterly financial report. Compare the results of the latest quarter available to you with the results in the Decision Point at the beginning of this chapter. Are Best Buy's revenue (sales) and operating income greater or less in the more recent quarter? What other information do you find in the quarterly report?

Group Activity Case

LO1 **Accounting Efficiency**

C 9. Way Heaters Company manufactures industrial heaters used in making candy. It sells its heaters to some customers on credit with generous terms specifying payment six months after purchase and an interest rate based on current bank rates. Because the interest on the loans accrues a little every day but is not paid until the note's due date, an adjusting entry must be made at the end of each accounting period to debit Interest Receivable and credit Interest Income for the amount of the interest accrued but not received to date. The company prepares financial statements every month. Keeping track of what has been accrued in the past is time-consuming because the notes carry different dates and interest rates. Form in-class groups to determine what the accountant can do to simplify the process of making the adjusting entry for accrued interest each month. Compare the groups' solutions with a class debriefing.

Business Communication Case

LO1, LO2, LO3, LO4 **Interview of Local Businessperson**

C 10. Arrange to spend about an hour interviewing the owner, manager, or accountant of a local service or retail business. Your goal is to learn as much as you can about the accounting cycle of the person's business. Ask the interviewee to show you his or her accounting records and to tell you how such transactions as sales, purchases, payments, and payroll are handled. Examine the documents used to support the transactions. Look at any journals, ledgers, or work sheets. Does the business use a computer? Does it use its own accounting system, or does it use an outside or centralized service? Does it use the cash or the accrual basis of accounting? When does it prepare adjusting entries? When does it prepare closing entries? How often does it prepare financial statements? Does it prepare reversing entries? How do its procedures differ from those described in the text? When the interview is finished, organize and write up your findings and be prepared to present them in class.

COMPREHENSIVE Problem: Treadle Website Design

This comprehensive problem involving Treadle Website Design covers all the learning objectives in this chapter and in the chapters on measuring business transactions and measuring business income. To complete the problem, you may sometimes have to refer to this material.

The July 31, 20xx, post-closing trial balance for the Treadle Website Design appears below.

Treadle Website Design
Post-Closing Trial Balance
July 31, 20xx

Cash	$22,480	
Accounts Receivable	5,000	
Office Supplies	3,660	
Prepaid Rent	1,600	
Office Equipment	16,320	
Accumulated Depreciation–Office Equipment		$ 300
Accounts Payable		6,280
Unearned Design Revenue		600
Wages Payable		720
P. Treadle, Capital		41,160
	$49,060	$49,060

During August, the agency engaged in these transactions:

Aug. 1 Received an additional investment of cash from P. Treadle, $20,000.
2 Purchased additional office equipment with cash, $4,700.
7 Purchased additional office supplies for cash, $540.
8 Completed the series of designs that began on July 31 and billed for the total design services performed, including the accrued revenues of $800 that had been recognized in an adjusting entry in July, $1,400.
12 Paid the amount due for the office equipment purchased last month, $3,000.
13 Accepted an advance in cash for design work to be done, $2,400.
15 Performed design services and received a cash fee, $2,900.
16 Received payment on account for design services performed last month, $2,800.
19 Made a partial payment on the utilities bill that was received and recorded at the end of July, $140.
20 Performed design services for Ward Department Stores and agreed to accept payment next month, $3,200.

Aug. 21 Performed design services for cash, $1,160.
  22 Received and paid the utilities bill for August, $900.
  23 Paid the assistant for four weeks' wages, $4,800.
  26 Paid the rent for September in advance, $1,600.
  30 Paid cash to P. Treadle as a withdrawal for personal expenses, $2,800.

Required

1. Record entries in journal form and post to the ledger accounts the optional reversing entries on August 1 for Wages Payable and Accounts Receivable (see adjustment for unrecorded wages on page 116 and adjustment for design revenue on page 119). (Begin the general journal on Page 5.)
2. Record the transactions for August in journal form.
3. Post the August transactions to the ledger accounts.
4. Prepare a trial balance in the Trial Balance columns of a work sheet.
5. Prepare adjusting entries and complete the work sheet using the information below.

   a. One month's prepaid rent has expired, $1,600.
   b. An inventory of supplies reveals $2,020 still on hand on August 31.
   c. Depreciation on equipment for August is calculated to be $300.
   d. Services performed for which payment had been received in advance totaled $1,300.
   e. Services performed that will not be billed until September totaled $580.
   f. Wages accrued by the end of August, $720.

6. From the work sheet prepare an income statement, a statement of owner's equity, and a balance sheet for August 31, 20xx.
7. Record the adjusting entries on August 31, 20xx in journal form, and post them to the ledger accounts.
8. Record the closing entries on August 31, 20xx in journal form, and post them to the ledger accounts.
9. Prepare a post-closing trial balance at August 31, 20xx.

Financial Reporting and Analysis

Owners, creditors, and other interested parties rely on the integrity of a company's financial reports. A company's managers and accountants therefore have a responsibility to act ethically in the reporting process. However, what is often overlooked is that the users of financial reports also have a responsibility to recognize and understand the types of judgments and estimates that underlie these reports.

LEARNING OBJECTIVES

Making a Statement

Balance
Sheet

Statement of
Cash Flows

Income
Statement

Grouping like accounts on the balance sheet and income statement aids analysis.

LO1 Describe the objectives and qualitative characteristics of financial reporting and the ethical responsibilities that financial reporting involves.

LO2 Define and describe the conventions of *comparability* and *consistency*, *materiality*, *conservatism*, *full disclosure*, and *cost-benefit*.

LO3 Identify and describe the basic components of a classified balance sheet.

LO4 Describe the features of multistep and single-step classified income statements.

LO5 Use classified financial statements to evaluate liquidity and profitability.

- How should financial statements be organized to provide the best information?

- What key measures best capture a company's financial performance?

In its annual report, **Dell's** management states that the company's objective is "to maximize stockholder value by executing a strategy based on ... a balance of three priorities: liquidity, profitability, and growth."[1] In judging whether a company has achieved its objectives, investors, creditors, managers, and others analyze relationships between key numbers in the financial statements that appear in the company's annual report.

Dell's annual report summarizes the company's financial performance by condensing a tremendous amount of information to a few numbers that managers and external users of financial statements consider most important. As shown in the Financial Highlights below, Dell uses just four measures to summarize its operating results and the change in those results from one fiscal year to the next.

DELL'S FINANCIAL HIGHLIGHTS: OPERATING RESULTS (In millions)			
	2005	2004	Change
Net revenue	$49,205	$41,444	18.7%
Gross profit	9,015	7,552	19.4%
Operating income	4,761	3,544	34.3%
Net income	3,043	2,645	15.0%

Foundations of Financial Reporting

LO1 Describe the objectives and qualitative characteristics of financial reporting and the ethical responsibilities that financial reporting involves.

By issuing stocks and bonds that are traded in financial markets, companies can raise the cash they need to carry out current and future business activities. Investors are interested mainly in returns from dividends and increases in the market value of their investment. Creditors want to know if the firm can repay a loan plus interest in accordance with specified terms. Very importantly, both investors and creditors need to know if the firm can generate adequate cash flows to maintain its liquidity. Financial statements are important to both groups in making that judgment. They offer valuable information that helps investors and creditors judge a company's ability to pay dividends or other distributions to owners and repay debts with interest.

In the following sections, we describe the objectives of financial reporting and the qualitative characteristics and ethical considerations that are involved. Figure 1 illustrates these factors.

Objectives of Financial Reporting

The Financial Accounting Standards Board (FASB) emphasizes the needs of users when it defines the objectives of financial reporting as follows:[2]

1. *To furnish information useful in making investment and credit decisions.* Financial reporting should offer information that can help current and potential investors (owners) and creditors make rational investment and credit deci-

---

■ **FIGURE 1**
Factors Affecting Financial Reporting

OBJECTIVES OF FINANCIAL REPORTING

1. To furnish information that is useful in making investment and credit decisions
2. To provide information useful in assessing cash flow prospects
3. To provide information about business resources, claims to those resources, and changes in them

QUALITATIVE CHARACTERISTICS		ETHICAL FINANCIAL REPORTING

QUALITATIVE CHARACTERISTICS

UNDERSTANDABILITY	USEFULNESS		ETHICAL FINANCIAL REPORTING
Decision makers must be able to interpret accounting information.	Accountants must provide information that is useful in making decisions.		**CERTIFICATION** Chief Executive Officer, Chief Financial Officer, and auditors must certify that financial statements are accurate, complete, and not misleading.

ACCOUNTING CONVENTIONS	RELEVANCE	RELIABILITY
• Comparability and consistency • Materiality • Conservatism • Full disclosure • Cost-benefit	• Feedback value • Predictive value • Timeliness	• Faithful representation • Verifiability • Neutrality

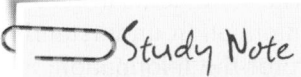

sions. The reports should be in a form that makes sense to anyone who has some understanding of business and is willing to study the information carefully.

2. *To provide information useful in assessing cash flow prospects.* Financial reporting should supply information that can help current and potential investors (owners) and creditors judge the amount, timing, and risk of expected cash receipts from dividends or interest and the proceeds from the sale, redemption, or maturity of stocks or loans.

3. *To provide information about business resources, claims to those resources, and changes in them.* Financial reporting should provide information about a company's assets, liabilities, and stockholders' (owner's) equity, and the effect that transactions have on them.

Financial statements periodically present to parties outside the business the information that has been gathered and processed in the accounting system. These statements—the balance sheet, the income statement, the statement of owner's equity, and the statement of cash flows—are the most important output of the accounting system. They are "general purpose" because of their wide audience. They are "external" because their users are outside the business. Because of a potential conflict of interest between managers, who must prepare the statements, and owners or creditors, who invest in or lend money to the business, financial statements are often audited by outside accountants to ensure their reliability.

Qualitative Characteristics of Accounting Information

Students in their first accounting course often get the idea that accounting is 100 percent accurate. Contributing to this perception is that introductory textbooks like this one present the basics of accounting in a simple form to help students understand them. All the problems can be solved, and all the numbers add up; what is supposed to equal something else does. Accounting seems very much like mathematics in its precision. In practice, however, accounting information is neither simple nor precise, and it rarely satisfies all criteria. The FASB emphasizes this fact in the following statement:

> The information provided by financial reporting often results from approximate, rather than exact, measures. The measures commonly involve numerous estimates, classifications, summarizations, judgments and allocations. The outcome of economic activity in a dynamic economy is uncertain and results from combinations of many factors. Thus, despite the aura of precision that may seem to surround financial reporting in general and financial statements in particular, with few exceptions the measures are approximations, which may be based on rules and conventions, rather than exact amounts.[3]

The goal of generating accounting information is to provide the data that different users need to make informed decisions for their unique situations. The ways this goal is accomplished provide much of the interest and controversy in accounting. To facilitate interpretation of accounting information, the FASB has established standards, or **qualitative characteristics**, by which to judge the information.

The most important qualitative characteristics are understandability and usefulness. **Understandability** depends not only on the accountant, but also on the decision maker. The accountant prepares the financial statements in accordance with practices that are intended to make the information understandable. But the decision maker must know how to interpret the information; in making decisions, he or she must judge what information to use, how to use it, and what it means. To understand accounting information, users must be familiar with the **accounting conventions**, or rules of thumb, used in preparing financial statements. These conventions, which we discuss later in the chapter, affect how and what information is presented in financial statements.

For accounting information to meet the standard of **usefulness**, it must have two major qualitative characteristics: relevance and reliability. **Relevance** means that the information has a direct bearing on a decision. In other words, if the information were not available, a different decision would be made. To be relevant, information must provide feedback, help predict future conditions, and be timely. For example, the income statement provides information about how a company performed over the past year (feedback), and it helps in planning for the next year (prediction). To be useful, however, it must be communicated soon enough after the end of the accounting period to enable the reader to make decisions (timeliness).

Reliability means that the user can depend on the information. To be reliable, information must represent what it is meant to represent. It must be credible and verifiable by independent parties using the same methods of measurement. It also must be neutral. Financial reports should convey information about a business as faithfully as possible without influencing anyone in a specific direction. For example, the balance sheet should represent the economic resources, obligations, and owner's equity of a business as accurately and completely as possible in accordance with generally accepted accounting principles, and it should be verifiable by an auditor.

The FASB is currently studying the potential tradeoff between relevance and reliability. For instance, some argue that fair value accounting is more relevant and therefore more valuable as information than historical cost even though it may be a less reliable measure. Others argue that historical cost is more valuable because of its reliability.[4]

Management's Certification of the Financial Statements

As we noted earlier in the text, in 2002, in the wake of accounting scandals at **Enron** and **WorldCom**, Congress passed the Sarbanes-Oxley Act. One of the important outcomes of this legislation was that the Securities and Exchange Commission instituted rules requiring the chief executive officers and chief financial officers of all publicly traded companies to certify that, to their knowledge, the quarterly and annual statements that their companies file with the SEC are accurate and complete. An example of this type of management certification appears in the 2006 10-K form that **Dell Computer Corporation** filed with the SEC. In that report, James M. Schneider, then the company's chief financial officer, made the following statement:

> Based on my knowledge, this annual report does not contain any untrue statement of material fact or omit to state a material fact necessary to make the statements . . . not misleading with respect to the period covered. . . . Based on my knowledge, the financial statements and other financial information . . . fairly present in all material respects the financial condition, results of operations and cash flows of the registrant as of, and for the periods presented in the annual report.[5]

As the Enron and WorldCom scandals demonstrated, fraudulent financial reporting can have high costs for investors, lenders, employees, and customers. It can also have high costs for the people who condone, authorize, or prepare misleading reports—even those at the highest corporate levels. In March 2005, Bernard J. Ebbers, former CEO of WorldCom, was convicted of seven counts of filing false reports with the SEC and one count each of securities fraud and conspiracy. Each count could carry a prison sentence of five to ten years[6]. In 2006, both Kenneth Lay, former chairman of Enron Corporation, and Jeffrey Skilling, Enron's former CEO, were found guilty of charges similar to the ones of which Ebbers was convicted.

STOP • REVIEW • APPLY

1-1. What are the three objectives of financial reporting?

1-2. What are the qualitative characteristics of accounting information? Explain their significance.

1-3. Who are the people responsible for preparing financial statements? What does the preparation of reliable financial statements entail?

Suggested answers to all Stop, Review, and Apply questions are available at http://college.hmco.com/accounting/needles/poa/10e/student_home.html.

Accounting Conventions

LO2 Define and describe the conventions of *comparability* and *consistency*, *materiality*, *conservatism*, *full disclosure*, and *cost-benefit*.

Financial statements are based largely on estimates and the application of accounting rules for recognition and allocation. To facilitate interpretation, accountants depend on five conventions, or rules of thumb, in recording transactions and preparing financial statements: comparability and consistency, materiality, conservatism, full disclosure, and cost-benefit.

Comparability and Consistency

Information about a company is more useful when it can be compared over several periods or when it can be compared with information about other companies. **Comparability** means that information is presented in such a way that a decision maker can recognize similarities, differences, and trends over different periods in the same company and among different companies.

Consistent use of accounting measures and procedures is important in achieving comparability. The **consistency** convention requires that once a company has adopted an accounting procedure, it must use it from one period to the next unless a note to the financial statements informs users of a change in procedure. Generally accepted accounting principles specify what the note must contain:

> The nature of and justification for a change in accounting principle and its effect on income should be disclosed in the financial statements of the period in which the change is made. The justification for the change

Like any other manufacturer, Goodyear must ensure that the quality of its products is consistent and that its accounting methods are as well. When a company changes an accounting method, it must inform users of its financial statements of the change. Such information is essential in making effective comparisons of a company's performance over several periods or in comparing its performance with that of other companies.

should explain clearly why the newly adopted accounting principle is preferable.[7]

For example, in the notes to its financial statements, **Goodyear Tire & Rubber Company** disclosed that it had changed its method of accounting for inventories because management felt the new method improved the matching of revenues and costs. Without such an acknowledgment, users of financial statements can assume that the treatment of a particular transaction, account, or item has not changed since the last period.

Materiality

Materiality refers to the relative importance of an item or event. In general, an item or event is material if there is a reasonable expectation that knowing about it would influence the decisions of users of financial statements. Some items or events are so small or insignificant that they would make little differ-

FOCUS ON BUSINESS PRACTICE

Are Yahoo! and Google Comparable? Can an Internet Company Be Conservative?

In a recent quarter, **Yahoo! Inc.**, reported revenue of $758 million, but looked at another way, the revenue could be $550 million. In the same quarter, Yahoo!'s rival, **Google Inc.**, reported revenue of $390 million, but that could be $652 million. What's going on?

Both Yahoo! and Google follow GAAP in reporting revenue, but their interpretations differ. The difference involves how they account for revenue from advertisements that they place on other companies' websites. Yahoo! and Google are paid each time an Internet user clicks on one of their ads, but they pay some of that money

to the company on whose site the ad appears. Yahoo! counts the revenue at the gross amount (and shows the payment as an operating expense); hence, its reported revenue of $758 million. Google counts the revenues at the net amount (gross minus the payment); hence, the reported revenue of $390 million. Analysts consider the way Google reports to be the more conservative practice, and in fact, when Yahoo! communicates with users, it shows the net amount also because it "conveys more transparent economic value to the investor."[8]

FOCUS ON BUSINESS PRACTICE
How Much Is Material? It's Not Only a Matter of Numbers.

The materiality issue was long a pet peeve of the SEC, which contended that companies were increasingly abusing the convention to protect their stocks from taking a pounding when earnings did not reach their targets. In consequence, the SEC issued a rule that put stricter requirements on the use of materiality. In addition to providing quantitative guides, the rule includes qualitative considerations. The percentage assessment of material-ity—the rule of thumb of 5 percent or more of net income that accountants and companies have traditionally used—is acceptable as an initial screening. However, the rule states that companies cannot decline to book items in the interest of meeting earnings estimates, preserving a growing earnings trend, converting a loss to a profit, increasing management compensation, or hiding an illegal transaction, such as a bribe.[9]

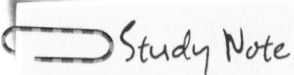

Theoretically, a $10 stapler is a long-term asset and should therefore be capitalized and depreciated over its useful life. However, the convention of materiality allows the stapler to be expensed entirely in the year of purchase because its cost is small and writing it off in one year will have no effect on anyone's decision making.

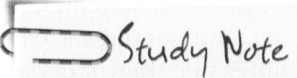

The purpose of conservatism is not to produce the lowest net income and lowest asset value. It is a guideline for choosing among GAAP alternatives, and it should be used with care.

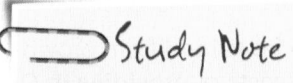

Expensing a long-term asset in the period of purchase is not an alternative allowed under GAAP.

ence to decision makers no matter how they are handled. Thus, a large company, like **Dell Computer Corporation**, may decide that expenditures for durable items of less than $500 should be charged as expenses rather than recorded as long-term assets and depreciated.

The materiality of an item normally is determined by relating its dollar value to an element of the financial statements, such as net income or total assets. As a rule, when an item is worth 5 percent or more of net income, accountants treat it as material. However, materiality depends not only on the value of an item, but also on its nature. For example, in a multimillion-dollar company, a mistake of $5,000 in recording an item may not be important, but the discovery of a $5,000 bribe or theft can be very important. Moreover, many small errors can add up to a material amount.

Conservatism

When accountants are uncertain about the judgments or estimates they must make, which is often the case, they look to the convention of **conservatism**. This convention holds that when faced with choosing between two equally acceptable procedures, accountants should choose the one that is least likely to overstate assets and income.

One of the most common applications of the conservatism convention is the use of the lower-of-cost-or-market method in accounting for inventories. Under this method, if an item's market value is greater than its original cost, the more conservative cost figure is used. If the market value is below the original cost, the more conservative market value is used. The latter situation often occurs in the computer industry.

Conservatism can be a useful tool in doubtful cases, but when it is abused, it can lead to incorrect and misleading financial statements. For example, there is no uncertainty about how a long-term asset of material cost should be treated. When conservatism is used to justify expensing such an asset in the period of purchase, income and assets for the current period will be understated, and income in future periods will be overstated. Its cost should be recorded as an asset and spread over the useful life of the asset, as explained in Chapter 3. Accountants therefore depend on the conservatism convention only when uncertain about which accounting procedure to use.

Full Disclosure

The convention of **full disclosure** requires that financial statements present all the information relevant to users' understanding of the statements. That is, the

statements must offer any explanation needed to keep them from being misleading. Explanatory notes are therefore an integral part of the financial statements. For instance, as we have already mentioned, the notes should disclose any change that a company has made in its accounting procedures.

A company must also disclose significant events arising after the balance sheet date in the financial statements. Suppose a firm has purchased a piece of land for a future subdivision. Shortly after the end of its fiscal year, the firm is served papers to halt construction because the Environmental Protection Agency asserts that the land was once a toxic waste dump. This information, which obviously affects the users of the financial statements, must be disclosed in the statements for the fiscal year just ended.

Additional note disclosures required by the FASB and other official bodies include the accounting procedures used in preparing the financial statements and important terms of a company's debt, commitments, and contingencies. However, the statements can become so cluttered with notes that they impede rather than help understanding. Beyond the required disclosures, the application of the full-disclosure convention is based on the judgment of management and of the accountants who prepare the financial statements.

In recent years, owners and creditors also have had an influence on full disclosure. To protect them, independent auditors, the stock exchanges, and the SEC have made more demands for disclosure by publicly owned companies. The SEC has pushed especially hard for the enforcement of full disclosure. As a result, more and better information about public companies is available to the public today than ever before.

Cost-Benefit

The **cost-benefit** convention holds that the benefits to be gained from providing accounting information should be greater than the costs of providing it. Of course, minimum levels of relevance and reliability must be reached if accounting information is to be useful. Beyond the minimum levels, however, it is up to the FASB and the SEC, which stipulate the information that must be reported, and the accountant, who provides the information, to judge the costs and benefits in each case.

Firms use the cost-benefit convention for both accounting and nonaccounting decisions. Department stores could almost completely eliminate shoplifting if they hired five times as many clerks as they now have and assigned them to watching customers. The benefit would be reduced shoplifting. The cost would be reduced sales (customers do not like being closely watched) and increased wages expense. Although shoplifting is a serious problem for department stores, the benefit of reducing shoplifting in this way does not outweigh the cost.

The costs and benefits of a requirement for accounting disclosure are both immediate and deferred. Judging the final costs and benefits of a far-reaching and costly requirement for accounting disclosure is difficult. For instance, the FASB allows certain large companies to make a supplemental disclosure in their financial statements of the effects of changes in consumer price levels. Most companies choose not to present this information because they believe the costs of producing and providing it exceed its benefits to the readers of their financial statements. Cost-benefit is a question that the FASB, the Securities and Exhange Commission, and all other regulators face. Even though there are no definitive ways of measuring costs and benefits, much of an accountant's work deals with these concepts.

STOP • REVIEW • APPLY

2-1. What are accounting conventions, and why are they important to users of financial statements?

2-2. Explain how each of the five accounting conventions helps users interpret financial information.

Examples of Accounting Conventions Each of the five accounting conventions below is described in one of the statements in the numbered list that follows. Match each statement to the letter of the appropriate convention.

a. Comparability and consistency
b. Materiality
c. Conservatism
d. Full disclosure
e. Cost-benefit

1. A note to the financial statements explains the company's method of revenue recognition.
2. Inventory is accounted for at its market value, which is less than its original cost.
3. A company uses the same method of revenue recognition year after year.
4. Several accounts are grouped into one category because the total amount of each account is small.
5. A company does not keep detailed records of certain operations because the information gained from the detail is not deemed useful.

SOLUTION
1. d   2. c   3. a   4. b   5. e

Classified Balance Sheet

LO3 Identify and describe the basic components of a classified balance sheet.

As you know, a balance sheet presents a company's financial position at a particular time. The balance sheets we have presented thus far categorize accounts as assets, liabilities, and owner's equity. Because even a fairly small company can have hundreds of accounts, simply listing accounts in these broad categories is not particularly helpful to a statement user. Setting up subcategories within the major categories can make financial statements much more useful. This format enables owners and creditors to study and evaluate relationships among the subcategories.

General-purpose external financial statements that are divided into subcategories are called **classified financial statements**. Figure 2 depicts the subcategories into which assets, liabilities, and owner's equity are usually broken down.

The subcategories of Ling Auto Supply Company's classified balance sheet, shown in Exhibit 1, typify those used by most corporations in the United States. The subcategories under owner's equity would, of course, be different if Ling Auto Supply was a corporation or partnership rather than a sole proprietorship.

Assets

As you can see in Exhibit 1, the classified balance sheet of a U.S. company typically divides assets into four categories:

1. Current assets
2. Investments
3. Property, plant, and equipment
4. Intangible assets

These categories are listed in the order of their presumed ease of conversion into cash. For example, current assets are usually more easily converted to cash than are property, plant, and equipment. For simplicity, some companies group investments, intangible assets, and other miscellaneous assets into a category called **other assets**.

Current Assets **Current assets** are cash and other assets that a company can reasonably expect to convert to cash, sell, or consume within one year or its *normal operating cycle*, whichever is longer. A company's **normal operating cycle** is the average time it needs to go from spending cash to receiving cash.

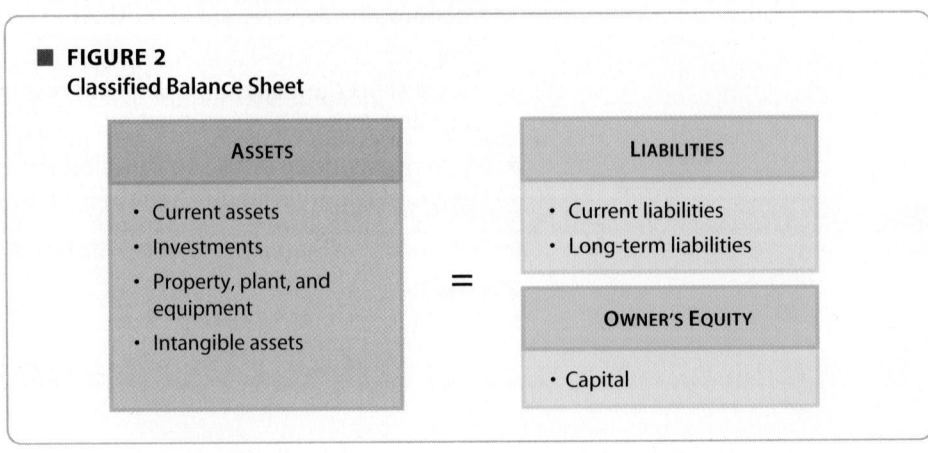

■ **FIGURE 2**
Classified Balance Sheet

EXHIBIT 1 ▶ | Classified Balance Sheet for Ling Auto Supply Company

Ling Auto Supply Company
Balance Sheet
December 31, 20xx

Assets

Current assets

Cash	$ 20,720	
Short-term investments	4,000	
Notes receivable	16,000	
Accounts receivable	70,600	
Merchandise inventory	120,800	
Prepaid insurance	13,200	
Supplies	3,392	
Total current assets		$248,712

Investments

Land held for future use	10,000

Property, plant, and equipment

Land		$ 9,000	
Building	$41,300		
Less accumulated depreciation	17,280	24,020	
Equipment	$54,000		
Less accumulated depreciation	28,900	25,100	
Total property, plant, and equipment			58,120

Intangible assets

Trademark	1,000
Total assets	$317,832

Liabilities

Current liabilities

Notes payable	$ 30,000	
Accounts payable	51,366	
Salaries payable	4,000	
Total current liabilities		$ 85,366

Long-term liabilities

Mortgage payable	35,600
Total liabilities	$120,966

Owner's Equity

J. Ling, Capital	$196,866	
Total owner's equity		196,866
Total liabilities and owner's equity		$317,832

For example, suppose a company uses cash to buy inventory and sells the inventory to a customer on credit. The resulting receivable must be collected in cash before the normal operating cycle ends.

The normal operating cycle for most companies is less than one year, but there are exceptions. For example, because of the length of time it takes **The Boeing Company** to build aircraft, its normal operating cycle exceeds one year. The inventory used in building the planes is nonetheless considered a current asset because the planes will be sold within the normal operating cycle. Another example is a company that sells on an installment basis. The payments for a television set or a refrigerator can extend over 24 or 36 months, but these receivables are still considered current assets.

Cash is obviously a current asset. Short-term investments, notes and accounts receivable, and inventory that a company expects to convert to cash within the next year or the normal operating cycle are also current assets. On the balance sheet, they are listed in order of their ease of conversion to cash.

Prepaid expenses, such as rent and insurance paid in advance, and inventories of supplies bought for use rather than for sale should be classified as current assets. These assets are current in the sense that if they had not been bought earlier, a current outlay of cash would be needed to obtain them.

In deciding whether an asset is current or noncurrent, the idea of "reasonable expectation" is important. For example, Short-Term Investments, also called *Marketable Securities*, is an account used for temporary investments, such as U.S. Treasury bills, of "idle" cash—that is, cash that is not immediately required for operating purposes. Management can reasonably expect to sell these securities as cash needs arise over the next year or within the company's current operating cycle. Investments in securities that management does not expect to sell within the next year and that do not involve the temporary use of idle cash should be shown in the investments category of a classified balance sheet.

Investments   The **investments** category includes assets, usually long term, that are not used in normal business operations and that management does not plan to convert to cash within the next year. Items in this category are securities held for long-term investment, long-term notes receivable, land held for future use, plant or equipment not used in the business, and special funds established to pay off a debt or buy a building. Also included are large permanent investments in another company for the purpose of controlling that company.

Property, Plant, and Equipment   **Property, plant, and equipment** are tangible long-term assets used in a business's day-to-day operations. They

⌐➔ Study Note

For an investment to be classified as current, management must expect to sell it within the next year or the current operating cycle, so it must be readily marketable.

represent a place to operate (land and buildings) and the equipment used to produce, sell, and deliver goods or services. They are therefore also called *operating assets* or, sometimes, *fixed assets, tangible assets, long-lived assets,* or *plant assets.* Through depreciation, the costs of these assets (except land) are spread over the periods they benefit. Past depreciation is recorded in the Accumulated Depreciation accounts.

To reduce clutter on the balance sheet, property, plant, and equipment are often combined—for example:

Property, plant, and equipment (net) $58,120

The company provides the details in a note to the financial statements.

The property, plant, and equipment category also includes natural resources owned by the company, such as forest lands, oil and gas properties, and coal mines, if they are used in the regular course of business. If they are not, they are listed in the investments category.

Intangible Assets   **Intangible assets** are long-term assets with no physical substance whose value stems from the rights or privileges they extend to their owners. Some of these assets, such as patents and copyrights, are recorded at cost, which is spread over the expected life of the right or privilege. Others with indefinite lives, such as trademarks and brands, are recorded at cost and remain at that amount unless it becomes apparent that they have lost their value. Also, goodwill, which arises in an acquisition of another company, is an intangible asset that is recorded at cost but is not amortized. It is reviewed each year for possible loss of value.

Liabilities

Liabilities are divided into two categories that are based on when the liabilities fall due: current liabilities and long-term liabilities.

Current Liabilities   **Current liabilities** are obligations that must be satisfied within one year or within the company's normal operating cycle, whichever is longer. These liabilities are typically paid out of current assets or by incurring new short-term liabilities. They include notes payable, accounts payable, the current portion of long-term debt, salaries and wages payable, and customer advances (unearned revenues).

Long-Term Liabilities   Debts that fall due more than one year in the future or beyond the normal operating cycle, which will be paid out of noncurrent assets, are **long-term liabilities**. Mortgages payable, long-term notes, bonds payable, employee pension obligations, and long-term lease liabilities generally fall into this category.

Owner's Equity

The terms *owner's equity, capital,* and *net worth* are used interchangeably. They all refer to the owner's interest in a company. The first two terms are preferred to *net worth* because most assets are recorded at original cost rather than at current value. For this reason, the ownership section will not represent "worth." It is really a claim against the assets of the company.

Although the form of business organization does not usually affect the accounting treatment of assets and liabilities, the equity section of the balance sheet differs depending on whether the business is a sole proprietorship, a partnership, or a corporation.

> **Study Note**
>
> The portion of a mortgage that is due during the next year or the current operating cycle would be classified as a current liability; the portion due after the next year or the current operating cycle would be classified as a long-term liability.

Sole Proprietorship

You are already familiar with the owner's equity section of a sole proprietorship, like the one shown in the balance sheet for Ling Auto Supply Company in Exhibit 1:

Owner's Equity

J. Ling, Capital $196,866

Partnership

The equity section of a partnership's balance sheet is called *partners' equity*. It might appear as follows:

Partners' Equity

A. J. Martin, Capital	$ 84,375	
J. Ling, Capital	112,491	
Total partners' equity		$196,866

Corporation

Corporations are by law separate, legal entities that are owned by their stockholders. The equity section of a balance sheet for a corporation is called stockholders' equity and has two parts: contributed, or paid-in, capital and retained earnings. It might appear like this:

Stockholders' Equity

Contributed capital		
Common stock, $10 par value, 10,000 shares authorized, issued, and outstanding	$100,000	
Additional paid-in capital	60,000	
Total contributed capital		$160,000
Retained earnings		36,866
Total stockholders' equity		$196,866

Remember that owner's equity accounts show the sources of and claims on assets. Of course, the claims are not on any particular asset but on the assets as a whole. It follows, then, that a corporation's contributed and earned capital accounts measure its stockholders' claims on assets and also indicate the sources of the assets. The **contributed capital** (also called *paid-in capital*) accounts reflect the amounts of assets invested by stockholders. Generally, contributed capital is shown on corporate balance sheets by two amounts: (1) the face, or par, value of issued stock and (2) the amounts paid in, or contributed, in excess of the par value per share. In the illustration above, stockholders invested amounts equal to the par value of the outstanding stock of $100,000 plus $60,000 in additional paid-in capital for a total of $160,000.

The **Retained Earnings** account is sometimes called *Earned Capital* because it represents the stockholders' claim to the assets that are earned from operations and reinvested in corporate operations. Distributions of assets to shareholders, which are called *dividends*, reduce the Retained Earnings account balance just as withdrawals of assets by the owner of a business reduce the Capital account balance. Thus the Retained Earnings account balance, in its simplest form, represents the earnings of the corporation less dividends paid to stockholders over the life of the business.

Dell's Balance Sheets

Although balance sheets generally resemble the one shown in Exhibit 1 for Ling Auto Supply Company, no two companies have financial statements that are exactly alike. The balance sheet of **Dell Computer Corporation** is a good example of some of the variations. As shown in Exhibit 2, it provides data for

EXHIBIT 2 ▶ **Classified Balance Sheet for Dell Computer Corporation**

Dell Computer Corporation
Consolidated Statements of Financial Position
(In millions)

	January 28, 2005	January 30, 2004
Assets		
Current assets:		
Cash and cash equivalents	$ 4,747	$ 4,317
Short-term investments	5,060	835
Accounts receivable, net	4,414	3,635
Inventories	459	327
Other	2,217	1,519
Total current assets	16,897	10,633
Property, plant, and equipment, net	1,691	1,517
Investments	4,319	6,770
Other non-current assets	308	391
Total assets	$23,215	$19,311
Liabilities and Stockholders' Equity		
Current liabilities:		
Accounts payable	8,895	7,316
Accrued and other	5,241	3,580
Total current liabilities	14,136	10,896
Long-term debt	505	505
Other non-current liabilities	2,089	1,630
Commitments and contingent liabilities (Note 8)	—	—
Total liabilities	16,730	13,031
Stockholders' equity:		
Preferred stock and capital in excess of $.01 par value; shares issued and outstanding: none	—	—
Common stock and capital in excess of $.01 par value; shares authorized: 7,000; shares issued: 2,769 and 2,721, respectively	8,195	6,823
Treasury stock, at cost; 284 and 165 shares, respectively	(10,758)	(6,539)
Retained earnings	9,174	6,131
Other comprehensive loss	(82)	(83)
Other	(44)	(52)
Total stockholders' equity	6,485	6,280
Total liabilities and stockholders' equity	$23,215	$19,311

Source: Dell Computer Corporation, *Annual Report*, 2005.

two years so that users can evaluate the change from one year to the next. Note that its major classifications are similar but not identical to those of Ling Auto Supply Company. For instance, Ling Auto Supply has asset categories for investments and intangibles, and Dell has an asset category called "other non-current assets," which is a small amount of its total assets. Also note that Dell has a category called "other non-current liabilities." Because this category is listed after long-term debt, it represents longer-term liabilities, due more than one year after the balance sheet date.

S T O P • R E V I E W • A P P L Y

3-1. What purpose do classified financial statements serve?

3-2. What are four common categories of assets on a classified balance sheet?

3-3. What criteria must an asset meet to be classified as current? Under what condition is an asset considered current even if it will not be realized as cash within a year? What are two examples of assets that fall into this category?

3-4. In what order should current assets be listed?

3-5. How does a short-term investment in the current assets section of a balance sheet differ from a security in the investments section?

3-6. What is an intangible asset? Give at least three examples.

3-7. Name the two major categories of liabilities.

3-8. What are the primary differences between the equity section of a partnership's or corporation's balance sheet and the equity section of a sole proprietorship's balance sheet?

Balance Sheet Classifications The lettered items below represent a classification scheme for a balance sheet. The numbered items are account titles. Match each account with the letter of the category in which it belongs, or indicate that it does not appear on the balance sheet.

a. Current assets

b. Investments

c. Property, plant, and equipment

d. Intangible assets

e. Current liabilities

f. Long-term liabilities

g. Owner's Capital

h. Not on balance sheet

1. Trademark
2. Marketable Securities
3. Land Held for Future Use
4. Property Taxes Payable
5. Note Payable in Five Years
6. Investment by Owner

7. Land Used in Operations
8. Accumulated Depreciation
9. Accounts Receivable
10. Interest Expense
11. Unearned Revenue
12. Prepaid Rent

SOLUTION		
1. d	5. f	9. a
2. a	6. g	10. h
3. b	7. c	11. e
4. e	8. c	12. a

Forms of the Income Statement

I n the income statements we have presented thus far, expenses have been deducted from revenue in a single step to arrive at net income. Here, we look at a multistep income statement and a single-step format more complex than the one we presented in earlier chapters.

Multistep Income Statement

A **multistep income statement** goes through a series of steps, or subtotals, to arrive at net income. Figure 3 compares the multistep income statement of a service company with that of a **merchandising company**, which buys and sells products, and a **manufacturing company**, which makes and sells products.

> **Study Note**
>
> The multistep income statement is a valuable analytical tool that is often overlooked. Analysts frequently convert a single-step statement into a multistep one because the latter separates operating sources of income from nonoperating ones. Owners want income to result primarily from operations, not from one-time gains or losses.

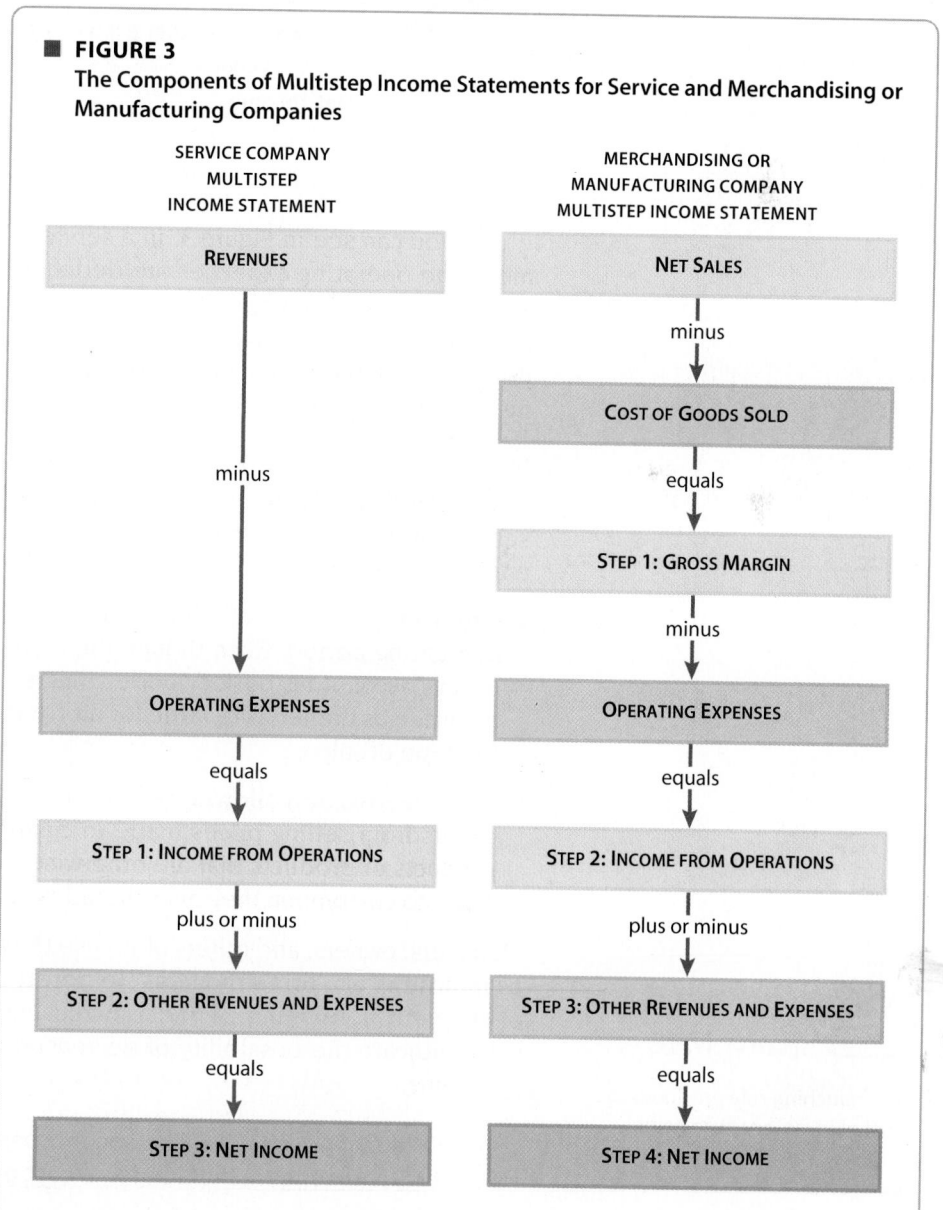

■ **FIGURE 3**
The Components of Multistep Income Statements for Service and Merchandising or Manufacturing Companies

EXHIBIT 3 ▶

Multistep Income Statement for Ling Auto Supply Company

Ling Auto Supply Company
Income Statement
For the Year Ended December 31, 20xx

Net sales		$579,312
Cost of goods sold		362,520
Gross margin		$216,792
Operating expenses		
Selling expenses	$109,560	
General and administrative expenses	69,008	
Total operating expenses		178,568
Income from operations		$ 38,224
Other revenues and expenses		
Interest income	$ 2,800	
Less interest expense	5,262	
Excess of other expenses over other revenues		2,462
Net income		$ 35,762

Step 1 — Net sales, Cost of goods sold, Gross margin
Step 2 — Operating expenses ... Income from operations
Step 3 — Other revenues and expenses
Step 4 — Net income

As you can see in Figure 3, in a service company's multistep income statement, the operating expenses are deducted from revenues in a single step to arrive at income from operations. In contrast, because manufacturing and merchandising companies make or buy goods for sale, they must include an additional step for the cost of goods sold. Exhibit 3 shows a multistep income statement for Ling Auto Supply Company, a merchandising company.

Net Sales   The first major part of a merchandising or manufacturing company's multistep income statement is **net sales**, often simply called *sales*. Net sales consist of the gross proceeds from sales (gross sales) less sales returns and allowances and any discounts allowed.

▶ **Gross sales** consist of total cash sales and total credit sales during an accounting period. Even though the cash may not be collected until the following accounting period, under the revenue recognition rule, revenue is recorded as earned when title for merchandise passes from seller to buyer at the time of sale.

▶ **Sales returns and allowances** are cash refunds, credits on account, and discounts from selling prices made to customers who have received defective products or products that are otherwise unsatisfactory. If other discounts are given to customers, they also should be deducted from gross sales.

Managers, owners, and others often use the amount of sales and trends in sales as indicators of a firm's progress. To detect trends, they compare the net sales of different accounting periods. Increasing sales suggest growth; decreasing sales indicate the possibility of decreased future earnings and other financial problems.

Cost of Goods Sold   The second part of a multistep income statement for a merchandiser or manufacturer is **cost of goods sold**, also called *cost of sales*.

Study Note

The matching rule precludes the cost of inventory from being expensed until the inventory has been sold.

Cost of goods sold (an expense) is the amount a merchandiser paid for the merchandise it sold during an accounting period. For a manufacturer, it is the cost of making the products it sold during an accounting period.

Gross Margin   The third major part of a multistep income statement for a merchandiser or manufacturer is **gross margin**, or *gross profit*, which is the difference between net sales and the cost of goods sold (Step 1 in Exhibit 3). To be successful, companies must achieve a gross margin sufficient to cover operating expenses and provide an adequate net income.

Managers are interested in both the amount and percentage of gross margin. The percentage is computed by dividing the amount of gross margin by net sales. In the case of Ling Auto Supply Company, the amount of gross margin is $216,792, and the percentage of gross margin is 37.4 percent ($216,792 ÷ $579,312). This information is useful in planning business operations. For instance, management may try to increase total sales by reducing the selling price. Although this strategy reduces the percentage of gross margin, it will work if the total of items sold increases enough to raise the absolute amount of gross margin. This is the strategy followed by discount warehouse stores like **Sam's Club** and **Costco Wholesale Corporation**.

On the other hand, management may decide to keep a high gross margin from sales and try to increase sales and the amount of gross margin by increasing operating expenses, such as advertising. This is the strategy used by upscale specialty stores like **Neiman Marcus** and **Tiffany & Co**.

Other strategies to increase gross margin from sales include using better purchasing methods to reduce cost of goods sold.

Operating Expenses   **Operating expenses**—expenses incurred in running a business other than the cost of goods sold—are the next major part of a multistep income statement. Operating expenses are often grouped into the categories of selling expenses and general and administrative expenses.

▸ Selling expenses include the costs of storing goods and preparing them for sale; preparing displays, advertising, and otherwise promoting sales; and delivering goods to a buyer if the seller has agreed to pay the cost of delivery.

▸ General and administrative expenses include expenses for accounting, personnel, credit checking, collections, and any other expenses that apply to overall operations. Although occupancy expenses, such as rent expense, insurance expense, and utilities expense, are often classified as general and administrative expenses, they can also be allocated between selling expenses and general and administrative expenses.

Careful planning and control of operating expenses can improve a company's profitability.

Income from Operations   **Income from operations**, or *operating income*, is the difference between gross margin and operating expenses (Step 2 in Exhibit 3). It represents the income from a company's main business. Income from operations is often used to compare the profitability of two or more companies or divisions within a company.

Other Revenues and Expenses   **Other revenues and expenses**, also called *nonoperating revenues and expenses*, are not related to a company's operating activities (Step 3 in Exhibit 3). This section of a multistep income statement includes revenues from investments (such as dividends and interest on stocks, bonds, and savings accounts) and interest earned on credit or notes extended to customers. It also includes interest expense and other expenses that result from borrowing money or from credit extended to the company. If a company has other kinds of revenues and expenses not related to its normal business operations, they, too, are included in this part of the income statement.

An analyst who wants to compare two companies independent of their financing methods—that is, *before* considering other revenues and expenses—would focus on income from operations.

Income Taxes **Income taxes**, also called *provision for income taxes*, represent the expense for federal, state, and local taxes on corporate income. Income taxes do not appear on the income statements of sole proprietorships and partnerships because the persons who own these businesses are the tax-paying units; they pay income taxes on their share of the business income. Corporations, however, must report and pay income taxes on their earnings. Income taxes are shown as a separate item on a corporation's income statement. Usually, the word *expense* is not used on the statement

Because federal, state, and local income taxes for corporations are substantial, they have a significant effect on business decisions. Current federal income tax rates for corporations vary from 15 percent to 35 percent depending on the amount of income before income taxes and other factors. Most other taxes, such as property and employment taxes, are included in operating expenses.

Net Income **Net income** is the final figure, or "bottom line," of an income statement. It is what remains of gross margin after operating expenses have been deducted, and other revenues and expenses have been added or deducted.(Step 4 in Exhibit 3).

▼ **EXHIBIT 4**

Multistep Income Statement for Dell Computer Corporation

Dell Computer Corporation
Consolidated Statement of Income
(In millions, except per share amounts)

	Fiscal Year Ended		
	January 28, 2005	January 30, 2004	January 31, 2003
Net revenue	$49,205	$41,444	$35,404
Cost of revenue	40,190	33,892	29,055
Gross margin	9,015	7,552	6,349
Operating expenses:			
Selling, general and administration	4,298	3,544	3,050
Research, development and engineering	463	464	455
Total operating expenses	4,761	4,008	3,505
Operating income	4,254	3,544	2,844
Investment and other income (loss), net	191	180	183
Income before income taxes	4,445	3,724	3,027
Income tax provision	1,402	1,079	905
Net income	$ 3,043	$ 2,645	$ 2,122

Source: Dell Computer Corporation, *Annual Report,* 2005.

EXHIBIT 5 ▶

Single-Step Income Statement for Ling Auto Supply Company

Ling Auto Supply Company
Income Statement
For the Year Ended December 31, 20xx

Revenues		
Net sales		$579,312
Interest income		2,800
Total revenues		$582,112
Costs and expenses		
Cost of goods sold	$362,520	
Selling expenses	109,560	
General and administrative expenses	69,008	
Interest expense	5,262	
Total costs and expenses		546,350
Net income		$ 35,762

Net income is an important performance measure because it represents the amount of earnings that accrue to owners. It is the amount transferred to owner's capital from all the income that business operations have generated during an accounting period. Both managers and owners often use net income to measure a business's financial performance over the past accounting period.

Dell's Income Statements

Like balance sheets, income statements vary among companies. You will rarely, if ever, find an income statement exactly like the one we have presented for Ling Auto Supply Company. Companies use both different terms and different structures. For example, as you can see in Exhibit 4, in its multistep income statement, **Dell Computer Corporation** provided three years of data for purposes of comparison.

Single-Step Income Statement

Exhibit 5 shows a **single-step income statement** for Ling Auto Supply Company. In this type of statement, net income is derived in a single step by putting the major categories of revenues in the first part of the statement and the major categories of costs and expenses in the second part. Both the multistep form and the single-step form have advantages: the multistep form shows the components used in deriving net income, and the single-step form has the advantage of simplicity.

Study Note

If you encounter income statement components not covered in this chapter, refer to the index at the end of the book to find the topic and read about it.

STOP • REVIEW • APPLY

4-1. What is the primary difference between the operations of a merchandising business and those of a service business? How is this difference reflected on the income statement?

4-2. Define *gross margin*. Why is it important?

4-3. Why are other revenues and expenses separated from operating revenues and expenses in a multistep income statement?

4-4. Explain how a multistep income statement differs from a single-step income statement. What are the merits of each form?

Income Statement Classification   A classification scheme for a multistep income statement and a list of accounts appear below. Match each account with the category in which it belongs, or indicate that it is not on the income statement.

a. Net sales

b. Cost of goods sold

c. Selling expenses

d. General and administrative expenses

e. Other revenues and expenses

f. Not on income statement

1. Sales Returns and Allowances

2. Cost of Sales

3. Dividend Income

4. Delivery Expense

5. Office Salaries Expense

6. Wages Payable

7. Sales Salaries Expense

8. Advertising Expense

9. Interest Expense

10. Commissions Expense

SOLUTION

1. a		6. f	
2. b		7. c	
3. e		8. c	
4. c		9. e	
5. d		10. c	

Using Classified Financial Statements

LO5   Use classified financial statements to evaluate liquidity and profitability.

Owners and creditors base their decisions largely on their assessments of a firm's potential liquidity and profitability, and in making those assessments, they often rely on ratios. As you will see in the following pages, ratios use the components of classified financial statements to reflect how well a firm has performed in terms of maintaining liquidity and achieving profitability.

Evaluation of Liquidity

As you know, *liquidity* means having enough money on hand to pay bills when they are due and to take care of unexpected needs for cash. In an earlier chapter, we introduced the cash return on assets ratio, a liquidity measure that is computed by dividing net cash flows from operating activities by average total assets. Here, we introduce two additional measures of liquidity: working capital and the current ratio.

Study Note

Accounts must be classified correctly before the ratios are computed. If they are not classified correctly, the ratios will be incorrect.

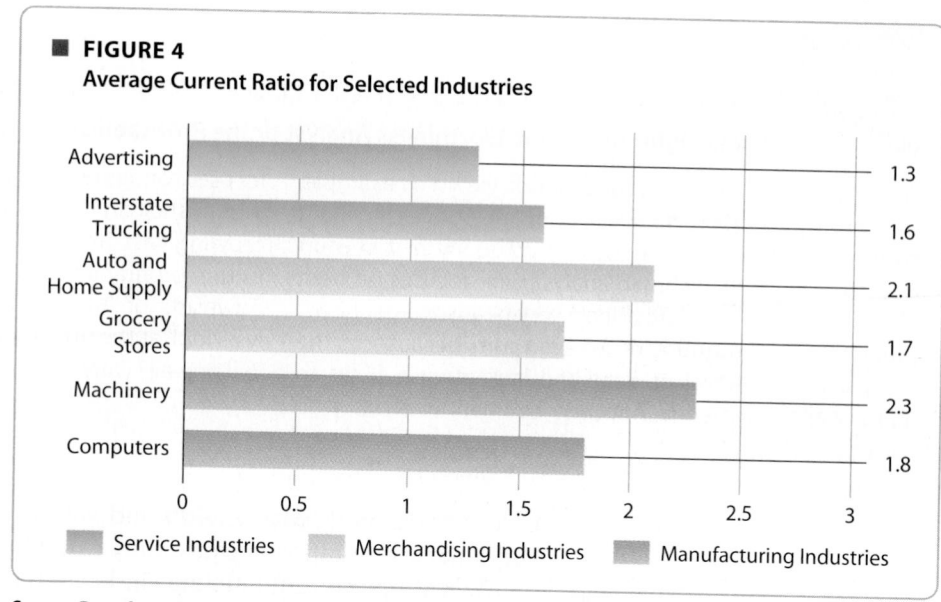

■ **FIGURE 4**
Average Current Ratio for Selected Industries

Industry	Ratio
Advertising	1.3
Interstate Trucking	1.6
Auto and Home Supply	2.1
Grocery Stores	1.7
Machinery	2.3
Computers	1.8

Service Industries   Merchandising Industries   Manufacturing Industries

Source: Data from Dun & Bradstreet, *Industry Norms and Key Business Ratios,* 2004–2005.

Working Capital

Working capital is the amount by which current assets exceed current liabilities. It is an important measure of liquidity because current liabilities must be satisfied within one year or one operating cycle, whichever is longer, and current assets are used to pay the current liabilities. Thus, the excess of current assets over current liabilities—the working capital—is what is on hand to continue business operations.

For Ling Auto Supply Company, working capital is computed as follows:

Current assets	$248,712
Less current liabilities	85,366
Working capital	$163,346

Working capital can be used to buy inventory, obtain credit, and finance expanded sales. Lack of working capital can lead to a company's failure.

Current Ratio

The current ratio is closely related to working capital. Many bankers and other creditors believe it is a good indicator of a company's ability to pay its debts on time. The **current ratio** is the ratio of current assets to current liabilities. For Ling Auto Supply Company, it is computed like this:

$$\text{Current Ratio} = \frac{\text{Current Assets}}{\text{Current Liabilities}} = \frac{\$248,712}{\$85,366} = 2.9$$

Thus, Ling Auto Supply has $2.90 of current assets for each $1.00 of current liabilities. Is that good or bad? The answer requires a comparison of this year's current ratio with ratios for earlier years and with similar measures for companies in the same industry.

As Figure 4 illustrates, the average current ratio varies from industry to industry. For the advertising industry, which has no merchandise inventory, the current ratio is 1.3. The auto and home supply industry, in which companies carry large merchandise inventories, has an average current ratio of 2.1. The current ratio for Ling Auto Supply Corporation, 2.9, exceeds the average for its industry.

A very low current ratio, of course, can be unfavorable, indicating that a company will not be able to pay its debts on time. But that is not always the

The answer depends on your point of view. For example, the future of **Amazon.com**, the online retailer, sparked controversy in the big investment company of **Lehman Brothers Inc.** One Lehman analyst, who focuses on debt and credit worthiness, provided a very bearish (pessimistic) prediction of the future of Amazon.com because of the company's high level of debt and lack of cash flows to make debt payments. Another Lehman analyst, who focuses on growth and future profitability, was bullish (optimistic) on Amazon.com because the company was growing fast and reducing costs, which should lead to future profitability. Credit analysts tend to look at the downside of future prospects, whereas profitability analysts look at the upside. Which view of Amazon.com's future will prevail? Only time will tell.[12]

case. For example, **McDonald's** and various other successful companies have very low current ratios because they carefully plan their cash flows.

A very high current ratio may indicate that a company is not using its assets to the best advantage. In other words, it could probably use its excess funds more effectively to increase its overall profit.

Evaluation of Profitability

Just as important as paying bills on time is *profitability*—the ability to earn a satisfactory income. As a goal, profitability competes with liquidity for managerial attention because liquid assets, although important, are not the best profit-producing resources. Cash, of course, means purchasing power, but a satisfactory profit can be made only if purchasing power is used to buy profit-producing (and less liquid) assets, such as inventory and long-term assets.

To evaluate a company's profitability, you must relate its current performance to its past performance and prospects for the future, as well as to the averages of other companies in the same industry. The following are the ratios commonly used to evaluate a company's ability to earn income:

1. Profit margin
2. Asset turnover
3. Return on assets
4. Debt to equity ratio
5. Return on equity

In previous chapters, we introduced the profit margin and return on assets ratios. Here, we review these ratios, introduce the other profitability ratios, and show their interrelationships.

Profit Margin The **profit margin** shows the percentage of each sales dollar that results in net income. It should not be confused with gross margin, which is not a ratio but rather the amount by which revenues exceed the cost of goods sold. Ling Auto Supply Company has a profit margin of 6.2 percent. It is computed as follows:

$$\text{Profit Margin} = \frac{\text{Net Income}}{\text{Net Sales}} = \frac{\$35,762}{\$579,312} = .062, \text{ or } 6.2\%$$

Thus, on each dollar of net sales, Ling Auto Supply makes 6.2 cents. A difference of 1 or 2 percent in a company's profit margin can be the difference between a fair year and a very profitable one.

Asset Turnover   The **asset turnover** ratio measures how efficiently assets are used to produce sales. In other words, it shows how many dollars of sales are generated by each dollar of assets. A company with a higher asset turnover uses its assets more productively than one with a lower asset turnover.

The asset turnover ratio is computed by dividing net sales by average total assets. Average total assets are the sum of assets at the beginning of an accounting period and at the end of the period divided by 2. For example, if Ling Auto Supply Company had assets of $297,240 at the beginning of the year, its asset turnover would be computed as follows:

$$\text{Asset Turnover} = \frac{\text{Net Sales}}{\text{Average Total Assets}}$$

$$= \frac{\$579,312}{(\$317,832 + \$297,240) \div 2} = \frac{\$579,312}{\$307,536} = 1.9 \text{ times}$$

Thus, Ling Auto Supply would produce $1.90 in sales for each dollar invested in assets. This ratio shows a relationship between an income statement figure (net sales) and a balance sheet figure (total assets).

Return on Assets   Both the profit margin and asset turnover ratios have limitations. The profit margin ratio does not consider the assets necessary to produce income, and the asset turnover ratio does not take into account the amount of income produced. The **return on assets** ratio overcomes these deficiencies by relating net income to average total assets. For Ling Auto Supply, it is computed like this:

$$\text{Return on Assets} = \frac{\text{Net Income}}{\text{Average Total Assets}}$$

$$= \frac{\$35,762}{(\$317,832 + \$297,240) \div 2} = \frac{\$35,762}{\$307,536} = .116, \text{ or } 11.6\%$$

For each dollar invested, Ling's assets generate 11.6 cents of net income. This ratio indicates the income-generating strength (profit margin) of the company's resources and how efficiently the company is using all its assets (asset turnover).

Return on assets, then, combines profit margin and asset turnover:

$\dfrac{\text{Net Income}}{\text{Net Sales}}$ $\times$	$\dfrac{\text{Net Sales}}{\text{Average Total Assets}}$ =	$\dfrac{\text{Net Income}}{\text{Average Total Assets}}$
Profit Margin $\times$	Asset Turnover =	Return on Assets
6.2% $\times$	1.9 times =	11.8%*

*The slight difference between 11.8 and 11.6 percent is due to rounding.

Thus, a company's management can improve overall profitability by increasing the profit margin, the asset turnover, or both. Similarly, in evaluating a company's overall profitability, a financial statement user must consider how these two ratios interact to produce return on assets.

By studying Figures 5, 6, and 7, you can see the different ways in which various industries combine profit margin and asset turnover to produce return on assets. For instance, by comparing the return on assets for grocery stores and computer companies, you can see how they achieve that return in very different ways. The grocery store industry has a profit margin of 1.6 percent, which when multiplied by an asset turnover of 4.9 times gives a return on assets of 7.8 percent. The computer industry has a higher profit margin, 4.3 percent, and a lower asset turnover, 1.7 times, and produces a return on assets of 7.3 percent, which is about the same as in the grocery industry.

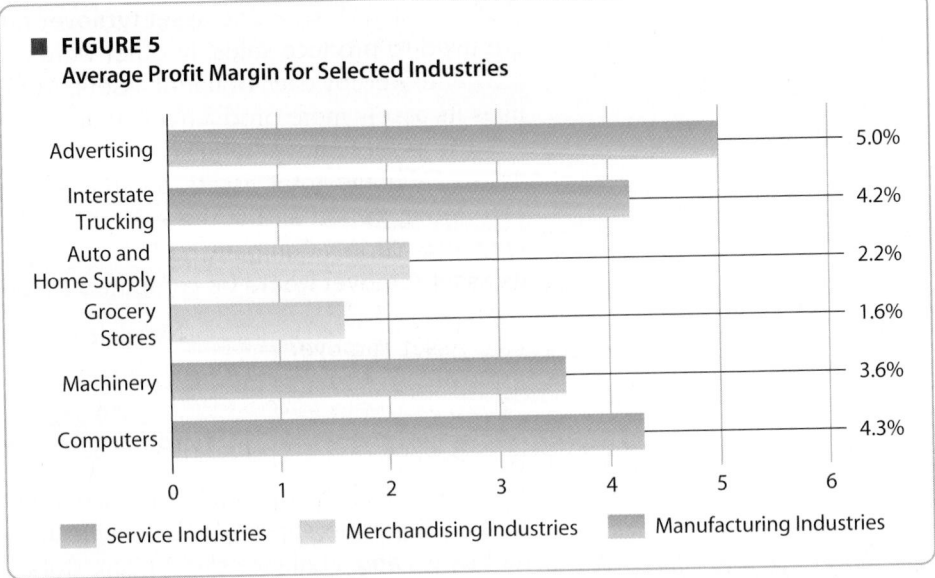

■ **FIGURE 5**
Average Profit Margin for Selected Industries

Source: Data from Dun & Bradstreet, *Industry Norms and Key Business Ratios,* 2004–2005.

Ling Auto Supply's profit margin of 6.2 percent is well above the auto and home supply industry's average, but its asset turnover of 1.9 times lags behind the industry average. Ling is sacrificing asset turnover to achieve a higher profit margin. This strategy is evidently working, because Ling's return on assets of 11.6 percent is much higher than the industry average.

Debt to Equity Ratio   Another useful measure of profitability is the **debt to equity ratio**, which shows the proportion of a company's assets that is financed by creditors and the proportion that is financed by the owner. This ratio is computed by dividing total liabilities by owner's equity. The balance sheets of most companies do not show total liabilities; a short way of determining them is to deduct the total owner's equity from total assets.

A debt to equity ratio of 1.0 means that total liabilities equal owner's equity—that half of a company's assets are financed by creditors. A ratio of 0.5

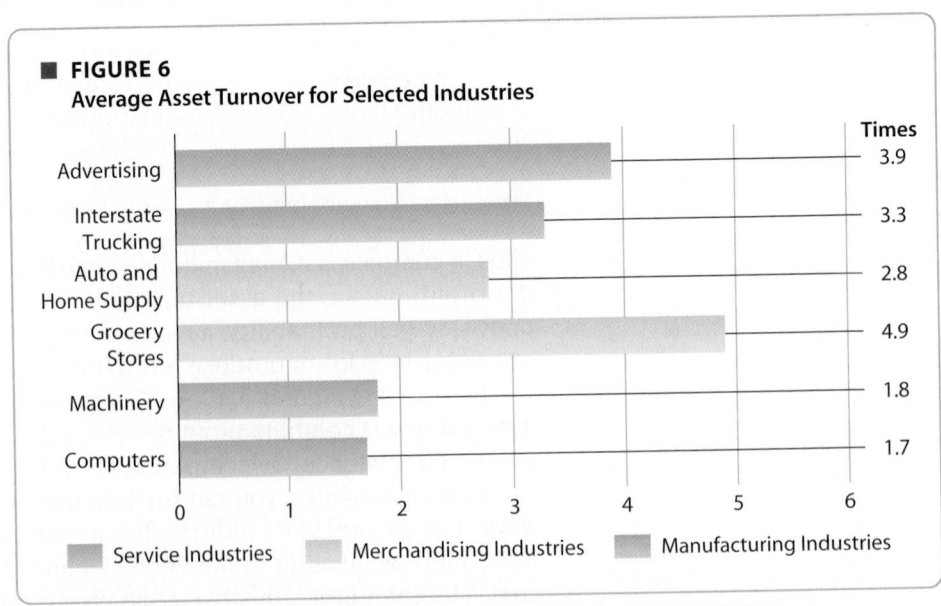

■ **FIGURE 6**
Average Asset Turnover for Selected Industries

Source: Data from Dun & Bradstreet, *Industry Norms and Key Business Ratios,* 2004–2005.

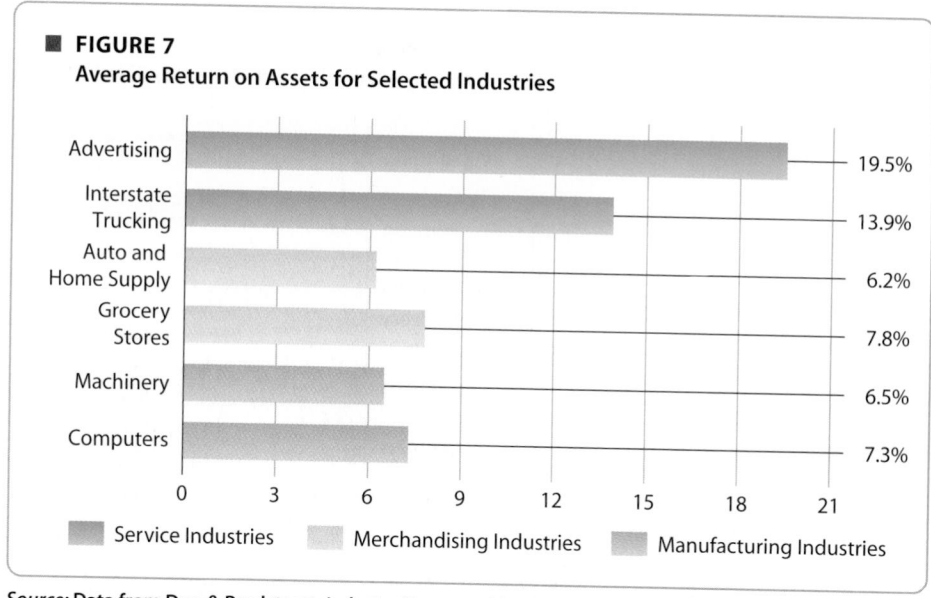

■ **FIGURE 7**
Average Return on Assets for Selected Industries

- Advertising — 19.5%
- Interstate Trucking — 13.9%
- Auto and Home Supply — 6.2%
- Grocery Stores — 7.8%
- Machinery — 6.5%
- Computers — 7.3%

Service Industries   Merchandising Industries   Manufacturing Industries

Source: Data from Dun & Bradstreet, *Industry Norms and Key Business Ratios,* 2004–2005.

means that one-third of a company's total assets are financed by creditors. A company with a high debt to equity ratio is at risk in poor economic times because it must continue to repay creditors. Owner's investments, on the other hand, do not have to be repaid, and withdrawals can be deferred when a company suffers because of a poor economy.

Ling Auto Supply's debt to equity ratio is computed as follows:

$$\text{Debt to Equity Ratio} = \frac{\text{Total Liabilities}}{\text{Owner's Equity}} = \frac{\$120,966}{\$196,866} = .614, \text{ or } 61.4\%$$

The debt to equity ratio of 61.4 percent means that Ling Auto Supply receives less than half of its financing from creditors and that it receives more than half from the owner.

The debt to equity ratio does not fit neatly into either the liquidity or profitability category. It is clearly very important to liquidity analysis because it relates to debt and its repayment. It is also relevant to profitability for two reasons:

1. Creditors are interested in the proportion of the business that is debt-financed because the more debt a company has, the more profit it must earn to ensure the payment of interest to creditors.

2. Owners are interested in the proportion of the business that is debt-financed because the amount of interest paid on debt affects the amount of profit left to provide a return on the owner's investment.

The debt to equity ratio also shows how much expansion is possible through borrowing additional long-term funds.

Figure 8 shows that the debt to equity ratio in selected industries varies from a low of 112.3 percent in the auto and home supply industry to a high of 241.3 percent in the advertising industry.

Return on Equity   Of course, owners are interested in how much they have earned on their investment in the business. Their **return on equity** is measured by the ratio of net income to average owner's equity. Taking the ending owner's equity from the balance sheet and assuming that beginning owner's

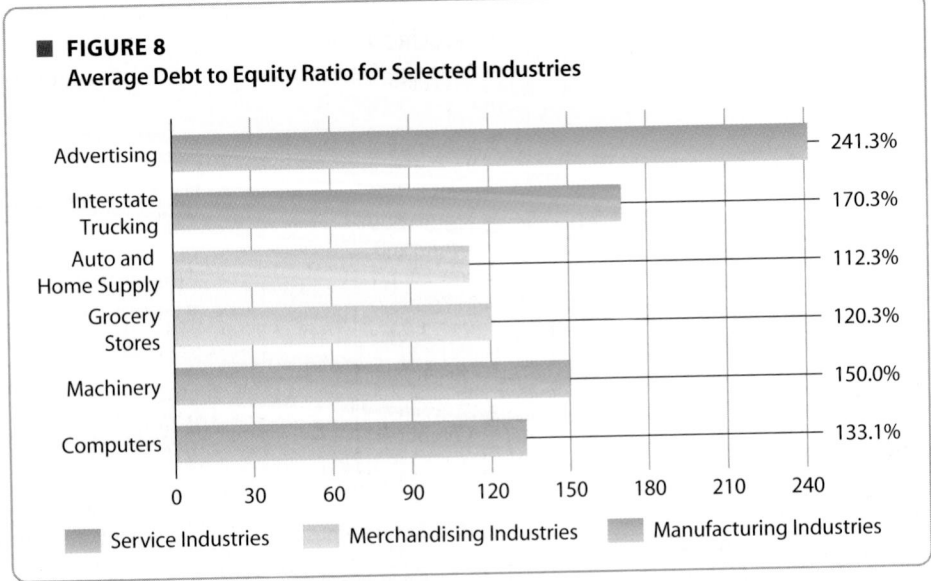

■ FIGURE 8
Average Debt to Equity Ratio for Selected Industries

Source: Data from Dun & Bradstreet, *Industry Norms and Key Business Ratios*, 2004–2005.

equity is $201,106, Ling Auto Supply Company's return on equity is computed as follows:

$$\text{Return on Equity} = \frac{\text{Net Income}}{\text{Average Owner's Equity}}$$

$$= \frac{\$35,762}{(\$196,866 + \$201,106) \div 2} = \frac{\$35,762}{\$198,986} = .180, \text{ or } 18.0\%$$

Thus, in 20xx, Ling earned 18.0 cents for every dollar invested by the owner. Whether this is an acceptable return depends on several factors, such as how much the company earned in previous years and how much other companies in the same industry earned. As measured by return on equity, the advertising industry is the most profitable of our sample industries, with a return on equity of 66.5 percent (see Figure 9). Ling Auto Supply Company's average return on equity of 18.0 percent is better than the average of 13.1 percent for the auto and home supply industry.

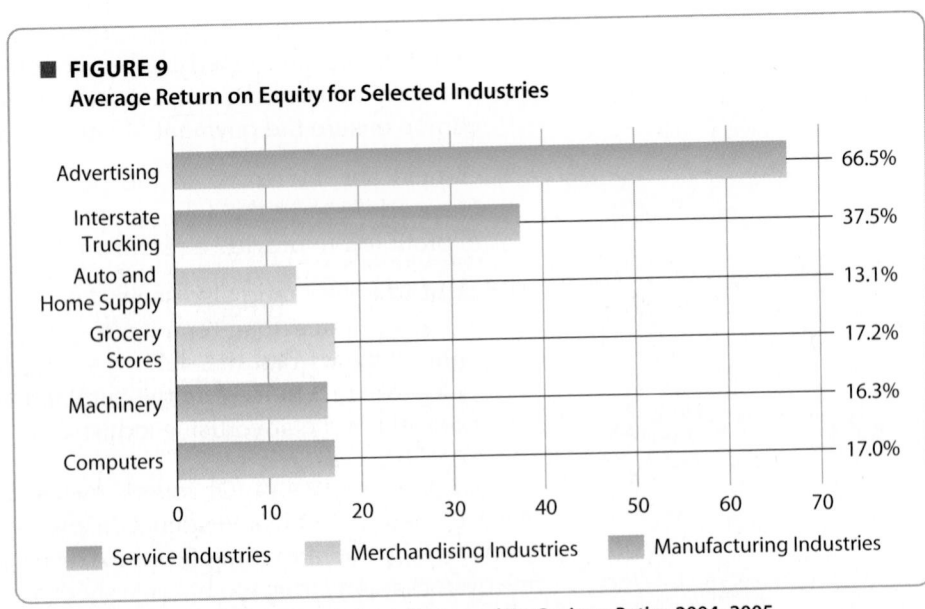

■ FIGURE 9
Average Return on Equity for Selected Industries

Source: Data from Dun & Bradstreet, *Industry Norms and Key Business Ratios*, 2004–2005.

Return on equity—the ratio of net income to average owner's equity—is an important measure of a company's profitability. It indicates how much owners or stockholders have earned on their investments. At one time, Coca-Cola Company was among a few companies that earned a 20 percent return on equity.

FOCUS ON BUSINESS PRACTICE
To What Level of Profitability Should a Company Aspire?

At one time, a company earning a 20 percent return on equity ranked among the elite. Only **Disney**, **Wal-Mart**, **Coca-Cola**, and a few other companies were able to achieve this level of profitability. However, in the first quarter of 1995, for the first time, the average company of the Standard & Poor's 500 companies made a return on equity of 20.12 percent. *The Wall Street Journal* described this performance as "akin to the average ball player hitting .350."[13] This meant that stockholders' equity would double every four years.

Why did this happen? First, a good business environment and cost cutting led to more profitable operations. Second, special charges and other accounting transactions reduced stockholders' equity for many companies. In this way, the denominator of the return on equity was reduced, thus increasing the ratio. This strategy of manipulating the denominator cannot last forever. After the economy dropped after 9/11, the return on equity for the S&P 500 dropped to half its former level.

Until 2000, the number of companies with a return on equity of more than 20 percent continued to increase, but during 2001, 2002, and 2003 this number declined. When earnings are declining, companies tend to emphasize measures of performance other than those related to profitability.

S T O P • R E V I E W • A P P L Y

5-1. Define *liquidity*, and name two measures of liquidity.

5-2. How is the current ratio computed, and why is it important?

5-3. Which is the more important goal, liquidity or profitability? Explain your answer.

5-4. Name five measures of profitability.

5-5. What is the relationship among profit margin, asset turnover, and return on assets?

A LOOK BACK AT

DELL COMPUTER CORPORATION

In the Decision Point at the beginning of the chapter, we noted that **Dell's** objective is "to maximize stockholder value by executing a strategy based on ...a balance of three priorities: liquidity, profitability, and growth."[14] We also noted that in judging whether a company has achieved its objectives, investors, creditors, and others analyze relationships between key numbers in the company's financial statements. We asked these questions:

- **How should financial statements be organized to provide the best information?**
- **What key measures best capture a company's financial performance?**

As you saw in Exhibits 2 and 4, Dell uses a classified balance sheet and a multistep income statement to communicate its financial results to users. The Financial Highlights from Dell's annual report that we presented in the Decision Point show that the company increased its revenues by 18.7 percent between 2004 and 2005. More significantly, it increased its operating income by 34.3 percent. Net income increased by only 15.0 percent, due to increases in income taxes.

Using data from Dell's balance sheets and income statements, we can analyze how the company achieved this growth by computing its profitability ratios (dollars are in millions):

	2005	**2004**
$\dfrac{\text{Net Income}}{\text{Net Revenues}}$	$\dfrac{\$3,043}{\$49,205}$	$\dfrac{\$2,645}{\$41,444}$
K/R Profit Margin:	6.2%	6.4%
$\dfrac{\text{Net Revenues}}{\text{Average Total Assets}}$	$\dfrac{\$49,205}{(\$23,215 + \$19,311) \div 2}$	$\dfrac{\$41,444}{(\$19,311 + \$15,470^*) \div 2}$
	$\dfrac{\$49,205}{\$21,263}$	$\dfrac{\$41,444}{\$17,390.5}$
K/R Asset Turnover:	2.3 times	2.4 times
$\dfrac{\text{Net Income}}{\text{Average Total Assets}}$	$\dfrac{\$3,043}{(\$23,215 + \$19,311) \div 2}$	$\dfrac{\$2,645}{(\$19,311 + \$15,470^*) \div 2}$
	$\dfrac{\$3,043}{\$21,263}$	$\dfrac{\$2,645}{\$17,390.5}$
K/R Return on Assets:	14.3, or 14.3%	15.2, or 15.2%

*From Dell Computer Corporation's 2004 annual report.

By relating these three ratios to each other and to the computer industry averages in Figures 5, 6, and 7, we can see that Dell's profitability is clearly superior:

	Profit Margin	×	Asset Turnover	=	Return on Assets
2005:	6.2%	×	2.3 times	=	14.3%
2004:	6.4%	×	2.4 times	=	15.2%*
Industry average	4.3%	×	1.7 times	=	7.3%

*The differences are due to rounding.

Dell's return on assets declined in 2005 by small decreases in both profit margin and asset turnover. It did better than its industry competitors by a substantial margin on both its profit margin and return on assets. Its asset turnover was stable and close to the industry average.

Dell also took advantage of debt financing to leverage its profitability into a very high return on equity, as shown by its debt to equity and return on equity ratios:

	2005	2004
$\dfrac{\text{Total Liabilities}}{\text{Total Stockholders' Equity}}$	$\dfrac{\$16,730}{\$6,485}$	$\dfrac{\$13,031}{\$6,280}$
K/R Debt to Equity Ratio:	2.58, or 258%	2.08, or 208%
Industry Average:	133.1%	
$\dfrac{\text{Net Income}}{\text{Average Stockholders' Equity}}$	$\dfrac{\$3,043}{(\$6,485 + \$6,280) \div 2}$	$\dfrac{\$2,645}{(\$6,280 + \$4,873^*) \div 2}$
	$\dfrac{\$3,043}{\$6,382.5}$	$\dfrac{\$2,645}{\$5,576.5}$
K/R Return on Equity:	47.7%	47.4%
Industry average:	17.0%	

*From Dell Computer Corporation's 2004 annual report.

By astute management of average assets, debt, and equity, Dell transformed a profit margin of 6.2 percent into a return to its stockholders of 47.7 percent, a performance almost 3 times better than that of its competitors.

CHAPTER REVIEW

REVIEW of Learning Objectives

LO1 Describe the objectives and qualitative characteristics of financial reporting and the ethical responsibilities that financial reporting involves.

The objectives of financial reporting are to provide information useful in making investment and credit decisions, judging cash flow prospects, and understanding business resources, claims to those resources, and changes in them.

The most important qualitative characteristics of accounting information are understandability and usefulness. Understandability depends on the knowledge of the user and the ability of the accountant to provide useful information. Usefulness is a function of two primary characteristics, relevance and reliability. Information is relevant when it has an effect on a decision. Information that is relevant has both feedback and predictive value and is timely. To be reliable, information must represent what it is supposed to represent and be verifiable and neutral. Since the passage of the Sarbanes-Oxley Act in 2002, CEOs and CFOs have been required to certify to the accuracy and completeness of their companies' financial statements.

LO2 Define and describe the conventions of *comparability* and *consistency, materiality, conservatism, full disclosure,* and *cost-benefit.*

Because accountants' measurements are not exact, certain conventions are applied to help users interpret financial statements. The first of these conventions is comparability and consistency. Consistency requires the use of the same accounting procedures from period to period and enhances the comparability of financial statements. The materiality convention has to do with determining the relative importance of an item. Conservatism entails using the procedure that is least likely to overstate assets and income. Full disclosure means including all relevant information in the financial statements. The cost-benefit convention holds that the benefits to be gained from providing accounting information should be greater than the costs of providing it.

LO3 Identify and describe the basic components of a classified balance sheet.

The basic components of a classified balance sheet are as follows:

Assets	Liabilities	Owner's Equity
Current assets	Current liabilities	Owner's Capital
Investments	Long-term liabilities	
Property, plant, and equipment		
Intangible assets		

Current assets are cash and other assets that a firm can reasonably expect to convert to cash or use up during the next year or the normal operating cycle, whichever is longer. Investments are assets, usually long term, that are not used in the normal operation of a business. Property, plant, and equipment are tangible long-term assets used in day-to-day operations. Intangible assets are long-term assets with no physical substance whose value stems from the rights or privileges they extend to owners.

A current liability is an obligation due to be paid or performed during the next year or the normal operating cycle, whichever is longer. Long-term liabilities are debts that fall due more than one year in the future or beyond the normal operating cycle.

The equity section of a sole proprietorship's balance sheet differs from the equity section of a partnership's or corporation's balance sheet in that it does not have subcategories for contributed capital (the assets invested by stockholders) and retained earnings (stockholders' claim to assets earned from operations and reinvested in operations).

LO4 Describe the features of multistep and single-step classified income statements.

Classified income statements for external reporting can be in multistep or single-step form. The multistep form arrives at net income through a series of steps; the single-step form arrives at it in a single step. A multistep income statement usually has a separate section for other revenues and expenses.

LO5 Use classified financial statements to evaluate liquidity and profitability.

In evaluating a company's liquidity and profitability, investors (owners) and creditors rely on the data provided in classified financial statements. Two measures of liquidity are working capital and the current ratio. Five measures of profitability are profit margin, asset turnover, return on assets, debt to equity ratio, and return on equity. Industry averages are useful in interpreting these ratios.

REVIEW of Concepts and Terminology

The following concepts and terms were introduced in this chapter:

Accounting conventions: Rules of thumb, or general principles, for recording transactions and preparing financial statements. **(LO1)**

Classified financial statements: General-purpose external financial statements that are divided into subcategories. **(LO3)**

Comparability: The convention of presenting information in a way that enables decision makers to recognize similarities, differences, and trends over different periods in the same company and among different companies. **(LO2)**

Conservatism: The convention that when faced with two equally acceptable alternatives, the accountant chooses the one least likely to overstate assets and income. **(LO2)**

Consistency: The convention requiring that once a company has adopted an accounting procedure, it must use it from one period to the next unless a note to the financial statements informs users of a change in procedure. **(LO2)**

Contributed capital: Assets that stockholders have invested in a corporation. **(LO3)**

Cost-benefit: The convention that the benefits gained from providing accounting information should be greater than the costs of providing that information. **(LO2)**

Cost of goods sold: The amount a merchandiser paid for the merchandise it sold during an accounting period or the cost to a manufacturer of making the products it sold during an accounting period. Also called *cost of sales*. **(LO4)**

Current assets: Cash and other assets that a company can reasonably expect to convert to cash, sell, or consume within one year or its normal operating cycle, whichever is longer. **(LO3)**

Current liabilities: Obligations due to be paid or performed within one year or within the normal operating cycle, whichever is longer. **(LO3)**

Full disclosure: The convention requiring that a company's financial statements and the accompanying notes present all information relevant to the users' understanding of the statements. **(LO2)**

Gross margin: The difference between net sales and cost of goods sold. Also called *gross profit*. **(LO4)**

Gross sales: Total sales for cash and on credit during an accounting period. **(LO4)**

Income from operations: Gross margin minus operating expenses. Also called *operating income*. **(LO4)**

Income taxes: A category for the expense of federal, state, and local taxes that appears only on the income statements of corporations. Also called *provision for income taxes*. **(LO4)**

Intangible assets: Long-term assets with no physical substance whose value stems from the rights or privileges they extend to their owners. **(LO3)**

Investments: Assets, usually long term, that are not used in the normal operation of a business and that management does not intend to convert to cash within the next year. **(LO3)**

Long-term liabilities: Debts that fall due more than one year in the future or beyond the normal operating cycle. **(LO3)**

Manufacturing company: A company that makes and sells products. **(LO4)**

Materiality: The convention that refers to the relative importance of an item or event in a financial statement and its influence on the decisions of the users of financial statements. **(LO2)**

Merchandising company: A company, either a wholesaler or retailer, that buys and sells products. **(LO4)**

Multistep income statement: An income statement that goes through a series of steps to arrive at net income. **(LO4)**

Net income: What remains of gross margin after operating expenses have been deducted, and other revenues and expenses have been added or deducted. **(LO4)**

Net sales: The gross proceeds from sales of merchandise (gross sales) less sales returns and allowances and any discounts allowed. Often called *sales.* **(LO4)**

Normal operating cycle: The average time a company needs to go from spending cash to receiving cash. **(LO3)**

Operating expenses: Expenses other than cost of goods sold incurred in running a business. **(LO4)**

Other assets: A balance sheet category that some companies use to group all assets other than current assets and property, plant, and equipment. **(LO3)**

Other revenues and expenses: The section of a multistep income statement that includes revenues and expenses not related to business operations. Also called *nonoperating revenues and expenses.* **(LO4)**

Property, plant, and equipment: Tangible long-term assets used in the continuing operation of a business. Also called *operating assets, fixed assets, tangible assets, long-lived assets,* or *plant assets.* **(LO3)**

Qualitative characteristics: Standards for judging accounting information. **(LO1)**

Relevance: The qualitative characteristic of information that has a direct effect on a decision. **(LO1)**

Reliability: The qualitative characteristic of information that represents what it is supposed to represent and is verifiable and neutral. **(LO1)**

Retained Earnings: The account that reflects stockholders' claims to the assets that are earned from corporate operations and that are reinvested in operations. Also called *Earned Capital.* **(LO3)**

Sales returns and allowances: Refunds, credits, and discounts given to customers who have received defective goods. **(LO4)**

Single-step income statement: An income statement that arrives at net income in a single step. **(LO4)**

Understandability: The qualitative characteristic of information that enables users to perceive its meaning. **(LO1)**

Usefulness: The qualitative characteristic of information that is relevant and reliable. **(LO1)**

Working capital: A measure of liquidity that shows the net current assets on hand to continue business operations; Total Current Assets − Total Current Liabilities. **(LO5)**

Key Ratios

Asset turnover: A measure of profitability that shows how efficiently assets are used to produce sales; Net Sales ÷ Average Total Assets. **(LO5)**

Current ratio: A measure of liquidity; Current Assets ÷ Current Liabilities. **(LO5)**

Debt to equity ratio: A measure of profitability that shows the proportion of a company's assets that is financed by creditors and the proportion financed by the owner; Total Liabilities ÷ Owner's Equity. **(LO5)**

Profit margin: A measure of profitability that shows the percentage of each sales dollar that results in net income; Net Income ÷ Net Sales. **(LO5)**

Return on assets: A measure of profitability that shows how efficiently a company uses its assets to produce income; Net Income ÷ Average Total Assets. **(LO5)**

Return on equity: A measure of profitability that relates the amount earned by a business to the owner's investment in the business; Net Income ÷ Average Owner's Equity. **(LO5)**

REVIEW Problem

LO5 **Using Ratios to Analyze Liquidity and Profitability**

%/® Flavin Shirt Company has been facing increased competition from overseas shirtmakers. Its total assets and owner's equity at the beginning of 20x7 were $690,000 and $590,000, respectively. A summary of the firm's data for 20x7 and 20x8 follows.

	20x8	20x7
Current assets	$ 200,000	$ 170,000
Total assets	880,000	710,000
Current liabilities	90,000	50,000
Long-term liabilities	150,000	50,000

	20x8	20x7
Owner's equity	$ 640,000	$ 610,000
Sales	1,200,000	1,050,000
Net income	60,000	80,000

Required

Use (1) liquidity analysis and (2) profitability analysis to document the Flavin Shirt Company's declining financial position.

Answer to Review Problem

1. Liquidity analysis

	A	B	C	D	E
1		Current Assets	Current Liabilities	Working Capital	Current Ratio
2	20x7	$170,000	$50,000	$120,000	3.40
3	20x8	200,000	90,000	110,000	2.22
4	Decrease in working capital			$ 10,000	
5	Decrease in current ratio				1.18
6					

Both working capital and the current ratio declined between 20x7 and 20x8 because the $40,000 increase in current liabilities ($90,000 − $50,000) was greater than the $30,000 increase in current assets.

2. Profitability analysis

A B C D	E Net Income	F G H Sales	I Profit Margin	J Average Total Assets	K Asset Turnover	L Return on Assets	M Average Stockholders' Equity	N Return on Equity
20x7	$80,000	$1,050,000	7.6%	$700,000[1]	1.50	11.4%	$600,000[3]	13.3%
20x8	60,000	1,200,000	5.0%	795,000[2]	1.51	7.5%	625,000[4]	9.6%
Increase (decrease)	($20,000)	$ 150,000	-2.6%	$ 95,000	0.01	-3.9%	$ 25,000	-3.7%
[1] ($710,000 + $690,000) ÷ 2 = $700,000								
[2] ($880,000 + $710,000) ÷ 2 = $795,000								
[3] ($610,000 + $590,000) ÷ 2 = $600,000								
[4] ($640,000 + $610,000) ÷ 2 = $625,000								

Net income decreased by $20,000 despite an increase in sales of $150,000 and an increase in average total assets of $95,000. Thus, the profit margin fell from 7.6 percent to 5.0 percent, and return on assets fell from 11.4 percent to 7.5 percent. Asset turnover showed almost no change and so did not contribute to the decline in profitability. The decrease in return on equity, from 13.3 percent to 9.6 percent, was not as great as the decrease in return on assets because the growth in total assets was financed mainly by debt rather than by owner's equity, as shown in the capital structure analysis below.

	A	B	C	D
1		Total Liabilities	Stockholders' Equity	Debt to Equity Ratio
2	20x7	$100,000	$610,000	16.4%
3	20x8	240,000	640,000	37.5%
4	Increase	$140,000	$ 30,000	21.1%
5				

Total liabilities increased by $140,000, while owner's equity increased by $30,000. Thus, the amount of the business financed by debt in relation to the amount financed by owner's equity increased between 20x7 and 20x8.

CHAPTER ASSIGNMENTS

BUILDING Your Basic Knowledge and Skills

Short Exercises

LO1 Objectives and Qualitative Characteristics

SE 1. Identify each of the following statements as either an objective (O) of financial information or as a qualitative (Q) characteristic of accounting information:

1. Information about business resources, claims to those resources, and changes in them should be provided.
2. Decision makers must be able to interpret accounting information.
3. Information that is useful in making investment and credit decisions should be furnished.
4. Accounting information must be relevant and reliable.
5. Information useful in assessing cash flow prospects should be provided.

LO2 Accounting Conventions

SE 2. State which of the accounting conventions—comparability and consistency, materiality, conservatism, full disclosure, or cost-benefit—is being followed in each case described below.

1. Management provides detailed information about the company's long-term debt in the notes to the financial statements.
2. A company does not account separately for discounts received for prompt payment of accounts payable because few of these transactions occur and the total amount of the discounts is small.
3. Management eliminates a weekly report on property, plant, and equipment acquisitions and disposals because no one finds it useful.
4. A company follows the policy of recognizing a loss on inventory when the market value of an item falls below its cost but does nothing if the market value rises.
5. When several accounting methods are acceptable, management chooses a single method and follows that method from year to year.

LO3 **Classification of Accounts: Balance Sheet**

SE 3. Tell whether each of the following accounts is a current asset; an investment; property, plant, and equipment; an intangible asset; a current liability; a long-term liability; owner's equity; or not on the balance sheet:

1. Delivery Trucks
2. Accounts Payable
3. Note Payable (due in 90 days)
4. Delivery Expense
5. Owner's Capital

6. Prepaid Insurance
7. Trademark
8. Investment to Be Held Six Months
9. Factory Not Used in Business

LO3 **Classified Balance Sheet**

SE 4. Using the following accounts, prepare a classified balance sheet at year end, May 31, 20xx: Accounts Payable, $800; Accounts Receivable, $1,100; Accumulated Depreciation–Equipment, $700; Cash, $200; Owner's Investment, $1,000; Equipment, $3,000; Franchise, $200; Investments (long-term), $500; Merchandise Inventory, $600; Notes Payable (long-term), $400; Owner's Capital, $?; Wages Payable, $100. Assume that this is the company's first year of operations.

LO4 **Classification of Accounts: Income Statement**

SE 5. Tell whether each of the following accounts is part of net sales, cost of goods sold, operating expenses, or other revenues and expenses, or is not on the income statement:

1. Delivery Expense
2. Interest Expense
3. Unearned Revenue
4. Sales Returns and Allowances

5. Cost of Sales
6. Depreciation Expense
7. Investment Income
8. Owner's Capital

LO4 **Single-Step Income Statement**

SE 6. Using the following accounts, prepare a single-step income statement at year end, May 31, 20xx: Cost of Goods Sold, $840; General Expenses, $450; Interest Expense, $210; Interest Income, $90; Net Sales, $2,400; Selling Expenses, $555.

LO4 **Multistep Income Statement**

SE 7. Using the accounts presented in **SE 6**, prepare a multistep income statement.

LO4 **Single-Step Income Statement**

SE 8. Using the following accounts and balances taken from a year-end balance sheet, compute working capital and the current ratio:

Accounts Payable	$ 3,500
Accounts Receivable	5,000
Cash	2,000
Marketable Securities	1,000
Merchandise Inventory	6,000
Notes Payable in Three Years	6,500
Property, Plant, and Equipment	20,000
Owner's Capital	24,000

LO5 **Liquidity Ratios**

SE 9. Using the following information from a balance sheet and an income statement, compute the (1) profit margin, (2) asset turnover, (3) return on assets, (4) debt to equity ratio, and (5) return on equity. (The previous year's total assets were $200,000, and owner's equity was $140,000.)

Total assets	$240,000
Total liabilities	60,000
Total owner's equity	180,000
Net sales	260,000
Cost of goods sold	140,000
Operating expenses	80,000

LO5 **Profitability Ratios**

SE 10. Assume that a company has a profit margin of 6.0 percent, an asset turnover of 3.2 times, and a debt to equity ratio of 50 percent. What are the company's return on assets and return on equity?

Exercises

LO1, LO2 **Discussion Questions**

E 1. Develop a brief answer to each of the following questions:

1. How do the four basic financial statements meet the third objective of financial reporting?
2. What are some areas that require estimates to record transactions under the matching rule?
3. How can financial information be consistent but not comparable?
4. When might an amount be material to management but not to the CPA auditing the financial statements?

LO3, LO4, LO5 **Discussion Questions**

E 2. Develop a brief answer to each of the following questions:

1. Why is it that land held for future use and equipment not currently used in the business are classified as investments rather than as property, plant, and equipment?
2. Which is the better measure of a company's performance—income from operations or net income?
3. Why is it important to compare a company's financial performance with industry standards?
4. Is the statement "Return on assets is a better measure of profitability than profit margin" true or false and why?

LO1, LO2 **Financial Accounting Concepts**

E 3. The lettered items below represent a classification scheme for the concepts of financial accounting. Match each numbered term in the list that follows with the letter of the category in which it belongs.

a. Decision makers (users of accounting information)
b. Business activities or entities relevant to accounting measurement
c. Objectives of accounting information
d. Accounting measurement considerations
e. Accounting processing considerations
f. Qualitative characteristics
g. Accounting conventions
h. Financial statements

1. Conservatism
2. Verifiability
3. Statement of cash flows
4. Materiality

5. Reliability
6. Recognition
7. Cost-benefit
8. Understandability
9. Business transactions
10. Consistency
11. Full disclosure
12. Furnishing information that is useful to owners and creditors
13. Specific business entities
14. Classification
15. Management
16. Neutrality
17. Internal accounting control
18. Valuation
19. Owners
20. Timeliness
21. Relevance
22. Furnishing information that is useful in assessing cash flow prospects

LO2 Accounting Concepts and Conventions

E 4. Each of the statements below violates a convention in accounting. State which of the following accounting conventions is violated: comparability and consistency, materiality, conservatism, full disclosure, or cost-benefit.

1. A series of reports that are time-consuming and expensive to prepare are presented to the owner each month, even though they are never used.
2. A company changes its method of accounting for depreciation.
3. The company in **2** does not indicate in the financial statements that the method of depreciation was changed; nor does it specify the effect of the change on net income.
4. A company's new office building, which is built next to the company's existing factory, is debited to the Factory account because it represents a fairly small dollar amount in relation to the factory.
5. The asset account for a pickup truck still used in the business is written down to what the truck could be sold for, even though the carrying value under conventional depreciation methods is higher.

LO3 Classification of Accounts: Balance Sheet

E 5. The lettered items below represent a classification scheme for a balance sheet, and the numbered items in the list below are account titles. Match each account with the letter of the category in which it belongs.

a. Current assets
b. Investments
c. Property, plant, and equipment
d. Intangible assets
e. Current liabilities
f. Long-term liabilities
g. Owner's equity
h. Not on balance sheet

1. Patent
2. Building Held for Sale
3. Prepaid Rent
4. Wages Payable
5. Note Payable in Five Years
6. Building Used in Operations
7. Fund Held to Pay Off Long-Term Debt
8. Inventory
9. Prepaid Insurance
10. Depreciation Expense
11. Accounts Receivable
12. Interest Expense
13. Unearned Revenue
14. Short-Term Investments
15. Accumulated Depreciation
16. Owner's Capital

LO3 Classified Balance Sheet Preparation

E 6. The following data pertain to Kabli Company: Accounts Payable, $20,400; Accounts Receivable, $15,200; Accumulated Depreciation–Building, $5,600; Accumulated Depreciation–Equipment, $6,800; Bonds Payable, $24,000; Building, $28,000; Cash, $12,480; Copyright, $2,480; Equipment, $60,800; Inventory, $16,000; Investment in Corporate Securities (long-term), $8,000; Investment in Six-Month Government Securities, $6,560; J. Kabli, Capital,

$95,280; Land, $3,200; Prepaid Rent, $480; and Revenue Received in Advance, $1,120.

Prepare a classified balance sheet at December 31, 20xx. Assume that this is Kabli Company's first year of operations.

LO4 **Classification of Accounts: Income Statement**

E 7. Using the classification scheme below for a multistep income statement, match each account with the letter of the category in which it belongs.

a. Net sales
b. Cost of sales
c. Selling expenses

d. General and administrative expenses
e. Other revenues and expenses
f. Not on income statement

1. Sales Discounts
2. Cost of Goods Sold
3. Dividend Income
4. Advertising Expense
5. Office Salaries Expense
6. Freight Out Expense
7. Prepaid Insurance

8. Utilities Expense
9. Sales Salaries Expense
10. Rent Expense
11. Depreciation Expense–Delivery Equipment
12. Interest Expense

LO4 **Preparation of Income Statements**

E 8. A company has the following data: net sales, $405,000; cost of goods sold, $220,000; selling expenses, $90,000; general and administrative expenses, $60,000; interest expense, $4,000; and interest income, $3,000.

1. Prepare a single-step income statement.
2. Prepare a multistep income statement.

LO4 **Multistep Income Statement**

E 9. A single-step income statement appears below. Present the information in a multistep income statement, and indicate what insights can be obtained from the multistep form as opposed to the single-step form.

Pasica Linens Company
Income Statement
For the Year Ended December 31, 20xx

Revenues		
Net sales		$1,197,132
Interest income		5,720
Total revenues		$1,202,852
Costs and expenses		
Cost of goods sold	$777,080	
Selling expenses	203,740	
General and administrative expenses	100,688	
Interest expense	13,560	
Total costs and expenses		1,095,068
Net income		$ 107,784

LO5 **Liquidity Ratios**

E 10. The accounts and balances that follow are from the general ledger of Fields Company. Compute the (1) working capital and (2) current ratio.

Accounts Payable	$13,280
Accounts Receivable	8,160

Cash	$ 1,200
Current Portion of Long-Term Debt	8,000
Long-Term Investments	8,320
Marketable Securities	10,080
Merchandise Inventory	20,320
Notes Payable (90 days)	12,000
Notes Payable (2 years)	16,000
Notes Receivable (90 days)	20,800
Notes Receivable (2 years)	8,000
Prepaid Insurance	320
Property, Plant, and Equipment	48,000
Property Taxes Payable	1,000
T. Fields, Capital	22,640
Salaries Payable	680
Supplies	280
Unearned Revenue	600

LO2 Profitability Ratios

E 11. The following end-of-year amounts are from the financial statements of Konstan Company: total assets, $213,000; total liabilities, $86,000; owner's equity, $127,000; net sales, $391,000; cost of goods sold, $243,000; operating expenses, $89,000; and withdrawals, $20,000. During the past year, total assets increased by $37,500. Total owner's equity was affected only by net income and withdrawals. Compute the (1) profit margin, (2) asset turnover, (3) return on assets, (4) debt to equity ratio, and (5) return on equity.

LO5 Liquidity and Profitability

E 12. The simplified balance sheet and income statement for a company appear below.

Balance Sheet
December 31, 20xx

Assets		Liabilities	
Current assets	$ 50,000	Current liabilities	$ 20,000
Investments	10,000	Long-term liabilities	30,000
Property, plant, and		Total liabilities	$ 50,000
equipment	146,500		
Intangible assets	13,500	**Owner's Equity**	
		Owner's capital	170,000
		Total liabilities and	
Total assets	$220,000	owner's equity	$220,000

Income Statement
For the Year Ended December 31, 20xx

Net sales	$410,000
Cost of goods sold	250,000
Gross margin	$160,000
Operating expenses	135,000
Net income	$ 25,000

Total assets and owner's equity at the beginning of 20xx were $180,000 and $145,000, respectively. The owner made no investments or withdrawals during the year.

1. Compute the following liquidity measures: (a) working capital and (b) current ratio.
2. Compute the following profitability measures: (a) profit margin, (b) asset turnover, (c) return on assets, (d) debt to equity ratio, and (e) return on equity.

Problems

Accounting Conventions

LO2 **P 1.** In each case below, accounting conventions may have been violated.

1. Hastings Manufacturing Company uses the cost method for computing the balance sheet amount of inventory unless the market value of the inventory is less than the cost, in which case the market value is used. At the end of the current year, the market value is $154,000 and the cost is $160,000. Hastings Manufacturing Company uses the $154,000 figure to compute the value of inventory because management believes it is the more cautious approach.

2. Gormanus Company has annual sales of $20,000,000. It follows the practice of recording any items costing less than $500 as expenses in the year purchased. During the current year, it purchased several chairs for the executive conference room at $490 each, including freight. Although the chairs were expected to last for at least ten years, they were recorded as an expense in accordance with company policy.

3. Nogel Company closed its books on October 31, 20x7, before preparing its annual report. On November 3, 20x7, a fire destroyed one of the company's two factories. Although the company had fire insurance and would not suffer a loss on the building, it seemed likely that it would suffer a significant decrease in sales in 20x8 because of the fire. It did not report the fire damage in its 20x7 financial statements because the fire had not affected its operations during that year.

4. Ex-Act Drug Company spends a substantial portion of its profits on research and development. The company had been reporting its $5,000,000 expenditure for research and development as a lump sum, but management recently decided to begin classifying the expenditures by project, even though its recordkeeping costs will increase.

5. During the current year, Rutherford Bennett Ives (RBI) Company changed from one generally accepted method of accounting for inventories to another method.

Required

For each of these cases, identify the accounting convention that applies, state whether or not the treatment is in accord with the convention and GAAP, and briefly explain why.

LO4 **Forms of the Income Statement**

P 2. Ramos Nursery Company's single-step income statements for 20x8 and 20x7 follow.

Ramos Nursery Company
Income Statements
For the Years Ended April 30, 20x8 and 20x7

	20x8	20x7
Revenues		
Net sales	$525,932	$475,264
Interest income	800	700
Total revenues	$526,732	$475,964
Costs and expenses		
Cost of goods sold	$234,948	$171,850
Selling expenses	161,692	150,700
General and administrative expenses	62,866	42,086
Interest expense	3,600	850
Total costs and expenses	$463,106	$365,486
Net income	$ 63,626	$110,478

Required

1. From the information provided, prepare multistep income statements for 20x7 and 20x8 showing percentages of net sales for each component.
2. User Insight: Did income from operations increase or decrease from 20x7 to 20x8? Write a short explanation of why this change occurred.

LO3, LO5 **Classified Balance Sheet**

P 3. The following information is from the June 30, 20x8, post-closing trial balance of Kissell Hardware Company.

Account Name	Debit	Credit
Cash	$ 31,000	
Short-Term Investments	33,000	
Notes Receivable	10,000	
Accounts Receivable	276,000	
Merchandise Inventory	145,000	
Prepaid Rent	1,600	
Prepaid Insurance	4,800	
Sales Supplies	1,280	
Office Supplies	440	
Deposit for Future Advertising	3,680	
Building, Not in Use	49,600	
Land	22,400	
Delivery Equipment	41,200	
Accumulated Depreciation–Delivery Equipment		$ 28,400
Trademark	4,000	
Accounts Payable		114,600
Salaries Payable		5,200
Interest Payable		840
Long-Term Notes Payable		80,000
J. Kissell, Capital		394,960

Required

1. From the information provided, prepare a classified balance sheet for Kissell Hardware Company.
2. Compute Kissell Hardware's current ratio and debt to equity ratio.
3. **User Insight:** As a user of the classified balance sheet, why would you want to know the current ratio or the debt to equity ratio?

LO5   Liquidity and Profitability

P 4. A summary of data from the income statements and balance sheets for Okumura Construction Supply Company for 20x8 and 20x7 appears below.

	20x8	20x7
Current assets	$ 366,000	$ 310,000
Total assets	2,320,000	1,740,000
Current liabilities	180,000	120,000
Long-term liabilities	800,000	580,000
Owner's equity	1,340,000	1,040,000
Net sales	4,600,000	3,480,000
Net income	300,000	204,000

Total assets and owner's equity at the beginning of 20x7 were $1,360,000 and $840,000, respectively.

Required

1. **User Insight:** Compute the following liquidity measures for 20x7 and 20x8: (a) working capital and (b) current ratio. Comment on the differences between the years.
2. **User Insight:** Compute the following measures of profitability for 20x7 and 20x8: (a) profit margin, (b) asset turnover, (c) return on assets, (d) debt to equity ratio, and (e) return on equity. Comment on the change in performance from 20x7 to 20x8.

LO3, LO4, LO5   Classified Financial Statement Preparation and Analysis

P 5. Wu Company sells outdoor sports equipment. At the December 31, 20x7, year end, the following financial information was available from the income statement: administrative expenses, $161,600; cost of goods sold, $700,840; interest expense, $45,280; interest income, $5,600; net sales, $1,428,780; and selling expenses, $440,400.

The following information was available from the balance sheet (after closing entries were made): accounts payable, $65,200; accounts receivable, $209,600; accumulated depreciation–delivery equipment, $34,200; accumulated depreciation–store fixtures, $84,440; cash, $56,800; delivery equipment, $177,000; inventory, $273,080; investment in securities (long-term), $112,000; investment in U.S. government securities (short-term), $79,200; long-term notes payable, $200,000; Y. Wu, Capital, $718,600 (ending balance); notes payable (short-term), $100,000; prepaid expenses (short-term), $11,520; and store fixtures, $283,240.

Total assets and total owner's equity at December 31, 20x6, were $1,048,800 and $752,340, respectively, and owner's withdrawals for the year were $120,000. The owner did not make any additional investments in the company during the year.

Required

1. From the information above, prepare (a) an income statement in single-step form, (b) a statement of owner's equity, and (c) a classified balance sheet.

2. From the statements you have prepared, compute the following measures: (a) working capital and current ratio (for liquidity); and (b) profit margin, asset turnover, return on assets, debt to equity ratio, and return on equity (for profitability).

3. **User Insight:** Using the industry averages for the auto and home supply business in Figures 4 through 9 in this chapter, determine whether Wu Company needs to improve its liquidity or its profitability. Explain your answer, making recommendations as to specific areas on which Wu Company should concentrate.

Alternate Problems

LO2   Accounting Conventions

P 6. In each case below, accounting conventions may have been violated.

1. After careful study, Kipling Company, which has offices in 40 states, has determined that its method of depreciating office furniture should be changed. The new method is adopted for the current year, and the change is noted in the financial statements.

2. In the past, Cortes Company has recorded operating expenses in general accounts (e.g., Salaries Expense and Utilities Expense). Management has determined that despite the additional recordkeeping costs, the company's income statement should break down each operating expense into its components of selling expense and administrative expense.

3. Fitz Company's auditor discovered that a company official had authorized the payment of an $800 bribe to a local official. Management argued that because the item was so small in relation to the size of the company ($1,500,000 in sales), the illegal payment should not be disclosed.

4. Glowacki's Bookstore built a small addition to its main building to house a new computer games section. Because no one could be sure that the computer games section would succeed, the accountant took a conservative approach and recorded the addition as an expense.

5. Since it began operations ten years ago, Xu Company has used the same generally accepted inventory method. The company does not disclose in its financial statements what inventory method it uses.

Required

In each of these cases, identify the accounting convention that applies, state whether or not the treatment is in accord with the convention and generally accepted accounting principles, and briefly explain why.

LO5   Liquidity and Profitability

P 7. Rollins Products Company has had poor operating results for the past two years. As the accountant for Rollins Products, you have the following information available to you:

	20x8	20x7
Current assets	$ 45,000	$ 35,000
Total assets	145,000	110,000
Current liabilities	20,000	10,000
Long-term liabilities	20,000	—
Owner's equity	105,000	100,000
Net sales	262,000	200,000
Net income	16,000	11,000

Total assets and owner's equity at the beginning of 20x7 were $90,000 and $80,000, respectively. The owner made no investments in 20x7 or 20x8.

Required

1. **User Insight:** Compute the following measures of liquidity for 20x7 and 20x8: (a) working capital and (b) current ratio. Comment on the differences between the years.
2. **User Insight:** Compute the following measures of profitability for 20x7 and 20x8: (a) profit margin, (b) asset turnover, (c) return on assets, (d) debt to equity ratio, and (e) return on equity. Comment on the change in performance from 20x7 to 20x8.

LO4 **Forms of the Income Statement**

P 8. The income statements that follow are for Loury Hardware Company.

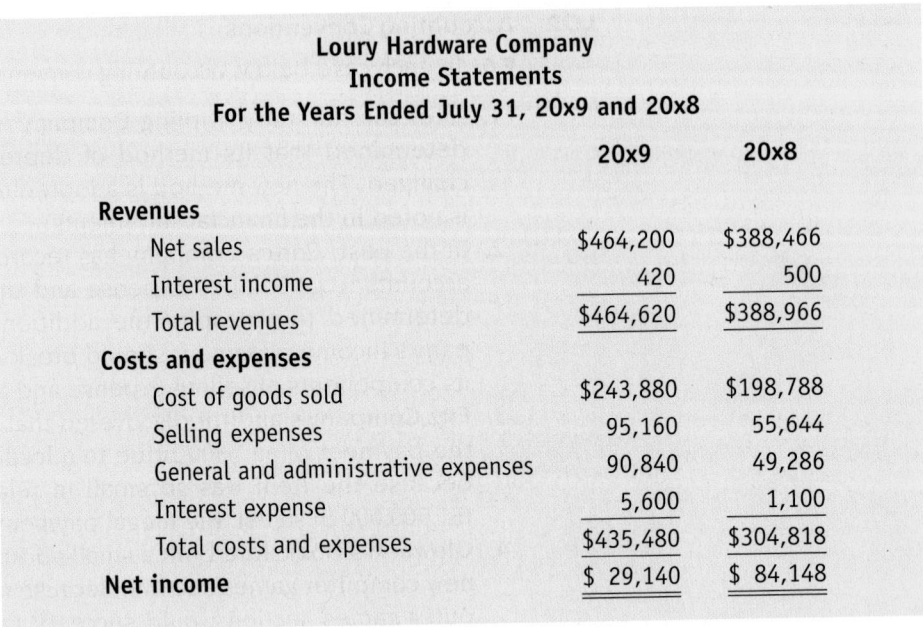

Loury Hardware Company Income Statements For the Years Ended July 31, 20x9 and 20x8		
	20x9	**20x8**
Revenues		
Net sales	$464,200	$388,466
Interest income	420	500
Total revenues	$464,620	$388,966
Costs and expenses		
Cost of goods sold	$243,880	$198,788
Selling expenses	95,160	55,644
General and administrative expenses	90,840	49,286
Interest expense	5,600	1,100
Total costs and expenses	$435,480	$304,818
Net income	$ 29,140	$ 84,148

Required

1. From the information provided, prepare a multistep income statement for 20x8 and 20x9 showing percentages of net sales for each component.
2. **User Insight:** Did income from operations increase or decrease between 20x8 and 20x9? Write a short explanation of why this change occurred.

ENHANCING Your Knowledge, Skills, and Critical Thinking

LO2 **Conceptual Understanding Cases**

Consistency and Full Disclosure

C 1. Cuyahoga Parking, which operates a seven-story parking building in downtown Cleveland, has a calendar year end. It serves daily and hourly parkers, as well as monthly parkers who pay a fixed monthly rate in advance. The company traditionally has recorded all cash receipts as revenues when received. Most monthly parkers pay in full during the month before they have the right to park. The company's auditors have said that beginning in 20x7, the company should consider recording the cash receipts from monthly parking on an accrual basis, crediting Unearned Revenues. Total cash receipts for 20x7 were $1,250,000, and the cash receipts received in 20x7 and applicable to January 20x8 were $62,500.

Discuss the relevance of the accounting conventions of consistency and full disclosure to the decision to record the monthly parking revenues on an accrual basis.

LO2 **Materiality**

C 2. Hagia Electronics operates a chain of consumer electronics stores in the Dallas area. This year the company achieved annual sales of $75 million, on which it earned a net income of $3 million. At the beginning of the year, management implemented a new inventory system that enabled it to track all purchases and sales. At the end of the year, a physical inventory reveals that the actual inventory was $120,000 below what the new system indicated it should be. The inventory loss, which probably resulted from shoplifting, is reflected in a higher cost of goods sold. The problem concerns management but seems to be less important to the company's auditors. What is materiality? Why might the inventory loss concern management more than it does the auditors? Do you think the amount of inventory loss is material?

Interpreting Financial Reports

LO5 **Comparison of Profitability**

C 3. Two of the largest chains of grocery stores in the United States are **Albertson's, Inc.**, and the **Great Atlantic & Pacific Tea Company (A&P).** In a recent fiscal year, Albertson's had a net income of $765 million, and A&P had a net income of $14 million. It is difficult to judge which company is more profitable from those figures alone because they do not take into account the relative sales, sizes, and investments of the companies. Data (in millions) needed to complete a financial analysis of the two companies follow:[15]

	Albertson's	A&P
Net sales	$36,762	$10,151
Beginning total assets	15,719	3,335
Ending total assets	16,078	3,309
Beginning total liabilities	10,017	2,489
Ending total liabilities	10,394	2,512
Beginning stockholders' equity	5,702	846
Ending stockholders' equity	5,684	797

1. Determine which company was more profitable by computing profit margin, asset turnover, return on assets, debt to equity ratio, and return on equity for the two companies. Comment on the relative profitability of the two companies.
2. What do the ratios tell you about the factors that go into achieving an adequate return on assets in the grocery industry? For industry data, refer to Figures 4 through 9 in this chapter.
3. How would you characterize the use of debt financing in the grocery industry and the use of debt by these two companies?

LO5 **Evaluation of Profitability**

C 4. Monique Smith is the owner of Monique Tapestries, which wholesales fine tapestries to retail stores. Because Smith was not satisfied with her company's earnings in 20x7, she raised prices in 20x8, thereby increasing gross margin from sales from 30 percent in 20x7 to 35 percent in 20x8. Smith is pleased that net income went up from 20x7 to 20x8, as shown in the comparative income statements that follow. Total assets for Monique Tapestries at year end for 20x6, 20x7, and 20x8 were $1,246,780, $1,386,810, and $1,536,910, respectively.

	20x8	20x7
Revenues		
Net sales	$1,222,600	$1,386,400
Costs and expenses		
Cost of goods sold	$ 794,690	$ 970,480
Selling and administrative expenses	338,398	333,008
Total costs and expenses	$1,133,088	$1,303,488
Net income	$ 89,512	$ 82,912

Has Monique Tapestries' profitability really improved? (**Hint:** Compute profit margin and return on assets.) What factors has Smith overlooked in evaluating the profitability of the company? (**Hint:** Compute asset turnover and comment on the role it plays in profitability.)

Decision Analysis Using Excel

LO5 **Financial Analysis for Loan Decision**

C 5. Esteban Almada was recently promoted to loan officer at First Federal Bank. He has authority to issue loans up to $75,000 without approval from a higher bank official. This week, two small companies—Dubrovnik Supplies and Shimano Fashions—have submitted proposals for a six-month, $75,000 loan. To prepare financial analyses of the two companies, Almada has obtained the information summarized below.

Dubrovnik Supplies is a local lumber and home improvement company. Because its sales have increased so much during the past two years, it has had to raise additional working capital, especially as represented by receivables and inventory. The $75,000 loan is needed to assure the company of enough working capital for the next year. Dubrovnik Supplies began the year with total assets of $1,110,000 and owner's equity of $390,000. During the past year, it had a net income of $60,000 on net sales of $1,140,000. Dubrovnik Supplies' unclassified balance sheet as of the current date is as follows:

Assets		Liabilities and Owner's Equity	
Cash	$ 45,000	Accounts payable	$ 300,000
Accounts receivable (net)	225,000	Notes payable (short-term)	150,000
Inventory	375,000	Notes payable (long-term)	300,000
Land	75,000	J. Dubrovnik, Capital	450,000
Buildings (net)	375,000		
Equipment (net)	105,000	Total liabilities and	
Total assets	$1,200,000	owner's equity	$1,200,000

Shimano Fashions has for three years been a successful clothing store for young professional women. The leased store is located in the downtown financial district. Shimano's loan proposal asks for $75,000 to pay for stocking a new line of women's suits during the coming season. At the beginning of the year, the company had total assets of $300,000 and total owner's equity of $171,000. Over the past year, the company earned a net income of $54,000 on net sales of $720,000. The firm's unclassified balance sheet at the current date is as follows:

Assets		Liabilities and Owner's Equity	
Cash	$ 15,000	Accounts payable	$120,000
Accounts receivable (net)	75,000	Accrued liabilities	15,000
Inventory	202,500	L. Shimano, Capital	225,000
Prepaid expenses	7,500		
Equipment (net)	60,000	Total liabilities and	
Total assets	$360,000	owner's equity	$360,000

1. Prepare a financial analysis of each company's liquidity before and after receiving the proposed loan. Also compute profitability ratios before and after, as appropriate. Write a brief summary of the effect of the proposed loan on each company's financial position.
2. Assume you are Esteban Almada and can make a loan to only one of these companies. Write a memorandum to the bank's vice president outlining your decision and naming the company to which you would lend $75,000. Be sure to state what positive and negative factors could affect each company's ability to pay back the loan in the next year. Also indicate what other information of a financial or nonfinancial nature would be helpful in making a final decision.

LO3, LO4 Annual Report Case: CVS Corporation

Classified Balance Sheet and Multistep Income Statement

C 6. Refer to **CVS Corporation's** annual report in the Supplement to Chapter 5 to answer the following questions. (Note that 2005 refers to the year ended December 31, 2005, and that 2004 refers to the year ended January 1, 2005.)

1. Consolidated balance sheets: (a) Did CVS's amount of working capital increase or decrease from 2004 to 2005? By how much? (b) Did the current ratio improve from 2004 to 2005? (c) Does the company have long-term investments or intangible assets? (d) Did CVS's debt to equity ratio change from 2004 to 2005? (e) What is the owner's (shareholders') equity for 2005? How does this amount compare with retained earnings?
2. Consolidated statements of earnings: (a) Does CVS use a multistep or single-step income statement? (b) Is it a comparative statement? (c) What is the trend of net earnings? (d) How significant are income taxes for CVS?

LO5 Comparison Case: CVS Versus Southwest

Financial Analysis

C 7. Compare the financial performance of **CVS** and **Southwest Airlines** on the basis of liquidity and profitability for 2005 and 2004. Use the following ratios: working capital, current ratio, debt to equity ratio, profit margin, asset turnover, return on assets, and return on equity. In 2003, total assets and total stockholders' equity for CVS were $10,543.1 million and $6,021.8 million, respectively. In 2003, Southwest's total assets were $9,878 million, and its total stockholders' equity was $5,052 million.

1. In general, how does Southwest's performance compare to CVS's performance with respect to liquidity and profitability?
2. What distinguishes Southwest's profitability performance from that of CVS?

Ethical Dilemma Case

LO1   **Ethics and Financial Reporting**

C 8. Beacon Systems, located outside Atlanta, develops computer software and licenses it to financial institutions. The firm uses an aggressive accounting method that records revenues from the software it has developed on a percentage of completion basis. Consequently, revenue for partially completed projects is recognized based on the portion of the project that has been completed. If a project is 50 percent completed, then 50 percent of the contracted revenue is recognized. In 20x8, preliminary estimates for a $7 million project are that the project is 75 percent complete. Because the estimate of completion is a matter of judgment, management asks for a new report showing the project to be 90 percent complete. The change will enable senior managers to meet their financial goals for the year and thus receive substantial year-end bonuses. Do you think management's action is ethical? If you were the company controller and were asked to prepare the new report, would you do it? What action would you take?

Internet Case

LO5   **Annual Reports and Financial Analysis**

C 9. Select a large, well-known company and access its annual report online. In its annual report, find the four basic financial statements and the notes to the financial statements. Perform a liquidity analysis, including the calculation of working capital and the current ratio. Perform a profitability analysis, calculating profit margin, asset turnover, return on assets, debt to equity ratio, and return on equity. Be prepared to present your findings in class.

Group Activity Case

LO1   **Qualitative Characteristics of Accounting Information**

C 10. Review the multistep income statement presented in Exhibits 3 and 4. In your group, discuss how this form of the income statement meets each of these qualitative characteristics of accounting information: understandability, usefulness, relevance, and reliability. Be prepared to present your conclusions in class.

Business Communication Case

LO5   **Financial Analysis with Industry Comparison**

C 11. Refer to the Look Back section at the end of the chapter and to Dell's classified balance sheet in Exhibit 2. Write a memorandum to the board of directors in executive summary form that summarizes Dell's profitability performance from 2004 to 2005. (Total assets and total stockholders' equity for Dell in 2003 were $15,470 million and $4,873 million, respectively.) Include an assessment of that performance and compare Dell's performance with the industry averages in Figures 4 through 9.

How to Read an Annual Report

More than 4 million corporations are chartered in the United States. Most of them are small, family-owned businesses. They are called *private* or *closely held corporations* because their common stock is held by only a few people and is not for sale to the public. Larger companies usually find it desirable to raise investment funds from many investors by issuing common stock to the public. These companies are called *public companies*. Although they are fewer in number than private companies, their total economic impact is much greater.

Public companies must register their common stock with the Securities and Exchange Commission (SEC), which regulates the issuance and subsequent trading of the stock of public companies. The SEC requires the management of public companies to report each year to stockholders on their companies' financial performance. This report, called an *annual report*, contains the company's annual financial statements and other pertinent data. Annual reports are a primary source of financial information about public companies and are distributed to all of a company's stockholders. They must also be filed with the SEC on a Form 10-K.

The general public may obtain an annual report by calling or writing the company or accessing the report online at the company's website. If a company has filed its 10-K electronically with the SEC, it can be accessed at http://www.sec.gov/edgar.shtml. Many libraries also maintain files of annual reports or have them available on electronic media, such as *Compact Disclosure*.

This supplement describes the major components of the typical annual report. To illustrate these components, the supplement includes the annual report of **CVS Corporation**, one of the country's most successful retailers. Case assignments in Chapters 1–17 refer to this annual report. For purposes of comparison, the supplement also includes the financial statements and summary of significant accounting policies (Note 1) of **Southwest Airlines Co.**, one of the largest and most successful airlines in the United States.

The Components of an Annual Report

In addition to listing the corporation's directors and officers, an annual report usually contains a letter to the stockholders (also called *shareholders*), a multi-year summary of financial highlights, a description of the company, management's discussion and analysis of the company's operating results and financial condition, the financial statements, notes to the financial statements, a statement about management's responsibilities, and the auditors' report.

Letter to the Stockholders

Traditionally, an annual report begins with a letter in which the top officers of the corporation tell stockholders about the company's performance and prospects. In CVS's 2005 annual report, the chairman and chief executive officer wrote to the stockholders about the highlights of the past year, the key priorities for the new year, and other aspects of the business. He reported as follows:

> This past year will certainly be remembered as one of considerable accomplishment for our company. We swiftly and successfully completed the integration of nearly 1,100 former Eckerd stores, along with the former Eckerd Health Services, acquired in 2004. At the same time, we opened

approximately 300 new or relocated stores in both existing and new markets. Throughout this activity, we never lost focus on our core business, as evidenced by our same store sales growth and market share gains.

Financial Highlights

The financial highlights section of an annual report presents key statistics for at least a five-year period but often for a ten-year period. It is often accompanied by graphs. CVS's annual report, for example, gives key figures for sales, operating profits, and other key measures. Note that the financial highlights section often includes nonfinancial data and graphs, such as the number of stores in CVS's case.

Description of the Company

An annual report contains a detailed description of the company's products and divisions. Some analysts tend to scoff at this section of the annual report because it often contains glossy photographs and other image-building material, but it should not be overlooked because it may provide useful information about past results and future plans.

Management's Discussion and Analysis

In this section, management describes the company's financial condition and results of operations and explains the difference in results from one year to the next. For example, CVS's management lists several factors contributing to its net sales performance, among them the following:

> Pharmacy sales growth continued to benefit from new market expansions, increased penetration in existing markets, our ability to attract and retain managed care customers and favorable industry trends. These trends include an aging American population: many "baby boomers" are now in their fifties and are consuming a greater number of prescription drugs. The increased use of pharmaceuticals as the first line of defense for individual healthcare also contributed to the growing demand for pharmacy services. We believe these favorable industry trends will continue.

CVS's management also describes the increase in cash flows from operating activities:

> The increase in net cash provided by operations during 2005 primarily resulted from increased revenue and improved inventory management. Fiscal 2004 reflected increased inventory payments as a result of higher inventory levels, and higher operating costs associated with the Acquired Businesses and investments, including the cost of extending store hours. The elevated inventory levels during 2004 were primarily the result of inventory purchased to reset the acquired stores with the CVS/pharmacy product mix.

Financial Statements

All companies present the same four basic financial statements in their annual reports, but the names they use may vary. As you can see in Exhibits S-I to S-4, CVS presents statements of operations (income statements), balance sheets, statements of shareholders' equity (includes retained earnings), and state-

▼ **EXHIBIT S-1**

CVS's Income Statements

| | CVS Corporation Consolidated Statements of Operations | | |

Consolidated means that data from all companies owned by CVS are combined.

CVS's fiscal year ends on the Saturday closest to December 31.

Fiscal year ended

(In millions, except per share amounts)	Dec. 31, 2005 (52 WEEKS)	Jan. 1, 2005 (52 WEEKS)	Jan. 3, 2004 (53 WEEKS)
Net sales	$37,006.2	$30,594.3	$26,588.0
Cost of goods sold, buying and warehousing costs	27,105.0	22,563.1	19,725.0
Gross margin	9,901.2	8,031.2	6,863.0
Selling, general and administrative expenses	7,292.6	6,079.7	5,097.7
Depreciation and amortization	589.1	496.8	341.7
Total operating expenses	7,881.7	6,576.5	5,439.4
Operating profit[1]	2,019.5	1,454.7	1,423.6
Interest expense, net[2]	110.5	58.3	48.1
Earnings before income tax provision	1,909.0	1,396.4	1,375.5
Income tax provision	684.3	477.6	528.2
Net earnings[3]	1,224.7	918.8	847.3
Preference dividends, net of income tax benefit[4]	14.1	14.2	14.6
Net earnings available to common shareholders	$ 1,210.6	$ 904.6	$ 832.7
BASIC EARNINGS PER COMMON SHARE:[5]			
Net earnings	$ 1.49	$ 1.13	$ 1.06
Weighted average common shares outstanding	811.4	797.2	788.8
DILUTED EARNINGS PER COMMON SHARE:			
Net earnings	$ 1.45	$ 1.10	$ 1.03
Weighted average common shares outstanding	841.6	830.8	815.4
DIVIDENDS DECLARED PER COMMON SHARE	$ 0.1450	$ 0.1325	$ 0.1150

1. This section shows earnings from ongoing operations.
2. CVS shows interest expense and income taxes separately.
3. The net earnings figure moves to the statements of shareholders' equity.
4. CVS shows the dividends distributed to preferred shareholders. This distribution is not an expense.
5. CVS discloses various breakdowns of earnings per share.

ments of cash flows. (Note that the numbers given in the statements are in millions, but the last six digits are omitted. For example, $2,019,500,000 is shown as $2,019.5.)

The headings of CVS's financial statements are preceded by the word *consolidated*. A corporation issues *consolidated* financial statements when it consists of more than one company and has combined the companies' data for reporting purposes.

CVS provides several years of data for each financial statement: two years for the balance sheet and three years for the others. Financial statements presented in this fashion are called *comparative financial statements*. Such statements are in accordance with generally accepted accounting principles and help readers assess the company's performance over several years.

▼ **EXHIBIT S-2**

CVS's Balance Sheets

CVS Corporation
Consolidated Balance Sheets

(In millions, except shares and per share amounts)	Dec. 31, 2005	Jan. 1, 2005
ASSETS:		
Cash and cash equivalents	$ 513.4	$ 392.3
Accounts receivable, net	1,839.6	1,764.2
Inventories	5,719.8	5,453.9
Deferred income taxes	241.1	243.1
Other current assets	78.8	66.0
Total current assets	8,392.7	7,919.5
Property and equipment, net	3,952.6	3,505.9
Goodwill	1,789.9	1,898.5
Intangible assets, net	802.2	867.9
Deferred income taxes	122.5	137.6
Other assets	223.5	217.4
Total assets	$15,283.4	$14,546.8
LIABILITIES:		
Accounts payable	$ 2,467.5	$ 2,275.9
Accrued expenses	1,521.4	1,666.7
Short-term debt	253.4	885.6
Current portion of long-term debt	341.6	30.6
Total current liabilities	4,583.9	4,858.8
Long-term debt	1,594.1	1,925.9
Other long-term liabilities	774.2	774.9
Commitments and contingencies (Note 10)		
SHAREHOLDERS' EQUITY:		
Preferred stock, $0.01 par value: authorized 120,619 shares; no shares issued or outstanding	—	—
Preference stock, series one ESOP convertible, par value $1.00: authorized 50,000,000 shares; issued and outstanding 4,165,000 shares at December 31, 2005 and 4,273,000 shares at January 1, 2005	222.6	228.4
Common stock, par value $0.01: authorized 1,000,000,000 shares; issued 838,841,000 shares at December 31, 2005 and 828,552,000 shares at January 1, 2005	8.4	8.3
Treasury stock, at cost: 24,533,000 shares at December 31, 2005 and 26,634,000 shares at January 1, 2005	(356.5)	(385.9)
Guaranteed ESOP obligation	(114.0)	(140.9)
Capital surplus	1,922.4	1,687.3
Retained earnings	6,738.6	5,645.5
Accumulated other comprehensive loss	(90.3)	(55.5)
Total shareholders' equity	8,331.2	6,987.2
Total liabilities and shareholders' equity	$15,283.4	$14,546.8

Callout notes:
- CVS categorizes certain assets as current assets.
- These are noncurrent or long-term assets.
- CVS categorizes certain liabilities as current liabilities.
- These are noncurrent or long-term liabilities.
- Balances in the shareholders' equity section are from the statements of shareholders' equity.

▼ **EXHIBIT S-3**

CVS's Statements of Shareholders' Equity

CVS Corporation
Consolidated Statements of Shareholders' Equity

> Each component of shareholders' equity is explained.

(In millions)	Shares Dec. 31, 2005	Shares Jan. 1, 2005	Shares Jan. 3, 2004	Dollars Dec. 31, 2005	Dollars Jan. 1, 2005	Dollars Jan. 3, 2004
PREFERENCE STOCK:						
Beginning of year	4.3	4.5	4.7	$ 228.4	$ 242.7	$ 250.4
Conversion to common stock	(0.1)	(0.2)	(0.2)	(5.8)	(14.3)	(7.7)
End of year	4.2	4.3	4.5	222.6	228.4	242.7
COMMON STOCK:						
Beginning of year	828.6	820.4	818.6	8.3	8.2	8.2
Stock options exercised and awards	10.2	8.2	1.8	0.1	0.1	—
End of year	838.8	828.6	820.4	8.4	8.3	8.2
TREASURY STOCK:						
Beginning of year	(26.6)	(29.6)	(32.4)	(385.9)	(428.6)	(469.5)
Purchase of treasury shares	—	—	—	(1.7)	(0.8)	(0.5)
Conversion of preference stock	0.5	1.2	0.6	7.3	17.9	9.6
Employee stock purchase plan issuance	1.6	1.8	2.2	23.8	25.6	31.8
End of year	(24.5)	(26.6)	(29.6)	(356.5)	(385.9)	(428.6)
GUARANTEED ESOP OBLIGATION:						
Beginning of year				(140.9)	(163.2)	(194.4)
Reduction of guaranteed ESOP obligation				26.9	22.3	31.2
End of year				(114.0)	(140.9)	(163.2)
CAPITAL SURPLUS:						
Beginning of year				1,687.3	1,553.1	1,542.5
Conversion of preference stock				(1.5)	(3.6)	(1.9)
Stock option activity and awards				188.8	119.4	9.2
Tax benefit on stock options and awards				47.8	18.4	3.3
End of year				1,922.4	1,687.3	1,553.1
ACCUMULATED OTHER COMPREHENSIVE LOSS:						
Beginning of year				(55.5)	(36.9)	(44.6)
Unrealized loss on derivatives				(2.9)	(19.8)	—
Minimum pension liability adjustment				(37.7)	1.2	7.7
End of year				(90.3)	(55.5)	(36.9)
RETAINED EARNINGS:						
Beginning of year				5,645.5	4,846.5	4,104.4
Net earnings				1,224.7	918.8	847.3
Preference stock dividends				(16.2)	(16.6)	(17.7)
Tax benefit on preference stock dividends				2.1	2.4	3.1
Common stock dividends				(117.5)	(105.6)	(90.6)
End of year				6,738.6	5,645.5	4,846.5
TOTAL SHAREHOLDERS' EQUITY				$8,331.2	$6,987.2	$6,021.8
COMPREHENSIVE INCOME:						
Net earnings				$1,224.7	$ 918.8	$ 847.3
Unrealized gain (loss) on derivatives				2.9	(19.8)	—
Minimum pension liability, net of income tax				(37.7)	1.2	7.7
COMPREHENSIVE INCOME				$1,189.9	$ 900.2	$ 855.0

> Net earnings are from the income statement.

▼ **EXHIBIT S-4**

CVS's Statements of Cash Flows

CVS Corporation
Consolidated Statements of Cash Flows

Cash flows are shown for operating activities, investing activities, and financing activities.

(In millions)	Dec. 31, 2005 (52 weeks)	Jan. 1, 2005 (52 weeks)	Jan. 3, 2004 (53 weeks)
Fiscal year ended			
CASH FLOWS FROM OPERATING ACTIVITIES:			
Cash receipts from sales	$36,923.1	$30,545.8	$26,276.9
Cash paid for inventory	(26,403.9)	(22,469.2)	(19,262.9)
Cash paid to other suppliers and employees	(8,186.7)	(6,528.5)	(5,475.5)
Interest and dividends received	6.5	5.7	5.7
Interest paid	(135.9)	(70.4)	(64.9)
Income taxes paid	(591.0)	(569.2)	(510.4)
NET CASH PROVIDED BY OPERATING ACTIVITIES	1,612.1	914.2	968.9
CASH FLOWS FROM INVESTING ACTIVITIES:			
Additions to property and equipment	(1,495.4)	(1,347.7)	(1,121.7)
Proceeds from sale-leaseback transactions	539.9	496.6	487.8
Acquisitions, net of cash and investments	12.1	(2,293.7)	(133.1)
Cash outflow from hedging activities	—	(32.8)	—
Proceeds from sale or disposal of assets	31.8	14.3	13.4
NET CASH USED IN INVESTING ACTIVITIES	(911.6)	(3,163.3)	(753.6)
CASH FLOWS FROM FINANCING ACTIVITIES:			
Reductions in long-term debt	(10.5)	(301.5)	(0.8)
Additions to long-term debt	16.5	1,204.1	—
Proceeds from exercise of stock options	178.4	129.8	38.3
Dividends paid	(131.6)	(119.8)	(105.2)
Additions to/(reductions in) short-term debt	(632.2)	885.6	(4.8)
NET CASH (USED IN) PROVIDED BY FINANCING ACTIVITIES	(579.4)	1,798.2	(72.5)
Net increase (decrease) in cash and cash equivalents	121.1	(450.9)	142.8
Cash and cash equivalents at beginning of year	392.3	843.2	700.4
CASH AND CASH EQUIVALENTS AT END OF YEAR	$ 513.4	$ 392.3	$ 843.2
RECONCILIATION OF NET EARNINGS TO NET CASH PROVIDED BY OPERATING ACTIVITIES			
Net earnings	$1,224.7	$ 918.8	$ 847.3
Adjustments required to reconcile net earnings to net cash provided by operating activities:			
Depreciation and amortization	589.1	496.8	341.7
Deferred income taxes and other non-cash items	13.5	(23.6)	41.1
Change in operating assets and liabilities providing/(requiring) cash, net of effects from acquisitions:			
Accounts receivable, net	(83.1)	(48.4)	(311.1)
Inventories	(265.2)	(509.8)	2.1
Other current assets	(13.2)	35.7	(3.0)
Other assets	(0.1)	8.5	(0.4)
Accounts payable	192.2	109.4	(41.5)
Accrued expenses	(43.8)	(144.2)	116.5
Other long-term liabilities	(2.0)	71.0	(23.8)
NET CASH PROVIDED BY OPERATING ACTIVITIES	$1,612.1	$ 914.2	$ 968.9

Cash and cash equivalents move to balance sheets.

CVS's fiscal year ends on the Saturday nearest the end of December (December 31, 2005 in the latest year). Retailers commonly end their fiscal years during a slow period, usually the end of January, which is in contrast to CVS's choosing the end of December.

Income Statements   CVS uses a multistep form of the income statement in that results are shown in several steps (in contrast to the single-step form illustrated in the chapter). The steps are gross margin, operating profit, earnings before income tax provision, and net earnings (see Exhibit S-1). The company also shows net earnings available to common shareholders, and it discloses the basic earnings per share and diluted earnings per share. Basic earnings per share is used for most analysis. Diluted earnings per share assumes that all rights that could be exchanged for common shares, such as stock options, are in fact exchanged. The weighted average number of shares of common stock, used in calculating the per share figures, are shown at the bottom of the income statement.

Balance Sheets   CVS has a typical balance sheet for a retail company (see Exhibit S-2). In the assets and liabilities sections, the company separates out the current assets and the current liabilities. Current assets will become available as cash or will be used up in the next year; current liabilities will have to be paid or satisfied in the next year. These groupings are useful in assessing a company's liquidity.

Several items in the shareholders' equity section of the balance sheet may need explanation. Common stock represents the number of shares outstanding at par value. Capital surplus (additional paid-in capital) represents amounts invested by stockholders in excess of the par value of the common stock. Preferred stock is capital stock that has certain features that distinguish it from common stock. Treasury stock represents shares of common stock the company repurchased.

Statements of Shareholders' Equity   Instead of a simple statement of retained earnings, CVS presents consolidated statements of shareholders' equity (Exhibit S-3). These statements explain the changes in components of stockholders' equity, including retained earnings.

Statements of Cash Flows   Whereas the income statement reflects CVS's profitability, the statement of cash flows reflects its liquidity (see Exhibit S-4). This statement provides information about a company's cash receipts, cash payments, and investing and financing activities during an accounting period.

The first major section of CVS's consolidated statements of cash flows shows cash flows from operating activities. It shows the cash received and paid for various items related to the company's operations. The second major section is cash flows from investing activities. Except for the acquisition in 2004, the largest outflow in this category is additions for property and equipment. This figure demonstrates that CVS is a growing company. The third major section is cash flows from financing activities. You can see here that CVS's largest cash inflow consists of proceeds from the exercise of stock options, and the largest outflow is reduction (repayment) of short-term debt.

At the bottom of the statements of cash flows, you can see a reconciliation of net earnings to net cash provided by operating activities. This disclosure is important to the user because it relates the goal of profitability (net earnings) to liquidity (net cash provided). Most companies substitute this disclosure for the operating activities at the beginning of their statement of cash flows.

Notes to the Financial Statements

To meet the requirements of full disclosure and help users interpret complex items, a company must add notes to the financial statements. The notes are considered an integral part of the statements. In recent years, the need for explanation and further details has become so great that the notes are often longer than the statements themselves. The notes to the financial statements include a summary of significant accounting policies and explanatory notes.

Summary of Significant Accounting Policies Generally accepted accounting principles require that the financial statements include a *Summary of Significant Accounting Policies*. In most cases, this summary is presented in the first note to the financial statements or as a separate section just before the notes. In this summary, the company tells which generally accepted accounting principles it has followed in preparing the statements. For example, in CVS's report, the company states the principles followed for revenue recognition:

> The Company recognizes revenue from the sale of merchandise at the time the merchandise is sold. . . . Service revenue from the Company's pharmacy benefit management segment, which is recognized using the net method. . . .

Explanatory Notes Other notes explain some of the items in the financial statements. For example, CVS describes its commitments for future lease payments as follows:

> Following is a summary of the future minimum lease payments under capital and operating leases as of December 31, 2005:

(In millions)	Capital Leases	Operating Leases
2006	$0.2	$1,233.0
2007	0.2	1,178.6
2008	0.2	1,127.5
2009	0.2	1,090.4
2010	0.1	1,205.4
Thereafter	0.0	10,492.8
	$0.9	$16,327.7

Information like this is very useful in determining the full scope of a company's liabilities and other commitments.

Supplementary Information Notes In recent years, the FASB and the SEC have ruled that certain supplemental information must be presented with financial statements. Examples are the quarterly reports that most companies present to their stockholders and to the SEC. These quarterly reports, called *interim financial statements*, are in most cases reviewed but not audited by a company's independent CPA firm. In its annual report, CVS presents unaudited quarterly financial data from its 2004 and 2005 quarterly statements. The quarterly data also includes the high and low price for the company's common stock during each quarter.

Reports of Management's Responsibilities

Separate statements of management's responsibility for the financial statements and for internal control structure accompany the financial statements as

■ **FIGURE S-1**
Auditor's Report for CVS Corporation

Report of Independent Registered Public Accounting Firm KPMG
The Board of Directors and Shareholders
CVS Corporation

① We have audited the accompanying consolidated balance sheets of CVS Corporation and subsidiaries as of December 31, 2005 and January 1, 2005, and the related consolidated statements of operations, shareholders' equity and cash flows for the fifty-two week periods ended December 31, 2005 and January 1, 2005 and the fifty-three week period ended January 3, 2004. These consolidated financial statements are the responsibility of the Company's management. Our responsibility is to express an opinion on these consolidated financial statements based on our audits.

② We conducted our audits in accordance with the standards of the Public Company Accounting Oversight Board (United States). Those standards require that we plan and perform the audit to obtain reasonable assurance about whether the financial statements are free of material misstatement. An audit includes examining, on a test basis, evidence supporting the amounts and disclosures in the financial statements. An audit also includes assessing the accounting principles used and significant estimates made by management, as well as evaluating the overall financial statement presentation. We believe that our audits provide a reasonable basis for our opinion.

③ In our opinion, the consolidated financial statements referred to above present fairly, in all material respects, the financial position of CVS Corporation and subsidiaries as of December 31, 2005 and January 1, 2005, and the results of their operations and their cash flows for the fifty-two week periods ended December 31, 2005 and January 1, 2005, and the fifty-three week period ended January 3, 2004, in conformity with accounting principles generally accepted in the United States of America.

④ We also have audited, in accordance with the standards of the Public Company Accounting Oversight Board (United States), the effectiveness of CVS Corporation's internal control over financial reporting as of December 31, 2005, based on criteria established in *Internal Control—Integrated Framework* issued by the Committee of Sponsoring Organizations of the Treadway Commission (COSO), and our report dated March 14, 2006 expressed an unqualified opinion on management's assessment of, and the effective operation of, internal control over financial reporting.

KPMG LLP

KPMG LLP
Providence, Rhode Island
March 14, 2006

required by the Sarbanes-Oxley Act of 2002. In its reports, CVS's management acknowledges its responsibility for establishing and maintaining effective internal control over financial reporting.

Reports of Certified Public Accountants

The *registered independent auditors' report* deals with the credibility of the financial statements. This report, prepared by independent certified public accountants, gives the accountants' opinion about how fairly the statements have been presented. Because management is responsible for preparing the financial statements, issuing statements that have not been independently audited would be like having a judge hear a case in which he or she was personally involved. The certified public accountants, acting independently, add the necessary credibility to management's figures for interested third parties. They report to the board of directors and the stockholders rather than to the company's management.

In form and language, most auditors' reports are like the one shown in Figure S-1. Usually, such a report is short, but its language is very important. It normally has four parts, but it can have a fifth part if an explanation is needed.

1. The first paragraph identifies the financial statements that have been audited. This paragraph also identifies responsibilities. The company's management is responsible for the financial statements, and the auditor is responsible for expressing an opinion on the financial statements based on the audit.

2. The second paragraph, or *scope section*, states that the examination was made in accordance with standards of the Public Company Accounting Oversight Board (PCAOB). This paragraph also contains a brief description of the objectives and nature of the audit.

3. The third paragraph, or *opinion section*, states the results of the auditors' examination. The use of the word *opinion* is very important because the auditor does not certify or guarantee that the statements are absolutely correct. To do so would go beyond the truth, because many items, such as depreciation, are based on estimates. Instead, the auditors simply give an opinion about whether, overall, the financial statements "present fairly," in all material respects, the company's financial position, results of operations, and cash flows. This means that the statements are prepared in accordance with generally accepted accounting principles. If, in the auditors' opinion, the statements do not meet accepted standards, the auditors must explain why and to what extent.

4. The fourth paragraph says the company's internal controls are effective.

At CVS, All Signs Point to Growth
CVS CORPORATION ANNUAL REPORT
2005

·· Financial Highlights

In millions, except per share

	2005	2004	% Change
	52 weeks	52 weeks	
Sales	$37,006.2	$30,594.3	21.0
Operating profit	2,019.5	1,454.7	38.8
Net earnings	1,224.7	918.8	33.3
Diluted earnings per common share	1.45	1.10	31.8
Stock price at calendar year end	26.42	22.54	17.2
Market capitalization at calendar year end	21,514.0	18,071.0	19.1

About Our Company

America's No. 1 drugstore chain, CVS operates more than 5,400 CVS/pharmacy stores in 34 states and the District of Columbia. Our PharmaCare subsidiary operates 51 specialty pharmacies and is the nation's fourth-largest, full-service pharmacy benefits manager. Total CVS revenues exceeded $37 billion in 2005, with more than 70 percent generated through pharmacy sales. In fact, our CVS/pharmacy stores fill more than one in every eight retail prescriptions in the United States. We remain committed to being the easiest pharmacy for customers to use. Our 148,000 colleagues work hard so that everyone can "expect something extra" whether entering one of our stores, shopping at CVS.com, or using PharmaCare's services.

Our company trades on the New York Stock Exchange under the ticker "CVS."

Chairman, President, and CEO Tom Ryan

To Our Shareholders:

The past year will certainly be remembered as one of considerable accomplishment for our company. We swiftly and successfully completed the integration of nearly 1,100 former Eckerd stores, along with the former Eckerd Health Services, acquired in 2004. At the same time, we opened approximately 300 new or relocated stores in both existing and new markets. Throughout this activity, we never lost focus on our core business, as evidenced by our same store sales growth and market share gains. Our PharmaCare pharmacy benefits manager (PBM) also hit new heights, recording total revenue of just under $3 billion.

Our company's total sales rose 21 percent to a record $37 billion, while diluted earnings per share climbed 32 percent, to $1.45. Same store sales, which now include the 2004 acquired stores, increased 6.5 percent, with front-end same store sales up a stellar 5.5 percent and pharmacy same store sales up 7.0 percent. I'm also pleased to report that we generated more than $650 million in free cash flow, reflecting the quality of our growth. Our shares produced a 17.9 percent total return, far outdistancing the 4.9 percent return posted by the S&P 500 Index.

All signs point to growth in 2006 and beyond

The nation's largest pharmacy chain by store count, we were operating 5,420 CVS/pharmacy® locations by year-end plus 51 PharmaCare specialty pharmacies. We opened many of our new stores in important growth markets such as Chicago, Minneapolis, Las Vegas, Los Angeles, Orange County, and Phoenix. All of those are newer markets entered by CVS during the past five years.

Our shares produced a 17.9 percent total return, far outdistancing the 4.9 percent return posted by the S&P 500 Index.

1

Stock Price at Year End*

05	$26.42
04	$22.54
03	$18.06

*Calendar year end

As far and as fast as we've come, it's important to note that much of the 2004 acquisition's benefits still lie ahead of us.

I'm happy to report that we surpassed our sales and profitability targets in all of them. We expect to open 250 to 275 new or relocated stores in 2006, adding 100 to 125 net new locations.

Meanwhile, we're delighted with the performance of the former Eckerd stores acquired in 2004. Concentrated largely in Florida and Texas, they have met or exceeded expectations on every front. All operations have been fully integrated, from marketing, distribution, and human resources to information systems and the successful combination of the acquired PBM operations under the PharmaCare banner. Yet, as far and as fast as we've come, it's important to note that we believe much of the acquisition's benefits still lie ahead of us. By employing our operational expertise and technology, we are taking advantage of a multi-year opportunity to drive top-line growth, improve margins, and reduce inventory shrinkage. Furthermore, a new distribution center similar to our Ennis, Texas, facility is set to open in Florida during the second half of 2006. Highly cost-effective, its storage and retrieval systems will be capable of servicing the same volume and number of stores as a facility twice its size.

Our planned acquisition of 700 standalone Sav-on® and Osco® drugstores from Albertson's, Inc., announced in January 2006, will further strengthen our position as America's No. 1 retail pharmacy. Upon completion of the transaction, which is expected to occur mid-2006, we will operate approximately 6,100 stores across 42 states. Almost half the stores we are acquiring are located in Southern California, which will make us the No. 1 drugstore in that fast-growing region. Most of the rest are high-volume stores in states where we already have a presence, providing many No. 1 or No. 2 market positions. We will also acquire a distribution center in La Habra, California. The transaction is expected to be accretive to both earnings and cash flow in its first full year.

Leveraging new opportunities in pharmacy

CVS now fills 14 percent of all U.S. retail drug prescriptions. Generics account for well over half of all the prescriptions we fill. With several blockbuster drugs poised to lose patent protection over the next several years, the demand for generics should continue to climb. While depressing top-line growth, the increasing adoption of generic pharmaceuticals is helping drive margin gains.

The Medicare Part D Prescription Drug Plan, launched in January 2006, should increase usage of pharmaceuticals over time by making them more affordable for seniors. Some 42 million Medicare beneficiaries are eligible for the new plan, and we've worked

Dividends Declared

- 05: $0.145
- 04: $0.133
- 03: $0.115

Our ExtraCare® loyalty card has become a powerful tool, and customers tell us that they love the benefits.

hard to position ourselves as a key information source. More than 15,000 CVS pharmacists have undergone extensive training to help seniors navigate the variety of options available to them. We've formed marketing alliances with three of the nation's leading managed care organizations: UnitedHealth Group, through its Ovations business unit, Aetna, and Humana. We've also hosted free educational seminars and set up Medicare Information Centers in stores across the country. As a result, we are already seeing new customers in our stores.

With the industry's leading retail presence and our PBM, we are in an excellent position to benefit from Medicare Part D. Our PharmaCare subsidiary has grown into the nation's fourth-largest, full-service PBM since its launch in 1994. An attractive business, it has low capital requirements and high return characteristics. PharmaCare has focused from the outset on providing clients with high-quality, low-cost solutions. It has also been at the leading edge of providing an integrated PBM/specialty pharmacy offering. In addition to its significant mail order pharmacy business, PharmaCare operates specialty stores across the country as well as a state-of-the-art specialty mail order facility. During 2005, PharmaCare announced a strategic alliance with Universal American Financial Corp., a leading health insurance company, under which PharmaCare will provide a full array of PBM services to Universal American-sponsored Medicare prescription plans.

Gaining share in all key, front-store categories

CVS gained share in the front of the store in all key categories, including health, beauty, vitamins, greeting cards, and general merchandise, while also increasing sales of private label products. Our ExtraCare® loyalty card has become a powerful tool, and customers tell us that they love the benefits. Impressively, they use the card for approximately 60 percent of front-store transactions. A laser focus on customer service is at the heart of our front-store strategy. Along with our loyalty program, new proprietary and exclusive products, and smarter promotions, our focus on making things "CVS easy®" for customers is driving our growth. Our customer research tells us that our service profile has strengthened. We are earning high marks for shopability, value, hours of operation, being in-stock, and overall customer service. Among our latest "CVS easy" initiatives, we've teamed up with MinuteClinic to offer in-store treatment for common family ailments through certified nurse practitioners and physician's assistants. As of February 2006, approximately 50 CVS/pharmacy stores included these independently operated clinics, and we expect that number to rise as the year progresses. Early reports indicate that customers enjoy the convenience.

Total Sales

05 $370
04 30.6
03 $26.6

In billions

Pharmacy Sales

05 $26.3
04 $21.5
03 $18.3

In billions

The combination of our stores and our PharmaCare PBM business offers payors a pharmacy solution unmatched by any competitor.

On the pages that follow, you can read about our growth opportunities in more detail. Before signing off, though, I want to thank our 148,000 CVS colleagues and our board of directors for their invaluable contributions. We could not have accomplished all we did without their tremendous dedication. They waged an impressive group effort around the integration of our 2004 acquisition while never losing focus on our existing business. Above and beyond their official responsibilities, CVS colleagues also took their civic responsibilities seriously. Their response to the devastation caused by Hurricane Katrina was quick, effective, and passionate, as they tried to make life easier for the many victims. I couldn't be more proud of the many contributions made by our team.

I also want to pay tribute to my friend and mentor Stanley Goldstein, who is stepping down from our board in May 2006. Stanley, along with his late brother Sid and Ralph Hoagland, had the vision to open the first CVS store in Lowell, Massachusetts, back in 1963. During his tenure as President of CVS/pharmacy and then President of Melville Corporation, Stanley helped transform the retail landscape. After stepping down as Chairman of CVS Corporation in 1999 and right up to the present, he has continued to provide valuable perspective and sage counsel. It has been my pleasure and privilege to know Stanley and work alongside him for nearly three decades. He has left a legacy that will help guide our company well into the future.

In closing, the bright opportunities before us mean that all signs point to growth for CVS. We expect to reap multi-year benefits from the turnaround of our acquired properties. Our retail pharmacies will leverage our leadership in the industry as well as the broader healthcare trends working in our favor. Furthermore, the combination of our stores and our PharmaCare PBM business offers payors a pharmacy solution unmatched by any competitor. Finally, our strong cash flow means that more CVS/pharmacy stores in more markets are on the way. Thank you for your confidence.

Thomas M. Ryan
Chairman of the Board, President, and Chief Executive Officer

March 14, 2006

2005 Financial Report

MANAGEMENT'S DISCUSSION AND ANALYSIS OF FINANCIAL CONDITION AND RESULTS OF OPERATIONS

The following discussion should be read in conjunction with our audited consolidated financial statements and our Cautionary Statement Concerning Forward-Looking Statements that are presented in this Annual Report.

Our Business

Our Company is a leader in the retail drugstore industry in the United States. We sell prescription drugs and a wide assortment of general merchandise, including over-the-counter drugs, beauty products and cosmetics, film and photofinishing services, seasonal merchandise, greeting cards and convenience foods through our CVS/pharmacy® retail stores and online through CVS.com.® We also provide pharmacy benefit management, mail order services and specialty pharmacy services through PharmaCare Management Services and PharmaCare Pharmacy® stores. As of December 31, 2005, we operated 5,471 retail and specialty pharmacy stores in 37 states and the District of Columbia.

Recent Development

On January 22, 2006, we entered into a definitive agreement under which we will acquire approximately 700 standalone Sav-on and Osco drugstores, as well as a distribution center located in La Habra, California, from Albertson's, Inc. ("Albertson's"), for $2.93 billion in cash immediately preceding the planned merger of Albertson's and Supervalu, Inc. ("Supervalu"). Approximately half of the drugstores are located in southern California, with others in our existing markets in numerous states across the Midwest and Southwest. We will also acquire Albertson's owned real estate interests in the drugstores for $1.0 billion in cash. Closing of the transaction, which is expected to occur in mid-2006, is subject to review under the Hart-Scott-Rodino Act, as well as other customary closing conditions. Further, closing is also conditioned on consummation of the merger between Albertson's and Supervalu, which is also subject to review under the Hart-Scott-Rodino Act and other customary closing conditions, as well as approval by the shareholders of Albertson's and Supervalu. We expect to finance the transaction through a combination of cash, short-term and long-term debt and proceeds from the subsequent sale-leaseback of owned real estate interests. Closing of the transaction is not subject to such financing.

Acquired Business

On July 31, 2004, the Company acquired certain assets and assumed certain liabilities from J.C. Penney Company, Inc. and certain of its subsidiaries, including Eckerd Corporation ("Eckerd"). The acquisition included more than 1,200 Eckerd retail drugstores and Eckerd Health Services, which included Eckerd's mail order and pharmacy benefit management businesses (collectively, the "Acquired Businesses"). The Company believes that the acquisition of the Acquired Businesses is consistent with its long-term strategy of expanding its retail drugstore business in high-growth markets and increasing the size and product offerings of its pharmacy benefit management business. Please see Note 2 to the consolidated financial statements for additional information.

Results of Operations and Industry Analysis

The Company's fiscal year is a 52 or 53 week period ending on the Saturday closest to December 31. Fiscal 2005, which ended on December 31, 2005 and fiscal 2004, which ended on January 1, 2005, each included 52 weeks. Fiscal 2003, which ended on January 3, 2004, included 53 weeks. Unless otherwise noted, all references to 2005, 2004 and 2003 relate to these fiscal years.

NET SALES-The following table summarizes our sales performance:

	2005	2004	2003
Net sales *(in billions)*	$ 37.0	$ 30.6	$ 26.6
Net sales increase:			
Total	21.0%	15.1%	10.0%
Pharmacy	22.0%	17.1%	11.9%
Front store	18.4%	10.5%	5.7%
Same store sales increase:			
Total	6.5%	5.5%	5.8%
Pharmacy	7.0%	7.0%	8.1%
Front store	5.5%	2.3%	1.2%
Pharmacy % of total sales	70.2%	70.0%	68.8%
Third party % of pharmacy sales	94.1%	94.1%	93.2%
Prescriptions filled *(in millions)*	434	366	335

As you review our net sales performance, we believe you should consider the following important information:

◇ Total net sales were significantly affected by the July 31, 2004 acquisition of the Acquired Businesses. Excluding the sales from the Acquired Businesses, total sales increased approximately 8.4% and 5.2% during 2005 and 2004, respectively. Beginning in August 2005, same store sales include the acquired stores, which increased total same store sales by approximately 60 basis points in 2005.

◇ Total net sales from new stores accounted for approximately 160 basis points of our total net sales percentage increase in 2005, and 190 basis points in 2004.

◇ Total net sales continued to benefit from our ongoing relocation program, which moves existing in-line shopping center stores to larger, more convenient, freestanding locations. Historically, we have achieved significant improvements in customer count and net sales when we do this. Although the number of annual relocations has decreased, our relocation strategy remains an important component of our overall growth strategy. As of December 31, 2005, approximately 59% of our existing stores were freestanding, compared to approximately 55% at January 1, 2005.

◇ The increase in total net sales in 2004 was negatively affected by the 53rd week in 2003, which generated $530.8 million in net sales.

◇ Pharmacy sales growth continued to benefit from new market expansions, increased penetration in existing markets, our ability to attract and retain managed care customers and favorable industry trends. These trends include an aging American population; many "baby boomers" are now in their fifties and are consuming a greater number of prescription drugs. The increased use of pharmaceuticals as the first line of defense for individual healthcare also contributed to the growing demand for pharmacy services. We believe these favorable industry trends will continue.

◇ Pharmacy sales were negatively impacted in all years by the conversion of brand named drugs to equivalent generic drugs, which typically have a lower selling price. However, our gross margins on generic drug sales are generally higher than our gross margins on equivalent brand named drug sales.

◊ Our pharmacy sales growth has also been adversely affected by the growth of the mail order channel, a decline in the number of significant new drug introductions, higher consumer co-payments and co-insurance arrangements and an increase in the number of over-the-counter remedies that had historically only been available by prescription. To address the growth in mail order, we may choose not to participate in certain prescription benefit programs that mandate filling maintenance prescriptions through a mail order service facility. In the event we elect to, for any reason, withdraw from current programs and/or decide not to participate in future programs, we may not be able to sustain our current rate of sales growth.

GROSS MARGIN, which includes net sales less the cost of merchandise sold during the reporting period and the related purchasing costs, warehousing costs, delivery costs and actual and estimated inventory losses, as a percentage of net sales was 26.8% in 2005. This compares to 26.3% in 2004 and 25.8% in 2003. As you review our gross margin performance, we believe you should consider the following important information:

◊ Our pharmacy gross margin rate continued to benefit from an increase in generic drug sales in 2005, which normally yield a higher gross margin than equivalent brand name drug sales.

◊ Our gross margin rate continued to benefit from reduced inventory losses as a result of new and continuing programs implemented in our existing stores and the Acquired Businesses. While we believe these programs will continue to provide operational benefits, particularly for the Acquired Businesses, we expect the future financial improvement to be less significant. In addition, we cannot guarantee that our programs will continue to reduce inventory losses.

◊ Our gross margin rate continues to be adversely affected by pharmacy sales growing at a faster pace than front store sales. On average, our gross margin on pharmacy sales is lower than our gross margin on front store sales. Pharmacy sales were 70.2% of total sales in 2005, compared to 70.0% in 2004 and 68.8% in 2003.

◊ Sales to customers covered by third party insurance programs have continued to increase and, thus, have become a larger component of our total pharmacy business. On average, our gross margin on third party pharmacy sales is lower than our gross margin on non-third party pharmacy sales. Third party pharmacy sales were 94.1% of pharmacy sales in 2005 and 2004, compared to 93.2% in 2003. We expect these negative trends to continue. In particular, the introduction of the new Medicare Part D benefit is anticipated to increase utilization and decrease pharmacy gross margin rates as higher margin business (such as cash and state Medicaid customers) migrate to Part D coverage. Further, on February 8, 2006, the President signed into law the Deficit Reduction Act of 2005 (the "Act"). The Act seeks to reduce federal spending by $3.6 billion over a five-year period by altering the Medicaid reimbursement formula for multi-source (i.e., generic) drugs. According to the Congressional Budget Office, retail pharmacies are expected to negotiate with individual states for higher dispensing fees to mitigate the adverse effect of these changes. These changes take effect January 1, 2007 and are expected to result in reduced Medicaid reimbursement rates for retail pharmacies. In addition, the President's proposed budget for fiscal year 2007 contains further reductions in the Medicaid reimbursement formula for multi-source drugs. The extent of these reductions cannot be determined at this time.

TOTAL OPERATING EXPENSES, which include store and administrative payroll, employee benefits, store and administrative occupancy costs, selling expenses, advertising expenses, administrative expenses and depreciation and amortization expense were 21.3% of net sales in 2005. This compares to 21.5% of net sales in 2004 and 20.5% in 2003. As you review our total operating expenses, we believe you should consider the following important information:

◊ Total operating expenses as a percentage of net sales continued to be impacted by an increase in the sale of generic drugs, which typically have a lower selling price than their brand named equivalents. Fiscal 2005 was also impacted by higher payroll and benefit costs.

◊ During the fourth quarter of 2004, we conformed our accounting for operating leases and leasehold improvements to the views expressed by the Office of the Chief Accountant of the Securities and Exchange Commission to the American Institute of Certified Public Accountants on February 7, 2005. As a result, we recorded a $65.9 million non-cash pre-tax adjustment to total operating expenses, which represents the cumulative effect of the adjustment for a period of approximately 20 years (the "Lease Adjustment"). Since the Lease Adjustment was not material to 2004 or any previously reported fiscal year, the cumulative effect was recorded in the fourth quarter of 2004. For internal comparisons, management finds it useful to assess year-to-year performance excluding the Lease Adjustment, which results in comparable 2004 total operating expenses as a percentage of net sales of 21.3%.

◊ Total operating expenses as a percentage of net sales also increased during 2004 due to integration and incremental costs as a result of the acquisition of the Acquired Businesses. In addition, the acquired stores had lower average sales per store during 2004, increasing operating expenses as a percentage of net sales.

◊ Fiscal 2004 and 2003 were impacted by an increase in payroll and benefit costs driven by an increase in the number of 24-hour and extended hour stores, as well as new stores.

INTEREST EXPENSE, NET consisted of the following:

In millions	2005	2004	2003
Interest expense	$ 117.0	$ 64.0	$ 53.9
Interest income	(6.5)	(5.7)	(5.8)
Interest expense, net	$ 110.5	$ 58.3	$ 48.1

The increase in interest expense, net during 2005 and 2004 was primarily driven by the increase in debt used to fund the acquisition of the Acquired Businesses, which occurred during the third quarter of 2004.

INCOME TAX PROVISION– Our effective income tax rate was 35.8% in 2005, 34.2% in 2004 and 38.4% in 2003. As you review our income tax provision, we believe you should consider the following important information:

◊ During the fourth quarter of 2005, an assessment of tax reserves resulted in a reduction that was principally based on resolving certain state tax matters. As a result, the Company reversed $52.6 million of previously recorded tax reserves through the income tax provision.

MANAGEMENT'S DISCUSSION AND ANALYSIS OF FINANCIAL CONDITION AND RESULTS OF OPERATIONS

Following is a summary of our store development activity for the respective years:

	2005	2004	2003
Total stores (beginning of year)	5,375	4,179	4,087
New and acquired stores	166	1,397	150
Closed stores	(70)	(201)	(58)
Total stores (end of year)	5,471	5,375	4,179
Relocated stores(1)	131	96	125

(1) Relocated stores are not included in new or closed store totals.

● During the fourth quarter of 2004, an assessment of tax reserves resulted in a reduction that was principally based on finalizing certain tax return years and on a 2004 court decision that was relevant to the industry. As a result, the Company reversed $60.0 million of previously recorded tax reserves through the income tax provision.

● For internal comparisons, management finds it useful to assess year-to-year performance excluding the impact of the tax benefit in 2005 and 2004 discussed above, and uses 38.6%, 38.5% and 38.4% as comparable effective tax rates for 2005, 2004 and 2003, respectively.

NET EARNINGS increased $305.9 million or 33.3% to $1.2 billion (or $1.45 per diluted share) in 2005. This compares to $918.8 million (or $1.10 per diluted share) in 2004, and $847.3 million (or $1.03 per diluted share) in 2003. For internal comparisons, management finds it useful to assess year-to-year performance excluding the $52.6 million tax reserve reversal discussed above, and uses $1.2 billion (or $1.39 per diluted share) for comparable net earnings in 2005. In addition, management finds it useful to remove the $40.5 million after-tax effect of the $65.9 million Lease Adjustment to total operating expense and the $60.0 million tax reserve reversal, discussed above, and uses $899.3 million (or $1.08 per diluted share) for its internal comparisons in 2004.

Liquidity & Capital Resources

We anticipate that our cash flow from operations, supplemented by short-term commercial paper and long-term borrowings, will continue to fund the future growth of our business.

NET CASH PROVIDED BY OPERATING ACTIVITIES increased to $1,612.1 million in 2005. This compares to $914.2 million in 2004 and $968.9 million in 2003. The increase in net cash provided by operations during 2005 primarily resulted from increased revenues and improved inventory management. Fiscal 2004 reflected increased inventory payments as a result of higher inventory levels, and higher operating costs associated with the Acquired Businesses and investments, including the cost of extending store hours. The elevated inventory levels during 2004 were primarily the result of inventory purchased to reset the acquired stores with the CVS/pharmacy product mix.

NET CASH USED IN INVESTING ACTIVITIES decreased to $911.6 million in 2005. The decrease in net cash used in investing activities during 2005 related to a decrease in acquisitions, as 2004 included the acquisition of the Acquired Businesses. Gross capital expenditures totaled $1,495.4 million during 2005, compared to $1,347.7 million in 2004 and $1,121.7 million in 2003. During 2005, approximately 56% of our total capital expenditures were for new store construction, 29% for store expansion and improvements and 15% for technology and other corporate initiatives, including a new distribution center in Florida, which is expected to be completed during 2006.

During 2006, we currently plan to invest over $1.4 billion in gross capital expenditures, which will include spending for approximately 250–275 new or relocated stores.

NET CASH USED IN FINANCING ACTIVITIES was $579.4 million in 2005, compared to net cash provided by financing activities of $1,798.2 million in 2004 and net cash used in financing activities of $72.5 million in 2003. The increase in net cash used in financing activities during 2005 was primarily due to a reduction in short-term borrowings. Fiscal 2004 reflected the financing of the acquisition of the Acquired Businesses, including the issuance of the Notes (defined below) during the third quarter of 2004. The increase was offset, in part, by the repayment of the $300 million, 5.5% unsecured senior notes, which matured during the first quarter of 2004. During 2005, we paid common stock dividends totaling $117.5 million, or $0.145 per common share. In January 2006, our Board of Directors authorized a 7% increase in our common stock dividend to $0.155 per share for 2006.

We believe that our current cash on hand and cash provided by operations, together with our ability to obtain additional short-term and long-term financing, will be sufficient to cover our working capital needs, capital expenditures, debt service and dividend requirements for at least the next several years.

We had $253.4 million of commercial paper outstanding at a weighted average interest rate of 3.3% as of December 31, 2005. In connection with our commercial paper program, we maintain a $650 million, five-year unsecured back-up credit facility, which expires on May 21, 2006, and a $675 million, five-year unsecured back-up credit facility, which expires on June 2, 2010. In addition, we maintain a $675 million, five-year unsecured back-up credit facility, which expires on June 11, 2009. The credit facilities allow for borrowings at various rates that are dependent in part on our public debt rating. As of December 31, 2005, we had no outstanding borrowings against the credit facilities.

On September 14, 2004, we issued $650 million of 4.0% unsecured senior notes due September 15, 2009, and $550 million of 4.875% unsecured senior notes due September 15, 2014 (collectively the "Notes"). The Notes pay interest semi-annually and may be redeemed at any time, in whole or in part at a defined redemption price plus accrued interest. Net proceeds from the Notes were used to repay a portion of the outstanding commercial paper issued to finance the acquisition of the Acquired Businesses. As of December 31, 2005, we had no freestanding derivatives in place.

Our credit facilities and unsecured senior notes contain customary restrictive financial and operating covenants. These covenants do not include a requirement for the acceleration of our debt maturities in the event of a downgrade in our credit rating. We do not believe that the restrictions contained in these covenants materially affect our financial or operating flexibility.

Our liquidity is based, in part, on maintaining investment-grade debt ratings. As of December 31, 2005, our long-term debt was rated "A3" by Moody's and "A-" by Standard & Poor's, and our commercial paper program was rated "P-2" by Moody's and "A-2" by Standard & Poor's. In assessing our credit strength, we believe that both Moody's and Standard & Poor's considered, among other things, our capital structure and financial policies as well as our consolidated balance sheet and other financial information. Our debt ratings have a direct impact on our future borrowing costs, access to capital markets and new store operating lease costs. Subsequent to our entry into the definitive agreement with Albertson's in January 2006, Standard & Poor's placed our long-term debt on a negative outlook, while Moody's placed all our ratings under review for possible downgrade. While a downgrade is possible, our long-term debt ratings are expected to remain investment grade.

Off-Balance Sheet Arrangements

In connection with executing operating leases, we provide a guarantee of the lease payments. We finance a portion of our new store development through sale-leaseback transactions, which involve selling stores to unrelated parties and then leasing the stores back under leases that qualify and are accounted for as operating leases. We do not have any retained or contingent interests in the stores, nor do we provide any guarantees, other than a guarantee of the lease payments, in connection with the transactions. In accordance with generally accepted accounting principles, our operating leases are not reflected in our consolidated balance sheet.

Between 1991 and 1997, we sold or spun off a number of subsidiaries, including Bob's Stores, Linens 'n Things, Marshalls, Kay-Bee Toys, Wilsons, This End Up and Footstar. In many cases, when a former subsidiary leased a store, we provided a guarantee of the store's lease obligations. When the subsidiaries were disposed of, the guarantees remained in place, although each initial purchaser agreed to indemnify us for any lease obligations we were required to satisfy. If any of the purchasers were to become insolvent and failed to make the required payments under a store lease, we could be required to satisfy these obligations. Assuming that each respective purchaser became insolvent, and we were required to satisfy all of these lease obligations, we estimate that we could settle the obligations for approximately $400 to $450 million as of December 31, 2005. As of December 31, 2005, we guaranteed approximately 360 such store leases, with the maximum remaining lease term extending through 2018.

We currently believe that the ultimate disposition of any of the lease guarantees will not have a material adverse effect on our consolidated financial condition, results of operations or future cash flows.

Following is a summary of our significant contractual obligations as of December 31, 2005:

In millions

		PAYMENTS DUE BY PERIOD			
	Total	*Within 1 Year*	*1-3 Years*	*3-5 Years*	*After 5 Years*
Operating leases	$16,327.7	$1,233.0	$2,306.1	$2,295.8	$10,492.8
Long-term debt	1,935.0	341.4	387.3	652.4	553.9
Purchase obligations	70.5	24.5	46.0	–	–
Other long-term liabilities reflected in our consolidated balance sheet	284.5	61.6	170.6	40.9	11.4
Capital lease obligations	0.7	0.2	0.2	0.3	–
	$18,618.4	$1,660.7	$2,910.2	$2,989.4	$11,058.1

Critical Accounting Policies

We prepare our consolidated financial statements in conformity with generally accepted accounting principles, which require management to make certain estimates and apply judgment. We base our estimates and judgments on historical experience, current trends and other factors that management believes to be important at the time the consolidated financial statements are prepared. On a regular basis, we review our accounting policies and how they are applied and disclosed in our consolidated financial statements. While we believe that the historical experience, current trends and other factors considered support the preparation of our consolidated financial statements in conformity with generally accepted accounting principles, actual results could differ from our estimates, and such differences could be material.

Our significant accounting policies are discussed in Note 1 to our consolidated financial statements. We believe the following accounting policies include a higher degree of judgment and/or complexity and, thus,

are considered to be critical accounting policies. The critical accounting policies discussed below are applicable to both of our business segments. We have discussed the development and selection of our critical accounting policies with the Audit Committee of our Board of Directors and the Audit Committee has reviewed our disclosures relating to them.

Impairment of Long-Lived Assets

We account for the impairment of long-lived assets in accordance with Statement of Financial Accounting Standards ("SFAS") No. 144, "Accounting for Impairment or Disposal of Long-Lived Assets." As such, we evaluate the recoverability of long-lived assets, including intangible assets with finite lives, but excluding goodwill, which is tested for impairment using a separate test, whenever events or changes in circumstances indicate that the carrying value of an asset may not be recoverable. We group and evaluate long-lived assets for impairment at the individual store level, which is the lowest level at which individual cash flows

MANAGEMENT'S DISCUSSION AND ANALYSIS OF FINANCIAL CONDITION AND RESULTS OF OPERATIONS can be identified. When evaluating long-lived assets for potential impairment, we first compare the carrying amount of the asset group to the individual store's estimated future cash flows (undiscounted and without interest charges). If the estimated future cash flows are less than the carrying amount of the asset group, an impairment loss calculation is prepared. The impairment loss calculation compares the carrying amount of the asset group to the individual store's estimated future cash flows (discounted and with interest charges). If required, an impairment loss is recorded for the portion of the asset group's carrying value that exceeds the individual store's estimated future cash flows (discounted and with interest charges).

Our impairment loss calculation contains uncertainty since we must use judgment to estimate each store's future sales, profitability and cash flows. When preparing these estimates, we consider each store's historical results and current operating trends and our consolidated sales, profitability and cash flow results and forecasts. These estimates can be affected by a number of factors including, but not limited to, general economic conditions, the cost of real estate, the continued efforts of third party organizations to reduce their prescription drug costs, the continued efforts of competitors to gain market share and consumer spending patterns. We have not made any material changes to our impairment loss assessment methodology during the past three years.

Closed Store Lease Liability
We account for closed store lease termination costs in accordance with SFAS No. 146, "Accounting for Costs Associated with Exit or Disposal Activities." As such, when a leased store is closed, we record a liability for the estimated present value of the remaining obligation under the non-cancelable lease, which includes future real estate taxes, common area maintenance and other charges, if applicable. The liability is reduced by estimated future sublease income.

The initial calculation and subsequent evaluations of our closed store lease liability contains uncertainty since we must use judgment to estimate the timing and duration of future vacancy periods, the amount and timing of future lump sum settlement payments and the amount and timing of potential future sublease income. When estimating these potential termination costs and their related timing, we consider a number of factors, which include, but are not limited to, historical settlement experience, the owner of the property, the location and condition of the property, the terms of the underlying lease, the specific marketplace demand and general economic conditions. We have not made any material changes in the reserve methodology used to record closed store lease reserves during the past three years.

Self-Insurance Liabilities
We are self-insured for certain losses related to general liability, workers' compensation and auto liability although we maintain stop loss coverage with third party insurers to limit our total liability exposure. We are also self-insured for certain losses related to health and medical liabilities.

The estimate of our self-insurance liability contains uncertainty since we must use judgment to estimate the ultimate cost that will be incurred to settle reported claims and unreported claims for incidents incurred but not reported as of the balance sheet date. When estimating our self-insurance liability we consider a number of factors, which include, but are not limited to, historical claim experience, demographic factors, severity factors and valuations provided by independent third party actuaries.

On a quarterly basis, we review our assumptions with our independent third party actuaries to determine that our self-insurance liability is adequate. We have not made any material changes in the accounting methodology used to establish our self-insurance liability during the past three years.

Inventory
Our inventory is stated at the lower of cost or market on a first-in, first-out basis using the retail method of accounting to determine cost of sales and inventory in our stores, and the cost method of accounting to determine inventory in our distribution centers. Under the retail method, inventory is stated at cost, which is determined by applying a cost-to-retail ratio to the ending retail value of our inventory. Since the retail value of our inventory is adjusted on a regular basis to reflect current market conditions, our carrying value should approximate the lower of cost or market. In addition, we reduce the value of our ending inventory for estimated inventory losses that have occurred during the interim period between physical inventory counts. Physical inventory counts are taken on a regular basis in each location to ensure that the amounts reflected in the consolidated financial statements are properly stated.

The accounting for inventory contains uncertainty since we must use judgment to estimate the inventory losses that have occurred during the interim period between physical inventory counts. When estimating these losses, we consider a number of factors, which include but are not limited to, historical physical inventory results on a location-by-location basis and current inventory loss trends. We have not made any material changes in the accounting methodology used to establish our inventory loss reserves during the past three years.

Although we believe that the estimates discussed above are reasonable and the related calculations conform to generally accepted accounting principles, actual results could differ from our estimates, and such differences could be material.

Recent Accounting Pronouncements

In December 2004, SFAS No. 123(R), "Share-Based Payment," was issued. This statement establishes standards for the accounting for transactions in which an entity exchanges its equity instruments for goods or services. The statement focuses primarily on accounting for transactions in which an entity obtains employee services in share-based payment transactions. The provisions of this statement are required to be adopted for annual periods beginning after June 15, 2005. We believe the adoption of this statement will decrease our diluted earnings per share by approximately $0.05 in 2006; however, we continue to evaluate the potential impact as the amount is subject to variation based on the granting of stock compensation during 2006. Please see Note 7 to our consolidated financial statements for additional information regarding stock-based compensation.

In October 2005, the Financial Accounting Standards Board ("FASB") issued FASB Staff Position ("FSP") No. FAS 13-1, "Accounting for Rental Costs Incurred during a Construction Period." The FSP addresses the accounting for rental costs associated with operating leases that are incurred during a construction period and requires rental costs associated with ground or building operating leases that are incurred during a construction period to be recognized as rental expense. The provisions of the FSP are required to be applied to the first reporting period beginning after December 15, 2005. We do not expect that the adoption of this position will have a material impact on our consolidated results of operations or financial position.

Cautionary Statement Concerning Forward-Looking Statements

The Private Securities Litigation Reform Act of 1995 (the "Reform Act") provides a safe harbor for forward-looking statements made by or on behalf of CVS Corporation. The Company and its representatives may, from time to time, make written or verbal forward-looking statements, including statements contained in the Company's filings with the Securities and Exchange Commission and in its reports to stockholders. Generally, the inclusion of the words "believe," "expect," "intend," "estimate," "project," "anticipate," "will" and similar expressions identify statements that constitute forward-looking statements. All statements addressing operating performance of CVS Corporation or any subsidiary, events or developments that the Company expects or anticipates will occur in the future, including statements relating to sales growth, earnings or earnings per common share growth, free cash flow, debt rating, inventory levels, inventory turn and loss rates, store development, relocations and new market entries, as well as statements expressing optimism or pessimism about future operating results or events, are forward-looking statements within the meaning of the Reform Act.

The forward-looking statements are and will be based upon management's then-current views and assumptions regarding future events and operating performance, and are applicable only as of the dates of such statements. The Company undertakes no obligation to update or revise any forward-looking statements, whether as a result of new information, future events, or otherwise.

By their nature, all forward-looking statements involve risks and uncertainties. Actual results may differ materially from those contemplated by the forward-looking statements for a number of reasons, including, but not limited to:

◇ The continued efforts of health maintenance organizations, managed care organizations, pharmacy benefit management companies and other third party payors to reduce prescription drug costs and pharmacy reimbursement rates;

◇ The potential effect on pharmacy sales and gross margin rates attributable to the introduction in 2006 of a new Medicare prescription drug benefit and the continued efforts by various government entities to reduce state Medicaid pharmacy reimbursement rates;

◇ The growth of mail order pharmacies and changes to pharmacy benefit plans requiring maintenance medications to be filled exclusively through mail order pharmacies;

◇ The effect on PharmaCare of increased competition in the pharmacy benefit management industry, a declining margin environment attributable to increased client demands for lower prices, enhanced service offerings and/or higher service levels and the possible termination of, or unfavorable modification to, contractual arrangements with key clients or providers;

◇ Our ability to continue to improve the operating results of the Acquired Businesses;

◇ Our ability to consummate the recently announced Albertson's transaction and successfully integrate the business to be acquired;

◇ Increased competition from other drugstore chains, supermarkets, discount retailers, membership clubs and Internet companies, as well as changes in consumer preferences or loyalties;

◇ The frequency and rate of introduction of successful new prescription drugs;

◇ Our ability to generate sufficient cash flows to support capital expansion and general operating activities;

◇ Interest rate fluctuations and changes in capital market conditions or other events affecting our ability to obtain necessary financing on favorable terms;

◇ Our ability to identify, implement and successfully manage and finance strategic expansion opportunities including entering new markets, acquisitions and joint ventures;

◇ Our ability to establish effective advertising, marketing and promotional programs (including pricing strategies and price reduction programs implemented in response to competitive pressures and/or to drive demand);

◇ Our ability to continue to secure suitable new store locations under acceptable lease terms;

◇ Our ability to attract, hire and retain suitable pharmacists and management personnel;

◇ Our ability to achieve cost efficiencies and other benefits from various operational initiatives and technological enhancements;

◇ Litigation risks as well as changes in laws and regulations, including changes in accounting standards and taxation requirements (including tax rate changes, new tax laws and revised tax law interpretations);

◇ The creditworthiness of the purchasers of businesses formerly owned by CVS and whose leases are guaranteed by CVS;

◇ Fluctuations in inventory cost, availability and loss levels and our ability to maintain relationships with suppliers on favorable terms;

◇ Our ability to implement successfully and to manage new computer systems and technologies;

◇ The strength of the economy in general or in the markets served by CVS, including changes in consumer purchasing power and/or spending patterns; and

◇ Other risks and uncertainties detailed from time to time in our filings with the Securities and Exchange Commission.

The foregoing list is not exhaustive. There can be no assurance that the Company has correctly identified and appropriately assessed all factors affecting its business. Additional risks and uncertainties not presently known to the Company or that it currently believes to be immaterial also may adversely impact the Company. Should any risks and uncertainties develop into actual events, these developments could have material adverse effects on the Company's business, financial condition and results of operations. For these reasons, you are cautioned not to place undue reliance on the Company's forward-looking statements.

MANAGEMENT'S REPORT ON INTERNAL CONTROL OVER FINANCIAL REPORTING

We are responsible for establishing and maintaining effective internal control over financial reporting. Our Company's internal control over financial reporting includes those policies and procedures that pertain to the Company's ability to record, process, summarize and report a system of internal accounting controls and procedures to provide reasonable assurance, at an appropriate cost/benefit relationship, that the unauthorized acquisition, use or disposition of assets are prevented or timely detected and that transactions are authorized, recorded and reported properly to permit the preparation of financial statements in accordance with generally accepted accounting principles (GAAP) and receipt and expenditures are duly authorized. In order to ensure the Company's internal control over financial reporting is effective, management regularly assesses such controls and did so most recently for its financial reporting as of December 31, 2005.

We conduct an evaluation of the effectiveness of our internal controls over financial reporting based on the framework in *Internal Control — Integrated Framework* issued by the Committee of Sponsoring Organizations of the Treadway Commission. This evaluation included review of the documentation, evaluation of the design effectiveness and testing of the operating effectiveness of controls. Our system of internal control over financial reporting is enhanced by periodic reviews by our internal auditors, written policies and procedures and a written Code of Conduct adopted by our Company's Board of Directors, applicable to all employees of our Company.

In addition, we have an internal Disclosure Committee, comprised of management from each functional area within the Company, which performs a separate review of our disclosure control and procedures. There are inherent limitations in the effectiveness of any system of internal controls over financial reporting.

Based on our evaluation, we conclude our Company's internal control over financial reporting is effective and provides reasonable assurance that assets are safeguarded and that the financial records are reliable for preparing financial statements as of December 31, 2005.

KPMG LLP, independent registered public accounting firm, is appointed by the Board of Directors and ratified by our Company's shareholders. They were engaged to render an opinion regarding the fair presentation of our consolidated financial statements as well as conducting a review of the system of internal accounting controls. Their accompanying report is based upon an audit conducted in accordance with the Public Company Accounting Oversight Board (United States) and includes an attestation on management's assessment of internal controls over financial reporting.

March 14, 2006

REPORT OF INDEPENDENT REGISTERED PUBLIC ACCOUNTING FIRM

The Board of Directors and Shareholders
CVS Corporation

We have audited management's assessment, included in the accompanying Management's Report on Internal Control Over Financial Reporting, that CVS Corporation and subsidiaries maintained effective internal control over financial reporting as of December 31, 2005, based on criteria established in *Internal Control—Integrated Framework* issued by the Committee of Sponsoring Organizations of the Treadway Commission (COSO). The Company's management is responsible for maintaining effective internal control over financial reporting and for its assessment of the effectiveness of internal control over financial reporting. Our responsibility is to express an opinion on management's assessment and an opinion on the effectiveness of the Company's internal control over financial reporting based on our audit.

We conducted our audit in accordance with the standards of the Public Company Accounting Oversight Board (United States). Those standards require that we plan and perform the audit to obtain reasonable assurance about whether effective internal control over financial reporting was maintained in all material respects. Our audit included obtaining an understanding of internal control over financial reporting, evaluating management's assessment, testing and evaluating the design and operating effectiveness of internal control, and performing such other procedures as we considered necessary in the circumstances. We believe that our audit provides a reasonable basis for our opinion.

A company's internal control over financial reporting is a process designed to provide reasonable assurance regarding the reliability of financial reporting and the preparation of financial statements for external purposes in accordance with generally accepted accounting principles. A company's internal control over financial reporting includes those policies and procedures that (1) pertain to the maintenance of records that, in reasonable detail, accurately and fairly reflect the transactions and dispositions of the assets of the company; (2) provide reasonable assurance that transactions are recorded as necessary to permit preparation of financial statements in accordance with generally accepted accounting principles, and that receipts and expenditures of the company are being made only in accordance with authorizations

of management and directors of the company; and (3) provide reasonable assurance regarding prevention or timely detection of unauthorized acquisition, use, or disposition of the company's assets that could have a material effect on the financial statements.

Because of its inherent limitations, internal control over financial reporting may not prevent or detect misstatements. Also, projections of any evaluation of effectiveness to future periods are subject to the risk that controls may become inadequate because of changes in conditions, or that the degree of compliance with the policies or procedures may deteriorate.

In our opinion, management's assessment that CVS Corporation and subsidiaries maintained effective internal control over financial reporting as of December 31, 2005, is fairly stated, in all material respects, based on criteria established in *Internal Control—Integrated Framework* issued by COSO. Also, in our opinion, CVS Corporation and subsidiaries maintained, in all material respects, effective internal control over financial reporting as of December 31, 2005, based on criteria established in *Internal Control—Integrated Framework* issued by COSO.

We also have audited, in accordance with the standards of the Public Company Accounting Oversight Board (United States), the consolidated balance sheets of CVS Corporation and subsidiaries as of December 31, 2005 and January 1, 2005, and the related consolidated statements of operations, shareholders' equity, and cash flows for the fifty-two week periods ended December 31, 2005 and January 1, 2005 and the fifty-three week period ended January 3, 2004, and our report dated March 14, 2006, expressed an unqualified opinion on those consolidated financial statements.

KPMG LLP
Providence, Rhode Island
March 14, 2006

CONSOLIDATED STATEMENTS OF OPERATIONS

In millions, except per share amounts	fiscal year ended Dec. 31, 2005 (52 weeks)	fiscal year ended Jan. 1, 2005 (52 weeks)	fiscal year ended Jan. 3, 2004 (53 weeks)
Net sales	$ 37,006.2	$ 30,594.3	$ 26,588.0
Cost of goods sold, buying and warehousing costs	27,105.0	22,563.1	19,725.0
Gross margin	9,901.2	8,031.2	6,863.0
Selling, general and administrative expenses	7,292.6	6,079.7	5,097.7
Depreciation and amortization	589.1	496.8	341.7
Total operating expenses	7,881.7	6,576.5	5,439.4
Operating profit	2,019.5	1,454.7	1,423.6
Interest expense, net	110.5	58.3	48.1
Earnings before income tax provision	1,909.0	1,396.4	1,375.5
Income tax provision	684.3	477.6	528.2
Net earnings	1,224.7	918.8	847.3
Preference dividends, net of income tax benefit	14.1	14.2	14.6
Net earnings available to common shareholders	$ 1,210.6	$ 904.6	$ 832.7
Basic earnings per common share:			
Net earnings	$ 1.49	$ 1.13	$ 1.06
Weighted average common shares outstanding	811.4	797.2	788.8
Diluted earnings per common share:			
Net earnings	$ 1.45	$ 1.10	$ 1.03
Weighted average common shares outstanding	841.6	830.8	815.4
Dividends declared per common share	$ 0.1450	$ 0.1325	$ 0.1150

See accompanying notes to consolidated financial statements.

CONSOLIDATED BALANCE SHEETS

In millions, except shares and per share amounts

	Dec. 31, 2005	Jan. 1, 2005
Assets:		
Cash and cash equivalents	$ 513.4	$ 392.3
Accounts receivable, net	1,839.6	1,764.2
Inventories	5,719.8	5,453.9
Deferred income taxes	241.1	243.1
Other current assets	78.8	66.0
Total current assets	8,392.7	7,919.5
Property and equipment, net	3,952.6	3,505.9
Goodwill	1,789.9	1,898.5
Intangible assets, net	802.2	867.9
Deferred income taxes	122.5	137.6
Other assets	223.5	217.4
Total assets	$ 15,283.4	$ 14,546.8
Liabilities:		
Accounts payable	$ 2,467.5	$ 2,275.9
Accrued expenses	1,521.4	1,666.7
Short-term debt	253.4	885.6
Current portion of long-term debt	341.6	30.6
Total current liabilities	4,583.9	4,858.8
Long-term debt	1,594.1	1,925.9
Other long-term liabilities	774.2	774.9
Commitments and contingencies (Note 10)		
Shareholders' equity:		
Preferred stock, $0.01 par value: authorized 120,619 shares; no shares issued or outstanding	—	—
Preference stock, series one ESOP convertible, par value $1.00: authorized 50,000,000 shares; issued and outstanding 4,165,000 shares December 31, 2005 and 4,273,000 shares at January 1, 2005	222.6	228.4
Common stock, par value $0.01: authorized 1,000,000,000 shares; issued 838,841,000 shares at December 31, 2005 and 828,552,000 shares at January 1, 2005	8.4	8.3
Treasury stock, at cost: 24,533,000 shares at December 31, 2005 and 26,634,000 shares at January 1, 2005	(356.5)	(385.9)
Guaranteed ESOP obligation	(114.0)	(140.9)
Capital surplus	1,922.4	1,687.3
Retained earnings	6,738.6	5,645.5
Accumulated other comprehensive loss	(90.3)	(55.5)
Total shareholders' equity	8,331.2	6,987.2
Total liabilities and shareholders' equity	$ 15,283.4	$ 14,546.8

See accompanying notes to consolidated financial statements.

CONSOLIDATED STATEMENTS OF SHAREHOLDERS' EQUITY

In millions	SHARES			DOLLARS		
	Dec. 31, 2005	Jan. 1, 2005	Jan. 3, 2004	Dec. 31, 2005	Jan. 1, 2005	Jan. 3, 2004
Preference stock:						
Beginning of year	4.3	4.5	4.7	$ 228.4	$ 242.7	$ 250.4
Conversion to common stock	(0.1)	(0.2)	(0.2)	(5.8)	(14.3)	(7.7)
End of year	4.2	4.3	4.5	222.6	228.4	242.7
Common stock:						
Beginning of year	828.6	820.4	818.6	8.3	8.2	8.2
Stock options exercised and awards	10.2	8.2	1.8	0.1	0.1	–
End of year	838.8	828.6	820.4	8.4	8.3	8.2
Treasury stock:						
Beginning of year	(26.6)	(29.6)	(32.4)	(385.9)	(428.6)	(469.5)
Purchase of treasury shares	–	–	–	(1.7)	(0.8)	(0.5)
Conversion of preference stock	0.5	1.2	0.6	7.3	17.9	9.6
Employee stock purchase plan issuance	1.6	1.8	2.2	23.8	25.6	31.8
End of year	(24.5)	(26.6)	(29.6)	(356.5)	(385.9)	(428.6)
Guaranteed ESOP obligation:						
Beginning of year				(140.9)	(163.2)	(194.4)
Reduction of guaranteed ESOP obligation				26.9	22.3	31.2
End of year				(114.0)	(140.9)	(163.2)
Capital surplus:						
Beginning of year				1,687.3	1,553.1	1,542.5
Conversion of preference stock				(1.5)	(3.6)	(1.9)
Stock option activity and awards				188.8	119.4	9.2
Tax benefit on stock options and awards				47.8	18.4	3.3
End of year				1,922.4	1,687.3	1,553.1
Accumulated other comprehensive loss:						
Beginning of year				(55.5)	(36.9)	(44.6)
Recognition of unrealized gain/(loss) on derivatives				2.9	(19.8)	–
Minimum pension liability adjustment				(37.7)	1.2	7.7
End of year				(90.3)	(55.5)	(36.9)
Retained earnings:						
Beginning of year				5,645.5	4,846.5	4,104.4
Net earnings				1,224.7	918.8	847.3
Preference stock dividends				(16.2)	(16.6)	(17.7)
Tax benefit on preference stock dividends				2.1	2.4	3.1
Common stock dividends				(117.5)	(105.6)	(90.6)
End of year				6,738.6	5,645.5	4,846.5
Total shareholders' equity				$ 8,331.2	$ 6,987.2	$ 6,021.8
Comprehensive income:						
Net earnings				$ 1,224.7	$ 918.8	$ 847.3
Recognition of unrealized gain/(loss) on derivatives				2.9	(19.8)	–
Minimum pension liability, net of income tax				(37.7)	1.2	7.7
Comprehensive income				$ 1,189.9	$ 900.2	$ 855.0

See accompanying notes to consolidated financial statements.

CONSOLIDATED STATEMENTS OF CASH FLOWS

In millions	fiscal year ended Dec. 31, 2005 (52 weeks)	fiscal year ended Jan. 1, 2005 (52 weeks)	fiscal year ended Jan. 3, 2004 (53 weeks)
Cash flows from operating activities:			
Cash receipts from sales	$ 36,923.1	$ 30,545.8	$ 26,276.9
Cash paid for inventory	(26,403.9)	(22,469.2)	(19,262.9)
Cash paid to other suppliers and employees	(8,186.7)	(6,528.5)	(5,475.5)
Interest and dividends received	6.5	5.7	5.7
Interest paid	(135.9)	(70.4)	(64.9)
Income taxes paid	(591.0)	(569.2)	(510.4)
Net cash provided by operating activities	1,612.1	914.2	968.9
Cash flows from investing activities:			
Additions to property and equipment	(1,495.4)	(1,347.7)	(1,121.7)
Proceeds from sale-leaseback transactions	539.9	496.6	487.8
Acquisitions, net of cash and investments	12.1	(2,293.7)	(133.1)
Cash outflow from hedging activities	—	(32.8)	—
Proceeds from sale or disposal of assets	31.8	14.3	13.4
Net cash used in investing activities	(911.6)	(3,163.3)	(753.6)
Cash flows from financing activities:			
Reductions in long-term debt	(10.5)	(301.5)	(0.8)
Additions to long-term debt	16.5	1,204.1	—
Proceeds from exercise of stock options	178.4	129.8	38.3
Dividends paid	(131.6)	(119.8)	(105.2)
Additions to/(reductions in) short-term debt	(632.2)	885.6	(4.8)
Net cash (used in) provided by financing activities	(579.4)	1,798.2	(72.5)
Net increase (decrease) in cash and cash equivalents	121.1	(450.9)	142.8
Cash and cash equivalents at beginning of year	392.3	843.2	700.4
Cash and cash equivalents at end of year	$ 513.4	$ 392.3	$ 843.2
Reconciliation of net earnings to net cash provided by operating activities:			
Net earnings	$ 1,224.7	$ 918.8	$ 847.3
Adjustments required to reconcile net earnings to net cash provided by operating activities:			
Depreciation and amortization	589.1	496.8	341.7
Deferred income taxes and other non-cash items	13.5	(23.6)	41.1
Change in operating assets and liabilities providing/(requiring) cash, net of effects from acquisitions:			
Accounts receivable, net	(83.1)	(48.4)	(311.1)
Inventories	(265.2)	(509.8)	2.1
Other current assets	(13.2)	35.7	(3.0)
Other assets	(0.1)	8.5	(0.4)
Accounts payable	192.2	109.4	(41.5)
Accrued expenses	(43.8)	(144.2)	116.5
Other long-term liabilities	(2.0)	71.0	(23.8)
Net cash provided by operating activities	$ 1,612.1	$ 914.2	$ 968.9

See accompanying notes to consolidated financial statements.

NOTES TO CONSOLIDATED FINANCIAL STATEMENTS

1 Significant Accounting Policies

DESCRIPTION OF BUSINESS–CVS Corporation (the "Company") is a leader in the retail drugstore industry in the United States. The Company sells prescription drugs and a wide assortment of general merchandise, including over-the-counter drugs, beauty products and cosmetics, film and photofinishing services, seasonal merchandise, greeting cards and convenience foods, through its CVS/pharmacy® retail stores and online through CVS.com.® The Company also provides pharmacy benefit management, mail order services and specialty pharmacy services through PharmaCare Management Services and PharmaCare Pharmacy® stores. As of December 31, 2005, the Company operated 5,471 retail and specialty pharmacy stores in 37 states and the District of Columbia.

BASIS OF PRESENTATION–The consolidated financial statements include the accounts of the Company and its wholly-owned subsidiaries. All material intercompany balances and transactions have been eliminated.

STOCK SPLIT–On May 12, 2005, the Company's Board of Directors authorized a two-for-one stock split, which was effected in the form of a dividend by the issuance of one additional share of common stock for each share of common stock outstanding. These shares were distributed on June 6, 2005 to shareholders of record as of May 23, 2005. All share and per share amounts presented herein have been restated to reflect the effect of the stock split.

FISCAL YEAR–The Company's fiscal year is a 52 or 53 week period ending on the Saturday nearest to December 31. Fiscal 2005, which ended on December 31, 2005, and fiscal 2004, which ended on January 1, 2005, each included 52 weeks. Fiscal 2003, which ended on January 3, 2004, included 53 weeks. Unless otherwise noted, all references to years relate to these fiscal years.

RECLASSIFICATIONS–Certain reclassifications have been made to the consolidated financial statements of prior years to conform to the current year presentation.

USE OF ESTIMATES–The preparation of financial statements in conformity with generally accepted accounting principles requires management to make estimates and assumptions that affect the reported amounts in the consolidated financial statements and accompanying notes. Actual results could differ from those estimates.

CASH AND CASH EQUIVALENTS–Cash and cash equivalents consist of cash and temporary investments with maturities of three months or less when purchased.

ACCOUNTS RECEIVABLE–Accounts receivable are stated net of an allowance for uncollectible accounts of $53.2 million and $57.3 million as of December 31, 2005 and January 1, 2005, respectively. The balance primarily includes amounts due from third party providers (e.g., pharmacy benefit managers, insurance companies and governmental agencies) and vendors.

FAIR VALUE OF FINANCIAL INSTRUMENTS–As of December 31, 2005, the Company's financial instruments include cash and cash equivalents, accounts receivable, accounts payable and short-term debt. Due to the short-term nature of these instruments, the Company's carrying value approximates fair value. The carrying amount of long-term debt was $1.9 billion, and the estimated fair value was $1.9 billion as of December 31,

2005 and January 1, 2005. The fair value of long-term debt was estimated based on rates currently offered to the Company for debt with similar terms and maturities. The Company had outstanding letters of credit, which guaranteed foreign trade purchases, with a fair value of $9.5 million as of December 31, 2005, and $7.8 million as of January 1, 2005. There were no outstanding investments in derivative financial instruments as of December 31, 2005 or January 1, 2005.

INVENTORIES–Inventory is stated at the lower of cost or market on a first-in, first-out basis using the retail method of accounting to determine cost of sales and inventory in our stores, and the cost method of accounting to determine inventory in our distribution centers. Independent physical inventory counts are taken on a regular basis in each store and distribution center location to ensure that the amounts reflected in the accompanying consolidated financial statements are properly stated. During the interim period between physical inventory counts, the Company accrues for anticipated physical inventory losses on a location-by-location basis based on historical results and current trends.

PROPERTY AND EQUIPMENT–Property, equipment and improvements to leased premises are depreciated using the straight-line method over the estimated useful lives of the assets, or when applicable, the term of the lease, whichever is shorter. Estimated useful lives generally range from 10 to 40 years for buildings, building improvements and leasehold improvements and 5 to 10 years for fixtures and equipment. Repair and maintenance costs are charged directly to expense as incurred. Major renewals or replacements that substantially extend the useful life of an asset are capitalized and depreciated.

Following are the components of property and equipment included in the consolidated balance sheets as of the respective balance sheet dates:

In millions	Dec. 31, 2005	Jan. 1, 2005
Land	$ 322.4	$ 262.6
Building and improvements	631.0	612.6
Fixtures and equipment	3,484.1	2,943.8
Leasehold improvements	1,496.7	1,286.5
Capitalized software	198.6	168.2
Capital leases	1.3	1.3
	6,134.1	5,275.0
Accumulated depreciation and amortization	(2,181.5)	(1,769.1)
	$ 3,952.6	$ 3,505.9

The Company capitalizes application development stage costs for significant internally developed software projects. These costs are amortized over a five-year period. Unamortized costs were $84.3 million as of December 31, 2005 and $78.6 million as of January 1, 2005.

IMPAIRMENT OF LONG-LIVED ASSETS–The Company accounts for the impairment of long-lived assets in accordance with Statement of Financial Accounting Standards ("SFAS") No. 144, "Accounting for Impairment or Disposal of Long-Lived Assets." As such, the Company groups and evaluates fixed and finite-lived intangible assets excluding goodwill, for impairment at the individual store level, which is the lowest level at which individual cash flows can be identified. When evaluating assets for potential impairment, the Company first compares the carrying amount of the asset group to the individual store's estimated future cash flows (undiscounted and without interest charges). If the estimated future cash flows used in this analysis are less than the carrying amount of the asset group, an impairment loss calculation is prepared. The impairment loss calculation compares the carrying amount of the asset group to the individual store's estimated fair value based on estimated future cash flows (discounted and with interest charges). If the carrying amount exceeds the individual store's estimated future cash flows (discounted and with interest charges), the loss is allocated to the long-lived assets of the group on a pro rata basis using the relative carrying amounts of those assets.

GOODWILL—The Company accounts for goodwill and intangibles under SFAS No. 142, "Goodwill and Other Intangible Assets." As such, goodwill and other indefinite-lived assets are not amortized, but are subject to annual impairment reviews. See Note 3 for further information on goodwill.

INTANGIBLE ASSETS—Purchased customer lists are amortized on a straight-line basis over their estimated useful lives of up to 10 years. Purchased leases are amortized on a straight-line basis over the remaining life of the lease. See Note 3 for further information on intangible assets.

REVENUE RECOGNITION—The Company recognizes revenue from the sale of merchandise at the time the merchandise is sold. Customer returns are immaterial. Service revenue from the Company's pharmacy benefit management segment, which is recognized using the net method under Emerging Issues Task Force ("EITF") Issue No. 99-19, "Reporting Revenue Gross as a Principal Versus Net as an Agent," is recognized at the time the service is provided. Service revenue totaled $201.8 million in 2005, $129.3 million in 2004 and $96.0 million in 2003. Premium revenue from the Company's pharmacy benefit management segment is accounted for under SFAS No. 113, "Accounting and Reporting for Reinsurance of Short-Duration and Long-Duration Contracts," and is recognized over the period of the contract in proportion to the amount of insurance coverage provided. Premiums collected in advance are deferred. Premium revenue totaled $91.6 million in 2005. There was no premium revenue in 2004 or 2003.

INSURANCE—The Company is self-insured for certain losses related to general liability, workers' compensation and automobile liability. The Company obtains third party insurance coverage to limit exposure from these claims. The Company is also self-insured for certain losses related to health and medical liabilities.

The Company's self-insurance accruals, which include reported claims and claims incurred but not reported, are calculated using standard insurance industry actuarial assumptions and the Company's historical claims experience. During 2005, PharmaCare Management Services entered into certain risk-based or reinsurance arrangements in connection with providing pharmacy plan management services. Policies and contract claims include actual claims reported but not paid and estimates of health care services incurred but not reported. The estimated claims incurred but not reported are calculated using standard insurance industry actuarial assumptions based on historical data, current enrollment, health service utilization statistics and other related information and are provided by third party actuaries.

VENDOR ALLOWANCES—The Company accounts for vendor allowances under the guidance provided by EITF Issue No. 02-16, "Accounting by a Customer (Including a Reseller) for Certain Consideration Received from a Vendor," and EITF Issue No. 03-10, "Application of EITF Issue No. 02-16 by Resellers to Sales Incentives Offered to Consumers by Manufacturers." Vendor allowances reduce the carrying cost of inventory unless they are specifically identified as a reimbursement for promotional programs and/or other services provided. Funds that are directly linked to advertising commitments are recognized as a reduction of advertising expense in the selling, general and administrative expenses line when the related advertising commitment is satisfied. Any such allowances received in excess of the actual cost incurred also reduce the carrying cost of inventory. The total value of any upfront payments received from vendors that are linked to purchase commitments is initially deferred. The deferred amounts are then amortized to reduce cost of goods sold over the life of the contract based upon purchase volume. The total value of any upfront payments received from vendors that are not linked to purchase commitments is also initially deferred. The deferred amounts are then amortized to reduce cost of goods sold on a straight-line basis over the life of the related contract. The total amortization of these upfront payments was not material to the accompanying consolidated financial statements.

STORE OPENING AND CLOSING COSTS—New store opening costs, other than capital expenditures, are charged directly to expense when incurred. When the Company closes a store, the present value of estimated unrecoverable costs, including the remaining lease obligation less estimated sublease income and the book value of abandoned property and equipment, are charged to expense. The long-term portion of the lease obligations associated with store closings was $406.3 million in 2005 and $507.1 million in 2005 and 2004, respectively.

ACCUMULATED OTHER COMPREHENSIVE LOSS—Accumulated other comprehensive loss consists of a minimum pension liability and unrealized losses on derivatives. The minimum pension liability totaled $117.0 million pre-tax ($73.4 million after-tax) as of December 31, 2005. The unrealized loss on derivatives totaled $26.7 million pre-tax ($16.9 million after-tax) as of December 31, 2005. The minimum pension liability totaled $57.7 million pre-tax ($35.7 million after-tax) and $59.4 million pre-tax ($36.9 million after-tax) as of January 1, 2005 and January 3, 2004, respectively. The unrealized loss on derivatives totaled $31.2 million pre-tax ($19.8 million after-tax) as of January 1, 2005.

STOCK-BASED COMPENSATION—The Company accounts for its stock-based compensation plans under the recognition and measurement principles of Accounting Principles Board ("APB") Opinion No. 25, "Accounting for Stock Issued to Employees," and related interpretations. As such, no stock-based employee compensation cost is reflected in net earnings for options granted under those plans since they had an exercise price equal to the market value of the underlying common stock on the date of grant. See Note 7 for further information on stock-based compensation.

The following table summarizes the effect on net earnings and earnings per common share if the Company had applied the fair value recognition provisions of SFAS No. 123, "Accounting for Stock-Based Compensation," to stock-based employee compensation for the respective years:

In millions, except per share amounts		2005	2004	2003
Net earnings, as reported		$ 1,224.7	$ 918.8	$ 847.3
Add: Stock-based employee compensation expense included in reported net earnings, net of related tax effects(1)		4.8	1.5	2.2
Deduct: Total stock-based employee compensation expense determined under fair value based method for all awards, net of related tax effects		48.6	40.2	52.4
Pro forma net earnings		$ 1,180.9	$ 880.1	$ 797.1
Basic EPS:	As reported	$ 1.49	$ 1.13	$ 1.06
	Pro forma	1.44	1.09	0.99
Diluted EPS:	As reported	$ 1.45	$ 1.10	$ 1.03
	Pro forma	1.40	1.06	0.97

(1) Amounts represent the after-tax compensation costs for restricted stock grants and expense related to the acceleration of vesting of stock options on certain terminated employees.

ADVERTISING COSTS—Advertising costs are expensed when the related advertising takes place. Advertising costs, net of vendor funding, which is included in selling, general and administrative expenses, were $206.6 million in 2005, $205.7 million in 2004 and $178.2 million in 2003.

INTEREST EXPENSE, NET—Interest expense was $117.0 million, $64.0 million and $53.9 million, and interest income was $6.5 million, $5.7 million and $5.8 million in 2005, 2004 and 2003, respectively. Capitalized interest totaled $12.7 million in 2005, $10.4 million in 2004 and $11.0 million in 2003.

INCOME TAXES—The Company provides for federal and state income taxes currently payable, as well as for those deferred because of timing differences between reporting income and expenses for financial statement purposes versus tax purposes. Federal and state incentive tax credits are recorded as a reduction of income taxes. Deferred tax assets and liabilities are recognized for the future tax consequences attributable to differences between the carrying amount of assets and liabilities for financial reporting purposes and the amounts used for income tax purposes. Deferred tax assets and liabilities are measured using the enacted tax rates expected to apply to taxable income in the years in which those temporary differences are expected to be recoverable or settled. The effect of a change in tax rates is recognized as income or expense in the period of the change.

EARNINGS PER COMMON SHARE—Basic earnings per common share is computed by dividing: (i) net earnings, after deducting the after-tax Employee Stock Ownership Plan ("ESOP") preference dividends, by (ii) the weighted average number of common shares outstanding during the year (the "Basic Shares").

When computing diluted earnings per common share, the Company assumes that the ESOP preference stock is converted into common stock and all dilutive stock options are exercised. After the assumed ESOP preference stock conversion, the ESOP Trust would hold common stock rather than ESOP preference stock and would receive common stock dividends ($0.145 per share in 2005, $0.1325 per share in 2004 and $0.115 per share in 2003) rather than ESOP preference stock dividends (currently $3.90 per share). Since the ESOP Trust uses the dividends it receives to service its debt, the Company would have to increase its contribution to the ESOP Trust to compensate it for the lower dividends. This additional contribution would reduce the Company's net earnings, which in turn, would reduce the amounts that would be accrued under the Company's incentive compensation plans.

Diluted earnings per common share is computed by dividing: (i) net earnings, after accounting for the difference between the dividends on the ESOP preference stock and common stock and after making adjustments for the incentive compensation plans, by (ii) Basic Shares plus the additional shares that would be issued assuming that all dilutive stock options are exercised and the ESOP preference stock is converted into common stock. Options to purchase 6.9 million and 9.4 million shares of common stock were outstanding as of December 31, 2005 and January 1, 2005, respectively, but were not included in the calculation of diluted earnings per share because the options' exercise prices were greater than the average market price of the common shares and, therefore, the effect would be antidilutive.

NEW ACCOUNTING PRONOUNCEMENTS—In December 2004, SFAS No. 123(R), "Share-Based Payment," was issued. This statement establishes standards for the accounting for transactions in which an entity exchanges its equity instruments for goods or services. The statement focuses primarily on accounting for transactions in which an entity obtains employee services in share-based payment transactions. The provisions of this statement are required to be adopted for annual periods beginning after June 15, 2005. The Company believes the adoption of this statement will decrease diluted earnings per share by approximately $0.05 in 2006, however, the Company continues to evaluate the potential impact as the amount is subject to variation based on the granting of stock compensation during 2006. Please see Note 7 to the Company's consolidated financial statements for additional information regarding stock-based compensation.

In October 2005, the Financial Accounting Standards Board ("FASB") issued FASB Staff Position ("FSP") No. FAS 13-1, "Accounting for Rental Costs Incurred during a Construction Period." The FSP addresses the accounting for rental costs associated with operating leases that are incurred during a construction period and requires rental costs associated with ground or building operating leases that are incurred during a construction period to be recognized as rental expense. The provisions of the FSP are required to be applied to the first reporting period beginning after December 15, 2005. The Company does not expect that the adoption of this position will have a material impact on the Company's consolidated results of operations or financial position.

2 Acquisition

On July 31, 2004, the Company acquired certain assets and assumed certain liabilities from J.C. Penney Company, Inc. and certain of its subsidiaries, including Eckerd Corporation ("Eckerd"). The acquisition included more than 1,200 Eckerd retail drugstores and Eckerd Health Services, which includes Eckerd's mail order and pharmacy benefit management businesses (collectively, the "Acquired Businesses"). The final purchase price, including transaction costs, was $2.1 billion.

Following is the allocation of the final purchase price and transaction costs:

ASSETS ACQUIRED AND LIABILITIES ASSUMED AS OF JULY 31, 2004

In millions

Cash and cash equivalents	$ 3.0
Accounts receivable	358.5
Inventories	928.4
Other current assets	67.2
Total current assets	1,357.1
Property and equipment	477.2
Goodwill	903.3
Intangible assets	500.0
Other assets	135.3
Total assets acquired	3,372.9
Accounts payable	499.5
Accrued expenses(1)(2)(3)	268.4
Total current liabilities	767.9
Other long-term liabilities(2)(3)	471.0
Total liabilities	1,238.9
Net assets acquired	2,134.0

(1) Accrued expenses include $54.7 million for the estimated costs associated with terminating various Eckerd contracts that were in place at the time of acquisition. As of December 31, 2005, $40.1 million of this liability has been settled with cash payments. The $14.6 million remaining liability will require future cash payments through 2009. Accrued expenses also include $10.5 million for the estimated severance, benefits and outplacement costs for 1,090 Eckerd employees that will be terminated. As of December 31, 2005, $8.0 million of this liability has been settled with cash payments. The $2.5 million remaining liability will require future cash payments through 2007.

(2) Accrued expenses include $23.0 million and Other long-term liabilities include $326.8 million for the estimated costs associated with the non-cancelable lease obligations of 302 Eckerd locations that the Company does not intend to operate. As of December 31, 2005, 275 of these locations have been closed and $100.8 million of this liability has been settled with cash payments. The $264.4 million remaining liability, which includes $9.2 of interest accretion, will require future cash payments through 2030.

(3) The Company believes that the remaining liability balances discussed above are adequate to cover the remaining costs associated with the related activities.

The following pro forma combined results of operations have been provided for illustrative purposes only and do not purport to be indicative of the actual results that would have been achieved by the combined companies for the periods presented or that will be achieved by the combined companies in the future:

In millions, except per share amounts

	2004
Net sales	$ 34,564.3
Net earnings	907.0
Basic earnings per share	$ 1.12
Diluted earnings per share	1.11

(1) The pro forma combined results of operations assume that the acquisition of the Acquired Businesses occurred at the beginning of the period presented. Such results have been prepared by adjusting the historical results of the Company to include the historical results of the Acquired Businesses, the incremental interest expense and the impact of the purchase price allocation discussed above.

(2) The pro forma combined results of operations do not include any cost savings that resulted from the combination of the Company and the Acquired Businesses or any costs that were incurred by the Company to integrate the Acquired Businesses.

3 Goodwill and Other Intangibles

Goodwill represents the excess of the purchase price over the fair value of net assets acquired. The Company accounts for goodwill and intangibles under SFAS No. 142, "Goodwill and Other Intangible Assets." As such, goodwill and other indefinite-lived assets are not amortized, but are subject to annual impairment reviews, or more frequent reviews if events or circumstances indicate there may be an impairment. When evaluating goodwill for potential impairment, the Company first compares the fair value of the reporting unit, based on estimated future discounted cash flows, with its carrying amount. If the estimated fair value of the reporting unit is less than its carrying amount, an impairment loss calculation is prepared. The impairment loss calculation compares the implied fair value of reporting unit goodwill with the carrying amount of that goodwill. If the carrying amount of reporting unit goodwill exceeds the implied fair value of that goodwill, an impairment loss is recognized in an amount equal to that excess. During the third quarter of 2005, the Company performed its required annual goodwill impairment test, which concluded there was no impairment of goodwill.

The carrying amount of goodwill was $1,789.9 million and $1,898.5 million as of December 31, 2005 and January 1, 2005, respectively. During 2005, gross goodwill decreased $108.6 million due to an $85.0 million favorable post-closing adjustment to the purchase price paid for the Acquired Businesses and $23.6 million in adjustments recorded to finalize the purchase price allocation. There was no impairment of goodwill during 2005.

Intangible assets other than goodwill are required to be separated into two categories: finite-lived and indefinite-lived. Intangible assets with finite useful lives are amortized over their estimated useful life, while indefinite-lived. Intangible assets with indefinite useful lives are not amortized. The Company currently has no intangible assets with indefinite lives.

Following is a summary of the Company's amortizable intangible assets as of the respective balance sheet dates:

In millions	Dec. 31, 2005		Jan. 1, 2005	
	Gross Carrying Amount	Accumulated Amortization	Gross Carrying Amount	Accumulated Amortization
Customer lists and Covenants not to compete	$ 1,152.4	$ (435.9)	$ 1,102.8	$ (321.8)
Favorable leases and Other	185.5	(99.8)	173.8	(86.9)
	$ 1,337.9	$ (535.7)	$ 1,276.6	$ (408.7)

The amortization expense for these intangible assets totaled $128.6 million in 2005, $95.9 million in 2004 and $63.2 million in 2003. The anticipated annual amortization expense for these intangible assets is $126.1 million in 2006, $119.7 million in 2007, $111.0 million in 2008, $102.7 million in 2009 and $93.3 million in 2010.

4 Borrowing and Credit Agreements

Following is a summary of the Company's borrowings as of the respective balance sheet dates:

In millions	Dec. 31, 2005	Jan. 1, 2005
Commercial paper	$ 253.4	$ 885.6
5.625% senior notes due 2006	300.0	300.0
3.875% senior notes due 2007	300.0	300.0
4.0% senior notes due 2009	650.0	650.0
4.875% senior notes due 2014	550.0	550.0
8.52% ESOP notes due 2008[1]	114.0	140.9
Mortgage notes payable	21.0	14.8
Capital lease obligations	0.7	0.8
	2,189.1	2,842.1
Less:		
Short-term debt	(253.4)	(885.6)
Current portion of long-term debt	(341.6)	(30.6)
	$ 1,594.1	$ 1,925.9

(1) See Note 8 for further information about the Company's ESOP Plan.

In connection with our commercial paper program, we maintain a $650 million, five-year unsecured back-up credit facility, which expires on May 21, 2006, and a $675 million, five-year unsecured back-up credit facility, which expires on June 2, 2010. In addition, we maintain a $675 million, five-year unsecured back-up credit facility, which expires on June 11, 2009. The credit facilities allow for borrowings at various rates depending on the Company's public debt ratings and require the Company to pay a quarterly facility fee of 0.1%, regardless of usage. As of December 31, 2005, the Company had no outstanding borrowings against the credit facilities. The weighted average interest rate for short-term debt was 3.3% and 1.8% as of December 31, 2005 and January 1, 2005, respectively.

In September 2004, the Company issued $650 million of 4.0% unsecured senior notes due September 15, 2009 and $550 million of 4.875% unsecured senior notes due September 15, 2014 (collectively the "Notes"). The Notes pay interest semi-annually and may be redeemed at any time, in whole or in part at a defined redemption price plus accrued interest. Net proceeds from the Notes were used to repay a portion of the outstanding commercial paper issued to finance the acquisition of the Acquired Businesses.

To manage a portion of the risk associated with potential changes in market interest rates between the Company entering into a definitive agreement to purchase the Acquired Businesses and the placement of the long-term financing, the Company entered into Treasury-Lock Contracts (the "Contracts") with total notional amounts of $600 million. The Company settled these Contracts at a loss of $32.8 million during the third quarter of 2004 in conjunction with the placement of the long-term financing. The Company accounts for the above derivatives in accordance with SFAS No. 133, "Accounting for Derivative Instruments and Hedging Activities," as modified by SFAS No. 138, "Accounting for Derivative Instruments and Certain Hedging Activities," which requires the resulting loss to be recorded in shareholders' equity as a component of accumulated other comprehensive loss. This unrealized loss will be amortized as a component of interest expense over the life of the related long-term financing. As of December 31, 2005, the Company had no freestanding derivatives in place.

The credit facilities and unsecured senior notes contain customary restrictive financial and operating covenants. The covenants do not materially affect the Company's financial or operating flexibility.

The aggregate maturities of long-term debt for each of the five years subsequent to December 31, 2005 are $341.6 million in 2006, $341.9 million in 2007, $45.7 million in 2008, $651.3 million in 2009 and $1.4 million in 2010.

5 Leases

The Company leases most of its retail locations and eight of its distribution centers under non-cancelable operating leases, whose initial terms typically range from 15 to 25 years, along with options that permit renewals for additional periods. The Company also leases certain equipment and other assets under non-cancelable operating leases, whose initial terms typically range from 3 to 10 years. During 2004, the Company conformed its accounting for operating leases and leasehold improvements to the views expressed by the Office of the Chief Accountant of the Securities and Exchange Commission to the American Institute of Certified Public Accountants on February 7, 2005. As a result, the Company recorded a $65.9 million non-cash pre-tax ($40.5 million after-tax) adjustment to total operating expenses, which represents the cumulative effect of the adjustment for a period of approximately 20 years (the "Lease Adjustment"). Since the effect of the Lease Adjustment was not material to 2004 or any previously reported fiscal year, the cumulative effect was recorded in the fourth quarter of 2004. Minimum rent is expensed on a straight-line basis over the term of the lease. In addition to minimum rental payments, certain leases require additional payments based on sales volume, as well as reimbursement for real estate taxes, common area maintenance and insurance, which are expensed when incurred.

Following is a summary of the Company's net rental expense for operating leases for the respective years:

In millions	2005	2004	2003
Minimum rentals	$ 1,213.2	$ 1,020.6	$ 838.4
Contingent rentals	63.3	61.7	62.0
	1,276.5	1,082.3	900.4
Less: sublease income	(18.8)	(14.0)	(10.1)
	$ 1,257.7	$ 1,068.3	$ 890.3

Following is a summary of the future minimum lease payments under capital and operating leases as of December 31, 2005:

In millions	Capital Leases	Operating Leases
2006	$ 0.2	$ 1,233.0
2007	0.2	1,178.6
2008	0.2	1,127.5
2009	0.2	1,090.4
2010	0.1	1,205.4
Thereafter	0.0	10,492.8
	0.9	$ 16,327.7
Less: imputed interest	(0.2)	
Present value of capital lease obligations	$ 0.7	

The Company finances a portion of its store development program through sale-leaseback transactions. The properties are sold and the resulting leases qualify and are accounted for as operating leases. The Company does not have any retained or contingent interests in the stores, nor does the Company provide any guarantees, other than a guarantee of lease payments, in connection with the sale-leasebacks. Proceeds from sale-leaseback transactions totaled $539.9 million in 2005, $496.6 million in 2004 and $487.8 million in 2003. The operating leases that resulted from these transactions are included in the above table.

6 Pension Plans and Other Postretirement Benefits

Defined Contribution Plans

The Company sponsors a voluntary 401(k) Savings Plan that covers substantially all employees who meet plan eligibility requirements. The Company makes matching contributions consistent with the provisions of the plan. At the participant's option, account balances, including the Company's matching contribution, can be moved without restriction among various investment options, including the Company's common stock. The Company also maintains a nonqualified, unfunded Deferred Compensation Plan for certain key employees. This plan provides participants the opportunity to defer portions of their compensation and receive matching contributions that they would have otherwise received under the 401(k) Savings Plan if not for certain restrictions and limitations under the Internal Revenue Code. The Company's contributions under the above defined contribution plans totaled $64.9 million in 2005, $52.1 million in 2004 and $46.9 million in 2003. The Company also sponsors an Employee Stock Ownership Plan. See Note 8 for further information about this plan.

Other Postretirement Benefits

The Company provides postretirement healthcare and life insurance benefits to certain retirees who meet eligibility requirements. The Company's funding policy is generally to pay covered expenses as they are incurred. For retiree medical plan accounting, the Company reviews external data and its own historical trends for healthcare costs to determine the healthcare cost trend rates.

For measurement purposes, future healthcare costs are assumed to increase at an annual rate of 10.0%, decreasing to an annual growth rate of 5.0% in 2011 and thereafter. A one percent change in the assumed healthcare cost trend rate would change the accumulated postretirement benefit obligation by $0.6 million and the total service and interest costs by $0.1 million.

During 2004, the Company adopted FAS 106-2, "Accounting and Disclosure Requirements Related to the Medicare Prescription Drug, Improvement and Modernization Act of 2003." This statement requires disclosure of the effects of the Medicare Prescription Drug, Improvement and Modernization Act and an assessment of the impact of the federal subsidy on the accumulated postretirement benefit obligation and net periodic postretirement benefit cost. The adoption of this statement did not have a material impact on the Company's consolidated results of operations, financial position or related disclosures.

Pension Plans

The Company sponsors a non-contributory defined benefit pension plan that covers certain full-time employees of Revco, D.S., Inc. who were not covered by collective bargaining agreements. On September 20, 1997, the Company suspended future benefit accruals under this plan. Benefits paid to retirees are based upon age at retirement, years of credited service and average compensation during the five-year period ended September 20, 1997. The plan is funded based on actuarial calculations and applicable federal regulations.

Pursuant to various labor agreements, the Company is also required to make contributions to certain union-administered pension and health and welfare plans that totaled $15.4 million in 2005, $15.0 million in 2004 and $13.2 million in 2003. The Company also has nonqualified supplemental executive retirement plans in place for certain key employees for whom it has purchased cost recovery variable life insurance.

The Company uses an investment strategy, which emphasizes equities in order to produce higher expected returns, and in the long run, lower expected expense and cash contribution requirements. The pension plan assets allocation targets 70% equity and 30% fixed income.

Following is a summary of the net periodic pension cost for the defined benefit and other postretirement benefit plans for the respective years:

In millions	DEFINED BENEFIT PLANS			OTHER POSTRETIREMENT BENEFITS		
	2005	2004	2003	2005	2004	2003
Service cost	$ 0.7	$ 0.9	$ 0.8	$ —	$ —	$ —
Interest cost on benefit obligation	21.4	20.5	20.5	0.6	0.7	0.8
Expected return on plan assets	(19.4)	(18.6)	(18.4)	(0.2)	—	—
Amortization of net loss (gain)	6.6	3.3	1.5	(0.1)	(0.1)	(0.1)
Amortization of prior service cost	0.1	0.1	0.1	(0.1)	(0.1)	(0.1)
Net periodic pension cost	$ 9.4	$ 6.2	$ 4.5	$ 0.3	$ 0.6	$ 0.6
Actuarial assumptions used to determine net period pension cost:						
Discount rate	6.00%	6.25%	6.50%	6.00%	6.25%	6.50%
Expected return on plan assets	8.50%	8.50%	8.75%	—	—	—
Actuarial assumptions used to determine benefit obligations:						
Discount rate	5.75%	6.00%	6.25%	5.75%	6.00%	6.25%
Expected return on plan assets	8.50%	8.50%	8.50%	—	—	—
Rate of compensation increase	4.00%	4.00%	4.00%	—	—	—

Following is the pension plan assets allocation by major category for the respective years:

	2005	2004
Equity	70%	70%
Fixed income	29%	29%
Other	1%	1%
	100%	100%

The equity investments primarily consist of large cap value and international value equity funds. The fixed income investments primarily consist of intermediate-term bond funds. The other category consists of cash and cash equivalents held for benefit payments.

Following is a reconciliation of the projected benefit obligation, fair value of plan assets and funded status of the Company's defined benefit and other postretirement benefit plans as of the respective balance sheet dates:

In millions	DEFINED BENEFIT PLANS		OTHER POSTRETIREMENT BENEFITS	
	Dec. 31, 2005	Jan. 1, 2005	Dec. 31, 2005	Jan. 1, 2005
Change in benefit obligation:				
Benefit obligation at beginning of year	$ 352.9	$ 339.1	$ 12.1	$ 13.3
Service cost	0.7	0.8	—	—
Interest cost	21.4	20.5	0.6	0.7
Actuarial loss (gain)	65.1	10.1	(0.7)	(0.5)
Benefits paid	(18.9)	(17.6)	(1.3)	(1.4)
Benefit obligation at end of year	$ 421.2	$ 352.9	$ 10.7	$ 12.1
Change in plan assets:				
Fair value at beginning of year	$ 255.2	$ 226.6	$ —	$ —
Actual return on plan assets	19.2	25.8	—	—
Company contributions	20.1	20.4	1.3	1.4
Benefits paid	(18.9)	(17.6)	(1.3)	(1.4)
Fair value at end of year	$ 275.6	$ 255.2	$ —	$ —
Funded status:				
Funded status	$ (145.6)	$ (97.7)	$ (10.7)	$ (12.1)
Unrecognized prior service cost	0.3	0.5	(0.3)	(0.4)
Unrecognized loss (gain)	122.6	63.8	(0.2)	0.3
Net liability recognized	$ (22.7)	$ (33.4)	$ (11.2)	$ (12.2)
Amounts recognized in the consolidated balance sheet:				
Accrued benefit liability	$ (139.7)	$ (91.1)	$ (11.2)	$ (12.2)
Minimum pension liability	117.0	57.7	—	—
Net liability recognized	$ (22.7)	$ (33.4)	$ (11.2)	$ (12.2)

The discount rate is determined by examining the current yields observed on the measurement date of fixed-interest, high quality investments expected to be available during the period to maturity of the related benefits. The expected long-term rate of return is determined by using the target allocation and historical returns for each asset class.

The Company utilized a measurement date of December 31 to determine pension and other postretirement benefit measurements. The Company included $17.1 million of accrued benefit liability in accrued expenses, while the remaining benefit liability was recorded in other long-term liabilities, as of December 31, 2005 and January 1, 2005. The accumulated benefit obligation for the defined benefit pension plans was $415.3 million and $345.9 million as of December 31, 2005 and January 1, 2005, respectively. The Company estimates it will make cash contributions to the pension plan during the next fiscal year of approximately $16.4 million, however, actual contributions will depend on the outcome of funding reform legislation. Estimated future benefit payments for the defined benefit plans and other postretirement benefit plans, respectively, are $19.1 million and $1.3 million in 2006, $19.8 million and $1.3 million in 2007, $20.6 million and $1.3 million in 2008, $21.3 million and $1.2 million in 2009, $22.2 million and $1.2 million in 2010 and $133.6 million and $4.9 million in aggregate for the following five years.

The Company recorded a minimum pension liability of $117.0 million as of December 31, 2005, and $57.7 million as of January 1, 2005, as required by SFAS No. 87. During 2005, the Company engaged its actuaries to perform a study to review the mortality experience of its defined benefit plans. As a result of the study, the Company changed the mortality table used to the 1994 Group Annuity Basic Table, projected to 2002 with Scale AA (the "2002 GATT Table"), which increased the minimum pension liability during 2005. A minimum pension liability is required when the accumulated benefit obligation exceeds the combined fair value of the underlying plan assets and accrued pension costs. The minimum pension liability adjustment is reflected in other long-term liabilities, long-term deferred income taxes and accumulated other comprehensive loss, which is included in shareholders' equity, in the accompanying consolidated balance sheets.

7 Stock Incentive Plans

The Company's 1997 Incentive Compensation Plan (the "ICP") provides for the granting of up to 85.8 million shares of common stock in the form of stock options and other awards to selected officers, employees and directors of the Company. All grants under the ICP are awarded at fair market value on the date of grant. Options granted prior to 2004 generally become exercisable over a four-year period from the grant date and expire ten years after the date of grant. Options granted during fiscal 2004 and 2005 generally become exercisable over a three-year period from the grant date and expire seven years after the date of grant. As of December 31, 2005, there were 25.0 million shares available for future grants under the ICP.

The ICP allows for up to 7.2 million restricted shares to be issued. The Company granted 427,000, 824,000 and 426,000 shares of restricted stock with a weighted average per share grant date fair value of $24.80, $18.41 and $12.63, in 2005, 2004 and 2003, respectively. In addition, the Company granted 812,000 restricted stock units with a weighted average fair value of $26.02 in 2005. The fair value of the restricted shares and units are expensed over the period during which the restrictions lapse. Compensation costs for restricted shares and units totaled $5.9 million in 2005, $2.4 million in 2004 and $3.6 million in 2003.

In 2004, an amendment to the Company's ICP was approved by shareholders, allowing non-employee directors to receive awards under the ICP. Upon approval of this amendment to the ICP, all authority to make future grants under the Company's 1996 Directors Stock Plan was terminated, although previously granted awards remain outstanding in accordance with their terms and the terms of the 1996 Directors Stock Plan.

Following is a summary of the stock option activity for the respective years:

Shares in thousands	2005		2004		2003	
	shares	weighted average exercise price	shares	weighted average exercise price	shares	weighted average exercise price
Outstanding at beginning of year	49,828	$ 17.58	54,158	$ 17.11	46,780	$ 18.21
Granted	5,790	22.53	5,864	17.75	12,802	12.61
Exercised	(10,072)	14.47	(7,564)	13.88	(1,414)	10.13
Cancelled	(1,929)	19.41	(2,630)	19.09	(4,010)	17.92
Outstanding at end of year	43,617	18.82	49,828	17.58	54,158	17.11
Exercisable at end of year	26,408	$ 19.82	25,098	$ 19.49	29,740	$ 17.77

Following is a summary of the stock options outstanding and exercisable as of December 31, 2005:

Shares in thousands	OPTIONS OUTSTANDING			OPTIONS EXERCISABLE	
Range of Exercise Prices	number outstanding	weighted average remaining life	weighted average exercise price	number exercisable	weighted average exercise price
$ 6.87 to $ 12.48	1,321	1.4	$ 11.25	1,252	$ 11.18
12.49 to 12.56	8,180	7.0	12.56	3,152	12.56
12.57 to 14.96	8,273	6.0	14.91	5,446	14.93
14.97 to 17.67	7,493	6.5	17.01	3,906	16.46
17.68 to 22.45	10,107	6.3	20.86	4,502	18.94
22.46 to 30.61	8,243	4.9	29.29	8,150	29.30
Total	43,617	6.0	$ 18.82	26,408	$ 19.82

The Company applies APB Opinion No. 25 to account for its stock incentive plans. Accordingly, no compensation cost has been recognized for stock options granted. Had compensation cost been recognized based on the fair value of stock options granted, consistent with SFAS No. 123, net earnings and net earnings per common share ("EPS") would approximate the pro forma amounts shown below:

In millions, except per share amounts	2005	2004	2003
Net earnings:			
As reported	$ 1,224.7	$ 918.8	$ 847.3
Pro forma	1,180.9	880.1	797.1
Basic EPS:			
As reported	$ 1.49	$ 1.13	$ 1.06
Pro forma	1.44	1.09	0.99
Diluted EPS:			
As reported	$ 1.45	$ 1.10	$ 1.03
Pro forma	1.40	1.06	0.97

The per share weighted average fair value of stock options granted during 2005, 2004 and 2003 was $8.46, $6.47 and $4.51, respectively.

The fair value of each stock option grant was estimated using the Black-Scholes Option Pricing Model with the following assumptions:

	2005	2004	2003
Dividend yield	0.56%	0.65%	0.85%
Expected volatility	34.00%	30.50%	29.63%
Risk-free interest rate	4.3%	3.9%	3.5%
Expected life	5.7	6.6	7.0

The 1999 Employee Stock Purchase Plan provides for the purchase of up to 14.8 million shares of common stock. Under the plan, eligible employees may purchase common stock at the end of each six-month offering period, at a purchase price equal to 85% of the lower of the fair market value on the first day or the last day of the offering period. During 2005, 1.3 million shares of common stock were purchased at an average price of $18.88 per share. As of December 31, 2005, 10.0 million shares of common stock have been issued since inception of the plan.

8 Employee Stock Ownership Plan

The Company sponsors a defined contribution Employee Stock Ownership Plan (the "ESOP") that covers full-time employees with at least one year of service.

In 1989, the ESOP Trust issued and sold $357.5 million of 20-year, 8.52% notes due December 31, 2008 (the "ESOP Notes"). The proceeds from the ESOP Notes were used to purchase 6.7 million shares of Series One ESOP Convertible Preference Stock (the "ESOP Preference Stock") from the Company. Since the ESOP Notes are guaranteed by the Company, the outstanding balance is reflected as long-term debt, and a corresponding guaranteed ESOP obligation is reflected in shareholders' equity in the accompanying consolidated balance sheets.

Each share of ESOP Preference Stock has a guaranteed minimum liquidation value of $53.45, is convertible into 4.628 shares of common stock and is entitled to receive an annual dividend of $3.90 per share. The ESOP Trust uses the dividends received and contributions from the Company to repay the ESOP Notes. As the ESOP Notes are repaid, ESOP Preference Stock is allocated to participants based on (i) the ratio of each year's debt service payment to total current and future debt service payments multiplied by (ii) the number of unallocated shares of ESOP Preference Stock in the plan.

As of December 31, 2005, 4.2 million shares of ESOP Preference Stock were outstanding, of which 3.0 million shares were allocated to participants and the remaining 1.2 million shares were held in the ESOP Trust for future allocations.

Annual ESOP expense recognized is equal to (i) the interest incurred on the ESOP Notes plus (ii) the higher of (a) the principal repayments or (b) the cost of the shares allocated, less (iii) the dividends paid. Similarly, the guaranteed ESOP obligation is reduced by the higher of (i) the principal payments or (ii) the cost of shares allocated.

Following is a summary of the ESOP activity for the respective years:

In millions	2005	2004	2003
ESOP expense recognized	$ 22.7	$ 19.5	$ 30.1
Dividends paid	16.2	16.6	17.7
Cash contributions	22.7	19.5	30.1
Interest payments	12.0	13.9	16.6
ESOP shares allocated	0.3	0.3	0.4

9 Income Taxes

The provision for income taxes consisted of the following for the respective years:

In millions	2005	2004	2003
Current:			
Federal	$ 632.8	$ 397.7	$ 421.5
State	31.7	62.6	77.3
	664.5	460.3	498.8
Deferred:			
Federal	17.9	22.5	31.0
State	1.9	(5.2)	(1.6)
	19.8	17.3	29.4
Total	$ 684.3	$ 477.6	$ 528.2

Following is a reconciliation of the statutory income tax rate to the Company's effective tax rate for the respective years:

	2005	2004	2003
Statutory income tax rate	35.0%	35.0%	35.0%
State income taxes, net of federal tax benefit	3.9	3.8	3.6
Other	(0.3)	(0.3)	(0.2)
Reversal of previously recorded tax reserves	(2.8)	(4.3)	—
Effective tax rate	35.8%	34.2%	38.4%

Following is a summary of the significant components of the Company's deferred tax assets and liabilities as of the respective balance sheet dates:

In millions	Dec. 31, 2005	Jan. 1, 2005
Deferred tax assets:		
Lease and rents	$ 258.3	$ 298.7
Inventory	124.0	111.3
Employee benefits	60.8	51.8
Accumulated other comprehensive items	53.5	33.4
Retirement benefits	11.0	15.0
Allowance for bad debt	22.1	20.8
Amortization method	16.9	19.9
Other	43.4	61.3
Total deferred tax assets	590.0	612.2
Deferred tax liabilities:		
Accelerated depreciation	(226.3)	(231.5)
Total deferred tax liabilities	(226.3)	(231.5)
Net deferred tax assets	$ 363.7	$ 380.7

During the fourth quarter of 2005, an assessment of tax reserves resulted in a reduction that was principally based on resolving certain state tax matters. As a result, the Company reversed $52.6 million of previously recorded tax reserves through the income tax provision. During the fourth quarter of 2004, an assessment of tax reserves resulted in a reduction that was principally based on finalizing certain tax return years and on a 2004 court decision that was relevant to the industry. As a result, the Company reversed $60.0 million of previously recorded tax reserves through the income tax provision. The Company believes it is more likely than not that the deferred tax assets included in the above table will be realized during future periods.

10 Commitments & Contingencies

Between 1991 and 1997, the Company sold or spun off a number of subsidiaries, including Bob's Stores, Linens 'n Things, Marshalls, Kay-Bee Toys, Wilsons, This End Up and Footstar. In many cases, when a former subsidiary leased a store, the Company provided a guarantee of the store's lease obligations. When the subsidiaries were disposed of, the Company's guarantees remained in place, although each initial purchaser has indemnified the Company for any lease obligations the Company was required to satisfy. If any of the purchasers or any of the former subsidiaries were to become insolvent and failed to make the required payments under a store lease, the Company could be required to satisfy these obligations. As of December 31, 2005, the Company guaranteed approximately 360 such store leases, with the maximum remaining lease term extending through 2018. Assuming that each respective purchaser became insolvent, and the Company was required to assume all of these lease obligations, management estimates that the Company could settle the obligations for approximately $400 to $450 million as of December 31, 2005.

Management believes the ultimate disposition of any of the guarantees will not have a material adverse effect on the Company's consolidated financial condition, results of operations or future cash flows.

As of December 31, 2005, the Company had outstanding commitments to purchase $70.5 million of merchandise inventory for use in the normal course of business. The Company currently expects to satisfy these purchase commitments by 2008.

The Rhode Island Attorney General's Office, the Rhode Island Ethics Commission and the United States Attorney's Office for the District of Rhode Island have been investigating the business relationships between certain former members of the Rhode Island General Assembly and various Rhode Island companies, including the Company. In connection with the investigation of these business relationships, a former state senator has been criminally charged by state and federal authorities, and has pled guilty to the federal charges. The Company will continue to cooperate fully with these investigations.

The United States Department of Justice and several state attorneys general are investigating whether any civil or criminal violations resulted from certain practices engaged in by CVS and others in the pharmacy industry with regard to dispensing one of two different dosage forms of a generic drug under circumstances in which some state Medicaid programs at various times reimbursed one dosage form at a different rate from the other. The Company is in discussions with various governmental agencies involved and believes its conduct was lawful and justified.

The enforcement staff of the United States Securities and Exchange Commission (the "SEC") has commenced an informal inquiry into matters related to the accounting for a transaction that occurred in 2000 (the "2000 Transaction"). Pursuant to the 2000 Transaction, the Company (i) made accounting entries reflecting the conveyance of certain excess plush toy collectible inventory to a third party; (ii) received a total of $42.5 million in barter credits; and (iii) made a cash payment of $12.5 million to the same third party. The inquiry is ongoing and the Company is continuing to respond to the SEC staff's requests. In December 2005, the Audit Committee of the Company's Board of Directors engaged independent outside counsel to undertake an internal review of the matter (the "Internal Review"). In March 2006, based on the findings from the Internal Review, the Audit Committee reached certain conclusions regarding the 2000 Transaction. The Audit Committee concluded that various aspects of the Company's accounting for the 2000 Transaction were incorrect, although the Internal Review did not result in any adjustments to the financial statements included in this Annual Report. On March 10, 2006, the Audit Committee reported its findings to the Company's Board of Directors, which adopted those findings. Subsequent to the Audit Committee reaching these conclusions, the Company's Controller (who was also the Principal Accounting Officer) and the Company's Treasurer resigned their positions. David B. Rickard, the Company's Executive Vice President, Chief Financial Officer and Chief Administrative Officer, will be acting as Principal Accounting Officer on an interim basis. The Company cannot predict the outcome or timing of the SEC inquiry, or of any related proceedings, although the Company does not believe that any of the above matters will have any material effect on the Company's results of operations or financial condition.

The Company is also a party to other litigation arising in the normal course of its business, none of which is expected to be material to the Company.

11 Business Segments

The Company currently operates two business segments, Retail Pharmacy and Pharmacy Benefit Management ("PBM"). The operating segments are segments of the Company for which separate financial information is available and for which operating results are evaluated regularly by executive management in deciding how to allocate resources and in assessing performance.

As of December 31, 2005, the Retail Pharmacy segment included 5,420 retail drugstores and the Company's online retail website, CVS.com®. The retail drugstores are located in 34 states and the District of Columbia and operate under the CVS® or CVS/pharmacy® name.

The PBM segment provides a full range of prescription benefit management services to managed care providers and other organizations. These services include mail order pharmacy services, specialty pharmacy services, plan design and administration, formulary management and claims processing. The specialty pharmacy business focuses on supporting individuals that require complex and expensive drug therapies.

The PBM segment operates under the PharmaCare Management Services and PharmaCare Pharmacy® names and includes 51 retail pharmacies, located in 21 states and the District of Columbia.

The Company evaluates segment performance based on operating profit before the effect of non-recurring charges and gains and certain intersegment activities and charges, including pharmacy revenues reported by the retail segment that are directly related to premium revenues that are reported by the PBM segment. The accounting policies of the segments are substantially the same as those described in Note 1.

Following is a reconciliation of the significant components of the Company's net sales for the respective years:

	2005	2004	2003
Pharmacy	70.2%	70.0%	68.8%
Front store	29.8	30.0	31.2
	100.0%	100.0%	100.0%

Following is a reconciliation of the Company's business segments to the consolidated financial statements:

In millions	Retail Pharmacy Segment	PBM Segment	Intersegment Eliminations	Consolidated Totals
2005: Net sales	$ 34,094.6	$ 2,956.2	$ (44.6)	$ 37,006.2
Operating profit	1,797.1	222.4	—	2,019.5
Depreciation and amortization	548.5	40.6	—	589.1
Total assets	13,878.5	1,404.9	—	15,283.4
Goodwill	1,152.4	637.5	—	1,789.9
Additions to property and equipment	1,471.3	24.1	—	1,495.4
2004: Net sales	$ 28,728.7	$ 1,865.6	$ —	$ 30,594.3
Operating profit	1,320.8	133.9	—	1,454.7
Depreciation and amortization	471.1	25.7	—	496.8
Total assets	13,118.5	1,428.3	—	14,546.8
Goodwill	1,257.4	641.1	—	1,898.5
Additions to property and equipment	1,341.5	6.2	—	1,347.7
2003: Net sales	$ 25,280.7	$ 1,307.3	$ —	$ 26,588.0
Operating profit	1,323.1	100.5	—	1,423.6
Depreciation and amortization	326.5	15.2	—	341.7
Total assets	9,975.0	568.1	—	10,543.1
Goodwill	690.4	198.6	—	889.0
Additions to property and equipment	1,114.2	7.5	—	1,121.7

12 Reconciliation of Earnings Per Common Share

Following is a reconciliation of basic and diluted earnings per common share for the respective years:

In millions, except per share amounts	2005	2004	2003
Numerator for earnings per common share calculation:			
Net earnings	$ 1,224.7	$ 918.8	$ 847.3
Preference dividends, net of income tax benefit	(14.1)	(14.2)	(14.6)
Net earnings available to common shareholders, basic	$ 1,210.6	$ 904.6	$ 832.7
Net earnings	$ 1,224.7	$ 918.8	$ 847.3
Dilutive earnings adjustment	(4.4)	(5.2)	(6.3)
Net earnings available to common shareholders, diluted	$ 1,220.3	$ 913.6	$ 841.0
Denominator for earnings per common share calculation:			
Weighted average common shares, basic	811.4	797.2	788.8
Preference stock	19.5	20.4	21.2
Stock options	9.9	13.2	5.4
Restricted stock units	0.8	–	–
Weighted average common shares, diluted	841.6	830.8	815.4
Basic earnings per common share:			
Net earnings	$ 1.49	$ 1.13	$ 1.06
Diluted earnings per common share:			
Net earnings	$ 1.45	$ 1.10	$ 1.03

13 Subsequent Event

On January 22, 2006, the Company entered into a definitive agreement under which it will acquire approximately 700 standalone Sav-on and Osco drugstores, as well as a distribution center located in La Habra, California, from Albertson's, Inc. ("Albertson's"), for $2.93 billion in cash immediately preceding the planned merger of Albertson's and Supervalu, Inc. ("Supervalu"). Approximately half of the drugstores are located in southern California, with others in the Company's existing markets in numerous states across the Midwest and Southwest. The Company will also acquire Albertson's owned real estate interests in the drugstores for $1.0 billion in cash. Closing of the transaction, which is expected to occur in mid-2006, is subject to review under the Hart-Scott-Rodino Act, as well as other customary closing conditions. Further, closing is also conditioned on consummation of the merger between Albertson's and Supervalu, which is also subject to review under the Hart-Scott-Rodino Act and other customary closing conditions, as well as approval by the shareholders of Albertson's and Supervalu. The Company expects to finance the transaction through a combination of cash, short-term and long-term debt and proceeds from the subsequent sale-leaseback of the owned real estate interests. Closing of the transaction is not subject to such financing.

14 Quarterly Financial Information (Unaudited)

In millions, except per share amounts

	First Quarter	Second Quarter	Third Quarter	Fourth Quarter	Fiscal Year
2005:					
Net sales	$ 9,182.2	$ 9,121.6	$ 8,970.4	$ 9,732.0	$ 37,006.2
Gross margin	2,380.8	2,417.4	2,401.0	2,702.0	9,901.2
Operating profit	499.8	477.7	438.9	603.1	2,019.5
Net earnings(2)	289.7	275.9	252.7	406.4	1,224.7
Net earnings per common share, basic(2)	0.35	0.34	0.31	0.49	1.49
Net earnings per common share, diluted(2)	0.34	0.33	0.30	0.48	1.45
Dividends per common share	0.03625	0.03625	0.03625	0.03625	0.1450
Stock price: (New York Stock Exchange)					
High	26.89	29.68	31.60	29.30	31.60
Low	22.02	25.02	27.67	23.89	22.02
Registered shareholders at year-end					12,067
2004:					
Net sales	$ 6,818.6	$ 6,943.1	$ 7,909.4	$ 8,923.2	$ 30,594.3
Gross margin	1,771.7	1,826.5	2,070.8	2,362.2	8,031.2
Operating profit(1)	405.6	387.2	316.0	345.9	1,454.7
Net earnings(2)	244.6	234.5	184.6	255.1	918.8
Net earnings per common share, basic(2)	0.30	0.29	0.23	0.31	1.13
Net earnings per common share, diluted(2)	0.30	0.28	0.22	0.30	1.10
Dividends per common share	0.033125	0.033125	0.033125	0.033125	0.1325
Stock price: (New York Stock Exchange)					
High	19.26	21.50	22.07	23.67	23.67
Low	16.98	17.85	19.31	20.86	16.98

(1) Operating profit for the fourth quarter and fiscal year 2004 includes the pre-tax effect of a $65.9 million Lease Adjustment. Please see Note 5 for additional information regarding the Lease Adjustment.

(2) Net earnings and net earnings per common share for the fourth quarter and fiscal year 2005 include the after-tax effect of the reversal of $52.6 million of previously recorded tax reserves as discussed in Note 9 above. Net earnings and net earnings per common share for the fourth quarter and fiscal year 2004 include the after-tax effect of the Lease Adjustment discussed in (1) above, and the reversal of $60.0 million of previously recorded tax reserves as discussed in Note 9 above.

FIVE-YEAR FINANCIAL SUMMARY

43

In millions, except per share amounts	2005 (52 weeks)	2004 (52 weeks)	2003 (53 weeks)	2002 (52 weeks)	2001 (52 weeks)
Statement of operations data:					
Net sales	$ 37,006.2	$ 30,594.3	$ 26,588.0	$ 24,181.5	$ 22,241.4
Gross margin(1)	9,901.2	8,031.2	6,863.0	6,068.8	5,691.0
Selling, general and administrative expenses(2)	7,292.6	6,079.7	5,097.7	4,552.3	4,256.3
Depreciation and amortization(2)(3)	589.1	496.8	341.7	310.3	320.8
Merger, restructuring and other non-recurring charges	—	—	—	—	343.3
Total operating expenses	7,881.7	6,576.5	5,439.4	4,862.6	4,920.4
Operating profit(4)	2,019.5	1,454.7	1,423.6	1,206.2	770.6
Interest expense, net	110.5	58.3	48.1	50.4	61.0
Income tax provision(5)	684.3	477.6	528.2	439.2	296.4
Net earnings(6)	$ 1,224.7	$ 918.8	$ 847.3	$ 716.6	$ 413.2
Per common share data:					
Net earnings:(6)					
Basic	$ 1.49	$ 1.13	$ 1.06	$ 0.89	$ 0.51
Diluted	1.45	1.10	1.03	0.88	0.50
Cash dividends per common share	0.1450	0.1325	0.1150	0.1150	0.1150
Balance sheet and other data:					
Total assets	$ 15,283.4	$ 14,546.8	$ 10,543.1	$ 9,645.3	$ 8,636.3
Long-term debt	1,594.1	1,925.9	753.1	1,076.3	810.4
Total shareholders' equity	8,331.2	6,987.2	6,021.8	5,197.0	4,566.9
Number of stores (at end of period)	5,471	5,375	4,179	4,087	4,191

(1) Gross margin includes the pre-tax effect of a $5.7 million ($3.6 million after-tax) non-recurring charge in 2001 related to the markdown of certain inventory contained in stores closed as part of a strategic restructuring program.

(2) In 2004, the Company conformed its accounting for operating leases and leasehold improvements to the views expressed by the Office of the Chief Accountant of the Securities and Exchange Commission to the American Institute of Certified Public Accountants on February 7, 2005. As a result, the Company recorded a non-cash pre-tax adjustment of $9.0 million ($5.4 million after-tax) to selling, general and administrative expenses and $56.9 million ($35.1 million after-tax) to depreciation and amortization, which represents the cumulative effect of the adjustment for a period of approximately 20 years. Since the effect of this non-cash adjustment was not material to 2004, or any previously reported fiscal year, the cumulative effect was recorded in the fourth quarter of 2004.

(3) As a result of adopting SFAS No. 142, "Goodwill and Other Intangible Assets," at the beginning of 2002, the Company no longer amortizes goodwill and other indefinite-lived intangible assets. Goodwill amortization totaled $31.4 million pre-tax ($28.2 million after-tax) in 2001.

(4) Operating profit includes the pre-tax effect of the charge discussed in Note (1) above and the following merger, restructuring and other non-recurring charges and gains: (i) in 2004, $65.9 million ($40.5 million after-tax) charge relating to conforming the Company's accounting for operating leases and leasehold improvements, and (ii) in 2001, $346.8 million ($226.9 million after-tax) charge related to restructuring and asset impairment costs associated with the 2001 strategic restructuring and $3.5 million ($2.1 million after-tax) net non-recurring gain resulting from $50.3 million of settlement proceeds received from various lawsuits against certain manufacturers of brand name prescription drugs and offset in part, by the Company's contribution of $46.8 million of these settlement proceeds to the CVS/pharmacy Charitable Trust, Inc. to fund future charitable giving.

(5) Income tax provision includes the effect of the following: (i) in 2005, a $52.6 million reversal of previously recorded tax reserves through the tax provision principally based on resolving certain state tax matters, and (ii) in 2004, a $60.0 million reversal of previously recorded tax reserves through the tax provision principally based on finalizing certain tax return years and on a 2004 court decision relevant to the industry.

(6) Net earnings and net earnings per common share include the after-tax effect of the charges and gains discussed in Notes (1), (2), (3), (4) and (5) above.

REPORT OF INDEPENDENT REGISTERED PUBLIC ACCOUNTING FIRM

KPMG

**The Board of Directors and Shareholders
CVS Corporation**

We have audited the accompanying consolidated balance sheets of CVS Corporation and subsidiaries as of December 31, 2005 and January 1, 2005, and the related consolidated statements of operations, shareholders' equity and cash flows for the fifty-two week periods ended December 31, 2005 and January 1, 2005 and the fifty-three week period ended January 3, 2004. These consolidated financial statements are the responsibility of the Company's management. Our responsibility is to express an opinion on these consolidated financial statements based on our audits.

We conducted our audits in accordance with the standards of the Public Company Accounting Oversight Board (United States). Those standards require that we plan and perform the audit to obtain reasonable assurance about whether the financial statements are free of material misstatement. An audit includes examining, on a test basis, evidence supporting the amounts and disclosures in the financial statements. An audit also includes assessing the accounting principles used and significant estimates made by management, as well as evaluating the overall financial statement presentation. We believe that our audits provide a reasonable basis for our opinion.

In our opinion, the consolidated financial statements referred to above present fairly, in all material respects, the financial position of CVS Corporation and subsidiaries as of December 31, 2005 and January 1, 2005, and the results of their operations and their cash flows for the fifty-two week periods ended December 31, 2005 and January 1, 2005, and the fifty-three week period ended January 3, 2004, in conformity with accounting principles generally accepted in the United States of America.

We also have audited, in accordance with the standards of the Public Company Accounting Oversight Board (United States), the effectiveness of CVS Corporation's internal control over financial reporting as of December 31, 2005, based on criteria established in *Internal Control — Integrated Framework* issued by the Committee of Sponsoring Organizations of the Treadway Commission (COSO), and our report dated March 14, 2006 expressed an unqualified opinion on management's assessment of, and the effective operation of, internal control over financial reporting.

KPMG LLP

KPMG LLP
Providence, Rhode Island
March 14, 2006

Officers

Thomas M. Ryan
Chairman of the Board, President and Chief Executive Officer

David B. Rickard
Executive Vice President, Chief Financial Officer and Chief Administrative Officer

Chris W. Bodine
Executive Vice President—Merchandising and Marketing

Larry J. Merlo
Executive Vice President—Stores

Douglas A. Sgarro
*Executive Vice President—Strategy and Chief Legal Officer
President CVS Realty Co.*

V. Michael Ferdinandi
Senior Vice President—Human Resources and Corporate Communications

Nancy R. Christal
Vice President—Investor Relations

Gregory S. Weishar
*Vice President
President and Chief Executive Officer PharmaCare*

Zenon P. Lankowsky
Secretary

Officer Certifications

The Company has filed the required certifications under Section 302 of the Sarbanes-Oxley Act of 2002 regarding the quality of our public disclosures as Exhibits 31.1 and 31.2 to our annual report on Form 10-K for the fiscal year ended December 31, 2005. After our 2005 annual meeting of stockholders, the Company filed with the New York Stock Exchange the CEO certification regarding its compliance with the NYSE corporate governance listing standards as required by NYSE Rule 303A.12(a).

Directors

W. Don Cornwell[2]
*Chairman of the Board and Chief Executive Officer
Granite Broadcasting Corporation*

Thomas P. Gerrity[1]
*Professor of Management
The Wharton School of the University of Pennsylvania*

Stanley P. Goldstein
*Retired; formerly Chairman of the Board and Chief Executive Officer
CVS Corporation*

Marian L. Heard[1][2][3]
*President and Chief Executive Officer
Oxen Hill Partners*

William H. Joyce[1][3]
*Chairman of the Board and Chief Executive Officer
Nalco Company*

Terrence Murray
*Retired; formerly Chairman of the Board and Chief Executive Officer
FleetBoston Financial Corporation*

Sheli Z. Rosenberg[2][3]
*Retired; formerly President, Chief Executive Officer and Vice Chairman
Equity Group Investments, LLC*

Thomas M. Ryan
*Chairman of the Board, President and Chief Executive Officer
CVS Corporation*

Alfred J. Verrecchia[1]
*President and Chief Executive Officer
Hasbro, Inc.*

(1) Member of the Audit Committee.
(2) Member of the Management Planning and Development Committee.
(3) Member of the Nominating and Corporate Governance Committee.

Shareholder Information

Corporate Headquarters
*CVS Corporation
One CVS Drive, Woonsocket, RI 02895
(401) 765-1500*

Annual Shareholders' Meeting
*11:00 a.m. May 11, 2006
CVS Corporate Headquarters*

Stock Market Listing
*New York Stock Exchange
Symbol: CVS*

Transfer Agent and Registrar
Questions regarding stock holdings, certificate replacement/transfer, dividends and address changes should be directed to:
*The Bank of New York
Shareholder Relations Department
P.O. Box 11258
Church Street Station
New York, NY 10286
Toll-free: (877) CVSPLAN (287-7526)
E-mail: shareowner-svcs@bankofny.com*

Direct Stock Purchase/Dividend Reinvestment Program
BuyDIRECT™ provides a convenient and economical way for you to purchase your first shares or additional shares of CVS common stock. The program is sponsored and administered by The Bank of New York. For more information, including an enrollment form, please contact:
The Bank of New York at (877) 287-7526

Financial and Other Company Information
The Company's Annual Report on Form 10-K will be sent without charge to any shareholder upon request by contacting:
*Nancy R. Christal
Vice President—Investor Relations
CVS Corporation
670 White Plains Road—Suite 210
Scarsdale, NY 10583
(800) 201-0938*

In addition, financial reports and recent filings with the Securities and Exchange Commission, including our Form 10-K, as well as other Company information, are available via the Internet at http://investor.cvs.com.

SOUTHWEST AIRLINES CO. ANNUAL REPORT 2005

Item 8. *Financial Statements and Supplementary Data*

SOUTHWEST AIRLINES CO.

CONSOLIDATED BALANCE SHEET

	December 31,	
	2005	2004
	(In millions, except share data)	
ASSETS		
Current assets:		
Cash and cash equivalents	$ 2,280	$ 1,048
Short-term investments	251	257
Accounts and other receivables	258	248
Inventories of parts and supplies, at cost	150	137
Fuel hedge contracts	641	428
Prepaid expenses and other current assets	40	54
Total current assets	3,620	2,172
Property and equipment, at cost:		
Flight equipment	10,999	10,037
Ground property and equipment	1,256	1,202
Deposits on flight equipment purchase contracts	660	682
	12,915	11,921
Less allowance for depreciation and amortization	3,488	3,198
	9,427	8,723
Other assets	1,171	442
	$14,218	$11,337
LIABILITIES AND STOCKHOLDERS' EQUITY		
Current liabilities:		
Accounts payable	$ 524	$ 420
Accrued liabilities	2,074	1,047
Air traffic liability	649	529
Current maturities of long-term debt	601	146
Total current liabilities	3,848	2,142
Long-term debt less current maturities	1,394	1,700
Deferred income taxes	1,896	1,610
Deferred gains from sale and leaseback of aircraft	136	152
Other deferred liabilities	269	209
Commitments and contingencies		
Stockholders' equity:		
Common stock, $1.00 par value: 2,000,000,000 shares authorized; 801,641,645 and 790,181,982 shares issued in 2005 and 2004, respectively	802	790
Capital in excess of par value	424	299
Retained earnings	4,557	4,089
Accumulated other comprehensive income	892	417
Treasury stock, at cost: 5,199,192 shares in 2004	—	(71)
Total stockholders' equity	6,675	5,524
	$14,218	$11,337

See accompanying notes.

28

SOUTHWEST AIRLINES CO.

CONSOLIDATED STATEMENT OF INCOME

| | Years Ended December 31, | | |
	2005	2004	2003
	(In millions, except per share amounts)		
OPERATING REVENUES:			
Passenger	$7,279	$6,280	$5,741
Freight	133	117	94
Other	172	133	102
Total operating revenues	7,584	6,530	5,937
OPERATING EXPENSES:			
Salaries, wages, and benefits	2,702	2,443	2,224
Fuel and oil	1,342	1,000	830
Maintenance materials and repairs	430	457	430
Aircraft rentals	163	179	183
Landing fees and other rentals	454	408	372
Depreciation and amortization	469	431	384
Other operating expenses	1,204	1,058	1,031
Total operating expenses	6,764	5,976	5,454
OPERATING INCOME	820	554	483
OTHER EXPENSES (INCOME):			
Interest expense	122	88	91
Capitalized interest	(39)	(39)	(33)
Interest income	(47)	(21)	(24)
Other (gains) losses, net	(90)	37	(259)
Total other expenses (income)	(54)	65	(225)
INCOME BEFORE INCOME TAXES	874	489	708
PROVISION FOR INCOME TAXES	326	176	266
NET INCOME	$ 548	$ 313	$ 442
NET INCOME PER SHARE, BASIC	$ .70	$ .40	$ .56
NET INCOME PER SHARE, DILUTED	$ .67	$ .38	$ .54

See accompanying notes.

29

SOUTHWEST AIRLINES CO.

CONSOLIDATED STATEMENT OF STOCKHOLDERS' EQUITY

Years Ended December 31, 2005, 2004, and 2003

	Common Stock	Capital in Excess of Par Value	Retained Earnings	Accumulated Other Comprehensive Income (Loss)	Treasury Stock	Total
	(In millions, except per share amounts)					
Balance at December 31, 2002	$777	$136	$3,455	$ 54	$ —	$4,422
Issuance of common stock pursuant to Employee stock plans	12	81	—	—	—	93
Tax benefit of options exercised	—	41	—	—	—	41
Cash dividends, $.018 per share	—	—	(14)	—	—	(14)
Comprehensive income (loss)						
Net income	—	—	442	—	—	442
Unrealized gain on derivative instruments	—	—	—	66	—	66
Other	—	—	—	2	—	2
Total comprehensive income						510
Balance at December 31, 2003	$789	$258	$3,883	$122	$ —	$5,052
Purchase of shares of treasury stock	—	—	—	—	(246)	(246)
Issuance of common and treasury stock pursuant to Employee stock plans	1	6	(93)	—	175	89
Tax benefit of options exercised	—	35	—	—	—	35
Cash dividends, $.018 per share	—	—	(14)	—	—	(14)
Comprehensive income (loss)						
Net income	—	—	313	—	—	313
Unrealized gain on derivative instruments	—	—	—	293	—	293
Other	—	—	—	2	—	2
Total comprehensive income						608
Balance at December 31, 2004	$790	$299	$4,089	$417	$ (71)	$5,524
Purchase of shares of treasury stock . . .	—	—	—	—	(55)	(55)
Issuance of common and treasury stock pursuant to Employee stock plans . . .	12	60	(66)	—	126	132
Tax benefit of options exercised	—	65	—	—	—	65
Cash dividends, $.018 per share	—	—	(14)	—	—	(14)
Comprehensive income (loss)						
Net income	—	—	548	—	—	548
Unrealized gain on derivative instruments	—	—	—	474	—	474
Other	—	—	—	1	—	1
Total comprehensive income						1,023
Balance at December 31, 2005	$802	$424	$4,557	$892	$ —	$6,675

See accompanying notes.

30

SOUTHWEST AIRLINES CO.

CONSOLIDATED STATEMENT OF CASH FLOWS

| | Years Ended December 31, | | |
	2005	2004	2003
	(In millions)		
CASH FLOWS FROM OPERATING ACTIVITIES:			
Net income	$ 548	$ 313	$ 442
Adjustments to reconcile net income to net cash provided by operating activities:			
Depreciation and amortization	469	431	384
Deferred income taxes	257	184	183
Amortization of deferred gains on sale and leaseback of aircraft	(16)	(16)	(16)
Amortization of scheduled airframe inspections and repairs	49	52	49
Income tax benefit from Employee stock option exercises	65	35	41
Changes in certain assets and liabilities:			
Accounts and other receivables	(9)	(75)	43
Other current assets	(59)	(44)	(19)
Accounts payable and accrued liabilities	855	231	129
Air traffic liability	120	68	50
Other	(50)	(22)	50
Net cash provided by operating activities	2,229	1,157	1,336
CASH FLOWS FROM INVESTING ACTIVITIES:			
Purchases of property and equipment, net	(1,210)	(1,775)	(1,238)
Change in short-term investments, net	6	124	(381)
Payment for assets of ATA Airlines, Inc.	(6)	(34)	—
Debtor in possession loan to ATA Airlines, Inc.	—	(40)	—
Other	—	(1)	—
Net cash used in investing activities	(1,210)	(1,726)	(1,619)
CASH FLOWS FROM FINANCING ACTIVITIES:			
Issuance of long-term debt	300	520	—
Proceeds from Employee stock plans	132	88	93
Payments of long-term debt and capital lease obligations	(149)	(207)	(130)
Payments of cash dividends	(14)	(14)	(14)
Repurchase of common stock	(55)	(246)	—
Other, net	(1)	(8)	3
Net cash provided by (used in) financing activities	213	133	(48)
NET INCREASE (DECREASE) IN CASH AND CASH EQUIVALENTS	1,232	(436)	(331)
CASH AND CASH EQUIVALENTS AT BEGINNING OF PERIOD	1,048	1,484	1,815
CASH AND CASH EQUIVALENTS AT END OF PERIOD	$ 2,280	$ 1,048	$ 1,484
CASH PAYMENTS FOR:			
Interest, net of amount capitalized	$ 71	$ 38	$ 62
Income taxes	$ 8	$ 2	$ 51

SUPPLEMENTAL SCHEDULE OF NONCASH INVESTING ACTIVITIES:

In December 2005, the Company obtained the rights to four of ATA Airlines, Inc. (ATA) leased Chicago Midway Airport gates in exchange for a $20 million reduction of the Debtor in possession loan to ATA:

Rights to Chicago Midway Gates acquired	$ 20
Debtor in possession loan to ATA reduction	$(20)

See accompanying notes.

31

SOUTHWEST AIRLINES CO.

NOTES TO CONSOLIDATED FINANCIAL STATEMENTS
December 31, 2005

1. Summary of Significant Accounting Policies

Basis Of Presentation. Southwest Airlines Co. (Southwest) is a major domestic airline that provides point-to-point, low-fare service. The Consolidated Financial Statements include the accounts of Southwest and its wholly owned subsidiaries (the Company). All significant intercompany balances and transactions have been eliminated. The preparation of financial statements in conformity with accounting principles generally accepted in the United States (GAAP) requires management to make estimates and assumptions that affect the amounts reported in the financial statements and accompanying notes. Actual results could differ from these estimates.

Certain prior period amounts have been reclassified to conform to the current presentation. In the Consolidated Balance Sheet as of December 31, 2004, the Company has reclassified certain amounts as "Short-term investments", that were previously classified as "Cash and cash equivalents." In the Consolidated Statement of Cash Flows for 2004 and 2003, changes in the amounts of "Short-term investments" are classified as cash flows from investing activities. In the Consolidated Statement of Income for 2004 and 2003, amounts previously classified as "Agency commissions" are now classified in "Other operating expenses."

Cash And Cash Equivalents. Cash in excess of that necessary for operating requirements is invested in short-term, highly liquid, income-producing investments. Investments with maturities of three months or less are classified as cash and cash equivalents, which primarily consist of certificates of deposit, money market funds, and investment grade commercial paper issued by major corporations and financial institutions. Cash and cash equivalents are stated at cost, which approximates market value.

Short-Term Investments. Short-term investments consist of auction rate securities with auction reset periods of less than 12 months. These investments are classified as available-for-sale securities and are stated at fair value. Unrealized gains and losses, net of tax, are recognized in "Accumulated other comprehensive income (loss)" in the accompanying Consolidated Balance Sheet. Realized gains and losses are reflected in "Interest income" in the accompanying Consolidated Income Statement.

Inventories. Inventories of flight equipment expendable parts, materials, and supplies are carried at average cost. These items are generally charged to expense when issued for use.

Property And Equipment. Depreciation is provided by the straight-line method to estimated residual values over periods generally ranging from 23 to 25 years for flight equipment and 5 to 30 years for ground property and equipment once the asset is placed in service. Residual values estimated for aircraft are 15 percent and for ground property and equipment range from zero to 10 percent. Property under capital leases and related obligations are recorded at an amount equal to the present value of future minimum lease payments computed on the basis of the Company's incremental borrowing rate or, when known, the interest rate implicit in the lease. Amortization of property under capital leases is on a straight-line basis over the lease term and is included in depreciation expense.

In estimating the lives and expected residual values of its aircraft, the Company primarily has relied upon actual experience with the same or similar aircraft types and recommendations from Boeing, the manufacturer of the Company's aircraft. Subsequent revisions to these estimates, which can be significant, could be caused by changes to the Company's maintenance program, modifications or improvements to the aircraft, changes in utilization of the aircraft (actual flight hours or cycles during a given period of time), governmental regulations on aging aircraft, changing market prices of new and used aircraft of the same or similar types, etc. The Company evaluates its estimates and assumptions each reporting period and, when warranted, adjusts these estimates and assumptions. Generally, these adjustments are accounted for on a prospective basis through depreciation and amortization expense, as required by GAAP.

When appropriate, the Company evaluates its long-lived assets used in operations for impairment. Impairment losses would be recorded when events and circumstances indicate that an asset might be impaired and the undiscounted cash flows to be generated by that asset are less than the carrying amounts of the asset. Factors that would indicate potential impairment include, but are not limited to, significant decreases in the market value of the long-lived asset(s), a significant change in the long-lived asset's physical condition,

SOUTHWEST AIRLINES CO.

NOTES TO CONSOLIDATED FINANCIAL STATEMENTS — (Continued)

operating or cash flow losses associated with the use of the long-lived asset, etc. While the airline industry as a whole has experienced many of these indicators, Southwest has continued to operate all of its aircraft and continues to experience positive cash flow.

Aircraft And Engine Maintenance. The cost of scheduled engine inspections and repairs and routine maintenance costs for all aircraft and engines are charged to maintenance expense as incurred. For the Company's 737-300 and 737-500 aircraft fleet types, scheduled airframe inspections and repairs, known as D checks, are generally performed every ten years. Costs related to D checks are capitalized and amortized over the estimated period benefited, presently the least of ten years, the time until the next D check, or the remaining life of the aircraft. Modifications that significantly enhance the operating performance or extend the useful lives of aircraft or engines are capitalized and amortized over the remaining life of the asset.

As of December 31, 2005, the majority of the Company's fleet was made up of its newest aircraft type, the 737-700. This aircraft type is maintained under a "next-generation" maintenance program, called MSG-3, in which tasks are bundled based on data gathered relative to fleet performance. Scheduled maintenance is still performed at recommended intervals; however, this program does not contain a D check. The costs of scheduled airframe inspections and repairs under this maintenance program are expensed as incurred, as those expenses more readily approximate the underlying scheduled maintenance tasks. See Note 2 regarding a 2006 change in the Company's maintenance program for 737-300 and 737-500 aircraft.

Intangible Assets. Intangible assets primarily consist of leasehold rights to airport owned gates acquired by the Company during 2004 and 2005. These assets are amortized on a straight-line basis over the expected useful life of the lease, approximately 20 years. The accumulated amortization related to the Company's intangible assets at December 31, 2004, and 2005, was not material. The Company periodically assesses its intangible assets for impairment in accordance with SFAS 142, *Goodwill and Other Intangible Assets;* however, no impairments have been noted.

Revenue Recognition. Tickets sold are initially deferred as "Air traffic liability". Passenger revenue is recognized when transportation is provided. "Air traffic liability" primarily represents tickets sold for future travel dates and estimated refunds and exchanges of tickets sold for past travel dates. The majority of the Company's tickets sold are nonrefundable. Tickets that are sold but not flown on the travel date can be reused for another flight, up to a year from the date of sale, or refunded (if the ticket is refundable). A small percentage of tickets (or partial tickets) expire unused. The Company estimates the amount of future refunds and exchanges, net of forfeitures, for all unused tickets once the flight date has passed. These estimates are based on historical experience over many years. The Company and members of the airline industry have consistently applied this accounting method to estimate revenue from forfeited tickets at the date travel is provided. Estimated future refunds and exchanges included in the air traffic liability account are constantly evaluated based on subsequent refund and exchange activity to validate the accuracy of the Company's revenue recognition method with respect to forfeited tickets.

Events and circumstances outside of historical fare sale activity or historical Customer travel patterns can result in actual refunds, exchanges or forfeited tickets differing significantly from estimates; however, these differences have historically not been material. Additional factors that may affect estimated refunds, exchanges, and forfeitures include, but may not be limited to, the Company's refund and exchange policy, the mix of refundable and nonrefundable fares, and fare sale activity. The Company's estimation techniques have been consistently applied from year to year; however, as with any estimates, actual refund and exchange activity may vary from estimated amounts.

Frequent Flyer Program. The Company accrues the estimated incremental cost of providing free travel for awards earned under its Rapid Rewards frequent flyer program. The Company also sells frequent flyer credits and related services to companies participating in its Rapid Rewards frequent flyer program. Funds received from the sale of flight segment credits are accounted for under the residual value method. The portion of those funds associated with future travel are deferred and recognized as "Passenger revenue" when the ultimate free travel awards are flown or the credits expire unused. The portion of the funds not associated with future travel are recognized in "Other revenue" in the period earned.

SOUTHWEST AIRLINES CO.

NOTES TO CONSOLIDATED FINANCIAL STATEMENTS — (Continued)

Advertising. The Company expenses the costs of advertising as incurred. Advertising expense for the years ended December 31, 2005, 2004, and 2003 was $173 million, $158 million, and $155 million, respectively.

Stock-based Employee Compensation. The Company has stock-based compensation plans covering the majority of its Employee groups, including a plan covering the Company's Board of Directors and plans related to employment contracts with certain Executive Officers of the Company. The Company accounts for stock-based compensation utilizing the intrinsic value method in accordance with the provisions of Accounting Principles Board Opinion No. 25 (APB 25), "Accounting for Stock Issued to Employees" and related Interpretations. Accordingly, no compensation expense is recognized for fixed option plans because the exercise prices of Employee stock options equal or exceed the market prices of the underlying stock on the dates of grant. Compensation expense for other stock options is not material.

The following table represents the effect on net income and earnings per share if the Company had applied the fair value based method and recognition provisions of Statement of Financial Accounting Standards (SFAS) No. 123, "Accounting for Stock-Based Compensation", to stock-based Employee compensation:

	2005	2004	2003
	(In millions, except per share amounts)		
Net income, as reported	$548	$313	$442
Add: Stock-based Employee compensation expense included in reported income, net of related tax effects	—	—	—
Deduct: Stock-based Employee compensation expense determined under fair value based methods for all awards, net of related tax effects	(43)	(74)	(57)
Pro forma net income	$505	$239	$385
Net income per share			
Basic, as reported	$ .70	$ .40	$ .56
Basic, pro forma	$ .63	$ .31	$ .49
Diluted, as reported	$ .67	$ .38	$ .54
Diluted, pro forma	$ .62	$ .30	$ .48

As required, the pro forma disclosures above include options granted since January 1, 1995. For purposes of pro forma disclosures, the estimated fair value of stock-based compensation plans and other options is amortized to expense primarily over the vesting period. For options with graded vesting, expense is recognized on a straight-line basis over the vesting period. See Note 13 for further discussion of the Company's stock-based Employee compensation and Note 2 for further information regarding the Company's January 1, 2006, adoption of SFAS 123R.

Financial Derivative Instruments. The Company accounts for financial derivative instruments utilizing Statement of Financial Accounting Standards No. 133 (SFAS 133), "Accounting for Derivative Instruments and Hedging Activities", as amended. The Company utilizes various derivative instruments, including crude oil, unleaded gasoline, and heating oil-based derivatives, to hedge a portion of its exposure to jet fuel price increases. These instruments primarily consist of purchased call options, collar structures, and fixed-price swap agreements, and are accounted for as cash-flow hedges, as defined by SFAS 133. The Company has also entered into interest rate swap agreements to convert a portion of its fixed-rate debt to floating rates. These interest rate hedges are accounted for as fair value hedges, as defined by SFAS 133.

Since the majority of the Company's financial derivative instruments are not traded on a market exchange, the Company estimates their fair values. Depending on the type of instrument, the values are determined by the use of present value methods or standard option value models with assumptions about commodity prices based on those observed in underlying

34

SOUTHWEST AIRLINES CO.

NOTES TO CONSOLIDATED FINANCIAL STATEMENTS — (Continued)

markets. Also, since there is not a reliable forward market for jet fuel, the Company must estimate the future prices of jet fuel in order to measure the effectiveness of the hedging instruments in offsetting changes to those prices, as required by SFAS 133. Forward jet fuel prices are estimated through the observation of similar commodity futures prices (such as crude oil, heating oil, and unleaded gasoline) and adjusted based on historical variations to those like commodities. See Note 10 for further information on SFAS 133 and financial derivative instruments.

Income Taxes. The Company accounts for deferred income taxes utilizing Statement of Financial Accounting Standards No. 109 (SFAS 109), "Accounting for Income Taxes", as amended. SFAS 109 requires an asset and liability method, whereby deferred tax assets and liabilities are recognized based on the tax effects of temporary differences between the financial statements and the tax bases of assets and liabilities, as measured by current enacted tax rates. When appropriate, in accordance with SFAS 109, the Company evaluates the need for a valuation allowance to reduce deferred tax assets.

The Operating Cycle and Merchandising Operations

Buying and selling goods and services is fundamental to the operation of retail and wholesale merchandising businesses. Managers who do not understand the dynamics of the cash flows of buying and selling merchandise and collecting from customers run the risk of putting their company in bankruptcy. Today's global environment, in which many goods are purchased and sold overseas, presents managers with additional challenges. In this chapter, we address the management of the operating cycle, the choice of inventory systems, merchandising income statements, and the recording of merchandising transactions.

LEARNING OBJECTIVES

Making a Statement

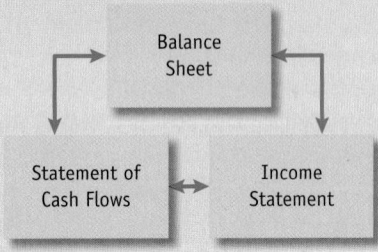

Merchandising transactions can affect all the financial statements.

LO1 Identify the management issues related to merchandising businesses.

LO2 Describe the terms of sale related to merchandising transactions.

LO3 Prepare an income statement and record merchandising transactions under the perpetual inventory system.

LO4 Prepare an income statement and record merchandising transactions under the periodic inventory system.

- How can the company efficiently manage its cycle of merchandising operations?

- How can merchandising transactions be recorded to reflect the company's performance?

Costco is a highly successful and fast-growing merchandising company. Like all other merchandisers, Costco has two key decisions to make: the price at which it will sell goods and the level of service it will provide. A department store may set the price of its merchandise at a relatively high level and provide a great deal of service. A discount store, on the other hand, may price its merchandise at a relatively low level and provide limited service. In the type of discount stores that Costco operates, customers buy memberships that allow them to buy in bulk at wholesale prices. Costco purchases merchandise in large quantities from many suppliers, places the goods on racks in its warehouse-like stores, and sells the goods to customers at very low prices, with minimal personal service.

Costco's large scale, reflected in its Financial Highlights,[1] presents management with many challenges.

COSTCO'S FINANCIAL HIGHLIGHTS

Operating Results (In millions)

Fiscal-Year Ended	August 28, 2005	August 29, 2004	Change
Net revenue	$52,935	$48,107	10.0%
Cost of sales	46,347	42,092	10.1
Gross margin	$ 6,588	$ 6,015	9.5
Operating expenses	5,114	4,630	10.5
Operating income	$ 1,474	$ 1,385	6.4

Managing Merchandising Businesses

LO1 Identify the management issues related to merchandising businesses.

A **merchandising business** earns income by buying and selling goods, which are called **merchandise inventory**. Whether a merchandiser is a wholesaler or a retailer, it uses the same basic accounting methods as a service company. However, the buying and selling of goods adds to the complexity of the business and of the accounting process. To understand the issues involved in accounting for a merchandising business, one must be familiar with the issues involved in managing such a business.

Operating Cycle

Merchandising businesses engage in a series of transactions called the **operating cycle**. Figure 1 shows the transactions that make up this cycle:

1. Purchase of merchandise inventory for cash or on credit

2. Payment for purchases made on credit

3. Sales of merchandise inventory for cash or on credit

4. Collection of cash from credit sales

Study Note

The operating cycle is the average days' inventory on hand plus the average number of days to collect credit sales.

When merchandisers purchase inventory on credit, which they usually do, they have a period of time before payment is due. However, this period is generally less than the time it takes them to sell the goods. To finance the inventory until they sell it and collect payment for it, merchandisers must rely on cash flows from within the company or from borrowing. If they lack the cash to pay bills when they come due, they can be forced out of business. Thus, managing cash flow is a critical concern.

A merchandiser's need to manage cash flow is demonstrated in Figure 2, which shows the financing period. Sometimes referred to as the *cash gap*, the

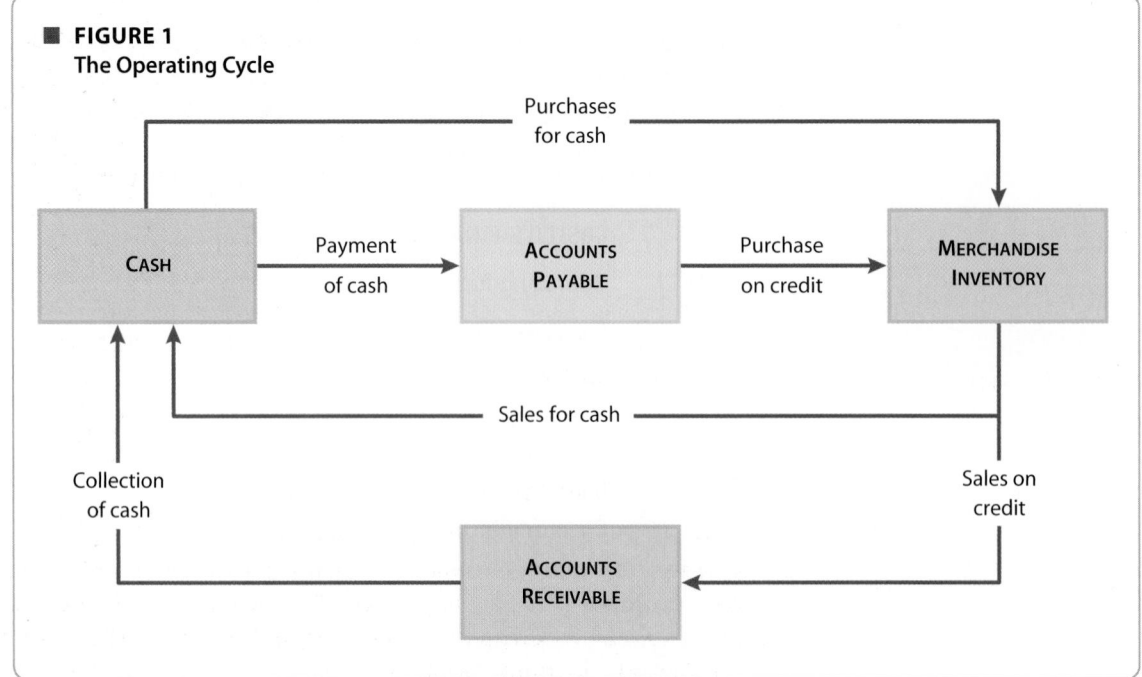

■ **FIGURE 1**
The Operating Cycle

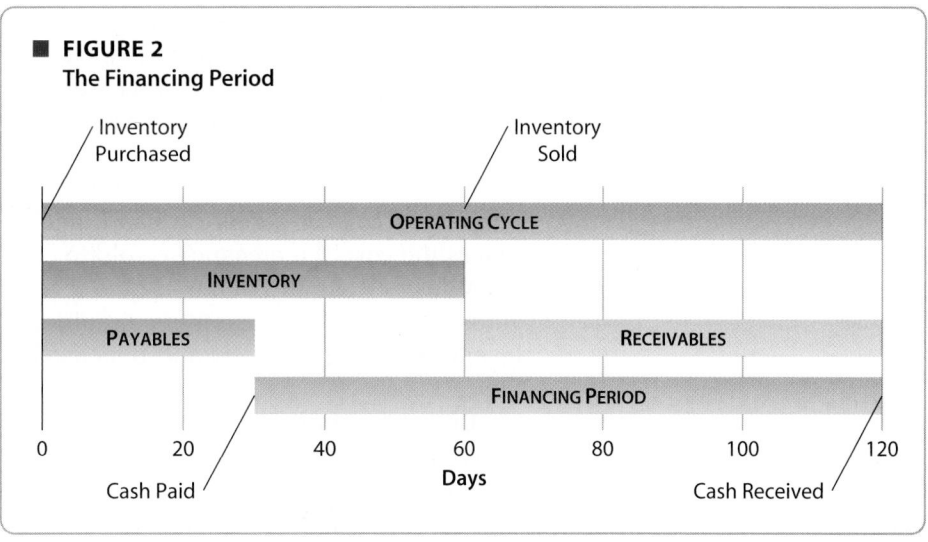

■ **FIGURE 2**
The Financing Period

financing period is the amount of time from the purchase of inventory until it is sold and payment is collected, less the amount of time creditors give the company to pay for the inventory. Thus, if it takes 60 days to sell the inventory, 60 days to collect for the sale, and creditors' payment terms are 30 days, the financing period is 90 days. During the financing period, the company will be without cash from this series of transactions and will need either to have funds available internally or to borrow from a bank.

The type of merchandising operation in which a company engages can affect the financing period. For example, compare **Costco's** financing period with that of a traditional department store chain, **Dillard's, Inc.:**

	Dillard's	Costco	Difference
Days' inventory on hand	101 days	29 days	−72 days
Days' receivable	43	5	−38
Less days' payable	−44	−31	−(13)
Financing period	**100 days**	**3 days**	**−97 days**

Costco has a significant advantage over Dillard's because it holds its inventory for a far shorter period before it sells it and collects receivables much faster. Its very short financing period is one of the reasons Costco can charge such low prices.

By reducing its financing period, a company can improve its cash flow. Many merchandisers, including Costco, do this by selling as much as possible for cash. Cash sales include sales made on bank *credit cards*, such as Visa or MasterCard, and on *debit cards*, which draw directly on the purchaser's bank account. They are considered cash sales because funds from them are available to the merchandiser immediately. Small retail stores may have mostly cash sales and very few credit sales, whereas large wholesale concerns may have almost all credit sales.

Choice of Inventory System

Another issue in managing a merchandising business is the choice of inventory system. Management must choose the system or combination of systems that best achieves the company's goals. The two basic systems of accounting for the many items in merchandise inventory are the perpetual inventory system and the periodic inventory system.

Study Note

A sale takes place when title to the goods transfers to the buyer.

Under the **perpetual inventory system**, continuous records are kept of the quantity and, usually, the cost of individual items as they are bought and sold. Under this system, the cost of each item is recorded in the Merchandise Inventory account when it is purchased. As merchandise is sold, its cost is transferred from the Merchandise Inventory account to the Cost of Goods Sold account. Thus, at all times the balance of the Merchandise Inventory account equals the cost of goods on hand, and the balance in Cost of Goods Sold equals the cost of merchandise sold to customers.

Managers use the detailed data that the perpetual inventory system provides to respond to customers' inquiries about product availability, to order inventory more effectively and thus avoid running out of stock, and to control the costs associated with investments in inventory.

Under the **periodic inventory system**, the inventory not yet sold, or on hand, is counted periodically. This physical count is usually taken at the end of the accounting period. No detailed records of the inventory on hand are maintained during the accounting period. The figure for inventory on hand is accurate only on the balance sheet date. As soon as any purchases or sales are made, the inventory figure becomes a historical amount, and it remains so until the new ending inventory amount is entered at the end of the next accounting period.

Some retail and wholesale businesses use the periodic inventory system because it reduces the amount of clerical work. If a business is fairly small, management can maintain control over its inventory simply through observation or by using an offline system of cards or computer records. But for larger businesses, the lack of detailed records may lead to lost sales or high operating costs.

Because of the difficulty and expense of accounting for the purchase and sale of each item, companies that sell items of low value in high volume have traditionally used the periodic inventory system. Examples of such companies include drugstores, automobile parts stores, department stores, and discount stores. In contrast, companies that sell items that have a high unit value, such as appliances or automobiles, have tended to use the perpetual inventory system.

The distinction between high and low unit value for inventory systems has blurred considerably in recent years. Although the periodic inventory system is still widely used, computerization has led to a large increase in the use of the perpetual inventory system. It is important to note that the perpetual inventory system does not eliminate the need for a physical count of the inventory. A physical count of inventory should be taken periodically to ensure that the actual number of goods on hand matches the quantity indicated by the computer records.

FOCUS ON BUSINESS PRACTICE

How Have Bar Codes Influenced the Choice of Inventory Systems?

Most grocery stores, which traditionally used the periodic inventory system, now employ bar coding to update the physical inventory as items are sold. At the checkout counter, the cashier scans the electronic marking on each product, called a *bar code* or *universal product code* (UPC), into the cash register, which is linked to a computer that records the sale. Bar coding has become common in all types of retail companies, and in manufacturing firms and hospitals as well. It has also become a major factor in the increased use of the perpetual inventory system. Interestingly, some retail businesses now use the perpetual inventory system for keeping track of the physical flow of inventory and the periodic inventory system for preparing their financial statements.

Foreign Business Transactions

Most large merchandising and manufacturing firms and even many small ones transact some of their business overseas. For example, a U.S. manufacturer may expand by selling its product to foreign customers, or it may lower its product cost by buying a less expensive part from a source in another country. Such sales and purchase transactions may take place in Japanese yen, British pounds, or some other foreign currency.

When an international transaction involves two different currencies, as most such transactions do, one currency has to be translated into another by using an exchange rate. As we noted earlier in the text, an *exchange rate* is the value of one currency stated in terms of another. We also noted that the values of other currencies in relation to the dollar rise and fall daily according to supply and demand. Thus, if there is a delay between the date of sale or purchase and the date of receipt of payment, the amount of cash involved in an international transaction may differ from the amount originally agreed on.

If the billing of an international sale and the payment for it are both in the domestic currency, no accounting problem arises. For example, if a U.S. maker of precision tools sells $160,000 worth of its products to a British company and bills the British company in dollars, the U.S. company will receive $160,000 when it collects payment. However, if the U.S. company bills the British company in British pounds and accepts payment in pounds, it will incur an **exchange gain or loss** if the exchange rate between dollars and pounds changes between the date of sale and the date of payment.

For example, assume that the U.S. company billed the sale of $160,000 at £100,000, reflecting an exchange rate of 1.60 (that is, $1.60 per pound) on the sale date. Now assume that by the date of payment, the exchange rate has fallen to 1.50. When the U.S. company receives its £100,000, it will be worth only $150,000 (£100,000 × $1.50 = $150,000). It will have incurred an exchange loss of $10,000 because it agreed to accept a fixed number of British pounds in payment for its products, and the value of each pound dropped before the payment was made. Had the value of the pound in relation to the dollar increased, the company would have made an exchange gain.

The same logic applies to purchases as to sales, except that the relationship of exchange gains and losses to changes in exchange rates is reversed. For example, assume that the U.S company purchases products from the British company for $160,000. If the payment is to be made in U.S. dollars, no accounting problem arises. However, if the British company expects to be paid in pounds, the U.S. company will have an exchange gain of $10,000 because it agreed to pay a fixed £100,000, and between the dates of purchase and payment, the exchange value of the pound decreased from $1.60 to $1.50. To make the £100,000 payment, the U.S. company has to expend only $150,000.

Exchange gains and losses are reported on the income statement. Because of their bearing on a company's financial performance, they are of considerable interest to managers and investors. Lack of uniformity in international accounting standards is another matter of which investors must be wary.

S T O P • R E V I E W • A P P L Y

1-1. What is the operating cycle of a merchandising business, and why is it important?

1-2. What is the financing period, and what are its components?

1-3. What is the difference between the perpetual inventory system and the periodic inventory system?

1-4. What conditions cause an exchange gain or loss?

Suggested answers to all Stop, Review, and Apply questions are available at http://college.hmco.com/accounting/needles/poa/10e/student_home.html.

Terms of Sale

LO2 Describe the terms of sale related to merchandising transactions.

When goods are sold on credit, both parties should understand the amount and timing of payment as well as other terms of the purchase, such as who pays delivery charges and what warranties or rights of return apply. Sellers quote prices in different ways. Many merchants quote the price at which they expect to sell their goods. Others, particularly manufacturers and wholesalers, quote prices as a percentage (usually 30 percent or more) off their list or catalogue prices. Such a reduction is called a **trade discount**.

For example, if an article is listed at $1,000 with a trade discount of 40 percent, or $400, the seller records the sale at $600, and the buyer records the purchase at $600. The seller may raise or lower the trade discount depending on the quantity purchased. The list or catalogue price and related trade discount are used only to arrive at an agreed-on price; they do not appear in the accounting records.

Sales and Purchases Discounts

The terms of sale are usually printed on the sales invoice and thus constitute part of the sales agreement. Terms differ from industry to industry. In some industries, payment is expected in a short period of time, such as 10 or 30 days. In these cases, the invoice is marked "n/10" ("net 10") or "n/30" ("net 30"), meaning that the amount of the invoice is due either 10 days or 30 days after the invoice date. If the invoice is due 10 days after the end of the month, it is marked "n/10 eom."

In some industries, it is customary to give a discount for early payment. This discount, called a **sales discount**, is intended to increase the seller's liquidity by reducing the amount of money tied up in accounts receivable. An invoice that offers a sales discount might be labeled "2/10, n/30," which means that the buyer either can pay the invoice within 10 days of the invoice date and take a 2 percent discount or can wait 30 days and pay the full amount of the invoice. It is often advantageous for a buyer to take the discount because the saving of 2 percent over a period of 20 days (from the 11th day to the 30th day) represents an effective annual rate of 36.5 percent (365 days ÷ 20 days × 2% = 36.5%). Most companies would be better off borrowing money to take the discount. The practice of giving sales discounts has been declining because it is costly to the seller and because, from the buyer's viewpoint, the amount of the discount is usually very small in relation to the price of the purchase.

Because it is not possible to know at the time of a sale whether the customer will pay in time to take advantage of a sales discount, the discounts are recorded only at the time the customer pays. For example, suppose Laboda Sportswear Company sells merchandise to a customer on September 20 for

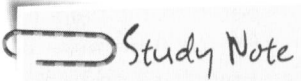

Study Note

A trade discount applies to the list or catalogue price. A sales discount applies to the sales price.

Study Note

Early collection also has the advantage of reducing the probability of a customer's defaulting.

$600 on terms of 2/10, n/30. Laboda records the sale on September 20 for the full amount of $600. If the customer takes advantage of the discount by paying on or before September 30, Laboda will receive $588 in cash and will reduce its accounts receivable by $600. The difference of $12 ($600 × .02) will be debited to an account called *Sales Discounts*. Sales Discounts is a contra-revenue account with a normal debit balance that is deducted from sales on the income statement.

The same logic applies to **purchases discounts**, which are discounts that a buyer takes for the early payment of merchandise. For example, the buyer in the transaction described above will record the purchase on September 20 at $600. If the buyer pays on or before September 30, it will record cash paid of $588 and reduce its accounts payable by $600. The difference of $12 is recorded as a credit to an account called *Purchases Discounts*. The Purchases Discounts account reduces cost of goods sold or purchases depending on the inventory method used.

Transportation Costs

In some industries, the seller usually pays transportation costs and charges a price that includes those costs. In other industries, it is customary for the purchaser to pay transportation charges. Special terms designate whether the seller or the purchaser pays the freight charges.

FOB shipping point means that the seller places the merchandise "free on board" at the point of origin and the buyer bears the shipping costs. The title to the merchandise passes to the buyer at that point. For example, when the sales agreement for the purchase of a car says "FOB factory," the buyer must pay the freight from the factory where the car was made to wherever he or she is located, and the buyer owns the car from the time it leaves the factory.

FOB destination means that the seller bears the transportation costs to the place where the merchandise is delivered. The seller retains title until the merchandise reaches its destination and usually prepays the shipping costs, in which case the buyer makes no accounting entry for freight.

Shipping terms affect the financial statements. *FOB shipping point* means the buyer pays the freight charges; when relatively small, these charges are usually included in cost of goods sold on the buyer's income statement. *FOB destination* means the seller pays the freight charges; they are included in selling expenses on the seller's income statement.

The effects of these special shipping terms are summarized as follows:

Shipping Term	Where Title Passes	Who Pays the Cost of Transportation
FOB shipping point	At origin	Buyer
FOB destination	At destination	Seller

When the buyer pays the transportation charge, it is called **freight-in**, and it is added to the cost of merchandise purchased. Thus, freight-in increases the buyer's cost of merchandise inventory, as well as the cost of goods sold after the product is sold. When freight-in is a relatively small amount, most companies include the cost in the cost of goods sold on the income statement rather than going to the trouble of allocating part of it to merchandise inventory.

When the seller pays the transportation charge, it is called **delivery expense**, or *freight-out*. Because the seller incurs this cost to facilitate the sale of its product, the cost is included in selling expenses on the income statement.

Terms of Debit and Credit Card Sales

Many retailers allow customers to use debit or credit cards to charge their purchases. Debit cards deduct directly from a person's bank account, whereas a credit card allows for payment later. Five of the most widely used credit cards are American Express, Discover Card, Diners Club, MasterCard, and Visa. The customer establishes credit with the lender (the credit card issuer) and receives a plastic card to use in making charges. If a seller accepts the card, the customer signs an invoice at the time of the sale. The sale is communicated to the seller's bank, resulting in a cash deposit in the seller's bank account. Thus, the seller does not have to establish the customer's credit, collect from the customer, or tie up money in accounts receivable. As payment, the lender, rather than paying the total amount of the credit card sales, takes a discount of 2 to 6 percent. The discount is a selling expense for the merchandiser. For example, if a restaurant makes sales of $1,000 on Visa credit cards and Visa takes a 4 percent discount on the sales, the restaurant would record Cash in the amount of $960 and Credit Card Expense in the amount of $40.

STOP • REVIEW • APPLY

2-1. What is the difference between a trade discount and a sales discount?

2-2. Is Sales Discounts an asset, liability, expense, or contra-revenue account? Is the normal balance of the Sales Discounts account a debit or a credit balance?

2-3. Two suppliers quoted these prices and terms on 50 units of a product:

	Price	Terms
Supplier A	$20 per unit	FOB shipping point
Supplier B	$21 per unit	FOB destination

Which supplier is quoting the better deal? Explain your answer.

2-4. Is freight-in an operating expense? Explain your answer.

Perpetual Inventory System

LO3 Prepare an income statement and record merchandising transactions under the perpetual inventory system.

Exhibit 1 shows how an income statement appears when a company uses the perpetual inventory system. The focal point of the statement is cost of goods sold, which is deducted from net sales to arrive at gross margin. Under the perpetual inventory system, the Merchandise Inventory and Cost of Goods Sold accounts are continually updated during the accounting period as purchases, sales, and other inventory transactions that affect these accounts occur.

Purchases of Merchandise

Figure 3 shows how transactions involving purchases of merchandise are recorded under the perpetual inventory system. As you can see, the focus of these journal entries is Accounts Payable. These entries are summarized below. (For a comparison of complete journal entries made under the perpetual and periodic inventory systems, see the Review Problem in this chapter.)

Purchases on Credit
Oct. 3: Received merchandise purchased on credit, invoice dated Oct. 1, terms n/10, $9,780.

Comment: Under the perpetual inventory system, the cost of merchandise is recorded in the Merchandise Inventory account at the time of purchase. In the

EXHIBIT 1 ▶

Income Statement Under the Perpetual Inventory System

Laboda Sportswear Company
Income Statement
For the Year Ended December 31, 20x8

Net sales	$478,650
Cost of goods sold*	262,720
Gross margin	$215,930
Operating expenses	156,968
Net income	$ 58,962

*Freight-in has been included in cost of goods sold.

Study Note

On the income statement, freight-in is included as part of cost of goods sold, and delivery expense (freight-out) is included as an operating (selling) expense.

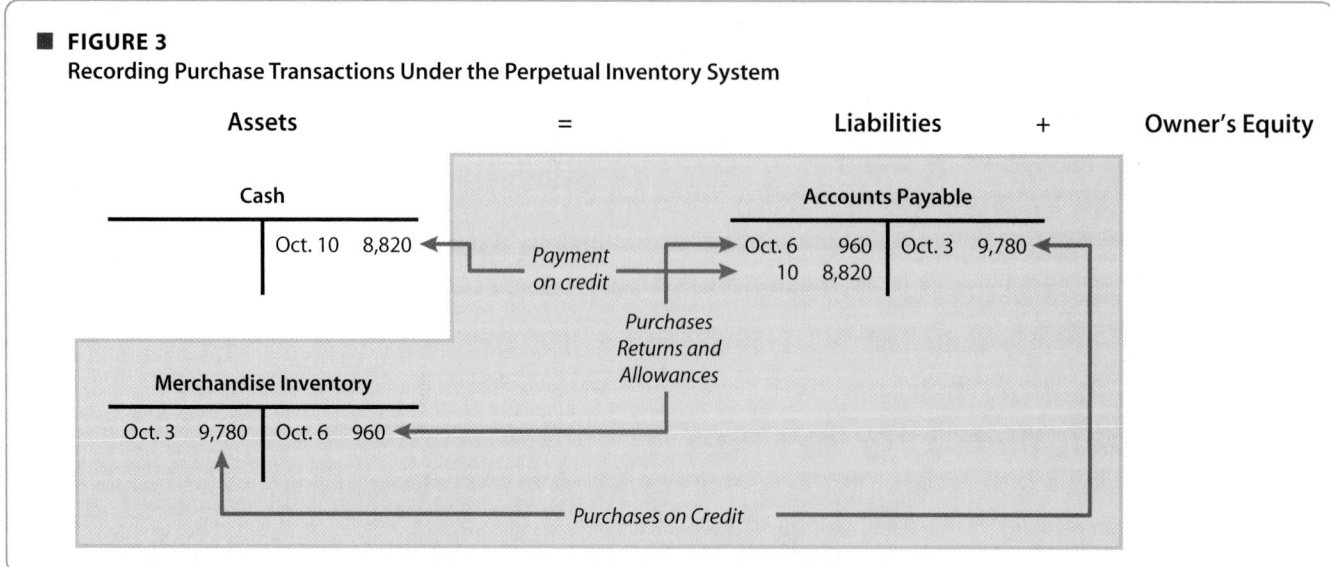

■ **FIGURE 3**
Recording Purchase Transactions Under the Perpetual Inventory System

The Merchandise Inventory account increases when a purchase is made.

transaction described here, payment is due ten days from the invoice date. If an invoice includes a charge for shipping or if shipping is billed separately, it should be debited to Freight-In.

Purchases Returns and Allowances
Oct. 6: Returned part of merchandise received on Oct. 3 for credit, $960.

Comment: Under the perpetual inventory system, when a buyer is allowed to return all or part of a purchase or is given an allowance—a reduction in the amount to be paid, Merchandise Inventory is reduced, as is Accounts Payable.

Payments on Account
Oct. 10: Paid amount in full due for the purchase of Oct. 3, part of which was returned on Oct. 6, $8,820.

Comment: Payment is made for the net amount due of $8,820 ($9,780 − $960).

Sales of Merchandise

Figure 4 shows how transactions involving sales of merchandise are recorded under the perpetual inventory system. These transactions involve several

FOCUS ON BUSINESS PRACTICE

Are Purchases Allowances Revenues?

Food companies like Sara Lee, Kraft, Georgia-Pacific, and Nestlé commonly give rebates, a type of purchases allowance, to supermarket chains that allow them more room to display their products. Another common practice among companies in the food industry is to grant customers rebates ranging from 8.5 percent to 48 percent depending on the customer's annual volume of purchases. A division of Ahold, the large Dutch supermarket operator, booked the rebates it anticipated receiving from food companies as revenue at the time it placed its orders. Sim- ply by buying more, which it did—to the point that its warehouses were filled with unsold goods—it was able to inflate revenues. Regional managers said it was clear that if they didn't place large orders, their jobs would be on the line. As it turned out, by prematurely recognizing the rebates, Ahold overstated it profits over two years by more than $500 million. The correct accounting practice would have been to wait until the rebate was granted at the time of payment and to show it as a reduction in cost of goods sold, not as an increase in revenue.[3]

FOCUS ON BUSINESS PRACTICE

How Are Web Sales Doing?

In spite of the well-publicized dot.com meltdown and the demise of many Internet retailers, merchandise sales over the Internet continue to thrive. Internet sales amounted to more than $170 billion in 2005[4]—up from $44.5 billion in 2001—and were expected to continue to grow rapidly in the near future. To date, the companies that have been most successful in using the Internet to enhance their operations have been established mail-order retailers like **Lands' End** and **L.L. Bean.** Other retailers, such as **Circuit City** and **Office Depot,** have also benefited from their use of the Internet. Circuit City allows customers to purchase online and pick up the products at stores near their homes. Office Depot, which focuses primarily on business-to-business Internet sales, has set up customized web pages for tens of thousands of corporate clients. These websites allow customers to make online purchases and check store inventories. Although Internet transactions are recorded in the same way as on-site transactions, the technology adds a level of complexity to the transactions.

Study Note

The Cost of Goods Sold account is increased and the Merchandise Inventory account is decreased when a sale is made.

accounts, including Cash, Accounts Receivable, Merchandise Inventory, and Cost of Goods Sold.

Sales on Credit

Oct. 7: Sold merchandise on credit, terms n/30, FOB destination, $2,400; the cost of the merchandise was $1,440.

Comment: Under the perpetual inventory system, sales always require two entries, as shown in Figure 4. First, the sale is recorded by increasing Accounts Receivable and Sales. Second, Cost of Goods Sold is updated by a transfer from Merchandise Inventory. In the case of cash sales, Cash rather than Accounts Receivable is debited for the amount of the sale. If the seller pays for the shipping, it should be debited to Delivery Expense.

■ **FIGURE 4**
Recording Sales Transactions Under the Perpetual Inventory System

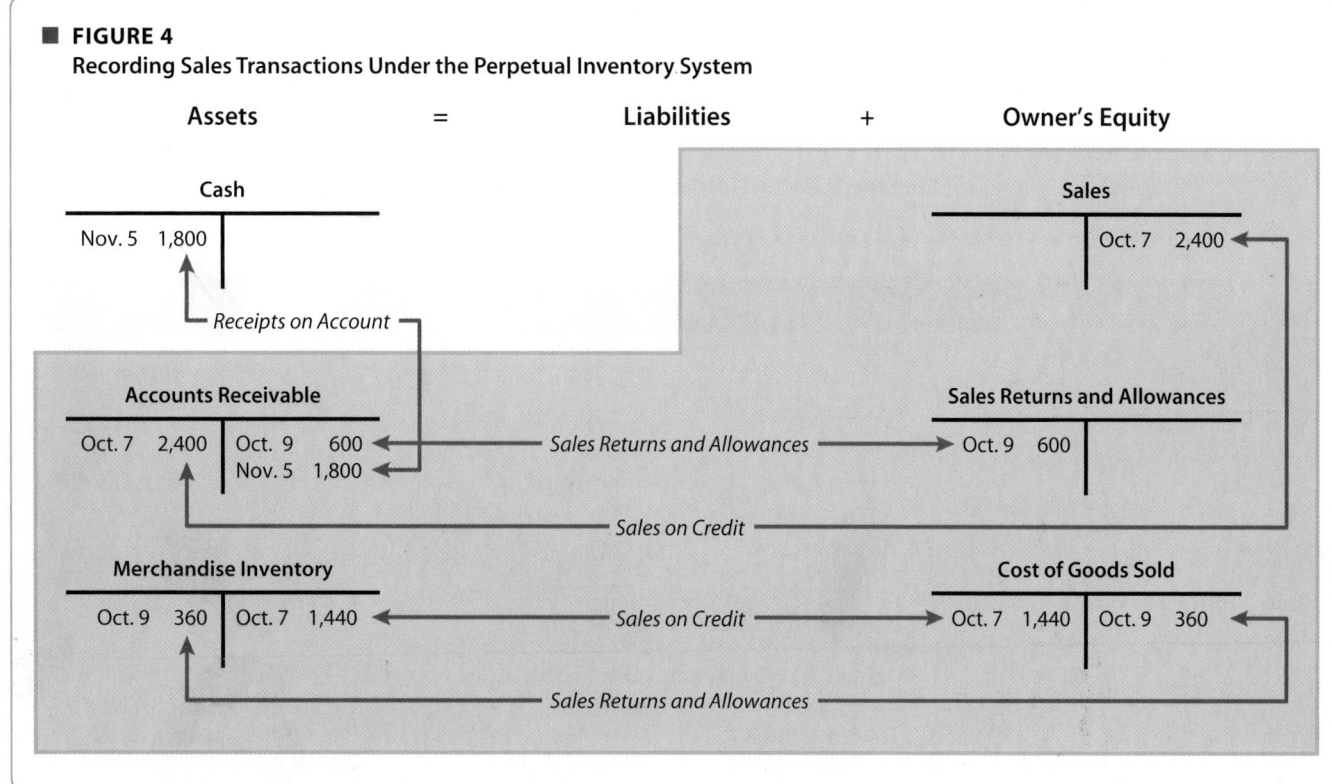

FOCUS ON BUSINESS PRACTICE

Are Sales Returns Worth Accounting For?

Some industries routinely have a high percentage of sales returns. More than 6 percent of all nonfood items sold in stores are eventually returned to vendors. This amounts to over $100 billion a year, or more than the gross national product of two-thirds of the world's nations.[5] Book publishers like **Simon & Schuster** often have returns as high as 30 to 50 percent because to gain the attention of potential buyers, they must distribute large numbers of copies to many outlets. Magazine publishers like **AOL Time Warner** expect to sell no more than 35 to 38 percent of the magazines they send to newsstands and other outlets.[6] In all these businesses, it pays management to scrutinize the Sales Returns and Allowances account for ways to reduce returns and increase profitability.

Sales Returns and Allowances

Oct. 9: Accepted for full credit return of part of merchandise sold on Oct. 7 and returned it to merchandise inventory, $600; the cost of the merchandise was $360.

Comment: Under the perpetual inventory system, when a seller allows the buyer to return all or part of a sale or gives an allowance—a reduction in amount, two entries are again necessary. First, the original sale is reversed by reducing Accounts Receivable and debiting Sales Returns and Allowances. The **Sales Returns and Allowances account** gives management a readily available measure of unsatisfactory products and dissatisfied customers. It is a contra-revenue account with a normal debit balance and is deducted from sales on the income statement. Second, the cost of the merchandise must also be transferred from the Cost of Goods Sold account back into the Merchandise Inventory account. If the company makes an allowance instead of accepting a return, or if the merchandise cannot be returned to inventory and resold, this transfer is not made.

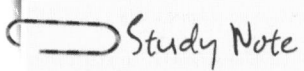

Study Note

Because the Sales account is established with a credit, its contra account, Sales Returns and Allowances, is established with a debit.

Receipts on Account

Nov. 5: Collected in full for sale of merchandise on Oct. 7, less the return on Oct. 9, $1,800.

Comment: Collection is made for the net amount due: $1,800 ($2,400 − $600). ●

S T O P • R E V I E W • A P P L Y

3-1. Under which inventory system is a Cost of Goods Sold account maintained? Explain why.

3-2. Discuss this statement: "The perpetual inventory system is the best system because management always needs to know how much inventory is on hand."

3-3. Why is it advisable to maintain a Sales Returns and Allowances account when the same result could be obtained by debiting each return or allowance to the Sales account?

Merchandising Transactions: Perpetual Inventory System The numbered items that follow are account titles, and the lettered items are types of merchandising transactions. For each transaction, indicate which accounts are debited or credited by placing the account numbers in the appropriate columns.

1. Cash
2. Accounts Receivable
3. Merchandise Inventory
4. Accounts Payable

5. Sales
6. Sales Returns and Allowances
7. Cost of Goods Sold

	Account Debited	Account Credited
a. Purchase on credit	___	___
b. Purchase return for credit	___	___
c. Purchase for cash	___	___
d. Sale on credit	___	___
e. Sale for cash	___	___
f. Sales return for credit	___	___
g. Payment on account	___	___
h. Receipt on account	___	___

SOLUTION

	Account Debited	Account Credited
a. Purchase on credit	3	4
b. Purchase return for credit	4	3
c. Purchase for cash	3	1
d. Sale on credit	2	5
	7	3
e. Sale for cash	1	5
	7	3
f. Sales return for credit	6	2
	3	7
g. Payment on account	4	1
h. Receipt on account	1	2

Periodic Inventory System

LO4 Prepare an income statement and record merchandising transactions under the periodic inventory system.

Exhibit 2 shows how an income statement appears when a company uses the periodic inventory system. A major feature of this statement is the computation of cost of goods sold. Cost of goods sold must be computed on the income statement because it is not updated for purchases, sales, and other transactions during the accounting period, as it is under the perpetual inventory system. Figure 5 illustrates the components of cost of goods sold.

EXHIBIT 2 ▶

Income Statement Under the Periodic Inventory System

Study Note

Most published financial statements are condensed, eliminating the detail shown here under cost of goods sold.

Laboda Sportswear Company
Income Statement
For the Year Ended December 31, 20x8

Net sales			$478,650
Cost of goods sold			
Merchandise inventory,			
December 31, 20x7		$105,600	
Purchases	$252,800		
Less purchases returns and			
allowances	15,552		
Net purchases	$237,248		
Freight-in	16,472		
Net cost of purchases		253,720	
Cost of goods available for sale		$359,320	
Less merchandise inventory,			
December 31, 20x8		96,600	
Cost of goods sold			262,720
Gross margin			$215,930
Operating expenses			156,968
Net income			$ 58,962

To calculate cost of goods sold, the **cost of goods available for sale** must first be determined. The cost of goods available for sale during an accounting period is the sum of two factors: beginning inventory and the net cost of purchases during the period. As you can see in Exhibit 2, the cost of the goods that Laboda Sportswear Company has available for sale during the period amounts to $359,320 ($105,600 + $253,720).

If a company sold all the goods available for sale during an accounting period, the cost of goods sold would equal the cost of goods available for sale.

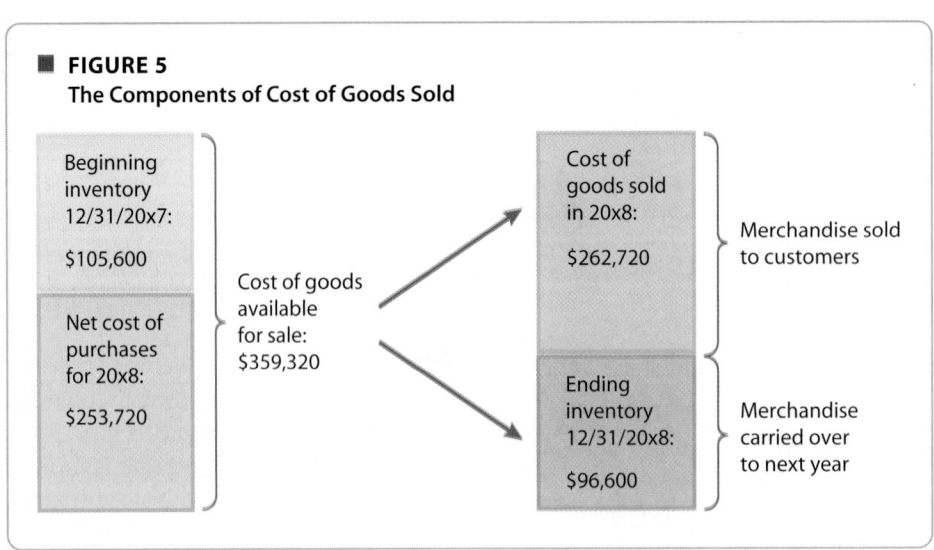

■ **FIGURE 5**
The Components of Cost of Goods Sold

In most businesses, however, some merchandise remains unsold and on hand at the end of the period. This ending inventory must be deducted from the cost of goods available for sale to determine the cost of goods sold. In Exhibit 2, the company's ending inventory on December 31, 20x8, is $96,600. Thus, its cost of goods sold is $262,720 ($359,320 − $96,600).

An important component of the cost of goods sold section is **net cost of purchases**. As you can see in the income statement in Exhibit 2, net cost of purchases is the sum of net purchases and freight-in. **Net purchases** equal total purchases less any deductions, such as purchases returns and allowances and any discounts allowed by suppliers for early payment. Freight-in is added to net purchases because transportation charges are a necessary cost of receiving merchandise for sale.

Purchases of Merchandise

Figure 6 shows how transactions involving purchases of merchandise are recorded under the periodic inventory system. A primary difference between the perpetual and periodic inventory systems is that in the perpetual inventory system, the Merchandise Inventory account is adjusted each time a purchase, sale, or other inventory transaction occurs, whereas in the periodic inventory system, the Merchandise Inventory account stays at its beginning balance until the physical inventory is recorded at the end of the period. The periodic system uses a Purchases account to accumulate purchases during an accounting period and a Purchases Returns and Allowances account to accumulate returns of and allowances on purchases.

We will now illustrate how Laboda Sportswear Company would record purchase transactions under the periodic inventory system.

Purchases on Credit

Oct. 3: Received merchandise purchased on credit, invoice dated Oct. 1, terms n/10, $9,780.

Comment: Under the periodic inventory system, the cost of merchandise is recorded in the **Purchases account** at the time of purchase. This account is a temporary one used only with the periodic inventory system. Its sole purpose is to accumulate the total cost of merchandise purchased for resale during an

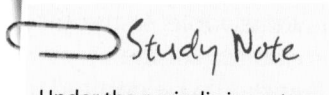

Study Note

Under the periodic inventory system, the Purchases account increases when a company makes a purchase.

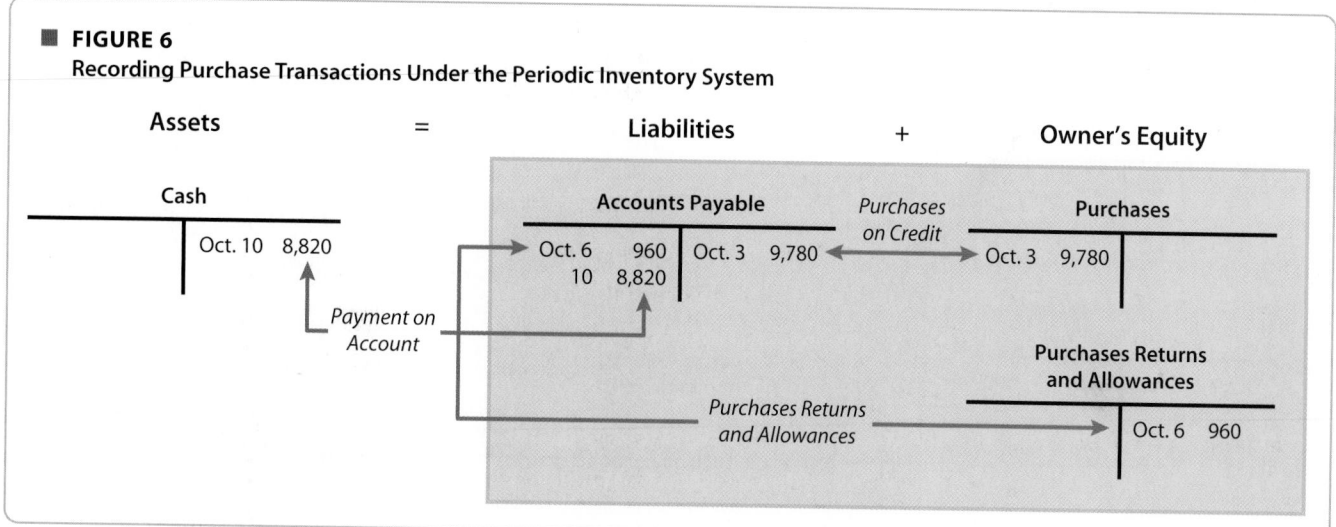

■ **FIGURE 6**
Recording Purchase Transactions Under the Periodic Inventory System

Study Note

Purchases accounts and Purchases Returns and Allowances accounts are used only in conjunction with a periodic inventory system.

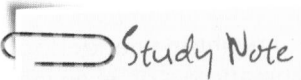

Study Note

Because the Purchases account is established with a debit, its contra account, Purchases Returns and Allowances, is established with a credit.

accounting period. (Purchases of other assets, such as equipment, are recorded in the appropriate asset account, not in the Purchases account.) The Purchases account does not indicate whether merchandise has been sold or is still on hand.

Purchases Returns and Allowances

Oct. 6: Returned part of merchandise received on Oct. 3 for credit, $960.

Comment: Under the periodic inventory system, the amount of a return or allowance is recorded in the **Purchases Returns and Allowances account**. This account is a contra-purchases account with a normal credit balance, and it is deducted from purchases on the income statement. Accounts Payable is also reduced.

Payments on Account

Oct. 10: Paid amount in full due for the purchase of Oct. 3, part of which was returned on Oct. 6, $8,820.

Comment: Payment is made for the net amount due of $8,820 ($9,780 − $960).

Sales of Merchandise

Figure 7 shows how transactions involving sales of merchandise are recorded under the periodic inventory system.

Sales on Credit

Oct. 7: Sold merchandise on credit, terms n/30, FOB destination, $2,400; the cost of the merchandise was $1,440.

Comment: As shown in Figure 7, under the periodic inventory system, sales require only one entry to increase Sales and Accounts Receivable. In the case of cash sales, Cash rather than Accounts Receivable is debited for the amount of the sale. If the seller pays for the shipping, the amount should be debited to Delivery Expense.

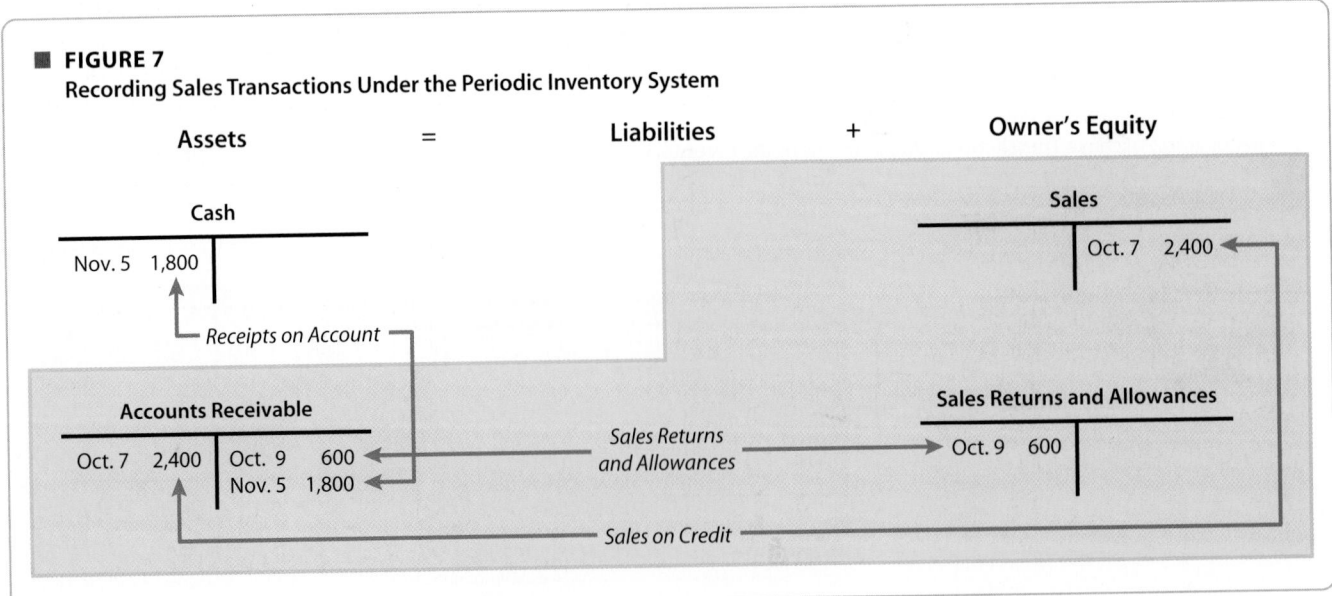

■ **FIGURE 7**
Recording Sales Transactions Under the Periodic Inventory System

Sales Returns and Allowances
Oct. 9: Accepted for full credit return of part of merchandise sold on Oct. 7 and returned it to merchandise inventory, $600; the cost of the merchandise was $360.

Comment: Under the periodic inventory system, when a seller allows the buyer to return all or part of a sale or gives an allowance, only one entry is needed to reduce Accounts Receivable and debit Sales Returns and Allowances. The Sales Returns and Allowances account is a contra-revenue account with a normal debit balance and is deducted from sales on the income statement.

Receipts on Account
Nov. 5: Collected in full for sale of merchandise on Oct. 7, less the return on Oct. 9, $1,800.

Comment: Collection is made for the net amount due: $1,800 ($2,400 − $600).

STOP • REVIEW • APPLY

4-1. Under the periodic inventory system, an important figure in computing cost of goods sold is cost of goods available for sale. What are the two main components of cost of goods available for sale, and what is the relationship of ending inventory to cost of goods available for sale?

4-2. Under the periodic inventory system, how must the amount of inventory at the end of the year be determined?

4-3. Hornberger Hardware purchased the following items: (a) a delivery truck, (b) two dozen hammers, (c) supplies for its office workers, and (d) a broom for the janitor. Which items should be debited to the Purchases account under the periodic inventory system?

4-4. What are the principal differences in the way merchandise transactions are recorded under the perpetual inventory system and the periodic inventory system?

Merchandising Transactions: Periodic Inventory System The numbered items below are account titles, and the lettered items are types of merchandising transactions. For each transaction, indicate which accounts are debited or credited by placing the account numbers in the appropriate columns.

1. Cash
2. Accounts Receivable
3. Merchandise Inventory
4. Accounts Payable
5. Sales
6. Sales Returns and Allowances
7. Purchases
8. Purchases Returns and Allowances

	Account Debited	Account Credited
a. Purchase on credit		
b. Purchase return for credit		
c. Purchase for cash		
d. Sale on credit		
e. Sale for cash		

	Account Debited	Account Credited
f. Sales return for credit	_____	_____
g. Payment on account	_____	_____
h. Receipt on account	_____	_____

SOLUTION

	Account Debited	Account Credited
a. Purchase on credit	7	4
b. Purchase return for credit	4	8
c. Purchase for cash	7	1
d. Sale on credit	2	5
e. Sale for cash	1	5
f. Sales return for credit	6	2
g. Payment on account	4	1
h. Receipt on account	1	2

A LOOK BACK AT

COSTCO WHOLESALE CORPORATION

In this chapter's Decision Point, we noted that **Costco's** managers face many challenges. To ensure the company's success, they must address the following questions:

- **How can the company efficiently manage its cycle of merchandising operations?**
- **How can merchandising transactions be recorded to reflect the company's performance?**

Costco is a very efficiently run organization, as its operating cycle attests. It sells its inventory every 30 days on average and has almost no receivables. The Financial Highlights at the beginning of the chapter also demonstrate operating efficiency. They show that Costco's operating expenses increased by 10.5 percent while its net revenue and gross margin increased by only 10 percent and 9.5 percent, respectively. Costco's chief executive officer had this to say about the company's performance:

> Our continued emphasis on cost controls and expense reduction enabled us to reduce our selling, general and administrative (SG&A) expenses as a percent of sales for the second year in a row.[7]

By buying and selling merchandise in bulk, providing very little service, and keeping its financing period to a minimum, Costco is able to offer its customers wholesale prices. A comparison of gross margin with net revenue in fiscal 2005 shows that Costco made only 12.4 percent ($6,588 ÷ $52,935) on each dollar of sales.

CHAPTER REVIEW

REVIEW of Learning Objectives

LO1 Identify the management issues related to merchandising businesses.

Merchandising companies differ from service companies in that they earn income by buying and selling goods. The buying and selling of goods adds to the complexity of the business and raises three issues that management must address. First, the series of transactions in which merchandising companies engage (the operating cycle) requires careful cash flow management. Second, management must choose whether to use the perpetual or the periodic inventory system. Third, if a company has international transactions, it must deal with changing exchange rates.

LO2 Describe the terms of sale related to merchandising transactions.

A trade discount is a reduction from the list or catalogue price of a product. A sales discount is a discount given for early payment of a sale on credit. Terms of 2/10, n/30 mean that the buyer can take a 2 percent discount if the invoice is paid within ten days of the invoice date. Otherwise, the buyer is obligated to pay the full amount in 30 days. Discounts on sales are recorded in the Sales Discounts account, and discounts on purchases are recorded in the Purchases Discounts account. FOB shipping point means that the buyer bears the cost of transportation and that title to the goods passes to the buyer at the shipping origin. FOB destination means that the seller bears the cost of transportation and that title does not pass to the buyer until the goods reach their destination. To the seller, debit and credit card sales are similar to cash sales.

LO3 Prepare an income statement and record merchandising transactions under the perpetual inventory system.

Under the perpetual inventory system, the Merchandise Inventory account is continuously adjusted by entering purchases, sales, and other inventory transactions as they occur. Purchases increase the Merchandise Inventory account, and purchases returns decrease it. As goods are sold, their cost is transferred from the Merchandise Inventory account to the Cost of Goods Sold account.

LO4 Prepare an income statement and record merchandising transactions under the periodic inventory system.

When the periodic inventory system is used, the cost of goods sold section of the income statement must include the following elements:

$$\text{Purchases} - \frac{\text{Purchases Returns}}{\text{and Allowances}} + \text{Freight-in} = \frac{\text{Net cost of}}{\text{Purchases}}$$

$$\frac{\text{Beginning}}{\text{Merchandise Inventory}} + \frac{\text{Net Cost}}{\text{of}}_{\text{Purchases}} = \frac{\text{Cost of Goods}}{\text{Available for}}_{\text{Sale}}$$

$$\frac{\text{Cost of Goods}}{\text{Available for}}_{\text{Sale}} - \frac{\text{Ending}}{\text{Merchandise Inventory}} = \frac{\text{Cost of}}{\text{Goods}}_{\text{Sold}}$$

Under the periodic inventory system, the Merchandise Inventory account stays at the beginning level until the physical inventory is recorded at the end of the accounting period. A Purchases account is used to accumulate purchases of merchandise during the accounting period, and a Purchases Returns and Allowances account is used to accumulate returns of purchases and allowances on purchases.

REVIEW of Concepts and Terminology

The following concepts and terms were introduced in this chapter:

Cost of goods available for sale: The sum of beginning inventory and the net cost of purchases during an accounting period. **(LO4)**

Delivery expense: The transportation cost of delivering merchandise. Also called *freight-out*. **(LO2)**

Exchange gain or loss: A gain or loss due to exchange rate fluctuation, which is reported on the income statement. **(LO1)**

Financing period: The amount of time from the purchase of inventory until it is sold and payment is collected, less the amount of time creditors give the company to pay for the inventory. **(LO1)**

FOB destination: A term indicating that the seller retains title to the merchandise until it reaches its destination and that the seller bears the shipping costs. **(LO2)**

FOB shipping point: A term indicating that the buyer assumes title to the merchandise at the shipping point and bears the shipping costs. **(LO2)**

Freight-in: The transportation cost of receiving merchandise. **(LO2)**

Merchandise inventory: The goods on hand at any one time that are available for sale to customers. **(LO1)**

Merchandising business: A business that earns income by buying and selling goods. **(LO1)**

Net cost of purchases: Net purchases plus any freight charges on the purchases. **(LO4)**

Net purchases: Total purchases less any deductions, such as purchases returns and allowances and discounts on purchases. **(LO4)**

Operating cycle: A series of transactions that includes purchases of merchandise inventory for cash or on credit, payment for purchases made on credit, sales of merchandise inventory for cash or on credit, and collection of cash from credit sales. **(LO1)**

Periodic inventory system: A system for determining inventory on hand by periodically taking a physical count. **(LO1)**

Perpetual inventory system: A system for determining inventory on hand by keeping continuous records of the quantity and, usually, the cost of individual items as they are bought and sold. **(LO1)**

Purchases account: A temporary account used under the periodic inventory system to accumulate the cost of merchandise purchased for resale during an accounting period. **(LO4)**

Purchases discounts: Discounts that buyers take for early payment of merchandise; the Purchases Discounts account is a contra-purchases account used under the periodic inventory system. **(LO2)**

Purchases Returns and Allowances account: A contra-purchases account used under the periodic inventory system to accumulate cash refunds, credits on account, and other allowances made by suppliers. **(LO4)**

Sales discount: A discount given to a buyer for early payment of a sale made on credit; the Sales Discounts account is a contra-revenue account. **(LO2)**

Sales Returns and Allowances account: A contra-revenue account used to accumulate cash refunds, credits on account, and other allowances made to customers who have received defective or otherwise unsatisfactory products. **(LO3)**

Trade discount: A deduction (usually 30 percent or more) off a list or catalogue price, which is not recorded in the accounting records. **(LO2)**

REVIEW Problem

LO3, LO4 **Merchandising Transactions: Perpetual and Periodic Inventory Systems**

Dawkins Company engaged in the following transactions during October:

Oct. 1 Sold merchandise to Ernie Devlin on credit, terms n/30, FOB shipping point, $1,050 (cost, $630).

2 Purchased merchandise on credit from Ruland Company, terms n/30, FOB shipping point, $1,900.

2 Paid Custom Freight $145 for freight charges on merchandise received.

Oct. 9 Purchased merchandise on credit from LNP Company, terms n/30, FOB shipping point, $1,800, including $100 freight costs paid by LNP Company.

    11 Accepted from Ernie Devlin a return of merchandise, which was returned to inventory, $150 (cost, $90).

    14 Returned for credit $300 of merchandise purchased on October 2.

    16 Sold merchandise for cash, $500 (cost, $300).

    22 Paid Ruland Company for purchase of October 2 less return of October 14.

    23 Received full payment from Ernie Devlin for his October 1 purchase, less return on October 11.

Required

1. Record these transactions in journal form, assuming Dawkins Company uses the perpetual inventory system.
2. Record the transactions in journal form, assuming Dawkins Company uses the periodic inventory system.

Answer to Review Problem

Accounts that differ under the two systems are highlighted.

				F	G	H					L	M	N
	A	B	C D E	**1. Perpetual Inventory System**			I	J	K		**2. Periodic Inventory System**		
2	Oct.	1		Accounts Receivable	1,050					Accounts Receivable		1,050	
3				Sales		1,050					Sales			1,050
4				Sold merchandise on							Sold merchandise on			
5				account to Ernie Devlin,							account to Ernie Devlin,			
6				terms n/30, FOB shipping							terms n/30. FOB shipping			
7				point							point			
8		1		Cost of Goods Sold	630									
9				Merchandise Inventory		630								
10				Transferred cost of										
11				merchandise sold to Cost										
12				of Goods Sold account										
13		2		Merchandise Inventory	1,900						Purchases		1,900	
14				Accounts Payable		1,900					Accounts Payable			1,900
15				Purchased merchandise							Purchased merchandise			
16				on account from Ruland							on account from Ruland			
17				Company, terms n/30, FOB							Company, terms n/30, FOB			
18				shipping point							shipping point			
19		2		Freight-In	145						Freight-In		145	
20				Cash		145					Cash			145
21				Paid freight on previous							Paid freight on previous			
22				purchase							purchase			
23		9		Merchandise Inventory	1,700						Purchases		1,700	
24				Freight-In	100						Freight-In		100	
25				Accounts Payable		1,800					Accounts Payable			1,800
26				Purchased merchandise on							Purchased merchandise on			
27				account from LNP Company,							account from LNP Company,			
28				terms n/30, FOB shipping							terms n/30, FOB shipping			
29				point, freight paid by supplier							point, freight paid by supplier			
30		11		Sales Returns and Allowances	150						Sales Returns and Allowances		150	
31				Accounts Receivable		150					Accounts Receivable			150
32				Accepted return of							Accepted return of			
33				merchandise from Ernie							merchandise from Ernie			
34				Devlin							Devlin			

(Continued)

	A	B	C	D	E	F	G	H	I	J	K	L	M	N
35						**1. Perpetual Inventory System**						**2. Periodic Inventory System**		
36	Oct.	11				Merchandise Inventory	90							
37						Cost of Goods Sold		90						
38						Transferred cost of								
39						merchandise returned to								
40						Merchandise Inventory								
41						account								
42		14			Accounts Payable		300				Accounts Payable		300	
43						Merchandise Inventory		300				Purchases Returns and Allowances		300
44						Returned portion of						Returned portion of		
45						merchandise purchased						merchandise purchased		
46						from Ruland Company						from Ruland Company		
47		16			Cash		500				Cash		500	
48						Sales		500				Sales		500
49						Sold merchandise for cash						Sold merchandise for cash		
50		16			Cost of Goods Sold		300							
51						Merchandise Inventory		300						
52						Transferred cost of								
53						merchandise sold to Cost of								
54						Goods Sold account								
55		22			Accounts Payable		1,600				Accounts Payable		1,600	
56						Cash		1,600				Cash		1,600
57						Made payment on account to						Made payment on account to		
58						Ruland Company						Ruland Company		
59						$1,900 − $300 = $1,600						$1,900 − $300 = $1,600		
60		23			Cash		900				Cash		900	
61						Accounts Receivable		900				Accounts Receivable		900
62						Received payment on						Received payment on		
63						account of Ernie Devlin						account of Ernie Devlin		
64						$1,050 − $150 = $900						$1,050 − $150 = $900		
65														

CHAPTER ASSIGNMENTS

BUILDING Your Knowledge and Skills

Short Exercises

LO1 Identification of Management Issues

SE 1. Identify each of the following decisions as most directly related to (a) cash flow management, (b) choice of inventory system, or (c) foreign merchandising transactions:

1. Determination of the amount of time from the purchase of inventory until it is sold and the amount due is collected
2. Determination of the effects of changes in exchange rates
3. Determination of policies governing sales of merchandise on credit
4. Determination of whether to use the periodic or the perpetual inventory system

LO1 Operating Cycle

SE 2. On average, Mason Company holds its inventory 40 days before it is sold, waits 25 days for customers' payments, and takes 33 days to pay suppliers. For how many days must it provide financing in its operating cycle?

LO2 **Terms of Sale**

SE 3. A dealer buys tooling machines from a manufacturer and resells them to its customers.

a. The manufacturer sets a list or catalogue price of $12,000 for a machine. The manufacturer offers its dealers a 40 percent trade discount.
b. The manufacturer sells the machine under terms of FOB shipping point. The cost of shipping is $700.
c. The manufacturer offers a sales discount of 2/10, n/30. The sales discount does not apply to shipping costs.

What is the net cost of the machine to the dealer, assuming it is paid for within ten days of purchase?

LO2 **Sales and Purchases Discounts**

SE 4. On April 15, Campeche Company sold merchandise to Walters Company for $3,000 on terms of 2/10, n/30. Assume a return of merchandise on April 20 of $600, and collection in full on April 25. What is the amount collected by Campeche on April 25?

LO3 **Purchases of Merchandise: Perpetual Inventory System**

SE 5. Record in T account form each of the following transactions, assuming the perpetual inventory system is used:

Aug. 2 Purchased merchandise on credit from Indio Company, invoice dated August 1, terms n/10, FOB shipping point, $1,150.
3 Received bill from Lee Shipping Company for transportation costs on August 2 shipment, invoice dated August 1, terms n/30, $105.
7 Returned damaged merchandise received from Indio Company on August 2 for credit, $180.
10 Paid in full the amount due to Indio Company for the purchase of August 2, part of which was returned on August 7.

LO4 **Purchases of Merchandise: Periodic Inventory System**

SE 6. Record in T account form the transactions in **SE 5**, assuming the periodic inventory system is used.

LO4 **Cost of Goods Sold: Periodic Inventory System**

SE 7. Using the following data and assuming cost of goods sold is $273,700, prepare the cost of goods sold section of a merchandising income statement (periodic inventory system). Include the amount of purchases for the month of October.

Freight-in	$13,800
Merchandise inventory, Sept. 30, 20xx	37,950
Merchandise inventory, Oct. 31, 20xx	50,600
Purchases	?
Purchases returns and allowances	10,350

LO4 **Sales of Merchandise: Periodic Inventory System**

SE 8. Record in T account form the following transactions, assuming the periodic inventory system is used:

Aug. 4 Sold merchandise on credit to Jing Company, terms n/30, FOB destination, $2,520.
5 Paid transportation costs for sale of August 4, $231.
9 Part of the merchandise sold on August 4 was accepted back from Jing Company for full credit and returned to the merchandise inventory, $735.

Sept. 3 Collected in full the amount due from Jing Company for merchandise sold on August 4, less the return on August 9.

Exercises

LO1, LO2   **Discussion Questions**

E 1. Develop a brief answer to each of the following questions:

1. Can a company have a "negative" financing period?
2. Suppose you sold goods to a company in Europe at a time when the exchange rate for the dollar was declining in relation to the euro. Would you want the European company to pay you in dollars or euros?
3. Which inventory system—the perpetual or periodic—is more useful to management? Why?

LO2, LO3, LO4   **Discussion Questions**

E 2. Develop a brief answer to each of the following questions:

1. Assume a large shipment of uninsured merchandise to your company is destroyed when the delivery truck has an accident and burns. Would you want the terms to be FOB shipping point or FOB destination?
2. Under the perpetual inventory system, the Merchandise Inventory account is constantly updated. What would cause it to have the wrong balance?
3. Why is a physical inventory needed under both the periodic and perpetual inventory systems?

LO1   **Management Issues and Decisions**

E 3. The management of Posad Cotton Company made the following decisions. Indicate whether each decision pertains primarily to (a) cash flow management, (b) choice of inventory system, or (c) foreign transactions.

1. Decided to reduce the credit terms offered to customers from 30 days to 20 days to speed up collection of accounts.
2. Decided that the benefits of keeping track of each item of inventory as it is bought and sold would exceed the costs of such a system.
3. Decided to purchase goods made by a Chinese supplier.
4. Decided to switch to a new cleaning service that will provide the same service at a lower cost with payment due in 30 days instead of 20 days.

LO1   **Foreign Merchandising Transactions**

E 4. Wooster Company purchased a special-purpose machine from Konigsberg Company on credit for €50,000. At the date of purchase, the exchange rate was $1.00 per euro. On the date of the payment, which was made in euros, the value of the euro was $1.25. Did Wooster incur an exchange gain or loss? How much was it?

LO2   **Terms of Sale**

E 5. A household appliance dealer buys refrigerators from a manufacturer and resells them to its customers.

a. The manufacturer sets a list or catalogue price of $1,500 for a refrigerator. The manufacturer offers its dealers a 30 percent trade discount.
b. The manufacturer sells the machine under terms of FOB destination. The cost of shipping is $150.
c. The manufacturer offers a sales discount of 2/10, n/30. Sales discounts do not apply to shipping costs.

What is the net cost of the refrigerator to the dealer, assuming it is paid for within ten days of purchase?

LO2, LO4   Sales Involving Discounts: Periodic Inventory System

E 6. Given the following transactions engaged in by Sasina Company, prepare journal entries and, assuming the periodic inventory system, determine the total amount received from Borsa Company.

Mar. 1   Sold merchandise on credit to Borsa Company, terms 2/10, n/30, FOB shipping point, $500.
       3   Accepted a return from Borsa Company for full credit, $200.
      10   Collected amount due from Borsa Company for the sale, less the return and discount.
      11   Sold merchandise on credit to Borsa Company, terms 2/10, n/30, FOB shipping point, $800.
      31   Collected amount due from Borsa Company for the sale of March 11.

LO2, LO3   Purchases Involving Discounts: Perpetual Inventory System

E 7. Washington Company engaged in the following transactions:

July   2   Purchased merchandise on credit from Zapala Company, terms 2/10, n/30, FOB destination, invoice dated July 1, $2,000.
       6   Returned some merchandise to Zapala Company for full credit, $250.
      11   Paid Zapala Company for purchase of July 2 less return and discount.
      14   Purchased merchandise on credit from Zapala Company, terms 2/10, n/30, FOB destination, invoice dated July 12, $2,250.
      31   Paid amount owed Zapala Company for purchase of July 14.

Prepare journal entries and, assuming the perpetual inventory system, determine the total amount paid to Zapala Company.

LO3   Preparation of the Income Statement: Perpetual Inventory System

E 8. Selected account balances at December 31, 20xx, for Weddings, Etc., are listed below. Prepare an income statement for the year ended December 31, 20xx. Show detail of net sales. The company uses the perpetual inventory system, and Freight-In has not been included in Cost of Goods Sold.

Account Name	Debit	Credit
Sales		$475,000
Sales Returns and Allowances	$ 23,500	
Cost of Goods Sold	280,000	
Freight-In	13,500	
Selling Expenses	43,000	
General and Administrative Expenses	87,000	

LO3   Recording Purchases: Perpetual Inventory System

E 9. The following transactions took place under the perpetual inventory system. Record each transaction in T account form.

a. Purchased merchandise on credit, terms n/30, FOB shipping point, $5,000.
b. Paid freight on the shipment in transaction **a**, $270.
c. Purchased merchandise on credit, terms n/30, FOB destination, $2,800.
d. Purchased merchandise on credit, terms n/30, FOB shipping point, $5,200, which includes freight paid by the supplier of $400.
e. Returned part of the merchandise purchased in transaction **c**, $1,000.
f. Paid the amount owed on the purchase in transaction **a**.
g. Paid the amount owed on the purchase in transaction **d**.
h. Paid the amount owed on the purchase in transaction **c** less the return in **e**.

LO3 Recording Sales: Perpetual Inventory System

E 10. On June 15, Dej Company sold merchandise for $2,600 on terms of n/30 to Musan Company. On June 20, Musan Company returned some of the merchandise for a credit of $600, and on June 25, Musan paid the balance owed. Give Dej's entries in T account form to record the sale, return, and receipt of cash under the perpetual inventory system. The cost of the merchandise sold on June 15 was $1,500, and the cost of the merchandise returned to inventory on June 20 was $350.

LO4 Preparation of the Income Statement: Periodic Inventory System

E 11. Using the selected year-end account balances at December 31, 20x7, for the Yacuma General Store shown below, prepare a 20x7 income statement. Show detail of net sales. The company uses the periodic inventory system. Beginning merchandise inventory was $26,000; ending merchandise inventory is $22,000.

Account Name	Debit	Credit
Sales		$297,000
Sales Returns and Allowances	$ 15,200	
Purchases	114,800	
Purchases Returns and Allowances		4,000
Freight-In	5,600	
Selling Expenses	48,500	
General and Administrative Expenses	37,200	

LO4 Merchandising Income Statement: Missing Data, Multiple Years

E 12. Determine the missing data for each letter in the following three income statements for Sampson Paper Company (in thousands):

	20x8	20x7	20x6
Sales	$p	$h	$572
Sales returns and allowances	48	38	a
Net sales	q	634	b
Merchandise inventory, beginning	r	i	76
Purchases	384	338	c
Purchases returns and allowances	62	j	34
Freight-in	s	58	44
Net cost of purchases	378	k	d
Cost of goods available for sale	444	424	364
Merchandise inventory, ending	78	l	84
Cost of goods sold	t	358	e
Gross margin	284	m	252
Selling expenses	u	156	f
General and administrative expenses	78	n	66
Total operating expenses	260	256	g
Net income	v	o	54

LO4 Recording Purchases: Periodic Inventory System

E 13. Using the data in **E 9**, give the entries in T-account form to record each of the transactions under the periodic inventory system.

LO4 Recording Sales: Periodic Inventory System

E 14. Using the relevant data in **E 10**, give the entries in T-account form to record each of the transactions under the periodic inventory system.

Problems

LO1, LO3 **Merchandising Income Statement: Perpetual Inventory System**

P 1. At the end of the fiscal year, August 31, 20x7, selected accounts from the adjusted trial balance for Mikhail's Patio Furniture were as follows:

Mikhail's Patio Furniture Partial Adjusted Trial Balance August 31, 20x7		
Sales		$162,000
Sales Returns and Allowances	$ 2,000	
Cost of Goods Sold	61,400	
Freight-In	2,300	
Store Salaries Expense	32,625	
Office Salaries Expense	12,875	
Advertising Expense	24,300	
Rent Expense	2,400	
Insurance Expense	1,200	
Utilities Expense	1,560	
Store Supplies Expense	2,880	
Office Supplies Expense	1,175	
Depreciation Expense–Store Equipment	1,050	
Depreciation Expense–Office Equipment	800	

Required

1. Using the information given, prepare a multistep income statement for Mikhail's Patio Furniture. Store Salaries Expense; Advertising Expense; Store Supplies Expense; and Depreciation Expense–Store Equipment are selling expenses. The other expenses are general and administrative expenses. The company uses the perpetual inventory system. Show details of net sales and operating expenses.

2. **User Insight:** Based on your knowledge at this point in the course, how would you use the income statement for Mikhail's Patio Furniture to evaluate the company's profitability? What other financial statement should be considered, and why?

LO3 **Merchandising Transactions: Perpetual Inventory System**

P 2. Tonia Company engaged in the following transactions in July 20xx:

July 1   Sold merchandise to Su Long on credit, terms n/30, FOB shipping point, $4,200 (cost, $2,520).

3   Purchased merchandise on credit from Angier Company, terms n/30, FOB shipping point, $7,600.

5   Paid Mix Freight for freight charges on merchandise received, $580.

8   Purchased merchandise on credit from Exto Supply Company, terms n/30, FOB shipping point, $7,200, which includes $400 freight costs paid by Exto Supply Company.

12   Returned some of the merchandise purchased on July 3 for credit, $1,200.

July 15   Sold merchandise on credit to Pete Smith, terms n/30, FOB shipping point, $2,400 (cost, $1,440).
17   Sold merchandise for cash, $2,000 (cost, $1,200).
18   Accepted for full credit a return from Su Long and returned merchandise to inventory, $400 (cost, $240).
24   Paid Angier Company for purchase of July 3 less return of July 12.
25   Received check from Su Long for July 1 purchase less the return on July 18.

Required

1. Prepare entries in journal form to record the transactions, assuming use of the perpetual inventory system. (Use the Review Problem in this chapter as a model.)

2. **User Insight:** Most companies call the first line of the income statement *net sales*. Other companies call it *sales*. Do you think these terms are equivalent and comparable? What would be the content of net sales? Why might a company use *sales* instead of *net sales*?

LO1, LO4   **Merchandising Income Statement: Periodic Inventory System**

 P 3. The data below are selected accounts from the adjusted trial balance of Dan's Sports Equipment on September 30, 20x7, the fiscal year end. The company's beginning merchandise inventory was $81,222 and ending merchandise inventory is $76,664 for the period.

Dan's Sports Equipment
Partial Adjusted Trial Balance
September 30, 20x7

Sales		$433,912
Sales Returns and Allowances	$ 11,250	
Purchases	221,185	
Purchases Returns and Allowances		30,238
Freight-In	10,078	
Store Salaries Expense	107,550	
Office Salaries Expense	26,500	
Advertising Expense	18,200	
Rent Expense	14,400	
Insurance Expense	2,800	
Utilities Expense	18,760	
Store Supplies Expense	464	
Office Supplies Expense	814	
Depreciation Expense–Store Equipment	1,800	
Depreciation Expense–Office Equipment	1,850	

Required

1. Prepare a multistep income statement for Dan's Sports Equipment. Store Salaries Expense; Advertising Expense; Store Supplies Expense; and Depreciation Expense–Store Equipment are selling expenses. The other expenses are general and administrative expenses. The company uses the periodic inventory system. Show details of net sales and operating expenses.

2. **User Insight:** Based on your knowledge at this point in the course, how would you use the income statement for Dan's Sports Equipment to evaluate the company's profitability? What other financial statements should you consider and why?

LO4 **Merchandising Transactions: Periodic Inventory System**

P 4. Use the data in **P 2** for this problem.

Required

1. Prepare entries in journal form to record the transactions, assuming use of the periodic inventory system. (Use the Review Problem in this chapter as a model.)

2. **User Insight:** Receiving cash rebates from suppliers based on the past year's purchases is common in some industries. If at the end of the year, Tonia Company receives rebates in cash from a supplier, should these cash rebates be reported as revenue? Why or why not?

Alternate Problems

LO1, LO3 **Merchandising Income Statement: Perpetual Inventory System**

P 5. At the end of the fiscal year, June 30, 20x7, selected accounts from the adjusted trial balance for Hans' Video Store were as follows:

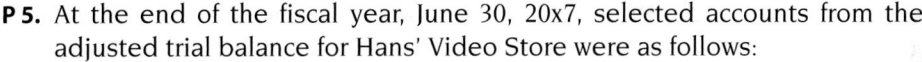

Hans' Video Store
Partial Adjusted Trial Balance
June 30, 20x7

Sales		$867,824
Sales Returns and Allowances	$ 22,500	
Cost of Goods Sold	442,370	
Freight-In	20,156	
Store Salaries Expense	215,100	
Office Salaries Expense	53,000	
Advertising Expense	36,400	
Rent Expense	28,800	
Insurance Expense	5,600	
Utilities Expense	17,520	
Store Supplies Expense	4,928	
Office Supplies Expense	3,628	
Depreciation Expense–Store Equipment	3,600	
Depreciation Expense–Office Equipment	3,700	

Required

1. Prepare a multistep income statement for Hans' Video Store. Freight-In should be combined with Cost of Goods Sold. Store Salaries Expense; Advertising Expense; Store Supplies Expense; and Depreciation Expense–Store Equipment are selling expenses. The other expenses are general and administrative expenses. The company uses the perpetual inventory system. Show details of net sales and operating expenses.

2. **User Insight:** Based on your knowledge at this point in the course, how would you use the income statement for Hans' Video Store to evaluate the

company's profitability? What other financial statement should you consider and why?

LO3 **Merchandising Transactions: Perpetual Inventory System**

 P 6. Tattle Company engaged in the following transactions in October 20xx:

Oct. 7 Sold merchandise on credit to Lina Ortiz, terms n/30, FOB shipping point, $6,000 (cost, $3,600).

 8 Purchased merchandise on credit from Ruff Company, terms n/30, FOB shipping point, $12,000.

 9 Paid Curry Company for shipping charges on merchandise purchased on October 8, $508.

 10 Purchased merchandise on credit from Sewall Company, terms n/30, FOB shipping point, $19,200, including $1,200 freight costs paid by Sewall.

 14 Sold merchandise on credit to Peter Watts, terms n/30, FOB shipping point, $4,800 (cost, $2,880).

 14 Returned damaged merchandise received from Ruff Company on October 8 for credit, $1,200.

 17 Received check from Lina Ortiz for her purchase of October 7.

 19 Sold merchandise for cash, $3,600 (cost, $2,160).

 20 Paid Sewall Company for purchase of October 10.

 21 Paid Ruff Company the balance from the transactions of October 8 and October 14.

 24 Accepted from Peter Watts a return of merchandise, which was put back in inventory, $400 (cost, $240).

Required

1. Prepare entries in journal form (refer to the Review Problem) to record the transactions, assuming use of the perpetual inventory system.
2. **User Insight:** Receiving cash rebates from suppliers based on the past year's purchases is a common practice in some industries. If at the end of the year Tattle Company receives rebates in cash from a supplier, should these cash rebates be reported as revenue? Why or why not?

LO1, LO4 **Merchandising Income Statement: Periodic Inventory System**

 P 7. Selected accounts from the adjusted trial balance for Pierre's Gourmet Shop as of March 31, 20x8, the end of the current fiscal year, appear at the top of the opposite page. The merchandise inventory for Pierre's Gourmet Shop was $38,200 at the beginning of the year and $29,400 at the end of the year.

Required

1. Using the information given, prepare a multistep income statement for Pierre's Gourmet Shop. Store Salaries Expense; Advertising Expense; Store Supplies Expense; and Depreciation Expense–Store Equipment are selling expenses. The other expenses are general and administrative expenses. The company uses the periodic inventory system. Show details of net sales and operating expenses.
2. **User Insight:** Based on your knowledge at this point in the course, how would you use the income statement for Pierre's Gourmet Shop to evaluate the company's profitability? What other financial statements should you consider, and why?

Pierre's Gourmet Shop
Partial Adjusted Trial Balance
March 31, 20x8

Sales		$165,000
Sales Returns and Allowances	$ 2,000	
Purchases	70,200	
Purchases Returns and Allowances		2,600
Freight-In	2,300	
Store Salaries Expense	32,625	
Office Salaries Expense	12,875	
Advertising Expense	24,300	
Rent Expense	2,400	
Insurance Expense	1,200	
Utilities Expense	1,560	
Store Supplies Expense	2,880	
Office Supplies Expense	1,175	
Depreciation Expense–Store Equipment	1,050	
Depreciation Expense–Office Equipment	800	

LO4 **Merchandising Transactions: Periodic Inventory System**

P 8. Use the data in **P 6** for this problem.

Required

1. Prepare entries in journal form to record the transactions, assuming use of the periodic inventory system. (Use the Review Problem in this chapter as a model.)

2. **User Insight:** Most companies call the first line of the income statement *net sales*. Other companies call it *sales*. Do you think these terms are equivalent and comparable? What would be the content of net sales? Why might a company use *sales* instead of *net sales*?

ENHANCING Your Knowledge, Skills, and Critical Thinking

Conceptual Understanding Cases

LO1 **Cash Flow Management**

C 1. Roman Sound Source has operated in Kansas for 30 years. The company has always prided itself on giving customers individual attention. It carries a large inventory so it can offer a good selection and deliver purchases quickly. It accepts credit cards and checks but also provides 90 days of credit to reliable customers who have purchased from the company in the past. It maintains good relations with suppliers by paying invoices quickly.

During the past year, the company has been strapped for cash and has had to borrow from the bank to pay its bills. An analysis of its financial statements reveals that, on average, inventory is on hand for 70 days before being sold, and receivables are held for 90 days before being collected. Accounts payable are paid, on average, in 20 days.

What are the operating cycle and the financing period? How long are Roman's operating cycle and financing period? Describe three ways in which Roman can improve its management of cash flow.

LO1 Periodic Versus Perpetual Inventory Systems

C 2. Books Unlimited is a well-established chain of 20 bookstores in western Ohio. In recent years, the company has grown rapidly, adding five new stores in regional malls. The manager of each store selects stock based on the market in his or her region. Managers select items from a master list of available titles that the central office provides. Every six months, a physical inventory is taken, and financial statements are prepared using the periodic inventory system. At that time, books that have not sold well are placed on sale or, whenever possible, returned to the publisher.

Management has found that when selecting books, the new managers are not judging the market as well as the managers of the older, established stores. Thus, management is thinking about implementing a perpetual inventory system and carefully monitoring sales from the central office. Do you think Books Unlimited should switch to the perpetual inventory system or stay with the periodic inventory system? Discuss the advantages and disadvantages of each system.

Interpreting Financial Reports

LO1 Effects of a Weak Dollar

C 3. In 2004, McDonald's reported that its sales in Europe exceeded its sales in the United States for the first time. This result, while reflective of the company's phenomenal success in Europe, was also attributed to the weak dollar in relation to the euro in 2004. McDonald's reports its sales wherever they take place in U.S. dollars. Explain why a weak dollar relative to the euro would lead to an increase in McDonald's reported European sales. Why is a weak dollar not relevant to a discussion of McDonald's sales in the United States?

Decision Analysis Using Excel

LO1, LO3, LO4 Analysis of Merchandising Income Statement

C 4. In 20x7, Alisa Harper opened a small retail store in a suburban mall. Called Harper Jeans Company, the shop sold designer jeans. Alisa Harper worked 14 hours a day and controlled all aspects of the operation. All sales were for cash or bank credit card. Harper Jeans Company was such a success that in 20x8, Harper decided to open a second store in another mall. Because the new shop needed her attention, she hired a manager to work in the original store with its two existing sales clerks. During 20x8, the new store was successful, but the operations of the original store did not match the first year's performance.

Concerned about this turn of events, Harper compared the two years' results for the original store. The figures are as follows:

	20x8	20x7
Net sales	$325,000	$350,000
Cost of goods sold	225,000	225,000
Gross margin	$100,000	$125,000
Operating expenses	75,000	50,000
Net income	$ 25,000	$ 75,000

In addition, Harper's analysis revealed that the cost and selling price of jeans were about the same in both years and that the level of operating expenses was roughly the same in both years, except for the new manager's $25,000 salary. Sales returns and allowances were insignificant amounts in both years.

Studying the situation further, Harper discovered the following facts about the cost of goods sold:

	20x8	20x7
Purchases	$200,000	$271,000
Total purchases allowances	15,000	20,000
Freight-in	19,000	27,000
Physical inventory, end of year	32,000	53,000

Still not satisfied, Harper went through all the individual sales and purchase records for the year. Both sales and purchases were verified. However, the 20x8 ending inventory should have been $57,000, given the unit purchases and sales during the year. After puzzling over all this information, Harper comes to you for accounting help.

1. Using Harper's new information, recompute the cost of goods sold for 20x7 and 20x8, and account for the difference in net income between 20x7 and 20x8.

2. Suggest at least two reasons for the discrepancy in the company's 20x8 ending inventory.

Annual Report Case: CVS Corporation

LO1 **Operating Cycle and Financing Period**

C 5. Refer to **CVS's** annual report in the Supplement to Chapter 5 and to Figures 1 and 2 in this chapter. Assume that at any one time CVS has about 76 days of merchandise inventory available for sale, takes about 18 days to collect its receivables, and takes about 40 days to pay its creditors. Write a memorandum to your instructor briefly describing CVS's operating cycle and financing period. The memorandum should identify the most common transactions in CVS's operating cycle. It should also refer to the importance of accounts receivable, accounts payable, and merchandise inventory in CVS's financial statements. Complete the memorandum by explaining why the operating cycle and financing period are favorable to the company.

Comparison Case: CVS Versus Walgreens

LO1 **Income Statement Analysis**

C 6. Refer to **CVS's** annual report in the Supplement to Chapter 5 and to the following data (in millions) for **Walgreens**: net sales, $42,201.6; cost of sales, $30,413.8; total operating expenses, $9,363.8; and inventory, $5,592.7. Determine which company—CVS or Walgreens—had more profitable merchandising operations in 2005 by preparing a schedule that compares the companies in terms of net sales, cost of sales, gross margin, total operating expenses, and income from operations as a percentage of sales. (**Hint:** Put the income statements in comparable formats.) In addition, for each company, compute inventory as a percentage of the cost of goods sold. Which company has the highest prices in relation to costs of sales? Which company is more efficient in its operating expenses? Which company manages its inventory better? Overall, on the basis of the income statement, which company is more profitable? Explain your answers.

Ethical Dilemma Case

LO1, LO3 **Barter Transactions**

C 7. Barter transactions in which one company trades goods or services to another company for other goods and services are becoming more common. Broadcasters, for example, often barter advertising air time for goods or services. In such good-faith transactions, the broadcaster will credit revenue for the fair value of on-air advertising while debiting accounts in equal amounts for the nonmonetary goods and services it receives. **Dynergy,** an energy company, and another company agreed to buy and sell power to each other for the same price, terms, and volume. This resulted in no profit for Dynergy but increased its sales for the year, which perhaps helped it meet its sales goals and management's annual incentive bonus plans.[8] Do you think barter transactions that result in little or no profit for either company are ethical? Are they ethical in certain situations but not in others? How could you tell the difference?

Internet Case

LO1, LO3 **Comparison of Traditional Merchandising with Ecommerce**

C 8. *Ecommerce* is a word coined to describe business conducted over the Internet. Ecommerce is similar in some ways to traditional retailing, but it presents new challenges. Go to the website of **Amazon.com.** Investigate and list the steps a customer takes to purchase an item on the site. How do these steps differ from those in a traditional retail store such as **Borders** or **Barnes & Noble**? What are some of the accounting challenges in recording Internet transactions? Be prepared to discuss your results in class.

Group Activity Case

LO1, LO2 **Merchandise Accounting and Inventory Systems**

C 9. Go to a retail business, such as a bookstore, clothing shop, gift shop, grocery store, hardware store, or car dealership in your local shopping area or a shopping mall. Ask to speak to someone who is knowledgeable about the store's inventory methods. Your instructor will assign groups to find the answers to the following questions. Be prepared to discuss your findings in class.

1. *Merchandising Accounting* Is the company a part of a chain or is it a small business? Does the company sell only merchandise or a combination of merchandise and services? How are sales recorded? Does the company sell on credit? If so, who decides who gets credit and what are the typical terms? Does the company buy any merchandise or in the case of a chain, does it order merchandise? If it purchases merchandise, how are purchases recorded?
2. *Inventory systems* How is each item of inventory identified? Does the business have a computerized or a manual inventory system? Which inventory system, periodic or perpetual, is used? How often do employees take a physical inventory? What procedures are followed in taking a physical inventory? What kinds of inventory reports are prepared or received?

Business Communication Case

LO1 **Operating Cycle in a Small Business**

C 10. Cara Westerman recently inherited the family business, Westerman Furniture Company. The company had built its reputation by selling to young couples, often newlyweds, who had little money to put down and often made monthly payments over one or two years to pay off the balance.

Cara notices that the company has a lot of past due bills from furniture companies and little cash, even though sales are at record levels. She has asked you, the company's accountant, to write a short memorandum to help her understand why the company is short on cash. One of the first things you note is that it takes about four months on average to sell the furniture after receiving it, and the furniture companies expect payment in 60 days. In your memo, include an explanation of the operating cycle as it applies to Westerman Furniture Company.

Inventories

For any company that makes or sells merchandise, inventory is an extremely important asset. Managing this asset is a challenging task. It requires not only protecting goods from theft or loss, but also ensuring that operations are highly efficient. Further, as you will see in this chapter, proper accounting of inventory is essential because misstatements will affect net income in at least two years.

LEARNING OBJECTIVES

LO1 Explain the management decisions related to inventory accounting, evaluation of inventory level, and the effects of inventory misstatements on income measurement.

LO2 Define *inventory cost,* contrast goods flow and cost flow, and explain the lower-of-cost-or-market (LCM) rule.

LO3 Calculate inventory cost under the periodic inventory system using various costing methods.

LO4 Explain the effects of inventory costing methods on income determination and income taxes.

SUPPLEMENTAL OBJECTIVES

Making a Statement

Balance
Sheet

Statement of
Cash Flows

Income
Statement

Valuation of inventories affects the amount of inventories on the balance sheet and the cost of goods sold on the income statement.

SO5 Calculate inventory cost under the perpetual inventory system using various costing methods.

SO6 Use the retail method and gross profit method to estimate the cost of ending inventory.

- What is the impact of inventory decisions on operating results?

- How should inventory be valued?

- How should the level of inventory be evaluated?

Cisco Systems manufactures and sells networking and communications products. It is the world's leading producer of the switches, hubs, gateways, and firewalls that make the Internet possible. As you can see in Cisco's Financial Highlights,[1] inventory is an important component of the company's total assets.

CISCO'S FINANCIAL HIGHLIGHTS
(In millions)

	2005	2004	2003
Product sales	$20,853	$18,550	$15,565
Cost of goods sold	6,758	5,766	4,594
Operating income	7,416	6,292	4,882
Inventories	1,297	1,207	873
Total assets	33,883	35,594	37,107

Managing Inventories

Inventory is considered a current asset because a company normally sells it within a year or within its operating cycle. For a merchandising company like **CVS** or **Walgreens**, inventory consists of all goods owned and held for sale in the regular course of business. Because manufacturing companies like **Cisco** are engaged in making products, they have three kinds of inventory:

- Raw materials (goods used in making products)
- Work in process (partially completed products)
- Finished goods ready for sale

In a note to its financial statements, Cisco showed the following breakdown of its inventories (figures are in millions):[2]

Inventories	2005	2004
Raw materials	$ 82	$ 58
Work in process	431	416
Finished goods	569	522
Other	215	211
Total inventories	$1,297	$1,207

The work in process and the finished goods inventories have three cost components:

- Cost of the raw materials that go into the product
- Cost of the labor used to convert the raw materials to finished goods
- Overhead costs that support the production process

Overhead costs include the costs of indirect materials (such as packing materials), indirect labor (such as the salaries of supervisors), factory rent, depreciation of plant assets, utilities, and insurance.

Inventory Decisions

Study Note

Management considers the behavior of inventory prices over time when selecting inventory costing methods.

The primary objective of inventory accounting is to determine income properly by matching costs of the period against revenues for the period. As you can see in Figure 1, in accounting for inventory, management must choose among different processing systems, costing methods, and valuation methods. These different systems and methods usually result in different amounts of reported net income. Thus, management's choices affect investors' and creditors' evaluations of a company, as well as internal evaluations, such as the performance reviews on which bonuses and executive compensation are based.

The consistency convention requires that once a company has decided on the systems and methods it will use in accounting for inventory, it must use them from one accounting period to the next unless management can justify a change. If a change is justifiable, the full disclosure convention requires that the notes to the financial statements clearly explain the change and its effects.

Because the valuation of inventory affects income, it can have a considerable impact on the amount of income taxes a company pays—and the amount of taxes it pays can have a considerable impact on its cash flows. Federal

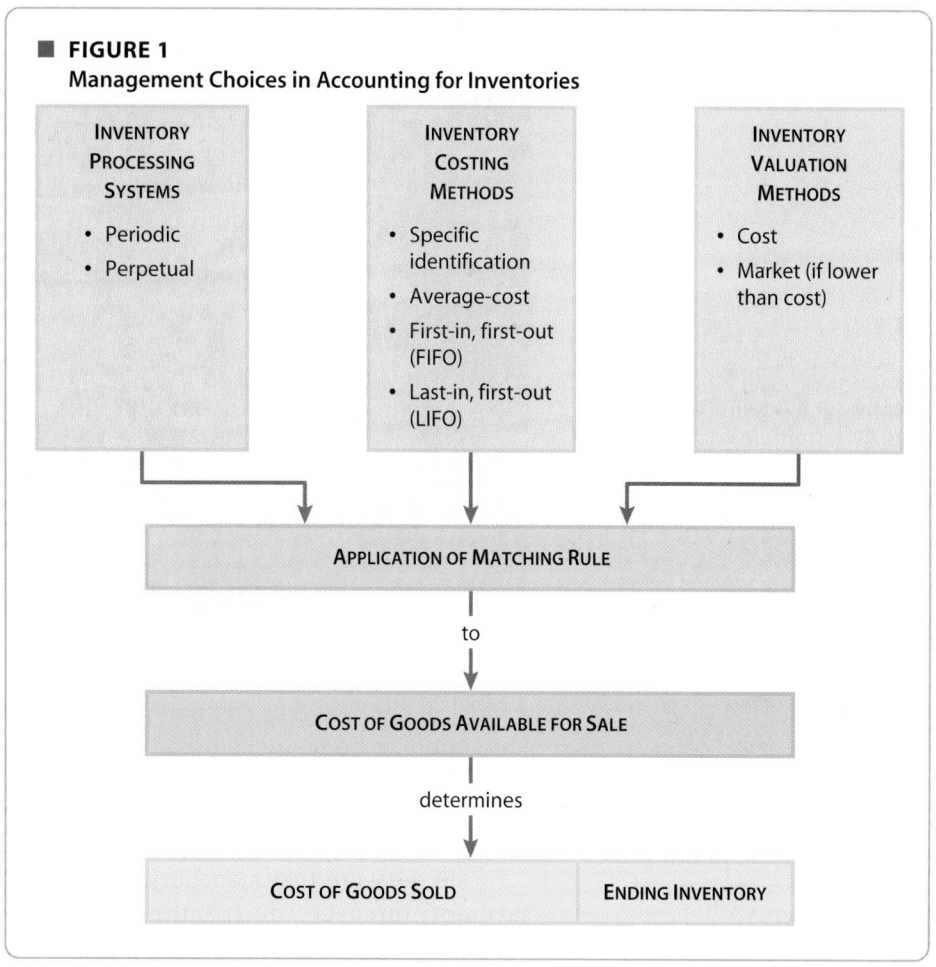

■ FIGURE 1
Management Choices in Accounting for Inventories

income tax regulations are specific about the valuation methods a company may use. As a result, management is sometimes faced with the dilemma of how to apply GAAP to income determination and still minimize income taxes.

Evaluating the Level of Inventory

The level of inventory a company maintains has important economic consequences. Ideally, management wants to have a great variety and quantity of

FOCUS ON BUSINESS PRACTICE

A Whirlwind Inventory Turnover—How Does Dell Do It?

Dell Computer Corporation turns its inventory over every six days. How can it do this when other computer companies have inventory on hand for 60 days or even longer? Technology and good inventory management are a big part of the answer.

Dell's speed from order to delivery sets the standard for the computer industry. Consider that a computer ordered by 9 A.M. can be delivered the next day by 9 P.M. How can Dell do this when it does not start ordering components and assembling computers until a customer places an order? First, Dell's suppliers keep components warehoused just

minutes from Dell's factories, making efficient, just-in-time operations possible. Another time and money saver is the handling of computer monitors. Monitors are no longer shipped first to Dell and then on to buyers. Dell sends an email message to a shipper, such as **United Parcel Service**, and the shipper picks up a monitor from a supplier and schedules it to arrive with the PC. In addition to contributing to a high inventory turnover, this practice saves Dell about $30 per monitor in freight costs. Dell is showing the world how to run a business in the cyber age by selling more than $1 million worth of computers a day on its website.[3]

Shoppers at this well-stocked Toys "R" Us store are very likely to find the items they want. Maintaining such a high level of inventory reduces the risk that a company will lose sales, but this policy has a price. The handling, storage, and interest costs involved can be substantial.

 Study Note

Some of the costs of carrying inventory are insurance, property tax, and storage costs. Other costs may result from spoilage and employee theft.

goods on hand so that customers have a large choice and do not have to wait for an item to be restocked. But implementing such a policy can be expensive. Handling and storage costs and the interest cost of the funds needed to maintain high inventory levels are usually substantial. On the other hand, low inventory levels can result in disgruntled customers and lost sales.

One measure that managers commonly use to evaluate inventory levels is **inventory turnover**, which is the average number of times a company sells its inventory during an accounting period. It is computed by dividing cost of goods sold by average inventory. For example, using the data presented in this chapter's Decision Point, we can compute **Cisco's** inventory turnover for 2005 as follows (figures are in millions):

$$\text{Inventory Turnover} = \frac{\text{Cost of Goods Sold}}{\text{Average Inventory}}$$

$$= \frac{\$6,758}{(\$1,297 + \$1,207) \div 2}$$

$$= \frac{\$6,758}{\$1,252} = 5.4 \text{ times}$$

Another common measure of inventory levels is **days' inventory on hand**, which is the average number of days it takes a company to sell the inventory it has in stock. For Cisco, it is computed as follows:

$$\text{Days' Inventory on Hand} = \frac{\text{Number of Days in a Year}}{\text{Inventory Turnover}}$$

$$= \frac{365 \text{ days}}{5.4 \text{ times}} = 67.6 \text{ days}$$

Cisco turned its inventory over 5.4 times in 2005 or, on average, every 67.6 days. Thus, it had to provide financing for the inventory for more than two months before it sold it.

As you can see in Figures 2 and 3, inventory turnover and days' inventory on hand vary by industry. Nonetheless, companies that maintain their inventories at low levels and still satisfy customers' needs are the most successful.

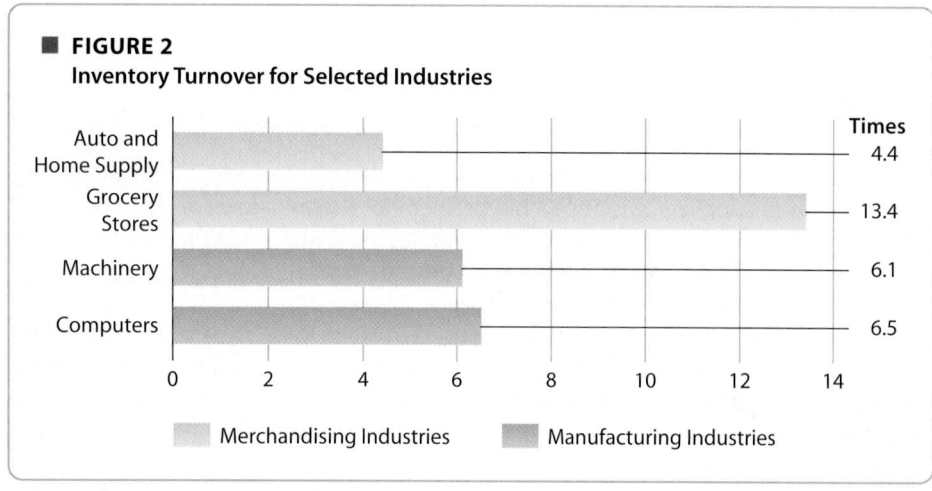

FIGURE 2
Inventory Turnover for Selected Industries

Source: Data from Dun & Bradstreet, *Industry Norms and Key Business Ratios*, 2004–2005

To reduce their levels of inventory, many merchandisers and manufacturers use supply-chain management in conjunction with a just-in-time operating environment. With **supply-chain management**, a company uses the Internet to order and track goods that it needs immediately. A **just-in-time operating environment** is one in which goods arrive just at the time they are needed.

Cisco uses supply-chain management to increase inventory turnover. It manages its inventory purchases through business-to-business transactions that it conducts over the Internet. It also uses a just-in-time operating environment in which it works closely with suppliers to coordinate and schedule shipments so that the shipments arrive exactly when needed. The benefits of using supply-chain management in a just-in-time operating environment are that Cisco has less money tied up in inventory and its cost of carrying inventory is reduced.

Effects of Inventory Misstatements on Income Measurement

The reason inventory accounting is so important to income measurement is the way income is measured on the income statement. Recall that gross margin is the difference between net sales and cost of goods sold and that cost of goods

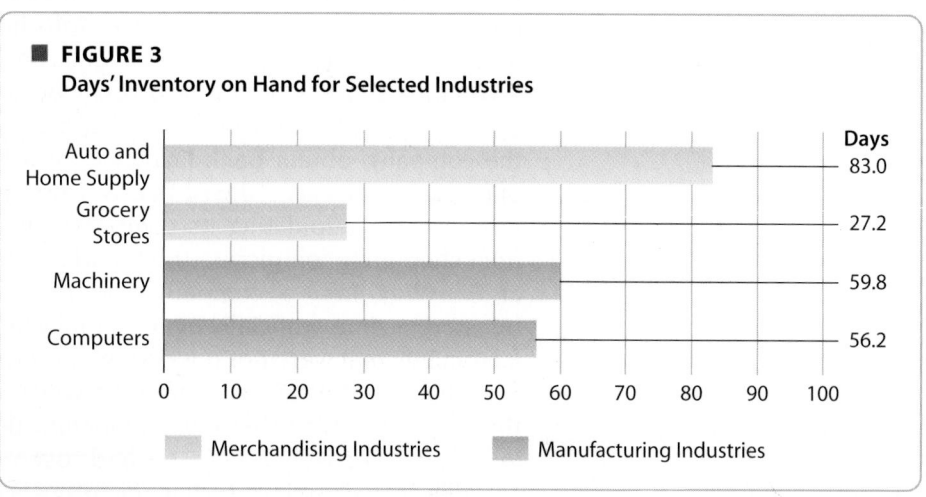

FIGURE 3
Days' Inventory on Hand for Selected Industries

Source: Data from Dun & Bradstreet, *Industry Norms and Key Business Ratios*, 2004–2005

FOCUS ON BUSINESS PRACTICE
What Do You Do to Cure a Bottleneck Headache?

A single seat belt can have as many as 50 parts, and getting the parts from suppliers was once a big problem for **Autoliv, Inc.,** a Swedish maker of auto safety devices. Autoliv's plant in Indianapolis was encountering constant bottlenecks in dealing with 125 different suppliers. To keep the production lines going required high-priced, rush shipments on a daily basis. To solve the problem, the company began using supply-chain management, keeping in touch with suppliers through the Internet rather than through faxes and phone calls. This system allowed suppliers to monitor the inventory at Autoliv and thus to anticipate problems. It also provided information on quantity and time of recent shipments, as well as continuously updated forecasts of parts that would be needed in the next 12 weeks. With supply-chain management, Autoliv reduced inventory by 75 percent and rush freight costs by 95 percent.[4]

sold depends on the portion of cost of goods available for sale assigned to ending inventory. These relationships lead to the following conclusions:

▶ The higher the value of ending inventory, the lower the cost of goods sold and the higher the gross margin.

▶ Conversely, the lower the value of ending inventory, the higher the cost of goods sold and the lower the gross margin.

Because the amount of gross margin has a direct effect on net income, the value assigned to ending inventory also affects net income. In effect, the value of ending inventory determines what portion of the cost of goods available for sale is assigned to cost of goods sold and what portion is assigned to the balance sheet as inventory to be carried over into the next accounting period.

The basic issue in separating goods available for sale into two components—goods sold and goods not sold—is to assign a value to the goods not sold, the ending inventory. The portion of goods available for sale not assigned to the ending inventory is used to determine the cost of goods sold. Because the figures for ending inventory and cost of goods sold are related, a misstatement in the inventory figure at the end of an accounting period will cause an equal misstatement in gross margin and income before income taxes in the income statement. The amount of assets and stockholders' equity on the balance sheet will be misstated by the same amount.

Inventory is particularly susceptible to fraudulent financial reporting. For example, it is easy to overstate or understate inventory by including end-of-the-year purchase and sales transactions in the wrong fiscal year or by simply misstating inventory. A misstatement can occur because of mistakes in the accounting process. It can also occur because of deliberate manipulation of operating results motivated by a desire to enhance the market's perception of the company, obtain bank financing, or achieve compensation incentives. In one spectacular case, **Rite Aid Corporation**, the large drugstore chain, falsified income by manipulating its computerized inventory system to cover losses from shoplifting, employee theft, and spoilage. In another case, bookkeepers at **RentWay, Inc.,** a company that rents furniture to apartment dwellers, boosted income artificially over several years by overstating inventory in small increments that were not noticed by top management.

Whatever the causes of an overstatement or understatement of inventory, the three examples that follow illustrate the effects. In each case, beginning inventory, net cost of purchases, and cost of goods available for sale are stated correctly. In Example 1, ending inventory is correctly stated; in Example 2, it is overstated by $6,000; and in Example 3, it is understated by $6,000.

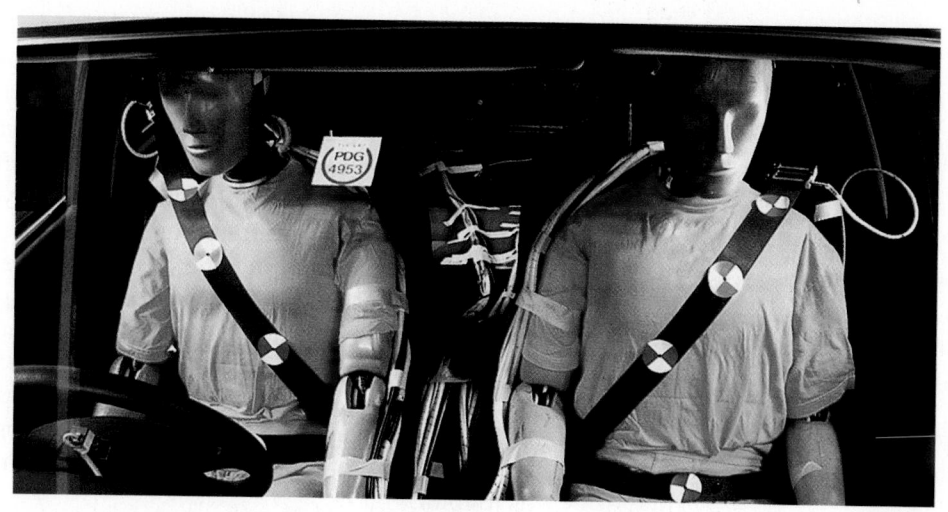

Autoliv's use of supply-chain management is an example of how this system has benefited businesses. By using the Internet to order and track the numerous parts involved in the manufacture of the seat belts pictured here, Autoliv prevented delays in the shipments of parts by allowing its suppliers to monitor inventory and thus to anticipate problems. The firm also drastically reduced its inventory and freight costs.

Example 1. Ending Inventory Correctly Stated at $10,000

Cost of Goods Sold for the Year		*Income Statement for the Year*	
Beginning inventory	$12,000	Net sales	$100,000
Net cost of purchases	58,000	Cost of goods sold	60,000
Cost of goods available for sale	$70,000		
Ending inventory	10,000	Gross margin	$ 40,000
		Operating expenses	32,000
		Income before income	
Cost of goods sold	$60,000	taxes	$ 8,000

Example 2. Ending Inventory Overstated by $6,000

Cost of Goods Sold for the Year		*Income Statement for the Year*	
Beginning inventory	$12,000	Net sales	$100,000
Net cost of purchases	58,000	Cost of goods sold	54,000
Cost of goods available for sale	$70,000		
Ending inventory	16,000	Gross margin	$ 46,000
		Operating expenses	32,000
		Income before income	
Cost of goods sold	$54,000	taxes	$ 14,000

Example 3. Ending Inventory Understated by $6,000

Cost of Goods Sold for the Year		*Income Statement for the Year*	
Beginning inventory	$12,000	Net sales	$100,000
Net cost of purchases	58,000	Cost of goods sold	66,000
Cost of goods available for sale	$70,000		
Ending inventory	4,000	Gross margin	$ 34,000
		Operating expenses	32,000
		Income before income	
Cost of goods sold	$66,000	taxes	$ 2,000

In all three examples, the cost of goods available for sale was $70,000. The difference in income before income taxes resulted from how this $70,000 was divided between ending inventory and cost of goods sold.

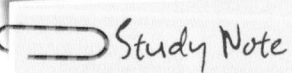

Study Note

A misstatement of inventory has the opposite effect in two successive accounting periods.

Because the ending inventory in one period becomes the beginning inventory in the following period, a misstatement in inventory valuation affects not only the current period but the following period as well. Over two periods, the errors in income before income taxes will offset, or counterbalance, each other. For instance, in Example 2, the overstatement of ending inventory will cause a $6,000 overstatement of beginning inventory in the following year, which will result in a $6,000 understatement of income.

Because the total income before income taxes for the two periods is the same, it may appear that one need not worry about inventory misstatements. However, the misstatements violate the matching rule. In addition, management, creditors, and investors base many decisions on the accountant's determination of net income. The accountant has an obligation to make the net income figure for each period as useful as possible.

The effects of inventory misstatements on income before income taxes are as follows:

Year 1	*Year 2*
Ending inventory overstated	**Beginning inventory overstated**
Cost of goods sold understated	Cost of goods sold overstated
Income before income taxes overstated	Income before income taxes understated
Ending inventory understated	**Beginning inventory understated**
Cost of goods sold overstated	Cost of goods sold understated
Income before income taxes understated	Income before income taxes overstated

S T O P • R E V I E W • A P P L Y

1-1. How does a manufacturing company's inventory differ from that of a merchandising company?

1-2. What is the primary objective of inventory accounting?

1-3. Why is the level of inventory important, and what are two common measures of inventory level?

1-4. Why is inventory particularly vulnerable to fraudulent financial reporting?

1-5. If inventory is overstated at the end of 20x7, what is the effect on the (a) 20x7 net income, (b) 20x7 year-end balance sheet value, (c) 20x8 net income, and (d) 20x8 year-end balance sheet value?

Suggested answers to all Stop, Review, and Apply questions are available at http://college.hmco.com/accounting/needles/poa/10e/student_home.html.

Inventory Cost and Valuation

LO2 Define *inventory cost,* contrast goods flow and cost flow, and explain the lower-of-cost-or-market (LCM) rule.

The primary basis of accounting for inventories is cost, the price paid to acquire an asset. **Inventory cost** includes the following:

- Invoice price less purchases discounts

◆ Freight-in, including insurance in transit

◆ Applicable taxes and tariffs

Other costs—for ordering, receiving, and storing—should in principle be included in inventory cost. In practice, however, it is so difficult to allocate such costs to specific inventory items that they are usually considered expenses of the accounting period rather than inventory costs.

Inventory costing and valuation depend on the prices of the goods in inventory. The prices of most goods vary during the year. A company may have purchased identical lots of merchandise at different prices. Also, when a company deals in identical items, it is often impossible to tell which have been sold and which are still in inventory. When that is the case, it is necessary to make an assumption about the order in which items have been sold. Because the assumed order of sale may or may not be the same as the actual order of sale, the assumption is really about the *flow of costs* rather than the *flow of physical inventory*.

Goods Flows and Cost Flows

Study Note

The assumed flow of inventory costs does not have to correspond to the physical flow of goods.

Goods flow refers to the actual physical movement of goods in the operations of a company. **Cost flow** refers to the association of costs with their *assumed* flow in the operations of a company. The assumed cost flow may or may not be the same as the actual goods flow. The possibility of a difference between cost flow and goods flow may seem strange at first, but it arises because several choices of assumed cost flow are available under generally accepted accounting principles. In fact, it is sometimes preferable to use an assumed cost flow that bears no relationship to goods flow because it gives a better estimate of income, which is the main goal of inventory valuation.

Merchandise in Transit Because merchandise inventory includes all items that a company owns and holds for sale, the status of any merchandise in transit, whether the company is selling it or buying it, must be evaluated to see if the merchandise should be included in the inventory count. Neither the seller nor the buyer has *physical* possession of merchandise in transit. As Figure 4 shows, ownership is determined by the terms of the shipping agreement,

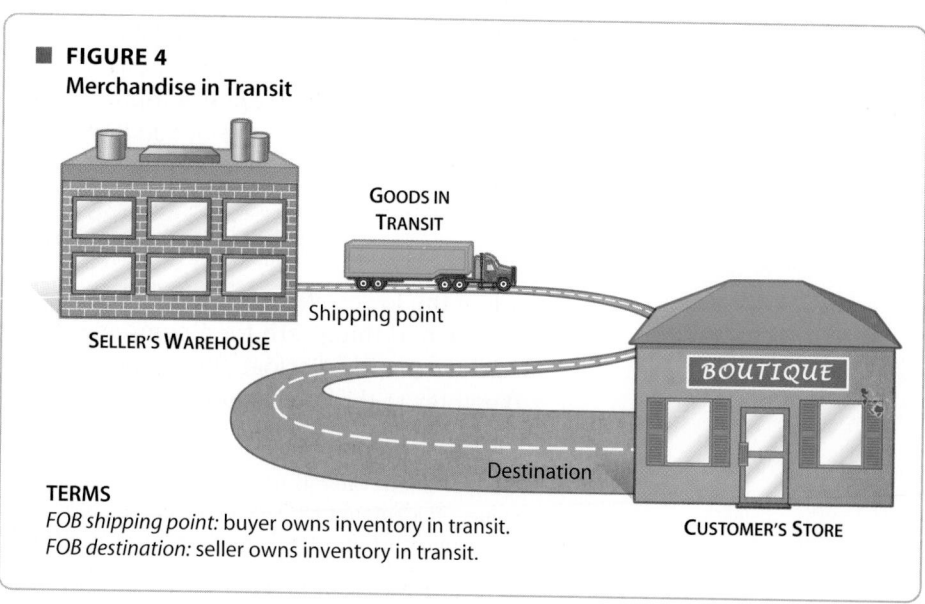

■ **FIGURE 4**
Merchandise in Transit

GOODS IN TRANSIT

Shipping point

SELLER'S WAREHOUSE

Destination

BOUTIQUE

CUSTOMER'S STORE

TERMS
FOB shipping point: buyer owns inventory in transit.
FOB destination: seller owns inventory in transit.

which indicate when title passes. Outgoing goods shipped FOB (free on board) destination are included in the seller's merchandise inventory, whereas those shipped FOB shipping point are not. Conversely, incoming goods shipped FOB shipping point are included in the buyer's merchandise inventory, but those shipped FOB destination are not.

Merchandise on Hand Not Included in Inventory   At the time a company takes a physical inventory, it may have merchandise on hand to which it does not hold title. For example, it may have sold goods but not yet delivered them to the buyer, but because the sale has been completed, title has passed to the buyer. Thus, the merchandise should be included in the buyer's inventory, not the seller's. Goods held on consignment also fall into this category.

A **consignment** is merchandise that its owner (the consignor) places on the premises of another company (the consignee) with the understanding that payment is expected only when the merchandise is sold and that unsold items may be returned to the consignor. Title to consigned goods remains with the consignor until the consignee sells the goods. Consigned goods should not be included in the consignee's physical inventory because they still belong to the consignor.

Lower-of-Cost-or-Market (LCM) Rule

Although cost is usually the most appropriate basis for valuation of inventory, inventory may at times be properly shown in the financial statements at less than its historical, or original, cost. If the market value of inventory falls below its historical cost because of physical deterioration, obsolescence, or decline in price level, a loss has occurred. This loss is recognized by writing the inventory down to **market**—that is, to its current replacement cost. For a merchandising company, market is the amount that it would pay at the present time for the same goods, purchased from the usual suppliers and in the usual quantities.

When the replacement cost of inventory falls below its historical cost (as determined by an inventory costing method), the **lower-of-cost-or-market (LCM) rule** requires that the inventory be written down to the lower value and that a loss be recorded. This rule is an example of the application of the conservatism convention because the loss is recognized before an actual transaction takes place. Under historical cost accounting, the inventory would remain at cost until it is sold. It may help in applying the LCM rule to think of it as the "lower-of-cost-or-replacement-cost" rule.* According to an AICPA survey, approximately 83 percent of 600 large companies apply the LCM rule to their inventories for financial reporting.[5]

Disclosure of Inventory Methods

When the lower-of-cost-or-market rule comes into play, it can be an indication of how bad things are for a company. The full disclosure convention requires that companies disclose their inventory methods, including the use of LCM, in the notes to their financial statements, and users should pay close attention to

Study Note

Cost must be determined by one of the inventory costing methods before it can be compared with the market value.

---

*Replacement value is normally used to value inventory, but in some cases, the realizable value—the amount for which it can be resold—is used. The circumstances in which this occurs are encountered in practice only occasionally. The valuation procedures are quite technical and are addressed in more advanced accounting courses.

them. For example, in 2001, when the market for Internet and telecommunications equipment had soured, **Cisco's** annual report contained this note:

> Inventories are stated at the lower of cost or market. Cost is computed . . . on a first-in, first-out basis. The company provides allowances on excess and obsolete inventories.[6]

In 2001, Cisco found itself faced with probably the largest inventory loss in history. It had to write down to zero almost two-thirds of its $2.5 billion inventory, 80 percent of which consisted of raw materials that would never be made into final product.[7]

In another case in which the LCM rule came into play, **Kmart**, through poor management, a downturn in the economy, and underperforming stores, found itself with a huge amount of excess merchandise, including more than 5,000 truckloads of goods stored in parking lots, which it could not sell except at drastically reduced prices. The company had to mark down its inventory by $1 billion in order to sell it, which resulted in a debilitating loss.[8]

S T O P • R E V I E W • A P P L Y

2-1. What items should be included in the cost of inventory?

2-2. What is the difference between goods flow and cost flow?

2-3. At the end of its fiscal year on June 30, Fargo Sales Company has an order for 130 units of product in its warehouse. Although the shipping department tries, it cannot ship the product by June 30, and title to the goods has not yet passed. Should the 130 units be included in the year-end count of inventory? Why or why not?

2-4. In the phrase *lower of cost or market*, what does *market* mean?

2-5. Why is it important for a company to disclose its method of accounting for inventory costs?

Inventory Costs and Valuation Concepts   Match the letter of each item below with the numbers of the related items:

a. An inventory cost

b. An assumption used in the valuation of inventory

c. Full disclosure convention

d. Conservatism convention

e. Consistency convention

f. Not an inventory cost or assumed flow

1. Cost of consigned goods

2. A note to the financial statements explaining inventory policies

3. Application of the LCM rule

4. Goods flow

5. Transportation charge for merchandise shipped FOB shipping point

6. Cost flow

7. Choosing a method and sticking with it

8. Transportation charge for merchandise shipped FOB destination

Inventory Cost Under the Periodic Inventory System

LO3 Calculate inventory cost under the periodic inventory system using various costing methods.

The value assigned to ending inventory is the result of two measurements: quantity and cost. As you know, under the periodic inventory system, quantity is determined by taking a physical inventory; under the perpetual inventory system, quantities are updated as purchases and sales take place. Cost is determined by using one of the following methods, each based on a different assumption of cost flow:

1. Specific identification method

2. Average-cost method

3. First-in, first-out (FIFO) method

4. Last-in, first-out (LIFO) method

The choice of method depends on the nature of the business, the financial effects of the method, and the cost of implementing the method.

To illustrate how each method is used under the periodic inventory system, we use the following data for June, a month in which prices were rising:

June 1	Inventory	80 units @ $10.00	$ 800
6	Purchase	220 units @ $12.50	2,750
25	Purchase	200 units @ $14.00	2,800
	Goods available for sale	500 units	$6,350
	Sales	280 units	
	On hand June 30	220 units	

The problem of inventory costing is to divide the cost of the goods available for sale ($6,350) between the 280 units sold and the 220 units on hand.

Specific Identification Method

The **specific identification method** identifies the cost of each item in ending inventory. It can be used only when it is possible to identify the units in ending inventory as coming from specific purchases. For instance, if the June 30 inventory consisted of 50 units from the June 1 inventory, 100 units from the June 6 purchase, and 70 units from the June 25 purchase, the specific identification method would assign the costs as follows:

Periodic Inventory System—Specific Identification Method

50 units @ $10.00	$ 500	Cost of goods available	
100 units @ $12.50	1,250	for sale	$6,350
70 units @ $14.00	980	Less June 30 inventory	2,730
220 units at a cost of	$2,730	Cost of goods sold	$3,620

The specific identification method may appear logical, and it can be used by companies that deal in high-priced articles, such as works of art, precious gems, or rare antiques. However, most companies do not use it for the following reasons:

1. It is usually impractical, if not impossible, to keep track of the purchase and sale of individual items.

2. When a company deals in items that are identical but that it bought at different prices, deciding which items were sold becomes arbitrary. If the company were to use the specific identification method, it could raise or lower income by choosing the lower- or higher-priced items.

Average-Cost Method

Under the **average-cost method**, inventory is priced at the average cost of the goods available for sale during the accounting period. Average cost is computed by dividing the total cost of goods available for sale by the total units available for sale. This gives an average unit cost that is applied to the units in ending inventory.

In our illustration, the ending inventory would be $2,794, or $12.70 per unit, determined as follows:

Periodic Inventory System—Average-Cost Method

Cost of Goods Available for Sale ÷ Units Available for Sale = Average Unit Cost

$6,350 ÷ 500 units = $12.70

Ending inventory: 220 units @ $12.70 =	$2,794
Cost of goods available for sale	$6,350
Less June 30 inventory	2,794
Cost of goods sold	$3,556

The average-cost method tends to level out the effects of cost increases and decreases because the cost of the ending inventory is influenced by all the prices paid during the year and by the cost of beginning inventory. Some analysts, however, criticize this method because they believe recent costs are more relevant for income measurement and decision making.

First-In, First-Out (FIFO) Method

The **first-in, first-out (FIFO) method** assumes that the costs of the first items acquired should be assigned to the first items sold. The costs of the goods on hand at the end of a period are assumed to be from the most recent purchases, and the costs assigned to goods that have been sold are assumed to be from the earliest purchases. Any business, regardless of its goods flow, can use the FIFO method because the assumption underlying it is based on the flow of costs, not the flow of goods.

In our illustration, the FIFO method would result in an ending inventory of $3,050, computed as follows:

Periodic Inventory System—FIFO Method

200 units @ $14.00 from purchase of June 25	$2,800
20 units @ $12.50 from purchase of June 6	250
220 units at a cost of	$3,050
Cost of goods available for sale	$6,350
Less June 30 inventory	3,050
Cost of goods sold	$3,300

Thus, the FIFO method values ending inventory at the most recent costs and includes earlier costs in cost of goods sold. During periods of rising prices, FIFO yields the highest possible amount of net income because cost of goods sold shows the earliest costs incurred, which are lower during periods of inflation. Another reason for this is that businesses tend to raise selling prices as costs increase, even when they purchased the goods before the cost increase. In periods of declining prices, FIFO tends to charge the older and higher prices against revenues, thus reducing income. Consequently, a major criticism of FIFO is that it magnifies the effects of the business cycle on income.

Last-In, First-Out (LIFO) Method

The **last-in, first-out (LIFO) method** of costing inventories assumes that the costs of the last items purchased should be assigned to the first items sold and that the cost of ending inventory should reflect the cost of the goods purchased earliest. Under LIFO, the June 30 inventory would be $2,550:

Periodic Inventory System—LIFO Method

80 units @ $10.00 from June 1 inventory	$ 800
140 units @ $12.50 from purchase of June 6	1,750
220 units at a cost of	$2,550
Cost of goods available for sale	$6,350
Less June 30 inventory	2,550
Cost of goods sold	$3,800

The effect of LIFO is to value inventory at the earliest prices and to include the cost of the most recently purchased goods in the cost of goods sold. This assumption, of course, does not agree with the actual physical movement of goods in most businesses.

There is, however, a strong logical argument to support LIFO. A certain size of inventory is necessary in a going concern—when inventory is sold, it must be replaced with more goods. The supporters of LIFO reason that the fairest determination of income occurs if the current costs of merchandise are matched against current sales prices, regardless of which physical units of merchandise are sold. When prices are moving either up or down, the cost of goods sold will, under LIFO, show costs closer to the price level at the time the goods are sold. Thus, the LIFO method tends to show a smaller net income during inflationary times and a larger net income during deflationary times than other methods of inventory valuation. The peaks and valleys of the business cycle tend to be smoothed out. In inventory valuation, the flow of costs—and hence

FOCUS ON BUSINESS PRACTICE
What's a "Category Killer"?

A type of retail company called the "category killer" seems to ignore the tenets of good inventory management. The category killers include **Home Depot, Barnes & Noble, Wal-Mart, Toys "R" Us,** and **Blockbuster Entertainment Corporation.** These retailers maintain huge inventories of the goods in which they specialize and sell them at such low prices that other firms find it hard to compete. Although the category killers have large amounts of money tied up in inventories, they maintain very sophisticated just-in-time operating environments that require suppliers to meet demanding standards for delivery of products and reduction of inventory costs. Some suppliers are required to stock the shelves and keep track of inventory levels. By minimizing handling and overhead costs and buying at favorably low prices, the category killers have realized large profits.

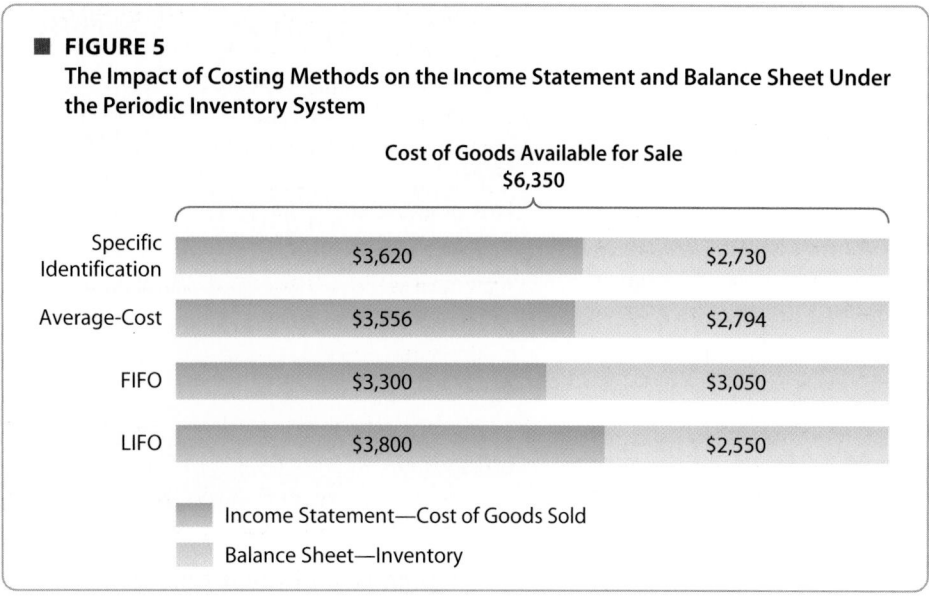

■ **FIGURE 5**
The Impact of Costing Methods on the Income Statement and Balance Sheet Under the Periodic Inventory System

Cost of Goods Available for Sale
$6,350

	Income Statement—Cost of Goods Sold	Balance Sheet—Inventory
Specific Identification	$3,620	$2,730
Average-Cost	$3,556	$2,794
FIFO	$3,300	$3,050
LIFO	$3,800	$2,550

■ Income Statement—Cost of Goods Sold
□ Balance Sheet—Inventory

income determination—is more important than the physical movement of goods and balance sheet valuation.

An argument can also be made against LIFO. Because the inventory valuation on the balance sheet reflects earlier prices, it often gives an unrealistic picture of the inventory's current value. Balance sheet measures like working capital and current ratio may be distorted and must be interpreted carefully.

Figure 5 summarizes how the four inventory costing methods affect the cost of goods sold on the income statement and inventory on the balance sheet when a company uses the periodic inventory system. In periods of rising prices, FIFO yields the highest inventory valuation, the lowest cost of goods sold, and hence a higher net income; LIFO yields the lowest inventory valuation, the highest cost of goods sold, and thus a lower net income.

S T O P • R E V I E W • A P P L Y

3-1. Do the FIFO and LIFO inventory costing methods result in different quantities of ending inventory? Explain your answer.

3-2. Under which inventory costing methods are (a) the earliest costs assigned to inventory, (b) the latest costs assigned to inventory, and (c) the average costs assigned to inventory?

3-3. What are the relative advantages and disadvantages of FIFO and LIFO from management's point of view?

Impact of Inventory Decisions

LO4 Explain the effects of inventory costing methods on income determination and income taxes

Table 1 shows how the specific identification, average-cost, FIFO, and LIFO methods of pricing inventory affect gross margin. The table uses the same data as in the previous section and assumes June sales of $5,000.

TABLE 1.   Effects of Inventory Costing Methods on Gross Margin

	Specific Identification Method	Average-Cost Method	FIFO Method	LIFO Method
Sales	$5,000	$5,000	$5,000	$5,000
Cost of goods sold				
Beginning inventory	$ 800	$ 800	$ 800	$ 800
Purchases	5,550	5,550	5,550	5,550
Cost of goods available for sale	$6,350	$6,350	$6,350	$6,350
Less ending inventory	2,730	2,794	3,050	2,550
Cost of goods sold	$3,620	$3,556	$3,300	$3,800
Gross margin	$1,380	$1,444	$1,700	$1,200

Keeping in mind that June was a period of rising prices, you can see in Table 1 that LIFO, which charges the most recent—and, in this case, the highest—prices to cost of goods sold, resulted in the lowest gross margin. Conversely, FIFO, which charges the earliest—and, in this case, the lowest—prices to cost of goods sold, produced the highest gross margin. The gross margin under the average-cost method falls between the gross margins produced by LIFO and FIFO, so this method clearly has a less pronounced effect.

During a period of declining prices, the LIFO method would produce a higher gross margin than the FIFO method. It is apparent that both these methods have the greatest impact on gross margin during prolonged periods of price changes, whether up or down. Because the specific identification method depends on the particular items sold, no generalization can be made about the effect of changing prices on gross margin.

Effects on the Financial Statements

As Figure 6 shows, the FIFO, LIFO, and average-cost methods of inventory costing are widely used. Each method has its advantages and disadvantages—none is perfect. Among the factors managers should consider in choosing an inventory costing method are the trend of prices and the effects of each method on financial statements, income taxes, and cash flows.

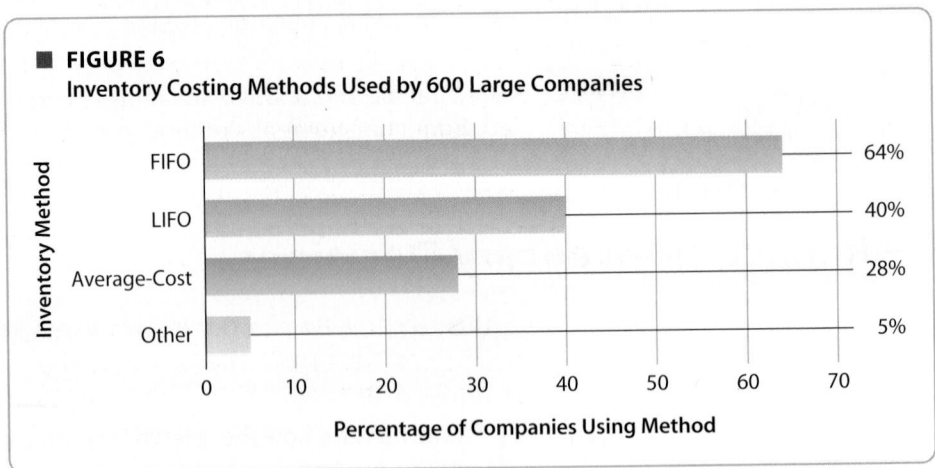

■ FIGURE 6
Inventory Costing Methods Used by 600 Large Companies

Source: Reprinted with permission from *Accounting Trends & Techniques.* Copyright © 2005 by American Institute of Certified Public Accountants.

As we have pointed out, inventory costing methods have different effects on the income statement and balance sheet. The LIFO method is best suited for the income statement because it matches revenues and cost of goods sold. But it is not the best method for valuation of inventory on the balance sheet, particularly during a prolonged period of price increases or decreases. FIFO, on the other hand, is well suited to the balance sheet because the ending inventory is closest to current values and thus gives a more realistic view of a company's current assets. Readers of financial statements must be alert to the inventory methods a company uses and be able to assess their effects.

Effects on Income Taxes

The Internal Revenue Service governs how inventories must be valued for federal income tax purposes. IRS regulations give companies a wide choice of inventory costing methods, including specific identification, average-cost, FIFO, and LIFO, and, except when the LIFO method is used, it allows them to apply the lower-of-cost-or-market rule. However, if a company wants to change the valuation method it uses for income tax purposes, it must have advance approval from the IRS.* This requirement conforms to the consistency convention. Because changes in inventory costing method can cause sizable fluctuations in income and make income statements hard to interpret from year to year, a company should change its inventory method only if there is a good reason to do so. The company must show the nature and effect of the change in its financial statements.

Many accountants believe that using the FIFO and average-cost methods in periods of rising prices causes businesses to report more than their actual profit, resulting in excess payment of income tax. Profit is overstated because cost of goods sold is understated relative to current prices. Thus, the company must buy replacement inventory at higher prices, while additional funds are needed to pay income taxes. During the rapid inflation of 1979 to 1982, billions of dollars reported as profits and paid in income taxes were believed to be the result of poor matching of current costs and revenues under the FIFO and average-cost methods. Consequently, many companies, believing that prices would continue to rise, switched to the LIFO inventory method.

When a company uses the LIFO method to report income for tax purposes, the IRS requires that it use the same method in its accounting records, and, as we have noted, it disallows use of the LCM rule. The company may, however, use the LCM rule for financial reporting purposes.

Over a period of rising prices, a business that uses the LIFO method may find that for balance sheet purposes, its inventory is valued at a figure far below what it currently pays for the same items. Management must monitor such a situation carefully, because if it lets the inventory quantity at year end fall below the level at the beginning of the year, the company will find itself paying higher income taxes. Higher income before taxes results because the company expenses the historical costs of inventory, which are below current costs. When sales have reduced inventories below the levels set in prior years, it is called a **LIFO liquidation**—that is, units sold exceed units purchased for the period.

Managers can prevent a LIFO liquidation by making enough purchases before the end of the year to restore the desired inventory level. Sometimes, however, a LIFO liquidation cannot be avoided because products are discontinued or supplies are interrupted, as in the case of a strike. In 2005, 31 out of

Study Note

In periods of rising prices, LIFO results in lower net income and thus lower taxes.

---

* A single exception to this rule is that when companies change to LIFO from another method, they do not need advance approval from the IRS.

FOCUS ON BUSINESS PRACTICE

Does a Company's Inventory Costing Method Affect Its Operating Decisions?

It certainly does when taxes are involved. Research has shown that among firms that use the LIFO inventory method, those with high tax rates are more likely to buy extra inventory at year end than are those with low tax rates.[9] This behavior is predictable because in determining taxable income, LIFO deducts the costs of the most recent purchases, which are likely to be higher than the costs of earlier purchases. By buying extra inventory at year end, a company can lower its income taxes.

600 large companies reported a LIFO liquidation in which their net income increased due to the matching of historical costs with present sales dollars.[10]

Effects on Cash Flows

Generally speaking, the choice of accounting methods does not affect cash flows. For example, a company's choice of average cost, FIFO, or LIFO does not affect what it pays for goods or the price at which it sells them. However, the fact that income tax law requires a company to use the same method for income tax purposes and financial reporting means that the choice of inventory method will affect the amount of income tax paid. Therefore, choosing a method that results in lower income will result in lower income taxes due. In most other cases where there is a choice of accounting method, a company may choose different methods for income tax computations and financial reporting.

STOP • REVIEW • APPLY

4-1. In periods of steadily rising prices, which inventory method—average-cost, FIFO, or LIFO—will give the (a) highest ending inventory cost, (b) lowest ending inventory cost, (c) highest net income, and (d) lowest net income?

4-2. What is the relationship between income tax rules and the inventory valuation methods?

Characteristics of Inventory Costing Methods   Match each of the descriptions listed below to these inventory costing methods:

a. Specific identification

b. Average-cost

c. First-in, first-out (FIFO)

d. Last-in, first-out (LIFO)

1. Matches recent costs with recent revenues   *d*

2. Assumes that each item of inventory is identifiable   *a*

3. Results in the most realistic balance sheet valuation   *c*

4. Results in the lowest net income in periods of deflation   *c*

5. Results in the lowest net income in periods of inflation   *d*

6. Matches the oldest costs with recent revenues   *c*

7. Results in the highest net income in periods of inflation   *c*

8. Results in the highest net income in periods of deflation   *d*

9. Tends to level out the effects of inflation   *b*

10. Is unpredictable as to the effects of inflation   *a*

Inventory Cost Under the Perpetual Inventory System

SO5 Calculate inventory cost under the perpetual inventory system using various costing methods.

Under the perpetual inventory system, cost of goods sold is accumulated as sales are made and costs are transferred from the Inventory account to the Cost of Goods Sold account. The cost of the ending inventory is the balance of the Inventory account. To illustrate costing methods under the perpetual inventory system, we use the following data:

Inventory Data—June 30

June			
	1	Inventory	80 units @ $10.00
	6	Purchase	220 units @ $12.50
	10	Sale	280 units
	25	Purchase	200 units @ $14.00
	30	Inventory	220 units

The specific identification method produces the same inventory cost and cost of goods sold under the perpetual system as under the periodic system because cost of goods sold and ending inventory are based on the cost of the identified items sold and on hand. The detailed records of purchases and sales maintained under the perpetual system facilitate the use of the specific identification method.

The average-cost method uses a different approach under the perpetual and periodic systems, and it produces different results. Under the periodic system, the average cost is computed for all goods available for sale during the period. Under the perpetual system, an average is computed after each purchase or series of purchases, as follows:

Perpetual Inventory System—Average-Cost Method

June				
	1	Inventory	80 units @ $10.00	$ 800
	6	Purchase	220 units @ $12.50	2,750
	6	Balance	300 units @ $11.83*	$3,550
				(new average computed)
	10	Sale	280 units @ $11.83*	(3,313)
	10	Balance	20 units @ $11.83*	$ 237
	25	Purchase	200 units @ $14.00	2,800
	30	Inventory	220 units @ $13.80*	$3,037
				(new average computed)
		Cost of goods sold		$3,313

*Rounded.

The costs applied to sales become the cost of goods sold, $3,313. The ending inventory is the balance, $3,037.

When costing inventory with the FIFO and LIFO methods, it is necessary to keep track of the components of inventory at each step of the way because as sales are made, the costs must be assigned in the proper order. The FIFO method is applied as follows:

Perpetual Inventory System—FIFO Method

June	1	Inventory	80 units @ $10.00		$ 800
	6	Purchase	220 units @ $12.50		2,750
	10	Sale	80 units @ $10.00	($ 800)	
			200 units @ $12.50	(2,500)	(3,300)
	10	Balance	20 units @ $12.50		$ 250
	25	Purchase	200 units @ $14.00		2,800
	30	Inventory	20 units @ $12.50	$ 250	
			200 units @ $14.00	2,800	$3,050
		Cost of goods sold			$3,300

Note that the ending inventory of $3,050 and the cost of goods sold of $3,300 are the same as the figures computed earlier under the periodic inventory system. This will always occur because the ending inventory under both systems consists of the last items purchased—in this case, the entire purchase of June 25 and 20 units from the purchase of June 6.

The LIFO method is applied as follows:

Perpetual Inventory System—LIFO Method

June	1	Inventory	80 units @ $10.00		$ 800
	6	Purchase	220 units @ $12.50		2,750
	10	Sale	220 units @ $12.50	($2,750)	
			60 units @ $10.00	(600)	(3,350)
	10	Balance	20 units @ $10.00		$ 200
	25	Purchase	200 units @ $14.00		2,800
	30	Inventory	20 units @ $10.00	$ 200	
			200 units @ $14.00	2,800	$3,000
		Cost of goods sold			$3,350

Notice that the ending inventory of $3,000 includes 20 units from the beginning inventory and 200 units from the June 25 purchase.

Figure 7 compares the average-cost, FIFO, and LIFO methods under the perpetual inventory system. The rank of the results is the same as under the periodic inventory system, but some amounts have changed. For example, LIFO has the lowest balance sheet inventory valuation regardless of the inven-

FOCUS ON BUSINESS PRACTICE

More Companies Enjoy LIFO!

The availability of better technology may partially account for the increasing use of LIFO in the United States. Using the LIFO method under the perpetual inventory system has always been a tedious process, especially if done man- ually. The development of faster and less expensive computer systems has made it easier for companies that use the perpetual inventory system to switch to LIFO and enjoy that method's economic benefits.

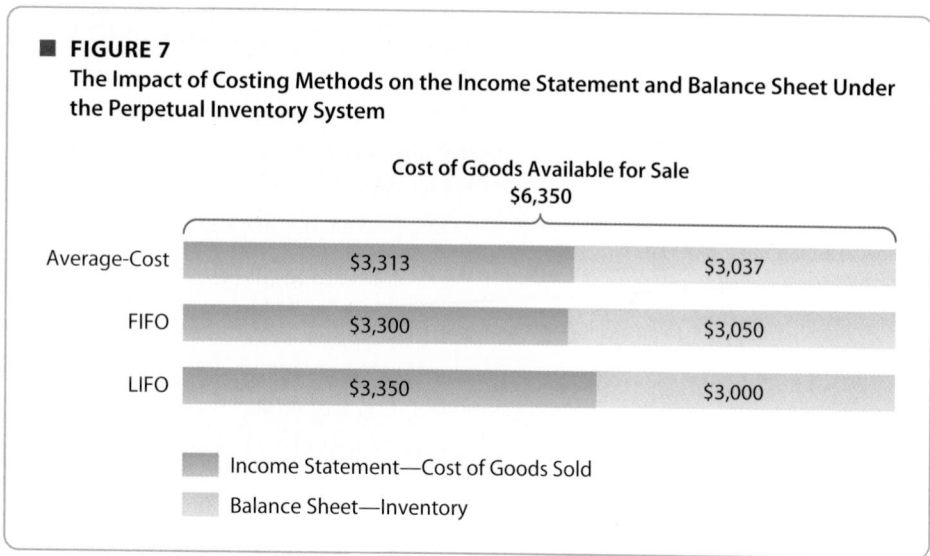

■ **FIGURE 7**
The Impact of Costing Methods on the Income Statement and Balance Sheet Under the Perpetual Inventory System

tory system used, but the amount is $3,000 using the perpetual system versus $2,550 using the periodic system.

S T O P • R E V I E W • A P P L Y

5-1. Why would it be more expensive to maintain a perpetual inventory system than a periodic inventory system?

5-2. Under the perpetual inventory system, why should a physical inventory be taken periodically?

Valuing Inventory by Estimation

> **SO6** Use the retail method and gross profit method to estimate the cost of ending inventory.

t is sometimes necessary or desirable to estimate the value of ending inventory. The retail method and gross profit method are most commonly used for this purpose.

Retail Method

The **retail method** estimates the cost of ending inventory by using the ratio of cost to retail price. Retail merchandising businesses use this method for two main reasons:

1. To prepare financial statements for each accounting period, one must know the cost of inventory; the retail method can be used to estimate the cost without taking the time or going to the expense of determining the cost of each item in the inventory.

2. Because items in a retail store normally have a price tag or a universal product code, it is common practice to take the physical inventory at retail

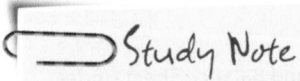

> **Study Note**
>
> Freight-in does not appear in the Retail column because retailers automatically price their goods high enough to cover freight charges.

TABLE 2.   Retail Method of Inventory Estimation

	Cost	Retail
Beginning inventory	$ 40,000	$ 55,000
Net purchases for the period (excluding freight-in)	107,000	145,000
Freight-in	3,000	
Goods available for sale	$150,000	$200,000
Ratio of cost to retail price: $\frac{\$150,000}{\$200,000} = 75\%$		
Net sales during the period		160,000
Estimated ending inventory at retail		$ 40,000
Ratio of cost to retail		75%
Estimated cost of ending inventory	$ 30,000	

from these price tags or codes and to reduce the total value to cost by using the retail method. The term *at retail* means the amount of the inventory at the marked selling prices of the inventory items.

When the retail method is used to estimate ending inventory, the records must show the beginning inventory at cost and at retail. They must also show the amount of goods purchased during the period at cost and at retail. The net sales at retail is the balance of the Sales account less returns and allowances. A simple example of the retail method is shown in Table 2.

Goods available for sale is determined at cost and at retail by listing beginning inventory and net purchases for the period at cost and at their expected selling price, adding freight-in to the cost column, and totaling. The ratio of these two amounts (cost to retail price) provides an estimate of the cost of each dollar of retail sales value. The estimated ending inventory at retail is then determined by deducting sales for the period from the retail price of the goods that were available for sale during the period. The inventory at retail is then converted to cost on the basis of the ratio of cost to retail.

The cost of ending inventory can also be estimated by applying the ratio of cost to retail price to the total retail value of the physical count of the ending inventory. Applying the retail method in practice is often more difficult than this simple example because of such complications as changes in retail price during the period, different markups on different types of merchandise, and varying volumes of sales for different types of merchandise.

> **Study Note**
>
> When estimating inventory by the retail method, the inventory need not be counted.

Gross Profit Method

The **gross profit method** (also known as the *gross margin method*) assumes that the ratio of gross margin for a business remains relatively stable from year to year. The gross profit method is used in place of the retail method when records of the retail prices of beginning inventory and purchases are not available. It is a useful way of estimating the amount of inventory lost or destroyed by theft, fire, or other hazards; insurance companies often use it to verify loss claims. The gross profit method is acceptable for estimating the cost of inventory for interim reports, but it is not acceptable for valuing inventory in the annual financial statements.

As Table 3 shows, the gross profit method is simple to use. First, figure the cost of goods available for sale in the usual way (add purchases to beginning

> **Study Note**
>
> It is highly desirable to maintain financial records off site. If records are destroyed, it can be difficult, if not impossible, to reconstruct the data necessary for an insurance claim.

TABLE 3. Gross Profit Method of Inventory Estimation

1. Beginning inventory at cost		$ 50,000
Purchases at cost (including freight-in)		290,000
Cost of goods available for sale		$340,000
2. Less estimated cost of goods sold		
Sales at selling price	$400,000	
Less estimated gross margin		
(400,000 × 30%)	120,000	
Estimated cost of goods sold		280,000
3. Estimated cost of ending inventory		$ 60,000

inventory). Second, estimate the cost of goods sold by deducting the estimated gross margin of 30 percent from sales. Finally, deduct the estimated cost of goods sold from the goods available for sale to arrive at the estimated cost of ending inventory.

STOP • REVIEW • APPLY

6-1. Does using the retail method mean that inventories are measured at retail value on the balance sheet? Explain your answer.

6-2. For what reasons might managers use the gross profit method of estimating inventory?

A LOOK BACK AT

CISCO SYSTEMS, INC.

In this chapter's Decision Point, we posed the following questions:

- **What is the impact of inventory decisions on operating results?**
- **How should inventory be valued?**
- **How should the level of inventory be evaluated?**

As we pointed out in the chapter, Cisco uses supply-chain management and a just-in-time operating environment to manage its inventory. By doing so, it reduces its operating costs. We also pointed out that in 2001, a time when the market for Cisco's products had soured, a note in Cisco's annual report disclosed that the company used the first-in, first-out costing method and applied the lower-of-cost-or-market rule to its inventories. Cisco's approach to valuation adheres to the conservatism convention because it recognizes losses in value before the products are sold. As a result, Cisco recognized a loss of more than $1.5 billion. Such losses are common in the rapidly changing Internet environment in which Cisco operates.

Using data from Cisco's Financial Highlights, we can evaluate the company's success in managing its inventories by comparing its inventory turnover ratio and days' inventory on hand in 2005 and 2004 (dollar amounts are in millions):

	2005	**2004**
$\dfrac{\text{Cost of Goods Sold}}{\text{Average Inventory}}$	$\dfrac{\$6{,}758}{(\$1{,}297 + \$1{,}207) \div 2}$	$\dfrac{\$5{,}766}{(\$1{,}207 + \$873) \div 2}$
	$\dfrac{\$6{,}758}{\$1{,}252}$	$\dfrac{\$5{,}766}{\$1{,}040}$
Ⓚ/Ⓡ Inventory Turnover:	5.4 times	5.5 times
$\dfrac{\text{Number of Days in a Year}}{\text{Inventory Turnover}}$	$\dfrac{365 \text{ days}}{5.4 \text{ times}}$	$\dfrac{365 \text{ days}}{5.5 \text{ times}}$
Ⓚ/Ⓡ Days' Inventory on Hand:	67.6 days	66.4 days

Thus, in 2005, Cisco experienced a slight decrease in its inventory turnover and a slight increase in the number of days it had inventory on hand.

CHAPTER REVIEW

REVIEW of Learning Objectives

LO1 Explain the management decisions related to inventory accounting, evaluation of inventory level, and the effects of inventory misstatements on income measurement.

The objective of inventory accounting is the proper determination of income through the matching of costs and revenues. In accounting for inventories, management must choose the type of processing system, costing method, and valuation method the company will use. Because the value of inventory affects a company's net income, management's choices will affect not only external and internal evaluations of the company, but also the amount of income taxes the company pays and its cash flows.

The level of inventory a company maintains has important economic consequences. To evaluate inventory levels, managers commonly use inventory turnover and its related measure, days' inventory on hand. Supply-chain management and a just-in-time operating environment are a means of increasing inventory turnover and reducing inventory carrying costs.

If the value of ending inventory is understated or overstated, a corresponding error—dollar for dollar—will be made in income before income taxes. Furthermore, because the ending inventory of one period is the beginning inventory of the next, the misstatement affects two accounting periods, although the effects are opposite.

LO2 Define *inventory cost,* contrast goods flow and cost flow, and explain the lower-of-cost-or-market (LCM) rule.

Inventory cost includes the invoice price less purchases discounts; freight-in, including insurance in transit; and applicable taxes and tariffs. Goods flow refers to the actual physical flow of merchandise in a business, whereas cost flow refers to the assumed flow of costs. The lower-of-cost-or-market rule states that if the replacement cost (market cost) of the inventory is lower than the original cost, the lower figure should be used.

LO3 Calculate inventory cost under the periodic inventory system using various costing methods.

The value assigned to ending inventory is the result of two measurements: quantity and cost. Quantity is determined by taking a physical inventory. Cost is determined by using one of four inventory methods, each based on a different assumption of cost flow. Under the periodic inventory system, the specific identification method identifies the actual cost of each item in inventory. The average-cost method assumes that the cost of inventory is the average cost of goods available for sale during the period. The first-in, first-out (FIFO) method assumes that the costs of the first items acquired should be assigned to the first items sold. The last-in, first-out (LIFO) method assumes that the costs of the last items acquired should be assigned to the first items sold. The inventory method used may or may not correspond to the actual physical flow of goods.

LO4 Explain the effects of inventory costing methods on income determination and income taxes.

During periods of rising prices, the LIFO method will show the lowest net income; FIFO, the highest; and average-cost, in between. LIFO and FIFO have the opposite effects in periods of falling prices. No generalization can be made regarding the specific identification method. The Internal Revenue Service requires that if LIFO is used for tax purposes, it must be used for financial statements; it also does not allow the lower-of-cost-or-market rule to be applied to the LIFO method.

Supplemental Objectives

SO5 Calculate inventory cost under the perpetual inventory system using various costing methods.

Under the perpetual inventory system, cost of goods sold is accumulated as sales are made and costs are transferred from the Inventory account to the Cost of Goods Sold account. The cost of the ending inventory is the balance of the Inventory account. The specific identification method and the FIFO method produce the same results under both the perpetual and periodic inventory systems. The results differ for the average-cost method because an average is calculated after each sale rather than at the end of the accounting period. Results also differ for the LIFO method because the cost components of inventory change constantly as goods are bought and sold.

SO6 Use the retail method and gross profit method to estimate the cost of ending inventory.

Two methods of estimating the value of inventory are the retail method and the gross profit method. Under the retail method, inventory is determined at retail prices and is then reduced to estimated cost by applying a ratio of cost to retail price. Under the gross profit method, cost of goods sold is estimated by reducing sales by estimated gross margin. The estimated cost of goods sold is then deducted from the cost of goods available for sale to estimate the cost of ending inventory.

REVIEW of Concepts and Terminology

The following concepts and terms were introduced in this chapter:

Average-cost method: An inventory costing method in which inventory is priced at the average cost of the goods available for sale during the period. **(LO3)**

Consignment: Merchandise that its owner (the consignor) places on the premises of another company (the consignee) with the understanding that payment is expected only when the merchandise is sold and that unsold items may be returned to the consignor. **(LO2)**

Cost flow: The association of costs with their assumed flow in the operations of a company. **(LO2)**

First-in, first-out (FIFO) method: An inventory costing method based on the assumption that the costs of the first items acquired should be assigned to the first items sold. **(LO3)**

Goods flow: The actual physical movement of goods in the operations of a company. **(LO2)**

Gross profit method: A method of inventory estimation based on the assumption that the ratio of gross margin for a business remains relatively stable from year to year. Also called *gross margin method*. **(SO6)**

Inventory cost: The invoice price of an asset less purchases discounts, plus freight in, plus applicable taxes and tariffs. **(LO2)**

Just-in-time operating environment: A method of reducing levels of inventory by working closely with suppliers to coordinate and schedule deliveries so that goods arrive just at the time they are needed. **(LO1)**

Last-in, first-out (LIFO) method: An inventory costing method based on the assumption that the costs of

the last items purchased should be assigned to the first items sold. **(LO3)**

LIFO liquidation: The reduction of inventory below previous levels because sales of older, lower-priced units have exceeded the purchases of units for the current period. **(LO4)**

Lower-of-cost-or-market (LCM) rule: A method of valuing inventory at an amount less than cost when the replacement cost falls below historical cost. **(LO2)**

Market: Current replacement cost of inventory. **(LO2)**

Retail method: A method of inventory estimation, used in retail merchandising businesses, in which inventory at retail value is reduced by the ratio of cost to retail price. **(SO6)**

Specific identification method: An inventory costing method in which the cost of each item in ending inventory is identified as coming from a specific purchase. **(LO3)**

Supply-chain management: A system of managing inventory and purchasing through business-to-business transactions conducted over the Internet. **(LO1)**

Key Ratios

Days' inventory on hand: The average number of days required to sell the inventory on hand; Number of Days in a Year ÷ Inventory Turnover. **(LO1)**

Inventory turnover: A ratio indicating the number of times a company's average inventory is sold during an accounting period; Cost of Goods Sold ÷ Average Inventory. **(LO1)**

REVIEW Problem

LO1, LO3, SO5   **Periodic and Perpetual Inventory Systems**

The following table summarizes the beginning inventory, purchases, and sales of Psi Company's single product during January:

	A	B	C	D	E	F	G	H
1					**Beginning Inventory and Purchases**			
2	Date				Units	Cost	Total	Sales Units
3	Jan.	1		Inventory	1,400	$20	$28,000	
4		8		Purchase	600	22	13,200	
5		10		Sale				1,600
6		24		Purchase	800	24	19,200	
8	Totals				2,800		$60,400	1,600

Required

1. Assuming that the company uses the periodic inventory system, compute the cost that should be assigned to ending inventory and to cost of goods sold using (a) the average-cost method, (b) the FIFO method, and (c) the LIFO method.
2. Assuming that the company uses the perpetual inventory system, compute the cost that should be assigned to ending inventory and to cost of goods sold using (a) the average-cost method, (b) the FIFO method, and (c) the LIFO method.
3. Compute inventory turnover and days' inventory on hand under each of the inventory cost flow assumptions in 1. What conclusion can you draw from this comparison?

Answer to Review Problem

	Units	Amount
Beginning inventory	1,400	$28,000
Purchases	1,400	32,400
Available for sale	2,800	$60,400
Sales	1,600	
Ending inventory	1,200	

1. Periodic inventory system:

   a. Average-cost method

Cost of goods available for sale	$60,400
Less ending inventory consisting of	
1,200 units at $21.57*	25,884
Cost of goods sold	$34,516

   *$60,400 ÷ 2,800 units = $21.57 (rounded).

   b. FIFO method

Cost of goods available for sale		$60,400
Less ending inventory consisting of		
Jan. 24 purchase (800 × $24)	$19,200	
Jan. 8 purchase (400 × $22)	8,800	28,000
Cost of goods sold		$32,400

c. LIFO method

Cost of goods available for sale	$60,400
Less ending inventory consisting of beginning inventory (1,200 × $20)	24,000
Cost of goods sold	$36,400

2. Perpetual inventory system:

a. Average-cost method

Date			Units	Cost	Amount
Jan.	1	Inventory	1,400	$20.00	$28,000
	8	Purchase	600	22.00	13,200
	8	Balance	2,000	20.60	$41,200
	10	Sale	(1,600)	20.60	(32,960)
	10	Balance	400	20.60	$ 8,240
	24	Purchase	800	24.00	19,200
	31	Inventory	1,200	22.87*	$27,440
Cost of goods sold					$32,960

*Rounded.

b. FIFO method

Date			Units	Cost	Amount
Jan.	1	Inventory	1,400	$20	$28,000
	8	Purchase	600	22	13,200
	8	Balance	1,400	20	
			600	22	$41,200
	10	Sale	(1,400)	20	
			(200)	22	(32,400)
	10	Balance	400	22	$ 8,800
	24	Purchase	800	24	19,200
	31	Inventory	400	22	
			800	24	$28,000
Cost of goods sold					$32,400

c. LIFO method

Date			Units	Cost	Amount
Jan.	1	Inventory	1,400	$20	$28,000
	8	Purchase	600	22	13,200
	8	Balance	1,400	20	
			600	22	$41,200
	10	Sale	(600)	22	
			(1,000)	20	(33,200)
	10	Balance	400	20	$ 8,000
	24	Purchase	800	24	19,200
	31	Inventory	400	20	
			800	24	$27,200
Cost of goods sold					$33,200

3. Ratios computed:

	Average-Cost	FIFO	LIFO
Cost of Goods Sold	$34,516	$32,400	$36,400
Average Inventory	$26,942	$28,000	$26,000
	($25,884 + $28,000) ÷ 2	($28,000 + $28,000) ÷ 2	($24,000 + $28,000) ÷ 2
Inventory Turnover:	1.3 times	1.2 times	1.4 times
Days' Inventory on Hand:	(365 days ÷ 1.3 times)	(365 days ÷ 1.2 times)	(365 days ÷ 1.4 times)
	280.8 days	304.2 days	260.7 days

In periods of rising prices, the LIFO method will always result in a higher inventory turnover and lower days' inventory on hand than the other costing methods. When comparing inventory ratios for two or more companies, their inventory methods should be considered.

CHAPTER ASSIGNMENTS

BUILDING Your Basic Knowledge and Skills

Short Exercises

LO1 Management Issues

SE 1. Indicate whether each of the following items is associated with (a) allocating the cost of inventories in accordance with the matching rule, (b) assessing the impact of inventory decisions, (c) evaluating the level of inventory, or (d) engaging in an unethical practice.

1. Calculating days' inventory on hand
2. Ordering a supply of inventory to satisfy customer needs
3. Valuing inventory at an amount to achieve a specific profit objective
4. Calculating the income tax effect of an inventory method
5. Deciding the cost to place on ending inventory

LO1 Inventory Turnover and Days' Inventory on Hand

SE 2. During 20x7, Chauncey Clothiers had beginning inventory of $480,000, ending inventory of $560,000, and cost of goods sold of $2,200,000. Compute the inventory turnover and days' inventory on hand.

LO3 Specific Identification Method

SE 3. Assume the following data with regard to inventory for Caciato Company:

Aug.	1	Inventory	40 units @ $10 per unit	$ 400
	8	Purchase	50 units @ $11 per unit	550
	22	Purchase	35 units @ $12 per unit	420
Goods available for sale			125 units	$1,370
Aug.	15	Sale	45 units	
	28	Sale	25 units	
Inventory, Aug. 31			55 units	

Assuming that the inventory consists of 30 units from the August 8 purchase and 25 units from the purchase of August 22, calculate the cost of ending inventory and cost of goods sold.

LO3 **Average-Cost Method: Periodic Inventory System**

SE 4. Using the data in **SE 3**, calculate the cost of ending inventory and cost of goods sold according to the average-cost method under the periodic inventory system.

LO3 **FIFO Method: Periodic Inventory System**

SE 5. Using the data in **SE 3**, calculate the cost of ending inventory and cost of goods sold according to the FIFO method under the periodic inventory system.

LO3 **LIFO Method: Periodic Inventory System**

SE 6. Using the data in **SE 3**, calculate the cost of ending inventory and cost of goods sold according to the LIFO method under the periodic inventory system.

LO4 **Effects of Inventory Costing Methods and Changing Prices**

SE 7. Using Table 1 as an example, prepare a table with four columns that shows the ending inventory and cost of goods sold for each of the results from your calculations in **SE 3** through **SE 6**, including the effects of the different prices at which the merchandise was purchased. Which method(s) would result in the lowest income taxes?

SO5 **Average-Cost Method: Perpetual Inventory System**

SE 8. Using the data in **SE 3**, calculate the cost of ending inventory and cost of goods sold according to the average-cost method under the perpetual inventory system.

SO5 **FIFO Method: Perpetual Inventory System**

SE 9. Using the data in **SE 3**, calculate the cost of ending inventory and cost of goods sold according to the FIFO method under the perpetual inventory system.

SO5 **LIFO Method: Perpetual Inventory System**

SE 10. Using the data in **SE 3**, calculate the cost of ending inventory and cost of goods sold according to the LIFO method under the perpetual inventory system.

Exercises

LO1, LO2 **Discussion Questions**

E 1. Develop a brief answer to each of the following questions:

1. Is it good or bad for a retail store to have a large inventory?
2. Which is more important from the standpoint of inventory costing: the flow of goods or the flow of costs?
3. Why is misstatement of inventory one of the most common means of financial statement fraud?
4. Given that the LCM rule is an application of the conservatism convention in the current accounting period, is the effect of this application also conservative in the next period?

LO4, SO5, SO6   Discussion Questions

E 2. Develop a brief answer to each of the following questions:

1. Under what condition would all four methods of inventory pricing produce exactly the same results?
2. Under the perpetual inventory system, why is the cost of goods sold not determined by deducting the ending inventory from goods available for sale, as it is under the periodic method?
3. Which of the following methods do not require a physical inventory: periodic inventory system, perpetual inventory method, retail method, or gross profit method?

LO1   Management Issues

E 3. Indicate whether each of the following items is associated with (a) allocating the cost of inventories in accordance with the matching rule, (b) assessing the impact of inventory decisions, (c) evaluating the level of inventory, or (d) engaging in an unethical action.

1. Computing inventory turnover
2. Valuing inventory at an amount to meet management's targeted net income
3. Application of the just-in-time operating environment
4. Determining the effects of inventory decisions on cash flows
5. Apportioning the cost of goods available for sale to ending inventory and cost of goods sold
6. Determining the effects of inventory methods on income taxes
7. Determining the assumption about the flow of costs into and out of the company

LO1   Inventory Ratios

E 4. Just a Buck Discount Stores is assessing its levels of inventory for 20x7 and 20x8 and has gathered the following data:

	20x8	20x7	20x6
Ending inventory	$ 96,000	$ 81,000	$69,000
Cost of goods sold	480,000	450,000	

Compute the inventory turnover and days' inventory on hand for 20x7 and 20x8 and comment on the results.

LO1   Effects of Inventory Errors

E 5. Condensed income statements for Cozumel Company for two years are shown below.

	20x8	20x7
Sales	$252,000	$210,000
Cost of goods sold	150,000	108,000
Gross margin	$102,000	$102,000
Operating expenses	60,000	60,000
Operating income	$ 42,000	$ 42,000

After the end of 20x8, the company discovered that an error had resulted in an $18,000 understatement of the 20x7 ending inventory.

Compute the corrected operating income for 20x7 and 20x8. What effect will the error have on operating income and owner's equity for 20x9?

LO1, LO2, LO3 **Accounting Conventions and Inventory Valuation**

E 6. Turnbow Company, a telecommunications equipment company, has used the LIFO method adjusted for lower of cost or market for a number of years. Due to falling prices of its equipment, it has had to adjust (reduce) the cost of inventory to market each year for two years. The company is considering changing its method to FIFO adjusted for lower of cost or market in the future. Explain how the accounting conventions of consistency, full disclosure, and conservatism apply to this decision. If the change were made, why would management expect fewer adjustments to market in the future?

LO3 **Periodic Inventory System and Inventory Costing Methods**

E 7. Martha's Grain Shop recorded the following purchases and sales of fertilizer during the past year:

Jan. 1	Beginning inventory	125 cases @ $23	$ 2,875
Feb. 25	Purchase	100 cases @ $26	2,600
June 15	Purchase	200 cases @ $28	5,600
Oct. 15	Purchase	150 cases @ $28	4,200
Dec. 15	Purchase	100 cases @ $30	3,000
	Goods available for sale	675	$18,275
	Total sales	500 cases	
Dec. 31	Ending inventory	175 cases	

Assume that Martha's Grain Shop sold all of the June 15 purchase and 100 cases each from the January 1 beginning inventory, the October 15 purchase, and the December 15 purchase.

Determine the costs that should be assigned to ending inventory and cost of goods sold under each of the following assumptions: (1) costs are assigned by the specific identification method; (2) costs are assigned by the average-cost method; (3) costs are assigned by the FIFO method; (4) costs are assigned by the LIFO method. What conclusions can be drawn about the effect of each method on the income statement and the balance sheet of Martha's Grain Shop? Round your answers to the nearest whole number and assume the periodic inventory system.

LO3 **Periodic Inventory System and Inventory Costing Methods**

E 8. During its first year of operation, Krabna Company purchased 5,600 units of a product at $42 per unit. During the second year, it purchased 6,000 units of the same product at $48 per unit. During the third year, it purchased 5,000 units at $60 per unit. Krabna Company managed to have an ending inventory each year of 1,000 units. The company uses the periodic inventory system.

Prepare cost of goods sold statements that compare the value of ending inventory and the cost of goods sold for each of the three years using (1) the FIFO inventory costing method and (2) the LIFO method. From the resulting data, what conclusions can you draw about the relationships between the changes in unit price and the changes in the value of ending inventory?

LO3 **Periodic Inventory System and Inventory Costing Methods**

E 9. In chronological order, the inventory, purchases, and sales of a single product for a recent month are as follows:

		Units	Amount per Unit
June 1	Beginning inventory	150	$30
4	Purchase	400	33
12	Purchase	800	36
16	Sales	1,300	60
24	Purchase	300	39

Using the periodic inventory system, compute the cost of ending inventory, cost of goods sold, and gross margin. Use the average-cost, FIFO, and LIFO inventory costing methods. Explain the differences in gross margin produced by the three methods. Round unit costs to cents and totals to dollars.

LO4 **Effects of Inventory Costing Methods on Cash Flows**

E 10. Hart Products, Inc., sold 120,000 cases of glue at $20 per case during 20x7. Its beginning inventory consisted of 20,000 cases at a cost of $12 per case. During 20x7, it purchased 60,000 cases at $14 per case and later 50,000 cases at $15 per case. Operating expenses were $550,000, and the applicable income tax rate was 30 percent.

Using the periodic inventory system, compute net income using the FIFO method and the LIFO method for costing inventory. Which alternative produces the larger cash flow? The company is considering a purchase of 10,000 cases at $15 per case just before the year end. What effect on net income and on cash flow will this proposed purchase have under each method? (**Hint:** What are the income tax consequences?)

SO5 **Perpetual Inventory System and Inventory Costing Methods**

E 11. Referring to the data provided in **E 9** and using the perpetual inventory system, compute the cost of ending inventory, cost of goods sold, and gross margin. Use the average-cost, FIFO, and LIFO inventory costing methods. Explain the reasons for the differences in gross margin produced by the three methods. Round unit costs to cents and totals to dollars.

LO3, SO5 **Periodic and Perpetual Systems and Inventory Costing Methods**

E 12. During July 20x7, Fan-Qi, Inc., sold 500 units of its product Ultima for $8,000. The following units were available:

	Units	Cost
Beginning inventory	200	$ 2
Purchase 1	80	4
Purchase 2	120	6
Purchase 3	300	9
Purchase 4	180	12

A sale of 500 units was made after purchase 3. Of the units sold, 200 came from beginning inventory and 300 came from purchase 3.

Determine cost of goods available for sale and ending inventory in units. Then determine the costs that should be assigned to cost of goods sold and ending inventory under each of the following assumptions: (1) Costs are assigned under the periodic inventory system using (a) the specific identification method, (b) the average-cost method, (c) the FIFO method, and (d) the LIFO method. (2) Costs are assigned under the perpetual inventory system using (a) the average-cost method, (b) the FIFO method, and (c) the LIFO method. For each alternative, show the gross margin. Round unit costs to cents and totals to dollars.

SO6   Retail Method

E 13. Corabia Dress Shop had net retail sales of $250,000 during the current year. The following additional information was obtained from the company's accounting records:

	At Cost	At Retail
Beginning inventory	$ 40,000	$ 60,000
Net purchases (excluding freight-in)	140,000	220,000
Freight-in	10,400	

1. Using the retail method, estimate the company's ending inventory at cost.
2. Assume that a physical inventory taken at year end revealed an inventory on hand of $18,000 at retail value. What is the estimated amount of inventory shrinkage (loss due to theft, damage, etc.) at cost using the retail method?

SO6   Gross Profit Method

E 14. Chen Mo-Wan was at home when he received a call from the fire department telling him his store had burned. His business was a total loss. The insurance company asked him to prove his inventory loss. For the year, until the date of the fire, Chen's company had sales of $900,000 and purchases of $560,000. Freight-in amounted to $27,400, and beginning inventory was $90,000. Chen always priced his goods to achieve a gross margin of 40 percent. Compute Chen's estimated inventory loss.

Problems

LO1, LO3   Periodic Inventory System and Inventory Costing Methods

P 1. The Midori Cabinet Company sold 2,200 cabinets during 20x7 at $160 per cabinet. Its beginning inventory on January 1 was 130 cabinets at $56. Purchases made during the year were as follows:

February	225 cabinets @ $62
April	350 cabinets @ $65
June	700 cabinets @ $70
August	300 cabinets @ $66
October	400 cabinets @ $68
November	250 cabinets @ $72

The company's selling and administrative expenses for the year were $101,000. The company uses the periodic inventory system.

Required

1. Prepare a schedule to compute the cost of goods available for sale.
2. Compute income before income taxes under each of the following inventory cost flow assumptions: (a) the average-cost method, (b) the FIFO method, and (c) the LIFO method.
3. **User Insight:** Compute inventory turnover and days' inventory on hand under each of the inventory cost flow assumptions in requirement **2**. What conclusion can you draw from this comparison?

LO1, LO3   Periodic Inventory System and Inventory Costing Methods

P 2. The inventory, purchases, and sales of Product ISO for March and April are listed below. The company closes its books at the end of each month. It uses the periodic inventory system.

Mar.	1	Beginning inventory	60 units @ $49
	10	Purchase	100 units @ $52

Mar.	19	Sale	90 units
	31	Ending inventory	70 units
Apr.	4	Purchase	120 units @ $53
	15	Purchase	50 units @ $54
	23	Sale	200 units
	25	Purchase	100 units @ $55
	30	Ending inventory	140 units

Required

1. Compute the cost of the ending inventory on March 31 and April 30 using the average-cost method. In addition, determine cost of goods sold for March and April. Round unit costs to cents and totals to dollars.
2. Compute the cost of the ending inventory on March 31 and April 30 using the FIFO method. Also determine cost of goods sold for March and April.
3. Compute the cost of the ending inventory on March 31 and April 30 using the LIFO method. Also determine cost of goods sold for March and April.
4. **User Insight:** Do the cash flows from operations for March and April differ depending on which inventory costing method is used—average-cost, FIFO, or LIFO? Explain.

LO4, SO5 **Perpetual Inventory System and Inventory Costing Methods**

K/R **P 3.** Use the data provided in **P 2**, but assume that the company uses the perpetual inventory system. (**Hint:** In preparing the solutions required below, it is helpful to determine the balance of inventory after each transaction, as shown in the Review Problem in this chapter.)

Required

1. Determine the cost of ending inventory and cost of goods sold for March and April using the average-cost method. Round unit costs to cents and totals to dollars.
2. Determine the cost of ending inventory and cost of goods sold for March and April using the FIFO method.
3. Determine the cost of ending inventory and cost of goods sold for March and April using the LIFO method.
4. **User Insight:** Assume that this company grows for many years in a long period of rising prices. How realistic do you think the balance sheet value for inventory would be and what effect would it have on the inventory turnover ratio?

SO6 **Retail Method**

P 4. Fuentes Company operates a large discount store and uses the retail method to estimate the cost of ending inventory. Management suspects that in recent weeks there have been unusually heavy losses from shoplifting or employee pilferage. To estimate the amount of the loss, the company has taken a physical inventory and will compare the results with the estimated cost of inventory. Data from the accounting records of Fuentes Company are as follows:

	At Cost	At Retail
October 1 beginning inventory	$51,488	$ 74,300
Purchases	71,733	108,500
Purchases returns and allowances	(2,043)	(3,200)
Freight-in	950	
Sales		109,183
Sales returns and allowances		(933)
October 31 physical inventory at retail		62,450

Required

1. Using the retail method, prepare a schedule to estimate the dollar amount of the store's month-end inventory at cost.
2. Use the store's cost to retail ratio to reduce the retail value of the physical inventory to cost.
3. Calculate the estimated amount of inventory shortage at cost and at retail.
4. **User Insight:** Many retail chains use the retail method because it is efficient. Why do you think using this method is an efficient way for these companies to operate?

SO6 **Gross Profit Method**

P 5. Oakley Sisters is a large retail furniture company that operates in two adjacent warehouses. One warehouse is a showroom, and the other is used to store merchandise. On the night of April 22, 20x8, a fire broke out in the storage warehouse and destroyed the merchandise stored there. Fortunately, the fire did not reach the showroom, so all the merchandise on display was saved.

Although the company maintained a perpetual inventory system, its records were rather haphazard, and the last reliable physical inventory had been taken on December 31. In addition, there was no control of the flow of goods between the showroom and the warehouse. Thus, it was impossible to tell what goods should have been in either place. As a result, the insurance company required an independent estimate of the amount of loss. The insurance company examiners were satisfied when they received the following information:

Merchandise inventory on December 31, 20x7	$ 727,400
Purchases, January 1 to April 22, 20x8	1,206,100
Purchases returns, January 1 to April 22, 20x8	(5,353)
Freight-in, January 1 to April 22, 20x8	26,550
Sales, January 1 to April 22, 20x8	1,979,525
Sales returns, January 1 to April 22, 20x8	(14,900)
Merchandise inventory in showroom on April 22, 20x8	201,480
Average gross margin	44%

Required

1. Prepare a schedule that estimates the amount of the inventory lost in the fire.
2. **User Insight:** What are some other reasons management might need to estimate the amount of inventory?

Alternate Problems

LO1, LO3 **Periodic Inventory System and Inventory Costing Methods**

P 6. MacRae Company merchandises a single product called Sooto. The following data represent beginning inventory and purchases of Sooto during the past year: January 1 inventory, 68,000 units at $11.00; February purchases, 80,000 units at $12.00; March purchases, 160,000 units at $12.40; May purchases, 120,000 units at $12.60; July purchases, 200,000 units at $12.80; September purchases, 160,000 units at $12.60; and November purchases, 60,000 units at $13.00. Sales of Sooto totaled 786,000 units at $20.00 per unit. Selling and administrative expenses totaled $5,102,000 for the year. MacRae Company uses the periodic inventory system.

Required

1. Prepare a schedule to compute the cost of goods available for sale.
2. Compute income before income taxes under each of the following inventory cost flow assumptions: (a) the average-cost method; (b) the FIFO method; and (c) the LIFO method.
3. **User Insight:** Compute inventory turnover and days' inventory on hand under each of the inventory cost flow assumptions listed in requirement **2**. What conclusion can you draw?

LO1, LO3   Periodic Inventory System and Inventory Costing Methods

P 7. The inventory of Product B and data on purchases and sales for a two-month period follow. The company closes its books at the end of each month. It uses the periodic inventory system.

Apr.	1	Beginning inventory	50 units @ $102
	10	Purchase	100 units @ $110
	17	Sale	90 units
	30	Ending inventory	60 units
May	2	Purchase	100 units @ $108
	14	Purchase	50 units @ $112
	22	Purchase	60 units @ $117
	30	Sale	200 units
	31	Ending inventory	70 units

Required

1. Compute the cost of ending inventory of Product B on April 30 and May 31 using the average-cost method. In addition, determine cost of goods sold for April and May. Round unit costs to cents and totals to dollars.
2. Compute the cost of the ending inventory on April 30 and May 31 using the FIFO method. In addition, determine cost of goods sold for April and May.
3. Compute the cost of the ending inventory on April 30 and May 31 using the LIFO method. In addition, determine cost of goods sold for April and May.
4. **User Insight:** Do the cash flows from operations for April and May differ depending on which inventory costing method is used—average-cost, FIFO, or LIFO? Explain.

LO4, SO5   Perpetual Inventory System and Inventory Costing Methods

P 8. Use the data provided in **P 7**, but assume that the company uses the perpetual inventory system. (**Hint:** In preparing the solutions required below, it is helpful to determine the balance of inventory after each transaction, as shown in the Review Problem in this chapter.)

Required

1. Determine the cost of ending inventory and cost of goods sold for April and May using the average-cost method. Round unit costs to cents and totals to dollars.
2. Determine the cost of ending inventory and cost of goods sold for April and May using the FIFO method.
3. Determine the cost of ending inventory and cost of goods sold for April and May using the LIFO method.
4. **User Insight:** Do the cash flows from operations for April and May differ depending on which inventory costing method is used—average-cost, FIFO, or LIFO? Explain.

≡ ENHANCING Your Knowledge, Skills, and Critical Thinking

Conceptual Understanding Cases

LO1 **Evaluation of Inventory Levels**

C 1. **J. C. Penney,** a large retail company with many stores, has an inventory turnover of 4.1 times. **Dell Computer Corporation,** an Internet mail-order company, has an inventory turnover of about 100.0. Dell achieves its high turnover through supply-chain management in a just-in-time operating environment. Why is inventory turnover important to companies like J. C. Penney and Dell? Why are comparisons among companies important? Are J. C. Penney and Dell a good match for comparison? Describe supply-chain management and a just-in-time operating environment. Why are they important to achieving a favorable inventory turnover?

LO1 **Misstatement of Inventory**

C 2. **Crazy Eddie, Inc.,** a discount consumer electronics chain, seemed to be missing $52 million in merchandise inventory. "It was a shock," the new management was quoted as saying. It was also one of the nation's largest swindles. Investors lost $145.6 million when the company declared bankruptcy. A count turned up only $75 million in inventory, compared with $126.7 million reported by former management. Net sales could account for only $6.7 million of the difference. At the time, it was not clear whether bookkeeping errors in prior years or an actual physical loss created the shortfall, although at least one store manager felt it was a bookkeeping error because security was strong. "It would be hard for someone to steal anything," he said. Former management was eventually fined $72.7 million.[11]

1. What is the effect of the misstatement of inventory on Crazy Eddie's reported earnings in prior accounting periods?
2. Is this a situation you would expect in a company that is experiencing financial difficulty? Explain.

LO4 **LIFO Inventory Method**

C 3. Eighty-five percent of chemical companies use the LIFO inventory method for the costing of inventories, whereas only 9 percent of computer equipment companies use LIFO.[12] Describe the LIFO inventory method. What effects does it have on reported income, cash flows, and income taxes during periods of price changes? Why do you think so many chemical companies use LIFO while most companies in the computer industry do not?

Interpreting Financial Reports

LO2 **LCM and Conservatism**

C 4. **Exxon Mobil Corporation,** the world's largest company, uses the LIFO inventory method for most of its inventories. Its inventory costs are heavily dependent on the cost of oil. In a recent year when the price of oil was down, Exxon Mobil, following the lower-of-cost-or-market (LCM) rule, wrote down its inventory by $325 million. In the next year, when the price of oil recovered, the company reported that market price exceeded the LIFO carrying values by $6.8 billion.[13] Explain why the LCM rule resulted in a write-down in the first year. What is the inconsistency between the first- and second-year treatments of the change in the price of oil? How does the accounting convention of conservatism explain the inconsistency? If the price of oil declined substantially in a third year, what would be the likely consequence?

LO1, LO4   **FIFO and LIFO**

C 5. **Exxon Mobil Corporation** had net sales of $237,054 million, cost of goods sold of $107,658 million, and net income of $21,510 million in 2003. Inventories under the LIFO method used by the company were $8,136 million in 2004 and $7,665 million in 2003. Inventory would have been considerably higher in both years if the company had used FIFO.[14] Why do you suppose Exxon Mobil's management chooses to use the LIFO inventory method? On what economic conditions, if any, do those reasons depend?

Decision Analysis Using Excel

LO3, LO4   **FIFO versus LIFO Analysis**

C 6. Refrigerated Truck Sales Company (RTS Company) buys large refrigerated trucks from the manufacturer and sells them to companies and independent truckers who haul perishable goods over long distances. RTS has been successful in this specialized niche of the industry. Because of the high cost of the trucks and of financing inventory, RTS tries to maintain as small an inventory as possible. In fact, at the beginning of July the company had no inventory or liabilities, as shown on the balance sheet below.

On July 9, RTS took delivery of a truck at a price of $150,000. On July 19, an identical truck was delivered to the company at a price of $160,000. On July 28, the company sold one of the trucks for $195,000. During July, expenses totaled $15,000. All transactions were paid in cash.

RTS Company
Balance Sheet
July 1, 20x7

Assets		Stockholders' Equity	
Cash	$400,000	Common stock	$400,000
Total assets	$400,000	Total stockholders' equity	$400,000

1. Prepare income statements and balance sheets for RTS on July 31 using (a) the FIFO method of inventory valuation and (b) the LIFO method of inventory valuation. Assume an income tax rate of 40 percent. Explain the effects of each method on the financial statements.
2. Assume that the management of RTS Company has a policy of declaring a cash dividend each period that is exactly equal to net income. What effects does this action have on each balance sheet prepared in requirement 1? How do the resulting balance sheets compare with the balance sheet at the beginning of the month? Which inventory method, if either, do you feel is more realistic in representing RTS's income?
3. Assume that RTS receives notice of another price increase of $10,000 on refrigerated trucks, to take effect on August 1. How does this information relate to management's dividend policy, and how will it affect next month's operations?

Annual Report Case: CVS Corporation

LO1, LO4, SO5, SO6   **Inventory Costing Methods and Ratios**

C 7. Refer to the note related to inventories in **CVS Corporation's** annual report in the Supplement to Chapter 5 to answer the following questions: What inventory method(s) does CVS use? If LIFO inventories had been valued at FIFO, why would there be no difference? Do you think many of the company's inventories are valued at market? Few companies use the retail method, so why do you think CVS uses it? Compute and compare the inventory turnover and days' inventory on hand for CVS for 2005 and 2004. Ending 2003 inventories were $4,016.5 million.

Comparison Case: CVS Versus Walgreens

LO1   **Inventory Efficiency**

 C 8. Refer to **CVS's** annual report in the Supplement to Chapter 5 and to the following data (in millions) for **Walgreens**: cost of goods sold, $30,413.8 and $27,310.4 for 2005 and 2004, respectively; inventories, $5,592.7, $4,738.6, and $4,202.7 for 2005, 2004, and 2003, respectively. Ending inventories for 2003 for CVS were $4,016.5 million. Calculate inventory turnover and days' inventory on hand for 2005 and 2004. If you did **C 7**, refer to your answer there for CVS. Has either company improved its performance over the past two years? What advantage does the superior company's performance provide to it? Which company appears to make the most efficient use of inventories? Explain your answers.

Ethical Dilemma Case

LO1, LO4   **Inventories, Income Determination, and Ethics**

C 9. Flare, Inc., which has a December 31 year end, designs and sells fashions for young professional women. Sandra Mason, president of the company, fears that the forecasted 20x7 profitability goals will not be reached. She is pleased when Flare receives a large order on December 30 from The Executive Woman, a retail chain of upscale stores for businesswomen. Mason immediately directs the controller to record the sale, which represents 13 percent of Flare's annual sales. At the same time, she directs the inventory control department not to separate the goods for shipment until after January 1. Separated goods are not included in inventory because they have been sold.

On December 31, the company's auditors arrive to observe the year-end taking of the physical inventory under the periodic inventory system. How will Sandra Mason's actions affect Flare's 20x7 profitability? How will they affect Flare's 20x8 profitability? Were Mason's actions ethical? Why or why not?

Internet Case

LO4, SO5   **Effect of LIFO on Income and Cash Flows**

 **C 10. Maytag Corporation,** an appliance manufacturer, uses the LIFO inventory method. Go to its website and select "About Maytag." Then select "Financial Center." After finding the income statement and inventory note, calculate what net income would have been had the company used FIFO. Calculate how much cash the company saved for the year and cumulatively by using LIFO. What is the difference between the LIFO and FIFO gross margin and profit margin results? Which reporting alternative is better for the company?

Group Activity Case

LO2, LO4   **Retail Business Inventories**

C 11. Assign teams to various types of stores in your community—a grocery, clothing, book, music, or appliance store. Make an appointment to interview the manager for 30 minutes to discuss the company's inventory accounting system. The store may be a branch of a larger company. Ask the following questions, summarize your findings in a paper, and be prepared to discuss your results in class:

1. What is the physical flow of merchandise into the store, and what documents are used in connection with this flow?
2. What documents are prepared when merchandise is sold?
3. Does the store keep perpetual inventory records? If so, does it keep the records in units only, or does it keep track of cost as well? If not, what system does the store use?
4. How often does the company take a physical inventory?
5. How are financial statements generated for the store?
6. What method does the company use to cost its inventory for financial statements?

Business Communication Case

LO1, LO2, LO3   **Inventory Ratio Analysis**

C 12. Yamaha Corporation and **Pioneer Corporation** are two large, diversified Japanese electronics companies. Both use the average-cost method and the lower-of-cost-or-market rule to account for inventories. The following data are for their 2005 fiscal years (in millions of yen):[15]

	Yamaha	Pioneer
Beginning inventory	¥ 72,146	¥107,806
Ending inventory	78,434	109,015
Cost of goods sold	335,483	584,060

Assume you have been asked to analyze the inventory efficiency of the two companies. Prepare a memorandum to your boss that compares the inventory efficiency of Yamaha and Pioneer by computing the inventory turnover and days' inventory on hand for both companies in 2005. Show and comment on the relative efficiency of the two companies. Also comment on how the inventory method would affect your evaluation if you were to compare Yamaha and Pioneer to each other and to a U.S. company given the fact that most companies in the United States use the LIFO inventory method. Mention what could be done to make the results comparable.

Cash and Receivables

ash and receivables require careful oversight to ensure that they are ethically handled. If cash is mismanaged or stolen, it can bring about the downfall of a business. Because accounts receivable and notes receivable require estimates of future losses, they can be easily manipulated to show improvement in reported earnings. Improved earnings can, of course, enhance a company's stock price, as well as the bonuses of its executives. In this chapter, we address the management of cash and demonstrate the importance of estimates in accounting for receivables.

LEARNING OBJECTIVES

Making a Statement

Balance
Sheet

Statement of
Cash Flows

Income
Statement

Estimation of uncollectible credit sales affects the amount of accounts receivable on the balance sheet and operating expenses on the income statement.

LO1 Identify and explain the management and ethical issues related to cash and receivables.

LO2 Define *cash equivalents,* and explain methods of controlling cash, including bank reconciliations.

LO3 Apply the allowance method of accounting for uncollectible accounts.

LO4 Define *promissory note,* and make common calculations for promissory notes receivable.

- How can the company control its cash needs?

- How can the company evaluate credit policies and the level of its receivables?

- How should the company estimate the value of its receivables?

Nike, one of the world's largest and best-known athletic sportswear companies, must give the retail stores that buy its products time to pay for their purchases. At the same time, however, Nike must have enough cash on hand to pay its suppliers. As you can see in Nike's Financial Highlights, cash and accounts receivable have made up 53 to 57 percent of its current assets in recent years.[1] The company must therefore plan and control its cash flows very carefully.

NIKE'S FINANCIAL HIGHLIGHTS (In millions)			
	2005	**2004**	**2003**
Cash	$ 1,388.1	$ 828.0	$ 634.0
Accounts receivable, net	2,262.1	2,120.2	2,083.9
Total current assets	6,351.1	5,528.6	4,787.1
Net sales	13,739.7	12,253.1	10,697.0

Management Issues Related to Cash and Receivables

The management of cash and accounts and notes receivable is critical to maintaining adequate liquidity. These assets are important components of the operating cycle, which also includes inventories and accounts payable. In dealing with cash and receivables, management must address five key issues: managing cash needs, setting credit policies, evaluating the level of accounts receivable, financing receivables, and making ethical estimates of credit losses.

Cash Needs

On the balance sheet, **cash** usually consists of currency and coins on hand, checks and money orders from customers, and deposits in checking and savings accounts. Cash is the most liquid of all assets and the most readily available to pay debts. It is central to the operating cycle because all operating transactions eventually use or generate cash.

Cash may include a *compensating balance*, an amount that is not entirely free to be spent. A **compensating balance** is a minimum amount that a bank requires a company to keep in its bank account as part of a credit-granting arrangement. Such an arrangement restricts cash; in effect, it increases the interest on the loan and reduces a company's liquidity. The Securities and Exchange Commission therefore requires companies that have compensating balances to disclose the amounts involved.

Most companies experience seasonal cycles of business activity during the year. During some periods, sales are weak; during others, they are strong. There are also periods when expenditures are high, and periods when they are low. For toy companies, college textbook publishers, amusement parks, construction companies, and manufacturers of sports equipment, the cycles are dramatic, but all companies experience them to some degree.

Seasonal cycles require careful planning of cash inflows, cash outflows, borrowing, and investing. Figure 1 shows the seasonal cycles typical of an athletic sportswear company like **Nike**. As you can see, cash receipts from sales are highest in the late spring and summer because that is when most people engage in outdoor sports. Sales are relatively low in the winter months. On the other hand, cash expenditures are highest in late winter and spring as the com-

FOCUS ON BUSINESS PRACTICE

How Do Good Companies Deal with Bad Times?

Good companies manage their cash well even in bad times. When a slump in the technology market caused **Texas Instrument's** sales to decline by more than 40 percent, resulting in a loss of nearly $120 million, this large electronics firm actually increased its cash by acting quickly to cut its purchases of plant assets by two-thirds. It also reduced its payroll and lowered the average number of days it had inventory on hand from 71 to 58.[2]

In similar circumstances, some companies have not reacted as quickly as Texas Instruments. For example,

before 9/11, the Big Three automakers—**General Motors**, **Ford**, and **DaimlerChrysler**—were awash in cash. However, in little over a year, the three companies went through $28 billion in cash through various purchases, losses, dividends, and share buybacks. Then, with increasing losses from rising costs, big rebates, and zero percent financing, they were suddenly faced with a shortage of cash. As a result, Standard & Poor's lowered their credit ratings, which raises the interest cost of borrowing money. Perhaps the Big Three should have held on to some of that cash.[3]

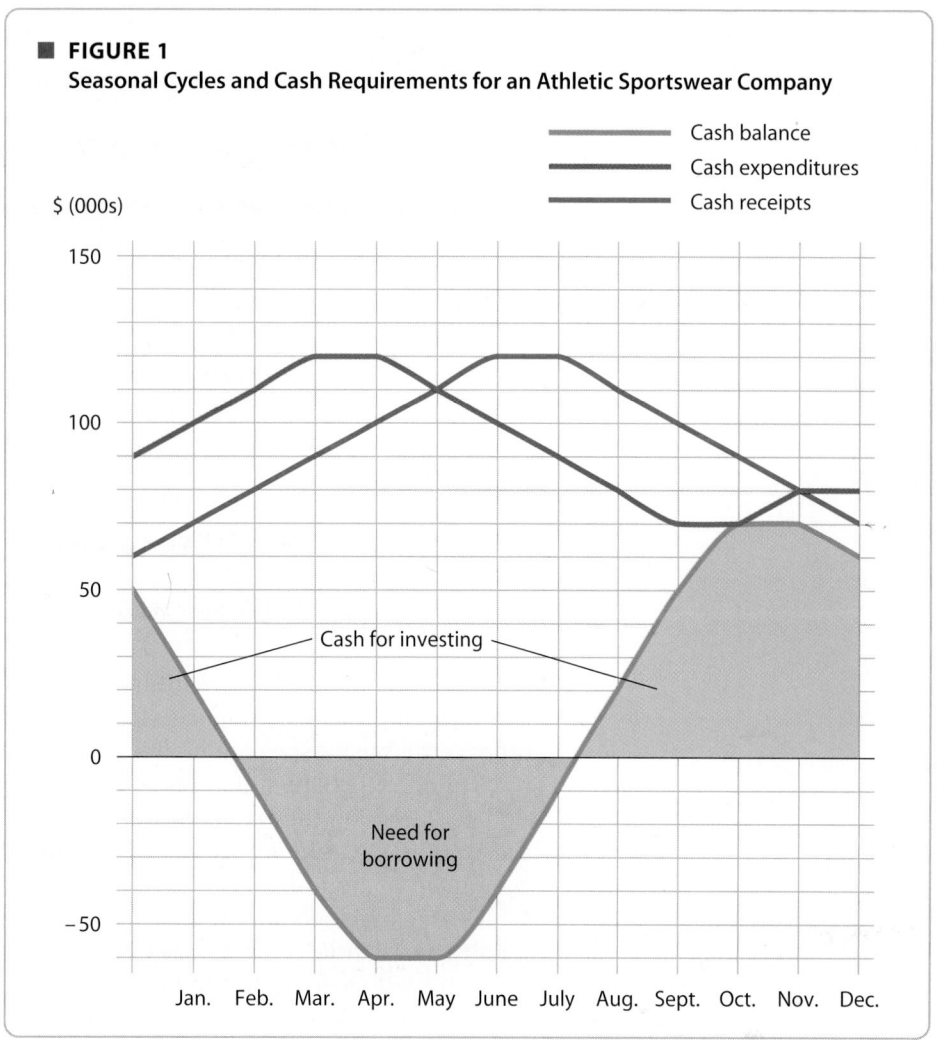

■ FIGURE 1
Seasonal Cycles and Cash Requirements for an Athletic Sportswear Company

pany builds up inventory for spring and summer selling. During the late summer, fall, and winter, the company has excess cash on hand that it needs to invest in a way that will earn a return but still permit access to cash as needed. During spring and early summer, the company needs to plan for short-term borrowing to tide it over until cash receipts pick up later in the year.

Accounts Receivable and Credit Policies

Like cash, accounts receivable and notes receivable are major types of **short-term financial assets**. Both kinds of receivables result from extending credit to individual customers or to other companies. Retailers like **Sears** (recently merged with **Kmart**) have made credit available to nearly every responsible person in the United States. Every field of retail trade has expanded by allowing customers to make payments a month or more after the date of sale. What is not so apparent is that credit has expanded even more among wholesalers and manufacturers like **Nike** than at the retail level. Figure 2 shows the levels of accounts receivable in selected industries.

As we have indicated, **accounts receivable** are the short-term financial assets of a wholesaler or retailer that arise from sales on credit. This type of credit is often called **trade credit**. Terms of trade credit usually range from 5 to 60 days, depending on industry practice. For some companies that sell to consumers, **installment accounts receivable**, which allow the buyer to make a

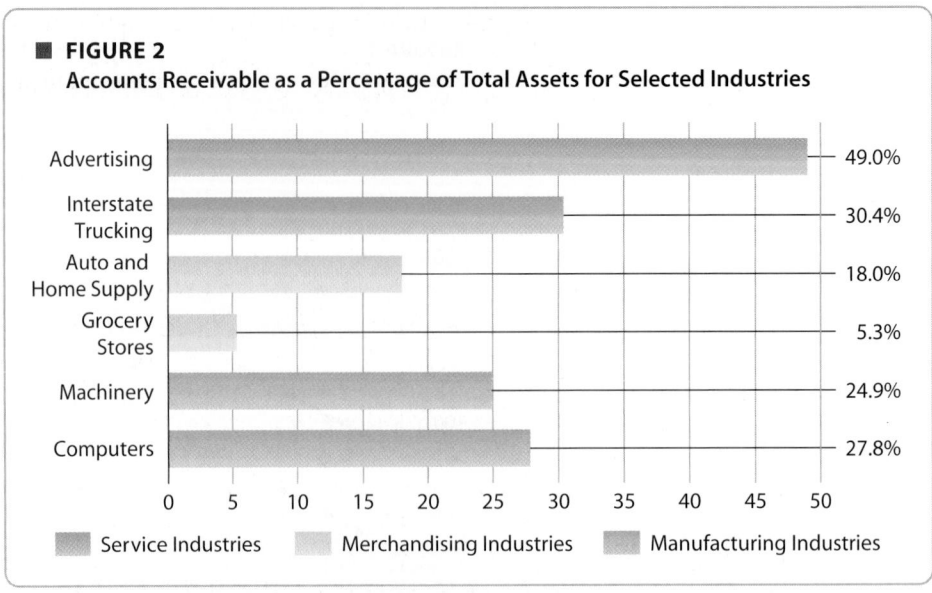

■ **FIGURE 2**
Accounts Receivable as a Percentage of Total Assets for Selected Industries

Source: Data from Dun & Bradstreet, *Industry Norms and Key Business Ratios,* 2004–2005.

series of time payments, constitute a significant portion of accounts receivable. Department stores, appliance stores, furniture stores, used car dealers, and other retail businesses often offer installment credit. The installment accounts receivable of retailers like **Sears** and **J. C. Penney** can amount to millions of dollars. Although the payment period may be 24 months or more, installment accounts receivable are classified as current assets if such credit policies are customary in the industry.

On the balance sheet, *accounts receivable* designates amounts arising from credit sales made to customers in the ordinary course of business. Because loans or credit sales made to employees, officers, or owners of the corporation increase the risk of uncollectibility and conflict of interest, they appear separately on the balance sheet under asset titles like *receivables from employees*.

Normally, individual accounts receivable have debit balances, but sometimes customers overpay their accounts either by mistake or in anticipation of making future purchases. When these accounts show credit balances, the company should show the total credits on its balance sheet as a current liability. The reason for this is that if the customers make no future purchases, the company will have to grant them refunds.

Companies that sell on credit do so to be competitive and to increase sales. In setting credit terms, a company must keep in mind the credit terms of its competitors and the needs of its customers. Obviously, any company that sells on credit wants customers who will pay their bills on time. To increase the likelihood of selling only to customers who will pay on time, most companies develop control procedures and maintain a credit department. The credit department's responsibilities include examining each person or company that applies for credit and approving or rejecting a credit sale to that customer. Typically, the credit department asks for information about the customer's financial resources and debts. It may also check personal references and credit bureaus for further information. Then, based on the information it has gathered, it decides whether to extend credit to the customer.

Companies that are too lenient in granting credit can run into difficulties when customers don't pay. For example, **Capital One**, an aggressive credit card company, attracted 8.1 million new customers, but many of them had poor credit ratings. As a result, the company's unpaid accounts rose from less than 4 percent to 4.96 percent and in 2004 were headed toward 6 percent.[4] **Sprint**, one of the weaker companies in the highly competitive cell phone industry, targeted customers with poor credit histories. It attracted so many who failed to pay their bills that its stock dropped by 50 percent to $2.50 because of the losses that resulted.[5]

Evaluating the Level of Accounts Receivable

Two common measures of the effect of a company's credit policies are receivable turnover and days' sales uncollected. The **receivable turnover** shows how many times, on average, a company turned its receivables into cash during an accounting period. It reflects the relative size of a company's accounts receivable and the success of its credit and collection policies. It may also be affected by external factors, such as seasonal conditions and interest rates. **Days' sales uncollected** is a related measure that shows, on average, how long it takes to collect accounts receivable.

The receivable turnover is computed by dividing net sales by average accounts receivable (net of allowances). Theoretically, the numerator should be net credit sales, but the amount of net credit sales is rarely available in public reports, so investors use total net sales. Using data from **Nike's** Financial Highlights at the beginning of the chapter, we can compute the company's receivable turnover as follows (dollar amounts are in millions):

$$\text{Receivable Turnover} = \frac{\text{Net Sales}}{\text{Average Accounts Receivable}}$$

$$= \frac{\$13,739.7}{(\$2,262.1 + \$2,120.2) \div 2}$$

$$= \frac{\$13,739.7}{\$2,191.2} = 6.3 \text{ times}$$

To find days' sales uncollected, the number of days in a year is divided by the receivable turnover, as follows:

$$\text{Days' Sales Uncollected} = \frac{365 \text{ days}}{\text{Receivable Turnover}} = \frac{365 \text{ days}}{6.3 \text{ times}} = 57.9 \text{ days}$$

Thus, Nike turned its receivables 6.3 times a year, or an average of every 57.9 days. A turnover period of this length is not unusual among apparel companies because their credit terms allow retail outlets time to sell products before paying for them. However, it is longer than the turnover period of many companies in other industries. To interpret a company's ratios, you must take into consideration the norms of the industry in which it operates.

FOCUS ON BUSINESS PRACTICE

How Do Powerful Buyers Cause Problems for Small Suppliers?

Big buyers often have significant power over small suppliers, and their cash management decisions can cause severe cash flow problems for the little companies that depend on them. For instance, in an effort to control costs and optimize cash flow, **Ameritech Corp.** told 70,000 suppliers that it would begin paying its bills in 45 days instead of 30. Other large companies routinely take 90 days or more to pay. Some small suppliers are so anxious to get the big companies' business that they fail to realize the implications of the deals they make until it is too late. When **Earthly Elements, Inc.,** accepted a $10,000 order for dried floral gifts from a national home shopping network, its management was ecstatic because the deal increased sales by 25 percent. But in four months, the resulting cash crunch forced the company to close down. When the shopping network finally paid for the order six months later, it was too late to revive Earthly Elements.[6]

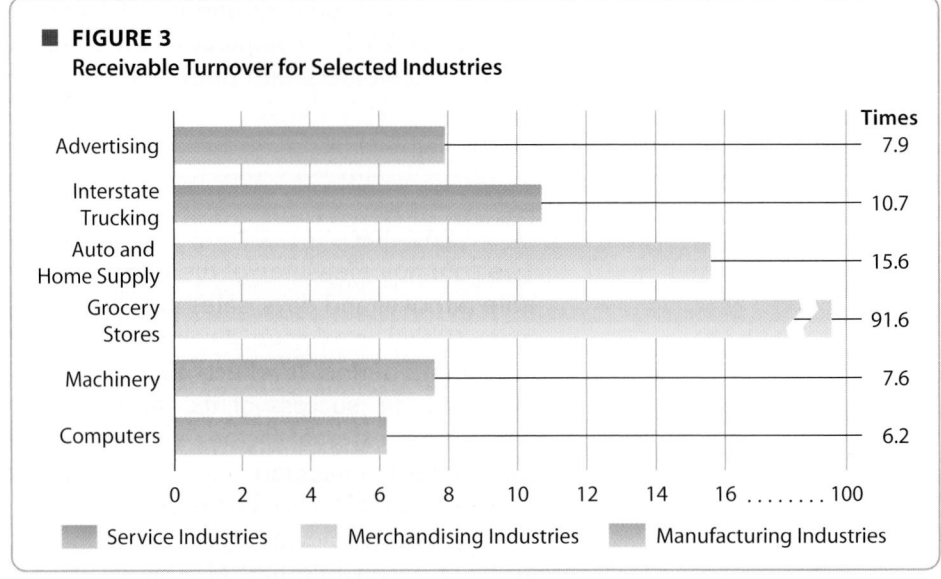

■ FIGURE 3
Receivable Turnover for Selected Industries

Source: Data from Dun & Bradstreet, *Industry Norms and Key Business Ratios,* 2004–2005.

As Figure 3 shows, the receivable turnover ratio varies substantially from industry to industry. Because grocery stores have few receivables, they have a very quick turnover. The turnover in interstate trucking is 10.7 times because the typical credit terms in that industry are 30 days. The turnover in the machinery and computer industries is lower because those industries tend to have longer credit terms.

Figure 4 shows the days' sales uncollected for the industries listed in Figure 3. Grocery stores, which have the lowest ratio (4.0 days) require the least amount of receivables financing; the computer industry, with days' sales uncollected of 58.9 days, requires the most.

Financing Receivables

Financial flexibility is important to most companies. Companies that have significant amounts of assets tied up in accounts receivable may be unwilling or

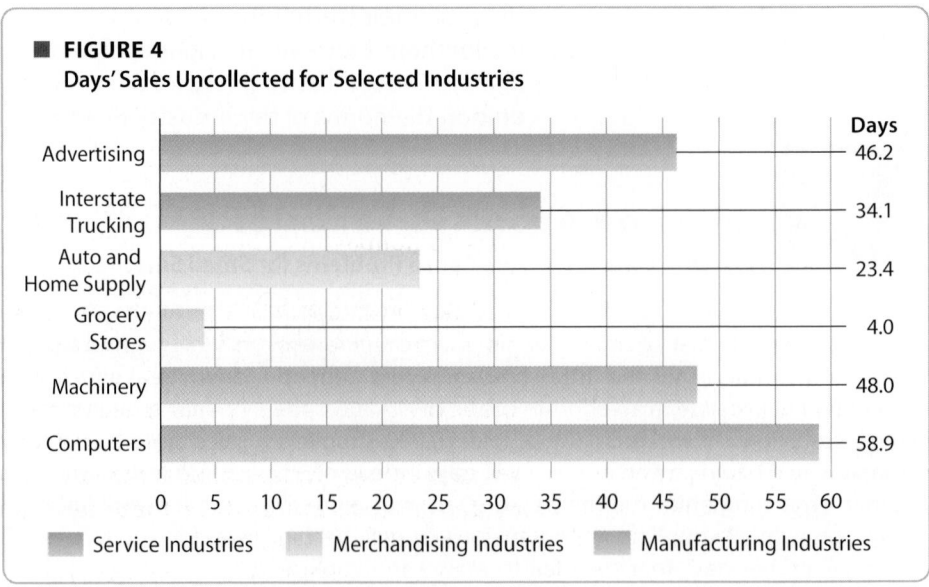

■ FIGURE 4
Days' Sales Uncollected for Selected Industries

Source: Data from Dun & Bradstreet, *Industry Norms and Key Business Ratios,* 2004–2005.

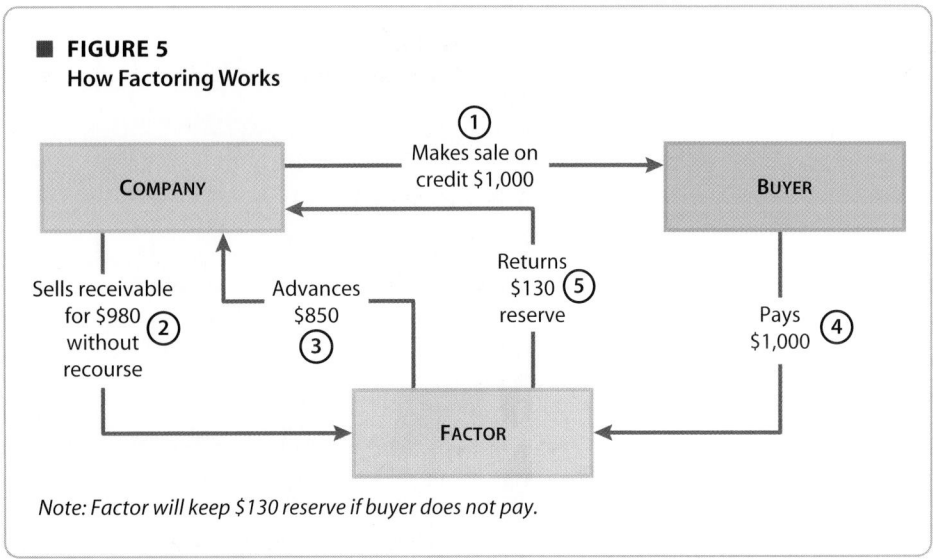

■ **FIGURE 5**
How Factoring Works

Note: Factor will keep $130 reserve if buyer does not pay.

unable to wait until they collect cash from their receivables. Many corporations have set up finance companies to help their customers pay for the purchase of their products. For example, **Ford** has set up Ford Motor Credit Company (FMCC), **General Motors** has set up General Motors Acceptance Corporation (GMAC), and **Sears** has set up Sears Roebuck Acceptance Corporation (SRAC). Other companies borrow funds by pledging their accounts receivable as collateral. If a company does not pay back its loan, the creditor can take the collateral (in this case, the accounts receivable) and convert it to cash to satisfy the loan.

Companies can also raise funds by selling or transferring accounts receivable to another entity, called a **factor**, as illustrated in Figure 5. The sale or transfer of accounts receivable, called **factoring**, can be done with or without recourse. *With recourse* means that the seller of the receivables is liable to the factor (i.e., the purchaser) if a receivable cannot be collected. *Without recourse* means that the factor bears any losses from unpaid accounts. A company's acceptance of credit cards like Visa, MasterCard, or American Express is an example of factoring without recourse because the issuers of the cards accept the risk of nonpayment.

The factor, of course, charges a fee for its service. The fee for sales with recourse is usually about 2 percent of the accounts receivable. The fee is higher for sales without recourse because the factor's risk is greater. In accounting terminology, a seller of receivables with recourse is said to be contingently liable. A **contingent liability** is a potential liability that can develop into a real liability if a particular event occurs. In this case, the event would be a customer's nonpayment of a receivable. A contingent liability generally requires disclosure in the notes to the financial statements.

Nike does not factor or otherwise directly finance its receivables, but **Circuit City Stores**, one of the nation's largest electronics and appliance retailers, does. To promote sales, Circuit City offers generous terms through its installment programs, under which customers pay over a number of months. However, because of its rapid growth, the company needs the cash from these installment receivables sooner than the customers have agreed to pay. To generate cash immediately from these receivables, Circuit City sells them through a process called *securitization*.

Under **securitization**, a company groups its receivables in batches and sells them at a discount to companies and investors. When the receivables are

> **Study Note**
>
> A company that factors its receivables will have a better receivable turnover and days' sales uncollected than a company that does not factor them.

To encourage sales, Circuit City offers installment programs, under which customers pay over time. When the company needs cash from these installment receivables sooner than customers have agreed to pay, Circuit City sells the receivables in batches at a discount to companies and investors—a process called *securitization*.

paid, the buyers get the full amount; their profit depends on the amount of the discount. Circuit City sells all its receivables without recourse, which means that after selling them, it has no further liability, even if no customers were to pay. If Circuit City sold its receivables with recourse and a customer did not pay, it would have to make good on the debt.[7]

Another method of financing receivables is to sell promissory notes held as notes receivable to a financial lender, usually a bank. This practice is called **discounting** because the bank derives its profit by deducting the interest from the maturity value of the note. The holder of the note (usually the payee) endorses the note and turns it over it to the bank. The bank expects to collect the maturity value of the note (principal plus interest) on the maturity date, but it also has recourse against the note's endorser.

For example, if Company A holds a $10,000 note from Company B and the note will pay $600 in interest, a bank may be willing to buy the note for $9,600. If Company B pays, the bank will receive $10,600 at maturity and realize a $1,000 profit. If it fails to pay, Company A is liable to the bank for payment. In the meantime, Company A has a contingent liability in the amount of the discounted note plus interest that it must disclose in the notes to its financial statements.

Ethics and Estimates in Accounting for Receivables

As we have noted, companies extend credit to customers because they expect it will increase their sales and earnings, but they know they will always have some credit customers who cannot or will not pay. The accounts of such customers are called **uncollectible accounts**, or *bad debts*, and they are expenses of selling on credit. To match these expenses, or losses, to the revenues they help generate, they should be recognized at the time credit sales are made.

Of course, at the time a company makes credit sales, it cannot identify which customers will not pay their bills, nor can it predict the exact amount of money it will lose. Therefore, to adhere to the matching rule, it must estimate losses from uncollectible accounts. The estimate becomes an expense in the fiscal year in which the sales are made.

Because the amount of uncollectible accounts can only be estimated and the exact amount will not be known until later, a company's earnings can be easily manipulated. Earnings can be overstated by underestimating the amount of losses from uncollectible accounts, and they can be understated by overestimating the amount of the losses. Misstatements of earnings can occur simply because of a bad estimate. But, as we have noted elsewhere, they can be deliberately made to meet analysts' estimates of earnings, reduce income taxes, or meet benchmarks for bonuses.

Among the many examples of unethical or questionable practices in dealing with uncollectible accounts are the following:

▶ **WorldCom** (now **MCI**) increased revenues and hid losses by continuing to bill customers for service for years after the customers had quit paying.

▶ The policy of **Household International**, a large personal finance company, seems to be flexible about when to declare loans delinquent. As a result, the company can vary its estimates of uncollectible accounts from year to year.[8]

▶ By making large allowances for estimated uncollectible accounts and then gradually reducing them, **Bank One** improved its earnings over several years.[9]

▶ **HealthSouth** manipulated its income by varying its estimates of the difference between what it charged patients and what it could collect from insurance companies.[10]

Companies with high ethical standards try to be accurate in their estimates of uncollectible accounts, and they disclose the basis of their estimates. For example, **Nike's** management describes its estimates as follows:

> We make ongoing estimates relating to the collectibility of our accounts receivables and maintain |an allowance| for estimated losses resulting from the inability of our customers to make required payments. In determining the amount of the |allowance|, we consider our historical level of credit losses and make judgments about the creditworthiness of significant customers based on ongoing credit evaluations. Since we cannot predict future changes in the financial stability of our customers, actual future losses from uncollectible accounts may differ from our estimates.[11]

S T O P • R E V I E W • A P P L Y

1-1. What items are included in the Cash account? What is a compensating balance?

1-2. Why does a company sell on credit if it expects that some of its accounts receivable will not be paid? What role does a credit department play in selling on credit?

1-3. Indicate which of the following items should be included in accounts receivable on the balance sheet (if an item does not belong there, indicate where on the balance sheet it should appear): (a) installment accounts receivable from regular customers, due monthly for three years; (b) debit balances in customers' accounts; (c) receivables from employees; (d) credit balances in customers' accounts; and (e) receivables from officers of the company.

1-4. How does the receivable turnover ratio help in evaluating the level of receivables?

1-5. What is a factor, and what do the terms *factoring with recourse* and *factoring without recourse* mean?

1-6. How is accounting for receivables susceptible to unethical financial reporting?

Suggested answers to all Stop, Review, and Apply questions are available at http://college.hmco.com/accounting/needles/poa/10e/student_home.html.

Cash Equivalents and Cash Control

> **LO2** Define *cash equivalents,* and explain methods of controlling cash, including bank reconciliations.

Cash Equivalents

As we noted earlier, cash is the asset most readily available to pay debts, but at times a company may have more cash on hand than it needs to pay its debts. Excess cash should not remain idle, especially during periods of high interest rates. Management may decide to invest the excess cash in short-term interest-bearing accounts or certificates of deposit (CDs) at banks and other financial institutions, in government securities (such as U.S. Treasury notes), or in other securities. If these investments have a term of 90 days or less when they are purchased, they are called **cash equivalents** because the funds revert to cash so quickly they are treated as cash on the balance sheet.

Nike describes its treatment of cash and cash equivalents as follows:

> Cash and equivalents represent cash and short-term, highly liquid investments with original maturities of three months or less at the time of purchase. The carrying amounts reflected in the consolidated balance sheet for cash and equivalents approximate fair value due to their short maturities.[12]

According to a recent survey of 600 large U.S. corporations, 6 percent use the term *cash* as the balance sheet caption, and 89 percent use either *cash and cash equivalents* or *cash and equivalents*. The rest either combine cash with marketable securities or have no cash.[13]

Cash Control Methods

In an earlier chapter, we discussed the concept of internal control and how it applies to cash transactions. Here, we address three additional ways of controlling cash: imprest systems; banking services, including electronic funds transfer; and bank reconciliations.

Imprest Systems Most companies need to keep some currency and coins on hand. Currency and coins are needed for cash registers, for paying expenses that are impractical to pay by check, and for situations that require cash advances—for example, when sales representatives need cash for travel expenses. One way to control a cash fund and cash advances is by using an **imprest system**.

A common form of imprest system is a petty cash fund, which is established at a fixed amount. A receipt documents each cash payment made from the fund. The fund is periodically reimbursed, based on the documented expenditures, by the exact amount necessary to restore its original cash balance. The person responsible for the petty cash fund must always be able to account for its contents by showing that total cash and receipts equal the original fixed amount.

Banking Services   All businesses rely on banks to control cash receipts and cash disbursements. Banks serve as safe depositories for cash, negotiable instruments, and other valuable business documents, such as stocks and bonds. The checking accounts that banks provide improve control by minimizing the amount of currency a company needs to keep on hand and by supplying permanent records of all cash payments. Banks also serve as agents in a variety of transactions, such as the collection and payment of certain kinds of debts and the exchange of foreign currencies.

Electronic funds transfer (EFT) is a method of conducting business transactions that does not involve the actual transfer of cash. With EFT, a company electronically transfers cash from its bank to another company's bank. For the banks, the electronic transfer is simply a bookkeeping entry. Companies today rely heavily on this method of payment. **Wal-Mart**, for example, makes 75 percent of its payments to suppliers through EFT.

Because of EFT and other electronic banking services, we are rapidly becoming a cashless society. Automated teller machines (ATMs) allow bank customers to make deposits, withdraw cash, transfer funds among accounts, and pay bills. Large consumer banks like **Citibank**, **Chase**, and **Bank of America** process hundreds of thousands of ATM transactions each week. Many banks also give customers the option of paying bills over the telephone and with *debit cards*. In 2005, debit cards accounted for more than 23 billion transactions.[14] When a customer makes a retail purchase using a debit card, the amount of the purchase is deducted directly from the buyer's bank account. The bank usually documents debit card transactions for the retailer, but the retailer must develop new internal controls to ensure that the transactions are recorded properly and that unauthorized transfers do not occur. It is expected that within a few years, a majority of all retail activity will be handled electronically.

Bank Reconciliations

Rarely does the balance of a company's Cash account exactly equal the cash balance on its bank statement. The bank may not yet have recorded certain transactions that appear in the company's records, and the company may not yet have recorded certain bank transactions. A bank reconciliation is therefore a necessary step in internal control. A **bank reconciliation** is the process of accounting for the difference between the balance on a company's bank statement and the balance in its Cash account. This process involves making additions to and subtractions from both balances to arrive at the adjusted cash balance.

The following are the transactions that most commonly appear in a company's records but not on its bank statement :

1. *Outstanding checks*: These are checks that a company has issued and recorded but that do not yet appear on its bank statement.

2. *Deposits in transit*: These are deposits a company has sent to its bank but that the bank did not receive in time to enter on the bank statement.

Transactions that may appear on the bank statement but not in the company's records include the following:

1. *Service charges* (SC): Banks often charge a fee, or service charge, for the use of a checking account. Many banks base the service charge on a number of factors, such as the average balance of the account during the month or the number of checks drawn.

2. NSF (*nonsufficient funds*) *checks*: An NSF check is a check that a company has deposited but that is not paid when the bank presents it to the issuer's bank. The bank charges the company's account and returns the check so that the company can try to collect the amount due. If the bank has deducted the NSF check on the bank statement but the company has not deducted it from its book balance, an adjustment must be made in the bank reconciliation. The company usually reclassifies the NSF check from Cash to Accounts Receivable because it must now collect from the person or company that wrote the check.

3. *Miscellaneous debits and credits*: Banks also charge for other services, such as stopping payment on checks and printing checks. The bank notifies the depositor of each deduction by including a debit memorandum with the monthly statement. A bank also sometimes serves as an agent in collecting on promissory notes for the depositor. When it does, it includes a credit memorandum in the bank statement, along with a debit memorandum for the service charge.

4. *Interest income*: Banks commonly pay interest on a company's average balance. Accounts that pay interest are sometimes called NOW or money market accounts.

Study Note

A credit memorandum means that an amount was *added* to the bank balance; a debit memorandum means that an amount was *deducted*.

An error by either the bank or the depositor will, of course, require immediate correction.

To illustrate the preparation of a bank reconciliation, suppose that Kim Maintenance Company's bank statement for October shows a balance of $3,471.07 on October 31 and that on the same date, the company's records show a cash balance of $2,415.91. The purpose of a bank reconciliation is to identify the items that make up the difference between these amounts and to determine the correct cash balance. Exhibit 1 shows Kim Maintenance Company's bank reconciliation for October. The circled numbers in the exhibit refer to the following:

1. The bank has not recorded a deposit in the amount of $276.00 that the company mailed to the bank on October 31.

2. The bank has not paid the five checks that the company issued in September and October: Even though the September 14 check was deducted in the September 30 reconciliation, it must be deducted again in each subsequent month in which it remains outstanding.

3. The company incorrectly recorded a $300 deposit from cash sales as $330.00. On October 6, the bank received the deposit and corrected the amount.

4. Among the returned checks was a credit memorandum showing that the bank had collected a promissory note from A. Jacobs in the amount of $280.00, plus $20.00 in interest on the note. A debit memorandum was also

EXHIBIT 1 ▶

Bank Reconciliation

Kim Maintenance Company
Bank Reconciliation
October 31, 20xx

Balance per bank, October 31		$3,471.07
① Add deposit of October 31 in transit		276.00
		$3,747.07
② Less outstanding checks:		
No. 551, issued on Sept. 14	$150.00	
No. 576, issued on Oct. 30	40.68	
No. 578, issued on Oct. 31	500.00	
No. 579, issued on Oct. 31	370.00	
No. 580, issued on Oct. 31	130.50	1,191.18
Adjusted bank balance, October 31		**$2,555.89**
Balance per books, October 31		$2,415.91
Add:		
④ Note receivable collected by bank	$280.00	
④ Interest income on note	20.00	
⑦ Interest income	15.62	315.62
		$2,731.53
Less:		
③ Overstatement of deposit of October 6	$ 30.00	
④ Collection fee	5.00	
⑤ NSF check of Arthur Clubb	128.14	
⑥ Service charge	12.50	175.64
Adjusted book balance, October 31		**$2,555.89**

⌐▭ *Study Note*

It is possible to place an item in the wrong section of a bank reconciliation and still have it balance. The *correct* adjusted balance must be obtained.

enclosed for the $5.00 collection fee. The company had not entered these amounts in its records.

5. Also returned with the bank statement was an NSF check for $128.14 that the company had received from a customer named Arthur Clubb. The NSF check was not reflected in the company's records.

6. A debit memorandum was enclosed for the regular monthly service charge of $12.50. The company had not yet recorded this charge.

7. Interest earned on the company's average balance was $15.62.

As you can see in Exhibit 1, starting from their separate balances, both the bank and book amounts are adjusted to the amount of $2,555.89. This adjusted balance is the amount of cash the company owns on October 31 and thus is the amount that should appear on its October 31 balance sheet.

When outstanding checks are presented to the bank for payment and the bank receives and records the deposit in transit, the bank balance will automatically become correct. However, the company must update its book balance by recording all the items reported by the bank. Thus, Kim Maintenance Company would record an increase in Cash with the following items:

▶ Increase (debit) in Notes Receivable, $280

▶ Increase (credit) in Interest Income, $20.00 (interest on note)

◗ Increase (credit) in Interest Income, $15.62 (interest on average bank balance)

The company would record a reduction in Cash with these items:

◗ Decrease (debit) in Sales, $30 (error in recording deposit)

◗ Increase (debit) in Accounts Receivable, $128.14 (return of NSF check)

◗ Increase (debit) in Bank Service Charges, $17.50 ($12.50 + $5.00)

As the use of electronic funds transfer, automatic payments, and debit cards increases, the items that most businesses will have to deal with in their bank reconciliations will undoubtedly grow.

S T O P • R E V I E W • A P P L Y

2-1. How do cash equivalents differ from cash?

2-2. Why is an imprest system an effective control over cash?

2-3. What is a bank reconciliation? What two amounts need to be reconciled?

Uncollectible Accounts

LO3 Apply the allowance method of accounting for uncollectible accounts.

Study Note

The direct charge-off method does not conform to the matching rule.

Some companies recognize a loss at the time they determine that an account is uncollectible by reducing Accounts Receivable and increasing Uncollectible Accounts Expense. Federal regulations require companies to use this method of recognizing a loss—called the **direct charge-off method** —in computing taxable income. Although small companies may use this method for all purposes, companies that follow generally accepted accounting principles do not use it in their financial statements. The reason they do not is that a direct charge-off is usually recorded in a different accounting period from the one in which the sale takes place, and the method therefore does not conform to the matching rule. Companies that follow GAAP prefer the allowance method.

The Allowance Method

Study Note

The allowance method relies on an estimate of uncollectible accounts but is in accord with the matching rule.

Under the **allowance method**, losses from bad debts are matched against the sales they help to produce. As mentioned earlier, when management extends credit to increase sales, it knows it will incur some losses from uncollectible accounts. Losses from credit sales should be recognized at the time the sales are made so that they are matched to the revenues they help generate. Of course, at the time a company makes credit sales, management cannot identify which customers will not pay their debts, nor can it predict the exact amount of money the company will lose. Therefore, to observe the matching rule, losses from uncollectible accounts must be estimated, and the estimate becomes an expense in the period in which the sales are made.

For example, suppose that Cottage Sales Company made most of its sales on credit during its first year of operation, 20x8. At the end of the year, accounts receivable amounted to $100,000. On December 31, 20x8, management reviewed the collectible status of the accounts receivable. Approximately $6,000 of the $100,000 of accounts receivable were estimated to be uncollectible. The following adjusting entry would be made on December 31 of that year:

A	= L +	OE				
−6,000		−6,000	20x8			
			Dec. 31	Uncollectible Accounts Expense	6,000	
				Allowance for Uncollectible Accounts		6,000
				To record the estimated uncollectible accounts expense for the year		

Disclosure of Uncollectible Accounts

Study Note

The purpose of Allowance for Uncollectible Accounts is to reduce the gross accounts receivable to the amount estimated to be collectible (net realizable value). The purpose of another contra account, Accumulated Depreciation, is *not* to reduce the gross plant and equipment accounts to realizable value. Rather, its purpose is to show how much of the cost of the plant and equipment has been allocated as an expense to previous accounting periods.

Uncollectible Accounts Expense appears on the income statement as an operating expense. **Allowance for Uncollectible Accounts** appears on the balance sheet as a contra account that is deducted from accounts receivable. It reduces the accounts receivable to the amount expected to be collected in cash, as follows:

Current assets		
Cash		$ 10,000
Short-term investments		15,000
Accounts receivable	$100,000	
Less allowance for uncollectible accounts	6,000	94,000
Inventory		56,000
Total current assets		$175,000

Accounts receivable may also be shown on the balance sheet as follows:

Accounts receivable (net of allowance for uncollectible accounts of $6,000)	$94,000

Or accounts receivable may be shown at "net," with the amount of the allowance for uncollectible accounts identified in a note to the financial statements. The allowance account is necessary because the specific uncollectible accounts will not be identified until later.

The allowance account often has other titles, such as *Allowance for Doubtful Accounts* and *Allowance for Bad Debts*. Once in a while, the older phrase *Reserve for Bad Debts* will be seen, but in modern practice it should not be used. *Bad Debts Expense* is a title often used for Uncollectible Accounts Expense.

Estimating Uncollectible Accounts Expense

Study Note

The accountant looks at both local and national economic conditions in determining the estimated uncollectible accounts expense.

As noted, expected losses from uncollectible accounts must be estimated. Of course, estimates can vary widely. If management takes an optimistic view and projects a small loss from uncollectible accounts, the resulting net accounts receivable will be larger than if management takes a pessimistic view. The net income will also be larger under the optimistic view because the estimated expense will be smaller. The company's accountant makes an estimate based on past experience and current economic conditions. For example, losses from uncollectible accounts are normally expected to be greater in a recession than during a period of economic growth. The final decision, made by management, on the amount of the expense will depend on objective information, such as

the accountant's analyses, and on certain qualitative factors, such as how investors, bankers, creditors, and others view the performance of the debtor company. Regardless of the qualitative considerations, the estimated losses from uncollectible accounts should be realistic.

Two common methods of estimating uncollectible accounts expense are the percentage of net sales method and the accounts receivable aging method.

Percentage of Net Sales Method

The **percentage of net sales method** asks the question, How much of this year's *net sales* will not be collected? The answer determines the amount of uncollectible accounts expense for the year. For example, the following balances represent Hassel Company's ending figures for 20x9:

SALES		SALES RETURNS AND ALLOWANCES	
	Dec. 31 645,000	Dec. 31 40,000	

SALES DISCOUNTS		ALLOWANCE FOR UNCOLLECTIBLE ACCOUNTS	
Dec. 31 5,000			Dec. 31 3,600

The following are Hassel's actual losses from uncollectible accounts for the past three years:

Year	Net Sales	Losses from Uncollectible Accounts	Percentage
20x6	$ 520,000	$10,200	1.96
20x7	595,000	13,900	2.34
20x8	585,000	9,900	1.69
Total	$1,700,000	$34,000	2.00

Credit sales often constitute most of a company's sales. If a company has substantial cash sales, it should use only its net credit sales in estimating uncollectible accounts.

Hassel's management believes that its uncollectible accounts will continue to average about 2 percent of net sales. The uncollectible accounts expense for the year 20x9 is therefore estimated as follows:

$$.02 \times (\$645,000 - \$40,000 - \$5,000) = .02 \times \$600,000 = \$12,000$$

The following entry would be made to record the estimate:

Study Note

Unlike the direct charge-off method, the percentage of net sales method matches revenues with expenses.

A   = L +   OE
−12,000   −12,000

20x9			
Dec. 31	Uncollectible Accounts Expense	12,000	
	Allowance for Uncollectible Accounts		12,000
	To record uncollectible accounts expense		
	at 2 percent of $600,000 net sales		

After this entry is posted, Allowance for Uncollectible Accounts will have a balance of $15,600:

ALLOWANCE FOR UNCOLLECTIBLE ACCOUNTS		
	Dec. 31	3,600
	Dec. 31 Adj.	12,000
	Dec. 31 Bal.	**15,600**

The balance consists of the $12,000 estimated uncollectible accounts receivable from 20x9 sales and the $3,600 estimated uncollectible accounts receivable from previous years.

Accounts Receivable Aging Method

The **accounts receivable aging method** asks the question, How much of the *ending balance of accounts receivable* will not be collected? With this method, the ending balance of Allowance for Uncollectible Accounts is determined directly through an analysis of accounts receivable. The difference between the amount determined to be uncollectible and the actual balance of Allowance for Uncollectible Accounts is the expense for the period. In theory, this method should produce the same result as the percentage of net sales method, but in practice it rarely does.

The **aging of accounts receivable** is the process of listing each customer's receivable account according to the due date of the account. If the customer's account is past due, there is a possibility that the account will not be paid. And that possibility increases as the account extends further beyond the due date. The aging of accounts receivable helps management evaluate its credit and collection policies and alerts it to possible problems.

Exhibit 2 illustrates the aging of accounts receivable for Myer Company. Each account receivable is classified as being not yet due or as being 1–30 days, 31–60 days, 61–90 days, or over 90 days past due. Based on past experience, the estimated percentage for each category is determined and multiplied by the amount in each category to determine the estimated, or target, balance of Allowance for Uncollectible Accounts. In total, it is estimated that $2,459 of the $44,400 in accounts receivable will not be collected.

Once the target balance for Allowance for Uncollectible Accounts has been found, it is necessary to determine the amount of the adjustment. The amount depends on the current balance of the allowance account. Let us assume two cases for the December 31 balance of Myer Company's Allowance for Uncollectible Accounts: (1) a credit balance of $800 and (2) a debit balance of $800.

In the first case, an adjustment of $1,659 is needed to bring the balance of the allowance account to a $2,459 credit balance:

Targeted balance for allowance for uncollectible accounts	$2,459
Less current credit balance of allowance for uncollectible accounts	800
Uncollectible accounts expense	$1,659

> **Study Note**
>
> When the write-offs in an accounting period exceed the amount of the allowance, a debit balance in the Allowance for Uncollectible Accounts account results.

▼ **EXHIBIT 2**

Analysis of Accounts Receivable by Age

Myer Company
Analysis of Accounts Receivable by Age
December 31, 20x8

Customer	Total	Not Yet Due	1–30 Days Past Due	31–60 Days Past Due	61–90 Days Past Due	Over 90 Days Past Due
A. Arnold	$ 150		$ 150			
M. Benoit	400			$ 400		
J. Connolly	1,000	$ 900	100			
R. Deering	250				$ 250	
Others	42,600	21,000	14,000	3,800	2,200	$1,600
Totals	$44,400	$21,900	$14,250	$4,200	$2,450	$1,600
Estimated percentage uncollectible		1.0	2.0	10.0	30.0	50.0
Allowance for Uncollectible Accounts	$ 2,459	$ 219	$ 285	$ 420	$ 735	$ 800

The uncollectible accounts expense is recorded as follows:

A	= L +	OE	
−1,659		−1,659	

20x8			
Dec. 31	Uncollectible Accounts Expense	1,659	
	Allowance for Uncollectible Accounts		1,659
	To bring the allowance for uncollectible accounts to the level of estimated losses		

The resulting balance of Allowance for Uncollectible Accounts is $2,459:

ALLOWANCE FOR UNCOLLECTIBLE ACCOUNTS		
	Dec. 31	800
	Dec. 31 Adj.	1,659
	Dec. 31 Bal.	**2,459**

In the second case, because Allowance for Uncollectible Accounts has a debit balance of $800, the estimated uncollectible accounts expense for the year will have to be $3,259 to reach the targeted balance of $2,459. This calculation is as follows:

Targeted balance for allowance for uncollectible accounts	$2,459
Plus current debit balance of allowance for uncollectible accounts	800
Uncollectible accounts expense	$3,259

The uncollectible accounts expense is recorded as follows:

A	= L +	OE
−3,259		−3,259

20x8
Dec. 31 Uncollectible Accounts Expense   3,259
            Allowance for Uncollectible Accounts   3,259
                To bring the allowance for
                uncollectible accounts to the
                level of estimated losses

After this entry, Allowance for Uncollectible Accounts has a credit balance of $2,459:

ALLOWANCE FOR UNCOLLECTIBLE ACCOUNTS	
Dec. 31 800	Dec. 31 Adj. 3,259
	Dec. 31 Bal. 2,459

Study Note

Describing the aging method as the balance sheet method emphasizes that the computation is based on ending accounts receivable rather than on net sales for the period.

Comparison of the Two Methods   Both the percentage of net sales method and the accounts receivable aging method estimate the uncollectible accounts expense in accordance with the matching rule, but as shown in Figure 6, they do so in different ways. The percentage of net sales method is an income statement approach. It assumes that a certain proportion of sales will not be collected, and this proportion is the *amount of* Uncollectible Accounts Expense for the accounting period. The accounts receivable aging method is a balance sheet approach. It assumes that a certain proportion of accounts receivable outstanding will not be collected. This proportion is the *targeted balance of the* Allowance for Uncollectible Accounts *account*. The expense for the accounting period is

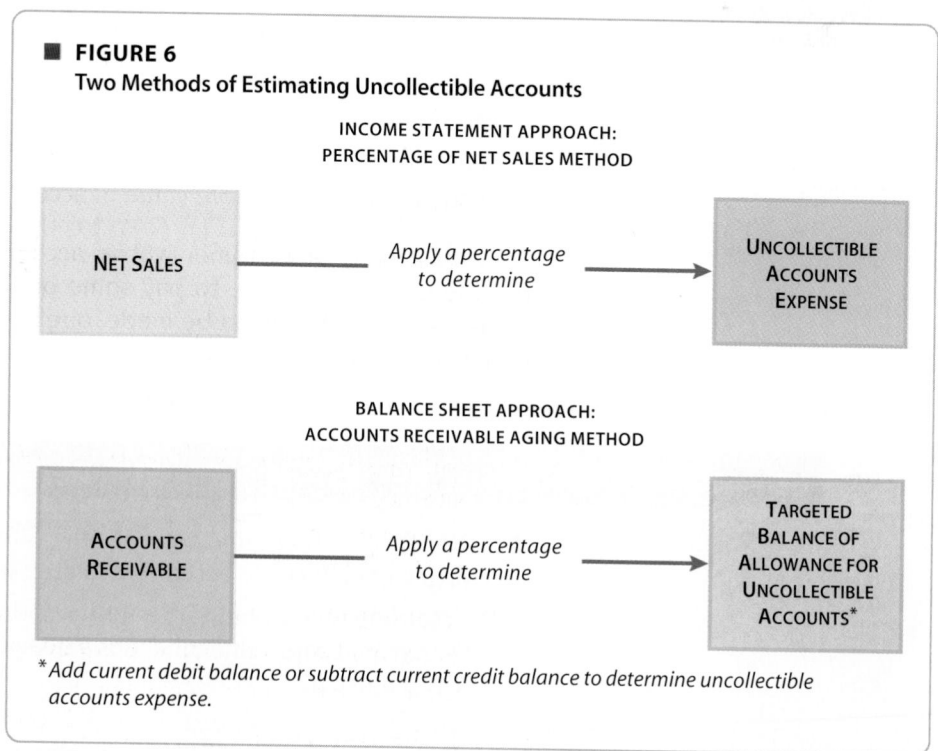

■ **FIGURE 6**
Two Methods of Estimating Uncollectible Accounts

INCOME STATEMENT APPROACH:
PERCENTAGE OF NET SALES METHOD

NET SALES → *Apply a percentage to determine* → UNCOLLECTIBLE ACCOUNTS EXPENSE

BALANCE SHEET APPROACH:
ACCOUNTS RECEIVABLE AGING METHOD

ACCOUNTS RECEIVABLE → *Apply a percentage to determine* → TARGETED BALANCE OF ALLOWANCE FOR UNCOLLECTIBLE ACCOUNTS*

*Add current debit balance or subtract current credit balance to determine uncollectible accounts expense.

the difference between the targeted balance and the current balance of the allowance account.

Writing Off Uncollectible Accounts

Regardless of the method used to estimate uncollectible accounts, the total of accounts receivable written off in an accounting period will rarely equal the estimated uncollectible amount. The allowance account will show a credit balance when the total of accounts written off is less than the estimated uncollectible amount. It will show a debit balance when the total of accounts written off is greater than the estimated uncollectible amount.

When it becomes clear that a specific account receivable will not be collected, the amount should be written off to Allowance for Uncollectible Accounts. Remember that the uncollectible amount was already accounted for as an expense when the allowance was established. For example, assume that on January 15, 20x9, R. Deering, who owes Myer Company $250, is declared bankrupt by a federal court. The entry to *write off* this account is as follows:

A = L + OE
+250
−250

20x9			
Jan. 15	Allowance for Uncollectible Accounts	250	
	Accounts Receivable		250
	To write off receivable		
	from R. Deering as uncollectible		
	because of his bankruptcy		

Although the write-off removes the uncollectible amount from Accounts Receivable, it does not affect the estimated net realizable value of accounts receivable. It simply reduces R. Deering's account to zero and reduces Allowance for Uncollectible Accounts by $250, as shown below:

> **Study Note**
>
> When writing off an individual account, debit Allowance for Uncollectible Accounts, not Uncollectible Accounts Expense.

	Balances Before Write-off	Balances After Write-off
Accounts receivable	$44,400	$44,150
Less allowance for uncollectible accounts	2,459	2,209
Estimated net realizable value of accounts receivable	$41,941	$41,941

Occasionally, a customer whose account has been written off as uncollectible will later be able to pay some or all of the amount owed. When that happens, two entries must be made: one to reverse the earlier write-off (which is now incorrect) and another to show the collection of the account.

S T O P • R E V I E W • A P P L Y

3-1. What accounting principle does the direct charge-off method of recognizing uncollectible accounts violate? Why?

3-2. According to generally accepted accounting principles, at what point in the cycle of sales and collections does a loss on an uncollectible account occur?

3-3. What is the effect on net income when management takes an optimistic rather than a pessimistic view of estimated uncollectible accounts?

3-4. Why is the percentage of net sales method of estimating uncollectible accounts called an income statement approach, and why is the accounts receivable aging method called a balance sheet approach?

3-5. What is the reasoning behind the percentage of net sales method and the accounts receivable aging method?

3-6. Suppose that after adjusting and closing accounts at the end of a fiscal year, Accounts Receivable is $176,000 and Allowance for Uncollectible Accounts is $14,500. (a) What is the collectible value of Accounts Receivable? (b) If the $450 account of a bankrupt customer is written off in the first month of the new year, what will the collectible value of Accounts Receivable be?

Aging and Net Sales Methods Contrasted A & A Musical Instrument, Inc., sells its merchandise on credit. In the company's last fiscal year, which ended July 31, it had net sales of $3,500,000. At the end of the fiscal year, it had Accounts Receivable of $900,000 and a credit balance in Allowance for Uncollectible Accounts of $5,600. In the past, the company has been unable to collect on approximately 1 percent of its net sales. An aging analysis of accounts receivable has indicated that $40,000 of current receivables are uncollectible.

1. Calculate the amount of uncollectible accounts expense, and use T accounts to determine the resulting balance of Allowance for Uncollectible Accounts under the percentage of net sales method and the accounts receivable aging method.

2. How would your answers change if Allowance for Uncollectible Accounts had a debit balance of $5,600 instead of a credit balance?

SOLUTION

1. **Percentage of net sales method:**

ALLOWANCE FOR UNCOLLECTIBLE ACCOUNTS

	July 31		5,600
	31	UA Exp.	35,000*
	July 31	Bal.	40,600

*Uncollectible Accounts Expense = $3,500,000 × .01

Aging Method:

ALLOWANCE FOR UNCOLLECTIBLE ACCOUNTS

	July 31		5,600
	31	UA Exp.	34,400*
	July 31	Bal.	40,000

*Uncollectible Accounts Expense = $40,000 − $5,600

2. Under the percentage of net sales method, the amount of the expense is the same in 1 and 2 but the ending balance will be $29,400 ($35,000 − $5,600). Under the aging method, the ending balance is the same, but the amount of the expense will be $45,600 ($40,000 + $5,600).

Notes Receivable

> **LO4**   Define *promissory note,* and make common calculations for promissory notes receivable.

A **promissory note** is an unconditional promise to pay a definite sum of money on demand or at a future date. The person or company that signs the note and thereby promises to pay is the *maker* of the note. The entity to whom payment is to be made is the *payee.*

The promissory note shown in Figure 7 is an unconditional promise by the maker, Samuel Mason, to pay a definite sum—or principal ($1,000)—to the payee, Cook County Bank & Trust, on August 18, 20x8. As you can see, this promissory note is dated May 20, 20x8, and bears an interest rate of 8 percent.

A payee includes all the promissory notes it holds that are due in less than one year in **notes receivable** in the current assets section of its balance sheet. A maker includes them in **notes payable** in the current liabilities section of its balance sheet.

The nature of a company's business generally determines how frequently it receives promissory notes from customers. Firms that sell durable goods of high value, such as farm machinery and automobiles, often accept promissory notes. Among the advantages of these notes are that they produce interest income and represent a stronger legal claim against a debtor than do accounts receivable. In addition, selling—or discounting—promissory notes to banks is a common financing method. Almost all companies occasionally accept promissory notes, and many companies obtain them in settlement of past-due accounts.

Maturity Date

The **maturity date** is the date on which a promissory note must be paid. This date must be stated on the note or be determinable from the facts stated on

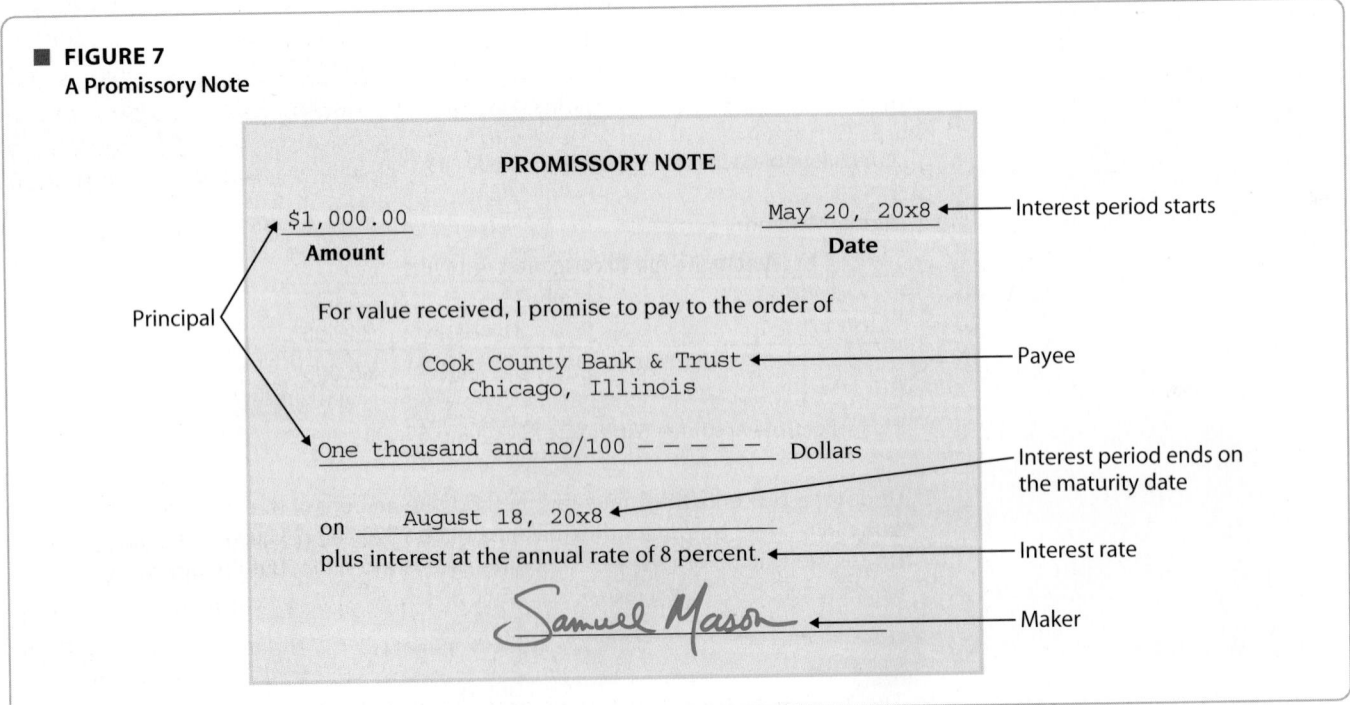

■ FIGURE 7
A Promissory Note

PROMISSORY NOTE

$1,000.00   May 20, 20x8 ← Interest period starts
Amount   **Date**

Principal

For value received, I promise to pay to the order of

    Cook County Bank & Trust ← Payee
       Chicago, Illinois

One thousand and no/100 – – – – – Dollars ← Interest period ends on the maturity date

on ____August 18, 20x8____ ← Interest period ends on the maturity date

plus interest at the annual rate of 8 percent. ← Interest rate

Samuel Mason ← Maker

Automobile manufacturers like Toyota, whose assembly line is pictured here, often accept promissory notes, which are unconditional promises to pay a definite sum of money on demand or at a future date. These notes produce interest income and represent a stronger legal claim against a debtor than do accounts receivable. In addition, firms commonly raise money by selling—or discounting—promissory notes to banks.

the note. The following are among the most common statements of maturity date:

1. A specific date, such as "November 14, 20xx"

2. A specific number of months after the date of the note, such as "three months after November 14, 20xx"

3. A specific number of days after the date of the note, such as "60 days after November 14, 20xx"

The maturity date is obvious when a specific date is stated. And when the maturity date is a number of months from the date of the note, one simply uses the same day in the appropriate future month. For example, a note dated January 20 that is due in two months would be due on March 20.

When the maturity date is a specific number of days from the date of the note, however, the exact maturity date must be determined. In computing the maturity date, it is important to exclude the date of the note. For example, a note dated May 20 and due in 90 days would be due on August 18, determined as follows:

Days remaining in May (31 − 20)	11
Days in June	30
Days in July	31
Days in August	18
Total days	90

Duration of a Note

The **duration of a note** is the time between a promissory note's issue date and its maturity date. Knowing the exact number of days in the duration of a note is important because interest is calculated on that basis. Identifying the duration is easy when the maturity date is stated as a specific number of days from the date of the note because the two numbers are the same. However, when the maturity date is stated as a specific date, the exact number of days must be

Another way to compute the duration of notes is to begin with the interest period, as in this example:

90	Interest period
−11	days remaining in May (31 − 20)
79	
−30	days in June
49	
−31	days in July
18	due date in August

determined. Assume that a note issued on May 10 matures on August 10. The duration of the note is 92 days:

Days remaining in May (31 − 10)	21
Days in June	30
Days in July	31
Days in August	10
Total days	92

Interest and Interest Rate

Interest is the cost of borrowing money or the return on lending money, depending on whether one is the borrower or the lender. The amount of interest is based on three factors: the principal (the amount of money borrowed or lent), the rate of interest, and the loan's length of time. The formula used in computing interest is as follows:

$$\text{Principal} \times \text{Rate of Interest} \times \text{Time} = \text{Interest}$$

Interest rates are usually stated on an annual basis. For example, the interest on a one-year, 8 percent, $1,000 note would be $80 ($1,000 × 8/100 × 1 = $80). If the term, or time period, of the note is three months instead of a year, the interest charge would be $20 ($1,000 × 8/100 × 3/12 = $20).

When the term of a note is expressed in days, the exact number of days must be used in computing the interest. Thus, if the term of the note described above was 45 days, the interest would be $10, computed as follows: $1,000 × 8/100 × 45/365 = $9.86.

Maturity Value

The **maturity value** is the total proceeds of a promissory note—face value plus interest—at the maturity date. The maturity value of a 90-day, 8 percent, $1,000 note is computed as follows:

$$
\begin{aligned}
\text{Maturity Value} &= \text{Principal} + \text{Interest} \\
&= \$1{,}000 + (\$1{,}000 \times 8/100 \times 90/365) \\
&= \$1{,}000 + \$19.73 \\
&= \$1{,}019.73
\end{aligned}
$$

There are also so-called non-interest-bearing notes. The maturity value is the face value, or principal amount. In this case, the principal includes an implied interest cost.

Accrued Interest

A promissory note received in one accounting period may not be due until a later period. The interest on a note accrues by a small amount each day of the note's duration. As we described in an earlier chapter, the matching rule requires that the accrued interest be apportioned to the periods in which it belongs. For example, assume that the $1,000, 90-day, 8 percent note discussed above was received on August 31 and that the fiscal year ended on September 30. In this case, 30 days interest, or $6.58 ($1,000 × 8/100 × 30/365 = $6.58), would be earned in the fiscal year that ends on September 30. An adjusting entry would be made to record the interest receivable as an asset and the interest income as revenue. The remainder of the interest income, $13.15

($1,000 $\times$ 8/100 $\times$ 60/365), would be recorded as income, and the interest receivable ($6.58) would be shown as received when the note is paid. Note that all the cash for the interest is received when the note is paid, but the interest income is apportioned to two fiscal years.

Dishonored Note

When the maker of a note does not pay the note at maturity, it is said to be a **dishonored note**. The holder, or payee, of a dishonored note should make an entry to transfer the total amount due (including interest income) from Notes Receivable to an account receivable from the debtor. Two objectives are accomplished by transferring a dishonored note into an Accounts Receivable account. First, it leaves only notes that have not matured and are presumably negotiable and collectible in the Notes Receivable account. Second, it establishes a record in the borrower's accounts receivable account that the customer has dishonored a note receivable. Such information may be helpful in deciding whether to extend credit to the customer in the future.

S T O P • R E V I E W • A P P L Y

4-1. What is a promissory note?

4-2. Who is the maker of a promissory note? Who is the payee?

4-3. What is the difference between interest and interest rate?

4-4. What are the maturity dates of the following notes: (a) a three-month note that is dated August 16, (b) a 90-day note that is dated August 16, and (c) a 60-day note that is dated March 25?

Promissory Note Calculations Assume that on December 1, 20x8, a company receives a 90-day, 8 percent, $5,000 note and that the company prepares financial statements monthly.

1. What is the maturity date of the note?

2. How much interest will be earned on the note if it is paid when due?

3. What is the maturity value of the note?

4. If the company's fiscal year ends on December 31, describe the adjusting entry that would be made, including the amount.

5. How much interest will be earned on this note in 20x9?

SOLUTION

1. Maturity date is March 1, 20x9, determined as follows:

Days remaining in December (31 − 1)	30
Days in January	31
Days in February	28
Days in March	1
Total days	90

2. Interest: $5,000 $\times$ 8/100 $\times$ 90/365 = $98.63

3. Maturity value: $5,000 + $98.63 = $5,098.63

4. An adjusting entry to accrue 30 days of interest income in the amount of $32.88 ($5,000 $\times$ 8/100 $\times$ 30/365) would be needed.

5. Interest earned in 20x9: $65.75 ($98.63 − $32.88)

NIKE, INC.

In this chapter's Decision Point, we noted that **Nike** must give the retailers that buy its products time to pay for their purchases, but at the same time, Nike must have enough cash on hand to pay its suppliers. To plan the company's cash flows, Nike's management must address the following questions:

- **How can the company control its cash needs?**
- **How can the company evaluate credit policies and the level of its receivables?**
- **How should the company estimate the value of its receivables?**

As you saw in Figure 1, companies like Nike go through seasonal cycles that affect their cash flows. At times, Nike may have excess cash available that it can invest in a way that earns a return but still permits ready access to cash. At other times, it may have to borrow funds. To ensure that it can borrow funds when it needs to, Nike maintains good relations with its banks.

To evaluate the company's credit policies and the level of its accounts receivable, management can compare the current year's receivable turnover and days' sales uncollected with those ratios in previous years. Using data from Nike's Financial Highlights, we can compute these ratios for 2004 and 2005 as follows (dollars are in millions):

		2005	2004
Receivable Turnover:	$\dfrac{\text{Net Sales}}{\text{Average Accounts Receivable}}$	$\dfrac{\$13,739.7}{(\$2,262.1 + \$2,120.2) \div 2}$	$\dfrac{\$12,253.1}{(\$2,120.2 + \$2,083.9) \div 2}$
		$= \dfrac{\$13,739.7}{\$2,191.2}$	$= \dfrac{\$12,253.1}{\$2,102.1}$
		$= 6.3$ times	$= 5.8$ times
Days' Sales Uncollected:	$\dfrac{\text{Number of Days in a Year}}{\text{Receivable Turnover}}$	$\dfrac{365 \text{ days}}{6.3 \text{ times}}$	$\dfrac{365 \text{ days}}{5.8 \text{ times}}$
		$= 57.9$ days	$= 62.9$ days

Thus, in 2005, Nike achieved a small improvement in its receivable turnover. It also reduced the number of days it takes to collect accounts receivable by 5.0 days.

A note in Nike's report to the SEC provides insight into management's ability to estimate losses from uncollectible accounts (amounts are in millions):

	2005	2004	2003	Totals
Uncollectible Accounts Expense	$33.5	$36.4	$25.8	$95.7
Write-offs net of recoveries	50.2	23.1	25.5	98.8
Difference	$(16.7)	$13.3	$ .3	$(3.1)

From this analysis, you can see the difficulty management has in estimating uncollectible accounts. For example, it overestimated the amount of loss from customers who did not pay in 2004 but underestimated the loss in 2005. Only in 2003 was the estimate close.

CHAPTER REVIEW

REVIEW of Learning Objectives

LO1 Identify and explain the management and ethical issues related to cash and receivables.

The management of cash and receivables is critical to maintaining adequate liquidity. In dealing with these assets, management must (1) consider the need for short-term investing and borrowing as the business's balance of cash fluctuates during seasonal cycles, (2) establish credit policies that balance the need for sales with the ability to collect, (3) evaluate the level of receivables using receivable turnover and days' sales uncollected, (4) assess the need to increase cash flows through the financing of receivables, and (5) understand the importance of ethics in estimating credit losses.

LO2 Define *cash equivalents*, and explain methods of controlling cash, including bank reconciliations.

Cash equivalents are investments that have a term of 90 days or less. Methods of controlling cash include imprest systems; banking services, including electronic funds transfer; and bank reconciliations. A bank reconciliation accounts for the difference between the balance on a company's bank statement and the balance in its Cash account. It involves adjusting for outstanding checks, deposits in transit, service charges, NSF checks, miscellaneous debits and credits, and interest income.

LO3 Apply the allowance method of accounting for uncollectible accounts.

Because of the time lag between credit sales and the time accounts are judged uncollectible, the allowance method is used to match the amount of uncollectible accounts against revenues in any given period. Uncollectible accounts expense is estimated by using either the percentage of net sales method or the accounts receivable aging method. When the first method is used, bad debts are judged to be a certain percentage of sales during the period. When the second method is used, certain percentages are applied to groups of accounts receivable that have been arranged by due dates.

Allowance for Uncollectible Accounts is a contra-asset account to Accounts Receivable. The estimate of uncollectible accounts is debited to Uncollectible Accounts Expense and credited to the allowance account. When an individual account is determined to be uncollectible, it is removed from Accounts Receivable by debiting the allowance account and crediting Accounts Receivable. If the written-off account is later collected, the earlier entry is reversed and the collection is recorded in the normal way.

LO4 Define *promissory note* and make common calculations for promissory notes receivable.

A promissory note is an unconditional promise to pay a definite sum of money on demand or at a future date. Companies that sell durable goods of high value, such as farm machinery and automobiles, often accept promissory notes. Selling these notes to banks is a common financing method. In accounting for promissory notes, it is important to know how to calculate the maturity date, duration of a note, interest and interest rate, and maturity value.

REVIEW of Concepts and Terminology

The following concepts and terms were introduced in this chapter:

Accounts receivable: Short-term financial assets that arise from sales on credit at the wholesale or retail level. **(LO1)**

Accounts receivable aging method: A method of estimating uncollectible accounts based on the assumption that a predictable proportion of each dollar of accounts receivable outstanding will not be collected. **(LO3)**

Aging of accounts receivable: The process of listing each customer's receivable account according to the due date of the account. **(LO3)**

Allowance for Uncollectible Accounts: A contra-asset account that reduces accounts receivable to the amount expected to be collected in cash. Also called *Allowance for Doubtful Accounts* and *Allowance for Bad Debts.* **(LO3)**

Allowance method: A method of accounting for uncollectible accounts by expensing estimated uncollectible accounts in the period in which the related sales take place. **(LO3)**

Bank reconciliation: The process of accounting for the difference between the balance appearing on a company's bank statement and the balance in its Cash account. **(LO2)**

Cash: Coins and currency on hand, checks and money orders from customers, and deposits in checking and savings accounts. **(LO1)**

Cash equivalents: Short-term investments that will revert to cash in 90 days or less from the time they are purchased. **(LO2)**

Compensating balance: A minimum amount that a bank requires a company to keep in its bank account as part of a credit-granting arrangement. **(LO1)**

Contingent liability: A potential liability that can develop into a real liability if a particular event occurs. **(LO1)**

Direct charge-off method: A method of accounting for uncollectible accounts by directly debiting an expense account when bad debts are discovered; it violates the matching rule but is required for computing federal income tax. **(LO3)**

Discounting: A method of selling notes receivable to a bank in which the bank derives its profit by deducting the interest from the maturity value of the note. **(LO1)**

Dishonored note: A promissory note that the maker cannot or will not pay at the maturity date. **(LO4)**

Duration of a note: The time between a promissory note's issue date and its maturity date. **(LO4)**

Electronic funds transfer (EFT): The transfer of funds from one bank to another through electronic communication. **(LO2)**

Factor: An entity that buys accounts receivable. **(LO1)**

Factoring: The sale or transfer of accounts receivable. **(LO1)**

Imprest system: A system for controlling small cash disbursements by establishing a fund at a fixed amount and periodically reimbursing the fund by the amount necessary to restore its original cash balance. **(LO2)**

Installment accounts receivable: Accounts receivable that are payable in a series of time payments. **(LO1)**

Interest: The cost of borrowing money or the return on lending money, depending on whether one is the borrower or the lender. **(LO4)**

Maturity date: The date on which a promissory note must be paid. **(LO4)**

Maturity value: The total proceeds of a promissory note—face value plus interest—at the maturity date. **(LO4)**

Notes payable: Collective term for promissory notes owed by the entity (maker) who promises payment to other entities. **(LO4)**

Notes receivable: Collective term for promissory notes held by the entity to whom payment is promised (payee). **(LO4)**

Percentage of net sales method: A method of estimating uncollectible accounts based on the assumption that a predictable proportion of each dollar of sales will not be collected. **(LO3)**

Promissory note: An unconditional promise to pay a definite sum of money on demand or at a future date. **(LO4)**

Securitization: The grouping of receivables into batches for sale at a discount to companies and investors. **(LO1)**

Short-term financial assets: Assets that arise from cash transactions, the investment of cash, and the extension of credit. **(LO1)**

Trade credit: Credit granted to customers by wholesalers or retailers. **(LO1)**

Uncollectible accounts: Accounts receivable owed by customers who cannot or will not pay. Also called *bad debts.* **(LO1)**

Key Ratios

Days' sales uncollected: A ratio that shows on average how long it takes to collect accounts receivable; 365 Days ÷ Receivable Turnover. **(LO1)**

Receivable turnover: A ratio for measuring the average number of times receivables are turned into cash during an accounting period; Net Sales ÷ Average Accounts Receivable. **(LO1)**

REVIEW Problem

LO1, LO3 **Estimating Uncollectible Accounts and Receivables Analysis**

 Farm Implement Corporation sells merchandise on credit and also accepts notes as payment. During the year ended June 30, the company had net sales of $1,200,000. At the end of the year, it had Accounts Receivable of $400,000 and a debit balance in Allowance for Uncollectible Accounts of $2,100. In the past, approximately 1.5 percent of net sales has been uncollectible. Also, an aging analysis of accounts receivable reveals that $17,000 in accounts receivable appears to be uncollectible.

Required

1. Compute Uncollectible Accounts Expense, and determine the ending balance of Allowance for Uncollectible Accounts and Accounts Receivable, Net, under (a) the percentage of net sales method and (b) the accounts receivable aging method.
2. Compute the receivable turnover and days' sales uncollected using the data from the accounts receivable aging method in requirement 1 and assuming that the prior year's net accounts receivable were $353,000.

Answer to Review Problem

1. Uncollectible Accounts Expense and ending account balances
    a. Percentage of net sales method:
       Uncollectible Accounts Expense = 1.5 percent × $1,200,000 = $18,000
       Allowance for Uncollectible Accounts = $18,000 − $2,100 = $15,900
       Accounts Receivable, Net = $400,000 − $15,900 = $384,100
    b. Accounts receivable aging method:
       Uncollectible Accounts Expense = $2,100 + $17,000 = $19,100
       Allowance for Uncollectible Accounts = $17,000
       Accounts Receivable, Net = $400,000 − $17,000 = $383,000
2. Receivable turnover and days' sales uncollected

$$\text{Receivable Turnover} = \frac{\$1,200,000}{(\$383,000 + \$353,000) \div 2} = 3.3 \text{ times}$$

$$\text{Days' Sales Uncollected} = \frac{365 \text{ days}}{3.3 \text{ times}} = 110.6 \text{ days}$$

CHAPTER ASSIGNMENTS

BUILDING Your Basic Knowledge and Skills

Short Exercises

LO1 **Management Issues**

SE 1. Indicate whether each of the following actions is related to (a) managing cash needs, (b) setting credit policies, (c) financing receivables, or (d) ethically reporting receivables:

1. Selling accounts receivable to a factor
2. Borrowing funds for short-term needs during slow periods
3. Conducting thorough checks of new customers' ability to pay
4. Making every effort to reflect possible future losses accurately

LO1   **Short-Term Liquidity Ratios**

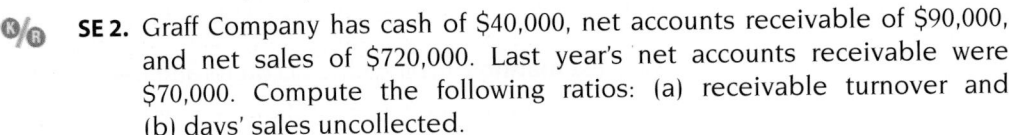

SE 2. Graff Company has cash of $40,000, net accounts receivable of $90,000, and net sales of $720,000. Last year's net accounts receivable were $70,000. Compute the following ratios: (a) receivable turnover and (b) days' sales uncollected.

LO2   **Cash and Cash Equivalents**

SE 3. Compute the amount of cash and cash equivalents on Balsas Company's balance sheet if, on the balance sheet date, it has currency and coins on hand of $250, deposits in checking accounts of $1,500, U.S. Treasury bills due in 80 days of $15,000, and U.S. Treasury bonds due in 200 days of $25,000.

LO2   **Bank Reconciliation**

SE 4. Prepare a bank reconciliation from the following information:

a. Balance per bank statement as of June 30, $4,862.77
b. Balance per books as of June 30, $2,479.48
c. Deposits in transit, $654.24
d. Outstanding checks, $3,028.89
e. Interest on average balance, $8.64

LO3   **Percentage of Net Sales Method**

SE 5. At the end of October, Murphy Company's management estimates the uncollectible accounts expense to be 1 percent of net sales of $1,385,000. Prepare the entry to record the uncollectible accounts expense, assuming the Allowance for Uncollectible Accounts has a debit balance of $7,000.

LO3   **Accounts Receivable Aging Method**

SE 6. An aging analysis on June 30 of the accounts receivable of Sung Corporation indicates that uncollectible accounts amount to $86,000. Prepare the entry to record uncollectible accounts expense under each of the following independent assumptions:

a. Allowance for Uncollectible Accounts has a credit balance of $18,000 before adjustment.
b. Allowance for Uncollectible Accounts has a debit balance of $14,000 before adjustment.

LO3   **Write-off of Accounts Receivable**

SE 7. Koude Corporation, which uses the allowance method, has accounts receivable of $25,400 and an allowance for uncollectible accounts of $4,900. An account receivable from Eva Stursa of $2,200 is deemed to be uncollectible and is written off. What is the amount of net accounts receivable before and after the write-off?

LO4   **Notes Receivable Calculations**

SE 8. On August 25, Champion Company received a 90-day, 9 percent note in settlement of an account receivable in the amount of $20,000. Determine the maturity date, amount of interest on the note, and maturity value.

Exercises

LO1, LO2   **Discussion Questions**

E 1. Develop a brief answer to each of the following questions:

1. Name some businesses whose needs for cash fluctuate during the year. Name some whose needs for cash are relatively stable over the year.

2. Why is it advantageous for a company to finance its receivables?

3. To increase its sales, a company decides to increase its credit terms from 15 to 30 days. What effect will this change in policy have on receivable turnover and days' sales uncollected?

4. How might the receivable turnover and days' sales uncollected reveal that management is consistently underestimating the amount of losses from uncollectible accounts? Is this action ethical?

LO3, LO4   Discussion Questions

E 2. Develop a brief answer to each of the following questions:

1. What accounting rule is violated by the direct charge-off method of recognizing uncollectible accounts? Why?

2. In what ways is Allowance for Uncollectible Accounts similar to Accumulated Depreciation? In what ways is it different?

3. Under what circumstances would an accrual of interest income on an interest-bearing note receivable not be required at the end of an accounting period?

LO1   Management Issues

E 3. Indicate whether each of the following actions is primarily related to (a) managing cash needs, (b) setting credit policies, (c) financing receivables, or (d) ethically reporting accounts receivable:

1. Buying a U.S. Treasury bill with cash that is not needed for a few months
2. Comparing receivable turnovers for two years
3. Setting a policy that allows customers to buy on credit
4. Selling notes receivable to a financing company
5. Making careful estimates of losses from uncollectible accounts
6. Borrowing funds for short-term needs in a period when sales are low
7. Changing the terms for credit sales in an effort to reduce the days' sales uncollected
8. Revising estimated credit losses in a timely manner when conditions change
9. Establishing a department whose responsibility is to approve customers' credit

LO1   Short-Term Liquidity Ratios

E 4. Using the following data from Kalel Corporation's financial statements, compute the receivable turnover and the days' sales uncollected:

Current assets	
Cash	$ 35,000
Short-term investments	85,000
Notes receivable	120,000
Accounts receivable, net	100,000
Inventory	250,000
Prepaid assets	25,000
Total current assets	$615,000
Current liabilities	
Notes payable	$150,000
Accounts payable	75,000
Accrued liabilities	10,000
Total current liabilities	$235,000
Net sales	$800,000
Last period's accounts receivable, net	$ 90,000

LO2 Cash and Cash Equivalents

E 5. At year end, Sarong Company had currency and coins in cash registers of $5,600, money orders from customers of $10,000, deposits in checking accounts of $64,000, U.S. Treasury bills due in 80 days of $180,000, certificates of deposit at the bank that mature in six months of $200,000, and U.S. Treasury bonds due in one year of $100,000. Calculate the amount of cash and cash equivalents that will be shown on the company's year-end balance sheet.

LO2 Bank Reconciliation

E 6. Prepare a bank reconciliation from the following information:

a. Balance per bank statement as of May 31, $16,655.44
b. Balance per books as of May 31, $12,091.94
c. Deposits in transit, $2,234.81
d. Outstanding checks, $6,808.16
e. Bank service charge, $9.85

LO3 Percentage of Net Sales Method

E 7. At the end of the year, Jung Enterprises estimates the uncollectible accounts expense to be .7 percent of net sales of $15,150,000. The current credit balance of Allowance for Uncollectible Accounts is $25,800. Prepare the entry to record the uncollectible accounts expense. What is the balance of Allowance for Uncollectible Accounts after this adjustment?

LO3 Accounts Receivable Aging Method

E 8. The Accounts Receivable account of Helmond Company shows a debit balance of $104,000 at the end of the year. An aging analysis of the individual accounts indicates estimated uncollectible accounts to be $6,700.

Prepare the entry to record the uncollectible accounts expense under each of the following independent assumptions: (a) Allowance for Uncollectible Accounts has a credit balance of $800 before adjustment, and (b) Allowance for Uncollectible Accounts has a debit balance of $800 before adjustment. What is the balance of Allowance for Uncollectible Accounts after each of these adjustments?

LO3 Aging Method and Net Sales Method Contrasted

E 9. At the beginning of 20xx, the balances for Accounts Receivable and Allowance for Uncollectible Accounts were $215,000 and $15,700 (credit), respectively. During the year, credit sales were $1,600,000, and collections on account were $1,475,000. In addition, $17,500 in uncollectible accounts was written off.

Using T accounts, determine the year-end balances of Accounts Receivable and Allowance for Uncollectible Accounts. Then prepare the year-end adjusting entry to record the uncollectible accounts expense under each of the following conditions. Also show the year-end balance sheet presentation of accounts receivable and allowance for uncollectible accounts.

a. Management estimates the percentage of uncollectible credit sales to be 1.2 percent of total credit sales.
b. Based on an aging of accounts receivable, management estimates the end-of-year uncollectible accounts receivable to be $19,350.

Post the results of each of the entries to the T account for Allowance for Uncollectible Accounts.

LO3 **Aging Method and Net Sales Method Contrasted**

E 10. During 20x7, Luna Supply Company had net sales of $5,700,000. Most of the sales were on credit. At the end of 20x7, the balance of Accounts Receivable was $700,000, and Allowance for Uncollectible Accounts had a debit balance of $24,000. Luna Supply Company's management uses two methods of estimating uncollectible accounts expense: the percentage of net sales method and the accounts receivable aging method. The percentage of uncollectible sales is 1.5 percent of net sales, and based on an aging of accounts receivable, the end-of-year uncollectible accounts total $70,000.

Prepare the end-of-year adjusting entry to record the uncollectible accounts expense under each method. What will the balance of Allowance for Uncollectible Accounts be after each adjustment? Why are the results different? Which method is likely to be more reliable? Why?

LO3 **Aging Method and Net Sales Method Contrasted**

E 11. The Rosewood Parts Company sells merchandise on credit. During the fiscal year ended July 31, the company had net sales of $2,300,000. At the end of the year, it had Accounts Receivable of $600,000 and a debit balance in Allowance for Uncollectible Accounts of $3,400. In the past, approximately 1.4 percent of net sales have proved to be uncollectible. Also, an aging analysis of accounts receivable reveals that $30,000 of the receivables appears to be uncollectible.

Prepare entries in journal form to record uncollectible accounts expense using (a) the percentage of net sales method and (b) the accounts receivable aging method. What is the resulting balance of Allowance for Uncollectible Accounts under each method? How would your answers under each method change if Allowance for Uncollectible Accounts had a credit balance of $3,400 instead of a debit balance? Why do the methods result in different balances?

LO3 **Write-off of Accounts Receivable**

E 12. Calvin Company, which uses the allowance method, has Accounts Receivable of $32,500 and an allowance for uncollectible accounts of $3,200 (credit). The company sold merchandise to Mariko Kimura for $3,600 and later received $1,200 from Kimura. The rest of the amount due from Kimura had to be written off as uncollectible. Using T accounts, show the beginning balances and the effects of the Kimura transactions on Accounts Receivable and Allowance for Uncollectible Accounts. What is the amount of net accounts receivable before and after the write-off?

LO4 **Interest Computations**

E 13. Determine the interest on the following notes:

a. $38,760 at 10 percent for 90 days
b. $27,200 at 12 percent for 60 days
c. $30,600 at 9 percent for 30 days
d. $51,000 at 15 percent for 120 days
e. $18,360 at 6 percent for 60 days

LO4 **Notes Receivable Calculations**

E 14. Determine the maturity date, interest at maturity, and maturity value for a 90-day, 10 percent, $18,000 note from Baptiste Corporation dated February 15.

LO4 **Notes Receivable Calculations**

E 15. Determine the maturity date, interest in 2007 and 2008, and maturity value for a 90-day, 12 percent, $15,000 note from a customer dated December 1, 20x7, assuming a December 31 year-end.

LO4 **Notes Receivable Calculations**

E 16. Determine the maturity date, interest at maturity, and maturity value for each of the following notes:

a. A 60-day, 10 percent, $2,400 note dated January 5 received from J. Gibbs for granting a time extension on a past-due account.

b. A 60-day, 12 percent, $1,500 note dated March 9 received from L. Varela for granting a time extension on a past-due account.

Problems

LO2 **Bank Reconciliation**

P 1. The following information is available for Rosemary Corporation as of April 30, 20xx:

a. Cash on the books as of April 30 amounted to $114,175.28. Cash on the bank statement for the same date was $141,717.08.

b. A deposit of $14,249.84, representing cash receipts of April 30, did not appear on the bank statement.

c. Outstanding checks totaled $7,293.64.

d. A check for $2,420.00 returned with the statement was recorded as $2,024.00. The check was for advertising.

e. The bank service charge for April amounted to $26.00.

f. The bank collected $36,400.00 for Rosemary Corporation on a note. The face value of the note was $36,000.00

g. An NSF check for $1,140.00 from a customer, Chad Altier, was returned with the statement.

h. The bank mistakenly deducted a check for $800.00 that was drawn by Fox Corporation.

i. The bank reported a credit of $460.00 for interest on the average balance.

Required

1. Prepare a bank reconciliation for Rosemary Corporation as of April 30, 20xx.

2. Prepare the necessary entries in journal form from the reconciliation.

3. State the amount of cash that should appear on Rosemary Corporation's balance sheet as of April 30.

4. User Insight: Why is a bank reconciliation a necessary internal control?

LO1, LO3 **Methods of Estimating Uncollectible Accounts and Receivables Analysis**

P 2. On December 31 of last year, the balance sheet of Vaslor Company had Accounts Receivable of $298,000 and a credit balance in Allowance for Uncollectible Accounts of $20,300. During the current year, Vaslor Company's records included the following selected activities: (a) sales on account, $1,195,000; (b) sales returns and allowances, $73,000; (c) collections from customers, $1,150,000; and (d) accounts written off as worthless, $16,000. In the past, 1.6 percent of Vaslor Company's net sales have been uncollectible.

Required

1. Prepare T accounts for Accounts Receivable and Allowance for Uncollectible Accounts. Enter the beginning balances, and show the effects on

these accounts of the items listed above, summarizing the year's activity. Determine the ending balance of each account.

2. Compute Uncollectible Accounts Expense and determine the ending balance of Allowance for Uncollectible Accounts under (a) the percentage of net sales method and (b) the accounts receivable aging method. Assume that an aging of the accounts receivable shows that $20,000 may be uncollectible.

3. Compute the receivable turnover and days' sales uncollected, using the data from the accounts receivable aging method in requirement **2**.

4. **User Insight:** How do you explain that the two methods used in requirement **2** result in different amounts for Uncollectible Accounts Expense? What rationale underlies each method?

LO3 **Accounts Receivable Aging Method**

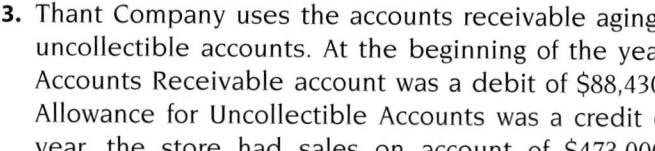

P 3. Thant Company uses the accounts receivable aging method to estimate uncollectible accounts. At the beginning of the year, the balance of the Accounts Receivable account was a debit of $88,430, and the balance of Allowance for Uncollectible Accounts was a credit of $7,200. During the year, the store had sales on account of $473,000, sales returns and allowances of $4,200, worthless accounts written off of $7,900, and collections from customers of $450,730. At the end of year (December 31), a junior accountant for Thant Company was preparing an aging analysis of accounts receivable. At the top of page 6 of the report, the following totals appeared:

Customer Account	Total	Not Yet Due	1–30 Days Past Due	31–60 Days Past Due	61–90 Days Past Due	Over 90 Days Past Due
Balance Forward	$89,640	$49,030	$24,110	$9,210	$3,990	$3,300

To finish the analysis, the following accounts need to be classified:

Account	Amount	Due Date
B. Singh	$ 930	Jan. 14 (next year)
L. Wells	620	Dec. 24
A. Roc	1,955	Sept. 28
T. Cila	2,100	Aug. 16
M. Mix	375	Dec. 14
S. Price	2,685	Jan. 23 (next year)
J. Wendt	295	Nov. 5
	$8,960	

From past experience, the company has found that the following rates are realistic for estimating uncollectible accounts:

Time	Percentage Considered Uncollectible
Not yet due	2
1–30 days past due	5
31–60 days past due	15
61–90 days past due	25
Over 90 days past due	50

Required

1. Complete the aging analysis of accounts receivable.
2. Compute the end-of-year balances (before adjustments) of Accounts Receivable and Allowance for Uncollectible Accounts.
3. Prepare an analysis computing the estimated uncollectible accounts.

4. Calculate Thant Company's estimated uncollectible accounts expense for the year (round the amount to the nearest whole dollar).
5. **User Insight:** What role do estimates play in applying the aging analysis? What factors might affect these estimates?

LO4 **Notes Receivable Calculations**

P 4. Abraham Importing Company engaged in the following transactions involving promissory notes:

May 3 Sold engines to Anton Company for $60,000 in exchange for a 90-day, 12 percent promissory note.
16 Sold engines to Yu Company for $32,000 in exchange for a 60-day, 13 percent note.
31 Sold engines to Yu Company for $30,000 in exchange for a 90-day, 11 percent note.

Required

1. For each of the notes, determine the (a) maturity date, (b) interest on the note, and (c) maturity value.
2. Assume that the fiscal year for Abraham Importing Company ends on June 30. How much interest income should be recorded on that date?
3. **User Insight:** What are the effects of the transactions in May on cash flows for the year ended June 30?

Alternate Problems

LO2 **Bank Reconciliation**

P 5. The following information is available for Abdul Saleem, Inc., as of May 31, 20xx:

a. Cash on the books as of May 31 amounted to $42,754.16. Cash on the bank statement for the same date was $52,351.46.
b. A deposit of $5,220.94, representing cash receipts of May 31, did not appear on the bank statement.
c. Outstanding checks totaled $3,936.80.
d. A check for $1,920.00 returned with the statement was recorded incorrectly in the check register as $1,380.00. The check was for a cash purchase of merchandise.
e. The bank service charge for May amounted to $25.
f. The bank collected $12,240.00 for Abdul Saleem, Inc., on a note. The face value of the note was $12,000.00.
g. An NSF check for $183.56 from a customer, Ann Greeno, was returned with the statement.
h. The bank mistakenly charged to the company account a check for $850.00 drawn by another company.
i. The bank reported that it had credited the account for $240.00 in interest on the average balance for May.

Required

1. Prepare a bank reconciliation for Abdul Saleem, Inc., as of May 31, 20xx.
2. Prepare the entries in journal form necessary to adjust the accounts.
3. What amount of cash should appear on Abdul Saleem, Inc.'s balance sheet as of May 31?
4. **User Insight:** Why is a bank reconciliation considered an important control over cash?

LO1, LO3 | **Methods of Estimating Uncollectible Accounts and Receivables Analysis**

P 6. Hernandez Company had an Accounts Receivable balance of $320,000 and a credit balance in Allowance for Uncollectible Accounts of $16,700 at January 1, 20xx. During the year, the company recorded the following transactions:

a. Sales on account, $1,052,000
b. Sales returns and allowances by credit customers, $53,400
c. Collections from customers, $993,000
d. Worthless accounts written off, $19,800

The company's past history indicates that 2.5 percent of its net credit sales will not be collected.

Required

1. Prepare T accounts for Accounts Receivable and Allowance for Uncollectible Accounts. Enter the beginning balances, and show the effects on these accounts of the items listed above, summarizing the year's activity. Determine the ending balance of each account.
2. Compute Uncollectible Accounts Expense and determine the ending balance of Allowance for Uncollectible Accounts under (a) the percentage of net sales method and (b) the accounts receivable aging method, assuming an aging of the accounts receivable shows that $24,000 may be uncollectible.
3. Compute the receivable turnover and days' sales uncollected, using the data from the accounts receivable aging method in requirement **2**.
4. **User Insight:** How do you explain that the two methods used in requirement **2** result in different amounts for Uncollectible Accounts Expense? What rationale underlies each method?

LO 3 | **Accounts Receivable Aging Method**

P 7. The Fossell Fashions Store uses the accounts receivable aging method to estimate uncollectible accounts. On February 1, 20x7, the balance of the Accounts Receivable account was a debit of $446,341, and the balance of Allowance for Uncollectible Accounts was a credit of $43,000. During the year, the store had sales on account of $3,724,000, sales returns and allowances of $63,000, worthless accounts written off of $44,300, and collections from customers of $3,214,000. As part of the end-of-year (January 31, 20x8) procedures, an aging analysis of accounts receivable is prepared. The analysis, which is partially complete, is as follows:

Customer Account	Total	Not Yet Due	1–30 Days Past Due	31–60 Days Past Due	61–90 Days Past Due	Over 90 Days Past Due
Balance Forward	$793,791	$438,933	$149,614	$106,400	$57,442	$41,402

To finish the analysis, the following accounts need to be classified:

Account	Amount	Due Date
J. Curtis	$10,977	Jan. 15
T. Dawson	9,314	Feb. 15 (next fiscal year)
L. Zapata	8,664	Dec. 20
R. Copa	780	Oct. 1
E. Land	14,810	Jan. 4
S. Qadri	6,316	Nov. 15
A. Rosenthal	4,389	Mar. 1 (next fiscal year)
	$55,250	

From past experience, the company has found that the following rates are realistic for estimating uncollectible accounts:

Time	Percentage Considered Uncollectible
Not yet due	2
1–30 days past due	5
31–60 days past due	15
61–90 days past due	25
Over 90 days past due	50

Required

1. Complete the aging analysis of accounts receivable.
2. Compute the end-of-year balances (before adjustments) of Accounts Receivable and Allowance for Uncollectible Accounts.
3. Prepare an analysis computing the estimated uncollectible accounts.
4. How much is Fossell Fashions Store's estimated uncollectible accounts expense for the year? (Round the adjustment to the nearest whole dollar.)
5. User Insight: What role do estimates play in applying the aging analysis? What factors might affect these estimates?

ENHANCING Your Knowledge, Skills, and Critical Thinking

Conceptual Understanding Cases

LO1   **Role of Credit Sales**

C 1. Mitsubishi Corp., a broadly diversified Japanese corporation, instituted a credit plan called Three Diamonds for customers who buy its major electronic products, such as large-screen televisions and videotape recorders, from specified retail dealers.[17] Under the plan, approved customers who make purchases in July of one year do not have to make any payments until September of the next year. Nor do they have to pay interest during the intervening months. Mitsubishi pays the dealer the full amount less a small fee, sends the customer a Mitsubishi credit card, and collects from the customer at the specified time.

What was Mitsubishi's motivation for establishing such generous credit terms? What costs are involved? What are the accounting implications?

LO1, LO3   **Role of Estimates in Accounting for Receivables**

C 2. CompuCredit is a credit card issuer in Atlanta. It prides itself on making credit cards available to almost anybody in a matter of seconds over the Internet. The cost to the consumer is an interest rate of 28 percent, about double that of companies that provide cards only to customers with good credit. Despite its high interest rate, CompuCredit has been successful, reporting 1.9 million accounts and an income of approximately $100 million in a recent year. To calculate its income, the company estimates that 10 percent of its $1.3 billion in accounts receivable will not be paid; the industry average is 7 percent. Some analysts have been critical of CompuCredit for being too optimistic in its projections of losses.[18]

Why are estimates necessary in accounting for receivables? If CompuCredit were to use the same estimate of losses as other companies in its industry, what would its income have been for the year? How would one determine if CompuCredit's estimate of losses is reasonable?

LO1 Receivables Financing

C 3. Gellis Appliances, Inc., located in central Michigan, is a small manufacturer of washing machines and dryers. Gellis sells most of its appliances to large, established discount retail companies that market the appliances under their own names. Gellis sells the appliances on trade credit terms of n/60. If a customer wants a longer term, however, Gellis will accept a note with a term of up to nine months. At present, the company is having cash flow troubles and needs $10 million immediately. Its cash balance is $400,000, its accounts receivable balance is $4.6 million, and its notes receivable balance is $7.4 million.

How might Gellis Appliance's management use its accounts receivable and notes receivable to raise the cash it needs? What are the company's prospects for raising the needed cash?

Interpreting Financial Reports

LO1 Comparison and Interpretation of Ratios

C 4. Fosters Group Limited and Heineken N.V. are two well-known beer companies. Fosters is an Australian company, and Heineken is Dutch. Fosters is about half the size of Heineken.

Ratios can help in comparing and understanding companies that are different in size and that use different currencies. For example, the receivable turnovers for Fosters and Heineken in 2005 and 2004 were as follows:[19]

	2005	2004
Fosters	5.6 times	3.2 times
Heineken	7.3 times	6.6 times

What do the ratios tell you about the credit policies of the two companies? How long does it take each, on average, to collect a receivable? What do the ratios tell you about the companies' relative needs for capital to finance receivables? Which company is improving? Can you tell which company has a better credit policy? Explain your answers.

Decision Analysis Using Excel

LO1, LO3 Accounting for Accounts Receivable

C 5. Mirador Products Co. is a major consumer goods company that sells over 3,000 products in 135 countries. The company's annual report to the Securities and Exchange Commission presented the following data (in thousands) pertaining to net sales and accounts related to accounts receivable for 2008, 2007, and 2006.

	2008	2007	2006
Net sales	$9,820,000	$9,730,000	$9,888,000
Accounts receivable	1,046,000	1,048,000	1,008,000
Allowance for uncollectible accounts	37,200	42,400	49,000
Uncollectible accounts expense	30,000	33,400	31,600
Uncollectible accounts written off	38,600	40,200	35,400
Recoveries of accounts previously written off	3,400	200	2,000

1. Compute the ratio of uncollectible accounts expense to net sales and to accounts receivable, and the ratio of allowance for uncollectible accounts to accounts receivable for 2008, 2007, and 2006.
2. Compute the receivable turnover and days' sales uncollected for each year, assuming 2005 net accounts receivable were $930,000,000.

3. What is your interpretation of the ratios? Describe management's attitude toward the collectibility of accounts receivable over the three-year period.

Annual Report Case: CVS Corporation

LO1, LO2, LO3   **Cash and Receivables**

C 6. Refer to **CVS Corporation's** annual report in the Supplement to Chapter 5 to answer the following questions:

1. What amount of cash and cash equivalents did CVS Corporation have in 2005? Do you suppose most of that amount is cash in the bank or cash equivalents?
2. CVS does not disclose an allowance for uncollectible accounts. How do you explain the lack of disclosure?
3. What do you think CVS's seasonal needs for cash are? Where in CVS's financial statements is the seasonality of sales discussed?

Comparison Case: CVS Versus Walgreens

LO1   **Accounts Receivable Analysis**

⊘/ℝ   **C 7.** Refer to the **CVS** annual report in the Supplement to Chapter 5 and to the following data (in millions) for Walgreens: net sales, $42,201.6 and $37,508.2 for 2005 and 2004, respectively; accounts receivable, net, $1,396.3 and $1,169.1 for 2005 and 2004, respectively.

1. Compute receivable turnover and days' sales uncollected for 2005 and 2004 for CVS and Walgreens. Accounts Receivable in 2003 were $1,349.6 million for CVS and $1,017.8 million for Walgreens.
2. Do you discern any differences in the two companies' credit policies? Explain your answer.

Ethical Dilemma Case

LO1, LO3   **Ethics and Uncollectible Accounts**

C 8. Anderson Interiors, a successful retail furniture company, is located in an affluent suburb where a major insurance company has just announced a restructuring that will lay off 4,000 employees. Anderson Interiors sells quality furniture, usually on credit. Accounts Receivable is one of its major assets. Although the company's annual uncollectible accounts losses are not out of line, they represent a sizable amount. The company depends on bank loans for its financing. Sales and net income have declined in the past year, and some customers are falling behind in paying their accounts.

Lucretia Anderson, the owner of the business, knows that the bank's loan officer likes to see a steady performance. She has therefore instructed the company's controller to underestimate the uncollectible accounts this year to show a small growth in earnings. Anderson believes this action is justified because earnings in future years will average out the losses, and since the company has a history of success, she believes the adjustments are meaningless accounting measures anyway.

Are Anderson's actions ethical? Would any parties be harmed by her actions? How important is it to try to be accurate in estimating losses from uncollectible accounts?

Internet Case

LO1, LO3   Comparison of J.C. Penney, Inc., and Dillard's, Inc.

C 9. Access the annual reports of **J.C. Penney** and **Dillard's**. Find the accounts receivable on each company's balance sheet and the notes to the financial statements that are related to those accounts. Which company has the most accounts receivable as a percentage of total assets? What is the percentage of the allowance account to gross accounts receivable for each company? Which company experienced the highest loss rate on its receivables? Why do you think there is a difference? Do the companies finance their receivables? Be prepared to discuss your findings in class.

Group Activity Case

LO1   Effects of Credit Policies

C 10. **Tenet Healthcare Corp.**, the second largest publicly traded hospital chain in the United States, had a large amount of uncollectible accounts expense because so many patients were unable to pay their medical bills. Its uncollectible accounts expense amounted to about 11 percent of its revenues. After management analyzed the problem, they found that 70 percent of the losses came from uninsured patients and 30 percent from those who had insurance. The company realized that many of the uninsured could not be expected to pay and that the large amount of the bills simply discouraged patients from seeking health care. The company decided to start charging these patients less, hoping it could eliminate 40 to 60 percent of its bad debts loss. The company's chief financial officer said, "A significant amount of the revenue will never be recorded in the first place due to this pricing, so that it will not have to be written off as bad debt.[20]

In informal groups in class, discuss and report on the following questions: What effect will the new pricing policy have on the company's reported earnings? Why would the company want to show lower uncollectible accounts expense? Do you think the new policy has ethical ramifications?

Business Communication Case

LO1, LO2   Cash Management and Cash Equivalents

C 11. Collegiate Publishing Company publishes college textbooks in the sciences and humanities. More than 50 percent of Collegiate Publishing's sales occur in July, August, and December. The company's cash balance builds up until sometime after the sales take place and the books are paid for. During the rest of the year, its sales are low. The company's treasurer keeps the cash in a bank checking account earning little or no interest and pays bills from this account as they come due. To survive periods when cash receipts are low, Collegiate Publishing Company sometimes borrows money, and it repays the loans in the months when cash receipts are largest.

The company is currently considering two plans of action. First, it would work with the bookstores to implement electronic funds transfer (EFT) for payment. Second, it would invest in short-term (less than 90 days) securities that pay a higher rate of interest than the checking account.

Write a memorandum to the president that lays out the advantages of EFT and states the accounting implications (if any) of the plan to invest in short-term securities.

9

Current Liabilities and the Time Value of Money

Although some current liabilities, such as accounts payable, are recorded when a company makes a purchase, others accrue during an accounting period and are not recorded until adjusting entries are made at the end of the period. In addition, the value of some accruals must be estimated. If accrued liabilities are not recognized and valued properly, both liabilities and expenses will be understated on the financial statements, making the company's performance look better than it actually is. The time value of money is a concept that underlies both assets and liabilities.

LEARNING OBJECTIVES

Making a Statement

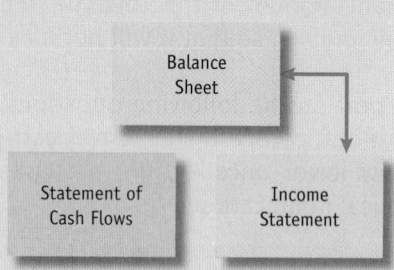

Measurement of unearned revenues and accrued expenses impacts the amount of current liabilities on the balance sheet and revenues and expenses on the income statement.

LO1 Identify the management issues related to current liabilities.

LO2 Identify, compute, and record definitely determinable and estimated current liabilities.

LO3 Distinguish *contingent liabilities* from *commitments*.

LO4 Define the *time value of money,* and apply it to future and present values.

LO5 Apply the time value of money to simple accounting situations.

- How does Amazon.com's decision to incur heavy debt relate to the goals of the business?

- Is the level of accounts payable in the operating cycle satisfactory?

- Has the company properly identified and accounted for all its current liabilities?

Amazon.com is one of the few Internet companies that survived the dot.com crash of 2001. Its management of cash flows and liabilities played a big role in its survival. As you can see in Amazon.com's Financial Highlights, its total liabilities in 2005 were almost $3.5 billion, approximately equal to its total assets of $3.7 billion. Thus, its stockholders' equity is quite small. This is due to an accumulated deficit (in retained earnings) of more than $2 billion from losses the high-flying company incurred in its start-up years.[1]

Managing liabilities is obviously important to achieving profitability and liquidity. A company must incur liabilities to support its operating and financing activities, but payment of these obligations requires an outflow of cash. Achieving the appropriate level of liabilities is critical to a company's success, especially for a new company. If a company has too few liabilities, it may not be earning up to its potential. If it has too many liabilities, it may be incurring excessive risks. A company with heavy debt is vulnerable to failure.

AMAZON.COM'S FINANCIAL HIGHLIGHTS
(In millions)

Current Liabilities	2005	2004
Accounts payable	$1,366	$1,142
Accrued expenses and other current liabilities	563	478
Total current liabilities	$1,929	$1,620
Long-term debt and other	1,521	1,855
Total liabilities	$3,450	$3,475

Management Issues Related to Current Liabilities

LO1 Identify the management issues related to current liabilities.

Current liabilities require careful management of liquidity and cash flows, as well as close monitoring of accounts payable. In reporting on current liabilities, managers must understand how they should be recognized, valued, classified, and disclosed.

Managing Liquidity and Cash Flows

The primary reason a company incurs current liabilities is to meet its needs for cash during the operating cycle. The operating cycle is the process of converting cash to cash through a series of purchases, sales, and collection of accounts receivable. Most current liabilities arise in support of this cycle, as when accounts payable arise from purchases of inventory, accrued expenses arise from operating costs, and unearned revenues arise from customers' advance payments. Companies incur short-term debt to raise cash during periods of inventory build-up or while waiting for collection of receivables. They use the cash to pay the portion of long-term debt that is currently due and to pay liabilities arising from operations.

Failure to manage the cash flows related to current liabilities can have serious consequences for a business. For instance, if suppliers are not paid on time, they may withhold shipments that are vital to a company's operations. Continued failure to pay current liabilities can lead to bankruptcy. To evaluate a company's ability to pay its current liabilities, analysts often use two measures of liquidity—working capital and the current ratio, both of which we defined in an earlier chapter. Current liabilities are a key component of both these measures. They typically equal from 25 to 50 percent of total assets.

As shown below (in thousands), **Amazon.com's** short-term liquidity as measured by working capital was positive in 2004 and improved in 2005 (in millions):

	Current Assets	−	Current Liabilities	=	Working Capital
2004	$2,539	−	$1,620	=	$919
2005	$2,929	−	$1,929	=	$1,000

 Amazon.com's current ratio (current assets divided by current liabilities) declined slightly, from 1.6 times in 2004 to 1.5 times in 2005.

Thus, despite its deficit in stockholders' equity, Amazon.com was able to maintain short-term liquidity. Companies commonly have problems maintaining liquidity in their early years, but Amazon.com managed its debt well. Further, as shown in its Financial Highlights, Amazon.com was able to raise funds by incurring long-term debt, which allowed it to acquire the facilities and software it needed in its operations.

Evaluating Accounts Payable

Another consideration in managing liquidity and cash flows is the time suppliers give a company to pay for purchases. Measures commonly used to assess a company's ability to pay within a certain time frame are **payables turnover** and **days' payable**. Payables turnover is the number of times, on average, that a company pays its accounts payable in an accounting period. Days' payable shows how long, on average, a company takes to pay its accounts payables.

To measure payables turnover for **Amazon.com**, we must first calculate purchases by adjusting cost of goods sold for the change in inventory. An increase in inventory means purchases were more than cost of goods sold; a

FOCUS ON BUSINESS PRACTICE
Debt Problems Can Plague Even Well-Known Companies.

In a Wall Street horror story that illustrates the importance of managing current liabilities, **Xerox Corporation**, one of the most storied names in American business, found itself combating rumors that it was facing bankruptcy. Following a statement by Xerox's CEO that the company's financial model was "unsustainable," management was forced to defend the company's liquidity by saying it had adequate funds to continue operations. But in a report filed with the SEC, management acknowledged that it had tapped into its $7 billion line of bank credit for more than $3 billion to pay off short-term debt that was coming due. Unable to secure more money from any other source to pay these debts, Xerox had no choice but to turn to the line of credit from its bank. Had it run out, the company might well have gone bankrupt.[2] Fortunately, Xerox was able to restructure its line of credit to stay in business.

decrease means purchases were less than cost of goods sold. Amazon.com's cost of goods sold in 2005 was $6,451 million, and its inventory increased by $86 million. Its payables turnover is computed as follows:

$$\text{Payables Turnover} = \frac{\text{Cost of Goods Sold} +/- \text{Change in Merchandise Inventory}}{\text{Average Accounts Payable}}$$

$$= \frac{\$6,451 + \$86}{(\$1,366 + \$1,142) \div 2}$$

$$= \frac{\$6,537}{\$1,254} = 5.2 \text{ times}$$

To find the days' payable, the number of days in a year is divided by the payables turnover:

$$\text{Days' Payable} = \frac{365 \text{ days}}{\text{Payables Turnover}} = \frac{365 \text{ days}}{5.2 \text{ times}} = 70.2 \text{ days}$$

The payables turnover of 5.2 times and days' payable of 70.2 days indicate that the credit terms Amazon.com receives from its suppliers are excellent. In other industries, the credit terms are not nearly as favorable. As you can see in Figures 1 and 2, companies in other industries have higher payables turnover and

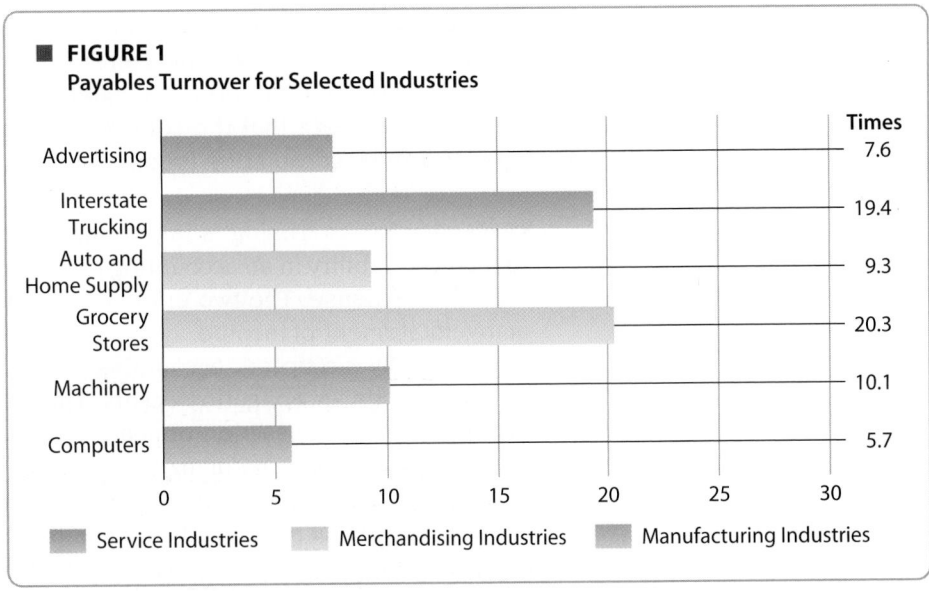

■ FIGURE 1
Payables Turnover for Selected Industries

Industry	Times
Advertising	7.6
Interstate Trucking	19.4
Auto and Home Supply	9.3
Grocery Stores	20.3
Machinery	10.1
Computers	5.7

Service Industries · Merchandising Industries · Manufacturing Industries

Source: Data from Dun & Bradstreet, *Industry Norms and Key Business Ratios,* 2004–2005.

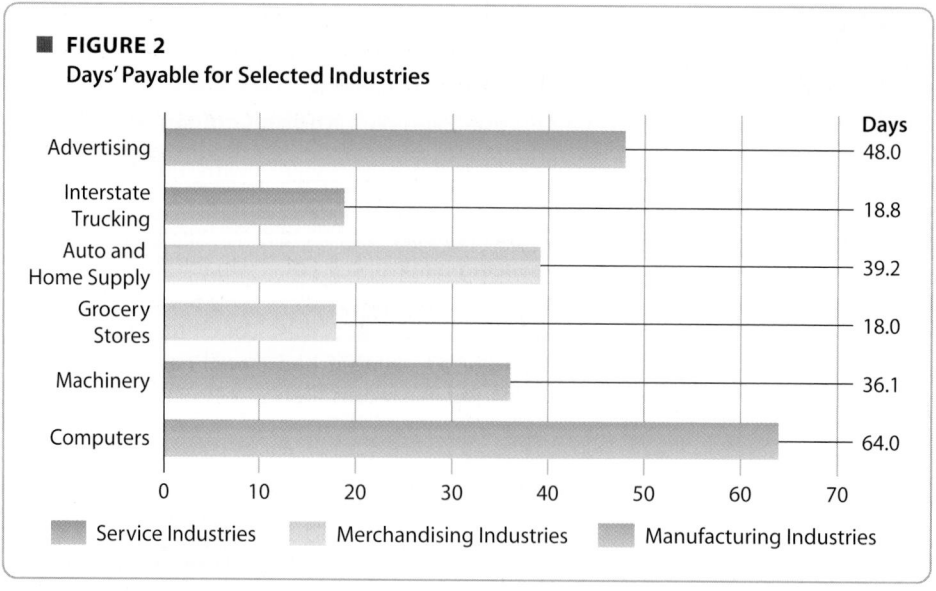

■ **FIGURE 2**
Days' Payable for Selected Industries

Source: Data from Dun & Bradstreet, *Industry Norms and Key Business Ratios,* 2004–2005.

lower days' payable than Amazon.com. The company's inventory turnover ratio of approximately 12.3 times is also extraordinary. These ratios have been a major factor in Amazon.com's ability to maintain adequate liquidity. To get a full picture of a company's operating cycle and liquidity, you should consider payables turnover and days' payable in relation to inventory and receivable turnovers and their related number of days' ratios.

Reporting Liabilities

In deciding whether to buy stock in a company or lend money to it, investors and creditors must evaluate not only the company's current liabilities, but its future obligations as well. In doing so, they have to rely on the integrity of the company's financial statements.

Ethical reporting of liabilities requires that they be properly recognized, valued, classified, and disclosed. In one notable case involving unethical reporting of liabilities, the CEO and other employees of **Nortel Networks Corporation**, a Canadian manufacturer of telecommunications equipment, understated accrued liabilities (and corresponding expenses) in order to report a profit and obtain salary bonuses. After all accrued liabilities had been identified, it was evident that the company was in fact losing money. The board of directors of the corporation fired all who had been involved.[3]

Recognition Timing is important in the recognition of liabilities. Failure to record a liability in an accounting period very often goes along with failure to record an expense. The two errors lead to an understatement of expense and an overstatement of income.

Generally accepted accounting principles require that a liability be recorded when an obligation occurs. This rule is harder to apply than it might appear. When a transaction obligates a company to make future payments, a liability arises and is recognized, as when goods are bought on credit. However, some current liabilities are not the result of direct transactions. One of the key reasons for making adjusting entries at the end of an accounting period is to recognize unrecorded liabilities that accrue during the period. Accrued liabilities include salaries payable and interest payable. Other liabilities that can only be estimated, such as taxes payable, must also be recognized through adjusting entries.

Agreements for future transactions do not have to be recognized. For instance, **Amazon.com** might agree to pay an executive $250,000 a year for a period of three years, or it might agree to buy an unspecified amount of advertising at a certain price over the next five years. Such contracts, though they are definite commitments, are not considered liabilities because they are for future—not past—transactions. Because there is no current obligation, no liability is recognized.

Valuation On the balance sheet, a liability is generally valued at the amount of money needed to pay the debt or at the fair market value of the goods or services to be delivered. Disclosure of the fair value of liabilities may be required in the notes to the financial statements.

The amount of most liabilities is definitely known. For example, **Amazon.com** sells a large number of gift certificates that are redeemable in the future. The amount of the liability (unearned revenue) is known, but the exact timing is not known.

Some companies, however, must estimate future liabilities. For example, an automobile dealer that sells a car with a one-year warranty must provide parts and service during the year. The obligation is definite because the sale has occurred, but the amount of the obligation can only be estimated. Such estimates are usually based on past experience and anticipated changes in the business environment.

Classification As you may recall from our discussion of classified balance sheets in an earlier chapter, **current liabilities** are debts and obligations that a company expects to satisfy within one year or within its normal operating cycle, whichever is longer. These liabilities are normally paid out of current assets or with cash generated by operations. **Long-term liabilities** are liabilities due beyond one year or beyond the normal operating cycle. The purpose of incurring long-term liabilities is to finance long-term assets. For example, **Amazon.com** incurs long-term debt to finance its warehouse and distribution system. The distinction between current and long-term liabilities is important because it affects the evaluation of a company's liquidity.

Disclosure A company may have to include additional explanation of some liability accounts in the notes to its financial statements. For example, if a company's Notes Payable account is large, it should disclose the balances, maturity dates, interest rates, and other features of the debts in an explanatory note. Any special credit arrangements should also be disclosed. For example, in a note to its financial statements, **Hershey Foods Corporation**, the famous candy company, discloses a portion of its credit arrangements:

> **Short-Term Debt**
> In September 2005, the Company entered into a new short-term credit agreement to establish an unsecured revolving credit facility to borrow up to $300 million.[4]

Unused lines of credit allow a company to borrow on short notice up to the credit limit, with little or no negotiation. Thus, the type of disclosure in Hershey's note is helpful in assessing whether a company has additional borrowing power.

S T O P • R E V I E W • A P P L Y

1-1. What are three examples of current liabilities?

1-2. What are two measures of liquidity used in evaluating a firm's ability to pay its current liabilities?

1-3. What does payables turnover tell you about a company's liquidity?

1-4. Why is the timing of liability recognition important?

1-5. What is the rule for classifying a liability as current?

1-6. Manly Company has an unused line of bank credit of $100,000. Should Manly record this line of credit as a liability and disclose it in its financial statements?

Suggested answers to all Stop, Review, and Apply questions are available at http://college.hmco.com/accounting/needles/poa/10e/student_home.html.

Common Types of Current Liabilities

> **LO2**   Identify, compute, and record definitely determinable and estimated current liabilities.

As noted earlier, a company incurs current liabilities to meet its needs for cash during the operating cycle. These liabilities fall into two major groups: definitely determinable liabilities and estimated liabilities.

Definitely Determinable Liabilities

Study Note

On the balance sheet, the order of presentation for current liabilities is not as strict as for current assets. Generally, accounts payable or notes payable appear first, and the rest of current liabilities follow.

Current liabilities that are set by contract or statute and that can be measured exactly are called **definitely determinable liabilities**. The problems in accounting for these liabilities are to determine their existence and amount and to see that they are recorded properly. The most common definitely determinable liabilities are described below.

Accounts Payable   Accounts payable (sometimes called *trade accounts payable*) are short-term obligations to suppliers for goods and services. The amount in the Accounts Payable account is generally supported by an accounts payable subsidiary ledger, which contains an individual account for each person or company to which money is owed. As shown in the Financial Highlights at the beginning of the chapter, accounts payable make up more than half of **Amazon.com's** current liabilities.

Bank Loans and Commercial Paper   Management often establishes a **line of credit** with a bank. This arrangement allows the company to borrow funds when they are needed to finance current operations. In a note to its financial statements, **Goodyear Tire & Rubber Company** describes its lines of credit as follows: "At December 31, 2005, we had credit arrangements totaling $7,112 million, of which $1,495 million were unused."[5]

Although a company signs a promissory note for the full amount of a line of credit, it has great flexibility in using the available funds. It can increase its borrowing up to the limit when it needs cash and reduce the amount borrowed when it generates enough cash of its own. Both the amount borrowed and the interest rate charged by the bank may change daily. The bank may require the company to meet certain financial goals (such as maintaining specific profit margins, current ratios, or debt to equity ratios) to retain its line of credit.

Companies with excellent credit ratings can borrow short-term funds by issuing **commercial paper**, which are unsecured loans (i.e., loans not backed up by any specific assets) that are sold to the public, usually through professionally managed investment firms. Highly rated companies rely heavily on commercial paper to raise short-term funds, but they can quickly lose access to this means of borrowing if their credit rating drops. Because of disappointing operating results in recent years, well-known companies like **DaimlerChrysler**, **Lucent Technologies**, and **Motorola** have lost some or all of their ability to issue commercial paper.

The portion of a line of credit currently borrowed and the amount of commercial paper issued are usually combined with notes payable in the current liabilities section of the balance sheet. Details are disclosed in a note to the financial statements.

Study Note

Only the used portion of a line of credit is recognized as a liability in the financial statements.

Notes Payable   Short-term notes payable are obligations represented by promissory notes. A company may sign promissory notes to obtain bank loans, pay suppliers for goods and services, or secure credit from other sources.

Interest is usually stated separately on the face of the note, as shown in Figure 3. The entries to record the note in Figure 3 are as follows:

ISSUANCE

A	=	L	+	OE
+5,000.00		+5,000.00		

Aug. 31	Cash	5,000.00	
	Notes Payable		5,000.00
	Issued 60-day,		
	12% promissory note		

PAYMENT

A	=	L	+	OE
−5,098.63		−5,000.00		−98.63

Oct. 30	Notes Payable	5,000.00	
	Interest Expense	98.63	
	Cash		5,098.63
	Payment of promissory		
	note with $100 interest		

$$\$5,000 \times \frac{12}{100} \times \frac{60}{365} = \$98.63$$

■ **FIGURE 3**
Promissory Note

Chicago, Illinois   August 31, 20xx

Sixty days after date I promise to pay First Federal Bank
the sum of $5,000 with interest at the rate of 12% per
annum.

                        Sandra Caron
                        Caron Corporation

Accrued Liabilities As we noted earlier, a key reason for making adjusting entries at the end of an accounting period is to recognize liabilities that are not already in the accounting records. This practice applies to any type of liability. As you will see, accrued liabilities (also called *accrued expenses*) can include estimated liabilities. As can be seen in **Amazon.com's** Financial Highlights, the company had accrued expenses and other current liabilities of about $500 million in both 2004 and 2005.

Here, we focus on interest payable, a definitely determinable liability. Interest accrues daily on interest-bearing notes. In accordance with the matching rule, an adjusting entry is made at the end of each accounting period to record the interest obligation up to that point. For example, if the accounting period of the maker of the note in Figure 3 ends on September 30, or 30 days after the issuance of the 60-day note, the adjusting entry would be as follows:

A =	L	+	OE
	+49.32		−49.32

Sept. 30	Interest Expense	49.32	
	Interest Payable		49.32
	To record 30 days' interest expense on promissory note		

$$\$5,000 \times \frac{12}{100} \times \frac{30}{365} = \$49.32$$

Dividends Payable As you know, cash dividends are a distribution of earnings to a corporation's stockholders, and a corporation's board of directors has the sole authority to declare them. The corporation has no liability for dividends until the date of declaration. The time between that date and the date of payment of dividends is usually short. During this brief interval, the dividends declared are considered current liabilities of the corporation.

Sales and Excise Taxes Payable Most states and many cities levy a sales tax on retail transactions, and the federal government imposes an excise tax on some products, such as gasoline. A merchant that sells goods subject to these taxes must collect the taxes and forward them periodically to the appropriate government agency. Until the merchant remits the amount it has collected to the government, that amount represents a current liability. For example, suppose a merchant makes a $100 sale that is subject to a 5 percent sales tax and a 10 percent excise tax. If the sale takes place on June 1, the entry to record it is as follows:

A =	L	+	OE
+115	+5		+100
	+10		

June 1	Cash	115	
	Sales		100
	Sales Tax Payable		5
	Excise Tax Payable		10
	Sales of merchandise and collection of sales and excise tax		

The sale is properly recorded at $100, and the taxes collected are recorded as liabilities to be remitted to the appropriate government agencies.

Companies that have a physical presence in many cities and states require a complex accounting system for sales taxes because the rates vary from state to state and city to city. Because **Amazon.com** is an Internet company without a physical presence in most states and thus does not always have to collect sales tax from its customers, its sales tax situation is simpler. This situation may change in the future, but so far Congress has exempted most Internet sales from sales tax.

Current Portion of Long-Term Debt

If a portion of long-term debt is due within the next year and is to be paid from current assets, that portion is classified as a current liability. For example, the notes to **Amazon.com's** financial statements show the following amounts (in millions):

Current liabilities:
    Current maturities of long-term debt $ 3
Long-term liabilities:
    Long-term debt   1,521

In this case, no journal entry is necessary. The total debt of $1,524 million is simply reclassified into two categories when the company prepares its financial statements.

Payroll Liabilities

For most organizations, the cost of labor and payroll taxes is a major expense. In the banking and airlines industries, payroll costs represent more than half of all operating costs. Payroll accounting is important because complex laws and significant liabilities are involved. The employer is liable to employees for wages and salaries and to various agencies for amounts withheld from wages and salaries and for related taxes. **Wages** are compensation of employees at an hourly rate; **salaries** are compensation of employees at a monthly or yearly rate.

Because payroll accounting applies only to an organization's employees, it is important to distinguish between employees and independent contractors. Employees are paid a wage or salary by the organization and are under its direct supervision and control. Independent contractors are not employees of the organization and so are not accounted for under the payroll system. They offer services to the organization for a fee, but they are not under its direct control or supervision. Certified public accountants, advertising agencies, and lawyers, for example, often act as independent contractors.

FOCUS ON BUSINESS PRACTICE

Small Businesses Offer Benefits, Too.

A survey of small business in the Midwest focused on the employee benefits that these companies offer. The graph at the right presents the results. As you can see, 77 percent of respondents provided both paid vacation and health/medical benefits, and 23 percent even offered their employees tuition reimbursement.[6]

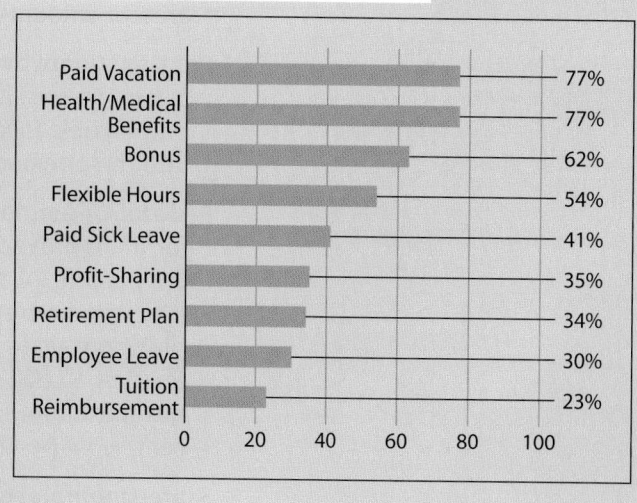

Figure 4 shows how payroll liabilities relate to employee earnings and employer taxes and other costs. When accounting for payroll liabilities, it is important to keep the following in mind:

▸ The amount payable to employees is less than the amount of their earnings. This occurs because employers are required by law or are requested by employees to withhold certain amounts from wages and send them directly to government agencies or other organizations.

▸ An employer's total liabilities exceed employees' earnings because the employer must pay additional taxes and make other contributions (e.g., for pensions and medical care) that increase the cost and liabilities.

The most common withholdings, taxes, and other payroll costs are described below.

Federal Income Taxes Employers are required to withhold federal income taxes from employees' paychecks and pay them to the United States Treasury. These taxes are collected each time an employee is paid.

State and Local Income Taxes Most states and some local governments levy income taxes. In most cases, the procedures for withholding are similar to those for federal income taxes.

Social Security (FICA) Tax The social security program (the Federal Insurance Contribution Act) provides retirement and disability benefits and survivor's benefits. About 90 percent of the people working in the United States fall under the provisions of this program. The 2005 social security tax rate of 6.2 percent was paid by *both* employee and employer on the first $90,000 earned by an employee during the calendar year. Both the rate and the base to which it applies are subject to change in future years.

Medicare Tax A major extension of the social security program is Medicare, which provides hospitalization and medical insurance for persons over age 65. In 2005, the Medicare tax rate was 1.45 percent of gross income, with no limit, paid by *both* employee and employer.

Medical Insurance Many organizations provide medical benefits to employees. Often, the employee contributes a portion of the cost through withholdings from income and the employer pays the rest—usually a greater amount—to the insurance company.

Pension Contributions Many organizations also provide pension benefits to employees. A portion of the pension contribution is withheld from the employee's income, and the organization pays the rest of the amount into the pension fund.

Federal Unemployment Insurance (FUTA) Tax This tax pays for programs for unemployed workers. It is paid *only* by employers and recently was 6.2 percent of the first $7,000 earned by each employee (this amount may vary from state to state). The employer is allowed a credit for unemployment taxes it pays to the state. The maximum credit is 5.4 percent of the first $7,000 earned by each employee. Most states set their rate at this maximum. Thus, the FUTA tax most often paid is .8 percent (6.2 percent − 5.4 percent) of the taxable wages.

State Unemployment Insurance Tax State unemployment programs provide compensation to eligible unemployed workers. The compensation

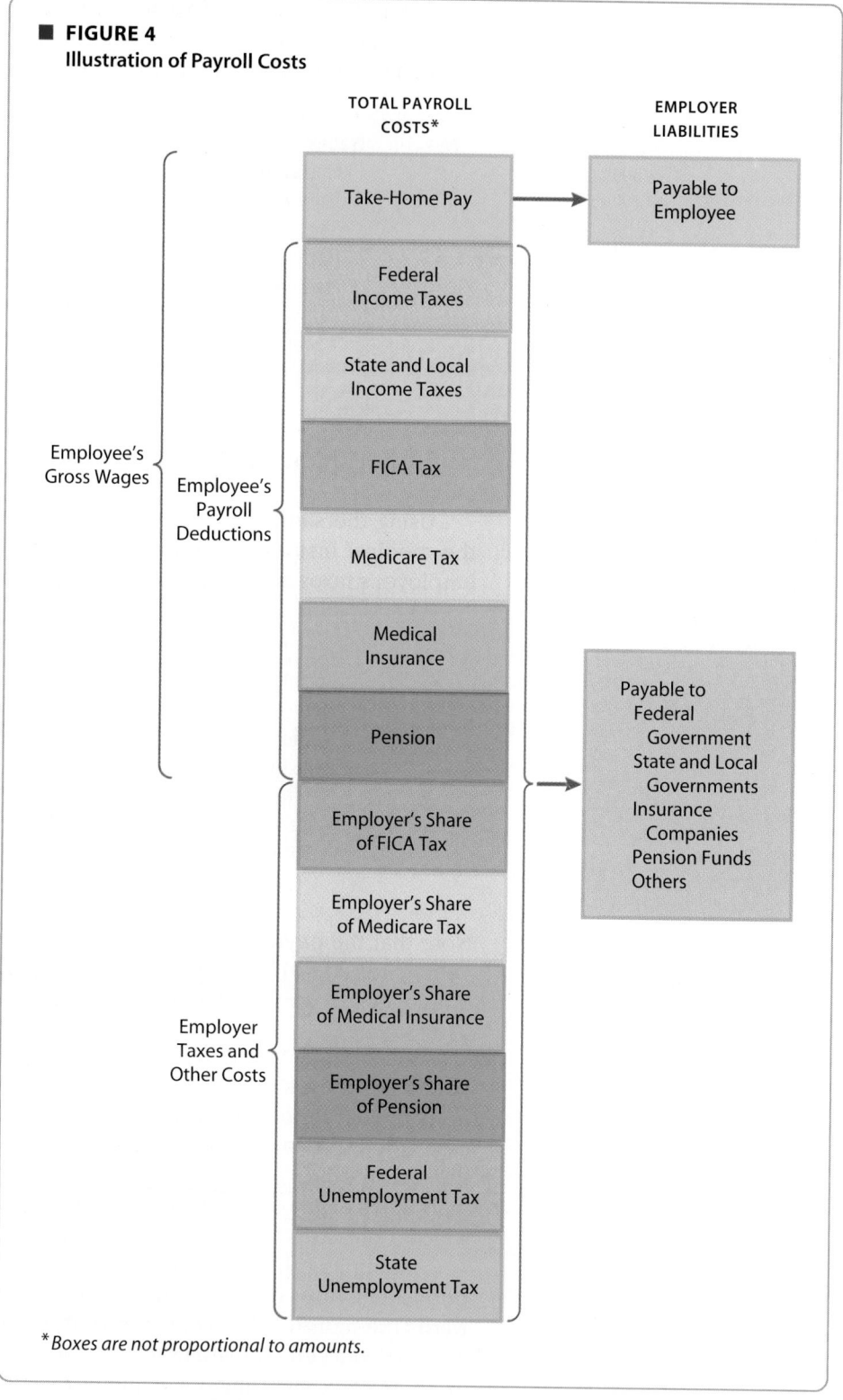

■ **FIGURE 4**
Illustration of Payroll Costs

TOTAL PAYROLL COSTS*

EMPLOYER LIABILITIES

Employee's Gross Wages

Employee's Payroll Deductions

Employer Taxes and Other Costs

Take-Home Pay

Federal Income Taxes

State and Local Income Taxes

FICA Tax

Medicare Tax

Medical Insurance

Pension

Employer's Share of FICA Tax

Employer's Share of Medicare Tax

Employer's Share of Medical Insurance

Employer's Share of Pension

Federal Unemployment Tax

State Unemployment Tax

Payable to Employee

Payable to Federal Government State and Local Governments Insurance Companies Pension Funds Others

Boxes are not proportional to amounts.

is paid out of the fund provided by the 5.4 percent of the first $7,000 (or whatever amount the state sets) earned by each employee. In some states, employers with favorable employment records may be entitled to pay less than 5.4 percent.

To illustrate the recording of a payroll, suppose that on February 15, a company's wages for employees are $32,500 and withholdings for employees are

$5,400 for federal income taxes, $1,200 for state income taxes, $2,015 for social security tax, $471 for Medicare tax, $900 for medical insurance, and $1,300 for pension contributions. The entry to record this payroll is as follows:

A = L + OE			
+5,400	−32,500		
+1,200			
+2,015			
+471			
+900			
+1,300			
+21,214			

Feb. 15	Wages Expense	32,500	
	Employees' Federal Income Taxes Payable		5,400
	Employees' State Income Taxes Payable		1,200
	Social Security Tax Payable		2,015
	Medicare Tax Payable		471
	Medical Insurance Premiums Payable		900
	Pension Contributions Payable		1,300
	Wages Payable		21,214
	To record payroll		

Note that although the employees earned $32,500, their take-home pay was only $21,214.

Using the same data but assuming that the employer pays 80 percent of the medical insurance premiums and half of the pension contributions, the employer's taxes and benefit costs would be recorded as follows:

A = L + OE			
+2,015	−9,401		
+471			
+3,600			
+1,300			
+260			
+1,755			

Feb. 15	Payroll Taxes and Benefits Expense	9,401	
	Social Security Tax Payable		2,015
	Medicare Tax Payable		471
	Medical Insurance Premiums Payable		3,600
	Pension Contributions Payable		1,300
	Federal Unemployment Tax Payable		260
	State Unemployment Tax Payable		1,755
	To record payroll taxes and other costs		

Note that the payroll taxes and benefits expense increase the total cost of the payroll to $41,901 ($9,401 + $32,500), which exceeds the amount earned by employees by almost 29 percent. This is a typical situation.

Unearned Revenues **Unearned revenues** are advance payments for goods or services that a company must provide in a future accounting period. In its annual report, **Amazon.com** states that it records unearned revenue as cash when it receives payments in advance and as accounts receivable when the unearned revenue represents a legally enforceable contract, as is the case in its sales of gift certificates. It then recognizes the revenue over the period in which it provides the products or services.

Among its other endeavors, Amazon.com sells subscriptions for magazine publishers. After deducting its commission for selling the subscriptions, it forwards the money it has collected to the publisher. Suppose, for example, that Amazon.com sells some annual subscriptions for a publisher of a monthly magazine. After deducting its commission, it forwards $240 to the publisher. Because the publisher has not yet delivered the 12 issues of the magazine, the $240 is unearned revenue. The publisher would make the following entry:

A = L + OE		
+240	+240	

Cash	240	
Unearned Subscriptions		240
Receipt of annual subscriptions in advance		

The publisher now has a liability of $240 that will be gradually reduced over the year as it sends out monthly issues of the magazine, which it will record as follows:

A = L + OE
   −20 +20

Unearned Subscriptions	20	
Subscription Revenues		20
Delivery of monthly magazine issues		

Many businesses, including repair companies, construction companies, and special-order firms, ask for a deposit before they will begin work. Until they deliver the goods or services, these deposits are current liabilities.

Estimated Liabilities

Study Note

Estimated liabilities are recorded and presented on the financial statements in the same way as definitely determinable liabilities. The only difference is that the computation of estimated liabilities involves some uncertainty.

Estimated liabilities are definite debts or obligations whose exact dollar amount cannot be known until a later date. Because there is no doubt that a legal obligation exists, the primary accounting problem is to estimate and record the amount of the liability. Examples of estimated liabilities are described below.

Income Taxes Payable The federal government, most state governments, and some cities and towns levy a tax on a corporation's income. The amount of the liability depends on the results of a corporation's operations, which are often not known until after the end of the corporation's fiscal year. However, because income taxes are an expense in the year in which income is earned, an adjusting entry is necessary to record the estimated tax liability. The format of a typical entry is as follows:

A = L + OE
   +53,000 −53,000

Dec. 31	Income Taxes Expense	53,000	
	Income Taxes Payable		53,000
	To record estimated federal		
	income taxes		

Sole proprietorships and partnerships do *not* pay income taxes. However, their owners must report their share of the firm's income on their individual tax returns.

Property Taxes Payable Property taxes are a main source of revenue for local governments. They are levied annually on real property, such as land and buildings, and on personal property, such as inventory and equipment. Because the fiscal years of local governments rarely correspond to a company's fiscal year, it is necessary to estimate the amount of property taxes that applies to each month of the year.

Promotional Costs You are no doubt familiar with the coupons and rebates that are part of many companies' marketing programs and with the frequent flyer programs that airlines have been offering for more than 20 years. Companies usually record the costs of these programs as a reduction in sales (a contra-sales account) rather than as an expense with a corresponding current liability. As **Hershey Foods Corporation** acknowledges in its annual report, promotional costs are hard to estimate:

FOCUS ON BUSINESS PRACTICE

Those Little Coupons Can Add Up.

Many companies promote their products by issuing coupons that offer "cents off" or other enticements. Because four out of five shoppers use coupons, companies are forced by competition to distribute them. The total value of unredeemed coupons, each of which represents a potential liability for the issuing company, is staggering. *PROMO Magazine* estimates that almost 300 billion coupons are issued annually. Of course, the liability depends on how many coupons will actually be redeemed. *PROMO* estimates that number at approximately 3.6 billion, or about 1.2 percent. Thus, a big advertiser that puts a cents-off coupon in Sunday papers to reach 60 million people can be faced with liability for 720,000 coupons. The total value of coupons redeemed each year is estimated at more than $3.6 billion.[7]

Accrued liabilities requiring the most difficult or subjective judgments include liabilities associated with marketing promotion programs and potentially unsaleable products. The Company utilizes numerous trade promotion programs. The costs of such programs are recognized as a reduction to net sales with the recording of the corresponding liability based on estimates at the time of product shipment. The accrued liability for marketing promotions is determined through analysis of programs offered, historical trends, [and other means].[8]

Hershey accrues between $550 million and $580 million in promotional costs each year and reports that its estimates are usually accurate within about 6 percent.

Study Note

Recording a product warranty expense in the period of the sale is an application of the matching rule.

Product Warranty Liability When a firm sells a product or service with a warranty, it has a liability for the length of the warranty. The warranty is a feature of the product and is included in the selling price; its cost should therefore be debited to an expense account in the period of the sale. Based on past experience, it should be possible to estimate the amount the warranty will cost in the future. Some products will require little warranty service; others may require much. Thus, there will be an average cost per product.

For example, suppose a muffler company like **Midas** guarantees that it will replace free of charge any muffler it sells that fails during the time the buyer owns the car. The company charges a small service fee for replacing the muffler. In the past, 6 percent of the mufflers sold have been returned for replacement under the warranty. The average cost of a muffler is $50. If the company sold 350 mufflers during July, the accrued liability would be recorded as an adjustment at the end of July, as shown below:

A =	L	+	OE
	+1,050		−1,050

July 31	Product Warranty Expense	1,050	
	Estimated Product Warranty Liability		1,050
	To record estimated product warranty expense:		

Number of units sold	350
Rate of replacement under warranty	× .06
Estimated units to be replaced	21
Estimated cost per unit	$50
Estimated liability for product warranty	$1,050

When a muffler is returned for replacement under the warranty, the cost of the muffler is charged against the Estimated Product Warranty Liability

Today, because of frequent flyer programs, U.S. airlines have more than 4 trillion "free miles" outstanding. What are the accounting implications of these programs? Companies usually record the costs as a reduction in sales (a contra-sales account) rather than as an expense with a corresponding current liability.

account. For example, suppose that on December 5, a customer returns with a defective muffler, which cost $40, and pays a $20 service fee to have it replaced. The entry is as follows:

A = L + OE
+20 −40 +20
−40

Dec. 5	Cash	20	
	Estimated Product Warranty Liability	40	
	Service Revenue		20
	Merchandise Inventory		40
	Replacement of muffler under warranty		

Vacation Pay Liability In most companies, employees accrue paid vacation as they work during the year. For example, an employee may earn two weeks of paid vacation for each 50 weeks of work. Thus, the person is paid 52 weeks' salary for 50 weeks' work. The cost of the two weeks' vacation should be allocated as an expense over the whole year so that month-to-month costs will not be distorted. The vacation pay represents 4 percent (two weeks' vacation divided by 50 weeks) of a worker's pay. Every week worked earns the employee a small fraction (2 percent) of vacation pay, which is 4 percent of total annual salary.

FOCUS ON BUSINESS PRACTICE

What Is the Cost of Frequent Flyer Miles?

In the early 1980s, **American Airlines** developed a frequent flyer program that awards free trips and other bonuses to customers based on the number of miles they fly on the airline. Since then, many other airlines have instituted similar programs, and it is estimated that 40 million people now participate in them. Today, U.S. airlines have more than 4 trillion "free miles" outstanding, and 8 percent

of passengers travel on "free" tickets. Estimated liabilities for these tickets have become an important consideration in evaluating an airline's financial position. Complicating the estimate is that almost half the miles have been earned through purchases from hotels, car rental and telephone companies, Internet service providers like **AOL**, and bank credit cards.[9]

Vacation pay liability can represent a substantial amount of money. For example, in the 10-K form that it submitted to the SEC for 2004, **US Airways** reported accrued salaries, wages, and vacation liabilities of $167 million.

Suppose that a company with a vacation policy of two weeks of paid vacation for each 50 weeks of work has a payroll of $21,000 and that it paid $1,000 of that amount to employees on vacation for the week ended April 20. Because of turnover and rules regarding term of employment, the company assumes that only 75 percent of employees will ultimately collect vacation pay. The computation of vacation pay expense based on the payroll of employees not on vacation ($21,000 − $1,000) is as follows: $20,000 × 4 percent × 75 percent = $600. The company would make the following entry to record vacation pay expense for the week ended April 20:

A = L + OE
    +600 −600

Apr. 20	Vacation Pay Expense	600	
	Estimated Liability for Vacation Pay		600
	Estimated vacation pay expense		

At the time employees receive their vacation pay, an entry is made debiting Estimated Liability for Vacation Pay and crediting Cash or Wages Payable. This entry records the $1,000 paid to employees on vacation during August:

A* = L + OE
−1,000 −1,000

* Assumes cash paid.

Aug. 31	Estimated Liability for Vacation Pay	1,000	
	Cash (or Wages Payable)		1,000
	Wages of employees on vacation		

The treatment of vacation pay presented here can also be applied to other payroll costs, such as bonus plans and contributions to pension plans.

STOP • REVIEW • APPLY

2-1. What is the difference between a line of credit and commercial paper?

2-2. When can a portion of long-term debt be classified as a current liability?

2-3. What are three types of employer-related payroll liabilities?

2-4. Who pays social security and Medicare taxes?

2-5. Why are unearned revenues classified as liabilities?

2-6. What is definite about an estimated liability?

2-7. Why are income taxes payable considered to be estimated liabilities?

2-8. In accounting for discount coupons, how is recording the estimate of how much will be redeemed as a contra-sales account similar to and different from recording it as a promotional expense?

2-9. When does a company incur a liability for a product warranty?

Identification of Current Liabilities Identify each of the following as either (1) a definitely determinable liability or (2) an estimated liability:

____ a. Bank loan

____ b. Dividends payable

__2__ c. Product warranty liabilities

___1___ d. Interest payable

___2___ e. Income taxes payable

___2___ f. Vacation pay liability

___1___ g. Notes payable

___2___ h. Property taxes payable

___1___ i. Commercial paper

___2___ j. Gift certificate liability

SOLUTION			
a.	1	f.	2
b.	1	g.	1
c.	2	h.	2
d.	1	i.	1
e.	2	j.	2

Contingent Liabilities and Commitments

LO3 Distinguish *contingent liabilities* from *commitments*.

The FASB requires companies to disclose in a note to their financial statements any contingent liabilities and commitments they may have. A **contingent liability** is not an *existing* obligation. Rather, it is a *potential* liability because it depends on a future event arising out of a past transaction. Contingent liabilities often involve lawsuits, income tax disputes, discounted notes receivable, guarantees of debt, and failure to follow government regulations. For instance, a construction company that built a bridge may have been sued by the state for using poor materials. The past transaction is the building of the bridge under contract. The future event is the outcome of the lawsuit, which is not yet known.

The FASB has established two conditions for determining when a contingency should be entered in the accounting records:

1. The liability must be probable.

2. The liability can be reasonably estimated.[10]

Estimated liabilities like the income tax, warranty, and vacation pay liabilities that we have described meet those conditions. They are therefore accrued in the accounting records.

In a survey of 600 large companies, the most common types of contingencies reported were litigation, which can involve many different issues, and environmental concerns, such as toxic waste cleanup.[11] In a note to its 2005 annual report, **Amazon.com** described a contingent liability involving litigation:

> In May 2004, Toysrus.com LLC filed a complaint against us for breach of contract. . . . We dispute the allegations of wrongdoing in this complaint and have brought counterclaims. . . .

A **commitment** is a legal obligation that does not meet the technical requirements for recognition as a liability and so is not recorded. The most common examples are purchase agreements and leases.[12] For example, in its

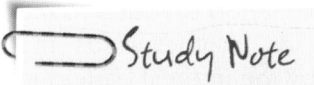
Study Note

Contingencies are recorded when they are probable and can be reasonably estimated.

2005 annual report, Amazon.com notes that "we currently lease office and fulfillment center facilities and fixed assets under non-cancelable operating and capital leases."

S T O P • R E V I E W • A P P L Y

3-1. What is a contingent liability, and how does it differ from a commitment?

3-2. What are two examples of contingent liabilities? Why is each a contingent liability?

3-3. What is an example of a commitment?

The Time Value of Money

LO4 Define the *time value of money,* and apply it to future and present values.

"Time is money" is a common expression. It derives from the concept of the **time value of money**, which refers to the costs or benefits derived from holding or not holding money over time. **Interest** is the cost of using money for a specific period.

The interest associated with the time value of money is an important consideration in any kind of business decision. For example, if you sell a bicycle for $100 and hold that amount for one year without putting it in a savings account, you have forgone the interest that the money would have earned. However, if you accept a note payable instead of cash and add the interest to the price of the bicycle, you will not forgo the interest that the cash could have earned.

Simple interest is the interest cost for one or more periods when the principal sum—the amount on which interest is computed—stays the same from period to period. **Compound interest** is the interest cost for two or more periods when after each period, the interest earned in that period is added to the amount on which interest is computed in future periods. In other words, the principal sum is increased at the end of each period by the interest earned in that period. The following two examples illustrate these concepts:

Study Note

In business, compound interest is the most useful concept of interest because it helps decision makers choose among alternative courses of action.

Example of Simple Interest Joe Sanchez accepts an 8 percent, $30,000 note due in 90 days. How much will he receive at that time? The interest is calculated as follows:

$$\text{Interest} = \text{Principal} \times \text{Rate} \times \text{Time}$$
$$= \$30{,}000.00 \times 8/100 \times 90/365$$
$$= \$591.78$$

Therefore, the total that Sanchez will receive is $30,591.78, calculated as follows:

$$\text{Total} = \text{Principal} + \text{Interest}$$
$$= \$30{,}000.00 + \$591.78$$
$$= \$30{,}591.78$$

Example of Compound Interest Anna Wang deposits $5,000 in an account that pays 6 percent interest. She expects to leave the principal and accumulated interest in the account for three years. How much will the account total at the end of three years? Assume that the interest is paid at the end of the year and is added to the principal at that time, and that this total in turn earns interest. The amount at the end of three years is computed as follows:

Year	(1) Principal Amount at Beginning of Year	(2) Annual Amount of Interest (Col. 2 × 6%)	(3) Accumulated Amount at End of Year (Col. 2 + Col. 3)
1	$5,000.00	$300.00	$5,300.00
2	5,300.00	318.00	5,618.00
3	5,618.00	337.08	5,955.08

At the end of three years, Wang will have $5,955.08 in her account. Note that the amount of interest increases each year by the interest rate times the interest of the previous year. For example, between year 1 and year 2, the interest increased by $18, which equals 6 percent times $300.

Future Value

Another way to ask the question we posed in our example of compound interest is, What is the future value of a single sum ($5,000) at compound interest (6 percent) for three years? **Future value** is the amount an investment will be worth at a future date if invested at compound interest. Managers often want to know future value, but the method of computing future value that we just illustrated is too time-consuming in practice. Imagine how tedious the calculation would be if the example were ten years instead of three. Fortunately, there are tables that simplify solving problems involving compound interest. Table 1, which shows the future value of $1 after a given number of periods, is an example. This table and the others in this chapter are excerpts from larger tables in the appendix on future value and present value tables.

Future Value of a Single Sum Invested at Compound Interest
Using Table 1 to compute the future value of Anna Wang's savings account, we simply look down the 6 percent column until we reach the line for three periods and find the factor 1.191. This factor, when multiplied by $1, gives the

TABLE 1.	**Future Value of $1 After a Given Number of Periods**												
Period	**1%**	**2%**	**3%**	**4%**	**5%**	**6%**	**7%**	**8%**	**9%**	**10%**	**12%**	**14%**	**15%**
1	1.010	1.020	1.030	1.040	1.050	1.060	1.070	1.080	1.090	1.100	1.120	1.140	1.150
2	1.020	1.040	1.061	1.082	1.103	1.124	1.145	1.166	1.188	1.210	1.254	1.300	1.323
3	1.030	1.061	1.093	1.125	1.158	1.191	1.225	1.260	1.295	1.331	1.405	1.482	1.521
4	1.041	1.082	1.126	1.170	1.216	1.262	1.311	1.360	1.412	1.464	1.574	1.689	1.749
5	1.051	1.104	1.159	1.217	1.276	1.338	1.403	1.469	1.539	1.611	1.762	1.925	2.011
6	1.062	1.126	1.194	1.265	1.340	1.419	1.501	1.587	1.677	1.772	1.974	2.195	2.313
7	1.072	1.149	1.230	1.316	1.407	1.504	1.606	1.714	1.828	1.949	2.211	2.502	2.660
8	1.083	1.172	1.267	1.369	1.477	1.594	1.718	1.851	1.993	2.144	2.476	2.853	3.059
9	1.094	1.195	1.305	1.423	1.551	1.689	1.838	1.999	2.172	2.358	2.773	3.252	3.518
10	1.105	1.219	1.344	1.480	1.629	1.791	1.967	2.159	2.367	2.594	3.106	3.707	4.046

future value of that $1 at compound interest of 6 percent for three periods (years in this case). Thus, we solve the problem as follows:

Principal: $5,000

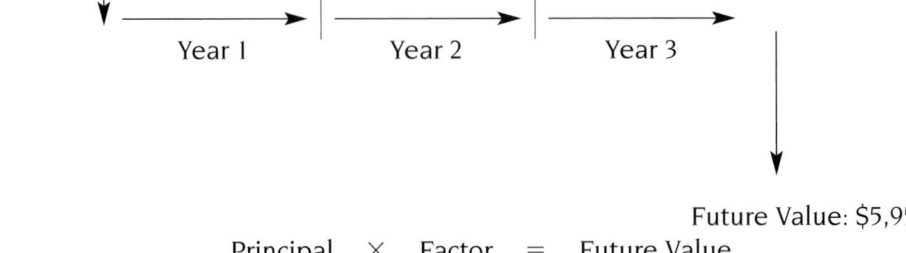

Future Value: $5,955

Principal	×	Factor	=	Future Value
$5,000	×	1.191	=	$5,955

Except for a rounding difference of $.08, the answer is the same as our earlier one.

Future Value of an Ordinary Annuity   Another common problem involves an **ordinary annuity**, which is a series of equal payments made at the end of equal intervals of time, with compound interest on these payments. For example, suppose that at the end of each of the next three years, Ben Katz puts $200 into a savings account that pays 5 percent interest. How much money will he have in his account at the end of the three years? The following is one way of computing the amount:

	(1)	(2)	(3) *Interest*	(4)	(5) *Accumulated at*
		Beginning	*Earned*	*Periodic*	*End of Period*
	Year	*Balance*	*(5% × Col. 2)*	*Payment*	*(Col. 2 + Col. 3 + Col. 4)*
	1	—	—	$200	$200.00
	2	$200.00	$10.00	200	410.00
	3	410.00	20.50	200	630.50

Katz would have $630.50 in his account at the end of three years, consisting of $600.00 in periodic payments and $30.50 in interest.

We can simplify this calculation by using Table 2. Looking down the 5 percent column and across the row for the third period, we find the factor 3.153. This factor, when multiplied by $1, gives the future value of a series of three $1 payments at compound interest of 5 percent. Thus, we solve the problem as follows:

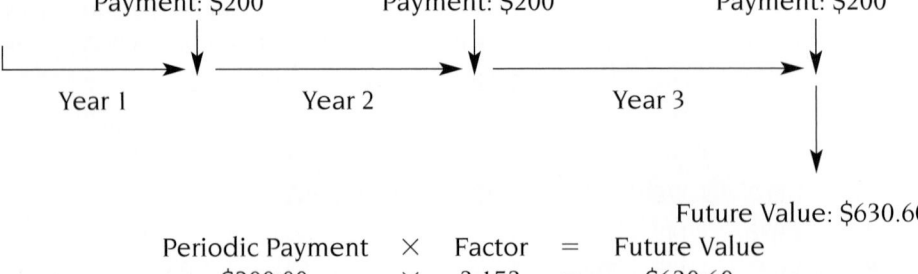

Payment: $200   Payment: $200   Payment: $200

Future Value: $630.60

Periodic Payment	×	Factor	=	Future Value
$200.00	×	3.153	=	$630.60

Except for a rounding difference of $.10, the result is the same as our earlier one.

TABLE 2. **Future Value of an Ordinary Annuity of $1 Paid in Each Period for a Given Number of Periods**

Period	1%	2%	3%	4%	5%	6%	7%	8%	9%	10%	12%	14%	15%
1	1.000	1.000	1.000	1.000	1.000	1.000	1.000	1.000	1.000	1.000	1.000	1.000	1.000
2	2.010	2.020	2.030	2.040	2.050	2.060	2.070	2.080	2.090	2.100	2.120	2.140	2.150
3	3.030	3.060	3.091	3.122	3.153	3.184	3.215	3.246	3.278	3.310	3.374	3.440	3.473
4	4.060	4.122	4.184	4.246	4.310	4.375	4.440	4.506	4.573	4.641	4.779	4.921	4.993
5	5.101	5.204	5.309	5.416	5.526	5.637	5.751	5.867	5.985	6.105	6.353	6.610	6.742
6	6.152	6.308	6.468	6.633	6.802	6.975	7.153	7.336	7.523	7.716	8.115	8.536	8.754
7	7.214	7.434	7.662	7.898	8.142	8.394	8.654	8.923	9.200	9.487	10.090	10.730	11.070
8	8.286	8.538	8.892	9.214	9.549	9.897	10.260	10.640	11.030	11.440	12.300	13.230	13.730
9	9.369	9.755	10.160	10.580	11.030	11.490	11.980	12.490	13.020	13.580	14.780	16.090	16.790
10	10.460	10.950	11.460	12.010	12.580	13.180	13.820	14.490	15.190	15.940	17.550	19.340	20.300

Present Value

Study Note

Present value is a method of valuing future cash flows. Financial analysts commonly compute present value to determine the value of potential investments.

Suppose you had the choice of receiving $100 today or one year from today. No doubt, you would choose to receive it today. Why? If you have the money today, you can put it in a savings account to earn interest so you will have more than $100 a year from today. In other words, an amount to be received in the future (future value) is not worth as much today as an amount received today (present value). **Present value** is the amount that must be invested today at a given rate of interest to produce a given future value. Thus, present value and future value are closely related.

For example, suppose Sue Dapper needs $1,000 one year from now. How much does she have to invest today to achieve that goal if the interest rate is 5 percent? From earlier examples, we can establish the following equation:

Present Value	×	(1.0 + Interest Rate)	=	Future Value
Present Value	×	1.05	=	$1,000.00
Present Value			=	$1,000.00 ÷ 1.05
Present Value			=	$952.38

To achieve a future value of $1,000, Dapper must invest a present value of $952.38. Interest of 5 percent on $952.38 for one year equals $47.62, and these two amounts added together equal $1,000.

Present Value of a Single Sum Due in the Future   When more than one period is involved, the calculation of present value is more complicated. For example, suppose Don Riley wants to be sure of having $4,000 at the end of three years. How much must he invest today in a 5 percent savings account to achieve this goal? We can compute the present value of $4,000 at compound interest of 5 percent for three years by adapting the above equation:

Year	Amount at End of Year	Divide by		Present Value at Beginning of Year
3	$4,000.00 ÷	1.05	=	$3,809.52
2	3,809.52 ÷	1.05	=	3,628.11
1	3,628.11 ÷	1.05	=	3,455.34

Riley must invest $3,455.34 today to achieve a value of $4,000 in three years.

TABLE 3. Present Value of $1 to Be Received at the End of a Given Number of Periods

Period	1%	2%	3%	4%	5%	6%	7%	8%	9%	10%
1	0.990	0.980	0.971	0.962	0.952	0.943	0.935	0.926	0.917	0.909
2	0.980	0.961	0.943	0.925	0.907	0.890	0.873	0.857	0.842	0.826
3	0.971	0.942	0.915	0.889	0.864	0.840	0.816	0.794	0.772	0.751
4	0.961	0.924	0.888	0.855	0.823	0.792	0.763	0.735	0.708	0.683
5	0.951	0.906	0.863	0.822	0.784	0.747	0.713	0.681	0.650	0.621
6	0.942	0.888	0.837	0.790	0.746	0.705	0.666	0.630	0.596	0.564
7	0.933	0.871	0.813	0.760	0.711	0.665	0.623	0.583	0.547	0.513
8	0.923	0.853	0.789	0.731	0.677	0.627	0.582	0.540	0.502	0.467
9	0.914	0.837	0.766	0.703	0.645	0.592	0.544	0.500	0.460	0.424
10	0.905	0.820	0.744	0.676	0.614	0.558	0.508	0.463	0.422	0.386

Again, we can simplify the calculation by using the appropriate table. In Table 3, the point at which the 5 percent column and the row for period 3 intersect shows a factor of .864. This factor, when multiplied by $1, gives the present value of $1 to be received three years from now at 5 percent interest. Thus, we solve the problem as follows:

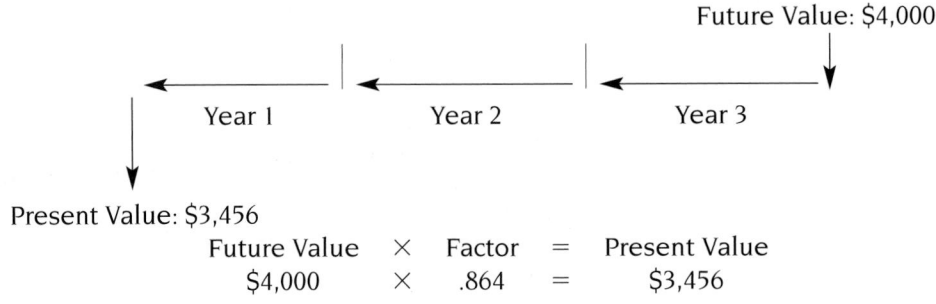

Future Value: $4,000

| Year 1 | Year 2 | Year 3 |

Present Value: $3,456

	Future Value	×	Factor	=	Present Value
	$4,000	×	.864	=	$3,456

Except for a rounding difference of $.66, this result is the same as our earlier one.

Present Value of an Ordinary Annuity   It is often necessary to compute the present value of a series of receipts or payments equally spaced over time—in other words, the present value of an ordinary annuity. For example, suppose Kathy Casal has sold a piece of property and is to receive $15,000 in three equal annual payments of $5,000 beginning one year from today. What is the present value of this sale if the current interest rate is 5 percent?

Using Table 3, we can compute the present value by calculating a separate value for each of the three payments and summing the results, as follows:

Future Receipts (Annuity)				Present Value Factor at 5 Percent (from Table 3)		Present Value
Year 1	Year 2	Year 3				
$5,000			×	.952	=	$ 4,760
	$5,000		×	.907	=	4,535
		$5,000	×	.864	=	4,320
Total Present Value						$13,615

The present value of the sale is $13,615. Thus, there is an implied interest cost (given the 5 percent rate) of $1,385 associated with the payment plan that allows the purchaser to pay in three installments.

TABLE 4. Present Value of an Ordinary $1 Annuity Received in Each Period for a Given Number of Periods

Period	1%	2%	3%	4%	5%	6%	7%	8%	9%	10%
1	0.990	0.980	0.971	0.962	0.952	0.943	0.935	0.926	0.917	0.909
2	1.970	1.942	1.913	1.886	1.859	1.833	1.808	1.783	1.759	1.736
3	2.941	2.884	2.829	2.775	2.723	2.673	2.624	2.577	2.531	2.487
4	3.902	3.808	3.717	3.630	3.546	3.465	3.387	3.312	3.240	3.170
5	4.853	4.713	4.580	4.452	4.329	4.212	4.100	3.993	3.890	3.791
6	5.795	5.601	5.417	5.242	5.076	4.917	4.767	4.623	4.486	4.355
7	6.728	6.472	6.230	6.002	5.786	5.582	5.389	5.206	5.033	4.868
8	7.652	7.325	7.020	6.733	6.463	6.210	5.971	5.747	5.535	5.335
9	8.566	8.162	7.786	7.435	7.108	6.802	6.515	6.247	5.995	5.759
10	9.471	8.983	8.530	8.111	7.722	7.360	7.024	6.710	6.418	6.145

We can make this calculation more easily by using Table 4. The point at which the 5 percent column intersects the row for period 3 shows a factor of 2.723. When multiplied by $1, this factor gives the present value of a series of three $1 payments (spaced one year apart) at compound interest of 5 percent. Thus, we solve the problem as follows:

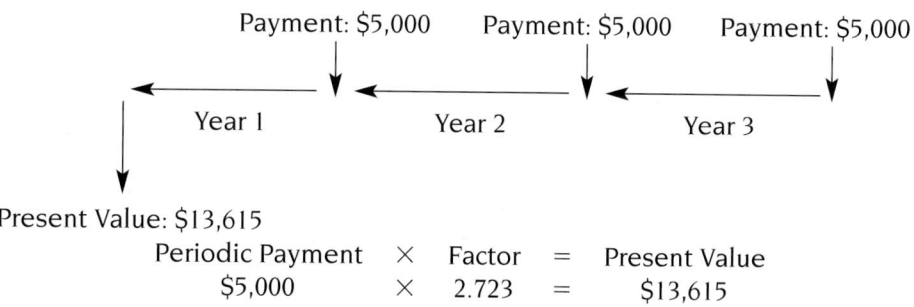

Periodic Payment	×	Factor	=	Present Value
$5,000	×	2.723	=	$13,615

This result is the same as the one we computed earlier.

Time Periods   As in all our examples, the compounding period is in most cases one year, and the interest rate is stated on an annual basis. However, the left-hand column in Tables 1 to 4 refers not to years but to periods. This wording accommodates compounding periods of less than one year. Savings accounts that record interest quarterly and bonds that pay interest semiannually are cases in which the compounding period is less than one year. To use the tables in these cases, it is necessary to (1) divide the annual interest rate by the number of periods in the year, and (2) multiply the number of periods in one year by the number of years.

For example, suppose we want to compute the future (maturity) value of a $6,000 note that is to be paid in two years and that carries an annual interest rate of 8 percent. The compounding period is semiannual. Before using Table 1 in this computation, we must compute the interest rate that applies to each compounding period and the total number of compounding periods. First, the interest rate to use is 4 percent (8% annual rate ÷ 2 periods per year). Second, the total number of compounding periods is 4 (2 periods per year × 2 years). From Table 1, therefore, the maturity value of the note is computed as follows:

Principal	×	Factor	=	Future Value
$6,000	×	1.170	=	$7,020

The note will be worth $7,020 in two years.

This method of determining the interest rate and the number of periods when the compounding period is less than one year can be used with all four tables.

STOP • REVIEW • APPLY

4-1. What is the time value of money?

4-2. What is the difference between simple and compound interest?

4-3. What is an ordinary annuity?

4-4. What is the key variable that relates present value to future value?

4-5. How does a compounding period of less than one year affect the computation of present value?

Applications of the Time Value of Money

LO5 Apply the time value of money to simple accounting situations.

The concepts of the future and present value of money are widely used in business decision making and financial reporting. The FASB has made them the foundation of its approach to using cash flow information in determining the fair value of assets and liabilities.[13] For example, the value of a long-term note receivable or payable can be determined by calculating the present value of the future interest payments.

As a rapidly growing company that makes many long-term investments in such things as distribution facilities, software, and the acquisition of other companies, **Amazon.com** finds many uses for the time value of money. For example, Amazon.com's management will compare the expected present value of the future cash flows of an investment with the current outlay that the investment requires, and it will use a target interest rate that it wants to earn on the investment. If the present value of the investment exceeds the current outlay, Amazon.com will earn at least its target interest rate if management's projections of cash are accurate.

In the sections that follow, we illustrate some simple, useful applications of the time value of money.

Valuing an Asset

An asset is something that will provide future benefits to the company that owns it. Usually, the purchase price of an asset represents the present value of those future benefits. It is possible to evaluate a proposed purchase price by comparing it with the present value of the asset to the company.

For example, Sam Hurst is thinking of buying a new machine that will reduce his annual labor cost by $700 per year. The machine will last eight years. The interest rate that Hurst assumes for making managerial decisions is 10 percent. What is the maximum amount (present value) that Hurst should pay for the machine?

Applications of the Time Value of Money

The present value of the machine to Hurst is equal to the present value of an ordinary annuity of $700 per year for eight years at compound interest of 10 percent. Using the factor from Table 4, we compute the value as follows:

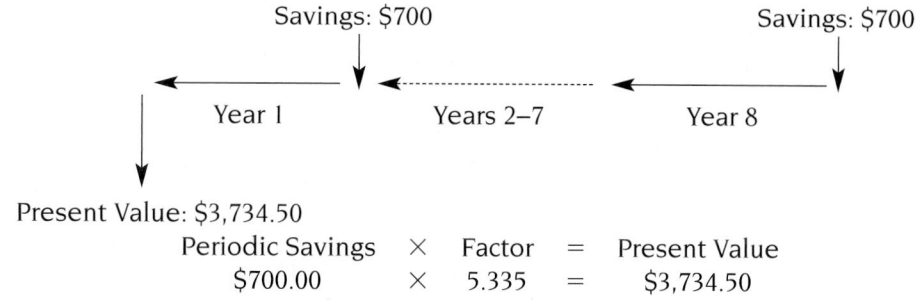

Savings: $700   Savings: $700

Year 1   Years 2–7   Year 8

Present Value: $3,734.50

Periodic Savings	×	Factor	=	Present Value
$700.00	×	5.335	=	$3,734.50

Hurst should not pay more than $3,734.50 for the machine because this amount equals the present value of the benefits he would receive from owning it.

Deferred Payment

To encourage buyers to make a purchase, sellers sometimes agree to defer payment for a sale. This practice is common among companies that sell agricultural equipment; to accommodate farmers who often need new equipment in the spring but cannot pay for it until they sell their crops in the fall, these companies are willing to defer payment.

Suppose Plains Implement Corporation sells a tractor to Dana Washington for $50,000 on February 1 and agrees to take payment ten months later, on December 1. When such an agreement is made, the future payment includes not only the selling price, but also an implied (imputed) interest cost. If the prevailing annual interest rate for such transactions is 12 percent compounded monthly, the actual price of the tractor would be the present value of the future

Companies that sell agricultural equipment like these combine harvesters often agree to defer payment for a sale. This practice is common because farmers often need new equipment in the spring but cannot pay for it until they sell their crops in the fall. Deferred payment is a useful application of the time value of money.

payment, computed using the factor from Table 3 (10 periods, 1 percent [12 percent divided by 12 months]), as follows:

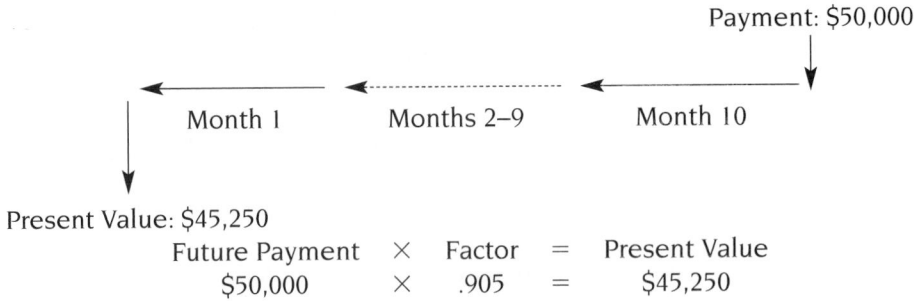

Present Value: $45,250

Future Payment	×	Factor	=	Present Value
$50,000	×	.905	=	$45,250

Washington records the present value, $45,250, in his purchase records, and Plains records it in its sales records. The balance consists of interest expense or interest income.

Investment of Idle Cash

Suppose Childware Corporation, a toy manufacturer, needs funds for a future expansion. At present, it has $10,000,000 in cash that it does not expect to need for one year. It places the cash in an account that pays 4 percent annual interest. Interest is compounded and credited to the company's account quarterly. How much cash will Childware have at the end of the year?

The future value factor from Table 1 is based on four quarterly periods of 1 percent (4 percent divided by 4 quarters), and the future value is computed as follows:

Principal: $10,000,000

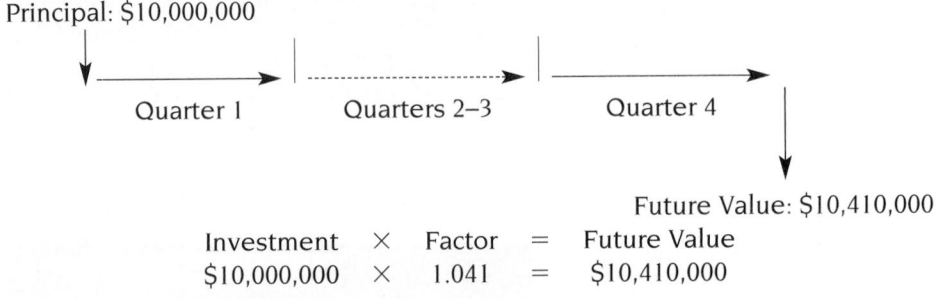

Future Value: $10,410,000

Investment	×	Factor	=	Future Value
$10,000,000	×	1.041	=	$10,410,000

The initial investment is recorded with a debit to Short-Term Investments. Each quarter, the company increases Short-Term Investments by the amount of the interest earned. Interest Income is credited. Similar entries would be made for four more months, at which time the balance of Short-Term Investments would be about $110,410,000. The actual amount accumulated might vary from this total because the interest rate paid may vary over time as a result of changes in market conditions.

Accumulation of a Fund for Loan Repayment

When a company owes a large fixed amount due in several years, management would be wise to accumulate a fund to pay off the debt at maturity. As part of a loan agreement, creditors sometimes require that such a fund be established. In establishing the fund, management must determine how much cash must be set aside each period to pay the debt. The amount will depend on the estimated rate of interest the fund will earn.

Suppose Aloha Corporation agrees with a creditor to set aside cash at the end of each year to accumulate enough to pay off a $100,000 note due in six years. It will make five annual contributions by the time the note is due. The fund is projected to earn 8 percent, compounded annually. We can calculate the amount of each annual payment by using Table 2 (5 periods, 8 percent):

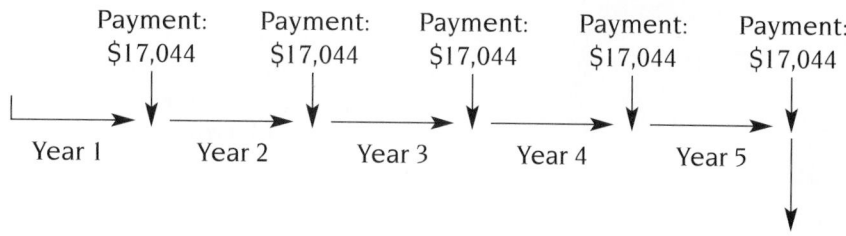

	Payment: $17,044	Payment: $17,044	Payment: $17,044	Payment: $17,044	Payment: $17,044
	Year 1	Year 2	Year 3	Year 4	Year 5

Future Value: $100,000

Future Value of Fund	÷	Factor	=	Annual Investment
$100,000	÷	5.867	=	$17,044 (rounded)

Other Applications

There are many other applications of present value in accounting, including computing imputed interest on non-interest-bearing notes, accounting for installment notes, valuing a bond, and recording lease obligations. Present value is also applied in accounting for pension obligations; valuing debt; depreciating property, plant, and equipment; making capital expenditure decisions; and generally in accounting for any item in which time is a factor. ●

STOP • REVIEW • APPLY

5-1. Why is the time value of money important in making business decisions?

5-2. What are the applications of present value to financial reporting?

5-3. What are some of the ways in which businesses use present value?

Valuing an Asset When Making a Purchasing Decision   Jerry owns a restaurant and has the opportunity to buy a high-quality espresso coffee machine for $5,000. After carefully studying projected costs and revenues, Jerry estimates that the machine will produce a net cash flow of $1,600 annually and will last for five years. He determines that an interest rate of 10 percent is an adequate return on investment for his business.

Calculate the present value of the machine to Jerry. Based on your calculation, do you think a decision to purchase the machine would be wise?

SOLUTION

Calculation of the present value:

Annual cash flow	$1,600.00
Factor from Table 4 (5 years at 10%)	× 3.791
Present value of net cash flows	$6,065.60
Less purchase price	− 5,000.00
Net present value	$1,065.60

The present value of the net cash flows from the machine exceeds the purchase price. Thus, the investment will return more than 10 percent to Jerry's business. A decision to purchase the machine would therefore be wise.

A LOOK BACK AT

AMAZON.COM, INC.

At the beginning of the chapter, we noted that **Amazon.com** has been an unusually successful Internet company. In its early years, it experienced operating losses of a magnitude that would have caused most companies to go bankrupt. Amazon.com, however, managed its cash flows and debt well enough to stay in business, and in 2003, it turned a profit for the first time. To accomplish this, the company had to provide investors and creditors with satisfactory answers to these questions:

- **How does Amazon.com's decision to incur heavy debt relate to the goals of the business?**
- **Is the level of accounts payable in the operating cycle satisfactory?**
- **Has the company properly identified and accounted for all its current liabilities?**

As a new company, Amazon.com had to make extensive investments in Internet software and distribution facilities. This required a lot of capital, much of which the company raised by borrowing money. It analyzed its future cash flows in terms of present value and carefully planned its cash needs by making very good use of the operating cycle. By selling mostly for cash, keeping inventories low, and making maximum use of credit from its suppliers, it was able to keep its cash needs to a minimum. This is particularly evident when we compare its payables turnover and days' payable for 2004 and 2005 (dollar amounts are in millions):

		2005	**2004**
$\dfrac{\text{Cost of Goods} \pm \text{Change in Merchandise}}{\text{Sold} \qquad \text{Inventory}}$	$=$	$\dfrac{\$6,451 + \$86}{(\$1,366 + \$1,142) \div 2}$	$\dfrac{\$5,319 + \$186}{(\$1,142 + \$820) \div 2}$
$\overline{\text{Average Accounts Payable}}$	$=$	$\dfrac{\$6,537}{\$1,254}$	$\dfrac{\$5,505}{\$981}$
Payables Turnover	$=$	5.2 times	5.6 times
$\dfrac{365 \text{ days}}{\text{Payables Turnover}}$		$\dfrac{365 \text{ days}}{5.2 \text{ times}}$	$\dfrac{365 \text{ days}}{5.6 \text{ times}}$
Days' Payable	$=$	70.2 days	65.2 days

Clearly, Amazon.com maintained a favorable payables turnover and days' payable ratio over the two-year period and experienced a small improvement in 2005. Now that Amazon.com has achieved profitable operations, it will be interesting to see how it manages it liabilities in the future.

CHAPTER REVIEW

REVIEW of Learning Objectives

LO1 Identify the management issues related to current liabilities.

Current liabilities are an important consideration in managing a company's liquidity and cash flows. Key measures of liquidity are working capital, payables turnover, and days' payable. Liabilities result from past transactions and should be recognized at the time a transaction obligates a company to make future payments. They are valued at the amount of money necessary to satisfy the obligation or at the fair value of the goods or services to be delivered. Liabilities are classified as current or long term. Supplemental disclosure is required when the nature or details of the obligations would help in understanding the liability.

LO2 Identify, compute, and record definitely determinable and estimated current liabilities.

The two major categories of current liabilities are definitely determinable liabilities and estimated liabilities. Definitely determinable liabilities can be measured exactly. They include accounts payable, bank loans and commercial paper, notes payable, accrued liabilities, dividends payable, sales and excise taxes payable, the current portion of long-term debt, payroll liabilities, and unearned revenues.

Estimated liabilities definitely exist, but their amounts are uncertain and must be estimated. They include liabilities for income taxes, property taxes, promotional costs, product warranties, and vacation pay.

LO3 Distinguish *contingent liabilities* from *commitments*.

A contingent liability is a potential liability that arises from a past transaction and is dependent on a future event. Contingent liabilities often involve lawsuits, income tax disputes, discounted notes receivable, guarantees of debt, and failure to follow government regulations. A commitment is a legal obligation, such as a purchase agreement, that is not recorded as a liability.

LO4 Define the *time value of money*, and apply it to future and present values.

The time value of money refers to the costs or benefits derived from holding or not holding money over time. Interest is the cost of using money for a specific period. In computing simple interest, the amount on which the interest is computed stays the same from period to period. In computing compound interest, the interest for a period is added to the principal amount before the interest for the next period is computed.

Future value is the amount an investment will be worth at a future date if invested at compound interest. An ordinary annuity is a series of equal payments made at the end of equal intervals of time, with compound interest on the payments. Present value is the amount that must be invested today at a given rate of interest to produce a given future value. The present value of an ordinary annuity is the present value of a series of payments. Calculations of future and present values are simplified by using the appropriate tables, which appear in an appendix to the book.

LO5 Apply the time value of money to simple accounting situations.

Present value may be used in evaluating the proposed purchase price of an asset, in computing the present value of deferred payments, in determining the future value of an investment of idle cash, in establishing a fund for loan repayment, and in numerous other accounting situations in which time is a factor.

REVIEW of Concepts and Terminology

The following concepts and terms were introduced in this chapter:

Commercial paper: Unsecured loans sold to the public, usually through professionally managed investment firms, as a means of borrowing short-term funds. **(LO2)**

Commitment: A legal obligation that does not meet the technical requirements for recognition as a liability. **(LO3)**

Compound interest: The interest cost for two or more periods when after each period, the interest of that period is added to the amount on which interest is computed in future periods. **(LO4)**

Contingent liability: A potential liability that arises from a past transaction and is dependent on a future event. **(LO3)**

Current liabilities: Debts and obligations that a company expects to satisfy within one year or within the normal operating cycle, whichever is longer. **(LO1)**

Definitely determinable liabilities: Current liabilities that are set by contract or statute and that can be measured exactly. **(LO2)**

Estimated liabilities: Definite debts or obligations whose exact amounts cannot be known until a later date. **(LO2)**

Future value: The amount an investment will be worth at a future date if invested at compound interest. **(LO4)**

Interest: The cost of using money for a specific period. **(LO4)**

Line of credit: An arrangement with a bank that allows a company to borrow funds as needed. **(LO2)**

Long-term liabilities: Debts and obligations due beyond one year or beyond the normal operating cycle. **(LO1)**

Ordinary annuity: A series of equal payments made at the end of equal intervals of time, with compound interest on the payments. **(LO4)**

Present value: The amount that must be invested today at a given rate of interest to produce a given future value. **(LO4)**

Salaries: Compensation of employees at a monthly or yearly rate. **(LO2)**

Simple interest: The interest cost for one or more periods when the amount on which the interest is computed stays the same from period to period. **(LO4)**

Time value of money: The costs or benefits derived from holding or not holding money over time. **(LO4)**

Unearned revenues: Revenues received in advance for goods or services that will not be delivered during the current accounting period. **(LO2)**

Wages: Compensation of employees at an hourly rate. **(LO2)**

Key Ratios

Days' payable: How long, on average, a company takes to pay its accounts payable; 365 days ÷ Payables Turnover. **(LO1)**

Payables turnover: The number of times, on average, that a company pays its accounts payable in an accounting period; (Cost of Goods Sold +/− Change in Merchandise Inventory) ÷ Average Accounts Payable. **(LO1)**

REVIEW Problem

LO1 **Identification and Evaluation of Current Liabilities**

 Sara Jones started a small fitness business, Sara's Fitness Center, last year. In addition to offering exercise classes, she sells nutritional supplements. She has not yet filed any tax reports for her business and therefore owes taxes. Because she has limited experience in running a business, she has brought you all her business records—a checkbook, canceled checks, deposit slips, suppliers' invoices, a notice of annual property taxes of $1,800 due to the city, and a promissory note to her bank for $8,000. She wants you to determine what her business owes the government and other parties.

You analyze all her records and determine the following as of December 31, 20x7:

Unpaid invoices for supplements	$ 6,000
Sales of supplements (excluding sales tax)	28,500
Cost of supplements sold	16,800
Exercise instructor salaries	11,400
Exercise revenues	40,700
Current assets	20,000
Supplements inventory (12/31/07)	13,500
Supplements inventory (12/31/06)	10,500

You learn that the company has sold gift certificates in the amount of $350 that have not been redeemed and that it has deducted $687 from its two employees' salaries for federal income taxes owed to the government. The current social security tax is 6.2 percent on maximum earnings of $90,000 for each employee, and the current Medicare tax is 1.45 percent (no maximum earnings). The FUTA tax is 5.4 percent to the state and .8 percent to the federal government on the first $7,000 earned by each employee; no employee earned more than $7,000. Jones has not filed a sales tax report to the state (6 percent of supplements sales).

Required

1. Given these facts, determine the company's current liabilities as of December 31, 20x7.
2. **User Insight:** Your analysis of the company's current liabilities has been based on documents that the owner showed you. What liabilities may be missing from your analysis?
3. **User Insight:** Evaluate the company's liquidity by calculating working capital, payables turnover, and days' payable. Comment on the results. (Assume average accounts payable were the same as year-end accounts payable.)

Answer to Review Problem

1. The current liabilities of Sara's Fitness Center as of December 31, 20x7, are as follows:

	A	B	C
1	Accounts payable		$ 6,000.00
2	Notes payable		8,000.00
3	Property tax liability		1,800.00
4	Sales tax payable	($28,500 x 0.06)	1,710.00
5	Social security tax payable	($11,400 x 0.062)	706.80
6	Medicare tax payable	($11,400 x 0.0145)	165.30
7	State unemployment tax payable	($11,400 x 0.054)	615.60
8	Federal unemployment tax payable	($11,400 x 0.008)	91.20
9	Federal income tax withholding		687.00
10	Unearned revenues		350.00
11	Total current liabilities		$ 20,125.90

2. The company may have current liabilities for which you have not seen any documentary evidence. For instance, invoices for accounts payable could be missing. In addition, the company may have accrued liabilities, such as vacation pay for its two employees, which would require establishing an

estimated liability. If the promissory note to Jones's bank is interest-bearing, it also would require an adjustment to accrue interest payable, and the company could have other loans outstanding for which you have not seen documentary evidence. Moreover, it may have to pay penalties and interest to the federal and state governments because of its failure to remit tax payments on a timely basis. City and state income tax withholding for the employees could be another overlooked liability.

3. Liquidity ratios computed and evaluated:

	A	B	C	D	E	F	G	H
1	Working Capital	=			Current Assets − Current Liabilities			
3		=			\$20,000.00 − \$20,125.90			
5		=			(\$125.90)			
6								
7	Payables Turnover	=		Cost of Goods Sold +/− Change in Merchandise Inventory				
8					Accounts Payable			
10		=			\$16,800 + \$3,000			
11					\$6,000			
13		=			\$19,800			
14					\$6,000			
16		=			3.3 times			
17								
18	Days' Payable	=			365 days			
19					Payables Turnover			
21		=			365 days			
22					3.3 times			
24		=			110.6 days			

Sara's Fitness Center has a negative working capital of \$125.90, its payables turnover is only 3.3 times, and it takes an average of 110.6 days to pay its accounts payable. Its liquidity is therefore highly questionable. Many of its current assets are inventory, which it must sell to generate cash, and it must pay most of its current liabilities sooner than the 110.6 days would indicate.

CHAPTER ASSIGNMENTS

BUILDING Your Basic Knowledge and Skills

Short Exercises

LO1   Issues in Accounting for Liabilities

SE 1. Indicate whether each of the following actions relates to (a) managing liquidity and cash flow, (b) recognition of liabilities, (c) valuation of liabilities, (d) classification of liabilities, or (e) disclosure of liabilities:

1. Determining that a liability will be paid in less than one year
2. Estimating the amount of a liability

3. Providing information about when liabilities are due and their interest rates
4. Determining when a liability arises
5. Assessing working capital and payables turnover

LO1 **Measuring Short-Term Liquidity**

SE 2. Robinson Company has current assets of $65,000 and current liabilities of $40,000, of which accounts payable are $35,000. Robinson's cost of goods sold is $230,000, its merchandise inventory increased by $10,000, and accounts payable were $25,000 the prior year. Calculate Robinson's working capital, payables turnover, and days' payable.

LO2, LO3 **Types of Liabilities**

SE 3. Indicate whether each of the following is (a) a definitely determinable liability, (b) an estimated liability, (c) a commitment, or (d) a contingent liability:

1. Dividends Payable
2. Pending litigation
3. Income Taxes Payable
4. Current portion of long-term debt
5. Vacation Pay Liability
6. Guaranteed loans of another company
7. Purchase agreement

LO2 **Interest Expense on Note Payable**

SE 4. On the last day of August, Navarro Company borrowed $120,000 on a bank note for 60 days at 10 percent interest. Assume that interest is stated separately. Prepare the following entries in journal form: (1) August 31, recording of note; and (2) October 30, payment of note plus interest.

LO2 **Payroll Expenses**

SE 5. The following payroll totals for the month of April are from the payroll register of Ha Corporation: salaries, $446,000; federal income taxes withheld, $62,880; social security tax withheld, $27,652; Medicare tax withheld, $6,467; medical insurance deductions, $13,160; and salaries subject to unemployment taxes, $313,200.

Determine the total and components of (1) the monthly payroll and (2) employer's payroll expense, assuming social security and Medicare taxes equal to the amounts for employees, a federal unemployment insurance tax of .8 percent, a state unemployment tax of 5.4 percent, and medical insurance premiums for which the employer pays 80 percent of the cost.

LO2 **Product Warranty Liability**

SE 6. Harper Corp. manufactures and sells travel clocks. Each clock costs $12.50 to produce and sells for $25. In addition, each clock carries a warranty that provides for free replacement if it fails during the two years following the sale. In the past, 5 percent of the clocks sold have had to be replaced under the warranty. During October, Harper sold 52,000 clocks, and 2,800 clocks were replaced under the warranty. Prepare entries in journal form to record the estimated liability for product warranties during the month and the clocks replaced under warranty during the month.

Note: Tables 1 to 4 in the appendix on future value and present value tables may be used where appropriate to solve **SE 7** through **SE 10.**

LO4 **Simple and Compound Interest**

SE 7. Murad Motors, Inc., receives a one-year note that carries a 12 percent annual interest rate on $3,000 for the sale of a used car. Compute the maturity value under each of the following assumptions: (1) Simple interest is charged. (2) The interest is compounded semiannually. (3) The interest is compounded quarterly. (4) The interest is compounded monthly.

LO4 **Future Value Calculations**

SE 8. Find the future value of (1) a single payment of $5,000 at 7 percent for ten years, (2) ten annual payments of $500 at 7 percent, (3) a single payment of $1,500 at 9 percent for seven years, and (4) seven annual payments of $1,500 at 9 percent.

LO4 **Present Value Calculations**

SE 9. Find the present value of (1) a single payment of $24,000 at 6 percent for 12 years, (2) 12 annual payments of $2,000 at 6 percent, (3) a single payment of $5,000 at 9 percent for five years, and (4) five annual payments of $5,000 at 9 percent.

LO5 **Valuing an Asset for the Purpose of Making a Purchasing Decision**

SE 10. Hogan Whitner owns a machine shop and has the opportunity to purchase a new machine for $30,000. After carefully studying projected costs and revenues, Whitner estimates that the new machine will produce a net cash flow of $7,200 annually and will last for eight years. Whitner believes that an interest rate of 10 percent is adequate for his business.

Calculate the present value of the machine to Whitner. Does the purchase appear to be a smart business decision?

Exercises

LO1, LO2, LO3 **Discussion Questions**

E 1. Develop a brief answer to each of the following questions:

1. Ned Johnson, a star college basketball player, received a contract from the Midwest Blazers to play professional basketball. The contract calls for a salary of $300,000 a year for four years, dependent on his making the team in each of those years. Should this contract be considered a liability and recorded on the books of the basketball team?
2. Is increasing payables turnover good or bad for a company? Why or why not?
3. Do adjusting entries involving estimated liabilities and accruals ever affect cash flows?
4. When would a commitment be recognized in the accounting records?

LO4 **Discussion Questions**

E 2. Develop a brief answer to each of the following questions:

1. Is a friend who borrows money from you for three years and agrees to pay you interest after each year paying you simple or compound interest?
2. Ordinary annuities assume that the first payment is made at the end of each year. In a transaction, who is better off in this arrangement, the payer or the receiver? Why?
3. Why is present value one of the most useful concepts in making business decisions?

LO1   Issues in Accounting for Liabilities

E 3. Indicate whether each of the following actions relates to (a) managing liquidity and cash flows, (b) recognition of liabilities, (c) valuation of liabilities, (d) classification of liabilities, or (e) disclosure of liabilities:

1. Setting a liability at the fair market value of goods to be delivered
2. Relating the payment date of a liability to the length of the operating cycle
3. Recording a liability in accordance with the matching rule
4. Providing information about financial instruments on the balance sheet
5. Estimating the amount of "cents-off" coupons that will be redeemed
6. Categorizing a liability as long-term debt
7. Measuring working capital
8. Comparing days' payable with last year

LO1   Measuring Short-Term Liquidity

E 4. In 20x7, Michaud Company had current assets of $155,000 and current liabilities of $100,000, of which accounts payable were $65,000. Cost of goods sold was $425,000, merchandise inventory increased by $40,000, and accounts payable were $55,000 in the prior year. In 20x8, Michaud had current assets of $210,000 and current liabilities of $160,000, of which accounts payable were $75,000. Cost of goods sold was $475,000, and merchandise inventory decreased by $15,000. Calculate Michaud working capital, payables turnover, and days' payable for 20x7 and 20x8. Assess Michaud liquidity and cash flows in relation to the change in payables turnover from 20x7 to 20x8.

LO2   Interest Expense on Note Payable

E 5. On the last day of October, Thornton Company borrows $60,000 on a bank note for 60 days at 12 percent interest. Interest is not included in the face amount. Prepare the following entries in journal form: (1) October 31, recording of note; (2) November 30, accrual of interest expense; and (3) December 30, payment of note plus interest.

LO2   Sales and Excise Taxes

E 6. Web Design Services billed its customers a total of $490,200 for the month of August, including 9 percent federal excise tax and 5 percent sales tax.

1. Determine the proper amount of service revenue to report for the month.
2. Prepare an entry in journal form to record the revenue and related liabilities for the month.

LO2   Payroll Expenses

E 7. At the end of October, the payroll register for Symphony Tool and Die Corporation contained the following totals: wages, $371,000; federal income taxes withheld, $94,884; state income taxes withheld, $15,636; social security tax withheld, $23,002; Medicare tax withheld, $5,379.50; medical insurance deductions, $12,870; and wages subject to unemployment taxes, $57,240.

   Determine the total and components of the (1) monthly payroll and (2) employer payroll expenses, assuming social security and Medicare taxes equal to the amount for employees, a federal unemployment insurance tax of .8 percent, a state unemployment tax of 5.4 percent, and medical insurance premiums for which the employer pays 80 percent of the cost.

LO2   Product Warranty Liability

E 8. Snapz Company manufactures and sells electronic games. Each game costs $25 to produce, sells for $45, and carries a warranty that provides for free replacement if it fails during the two years following the sale. In the past, 7 percent of the games sold had to be replaced under the warranty. During July, Snapz sold 13,000 games, and 1,400 games were replaced under the warranty.

1. Prepare an entry in journal form to record the estimated liability for product warranties during the month.
2. Prepare an entry in journal form to record the games replaced under warranty during the month.

LO2 **Vacation Pay Liability**

E 9. Bivens Corporation gives three weeks' paid vacation to each employee who has worked at the company for one year. Based on studies of employee turnover and previous experience, management estimates that 65 percent of the employees will qualify for vacation pay this year.

1. Assume that Bivens's July payroll is $300,000, of which $20,000 is paid to employees on vacation. Figure the estimated employee vacation benefit for the month.
2. Prepare an entry in journal form to record the employee benefit for July.
3. Prepare an entry in journal form to record the pay to employees on vacation.

Note: Tables 1 to 4 in the appendix on future value and present value tables may be used where appropriate to solve **E 10** through **E 20**.

LO4 **Future Value Calculations**

E 10. Song receives a one-year note for $6,000 that carries a 12 percent annual interest rate for the sale of a used car. Compute the maturity value under each of the following assumptions: (1) The interest is simple interest. (2) The interest is compounded semiannually. (3) The interest is compounded quarterly. (4) The interest is compounded monthly.

LO4 **Future Value Calculations**

E 11. Find the future value of (1) a single payment of $40,000 at 7 percent for ten years, (2) ten annual payments of $4,000 at 7 percent, (3) a single payment of $12,000 at 9 percent for seven years, and (4) seven annual payments of $12,000 at 9 percent.

LO4, LO5 **Determining an Advance Payment**

E 12. Denise Davis is contemplating paying five years' rent in advance. Her annual rent is $12,600. Calculate the single sum that would have to be paid now for the advance rent if we assume compound interest of 8 percent.

LO4 **Present Value Calculations**

E 13. Find the present value of (1) a single payment of $12,000 at 6 percent for 12 years, (2) 12 annual payments of $1,000 at 6 percent, (3) a single payment of $2,500 at 9 percent for five years, and (4) five annual payments of $2,500 at 9 percent.

LO4, LO5 **Present Value of a Lump-Sum Contract**

E 14. A contract calls for a lump-sum payment of $30,000. Find the present value of the contract, assuming that (1) the payment is due in five years, and the current interest rate is 9 percent; (2) the payment is due in ten years, and the current interest rate is 9 percent; (3) the payment is due in five years, and the current interest rate is 5 percent; and (4) the payment is due in ten years, and the current interest rate is 5 percent.

LO4, LO5   **Present Value of an Annuity Contract**

E 15. A contract calls for annual payments of $2,400. Find the present value of the contract, assuming that (1) the number of payments is seven, and the current interest rate is 6 percent; (2) the number of payments is 14, and the current interest rate is 6 percent; (3) the number of payments is seven, and the current interest rate is 8 percent; and (4) the number of payments is 14, and the current interest rate is 8 percent.

LO4, LO5   **Valuing an Asset for the Purpose of Making a Purchasing Decision**

E 16. Charles Ogden owns a service station and has the opportunity to purchase a car wash machine for $15,000. After carefully studying projected costs and revenues, Ogden estimates that the car wash machine will produce a net cash flow of $2,600 annually and will last for eight years. He determines that an interest rate of 14 percent is adequate for his business. Calculate the present value of the machine to Ogden. Does the purchase appear to be a smart business decision?

LO4, LO5   **Deferred Payment**

E 17. Antwone Equipment Corporation sold a precision tool machine with computer controls to Trudeau Corporation for $400,000 on January 2 and agreed to take payment nine months later on October 2. Assuming that the prevailing annual interest rate for such a transaction is 16 percent compounded quarterly, what is the actual sale (purchase) price of the machine tool?

LO4, LO5   **Investment of Idle Cash**

E 18. Playwright Publishing Company, a publisher of college textbooks, has just completed a successful fall selling season and has $2,500,000 in cash to invest for nine months, beginning on January 1. The company places the cash in an account that is expected to pay 4 percent annual interest compounded quarterly. Interest is credited to the company's account each quarter. How much cash will the company have at the end of nine months?

LO4, LO5   **Accumulation of a Fund**

E 19. Semma Corporation borrows $1,500,000 from an insurance company on a five-year note. Management agrees to set aside enough cash at the end of each year to accumulate the amount needed to pay off the note at maturity. Since the first contribution to the fund will be made in one year, four annual contributions are needed. Assuming that the fund will earn 10 percent compounded annually, how much will the annual contribution to the fund be? (Round to nearest dollar.)

LO4, LO5   **Negotiating the Sale of a Business**

E 20. Andrea Lima is attempting to sell her business to Alfonso Moreno. The company has assets of $1,800,000, liabilities of $1,600,000, and stockholders' equity of $200,000. Both parties agree that the proper rate of return to expect is 12 percent; however, they differ on other assumptions. Lima believes that the business will generate at least $200,000 per year of cash flows for 20 years. Moreno thinks that $160,000 in cash flows per year is more reasonable and that only ten years in the future should be considered. Using Table 4 in the appendix on future value and present value tables, determine the range for negotiation by computing the present value of Lima's offer to sell and of Moreno's offer to buy.

Problems

LO1, LO2, LO3 **Identification of Current Liabilities, Contingencies, and Commitments**

P 1. Listed below are common types of current liabilities, contingencies, and commitments:

a. Accounts payable
b. Bank loans and commercial paper
c. Notes payable
d. Dividends payable
e. Sales and excise taxes payable
f. Current portion of long-term debt
g. Payroll liabilities
h. Unearned revenues

i. Income taxes payable
j. Property taxes payable
k. Promotional costs
l. Product warranty liability
m. Vacation pay liability
n. Contingent liability
o. Commitment

Required

1. For each of the following statements, identify the category above to which it gives rise or with which it is most closely associated:

    1. A company agrees to replace parts of a product if they fail.
    2. An employee earns one day off for each month worked.
    3. A company signs a contract to lease a building for five years.
    4. A company puts discount coupons in the newspaper.
    5. A company agrees to pay insurance costs for employees.
    6. A portion of a mortgage on a building is due this year.
    7. The board of directors declares a dividend.
    8. A company has trade payables.
    9. A company has a pending lawsuit against it.
    10. A company arranges for a line of credit.
    11. A company signs a note due in 60 days.
    12. A company operates in a state that has a sales tax.
    13. A company earns a profit that is taxable.
    14. A company owns buildings that are subject to property taxes.

2. **User Insight:** Of the items listed from **a** to **o** above, which ones would you not expect to see listed on the balance sheet with a dollar amount? Of those items that would be listed on the balance sheet with a dollar amount, which ones would you consider to involve the most judgment or discretion on the part of management?

LO2 **Notes Payable and Wages Payable**

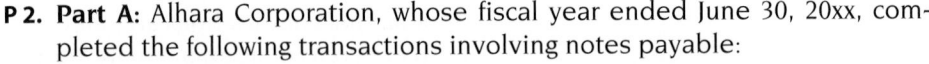

P 2. Part A: Alhara Corporation, whose fiscal year ended June 30, 20xx, completed the following transactions involving notes payable:

May 21 Obtained a 60-day extension on a $36,000 trade account payable owed to a supplier by signing a 60-day, $36,000 note. Interest is in addition to the face value, at the rate of 14 percent.

June 30 Made the end-of-year adjusting entry to accrue interest expense.

July 20 Paid off the note plus interest due the supplier.

Required

1. Prepare journal entries for the notes payable transactions.
2. **User Insight:** When notes payable appears on the balance sheet, what other current liability would you look for to be associated with the notes? What would it mean if this other current liability did not appear?

Part B: The payroll register for Alhara Corporation contained the following totals at the end of July: wages, $278,250; federal income taxes withheld,

$71,163; state income taxes withheld, $11,727; social security tax withheld, $17,253; Medicare tax withheld, $4,035; medical insurance deductions, $9,600; and wages subject to unemployment taxes, $171,720.

Required

Prepare entries to record the (1) monthly payroll and (2) employer payroll expenses, assuming social security and Medicare taxes equal to the amount for employees, a federal unemployment insurance tax of .8 percent, a state unemployment tax of 5.4 percent, and medical insurance premiums for which the employer pays 80 percent of the cost.

LO2 **Product Warranty Liability**

P 3. Visicorp Company is engaged in the retail sale of high-definition televisions (HDTVs). Each HDTV has a 24-month warranty on parts. If a repair under warranty is required, a charge for the labor is made. Management has found that 20 percent of the HDTVs sold require some work before the warranty expires. Furthermore, the average cost of replacement parts has been $120 per repair. At the beginning of January, the account for the estimated liability for product warranties had a credit balance of $28,600. During January, 112 HDTVs were returned under the warranty. The cost of the parts used in repairing the HDTVs was $17,530, and $18,884 was collected as service revenue for the labor involved. During January, the month before the Super Bowl, Visicorp Company sold 450 new HDTVs.

Required

1. Prepare entries in journal form to record each of the following: (a) the warranty work completed during the month, including related revenue; (b) the estimated liability for product warranties for HDTVs sold during the month.
2. Compute the balance of the Estimated Product Warranty Liability account at the end of the month.
3. **User Insight:** If the company's product warranty liability is overestimated, what are the effects on current and future years' income?

LO1 **Identification and Evaluation of Current Liabilities**

P 4. Jose Hernandez opened a small motorcycle repair shop, Hernandez Cycle Repair, on January 2, 20x7. The shop also sells a limited number of motorcycle parts. In January 20x8, Hernandez realized he had never filed any tax reports for his business and therefore probably owes a considerable amount of taxes. Since he has limited experience in running a business, he has brought you all his business records, including a checkbook, canceled checks, deposit slips, suppliers' invoices, a notice of annual property taxes of $4,620 due to the city, and a promissory note to his father-in-law for $5,000. He wants you to determine what his business owes the government and other parties.

You analyze all his records and determine the following as of December 31, 20x7:

Unpaid invoices for motorcycle parts	$ 18,000
Parts sales (excluding sales tax)	88,540
Cost of Parts Sold	62,250
Workers' salaries	20,400
Repair revenues	120,600
Current assets	32,600
Motorcycle parts inventory	23,500

You learn that the company has deducted $952 from the two employees' salaries for federal income taxes owed to the government. The current social security tax is 6.2 percent on maximum earnings of $90,000 for each employee, and the current Medicare tax is 1.45 percent (no maximum earnings). The FUTA tax is 5.4 percent to the state and .8 percent to the federal government on the first $7,000 earned by each employee, and each employee earned more than $7,000. Hernandez has not filed a sales tax report to the state (5 percent of sales).

Required

1. Given these limited facts, determine Hernandez Cycle Repair's current liabilities as of December 31, 20x7.
2. User Insight: What additional information would you want from Hernandez to satisfy yourself that all current liabilities have been identified?
3. User Insight: Evaluate Hernandez's liquidity by calculating working capital, payables turnover, and days' payable. Comment on the results. (Assume average accounts payable were the same as year-end accounts payable.)

LO4, LO5 **Applications of Time Value of Money**

P 5. The management of Pzazz, Inc., took the following actions that went into effect on January 2, 20x7. Each action involved an application of the time value of money.

a. Established in one payment of $50,000 a contingency fund for the possible settlement of a lawsuit. The suit is expected to be settled in two years.
b. Asked for another fund to be established by a single payment to accumulate to $150,000 in four years.
c. Approved the purchase of a parcel of land for future plant expansion. Payments are to start January 2, 20x8, at $100,000 per year for five years.
d. Determined that a new building to be built on the property in **c** would cost $800,000 and authorized five annual payments to be paid starting January 2, 20x8, into a fund for its construction.

Required

1. Assuming an annual interest rate of 8 percent and using Tables 1 to 4 in this chapter, answer the following questions:
   a. In action **a**, how much will the fund total in two years?
   b. In action **b**, how much will need to be deposited initially to accumulate the desired amount?
   c. In action **c**, what is the purchase price (present value) of the land?
   d. In action **d**, how much would the equal annual payments need to be to accumulate enough money to construct the building?
2. User Insight: What is the fundamental reason time value of money analysis is a useful tool in making business decisions?

Alternate Problems

LO2 **Notes Payable and Wages Payable**

P 6. Part A: Green T Company, whose fiscal year ends December 31, completed the following transactions involving notes payable:

20x7
Nov. 25 Purchased a new loading cart by issuing a 60-day, 10 percent note for $43,200.
Dec. 31 Made the end-of-year adjusting entry to accrue interest expense.

20x8
Jan.   24   Paid off the loading cart note.

Required

1. Prepare entries in journal form for Green T Company's notes payable transactions.
2. **User Insight:** When notes payable appears on the balance sheet, what other current liability would you look for to be associated with the notes? What would it mean if this other current liability did not appear?

   Part B: At the end of October, the payroll register for Green T Company contained the following totals: wages, $92,750; federal income taxes withheld, $23,721; state income taxes withheld, $3,909; social security tax withheld, $5,751; Medicare tax withheld, $1,345; medical insurance deductions, $3,200; and wages subject to unemployment taxes, $57,240.

Required

Prepare entries to record the (1) monthly payroll and (2) employer payroll expenses, assuming social security and Medicare taxes equal to the amount for employees, a federal unemployment insurance tax of .8 percent, a state unemployment tax of 5.4 percent, and medical insurance premiums for which the employer pays 80 percent of the cost.

LO2   **Product Warranty Liability**

 P 7. The Kow Long Products Company manufactures and sells wireless video cell phones, which it guarantees for five years. If a cell phone fails, it is replaced free, but the customer is charged a service fee for handling. In the past, management has found that only 3 percent of the cell phones sold required replacement under the warranty. The average cell phone costs the company $240. At the beginning of September, the account for estimated liability for product warranties had a credit balance of $208,000. During September, 250 cell phones were returned under the warranty. The company collected $9,860 of service fees for handling. During the month, the company sold 2,800 cell phones.

Required

1. Prepare entries in journal form to record (a) the cost of cell phones replaced under warranty and (b) the estimated liability for product warranties for cell phones sold during the month.
2. Compute the balance of the Estimated Product Warranty Liability account at the end of the month.
3. **User Insight:** If the company's product warranty liability is underestimated, what are the effects on current and future years' income?

LO4, LO5   **Applications of Time Value of Money**

P 8. Rothberg Corporation's management took the following actions, which went into effect on January 2, 20x7. Each action involved an application of the time value of money.

a. Established a new retirement plan to take effect in three years and authorized three annual payments of $1,000,000, starting January 2, 20x8, to establish the retirement fund.
b. Approved plans for a new distribution center to be built for $2,000,000 and authorized five annual payments, starting January 2, 20x8, to accumulate the funds for the new center.
c. Bought out the contract of a member of top management for a payment of $100,000 per year for four years beginning January 2, 20x8.

d. Set aside $600,000 for possible losses from lawsuits over a defective product. The lawsuits are not expected to be settled for three years.

Required

1. Assuming an annual interest rate of 10 percent and using Tables 1 to 4 in this chapter, answer the following questions:
   a. In action **a**, how much will the retirement fund total after the three payments are made?
   b. In action **b**, how much must the annual payment be to reach the goal?
   c. In action **c**, what is the cost (present value) of the buyout?
   d. In action **d**, how much will the fund total in three years?
2. **User Insight:** Many businesses analyze the time value of money extensively when making decisions about investing in long-term assets. Why is this type of analysis particularly appropriate for such decisions?

ENHANCING Your Knowledge, Skills, and Critical Thinking

Conceptual Understanding Cases

LO2 **Frequent Flyer Plan**

C 1. JetGreen Airways instituted a frequent flyer program in which passengers accumulate points toward a free flight based on the number of miles they fly on the airline. One point was awarded for each mile flown, with a minimum of 750 miles being given for any flight. Because of competition in 2008, the company began a bonus plan in which passengers receive triple the normal mileage points. In the past, about 1.5 percent of passenger miles were flown by passengers who had converted points to free flights. With the triple mileage program, JetGreen expects that a 2.5 percent rate will be more appropriate for future years.

During 2008, the company had passenger revenues of $966.3 million and passenger transportation operating expenses of $802.8 million before depreciation and amortization. Operating income was $86.1 million. What is the appropriate rate to use to estimate free miles? What would be the effect of the estimated liability for free travel by frequent fliers on 2008 net income? Describe several ways to estimate the amount of this liability. Be prepared to discuss the arguments for and against recognizing this liability.

LO3 **Lawsuits and Contingent Liabilities**

C 2. When faced with lawsuits, many companies recognize a loss and therefore credit a liability or reserve account for any future losses that may result. For instance, in the famous **WorldCom** case, **Citibank**, the world's largest financial services firm, announced it was setting up reserves or liabilities of $5.6 billion in connection with pending lawsuits related to its relationship with World-Com.[14] Are these lawsuits contingent liabilities? Using the two criteria established by the FASB for recording a contingency, what conditions must exist for Citibank to record these lawsuits when they have not yet been heard in court?

LO4, LO5 **Time Value of Money**

C 3. **Mitsubishi**, the large Japanese electronics company, advertised its $4,499 Diamond Series 65-inch-wide screen Projection TV with no payments and no interest for 12 months.[15] What role does the time value of money play in this promotion? Assuming that Mitsubishi is able to borrow funds at 8 percent interest, what is the cost to Mitsubishi of every customer who takes advantage of this offer? If you were able to borrow to pay cash for this TV, which rate would be more relevant in determining how much you might offer for the TV—the rate at which you borrow money or the rate Mitsubishi borrows money?

Interpreting Financial Reports

LO1   Comparison of Two Companies' Ratios with Industry Ratios

C 4. Both **Sun Microsystems Inc**. and **Cisco Systems** are in the computer industry. These data (in millions) are for their fiscal year ends:[16]

	Sun	Cisco
Average accounts payable	$1,112	$ 696
Cost of goods sold	6,481	8,130
Increase (decrease) in inventory	(33)	90

Compare the payables turnover ratio and days' payable for both companies. Comment on the results. How are cash flows affected by days' payable? How do Sun Microsystems' and Cisco Systems' ratios compare with the computer industry ratios shown in Figures 1 and 2 in this chapter? (Use year-end amounts for ratios.)

LO2   Nature and Recognition of an Estimated Liability

C 5. The decision to recognize and record a liability is sometimes a matter of judgment. People who use **General Motors** credit cards earn rebates toward the purchase or lease of GM vehicles in relation to the amount of purchases they make with their cards. General Motors chooses to treat these outstanding rebates as a commitment in the notes to its financial statements:

> GM sponsors a credit card program . . . which offers rebates that can be applied primarily against the purchase or lease of GM vehicles. The amount of rebates available to qualified cardholders (net of deferred program income) was $4.5 billion, $4.1 billion, and $4.0 billion at December 31, 2004, 2003, and 2002, respectively.[17]

Using the two criteria established by the FASB for recording a contingency, explain GM's reasoning in treating this liability as a commitment in the notes, where it will likely receive less attention by analysts, rather than including it on the income statement as an expense and on the balance sheet as an estimated liability. Do you agree with this position? (**Hint:** Apply the matching rule.)

Decision Analysis Using Excel

LO4, LO5   Baseball Contract

C 6. The St. Louis Titans' fifth-year shortstop Devon Turner made the All-Star team in 2007. Turner has three years left on a contract that is to pay him $2.4 million a year. He wants to renegotiate his contract because other players who have equally outstanding records (although they also have more experience) are receiving as much as $10.5 million per year for five years. Management has a policy of never renegotiating a current contract but is willing to consider extending the contract to additional years. In fact, the Titans have offered Turner an additional three years at $6.0 million, $9.0 million, and $12.0 million, respectively. In addition, they have added an option year at $15.0 million. Management points out that this package is worth $42.0 million, or $10.5 million per year on average. Turner is considering this offer and is also considering asking for a bonus to be paid upon signing the contract. Write a memorandum to Turner that comments on management's position and evaluates the offer, assuming a current interest rate of 10 percent. (**Hint:** Use present values.) Propose a range for the signing bonus. Finally, include other considerations that may affect the value of the offer.

Annual Report Case: CVS Corporation

LO1, LO3   **Short-Term Liabilities and Seasonality; Commitments and Contingencies**

C 7. Refer to the quarterly financial report near the end of the notes to the financial statements in **CVS's** annual report. Is CVS a seasonal business? Would you expect short-term borrowings and accounts payable to be unusually high or unusually low at the balance sheet date of December 31, 2005?

Read CVS's note on commitments and contingencies. What commitments and contingencies does the company have? Why is it important to consider this information in connection with payables analysis?

Comparison Case: CVS Corporation Versus Walgreens

LO1   **Payables Analysis**

C 8. Refer to **CVS's** financial statements in the Supplement to Chapter 5 and to the following data for **Walgreens**:

	2005	2004	2003
Cost of sales	$30,413.8	$27,310.4	$23,706.2
Trade accounts payable	2,918.2	2,641.5	2,407.8
Increase in inventories	854.1	536.0	557.5

Compute the payables turnover and days' payable for CVS and Walgreens for the past two years. In 2003, CVS had accounts payable of $1,666.4 million, and its inventories were $4,016.5. Which company do you think makes the most use of creditors for financing the needs of the operating cycle? Has the trend changed?

Ethical Dilemma Case

LO2   **Known Legal Violations**

C 9. Surf and Turf Restaurant is a large steak restaurant in the suburbs of Chicago. Don O'Shannon, an accounting student at a nearby college, recently secured a full-time accounting job at the restaurant. He felt fortunate to have a good job that accommodated his class schedule because the local economy was very bad. After a few weeks on the job, O'Shannon realized that his boss, the owner of the business, was paying the kitchen workers in cash and was not withholding federal and state income taxes or social security and Medicare taxes. O'Shannon understands that federal and state laws require these taxes to be withheld and paid to the appropriate agency in a timely manner. He also realizes that if he raises this issue, he could lose his job. What alternatives are available to O'Shannon? What action would you take if you were in his position? Why did you make this choice?

Internet Case

LO2, LO3   **Pain in the Drug Industry**

C 10. Pain medications have been in the news. The big drug company **Merck** had to withdraw its pain killer Vioxx from the market when it became known that the drug increased the risk of heart attacks. Other drugs are under scrutiny, like Celebrex from **Pfizer**. Do an Internet search on these terms and companies. Find out if any lawsuits have been initiated and how these companies are reacting. Access their annual reports and find out what they report under contingent liabilities in the notes to the financial statements and elsewhere. Have they set aside any reserves for liabilities? What are the criteria for recognizing potential liabilities in the accounting records?

Group Activity Case

LO2, LO5 **Nature and Recognition of an Estimated Liability**

C 11. Assume that you work for Relax-A-Pools, Inc., a retail company that sells backyard above-ground swimming pools for $10,000. Your boss is considering two types of promotions:

1. Offering customers a $1,000 coupon that they can apply to future purchases, including the purchase of annual pool maintenance.
2. Offering credit terms that allow payments of $2,000 down and $2,000 per year for four years starting one year after the purchase. Relax-A-Pools would have to borrow money at 7 percent interest to finance these credit arrangements.

Divide the class into groups. After discussing the relative merits of these two plans, including their implications for accounting and the time value of money, each group should decide on the best alternative. The groups may recommend changes in the plans. A representative of each group should report the group's findings to the class.

Business Communication Case

LO5 **Evaluation of an Auto Lease**

C 12. **Ford Credit** ran an advertisement offering three alternatives for a 24-month lease on a new Lincoln automobile. The three alternatives were zero dollars down and $587 per month for 24 months, $1,975 down and $499 per month for 24 months, or $12,283 down and no monthly payments.[18] Your boss asks you to prepare an analysis of the three alternatives assuming a 12 percent annual return compounded monthly is the relevant interest rate for the company. Present your analysis and make a recommendation to your boss in a one-page business memorandum. Use Table 4 in the appendix on future value and present value tables to determine which is the best deal. How would your recommendation change if the interest rate were higher? If it were lower?

Internal Control

In earlier chapters, we pointed out management's responsibility for ensuring the accuracy and fairness of financial statements. To fulfill that responsibility, management must see that transactions are properly recorded and that the company's assets are protected. That, in turn, requires a system of internal controls. In this chapter, we examine internal controls over the transactions of merchandising companies. These controls and the other issues that we describe apply not just to merchandisers, but to all types of companies.

LEARNING OBJECTIVES

LO1 Identify the management issues related to internal control.

LO2 Describe the components of internal control, control activities, and limitations on internal control.

LO3 Apply internal control activities to common merchandising transactions.

SUPPLEMENTAL OBJECTIVE

SO4 Demonstrate the use of a simple imprest (petty cash) system.

Making a Statement

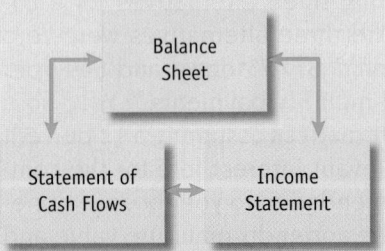

Internal control applies to all transactions and ensures the fair presentation of the financial statements.

HOME DEPOT, INC.

- How can Home Depot maintain control over its merchandising operations?

- How can the users of Home Depot's financial statements be confident that the company has achieved internal control?

Home Depot is the second largest retailer in the United States and the largest U.S. retailer specializing in home improvement. The company's sales total more than $81.5 billion per year. These sales take place in over 2,000 stores and involve 1.3 billion customer transactions. On average, each transaction amounts to about $58. In addition to cash and the other assets that it owns, Home Depot has inventory worth $11.4 billion.[1] Think for a moment of the enormous challenge the company faces in trying to protect its assets and ensure that all transactions are recorded properly.

Management Issues Related to Internal Control

LO1 Identify the management issues related to internal control.

nternal control is a process designed by a company to establish the reliability of the accounting records and financial statements in accordance with generally accepted accounting principles (GAAP) and to ensure that the company's assets are protected.[2] Management must assess its needs for internal controls, establish its responsibility for them, and engage auditors of them, if required.

The Need for Internal Controls

Buying and selling, the principal transactions of merchandising businesses, involve assets—cash, accounts receivable, and merchandise inventory—that are vulnerable to theft and embezzlement. Cash and inventory can, of course, be fairly easy to steal. The potential for embezzlement exists because the large number of transactions that are usually involved in a merchandising business (e.g., cash receipts, receipts on account, payments for purchases, and receipts and shipments of inventory) makes monitoring the accounting records difficult. If a merchandising company like **Home Depot** does not take steps to protect its assets, it can suffer high losses of both cash and inventory. Management's responsibility is to establish an environment, accounting systems, and internal control procedures that will protect the company's assets.

A company's merchandise inventory includes all goods intended for sale regardless of where they are located—on shelves, in storerooms, in warehouses, or in trucks between warehouses and stores. It also includes goods in transit from suppliers if title to the goods has passed to the merchandiser. Ending inventory does not include merchandise that a company has sold but not yet delivered to customers. Nor does it include goods that it cannot sell because they are damaged or obsolete. If damaged or obsolete goods can be sold at a reduced price, however, they should be included in ending inventory at their reduced value.

Merchandisers usually take a **physical inventory** after the close of business on the last day of their fiscal year. This process involves an actual count of all merchandise on hand. It can be a difficult task because it is easy to accidentally omit items or count them twice. A physical inventory must be taken under both the periodic and the perpetual inventory systems.

To facilitate the process, merchandisers often end the fiscal year in a slow season, when inventories are at relatively low levels. For example, many department stores end their fiscal year in January or February. After hours—at night, on a weekend, or when the store closes for all or part of a day for taking inventory—employees count all items and record the results on numbered inventory tickets or sheets, following procedures to ensure that no items will be missed. Using bar coding to take inventory electronically has greatly facilitated the process in many companies.

Most companies experience losses of merchandise inventory from spoilage, shoplifting, and theft by employees. When such losses occur, the periodic inventory system provides no means of identifying them because the costs are automatically included in the cost of goods sold. For example, suppose a company has lost $1,250 in stolen merchandise during an accounting period. When the physical inventory is taken, the missing items are not in

Study Note

Inventory shortages can result from honest mistakes, such as accidentally tagging inventory with the wrong number.

Merchandise inventory includes all goods intended for sale wherever they are located—on store shelves, in warehouses, on car lots, or in transit from suppliers if title to the goods has passed to the merchandiser. To prevent loss of inventory, a merchandiser must have an effective system of internal control.

stock, so they cannot be counted. Because the ending inventory does not contain these items, the amount subtracted from the cost of goods available for sale is less than it would be if the goods were in stock. The cost of goods sold, then, is overstated by $1,250. In a sense, the cost of goods sold is inflated by the amount of merchandise that has been lost.

The perpetual inventory system makes it easier to identify such losses. Because the Merchandise Inventory account is continuously updated for sales, purchases, and returns, the loss will show up as the difference between the inventory records and the physical inventory taken at the end of the accounting period. Once the amount of the loss has been identified, the ending inventory is updated by crediting the Merchandise Inventory account. The offsetting debit is usually an increase in Cost of Goods Sold because the loss is considered a cost that reduces the company's gross margin.

> **Study Note**
>
> An adjustment to the Merchandise Inventory account will be needed if the physical inventory reveals a difference between the actual inventory and the amount in the records.

Management's Responsibility for Internal Control

Management is responsible for establishing a satisfactory system of internal controls. Such a system includes all the policies and procedures needed to ensure the reliability of financial reporting, compliance with laws and regulations, and the effectiveness and efficiency of operations. In other words, management must safeguard the firm's assets, ensure the reliability of its accounting records, and see that its employees comply with all legal requirements and operate the firm to the best advantage of its owners.

Section 404 of the Sarbanes-Oxley Act of 2002 requires that the chief executive officer, the chief financial officer, and the auditors of a public company fully document and certify the company's system of internal controls. For example, in its annual report, **Home Depot** acknowledges management's responsibility for internal control as follows:

> Our management is responsible for establishing and maintaining adequate internal controls over financial reporting. . . . Under the supervision and

FOCUS ON BUSINESS PRACTICE
How Hard Is Financial Fraud to Detect When Its Effects Are Not Material?

In some companies, management works hard to fool the auditors. Several former chief financial officers of **Health-South** pleaded guilty to a massive fraud that did manage to fool the auditors for a number of years. To meet the expectations of financial analysts, these executives manipulated the company's revenue line so that revenue and earnings appeared greater than they were. The fraud involved making adjustments for the difference between what HealthSouth charged a patient and the amount the company could collect from the patient's health insurer. By improperly recording these amounts, HealthSouth's CFOs improved revenue and earnings. For every dollar of illicit revenue they recorded as a credit, they had to make a corresponding debit entry on the balance sheet. Knowing the materiality convention and that the auditors look for material differences, they spread the adjustments around the balance sheet in small pieces so that the auditors wouldn't notice. In effect, the balance sheet looked right because every account, even cash, was artificially increased by a small, or immaterial, amount. In the end, total assets were overstated by $1.5 billion.[3]

with the participation of our management, including our principal executive officer and principal financial officer, we conducted an evaluation of the effectiveness of our internal controls over financial reporting. . . . Based on our evaluation, our management concluded that our internal control over financial reporting was effective as of January 29, 2006.[4]

Independent Accountant's Audit of Internal Control

Although privately owned companies usually are not required to have an independent certified public accountant audit their financial statements, many companies choose to do so. These companies are also not required to have their internal control systems audited. Public companies like **Home Depot**, on the other hand, are required to have not only an independent audit of their financial statements; under the Sarbanes-Oxley Act, they must also have an audit of their internal control over financial reporting. This audit provides reasonable assurance of the adequacy of management's assessment that proper records are maintained, transactions are recorded in accordance with GAAP, and assets are protected. For instance, Home Depot's auditors state:

In our opinion, management's assessment that The Home Depot, Inc., and subsidiaries maintained effective internal control over financial reporting as of January 29, 2006, is fairly stated, in all material respects.[5]

S T O P • R E V I E W • A P P L Y

1-1. What is internal control?

1-2. Why are internal controls needed?

1-3. What is management's responsibility with regard to internal control?

1-4. What does the Sarbanes-Oxley Act require of the auditor of a public company?

Suggested answers to all Stop, Review, and Apply questions are available at http://college.hmco.com/accounting/needles/poa/10e/student_home.html.

Internal Control: Components, Activities, and Limitations

LO2 Describe the components of internal control, control activities, and limitations on internal control.

As mentioned earlier, if a merchandising company does not take steps to protect its assets, it can suffer high losses of cash and inventory through embezzlement and theft. To avoid such occurrences, management must set up and maintain a good system of internal control.

Components of Internal Control

An effective system of internal control has five interrelated components:[6]

1. **Control environment** The **control environment** is created by management's overall attitude, awareness, and actions. It encompasses a company's ethics, philosophy and operating style, organizational structure, method of assigning authority and responsibility, and personnel policies and practices. Personnel should be qualified to handle responsibilities, which means that they must be trained and informed about what is expected of them. For example, the manager of a retail store should train employees to follow prescribed procedures for handling cash sales, credit card sales, and returns and refunds.

2. **Risk assessment** **Risk assessment** involves identifying areas in which risks of loss of assets or inaccuracies in accounting records are high so that adequate controls can be implemented. Among the greater risks in a retail store are that employees may steal cash and customers may steal goods.

3. **Information and communication** **Information and communication** pertains to the accounting system established by management—to the way the system gathers and treats information about the company's transactions and to how it communicates individual responsibilities within the system. Employees must understand exactly what their functions are.

4. **Control activities** **Control activities** are the policies and procedures management puts in place to see that its directives are carried out. (Control activities are discussed in more detail below.)

5. **Monitoring** **Monitoring** involves management's regular assessment of the quality of internal control, including periodic review of compliance with all policies and procedures. Large companies often have a staff of internal auditors who review the company's system of internal control to determine if it is working properly and if procedures are being followed. In smaller businesses, owners and managers conduct these reviews.

Control Activities

Control activities are a very important way of implementing internal control. The goal of these activities is to safeguard a company's assets and ensure the reliability of its accounting records.

Control activities include the following:

1. **Authorization** Managers should authorize certain transactions and activities. In a retail store, for example, cashiers customarily authorize cash

sales, but other transactions, such as issuing a refund, may require a manager's approval.

2. **Recording transactions** To establish accountability for assets, all transactions should be recorded. For example, if a retail store uses a cash register that records sales, refunds, and other transactions on a paper tape or computer disk, the cashier can be held accountable for the cash received and the merchandise removed during his or her shift.

3. **Documents and records** Well-designed documents help ensure that transactions are properly recorded. For example, using prenumbered invoices and other documents is a way of ensuring that all transactions are recorded.

4. **Physical controls** Managers should specify who has access to assets. For example, in a retail store, only the person responsible for the cash register should have access to it. Other employees should not be able to open the cash drawer when the cashier is not present. Similarly, only authorized personnel should have access to warehouses and storerooms. Access to accounting records, including those stored in company computers, should also be controlled.

5. **Periodic independent verification** Someone other than the persons responsible for the accounting records and assets should periodically check the records against the assets. For example, at the end of each shift or day in a retail store, the owner or manager should count the cash in the cash drawer and compare the amount with the amount recorded on the tape or computer disk in the cash register. Other examples of independent verification are periodic counts of physical inventory and reconciliations of monthly bank statements.

6. **Separation of duties** No one person should be in charge of authorizing transactions, handling assets, or keeping records of assets. For example, in a well-managed electronics store, each employee oversees only a single part of a transaction. A sales employee takes the order and creates an invoice. Another employee receives the customer's cash or credit card payment and issues a receipt. Once the customer has a receipt, and only then, a third employee obtains the item from the warehouse and gives it to the customer. A person in the accounting department subsequently compares all sales recorded on the tape or disk in the cash register with the

FOCUS ON BUSINESS PRACTICE

Which Frauds Are Most Common?

A survey of 5,000 large U.S. businesses disclosed that 36 percent suffered losses in excess of $1 million (up from 21 percent in 1998) due to fraud or inventory theft. The frauds most commonly cited were credit card fraud, check fraud, false invoices and phantom vendors, and expense account abuse. The most common reasons for the occurrences of these frauds were poor internal controls, management override of internal controls, and collusion. The most common methods of detecting them were notification by an employee, internal controls, internal auditor review, notification by a customer, and accidental discovery.

Companies that are successful in preventing fraud have a good system of internal control, a formal code of ethics, and a program to monitor compliance that includes a system for reporting incidents of fraud. These companies routinely communicate the existence of the program to their employees.[7]

sales invoices and updates the inventory in the accounting records. The separation of duties means that a mistake, careless or not, cannot be made without being seen by at least one other person.

7. **Sound personnel practices**   Personnel practices that promote internal control include adequate supervision, rotation of key people among different jobs, insistence that employees take vacations, and bonding of personnel who handle cash or inventory. **Bonding** is the process of carefully checking an employee's background and insuring the company against theft by that person. Bonding does not guarantee against theft, but it does prevent or reduce loss if theft occurs. Prudent personnel practices help ensure that employees know their jobs, are honest, and will find it difficult to carry out and conceal embezzlement over time.

Limitations of Internal Control

No system of internal control is without weaknesses. As long as people perform control procedures, an internal control system will be vulnerable to human error. Errors can arise from misunderstandings, mistakes in judgment, carelessness, distraction, or fatigue. And separation of duties can be defeated through collusion by employees who secretly agree to deceive a company. In addition, established procedures may be ineffective against employees' errors or dishonesty, and controls that were initially effective may become ineffective when conditions change. In some cases, the costs of establishing and maintaining elaborate control systems may exceed the benefits. In a small business, for example, active involvement by the owner can be a practical substitute for the separation of some duties.

Study Note

No control procedure can guarantee the prevention of theft. However, the more procedures that are in place, the less likely it is that a theft will occur.

S T O P • R E V I E W • A P P L Y

2-1. Most people think of internal control as a means of making fraud harder to commit and easier to detect. What are some other important purposes of internal control?

2-2. What are the five components of internal control?

2-3. What are some examples of control activities?

2-4. Why is the separation of duties necessary to ensure sound internal control? What does this principle assume about the relationships of employees in a company and the possibility of two or more of them stealing from the company?

Internal Control over Merchandising Transactions

LO3   Apply internal control activities to common merchandising transactions.

Sound internal control activities are needed in all aspects of a business, but particularly when assets are involved. Assets are especially vulnerable when they enter and leave a business. When sales are made, for example, cash or other assets enter the business, and goods or services leave.

Controls must be set up to prevent theft during those transactions. Purchases of assets and payments of liabilities must also be controlled; adequate purchasing and payment systems can safeguard most such transactions. In addition, assets on hand, such as cash, investments, inventory, plant, and equipment, must be protected.

When a system of internal control is applied effectively to merchandising transactions, it can achieve important management goals. As we have noted, it can prevent losses of cash and inventory due to theft or fraud, and it can ensure that records of transactions and account balances are accurate. It can also help managers achieve three broader goals:

1. Keeping enough inventory on hand to sell to customers without overstocking merchandise

2. Keeping sufficient cash on hand to pay for purchases in time to receive discounts

3. Keeping credit losses as low as possible by making credit sales only to customers who are likely to pay on time

In this section of the text, you will see how merchandising companies apply internal control activities to such transactions as cash sales, receipts, purchases, and cash payments. Service and manufacturing businesses use similar procedures.

Control of Cash

One control that managers use to meet the broad goals listed above is the cash budget, which projects future cash receipts and disbursements. By maintaining adequate cash balances, a company is able to take advantage of discounts on purchases, prepare to borrow money when necessary, and avoid the damaging effects of being unable to pay bills when they are due. By investing excess cash, the company can earn interest until the cash is needed.

A more specific control is the separation of duties that involve the handling of cash. Such separation makes theft without detection extremely unlikely unless two or more employees conspire. The separation of duties is easier in large businesses than in small ones, where one person may have to carry out several duties. The effectiveness of internal control over cash varies, based on the size and nature of the company. Most firms, however, should use the following procedures:

1. Separate the functions of authorization, recordkeeping, and custodianship of cash.

2. Limit the number of people who have access to cash, and designate who those people are.

3. Bond all employees who have access to cash.

4. Keep the amount of cash on hand to a minimum by using banking facilities as much as possible.

5. Physically protect cash on hand by using cash registers, cashiers' cages, and safes.

6. Record and deposit all cash receipts promptly, and make payments by check rather than by currency.

7. Have a person who does not handle or record cash make unannounced audits of the cash on hand.

> **Study Note**
>
> Maintaining internal control is especially difficult for a merchandiser. Management must not only establish controls for cash sales, receipts, purchases, and cash payments, but also go to great lengths to manage and protect its inventory.

8. Have a person who does not authorize, handle, or record cash transactions reconcile the Cash account each month.

Notice that each of these procedures helps safeguard cash by making it more difficult for any one individual who has access to cash to steal or misuse it without being detected.

Control of Cash Receipts

Cash from sales of goods and services can be received by mail or over the counter in the form of checks, credit or debit cards, or currency. Whatever the source of the cash, it should be recorded immediately upon receipt in a cash receipts journal. Such a journal establishes a written record of cash receipts that should prevent errors and make theft more difficult.

Control of Cash Received by Mail
Cash received by mail is vulnerable to theft by the employees who handle it. For that reason, companies that deal in mail-order sales generally ask customers to pay by credit card, check, or money order instead of with currency.

When cash is received in the mail, two or more employees should handle it. The employee who opens the mail should make a list in triplicate of the money received. The list should contain each customer's name, the purpose for which the money was sent, and the amount. One copy goes with the cash to the cashier, who deposits the money. The second copy goes to the accounting department for recording. The person who opens the mail keeps the third copy. Errors can be easily caught because the amount deposited by the cashier must agree with the amount received and the amount recorded in the cash receipts journal.

Control of Cash Received over the Counter
Cash registers and prenumbered sales tickets are common tools for controlling cash received over the counter. The amount of a cash sale is rung up on the cash register at the time of the sale. The register should be placed so that the customer can see the amount recorded. Each cash register should have a locked-in tape on which it prints the day's transactions. At the end of the day, the cashier counts the cash in the register and turns it in to the cashier's office. Another employee takes the tape out of the cash register and records the cash receipts for the day in the cash receipts journal. The amount of cash turned in and the amount recorded on the tape should agree; if not, any differences must be explained.

Large retail chains like **Home Depot** commonly monitor cash receipts by having each cash register tied directly into a computer that records each transaction as it occurs. Whether the elements are performed manually or with a

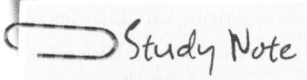

Study Note

The cashier should not be allowed to remove the cash register tape or to record the day's cash receipts.

FOCUS ON BUSINESS PRACTICE

How Do Computers Promote Internal Control?

One of the more difficult challenges facing computer programmers is to build good internal controls into accounting programs. Such programs must include controls that prevent unintentional errors, as well as unauthorized access and tampering. They prevent errors through reasonableness checks (such as not allowing any transactions over a specified amount), mathematical checks that verify the arithmetic of transactions, and sequence checks that require documents and transactions to be in proper order. They typically use passwords and questions about randomly selected personal data to prevent unauthorized access to computer records. They may also use firewalls, which are strong electronic barriers to unauthorized access, as well as data encryption. Data encryption is a way of coding data so that if they are stolen, they are useless to the thief.

■ **FIGURE 1**
Internal Controls in a Large Company: Separation of Duties and Documentation

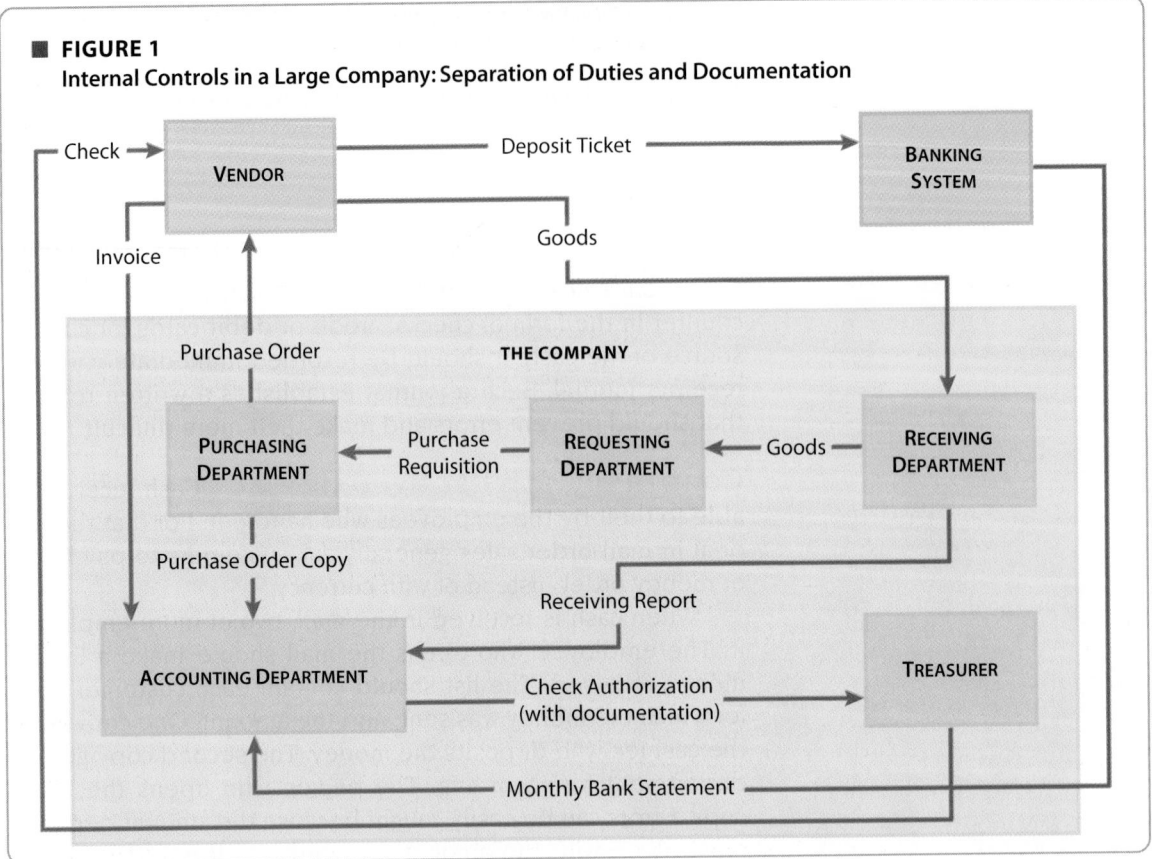

computer, separating responsibility for cash receipts, cash deposits, and recordkeeping is necessary to ensure good internal control.

In some stores, internal control is further strengthened by the use of prenumbered sales tickets and a central cash register or cashier's office, where all sales are rung up and collected by a person who does not participate in the sale. The salesperson completes a prenumbered sales ticket at the time of the sale, giving one copy to the customer and keeping a copy. At the end of the day, all sales tickets must be accounted for, and the sales total computed from the sales tickets must equal the total sales recorded on the cash register.

Control of Purchases and Cash Disbursements

Cash disbursements are particularly vulnerable to fraud and embezzlement. In one case, the treasurer of one of the nation's largest jewelry retailers was charged with having stolen over $500,000 by systematically overpaying the company's federal income taxes and keeping the refund checks as they came back to the company.

To avoid this type of theft, cash payments should be made only after they have been specifically authorized and supported by documents that establish the validity and amount of the claims. A company should also separate the duties involved in purchasing goods and services and the duties involved in paying for them. The degree of separation that is possible varies, depending on the size of the business.

Figure 1 shows how a large company can maximize the separation of duties. Five internal units (the requesting department, the purchasing department, the accounting department, the receiving department, and the treasurer) and two firms outside the company (the vendor and the bank) play a role in this control plan. Notice that business documents are crucial components of the plan.

Figure 2 illustrates the typical sequence in which documents are used in an internal control plan for purchases and cash disbursements. To begin, the credit office (requesting department) of Laboda Sportswear Company fills out a formal request for a purchase, or **purchase requisition**, for office supplies (item 1). The department head approves it and forwards it to the purchasing department. The people in the purchasing department prepare a **purchase order** (item 2). The purchase order is addressed to the vendor (seller) and contains a description of the quantity and type of items ordered, the expected price, the shipping date and terms, and other instructions. The purchase order indicates that Laboda Sportswear will not pay any bill that does not include a purchase order number.

After receiving the purchase order, the vendor, Henderson Supply Company, ships the goods and sends an **invoice** (item 3) to Laboda Sportswear. The invoice shows the quantity of goods delivered, describes what they are, and lists the price and terms of payment. If all the goods cannot be shipped immediately, the invoice indicates the estimated date of shipment for the remainder.

When the goods reach Laboda Sportswear's receiving department, an employee notes the quantity, type of goods, and their condition on a **receiving report** (item 4). The receiving department does not receive a copy of the purchase order or the invoice, so its employees don't know what should be received or its value. Thus, they are not tempted to steal any excess that may be delivered.

The receiving report goes to the accounting department, where it is compared with the purchase order and the invoice. If everything is correct, the accounting department completes a **check authorization** and attaches it to the three supporting documents. The check authorization form shown in item 5 has a space for each item to be checked off as it is examined. Notice that the accounting department has all the documentary evidence for the transaction but does not have access to the assets purchased. Nor does it write the check for payment. This means that the people doing the accounting cannot conceal fraud by falsifying documents.

Finally, the treasurer examines all the documents. If the treasurer approves them, he or she signs a check (item 6) made out to the vendor in the amount of the invoice less any applicable discount. In some systems, the accounting department fills out the check so that all the treasurer has to do is inspect and sign it. The check is then sent to the vendor, with a remittance advice showing what the check is for. A vendor that is not paid the proper amount will complain, of course, thus providing a form of outside control over the payment. The vendor deposits the check in its bank, and the canceled check appears in Laboda Sportswear's next bank statement (item 7). If the treasurer has made the check out for the wrong amount (or altered an amount that was already filled in), the problem will show up in the company's bank reconciliation.

As shown in Figure 2, every action is documented and verified by at least one other person. Thus, the requesting department cannot work out a kickback scheme to make illegal payments to the vendor because the receiving department independently records receipts and the accounting department verifies prices. The receiving department cannot steal goods because the receiving report must equal the invoice. For the same reason, the vendor cannot bill for

Study Note

A purchase requisition is not the same as a purchase order. A purchase requisition is sent to the purchasing department; a purchase order is sent to the vendor.

Study Note

Invoice is the business term for *bill*. Every business document must have a number for purposes of reference.

■ **FIGURE 2**

Internal Control Plan for Purchases and Cash Disbursements

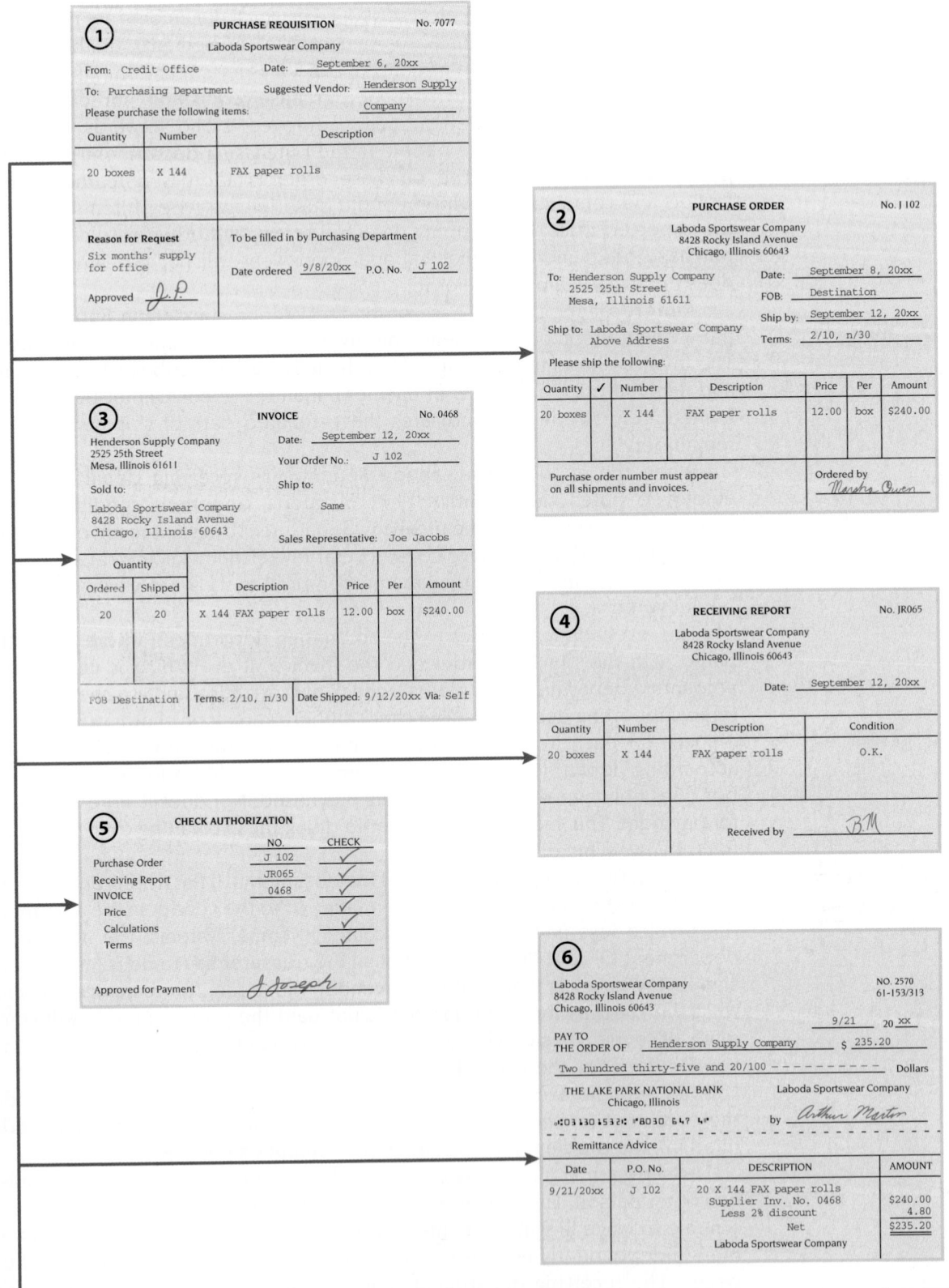

Business Document	Prepared by	Sent to	Verification and Related Procedures
① Purchase requisition	Requesting department	Purchasing department	Purchasing verifies authorization.
② Purchase order	Purchasing department	Vendor	Vendor sends goods or services in accordance with purchase order.
③ Invoice	Vendor	Accounting department	Accounting receives invoice from vendor.
④ Receiving report	Receiving department	Accounting department	Accounting compares invoice, purchase order, and receiving report. Accounting verifies prices.
⑤ Check authorization	Accounting department	Treasurer	Accounting attaches check authorization to invoice, purchase order, and receiving report.
⑥ Check	Treasurer	Vendor	Treasurer verifies all documents before preparing check.
⑦ Bank statement	Buyer's bank	Accounting department	Accounting compares amount and payee's name on returned check with check authorization.

⑦
Statement of Account with
THE LAKE PARK NATIONAL BANK
Chicago, Illinois

Laboda Sportswear Company
8428 Rocky Island Avenue
Chicago, Illinois 60643

Checking Acct No
8030-647-4
Period covered
Sept.30-Oct.31,20xx

Previous Balance	Checks/Debits—No.	Deposits/Credits—No.	S.C.	Current Balance
$2,645.78	$4,319.33 --16	$5,157.12 --7	$12.50	$3,471.07

CHECKS/DEBITS			DEPOSITS/CREDITS		DAILY BALANCES	
Posting Date	Check No.	Amount	Posting Date	Amount	Date	Amount
					09/30	2,645.78
10/01	2564	100.00	10/01	586.00	10/01	2,881.78
10/01	2565	250.00	10/05	1,500.00	10/04	2,825.60
10/04	2567	56.18	10/06	300.00	10/05	3,900.46
10/05	2566	425.14	10/16	1,845.50	10/06	4,183.34
10/06	2568	17.12	10/21	600.00	10/12	2,242.34
10/12	2569	1,705.80	10/24	300.00CM	10/16	3,687.84
10/12	2570	235.20	10/31	25.62IN	10/17	3,589.09
10/16	2571	400.00			10/21	4,189.09
10/17	2572	29.75			10/24	3,745.59
10/17	2573	69.00			10/25	3,586.09
10/24	2574	738.50			10/28	3,457.95
10/24		5.00DM			10/31	3,471.07
10/25	2575	7.50				
10/25	2577	152.00				
10/28		118.14NSF				
10/28		10.00DM				
10/31		12.50SC				

Explanation of Symbols:

CM – Credit Memo   SC – Service Charge   The last amount
DM – Debit Memo   EC – Error Correction   in this column
NSF – Non-Sufficient Funds OD – Overdraft   is your balance.
                          IN – Interest on Average Balance

Please examine; if no errors are reported within ten (10) days, the account will be considered to be correct.

more goods than it ships. The treasurer verifies the accounting department's work, and the accounting department ultimately checks the treasurer's work.

The system we have described is a simple one that provides adequate internal control. There are many variations on it.

STOP • REVIEW • APPLY

3-1. At Thrifty Variety Store, sales clerks count the currency in their cash registers at the end of each day. They then remove the tape from their registers and fill in a daily cash form, in which they note any discrepancies. An employee in the cashier's office counts the cash, compares the total with the daily cash form, and then gives the cash to the company's cashier. What is the weakness in this system of internal control?

3-2. How does a movie theater control cash receipts?

3-3. In a small business, it is sometimes impossible to separate duties completely. What are three other procedures that a small business can use to achieve internal control over cash?

Business Documents for Purchases and Cash Disbursements   Items **a–e** below are a company's departments. Items **f** and **g** are firms with which the company has transactions:

a. Requesting department
b. Purchasing department
c. Receiving department
d. Accounting department
e. Treasurer
f. Vendor
g. Bank

Use the letter of the department or firm to indicate which one prepares and sends the following business documents:

	Prepared by	Received by
1. Receiving report		
2. Purchase order		
3. Purchase requisition		
4. Check		
5. Invoice		
6. Check authorization		
7. Bank statement		

SOLUTION

	Prepared By	Received By
1. Receiving report	c	d
2. Purchase order	b	f
3. Purchase requisition	a	b
4. Check	d, e	f
5. Invoice	f	d
6. Check authorization	d	e
7. Bank statement	g	d

Petty Cash Funds

SO4 Demonstrate the use of a simple imprest (petty cash) system.

It is not always practical to make every disbursement by check. For example, it is sometimes necessary to make small payments of cash for such things as postage stamps, incoming postage, shipping charges due, or minor purchases of pens, paper, and the like.

For situations in which it is inconvenient to pay by check, most companies set up a **petty cash fund**. One of the best ways to control a petty cash fund is through an **imprest system**. Under this system, a petty cash fund is established for a fixed amount. A voucher documents each cash payment made from the fund. The fund is periodically reimbursed, based on the vouchers, by the exact amount necessary to restore its original cash balance.

Establishing the Petty Cash Fund

Some companies have a regular cashier or other employee who administers the petty cash fund. To establish the fund, the company issues a check for an amount intended to cover two to four weeks of small expenditures. The check is cashed and the money placed in the petty cash box, drawer, or envelope.

The only entry required when the fund is established is to record the check.

A = L + OE
±

Oct. 14	Petty Cash	100.00	
	Cash		100.00
	To establish the petty cash fund		

Making Disbursements from the Petty Cash Fund

The custodian of the petty cash fund should prepare a **petty cash voucher**, or written authorization, for each expenditure, as shown in Figure 3. On each petty cash voucher, the custodian enters the date, amount, and purpose of the expenditure. The person who receives the payment signs the voucher.

Study Note

Even though withdrawals from petty cash are generally small, the cumulative total over time can represent a substantial amount. Accordingly, an effective system of internal control must be established for the management of the fund.

■ **FIGURE 3**
Petty Cash Voucher

PETTY CASH VOUCHER

No. X 744

Date Oct. 23, 20xx

For _Postage due_
Charge to _Postage Expense_
Amount $2.86

_W.S._
Approved by

Tom L
Received by

The custodian should be informed that unannounced audits of the fund will be made occasionally. The cash in the fund plus the sum of the petty cash vouchers should at all times equal the amount shown in the Petty Cash account.

Reimbursing the Petty Cash Fund

At specified intervals, when the fund becomes low, and at the end of an accounting period, the petty cash fund is replenished by a check issued to the custodian for the exact amount of the expenditures. From time to time, there may be minor discrepancies in the amount of cash left in the fund at the time of reimbursement. In those cases, the amount of the discrepancy is recorded in a Cash Short or Over account—as a debit if short or as a credit if over.

Assume that after two weeks the petty cash fund established earlier has a cash balance of $14.27 and petty cash vouchers as follows: postage, $25.00; supplies, $30.55; and freight in, $30.00. The entry to replenish, or replace, the fund would be:

A = L + OE				
−	Oct. 28	Postage Expense	25.00	
−		Supplies	30.55	
−		Freight-In	30.00	
−		Cash Short or Over	0.18	
		Cash		85.73
		To replenish the petty cash fund		

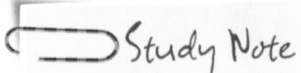

Study Note

When the petty cash fund is replenished, the Petty Cash account is neither debited nor credited. But if the size of the fund changes, there should be an entry to Petty Cash.

Notice that the Petty Cash account was not affected by the entry to replenish the fund. The Petty Cash account is debited when the fund is established or the fund level is changed. Expense or asset accounts are debited each time the fund is replenished, including in this case $0.18 to Cash Short or Over for a small cash shortage. In most cases, no further entries to the Petty Cash account are needed unless the firm wants to change the fixed amount of the fund.

The petty cash fund should be replenished at the end of an accounting period to bring it up to its fixed amount and ensure that changes in the other accounts involved are reflected in the current period's financial statements. If, through an oversight, the petty cash fund is not replenished at the end of the period, expenditures for the period still must appear on the income statement. They are shown through an adjusting entry debiting the expense accounts and crediting Petty Cash. The result is a reduction in the petty cash fund and the Petty Cash account by the amount of the adjusting entry. In the financial statements, the balance of the Petty Cash account is usually combined with other cash accounts.

STOP • REVIEW • APPLY

4-1. How does an imprest fund establish control over cash?

4-2. What should the total of receipts and cash in the imprest fund always be?

HOME DEPOT, INC.

In the Decision Point at the start of this chapter, we noted that as the second largest retailer in the United States, Home Depot faces a huge challenge in maintaining accurate records and protecting its assets at its many stores. We asked these questions:

- **How can Home Depot maintain control over its merchandising operations?**
- **How can the users of Home Depot's financial statements be confident that the company has achieved internal control?**

After reading this chapter, you know that to maintain control over its merchandising operations, Home Depot must have a system of internal controls that ensures that its records are maintained properly and that its assets are safeguarded. To do this, management must assess the risks of loss, establish an environment that encourages compliance with controls, implement a good accounting system that has a full set of control activities, and continuously monitor the system to see that it functions as planned.

Because Home Depot is a public company, users of its financial statements can determine whether the company's management meets its objectives by referring to the company's annual report. Section 404 of the Sarbanes-Oxley Act requires the top management of all public companies to state in their annual reports their responsibility for the company's system of internal control and their assessment of it. In addition, the report of the company's independent auditor will state the auditor's opinion on whether management's assessment of the system of internal controls is reasonable. Based on these two reports, users can have confidence in the company's financial statements.

CHAPTER REVIEW

REVIEW of Learning Objectives

LO1 Identify the management issues related to internal control.

Internal control is a process designed by a company to establish the reliability of the accounting records and financial statements in accordance with generally accepted accounting principles (GAAP) and to ensure that the company's assets are protected. Management's responsibility is to establish an environment, accounting systems, and internal control procedures that will protect the company's assets and to assess how well it meets these goals. Public companies must engage an independent CPA to verify that management is indeed meeting these goals.

LO2 Describe the components of internal control, control activities, and limitations on internal control.

Internal control consists of all the policies and procedures a company uses to ensure the reliability of financial reporting, compliance with laws and regulations, and the effectiveness and efficiency of operations. Internal control has five components: the control environment, risk assessment, information and communication, control activities, and monitoring. Control activities include having managers authorize certain transactions; recording all transactions to establish accountability for assets; using well-designed documents to ensure proper recording of transactions; instituting physical controls; periodically checking records and assets; separating duties; and using sound personnel practices. A system of internal control relies on the people who implement it. Thus, the effectiveness of internal control is limited by the people involved. Human error, collusion, and failure to recognize changed conditions can contribute to a system's failure.

LO3 Apply internal control activities to common merchandising transactions.

To implement internal control over cash sales, receipts, purchases, and disbursements, the functions of authorization, recordkeeping, and custodianship of cash should be kept separate. The people who have access to cash should be specifically designated and their number limited. Employees who have access to cash should be bonded. The control system should also provide for the use of banking services, physical protection of assets, prompt recording and deposit of cash receipts, and payment by check. A person who does not authorize, handle, or record cash transactions should make unannounced audits of the cash on hand, and the Cash account should be reconciled each month.

SO4 Demonstrate the use of a simple imprest (petty cash) system.

An imprest system is a method of controlling small cash expenditures by setting up a fund at a fixed amount and periodically reimbursing the fund by the amount necessary to restore the original balance. A petty cash fund, one example of an imprest system, is established by a debit to Petty Cash and a credit to Cash. It is replenished by debits to various expense or asset accounts and a credit to Cash. Each expenditure should be supported by a petty cash voucher.

REVIEW of Concepts and Terminology

The following concepts and terms were introduced in this chapter:

Bonding: The process of carefully checking an employee's background and insuring the company against theft by that person. **(LO2)**

Check authorization: A form that an accounting department prepares after it has compared a receiving report with a purchase order and invoice and that authorizes the issuance of a check to pay the invoice. **(LO3)**

Control activities: Policies and procedures that management establishes to ensure that the objectives of internal control are met. **(LO2)**

Control environment: A company's ethics, philosophy and operating style, organizational structure, method of assigning authority and responsibility, and personnel policies and practices. **(LO2)**

Imprest system: A system for controlling small cash disbursements by establishing a fund at a fixed amount and periodically reimbursing the fund by the amount necessary to restore the original cash balance. **(SO4)**

Information and communication: A component of internal control that refers to the way in which the accounting system gathers and treats information and how it communicates responsibilities within the system. **(LO2)**

Internal control: A process designed by a company to establish the reliability of the accounting records and financial statements in accordance with generally accepted accounting principles (GAAP) and to ensure that the company's assets are protected. **(LO1)**

Invoice: A form that a vendor sends to a purchaser describing the goods delivered and the quantity, price, and terms of payment. **(LO3)**

Monitoring: Management's regular assessment of the quality of internal control. **(LO2)**

Petty cash fund: A fund for making small payments of cash when it is inconvenient to pay by check. **(SO4)**

Petty cash voucher: A form signed by a person who receives cash from a petty cash fund; lists the date, amount, and purpose of the expenditure. **(SO4)**

Physical inventory: An actual count of all merchandise on hand. **(LO1)**

Purchase order: A form that a company's purchasing department sends to a vendor describing the items ordered and the quantity, price, terms, and shipping date. **(LO3)**

Purchase requisition: A formal written request for a purchase that a company's credit office (requesting department) sends to the purchasing department. **(LO3)**

Receiving report: A form on which an employee in a company's receiving department notes the quantity, type of goods, and their condition upon delivery from the vendor. **(LO3)**

Risk assessment: The identification of areas in which risk of loss of assets or inaccuracies in accounting records is high. **(LO2)**

REVIEW Problem

LO2, LO3   **Internal Control Procedures**

Jackson's Grill is a small neighborhood restaurant. The shop's owner, Rose Jackson, has set up a system of internal control over sales to prevent theft and to ensure the accuracy of the accounting records. Among the procedures related to cashiers are the following:

1. Jackson hires experienced cashiers who are bonded and checks the references of all new employees.
2. New cashiers are trained in all procedures before being allowed to handle cash.
3. All food bills are prenumbered sequentially.
4. When a customer finishes a meal, the waiter writes up a bill that describes the food items purchased, including the total price.
5. The waiters are not allowed to access the cash register.
6. If the sale is by credit card, the cashier runs the credit card through a scanner that verifies the customer's credit. The scanner prints out a receipt and a slip for the customer to sign. The signed slip is put in the cash register, and the customer is given the receipt and a copy of the sales invoice.
7. All sales, whether cash or credit, are rung up on the cash register.
8. The cash register may be locked with a key. The cashier is the only person other than Jackson who has a key. The cash register must be locked when the cashier is not present.

9. Refunds or discounts are made only with Jackson's approval.
10. At the end of each day, Jackson counts the cash and checks in the cash register and compares the total with the amount recorded on the tape inside the register. Jackson totals all the signed credit card slips and ensures that the total equals the amount recorded by the scanner.

Match the following control procedures to each of the above policies. (Some may have more than one answer.)

a. Authorization
b. Recording transactions
c. Documents and records
d. Physical controls

e. Periodic independent verification
f. Separation of duties
g. Sound personnel practices

Answer to Review Problem

1. g
2. g
3. c
4. a, c
5. d, f

6. b, c
7. b
8. d
9. a, f
10. e

CHAPTER ASSIGNMENTS

BUILDING Your Basic Knowledge and Skills

Short Exercises

LO1 Internal Control

SE 1. Match the following items with their related statements below:

a. Internal control
b. A need of internal control
c. Management's responsibility
d. Independent accountant's audit

1. Evaluates management's assessment of internal control over financial reporting
2. A process that establishes reliability of accounting records and financial statements in accordance with GAAP
3. Many assets such as cash and inventories are at risk of loss
4. Establishes a system of internal control and assesses its effectiveness

LO2 Components of Internal Control

SE 2. Match each of the following items with the related statement below:

a. Control environment
b. Risk assessment
c. Information and communication
d. Control activities
e. Monitoring

1. Policies and procedures management puts in place to see that its directives are carried out

2. Identifying areas where losses may occur
3. Regular assessment of the quality of internal controls
4. Management's overall attitude, awareness, and actions
5. Pertains to the accounting system

LO2   Limitations of Internal Control

SE 3. Internal control is subject to several inherent limitations. Indicate whether each of the following situations is an example of (a) human error, (b) collusion among employees, (c) changed conditions, or (d) cost-benefit considerations:

1. Effective separation of duties in a restaurant is impractical because the business is too small.
2. The cashier and the manager of a retail shoe store work together to avoid the internal controls for the purpose of embezzling funds.
3. The cashier in a pizza shop does not understand the procedures for operating the cash register and thus fails to ring up all the sales and count the cash at the end of the day.
4. At a law firm, computer supplies are mistakenly delivered to the reception area instead of the receiving area because the supplier began using a different system of shipment. As a result, the receipt of supplies is not recorded.

LO3   Separation of Duties

SE 4. Match the following functions for collecting cash by Acme Cleaners with the statements below:

a. Authorization   c. Recordkeeping
b. Custody

1. The cashier is responsible for funds in the cash register.
2. All sales are recorded on prenumbered invoices and rung up on the cash register.
3. All refunds must be approved by the manager.

LO3   Physical Controls

SE 5. Match the following assets of a small retail store with their related physical controls below:

a. Cash   c. Supplies
b. Merchandise inventory   d. Computers

1. An alarm that signals if unsold items leave the store
2. Cash register
3. A locked cabinet in the supplies closet
4. A cable with a lock
5. A locked showcase

LO2, LO3   Internal Control Activities

SE 6. Match the check-writing policies for a small business described below to the following control activities:

a. Authorization   e. Periodic independent verification
b. Recording transactions   f. Separation of duties
c. Documents and records   g. Sound personnel practices
d. Physical controls

1. The person who writes the checks to pay bills is different from the people who authorize the payments and keep records of the payments.

2. The checks are kept in a locked drawer. The only person who has the key is the person who writes the checks.

3. The person who writes the checks is bonded.

4. Once each month the owner compares and reconciles the amount of money shown in the accounting records with the amount in the bank account.

5. The owner of the business approves each check before it is mailed.

6. Information pertaining to each check is recorded on the check stub.

7. Every day, all checks are recorded in the accounting records, using the information on the check stubs.

LO3   Business Documents

SE 7. Arrange the following business documents in the normal order in which they would be prepared:

1. Invoice
2. Purchase order
3. Check
4. Receiving report
5. Bank statement
6. Purchase requisition
7. Check authorization

SO4   Petty Cash Fund

SE 8. A petty cash fund is established at $100. At the end of May, the fund has a cash balance of $36 and petty cash vouchers for postage, $29, and office supplies, $34. Prepare the entry on May 31 to replenish the fund.

Exercises

LO1, LO2   Discussion Questions

E 1. Develop a brief answer to each of the following questions:

1. Why is it important for public companies to have an audit of management's assessment of internal control?

2. Why is a system of internal control not able to overcome collusion by employees?

3. Which of the following accounts would be assigned a higher level of risk: Building or Merchandising Inventory?

LO2, LO3   Discussion Questions

E 2. Develop a brief answer to each of the following questions:

1. What role does the internal audit department play in internal control?

2. What role does a bank reconciliation play in internal control over cash?

3. Why is it important to write down the amount of cash received through the mail or over the counter?

LO2   Components of Internal Control

E 3. Match the following items with the related statements below:

a. Company environment   d. Control activities
b. Risk assessment   e. Monitoring
c. Information and communication

1. The company has an internal audit department.
2. Management encourages employees to follow the rules.

3. Management regularly considers what losses the company might face.
4. Management puts separation of duties in place.
5. The company gathers appropriate information and communicates it to employees.
6. Personnel are well trained and instructed in their duties.
7. The company employs good physical controls.
8. Managers are observant and review how procedures by those who report to them are carried out.
9. The company has a good accounting system.

LO2, LO3   **Control Procedures**

E 4. Alina Sadofsky, who operates a small grocery store, has established the following policies with regard to the checkout cashiers:

1. Each cashier has his or her own cash drawer, to which no one else has access.
2. Cashiers may accept checks for purchases under $50 with proper identification. For checks over $50, they must receive approval from Sadofsky.
3. Every sale must be rung up on the cash register and a receipt given to the customer. Each sale is recorded on a tape inside the cash register.
4. At the end of each day, Sadofsky counts the cash in the drawer and compares it with the amount on the tape inside the cash register.

Match the following conditions for internal control to each of the policies listed above:

a. Transactions are executed in accordance with management's general or specific authorization.
b. Transactions are recorded as necessary to permit preparation of financial statements and maintain accountability for assets.
c. Access to assets is permitted only as allowed by management.
d. At reasonable intervals, the records of assets are compared with the existing assets.

LO2, LO3   **Internal Control Procedures**

E 5. Adelphi Video Store maintains the following policies with regard to purchases of new videotapes at each of its branch stores:

1. Employees are required to take vacations, and the duties of employees are rotated periodically.
2. Once each month a person from the home office visits each branch store to examine the receiving records and to compare the inventory of videos with the accounting records.
3. Purchases of new videos must be authorized by purchase order in the home office and paid for by the treasurer in the home office. Receiving reports are prepared in each branch and sent to the home office.
4. All new personnel receive one hour of training in how to receive and catalogue new videos.
5. The company maintains a perpetual inventory system that keeps track of all videos purchased, sold, and on hand.

Match the following control procedures to each of the above policies. (Some may have several answers.)

a. Authorization
b. Recording transactions
c. Documents and records
d. Physical controls
e. Periodic independent verification
f. Separation of duties
g. Sound personnel practices

LO3 **Business Documents**

E 6. Items **a–e** below are a company's departments. Items **f** and **g** are firms with which the company has transactions:

a. Requesting department   e. Treasurer
b. Purchasing department   f. Vendor
c. Receiving department   g. Bank
d. Accounting department

Use the letter of the department or firm to indicate which one prepares and sends the following business documents:

	Prepared by	Received by
1. Bank statement	_____	_____
2. Purchase requisition	_____	_____
3. Purchase order	_____	_____
4. Check authorization	_____	_____
5. Invoice	_____	_____
6. Check	_____	_____
7. Receiving report	_____	_____

LO3 **Use of Accounting Records in Internal Control**

E 7. Careful scrutiny of accounting records and financial statements can lead to the discovery of fraud or embezzlement. Each of the situations that follow may indicate a breakdown in internal control. Indicate the nature of the possible fraud or embezzlement in each of these situations.

1. Wages expense for a branch office was 30 percent higher in 20x8 than in 20x7, even though the office was authorized to employ only the same four employees and raises were only 5 percent in 20x8.
2. Sales returns and allowances increased from 5 percent to 20 percent of sales in the first two months of 20x8, after record sales in 20x7 resulted in large bonuses for the sales staff.
3. Gross margin decreased from 40 percent of net sales in 20x7 to 20 percent in 20x8, even though there was no change in pricing. Ending inventory was 50 percent less at the end of 20x8 than it was at the beginning of the year. There is no immediate explanation for the decrease in inventory.
4. A review of daily records of cash register receipts shows that one cashier consistently accepts more discount coupons for purchases than do the other cashiers.

LO4 **Imprest System**

E 8. Developing a convenient means of providing sales representatives with cash for their incidental expenses, such as entertaining a client at lunch, is a problem many companies face. Under one company's plan, the sales representatives receive advances in cash from the petty cash fund. Each advance is supported by an authorization from the sales manager. The representative returns the receipt for the expenditure and any unused cash, which is replaced in the petty cash fund. The cashier of the petty cash fund is responsible for seeing that the receipt and the cash returned equal the advance. When the petty cash fund is reimbursed, the amount of the representative's expenditure is debited to Direct Sales Expense.

What is the weak point in this system? What fundamental principle of internal control is being ignored? What improvement in the procedure can you suggest?

SO4 **Petty Cash Transactions**

E 9. A small company maintains a petty cash fund for minor expenditures. In June and July, the following transactions took place:

a. The fund was established in the amount of $100.00 on June 1 from the proceeds of check no. 2707.

b. On June 30, the petty cash fund had cash of $15.46 and the following receipts on hand: postage, $40.00; supplies, $24.94; delivery service, $12.40; and rubber stamp, $7.20. Check no. 2778 was drawn to replenish the fund.

c. On July 31, the petty cash fund had cash of $22.06 and these receipts on hand: postage, $34.20; supplies, $32.84; and delivery service, $6.40. The petty cash custodian could not account for the shortage. Check no. 2847 was drawn to replenish the fund.

Prepare entries in journal form necessary to record each transaction.

Problems

LO2 **Internal Control Components**

P 1. Jason Company, a small electronics distributor, has experienced losses of inventory over the past year. Sara Jason, the owner, on the advice of her accountant, has adopted a set of internal controls in an effort to stop the losses. Jason has taken the following steps:

1. She encourages employees to follow the rules.
2. She regularly considers ways in which inventory losses might occur.
3. She put separation of duties in place.
4. She gathers appropriate information and communicates it to employees.
5. She sees that new and existing employees are well trained and instructed in their duties.
6. She makes sure inventories are physically protected with locked storage and electronic monitors.
7. She observes and reviews how procedures by those who report to her are carried out.
8. She had her accountant install a better accounting system over inventory.
9. She trains new employees in how to properly carry out control procedures.

Required

1. Show that Sara Jason's new system engages all the components of internal control by matching each of the above steps with one of the internal control components below:
   a. Control environment
   b. Risk assessment
   c. Information and communication
   d. Control activities
   e. Monitoring

2. **User Insight:** As the owner of a small company, why is it important that Sarah Jason take an active part in the management of the internal control system?

LO2, LO3 **Control Activities**

P 2. Industrial Services Company provides maintenance services to factories in and around West Bend, Wisconsin. The company, which buys a large amount of cleaning supplies, consistently has been over budget in its expenditures for these items. In the past, supplies were left out in the open in the warehouse to be taken each evening as needed by the onsite supervisors. A clerk in the accounting department periodically ordered additional supplies from a long-time supplier. No records were maintained other than to record purchases. Once a year, an inventory of supplies was made for the preparation of the financial statements.

To solve the budgetary problem, management decides to implement a new system for purchasing and controlling supplies. The following actions take place:

1. Management places a supplies clerk in charge of a secured storeroom for cleaning supplies.
2. Supervisors use a purchase requisition to request supplies for the jobs they oversee.
3. Each job receives a predetermined amount of supplies based on a study of each job's needs.
4. In the storeroom, the supplies clerk notes the levels of supplies and completes the purchase requisition when new supplies are needed.
5. The purchase requisition goes to the purchasing clerk, a new position. The purchasing clerk is solely responsible for authorizing purchases and preparing the purchase orders.
6. Supplier prices are monitored constantly by the purchasing clerk to ensure that the lowest price is obtained.
7. When supplies are received, the supplies clerk checks them in and prepares a receiving report. The supplies clerk sends the receiving report to accounting, where each payment to a supplier is documented by the purchase requisition, the purchase order, and the receiving report.
8. The accounting department also maintains a record of supplies inventory, supplies requisitioned by supervisors, and supplies received.
9. Once each month, the warehouse manager takes a physical inventory of cleaning supplies in the storeroom and compares it against the supplies inventory records that the accounting department maintains.

Required

1. Indicate which of the following control activities applies to each of the improvements in the internal control system (more than one may apply):
   a. Authorization
   b. Recording transactions
   c. Documents and records
   d. Physical controls
   e. Periodic independent verification
   f. Separation of duties
   g. Sound personnel practices

2. **User Insight:** Explain why each new control activity is an improvement over the activities of the old system.

LO2, LO3 **Internal Control Activities**

P3. Eyles Sports Shop is a small neighborhood sporting goods store. The shop's owner, Samantha Eyles, has set up a system of internal control over sales to prevent theft and to ensure the accuracy of the accounting records.

When a customer buys a product, the cashier writes up a sales invoice that describes the purchase, including the total price. All sales invoices are prenumbered sequentially.

If the sale is by credit card, the cashier runs the credit card through a scanner that verifies the customer's credit. The scanner prints out a receipt and a slip for the customer to sign. The signed slip is put in the cash register, and the customer is given the receipt and a copy of the sales invoice.

If the sale is by cash or check, the cashier rings it up on the cash register and gives change, if appropriate. Checks must be written for the exact amount of the purchase and must be accompanied by identification. The sale is recorded on a tape inside the cash register that cannot be accessed by the cashier. The cash register may be locked with a key. The cashier is the only person other than Eyles who has a key. The cash register must be locked when the cashier is not present. Refunds are made only with Eyles's approval, are recorded on prenumbered credit memorandum forms, and are rung up on the cash register.

At the end of each day, Eyles counts the cash and checks in the cash register and compares the total with the amount recorded on the tape inside the register. Eyles totals all the signed credit card slips and ensures that the total equals the amount recorded by the scanner. Eyles also makes sure that all sales invoices and credit memoranda are accounted for. Eyles prepares a bank deposit ticket for the cash, checks, and signed credit card slips, less $40 in change to be put in the cash register the next day, and removes the record of the day's credit card sales from the scanner. All the records are placed in an envelope that is sealed and sent to the company's accountant for verification and recording in the company records. On the way home, Eyles places the bank deposit in the night deposit box.

The company hires experienced cashiers who are bonded. The owner spends the first half-day with new cashiers, showing them the procedures and overlooking their work.

Required

1. Give an example of how each of the following control activities is applied to internal control over sales and cash at Eyles Sports Shop. (Do not address controls over inventory.)
   a. Authorization
   b. Recording transactions
   c. Documents and records
   d. Physical controls
   e. Periodic independent verification
   f. Separation of duties
   g. Sound personnel practices

2. **User Insight:** Can the system as described protect against a cashier who accepts cash for a sale but does not ring up the sale and pockets the cash? If so, how does it prevent this action?

SO4 **Imprest (Petty Cash) Fund Transactions**

 P 4. On July 1, Acton Company established an imprest (petty cash) fund in the amount of $400.00 in cash from a check drawn for the purpose of establishing the fund. On July 31, the petty cash fund has cash of $31.42 and the following receipts on hand: for merchandise received, $204.30; freight-in, $65.74; laundry service, $84.00; and miscellaneous expense, $14.54. A check was drawn to replenish the fund.

On Aug. 31, the petty cash fund has cash of $55.00 and the following receipts on hand: merchandise, $196.84; freight-in, $76.30; laundry service, $84.00; and miscellaneous expense, $7.86. The petty cash custodian is not able to account for the excess cash in the fund. A check is drawn to replenish the fund.

Required

1. In journal form, prepare the entries necessary to record each of these transactions. The company uses the periodic inventory system.
2. **User Insight:** What are two examples of why a local semi-professional baseball team might have need for an imprest (petty cash) system?

Alternate Problems

LO2   **Internal Control Components**

P 5. Dodge Company, a small retail bookstore, has experienced losses of inventory over the past year. George Dodge, the owner, on the advice of his accountant, has adopted a set of internal controls in an effort to stop the losses. Dodge has taken the following steps:

1. He regularly considers ways in which inventory losses might occur.
2. He had his accountant set up an accounting system over inventory.
3. He requires all new and existing employees to attend a training session in which they are instructed in their duties.
4. He makes sure that different employees perform the duties of authorization, custody, and recordkeeping.
5. He spends time "on the floor" encouraging employees to follows the procedures.
6. He periodically gathers appropriate information about inventory situations and communicates his findings to employees.
7. He had all items in inventory marked with an electronic bar code that signals an alarm if someone tries to take an item out of the store without paying for it.
8. He observes and reviews how internal control procedures are carried out.
9. He hires his accountant to periodically conduct internal audit work.

Required

1. Show that Dodge's new system engages all the components of internal control by matching each of the above steps with one of the internal control components below:
   a. Control environment
   b. Risk assessment
   c. Information and communication
   d. Control activities
   e. Monitoring
2. **User Insight:** As the owner of a small company, why is it important that George Dodge take an active part in the management of the internal control system?

LO3   **Internal Control Procedures**

P 6. VuWay Printers makes printers for personal computers and maintains a factory outlet showroom through which it sells its products to the public. The company's management has set up a system of internal controls over the inventory of printers to prevent theft and to ensure the accuracy of the accounting records.

All printers in inventory at the factory outlet are kept in a secured warehouse behind the showroom, except for the sample printers on display. Only authorized personnel may enter the warehouse. When a customer buys a printer, a sales invoice is written in triplicate by the cashier and is marked "paid." The sales invoices are sequentially numbered, and all must be accounted for. The cashier sends the pink copy of the completed invoice to the warehouse, gives the blue copy to the customer, and keeps the green copy. The customer drives around to the warehouse entrance. The warehouse attendant takes the blue copy of the invoice from the customer and gives the customer the printer and the pink copy of the invoice.

The company maintains a perpetual inventory system for the printers at the outlet. The warehouse attendant at the outlet signs an inventory transfer sheet for each printer received. An accountant at the factory is assigned responsibility for maintaining the inventory records based on copies of the inventory transfer sheets and the sales invoices. The records are updated daily and may be accessed by computer but not modified by the sales personnel and the warehouse attendant. The accountant also sees that all prenumbered inventory transfer sheets are accounted for and compares copies of them with the ones signed by the warehouse attendant. Once every three months, the company's internal auditor takes a physical count of the printer inventory and compares the results with the perpetual inventory records.

All new employees are required to read a sales and inventory manual and attend a two-hour training session about the internal controls. They must demonstrate that they can perform the functions required of them.

Required

1. Give an example of how each of the following control activities is applied to internal control over inventory at VuWay Printers:
   a. Authorization
   b. Recording transactions
   c. Documents and records
   d. Physical controls
   e. Periodic independent verification
   f. Separation of duties
   g. Sound personnel practices

2. **User Insight:** Can the described system protect against an employee who picks up a printer and carries it off when leaving work?

SO4   Imprest (Petty Cash) Transaction

P 7. A small company maintains a petty cash fund for minor expenditures. The following transactions occurred in June and July.

a. The fund was established in the amount of $300.00 on June 1 from the proceeds of check no. 1515.

b. On June 30, the petty cash fund had cash of $46.38 and the following receipts on hand: postage, $120.00; supplies, $74.82; delivery service, $37.20; and rubber stamp, $21.60. Check no. 1527 was drawn to replenish the fund.

c. On July 31, the petty cash fund had cash of $66.18 and the following receipts on hand: postage, $102.60; supplies, $98.52; and delivery service, $19.20. The petty cash custodian could not account for the shortage. Check no. 1621 was written to replenish the fund.

Required

1. In journal form, prepare the entries necessary to record each of these transactions.
2. **User Insight:** A charity reimburses volunteers for small out-of-pocket expenses such as parking and gasoline when the volunteers are carrying out the business of the charity. How might an imprest (petty cash) fund be helpful in controlling these expenditures?

ENHANCING Your Knowledge, Skills, and Critical Thinking

Conceptual Understanding Case

LO2, LO3 **Control Systems**

C 1. In the spring of each year, Steinbrook College's theater department puts on a contemporary play. Before the performance, the theater manager instructs student volunteers in their duties as cashier, ticket taker, and usher.

The cashier, who is located in a box office at the entrance to the auditorium, receives cash from customers and enters the number of tickets and the amount paid into a computer, which prints out serially numbered tickets. The cashier puts the cash in a locked cash drawer and gives the tickets to the customer.

Customers give their tickets to the ticket taker. The ticket taker tears each ticket in half, gives one half to the customer, and puts the other half in a locked box. When customers present their ticket stubs to an usher, the usher shows them to their seats.

1. Describe how the control activities discussed in this chapter (authorization; recording transactions; documents and records; physical controls; periodic independent verification; separation of duties; and sound personnel practices) apply to the cashier, ticket taker, and usher.
2. Could the cashier issue a ticket to a friend without taking in cash? Could the ticket taker allow friends to enter without a ticket? If not, how might they be caught?

Interpreting Financial Reports

LO2, LO3 **Internal Control Lapse**

C 2. Starbucks Corporation accused an employee and her husband of embezzling $3.7 million by billing the company for services from a fictitious consulting firm. The couple had created a phony company called RAD Services Inc. and charged Starbucks for work they never provided. The employee worked in Starbucks' Information Technology Department. RAD Services Inc. charged Starbucks as much as $492,800 for consulting services in a single week.[8] For such a fraud to have taken place, certain control activities were likely not implemented. Identify and describe these control activities.

Decision Analysis Using Excel

LO2, LO3

Identifying Internal Control Weaknesses

C 3. Fleet's is a retail store with several departments. Its internal control procedures for cash sales and purchases are as follows:

Cash sales. The sales clerk in each department rings up every cash sale on the department's cash register. The cash register produces a sales slip, which the clerk gives to the customer along with the merchandise. A continuous tape locked inside the cash register makes a carbon copy of the sales ticket. At the end of each day, the sales clerk presses a "total" key on the register, and it prints the total sales for the day on the continuous tape. The sales clerk then unlocks the tape, reads the total sales figure, and makes the entry in the accounting records for the day's cash sales. Next, she counts the cash in the drawer, places the $100 change fund back in the drawer, and gives the cash received to the cashier. Finally, she files the cash register tape and is ready for the next day's business.

Purchases. At the requests of the various department heads, the purchasing agent orders all goods. When the goods arrive, the receiving clerk prepares a receiving report in triplicate. The receiving clerk keeps one copy; the other two copies go to the purchasing agent and the department head. Invoices are forwarded immediately to the accounting department to ensure payment before the discount period elapses. After payment, the invoice is forwarded to the purchasing agent for comparison with the purchase order and the receiving report and is then returned to the accounting office for filing.

Fleet's president has asked you to evaluate these control procedures for cash sales and purchases. Write a memorandum to the president identifying the significant internal control weaknesses in each of the above situations, and in each case, recommend changes that would improve the system.

Annual Report Case: CVS Corporation

LO1 **Recognition, Valuation, and Classification**

C 4. To answer the following questions, refer to "Management's Report on Internal Control Over Financial Reporting" and the "Report of Independent Registered Public Accounting Firm" in **CVS's** annual report in the Supplement to Chapter 5:

1. What is management's responsibility with regard to internal control over financial reporting?
2. What is management's conclusion regarding its assessment of internal control over financial reporting?
3. Does CVS's auditor agree with management's assessment?
4. What does the auditor say about the limitations or risks associated with internal control?

Comparison Case: CVS Versus Southwest

LO2 **Contrasting Internal Control Needs**

C 5. In a typical **CVS** store, customers wheel carts down aisles to select items for purchase and take them to a checkout counter where they pay with cash or credit card. The company is concerned that customers might leave the store with merchandise that they have not paid for. Typically, customers of **Southwest Airlines** have already paid for their tickets when they arrive at the gate. The company is concerned that customers who do not have tickets might be allowed on the plane. (Southwest does not have assigned seating.) Compare the risks for each company in the situations just described and the internal control procedures that are needed.

Ethical Dilemma Case

LO1   **Personal Responsibility for Mistakes**

C 6. Suppose you have a part-time sales position over the winter break in a small clothing store that is part of a national chain. The store's one full-time employee, with whom you have become friendly, hired you. Explain what you would do in the situations described below, and identify two internal control problems that exist in each situation.

1. You arrive at the store at 6 P.M. to take over the evening shift from the full-time employee who hired you. You notice that this person takes a coat from a rack, puts it on, and leaves by the back door. You are not sure if the coat is one that was for sale or if it belonged to the employee.
2. You are the only person in the store on a busy evening. At closing time, you total the cash register and the receipts and discover that the cash register is $20 short of cash. You consider replacing the $20 out of your pocket because you think you may have made a mistake and are afraid you might lose your job if the company thinks you took the money.

Internet Case

LO1, LO2, LO3   **Internet Retailing**

C 7. You have undoubtedly made a purchase or know people who have made a purchase over the Internet from retailers like **Crate & Barrel**, **Eddie Bauer Inc.**, and **Amazon.com.** In what ways do Internet transactions differ from transactions in a retail store? What effect do these differences have on internal controls?

Group Activity Case

LO2, LO3   **Internal Controls**

C 8. Go to a local retail business, such as a bookstore, clothing shop, gift shop, grocery store, hardware store, or car dealership. Ask to speak to someone who is knowledgeable about the store's methods of internal control. After you and other members of the class have completed this step individually, your instructor will divide the class into groups. Group members will compare their findings and develop answers to the questions that follow. A member of each group will then present the group's answers to the class.

1. How does the company protect itself against inventory theft and loss?
2. What control activities, including authorization, recording transactions, documents and records, physical controls, periodic independent verification, separation of duties, and sound personnel practices, does the company use?
3. Can you see these control procedures in use?

Business Communication Case

LO2, LO3   **Internal Control in a Small Business**

C 9. Gina Limke runs a small business called Limke Construction Company. In the past, the company's site managers have been allowed to purchase construction materials for their own jobs. Gina Limke thinks that if she establishes a central purchasing department, it might help reduce waste and possibly theft. She has asked you, the company's accountant, to write a short memorandum describing how such a purchasing system and the accompanying internal controls would work, and what forms would be needed to implement it. Assume that the company has a central warehouse where materials can be received.

11

Long-Term Assets

ong-term assets include tangible assets, such as land, buildings, and equipment; natural resources, such as timberland and oil fields; and intangible assets, such as patents and copyrights. These assets represent a company's strategic commitments well into the future. The judgments related to their acquisition, operation, and disposal and to the allocation of their costs will affect a company's performance for years to come. Investors and creditors rely on accurate and full reporting of the assumptions and judgments that underlie the measurement of long-term assets.

LEARNING OBJECTIVES

Making a Statement

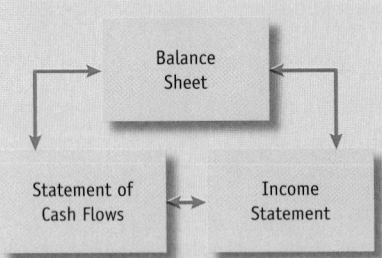

Purchase, use, and disposal of long-term assets affect all financial statements.

LO1 Define *long-term assets,* and explain the management issues related to them.

LO2 Distinguish between *capital expenditures* and *revenue expenditures,* and account for the cost of property, plant, and equipment.

LO3 Compute depreciation under the straight-line, production, and declining-balance methods.

LO4 Account for the disposal of depreciable assets.

LO5 Identify the issues related to accounting for natural resources, and compute depletion.

LO6 Identify the issues related to accounting for intangible assets, including research and development costs and goodwill.

- What are Apple's long-term assets?
- What are its policies in accounting for long-term assets?
- Does the company generate enough cash flow to finance its continued growth?

Long known for its innovative technology and design of computers, **Apple** revolutionized the music industry with its digital iPod music player. The company's success stems from its willingness to invest in research and development and long-term assets to create new products. Each year, it spends about $500 million on research and development and about $200 million on new long-term assets. Almost 40 percent of its tangible assets are long term. You can get an idea of the extent and importance of Apple's long-term assets by looking at the Financial Highlights from its balance sheet.[1]

APPLE COMPUTER'S FINANCIAL HIGHLIGHTS
(In millions)

	2005	2004
Property, Plant, and Equipment:		
Land and buildings	$ 361	$ 351
Machinery, equipment, and internal-use software	494	422
Office furniture and equipment	81	79
Leasehold improvements	545	446
	1,481	1,298
Less accumulated depreciation and amortization	664	591
Total property, plant, and equipment, net	$ 817	$ 707
Other Noncurrent Assets:		
Goodwill	$ 69	$ 80
Acquired intangible assets, net	27	17
Other noncurrent assets	338	191
Total other noncurrent assets	$ 434	$ 288

Management Issues Related to Long-Term Assets

LO1 Define *long-term assets,* and explain the management issues related to them.

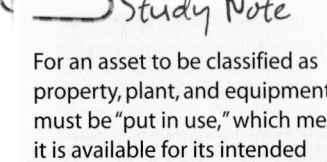

Study Note

For an asset to be classified as property, plant, and equipment, it must be "put in use," which means it is available for its intended purpose. An emergency generator is "put in use" when it is available for emergencies, even if it is never used.

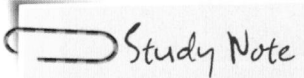

Study Note

A computer that a company uses in an office is a long-term plant asset. An identical computer that a company sells to customers is considered inventory.

Long-term assets were once called fixed assets, but this term has fallen out of favor because it implies that the assets last forever, which they do not. Long-term assets have the following characteristics:

▶ *They have a useful life of more than one year.* This distinguishes them from current assets, which a company expects to use up or convert to cash within one year or during its operating cycle, whichever is longer. They also differ from current assets in that they support the operating cycle, rather than being part of it. Although there is no strict rule for defining the useful life of a long-term asset, the most common criterion is that the asset be capable of repeated use for at least a year. Included in this category is equipment used only in peak or emergency periods, such as electric generators.

▶ *They are used in the operation of a business.* Assets not used in the normal course of business, such as land held for speculative reasons or buildings no longer used in ordinary business operations, should be classified as long-term investments, not as long-term assets.

▶ *They are not intended for resale to customers.* An asset that a company intends to resell to customers should be classified as inventory—not as a long-term asset—no matter how durable it is. For example, a printing press that a manufacturer offers for sale is part of the manufacturer's inventory, but it is a long-term asset for a printing company that buys it to use in its operations.

Figure 1 shows the relative importance of long-term assets in various industries. Figure 2 shows how long-term assets are classified and defines the methods of accounting for them. Plant assets, which are **tangible assets**, are accounted for through **depreciation**. (Although land is a tangible asset, it is not depreciated because it has an unlimited life.) **Natural resources**, which are also tangible assets, are accounted for through **depletion**. **Intangible assets**

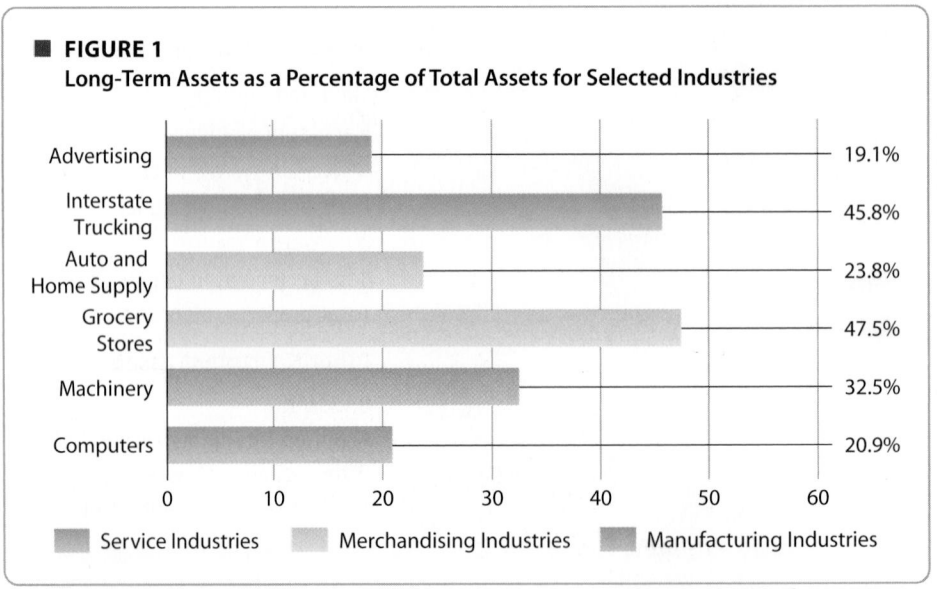

■ **FIGURE 1**
Long-Term Assets as a Percentage of Total Assets for Selected Industries

Industry	Percentage
Advertising	19.1%
Interstate Trucking	45.8%
Auto and Home Supply	23.8%
Grocery Stores	47.5%
Machinery	32.5%
Computers	20.9%

Service Industries   Merchandising Industries   Manufacturing Industries

Source: Data from Dun & Bradstreet, *Industry Norms and Key Business Ratios,* 2004–2005

■ **FIGURE 2**
Classification of Long-Term Assets and Methods of Accounting for Them

BALANCE SHEET	INCOME STATEMENT
Long-Term Assets	**Expenses**

 **Tangible Assets:** long-term assets that have physical substance

Land

Plant, Buildings, Equipment (plant assets)

Land is not expensed because it has an unlimited life.

Depreciation: periodic allocation of the cost of a tangible long-lived asset (other than land and natural resources) over its estimated useful life

 **Natural Resources:** long-term assets purchased for the economic value that can be taken from the land and used up, as with ore, lumber, oil, and gas or other resources contained in the land

Mines

Timberland

Oil and Gas Fields

Depletion: exhaustion of a natural resource through mining, cutting, pumping, or other extraction, and the way in which the cost is allocated

 **Intangible Assets:** long-term assets that have no physical substance but have a value based on rights or advantages accruing to the owner

Patents, Copyrights, Trademarks, Franchises, Leaseholds, Goodwill

Amortization: periodic allocation of the cost of an intangible asset to the periods it benefits

Some intangible assets with indefinite useful lives, such as goodwill, are not amortized but are reviewed annually for impairment.

Study Note

To be classified as intangible, an asset must lack physical substance, be long term, and represent a legal right or advantage.

are accounted for through **amortization**. (Although goodwill is an intangible asset, it is not expensed; however, it is reviewed for impairment each year.)

Long-term assets are generally reported at carrying value. As shown in Figure 3, **carrying value** (also called *book value*) is the unexpired part of an asset's cost. If a long-term asset loses some or all of its potential to generate revenue before the end of its useful life, it is deemed *impaired*, and its carrying value is reduced.

All long-term assets are subject to an annual impairment evaluation. **Asset impairment** occurs when the carrying value of a long-term asset exceeds

■ **FIGURE 3**
Carrying Value of Long-Term Assets on the Balance Sheet

Plant Assets	Natural Resources	Intangible Assets
Less Accumulated Depreciation	Less Accumulated Depletion	Less Accumulated Amortization
Carrying Value	Carrying Value	Carrying Value

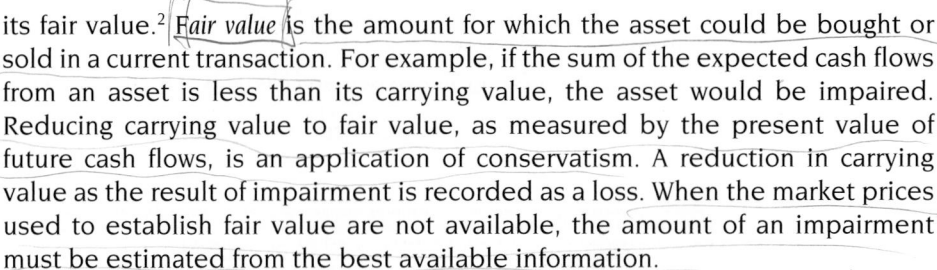

its fair value.[2] *Fair value* is the amount for which the asset could be bought or sold in a current transaction. For example, if the sum of the expected cash flows from an asset is less than its carrying value, the asset would be impaired. Reducing carrying value to fair value, as measured by the present value of future cash flows, is an application of conservatism. A reduction in carrying value as the result of impairment is recorded as a loss. When the market prices used to establish fair value are not available, the amount of an impairment must be estimated from the best available information.

Although **Apple** reported no asset impairments in 2005, in 2004 it recognized losses of $5.5 million in asset impairments. A few years earlier, in the midst of an economic slowdown in the telecommunications industry, **World-Com** recorded asset impairments that totaled $79.8 billion, the largest impairment write-down in history. Since then, other telecommunications companies, including **AT&T** and **Qwest Communications**, have taken large impairment write-downs. Due to these companies' declining revenues, the carrying value of some of their long-term assets no longer exceeded the cash flows that they were meant to help generate.[3] Because of the write-downs, these companies reported large operating losses.

Taking a large write-down in a bad year is often called "taking a big bath" because it "cleans" future years of the bad year's costs and thus can help a company return to a profitable status. In other words, by taking the largest possible loss on a long-term asset in a bad year, companies hope to reduce the costs of depreciation or amortization on the asset in subsequent years.

In the next few pages, we discuss the management issues related to long-term assets—how management decides whether it will acquire them, how it will finance them, and how it will account for them.

Acquiring Long-Term Assets

The decision to acquire a long-term asset is a complex process. For example, **Apple's** decision to invest capital in establishing its own retail stores throughout the country required very careful analysis. Methods of evaluating data to make rational decisions about acquiring long-term assets are grouped under a topic called capital budgeting, which is usually covered as a managerial accounting topic. However, an awareness of the general nature of the problem is helpful in understanding the management issues related to long-term assets.

To illustrate an acquisition decision, suppose that Apple's management is considering the purchase of a $50,000 customer-relations software package. Management estimates that the new software will save net cash flows of $20,000 per year for four years, the usual life of new software, and that the software will be worth $10,000 at the end of that period. These data are summarized as follows:

	20x5	20x6	20x7	20x8
Acquisition cost	($50,000)			
Net annual savings in cash flows	20,000	$20,000	$20,000	$20,000
Disposal price				10,000
Net cash flows	($30,000)	$20,000	$20,000	$30,000

To put the cash flows on a comparable basis, it is helpful to use present value tables, such as Tables 3 and 4 in the appendix on future value and present value tables. If the interest rate set by management as a desirable return is 10 percent compounded annually, the purchase decision would be evaluated as follows:

		Present Value
Acquisition cost	Present value factor = 1.000 1.000 × $50,000	($50,000)
Net annual savings in cash flows	Present value factor = 3.170 (Table 4: 4 periods, 10%) 3.170 × $20,000	63,400
Disposal price	Present value factor = .683 (Table 3: 4 periods, 10%) .683 × $10,000	6,830
Net present value		$20,230

As long as the net present value is positive, Apple will earn at least 10 percent on the investment. In this case, the return is greater than 10 percent because the net present value is a positive $20,230. Moreover, the net present value is large relative to the investment. Based on this analysis, it appears that Apple's management should make the decision to purchase. However, in making its decision, it should take other important considerations into account, including the costs of training personnel to use the software. It should also allow for the possibility that because of unforeseen circumstances, the savings may not be as great as expected.

Information about acquisitions of long-term assets appears in the investing activities section of the statement of cash flows. In referring to this section of its 2005 annual report, Apple's management makes the following statement:

> The Company's total capital expenditures were $260 million during fiscal 2005. . . . The Company currently anticipates it will utilize approximately $390 million for capital expenditures during 2006, approximately $210 million of which is expected to be utilized for further expansion of the Company's Retail segment and the remainder utilized to support normal replacement of existing capital assets and enhancements to general information technology infrastructure.

Financing Long-Term Assets

When management decides to acquire a long-term asset, it must also decide how to finance the purchase. Many financing arrangements are based on the life of the asset. For example, an automobile loan generally spans 4 or 5 years, whereas a mortgage on a house may span 30 years. For a major long-term acquisition, a company may issue stock, long-term notes, or bonds. Some companies are profitable enough to pay for long-term assets out of cash flows from operations. A good place to study a company's investing and financing activities is its statement of cash flows, and a good measure of its ability to finance long-term assets is free cash flow.

Free cash flow is the amount of cash that remains after deducting the funds a company must commit to continue operating at its planned level. The commitments to be covered include current or continuing operations, interest, income taxes, dividends, and net capital expenditures (purchases of plant assets minus sales of plant assets). If a company fails to pay for current or continuing operations, interest, and income taxes, its creditors and the government can take legal action. Although the payment of dividends is not strictly required, dividends normally represent a commitment to stockholders. If they are reduced or eliminated, stockholders will be unhappy, and the price of the company's stock will fall. Net capital expenditures represent management's plans for the future.

A positive free cash flow means that a company has met all its cash commitments and has cash available to reduce debt or to expand its operations. A negative free cash flow means that it will have to sell investments, borrow money, or issue stock in the short term to continue at its planned level. If free cash flow remains negative for several years, a company may not be able to raise cash by issuing stock or bonds.

Using data from **Apple's** statement of cash flows in its 2005 annual report, we can compute the company's free cash flow as follows (in millions):

$$\text{Free Cash Flow} = \text{Net Cash Flows from Operating Activities} - \text{Dividends} -$$
$$(\text{Purchases of Plant Assets} - \text{Sales of Plant Assets})$$
$$= \$2,535 - \$0 - (\$260 - \$0)$$
$$= \$2,275$$

Study Note

The computation of free cash flow uses *net capital expenditures* in place of (*purchases of plant assets − sales of plant assets*) when plant assets are small or immaterial.

This analysis confirms Apple's strong financial position. Its cash flow from operating activities far exceeds its net capital expenditures of $260 million. A factor that contributes to its positive free cash flow of $2,275 million is that the company pays no dividends. The financing activities section of Apple's statement of cash flows also indicates that the company raised an additional $543 million through an issuance of common stock.

Applying the Matching Rule

When a company records an expenditure as a long-term asset, it is deferring an expense until a later period. Thus, the current period's profitability looks better than it would if the expenditure had been expensed immediately. Management has considerable latitude in making the judgments and estimates necessary to account for all types and aspects of long-term assets. Sometimes, this latitude is used unwisely and unethically. For example, in the infamous **WorldCom** accounting fraud, management ordered that certain expenditures that should have been recorded as operating expenses be capitalized as long-term assets and written off over several years. The result was an overstatement of income by about $10 billion, which ultimately led to the largest bankruptcy in the history of U.S. business.

To avoid fraudulent reporting of long-term assets, a company's management must apply the matching rule in resolving two important issues. The first is how much of the total cost of a long-term asset to allocate to expense in the current accounting period. The second is how much to retain on the balance sheet as an asset that will benefit future periods. To resolve these issues, management must answer four important questions about the acquisition, use, and disposal of each long-term asset (see Figure 4):

1. How is the cost of the long-term asset determined?

2. How should the expired portion of the cost of the long-term asset be allocated against revenues over time?

3. How should subsequent expenditures, such as repairs and additions, be treated?

4. How should disposal of the long-term asset be recorded?

Management's answers to these questions can be found in the company's annual report under management's discussion and analysis and in the notes to the financial statements.

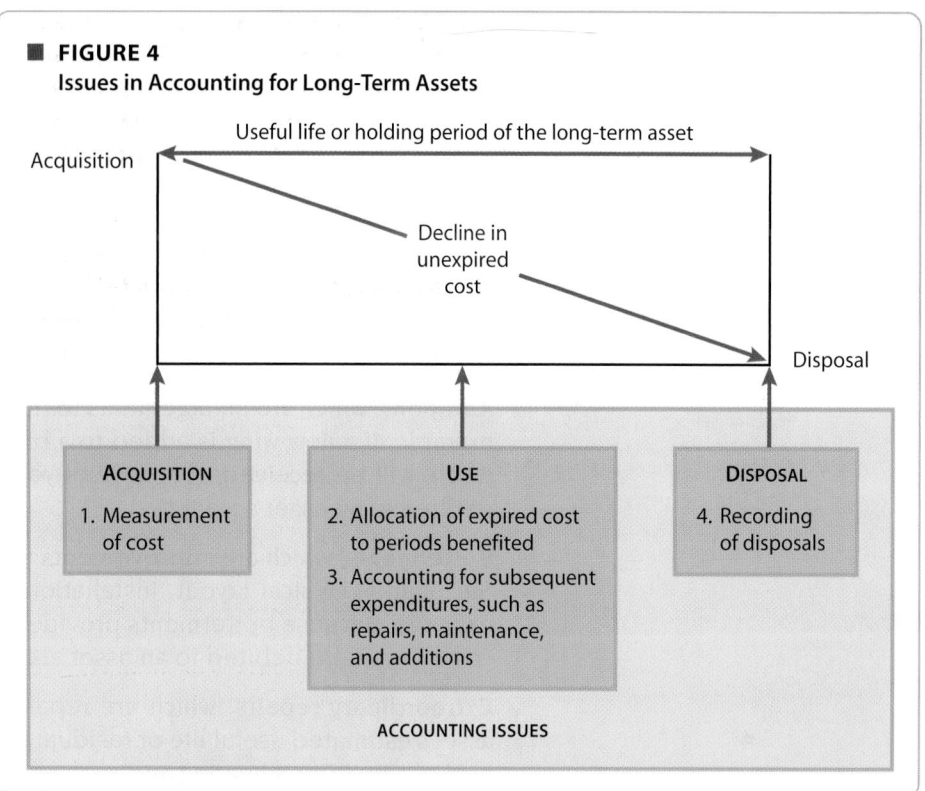

■ FIGURE 4
Issues in Accounting for Long-Term Assets

1-1. What are the characteristics of long-term assets?

1-2. Why is land different from other long-term assets?

1-3. What do accountants mean by *depreciation*, and how does depreciation differ from depletion and amortization?

1-4. What is asset impairment, and how does it affect the valuation of long-term assets?

1-5. How do cash flows relate to the decision to acquire a long-term asset, and how does an asset's useful life relate to the means of financing it?

1-6. Define *free cash flow*, and identify its components. What do *positive free cash flow* and *negative free cash flow* mean?

1-7. What four questions are important in accounting for long-term assets?

Suggested answers to all Stop, Review, and Apply questions are available at http://college.hmco.com/accounting/needles/poa/10e/student_home.html.

Acquisition Cost of Property, Plant, and Equipment

LO2 Distinguish between *capital expenditures* and *revenue expenditures,* and account for the cost of property, plant, and equipment.

Expenditure refers to a payment or an obligation to make a future payment for an asset, such as a truck, or for a service, such as a repair. Expenditures are classified as capital expenditures or revenue expenditures.

♦ A **capital expenditure** is an expenditure for the purchase or expansion of a long-term asset. Capital expenditures are recorded in asset accounts because they benefit several future accounting periods.

♦ A **revenue expenditure** is an expenditure made for the ordinary repairs and maintenance needed to keep a long-term asset in good operating condition. For example, trucks, machines, and other equipment require periodic tune-ups and routine repairs. Expenditures of this type are recorded in expense accounts because their benefits are realized in the current period.

Capital expenditures include outlays for plant assets, natural resources, and intangible assets. They also include expenditures for the following:

♦ **Additions**, which are enlargements to the physical layout of a plant asset. For example, if a new wing is added to a building, the benefits from the expenditure will be received over several years, and the amount paid should be debited to an asset account.

♦ **Betterments**, which are improvements to a plant asset but that do not add to the plant's physical layout. Installation of an air-conditioning system is an example. Because betterments provide benefits over a period of years, their costs should be debited to an asset account.

♦ **Extraordinary repairs**, which are repairs that significantly enhance a plant asset's estimated useful life or residual value. For example, a complete overhaul of a building's heating and cooling system may extend the system's useful life by five years. Extraordinary repairs are typically recorded by reducing the Accumulated Depreciation account; the assumption in doing so is that some of the depreciation previously recorded on the asset has now been eliminated. The effect of the reduction is to increase the asset's carrying value by the cost of the extraordinary repair. The new carrying value should be depreciated over the asset's new estimated useful life.

The distinction between capital and revenue expenditures is important in applying the matching rule. For example, if the purchase of a machine that will benefit a company for several years is mistakenly recorded as a revenue expenditure, the total cost of the machine becomes an expense on the income statement in the current period. As a result, current net income will be reported at a lower amount (understated), and in future periods, net income will be reported at a higher amount (overstated). If, on the other hand, a revenue expenditure, such as the routine overhaul of a piece of machinery, is charged to an asset account, the expense of the current period will be understated. Current net income will be overstated by the same amount, and the net income of future periods will be understated.

General Approach to Acquisition Costs

Study Note

Expenditures necessary to prepare an asset for its intended use are a cost of the asset.

The acquisition cost of property, plant, and equipment includes all expenditures reasonable and necessary to get an asset in place and ready for use. For example, the cost of installing and testing a machine is a legitimate cost of acquiring the machine. However, if the machine is damaged during installation, the cost of repairs is an operating expense, not an acquisition cost.

Acquisition cost is easiest to determine when a purchase is made for cash. In that case, the cost of the asset is equal to the cash paid for it plus expenditures for freight, insurance while in transit, installation, and other necessary related costs. Expenditures for freight, insurance while in transit, and installation are included in the cost of the asset because they are necessary if the asset is to function. In accordance with the matching rule, these expenditures are allocated over the asset's useful life rather than charged as expenses in the current period.

Any interest charges incurred in purchasing an asset are not a cost of the asset; they are a cost of borrowing the money to buy the asset and are therefore an operating expense. An exception to this rule is that interest costs incurred during the construction of an asset are properly included as a cost of the asset.[4]

As a matter of practicality, many companies establish policies that define when an expenditure should be recorded as an expense or as an asset. For example, small expenditures for items that qualify as long-term assets may be treated as expenses because the amounts involved are not material in relation to net income. Thus, although a wastebasket may last for years, it would be recorded as supplies expense rather than as a depreciable asset.

Specific Applications

In the sections that follow, we discuss some of the problems of determining the cost of long-term plant assets.

Study Note

Many costs may be incurred to prepare land for its intended use and condition. All such costs are a cost of the land.

Land   The purchase price of land should be debited to the Land account. Other expenditures that should be debited to the Land account include commissions to real estate agents; lawyers' fees; accrued taxes paid by the purchaser; costs of preparing the land to build on, such as the costs of tearing down old buildings and grading the land; and assessments for local improvements, such as putting in streets and sewage systems. The cost of landscaping is usually debited to the Land account because such improvements are relatively permanent. Land is not subject to depreciation because it has an unlimited useful life.

Let us assume that a company buys land for a new retail operation. The net purchase price is $170,000. The company also pays brokerage fees of $6,000, legal fees of $2,000, $10,000 to have an old building on the site torn down, and

To make way for its new headquarters in Birmingham, Alabama, Energen Corporation had this ten-story building imploded. Like other costs involved in preparing land for use, the cost of implosion is debited to the Land account. Other expenditures debited to the Land account include the purchase price of the land, brokerage and legal fees involved in the purchase, taxes paid by the purchaser, and landscaping.

$1,000 to have the site graded. It receives $4,000 in salvage from the old building. The cost of the land is $185,000, calculated as follows:

Net purchase price		$170,000
Brokerage fees		6,000
Legal fees		2,000
Tearing down old building	$10,000	
Less salvage	4,000	6,000
Grading		1,000
Total cost		$185,000

Land Improvements   Some improvements to real estate, such as driveways, parking lots, and fences, have a limited life and thus are subject to depreciation. They should be recorded in an account called Land Improvements rather than in the Land account.

Buildings   When a company buys a building, the cost includes the purchase price and all repairs and other expenditures required to put the building in usable condition. When a company uses a contractor to construct a building, the cost includes the net contract price plus other expenditures necessary to put the building in usable condition. When a company constructs its own building, the cost includes all reasonable and necessary expenditures, including the costs of materials, labor, part of the overhead and other indirect costs, architects' fees, insurance during construction, interest on construction loans during the period of construction, lawyers' fees, and building permits. Because buildings have a limited useful life, they are subject to depreciation.

Leasehold Improvements   Improvements to leased property that become the property of the lessor (the owner of the property) at the end of the lease are called **leasehold improvements**. For example, a tenant's installation of light fixtures, carpets, or walls would be considered a leasehold improvement. These improvements are usually classified as tangible assets in the property, plant, and equipment section of the balance sheet. Sometimes, they are included in the intangible assets section; the theory in reporting them as intangibles is that because they revert to the lessor at the end of the lease, they are more of a right than a tangible asset. The cost of a leasehold improvement is depreciated or amortized over the remaining term of the lease or the useful life of the improvement, whichever is shorter.

Leasehold improvements are fairly common in large businesses. A study of large companies showed that 19 percent report leasehold improvements. The percentage is likely to be much higher for small businesses because they generally operate in leased premises.[5]

Equipment   The cost of equipment includes all expenditures connected with purchasing the equipment and preparing it for use. Among these expenditures are the invoice price less cash discounts; freight, including insurance; excise taxes and tariffs; buying expenses; installation costs; and test runs to ready the equipment for operation. Equipment is subject to depreciation.

Group Purchases   Companies sometimes purchase land and other assets for a lump sum. Because land has an unlimited life and is a nondepreciable asset, it must have a separate ledger account, and the lump-sum purchase price must be apportioned between the land and the other assets. For example, suppose a company buys a building and the land on which it is situated for a lump sum of $85,000. The company can apportion the costs by determining what it would have paid for the building and for the land if it had purchased them separately and applying the appropriate percentages to the lump-sum price. Assume that appraisals yield estimates of $10,000 for the land and $90,000 for the building if purchased separately. In that case, 10 percent of the lump-sum price, or $8,500, would be allocated to the land, and 90 percent, or $76,500, would be allocated to the building, as follows:

	Appraisal	Percentage		Apportionment	
Land	$ 10,000	10%	($10,000 ÷ $100,000)	$ 8,500	($85,000 × 10%)
Building	90,000	90%	($90,000 ÷ $100,000)	76,500	($85,000 × 90%)
Totals	$100,000	100%		$85,000	

S T O P • R E V I E W • A P P L Y

2-1. What is the difference between revenue expenditures and capital expenditures, and why is it important?

2-2. In what ways do an addition, a betterment, and an extraordinary repair differ?

2-3. When an addition to a building is charged as a repair expense, how will it affect income in future years?

2-4. What, in general, is included in the acquisition cost of a long-term asset?

2-5. The following expenditures relate to the purchase of a computer system: (a) purchase price, (b) interest charges incurred in purchasing the equipment, (c) freight charges, (d) installation charges, (e) cost of special communications outlets at the computer site, (f) cost of repairing a part damaged during installation, and (g) cost of adjustments to the system during the first month of operation. Which of these expenditures should be charged to an asset account?

2-6. Hale's Grocery obtained bids on the construction of a receiving dock at the back of its store. The lowest bid was $22,000. The company decided to build the dock itself and was able to do so for $20,000, which it borrowed. It recorded the expenditures by debiting its Buildings account for $22,000 and crediting its Notes Payable account for $20,000 and its Gain on Construction account for $2,000. Do you agree with this entry? Why or why not?

Identification of Capital Expenditures Match each term below with the corresponding action in the list that follows by writing the appropriate numbers in the blanks:

1. Addition   **6.** Leasehold improvement

2. Betterment   **7.** Buildings

3. Extraordinary repair   **8.** Equipment

4. Land   **9.** Not a capital expenditure

5. Land improvement

___ a. Purchase of a computer

___ b. Purchase of a lighting system for a parking lot

___ c. Repainting of an existing building

3 d. Installation of a new roof that extends an existing building's useful life

7 e. Construction of a foundation for a new building

1 f. Erection of a new storage facility at the back of an existing building

6 g. Installation of partitions and shelves in a leased space

4 h. Clearing of land in preparation for construction of a new building

2 i. Installation of a new heating system in an existing building

---

SOLUTION

a.	8	f.	1
b.	5	g.	6
c.	9	h.	4
d.	3	i.	2
e.	7		

Depreciation

LO3 Compute depreciation under the straight-line, production, and declining-balance methods.

As we noted earlier, *depreciation* is the periodic allocation of the cost of a tangible asset (other than land and natural resources) over the asset's estimated useful life. In accounting for depreciation, it is important to keep the following points in mind:

▸ *All tangible assets except land have a limited useful life, and the costs of these assets must be distributed as expenses over the years they benefit.* Physical deterioration and obsolescence are the major factors in limiting a depreciable asset's useful life.

— **Physical deterioration** results from use and from exposure to the elements, such as wind and sun. Periodic repairs and a sound maintenance policy may keep buildings and equipment in good operating order and extract the maximum useful life from them, but every machine or building must at some point be discarded. Repairs do not eliminate the need for depreciation.

— **Obsolescence** refers to the process of going out of date. Because of fast-changing technology and fast-changing demands, machinery and even buildings often become obsolete before they wear out.

Accountants do not distinguish between physical deterioration and obsolescence because they are interested in the length of an asset's useful life, not in what limits its useful life.

▸ *Depreciation refers to the allocation of the cost of a plant asset to the periods that benefit from the asset, not to the asset's physical deterioration or decrease in market value.* The term *depreciation* describes the gradual conversion of the cost of the asset into an expense.

▸ *Depreciation is not a process of valuation.* Accounting records are not indicators of changing price levels; they are kept in accordance with the cost principle. Because of an advantageous purchase price and market conditions, the

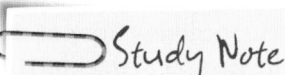

Study Note

A computer may be functioning as well as it did on the day it was purchased four years ago, but because much faster, more efficient computers have become available, the old computer is now obsolete.

Study Note

Depreciation is the allocation of the acquisition cost of a plant asset, and any similarity between undepreciated cost and current market value is pure coincidence.

FOCUS ON BUSINESS PRACTICE

How Long Is the Useful Life of an Airplane?

Most airlines depreciate their planes over an estimated useful life of 10 to 20 years. But how long will a properly maintained plane really last? Western Airlines paid $3.3 million for a new Boeing 737 in July 1968. More than 78,000 flights and 30 years later, this aircraft was still flying for Vanguard Airlines, a no-frills airline. Among the other airlines that have owned this plane are Piedmont, Delta, and US Airways. Virtually every part of the plane has been replaced over the years. Boeing believes the plane could theoretically make double the number of flights before it is retired.

The useful lives of many types of assets can be extended indefinitely if the assets are correctly maintained, but proper accounting in accordance with the matching rule requires depreciation over a "reasonable" useful life. Each airline that owned the plane would have accounted for the plane in this way.

value of a building may increase. Nevertheless, because depreciation is a process of allocation, not valuation, depreciation on the building must continue to be recorded. Eventually, the building will wear out or become obsolete regardless of interim fluctuations in market value.

Factors in Computing Depreciation

Four factors affect the computation of depreciation:

1. *Cost.* As explained earlier, cost is the net purchase price of an asset plus all reasonable and necessary expenditures to get it in place and ready for use.

2. *Residual value.* **Residual value** is an asset's estimated scrap, salvage, or trade-in value on the estimated date of its disposal. Other terms used to describe residual value are *salvage value* and *disposal value*.

3. *Depreciable cost.* **Depreciable cost** is an asset's cost less its residual value. For example, a truck that cost $12,000 and that has a residual value of $3,000 would have a depreciable cost of $9,000. Depreciable cost must be allocated over the useful life of the asset.

4. *Estimated useful life.* **Estimated useful life** is the total number of service units expected from a long-term asset. Service units may be measured in terms of the years an asset is expected to be used, the units it is expected to produce, the miles it is expected to be driven, or similar measures. In computing an asset's estimated useful life, an accountant should consider all relevant information, including past experience with similar assets, the asset's present condition, the company's repair and maintenance policy, and current technological and industry trends.

Depreciation is recorded at the end of an accounting period with an adjusting entry that takes the following form:

Study Note

Residual value is the portion of an asset's acquisition cost that a company expects to recover when it disposes of the asset.

Study Note

It is depreciable cost, not acquisition cost, that is allocated over a plant asset's useful life.

A = L + OE	
−XXX −XXX	

Depreciation Expense–Asset Name	XXX	
Accumulated Depreciation–Asset Name		XXX
To record depreciation for the period		

Methods of Computing Depreciation

Many methods are used to allocate the cost of plant assets to accounting periods through depreciation. Each is appropriate in certain circumstances. The most common methods are the straight-line method, the production method, and an accelerated method known as the declining-balance method.

Straight-Line Method

When the **straight-line method** is used to calculate depreciation, the asset's depreciable cost is spread evenly over the estimated useful life of the asset. The straight-line method is based on the assumption that depreciation depends only on the passage of time. The depreciation expense for each period is computed by dividing the depreciable cost (cost of the depreciating asset less its estimated residual value) by the number of accounting periods in the asset's estimated useful life. The rate of depreciation is the same in each year.

Suppose, for example, that a delivery truck cost $10,000 and has an estimated residual value of $1,000 at the end of its estimated useful life of five years. Under the straight-line method, the annual depreciation would be $1,800, calculated as follows:

$$\frac{\text{Cost} - \text{Residual Value}}{\text{Estimated Useful Life}} = \frac{\$10,000 - \$1,000}{5 \text{ years}} = \$1,800 \text{ per year}$$

The depreciation schedule for the five years would be as follows:

Depreciation Schedule, Straight-Line Method

	Cost	Annual Depreciation	Accumulated Depreciation	Carrying Value
Date of purchase	$10,000	—	—	$10,000
End of first year	10,000	$1,800	$1,800	8,200
End of second year	10,000	1,800	3,600	6,400
End of third year	10,000	1,800	5,400	4,600
End of fourth year	10,000	1,800	7,200	2,800
End of fifth year	10,000	1,800	9,000	1,000

Note that in addition to annual depreciation's being the same each year, the accumulated depreciation increases uniformly, and the carrying value decreases uniformly until it reaches the estimated residual value.

Production Method

The **production method** is based on the assumption that depreciation is solely the result of use and that the passage of time plays no role in the process. If we assume that the delivery truck in the previous example has an estimated useful life of 90,000 miles, the depreciation cost per mile would be determined as follows:

$$\frac{\text{Cost} - \text{Residual Value}}{\text{Estimated Units of Useful Life}} = \frac{\$10,000 - \$1,000}{90,000 \text{ miles}} = \$0.10 \text{ per mile}$$

If the truck was driven 20,000 miles in the first year, 30,000 miles in the second, 10,000 miles in the third, 20,000 miles in the fourth, and 10,000 miles in the fifth, the depreciation schedule for the truck would be as follows:

Depreciation Schedule, Production Method

	Cost	Miles	Annual Depreciation	Accumulated Depreciation	Carrying Value
Date of purchase	$10,000	—	—	—	$10,000
End of first year	10,000	20,000	$2,000	$2,000	8,000
End of second year	10,000	30,000	3,000	5,000	5,000
End of third year	10,000	10,000	1,000	6,000	4,000
End of fourth year	10,000	20,000	2,000	8,000	2,000
End of fifth year	10,000	10,000	1,000	9,000	1,000

As you can see, the amount of depreciation each year is directly related to the units of use. The accumulated depreciation increases annually in direct relation to these units, and the carrying value decreases each year until it reaches the estimated residual value.

The production method should be used only when the output of an asset over its useful life can be estimated with reasonable accuracy. In addition, the unit used to measure the estimated useful life of an asset should be appropriate for the asset. For example, the number of items produced may be an appropriate measure for one machine, but the number of hours of use may be a better measure for another.

Declining-Balance Method An **accelerated method** of depreciation results in relatively large amounts of depreciation in the early years of an asset's life and smaller amounts in later years. This type of method, which is based on the passage of time, assumes that many plant assets are most efficient when new and so provide the greatest benefits in their first years. It is consistent with the matching rule to allocate more depreciation to an asset in its earlier years than to later ones if the benefits it provides in its early years are greater than those it provides later on.

Fast-changing technologies often cause equipment to become obsolescent and lose service value rapidly. In such cases, using an accelerated method is appropriate because it allocates more depreciation to earlier years than to later ones. Another argument in favor of using an accelerated method is that repair expense is likely to increase as an asset ages. Thus, the total of repair and depreciation expense will remain fairly constant over the years. This result naturally assumes that the services received from the asset are roughly equal from year to year.

The **declining-balance method** is the most common accelerated method of depreciation. With this method, depreciation is computed by applying a fixed rate to the carrying value (the declining balance) of a tangible long-term asset. It therefore results in higher depreciation charges in the early years of the asset's life. Though any fixed rate can be used, the most common rate is a percentage equal to twice the straight-line depreciation percentage. When twice the straight-line rate is used, the method is usually called the **double-declining-balance method**.

In our example of the straight-line method, the delivery truck had an estimated useful life of five years, and the annual depreciation rate for the truck was therefore 20 percent (100 percent ÷ 5 years). Under the double-declining-balance method, the fixed rate would be 40 percent (2 × 20 percent). This fixed rate is applied to the carrying value that remains at the end of each year. With this method, the depreciation schedule would be as follows:

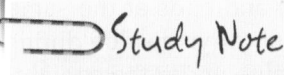
> Study Note

Accelerated depreciation is appropriate for assets that provide the greatest benefits in their early years. Under an accelerated method, depreciation charges will be highest in years when revenue generation from the asset is highest.

> Study Note

The double-declining-balance method is the only method presented here in which the residual value is not deducted before beginning the depreciation calculation.

Depreciation Schedule, Double-Declining-Balance Method

	Cost	Annual Depreciation		Accumulated Depreciation	Carrying Value
Date of purchase	$10,000		—	—	$10,000
End of first year	10,000	(40% × $10,000)	$4,000	$4,000	6,000
End of second year	10,000	(40% × $6,000)	2,400	6,400	3,600
End of third year	10,000	(40% × $3,600)	1,440	7,840	2,160
End of fourth year	10,000	(40% × $2,160)	864	8,704	1,296
End of fifth year	10,000		296*	9,000	1,000

*Depreciation is limited to the amount necessary to reduce carrying value to residual value: $296 = $1,296 (previous carrying value) − $1,000 (residual value).

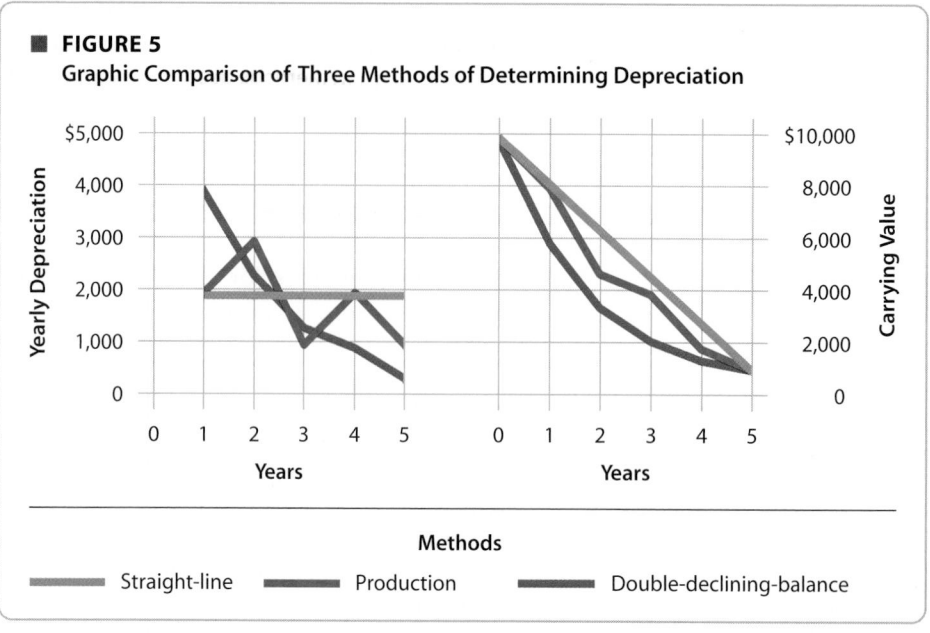

■ **FIGURE 5**
Graphic Comparison of Three Methods of Determining Depreciation

Methods

——— Straight-line ——— Production ——— Double-declining-balance

Note that the fixed rate is always applied to the carrying value at the end of the previous year. Depreciation is greatest in the first year and declines each year after that. The depreciation in the last year is limited to the amount necessary to reduce carrying value to residual value.

Comparison of the Three Methods Figure 5 compares yearly depreciation and carrying value under the three methods. The graph on the left shows yearly depreciation. As you can see, straight-line depreciation is uniform at $1,800 per year over the five-year period. The double-declining-balance method begins at $4,000 and decreases each year to amounts that are less than straight-line (ultimately, $296). The production method does not generate a regular pattern because of the random fluctuation of the depreciation from year to year.

The graph on the right shows the carrying value under the three methods. Each method starts in the same place (cost of $10,000) and ends at the same place (residual value of $1,000). However, the patterns of carrying value during the asset's useful life differ. For instance, the carrying value under the straight-line method is always greater than under the double-declining-balance method, except at the beginning and end of the asset's useful life.

FOCUS ON BUSINESS PRACTICE
Accelerated Methods Save Money!

As shown in Figure 6, an AICPA study of 600 large companies found that the overwhelming majority used the straight-line method of depreciation for financial reporting. Only about 9 percent used some type of accelerated method, and 4 percent used the production method. These figures tend to be misleading about the importance of accelerated depreciation methods, however, especially when it comes to income taxes. Federal income tax laws allow either the straight-line method or an accelerated method, and for tax purposes, about 75 percent of the 600 companies studied preferred an accelerated method. Companies use different methods of depreciation for good reason. The straight-line method can be advantageous for financial reporting because it can produce the highest net income, and an accelerated method can be beneficial for tax purposes because it can result in lower income taxes.

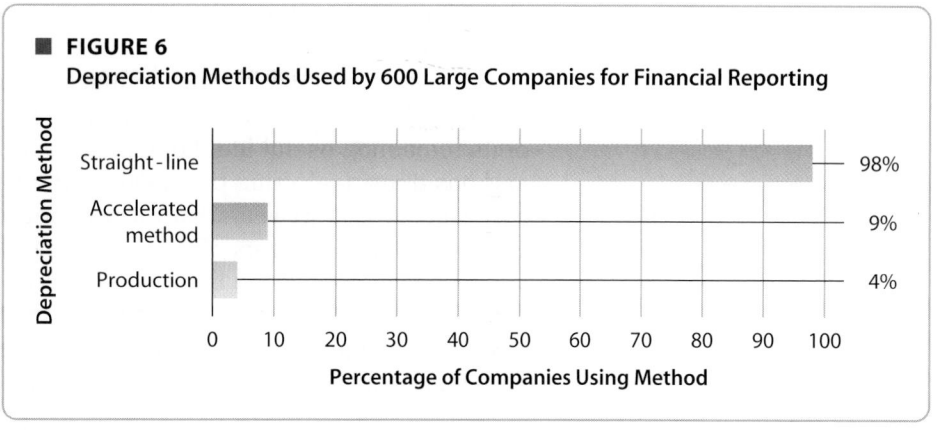

■ FIGURE 6
Depreciation Methods Used by 600 Large Companies for Financial Reporting

Total percentage exceeds 100 because some companies used different methods for different types of depreciable assets.

Source: "Depreciation Methods Used by 600 Large Companies." Reprinted with permission from *Accounting Trends & Techniques.* Copyright © 2005 by the American Institute of Certified Public Accountants, Inc.

Special Issues in Depreciation

Other issues in depreciating assets include group depreciation, depreciation for partial years, revision of depreciation rates, and accelerated cost recovery for tax purposes.

Group Depreciation   The estimated useful life of an asset is the average length of time assets of the same type are expected to last. For example, the average useful life of a particular type of machine may be six years, but some machines in this category may last only two or three years, while others may last eight or nine years or longer. For this reason, and for convenience, large companies group similar assets, such as machines, trucks, and pieces of office equipment, to calculate depreciation. This method, called **group depreciation**, is widely used in all fields of industry and business. A survey of large businesses indicated that 65 percent used group depreciation for all or part of their plant assets.[6]

Depreciation for Partial Years   To simplify our examples of depreciation, we have assumed that plant assets were purchased at the beginning or end of an accounting period. Usually, however, businesses buy assets when they are needed and sell or discard them when they are no longer needed or useful. The time of year is normally not a factor in the decision. Thus, it is often necessary to calculate depreciation for partial years. Some companies compute depreciation to the nearest month. Others use the half-year convention, in which one-half year of depreciation is taken in the year the asset is purchased and one-half year is taken in the year the asset is sold.

Revision of Depreciation Rates   Because a depreciation rate is based on an estimate of an asset's useful life, the periodic depreciation charge is seldom precise. It is sometimes very inadequate or excessive. Such a situation may result from an underestimate or overestimate of the asset's useful life or from a wrong estimate of its residual value. What should a company do when it discovers that a piece of equipment that it has used for several years will last a shorter—or longer—time than originally estimated? Sometimes, it is necessary to revise the estimate of useful life so that the periodic depreciation expense increases or decreases. Then, to reflect the revised situation, the remaining depreciable cost of the asset is spread over the remaining years of useful life.

With this technique, the annual depreciation expense is increased or decreased to reduce the asset's carrying value to its residual value at the end of its remaining useful life. For example, suppose a delivery truck cost $7,000 and has a residual value of $1,000. At the time of the purchase, the truck was expected to last six years, and it was depreciated on the straight-line basis. However, after two years of intensive use, it is determined that the truck will last only two more years, but its residual value at the end of the two years will still be $1,000. In other words, at the end of the second year, the truck's estimated useful life is reduced from six years to four years. At that time, the asset account and its related accumulated depreciation account would be as follows:

DELIVERY TRUCK		ACCUMULATED DEPRECIATION— DELIVERY TRUCK	
Cost 7,000		Depreciation, Year 1	1,000
		Depreciation, Year 2	1,000

The remaining depreciable cost is computed as follows:

Cost	−	**Depreciation Already Taken**	−	**Residual Value**	
$7,000	−	$2,000	−	$1,000	= $4,000

The new annual periodic depreciation charge is computed by dividing the remaining depreciable cost of $4,000 by the remaining useful life of two years. Therefore, the new periodic depreciation charge is $2,000. This method of revising depreciation is used widely in industry. It is also supported by *Opinion No. 9* and *Opinion No. 20* of the Accounting Principles Board of the AICPA.

Accelerated Cost Recovery for Tax Purposes Over the years, to encourage businesses to invest in new plant and equipment, Congress has revised the federal income tax law to allow rapid write-offs of plant assets. Depreciation allowed for tax purposes differs considerably from depreciation calculated for financial statements. Tax methods of depreciation are usually not acceptable for financial reporting because the periods over which deductions may be taken are often shorter than the assets' estimated useful lives.

Recent changes in the federal income tax law allow a small company to expense the first $100,000 of equipment expenditures rather than recording them as assets. The law also allows an accelerated method of writing off expenditures that are recorded as assets. This method discards the concepts of estimated useful life and residual value. For most property other than real estate, it uses a 200 percent declining balance with a half-year convention (only one half-year's depreciation is allowed in the year of purchase, and one half-year's depreciation is taken in the last year). This method enables businesses to recover most of the cost of their investments early in the depreciation process.

Study Note

For financial reporting purposes, the objective is to measure performance accurately. For tax purposes, the objective is to minimize tax liability.

STOP • REVIEW • APPLY

3-1. Why is it useful to think of a plant asset as a bundle of service units?

3-2. A firm buys technical equipment that is expected to last 12 years. Why might the firm have to depreciate the equipment over a shorter time?

3-3. A company purchased a building five years ago. The building's market value is now greater than when the building was purchased. Should the company stop depreciating the building?

3-4. Evaluate the following statement: "A parking lot should not be depreciated because adequate repairs will make it last for an indefinite period."

3-5. Is the purpose of depreciation to determine the value of equipment? Explain your answer.

3-6. How do the assumptions underlying the straight-line and production methods of depreciation differ?

3-7. What is the principal argument in favor of an accelerated depreciation method?

3-8. On what basis is depreciation taken on a group of assets rather than on individual items?

3-9. What procedure should be followed in revising a depreciation rate?

Disposal of Depreciable Assets

LO4 Account for the disposal of depreciable assets.

When plant assets are no longer useful because they have physically deteriorated or become obsolete, a company can dispose of them by discarding them, selling them for cash, or trading them in on the purchase of a new asset. Regardless of how a company disposes of a plant asset, it must record depreciation expense for the partial year up to the date of disposal. This step is required because the company used the asset until that date and, under the matching rule, the accounting period should receive the proper allocation of depreciation expense.

In the next sections, we show how a company records each type of disposal. As our example, we assume that MGC Company purchased a machine on January 2, 20x2, for $6,500 and planned to depreciate it on a straight-line basis over an estimated useful life of eight years. The machine's residual value at the end of eight years was estimated to be $300. On December 31, 20x7, the balances of the relevant accounts were as follows:

MACHINERY	ACCUMULATED DEPRECIATION—MACHINERY
6,500			4,650

On January 2, 20x8, management disposed of the asset.

Study Note

When it disposes of an asset, a company must bring the depreciation up to date and remove all evidence of ownership of the asset, including the contra account Accumulated Depreciation.

Discarded Plant Assets

A plant asset rarely lasts exactly as long as its estimated life. If it lasts longer than its estimated life, it is not depreciated past the point at which its carrying value equals its residual value. The purpose of depreciation is to spread the depreciable cost of an asset over its estimated life. Thus, the total accumulated depreciation should never exceed the total depreciable cost. If an asset remains in use beyond the end of its estimated life, its cost and accumulated depreciation remain in the ledger accounts. Proper records will thus be available for maintaining control over plant assets. If the residual value is zero, the carrying value of a fully depreciated asset is zero until the asset is disposed of. If such an asset is discarded, no gain or loss results.

In our example, however, the discarded equipment has a carrying value of $1,850 at the time of its disposal. The carrying value is computed from the T accounts above as machinery of $6,500 less accumulated depreciation of $4,650. A loss equal to the carrying value should be recorded when the machine is discarded, as follows:

A = L + OE
+ 4,650   −1,850
− 6,500

20x8			
Jan. 2	Accumulated Depreciation–Machinery	4,650	
	Loss on Disposal of Machinery	1,850	
	Machinery		6,500
	Discarded machine no longer		
	used in the business		

Gains and losses on disposals of plant assets are classified as other revenues and expenses on the income statement.

Plant Assets Sold for Cash

Study Note

When an asset is discarded or sold for cash, the gain or loss equals cash received minus the carrying value.

The entry to record a plant asset sold for cash is similar to the one just illustrated, except that the receipt of cash should also be recorded. The following entries show how to record the sale of a machine under three assumptions about the selling price. In the first case, the $1,850 cash received is exactly equal to the $1,850 carrying value of the machine; therefore, no gain or loss occurs:

A = L + OE
+ 1,850
+ 4,650
− 6,500

20x8			
Jan. 2	Cash	1,850	
	Accumulated Depreciation–Machinery	4,650	
	Machinery		6,500
	Sale of machine for carrying		
	value; no gain or loss		

In the second case, the $1,000 cash received is less than the carrying value of $1,850, so a loss of $850 is recorded:

A = L + OE
+ 1,000   −850
+ 4,650
− 6,500

20x8			
Jan. 2	Cash	1,000	
	Accumulated Depreciation–Machinery	4,650	
	Loss on Sale of Machinery	850	
	Machinery		6,500
	Sale of machine at less than		
	carrying value; loss of $850		
	($1,850 − $1,000) recorded		

In the third case, the $2,000 cash received exceeds the carrying value of $1,850, so a gain of $150 is recorded:

A	= L +	OE
+ 2,000		+150
+ 4,650		
− 6,500		

```
20x8
Jan. 2  Cash                                            2,000
        Accumulated Depreciation–Machinery             4,650
            Gain on Sale of Machinery                            150
            Machinery                                          6,500
            Sale of machine at more than the
            carrying value; gain of $150
            ($2,000 − $1,850) recorded
```

Exchanges of Plant Assets

As we have noted, businesses can dispose of plant assets by trading them in on the purchase of other plant assets. Exchanges may involve similar assets, such as an old machine traded in on a newer model, or dissimilar assets, such as a cement mixer traded in on a truck. In either case, the purchase price is reduced by the amount of the trade-in allowance.

Basically, accounting for exchanges of plant assets is similar to accounting for sales of plant assets for cash. If the trade-in allowance is greater than the asset's carrying value, the company realizes a gain. If the allowance is less, it suffers a loss. (Some special rules apply and are addressed in more advanced courses.)

STOP • REVIEW • APPLY

4-1. If a company sells a plant asset during its fiscal year, why should it compute depreciation on the asset for the part of the year that precedes the date of the sale?

4-2. If a plant asset is discarded before the end of its useful life, how is the amount of loss measured?

4-3. When a company sells an asset for cash, how is the gain or loss on the sale determined?

Natural Resources

LO5 Identify the issues related to accounting for natural resources, and compute depletion.

Study Note

Natural resources are not intangible assets. They are correctly classified as components of property, plant, and equipment.

Natural resources are long-term assets that appear on a balance sheet with descriptive titles like Timberlands, Oil and Gas Reserves, and Mineral Deposits. The distinguishing characteristic of these assets is that they are converted to inventory by cutting, pumping, mining, or other extraction methods. They are recorded at acquisition cost, which may include some costs of development. As a natural resource is extracted and converted to inventory, its asset account must be proportionally reduced. For example, the carrying value of oil reserves on the balance sheet is reduced by the proportional cost of the barrels pumped during the period. As a result, the original cost of the oil reserves is gradually reduced, and depletion is recognized in the amount of the decrease.

When you season your food with salt, you probably don't think of it as using a natural resource, but that is what salt is. Table salt is produced by evaporation methods; rock salt, which is used for highway maintenance, is mined. Natural resources are considered components of property, plant, and equipment. These long-term assets are recorded at acquistion cost, which may include some costs of development.

Depletion

Depletion refers not only to the exhaustion of a natural resource, but also to the proportional allocation of the cost of a natural resource to the units extracted. The way in which the cost of a natural resource is allocated closely resembles the production method of calculating depreciation. When a natural resource is purchased or developed, the total units that will be available, such as barrels of oil, tons of coal, or board-feet of lumber, must be estimated. The depletion cost per unit is determined by dividing the cost of the natural resource (less residual value, if any) by the estimated number of units available. The amount of the depletion cost for each accounting period is then computed by multiplying the depletion cost per unit by the number of units extracted and sold.

For example, suppose a mine was purchased for $1,800,000 and that it has an estimated residual value of $300,000 and contains an estimated 1,500,000 tons of coal. The depletion charge per ton of coal is $1, calculated as follows:

$$\frac{\$1,800,000 - \$300,000}{1,500,000 \text{ tons}} = \$1 \text{ per ton}$$

Thus, if 115,000 tons of coal are mined and sold during the first year, the depletion charge for the year is $115,000. This charge would be recorded as follows:

A	= L +	OE
−115,000		−115,000

Dec. 31	Depletion Expense–Coal Deposits	115,000	
	Accumulated Depletion–Coal Deposits		115,000
	To record depletion of coal mine:		
	$1 per ton for 115,000 tons		
	mined and sold		

On the balance sheet, data for the mine would be presented as follows:

Coal deposits	$1,800,000	
Less accumulated depletion	115,000	$1,685,000

Sometimes, a natural resource is not sold in the year it is extracted. It is important to note that it would then be recorded as a depletion *expense* in the year it is *sold*. The part not sold is considered inventory.

Depreciation of Related Plant Assets

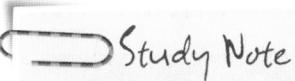

The extraction of natural resources generally requires special on-site buildings and equipment (e.g., conveyors, drills, and pumps). The useful life of these plant assets may be longer than the estimated time it will take to deplete the resources. However, a company may plan to abandon these assets after all the resources have been extracted because they no longer serve a useful purpose. In this case, they should be depreciated on the same basis as the depletion.

For example, if machinery with a useful life of ten years is installed on an oil field that is expected to be depleted in eight years, the machinery should be depreciated over the eight-year period, using the production method. That way, each year's depreciation will be proportional to the year's depletion. If one-sixth of the oil field's total reserves is pumped in one year, then the depreciation should be one-sixth of the machinery's cost minus the residual value.

If the useful life of a long-term plant asset is less than the expected life of the resource, the shorter life should be used to compute depreciation. In such cases, or when an asset will not be abandoned after all reserves have been depleted, other depreciation methods, such as straight-line or declining-balance, are appropriate.

Development and Exploration Costs in the Oil and Gas Industry

The costs of exploring and developing oil and gas resources can be accounted for under one of two methods. Under **successful efforts accounting**, the cost of successful exploration—for example, producing an oil well—is a cost of the resource. It should be recorded as an asset and depleted over the estimated life of the resource. The cost of an unsuccessful exploration—such as the cost of a dry well—is written off immediately as a loss. Because of these immediate write-offs, successful efforts accounting is considered the more conservative method and is used by most large oil companies.

On the other hand, smaller, independent oil companies argue that the cost of dry wells is part of the overall cost of the systematic development of an oil field and is thus a part of the cost of producing wells. Under the **full-costing method**, all costs, including the cost of dry wells, are recorded as assets and depleted over the estimated life of the producing resources. This method tends to improve a company's earnings performance in its early years.

The Financial Accounting Standards Board permits the use of either method.[7]

FOCUS ON BUSINESS PRACTICE

How Do You Measure What's Underground? With a Good Guess.

Accounting standards require publicly traded energy companies to disclose in their annual reports their production activities, estimates of their proven oil and gas reserves, and estimates of the present value of the future cash flows those reserves are expected to generate. The figures are not easy to estimate. After all, the reserves are often miles underground or beneath deep water. As a result, these figures considered "supplementary" and not reliable enough to be audited independently. Nevertheless, it appears that some companies, including **Royal Dutch/Shell Group**, have overestimated their reserves and thus overestimated their future prospects. Apparently, some managers at Royal Dutch/Shell Group receive bonuses based on the amount of new reserves added to the annual report. When the company recently announced that it was reducing its reported reserves by 20 percent, the price of its stock dropped.[8]

S T O P • R E V I E W • A P P L Y

5-1. What circumstance would cause the amount of annual depletion to differ from the amount of depletion expense?

5-2. Under what circumstances can a mining company depreciate its plant assets over a period that is less than the assets' useful lives?

5-3. What is the difference between successful efforts accounting and full-costing accounting?

Natural Resource Depletion and Depreciation of Related Plant Assets

Maase Mining Company paid $4,400,000 for land containing an estimated 20 million tons of ore. The land without the ore is estimated to be worth $1,000,000. The company spent $690,000 to erect buildings on the site and $1,200,000 on installing equipment. The buildings have an estimated useful life of 30 years, and the equipment has an estimated useful life of 10 years. Because of the remote location, neither the buildings nor the equipment has a residual value. The company expects that it can mine all the usable ore in 10 years. During its first year of operation, it mined and sold 1,400,000 tons of ore.

1. Compute the depletion charge per ton.

2. Compute the depletion expense that Maase Mining should record for its first year of operation.

3. Determine the depreciation expense for the year for the buildings, making it proportional to the depletion.

4. Determine the depreciation expense for the year for the equipment under two alternatives: (a) making the expense proportional to the depletion, and (b) using the straight-line method.

SOLUTION

1. $\dfrac{\$4,400,000 - \$1,000,000}{20,000,000 \text{ tons}} = \$.0.17 \text{ per ton}$

2. $1,400,000 \text{ tons} \times \$0.17 \text{ per ton} = \$238,000$

3. $\dfrac{1,400,000 \text{ tons}}{20,000,000 \text{ tons}} \times \$690,000 = \$48,300$

4. a. $\dfrac{1,400,000 \text{ tons}}{20,000,000 \text{ tons}} \times \$1,200,000 = \$84,000$

   b. $\dfrac{\$1,200,000}{10 \text{ years}} \times 1 \text{ year} = \$120,000$

Intangible Assets

LO6 Identify the issues related to accounting for intangible assets, including research and development costs and goodwill.

An intangible asset is both long term and nonphysical. Its value comes from the long-term rights or advantages it affords its owner. Table 1 describes the most common types of intangible assets—goodwill, trademarks and brand names, copyrights, patents, franchises and licenses, leaseholds, software, noncompete covenants, and customer lists—and their accounting treatment. Like intangible assets, some current assets—for exam-

TABLE 1. Accounting for Intangible Assets

Type	Description	Usual Accounting Treatment*
Goodwill	The excess of the amount paid for a business over the fair market value of the business's net assets	Debit Goodwill for the acquisition cost, and review impairment annually.
Trademark, brand name	A registered symbol or name that can be used only by its owner to identify a product or service	Debit Trademark or Brand Name for the acquisition cost, and review impairment annually.
Copyright	An exclusive right granted by the federal government to reproduce and sell literary, musical, and other artistic materials and computer programs for a period of the author's life plus 70 years	Record at acquisition cost, and amortize over the asset's useful life, which is often much shorter than its legal life. For example, the cost of paperback rights to a popular novel would typically be amortized over a useful life of two to four years.
Patent	An exclusive right granted by the federal government for a period of 20 years to make a particular product or use a specific process. A design may be granted a patent for 14 years.	The cost of successfully defending a patent in a patent infringement suit is added to the acquisition cost of the patent. Amortize over the asset's useful life, which may be less than its legal life.
Franchise, license	A right to an exclusive territory or market, or the right to use a formula, technique, process, or design	Debit Franchise or License for the acquisition cost, and amortize over the asset's useful life since it is likely that these types of assets would have a definite useful life; if an indefinite life is determined, review impairment annually.
Leasehold	A right to occupy land or buildings under a long-term rental contract. For example, if Company A sells or subleases its right to use a retail location to Company B for ten years in return for one or more rental payments, Company B has purchased a leasehold.	The lessor (Company A) debits Leasehold for the amount of the rental payment and amortizes it over the remaining life of the lease. The lessee (Company B) debits payments to Lease Expense.
Software	Capitalized costs of computer programs developed for sale, lease, or internal use	Record the amount of capitalizable production costs, and amortize over the estimated economic life of the product.
Noncompete covenant	A contract limiting the rights of others to compete in a specific industry or line of business for a specified period	Record at acquisition cost, and amortize over the contract period.
Customer list	A list of customers or subscribers	Debit Customer Lists for amount paid, and amortize over the asset's expected life.

*All intangible assets are subject to an annual impairment test.

ple, accounts receivable and certain prepaid expenses—have no physical substance, but because current assets are short term, they are not classified as intangible assets.

Figure 7 shows the percentage of companies that report the various types of intangible assets. For some companies, intangible assets make up a substantial portion of total assets. As noted in the Decision Point, **Apple Computer's** goodwill and other acquired intangible assets amounted to $96 million in 2005. How these assets are accounted for has a major effect on Apple's performance.

The purchase of an intangible asset is a special kind of capital expenditure. Such assets are accounted for at acquisition cost—that is, the amount that a company paid for them. Some intangible assets, such as goodwill and trademarks, may be acquired at little or no cost. Even though these assets may have

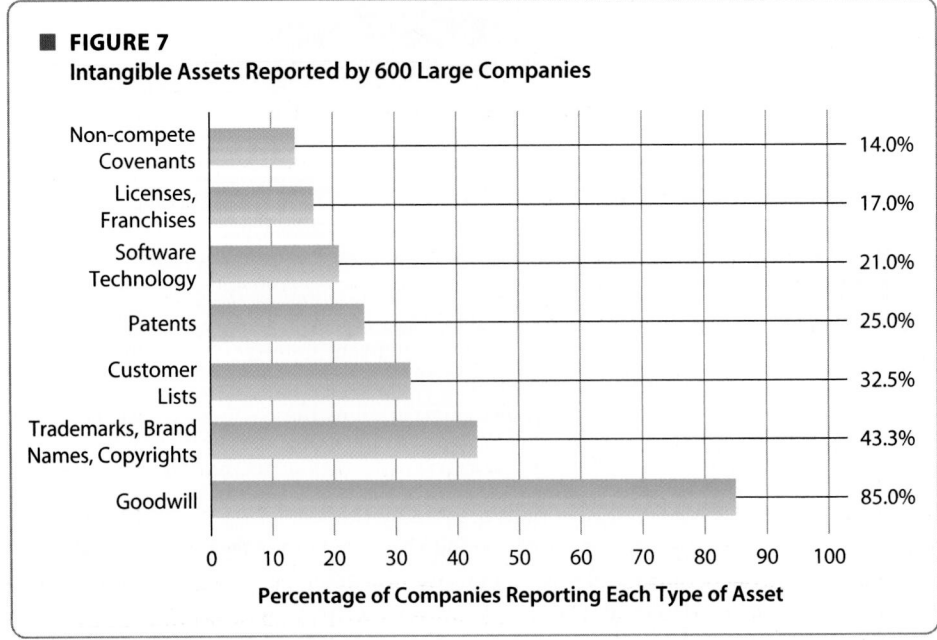

■ FIGURE 7
Intangible Assets Reported by 600 Large Companies

Source: Data from American Institute of Certified Public Accountants, *Accounting Trends & Techniques* (New York: AICPA, 2005).

great value and be needed for profitable operations, a company should include them on its balance sheet only if it purchased them from another party at a price established in the marketplace. When a company develops its own intangible assets, it should record the costs of development as expenses. An exception is the cost of internally developed computer software after a working prototype of the software has been developed.

Purchased intangible assets are recorded at cost, or at fair value when purchased as part of a group of assets. The useful life of an intangible asset is the period over which the asset is expected to contribute to future cash flows of the entity. The useful life may be definite or indefinite.[9]

▶ *Definite useful life.* A definite useful life means the useful life is subject to a legal limit or can be reasonably estimated. Examples include patents, copyrights, and leaseholds. Often the estimated useful lives of these assets are less than their legal limits. The cost of an intangible asset with a definite

FOCUS ON BUSINESS PRACTICE

Who's Number One in Brands?

Brands are intangible assets that often do not appear on a company's balance sheet because rather than purchasing them, the company has developed them over time. A recent report attempted to value brands by the discounted present value of future cash flows.[10] According to the report, the ten most valuable brands in the world were as follows:

Coca-Cola	Nokia
Microsoft	Disney
IBM	McDonald's
GE	Marlboro
Intel	Mercedes

Coca-Cola's brand was valued at almost $70 billion, whereas the Mercedes brand was valued at $21 billion. Where did **Apple** stand? It was number 50 at $5.3 billion, but this analysis was made before taking into account Apple's successful iPod, which has certainly increased its brand power.

One of the most valuable intangible assets some companies have is a list of customers. For example, the **Newark Morning Ledger Company**, a newspaper chain, purchased a chain of Michigan newspapers whose list of 460,000 subscribers was valued at $68 million. The U.S. Supreme Court upheld the company's right to amortize the value of the subscriber list because the company showed that the list had a limited useful life. The Internal Revenue Service had argued that the list had an indefinite life and therefore could not provide tax deductions through amortization. This ruling has benefited other types of businesses that purchase everything from bank deposits to pharmacy prescription files.[11]

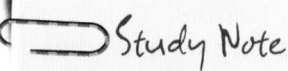
Study Note

The cost of mailing lists may be recorded as an asset because the mailing lists will be used over and over and will benefit future accounting periods.

useful life should be allocated to expense through periodic amortization over the asset's useful life in the same way that a building is depreciated.

▶ *Indefinite useful life.* An indefinite useful life means that the useful life of the asset is not limited by legal, regulatory, contractual, competitive, economic, or other factors. This definition does not imply that these assets last forever. Examples can include trademarks and brands. The costs of intangible assets with an indefinite life are not amortized as long as circumstances continue to support an indefinite life.

All intangible assets, whether definite or indefinite, are subject to an annual impairment test to determine if the assets justify their value on the balance sheet. If it is determined that they have lost some or all of their value in producing future cash flows, they should be written down to their fair value or to zero if they have no fair value. The amount of the write-down is shown on the income statement as an impairment charge (deduction) in income from operations.

To illustrate these procedures, suppose Soda Bottling Company purchases a patent on a unique bottle cap for $18,000. The purchase would be recorded with an entry of $18,000 in the asset account Patents. (Note that if the company developed the bottle cap internally instead of purchasing the patent, the costs of developing the cap—such as researchers' salaries and the costs of supplies and equipment used in testing—would be expensed as incurred.) Although the patent for the bottle cap will last for 20 years, Soda determines that it will sell the product that uses the cap for only six years.

The entry to record the annual amortization expense would be for $3,000 ($18,000 ÷ 6 years). The Patents account is reduced directly by the amount of the amortization expense. This is in contrast to the treatment of other long-term asset accounts, for which depreciation or depletion is accumulated in separate contra accounts.

If the patent becomes worthless before it is fully amortized, the remaining carrying value is written off as a loss by removing it from the Patents account.

Research and Development Costs

Most successful companies carry out research and development (R&D) activities, often within a separate department. Among these activities are development of new products, testing of existing and proposed products, and pure research. The costs of these activities are substantial for many companies. In a recent year, **General Motors** spent $6.7 billion, or about 3.5 percent of its revenues, on R&D.[12] R&D costs can be even greater in high-tech fields like pharmaceuticals. For example, **Abbott Laboratories** recently spent $1.8 billion, or 8.1 percent of its revenues, on R&D.[13]

The Financial Accounting Standards Board requires that all R&D costs be treated as revenue expenditures and charged to expense in the period in which they are incurred.[14] The reasoning behind this requirement is that it is too hard to trace specific costs to specific profitable developments. Also, the costs of research and development are continuous and necessary for the success of a business and so should be treated as current expenses. To support this conclusion, the FASB cited studies showing that 30 to 90 percent of all new products fail and that 75 percent of new-product expenses go to unsuccessful products. Thus, their costs do not represent future benefits.

Computer Software Costs

The costs that companies incur in developing computer software for sale or lease or for their own internal use are considered research and development costs until the product has proved technologically feasible. Thus, costs incurred before that point should be charged to expense as they are incurred. A product is deemed technologically feasible when a detailed working program has been designed. Once that occurs, all software production costs are recorded as assets and are amortized over the software's estimated economic life using the straight-line method. If at any time the company cannot expect to realize from the software the amount of the unamortized costs on the balance sheet, the asset should be written down to the amount expected to be realized.[15]

Goodwill

Goodwill means different things to different people. Generally, it refers to a company's good reputation. From an accounting standpoint, goodwill exists when a purchaser pays more for a business than the fair market value of the business's net assets. In other words, the purchaser would pay less if it bought the assets separately. Most businesses are worth more as going concerns than as collections of assets.

When the purchase price of a business is more than the fair market value of its physical assets, the business must have intangible assets. If it does not have patents, copyrights, trademarks, or other identifiable intangible assets of value, the excess payment is assumed to be for goodwill. Goodwill reflects all the factors that allow a company to earn a higher-than-market rate of return on its assets, including customer satisfaction, good management, manufacturing efficiency, the advantages of having a monopoly, good locations, and good employee relations. The payment above and beyond the fair market value of the tangible assets and other specific intangible assets is properly recorded in the Goodwill account.

FOCUS ON BUSINESS PRACTICE

Wake up, Goodwill Is Growing!

As Figure 7 shows, 85 percent of 600 large companies separately report goodwill as an asset. Because much of the growth of these companies has come through purchasing other companies, goodwill as a percentage of total assets has also grown. As the table at the right shows, the amount of goodwill can be material.[16]

	Goodwill (in billions)	Percentage of Total Assets
General Mills	$6,684	36
Heinz	$1,956	20
Tribune Company	$5,467	38

The FASB requires that purchased goodwill be reported as a separate line item on the balance sheet and that it be reviewed annually for impairment. If the fair value of goodwill is less than its carrying value on the balance sheet, goodwill is considered impaired. In that case, it is reduced to its fair value, and the impairment charge is reported on the income statement. A company can perform the fair value measurement for each reporting unit at any time as long as the measurement date is consistent from year to year.[17]

A company should record goodwill only when it acquires a controlling interest in another business. The amount to be recorded as goodwill can be determined by writing the identifiable net assets up to their fair market values at the time of purchase and subtracting the total from the purchase price. For example, suppose a company pays $11,400,000 to purchase another business. If the net assets of the business (total assets − total liabilities) are fairly valued at $10,000,000, then the amount of the goodwill is $1,400,000 ($11,400,000 − $10,000,000). If the fair market value of the net assets is more or less than $10,000,000, an entry is made in the accounting records to adjust the assets to the fair market value. The goodwill would then represent the difference between the adjusted net assets and the purchase price of $11,400,000.

STOP • REVIEW • APPLY

6-1. Accounts receivable have no physical substance. Why are they then not classified as intangible assets?

6-2. Under what circumstances can a company have intangible assets that do not appear on the balance sheet?

6-3. What is the FASB's rule for treating research and development costs?

6-4. How is accounting for software development costs similar to and different from accounting for research and development costs?

6-5. Under what conditions should goodwill be recorded? Should it remain in the records permanently once it is recorded?

A LOOK BACK AT

APPLE COMPUTER, INC.

We began the chapter by emphasizing that **Apple's** success as an innovator and marketer comes from wise and steady investments in long-term assets and related expenditures like research and development. In evaluating Apple's performance, investors and creditors look for answers to the following questions:

- What are Apple's long-term assets?
- What are its policies in accounting for long-term assets?
- Does the company generate enough cash flow to finance its continued growth?

Apple's tangible long-term assets include land, manufacturing facilities, office buildings, machinery, equipment, and leasehold improvements to its retail stores. Its balance sheet also includes goodwill and intangible assets that it acquired through acquisitions. Because internally developed intangible assets are not recorded as assets, the value of Apple's own brand name is not reflected on the balance sheet. Clearly, however, it far exceeds the value of the intangible assets that are listed.

In accordance with GAAP, Apple's accounting policies include using the straight-line depreciation method for tangible assets, amortizing intangible assets over a reasonable useful life, and expensing research and development costs. In addition, it evaluates its long-term assets for impairment each year to ensure that it is not carrying assets on its balance sheet at amounts that exceed their value.

A good measure of the funds that Apple has available for growth is its free cash flow:

Free Cash Flow = Net Cash Flows from Operating Activities − Dividends − (Purchases of Plant Assets − Sales of Plant Assets)

2005	**2004**
Free Cash Flow = $2,535 − $0 − ($260 − $0)	= $934 − $0 − ($176 − $0)
= $2,275	= $758

This two-year view of Apple's free cash flow shows great improvement in 2005. The company obviously generated enough cash to finance its continued growth. Its policy of not paying dividends contributes to the amount of cash it has available for this purpose. Although Apple may have sold some plant assets, the amounts were sufficiently immaterial that it did not report them separately.

CHAPTER REVIEW

REVIEW of Learning Objectives

LO1 Define *long-term assets,* and explain the management issues related to them.

Long-term assets have a useful life of more than one year, are used in the operation of a business, and are not intended for resale. They can be tangible or intangible. In the former category are land, plant assets, and natural resources. In the latter are patents, trademarks, franchises, and other rights, as well as goodwill. The management issues related to long-term assets include decisions about whether to acquire the assets, how to finance them, and how to account for them.

LO2 Distinguish between *capital expenditures* and *revenue expenditures,* and account for the cost of property, plant, and equipment.

Capital expenditures are recorded as assets, whereas revenue expenditures are recorded as expenses of the current period. Capital expenditures include not only outlays for plant assets, natural resources, and intangible assets, but also expenditures for additions, betterments, and extraordinary repairs that increase an asset's residual value or extend its useful life. Revenue expenditures are made for ordinary repairs and maintenance. The error of classifying a capital expenditure as a revenue expenditure, or vice versa, has an important effect on net income.

The acquisition cost of property, plant, and equipment includes all expenditures reasonable and necessary to get the asset in place and ready for use. Among these expenditures are purchase price, installation cost, freight charges, and insurance during transit. The acquisition cost of a plant asset is allocated over the asset's useful life.

LO3 Compute depreciation under the straight-line, production, and declining-balance methods.

Depreciation—the periodic allocation of the cost of a plant asset over its estimated useful life—is commonly computed by using the straight-line method, the production method, or an accelerated method. The straight-line method is related directly to the passage of time, whereas the production method is related directly to use or output. An accelerated method, which results in relatively large amounts of depreciation in earlier years and reduced amounts in later years, is based on the assumption that plant assets provide greater economic benefits in their earlier years than in later ones. The most common accelerated method is the declining-balance method.

LO4 Account for the disposal of depreciable assets.

A company can dispose of a long-term plant asset by discarding or selling it or exchanging it for another asset. Regardless of the way in which a company disposes of such an asset, it must record depreciation up to the date of disposal. To do so, it must remove the carrying value from the asset account and the depreciation to date from the accumulated depreciation account. When a company sells a depreciable long-term asset at a price that differs from its carrying value, it should report the gain or loss on its income statement. In recording exchanges of similar plant assets, a gain or loss may arise.

LO5 Identify the issues related to accounting for natural resources, and compute depletion.

Natural resources are depletable assets that are converted to inventory by cutting, pumping, mining, or other forms of extraction. They are recorded at cost as long-term assets. As natural resources are sold, their costs are allocated as expenses through depletion charges. The depletion charge is based on the ratio of the resource extracted to the total estimated resource. A major issue related to this subject is accounting for oil and gas reserves.

LO6 Identify the issues related to accounting for intangible assets, including research and development costs and goodwill.

The purchase of an intangible asset should be treated as a capital expenditure and recorded at acquisition cost. Intangible assets with a definite useful life are amortized over the useful life of the asset. Those with an indefinite life are reviewed annually for possible impairment. The FASB requires that research and development costs be treated as revenue expenditures and charged as expenses in the periods of expenditure. Software costs are treated as research and development costs and expensed until a feasible working program is developed, after which time the costs may be capitalized and amortized over a reasonable estimated life. Goodwill is the excess of the amount paid for a business over the fair market value of the net assets and is usually related to the business's superior earning potential. It should be recorded only when a company purchases an entire business, and it should be reviewed annually for possible impairment.

REVIEW of Concepts and Terminology

The following concepts and terms were introduced in this chapter:

Accelerated method: A method of depreciation that allocates relatively large amounts of the depreciable cost of an asset to earlier years and smaller amounts to later years. **(LO3)**

Additions: Enlargements to the physical layout of a plant asset. **(LO2)**

Amortization: The periodic allocation of the cost of an intangible asset to the periods it benefits. **(LO1)**

Asset impairment: Loss of revenue-generating potential of a long-lived asset before the end of its useful life; the difference between an asset's carrying value and its fair value, as measured by the present value of the expected cash flows. **(LO1)**

Betterments: Improvements that do not add to the physical layout of a plant asset. **(LO2)**

Brand name: A registered name that can be used only by its owner to identify a product or service. **(LO6)**

Capital expenditure: An expenditure for the purchase or expansion of a long-term asset, which is recorded in an asset account. **(LO2)**

Carrying value: The unexpired part of an asset's cost. Also called *book value*. **(LO1)**

Copyright: An exclusive right granted by the federal government to reproduce and sell literary, musical, and other artistic materials and computer programs for a period of the author's life plus 70 years. **(LO6)**

Customer list: A list of customers or subscribers. **(LO6)**

Declining-balance method: An accelerated method of depreciation in which depreciation is computed by applying a fixed rate to the carrying value (the declining balance) of a tangible long-lived asset. **(LO3)**

Depletion: The exhaustion of a natural resource through mining, cutting, pumping, or other extraction, and the way in which the cost is allocated. **(LO1)**

Depreciable cost: The cost of an asset less its residual value. **(LO3)**

Depreciation: The periodic allocation of the cost of a tangible long-lived asset (other than land and natural resources) over its estimated useful life. **(LO1)**

Double-declining-balance method: An accelerated method of depreciation in which a fixed rate equal to twice the straight-line percentage is applied to the carrying value (the declining balance) of a tangible long-lived asset. **(LO3)**

Estimated useful life: The total number of service units expected from a long-term asset. **(LO3)**

Expenditure: A payment or an obligation to make future payment for an asset or a service. **(LO2)**

Extraordinary repairs: Repairs that significantly enhance a plant asset's estimated useful life or residual value and thereby increase its carrying value. **(LO2)**

Franchise: The right to an exclusive territory or market. **(LO6)**

Free cash flow: Amount of cash that remains after deducting the funds a company must commit to continue operating at its planned level; Net Cash Flows from Operating Activities − Dividends − (Purchases of Plant Assets − Sales of Plant Assets). **(LO1)**

Full-costing method: A method of accounting for the costs of exploring and developing oil and gas resources in which all costs are recorded as assets and depleted over the estimated life of the producing resources. **(LO5)**

Goodwill: The excess of the amount paid for a business over the fair market value of the business's net assets. **(LO6)**

Group depreciation: The grouping of similar items to calculate depreciation. **(LO3)**

Intangible assets: Long-term assets with no physical substance whose value is based on rights or advantages accruing to the owner. **(LO1)**

Leasehold: A right to occupy land or buildings under a long-term rental contract. **(LO6)**

Leasehold improvements: Improvements to leased property that become the property of the lessor at the end of the lease. **(LO2)**

License: The right to use a formula, technique, process, or design. **(LO6)**

Long-term assets: Assets that have a useful life of more than one year, are used in the operation of a business, and are not intended for resale. Less commonly called *fixed assets*. **(LO1)**

Natural resources: Long-term assets purchased for the economic value that can be taken from the land and used up. **(LO1)**

Noncompete covenant: A contract limiting the rights of others to compete in a specific industry or line of business for a specified period. **(LO6)**

Obsolescence: The process of becoming out of date, which is a factor in the limited useful life of tangible assets. **(LO3)**

Patent: An exclusive right granted by the federal government for a period of 20 years to make a particular product or use a specific process. **(LO6)**

Physical deterioration: A decline in the useful life of a depreciable asset resulting from use and from exposure to the elements. **(LO3)**

Production method: A method of depreciation that assumes depreciation is solely the result of use and that allocates depreciation based on the units of use or output during each period of an asset's useful life. **(LO3)**

Residual value: The estimated net scrap, salvage, or trade-in value of a tangible asset at the estimated date of its disposal. Also called *salvage value* or *disposal value*. **(LO3)**

Revenue expenditure: An expenditure for ordinary repairs and maintenance of a long-term asset, which is recorded by a debit to an expense account. **(LO2)**

Software: Capitalized costs associated with computer programs developed for sale, lease, or internal use and amortized over the estimated economic life of the programs. **(LO6)**

Straight-line method: A method of depreciation that assumes depreciation depends only on the passage of time and that allocates an equal amount of depreciation to each accounting period in an asset's useful life. **(LO3)**

Successful efforts accounting: A method of accounting for the costs of exploring and developing oil and gas resources in which successful exploration is recorded as an asset and depleted over the estimated life of the resource and all unsuccessful efforts are immediately written off as losses. **(LO5)**

Tangible assets: Long-term assets that have physical substance. **(LO1)**

Trademark: A registered symbol that can be used only by its owner to identify a product or service. **(LO6)**

REVIEW Problem

LO3 Comparison of Depreciation Methods

Norton Construction Company purchased a cement mixer on January 2, 20x5, for $14,500. The mixer was expected to have a useful life of five years and a residual value of $1,000. The company's engineers estimated that the mixer would have a useful life of 7,500 hours. It was used for 1,500 hours in 20x5, 2,625 hours in 20x6, 2,250 hours in 20x7, 750 hours in 20x8, and 375 hours in 20x9. The company's fiscal year ends on December 31.

Required

1. Compute the depreciation expense and carrying value for 20x5 to 20x9, using the following methods: (a) straight-line, (b) production, and (c) double-declining-balance.

2. Show the balance sheet presentation for the cement mixer on December 31, 20x5. Assume the straight-line method.
3. What conclusions can you draw from the patterns of yearly depreciation?

Answer to Review Problem

1. Depreciation computed:

	A	B	C	D	E
1	Depreciation Method	Year	Computation	Depreciation	Carrying Value
2	a. Straight-line	20x5	$13,500 ÷ 5	$2,700	$11,800
3		20x6	13,500 ÷ 5	2,700	9,100
4		20x7	13,500 ÷ 5	2,700	6,400
5		20x8	13,500 ÷ 5	2,700	3,700
6		20x9	13,500 ÷ 5	2,700	1,000
7					
8	b. Production	20x5	$13,500 × 1,500/7,500	$2,700	$11,800
9		20x6	13,500 × 2,625/7,500	4,725	7,075
10		20x7	13,500 × 2,250/7,500	4,050	3,025
11		20x8	13,500 × 750/7,500	1,350	1,675
12		20x9	13,500 × 375/7,500	675	1,000
13					
14	c. Double-declining-balance	20x5	$14,500 × .4	$5,800	$8,700
15		20x6	8,700 × .4	3,480	5,220
16		20x7	5,220 × .4	2,088	3,132
17		20x8	3,132 × .4	1,253[*]	1,879
18		20x9		879[†]	1,000
19					
20	* Rounded.				
21	† Remaining depreciation to reduce carrying value to residual value ($1,879 – $879).				

2. Balance sheet presentation on December 31, 20x5:

Property, plant, and equipment
Cement mixer $14,500
Less accumulated depreciation   2,700
                                                       $11,800

3. The pattern of depreciation for the straight-line method differs significantly from the pattern for the double-declining-balance method. In the earlier years, the amount of depreciation under the double-declining-balance method is significantly greater than the amount under the straight-line method. In the later years, the opposite is true. The carrying value under the straight-line method is greater than under the double-declining-balance method at the end of all years except the fifth year. Depreciation under the production method differs from depreciation under the other methods in that it follows no regular pattern. It varies with the amount of use. Consequently, depreciation is greatest in 20x6 and 20x7, which are the years of greatest use. Use declined significantly in the last two years.

CHAPTER ASSIGNMENTS

BUILDING Your Basic Knowledge and Skills

Short Exercises

LO1 **Management Issues**

SE 1. Indicate whether each of the following actions is primarily related to (a) acquisition of long-term assets, (b) evaluating the adequacy of financing of long-term assets, or (c) applying the matching rule to long-term assets.

1. Deciding between common stock and long-term notes for the raising of funds
2. Relating the acquisition cost of a long-term asset to the cash flows generated by the asset
3. Determining how long an asset will benefit the company
4. Deciding to use cash flows from operations to purchase long-term assets
5. Determining how much an asset will sell for when it is no longer useful to the company
6. Calculating free cash flow

LO1 **Free Cash Flow**

SE 2. Sebel Corporation had cash flows from operating activities during the past year of $194,000. During the year, the company expended $25,000 for dividends; expended $158,000 for property, plant, and equipment; and sold property, plant, and equipment for $12,000. Calculate the company's free cash flow. What does the result tell you about the company?

LO2 **Determining Cost of Long-Term Assets**

SE 3. Watts Auto purchased a neighboring lot for a new building and parking lot. Indicate whether each of the following expenditures is properly charged to (a) Land, (b) Land Improvements, or (c) Buildings.

1. Paving costs
2. Architects' fee for building design
3. Cost of clearing the property
4. Cost of the property
5. Building construction costs
6. Lights around the property
7. Building permit
8. Interest on the construction loan

LO2 **Group Purchase**

SE 4. Lian Company purchased property with a warehouse and parking lot for $1,500,000. An appraiser valued the components of the property if purchased separately as follows:

Land	$ 400,000
Land improvements	200,000
Building	1,000,000
Total	$1,600,000

Determine the cost to be assigned to each component.

LO3 **Straight-Line Method**

SE 5. Willowbrook Fitness Center purchased a new step machine for $8,250. The apparatus is expected to last four years and have a residual value of $750. What will the depreciation expense be for each year under the straight-line method?

LO3   **Production Method**

SE 6. Assume that the step machine in **SE 5** has an estimated useful life of 8,000 hours and was used for 2,400 hours in year 1, 2,000 hours in year 2, 2,200 hours in year 3, and 1,400 hours in year 4. How much would depreciation expense be in each year?

LO3   **Double-Declining-Balance Method**

SE 7. Assume that the step machine in **SE 5** is depreciated using the double-declining-balance method. How much would depreciation expense be in each year?

LO4   **Disposal of Plant Assets: No Trade-In**

SE 8. Alarico Printing owned a piece of equipment that cost $16,200 and on which it had recorded $9,000 of accumulated depreciation. The company disposed of the equipment on January 2, the first day of business of the current year.

1. Calculate the carrying value of the equipment.
2. Calculate the gain or loss on the disposal under each of the following assumptions:
   a. The equipment was discarded as having no value.
   b. The equipment was sold for $3,000 cash.
   c. The equipment was sold for $8,000 cash.

LO5   **Natural Resources**

SE 9. Narda Company purchased land containing an estimated 4,000,000 tons of ore for $16,000,000. The land will be worth $2,400,000 without the ore after eight years of active mining. Although the equipment needed for the mining will have a useful life of 20 years, it is not expected to be usable and will have no value after the mining on this site is complete. Compute the depletion charge per ton and the amount of depletion expense for the first year of operation, assuming that 600,000 tons of ore are mined and sold. Also, compute the first-year depreciation on the mining equipment using the production method, assuming a cost of $19,200,000 with no residual value.

LO6   **Intangible Assets: Computer Software**

SE 10. Danya Company has created a new software application for PCs. Its costs during research and development were $250,000. Its costs after the working program was developed were $175,000. Although the company's copyright may be amortized over 40 years, management believes that the product will be viable for only five years. How should the costs be accounted for? At what value will the software appear on the balance sheet after one year?

Exercises

LO1, LO2, LO3   **Discussion Questions**

E 1. Develop a brief answer for each of the following questions:

1. Is carrying value ever the same as market value?
2. What major advantage does a company that has positive free cash flow have over a company that has negative free cash flow?
3. What incentive does a company have to allocate more of a group purchase price to land than to building?

4. Which depreciation method would best reflect the risk of obsolescence from rapid technological changes?

LO4, LO5, LO6 **Discussion Questions**

E 2. Develop a brief answer for each of the following questions:

1. When would the disposal of a long-term asset result in no gain or loss?
2. When would annual depletion not equal depletion expense?
3. Why would a firm amortize a patent over fewer years than the patent's life?
4. Why would a company spend millions of dollars on goodwill?

LO1 **Management Issues**

E 3. Indicate whether each of the following actions is primarily related to (a) acquisition of long-term assets, (b) evaluating the financing of long-term assets, or (c) applying the matching rule to long-term assets.

1. Deciding to use the production method of depreciation
2. Allocating costs on a group purchase
3. Determining the total units a machine will produce
4. Deciding to borrow funds to purchase equipment
5. Estimating the savings a new machine will produce and comparing that amount to cost
6. Examining the trend of free cash flow over several years
7. Deciding whether to rent or buy a piece of equipment

LO1 **Purchase Decision—Present Value Analysis**

E 4. Management is considering the purchase of a new machine for a cost of $6,000. It is estimated that the machine will generate positive net cash flows of $1,500 per year for five years and will have a disposal price at the end of that time of $500. Assuming an interest rate of 9 percent, determine if management should purchase the machine. Use Tables 3 and 4 in the appendix on future value and present value tables to determine the net present value of the new machine.

LO1 **Free Cash Flow**

E 5. Zedek Corporation had cash flows from operating activities during the past year of $216,000. During the year, the company expended $462,000 for property, plant, and equipment; sold property, plant, and equipment for $54,000; and paid dividends of $50,000. Calculate the company's free cash flow. What does the result tell you about the company?

LO2 **Special Types of Capital Expenditures**

E 6. Tell whether each of the following transactions related to an office building is a revenue expenditure (RE) or a capital expenditure (CE). In addition, indicate whether each transaction is an ordinary repair (OR), an extraordinary repair (ER), an addition (A), a betterment (B), or none of these (N).

1. The hallways and ceilings in the building are repainted at a cost of $4,150.
2. The hallways, which have tile floors, are carpeted at a cost of $14,000.
3. A new wing is added to the building at a cost of $87,500.
4. Furniture is purchased for the entrance to the building at a cost of $8,250.
5. The air-conditioning system is overhauled at a cost of $14,250. The overhaul extends the useful life of the air-conditioning system by ten years.
6. A cleaning firm is paid $100 per week to clean the newly installed carpets.

LO2 **Determining Cost of Long-Term Assets**

E 7. Sakai Manufacturing purchased land next to its factory to be used as a parking lot. The expenditures incurred by the company were as follows:

purchase price, $300,000; broker's fees, $24,000; title search and other fees, $2,200; demolition of a cottage on the property, $8,000; general grading of property, $4,200; paving parking lots, $40,000; lighting for parking lots, $32,000; and signs for parking lots, $6,400. Determine the amounts that should be debited to the Land account and the Land Improvements account.

LO2 **Group Purchase**

E 8. Ebra Allen purchased a car wash for $240,000. If purchased separately, the land would have cost $60,000, the building $135,000, and the equipment $105,000. Determine the amount that should be recorded in the new business's records for land, building, and equipment.

LO2, LO3 **Cost of Long-Term Asset and Depreciation**

E 9. Demarco Phipps purchased a used tractor for $17,500. Before the tractor could be used, it required new tires, which cost $1,100, and an overhaul, which cost $1,400. Its first tank of fuel cost $75. The tractor is expected to last six years and have a residual value of $2,000. Determine the cost and depreciable cost of the tractor and calculate the first year's depreciation under the straight-line method.

LO3 **Depreciation Methods**

E 10. On January 13, 20x8, Silverio Oil Company purchased a drilling truck for $45,000. Silverio expects the truck to last five years or 200,000 miles, with an estimated residual value of $7,500 at the end of that time. During 20x9, the truck is driven 48,000 miles. Silverio's year end is December 31. Compute the depreciation for 20x9 under each of the following methods: (1) straight-line, (2) production, and (3) double-declining-balance. Using the amount computed in **(3)**, prepare the entry in journal form to record depreciation expense for the second year, and show how the Drilling Truck account would appear on the balance sheet.

LO3 **Double-Declining-Balance Method**

E 11. Percival Burglar Alarm Systems Company purchased a computer for $1,120. It has an estimated useful life of four years and an estimated residual value of $120. Compute the depreciation charge for each of the four years using the double-declining-balance method.

LO3 **Revision of Depreciation Rates**

E 12. Feld Hospital purchased a special x-ray machine. The machine, which cost $623,120, was expected to last ten years, with an estimated residual value of $63,120. After two years of operation (and depreciation charges using the straight-line method), it became evident that the x-ray machine would last a total of only seven years. The estimated residual value, however, would remain the same. Given this information, determine the new depreciation charge for the third year on the basis of the revised estimated useful life.

LO4 **Disposal of Plant Assets**

E 13. A piece of equipment that cost $64,800 and on which $36,000 of accumulated depreciation had been recorded was disposed of on January 2, the first day of business of the current year. For each of the following assumptions, compute the gain or loss on the disposal.

1. The equipment was discarded as having no value.
2. The equipment was sold for $12,000 cash.
3. The equipment was sold for $36,000 cash.

LO4 **Disposal of Plant Assets**

E 14. King Company purchased a computer on January 2, 20x6, at a cost of $2,500. The computer is expected to have a useful life of five years and a residual value of $250. Assume that the computer is disposed of on July 1, 20x9. Record the depreciation expense for half a year and the disposal under each of the following assumptions:

1. The computer is discarded.
2. The computer is sold for $400.
3. The computer is sold for $1,100.

LO5 **Natural Resource Depletion and Depreciation of Related Plant Assets**

E 15. Cooby Company purchased land containing an estimated 5 million tons of ore for a cost of $8,800,000. The land without the ore is estimated to be worth $500,000. During its first year of operation, the company mined and sold 750,000 tons of ore. Compute the depletion charge per ton. Compute the depletion expense that Cooby should record for the year.

LO6 **Amortization of Copyrights and Trademarks**

E 16. The following exercise is about amortizing copyrights and trademarks.

1. Akram Publishing Company purchased the copyright to a basic computer textbook for $40,000. The usual life of a textbook is about four years. However, the copyright will remain in effect for another 50 years. Calculate the annual amortization of the copyright.
2. Saui Company purchased a trademark from a well-known supermarket for $320,000. The management of the company argued that the trademark's useful life was indefinite. Explain how the cost should be accounted for.

LO6 **Accounting for a Patent**

E 17. At the beginning of the fiscal year, Ricks Company purchased for $1,030,000 a patent that applies to the manufacture of a unique tamper-proof lid for medicine bottles. Ricks incurred legal costs of $450,000 in successfully defending use of the lid by a competitor. Ricks estimated that the patent would be valuable for at least ten years.

During the first two years of operations, Ricks Company successfully marketed the lid. At the beginning of the third year, a study appeared in a consumer magazine showing that children could in fact remove the lid. As a result, all orders for the lids were canceled, and the patent was rendered worthless.

Prepare entries in journal form to record the following: (a) purchase of the patent; (b) successful defense of the patent; (c) amortization expense for the first year; and (d) write-off of the patent as worthless.

Problems

LO1, LO2 **Identification of Long-Term Assets Terminology**

P 1. Listed below are common terms associated with long-term assets:

a. Tangible assets
b. Natural resources
c. Intangible assets
d. Additions
e. Betterments
f. Extraordinary repair

g. Depreciation
h. Depletion
i. Amortization
j. Revenue expenditure
k. Free cash flow

Required

1. For each of the following statements, identify the term listed above with which it is associated. (If two terms apply, choose the one that is most closely associated.)

   1. Periodic cost associated with intangible assets
   2. Cost of constructing a new wing on a building
   3. A measure of funds available for expansion
   4. A group of assets encompassing property, plant, and equipment
   5. Cost associated with enhancing a building but not expanding it
   6. Periodic cost associated with tangible assets
   7. A group of assets that gain their value from contracts or rights
   8. Cost of normal repairs to a building
   9. Assets whose value derives from what can be extracted from them
   10. Periodic cost associated with natural resources
   11. Cost of a repair that extends the useful life of a building

2. **User Insight:** Assuming the company uses cash for all its expenditures, which of the items listed above would you expect to see on the income statement? Which ones would not result in an outlay of cash?

LO2 Determining Cost of Assets

P 2. Oslo Company was formed on January 1, 2007, and began constructing a new plant. At the end of 2007, its auditor discovered that all expenditures involving long-term assets had been debited to an account called Fixed Assets. An analysis of the Fixed Assets account, which had a year-end balance of $2,644,972, disclosed that it contained the following items:

Cost of land	$ 316,600
Surveying costs	4,100
Transfer of title and other fees required by the county	920
Broker's fees for land	21,144
Attorney's fees associated with land acquisition	7,048
Cost of removing timber from land	50,400
Cost of grading land	4,200
Cost of digging building foundation	34,600
Architect's fee for building and land improvements (80 percent building)	64,800
Cost of building construction	710,000
Cost of sidewalks	11,400
Cost of parking lots	54,400
Cost of lighting for grounds	80,300
Cost of landscaping	11,800
Cost of machinery	989,000
Shipping cost on machinery	55,300
Cost of installing machinery	176,200
Cost of testing machinery	22,100
Cost of changes in building to comply with safety regulations pertaining to machinery	12,540
Cost of repairing building that was damaged in the installation of machinery	8,900
Cost of medical bill for injury received by employee while installing machinery	2,400
Cost of water damage to building during heavy rains prior to opening the plant for operation	6,820
Account balance	$2,644,972

Oslo Company sold the timber it cleared from the land to a firewood dealer for $5,000. This amount was credited to Miscellaneous Income.

During the construction period, two of Oslo's supervisors devoted full time to the construction project. Their annual salaries were $48,000 and $42,000, respectively. They spent two months on the purchase and preparation of the land, six months on the construction of the building (approximately one-sixth of which was devoted to improvements on the grounds), and one month on machinery installation. When the plant began operation on October 1, the supervisors returned to their regular duties. Their salaries were debited to Factory Salaries Expense.

Required

1. Prepare a schedule with the following column headings: Land, Land Improvements, Buildings, Machinery, and Expense. Place each of the above expenditures in the appropriate column. Negative amounts should be shown in parentheses. Total the columns.
2. User Insight: What impact does the classification of the items among several accounts have on evaluating the profitability performance of the company?

LO3, LO4   **Comparison of Depreciation Methods**

P 3. Laughlin Designs, Inc., purchased a computerized blueprint printer that will assist in the design and display of plans for factory layouts. The cost of the printer was $22,500, and its expected useful life is four years. The company can probably sell the printer for $2,500 at the end of six years. The printer is expected to last 6,000 hours. It was used 1,200 hours in year 1; 1,800 hours in year 2; 2,400 hours in year 3; and 600 hours in year 4.

Required

1. Compute the annual depreciation and carrying value for the new blueprint printer for each of the four years (round to the nearest dollar where necessary) under each of the following methods: (a) straight-line, (b) production, and (c) double-declining-balance.
2. If the printer is sold for $12,000 after year 2, what would be the gain or loss under each method?
3. User Insight: What conclusions can you draw from the patterns of yearly depreciation and carrying value in requirement 1? Do the three methods differ in their impact on profitability? Do they differ in their effect on the company's operating cash flows? Explain.

LO3, LO4   **Comparison of Depreciation Methods**

P 4. Myles Construction Company purchased a new crane for $360,500 at the beginning of year 1. The crane has an estimated residual value of $35,000 and an estimated useful life of six years. The crane is expected to last 10,000 hours. It was used 1,800 hours in year 1; 2,000 in year 2; 2,500 in year 3; 1,500 in year 4; 1,200 in year 5; and 1,000 in year 6.

Required

1. Compute the annual depreciation and carrying value for the new crane for each of the six years (round to the nearest dollar where necessary) under each of the following methods: (a) straight-line, (b) production, and (c) double-declining-balance.
2. If the crane is sold for $250,000 after year 3, what would be the amount of gain or loss under each method?

3. **User Insight:** Do the three methods differ in their effect on the company's profitability? Do they differ in their effect on the company's operating cash flows? Explain.

LO5 Natural Resource Depletion and Depreciation of Related Plant Assets

P 5. Dombrad Mining Company purchased land containing an estimated 10 million tons of ore for a cost of $4,400,000. The land without the ore is estimated to be worth $800,000. The company expects that all the usable ore can be mined in 10 years. Buildings costing $400,000 with an estimated useful life of 30 years were erected on the site. Equipment costing $480,000 with an estimated useful life of 10 years was installed. Because of the remote location, neither the buildings nor the equipment has an estimated residual value. During its first year of operation, the company mined and sold 800,000 tons of ore.

Required

1. Compute the depletion charge per ton.
2. Compute the depletion expense that Dombrad Mining should record for the year.
3. Determine the depreciation expense for the year for the buildings, making it proportional to the depletion.
4. Determine the depreciation expense for the year for the equipment under two alternatives: (a) making the expense proportional to the depletion and (b) using the straight-line method.
5. **User Insight:** Suppose the company mined and sold 1,000,000 tons of ore (instead of 800,000) during the first year. Would the change in the results in requirements **2** or **3** affect earnings or cash flows? Explain.

Alternate Problems

LO2 Determining Cost of Assets

P 6. Pappas Computers constructed a new training center in 20x7. You have been hired to manage the training center. A review of the accounting records shows the following expenditures debited to an asset account called Training Center:

Attorney's fee, land acquisition	$ 34,900
Cost of land	598,000
Architect's fee, building design	102,000
Building	1,020,000
Parking lot and sidewalk	135,600
Electrical wiring, building	164,000
Landscaping	55,000
Cost of surveying land	9,200
Training equipment, tables, and chairs	136,400
Installation of training equipment	68,000
Cost of grading the land	14,000
Cost of changes in building to soundproof rooms	59,200
Total account balance	$2,396,300

During the center's construction, an employee of Pappas Computers worked full time overseeing the project. He spent two months on the purchase and preparation of the site, six months on the construction, one month on land improvements, and one month on equipment installation and training room furniture purchase and setup. His salary of $64,000 during this ten-month period was charged to Administrative Expense. The training center was placed in operation on November 1.

Required

1. Prepare a schedule with the following four column (account) headings: Land, Land Improvements, Building, and Equipment. Place each of the above expenditures in the appropriate column. Total the columns.
2. **User Insight:** What impact does the classification of the items among several accounts have on evaluating the profitability performance of the company?

LO3, LO4   **Comparison of Depreciation Methods**

P 7. Gent Manufacturing Company purchased a robot for $720,000 at the beginning of year 1. The robot has an estimated useful life of four years and an estimated residual value of $60,000. The robot, which should last 20,000 hours, was operated 6,000 hours in year 1; 8,000 hours in year 2; 4,000 hours in year 3; and 2,000 hours in year 4.

Required

1. Compute the annual depreciation and carrying value for the robot for each year assuming the following depreciation methods: (a) straight-line, (b) production, and (c) double-declining-balance.
2. If the robot is sold for $750,000 after year 2, what would be the amount of gain or loss under each method?
3. **User Insight:** What conclusions can you draw from the patterns of yearly depreciation and carrying value in requirement 1? Do the three methods differ in their effect on the company's profitability? Do they differ in their effect on the company's operating cash flows? Explain.

LO5   **Natural Resource Depletion and Depreciation of Related Plant Assets**

P 8. Karanga Company purchased land containing an estimated 20 million tons of ore for a cost of $6,600,000. The land without the ore is estimated to be worth $1,200,000. The company expects that all the usable ore can be mined in 10 years. Buildings costing $600,000 with an estimated useful life of 20 years were erected on the site. Equipment costing $720,000 with an estimated useful life of 10 years was installed. Because of the remote location, neither the buildings nor the equipment has an estimated residual value. During its first year of operation, the company mined and sold 900,000 tons of ore.

Required

1. Compute the depletion charge per ton.
2. Compute the depletion expense that Karanga should record for the year.
3. Determine the depreciation expense for the year for the buildings, making it proportional to the depletion.
4. Determine the depreciation expense for the year for the equipment under two alternatives: (a) making the expense proportional to the depletion and (b) using the straight-line method.
5. **User Insight:** Suppose the company mined and sold 500,000 tons of ore (instead of 900,000) during the first year. Would the change in the results in requirement **2** or **3** affect earnings or cash flows? Explain.

≡ ENHANCING Your Knowledge, Skills, and Critical Thinking

Conceptual Understanding Cases

LO1 Effect of Change in Estimates

C 1. The airline industry was hit particularly hard after the 9/11 attacks on the World Trade Center in 2001. In 2002, **Southwest Airlines**, one of the healthier airlines companies, made a decision to lengthen the useful lives of its aircraft from 22 to 27 years. Shortly thereafter, following Southwest's leadership, other airlines made the same move.[18]

What advantage, if any, can the airlines gain by making this change in estimate? Will it change earnings or cash flows and, if it does, will the change be favorable or negative?

Some people argue that the useful lives and depreciation of airplanes are irrelevant. They claim that because of the extensive maintenance and testing that airline companies are required by law to perform, the planes theoretically can be in service for an indefinite future period. What is wrong with this argument?

LO1 Impairment Test

C 2. The annual report for **Costco Wholesale Corporation**, the large discount company, contains the following statement:

> The company periodically evaluates the realizability of long-lived assets for impairment when [circumstances] may indicate the carrying amount of the asset may not be recoverable.[19]

What does the concept of impairment mean in accounting? What effect does impairment have on profitability and cash flows? Why would the concept of impairment be referred to as a conservative accounting approach?

LO3 Accounting Policies

C 3. **IBM**, the large computer equipment and services company, states in its annual report that "plant, rental machines and other property are carried at cost and depreciated over their useful lives using the straight-line method."[20] What estimates are necessary to carry out this policy? What factors should be considered in making each of the estimates?

Interpreting Financial Reports

LO6 Brands

C 4. **Hilton Hotels Corporation** and **Marriott International** provide hospitality services. Hilton Hotels' well-known brands include Hilton, Doubletree, Hampton Inn, Embassy Suites, Red Lion Hotels and Inns, and Homewood Suites. Marriott also owns or manages properties with recognizable brand names, such as Marriott Hotels, Resorts and Suites; Ritz-Carlton; Renaissance Hotels; Residence Inn; Courtyard; and Fairfield Inn.

On its balance sheet, Hilton Hotels Corporation includes brands (net of amortization) of $970 million, or 11.8 percent of total assets. Marriott International, however, does not list brands among its intangible assets.[21] What principles of accounting for intangibles would cause Hilton to record brands as an asset while Marriott does not? How will these differences in accounting for brands generally affect the net income and return on assets of these two competitors?

LO3 Effects of Change in Accounting Method

C 5. Depreciation expense is a significant cost for companies in which plant assets are a high proportion of assets. The amount of depreciation expense in a given year is affected by estimates of useful life and choice of depreciation method. In 2007, Century Steelworks Company, a major integrated steel producer, changed the estimated useful lives for its major production assets. It also changed the method of depreciation for other steel-making assets from straight-line to the production method.

In its 2007 annual report, Century Steelworks Company makes the following statement:

> A recent study conducted by management shows that actual years-in-service figures for our major production equipment and machinery are, in most cases, higher than the estimated useful lives assigned to these assets. We have recast the depreciable lives of such assets so that equipment previously assigned a useful life of 8 to 26 years now has an extended depreciable life of 10 to 32 years.

The report goes on to explain the new production method of depreciation, as follows:

> [The method] recognizes that depreciation of production equipment and machinery correlates directly to both physical wear and tear and the passage of time. The production method of depreciation, which we have now initiated, more closely allocates the cost of these assets to the periods in which products are manufactured.

The report summarizes the effects of the changes in estimated useful lives and depreciation method on the year 2007 as shown in the following table:

Incremental Increase in Net Income	In Millions	Per Share
Lengthened lives	$11.0	$ .80
Production method		
Current year	7.3	.53
Prior years	2.8	.20
Total increase	$21.1	$1.53

During 2007, Century Steelworks reported a net loss of $83,156,500 ($6.03 per share). Depreciation expense for 2007 was $87,707,200.

In explaining the changes the company has made, the controller of Century Steelworks was quoted in an article in *Business Journal* as follows: "There is no reason for Century Steelworks to continue to depreciate our assets more conservatively than our competitors do." But the article also quotes an industry analyst who argues that by slowing its method of depreciation, Century Steelworks could be viewed as reporting lower-quality earnings.

1. Explain the accounting treatment when there is a change in the estimated lives of depreciable assets. What circumstances must exist for the production method to produce the effect it did in relation to the straight-line method? What would Century Steelworks' net income or loss have been if the changes had not been made? What might have motivated management to make the changes?

2. What does the controller of Century Steelworks mean when he says that Century had been depreciating "more conservatively than our competitors do"? Why might the changes at Century Steelworks indicate, as the analyst

asserts, "lower-quality earnings"? What risks might Century face as a result of its decision to use the production method of depreciation?

Decision Analysis Using Excel

LO1 **Purchase Decision and Time Value of Money**

C 6. Morningside Machine Works has obtained a subcontract from the government to manufacture special parts for a new military aircraft. The parts are to be delivered over the next five years, and the company will be paid as the parts are delivered.

To make the parts, Morningside Machine Works will have to purchase new equipment. Two types are available. Type A is conventional equipment that can be put into service immediately; Type B requires one year to be put into service but is more efficient than Type A. Type A requires an immediate cash investment of $1,000,000 and will produce enough parts to provide net cash receipts of $340,000 each year for the five years. Type B may be purchased by signing a two-year non-interest-bearing note for $1,346,000. It is projected that Type B will produce net cash receipts of zero in year 1, $500,000 in year 2, $600,000 in year 3, $600,000 in year 4, and $200,000 in year 5. Neither type of equipment can be used on other contracts, and neither type will have any useful life remaining at the end of the contract. Morningside currently pays an interest rate of 16 percent to borrow money.

1. What is the present value of the investment required for each type of equipment? (Use Table 3 in the appendix on future value and present value tables.)
2. Compute the net present value of each type of equipment based on your answer in **1** and the present value of the net cash receipts projected to be received. (Use Tables 3 and 4 in the appendix on future value and present value tables.)
3. Write a memorandum to the board of directors that recommends the option that appears to be best for Morningside. Explain your reasoning and include **1** and **2** as attachments.

Annual Report Case: CVS Corporation

LO1, LO2, LO3, LO6 **Long-Term Assets**

C 7. To answer the following questions, refer to **CVS Corporation's** annual report in the Supplement to Chapter 5. Examine the balance sheets and the summary of significant accounting policies on property and equipment in the notes to the financial statements.

1. What percentage of total assets in the most recent year was property and equipment, net? What are the major categories of CVS's property and equipment, and which is the most significant type of property and equipment? What are leasehold improvements? How significant are these items, and what are their effects on the earnings of the company?
2. Continue with the summary of significant accounting policies item on property and equipment in the CVS annual report. What method of depreciation does CVS use? How long does management estimate its buildings will last as compared with furniture and equipment? What does this say about the company's need to remodel its stores?
3. Refer to the note on impairment of long-lived assets in the summary of sig-

nificant accounting policies in CVS Corporation's annual report. How does the company determine if it has impaired assets?

Comparison Case: CVS Versus Southwest

LO1

Long-Term Assets and Free Cash Flows

C 8. Refer to the annual report of **CVS Corporation** and to the financial statements of **Southwest Airlines Co**. in the Supplement to Chapter 5 to answer the following questions:

1. Prepare a table that shows the net amount each company spent on property and equipment (from the statement of cash flows), the total property and equipment (from the balance sheet), and the percentage of the first figure to the second for each of the past two years. Which company grew its property and equipment at a faster rate?
2. Calculate free cash flow for each company for the past two years. What conclusions can you draw about the need for each company to raise funds from debt and equity and the ability of each company to grow?

Ethical Dilemma Case

LO2

Ethics and Allocation of Acquisition Costs

C 9. Signal Company has purchased land and a warehouse for $18,000,000. The warehouse is expected to last 20 years and to have a residual value equal to 10 percent of its cost. The chief financial officer (CFO) and the controller are discussing the allocation of the purchase price. The CFO believes that the largest amount possible should be assigned to the land because this action will improve reported net income in the future. Depreciation expense will be lower because land is not depreciated. He suggests allocating one-third, or $6,000,000, of the cost to the land. This results in depreciation expense each year of $540,000 [($12,000,000 − $1,200,000) ÷ 20 years].

The controller disagrees. She argues that the smallest amount possible, say one-fifth of the purchase price, should be allocated to the land, thereby saving income taxes, since the depreciation, which is tax-deductible, will be greater. Under this plan, annual depreciation would be $648,000 [($14,400,000 − $1,440,000) ÷ 20 years]. The annual tax savings at a 30 percent tax rate is $32,400 [($648,000 − $540,000) × .30]. How would each decision affect the company's cash flows? Ethically, how should the purchase cost be allocated? Who will be affected by the decision?

Internet Case

LO3, LO4, LO6

SEC and Forms 10-K

C 10. Public corporations are required not only to communicate with their stockholders by means of an annual report but also to submit an annual report to the Securities and Exchange Commission (SEC). The annual report to the SEC is called a Form 10-K and is a source of the latest information about a company. Access the SEC's EDGAR files to locate either **H.J. Heinz Company's** or **Ford Motor Company's** Form 10-K. Find the financial statements and the notes to the financial statements. Scan through the notes to the financial statements and prepare a list of information related to long-term assets, including intangibles. For instance, what depreciation methods does the company use?

What are the useful lives of its property, plant, and equipment? What intangible assets does the company have? Does the company have goodwill? How much does the company spend on research and development? In the statement of cash flows, how much did the company spend on new property, plant, and equipment (capital expenditures)? Summarize your results and be prepared to discuss them in class as well as your experience in using the SEC's EDGAR database.

Group Activity Case

LO2, LO6 **Ethics of Aggressive Accounting Policies**

C 11. Is it ethical to choose aggressive accounting practices to advance a company's business? During the 1990s, **America Online (AOL)**, the largest Internet service provider in the United States, was one of the hottest stocks on Wall Street. After its initial stock offering in 1992, AOL's stock price shot up by several thousand percent.

Accounting is very important to a company like AOL because earnings enable it to sell shares of stock and raise more cash to fund its growth. In its early years, AOL was one of the most aggressive companies in its choice of accounting principles. AOL's strategy called for building the largest customer base in the industry. Consequently, it spent many millions of dollars each year marketing its services to new customers. Such costs are usually recognized as operating expenses in the year in which they are incurred. However, AOL treated these costs as long-term assets, called "deferred subscriber acquisition costs," and expensed them over several years, because it said the average customer was going to stay with the company for three years or more. The company also recorded research and development costs as "product development costs" and amortized them over five years.

Both of these practices are justifiable theoretically, but they are not common practice. If the standard, more conservative practice had been followed, the company would have had a net loss in every year it has been in business.[22] This result would have greatly limited AOL's ability to raise money and grow.

Form groups to discuss this case. Determine whether your group thinks AOL was or was not justified in adopting the "aggressive" accounting techniques. In your group, answers to the following questions may help you reach a conclusion: What was "aggressive" about AOL's accounting techniques? What was management's rationale for adopting the accounting policies that it did? What could go wrong with such a plan? How would you evaluate the ethics of AOL's actions? Who benefits from the actions? Who is harmed by these actions? Be prepared to support your conclusion in class.

Business Communication Case

LO3 **Motivation for Change of Depreciation Method**

C 12. **Polaroid Corporation**, a manufacturer of instant cameras and film, changed from an accelerated depreciation method for financial reporting purposes to the straight-line method for assets acquired after January 1, 1997. As noted in Polaroid's 1997 annual report:

> The company changed its method of depreciation for financial reporting for the cost of buildings, machinery, and equipment acquired on or after January 1, 1997, from a primarily accelerated method to the straight-line method.[23]

Polaroid's deteriorating financial position led it to declare bankruptcy in 2001. Write a one-page memorandum that argues that the change in accounting method may have been a signal that the company was in financial trouble. In your memorandum, discuss the effects of the change on future earnings and cash flows. In addition, discuss which of the two depreciation methods is more conservative.

12

Contributed Capital

In this chapter, we focus on long-term *equity* financing—that is, on the capital that stockholders contribute to a corporation. The issues involved in equity financing include the type of stock a corporation issues, the dividends that it pays, and the treasury stock that it purchases. These issues can significantly affect return on equity and other measures of profitability on which management's compensation is based. Thus, ethics is a major concern. Management's decisions must be based not on personal gain, but on the value created for the corporation's owners.

LEARNING OBJECTIVES

Making a Statement

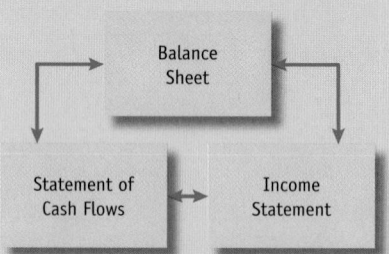

Stock transactions only impact the balance sheet and the statement of cash flows.

LO1 Identify and explain the management issues related to contributed capital.

LO2 Identify the components of stockholders' equity.

LO3 Identify the characteristics of preferred stock.

LO4 Account for the issuance of stock for cash and other assets.

LO5 Account for treasury stock.

- Why did Google's management choose to issue common stock to satisfy its needs for new capital?

- What are some of the advantages and disadvantages of this approach to financing a business?

- What measures should an investor use in evaluating management's performance?

When a company issues stock to the public for the first time, it is called an **initial public offering (IPO)**. There are many initial public offerings in any given year, but when Google, the popular Internet search engine company, went to market with its IPO in August 2004, it created a national sensation for several reasons. First, it was the largest IPO by an Internet company after the tech-bust in 2001 and 2002. Second, Google provides a very well known and widely used search service. Third, rather than allocating shares of stock to a few insiders, Google used an auction system that allowed anyone to partici-pate in its IPO. In the end, the company issued approximately 22.5 million shares at $85 per share for a total of $1.9 billion. Those who were fortunate enough to get shares saw the price per share soar to $135 in a few days and reach $400 per share in 2006. Google's Financial Highlights show the effect of the IPO and other related stock transactions on stockholders' equity.[1]

GOOGLE'S FINANCIAL HIGHLIGHTS
(In thousands)

	Sept. 30 2004	June 30 2004
Stockholders' equity		
Preferred stock	$ —	$ 79,860
Common stock	273	165
Additional paid-in capital	2,497,299	956,882
Retained earnings	386,371	334,388
Other items	(294,920)	(354,596)
Total stockholders' equity	$2,589,023	$1,016,699
Total assets	$2,888,518	$1,328,022

Management Issues Related to Contributed Capital

In Chapter 1, we defined a *corporation* as a business unit chartered by the state and legally separate from its owners—that is, its stockholders. *Contributed capital*, which refers to stockholders' investments in a corporation, is a major means of financing a corporation. Managing contributed capital requires an understanding of the corporate organization, its advantages and disadvantages, and the issues involved in equity financing. It also requires familiarity with dividend policies, with how to use return on equity to evaluate performance, and with stock option plans.

The Corporate Organization

The corporate form of business is well suited to today's trends toward large organizations, international trade, and professional management. Although fewer in number than sole proprietorships and partnerships, corporations dominate the U.S. economy, in part because of their ability to raise large amounts of capital. In 2004, the amount of new capital that corporations raised was $2,860 billion. Of this amount, $2,656 billion, or 92.9 percent, came from new bond issues; $170 billion, or 5.9 percent, came from new common stock issues; and $33 billion, or 1.2 percent, came from preferred stock issues.[2]

To form a corporation, most states require persons (called incorporators) to sign an application and file it with the proper state official. This application contains the **articles of incorporation**. If approved by the state, these articles, which form the company charter, become a contract between the state and the incorporators. The company is then authorized to do business as a corporation.

The authority to manage a corporation is delegated by its stockholders to a board of directors and by the board of directors to the corporation's officers (see Figure 1). That is, the stockholders elect a board of directors, which sets corporate policies and chooses the corporation's officers, who in turn carry out the corporate policies in their management of the business.

Stockholders A unit of ownership in a corporation is called a **share of stock**. The articles of incorporation state the maximum number of shares that a corporation is authorized to issue. The number of shares held by stockholders is the outstanding stock; this may be less than the number authorized in the articles of incorporation. To invest in a corporation, a stockholder transfers cash or other resources to the corporation. In return, the stockholder receives shares of stock representing a proportionate share of ownership in the corporation.

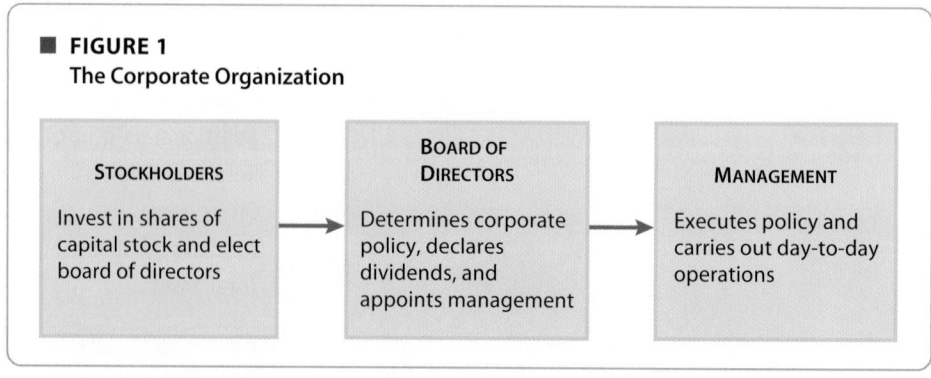

■ **FIGURE 1**
The Corporate Organization

STOCKHOLDERS	BOARD OF DIRECTORS	MANAGEMENT
Invest in shares of capital stock and elect board of directors	Determines corporate policy, declares dividends, and appoints management	Executes policy and carries out day-to-day operations

Afterward, the stockholder may transfer the shares at will. Corporations may have more than one kind of stock.

Board of Directors As noted, a corporation's board of directors decides on major business policies. Among the board's specific duties are authorizing contracts, setting executive salaries, and arranging major loans with banks. The declaration of dividends is also an important function of the board of directors. **Dividends** are distributions of resources, generally in the form of cash, to stockholders, and only the board of directors has the authority to declare them. Paying dividends is one way of rewarding stockholders for their investment when the corporation has been successful in earning a profit. (The other way is through a rise in the market value of the stock.) Although there is usually a delay of two or three weeks between the time the board declares a dividend and the date of the actual payment, we assume in the early chapters of this book that declaration and payment are made on the same day.

The composition of the board of directors varies from company to company, but generally it includes several officers of the corporation and several outsiders. The outsiders are called *independent directors* because they do not directly participate in managing the business.

Management Management, appointed by the board of directors to carry out corporate polices and run day-to-day operations, consists of the operating officers—generally the president, or chief executive officer; vice presidents; chief financial officer; and chief operating officer. Besides being responsible for running the business, management has the duty of reporting the financial results of its administration to the board of directors and the stockholders. Though management must, at a minimum, make a comprehensive annual report, it generally reports more often. The annual reports of large public corporations are available to the public. Excerpts from many of them appear throughout this book.

Advantages and Disadvantages of Incorporation

Managers of a corporation must be familiar with the advantages and disadvantages of this form of business. Some of the advantages are as follows:

- **Separate Legal Entity** As a separate legal entity, a corporation can buy and sell property, sue other parties, enter into contracts, hire and fire employees, and be taxed.

- **Limited Liability** Because a corporation is a legal entity, separate from its owners, its creditors can satisfy their claims only against the assets of the corporation, not against the personal property of the corporation's owners. Because the owners are not responsible for the corporation's debts, their liability is limited to the amount of their investment. In contrast, the personal property of sole proprietors and partners generally is available to creditors.

- **Ease of Capital Generation** It is fairly easy for a corporation to raise capital because shares of ownership in the business are available to a great number of potential investors for a small amount of money. As a result, a single corporation can have many owners.

- **Ease of Transfer of Ownership** A share of stock, a unit of ownership in a corporation, is easily transferable. A stockholder can normally buy and sell shares without affecting the corporation's activities or needing the approval of other owners.

▶ **Lack of Mutual Agency**   Mutual agency is not a characteristic of corporations. If a stockholder tries to enter into a contract for the corporation, the corporation is not bound by the contract. But in a partnership, because of mutual agency, all the partners can be bound by one partner's actions.

▶ **Continuous Existence**   Because a corporation is a separate legal entity, an owner's death, incapacity, or withdrawal does not affect the life of the corporation. A corporation's life is set by its charter and regulated by state laws.

▶ **Centralized Authority and Responsibility**   The board of directors represents the stockholders and delegates the responsibility and authority for the day-to-day operation of the corporation to a single person, usually the president. Operating power is not divided among the many owners of the business. The president may delegate authority over certain segments of the business to others, but he or she is held accountable to the board of directors. If the board is dissatisfied with the performance of the president, it can replace that person.

▶ **Professional Management**   Large corporations have many owners, most of whom are unequipped to make timely decisions about business operations. So, management and ownership are usually separate. This allows a corporation to hire the best talent available to manage the business.

The disadvantages of corporations include the following:

▶ **Government Regulation**   Corporations must meet the requirements of state laws. As "creatures of the state," they are subject to greater state control and regulation than are other forms of business. They must file many reports with the state in which they are chartered. Publicly held corporations must also file reports with the Securities and Exchange Commission and with the stock exchanges on which they are listed. Meeting these requirements is very costly.

▶ **Taxation**   A major disadvantage of the corporate form of business is **double taxation**. Because a corporation is a separate legal entity, its earnings are subject to federal and state income taxes, which may be as much as 35 percent of corporate earnings. If any of the corporation's after-tax earnings are paid out as dividends, the earnings are taxed again as income to the stockholders. In contrast, the earnings of sole proprietorships and partnerships are taxed only once, as personal income to the owners.

▶ **Limited Liability**   Although limited liability is an advantage of incorporation, it can also be a disadvantage. Limited liability restricts the ability of a small corporation to borrow money. Because creditors can lay claim only to the assets of a corporation, they may limit their loans to the level secured by those assets or require stockholders to guarantee the loans personally.

▶ **Separation of Ownership and Control**   Just as limited liability can be a drawback of incorporation, so can the separation of ownership and control. Management sometimes makes decisions that are not good for the corporation as a whole. Poor communication can also make it hard for stockholders to exercise control over the corporation or even to recognize that management's decisions are harmful.

Equity Financing

Equity financing is accomplished through the issuance of stock to investors in exchange for assets, usually cash. Once the stock has been issued to them, the

Study Note

Among the agencies that regulate corporations are the Public Company Accounting Oversight Board (PCAOB), Securities and Exchange Commission (SEC), the Occupational Safety and Health Administration (OSHA), the Federal Trade Commission (FTC), the Environmental Protection Agency (EPA), the Nuclear Regulatory Commission (NRC), the Equal Employment Opportunity Commission (EEOC), the Interstate Commerce Commission (ICC), the National Transportation Safety Board (NTSB), the Federal Aviation Administration (FAA), and the Federal Communications Commission (FCC).

Study Note

Lenders to a small corporation may require the corporation's officers to sign a promissory note, which makes them personally liable for the debt.

stockholders can transfer their ownership at will. When they do, they must sign their **stock certificates**, documents showing the number of shares that they own, and send them to the corporation's secretary. In large corporations that are listed on the stock exchanges, stockholders' records are hard to maintain. Such companies can have millions of shares of stock, thousands of which change ownership every day. Therefore, they often appoint independent registrars and transfer agents (usually banks and trust companies) to help perform the secretary's duties. The outside agents are responsible for transferring the corporation's stock, maintaining stockholders' records, preparing a list of stockholders for stockholders' meetings, and paying dividends.

Par value and *legal capital* are important terms in equity financing. **Par value** is an arbitrary amount assigned to each share of stock. It must be recorded in the capital stock accounts, and it constitutes a corporation's legal capital. **Legal capital** is the number of shares issued times the par value. It is the minimum amount that a corporation can report as contributed capital.

Par value usually bears little if any relationship to the shares' market value or book value. For example, although **Google's** stock initially sold for $85 per share and the market value is now much higher, its par value per share is only $.001. Google's legal capital is only about $293,000 (293 million shares × $.001) even though the total market value of its shares exceeds $100 billion.

To help with its initial public offering (IPO), a corporation often uses an **underwriter**—an intermediary between the corporation and the investing public. For a fee—usually less than 1 percent of the selling price—the underwriter guarantees the sale of the stock. The corporation records the amount of the net proceeds of the offering—what the public paid less the underwriter's fees, legal and printing expenses, and any other direct costs of the offering—in its capital stock and additional paid-in capital accounts. Because of the size of its IPO, Google used a group of investment banks headed by two well-known investment bankers, **Morgan Stanley** and **Credit Suisse First Boston**.

The costs of forming a corporation are called **start-up and organization costs**. These costs, which are incurred before a corporation begins operations, include state incorporation fees and attorneys' fees for drawing up the articles of incorporation. They also include the cost of printing stock certificates, accountants' fees for registering the firm's initial stock, and other expenditures necessary for the formation of the corporation. Because Google's IPO was so large, the fees of the lawyers, accountants, and underwriters who helped arrange the IPO amounted to millions of dollars.

Theoretically, start-up and organization costs benefit the entire life of a corporation. For that reason, a case can be made for recording them as intangible assets and amortizing them over the life of the corporation. However, a corporation's life normally is not known, so accountants expense start-up and organization costs as they are incurred.

Advantages of Equity Financing

Financing a business by issuing common stock has several advantages:

- It is less risky than financing with bonds because a company does not pay dividends on common stock unless the board of directors decides to pay them. In contrast, if a company does not pay interest on bonds, it can be forced into bankruptcy.

- When a company does not pay a cash dividend, it can plow the cash generated by profitable operations back into the company's operations. **Google**, for instance, does not currently pay any dividends, and its issuance of common stock provides it with funds for expansion.

- A company can use the proceeds of a common stock issue to maintain or improve its debt to equity ratio.

Disadvantages of Equity Financing   Issuing common stock also has certain disadvantages:

- Unlike interest on bonds, dividends paid on stock are not tax-deductible.

- When a corporation issues more stock, it dilutes its ownership. Thus, the current stockholders must yield some control to the new stockholders.

Dividend Policies

A corporation's board of directors has sole authority to declare dividends, but senior managers, who usually serve as members of the board, influence dividend policies. Receiving dividends is one of two ways in which stockholders can earn a return on their investment in a corporation. The other way is to sell their shares for more than they paid for them.

Although a corporation may have sufficient cash and retained earnings to pay a dividend, its board of directors may not declare one for several reasons. The corporation may need the cash for expansion; it may want to improve its overall financial position by liquidating debt; or it may be facing major uncertainties, such as a pending lawsuit or strike or a projected decline in the economy, which makes it prudent to preserve resources.

A corporation pays dividends quarterly, semiannually, annually, or at other times declared by its board of directors. Most states do not allow a corporation to declare a dividend that exceeds its retained earnings. When a corporation does declare a dividend that exceeds retained earnings, it is, in essence, returning to the stockholders part of their contributed capital. This is called a **liquidating dividend**. A corporation usually pays a liquidating dividend only when it is going out of business or reducing its operations.

Having sufficient retained earnings in itself does not justify the declaration of a dividend. If a corporation does not have cash or other assets readily available for distribution, it might have to borrow money to pay the dividend—an action most boards of directors want to avoid.

Dividend Dates   Three important dates are associated with dividends:

- The **declaration date** is the date on which the board of directors formally declares that the corporation is going to pay a dividend. Because the legal obligation to pay the dividend arises at this time, a liability for Dividends Payable is recorded and the Dividends account is debited on this date. In the accounting process, Retained Earnings will be reduced by the total dividends declared during the period.

- The **record date** is the date on which ownership of stock, and therefore the right to receive a dividend, is determined. Persons who own the stock on the record date will receive the dividend. No journal entry is made on this date. Between the record date and the date of payment, the stock is said to be **ex-dividend**. If the owner on the date of record sells the shares of stock before the date of payment, the right to the dividend remains with that person; it does not transfer with the shares to the second owner.

- The **date of payment** is the date on which the dividend is paid to the stockholders of record. On this date, the Dividends Payable account is eliminated, and the Cash account is reduced.

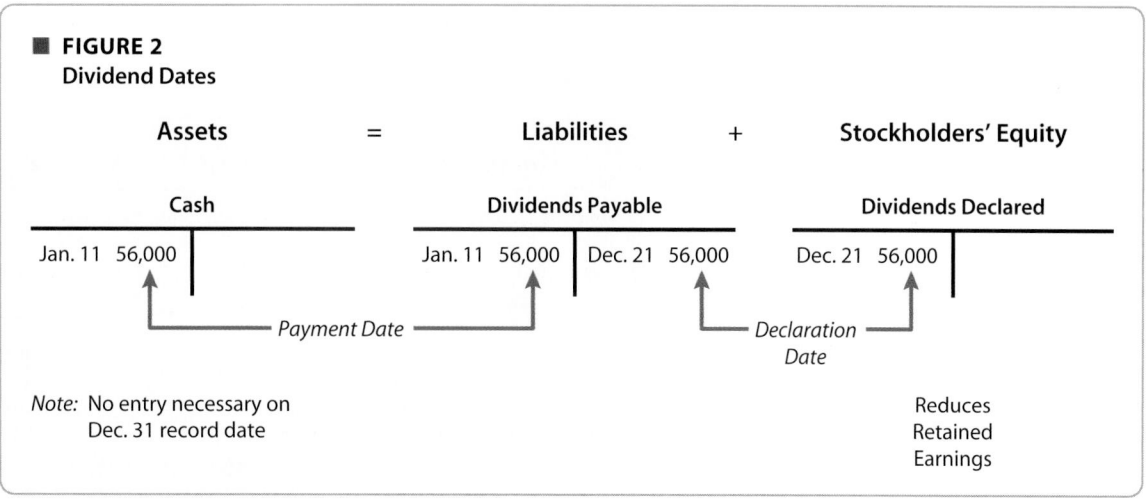

■ **FIGURE 2**
Dividend Dates

Because an accounting period may end between the record date and the payment date, dividends declared during the period may exceed the amount paid for dividends. For example, in Figure 2, the accounting period ends on December 31. The declaration date for the dividends is December 21, the record date is December 31, and the payment date is January 11. In this case, the statement of retained earnings for the accounting period will show a decrease in the dividends declared, but the statement of cash flows will not show the dividends because the cash has not yet been paid out.

Evaluating Dividend Policies   To evaluate the amount of dividends they receive, investors use the **dividends yield** ratio. Dividends yield is computed by dividing the dividends per share by the market price per share. **Microsoft's** history of dividend payments provides an interesting example. Having built up a large cash balance through its years of profitable operations, Microsoft increased its annual dividend to $4.0 billion ($.36 per share) in 2006. The company declared a special dividend of $32 billion ($3 per share) in 2004.[3] Using Microsoft's regular annual dividend as a more realistic measure of what investors can expect in the future, its dividends yield is computed as follows:

$$\text{Dividends Yield} = \frac{\text{Dividends per Share}}{\text{Market Price per Share}} = \frac{\$.36}{\$23.17} = = 1.6\%$$

Figure 3 shows how Microsoft's dividends yield and last price are quoted on NASDAQ. Because the yield on corporate bonds exceeds 7 percent, Microsoft shareholders must expect some of their return to come from increases in the price of the shares.

Companies usually pay dividends only when they have had profitable operations. For example, **Apple Computer** began paying dividends in 1987, but it stopped those payments in 1996 to conserve cash after it suffered large operating losses in 1995. However, factors other than earnings affect the decision to pay dividends. Among them are the following:

 ▶ **Industry policies**   A company may change its dividend policy to bring it into line with the prevailing policy in its industry. For example, despite positive earnings, **AT&T Corporation** slashed its dividends by 83 percent. This action put AT&T's policy more in line with the policies of its peers in the telecommunications industry, most of which do not pay dividends.[4]

 ▶ **Volatility of earnings**   If a company has years of good earnings followed by years of poor earnings, it may want to keep dividends low to avoid giving a

■ **FIGURE 3**
Stock Quotations on NASDAQ

NASDAQ NATIONAL MARKET EXCHANGE

YTD % CHG	52 WEEKS HI	52 WEEKS LO	STOCK (SYM)		DIV	YLD %	PE	VOL 100S	LAST	NET CHG
−18.2	55.35	38.21	✦ MicrosSys	MCRS	...		27	3803	39.53	− 0.81
− 8.1	31.85	18.13	Microsemi	MSCC	...		38	9280	25.41	− 0.28
−11.4	28.38	23.14	Microsoft	MSFT	.36	1.6	18	821968	23.17	− 0.05
+24.9	109.50	49.50	MicroStrat	MSTR	...		24	2263	103.24	− 2.00
+ 5.5	4.11	3.25	MicrotekMed	MTMD	...		11	1290	3.67	+ 0.04
+42.4	7.19	3.39	Microtune	TUNE	...	...		6373	5.94	− 0.04
+65.2	14.45	6.34	McrsEndovasc	MEND n	...		dd	z84487	14.37	+ 0.94
− 0.1	31.44	25.41	MidStBcsh	MDST	.72	2.7	17	z61085	26.71	− 0.43
+ 2.2	98.36	51.26	Middleby	MIDD	...		21	z75435	88.43	− 3.07
+ 5.4	23.47	17.03	MidsexWtr	MSEX	.68	3.7	25	z22626	18.28	− 0.15
+ 2.0	40.42	31.06	✦ Midland	MLAN	.25	0.7	11	z12342	36.76	− 0.40

Source: Stock quotations on the NASDAQ from *Wall Street Journal,* May 13, 2006. Copyright © Dow Jones & Co., Inc. Reprinted by permission of Dow Jones & Company via Copyright Clearance Center.

false impression of sustained high earnings. For example, for years, **General Motors** paid a fairly low but stable dividend but declared a bonus dividend in especially good years.

▸ **Effect on cash flows**   A company may not pay dividends because its operations do not generate enough cash to do so or because it wants to invest cash in future operations. For instance, **Abbott Laboratories** pays a dividend of only $1.10 per share on earnings of $2.17 per share. Abbott believes a portion of the cash generated by the earnings is better spent for other purposes, such as researching and developing new drugs that will generate revenue in the future. It is partly due to Abbott's investment in new products that stockholders are willing to pay a high price for its stock.[5]

Recently, because of a 15 percent reduction in the tax rate on dividends, attitudes toward dividends have changed. Many firms have either increased their dividends or started to pay dividends for the first time. The special dividend by Microsoft mentioned earlier is a good example of this effect.

Using Return on Equity to Measure Performance

Return on equity is the most important ratio associated with stockholders' equity. It is also a common measure of management's performance. For instance, when *BusinessWeek* and *Forbes* rate companies on their success, return on equity is the major basis of their evaluations. In addition, the compensation of top executives is often tied to return on equity benchmarks.

Google's return on equity before its IPO is computed as follows:[6]

$$\text{Return on Equity} = \frac{\text{Net Income}}{\text{Average Stockholders' Equity}}$$

$$= \frac{\$105,548}{(\$588,770 + \$173,953) \div 2}$$

$$= \frac{\$105,548}{\$381,362}$$

$$= 27.7\%$$

Google's healthy return on equity of 27.7 percent depends, of course, on the amount of net income the company earns. But it also depends on the level of stockholders' equity, which in turn depends on management decisions about the amount of stock the company sells to the public. As more shares are sold, stockholders' equity increases, and as a result, return on equity decreases. Management can keep stockholders' equity at a minimum by financing the business with cash flows from operations and by issuing debt instead of stock. But, as we have noted, issuing bonds and other types of debt increases a firm's risk because the interest and principal of the debt must be paid on time.

Management can also reduce the number of shares in the hands of the public by buying back the company's shares on the open market. The cost of these shares, which are called **treasury stock**, has the effect of reducing stockholders' equity and thereby increasing return on equity. Many companies follow this practice instead of paying or increasing dividends. Their reason for doing so is that it puts money into the hands of stockholders in the form of market price appreciation without creating a commitment to higher dividends in the future. For instance, **Microsoft** is in the process of purchasing its common stock on the open market at a cost of $30 billion over a four-year period.[7] Microsoft's stock repurchases will improve the company's return on equity, increase its earnings per share, and lower its price/earnings ratio.

The **price/earnings (P/E) ratio** is a measure of investors' confidence in a company's future. It is calculated by dividing the market price per share by the earnings per share. The price/earnings ratio will vary as market price per share fluctuates daily and the amount of earnings per share changes. If you look back at Figure 3, you will see that it shows a P/E ratio of 18.0 for Microsoft. It was computed using the annual earnings per share from Microsoft's most recent income statement, as follows:

$$\frac{\text{Price/Earnings (P/E)}}{\text{Ratio}} = \frac{\text{Market Price per Share}}{\text{Earnings per Share}} = \frac{\$23.17}{\$1.29} = 18.0 \text{ times}$$

Because the market price is 18.0 times earnings, investors are paying a relatively high price in relation to earnings. They do so in the expectation that this software company will continue to be successful. High P/E ratios should be interpreted cautiously because unusually low earnings can produce an artificially high P/E ratio.

Stock Options as Compensation

More than 97 percent of public companies encourage employees to invest in their common stock through **stock option plans**.[8] Most such plans give employees the right to purchase stock in the future at a fixed price. Some companies offer stock option plans only to management personnel, but others, including **Google**, make them available to all employees. Because the market value of a company's stock is tied to a company's performance, these plans are a means of both motivating and compensating employees. As the market value of the stock goes up, the difference between the option price and the market price grows, which increases the amount of compensation. Another key benefit of stock option plans is that compensation expense is tax-deductible.

On the date stock options are granted, the fair value of the options must be estimated. The amount in excess of the exercise price is recorded as compensation expense over the grant period.[9] For example, suppose that on July 1, 20X6, a company grants its top executives the option to purchase 50,000 shares of $10 par value common stock at its current market value of $15 per share. On March 30, 20X9, when the market price is $25 per share, one of the firm's vice presidents exercises her option and purchases 2,000 shares. Although the vice

FOCUS ON BUSINESS PRACTICE

How Did Accounting for Stock Options Become Political?

During the past decade, stock options have generated more controversy than any other single issue in accounting. Even the U.S. Congress has been involved on several occasions. The issue is whether the value of stock options should be counted as an expense on the income statement or buried in a note to the financial statements. The FASB has long held that options should be treated as expense, but in trying to pass this rule, it has encountered heavy opposition from the technology industry, which is the largest user of stock options.

Leaders of the technology industry maintain that expensing stock options would hurt their companies' profits and growth. They also maintain that the value of stock options is too hard to measure and that the options could turn out to be worthless. Proponents of expensing argue that stock options are a form of compensation and therefore must have value. They also point out that many items in the financial statements are based on estimates and that if all companies reported options as expense, their financial statements would be more comparable.

The FASB finally ruled that as of 2005, all publicly traded companies must expense stock options. However, even before the FASB's ruling, more than 750 companies, including **Boeing Corporation** and **BankOne** (now part of **JP Morgan/Chase**), accepted the eventual expensing of stock options and voluntarily started expensing them.[10]

president has a gain of $20,000 (the $50,000 market value less the $30,000 option price), no compensation expense is recorded because the company receives only the option price, not the market value. Any one of several methods of estimating the fair value of options at the grant date may be used; they are dealt with in more advanced courses.

STOP • REVIEW • APPLY

1-1. What are the functions of a corporation's stockholders, board of directors, and management?

1-2. Identify and explain the advantages and disadvantages of the corporate form of business.

1-3. What three dates are important in paying dividends?

1-4. What is the dividends yield ratio, and what do investors learn from it?

1-5. What are two general ways in which management can improve a company's return on equity?

1-6. What is the price/earnings (P/E) ratio, and what does it measure?

1-7. What is a stock option plan, and why would a company want to have one?

Suggested answers to all Stop, Review, and Apply questions are available at http://college.hmco.com/accounting/needles/poa/10e/student_home.html.

Components of Stockholders' Equity

LO2 Identify the components of stockholders' equity.

In a corporation's balance sheet, the owners' claims to the business are called *stockholders' equity.* As shown in Exhibit 1, this section of a corporate balance sheet usually has at least three components.

EXHIBIT 1 ▶

Stockholders' Equity Section of a Balance Sheet		
Stockholders' Equity		
Contributed capital		
Preferred stock, $50 par value, 1,000 shares authorized, issued, and outstanding		$ 50,000
Common stock, $5 par value, 30,000 shares authorized, 20,000 shares issued, 18,000 shares outstanding	$100,000	
Additional paid-in capital	50,000	150,000
Total contributed capital		$200,000
Retained earnings		60,000
Total contributed capital and retained earnings		$260,000
Less treasury stock, common (2,000 shares at cost)		20,000
Total stockholders' equity		$240,000

▶ **Contributed capital**—the stockholders' investments in the corporation

▶ **Retained earnings**—the earnings of the corporation since its inception, less any losses, dividends, or transfers to contributed capital. Retained earnings are reinvested in the business. They are not a pool of funds to be distributed to the stockholders; instead, they represent the stockholders' claim to assets resulting from profitable operations.

▶ **Treasury stock**—shares of its own stock that the corporation has bought back on the open market. The cost of these shares is treated not as an investment, but as a reduction in stockholders' equity. By buying back the shares, the corporation reduces the ownership of the business.

As you can see in **Google's** Financial Highlights at the beginning of the chapter, "other items" may also appear in the stockholders' equity section. We discuss these items in a later chapter.

BUSINESS FOCUS ON PRACTICE
Are You a First-Class or Second-Class Stockholder?

When companies go public, insiders—usually the founders of the company or top management—often get first-class shares with extra votes, while outsiders get second-class shares with fewer votes. The class A and class B shares of **Adolph Coors Company**, the large brewing firm, are an extreme example. The company's class B shares, owned by the public, have no votes except in the case of a merger. Its class A shares, held by the Coors family trust, have all the votes on other issues.

Google also has two classes of common shares. Both classes are identical except that each class B share is entitled to ten votes and each class A share is entitled to only one vote. Class A shares are the ones that Google offered to the public in its IPO.

Shareholder advocates denounce the class division of shares as undemocratic. They maintain that this practice gives a privileged few shareholders all or most of the control of a company and that it denies other shareholders voting power consistent with the risk they are taking. Defenders of the practice argue that it shields top executives from the market's obsession with short-term results and allows them to make better long-term decisions. They also point out that many investors don't care about voting rights as long as the stock performs well.[11]

Larry Page *(left)* and Sergey Brin, who founded Google, Inc., in 1998, have a lot to look happy about. In its IPO in August 2004, Google issued about 22.5 million shares at $85 per share for a total of $1.9 billion. The price per share soared to $135 in a few days and reached $400 in 2006. The ability to raise large amounts of capital by issuing stocks and bonds is part of the reason corporations dominate the U.S. economy.

A corporation can issue two types of stock:

▸ **Common stock** is the basic form of stock that a corporation issues; that is, if a corporation issues only one type of stock, it is common stock. Because shares of common stock carry voting rights, they generally provide their owners with the means of controlling the corporation. Common stock is also called **residual equity**, which means that if the corporation is liquidated, the claims of all creditors and usually those of preferred stockholders rank ahead of the claims of common stockholders.

▸ To attract investors whose goals differ from those of common stockholders, a corporation may also issue **preferred stock**. Preferred stock gives its owners preference over common stockholders, usually in terms of receiving dividends and in terms of claims to assets if the corporation is liquidated. (We describe these preferences in more detail later in the chapter.)

In keeping with the convention of full disclosure, the stockholders' equity section of a corporate balance sheet gives a great deal of information about the corporation's stock. Under contributed capital, it lists the kinds of stock; their par value; and the number of shares authorized, issued, and outstanding.

▸ **Authorized shares** are the maximum number of shares that a corporation's state charter allows it to issue. Most corporations are authorized to issue more shares than they need to issue at the time they are formed. Thus, they are able to raise more capital in the future by issuing additional shares. When a corporation issues all of its authorized shares, it cannot issue more without a change in its state charter.

▸ **Issued shares** are those that a corporation sells or otherwise transfers to stockholders. The owners of a corporation's issued shares own 100 percent of the business. Unissued shares have no rights or privileges until they are issued.

▸ **Outstanding shares** are shares that a corporation has issued and that are still in circulation. Treasury stock is not outstanding because it consists of

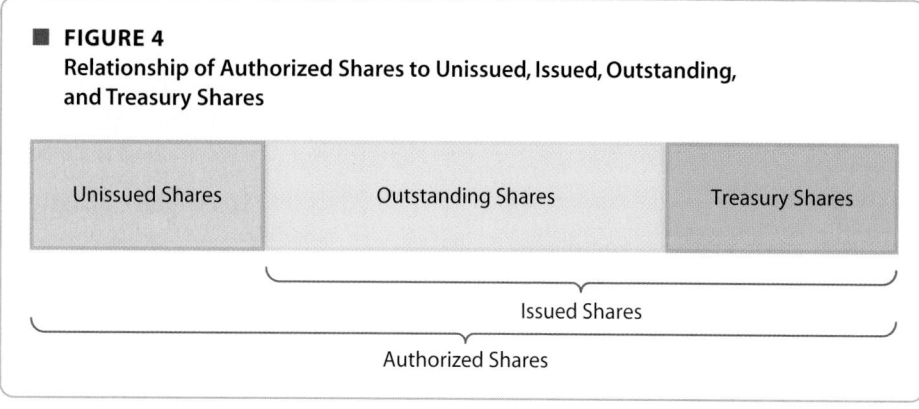

■ **FIGURE 4**
Relationship of Authorized Shares to Unissued, Issued, Outstanding, and Treasury Shares

shares that a corporation has issued but that it has bought back and thereby put out of circulation. Thus, a corporation can have more shares issued than are currently outstanding.

Figure 4 shows the relationship of authorized shares to issued, unissued, outstanding, and treasury shares. In this regard, Google is an interesting example. The company has 9 billion authorized shares of stock and only about 293 million shares issued, even after its initial public offering. With its excess of authorized issues, Google obviously has plenty of flexibility for future stock transactions.

STOP • REVIEW • APPLY

2-1. Why is common stock called *residual equity*?

2-2. How does preferred stock differ from common stock?

2-3. What distinguishes authorized shares from issued shares and outstanding shares?

2-4. What is the difference between issued shares and outstanding shares?

Components of Stockholders' Equity   The following data are from the records of Taupo Corporation on December 31, 20xx:

	Balance
Preferred stock, $100 par value, 6 percent noncumulative, 10,000 shares authorized, issued, and outstanding	$1,000,000
Common stock, $2 par value, 200,000 shares authorized, 180,000 shares issued, and 170,000 shares outstanding	360,000
Additional paid-in capital	978,000
Retained earnings	345,000
Treasury stock, common (10,000 shares, at cost)	220,000

Prepare a stockholders' equity section for Taupo Corporation's balance sheet.

SOLUTION

Taupo Corporation
Balance Sheet
December 31, 20xx

Stockholders' Equity

Contributed capital		
Preferred stock, $100 par value, 6 percent noncumulative, 10,000 shares authorized, issued, and outstanding		$1,000,000
Common stock, $2 par value, 200,000 shares authorized, 180,000 shares issued, 170,000 shares outstanding	$ 360,000	
Additional paid-in capital	978,000	1,338,000
Total contributed capital		$2,338,000
Retained earnings		345,000
Total contributed capital and retained earnings		$2,683,000
Less treasury stock, common (10,000 shares at cost)		220,000
Total stockholders' equity		$2,463,000

Preferred Stock

LO3   Identify the characteristics of preferred stock.

Most preferred stock has one or more of the following characteristics: preference as to dividends, preference as to assets if a corporation is liquidated, convertibility, and a callable option. A corporation may offer several different classes of preferred stock, each with distinctive characteristics to attract different investors.

Preference as to Dividends

Preferred stockholders ordinarily must receive a certain amount of dividends before common stockholders receive anything. The amount that preferred stockholders must be paid before common stockholders can be paid is usually stated in dollars per share or as a percentage of the par value of the preferred shares. For example, a company might pay an annual dividend of $4 per share on preferred stock, or it might issue preferred stock at $50 par value and pay an annual dividend of 8 percent of par value, which would also be $4 per share.

Preferred stockholders have no guarantee of ever receiving dividends. A company must have earnings and its board of directors must declare dividends on preferred stock before any liability arises. The consequences of not granting an annual dividend on preferred stock vary according to whether the stock is noncumulative or cumulative:

▸ If the stock is **noncumulative preferred stock** and the board of directors fails to declare a dividend on it in any given year, the company is under no obligation to make up the missed dividend in future years.

▸ If the stock is **cumulative preferred stock**, the dividend amount per share accumulates from year to year, and the company must pay the whole amount before it pays any dividends on common stock.

Dividends not paid in the year they are due are called **dividends in arrears**. For example, suppose that a corporation has 10,000 shares of $100 par value, 5 percent cumulative preferred stock outstanding. If the corporation pays no dividends in 20x7, preferred dividends in arrears at the end of the year would amount to $50,000 (10,000 shares × $100 × .05 = $50,000). If the corporation's board declares dividends in 20x8, the corporation must pay preferred stockholders the dividends in arrears plus their current year's dividends before paying any dividends on common stock.

Dividends in arrears are not recognized as liabilities because no liability exists until the board of directors declares a dividend. A corporation cannot be sure it is going to make a profit, so, of course, it cannot promise dividends to stockholders. However, if it has dividends in arrears, it should report the amount either in the body of its financial statements or in a note to its financial statements.

The following note is typical of one that might appear in a company's annual report:

> On December 31, 20xx, the company was in arrears by $37,851,000 ($1.25 per share) on dividends to its preferred stockholders. The company must pay all dividends in arrears to preferred stockholders before paying any dividends to common stockholders.

Suppose that on January 1, 20x7, a corporation issued 10,000 shares of $10 par value, 6 percent cumulative preferred stock and 50,000 shares of common stock. Operations in 20x7 produced income of only $4,000. However, in the same year, the corporation's board of directors declared a $3,000 cash dividend to the preferred stockholders. Thus, the dividend picture at the end of 20x7 was as follows:

20x7 dividends due preferred stockholders ($100,000 × .06)	$6,000
Less 20x7 dividends declared to preferred stockholders	3,000
20x7 preferred stock dividends in arrears	$3,000

Now suppose that in 20x8, the corporation earns income of $30,000 and wants to pay dividends to both the preferred and the common stockholders. Because the preferred stock is cumulative, the corporation must pay the $3,000 in arrears on the preferred stock, plus the current year's dividends on the preferred stock, before it can distribute a dividend to the common stockholders. If the corporation's board of directors now declares a $12,000 dividend to be distributed to preferred and common stockholders, the distribution would be as follows:

20x8 declaration of dividends	$12,000
Less 20x7 preferred stock dividends in arrears	3,000
Amount available for 20x8 dividends	$ 9,000
Less 20x8 dividends due preferred stockholders ($100,000 × .06)	6,000
Remainder available to common stockholders	$ 3,000

Preference as to Assets

Preferred stockholders often have preference in terms of their claims to a corporation's assets if the corporation is liquidated. If a corporation does go out of

business, these preferred stockholders have a right to receive the par value of their stock or a larger stated liquidation value per share before the common stockholders receive any share of the corporation's assets. This preference can also extend to any dividends in arrears owed to the preferred stockholders.

Convertible Preferred Stock

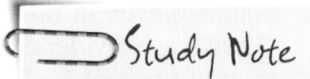

Study Note

When preferred stockholders convert their shares to common stock, they gain voting rights but lose the dividend and liquidation preference. Conversion back to preferred stock is not an option.

Like all preferred stockholders, owners of **convertible preferred stock** are more likely than common stockholders to receive regular dividends. In addition, they can exchange their shares of preferred stock for shares of common stock at a ratio stated in the company's preferred stock contract. If the market value of the company's common stock increases, the conversion feature allows these stockholders to share in the increase by converting their stock to common stock. For example, if you look back at **Google's** Financial Highlights at the beginning of the chapter, you will see that when Google went to market with its IPO, the company's preferred stockholders took advantage of the steep increase in the price of the common stock by converting their shares to common stock. Thus, by including the conversion feature, companies can make their preferred stock more attractive to investors.

Suppose, for instance, that a company issues 1,000 shares of 8 percent, $100 par value convertible preferred stock for $100 per share. Each share of stock can be converted to five shares of the company's common stock at any time. The market value of the common stock at the time the company issues the convertible preferred stock is $15 per share. In the past, an owner of the common stock could expect dividends of about $1 per share per year. The owner of one share of preferred stock, on the other hand, now holds an investment that has a market value of about $75 and is also more likely than a common stockholder to receive dividends.

Now suppose that in the next several years, the corporation's earnings increase, the dividends paid to common stockholders increase to $3 per share, and the market value of a share of common stock increases from $15 to $30. Preferred stockholders can convert each of their preferred shares to five common shares, thereby increasing their dividends from $8 on each preferred share to $15 ($3 on each of five common shares). Moreover, the market value of each share of preferred stock will be close to the $150 value of the five shares of common stock because each share can be converted to five shares of common stock.

Callable Preferred Stock

Most preferred stock is **callable preferred stock**—that is, the issuing corporation can redeem or retire it at a price stated in the preferred stock contract. An owner of nonconvertible preferred stock must surrender it to the issuing corporation when asked to do so. If the preferred stock is convertible, the stockholder can either surrender the stock to the corporation or convert it to common stock when the corporation calls the stock. The *call price*, or redemption price, is usually higher than the stock's par value. For example, preferred stock that has a $100 par value might be callable at $103 per share.

When preferred stock is called and surrendered, the stockholder is entitled to the following:

▶ The par value of the stock

▶ The call premium

▶ Any dividends in arrears

▶ The current period's dividend prorated by the proportion of the year to the call date

A corporation may decide to call its preferred stock for any of the following reasons:

▶ It may want to force conversion of the preferred stock to common stock because the dividend that it pays on preferred shares is higher than the dividend that it pays on the equivalent number of common shares.

▶ It may be able to replace the outstanding preferred stock with a preferred stock at a lower dividend rate or with long-term debt, which can have a lower after-tax cost.

▶ It may simply be profitable enough to retire the preferred stock.

STOP • REVIEW • APPLY

3-1. What does preferred stock's preference as to dividends and assets mean?

3-2. What is cumulative preferred stock, and how does it relate to dividends in arrears? How should dividends in arrears be disclosed in the financial statements?

3-3. Define the terms *convertible* and *callable* as they apply to preferred stock.

Cash Dividends with Dividends in Arrears   Peace Corporation has 1,000 shares of $100 par value, 7 percent cumulative preferred stock outstanding and 100,000 shares of $1 par value common stock outstanding. In the corporation's first three years of operation, its board of directors declared cash dividends as follows:

20x7, none
20x8, $10,000
20x9, $15,000

Determine the total cash dividends paid to the preferred and common stockholders during each of the three years.

SOLUTION

20x7:	None	
20x8:	Preferred dividends in arrears (1,000 shares × $100 × .07)	$ 7,000
	Current year remainder to preferred ($10,000 − $7,000)	3,000
	Total to preferred stockholders	$10,000
20x9:	Preferred dividends in arrears ($7,000 − $3,000)	$ 4,000
	Current year to preferred (1,000 shares × $100 × .07)	7,000
	Total to preferred stockholders	$11,000
	Total to common stockholders ($15,000 − $11,000)	4,000
	Total dividends in 20x9	$15,000

Issuance of Common Stock

LO4 Account for the issuance of stock for cash and other assets.

A share of capital stock may be either par or no-par. The value of par stock is stated in the corporate charter and must be printed on each stock certificate. It can be $.01, $1, $5, $100, or any other amount established by the organizers of the corporation. For instance, the par value of **Google's** common stock is $.001. The par values of common stocks tend to be lower than those of preferred stocks.

As noted earlier, par value is the amount per share that is recorded in a corporation's capital stock accounts, and it constitutes a corporation's legal capital. A corporation cannot declare a dividend that would cause stockholders' equity to fall below the firm's legal capital. Par value is thus a minimum cushion of capital that protects a corporation's creditors. Any amount in excess of par value that a corporation receives from a stock issue is recorded in its Additional Paid-in Capital account and represents a portion of its contributed capital.

No-par stock is capital stock that does not have a par value. A corporation may issue stock without a par value for several reasons. For one thing, rather than recognizing par value as an arbitrary figure, investors may confuse it with the stock's market value. For another, most states do not allow a stock issue below par value, and this limits a corporation's flexibility in obtaining capital.

State laws often require corporations to place a **stated value** on each share of stock that they issue, but even when this is not required, a corporation's board of directors may do so as a matter of convenience. The stated value can be any value set by the board unless the state specifies a minimum amount, which is sometimes the case. The stated value can be set before or after the shares are issued if the state law is not specific.

Study Note

Legal capital is the minimum amount a corporation can report as contributed capital. To protect creditors, a corporation cannot declare a dividend that would reduce capital below the amount of legal capital.

Par Value Stock

When a corporation issues par value stock, the appropriate capital stock account (usually Common Stock or Preferred Stock) is credited for the par value regardless of whether the proceeds are more or less than the par value.

When a corporation issues stock at a price greater than par value, as is usually the case, the proceeds in excess of par are credited to an account called Additional Paid-in Capital. For example, suppose Xon Corporation is authorized to issue 20,000 shares of $10 par value common stock and that it issues

10,000 shares at $12 each on January 1, 20xx. The entry to record the issuance of the stock at the price in excess of par value would be as follows:

A = L + OE
+120,000   +100,000
           +20,000

Jan. 1	Cash	120,000	
	Common Stock		100,000
	Additional Paid-in Capital		20,000
	Issued 10,000 shares of $10 par value common stock for $12 per share		

Cash is debited for the proceeds of $120,000 (10,000 shares × $12), and Common Stock is credited for the total par value of $100,000 (10,000 shares × $10). Additional Paid-in Capital is credited for the difference of $20,000 (10,000 shares × $2).

The amount in excess of par value is part of Xon Corporation's contributed capital and will be included in the stockholders' equity section of its balance sheet. Immediately after the stock issue, this section of Xon's balance sheet would appear as follows:

Contributed capital	
Common stock, $10 par value, 20,000 shares authorized, 10,000 shares issued and outstanding	$100,000
Additional paid-in capital	20,000
Total contributed capital	$120,000
Retained earnings	—
Total stockholders' equity	$120,000

If a corporation issues stock for less than par value, an account called Discount on Capital Stock is debited for the difference. The issuance of stock at a discount rarely occurs; it is illegal in many states.

No-Par Stock

Most states require that all or part of the proceeds from a corporation's issuance of no-par stock be designated as legal capital, which cannot be used unless the corporation is liquidated. The purpose of this requirement is to protect the corporation's assets for creditors.

Suppose that on January 1, 20xx, Xon Corporation issues 10,000 shares of no-par common stock at $15 per share. The $150,000 (10,000 shares × $15) in proceeds would be recorded as follows:

A = L + OE
+150,000   +150,000

Jan. 1	Cash	150,000	
	Common Stock		150,000
	Issued 10,000 shares of no-par common stock for $15 per share		

Because the stock does not have a stated or par value, all proceeds of the issue are credited to Common Stock and are part of the company's legal capital.

As noted earlier, state laws may require corporations to put a stated value on each share of stock that they issue. Assuming the same facts as above except that Xon puts a $10 stated value on each share of its no-par stock, the entry would be as follows:

A	= L +	OE
+150,000		+100,000
		50,000

Jan. 1	Cash	150,000	
	Common Stock		100,000
	Additional Paid-in Capital		50,000
	Issued 10,000 shares of no-par common stock with $10 stated value for $15 per share		

Notice that the legal capital credited to Common Stock is the stated value decided by Xon's board of directors. Also note that the Additional Paid-in Capital account is credited for $50,000, which is the difference between the proceeds ($150,000) and the total stated value ($100,000).

Issuance of Stock for Noncash Assets

A corporation may issue stock in return for assets or services other than cash. Transactions of this kind usually involve a corporation's exchange of stock for land or buildings or for the services of attorneys and others who help organize the corporation. In such cases, the problem is to determine the dollar amount at which the exchange should be recorded.

A corporation's board of directors has the right to determine the fair market value of the assets or services that the corporation receives in exchange for its stock. Generally, such a transaction is recorded at the fair market value of the stock that the corporation is giving up. If the stock's fair market value cannot be determined, the fair market value of the assets or services received can be used.

For example, suppose that when Xon Corporation was formed on January 1, 20xx, its attorney agreed to accept 100 shares of its $10 par value common stock for services rendered. At that time, the market value of the stock could not be determined. However, for similar services, the attorney would have charged Xon $1,500. The entry to record this noncash transaction is as follows:

> **Study Note**
>
> In establishing the fair market value of property that a corporation exchanges for stock, a board of directors cannot be arbitrary; it must use all the information at its disposal.

A	= L +	OE
		−1,500
		+1,000
		+500

Jan. 1	Start-Up and Organization Costs	1,500	
	Common Stock		1,000
	Additional Paid-in Capital		500
	Issued 100 shares of $10 par value common stock for attorney's services		

Now suppose that two years later, Xon Corporation exchanged 1,000 shares of its $10 par value common stock for a piece of land. At the time of the exchange, Xon's stock was selling on the market for $16 per share. The following entry records this exchange:

A	= L +	OE
+16,000		+10,000
		+6,000

Jan. 1	Land	16,000	
	Common Stock		10,000
	Additional Paid-in Capital		6,000
	Issued 1,000 shares of $10 par value common stock with a market value of $16 per share for a piece of land		

4-1. What is the significance of the following terms: *par value*, *no-par value*, and *stated value*?

4-2. Which is more relevant to the analyst: par value, additional paid-in capital, or the total of the two?

4-3. What two methods are used to value stock when it is issued for noncash assets, and when should each be used?

Accounting for Treasury Stock

LO5 Account for treasury stock.

> *Study Note*
>
> Treasury stock is not the same as unissued stock. Treasury stock represents shares that have been issued but are no longer outstanding. Unissued shares, on the other hand, have never been in circulation.

As we noted earlier, treasury stock is stock that the issuing company has reacquired, usually by purchasing shares on the open market. Although repurchasing its own stock can be a severe drain on a corporation's cash, it is common practice. In a recent year, 398, or 66 percent, of 600 large companies held treasury stock.[13]

Among the reasons a company may want to buy back its own stock are the following:

▶ It may want stock to distribute to employees through stock option plans.

▶ It may be trying to maintain a favorable market for its stock.

▶ It may want to increase its earnings per share or stock price per share.

▶ It may want to have additional shares of stock available for purchasing other companies.

▶ It may want to prevent a hostile takeover.

A purchase of treasury stock reduces a company's assets and stockholders' equity. It is not considered a purchase of assets, as the purchase of shares in another company would be. A company can hold treasury shares for an indefinite period or reissue or retire them. Treasury shares have no rights until they are reissued. Like unissued shares, they do not have voting rights, rights to dividends, or rights to assets during liquidation of the company. However, there is one major difference between unissued shares and treasury shares. A share of stock issued at par value or greater and that was reacquired as treasury stock can be reissued at less than par value without negative results.

Purchase of Treasury Stock

When treasury stock is purchased, it is recorded at cost. The par value, stated value, or original issue price of the stock is ignored. As noted above, the purchase reduces both a firm's assets and its stockholders' equity. For example, suppose that on September 15, Caprock Corporation purchases 1,000 shares of its common stock on the market at a price of $50 per share. The purchase would be recorded as follows:

A	= L +	OE			
−50,000		−50,000	Sept. 15	Treasury Stock, Common	50,000	
				Cash		50,000
				Acquired 1,000 shares of the company's common stock for $50 per share		

Study Note

Because treasury stock reduces stockholders' equity—the denominator of the return on equity ratio—the return on equity will increase when treasury shares are purchased even though there is no increase in earnings.

The stockholders' equity section of Caprock's balance sheet shows the cost of the treasury stock as a deduction from the total of contributed capital and retained earnings:

Contributed capital	
Common stock, $5 par value, 100,000 shares authorized, 30,000 shares issued, 29,000 shares outstanding	$ 150,000
Additional paid-in capital	30,000
Total contributed capital	$ 180,000
Retained earnings	900,000
Total contributed capital and retained earnings	$1,080,000
Less treasury stock, common (1,000 shares at cost)	50,000
Total stockholders' equity	$1,030,000

Notice that the number of shares issued, and therefore the legal capital, has not changed. However, the number of shares outstanding has decreased as a result of the transaction.

Sale of Treasury Stock

Treasury shares can be sold at cost, above cost, or below cost. For example, suppose that on November 15, Caprock Corporation sells its 1,000 treasury shares for $50 per share. The following entry records the transaction:

A	= L +	OE			
+50,000		+50,000	Nov. 15	Cash	50,000	
				Treasury Stock, Common		50,000
				Reissued 1,000 shares of treasury stock for $50 per share		

In 2004, Microsoft's board approved a plan to buy back $30 billion of the company's common stock over the next four years. When are share buybacks not a good idea? According to investor Warren Buffett, shown here offering his hand to Microsoft's Bill Gates, buybacks are ill-advised when a company buys high and sells low and when it borrows money to finance a buyback.

When treasury shares are sold for an amount greater than their cost, the excess of the sales price over cost should be credited to Paid-in Capital, Treasury Stock. No gain should be recorded.

For instance, suppose that on November 15, Caprock Corporation sells its 1,000 treasury shares for $60 per share. The entry for the reissue would be as follows:

A	= L +	OE
+60,000		+50,000
		+10,000

Nov. 15	Cash	60,000	
	Treasury Stock, Common		50,000
	Paid-in Capital, Treasury Stock		10,000
	Sold 1,000 shares of treasury stock for $60 per share; cost was $50 per share		

> **Study Note**
>
> Gains and losses on the reissue of treasury stock are never recognized as such. Instead, the Retained Earnings and Paid-in Capital, Treasury Stock accounts are used.

When treasury shares are sold below their cost, the difference is deducted from Paid-in Capital, Treasury Stock. If this account does not exist or if its balance is insufficient to cover the excess of cost over the reissue price, Retained Earnings absorbs the excess. No loss is recorded.

For example, suppose that on September 15, Caprock bought 1,000 shares of its common stock on the market at a price of $50 per share. On October 15, the company sold 400 shares for $60 per share, and on December 15, it sold the remaining 600 shares for $42 per share.

The entries for these three transactions are as follows:

A	= L +	OE
−50,000		−50,000

Sept. 15	Treasury Stock, Common	50,000	
	Cash		50,000
	Purchased 1,000 shares of treasury stock at $50 per share		

A = L +   OE
+24,000   +20,000
               +4,000

Oct. 15	Cash	24,000	
	Treasury Stock, Common		20,000
	Paid-in Capital, Treasury Stock		4,000
	Sold 400 shares of treasury stock for $60 per share; cost was $50 per share		

A = L +   OE
+25,200   −4,000
               −800
               +30,000

Dec. 15	Cash	25,200	
	Paid-in Capital, Treasury Stock	4,000	
	Retained Earnings	800	
	Treasury Stock, Common		30,000
	Sold 600 shares of treasury stock for $42 per share; cost was $50 per share		

⊃ *Study Note*

Retained Earnings is debited only when the Paid-in Capital, Treasury Stock account has been depleted. In this case, the credit balance of $4,000 is completely exhausted before Retained Earnings absorbs the excess.

In the entry for the December 15 transaction, Retained Earnings is debited for $800 because the 600 shares were sold for $4,800 less than cost. That amount is $800 greater than the $4,000 of paid-in capital generated by the sale of the 400 shares of treasury stock on October 15.

Retirement of Treasury Stock

If a company decides that it will not reissue treasury stock, it can, with the approval of its stockholders, retire the stock. When shares of stock are retired, all items related to those shares are removed from the associated capital accounts. If the cost of buying back the treasury stock is less than the company received when it issued the stock, the difference is recorded in Paid-in Capital, Retirement of Stock. If the reacquisition cost is more than was received when the stock was first issued, the difference is a reduction in stockholders' equity and is debited to Retained Earnings. For instance, suppose that on November 15, Caprock Corporation decides to retire the 1,000 shares of stock that it bought back for $50,000. If the $5 par value common stock was originally issued at $6 per share, this entry would record the retirement:

A = L +   OE
           −5,000
           −1,000
           −44,000
           +50,000

Nov. 15	Common Stock	5,000	
	Additional Paid-in Capital	1,000	
	Retained Earnings	44,000	
	Treasury Stock, Common		50,000
	Retired 1,000 shares that cost $50 per share and were issued originally at $6 per share		

S T O P • R E V I E W • A P P L Y

5-1. What is treasury stock?

5-2. What are some reasons a company would buy back its own stock?

5-3. What is the effect of treasury stock on the balance sheet?

A LOOK BACK AT

GOOGLE, INC.

This chapter's Decision Point focused on one of the most exciting financing events of recent history, **Google's** IPO. In evaluating Google's performance since its IPO, those who invested in its stock should consider the following questions:

- Why did Google's management choose to issue common stock to satisfy its needs for new capital?
- What are some of the advantages and disadvantages of this approach to financing a business?
- What measures should an investor use in evaluating management's performance?

As a relatively new company, Google needed to raise capital so that it could expand its operations. The company's management decided to do so by issuing common stock. This approach to financing does not burden a company with debt or interest payments. In addition, the company has the option of paying or not paying dividends. Because Google currently does not pay dividends, it can invest cash from its earnings in expanding the company. Issuing stock does, however, dilute the ownership of a company's current owners, and if the company pays dividends, they are not tax-deductible, as interest on debt is.

Return on equity is, of course, a key measure of management's performance. We showed in an earlier computation that Google's return on equity before its IPO was 27.7 percent. Using the same net income as in that computation and data from Google's Financial Highlights, we can compute the company's return on equity after the IPO as follows:

$$\text{Return on Equity} = \frac{\text{Net Income}}{\text{Average Stockholders' Equity}}$$

$$\text{Return on Equity} = \frac{\$105{,}548}{(\$2{,}589{,}023 + \$1{,}016{,}699) \div 2}$$

$$= 5.9\%$$

Obviously, the IPO significantly reduced Google's return on equity, from 27.7 percent to 5.9 percent. However, Google's price/earnings (P/E) ratios at the time of the IPO and six months later show that investors were counting on Google to continue to grow and be successful.

At the time of the IPO, when Google's stock sold for $85 per share, its P/E ratio was:

$$\text{P/E Ratio} = \frac{\text{Market Price per Share}}{\text{Earnings per Share}}$$

$$\text{P/E Ratio} = \frac{\$85}{\$1.14} = 74.6 \text{ times}$$

Six months later, when the price per share was $185, Google's P/E ratio had soared once again:

$$\text{P/E Ratio} = \frac{\$185}{\$1.14} = 162.3 \text{ times}$$

This is a very high P/E ratio; the average for the S&P 500 stocks at the time was about 16. Evidently, despite Google's not paying dividends, investors think the company's future is very bright. By 2006, Google's P/E ratio was up to 168, and the company's stock was added to the prestigious S&P 500, which is made up of the 500 largest companies in the United States.

CHAPTER REVIEW

REVIEW of Learning Objectives

LO1 Identify and explain the management issues related to contributed capital.

Contributed capital is a critical component in corporate financing. Managing contributed capital requires an understanding of the advantages and disadvantages of the corporate form of business and of the issues involved in using equity financing. Managers must also know how to determine dividend policies and how to evaluate these policies using dividends yield, return on equity, and the price/earnings ratio. The liability for payment of dividends arises on the date the board of directors declares a dividend. The declaration is recorded with a debit to Dividends and a credit to Dividends Payable. The record date—the date on which ownership of the stock, and thus of the right to receive a dividend, is determined—requires no entry. On the date of payment, the Dividends Payable account is eliminated, and the Cash account is reduced. Another issue involved in managing contributed capital is using stock options as compensation.

LO2 Identify the components of stockholders' equity.

The stockholders' equity section of a corporate balance usually has at least three components: contributed capital, retained earnings, and treasury stock. Contributed capital consists of money raised through stock issues. A corporation can issue two types of stock: common stock and preferred stock. Common stockholders have voting rights; they also share in the earnings of the corporation. Preferred stockholders usually have preference over common stockholders in one or more areas. Retained earnings are reinvested in the corporation; they represent stockholders' claims to assets resulting from profitable operations. Treasury stock is stock that the issuing corporation has reacquired. It is treated as a deduction from stockholders' equity.

LO3 Identify the characteristics of preferred stock.

Preferred stock generally gives its owners first right to dividend payments. Only after these stockholders have been paid can common stockholders receive any portion of a dividend. If the preferred stock is cumulative and dividends are in arrears, a corporation must pay the amount in arrears to preferred stockholders before it pays any dividends to common stockholders. Preferred stockholders also usually have preference over common stockholders in terms of their claims to corporate assets if the corporation is liquidated. In addition, preferred stock may be convertible to common stock, and it is often callable at the option of the corporation.

LO4 Account for the issuance of stock for cash and other assets.

Corporations normally issue their stock in exchange for cash or other assets. Most states require corporations to issue stock at a minimum value called *legal capital*. Legal capital is represented by the stock's par or stated value.

When stock is issued for cash at par or stated value, Cash is debited and Common Stock or Preferred Stock is credited. When stock is sold at an amount greater than par or stated value, the excess is recorded in Additional Paid-in Capital.

When stock is issued for noncash assets, the general rule is to record the stock at its market value. If this value cannot be determined, the fair market value of the asset received is used to record the transaction.

LO5 Account for treasury stock.

Treasury stock is stock that the issuing company has reacquired. A company may buy back its own stock for several reasons, including a desire to create stock option plans, maintain a favorable market for the stock, increase earnings per share, or purchase other companies. Treasury stock is recorded at cost and is deducted from stockholders' equity. It can be reissued or retired. It is similar to unissued stock in that it does not have rights until it is reissued.

REVIEW of Concepts and Terminology

The following concepts and terms were introduced in this chapter:

Articles of incorporation: An official document filed with and approved by a state that authorizes the incorporators to do business as a corporation. **(LO1)**

Authorized shares: The maximum number of shares a corporation can issue without a change in its state charter. **(LO2)**

Callable preferred stock: Preferred stock that the issuing corporation can redeem or retire at a stated price. **(LO3)**

Common stock: Shares of stock that carry voting rights but that rank below preferred stock in terms of dividends and the distribution of assets. **(LO2)**

Convertible preferred stock: Preferred stock that the owner can exchange for common stock. **(LO3)**

Cumulative preferred stock: Preferred stock on which unpaid dividends accumulate over time and that must be satisfied before a dividend can be paid to common stockholders. **(LO3)**

Date of payment: The date on which a dividend is paid. **(LO1)**

Declaration date: The date on which a board of directors declares a dividend. **(LO1)**

Dividend: A distribution of a corporation's assets (usually cash generated by past earnings) to its stockholders. **(LO1)**

Dividends in arrears: Past dividends on cumulative preferred stock that remain unpaid. **(LO3)**

Double taxation: Taxation of corporate earnings twice—once as income of the corporation and once as income to stockholders in the form of dividends. **(LO1)**

Ex-dividend: A description of stock between the record date and the date of payment, during which the right to the dividend remains with the person who owned the stock on the record date. **(LO1)**

Initial public offering (IPO): A company's first issue of capital stock to the public. **(Decision Point)**

Issued shares: The shares of stock sold or otherwise transferred to stockholders. **(LO2)**

Legal capital: The number of shares of stock issued times the par value; the minimum amount a corporation can report as contributed capital. **(LO1)**

Liquidating dividend: A dividend that exceeds retained earnings and that a corporation usually pays only when it is going out of business or reducing its operations. **(LO1)**

Noncumulative preferred stock: Preferred stock that does not oblige the issuer to make up a missed dividend in a subsequent year. **(LO3)**

No-par stock: Capital stock that does not have a par value. **(LO4)**

Outstanding shares: Shares that have been issued and that are still in circulation. **(LO2)**

Par value: An arbitrary amount assigned to each share of stock; constitutes a corporation's legal capital. **(LO1)**

Preferred stock: Stock that has preference over common stock, usually in terms of dividends and the distribution of assets. **(LO2)**

Record date: The date on which ownership of stock, and thus the right to receive a dividend, is determined. **(LO1)**

Residual equity: The equity of common stockholders after all other claims have been satisfied. **(LO2)**

Share of stock: A unit of ownership in a corporation. **(LO1)**

Start-up and organization costs: The costs of forming a corporation. **(LO1)**

Stated value: A value that a board of directors assigns to no-par stock. **(LO4)**

Stock certificates: Documents issued to stockholders showing the number of shares that they own. **(LO1)**

Stock option plans: Plans that give employees the right to purchase their companies' stock under specified terms. **(LO1)**

Treasury stock: Capital stock, either common or preferred, that the issuing company has reacquired and has not subsequently resold or retired. **(LO1)**

Underwriter: An intermediary between the corporation and the investing public who facilitates an issue of stock or other securities for a fee. **(LO1)**

Key Ratios

Dividends yield: Current return to stockholders in the form of dividends; Dividends per Share ÷ Market Price per Share. **(LO1)**

Price/earnings (P/E) ratio: A measure of confidence in a company's future; Market Price per Share ÷ Earnings per Share. **(LO1)**

Return on equity: A measure of management's performance; Net Income ÷ Average Stockholders' Equity. **(LO1)**

REVIEW Problem

LO1, LO2, LO3, LO4, LO5   **Recording Stock Issues and Calculating Related Ratios**

Beta Corporation was organized in 20x8 in Arizona. Its state charter authorized it to issue 1 million shares of $1 par value common stock and 25,000 shares of 4 percent, $20 par value cumulative and convertible preferred stock. Beta's stock transactions during 20x8 were as follows:

Feb. 1 Issued 100,000 shares of common stock for $125,000.
     15 Issued 3,000 shares of common stock for accounting and legal services. The bills for these services totaled $3,600.
Mar. 15 Issued 120,000 shares of common stock to Edward Jackson in exchange for a building and land appraised at $100,000 and $25,000, respectively.
Apr. 2 Purchased 20,000 shares of common stock for the treasury at $1.25 per share from a person who changed her mind about investing in the company.
July 1 Issued 25,000 shares of preferred stock for $500,000.
Sept. 30 Sold 10,000 of the shares in the treasury for $1.50 per share.
Dec. 31 Beta's board of directors declared dividends of $24,910 payable on January 15, 20x9, to stockholders of record on January 7. Dividends included preferred stock dividends of $10,000 for one-half year.

For the period ended December 31, 20x8, Beta reported net income of $40,000 and earnings per common share of $.14. At December 31, the market price per common share was $1.60.

Required

1. Record Beta's stock transactions in T accounts.
2. Prepare the stockholders' equity section of Beta's balance sheet as of December 31, 20x8. (**Hint:** Use net income and dividends to calculate retained earnings.)
3. Calculate Beta's dividends yield on common stock, price/earnings ratio of common stock, and return on equity.

Answer to Review Problem

1. Entries in T accounts:

	A	B	C	D	E	F	G	H	I	J	K	L	M	N	O	P	Q	R	S	T
1			Assets				=			Liabilities				+			Stockholders' Equity			
2																				
3			Cash							Dividends Payable							Preferred Stock			
4	Feb.	1	125,000	April	2	25,000					Dec.	31	24,910					July	1	500,000
5	July	1	500,000																	
6	Sept.	30	15,000														Common Stock			
7																	Feb.	1	100,000
8			Building															15	3,000
9	Mar.	15	100,000														Mar.	15	120,000
10																	Bal.		**223,000**

	A	B	C	D	E	F	G	H	I	J	K	L	M	N	O	P	Q	R	S	T
11			**Assets**				**=**			**Liabilities**				**+**			**Stockholders' Equity**			
12																				
13			**Land**														**Additional Paid-in Capital**			
14	Mar.	15	25,000														Feb.	1	25,000
15																		15	600
16																	Mar.	15	5,000
17																	Bal.		**30,600**
18																			
19																	**Paid-in Capital, Treasury Stock**			
20																	Sept.	30	2,500
21																			
22																	**Dividends**			
23															Dec.	31	24,910		
24																			
25																	**Treasury Stock**			
26															April	2	25,000	Sept.	30	12,500
27															Bal.		**12,500**		
28																			
29																	**Start-up and Organization Costs**			
30															Feb.	15	3,600		

2. Stockholders' equity section of the balance sheet:

	A	B	C
1	**Beta Corporation**		
2	**Balance Sheet**		
3	**December 31, 20x8**		
5	**Stockholders' Equity**		
7	Contributed capital		
8	Preferred stock, 4 percent cumulative convertible,		
9	$20 par value, 25,000 shares authorized, issued, and outstanding		$500,000
10	Common stock, $1 par value, 1,000,000 shares		
11	authorized, 223,000 shares issued, and 213,000 shares outstanding	$223,000	
12	Additional paid-in capital	30,600	
13	Paid-in capital, treasury stock	2,500	256,100
14	Total contributed capital		$756,100
15	Retained earnings		15,090*
16	Total contributed capital and retained earnings		$771,190
17	Less treasury stock (10,000 shares, at cost)		12,500
18	Total stockholders' equity		$758,690
19			
20	*Retained Earnings = Net Income - Cash Dividends Declared = $40,000 - $24,910 = $15,090		

3. Dividends yield on common stock, price/earnings ratio of common stock, and return on equity:

$$\text{Dividends per Share} = \frac{\text{Common Stock Dividend}}{\text{Common Shares Outstanding}} = \frac{\$14,910}{213,000} = \$.07$$

$$\text{Dividends Yield} = \frac{\text{Dividends per Share}}{\text{Market Price per Share}} = \frac{\$0.07}{\$1.60} = 4.4\%$$

$$\text{Price/Earnings Ratio} = \frac{\text{Market Price per Share}}{\text{Earnings per Share}} = \frac{\$1.60}{\$0.14} = 11.4 \text{ times}$$

The opening balance of stockholders' equity on February 1, 20x8, was $125,000.

$$\text{Return on Equity} = \frac{\text{Net Income}}{\text{Average Stockholders' Equity}}$$

$$= \frac{\$40,000}{(\$758,690 + \$125,000) \div 2}$$

$$= \frac{\$40,000}{\$441,845}$$

$$= 9.1\%$$

CHAPTER ASSIGNMENTS

BUILDING Your Basic Knowledge and Skills

Short Exercises

LO1 Management Issues

SE 1. Indicate whether each of the following actions is related to (a) managing under the corporate form of business, (b) using equity financing, (c) determining dividend policies, (d) evaluating performance using return on equity, or (e) issuing stock options:

1. Considering whether to make a distribution to stockholders
2. Controlling day-to-day operations
3. Determining whether to issue preferred or common stock
4. Compensating management based on the company's meeting or exceeding the targeted return on equity
5. Compensating employees by giving them the right to purchase shares at a given price
6. Transferring shares without the approval of other owners

LO1 Advantages and Disadvantages of a Corporation

SE 2. Identify whether each of the following characteristics is an advantage or a disadvantage of the corporate form of business:

1. Ease of transfer of ownership
2. Taxation
3. Separate legal entity
4. Lack of mutual agency
5. Government regulation
6. Continuous existence

LO2   Effect of Start-up and Organization Costs

SE 3. At the beginning of 20x8, Batson Company incurred the following start-up and organization costs: (1) attorneys' fees with a market value of $10,000, paid with 6,000 shares of $1 par value common stock, and (2) incorporation fees of $6,000. Calculate total start-up and organization costs. What will be the effect of these costs on the income statement and balance sheet?

LO1   Exercise of Stock Options

SE 4. On June 6, Aretha Dafoe exercised her option to purchase 20,000 shares of Shalom Company $1 par value common stock at an option price of $8. The market price per share was $8 on the grant date and $36 on the exercise date. Record the transaction on Shalom's books.

LO2   Stockholders' Equity

SE 5. Prepare the stockholders' equity section of Fina Corporation's balance sheet from the following accounts and balances on December 31, 20xx:

	Balance
Common Stock, $10 par value, 30,000 shares authorized, 20,000 shares issued, and 19,500 shares outstanding	$200,000
Additional paid-in Capital	100,000
Retained Earnings	15,000
Treasury Stock, Common (500 shares, at cost)	7,500

LO1   Cash Dividends

SE 6. Tone Corporation has authorized 200,000 shares of $1 par value common stock, of which 160,000 are issued and 140,000 are outstanding. On May 15, the board of directors declared a cash dividend of $.20 per share, payable on June 15 to stockholders of record on June 1. Prepare the entries in T accounts, as necessary, for each of the three dates.

LO3   Preferred Stock Dividends with Dividends in Arrears

SE 7. The Ferris Corporation has 2,000 shares of $100, 8 percent cumulative preferred stock outstanding and 40,000 shares of $1 par value common stock outstanding. In the company's first three years of operation, its board of directors paid cash dividends as follows: 20x7, none; 20x8, $40,000; and 20x9, $80,000. Determine the total cash dividends and dividends per share paid to the preferred and common stockholders during each of the three years.

LO4   Issuance of Stock

SE 8. Rattich Company is authorized to issue 50,000 shares of common stock. The company sold 2,500 shares at $12 per share. Prepare entries in journal form to record the sale of stock for cash under each of the following independent alternatives: (1) The stock has a par value of $5, and (2) the stock has no par value but a stated value of $1 per share.

LO4   Issuance of Stock for Noncash Assets

SE 9. Learner Corporation issued 16,000 shares of its $1 par value common stock in exchange for land that had a fair market value of $100,000. Prepare in journal form the entries necessary to record the issuance of the stock for the land under each of these conditions: (1) The stock was selling for $7 per share on the day of the transaction; (2) management attempted to place a value on the common stock but could not do so.

LO5 **Treasury Stock Transactions**

SE 10. Prepare in journal form the entries necessary to record the following stock transactions of the Seoul Company during 20xx:

Oct. 1 Purchased 2,000 shares of its own $2 par value common stock for $20 per share, the current market price.

17 Sold 500 shares of treasury stock purchased on October 1 for $25 per share.

21 Sold 800 shares of treasury stock purchased on October 1 for $18 per share.

LO5 **Retirement of Treasury Stock**

SE 11. On October 28, 20xx, the Seoul Company (**SE 10**) retired the remaining 700 shares of treasury stock. The shares were originally issued at $5 per share. Prepare the necessary entry in journal form.

Exercises

LO1, LO2 **Discussion Questions**

E 1. Develop brief answers to each of the following questions:

1. Why are most large companies established as corporations rather than as partnerships?
2. Why do many companies like to give stock options as compensation?
3. If an investor sells shares after the declaration date but before the date of record, does the seller still receive the dividend?
4. Why does a company usually not want to issue all its authorized shares?

LO3, LO4, LO5 **Discussion Questions**

E 2. Develop brief answers to each of the following questions:

1. Why would a company want to issue callable preferred stock?
2. What arguments can you give for treating preferred stock as debt rather than equity when carrying out financial analysis?
3. What relevance does par value or stated value have to a financial ratio, such as return on equity or debit to equity?
4. Why is treasury stock not considered an investment or an asset?

LO1 **Dividends Yield and Price/Earnings Ratio**

E 3. In 20x8, Rhinehart Corporation earned $4.40 per share and paid a dividend of $2.00 per share. At year end, the price of its stock was $66 per share. Calculate the dividends yield and the price/earnings ratio.

LO2 **Stockholders' Equity**

E 4. The following accounts and balances are from the records of Guard Corporation on December 31, 20xx:

	Balance
Preferred Stock, $100 par value, 9 percent cumulative, 10,000 shares authorized, 6,000 shares issued and outstanding	$600,000
Common Stock, $12 par value, 45,000 shares authorized, 30,000 shares issued, and 28,500 shares outstanding	360,000
Additional Paid-in Capital	194,000
Retained Earnings	23,000
Treasury Stock, Common (1,500 shares, at cost)	30,000

Prepare the stockholders' equity section for Guard Corporation's balance sheet as of December 31, 20xx.

LO2, LO3 Characteristics of Common and Preferred Stock

E 5. Indicate whether each of the following characteristics is more closely associated with common stock (C) or preferred stock (P):

1. Often receives dividends at a set rate
2. Is considered the residual equity of a company
3. Can be callable
4. Can be convertible
5. More likely to have dividends that vary in amount from year to year
6. Can be entitled to receive dividends not paid in past years
7. Likely to have full voting rights
8. Receives assets first in liquidation
9. Generally receives dividends before other classes of stock

LO2, LO4 Stock Entries Using T Accounts; Stockholders' Equity

E 6. Rath School Supply Corporation was organized in 20xx. It was authorized to issue 200,000 shares of no-par common stock with a stated value of $5 per share, and 40,000 shares of $100 par value, 6 percent noncumulative preferred stock. On March 1, the company issued 120,000 shares of its common stock for $15 per share and 16,000 shares of its preferred stock for $100 per share.

1. Record the issuance of the stock in T accounts.
2. Prepare the stockholders' equity section of Rath School Supply Corporation's balance sheet as it would appear immediately after the company issued the common and preferred stock.

LO1 Cash Dividends

E 7. Mendoza Corporation secured authorization from the state for 100,000 shares of $10 par value common stock. It has 80,000 shares issued and 70,000 shares outstanding. On June 5, the board of directors declared a $.50 per share cash dividend to be paid on June 25 to stockholders of record on June 15. Prepare entries in T accounts to record these events.

LO1, LO5 Cash Dividends

E 8. Martin Corporation has 250,000 authorized shares of $1 par value common stock, of which 200,000 are issued, including 20,000 shares of treasury stock. On October 15, the corporation's board of directors declared a cash dividend of $.25 per share payable on November 15 to stockholders of record on November 1. Prepare entries in T accounts for each of the three dates.

LO3 Cash Dividends with Dividends in Arrears

E 9. Canterbury Corporation has 20,000 shares of its $100 par value, 7 percent cumulative preferred stock outstanding, and 100,000 shares of its $1 par value common stock outstanding. In Canterbury's first four years of operation, its board of directors paid cash dividends as follows: 20x6, none; 20x7, $240,000; 20x8, $280,000; 20x9, $280,000. Determine the dividends per share and total cash dividends paid to the preferred and common stockholders during each of the four years.

LO3 Cash Dividends on Preferred and Common Stock

E 10. Khandi Corporation pays dividends at the end of each year. The dividends that it paid for 20x7, 20x8, and 20x9 were $160,000, $120,000, and

$360,000, respectively. Calculate the total amount of dividends Khandi Corporation paid in each of these years to its common and preferred stockholders under both of the following capital structures: (1) 40,000 shares of $100 par, 6 percent noncumulative preferred stock and 120,000 shares of $10 par common stock; (2) 20,000 shares of $100 par, 7 percent cumulative preferred stock and 120,000 shares of $10 par common stock. Khandi Corporation had no dividends in arrears at the beginning of 20x7.

LO4   Issuance of Stock

E 11. Red Valley Company is authorized to issue 100,000 shares of common stock. On August 1, the company issued 5,000 shares at $25 per share. Prepare entries in journal form to record the issuance of stock for cash under each of the following alternatives:

1. The stock has a par value of $25.
2. The stock has a par value of $10.
3. The stock has no par value.
4. The stock has a stated value of $1 per share.

LO4   Issuance of Stock for Noncash Assets

E 12. On July 1, 20xx, Gorlin, a new corporation, issued 40,000 shares of its common stock to finance a corporate headquarters building. The building has a fair market value of $1,200,000 and a book value of $800,000. Because Gorlin is a new corporation, it is not possible to establish a market value for its common stock. Record the issuance of stock for the building, assuming the following conditions: (1) the par value of the stock is $10 per share; (2) the stock is no-par stock; and (3) the stock has a stated value of $4 per share.

LO5   Treasury Stock Transactions

E 13. Record in T accounts the following stock transactions of Bornstein Company, which represent all the company's treasury stock transactions during 20xx:

May   5   Purchased 800 shares of its own $2 par value common stock for $20 per share, the current market price.
     17   Sold 300 shares of treasury stock purchased on May 5 for $22 per share.
     21   Sold 200 shares of treasury stock purchased on May 5 for $20 per share.
     28   Sold the remaining 300 shares of treasury stock purchased on May 5 for $19 per share.

LO5   Treasury Stock Transactions Including Retirement

E 14. Record in T accounts the following stock transactions of Adderly Corporation, which represent all its treasury stock transactions for the year:

June 1   Purchased 1,000 shares of its own $30 par value common stock for $70 per share, the current market price.
     10   Sold 250 shares of treasury stock purchased on June 1 for $80 per share.
     20   Sold 350 shares of treasury stock purchased on June 1 for $58 per share.

June 30   Retired the remaining shares purchased on June 1. The original issue price was $42 per share.

LO1, LO2, LO4, LO5   ## Problems

Common Stock Transactions and Stockholders' Equity

P 1. Sussex Corporation began operations on September 1, 20xx. The corporation's charter authorized 300,000 shares of $8 par value common stock. Sussex Corporation engaged in the following transactions during its first quarter:

Sept.   1   Issued 50,000 shares of common stock, $500,000.
       1   Paid an attorney $32,000 to help start up and organize the corporation and obtain a corporate charter from the state.
Oct.   2   Issued 80,000 shares of common stock, $960,000.
    15   Purchased 10,000 shares of common stock for $150,000.
Nov.   30   Declared a cash dividend of $.40 per share to be paid on December 15 to stockholders of record on December 10.

Required

1. Prepare entries in T accounts to record the above transactions.
2. Prepare the stockholders' equity section of Sussex Corporation's balance sheet on November 30, 20xx. Net income for the quarter was $80,000.
3. **User Insight:** What effect, if any, will the cash dividend declaration on November 30 have on net income, retained earnings, and cash flows?

LO1, LO3   ### Preferred and Common Stock Dividends and Dividend Yield

P 2. The DeMeo Corporation had both common stock and preferred stock outstanding from 20x7 through 20x9. Information about each stock for the three years is as follows:

Type	Par Value	Shares Outstanding	Other
Preferred	$100	40,000	7% cumulative
Common	20	600,000	

The company paid $140,000, $800,000, and $1,100,000 in dividends for 20x7 through 20x9, respectively. The market price per common share was $15 and $17 per share at the end of years 20x8 and 20x9, respectively.

Required

1. Determine the dividends per share and total dividends paid to the common and preferred stockholders each year.
2. Assuming that the preferred stock was noncumulative, repeat the computations performed in requirement **1**.
3. Calculate the 20x8 and 20x9 dividends yield for common stock using dividends per share computed in requirement **2**.
4. **User Insight:** How are cumulative preferred stock and noncumulative preferred stock similar to long-term bonds? How do they differ from long-term bonds?

LO1, LO2, LO3, LO4, LO5   ### Comprehensive Stockholders' Equity Transactions

P 3. In January 20xx, the Jones Corporation was organized and authorized to issue 2,000,000 shares of no-par common stock and 50,000 shares of 5 percent, $50 par value, noncumulative preferred stock. The stock-related transactions for the first year's operations were as follows:

| | | | Account | |
			Debited	Credited
Jan.	19	Sold 15,000 shares of common stock for $31,500. State law requires a minimum of $1 stated value per share.	110 ($31,500)	310 ($15,000) 312 ($16,500)
	21	Issued 5,000 shares of common stock to attorneys and accountants for services valued at $11,000 and provided during the organization of the corporation.	_____	_____
Feb.	7	Issued 30,000 shares of common stock for a building that had an appraised value of $78,000.	_____	_____
Mar.	22	Purchased 10,000 shares of its common stock at $3 per share.	_____	_____
July	15	Issued 5,000 shares of common stock to employees under a stock option plan that allows any employee to buy shares at the current market price, which is now $3 per share.	_____	_____
Aug.	1	Sold 2,500 shares of treasury stock for $4 per share.	_____	_____
Sept.	1	Declared a cash dividend of $.15 per common share to be paid on September 25 to stockholders of record on September 15.	_____	_____
	15	Date of record for cash dividends	_____	_____
	25	Paid cash dividends to stockholders of record on September 15.	_____	_____
Oct.	30	Issued 4,000 shares of common stock for a piece of land. The stock was selling for $3 per share, and the land had a fair market value of $12,000.	_____	_____
Dec.	15	Issued 2,200 shares of preferred stock for $50 per share.	_____	_____

Required

1. For each of the above transactions, enter in the blanks provided the account numbers and dollar amounts (as shown in the example) for the account(s) debited and credited. The account numbers are listed below.

110 Cash	312 Additional Paid-in Capital
120 Land	313 Paid-in Capital, Treasury Stock
121 Building	340 Retained Earnings
220 Dividends Payable	341 Dividends
305 Preferred Stock	350 Treasury Stock, Common
310 Common Stock	510 Start-up and Organization Costs

2. **User Insight:** Why is the stockholders' equity section of the balance sheet an important consideration in analyzing the performance of a company?

LO1, LO2, LO3, LO4, LO5 Comprehensive Stockholders' Equity Transactions and Financial Ratios

P 4. Kokaly Plastics Corporation was chartered in the state of Massachusetts. The company was authorized to issue 20,000 shares of $100 par value, 6 percent preferred stock and 100,000 shares of no-par common stock. The common stock has a $2 stated value. The stock-related transactions for the quarter ended October 31, 20xx, were as follows:

Aug. 3 Issued 20,000 shares of common stock at $22 per share.
      15 Issued 16,000 shares of common stock for land. Asking price for the land was $200,000. Common stock's market value was $12 per share.
      22 Issued 10,000 shares of preferred stock for $1,000,000.
Oct. 4 Issued 10,000 shares of common stock for $120,000.
      10 Purchased 5,000 shares of common stock for the treasury for $13,000.
      15 Declared a quarterly cash dividend on the outstanding preferred stock and $.10 per share on common stock outstanding, payable on October 31 to stockholders of record on October 25.
      25 Date of record for cash dividends.
      31 Paid cash dividends.

Required

1. Record transactions for the quarter ended October 31, 20xx, in T accounts.
2. Prepare the stockholders' equity section of the balance sheet as of October 31, 20xx. Net income for the quarter was $46,000.
3. **User Insight:** Calculate dividends yield, price/earnings ratio, and return on equity. Assume earnings per common share are $1.97 and market price per common share is $25. For beginning stockholders' equity, use the balance after the August transactions.
4. **User Insight:** Discuss the results in **3**, including the effect on investors' returns and the firm's profitability as it relates to stockholders' equity.

LO1, LO5 Treasury Stock

P 5. The Spivak Company was involved in the following treasury stock transactions during 20xx:

a. Purchased 80,000 shares of its $1 par value common stock on the market for $2.50 per share.
b. Purchased 16,000 shares of its $1 par value common stock on the market for $2.80 per share.
c. Sold 44,000 shares purchased in **a** for $131,000.
d. Sold the other 36,000 shares purchased in **a** for $72,000.
e. Sold 6,000 of the remaining shares of treasury stock for $1.60 per share.
f. Retired all the remaining shares of treasury stock. All shares originally were issued at $1.50 per share.

Required

1. Record the treasury stock transactions in T accounts.
2. **User Insight:** What is the reasoning behind treating the purchase of treasury stock as a reduction in stockholders' equity as opposed to treating it as an investment asset?

Alternate Problems

LO1, LO2, LO4 Common Stock Transactions and Stockholders' Equity

P 6. On March 1, 20xx, Carmel Corporation began operations with a charter from the state that authorized 100,000 shares of $4 par value common stock. Over the next quarter, the firm engaged in the transactions that follow.

Mar. 1 Issued 30,000 shares of common stock, $200,000.
2 Paid fees associated with obtaining the charter and starting up and organizing the corporation, $24,000.
Apr. 10 Issued 13,000 shares of common stock, $130,000.
15 Purchased 5,000 shares of common stock, $50,000
May 31 The board of directors declared a $.20 per share cash dividend to be paid on June 15 to shareholders of record on June 10.

Required

1. Record the above transactions in T accounts.
2. Prepare the stockholders' equity section of Carmel Corporation's balance sheet on May 31, 20xx. Net income earned during the first quarter was $30,000.
3. **User Insight:** What effect, if any, will the cash dividend declaration on May 31 have on Carmel Corporation's net income, retained earnings, and cash flows?

LO1, LO3 **Preferred and Common Stock Dividends and Dividends Yield**

 P 7. The Clockwork Corporation had the following stock outstanding from 20x6 through 20x9:

Preferred stock: $100 par value, 8 percent cumulative, 10,000 shares authorized, issued, and outstanding
Common stock: $10 par value, 200,000 shares authorized, issued, and outstanding

The company paid $60,000, $60,000, $188,000, and $260,000 in dividends during 20x6, 20x7, 20x8, and 20x9, respectively. The market price per common share was $7.25 and $8.00 per share at the end of years 20x8 and 20x9, respectively.

Required

1. Determine the dividends per share and the total dividends paid to common stockholders and preferred stockholders in 20x6, 20x7, 20x8, and 20x9.
2. Perform the same computations, with the assumption that the preferred stock was noncumulative.
3. Calculate the 20x8 and 20x9 dividends yield for common stock, using the dividends per share computed in requirement **2**.
4. **User Insight:** How are cumulative preferred stock and noncumulative preferred stock similar to long-term bonds? How do they differ from long-term bonds?

LO1, LO2, LO3, LO4, LO5 **Comprehensive Stockholders' Equity Transactions and Stockholders' Equity**

 **P 8.** Vanowski, Inc., was organized and authorized to issue 10,000 shares of $100 par value, 9 percent preferred stock and 100,000 shares of no-par, $5 stated value common stock on July 1, 20xx. Stock-related transactions for Vanowski are as follows:

July 1 Issued 20,000 shares of common stock at $11 per share.
1 Issued 1,000 shares of common stock at $11 per share for services rendered in connection with the organization of the company.
2 Issued 2,000 shares of preferred stock at par value for cash.
10 Issued 5,000 shares of common stock for land on which the asking price was $70,000. Market value of the stock was $12. Management wishes to record the land at full market value of the stock.
Aug. 2 Purchased 3,000 shares of its common stock at $13 per share.

Aug. 10 Declared a cash dividend for one month on the outstanding preferred stock and $.02 per share on common stock outstanding,
payable on August 22 to stockholders of record on August 12.

12 Date of record for cash dividends.

22 Paid cash dividends.

Required

1. Record the transactions in journal form.
2. Prepare the stockholders' equity section of the balance sheet as it would appear on August 31, 20xx. Net income for July and August was $23,000.
3. **User Insight:** Calculate dividends yield, price/earnings ratio, and return on equity. Assume earnings per common share are $1.00 and market price per common share is $20. For beginning stockholders' equity, use the balance after the July transactions.
4. **User Insight:** Discuss the results in requirement **3**, including the effect on investors' returns and the company's profitability as it relates to stockholders' equity.

ENHANCING Your Knowledge, Skills, and Critical Thinking

Conceptual Understanding Cases

LO1 **Reasons for Issuing Common Stock**

C 1. In a recent year, **Avaya, Inc.**, an East Coast telecommunications company, issued 34,300,000 shares of common stock for a total of $212,000,000.[15] As a growing company, Avaya could have raised this significant amount of money by issuing long-term bonds, but the company's bond rating had recently been lowered. What are some advantages of issuing common stock as opposed to bonds? What are some disadvantages?

LO3 **Reasons for Issuing Preferred Stock**

C 2. Preferred stock is a hybrid security; it has some of the characteristics of stock and some of the characteristics of bonds. Historically, preferred stock has not been a popular means of financing. In the past few years, however, it has become more attractive to companies and individual investors alike, and investors are buying large amounts because of high yields. Large preferred stock issues have been made by such banks as **Chase**, **Citibank**, **HSBC Bank USA**, and **Wells Fargo**, as well as by other companies. The dividends yields on these stocks are over 9 percent, higher than the interest rates on bonds of comparable risk.[16] Especially popular are preferred equity redemption convertible stocks, or PERCs, which are automatically convertible into common stock after three years if the company does not call them first and retire them. What reasons can you give for the popularity of preferred stock, and of PERCs in particular, when the tax-deductible interest on bonds is lower? Discuss from both the company's and the investor's standpoint.

LO5 **Purposes of Treasury Stock**

C 3. Many companies in recent years have bought back their common stock. For example, **IBM**, with large cash holdings, spent almost $27 billion over five years repurchasing its stock. What are the reasons companies buy back their own shares? What is the effect of common stock buybacks on earnings per share, return on equity, return on assets, debt to equity, and the current ratio?

Interpreting Financial Reports

LO4 **Effect of Stock Issue**

C 4. When **Netscape Communications Corporation** went public with an IPO, it issued stock at $28 per share. In its second year as a public company, Netscape (which later became a subsidiary of **AOL Time Warner**) announced a common stock issue in an ad in *The Wall Street Journal*:

6,440,000 Shares
NETSCAPE
Common Stock
Price $53¾ a share

If Netscape had sold all these shares at the offering price of $53.75, the net proceeds before issue costs would have been $346.15 million.

Shown below is a portion of the stockholders' equity section of the balance sheet adapted from Netscape's annual report, which was issued prior to this stock offering:

Stockholders' Equity (In thousands)	
Common Stock, $0.0001 par value, 200,000,000 shares authorized; 81,063,158 shares issued and outstanding	$ 8
Additional paid-in capital	196,749
Accumulated deficit	(16,314)

1. Assume the net proceeds from the sale of 6,440,000 shares at $53.75 were $342.6 million after issue costs. Record the stock issuance on Netscape's accounting records in journal form.
2. Prepare the portion of the stockholders' equity section of the balance sheet shown above after the issue of the common stock, based on the information given. Round all answers to the nearest thousand.
3. Based on your answer in **2**, did Netscape have to increase its authorized shares to undertake this stock issue?
4. What amount per share did Netscape receive and how much did Netscape's underwriters receive to help in issuing the stock if investors paid $53.75 per share? What do underwriters do to earn their fee?

LO3 **Effect of Deferring Preferred Dividends**

C 5. **US Airways** had indefinitely deferred the quarterly dividend on its $358 million of cumulative convertible 91¼ percent preferred stock.[17] According to a US Airways spokesperson, the company did not want to "continue to pay a dividend while the company is losing money." Others interpreted the action as "an indication of a cash crisis situation."

At the time, **Berkshire Hathaway**, the large company run by Warren Buffett and the owner of the preferred stock, was not happy. However, US Airways was able to turn around, become profitable, and return to paying its cumulative dividends on preferred stock. Berkshire Hathaway was able to convert the preferred stock into 9.24 million shares of US Airways' common stock at $38.74 per share at a time when the market value had risen to $62.[18]

What is cumulative convertible preferred stock? Why is deferring dividends on those shares a drastic action? What is the impact on profitability and liquidity? Why did using preferred stock instead of long-term bonds as a financing method probably save the company from bankruptcy? What was Berkshire Hathaway's gain on its investment at the time of the conversion?

LO1, LO2 ## Decision Analysis Using Excel

Analysis of Alternative Financing Methods

C 6. Northeast Servotech Corporation, which offers services to the computer industry, has expanded rapidly in recent years. Because of its profitability, the company has been able to grow without obtaining external financing. This fact is reflected in its current balance sheet, which contains no long-term debt. The liabilities and stockholders' equity sections of the balance sheet on March 31, 20xx, appear below.

Northeast Servotech Corporation
Balance Sheet
March 31, 20xx

Liabilities

Current liabilities		$ 500,000

Stockholders' Equity

Common stock, $10 par value, 500,000 shares authorized, 100,000 shares issued and outstanding	$1,000,000	
Additional paid-in capital	1,800,000	
Retained earnings	1,700,000	
Total stockholders' equity		4,500,000
Total liabilities and stockholders' equity		$5,000,000

The company now has the opportunity to double its size by purchasing the operations of a rival company for $4,000,000. If the purchase goes through, Northeast Servotech will become one of the top companies in its specialized industry. The problem for management is how to finance the purchase. After much study and discussion with bankers and underwriters, management has prepared the following three financing alternatives to present to the board of directors, which must authorize the purchase and the financing:

> *Alternative A* The company could issue $4,000,000 of long-term debt. Given the company's financial rating and the current market rates, management believes the company will have to pay an interest rate of 12 percent on the debt.
> *Alternative B* The company could issue 40,000 shares of 8 percent, $100 par value preferred stock.
> *Alternative C* The company could issue 100,000 additional shares of $10 par value common stock at $40 per share.

Management explains to the board that the interest on the long-term debt is tax-deductible and that the applicable income tax rate is 40 percent. The board members know that a dividend of $.80 per share of common stock was paid last year, up from $.60 and $.40 per share in the two years before that. The board has had a policy of regular increases in dividends of $.20 per share. The board believes each of the three financing alternatives is feasible and now wants to study the financial effects of each alternative.

1. Prepare a schedule to show how the liabilities and stockholders' equity sections of Northeast Servotech's balance sheet would look under each alternative, and compute the debt to equity ratio (total liabilities ÷ total stockholders' equity) for each.
2. Compute and compare the cash needed to pay the interest or dividends for each kind of new financing, net of income taxes, in the first year.
3. How might the cash needed to pay for the financing change in future years under each alternative?
4. Prepare a memorandum to the board of directors that evaluates the alternatives in order of preference based on cash flow effects, giving arguments for and against each one.

Annual Report Case: CVS Corporation

LO1, LO2, LO5 **Stockholders' Equity**

C 7. Refer to the **CVS Corporation** annual report in the Supplement to Chapter 5 to answer the following questions:

1. What type of capital stock does CVS have? What is the par value? How many shares were authorized, issued, and outstanding at the end of fiscal 2005?
2. What is the dividends yield (use average price of stock in last quarter) for CVS and its relationship to the investors' total return? Does the company rely mostly on stock or on earnings for its stockholders' equity?
3. Does the company have a stock option plan? To whom do the stock options apply? Do employees have significant stock options? Given the market price of the stock shown in the report, do these options represent significant value to the employees?

Comparison Case: CVS Versus Southwest

LO1, LO5 **Return on Equity, Treasury Stock, and Dividends Policy**

C 8. Refer to the annual report of **CVS Corporation** and the financial statements of **Southwest Airlines Co.** in the Supplement to Chapter 5.

1. Compute the return on equity for both companies for fiscal 2005 and 2004. Total stockholders' equity for CVS and Southwest in 2003 was $6,021.8 million and $5,052 million, respectively.
2. Did either company purchase treasury stock during these years? How will the purchase of treasury stock affect return on equity and earnings per share?
3. Did either company issue stock during these years? What are the details?
4. Compare the dividend policy of the two companies.

Ethical Dilemma Case

LO1, LO5 **Ethics, Management Compensation, and Treasury Stock**

C 9. Compensation of senior management is often tied to earnings per share or return on equity. Treasury stock purchases have a favorable impact on both these measures. In the recent buyback boom, many companies borrowed money to purchase treasury shares. In some cases, the motivation for the borrowing and repurchase of shares was the desire of executives to secure their year-end cash bonuses. Did these executives act ethically? Were their actions in the best interests of stockholders? Why or why not? How might such behavior be avoided in the future?

Internet Case

LO1, LO2, LO3, LO4, LO5   Comprehensive Analysis of Stockholders' Equity

C 10. Many Internet companies have gone public in recent years. These companies are generally unprofitable in their start-up years and require a great deal of cash to finance expansion. They also reward their employees with stock options. Choose any one of the following Internet companies: **Amazon.com**, **Yahoo!**, or **eBay**. Go to the website of the company you have selected. In the company's latest annual report, look at the financing section of the statement of cash flows for the last three years. How has the company financed its business? Has it issued stock or long-term debt? Has it purchased treasury stock, paid dividends, or issued stock under stock option plans? Is the company profitable (see net income or earnings at the top of the statement)? Are your findings in line with your expectations about Internet companies? Find the company's stock price, either on its website or in a newspaper, and compare it with the average issue price of the company's past stock issues. Summarize your findings and conclusions.

Group Activity Case

LO1, LO5   Treasury Stock or Dividends?

C 11. In your class, divide into small groups. Assume the president of a small company that has been profitable for several years but has not paid a dividend has hired your group. The company has built up a cash reserve. It has 20 stockholders, but the president owns 40 percent of the company's shares. Several of the stockholders with smaller numbers of shares would like to sell their shares, but there is no ready market. The president of the company has asked your group to determine whether it would be better to recommend to the board of directors that they pay a dividend to all stockholders or whether they should buy out the smaller stockholders to hold in the treasury shares and possibly retire them. In your group, decide which recommendation you will make to the president. Develop a series of points to support your argument. Participate in a class debate among teams who have chosen opposing positions.

Business Communication Case

LO1   Debt or Equity Financing

C 12. As noted in the Decision Point at the beginning of this chapter, **Google, Inc.**, announced a common stock issue:

22,500,000 Shares
.001 Par Value Common Stock
Price $85 a share

The net proceeds before issue costs were $1.9 billion.

Given Google's successful track record as a start-up company, it is likely the company could have borrowed $1.9 billion in debt financing rather than issue common stock. Write a one-page business memorandum that takes either the position that (1) Google should have issued debt at an interest rate of 8 percent or (2) Google is correct in issuing common stock. Be sure to include in your presentation the effect of your alternative on the debt to equity ratio and return on equity.

Long-Term Liabilities

Long-term liabilities can be an attractive means of financing the expansion of a business. By incurring long-term debt to fund growth, a company may be able to earn a return that exceeds the interest it pays on the debt. When it does, it increases earnings for stockholders—that is, return on equity. Many companies reward top managers with bonuses for improving return on equity. This incentive provides a temptation to incur too much debt, which increases a company's financial risk. Thus, in deciding on an appropriate level of debt, as in so many other management issues, ethics is a major concern.

LEARNING OBJECTIVES

LO1 Identify the management issues related to long-term debt.

LO2 Describe the features of a bond issue and the major characteristics of bonds.

LO3 Record bonds issued at face value and at a discount or premium.

LO4 Use present values to determine the value of bonds.

LO5 Amortize bond discounts and bond premiums using the straight-line and effective interest methods.

LO6 Account for the retirement of bonds and the conversion of bonds into stock.

SUPPLEMENTAL OBJECTIVE

Making a Statement

SO7 Record bonds issued between interest dates and year-end adjustments.

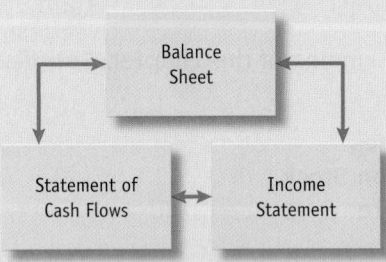

Long-term liability activities can impact all financial statements.

McDONALD'S CORPORATION

- What are McDonald's most important long-term debts?

- What are its considerations in deciding to issue long-term debt?

- How does one evaluate whether a company has too much debt?

McDonald's, the world's largest restaurant chain, passed a milestone in 2004 when it earned more revenues in Europe than in the United States. To finance its continued global expansion, the company raises funds by issuing both debt and capital stock. As you can see in its Financial Highlights, McDonald's relies heavily on debt financing. In 2005, its long-term liabilities were more than 71 percent of its shareholders' equity and, together with current liabilities, they almost equaled shareholders' equity. McDonald's long-term obligations include numerous leases on real estate, as well as employee pension and health plans.[1]

McDONALD'S FINANCIAL HIGHLIGHTS
(In millions)

	2005	2004
Total current liabilities	$ 4,036.3	$ 3,520.5
Long-term debt	$ 8,937.4	$ 8,357.3
Other long-term liabilities	892.3	976.7
Deferred income taxes	976.7	781.5
Total long-term liabilities	$10,806.4	$10,115.5
Total shareholders' equity	$15,146.1	$14,201.5
Total liabilities and shareholders' equity	$29,988.8	$27,837.5

Management Issues Related to Issuing Long-Term Debt

LO1 Identify the management issues related to long-term debt.

P rofitable operations and short-term credit seldom provide sufficient cash for a growing business. Growth usually requires investment in long-term assets and in research and development and other activities that will produce income in future years. To finance these assets and activities, a company needs funds that will be available for long periods. Two key sources of long-term funds are the issuance of capital stock and the issuance of long-term debt. The management issues related to long-term debt financing are whether to take on long-term debt, how much long-term debt to carry, and what types of long-term debt to incur.

Deciding to Issue Long-Term Debt

A key decision for management is whether to rely solely on stockholders' equity—capital stock issued and retained earnings—for long-term funds or to rely partially on long-term debt. Some companies, such as **Microsoft** and **Apple Computer**, do not issue long-term debt, but like **McDonald's**, most companies find it useful to do so.

Because long-term debt must be paid at maturity and usually requires periodic payments of interest, issuing common stock has two advantages over issuing long-term debt: (1) it does not have to be paid back, and (2) a company normally pays dividends on common stock only if it earns sufficient income. Issuing long-term debt, however, has the following advantages over issuing common stock:

▶ **No loss of stockholder control.** When a corporation issues long-term debt, common stockholders do not relinquish any of their control over the company because bondholders and other creditors do not have voting rights. But when a corporation issues additional shares of common stock, the votes of the new stockholders may force current stockholders and management to give up some control.

▶ **Tax effects.** The interest on debt is tax-deductible, whereas dividends on common stock are not. For example, if a corporation pays $100,000 in interest and its income tax rate is 30 percent, its net cost will be $70,000 because it will save $30,000 on income taxes. To pay $100,000 in dividends on common stock, the corporation would have to earn $142,857 before income taxes [($100,000 ÷ (1 − .30)].

▶ **Financial leverage.** If a corporation earns more from the funds it raises by incurring long-term debt than it pays in interest on the debt, the excess will increase its earnings for the stockholders. This concept is called **financial leverage**, or *trading on equity*. For example, if a company earns 12 percent on a $1,000,000 investment financed by long-term 10 percent notes, it will earn $20,000 before income taxes ($120,000 − $100,000). The debt to equity ratio is considered an overall measure of a company's financial leverage.

Despite these advantages, debt financing is not always in a company's best interest. It may entail the following:

▶ **Financial risk.** A high level of debt exposes a company to financial risk. A company whose plans for earnings do not pan out, whose operations are subject to the ups and downs of the economy, or whose cash flow is weak may be unable to pay the principal amount of its debt at the maturity date or even to make periodic interest payments. Creditors can then force the company into bankruptcy—something that has occurred often in the heavily debt-financed airline industry. **TWA**, **Continental Airlines**, and **United Airlines** filed for bankruptcy protection because they could not make payments on their long-term debt and other liabilities. (While in bankruptcy, they restructured their debt and interest payments: TWA sold off its assets, Continental survived, and United is still trying to come out of bankruptcy.)

◗ **Negative financial leverage.** Financial leverage can work against a company if the earnings from its investments do not exceed its interest payments. For example, many small Internet companies failed in recent years because they relied too heavily on debt financing before developing sufficient resources to ensure their survival.

Evaluating Long-Term Debt

The amount of long-term debt that companies carry varies widely. For many companies, it is less than 1.0 times stockholders' equity. However, as Figure 1 shows, the average debt to equity for selected industries often exceeds 1.0 times stockholders' equity. The range is from 1.1 to 2.4 times stockholders' equity.

To assess how much debt to carry, managers compute the debt to equity ratio. Using data from **McDonald's** Financial Highlights, we can compute its debt to equity ratio in 2005 as follows (in millions):

$$\text{Debt to Equity} = \frac{\text{Total Liabilities}}{\text{Total Stockholders' Equity}}$$

$$= \frac{\$4,036.3 + \$10,806.4}{\$15,146.1} = \frac{\$14,842.7}{\$15,146.1} = 1.0 \text{ times}$$

A debt to equity ratio of 1.0 is relatively large, but it does not tell the whole story. McDonald's also has long-term leases on property at about 15,000 locations. McDonald's structures these leases in such a way that they do not appear

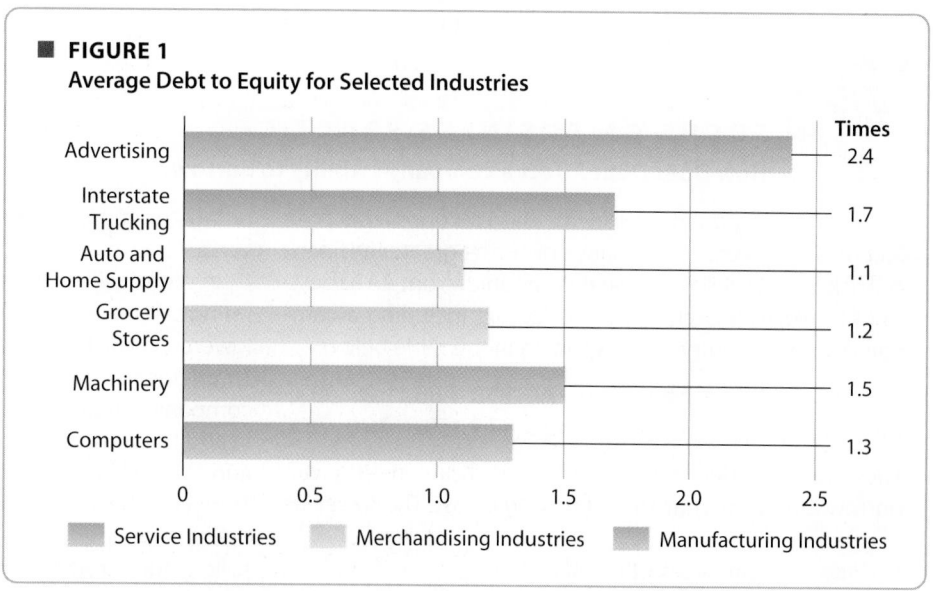

■ **FIGURE 1**
Average Debt to Equity for Selected Industries

Industry	Times
Advertising	2.4
Interstate Trucking	1.7
Auto and Home Supply	1.1
Grocery Stores	1.2
Machinery	1.5
Computers	1.3

Service Industries   Merchandising Industries   Manufacturing Industries

Source: Data from Dun & Bradstreet, *Industry Norms and Key Business Ratios, 2004–2005.*

as liabilities on its balance sheet. This practice is called **off-balance-sheet financing** and, as used by McDonald's, is entirely legal. The leases are, however, long-term commitments of cash payments and so have the effect of long-term liabilities. McDonald's total commitment for its leases, which are generally for 20 years, is $11,333.7 million.[2] If we add the discounted present value of these lease obligations to McDonald's balance sheet debt, it brings the total debt to about $25,000 million.

Financial leverage—using long-term debt to fund investments or operations that increase return on equity—is advantageous as long as a company is able to make timely interest payments and repay the debt at maturity. Because failure to do so can force a company into bankruptcy, companies must assess the financial risk involved. A common measure of how much risk a company undertakes by assuming long-term debt is the **interest coverage ratio**. It measures the degree of protection a company has from default on interest payments.

McDonald's 2005 annual report shows that the company had income before taxes of $3,701.6 million and interest expense of $356.1 million. Using these figures, we can compute McDonald's interest coverage ratio as follows:

$$\text{Interest Coverage Ratio} = \frac{\text{Income Before Income Taxes} + \text{Interest Expense}}{\text{Interest Expense}}$$

$$= \frac{\$3,701.6 + \$356.1}{\$356.1}$$

$$= \frac{\$4,057.7}{\$356.1}$$

$$= 11.4 \text{ times}$$

McDonald's strong interest coverage ratio of 11.4 times shows that it was in no danger of being unable to make interest payments. However, in computing this ratio, management will add the company's off-balance-sheet rent expense of $1,362.0 to its interest expense. This procedure decreases the coverage ratio to about 3.2 times. Although still adequate to cover interest payments, the adjusted coverage ratio is far less robust, which demonstrates the significant effect that off-balance-sheet financing for leases can have on a company's financial situation.

FOCUS ON BUSINESS PRACTICE

How Does Debt Affect a Company's Ability to Borrow?

Credit ratings by agencies like Standard & Poor's reflect the fact that the greater a company's debt, the greater its financial risk. Standard & Poor's rates companies from AAA (best) to CCC (worst) based on various factors, including a company's debt to equity ratio, as shown in the table below.

Rating	AAA	AA	A	BBB	BB	B	CCC
Debt/Equity Ratio*	4.5	34.1	42.9	47.9	59.8	76.0	75.7

These ratings affect not only how much a company can borrow, but also what the interest will cost. The lower its rating, the more a company must pay in interest, and vice versa.

In the heavily debt-laden auto industry, a change in debt rating can mean millions of dollars. For instance, when S & P lowered **General Motors'** and **Ford Motor Company's** credit ratings to "junk status"—BB—it meant that these companies might have to pay 1 or more percentage points in additional interest, which on a debt of $291 billion for GM and $161 billion for Ford would amount to about $2 billion.[3] Thus, companies must pay close attention to their financial risk as expressed by the debt to equity ratio. **McDonald's** solid credit is reflected in an A rating.

*Averages of companies with similar ratings.

Types of Long-Term Debt

To structure long-term financing to the best advantage of their companies, managers must know the characteristics of the various types of long-term debt. The most common are bonds payable, notes payable, mortgages payable, long-term leases, pension liabilities, other postretirement benefits, and deferred income taxes.

Bonds Payable   Long-term bonds are the most common type of long-term debt. They can have many different characteristics, including the amount of interest, whether the company can elect to repay them before their maturity date, and whether they can be converted to common stock. We cover bonds in detail in later sections of this chapter.

Notes Payable   Long-term notes payable, those that come due in more than one year, are also very common. They differ from bonds mainly in the way the contract with the creditor is structured. A long-term note is a promissory note that represents a loan from a bank or other creditor, whereas a bond is a more complex financial instrument that usually involves debt to many creditors. Analysts often do not distinguish between long-term notes and bonds because they have similar effects on the financial statements. Recently, in one of the largest debt offerings in history, **Deutsche Telekom International Finance** raised $14.6 billion by issuing a series of long-term notes denominated in dollars, Euros, pounds, and yen. Some notes were due in 2005, 2010, and 2030.[4]

Mortgages Payable   A **mortgage** is a long-term debt secured by real property. It is usually paid in equal monthly installments. Each monthly payment includes interest on the debt and a reduction in the debt. Table 1 shows the first three monthly payments on a $50,000, 12 percent mortgage. The mortgage was obtained on June 1, and the monthly payments are $800. The entry to record the July 1 payment would be as follows:

A = L + OE	July 1	Mortgage Payable	300	
−800 −300 −500		Mortgage Interest Expense	500	
		Cash		800
		Made monthly mortgage payment		

TABLE 1.   Monthly Payment Schedule on a $50,000, 12 Percent Mortgage

Payment Date	A Unpaid Balance at Beginning of Period	B Monthly Payment	C Interest for 1 Month at 1% on Unpaid Balance* ($1\% \times A$)	D Reduction in Debt (B − C)	E Unpaid Balance at End of Period (A − D)
June 1					$50,000
July 1	$50,000	$800	$500	$300	49,700
Aug. 1	49,700	800	497	303	49,397
Sept. 1	49,397	800	494	306	49,091

*Rounded to the nearest dollar.

Notice from the entry and from Table 1 that the July 1 payment represents interest expense of $500 ($50,000 × .12 × 1/12) and a reduction in the debt of $300 ($800 − $500). Therefore, the July payment reduces the unpaid balance to $49,700. August's interest expense is slightly less than July's because of the decrease in the debt.

Long-Term Leases   A company can obtain an operating asset in three ways:

1. By borrowing money and buying the asset

2. By renting the asset on a short-term lease

3. By obtaining the asset on a long-term lease

The first two methods do not create accounting problems. When a company uses the first method, it records the asset and liability at the amount paid, and the asset is subject to periodic depreciation.

When a company uses the second method, the lease is short in relation to the useful life of the asset, and the risks of ownership remain with the lessor. This type of agreement is called an **operating lease**. Payments on operating leases are properly treated as rent expense.

The third method is one of the fastest-growing ways of financing plant assets in the United States today. A long-term lease on a plant asset has several advantages. It requires no immediate cash payment, the rental payment is deducted in full for tax purposes, and it costs less than a short-term lease. Acquiring the use of plant assets under long-term leases does create several accounting challenges, however.

Long-term leases may be carefully structured, as they are by **McDonald's**, so that they can be accounted for as operating leases. Accounting standards require, however, that a long-term lease be treated as a **capital lease** when it meets the following conditions:

▸ It cannot be canceled.

▸ Its duration is about the same as the useful life of the asset.

▸ It stipulates that the lessee has the option to buy the asset at a nominal price at the end of the lease.

A capital lease is thus more like a purchase or sale on installment than a rental. The lessee in a capital lease should record an asset, depreciation on the asset, and a long-term liability equal to the present value of the total lease payments during the lease term.[5] Much like a mortgage payment, each lease payment consists partly of interest expense and partly of repayment of debt.

Suppose, for example, that Glenellen Manufacturing Company enters into a long-term lease for a machine. The lease terms call for an annual payment of $4,000 for six years, which approximates the useful life of the machine. At the end of the lease period, the title to the machine passes to Glenellen. This lease is clearly a capital lease and should be recorded as an asset and a liability.

Present value techniques can be used to place a value on the asset and on the corresponding liability in a capital lease. Suppose Glenellen's interest cost on the unpaid part of its obligation is 16 percent. Using the factor for 16 percent and six periods in Table 4 in the appendix on future value and present values tables, we can compute the present value of the lease payments as follows:

Periodic Payment × Factor = Present Value

$4,000 × 3.685 = $14,740

The entry to record the lease is as follows:

Study Note

Under a capital lease, the lessee should record depreciation, using any allowable method.

Study Note

A capital lease is in substance an installment purchase, and the leased asset and related liability must be recognized at their present value.

A   =   L   + OE
+ 14,740 + 14,740

Capital Lease Equipment	14,740	
Capital Lease Obligations		14,740
To record capital lease on machinery		

Capital Lease Equipment is classified as a long-term asset. Capital Lease Obligations is classified as a long-term liability.

Each year, Glenellen must record depreciation on the leased asset. Using straight-line depreciation, a six-year life, and no residual value, the following entry would record the depreciation:

A   = L +   OE
−2,457   −2,457

Depreciation Expense–Capital Lease Equipment	2,457	
Accumulated Depreciation–Capital Lease Equipment		2,457
To record depreciation expense on capital lease		

The interest expense for each year is computed by multiplying the interest rate (16 percent) by the amount of the remaining lease obligation. Table 2 shows these calculations. Using the data in the table, the first lease payment would be recorded as follows:

A   =   L   +   OE
−4,000   −1,642   −2,358

Interest Expense (Column B)	2,358	
Capital Lease Obligations (Column C)	1,642	
Cash (Column A)		4,000
Made payment on capital lease		

This example suggests why companies are motivated to engage in off-balance-sheet financing for leases. By structuring long-term leases so that they can be accounted for as operating leases, companies avoid recording them on the balance sheet as long-term assets and liabilities. This practice, which, as

TABLE 2. Payment Schedule on a 16 Percent Capital Lease

Year	A Lease Payment	B Interest (16%) on Unpaid Obligation* (D × 16%)	C Reduction of Lease Obligation (A − B)	D Balance of Lease Obligation (D − C)
Beginning				$14,740
1	$ 4,000	$2,358	$ 1,642	13,098
2	4,000	2,096	1,904	11,194
3	4,000	1,791	2,209	8,985
4	4,000	1,438	2,562	6,423
5	4,000	1,028	2,972	3,451
6	4,000	549†	3,451	—
	$24,000	$9,260	$14,740	

*Rounded to the nearest dollar.

†The last year's interest equals $549 ($4,000 − $3,451); it does not exactly equal $552 ($3,451 × $\frac{16}{100}$ × 1) because of the cumulative effect of rounding.

we have noted, is legal and which **McDonald's** uses with skill, not only improves the debt to equity ratio by showing less debt on the balance sheet; it also improves the return on assets by reducing the total assets.

Pension Liabilities   Most employees of medium-sized and large companies are covered by a **pension plan**, a contract that requires a company to pay benefits to its employees after they retire. Some companies pay the full cost of the pension plan, but in many companies, employees share the cost by contributing part of their salaries or wages. The contributions from employer and employees are usually paid into a **pension fund**, which is invested on behalf of the employees and from which benefits are paid to retirees. Pension benefits typically consist of monthly payments to retired employees and other payments upon disability or death.

Employers whose pension plans do not have sufficient assets to cover the present value of their pension obligations must record the amount of the shortfall as a liability on their balance sheets. If a pension plan has sufficient assets to cover its obligations, no balance sheet reporting is required or permitted.

There are two kinds of pension plans:

▶ *Defined contribution plan.* Under a defined contribution plan, the employer makes a fixed annual contribution, usually a percentage of the employee's gross pay; the amount of the contribution is specified in an agreement between the company and the employees. Retirement payments vary depending on how much the employee's retirement account earns. Employees usually control their own investment accounts, can make additional contributions of their own, and can transfer the funds if they leave the company. Examples of defined contribution plans include 401(k) plans, profit-sharing plans, and employee stock ownership plans (ESOPs).

▶ *Defined benefit plan.* Under a defined benefit plan, the employer contributes an amount annually required to fund estimated future pension liability arising from employment in the current year. The exact amount of the liability will not be known until the retirement and death of the current employees. Although the amount of future benefits is fixed, the annual contributions vary depending on assumptions about how much the pension fund will earn.

Annual pension expense under a defined contribution plan is simple and predictable. Pension expense equals the fixed amount of the annual contribution. In contrast, annual expense under a defined benefit plan is one of the most complex topics in accounting. The intricacies are reserved for advanced courses, but in concept, the procedure is simple. Computation of the annual expense takes into account the estimation of many factors, such as the average remaining service life of active employees, the long-run return on pension plan assets, and future salary increases.

Because pension expense under a defined benefit plan is not predictable and can vary from year to year, many companies are adopting the more predictable defined contribution plans. For example, in its 2005 annual report, **McDonald's** states that its plan "includes a 401(k) feature, an ESOP feature and a discretionary employer profit sharing match."

Other Postretirement Benefits   Many companies provide retired employees not only with pensions, but also with health care and other benefits. In the past, these **other postretirement benefits** were accounted for on a cash basis—that is, they were expensed when the benefits were paid, after an employee had retired. More recent accounting standards hold that employees earn these benefits during their employment and that, in accordance with the

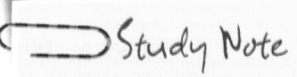

Study Note

Companies prefer defined contribution plans because the employees assume the risk that their pension assets will earn a sufficient return to meet their retirement needs.

Study Note

Accounting for a defined benefit plan is far more complex than accounting for a defined contribution plan. Fortunately, accountants can rely on the calculations of professional actuaries, whose expertise includes the mathematics of pension plans.

Postretirement benefits, such as health care, are a type of long-term debt for the company that provides them. Recent accounting standards hold that employees earn these benefits during their employment and that the benefits should therefore be estimated and accrued while the employee is working.

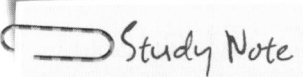

Other postretirement benefits should be expensed as the employee earns them, not when they are paid after the employee retires. This practice conforms to the matching rule.

matching rule, they should be estimated and accrued during the time the employee is working.[6]

The estimates must take into account assumptions about retirement age, mortality, and, most significantly, future trends in health care benefits. Like pension benefits, such future benefits should be discounted to the current period. A field test conducted by the Financial Executives Research Foundation determined that the change to accrual accounting increased postretirement benefits by two to seven times the amount recognized on a cash basis. **General Motors**, the nation's largest private purchaser of health care, recently reported that its future health care liabilities for retirees exceeded $60 billion.[7]

Deferred Income Taxes Among the long-term liabilities on the balance sheets of many companies, including **McDonald's**, is account called **Deferred Income Taxes**. Deferred income taxes are the result of using different accounting methods to calculate income taxes on the income statement and income tax liability on the income tax return. For instance, companies often use straight-line depreciation for financial reporting and an accelerated method to calculate income tax liability. Because straight-line depreciation is less than accelerated depreciation in the early years of an asset's life, the presumption is that the income taxes will eventually have to be paid. Thus, the difference is listed as a long-term liability, deferred income taxes. Because companies try to manage their affairs to minimize income taxes paid, deferred income taxes can become quite large. In McDonald's case, as shown in the company's Financial Highlights, they amounted to almost $1 billion in 2005. We cover deferred income taxes in greater detail in a later chapter.

S T O P • R E V I E W • A P P L Y

1-1. What are the advantages and disadvantages of issuing long-term debt?

1-2. Why is interest coverage important in evaluating long-term debt?

1-3. What are the two components of a uniform monthly mortgage payment?

1-4. What is a capital lease? Why should an accountant record both an asset and a liability in connection with this type of lease?

1-5. What is a pension plan? What is a pension fund?

1-6. What is the difference between a defined contribution plan and a defined benefit plan?

1-7. What are other postretirement benefits, and how is the matching rule applied to them?

Suggested answers to all Stop, Review, and Apply questions are available at http://college.hmco.com/accounting/needles/poa/10e/student_home.html.

Identification of Long-Term Debt   Each type of long-term liability below is closely related to one of the statements in the list that follows. Write the number of the liability next to the statement to which it applies.

1. Bonds payable   **5.** Pension liabilities

2. Long-term notes payable   **6.** Other postretirement benefits

3. Mortgage payable   **7.** Deferred income taxes

4. Long-term lease

____ a. Cost of health care after employees' retirement

____ b. The most common type of long-term debt

____ c. The result of differences between accounting income and taxable income

____ d. Debt that is secured by real estate

____ e. Promissory note that is due in more than one year

____ f. May be based on a percentage of employees' wages or on future benefits

____ g. Can be similar in form to an installment purchase

SOLUTION

a. 6	e. 2
b. 1	f. 5
c. 7	g. 4
d. 3	

The Nature of Bonds

LO2   Describe the features of a bond issue and the major characteristics of bonds.

A bond is a security, usually long term, representing money that a corporation borrows from the investing public. (The federal, state, and local governments also issue bonds to raise money, as do foreign countries.) A bond entails a promise to repay the amount borrowed, called the *principal*, on a specified date and to pay interest at a specified rate at specified times—usually semiannually. In contrast to stockholders, who are the owners of a corporation, bondholders are a corporation's creditors.

When a public corporation decides to issue bonds, it must submit the appropriate legal documents to the Securities and Exchange Commission for

FOCUS ON BUSINESS PRACTICE
Check Out Those Bond Prices!

The price of many bonds can be found daily in business publications like *The Wall Street Journal*. For instance, shown below are quotations for the bonds of Ford Motor Credit Company and General Electric (GE) Capital Corporation, two very active corporate bond traders:[8]

	Face Rate	Maturity	Last Price	Last Yield
Ford Motor Credit	7.0	10/1/13	97.375	7.427
GE Capital	5.875	2/15/12	107.364	4.579

GE Capital is one of the strongest companies financially, while Ford Motor Credit is one of the weaker ones. Note that the face rate on GE Capital's bond is lower than the face rate on Ford Motor Credit's (5.875 percent versus 7.0 percent). In addition, the last price on Ford Motor Credit's bond is less than 100 (97.375); thus, the market rate of interest on the bond (last yield of 7.427 percent) is greater than the face rate. This means that investors are not willing to settle for the 7.0 percent face rate and are demanding a higher rate by paying less than 100. Conversely, GE Capital's bond sells for more than 100 (107.364), which means that investors are willing to accept a market rate (4.579 percent) that is even less than the bond's face rate. The prices of bonds vary daily as companies' fortunes and interest rates change.

permission to borrow the funds. The SEC reviews the corporation's financial health and the specific terms of the **bond indenture**, which is a contract that defines the rights, privileges, and limitations of the bondholders. The bond indenture generally describes such things as the maturity date of the bonds, interest payment dates, and the interest rate. It may also cover repayment plans and restrictions. Once the bond issue is approved, the corporation has a limited time in which to issue the authorized bonds. As evidence of its debt to the bondholders, the corporation provides each of them with a **bond certificate**.

Bond Issue: Prices and Interest Rates

A **bond issue** is the total value of bonds issued at one time. For example, a $1,000,000 bond issue could consist of a thousand $1,000 bonds. The prices of bonds are stated in terms of a percentage of the face value, or principal, of the bonds. A bond issue quoted at 103 1/2 means that a $1,000 bond costs $1,035 ($1,000 × 1.035). When a bond sells at exactly 100, it is said to sell at face (or par) value. When it sells below 100, it is said to sell at a discount; above 100, at a premium. For instance, a $1,000 bond quoted at 87.62 would be selling at a discount and would cost the buyer $876.20.

Face Interest Rate and Market Interest Rate   Two interest rates relevant to bond prices are the face interest rate and market interest rate:

▶ The **face interest rate** is the fixed rate of interest paid to bondholders based on the face value of the bonds. The rate and amount are fixed over the life of the bond. To allow time to file with the SEC, publicize the bond issue, and print the bond certificates, a company must decide in advance what the face interest rate will be. Most companies try to set the face interest rate as close as possible to the market interest rate.

▶ The **market interest rate** is the rate of interest paid in the market on bonds of similar risk.* It is also called the *effective interest rate*. The market interest

> ### Study Note
> When bonds with an interest rate different from the market rate are issued, they sell at a discount or premium. The discount or premium acts as an equalizing factor.

> ### Study Note
> A bond sells at face value when the face interest rate of the bond is identical to the market interest rate for similar bonds on the date of issue.

---

*At the time this chapter was written, the market interest rates on corporate bonds were volatile. Therefore, we use a variety of interest rates in our examples.

rate fluctuates daily. Because a company has no control over it, the market interest rate often differs from the face interest rate on the issue date.

Discounts and Premiums   If the market interest rate fluctuates from the face interest rate before the issue date, the issue price of bonds will not equal their face value. This fluctuation in market interest rate causes the bonds to sell at either a discount or premium:

▶ A **discount** equals the excess of the face value over the issue price. The issue price will be less than the face value when the market interest rate is higher than the face interest rate.

▶ A **premium** equals the excess of the issue price over the face value. The issue price will be more than the face value when the market interest rate is lower than the face interest rate.

Discounts or premiums are contra-accounts that are subtracted from or added to bonds payable on the balance sheet.

Characteristics of Bonds

A bond indenture can be written to fit an organization's financing needs. As a result, the bonds issued in today's financial markets have many different features. We describe several of the more important features in the following paragraphs.

Study Note

Do not confuse the terms *indenture* and *debenture*. They sound alike, but an indenture is a bond contract, whereas a debenture is an unsecured bond. A debenture bond of a stable company actually might be a less risky investment than a secured bond of an unstable company.

Unsecured and Secured Bonds   Bonds can be either unsecured or secured. **Unsecured bonds** (also called *debenture bonds*) are issued on the basis of a corporation's general credit. **Secured bonds** carry a pledge of certain corporate assets as a guarantee of repayment. A pledged asset may be a specific asset, such as a truck, or a general category of asset, such as property, plant, or equipment.

Term and Serial Bonds   When all the bonds of an issue mature at the same time, they are called **term bonds**. For instance, a company may decide to issue $1,000,000 worth of bonds, all due 20 years from the date of issue.

When the bonds of an issue mature on different dates, they are called **serial bonds**. For example, suppose a $1,000,000 bond issue calls for paying $200,000 of the principal every five years. This arrangement means that after the first $200,000 payment is made, $800,000 of the bonds would remain outstanding for the next five years, $600,000 for the next five years, and so on. A company may issue serial bonds to ease the task of retiring its debt—that is, paying off what it owes on the bonds.

Study Note

An advantage of issuing serial bonds is that the organization retires the bonds over a period of years, rather than all at once.

Callable and Convertible Bonds   When bonds are callable and convertible, a company may be able to retire them before their maturity dates. When a company does retire a bond issue before its maturity date, it is called **early extinguishment of debt**. Doing so can be to a company's advantage.

Callable bonds give the issuer the right to buy back and retire the bonds before maturity at a specified **call price**, which is usually above face value. Callable bonds give a company flexibility in financing its operations. For example, if bond interest rates drop, the company can call the bonds and reissue debt at a lower interest rate. A company might also call its bonds if it has earned enough to pay off the debt, if the reason for having the debt no longer exists, or if it wants to restructure its debt to equity ratio. The bond indenture states the time period and the prices at which the bonds can be redeemed.

FOCUS ON BUSINESS PRACTICE
Some Companies Are Saying "Yes-Yes" to "No-Nos."

Some companies, especially those in the technology sector, have found it hard to resist issuing a new type of convertible bond. These bonds, which are called "zero coupon bonds," carry no interest and can be converted to common stock if the issuing company's stock price reaches a certain level. This is seemingly a great deal for the issuer. The issuer pays *no* interest, and *no* repayment is necessary if the bonds are converted to stock—hence, the term "No-Nos."

Convertible bond offerings have shot up, thanks to "No-Nos." For instance, **Sony Corporation**, the large Japanese electronics company, raised $2.29 billion by issuing "No-Nos" that offer no interest and mature in five years. If the company's stock goes up 47.5 percent, a bondholder will be better off by converting the bonds to stock rather than accepting repayment.[9]

What's the catch to these bonds? The catch is that if a company's stock does not go up, they are "debt bombs" for the issuers. Among the high flyers that have suffered as a result of saying "yes-yes" to "No-Nos" are **Tyco**, **Cox Communications**, and **Comcast**, which narrowly avoided bankruptcy when their stock prices dropped.

Convertible bonds allow the bondholder to exchange a bond for a specified number of shares of common stock. The face value of a convertible bond when issued is greater than the market value of the shares to which it can be converted. However, if the market price of the common stock rises above a certain level, the value of the bond rises in relation to the value of the common stock. Even if the stock price does not rise, the investor still holds the bond and receives both the periodic interest payments and the face value at the maturity date.

One advantage of issuing convertible bonds is that the interest rate is usually lower because investors are willing to give up some current interest in the hope that the value of the stock will increase and the value of the bonds will therefore also increase. In addition, if the bonds are both callable and convertible and the market value of the stock rises to a level at which the bond is worth more than face value, management can avoid repaying the bonds by calling them for redemption, thereby forcing the bondholders to convert their bonds into common stock. The bondholders will agree to convert because no gain or loss results from the transaction.

Registered and Coupon Bonds

Registered bonds are issued in the names of the bondholders. The issuing organization keeps a record of the bondholders' names and addresses and pays them interest by check on the interest payment date. Most bonds today are registered.

Coupon bonds are not registered with the organization. Instead, they bear coupons stating the amount of interest due and the payment date. The bondholder removes the coupons from the bonds on the interest payment dates and presents them at a bank for collection.

STOP • REVIEW • APPLY

2-1. What are a bond issue, a bond certificate, and a bond indenture? What information is in a bond indenture?

2-2. Napier Corporation sold a $500,000 bond issue of 5 percent, $1,000 bonds. What would the proceeds from the sale be if the bonds were issued at 95, at 100, and at 102?

2-3. If you were about to buy bonds on which the face interest rate was less than the market interest rate, would you expect to pay more or less than par value for the bonds?

2-4. What are the essential differences between (a) a discount and premium, (b) secured and unsecured (debenture) bonds, (c) term and serial bonds, (d) callable and convertible bonds, and (e) registered and coupon bonds?

Accounting for the Issuance of Bonds

LO3 Record bonds issued at face value and at a discount or premium.

When the board of directors of a public corporation decides to issue bonds, the company must submit the appropriate legal documents to the Securities and Exchange Commission for authorization to borrow the funds. It is not necessary to make a journal entry to record the authorization of a bond issue. However, most companies disclose the authorization in the notes to their financial statements. The note lists the number and value of bonds authorized, the interest rate, the interest payment dates, and the life of the bonds. In sections that follow, we show how to record bonds issued at face value, at a discount, and at a premium.

Bonds Issued at Face Value

Suppose Katakis Corporation issues $100,000 of 9 percent, five-year bonds on January 1, 2007, and sells them on the same date for their face value. The bond indenture states that interest is to be paid on January 1 and July 1 of each year. The entry to record the bond issue is as follows:

A	=	L	+ OE
+100,000		+100,000	

2007			
Jan. 1	Cash	100,000	
	Bonds Payable		100,000
	Sold $100,000 of 9%, 5-year bonds at face value		

Once a corporation issues bonds, it must pay interest to the bondholders over the life of the bonds, usually semiannually, and the principal of the bonds at maturity. In this example, interest is paid on January 1 and July 1 of each year. Thus, Katakis would owe the bondholders $4,500 interest on July 1, 2007:

$$\text{Interest} = \text{Principal} \times \text{Rate} \times \text{Time}$$
$$= \$100,000 \times \tfrac{9}{100} \times 6/12 \text{ year}$$
$$= \$4,500$$

Katakis would record the interest paid to the bondholders on each semiannual interest payment date (January 1 or July 1) as follows:

Study Note

When calculating semiannual interest, do not use the annual rate (9 percent in this case). Rather, use half the annual rate.

A*	= L +	OE
−4,500		−4,500

*Assumes cash paid.

Bond Interest Expense		4,500	
Cash (or Interest Payable)			4,500
Paid (or accrued) semiannual interest to bondholders of 9%, 5-year bonds			

In 1993, to take advantage of historically low interest rates on long-term debt, The Walt Disney Company issued $150 million of 100-year bonds at a yield of only 7.5 percent. At the time, some analysts wondered if even Mickey Mouse could survive 100 years. However, Mickey, who first appeared in 1928 in the animated short film *Steamboat Willie*, goes on. In 2003, he celebrated his 75th birthday.

Bonds Issued at a Discount

Suppose Katakis Corporation issues $100,000 of 9 percent, five-year bonds at 96.149 on January 1, 2007, when the market interest rate is 10 percent. In this case, the bonds are being issued at a discount because the market interest rate exceeds the face interest rate. The following entry records the issuance of the bonds at a discount:

A	=	L	+ OE
+96,149		−3,851	
		+100,000	

2007			
Jan. 1	Cash	96,149	
	Unamortized Bond Discount	3,851	
	Bonds Payable		100,000
	Sold $100,000 of 9%, 5-year		
	bonds at 96.149		

Face amount of bonds	$100,000	
Less purchase price of bonds		
($100,000 × .96149)	96,149	
Unamortized bond discount	$ 3,851	

FOCUS ON BUSINESS PRACTICE
100-Year Bonds Are Not for Everyone.

In 1993, interest rates on long-term debt were at historically low levels, which induced some companies to attempt to lock in those low costs for long periods. One of the most aggressive companies in that regard was **The Walt Disney Company**, which issued $150 million of 100-year bonds at a yield of only 7.5 percent. It was the first time since 1954 that 100-year bonds had been issued. Among the others that followed Walt Disney's lead by issuing 100-year bonds were the **Coca-Cola Company**, **Columbia HCA Healthcare**, **Bell South**, **IBM**, and even the People's Republic of China. Some analysts wondered if even Mickey Mouse could survive 100 years. Investors who purchase such bonds take a financial risk because if interest rates rise, which is always likely, the market value of the bonds will decrease.[10]

In this entry, Cash is debited for the amount received ($96,149), Bonds Payable is credited for the face amount ($100,000) of the bond liability, and the difference ($3,851) is debited to Unamortized Bond Discount. If a balance sheet is prepared right after the bonds are issued at a discount, the liability for bonds payable is reported as follows:

Long-term liabilities
    9% bonds payable, due 1/1/2012 $100,000
    Less unamortized bond discount   3,851 $96,149

Unamortized Bond Discount is a contra-liability account. Its balance is deducted from the face amount of the bonds to arrive at the carrying value, or present value, of the bonds. The bond discount is described as unamortized because it will be amortized (written off) over the life of the bonds.

Bonds Issued at a Premium

When bonds have a face interest rate above the market rate for similar investments, they are issued at a price above the face value, or at a premium. For example, suppose Katakis Corporation issues $100,000 of 9 percent, five-year bonds for $104,100 on January 1, 2007, when the market interest rate is 8 percent. This means that investors will purchase the bonds at 104.1 percent of their face value. The issuance would be recorded as follows:

A	=	L	+ OE
+104,100		+4,100	
		+100,000	

2007				
Jan. 1	Cash		104,100	
	Unamortized Bond Premium			4,100
	Bonds Payable			100,000
	Sold $100,000 of 9%, 5-year bonds			
	at 104.1 ($100,000 × 1.041)			

Right after this entry is made, bonds payable would be presented on the balance sheet as follows:

Long-term liabilities
    9% bonds payable, due 1/1/2012 $100,000
    Unamortized bond premium   4,100 $104,100

The carrying value of the bonds payable is $104,100, which equals the face value of the bonds plus the unamortized bond premium. The cash received from the bond issue is also $104,100. This means that the purchasers were willing to pay a premium of $4,100 to buy these bonds because their face interest rate was higher than the market interest rate.

Bond Issue Costs

The costs of issuing bonds can amount to as much as 5 percent of a bond issue. These costs often include the fees of underwriters, whom corporations hire to take care of the details of marketing a bond issue. Because the issue costs benefit the whole life of a bond issue, it makes sense to spread them over that period. It is generally accepted practice to establish a separate account for these costs and to amortize them over the life of the bonds.

    Because issue costs decrease the amount of money a company receives from a bond issue, they have the effect of raising the discount or lowering the premium on the issue. Thus, bond issue costs can be spread over the life of the bonds through the amortization of a discount or premium. This method simplifies recordkeeping. In the rest of our discussion, we assume that all bond issue costs increase the discounts or decrease the premiums on bond issues.

STOP • REVIEW • APPLY

3-1. When bonds are issued at a discount, will the market interest rate be more or less than the face interest rate?

3-2. When bonds are issued at a premium, how is the bond liability shown on the balance sheet?

3-3. Why do bond issue costs increase the discount on a bond issue?

Using Present Value to Value a Bond

LO4 Use present values to determine the value of bonds.

A bond's value is based on the present value of two components of cash flow: a series of fixed interest payments, and a single payment at maturity. The amount of interest a bond pays is fixed over its life. However, the market interest rate varies from day to day. Thus, the amount investors are willing to pay for a bond varies as well.

Case 1: Market Rate Above Face Rate

Suppose a bond has a face value of $10,000 and pays fixed interest of $450 every six months (a 9 percent annual rate). The bond is due in five years. If the market interest rate today is 12 percent, what is the present value of the bond?

To answer this question, we use Table 4 in the appendix on future value and present value tables to calculate the present value of the periodic interest payments of $450, and we use Table 3 in the same appendix to calculate the present value of the single payment of $10,000 at maturity. Because interest payments are made every six months, the compounding period is half a year. Thus, we have to convert the annual rate to a semiannual rate of 6 percent (12 percent divided by two six-month periods per year) and use ten periods (five years multiplied by two six-month periods per year). With this information, we can compute the present value of the bond as follows:

Present value of 10 periodic payments at 6%:	
$450 × 7.360 (from Table 4 in the appendix)	$3,312.00
Present value of a single payment at the end of	
10 periods at 6%: $10,000 × .558 (from	
Table 3 in the appendix):	5,580.00
Present value of $10,000 bond	$8,892.00

The market interest rate has increased so much since the bond was issued—from 9 percent to 12 percent—that the value of the bond today is only $8,892.00. That amount is all investors would be willing to pay at this time for a bond that provides income of $450 every six months and a return of the $10,000 principal in five years.

Case 2: Market Rate Below Face Rate

As Figure 2 shows, if the market interest rate on the bond described above falls below the face interest rate, say to 8 percent (4 percent semiannually), the present value of the bond will be greater than the face value of $10,000:

Present value of 10 periodic payments at 4%:		
$450 × 8.111 (from Table 4 in the appendix)		$ 3,649.95
Present value of a single payment at the end of		
10 periods at 4%: $10,000 × .676 (from		
Table 3 in the appendix)		6,760.00
Present value of $10,000 bond		$10,409.95

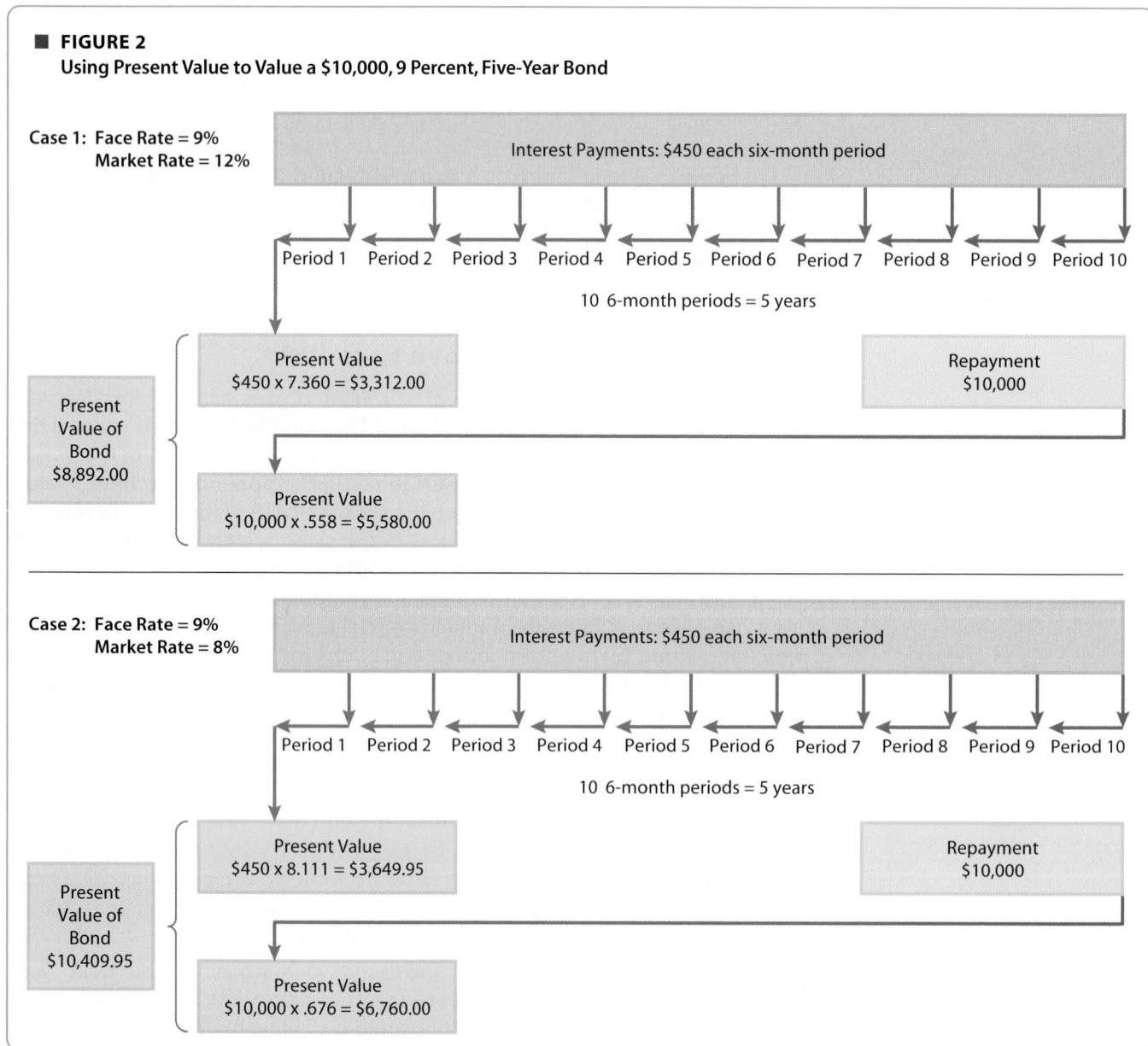

■ **FIGURE 2**
Using Present Value to Value a $10,000, 9 Percent, Five-Year Bond

Case 1: Face Rate = 9%
Market Rate = 12%

Interest Payments: $450 each six-month period

Period 1 Period 2 Period 3 Period 4 Period 5 Period 6 Period 7 Period 8 Period 9 Period 10

10 6-month periods = 5 years

Present Value
$450 x 7.360 = $3,312.00

Repayment
$10,000

Present Value of Bond $8,892.00

Present Value
$10,000 x .558 = $5,580.00

Case 2: Face Rate = 9%
Market Rate = 8%

Interest Payments: $450 each six-month period

Period 1 Period 2 Period 3 Period 4 Period 5 Period 6 Period 7 Period 8 Period 9 Period 10

10 6-month periods = 5 years

Present Value
$450 x 8.111 = $3,649.95

Repayment
$10,000

Present Value of Bond $10,409.95

Present Value
$10,000 x .676 = $6,760.00

4-1. When considering the value of bonds, what are the two future cash flows that must be considered?

4-2. How does present value apply to valuing the two cash flows referred to in the previous question?

Amortization of Bond Discounts and Premiums

LO5 Amortize bond discounts and bond premiums using the straight-line and effective interest methods.

> **Study Note**
>
> Whether a bond is sold at a discount or a premium, its carrying value will equal its face value on the maturity date.

A bond discount or premium represents the amount by which the total interest cost is higher or lower than the total interest payments. To record interest expense properly and ensure that the carrying value of bonds payable at maturity equals face value, it is necessary to systematically reduce the bond discount or premium—that is, to amortize them—over the life of the bonds. This is accomplished by using either the straight-line method or the effective interest method.

Amortizing a Bond Discount

In one of our earlier examples, Katakis Corporation issued $100,000 of five-year bonds at a time when the market interest rate of 10 percent exceeded the face interest rate of 9 percent. The bonds sold for $96,149, resulting in an unamortized bond discount of $3,851.

Because a bond discount affects interest expense in each year of a bond issue, the bond discount should be amortized over the life of the bond issue. In this way, the unamortized bond discount will decrease gradually over time, and the carrying value of the bond issue (face value less unamortized discount) will gradually increase. By the maturity date, the carrying value of the bond issue will equal its face value, and the unamortized bond discount will be zero.

In the following sections, we calculate Katakis Corporation's total interest cost and amortize its bond discount using the straight-line and the effective interest methods.

> **Study Note**
>
> A bond discount is a component of interest cost because it represents the amount in excess of the issue price that a corporation must pay on the maturity date.

Calculating Total Interest Cost   When a corporation issues bonds at a discount, the market (or effective) interest rate that it pays is greater than the face interest rate on the bonds. The reason is that the interest cost is the stated interest payments *plus* the amount of the bond discount. That is, although the company does not receive the full face value of the bonds on issue, it still must pay back the full face value at maturity. The difference between the issue price and the face value must be added to the total interest payments to arrive at the actual interest expense.

The full cost to Katakis Corporation of issuing its bonds at a discount is as follows:

Cash to be paid to bondholders

Face value at maturity	$100,000
Interest payments ($100,000 × .09 × 5 years)	45,000
Total cash paid to bondholders	$145,000
Less cash received from bondholders	96,149
Total interest cost	$ 48,851

Or, alternatively:

Interest payments ($100,000 × .09 × 5 years)	$ 45,000
Bond discount	3,851
Total interest cost	$ 48,851

The total interest cost of $48,851 is made up of $45,000 in interest payments and the $3,851 bond discount. Thus, the bond discount increases the interest paid on the bonds from the face interest rate to the market interest rate. The market (or effective) interest rate is the real interest cost of the bond over its life.

To have each year's interest expense reflect the market interest rate, the discount must be allocated over the remaining life of the bonds as an increase in the interest expense each period. Thus, interest expense for each period will exceed the actual payment of interest by the amount of the bond discount amortized over the period. This process of allocation is called *amortization of the bond discount*.

Some bonds do not require periodic interest payments. These bonds, called **zero coupon bonds**, are simply a promise to pay a fixed amount at the maturity date. They are issued at a large discount because the only interest that the buyer earns or the issuer pays is the discount. For example, a five-year, $100,000 zero coupon bond issued when the market rate is 14 percent, compounded semiannually, would sell for only $50,800. That amount is the present value of a single payment of $100,000 at the end of five years. The discount of $49,200 ($100,000 − $50,800) is the total interest cost, which is amortized over the life of the bond.

 **Study Note**

The discount on a zero coupon bond represents the interest that will be paid (in its entirety) on the maturity date.

Straight-Line Method   The **straight-line method** equalizes amortization of a bond discount for each interest period. Using our example of Katakis Corporation, the interest payment dates of the bond issue are January 1 and July 1 of each year, and the bonds mature in five years. With the straight-line method, the amount of the bond discount amortized and the interest expense for each semiannual period are calculated in four steps:

1. Total Interest Payments = Interest Payments per Year × Life of Bonds

$$= 2 \times 5 = 10$$

2. Amortization of Bond Discount per Interest Period = $\dfrac{\text{Bond Discount}}{\text{Total Interest Payments}}$

$$= \frac{\$3,851}{10}$$

$$= \$385^*$$

3. Cash Interest Payment = Face Value × Face Interest Rate × Time

$$= \$100,000 \times .09 \times 6/12 = \$4,500$$

---

*Rounded.

4. Interest Expense per Interest Period = Interest Payment + Amortization of Bond Discount

$$= \$4{,}500 + \$385 = \$4{,}885$$

On July 1, 2007, the first semiannual interest date, the entry would be as follows:

A*	=	L	+	OE
−4,500		+385		−4,885

*Assumes cash paid.

2007			
July 1	Bond Interest Expense	4,885	
	Unamortized Bond Discount		385
	Cash (or Interest Payable)		4,500
	Paid (or accrued) semiannual interest to bondholders and amortized the discount on 9%, 5-year bonds		

Notice that the bond interest expense is $4,885, but the amount paid to the bondholders is the $4,500 face interest payment. The difference of $385 is the credit to Unamortized Bond Discount. This lowers the debit balance of Unamortized Bond Discount and raises the carrying value of the bonds payable by $385 each interest period. If no changes occur in the bond issue, this entry will be made every six months for the life of the bonds. When the bond issue matures, the Unamortized Bond Discount account will have a zero balance, and the carrying value of the bonds will be $100,000—exactly equal to the amount due the bondholders.

Although the straight-line method has long been used, it has a certain weakness. When it is used to amortize a discount, the carrying value goes up each period, but the bond interest expense stays the same; thus, the rate of interest falls over time. Conversely, when this method is used to amortize a premium, the rate of interest rises over time. The Accounting Principles Board therefore holds that the straight-line method should be used only when it does not lead to a material difference from the effective interest method.[11] A material difference is one that affects the evaluation of a company.

Effective Interest Method When the **effective interest method** is used to compute the interest and amortization of a bond discount, a constant interest rate is applied to the carrying value of the bonds at the beginning of each interest period. This constant rate is the market rate (i.e., the effective rate) at the time the bonds were issued. The amount amortized each period is the difference between the interest computed by using the market rate and the actual interest paid to bondholders.

As an example, we use the same facts we used earlier—a $100,000 bond issue at 9 percent, with a five-year maturity and interest to be paid twice a year. The market rate at the time the bonds were issued was 10 percent, so the bonds sold for $96,149, a discount of $3,851. Table 3 shows the interest and amortization of the bond discount.

The amounts in the table for period 1 were computed as follows:

Column A: The carrying value of the bonds is their face value less the unamortized bond discount ($100,000 − $3,851 = $96,149).

Column B: The interest expense to be recorded is the effective interest. It is found by multiplying the carrying value of the bonds by the market interest rate for one-half year ($96,149 × .10 × 6/12 = $4,807).

TABLE 3. Interest and Amortization of a Bond Discount: Effective Interest Method

Semiannual Interest Period	A Carrying Value at Beginning of Period	B Semiannual Interest Expense at 10% to Be Recorded* (5% × A)	C Semiannual Interest Payment to Bondholders (4½% × $100,000)	D Amortization of Bond Discount (B − C)	E Unamortized Bond Discount at End of Period (E − D)	F Carrying Value at End of Period (A + D)
0					$3,851	$ 96,149
1	$96,149	$4,807	$4,500	$307	3,544	96,456
2	96,456	4,823	4,500	323	3,221	96,779
3	96,779	4,839	4,500	339	2,882	97,118
4	97,118	4,856	4,500	356	2,526	97,474
5	97,474	4,874	4,500	374	2,152	97,848
6	97,848	4,892	4,500	392	1,760	98,240
7	98,240	4,912	4,500	412	1,348	98,652
8	98,652	4,933	4,500	433	915	99,085
9	99,085	4,954	4,500	454	461	99,539
10	99,539	4,961†	4,500	461	—	100,000

*Rounded to the nearest dollar.

†Last period's interest expense equals $4,961 ($4,500 + $461); it does not equal $4,977 ($99,539 × .05) because of the cumulative effect of rounding.

Column C: The interest paid in the period is a constant amount computed by multiplying the face value of the bonds by their face interest rate by the interest time period ($100,000 × .09 × 6/12 = $4,500).

Column D: The discount amortized is the difference between the effective interest expense to be recorded and the interest to be paid on the interest payment date ($4,807 − $4,500 = $307).

Column E: The unamortized bond discount is the balance of the bond discount at the beginning of the period less the current period amortization of the discount ($3,851 − $307 = $3,544). The unamortized discount decreases in each interest payment period because it is amortized as a portion of interest expense.

Column F: The carrying value of the bonds at the end of the period is the carrying value at the beginning of the period plus the amortization during the period ($96,149 + $307 = $96,456). Notice that the sum of the carrying value and the unamortized discount (Column F + Column E) always equals the face value of the bonds ($96,456 + $3,544 = $100,000).

The entry to record the interest expense is exactly like the one when the straight-line method is used. However, the amounts debited and credited to the various accounts are different. Using the effective interest method, the entry for July 1, 2007, would be as follows:

Study Note

The bond interest expense recorded exceeds the amount of interest paid because of the amortization of the bond discount. The matching rule dictates that the discount be amortized over the life of the bond.

A*	=	L	+	OE
−4,500		+307		−4,807

*Assumes cash paid.

2007			
July 1	Bond Interest Expense	4,807	
	Unamortized Bond Discount		307
	Cash (or Interest Payable)		4,500
	Paid (or accrued) semiannual interest to bondholders and amortized the discount on 9%, 5-year bonds		

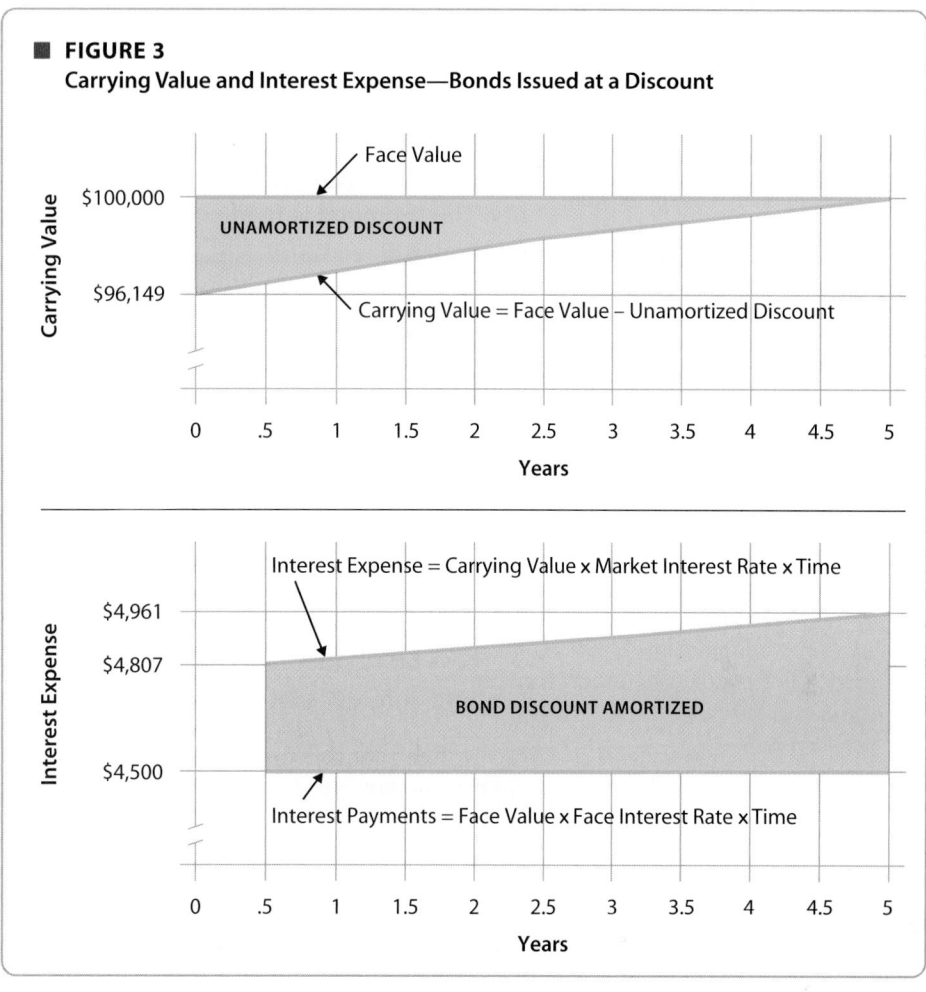

FIGURE 3
Carrying Value and Interest Expense—Bonds Issued at a Discount

Although an interest and amortization table is useful because it can be prepared in advance for all periods, it is not necessary to have one to determine the amortization of a discount for any one interest payment period. It is necessary only to multiply the carrying value by the effective interest rate and subtract the interest payment from the result. For example, the amount of discount to be amortized in the seventh interest payment period is $412, calculated as follows: ($98,240 $\times$ .05) − $4,500.

Figure 3, which is based on the data in Table 3, shows how the effective interest method affects the amortization of a bond discount. Notice that the carrying value (the issue price) is initially less than the face value, but that it gradually increases toward face value over the life of the bond issue. Notice also that interest expense exceeds interest payments by the amount of the bond discount amortized. Interest expense increases gradually over the life of the bond because it is based on the gradually increasing carrying value (multiplied by the market interest rate).

Amortizing a Bond Premium

In our earlier example of bonds issued at a premium, Katakis Corporation issued $100,000 of five-year bonds at a time when the market interest rate was 8 percent and the face interest rate was 9 percent. The bonds sold for $104,100, which resulted in an unamortized bond premium of $4,100. Like a discount, a premium must be amortized over the life of the bonds so that it can be matched to its effects on interest expense during that period. In the following

Study Note

The bond interest *increases* each period because the carrying value of the bonds (the principal on which the interest is calculated) increases each period.

sections, we calculate Katakis's total interest cost and amortize its bond premium using the straight-line and effective interest methods.

Calculation of Total Interest Cost

Because the bondholders paid more than face value for the bonds, the premium of $4,100 ($104,100 − $100,000) represents an amount that the bondholders will not receive at maturity. The premium is in effect a reduction, in advance, of the total interest paid on the bonds over the life of the bond issue. The total interest cost over the issue's life can be computed as follows:

Cash to be paid to bondholders		
Face value at maturity		$100,000
Interest payments ($100,000 × .09 × 5 years)		45,000
Total cash paid to bondholders		$145,000
Less cash received from bondholders		104,100
Total interest cost		$ 40,900

Or, alternatively:

Interest payments ($100,000 × .09 × 5 years)		$ 45,000
Less bond premium		4,100
Total interest cost		$ 40,900

Notice that the total interest payments of $45,000 exceed the total interest cost of $40,900 by $4,100, the amount of the bond premium.

Straight-Line Method

Under the straight-line method, the bond premium is spread evenly over the life of the bond issue. As with bond discounts, the amount of the bond premium amortized and the interest expense for each semiannual period are computed in four steps:

1. Total Interest Payments = Interest Payments per Year × Life of Bonds

$$= 2 \times 5 = 10$$

2. Amortization of Bond Premium per Interest Period $= \dfrac{\text{Bond Premium}}{\text{Total Interest Payments}}$

$$= \frac{\$4,100}{10}$$

$$= \$410$$

3. Cash Interest Payment = Face Value × Face Interest Rate × Time

$$= \$100,000 \times .09 \times 6/12 = \$4,500$$

4. Interest Expense per Interest Period = Interest Payment − Amortization of Bond Premium

$$= \$4,500 - \$410 = \$4,090$$

On July 1, 2007, the first semiannual interest date, the entry would be like this:

A*	=	L	+	OE
−4,500		−410		−4,090

*Assumes cash paid.

2007			
July 1	Bond Interest Expense	4,090	
	Unamortized Bond Premium	410	
	Cash (or Interest Payable)		4,500
	Paid (or accrued) semiannual interest		
	to bondholders and amortized the		
	premium on 9%, 5-year bonds		

Study Note

A bond premium is deducted from interest payments in calculating total interest because a bond premium represents an amount over the face value of a bond that the corporation never has to return to the bondholders. In effect, it reduces the higher-than-market interest the corporation is paying on the bond.

TABLE 4.   Interest and Amortization of a Bond Premium: Effective Interest Method

Semiannual Interest Period	A Carrying Value at Beginning of Period	B Semiannual Interest Expense at 8% to Be Recorded* (4% × A)	C Semiannual Interest Payment to Bondholders (4½% × $100,000)	D Amortization of Bond Premium (C − B)	E Unamortized Bond Premium at End of Period (E − D)	F Carrying Value at End of Period (A − D)
0					$4,100	$104,100
1	$104,100	$4,164	$4,500	$336	3,764	103,764
2	103,764	4,151	4,500	349	3,415	103,415
3	103,415	4,137	4,500	363	3,052	103,052
4	103,052	4,122	4,500	378	2,674	102,674
5	102,674	4,107	4,500	393	2,281	102,281
6	102,281	4,091	4,500	409	1,872	101,872
7	101,872	4,075	4,500	425	1,447	101,447
8	101,447	4,058	4,500	442	1,005	101,005
9	101,005	4,040	4,500	460	545	100,545
10	100,545	3,955†	4,500	545	—	100,000

*Rounded to the nearest dollar.

†Last period's interest expense equals $3,955 ($4,500 − $545); it does not equal $4,022 ($100,545 × .04) because of the cumulative effect of rounding.

Study Note

The bond interest expense recorded is less than the amount of the interest paid because of the amortization of the bond premium. The matching rule dictates that the premium be amortized over the life of the bond.

Note that the bond interest expense is $4,090, but the amount that bondholders receive is the $4,500 face interest payment. The difference of $410 is the debit to Unamortized Bond Premium. This lowers the credit balance of the Unamortized Bond Premium account and the carrying value of the bonds payable by $410 each interest period. If the bond issue remains unchanged, the same entry will be made on every semiannual interest date over the life of the bond issue. When the bond issue matures, the balance in the Unamortized Bond Premium account will be zero, and the carrying value of the bonds payable will be $100,000—exactly equal to the amount due the bondholders.

As noted earlier, the straight-line method should be used only when it does not lead to a material difference from the effective interest method.

Effective Interest Method   Under the straight-line method, the effective interest rate changes constantly, even though the interest expense is fixed, because the effective interest rate is determined by comparing the fixed interest expense with a carrying value that changes as a result of amortizing the discount or premium. To apply a fixed interest rate over the life of the bonds based on the actual market rate at the time of the bond issue, one must use the effective interest method. With this method, the interest expense decreases slightly each period (see Table 4, Column B) because the amount of the bond premium amortized increases slightly (Column D). This occurs

FOCUS ON BUSINESS PRACTICE

Speed Up the Calculations!

Interest and amortization tables like those in Tables 3 and 4 are ideal applications for computer spreadsheet software, such as Lotus and Microsoft Excel. Once the tables have been constructed with the proper formula in each cell, only

five variables must be entered to produce the entire table: the face value, selling price, maturity date, face interest rate, and market interest rate.

because a fixed rate is applied each period to the gradually decreasing carrying value (Column A). The first interest payment is recorded as follows:

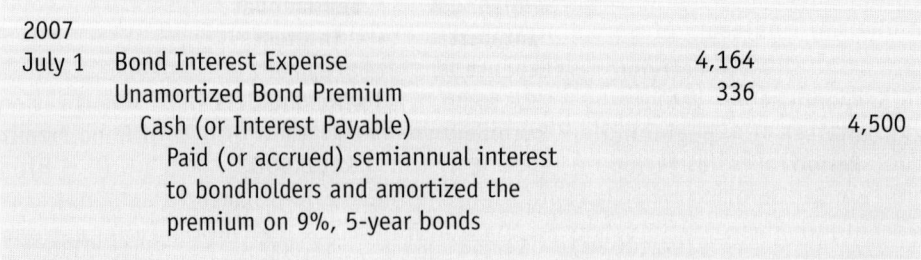

A*	=	L	+	OE
−4,500		−336		−4,164

*Assumes cash paid.

2007			
July 1	Bond Interest Expense	4,164	
	Unamortized Bond Premium	336	
	Cash (or Interest Payable)		4,500
	Paid (or accrued) semiannual interest		
	to bondholders and amortized the		
	premium on 9%, 5-year bonds		

Note that the unamortized bond premium (Column E) decreases gradually to zero as the carrying value decreases to the face value (Column F). To find the amount of premium amortized in any one interest payment period, subtract the effective interest expense (the carrying value times the effective interest rate, Column B) from the interest payment (Column C). In semiannual interest period 5, for example, the amortization of premium is $393, which is calculated in the following manner: $4,500 − ($102,674 × .04).

Figure 4, which is based on the data in Table 4, shows how the effective interest method affects the amortization of a bond premium. Notice that the carrying value (issue price) is initially greater than the face value, but that it gradually decreases toward the face value over the life of the bond issue. Notice also that interest payments exceed interest expense by the amount of

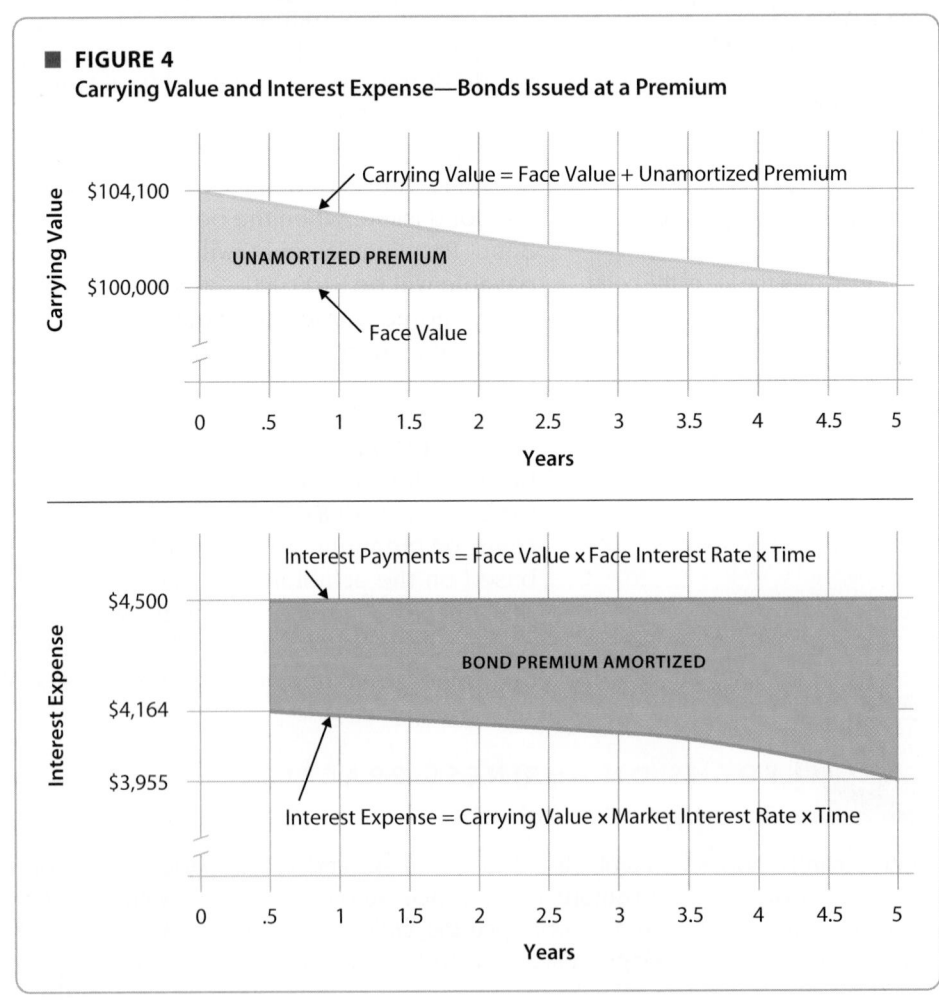

■ **FIGURE 4**
Carrying Value and Interest Expense—Bonds Issued at a Premium

the premium amortized. Interest expense decreases gradually over the life of the bond because it is based on the gradually decreasing carrying value (multiplied by the market interest rate).

S T O P • R E V I E W • A P P L Y

5-1. What is included in the calculation of the total interest cost fo a bond issue other than interest payments?

5-2. Why is the straight-line method of amortization usually acceptable even though it is not the most theoretically correct method?

5-3. Why does the amortization of a bond discount increase interest expense to an amount greater than interest paid? Why does the amortization of a premium have the opposite effect?

5-4. When the effective interest method of amortizing a bond discount or premium is used, why does the amount of interest expense change from period to period?

Bond Transactions On June 1, Bassi Corporation issues $8,000,000 of 8 percent, 20-year bonds at 97. Interest is payable semiannually, on May 31 and November 30. Bassi's fiscal year ends on November 30.

1. Using the straight-line method of amortization, prepare entries in journal form for June 1 and November 30.

2. Using the effective interest method and assuming the same facts as above except that the market rate of interest is 8.5 percent, prepare the entry for November 30.

SOLUTION

1. Straight-line method

June 1	Cash	7,760,000	
	Unamortized Bond Discount	240,000	
	Bonds Payable		8,000,000
	Issue of $8,000,000 of 8%,		
	20-year bonds at 97		
	$8,000,000 × .97 = $7,760,000		
Nov. 30	Bond Interest Expense	326,000	
	Unamortized Bond Discount		6,000
	Cash		320,000
	Paid bondholders semiannual interest and		
	amortized the discount on 8%, 20-year bonds		
	$240,000 ÷ 40 periods = $6,000		
	$8,000,000 × .04 = $320,000		

2. Effective interest method

Nov. 30	Bond Interest Expense	329,800	
	Unamortized Bond Interest		9,800
	Cash		320,000
	Paid bondholders semiannual interest and		
	amortized the discount on 8%, 20-year bonds		
	$7,760,000 × .0425 = $329,800		
	$8,000,000 × .04 = $320,000		

Retirement of Bonds

> **LO6** Account for the retirement of bonds and the conversion of bonds into stock.

Usually, companies pay bonds when they are due—on the maturity date. However, as we noted in our earlier discussion of callable and convertible bonds, retiring a bond issue before its maturity date can be to a company's advantage. For example, when interest rates drop, many companies refinance their bonds at the lower rate, much like homeowners who refinance their mortgage loans when interest rates go down. Even though companies usually pay a premium for early extinguishment of bond debt, what they save on interest can make the refinancing cost-effective.

Calling Bonds

Let's suppose that Katakis Corporation can call, or retire, at 105 the $100,000 of bonds it issued at a premium (104.1) on January 1, 2007, and that it decides to do so on July 1, 2010. The retirement thus takes place on the seventh interest payment date. Assume that the entry for the required interest payment and the amortization of the premium has been made. The entry to record the retirement of the bonds is as follows:

A	=	L	+	OE
−105,000		−100,000		−3,553
		−1,477		

2010			
July 1	Bonds Payable	100,000	
	Unamortized Bond Premium	1,447	
	Loss on Retirement of Bonds	3,553	
	Cash		105,000
	Retired 9% bonds at 105		

In this entry, the cash paid is the face value times the call price ($100,000 × 1.05 = $105,000). The unamortized bond premium can be found in Column E of Table 4. The loss on retirement of bonds occurs because the call price of the bonds is greater than the carrying value ($105,000 − $101,447 = $3,553).

Sometimes, a rise in the market interest rate can cause the market value of bonds to fall considerably below their face value. If it has the cash to do so, the company may find it advantageous to purchase the bonds on the open market and retire them, rather than wait and pay them off at face value. A gain is recognized for the difference between the purchase price of the bonds and the carrying value of the retired bonds.

For example, suppose that because of a rise in interest rates, Katakis Corporation is able to purchase the $100,000 bond issue on the open market at 85. The entry would be as follows:

A	=	L	+	OE
−85,000		−100,000		+16,447
		−1,447		

2010			
July 1	Bonds Payable	100,000	
	Unamortized Bond Premium	1,447	
	Cash		85,000
	Gain on Retirement of Bonds		16,447
	Purchased and retired		
	9% bonds at 85		

Converting Bonds

When a bondholder converts bonds to common stock, the company records the common stock at the carrying value of the bonds. The bond liability and the unamortized discount or premium are written off the books. For this reason, no gain or loss on the transaction is recorded. For example, suppose Katakis Corporation does not call its bonds on July 1, 2010. Instead, the corporation's bondholders decide to convert all their bonds to $8 par value common stock under a convertible provision of 40 shares of common stock for each $1,000 bond. The entry would be as follows:

A =	L	+	OE
	−100,000		+32,000
	−1,447		+69,447

2010			
July 1	Bonds Payable	100,000	
	Unamortized Bond Premium	1,447	
	Common Stock		32,000
	Additional Paid-in Capital		69,447
	Converted 9% bonds payable into		
	$8 par value common stock at a rate		
	of 40 shares for each $1,000 bond		

The unamortized bond premium is found in Column E of Table 4. At a rate of 40 shares for each $1,000 bond, 4,000 shares will be issued, with a total par value of $32,000 (4,000 × $8). The Common Stock account is credited for the amount of the par value of the stock issued. In addition, Additional Paid-in Capital is credited for the difference between the carrying value of the bonds and the par value of the stock issued ($101,447 − $32,000 = $69,447). No gain or loss is recorded.

S T O P • R E V I E W • A P P L Y

6-1. When may a company want to exercise the call provision of a bond?

6-2. Why are convertible bonds advantageous to both the company and the bondholder?

Other Bonds Payable Issues

> **SO7** Record bonds issued between interest dates and year-end adjustments.

Among the other issues involved in accounting for bonds payable are the sale of bonds between interest payment dates and the year-end accrual of bond interest expense.

Sale of Bonds Between Interest Dates

Although corporations may issue bonds on an interest payment date, as in our previous examples, they often issue them between interest payment dates. When that is the case, they generally collect from the investors the interest that would have accrued for the partial period preceding the issue date, and at the end of the first interest period, they pay the interest for the entire period. In other words, the interest collected when bonds are sold is returned to investors on the next interest payment date.

There are two reasons for following this procedure:

1. From a practical standpoint, if a company issued bonds on several different days and did not collect the accrued interest, records would have to be maintained for each bondholder and date of purchase. The interest due each bondholder would therefore have to be computed for a different time period. Clearly, this procedure would involve large bookkeeping costs. On the other hand, if accrued interest is collected when the bonds are sold, the corporation can pay the interest due for the entire period on the interest payment date, thereby eliminating the extra computations and costs.

2. When accrued interest is collected in advance, the amount is subtracted from the full interest paid on the interest payment date. Thus, the resulting interest expense represents the amount for the time the money was borrowed.

For example, suppose Katakis Corporation sold $100,000 of 9 percent, five-year bonds for face value on May 1, 2007, rather than on January 1, 2007. The entry to record the sale of the bonds is as follows:

A	=	L	+	OE
+103,000		+100,000		+3,000

2007			
May 1	Cash	103,000	
	Bond Interest Expense		3,000
	Bonds Payable		100,000
	Sold 9%, 5-year bonds at face value plus 4 months' accrued interest $100,000 × .09 × 4/12 = $3,000		

Cash is debited for the amount received, $103,000 (the face value of $100,000 plus four months' accrued interest of $3,000). Bond Interest Expense is credited for the $3,000 of accrued interest, and Bonds Payable is credited for the face value of $100,000.

When the first semiannual interest payment date arrives, this entry is made:

A*	=	L	+	OE
−4,500				−4,500

*Assumes cash paid.

2007			
July 1	Bond Interest Expense	4,500	
	Cash (or Interest Payable)		4,500
	Paid (or accrued) semiannual interest $100,000 × .09 × 6/12 = $4,500		

Notice that the entire half-year interest is debited to Bond Interest Expense and credited to Cash because the corporation pays bond interest every six months, in full six-month amounts. Figure 5 illustrates this process. The actual interest expense for the two months that the bonds were outstanding is $1,500. This amount is the net balance of the $4,500 debit to Bond Interest Expense on July 1 less the $3,000 credit to Bond Interest Expense on May 1. You can see these steps clearly in the following T account:

BOND INTEREST EXPENSE			
Bal.	0	May 1	3,000
July 1	4,500		
Bal.	**1,500**		

Year-End Accrual of Bond Interest Expense

Bond interest payment dates rarely correspond with a company's fiscal year. Therefore, an adjustment must be made to accrue the interest expense on the bonds from the last interest payment date to the end of the fiscal year. In addition, any discount or premium on the bonds must be amortized for the partial period.

In our example of bonds issued at a premium, Katakis Corporation issued $100,000 of bonds on January 1, 2007, at 104.1 percent of face value. Suppose Katakis's fiscal year ends on September 30, 2007. In the period since the interest payment and amortization of the premium on July 1, three months' worth of interest has accrued. Under the effective interest method, the following adjusting entry would be made:

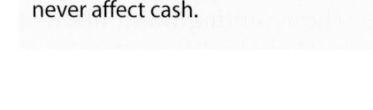

Study Note

Remember that adjusting entries never affect cash.

$$A = L + OE$$
$$-174.50 \quad -2,075.50$$
$$+2,250.00$$

2007			
Sept. 30	Bond Interest Expense	2,075.50	
	Unamortized Bond Premium	174.50	
	Bond Interest Payable		2,250.00
	To record accrual of interest		
	on 9% bonds payable for		
	3 months and amortization		
	of one-half of the premium		
	for the second interest		
	payment period		

Study Note

The matching rule dictates that both the accrued interest and the amortization of a premium or discount be recorded at year end.

This entry covers one-half of the second interest period. Unamortized Bond Premium is debited for $174.50, which is one-half of $349, the amortization of the premium for the second period from Table 4. Bond Interest Payable is credited for $2,250, three months' interest on the face value of the bonds ($100,000 × .09 × 3/12). The net debit figure of $2,075.50 ($2,250.00 − $174.50) is the bond interest expense for the three-month period.

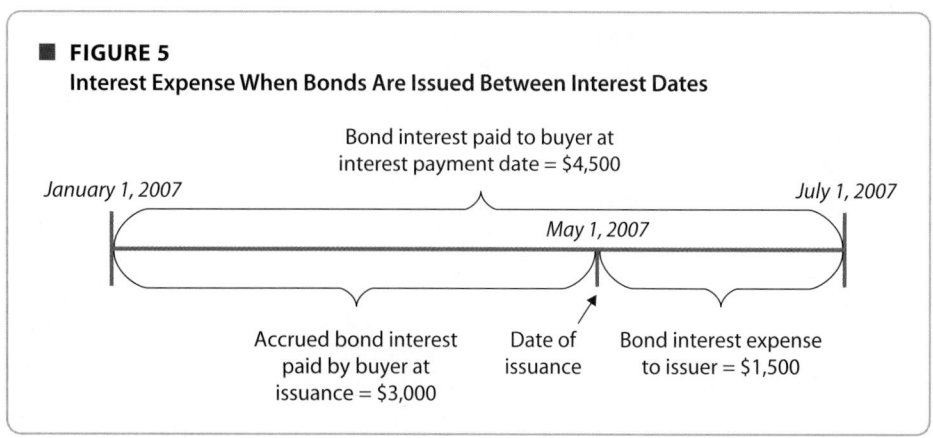

■ **FIGURE 5**
Interest Expense When Bonds Are Issued Between Interest Dates

On the interest payment date of January 1, 2008, the entry to pay the bond-holders and amortize the premium is as follows:

A	=	L	+	OE
−4,500.00		−2,250.00		−2,075.50
		−174.50		

2008			
Jan. 1	Bond Interest Expense	2,075.50	
	Bond Interest Payable	2,250.00	
	Unamortized Bond Premium	174.50	
	Cash		4,500.00
	Paid semiannual interest,		
	including interest previously		
	accrued, and amortized the		
	premium for the period since		
	the end of the fiscal year		

One-half ($2,250) of the amount paid ($4,500) was accrued on September 30. Unamortized Bond Premium is debited for $174.50, the remaining amount to be amortized for the period ($349.00 − $174.50). The resulting bond interest expense is the amount that applies to the three-month period from October 1 to December 31.

Bond discounts are recorded at year end in the same way as bond premiums. The difference is that the amortization of a bond discount increases interest expense instead of decreasing it.

S T O P • R E V I E W • A P P L Y

7-1. When a company issues bonds between interest dates, why does it collect an amount equal to accrued interest from the buyer?

7-2. In making the year-end accrual for interest on bonds payable, what two computations affect the amount of interest expense?

A LOOK BACK AT

McDONALD'S CORPORATION

As we noted in this chapter's Decision Point, McDonald's relies on both debt and equity financing to support its continued global expansion. Because of the extent of the company's long-term debt, potential investors and creditors need to address the following questions:

● **What are McDonald's most important long-term debts?**

● **What are its considerations in deciding to issue long-term debt?**

● **How does one evaluate whether a company has too much debt?**

In addition to bonds, notes, and mortgages, McDonald's long-term debt includes leases on numerous properties. The company also has deferred income taxes and pension and health plans. Its purpose in taking on long-term debt is to foster growth and increase earnings. By using financial leverage in this way, McDonald's, like any other company, assumes financial risk. In McDonald's case, the risk is partially offset because much of its long-term debt relates to leases on real estate, an area in which the company has long experience and great expertise. McDonald's management commits the company to long-term leases not only because it believes the company will stay in the leased locations for a long time, but also because it is a way of financing expansion.

McDonald's 2005 annual report includes a detailed description of management's approach to debt financing. It points out that Standard & Poor's gives the company an "A" credit rating and that management carefully monitors key credit ratios that "incorporate capitalized operating leases to estimate total adjusted debt."

We can evaluate whether McDonald's maintains an appropriate level of debt by computing its interest coverage ratio over a two-year period, as follows:

$$\text{Interest Coverage Ratio} = \frac{\text{Income Before Income Taxes} + \text{Interest Expense}}{\text{Interest Expense}}$$

2005	2004
$= \dfrac{\$3,701.6 + \$356.1}{\$356.1}$	$= \dfrac{\$3,202.4 + \$358.4}{\$358.4}$
$= \dfrac{\$4,057.7}{\$356.1}$	$= \dfrac{\$3,560.8}{\$358.4}$
$=$ 11.4 times	$=$ 9.9 times

This analysis shows that McDonald's can easily cover its interest payments and that its ability to do so increased over the two-year period. There is plenty of cushion in this ratio to cover all of McDonald's balance sheet commitments, including long-term leases.

CHAPTER REVIEW

REVIEW of Learning Objectives

LO1 Identify the management issues related to long-term debt.

Long-term debt is used to finance assets and business activities, such as research and development, that will produce income in future years. The management issues related to long-term debt are whether to take on long-term debt, how much debt to carry, and what types of debt to incur. The advantages of issuing long-term debt are that common stockholders do not relinquish any control, interest on debt is tax-deductible, and financial leverage can increase earnings. The disadvantages are that interest and principal must be paid on time and financial leverage can work against a company if an investment is not successful. The level of debt can be evaluated using the debt to equity ratio and the interest coverage ratio. Common types of long-term debt are bonds, notes, mortgages, long-term leases, pension liabilities, other postretirement benefits, and deferred income taxes.

LO2 Describe the features of a bond issue and the major characteristics of bonds.

A bond is a security that represents money borrowed from the investing public. When a corporation issues bonds, it enters into a contract, called a bond indenture, with the bondholders. The bond indenture defines the terms of the bond issue. A bond issue is the total value of bonds issued at one time. The prices of bonds are stated in terms of a percentage of the face value, or principal, of the bonds. The face interest rate is the fixed rate of interest paid to bondholders based on the face value. The market interest rate is the rate of interest paid in the market on bonds of similar risk. If the market rate fluctuates from the face interest rate before the bond issue date, the bonds will sell at either a discount or a premium.

A corporation can issue several types of bonds, each having different characteristics. For example, a bond issue may or may not require security (secured versus unsecured bonds). It may be payable at a single time (term bonds) or at several times (serial bonds). And the holder may receive interest automatically (registered bonds) or may have to return coupons to receive interest payable (coupon bonds). Bonds may also be callable and convertible.

LO3 Record bonds issued at face value and at a discount or premium.

Bondholders pay face value for bonds when the interest rate on the bonds approximates the market rate for similar investments. The issuing corporation records the bond issue at face value as a long-term liability in the Bonds Payable account. Bonds are issued at a discount when their face interest rate is lower than the market rate for similar investments. The difference between the face value and the issue price is debited to Unamortized Bond Discount. Bonds are issued at a premium when their face interest rate is greater than the market interest rate on similar investments. The difference between the issue price and the face value is credited to Unamortized Bond Premium.

LO4 Use present values to determine the value of bonds.

The value of a bond is determined by summing the present values of (1) the series of fixed interest payments of the bond issue and (2) the single payment of the face value at maturity. Tables 3 and 4 in the appendix on future value and present value tables should be used in making these computations.

LO5 Amortize bond discounts and bond premiums using the straight-line and effective interest methods.

The straight-line method allocates a fixed portion of a bond discount or premium each interest period to adjust the interest payment to interest expense. The effective interest method, which is used when the effects of amortization are material, applies a constant rate of interest to the carrying value of the bonds. To find interest and the amortization of discounts or premiums, the effective interest rate is applied to the carrying value of the bonds (face value minus the discount or plus the premium) at the beginning of the interest period. The amount of the discount or premium to be amortized is the difference between the interest figured by using the effective rate and that obtained by using the face rate. The results of using the effective interest method on bonds issued at a discount or a premium are summarized below and compared with issuance at face value:

	Bonds Issued at		
	Face Value	**Discount**	**Premium**
Trend in carrying value over bond term	Constant	Increasing	Decreasing
Trend in interest expense over bond term	Constant	Increasing	Decreasing
Interest expense versus interest payments	Interest expense = interest payments	Interest expense > interest payments	Interest expense < interest payments
Classification of bond discount or premium	Not applicable	Contra-liability (deducted from Bonds Payable)	Liability (added to Bonds Payable)

LO6 Account for the retirement of bonds and the conversion of bonds into stock.

Callable bonds can be retired before maturity at the option of the issuing corporation. The call price is usually an amount greater than the face value of the bonds, in which case the corporation recognizes a loss on the retirement of the bonds. Sometimes, a rise in the market interest rate causes the market value of the bonds to fall below face value. If a company purchases its bonds on the open market at a price below carrying value, it recognizes a gain on the transaction.

Convertible bonds allow the bondholder to convert bonds to the issuing corporation's common stock. When bondholders exercise this option, the common stock issued is recorded at the carrying value of the bonds being converted. No gain or loss is recognized.

Supplemental Objective

SO7 Record bonds issued between interest dates and year-end adjustments.

When bonds are sold between the interest payment dates, the issuing corporation collects from investors the interest that has accrued since the last interest payment date. When the next interest payment date arrives, the corporation pays the bondholders interest for the entire interest period.

When the end of a corporation's fiscal year does not fall on an interest payment date, the corporation must accrue bond interest expense from the last interest payment date to the end of its fiscal year. This accrual results in the inclusion of the interest expense in the year it is incurred.

REVIEW of Concepts and Terminology

The following concepts and terms were introduced in this chapter:

Bond: A security, usually long term, representing money that a corporation or other entity borrows from the investing public. **(LO2)**

Bond certificate: Evidence of an organization's debt to a bondholder. **(LO2)**

Bond indenture: A contract that defines the terms of a bond issue. **(LO2)**

Bond issue: The total value of bonds issued at one time. **(LO2)**

Callable bonds: Bonds that the issuing corporation can buy back and retire at a call price before their maturity dates. **(LO2)**

Call price: A specified price, usually above face value, at which a corporation can buy back its bonds before maturity. **(LO2)**

Capital lease: A long-term lease that resembles a purchase or sale on installment and in which the lessee assumes the risk of ownership. **(LO1)**

Convertible bonds: Bonds that can be exchanged for the issuing corporation's common stock. **(LO2)**

Coupon bonds: Bonds not registered with the issuing organization that bear coupons stating the amount of interest due and the payment date. **(LO2)**

Deferred income taxes: The result of using different methods to calculate income taxes for financial reporting and tax purposes. **(LO1)**

Discount: The amount by which a bond's face value exceeds its issue price, which occurs when the market interest rate is higher than the face interest rate. **(LO2)**

Early extinguishment of debt: The retirement of a bond issue before its maturity date. **(LO2)**

Effective interest method: A method of amortizing bond discounts or premiums that applies a constant interest rate (the market rate when the bonds were issued) to the bonds' carrying value at the beginning of each interest period. **(LO5)**

Face interest rate: The fixed rate of interest paid to bondholders based on the face value of the bonds. **(LO2)**

Financial leverage: A corporation's ability to increase earnings for stockholders by earning more on assets than it pays in interest on the debt it incurred to finance the assets. Also called *trading on equity*. **(LO1)**

Market interest rate: The rate of interest paid in the market on bonds of similar risk. Also called *effective interest rate*. **(LO2)**

Mortgage: A debt secured by real property. **(LO1)**

Off-balance-sheet financing: Structuring long-term debts in such a way that they do not appear as liabilities on the balance sheet. **(LO1)**

Operating lease: A short-term lease in which the risks of ownership remain with the lessor and for which payments are recorded as rent expense. **(LO1)**

Other postretirement benefits: Health care and other nonpension benefits paid after retirement but earned while the employee is still working. **(LO1)**

Pension fund: A fund established by the contributions of an employer and often of employees from which payments are made to employees after retirement or upon disability or death. **(LO1)**

Pension plan: A contract requiring a company to pay benefits to its employees after they retire. **(LO1)**

Premium: The amount by which a bond's issue price exceeds its face value, which occurs when the market interest rate is lower than the face interest rate. **(LO2)**

Registered bonds: Bonds that the issuing company registers in the names of the bondholders. **(LO2)**

Secured bonds: Bonds that carry a pledge of certain assets as a guarantee of repayment. **(LO2)**

Serial bonds: Bonds in one issue that mature on different dates. **(LO2)**

Straight-line method: A method of amortizing bond discounts or premiums that allocates the discount or premium equally over each interest period of the life of a bond. **(LO5)**

Term bonds: Bonds in one issue that mature at the same time. **(LO2)**

Unsecured bonds: Bonds issued on an organization's general credit. Also called *debenture bonds*. **(LO2)**

Zero coupon bonds: Bonds that do not pay periodic interest but that pay a fixed amount on the maturity date. **(LO5)**

Key Ratio

Interest coverage ratio: A measure of the degree of protection a company has from default on interest payments; (Income Before Income Taxes + Interest Expense) ÷ Interest Expense. **(LO1)**

≡ REVIEW Problem

LO3, LO5, LO6 **Accounting for a Bond Discount, Bond Retirement, and Bond Conversion**

When Merrill Manufacturing Company wanted to expand its metal window division, it did not have enough capital to finance the project. To fund it, management sought and received approval from the board of directors to issue bonds. The bond indenture stated that the company would issue $5,000,000 of 8 percent, five-year bonds on January 1, 2008, and would pay interest semiannually, on June 30 and December 31 of each of the five years. It also stated that the bonds would be callable at 104 and that each $1,000 bond would be convertible to 30 shares of $10 par value common stock. Merrill sold the bonds on January 1, 2008, at 96 because the market rate of interest for similar investments was 9 percent. It decided to amortize the bond discount by using the effective interest method. On July 1, 2010, management called and retired half the bonds, and investors converted the other half to common stock.

Required

1. Prepare an interest and amortization schedule for the first five interest periods.
2. Prepare entries in journal form to record the sale of the bonds, the first two interest payments, the bond retirement, and the bond conversion.

Answer to Review Problem

1. Schedule for the first five interest periods:

	A	B	C	D	E	F	G	H	I	J	K	L	M
1						Interest and Amortization of Bond Discount							
2	Semiannual Interest Payment Date		Carrying Value at Beginning of Period		Semiannual Interest Expense* (9% × ½)		Semiannual Interest Payment (8% × ½)		Amorti- zation of Discount		Unamortized Bond Discount at End of Period		Carrying Value at End of Period
3	Jan. 1, 2008											$200,000	$4,800,000
4	June 30, 2008		$4,800,000		$216,000		$200,000		$16,000		184,000		4,816,000
5	Dec. 31, 2008		4,816,000		216,720		200,000		16,720		167,280		4,832,720
6	June 30, 2009		4,832,720		217,472		200,000		17,472		149,808		4,850,192
7	Dec. 31, 2009		4,850,192		218,259		200,000		18,259		131,549		4,868,451
8	June 30, 2010		4,868,451		219,080		200,000		19,080		112,469		4,887,531
10	* Rounded to the nearest dollar.												

2. Entries in journal form:

	A	B	C	D	E	F
1	2008					
2	Jan.	1	Cash		4,800,000	
3			Unamortized Bond Discount		200,000	
4			Bonds Payable			5,000,000
5			Sold $5,000,000 of 8%, 5-year bonds at 96			
6	June	30	Bond Interest Expense		216,000	
7			Unamortized Bond Discount			16,000
8			Cash			200,000
9			Paid semiannual interest and amortized the discount on 8%, 5-year bonds			
10	Dec.	31	Bond Interest Expense		216,720	
11			Unamortized Bond Discount			16,720
12			Cash			200,000

14	2010					
15	July	1	Bonds Payable		2,500,000	
16			Loss on Retirement of Bonds		156,235	
17			Unamortized Bond Discount			56,235
18			Cash			2,600,000
19			Called $2,500,000 of 8% bonds and retired them at 104			
20			$112,469 × ½ = $56,235*			
21		1	Bonds Payable		2,500,000	
22			Unamortized Bond Discount			56,234
23			Common Stock			750,000
24			Additional paid-in Capital			1,693,766
25			Converted $2,500,000 of 8% bonds into common stock:			
26			2,500 × 30 shares = 75,000 shares			
27			75,000 shares × $10 = $750,000			
28			$112,469 - $56,235 = $56,234			
29			$2,500,000 - ($56,234 + $750,000) = $1,693,766			
30						
31	* Rounded.					

CHAPTER ASSIGNMENTS

BUILDING Your Basic Knowledge and Skills

Short Exercises

LO1 **Bond Versus Common Stock Financing**

SE 1. Indicate whether each of the following is an advantage or a disadvantage of using long-term bond financing rather than issuing common stock.

1. Interest paid on bonds is tax-deductible.
2. Investments are sometimes not as successful as planned.
3. Financial leverage can have a negative effect when investments do not earn as much as the interest payments on the related debt.
4. Bondholders do not have voting rights in a corporation.
5. Positive financial leverage may be achieved.

LO1 **Types of Long-Term Liabilities**

SE 2. Place the number of the liability next to the statement to which it applies.

1. Bonds payable   ____ a. May result in a capital lease
2. Long-term notes payable   ____ b. Differences in income taxes on accounting income and taxable income
3. Mortgage payable   ____ c. The most popular form of long-term financing
4. Long-term lease   ____ d. Often used to purchase land and buildings

5. Pension liabilities   ___ e. Often used interchangeably with bonds payable

6. Other post-retirement benefits   ___ f. Future health care costs are a major component

7. Deferred income taxes   ___ g. May include 401(k), ESOPs, or profit-sharing

LO1 Mortgage Payable

SE 3. Karib Corporation purchased a building by signing a $150,000 long-term mortgage with monthly payments of $1,200. The mortgage carries an interest rate of 8 percent. Prepare a monthly payment schedule showing the monthly payment, the interest for the month, the reduction in debt, and the unpaid balance for the first three months. (Round to the nearest dollar.)

LO4 Valuing Bonds Using Present Value

SE 4. Rogers Paints, Inc., is considering the sale of two bond issues. Choice A is a $600,000 bond issue that pays semiannual interest of $32,000 and is due in 20 years. Choice B is a $600,000 bond issue that pays semiannual interest of $30,000 and is due in 15 years. Assume that the market interest rate for each bond is 12 percent. Calculate the amount that Rogers Paints will receive if both bond issues occur. (Calculate the present value of each bond issue and sum.)

LO3, LO5 Straight-Line Method

SE 5. On April 1, 20x7, Morimoto Corporation issued $8,000,000 in 8.5 percent, five-year bonds at 98. The semiannual interest payment dates are April 1 and October 1. Prepare entries in journal form for the issue of the bonds by Morimoto on April 1, 20x7, and the first two interest payments on October 1, 20x7, and April 1, 20x8. Use the straight-line method and ignore year-end accruals.

LO3, LO5, SO7 Effective Interest Method

SE 6. On March 1, 20xx, Samsonite Freight Company sold $200,000 of its 9.5 percent, 20-year bonds at 106. The semiannual interest payment dates are March 1 and September 1. The market interest rate is 8.9 percent. The firm's fiscal year ends August 31. Prepare entries in journal form to record the sale of the bonds on March 1, the accrual of interest and amortization of premium on August 31, and the first interest payment on September 1. Use the effective interest method to amortize the premium.

LO6 Bond Retirement

SE 7. The Geller Corporation has outstanding $400,000 of 8 percent bonds callable at 104. On December 1, immediately after the payment of the semiannual interest and the amortization of the bond discount were recorded, the unamortized bond discount equaled $10,500. On that date, $240,000 of the bonds were called and retired. Prepare the entry to record the retirement of the bonds on December 1.

LO6 Bond Conversion

SE 8. The Tramot Corporation has $2,000,000 of 6 percent bonds outstanding. There is $40,000 of unamortized discount remaining on the bonds after the March 1, 20x8, semiannual interest payment. The bonds are convertible at the rate of 20 shares of $10 par value common stock for each $1,000 bond. On March 1, 20x8, bondholders presented $1,200,000 of the bonds for conversion. Prepare the entry to record the conversion of the bonds.

SO7   **Bond Issue Between Interest Dates**

SE 9. Downey Corporation sold $400,000 of 9 percent, ten-year bonds for face value on September 1, 20xx. The issue date of the bonds was May 1, 20xx. The company's fiscal year ends on December 31, and this is its only bond issue. Record the sale of the bonds on September 1 and the first semiannual interest payment on November 1, 20xx. What is the bond interest expense for the year ended December 31, 20xx?

LO3, LO5, SO7   **Year-End Accrual of Bond Interest**

SE 10. On October 1, 20x7, Winston Corporation issued $250,000 of 9 percent bonds at 96. The bonds are dated October 1 and pay interest semiannually. The market rate of interest is 10 percent, and the company's year end is December 31. Prepare the entries to record the issuance of the bonds, the accrual of the interest on December 31, 20x7, and the payment of the first semiannual interest on April 1, 20x8. Assume the company uses the effective interest method to amortize the bond discount.

Exercises

LO1, LO2, LO6   **Discussion Questions**

E 1. Develop brief answers to each of the following questions:

1. How does a lender assess the risk that a borrower may default—that is, not pay interest and principal when due?
2. If a company with a high debt to equity ratio wants to increase its debt when the economy is weak, what kind of bond might it issue?
3. Why might a company lease a long-term asset rather than buy it and issue long-term bonds?
4. Why are callable and convertible bonds considered to add to management's future flexibility in financing a business?

LO3, LO4, LO5, SO7   **Discussion Questions**

E 2. Develop brief answers to each of the following questions:

1. What determines whether bonds are issued at a discount, premium, or face value?
2. Why does the market price of a bond vary over time?
3. When is it acceptable to use the straight-line method to amortize a bond discount or premium?
4. Why must the accrual of bond interest be recorded at the end of an accounting period?

LO1   **Interest Coverage Ratio**

E 3. Compute the interest coverage ratios for 20x7 and 20x8 from the partial income statements of Wool Company that appear below. State whether the ratio improved or worsened over time.

	20x8	20x7
Income from operations	$47,780	$36,920
Interest expense	11,600	6,600
Income before income taxes	$36,180	$30,320
Income taxes	10,800	9,000
Net income	$25,380	$21,320

LO1 **Mortgage Payable**

E 4. Velocity Corporation purchased a building by signing a $75,000 long-term mortgage with monthly payments of $1,000. The mortgage carries an interest rate of 12 percent.

1. Prepare a monthly payment schedule showing the monthly payment, the interest for the month, the reduction in debt, and the unpaid balance for the first three months. (Round to the nearest dollar.)
2. Prepare entries in journal form to record the purchase and the first two monthly payments.

LO1 **Recording Lease Obligations**

E 5. Tubbs Corporation has leased a piece of equipment that has a useful life of 12 years. The terms of the lease are payments of $86,000 per year for 12 years. Tubbs currently is able to borrow money at a long-term interest rate of 15 percent. (Round answers to the nearest dollar.)

1. Calculate the present value of the lease.
2. Prepare the entry to record the lease agreement.
3. Prepare the entry to record depreciation of the equipment for the first year using the straight-line method.
4. Prepare the entries to record the lease payments for the first two years.

LO4 **Valuing Bonds Using Present Value**

E 6. Ames, Inc., is considering the sale of two bond issues. Choice A is a $1,600,000 bond issue that pays semiannual interest of $128,000 and is due in 20 years. Choice B is a $1,600,000 bond issue that pays semiannual interest of $120,000 and is due in 15 years. Assume that the market interest rate for each bond is 12 percent. Calculate the amount that Ames, Inc., will receive if both bond issues are made. (**Hint:** Calculate the present value of each bond issue and sum.)

LO4 **Valuing Bonds Using Present Value**

E 7. Use the present value tables in the appendix on future value and present value tables to calculate the issue price of a $600,000 bond issue in each of the following independent cases. Assume interest is paid semiannually.

a. A 10-year, 8 percent bond issue; the market interest rate is 10 percent.
b. A 10-year, 8 percent bond issue; the market interest rate is 6 percent.
c. A 10-year, 10 percent bond issue; the market interest rate is 8 percent.
d. A 20-year, 10 percent bond issue; the market interest rate is 12 percent.
e. A 20-year, 10 percent bond issue; the market interest rate is 6 percent.

LO4 **Zero Coupon Bonds**

E 8. The state of Idaho needs to raise $50,000,000 for highway repairs. Officials are considering issuing zero coupon bonds, which do not require periodic interest payments. The current market interest rate for the bonds is 10 percent. What face value of bonds must be issued to raise the needed funds, assuming the bonds will be due in 30 years and compounded annually? How would your answer change if the bonds were due in 50 years? How would both answers change if the market interest rate were 8 percent instead of 10 percent?

LO3, LO5 **Straight-Line Method**

E 9. Kigga Corporation issued $2,000,000 in 10.5 percent, ten-year bonds on February 1, 20x7, at 104. Semiannual interest payment dates are January 31 and July 31. Use the straight-line method and ignore year-end accruals.

1. With regard to the bond issue on February 1, 20x7:
   a. How much cash is received?
   b. How much is Bonds Payable?
   c. What is the difference between **a** and **b** called and how much is it?
2. With regard to the bond interest payment on July 31, 20x7:
   a. How much cash is paid in interest?
   b. How much is the amortization?
   c. How much is interest expense?
3. With regard to the bond interest payment on January 31, 20x8:
   a. How much cash is paid in interest?
   b. How much is the amortization?
   c. How much is interest expense?

LO3, LO5 **Straight-Line Method**

E 10. Bianca Corporation issued $16,000,000 in 8.5 percent, five-year bonds on March 1, 20x7, at 96. The semiannual interest payment dates are September 1 and March 1. Prepare entries in journal form for the issue of the bonds by Bianca on March 1, 20x7, and the first two interest payments on September 1, 20x7, and March 1, 20x8. Use the straight-line method and ignore year-end accruals.

LO3, LO5 **Effective Interest Method**

E 11. The Stream Toy Company sold $250,000 of 9.5 percent, 20-year bonds on April 1, 20x8, at 106. The semiannual interest payment dates are March 31 and September 30. The market interest rate is 8.9 percent. The company's fiscal year ends September 30. Use the effective interest method to calculate the amortization.

1. With regard to the bond issue on April 1, 20x8:
   a. How much cash is received?
   b. How much is Bonds Payable?
   c. What is the difference between **a** and **b** called and how much is it?
2. With regard to the bond interest payment on September 30, 20x8:
   a. How much cash is paid in interest?
   b. How much is the amortization?
   c. How much is interest expense?
3. With regard to the bond interest payment on March 31, 20x9:
   a. How much cash is paid in interest?
   b. How much is the amortization?
   c. How much is interest expense?

LO3, LO5 **Effective Interest Method**

E 12. On March 1, 20x7, the Van Wurt Corporation issued $600,000 of 10 percent, five-year bonds. The semiannual interest payment dates are February 28 and August 31. Because the market rate for similar investments was 11 percent, the bonds had to be issued at a discount. The discount on the issuance of the bonds was $24,335. The company's fiscal year ends February 28. Prepare entries in journal form to record the bond issue on March 1, 20x7, the payment of interest, and the amortization of the discount on August 31, 20x7 and on February 28, 20x8. Use the effective interest method. (Round answers to the nearest dollar.)

LO6 **Bond Retirement**

E 13. The Perusko Corporation has outstanding $800,000 of 8 percent bonds callable at 104. On September 1, immediately after recording the payment of the semiannual interest and the amortization of the discount, the unamortized bond discount equaled $21,000. On that date, $480,000 of the bonds was called and retired.

1. How much cash must be paid to retire the bonds?
2. Is there a gain or loss on retirement, and if so, how much is it?

LO6   **Bond Conversion**

E 14. The Manco Corporation has $800,000 of 6 percent bonds outstanding. There is $40,000 of unamortized discount remaining on these bonds after the July 1, 2008, semiannual interest payment. The bonds are convertible at the rate of 40 shares of $5 par value common stock for each $2,000 bond. On July 1, 2008, bondholders presented $600,000 of the bonds for conversion.

1. Is there a gain or loss on conversion, and if so, how much is it?
2. How many shares of common stock are issued in exchange for the bonds?
3. In dollar amounts, how does this transaction affect the total liabilities and the total stockholders' equity of the company? In your answer, show the effects on four accounts.

LO5, SO7   **Effective Interest Method and Interest Accrual**

E 15. The long-term debt section of the Panza Corporation's balance sheet at the end of its fiscal year, December 31, 2007, is as follows:

Long-term liabilities		
Bonds payable—8%, interest payable		
1/1 and 7/1, due 12/31/16	$500,000	
Less unamortized bond discount	40,000	$460,000

Prepare entries in journal form relevant to the interest payments on July 1, 2007, December 31, 2007, and January 1, 2008. Assume a market interest rate of 10 percent.

LO4, LO6   **Time Value of Money and Early Extinguishment of Debt**

E 16. Charles, Inc., has a $700,000, 8 percent bond issue that was issued a number of years ago at face value. There are now ten years left on the bond issue, and the market interest rate is 16 percent. Interest is paid semi-annually. The company purchases the bonds on the open market at the calculated current market value and retires the bonds.

1. Using present value tables, calculate the current market value of the bond issue.
2. Is there a gain or loss on retirement of bonds, and if so, how much is it?

LO3, SO7   **Bond Issue on and Between Interest Dates**

E 17. Agard Techtronics, Inc., is authorized to issue $3,600,000 in bonds on June 1. The bonds carry a face interest rate of 9 percent, which is to be paid on June 1 and December 1. Prepare entries in journal form for the issue of the bonds by Agard Techtronics, Inc., under the assumptions that (a) the bonds are issued on September 1 at 100 and (b) the bonds are issued on June 1 at 105.

SO7   **Bond Issue Between Interest Dates**

E 18. Plaka Corporation sold $800,000 of 12 percent, ten-year bonds at face value on September 1, 20xx. The issue date of the bonds was May 1, 20xx.

1. Record the sale of the bonds on September 1 and the first semiannual interest payment on November 1, 20xx.
2. The company's fiscal year ends on December 31, and this is its only bond issue. What is the bond interest expense for the year ended December 31, 20xx?

LO3, LO5, SO7 **Year-End Accrual of Bond Interest**

E 19. Chaney Corporation issued $2,000,000 of 9 percent bonds on October 1, 20x7, at 96. The bonds are dated October 1 and pay interest semiannually. The market interest rate is 10 percent, and Chaney's fiscal year ends on December 31. Prepare the entries to record the issuance of the bonds, the accrual of the interest on December 31, 20x7, and the first semiannual interest payment on April 1, 20x8. Assume the company uses the effective interest method to amortize the bond discount.

Problems

LO1, LO2, LO3 **Bond Terminology**

P 1. Listed below are common terms associated with bonds:

a. Bond certificate	j. Coupon bonds
b. Bond issue	k. Callable bonds
c. Bond indenture	l. Convertible bonds
d. Unsecured bonds	m. Face interest rate
e. Debenture bonds	n. Market interest rate
f. Secured bonds	o. Effective interest rate
g. Term bonds	p. Bond premium
h. Serial bonds	q. Bond discount
i. Registered bonds	

Required

1. For each of the following statements, identify the category above with which it is associated. (If two statements apply, choose the category with which it is most closely associated.)

   1. Occurs when bonds are sold at more than face value
   2. Rate of interest that will vary depending on economic conditions
   3. Bonds that may be exchanged for common stock
   4. Bonds that are not registered
   5. A bond issue in which all bonds are due on the same date
   6. Occurs when bonds are sold at less than face value
   7. Rate of interest that will be paid regardless of market conditions
   8. Bonds that may be retired at management's option
   9. A document that is evidence of a company's debt
   10. Same as market rate of interest
   11. Bonds for which the company knows who owns them
   12. A bond issue for which bonds are due at different dates
   13. The total value of bonds issued at one time
   14. Bonds whose payment involves a pledge of certain assets
   15. Same as debenture bonds
   16. Contains the terms of the bond issue
   17. Bonds issued on the general credit of the company

2. **User Insight:** What effect will a decrease in interest rates below the face interest rate and before a bond is issued have on the cash received from

the bond issue? What effect will the decrease have on interest expense? What effect will the decrease have on the amount of cash paid for interest?

LO3, LO5, LO6 **Bond Basics—Straight-line Method, Retirement, and Conversion**

P 2. Abel Corporation has $10,000,000 of 10.5 percent, 20-year bonds dated June 1, 20x7, with interest payment dates of May 31 and November 30. After ten years the bonds are callable at 104, and each $1,000 bond is convertible into 25 shares of $20 par value common stock. The company's fiscal year ends on December 31. It uses the straight-line method to amortize bond premiums or discounts.

Required

1. Assume the bonds are issued at 103 on June 1, 20x7.

    a. How much cash is received?
    b. How much is Bonds Payable?
    c. What is the difference between **a** and **b** called and how much is it?
    d. With regard to the bond interest payment on November 30, 20x7:
       (1) How much cash is paid in interest?
       (2) How much is the amortization?
       (3) How much is interest expense?

2. Assume the bonds are issued at 97 on June 1, 20x7.

    a. How much cash is received?
    b. How much is Bonds Payable?
    c. What is the difference between **a** and **b** called and how much is it?
    d. With regard to the bond interest payment on November 30, 20x7:
       (1) How much cash is paid in interest?
       (2) How much is the amortization?
       (3) How much is interest expense?

3. Assume the issue price in requirement **1** and that the bonds are called and retired ten years later.

    a. How much cash will have to be paid to retire the bonds?
    b. Is there a gain or loss on the retirement, and if so, how much is it?

4. Assume the issue price in requirement **2** and that the bonds are converted to common stock ten years later.

    a. Is there a gain or loss on the conversion, and if so, how much is it?
    b. How many shares of common stock are issued in exchange for the bonds?
    c. In dollar amounts, how does this transaction affect the total liabilities and the total stockholders' equity of the company? In your answer, show the effects on four accounts.

5. **User Insight:** Assume that after ten years, market interest rates have dropped significantly and that the price on the company's common stock has risen significantly. Also assume that management wants to improve its credit rating by reducing its debt to equity ratio and that it needs what cash it has for expansion. Which approach would management prefer—the approach and result in requirement **3** or **4**? Explain your answer. What would be a disadvantage of the approach you chose?

LO3, LO5 **Effective Interest Method**

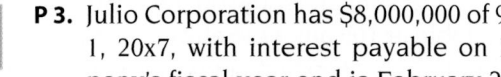

P 3. Julio Corporation has $8,000,000 of 9.5 percent, 25-year bonds dated March 1, 20x7, with interest payable on February 28 and August 31. The company's fiscal year end is February 28. It uses the effective interest method to amortize bond premiums or discounts. (Round amounts to the nearest dollar.)

Required

1. Assume the bonds are issued at 102.5 on March 1, 20x7, to yield an effective interest rate of 9.2 percent. Prepare entries in journal form for March 1, 20x7, August 31, 20x7, and February 28, 20x8.
2. Assume the bonds are issued at 97.5 on March 1, 2007, to yield an effective interest rate of 9.8 percent. Prepare entries in journal form for March 1, 20x7, August 31, 20x7, and February 28, 20x8.
3. User Insight: Explain the role that market interest rates play in causing a premium in requirement **1** and a discount in requirement **2**.

LO3, LO5, SO7   Bonds Issued at a Discount and a Premium—Effective Interest Method

P 4. Waxman Corporation issued bonds twice during 20x7. A summary of the transactions involving the bonds follows.

20x7

Jan.	1	Issued $6,000,000 of 9.9 percent, ten-year bonds dated January 1, 20x7, with interest payable on June 30 and December 31. The bonds were sold at 102.6, resulting in an effective interest rate of 9.4 percent.
Mar.	1	Issued $4,000,000 of 9.2 percent, ten-year bonds dated March 1, 20x7, with interest payable March 1 and September 1. The bonds were sold at 98.2, resulting in an effective interest rate of 9.5 percent.
June	30	Paid semiannual interest on the January 1 issue and amortized the premium, using the effective interest method.
Sept.	1	Paid semiannual interest on the March 1 issue and amortized the discount, using the effective interest method.
Dec.	31	Paid semiannual interest on the January 1 issue and amortized the premium, using the effective interest method.
	31	Made an end-of-year adjusting entry to accrue interest on the March 1 issue and to amortize two-thirds of the discount applicable to the second interest period.

20x8

Mar.	1	Paid semiannual interest on the March 1 issue and amortized the remainder of the discount applicable to the second interest period.

Required

1. Prepare entries in journal form to record the bond transactions. (Round amounts to the nearest dollar.)
2. User Insight: Describe the effect on profitability and liquidity by answering the following questions.

    a. What is the total interest expense in 20x7 for each of the bond issues?
    b. What is the total cash paid in 20x7 for each of the bond issues?
    c. What differences, if any, do you observe and how do you explain them?

LO3, LO5, LO6   Bond Interest and Amortization Table, Retirements, and Conversions

P 5. In 2008, the Fender Corporation was authorized to issue $60,000,000 of six-year unsecured bonds. The bonds carried a face interest rate of 9 percent, payable semiannually on June 30 and December 31. The bonds were callable at 105 any time after June 30, 2011. All of the bonds were issued on July 1, 2008 at 95.568, a price yielding an effective interest rate of 10 percent. On July 1, 2011, the company called and retired half the outstanding bonds.

Required

1. Prepare a table similar to Table 1 to show the interest and amortization of the bond discount for 12 interest payment periods, using the effective interest method. (Round results to the nearest dollar.)
2. Calculate the amount of loss on early retirement of one-half of the bonds on July 1, 2011.
3. Assume the bonds are also convertible at the rate of 25 shares of $10 par value common stock for each $1,000 bond and that the other half of the bonds were converted on July 1, 2011. Calculate the amounts at which Common Stock and Additional Paid-in Capital would be increased as a result of this transaction.
4. **User Insight:** Under the effective interest method used in this problem, does interest expense exceed cash paid for interest or is it less? Explain your answer. Also explain why interest expense differs for each six-month period. What role does materiality play in the choice of the effective interest method?

Alternate Problems

LO3, LO5, LO6   **Bond Basics—Straight-Line Method, Retirement and Conversion**

P 6. Bassi Corporation has $8,000,000 of 9.5 percent, 25-year bonds dated May 1, 20x8, with interest payable on April 30 and October 31. The company's fiscal year ends on December 31, and it uses the straight-line method to amortize bond premiums or discounts. The bonds are callable after ten years at 103 or convertible into 40 shares of $10 par value common stock.

Required

1. Assume the bonds are issued at 103.5 on May 1, 20x8.
   a. How much cash is received?
   b. How much is Bonds Payable?
   c. What is the difference between **a** and **b** called and how much is it?
   d. With regard to the bond interest payment on October 31, 20x8:
      (1) How much cash is paid in interest?
      (2) How much is the amortization?
      (3) How much is interest expense?
2. Assume the bonds are issued at 96.5 on May 1, 20x8.
   a. How much cash is received?
   b. How much is Bonds Payable?
   c. What is the difference between **a** and **b** called and how much is it?
   d. With regard to the bond interest payment on October 31, 20x8:
      (1) How much cash is paid in interest?
      (2) How much is the amortization?
      (3) How much is interest expense?
3. Assume the issue price in requirement **1** and that the bonds are called and retired ten years later.
   a. How much cash will have to be paid to retire the bonds?
   b. Is there a gain or loss on the retirement, and if so, how much is it?
4. Assume the issue price in requirement **2** and that the bonds are converted to common stock ten years later.

a. Is there a gain or loss on conversion, and if so, how much is it?

b. How many shares of common stock are issued in exchange for the bonds?

c. In dollar amounts, how does this transaction affect the total liabilities and the total stockholders' equity of the company? In your answer, show the effects on four accounts.

5. **User Insight:** Assume that after ten years market interest rates have dropped significantly and that the price of the company's common stock has risen significantly. Also assume that management wants to improve its credit rating by reducing its debt to equity ratio and that it needs what cash it currently has for expansion. Would management prefer the approach and result in requirement **3** or **4**? Explain your answer. What would be a disadvantage of the approach you chose?

LO3, LO5   **Bond Transactions—Effective Interest Method**

P 7. Khan Corporation has $20,000,000 of 10.5 percent, 20-year bonds dated June 1, 20x7 with interest payment dates of May 31 and November 30. The company's fiscal year ends November 30. It uses the effective interest method to amortize bond premiums or discounts.

Required

1. Assume the bonds are issued at 103 on June 1 to yield an effective interest rate of 10.1 percent. Prepare entries in journal form for June 1, 20x7, November 30, 20x7, and May 31, 20x8. (Round amounts to the nearest dollar.)

2. Assume the bonds are issued at 97 on June 1 to yield an effective interest rate of 10.9 percent. Prepare entries in journal form for June 1, 20x7, November 30, 20x7, and May 31, 20x8. (Round amounts to the nearest dollar.)

3. **User Insight:** Explain the role that market interest rates play in causing a premium in requirement **1** and a discount in requirement **2**.

LO3, LO5, SO7   **Bonds Issued at a Discount and a Premium—Effective Interest Method**

P 8. Pakesh Corporation issued bonds twice during 20x7. The transactions were as follows:

20x7

Jan.   1   Issued $2,000,000 of 9.2 percent, ten-year bonds dated January 1, 20x7, with interest payable on June 30 and December 31. The bonds were sold at 98.1, resulting in an effective interest rate of 9.5 percent.

Apr.   1   Issued $4,000,000 of 9.8 percent, ten-year bonds dated April 1, 20x7, with interest payable on March 31 and September 30. The bonds were sold at 101, resulting in an effective interest rate of 9.5 percent.

June   30   Paid semiannual interest on the January 1 issue and amortized the discount, using the effective interest method.

Sept.   30   Paid semiannual interest on the April 1 issue and amortized the premium, using the effective interest method.

Dec.   31   Paid semiannual interest on the January 1 issue and amortized the discount, using the effective interest method.

31   Made an end-of-year adjusting entry to accrue interest on the April 1 issue and to amortize half the premium applicable to the second interest period.

20x8

Mar. 31 Paid semiannual interest on the April 1 issue and amortized the premium applicable to the second half of the second interest period.

Required

1. Prepare entries in journal form to record the bond transactions. (Round amounts to the nearest dollar.)
2. **User Insight:** Describe the effect of the above transactions on profitability and liquidity by answering the following questions.
   a. What is the total interest expense in 20x7 for each of the bond issues?
   b. What is the total cash paid in 20x7 for each of the bond issues?
   c. What differences, if any, do you observe and how do you explain them?

ENHANCING Your Knowledge, Skills, and Critical Thinking

Conceptual Understanding Cases

LO1   **Effect of Long-Term Leases**

C1. Many companies use long-term leases to finance long-term assets. Although these leases are similar to mortgage payments, they are structured in such a way that they qualify as operating leases. As a result, the lease commitments do not appear on the companies' balance sheets. In a recent year, **Continental Airlines** had lease commitments of $324 million, and **Heinz** had lease commitments of $220 million.[12]

What effect do these types of leases have on the balance sheet? Why would the use of these long-term leases make a company's debt to equity ratio, interest coverage ratio, and free cash flow look better than they really are? What is a capital lease? How does the application of capital lease accounting provide insight into a company's financial health?

LO2, LO6   **Bond Issue**

C2. Eastman Kodak, the photography company, issued a $1 billion bond issue. Even though the company's credit rating was low, the bond issue was well received by the investment community because the company offered attractive terms. The offering comprised $500 million of 10-year unsecured notes and $500 million of 30-year convertible bonds. The convertibles were callable after seven years and would be convertible into common stock about 40 to 45 percent higher than the current price.[13]

What are unsecured notes? Why would they carry a relatively high interest rate? What are convertible securities? Why are they good for the investor and for the company? Why would they carry a relatively low interest rate? What does *callable* mean? What advantage does this feature give the company?

LO2, LO3   **Bond Interest Rates and Market Prices**

C3. Safeway Inc. is one of the largest food and drug retailers in North America. Among its long-term liabilities was a bond due in 2004 that carried a face interest rate of 9.65 percent.[14] This bond sold on the New York Stock Exchange at 108⅝. Did this bond sell at a discount or a premium? Assuming the bond was originally issued at face value, did interest rates rise or decline after the date of issue? Would you have expected the market rate of interest on this bond to be more or less than 9.65 percent? Did the current market price affect either the amount that the company paid in semiannual interest or the amount of interest expense for the same period? Explain your answers.

Interpreting Financial Reports

LO1 **Debt Repayment**

C 4. During economic recessions, occupancy rates of hotels generally decline, and as a result, the hotels are forced to reduce their room prices. The impact on a hotel's cash flows may be such that it is unable to pay its debts when they come due.

Some years ago, the Hospitality Research Group studied the financial statements of 3,300 hotels. It found that 16 percent of hotels were unable to generate enough cash from operations to make debt repayments in 2000. The study estimated that this figure would increase to 20.9 percent in 2001 and 36.5 percent in 2002.[15] What alternative sources of cash might be available to hotels whose cash flows from operations are inadequate to cover debt repayments?

LO2 **Characteristics of Convertible Debt**

C 5. Amazon.com, Inc., gained renown as an online marketplace for books, records, and other products. Although the increase in its stock price was initially meteoric, only recently has the company begun to earn a profit. To support its enormous growth, Amazon.com issued $1,250,000,000 in 4¾ percent convertible notes due in 2009 at face value. Interest is payable on February 1 and August 1. The notes are convertible into common stock at a price of $78 per share, which at the time of issue was 27 percent above the market price of $61.50. The market value of Amazon.com's common stock has been quite volatile, from $50 to $35 in early 2006.[16]

What reasons can you suggest for Amazon.com's management choosing notes that are convertible into common stock rather than simply issuing non-convertible notes or issuing common stock directly? Are there any disadvantages to this approach? If the price of the company's common stock goes to $100 per share, what would be the total theoretical value of the notes? If the holders of the notes were to elect to convert the notes into common stock, what would be the effect on the company's debt to equity ratio, and what would be the effect on the percentage ownership of the company by other stockholders?

Decision Analysis Using Excel

LO1, LO2 **Issuance of Long-Term Bonds Versus Leasing**

C 6. The Weiss Chemical Corporation plans to build or lease a new plant that will produce liquid fertilizer for the agricultural market. The plant is expected to cost $800,000,000 and will be located in the southwestern United States. The company's chief financial officer, Sharon Weiss, has spent the last several weeks studying different means of financing the plant. Following her talks with bankers and other financiers, she has decided that there are two basic choices: the plant can be financed through the issuance of a long-term bond or through a long-term lease. Details for the two options are as follows:

1. Issue $800,000,000 of 25-year, 16 percent bonds secured by the new plant. Interest on the bonds would be payable semiannually.

2. Sign a 25-year lease for an existing plant calling for lease payments of $65,400,000 on a semiannual basis.

Weiss wants to know what effect each choice would have on the company's financial statements. She estimates that the useful life of the plant is 25 years, at which time the plant is expected to have an estimated residual value of $80,000,000.

Weiss is planning a meeting to discuss the alternatives. Write a short memorandum to her identifying the issues that should be considered at this meeting. (**Note:** You are not asked to make any calculations, discuss the factors, or recommend an action.)

Annual Report Case: CVS Corporation

LO1 **Business Practice, Long-Term Debt, Leases, and Pensions**

C 7. To answer the following questions, refer to the financial statements and the notes to the financial statements in **CVS Corporation's** annual report in the Supplement to Chapter 5:

1. Is it the practice of CVS to own or lease most of its buildings?
2. Does CVS lease property predominantly under capital leases or under operating leases? How much was rental expense for operating leases in 2005?
3. Does CVS have a defined benefit pension plan? Does it offer postretirement benefits?

Comparison Case: CVS Versus Southwest

LO1 **Use of Debt Financing**

Ⓚ/Ⓡ **C 8.** Refer to the annual report of **CVS Corporation** and the financial statements of **Southwest Airlines Co.** in the Supplement to Chapter 5. Calculate the debt to equity ratio and the interest coverage ratio for both companies' two most recent years. Find the note to the financial statements that contains information on leases and lease commitments by CVS. Southwest's lease expenses were $403 million and $409 million in 2004 and 2005, respectively, and total lease commitments for future years were $2,533 million. What effect do the total lease commitments and lease expense have on your assessment of the ratios you calculated? Evaluate and comment on the relative performance of the two companies with regard to debt financing. Which company has more risk of not being able to meet its interest obligations? How does leasing affect the analysis? Explain.

Ethical Dilemma Case

LO2 **Bond Indenture and Ethical Reporting**

C 9. CellWorks Technology, Inc., a biotech company, has a $24,000,000 bond issue outstanding. The bond indenture has several restrictive provisions, including requirements that current assets exceed current liabilities by a ratio of 2 to 1 and that income before income taxes exceed the annual interest on the bonds by a ratio of 3 to 1. If those requirements are not met, the bondholders can force the company into bankruptcy. The company is still awaiting Food and Drug Administration (FDA) approval of its new product, CMZ-12, a cancer treatment drug. Management has been counting on sales of CMZ-12 this year to meet the provisions of the bond indenture. As the end of the fiscal year approaches, the company does not have sufficient current assets or income before income taxes to meet the requirements. Roger Landon, the chief financial officer, proposes, "Since we can assume that FDA approval will occur early next year, I suggest we book sales and receivables from our major customers now in anticipation of next year's sales. This action will increase our current assets and our income before income taxes. It is essential that we do this to save the company. Look at all the people who will be hurt if we don't do it."

Is Landon's proposal acceptable accounting? Is it ethical? Who could be harmed by it? What steps might management take?

Internet Case

LO2 **Bond Rating Changes**

C 10. During economic or industry recessions, it is common to see downward revisions of bond ratings. Access Standard & Poor's list of companies with lowered bond ratings and identify three whose names you recognize. Based on your general knowledge of these companies, give reasons that you believe contributed to the downgrade of the ratings.

Group Activity Case

LO4 **Nature of Zero Coupon Notes**

C 11. The *Wall Street Journal* reported, "Financially ailing **Trans World Airlines** has renegotiated its agreement to sell its 40 landing and takeoff slots and three gates at O'Hare International Airport to **American Airlines.**"[17] Instead of receiving a lump-sum cash payment in the amount of $162.5 million, TWA elected to receive a zero coupon note from American that would be paid off in monthly installments over a 20-year period. Since the 240 monthly payments totaled $500 million, TWA placed a value of $500 million on the note and indicated that the bankruptcy court would not have accepted the lower lump-sum cash payment.[18]

Divide into groups to discuss the following questions:

1. How does this zero coupon note differ from the zero coupon bonds that were described earlier in this chapter?

2. How do you explain the difference between the $162.5 million cash payment and the $500 million note?

3. Do you think TWA was right in placing a $500 million price on the sale?

Business Communication Case

LO1 **Comparison of Interest Coverage**

C 12. Japanese companies have historically relied more on debt financing and are more highly leveraged than U.S. companies. For instance, **NEC Corporation** and **Sanyo Electric Co.**, two large Japanese electronics companies, had debt to equity ratios of about 4.0 and 8.0, respectively, in 2005.[19] From the selected data from the companies' annual reports shown in the table that follows (in millions of yen), compute the interest coverage ratios for the two companies for the two years.

	NEC		Sanyo	
	2005	**2004**	**2005**	**2004**
Interest expense	18,632	27,510	17,118	14,868
Income (loss) before income taxes	115,664	160,546	(16,675)	45,992

Assume you are a financial analyst. Write a one-page memorandum that addresses the riskiness of these two companies and the trends they show. Include in your memorandum a summary of the advantages and disadvantages of a debt-laden capital structure.

The Corporate Income Statement and the Statement of Stockholders' Equity

As we pointed out in an earlier chapter, earnings management—the practice of manipulating revenues and expenses to achieve a specific outcome—is unethical when companies use it to create misleading financial statements. Users of financial statements consider the possibility of earnings management by assessing the quality, or sustainability, of a company's earnings. To do so, they evaluate how the components of the company's income statement affect earnings. In this chapter, we focus on those components. We also cover earnings per share, the statement of stockholders' equity, stock dividends and stock splits, and book value per share.

LEARNING OBJECTIVES

Making a Statement

Balance Sheet

Statement of Cash Flows

Income Statement

The corporate income statement aids in the analysis of profitability and links to stockholders' equity, a component of the balance sheet.

LO1 Define *quality of earnings,* and identify the components of a corporate income statement.

LO2 Show the relationships among income taxes expense, deferred income taxes, and net of taxes.

LO3 Describe the disclosure on the income statement of discontinued operations and extraordinary items.

LO4 Compute earnings per share.

LO5 Define *comprehensive income,* and describe the statement of stockholders' equity.

LO6 Account for stock dividends and stock splits.

LO7 Calculate book value per share.

- What items other than normal operating activities contributed to Motorola's performance?

- What does the company's income statement indicate about its quality of earnings?

- How does one put the various measures of performance (some of which are shown in Motorola's financial highlights) in perspective?

Motorola, a well-known maker of cell phones and other telecommunications equipment, has had its ups and downs in recent years. As shown in its Financial Highlights, the company had low earnings in 2003 but improved its earnings in 2004 and 2005.[1] Motorola's income statements reflect the changes the company has made to improve operations over this period.

How does one use complex income statements like Motorola's to evaluate a company's performance? It is not enough to simply look at the "bottom line" (i.e., net earnings) or even at net sales and operating income. To gain a proper perspective on a company's performance, one must examine the components of its income statement.

MOTOROLA'S FINANCIAL HIGHLIGHTS
(In millions, except per share data)

	2005	2004	2003
Net sales	$36,843	$31,323	$23,155
Operating earnings (loss)	4,696	3,132	1,273
Net earnings	4,578	1,532	893
Basic earnings per share	1.85	0.65	0.38
Cash flows from operating activities	4,605	3,066	1,991

Performance Measurement: Quality of Earnings Issues

LO1   Define *quality of earnings,* and identify the components of a corporate income statement.

N et income (net earnings) is the measure most commonly used to evaluate a company's performance. In fact, a survey of 2,000 members of the Association for Investment Management and Research indicated that the two most important economic measures in evaluating common stocks were expected changes in earnings per share and expected return on equity.[2] Net income is a key component of both measures.

Because of the importance of net income, or the "bottom line," in measuring a company's prospects, there is significant interest in evaluating the quality of the net income figure, or the **quality of earnings**. The quality of a company's earnings refers to the substance of earnings and their sustainability into future accounting periods. For example, if earnings increase because of a gain on the sale of an asset, this portion of earnings will not be sustained in the future.

The accounting estimates and methods that a company uses affect the quality of its earnings, as do these components of the income statement:

- Gains and losses on transactions

- Write-downs and restructurings

- Nonoperating items

Because management has choices in the content and positioning of these income statement components, there is a potential for managing earnings to achieve specific income targets. It is therefore critical for users of income statements to understand these factors and take them into consideration when evaluating a company's performance.

Exhibit 1 shows the components of a typical corporate income statement. Net income or loss (the "bottom line" of the income statement) includes all revenues, expenses, gains, and losses over the accounting period. When a company has both continuing and discontinued operations, the operating income section is called **income from continuing operations**. Income from continuing operations before income taxes may include gains or losses on the sale of assets, write-downs, and restructurings. The income taxes expense section of the statement is subject to special accounting rules.

As you can see in Exhibit 1, the section of a corporate income statement that follows income taxes contains such nonoperating items as discontinued operations and extraordinary gains (or losses). Another item that may appear

FOCUS ON BUSINESS PRACTICE
Why Do Investors Study Quality of Earnings?

Analysts for **Twentieth Century Mutual Funds**, a major investment company now merged with **American Century Investments Corporation**, make adjustments to a company's reported financial performance to create a more accurate picture of the company's ongoing operations. For example, suppose a paper manufacturer reports earnings of $1.30 per share. Further investigation, however, shows that the per share number includes a one-time gain on the sale of assets, which accounts for an increase of $.25 per share. Twentieth Century would list the company as earning only $1.05 per share. "These kinds of adjustments help assure long-term decisions aren't based on one-time events."[3]

▼ EXHIBIT 1

Corporate Income Statement

Envest Corporation
Income Statement
For the Year Ended December 31, 20x8

Operating items before income taxes	Revenues	$925,000
	Costs and expenses	(550,000)
	Gain on sale of assets	150,000
	Write-downs of assets	(25,000)
	Restructurings	(75,000)
	Income from continuing operations before income taxes	$425,000
Income taxes	Income taxes expense	144,500
	Income from continuing operations	$280,500
	Discontinued operations	
Nonoperating items	Income from operations of discontinued segment (net of taxes, $35,000)	$90,000
	Loss on disposal of segment (net of taxes, $42,000)	(73,000) 17,000
	Income before extraordinary items	$297,500
	Extraordinary gain (net of taxes, $12,000)	37,000
	Net income	$334,500
	Earnings per common share:	
	Income from continuing operations	$ 2.81
Earnings per share information	Discontinued operations (net of taxes)	.17
	Income before extraordinary items	$ 2.98
	Extraordinary gain (net of taxes)	.37
	Net income	$ 3.35

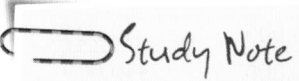

Study Note

It is important to know which items included in earnings are recurring and which are one-time items. Income from continuing operations before nonoperating items gives a clear signal about future results. In assessing a company's future earnings potential, nonoperating items are excluded because they are not expected to continue.

in this section is the write-off of goodwill when its value has been impaired. Earnings per share information appears at the bottom of the statement.

The Effect of Accounting Estimates and Methods

Users of financial statements need to be aware of the impact that accounting estimates and methods have on the income that a firm reports. As you know, to comply with the matching rule, accountants must assign revenues and expenses to the periods in which they occur. If they cannot establish a direct relationship between revenues and expenses, they systematically allocate the expenses among the accounting periods that benefit from them, and in doing so, they must make estimates and exercise judgment. An accounting estimate should be based on realistic assumptions, but there is latitude in making the estimate, and the final judgment will affect the net income that appears on a company's income statement.

For example, when a company acquires an asset, the accountant must estimate the asset's useful life. Technological obsolescence could shorten the asset's expected useful life, and regular maintenance and repairs could lengthen it. Although the actual useful life cannot be known with certainty until some future date, the accountant's estimate of it affects both current and future operating income. Other areas that require accounting estimates include the residual value of assets, uncollectible accounts receivable, sales returns, total units of production, total recoverable units of natural resources, amortization periods, warranty claims, and environmental cleanup costs.

Accounting estimates are not equally important to all firms. Their importance depends on the industry in which a firm operates. For example, estimated uncollectible receivables for a credit card firm, such as **American Express**, or for a financial services firm, such as **Bank of America**, can have a material impact on earnings, but estimated useful life may be less important because depreciable assets represent only a small percentage of the firm's total assets. **Walgreens** has very few receivables, but it has substantial investments in depreciable assets. Thus, estimates of useful life and residual value are much more important to Walgreens than an estimate of uncollectible accounts receivable.

The accounting methods a firm uses also affect its operating income. Generally accepted accounting methods include uncollectible receivable methods (percentage of net sales and aging of accounts receivable), inventory methods (LIFO, FIFO, and average-cost), depreciation methods (accelerated, production, and straight-line), and revenue recognition methods. All these methods are designed to match revenues and expenses, but the expenses are estimates, and the period or periods benefited cannot be demonstrated conclusively. In practice, it is hard to justify one method of estimation over another.

Different accounting methods have different effects on net income. Some methods are more conservative than others because they tend to produce a lower net income in the current period. For example, suppose that two companies have similar operations, but one uses FIFO for inventory costing and the straight-line (SL) method for computing depreciation, whereas the other uses LIFO for inventory costing and the double-declining-balance (DDB) method for computing depreciation. The income statements of the two companies might appear as follows:

	FIFO *and* SL	LIFO *and* DDB
Net sales	$925,000	$925,000
Goods available for sale	$400,000	$400,000
Less ending inventory	60,000	50,000
Cost of goods sold	$340,000	$350,000
Gross margin	$585,000	$575,000
Less depreciation expense	$ 40,000	$ 80,000
Less other expenses	170,000	170,000
Total operating expenses	$210,000	$250,000
Income from continuing operations before income taxes	$375,000	$325,000

The income from continuing operations before income taxes (operating income) for the firm that uses LIFO and DDB is lower because in periods of rising prices, the LIFO inventory costing method produces a higher cost of goods sold, and in the early years of an asset's useful life, accelerated depreciation yields a higher depreciation expense. The result is lower operating income. However, future operating income should be higher.

Although the choice of accounting method does not affect cash flows except for possible differences in income taxes, the $50,000 difference in operating income stems solely from the choice of accounting methods. Estimates of

FOCUS ON BUSINESS PRACTICE
Were Preussag's Year-End Results Really "Remarkable"?

The big German travel company **Preussag** reported that the year 2000 was "a remarkable year" in which the company achieved "all-time high" results and "profit rose by 16.5 percent." However, Preussag's financial reports reveal that profits would have been far less remarkable if the company had not made four voluntary accounting changes. Had these changes not been taken into account, profits would have increased by only 6.7 percent. The company began recognizing revenue from holiday packages at the beginning of the holiday instead of at the stage of completion, and it began deferring the cost of brochures over future tourist seasons. In addition, the cost of flying the planes empty at the beginning and end of each tourist season were amortized over the season. Finally, Preussag changed its inventory method from LIFO to the average-cost method. Cosmetic changes like these do not affect future cash flows or change a company's operations for the better.[4]

the useful lives and residual values of plant assets could lead to an even greater difference. In practice, of course, differences in net income occur for many reasons, but the user of financial statements must be aware of the discrepancies that can occur as a result of the accounting methods used in preparing the statements. In general, an accounting method or estimate that results in lower current earnings produces a better quality of operating income.

The latitude that companies have in their choice of accounting methods and estimates could cause problems in the interpretation of financial statements were it not for the conventions of full disclosure and consistency. As noted in an earlier chapter, full disclosure requires management to explain the significant accounting policies used in preparing the financial statements in a note to the statements. Consistency requires that the same accounting procedures be followed from year to year. If a change in procedure is made, the nature of the change and its monetary effect must be explained in a note. For instance, in a note to its financial statements, **Motorola** discloses that it uses the FIFO method for inventory accounting and a combination of straight-line and accelerated depreciation methods for various groups of long-term assets.

Gains and Losses

When a company sells or otherwise disposes of operating assets or marketable securities, a gain or loss generally results. Although these gains or losses appear in the operating section of the income statement, they usually represent one-time events. They are not sustainable, ongoing operations, and management often has some choice as to their timing. Thus, from an analyst's point of view, they should be ignored when considering operating income.

Write-downs and Restructurings

Management has considerable latitude in deciding when an asset is no longer of value to the company. When management makes this judgment, a write-down or restructuring occurs.

▶ A **write-down**, also called a *write-off*, is a reduction in the value of an asset below its carrying value on the balance sheet.

▶ A **restructuring** is the estimated cost of a change in a company's operations. It usually involves the closing of facilities and the laying off of personnel.

Both write-downs and restructurings reduce current operating income and boost future income by shifting future costs to the current accounting period.

They are often an indication of poor management decisions in the past, such as paying too much for the assets of another company or making operational changes that do not work out. Companies sometimes take all possible losses in the current year so that future years will be "clean" of these costs. Such "big baths," as they are called, commonly occur when a company is having a bad year. They also often occur in years when there is a change in management. The new management takes a "big bath" in the current year so it can show improved results in future years.

In a recent year, 32 percent of 600 large companies had write-downs of tangible assets, and 38 percent had restructurings. Another 52 percent had write-downs or charges related to intangible assets, often involving goodwill.[7]

Nonoperating Items

The nonoperating items that appear on the income statement,* such as discontinued operations and extraordinary gains and losses, can also significantly affect net income. In Exhibit 1, earnings per common share for income from continuing operations are $2.81, but when all the nonoperating items are taken into consideration, net income per share is $3.35.

Analysts base their calculations of trends and ratios on the assumption that the components of the income statement are comparable from year to year and from company to company. However, the astute analyst will always look beyond the ratios to the quality of these components. For example, write-downs, restructurings, and nonoperating items, if the charges are large enough, can have a significant effect on a company's return on equity.

Quality of Earnings and Cash Flows

The reason for considering quality of earnings issues is to assess how they affect cash flows and performance measures that are affected by earnings, such as profit margin, return on assets, and return on equity. Generally, except for their effect on income taxes, gains and losses, asset write-downs, restructurings, and nonoperating items have no effect on cash flows because the cash for

---

*In May 2005, the FASB issued a statement that removed an item from this category. The effects of changes in accounting principles are no longer reported on the income statement but are a direct adjustment to retained earnings.

Motorola provides communications equipment to the National Football League. Shown here wearing a Motorola headset is Bill Belichick, head coach of the New England Patriots. Despite Motorola's sluggish results in recent years, its CEO pointed out in 2005 that the company's quality of earnings had improved from year to year. *Quality of earnings* refers to the substance and sustainability of earnings into future accounting periods.

these items has already been expended. Thus, the focus of analysis is on sustainable earnings, which generally have a relationship to future cash flows.

Because **Motorola** has a history of reporting nonrecurring special items, including restructuring expenses and investment and inventory write-offs, analysts have questioned the quality of its earnings.[8] Recently, the company had 15 straight quarters of such items. As shown in Exhibit 2, the nonrecurring special

EXHIBIT 2 ▶

Motorola's Income Statement

	Year Ended December 31		
(In millions)	**2005**	2004	2003
Net sales	**$36,843**	$31,323	$23,155
Cost of sales	**25,066**	20,969	15,652
Gross margin	**11,777**	10,354	7,503
Selling, general, and administrative expenses	**3,859**	3,714	3,285
Research and development expenditures	**3,680**	3,412	2,979
Reorganization of businesses	—	(15)	23
Other charges (income)	(458)	111	(57)
Operating earnings	**4,696**	3,132	1,273
Other income (expense):			
Interest income (expense), net	**71**	(199)	(294)
Gains on sales of investments and businesses, net	1,861	460	539
Other	**(108)**	(141)	(142)
Total other income	**1,824**	120	103
Earnings from continuing operations	**6,520**	3,252	1,376
Income tax expense	**1,921**	1,061	448
Earnings from continuing operations	**4,599**	2,191	928
Loss from discontinued operations	(21)	(659)	(35)
Net earnings	**$ 4,578**	$ 1,532	$ 893

Note: Highlighted items are discussed in the text.
Source: Motorola, Inc., *Annual Report*, 2005.

items in Motorola's income statement include reorganization of businesses, other charges, gains on sales of investments and businesses, and losses from discontinued operations in 2003, 2004, and 2005. However, if you look back at Motorola's Financial Highlights at the start of this chapter, you will see that the company's cash flows from operating activities exceeded net earnings in all three years. By this measure, Motorola's earnings are of relatively high quality.

S T O P • R E V I E W • A P P L Y

1-1. What is quality of earnings? What are three components of the income statement that affect quality of earnings?

1-2. Why would the reader of financial statements be interested in management's choice of accounting methods and estimates? Give an example.

1-3. What is the difference between a write-down and a restructuring, and where do these items appear on a corporate income statement?

1-4. How do cash flows relate to quality of earnings?

Suggested Answers to all Stop, Review, and Apply questions are available at http://college.hmco.com/accounting/needles/poa/10e/student_home.html.

Income Taxes

LO2 Show the relationships among income taxes expense, deferred income taxes, and net of taxes.

Corporations determine their taxable income (the amount on which they pay taxes) by deducting allowable expenses from taxable income. The federal tax laws determine which expenses corporations may deduct. (Rules for calculating and reporting taxable income in specialized industries, such as banking, insurance, mutual funds, and cooperatives, are highly technical and may vary significantly from the ones we discuss in this chapter.)

Table 1 shows the tax rates that apply to a corporation's taxable income. A corporation with taxable income of $70,000 would have a federal income tax liability of $12,500: $7,500 (the tax on the first $50,000 of taxable income) plus $5,000 (25 percent of the $20,000 earned in excess of $50,000).

Income taxes expense is recognized in the accounting records on an accrual basis. It may or may not equal the amount of taxes a corporation actually pays. The amount a corporation pays is determined by the rules of the income tax code. As we noted earlier in the text, small businesses often keep both their accounting records and tax records on a cash basis, so that the income taxes expense on their income statements equals their income taxes. This practice is acceptable as long as the difference between the income calculated on an accounting basis and the income calculated for tax purposes is not material. However, the purpose of accounting is not to determine taxable income and tax liability, but to determine net income in accordance with GAAP.

Management has an incentive to use methods that minimize its firm's tax liability. But accountants, who are bound by accrual accounting and the materiality concept, cannot let tax procedures dictate their method of preparing financial statements if the result would be misleading. The difference between

> **Study Note**
>
> Many people think it is illegal to keep accounting records on a different basis from income tax records. However, the Internal Revenue Code and GAAP often do not agree. To work with two conflicting sets of guidelines, the accountant must keep two sets of records.

TABLE 1. Tax Rate Schedule for Corporations, 2006

Taxable Income		Tax Liability	
Over	But Not Over		Of the Amount Over
	$ 50,000	0 + 15%	—
$ 50,000	75,000	$ 7,500 + 25%	$ 50,000
75,000	100,000	13,750 + 34%	75,000
100,000	335,000	22,250 + 39%	100,000
335,000	10,000,000	113,900 + 34%	335,000
10,000,000	15,000,000	3,400,000 + 35%	10,000,000
15,000,000	18,333,333	5,150,000 + 38%	15,000,000
18,333,333	—	6,416,667 + 35%	18,333,333

Note: Tax rates are subject to change by Congress.

accounting income and taxable income, especially in large businesses, can be material. This discrepancy can result from differences in the timing of the recognition of revenues and expenses under accrual accounting and the tax method. The following table shows some possible variations:

	Accrual Accounting	*Tax Method*
Expense recognition	Accrual or deferral	At time of expenditure
Accounts receivable	Allowance	Direct charge-off
Inventories	Average-cost	FIFO
Depreciation	Straight-line	Accelerated cost recovery

Deferred Income Taxes

Income tax allocation is the method used to accrue income taxes expense on the basis of accounting income when accounting income and taxable income differ. The account used to record the difference between income taxes expense and income taxes payable is called **Deferred Income Taxes**. For example, in the income statement in Exhibit 1, Envest Corporation has income taxes expense of $144,500. Suppose, however, that Envest's actual income taxes payable are $92,000. The following entry shows how income tax allocation would treat this situation:

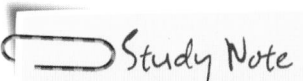

A =	L	+	OE
	+92,000		−144,500
	+52,500		

Dec. 31	Income Taxes Expense	144,500	
	Income Taxes Payable		92,000
	Deferred Income Taxes		52,500
	To record estimated current and deferred income taxes		

In other years, Envest's Income Taxes Payable may exceed its Income Taxes Expense. In this case, the entry is the same except that Deferred Income Taxes is debited.

The Financial Accounting Standards Board has issued specific rules for recording, measuring, and classifying deferred income taxes.[9] Deferred income taxes are recognized for the estimated future tax effects resulting from temporary differences in the valuation of assets, liabilities, equity, revenues,

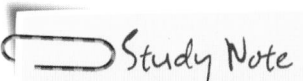
Study Note

The discrepancy between GAAP-based tax expense and Internal Revenue Code-based tax liability creates the need for the Deferred Income Taxes account.

Study Note

Deferred Income Taxes is classified as a liability when it has a credit balance and as an asset when it has a debit balance. It is further classified as either current or long-term depending on when it is expected to reverse.

expenses, gains, and losses for tax and financial reporting purposes. Temporary differences include revenues and expenses or gains and losses that are included in taxable income before or after they are included in financial income. In other words, the recognition point for revenues, expenses, gains, and losses is not the same for tax and financial reporting.

For example, advance payments for goods and services, such as magazine subscriptions, are not recognized as income until the products are shipped. However, for tax purposes, advance payments are usually recognized as revenue when cash is received. As a result, taxes paid exceed taxes expense, which creates a deferred income taxes asset (or prepaid taxes).

Classification of deferred income taxes as current or noncurrent depends on the classification of the asset or liability that created the temporary difference. For example, the deferred income taxes asset mentioned above would be classified as current if unearned subscription revenue were classified as a current liability. On the other hand, the temporary difference arising from depreciation is related to a long-term depreciable asset. Therefore, the resulting deferred income taxes would be classified as long-term. If a temporary difference is not related to an asset or liability, it is classified as current or noncurrent based on its expected date of reversal. (Temporary differences and the classification of deferred income taxes that results are covered in depth in more advanced courses.)

Each year, the balance of the Deferred Income Taxes account is evaluated to determine whether it still accurately represents the expected asset or liability in light of legislated changes in income tax laws and regulations.

In any given year, the amount a company pays in income taxes is determined by subtracting (or adding) the deferred income taxes for that year from (or to) income taxes expense. In subsequent years, the amount of deferred income taxes can vary based on changes in tax laws and rates.

A survey of the financial statements of 600 large companies indicates the importance of deferred income taxes to financial reporting. About 68 percent reported deferred income taxes with a credit balance in the long-term liability section of their balance sheets.[10]

Net of Taxes

The phrase **net of taxes** indicates that taxes (usually income taxes) have been taken into account in reporting an item in the financial statements. The phrase is used in a corporate income statement when a company has items that must be disclosed in a separate section. Each such item should be reported net of the applicable income taxes to avoid distorting the income taxes expense associated with ongoing operations and the resulting net operating income.

For example, assume that a corporation with operating income before income taxes of $120,000 has a total tax expense of $66,000 and that the total income includes a gain of $100,000 on which a tax of $30,000 is due. Also assume that the gain is not part of the corporation's normal operations and must be disclosed separately on the income statement as an extraordinary item. This is how the income taxes expense would be reported on the income statement:

Operating income before income taxes	$120,000
Income taxes expense	36,000
Income before extraordinary item	$ 84,000
Extraordinary gain (net of taxes, $30,000)	70,000
Net income	$154,000

If all the income taxes expense were deducted from operating income before income taxes, both the income before extraordinary item and the extraordinary gain would be distorted.

The procedure is the same in the case of an extraordinary loss. For example, given the same facts except that the income taxes expense is only $6,000 because of a $100,000 extraordinary loss, the result is a $30,000 tax savings:

Operating income before income taxes	$120,000
Income taxes expense	36,000
Income before extraordinary item	$ 84,000
Extraordinary loss (net of taxes, $30,000)	(70,000)
Net income	$ 14,000

In Exhibit 1, the total of the income tax items for Envest Corporation is $149,500. That amount is allocated among five statement components, as follows:

Income taxes expense on income from continuing operations	$144,500
Income taxes on income from a discontinued segment	35,000
Income tax savings on the loss on the disposal of the segment	(42,000)
Income taxes on extraordinary gain	12,000
Total income taxes expense	$149,500

S T O P • R E V I E W • A P P L Y

2-1. "Accounting income should be geared to the concept of taxable income because the public understands that concept." Comment on this statement, and explain why income tax allocation is necessary.

2-2. What are deferred income taxes?

2-3. How does the concept of net of taxes affect the income statement?

Income Tax Allocation   Jimenez Corporation reported the following accounting income before income taxes, income taxes expense, and net income for 20x8 and 20x9:

	20x8	20x9
Income before income taxes	$84,000	$84,000
Income taxes expense	26,490	26,490
Net income	$57,510	$57,510

On the balance sheet, deferred income taxes liability increased by $11,520 in 20x8 and decreased by $5,640 in 20x9.

1. How much was actually payable in income taxes for 20x8 and 20x9?

2. Prepare entries in journal form to record estimated current and deferred income taxes for 20x8 and 20x9.

SOLUTION
1. Income taxes calculated:

	20x8	20x9
Income taxes expense	$26,490	$26,490
Decrease (increase) in deferred income taxes	(11,520)	5,640
Income taxes payable	$14,970	$32,130

2. Entries prepared:

20x8	Income Taxes Expense		26,490	
	Deferred Income Taxes			11,520
	Income Taxes Payable			14,970
	To record estimated current and deferred income taxes for 20x8			
20x9	Income Taxes Expense		26,490	
	Deferred Income Taxes		5,640	
	Income Taxes Payable			32,130
	To record estimated current and deferred income taxes for 20x9			

Nonoperating Items

LO3 Describe the disclosure on the income statement of discontinued operations and extraordinary items.

Nonoperating items are items unrelated to a company's normal operations. They appear in a separate section of the income statement because they are considered one-time items that will not affect future results. The two principal kinds of nonoperating items are discontinued operations and extraordinary items.

Discontinued Operations

Large companies usually have many **segments**. A segment may be a separate major line of business or serve a separate class of customer. For example, a company that makes heavy drilling equipment may have another line of business, such as the manufacture of mobile homes. A company may discontinue or otherwise dispose of segments that do not fit its future plans or that are unprofitable. **Discontinued operations** are segments that are no longer part of a company's operations. To make it easier to evaluate a company's ongoing operations, generally accepted accounting principles require that gains and losses from discontinued operations be reported separately on the income statement.

In Exhibit 1, the disclosure of discontinued operations has two parts. One part shows that after the decision to discontinue, the income from operations of the disposed segment was $90,000 (net of $35,000 taxes). The other part shows that the loss from the disposal of the segment was $73,000 (net of $42,000 tax savings). (Computation of the gains or losses involved in discontinued operations is covered in more advanced accounting courses.)

Extraordinary Items

The Accounting Principles Board defines **extraordinary items** as "events or transactions that are distinguished by their unusual nature *and* by the infrequency of their occurrence."[11] The board describes unusual and infrequent occurrences as follows:

Unusual nature: The underlying event or transaction should be clearly unrelated to, or only incidentally related to, the ordinary and typical activities of the entity.

Infrequency of occurrence: The underlying event or transaction should not reasonably be expected to recur in the foreseeable future.

If an item is both unusual and infrequent (and material in amount), it should be reported separately from continuing operations on the income statement. The disclosure allows readers to identify gains or losses in income that would not be expected to happen again soon. Items usually treated as extraordinary include the following:

1. An uninsured loss from flood, earthquake, fire, or theft

2. A gain or loss resulting from the passage of a new law

3. The expropriation (taking) of property by a foreign government

In Exhibit 1, the extraordinary gain was $37,000 after taxes of $12,000.

S T O P • R E V I E W • A P P L Y

3-1. Why should a gain or loss on discontinued operations be disclosed separately on the income statement?

3-2. What are the two major criteria for extraordinary items? How should extraordinary items be disclosed in the financial statements?

Earnings per Share

LO4 Compute earnings per share.

> **Study Note**
>
> Earnings per share is a measure of a corporation's profitability. It is one of the most closely watched financial ratios in the business world. Its disclosure on the income statement is required.

Readers of financial statements use earnings per share to judge a company's performance and to compare it with the performance of other companies. Because this information is so important, the Accounting Principles Board concluded that earnings per share of common stock should be presented on the face of the income statement.[12] As shown in Exhibit 1, this information is usually disclosed just below net income.

A corporate income statement always shows earnings per share for income from continuing operations and other major components of net income. For example, if a company has a gain or loss on discontinued operations or on extraordinary items, its income statement may present earnings per share amounts for the gain or loss.

Exhibit 3 shows how **Motorola** presents earnings per share on its income statement. As you can see, the statement covers three years, and discontinued operations had a negative effect on earnings per share in all three years. However, the earnings per share for continuing operations is a better indicator of the company's future performance. Note that earnings per share are reported as basic and diluted.

Basic Earnings per Share

Basic earnings per share is the net income applicable to common stock divided by the weighted-average number of common shares outstanding. To compute this figure, one must determine if the number of common shares outstanding changed during the year and if the company paid dividends on preferred stock.

EXHIBIT 3 ▶

Motorola's Earnings Per Share Presentation			
	Years Ended December 31		
	2005	2004	2003
Earnings (loss) per common share:			
Basic:			
Continuing operations	**$1.86**	$0.93	$0.40
Discontinued operations	**(0.01)**	(0.28)	(0.02)
	$1.85	$0.65	$0.38
Diluted:			
Continuing operations	**$1.82**	$0.90	$0.39
Discontinued operations	**(0.01)**	(0.26)	(0.01)
	$1.81	$0.64	$0.38
Weighted average common shares outstanding:			
Basic	**2,471.3**	2,365.0	2,321.9
Diluted	**2,527.0**	2,472.0	2,351.2

Source: Motorola, Inc., *Annual Report,* 2005.

When a company has only common stock and the number of shares outstanding is the same throughout the year, the earnings per share computation is simple. Exhibit 1 shows that Envest Corporation had net income of $334,500. If Envest had 100,000 shares of common stock outstanding during the entire year, the earnings per share of common stock would be computed as follows:

$$\text{Earnings per Share} = \frac{\$334,500}{100,000} = \$3.35^* \text{ per share}$$

If the number of shares outstanding changes during the year, it is necessary to figure the weighted-average number of shares outstanding for the year. Suppose that from January 1 to March 31, Envest Corporation had 100,000 shares outstanding; from April 1 to September 30, it had 120,000 shares outstanding; and from October 31 to December 31, it had 130,000 shares outstanding. The weighted-average number of common shares outstanding and basic earnings per share would be determined this way:

100,000 shares $\times$ $\frac{3}{12}$ year	25,000
120,000 shares $\times$ $\frac{6}{12}$ year	60,000
130,000 shares $\times$ $\frac{3}{12}$ year	32,500
Weighted-average common shares outstanding	117,500

$$\text{Basic Earnings per Share} = \frac{\text{Net Income}}{\text{Weighted-Average Common Shares Outstanding}}$$

$$= \frac{\$334,500}{117,500 \text{ shares}} = \$2.85 \text{ per share}$$

If a company has nonconvertible preferred stock outstanding, the dividend for that stock must be subtracted from net income before earnings per share for common stock are computed. Suppose that Envest Corporation has preferred stock on which it pays an annual dividend of $23,500. Earnings per share on common stock would be $2.65 [($334,500 − $23,500) ÷ 117,500 shares].

*This number is rounded, as are some other results of computations that follow.

Diluted Earnings Per Share

Companies can have a simple capital structure or a complex capital structure.

⬧ A company has a **simple capital structure** if it has no preferred stocks, bonds, or stock options that can be converted to common stock. A company with a simple capital structure computes earnings per share as shown above.

⬧ A company that has issued securities or stock options that can be converted to common stock has a **complex capital structure**. These securities and options have the potential of diluting the earnings per share of common stock.

Potential dilution means that the conversion of stocks or bonds or the exercise of stock options can increase the total number of shares of common stock that a company has outstanding and thereby reduce a current stockholder's proportionate share of ownership in the company. For example, suppose that a person owns 10,000 shares of a company's common stock, which equals 2 percent of the outstanding shares of 500,000. Now suppose that holders of convertible bonds convert the bonds into 100,000 shares of stock. The person's 10,000 shares would then equal only 1.67 percent (10,000 ÷ 600,000) of the outstanding shares. In addition, the added shares outstanding would lower earnings per share and would most likely lower market price per share.

 When a company has a complex capital structure, it must report two earnings per share figures: basic earnings per share and diluted earnings per share.[13] **Diluted earnings per share** are calculated by adding all potentially dilutive securities to the denominator of the basic earnings per share calculation. This figure shows stockholders the maximum potential effect of dilution on their ownership position. As you can see in Exhibit 3, the dilution effect for **Motorola** is not large, only 4 cents per share in 2005 ($1.85 − $1.81), because the company's only dilutive securities are a relatively few stock options.

S T O P • R E V I E W • A P P L Y

4-1. Where are earnings per share disclosed in the financial statements?

4-2. When does a company have a simple capital structure? A complex capital structure?

4-3. What is the difference between basic and diluted earnings per share?

Earnings per Share   During 20x7, Chester Corporation reported a net income of $3,059,000. On January 1, 20x7, Chester had 700,000 shares of common stock outstanding, and it issued an additional 420,000 shares of common stock on October 1. The company has a simple capital structure.

1. Determine the weighted-average number of common shares outstanding.

2. Compute earnings per share.

SOLUTION

1. Weighted-average number of common shares outstanding:

700,000 shares × 9/12	525,000
1,120,000 shares × 3/12	280,000
Weighted-average number of common shares outstanding	805,000

2. Earnings per share:
   $3,059,000 ÷ 805,000 shares = $3.80

Comprehensive Income and the Statement of Stockholders' Equity

LO5 Define *comprehensive income,* and describe the statement of stockholders' equity.

The concept of comprehensive income and the statement of stockholders' equity provide further explanation of the income statement and the balance sheet and serve as links between those two statements.

Comprehensive Income

Some items that are not stock transactions affect stockholders' equity. These items, which come from sources other than stockholders and that account for the change in a company's equity during an accounting period, are called **comprehensive income**. Comprehensive income includes net income, changes in unrealized investment gains and losses, and other items affecting equity, such as foreign currency translation adjustments. The FASB takes the position that these changes in stockholders' equity should be summarized as income for a period.[14] Companies may report comprehensive income and its components in a separate financial statement, as **eBay** does in Exhibit 4, or as a part of another financial statement.

In a recent survey of 600 large companies, 575 reported comprehensive income. Of these, 84 percent reported comprehensive income in the statement of stockholders' equity, 12 percent reported it in a separate statement, and only 4 percent reported it in the income statement.[15] In Exhibit 5, we follow the most common practice and show it as a part of the statement of stockholders' equity.

The Statement of Stockholders' Equity

Study Note

The statement of stockholders' equity is a labeled calculation of the change in each stockholders' equity account over an accounting period.

Study Note

The ending balances on the statement of stockholders' equity are transferred to the stockholders' equity section of the balance sheet.

The **statement of stockholders' equity**, also called the *statement of changes in stockholders' equity*, summarizes changes in the components of the stockholders' equity section of the balance sheet. Most companies use this statement in place of the statement of retained earnings because it reveals much more about the stockholders' equity transactions that took place during the accounting period.

For example, in Kavra Corporation's statement of stockholders' equity in Exhibit 5, the first line shows the beginning balance of each account in the stockholders' equity section of the balance sheet. Each subsequent line discloses the effects of transactions on those accounts. Kavra had a net income of $270,000 and a foreign currency translation loss of $10,000, which it reported as accumulated other comprehensive income. These two items together resulted in comprehensive income of $260,000.

Kavra's statement of stockholders' equity also shows that during 20x8, the firm issued 5,000 shares of common stock for $250,000, had a conversion of $100,000 of preferred stock to common stock, declared and issued a 10 percent stock dividend on common stock, purchased treasury stock for $24,000, and paid cash dividends on both preferred and common stock. The ending balances of the accounts appear at the bottom of the statement. Those accounts and balances make up the stockholders' equity section of Kavra's balance sheet on December 31, 20x8, as shown in Exhibit 6.

EXHIBIT 4 ▶ | **eBay's Statement of Comprehensive Income**

	Year Ended December 31		
(In thousands)	**2005**	**2004**	**2003**
Net income	$1,082,043	$778,223	$441,771
Other comprehensive income (loss)			
Foreign currency translation	(140,459)	139,523	66,326
Unrealized gains (losses) on investments, net	1,922	(8,703)	(5,497)
Unrealized gains on cash flow hedges	1,297	5,525	4,249
Estimated tax benefit/(provision)	(1,272)	1,102	620
Other comprehensive income (loss)	(138,512)	137,447	65,698
Comprehensive income	943,531	$915,670	$507,469

Source: eBay Inc., *Annual Report*, 2005.

▼ EXHIBIT 5

Statement of Stockholders' Equity

Kavra Corporation
Statement of Stockholders' Equity
For the Year Ended December 31, 20x8

	Preferred Stock $100 Par Value 8% Convertible	Common Stock $10 Par Value	Additional Paid-in Capital	Retained Earnings	Treasury Stock	Accumulated Other Comprehensive Income	Total
Balance, December 31, 20x7	$400,000	$300,000	$300,000	$600,000	—		$1,600,000
Net income				270,000			270,000
Foreign currency translation adjustment						($10,000)	(10,000)
Issuance of 5,000 shares of common stock		50,000	200,000				250,000
Conversion of 1,000 shares of preferred stock to 3,000 shares of common stock	(100,000)	30,000	70,000				—
10 percent stock dividend on common stock, 3,800 shares		38,000	152,000	(190,000)			—
Purchase of 500 shares of treasury stock					($24,000)		(24,000)
Cash dividends							
Preferred stock				(24,000)			(24,000)
Common stock				(47,600)			(47,600)
Balance, December 31, 20x8	$300,000	$418,000	$722,000	$608,400	($24,000)	($10,000)	$2,014,000

EXHIBIT 6 ▶

Stockholders' Equity Section of a Balance Sheet

Kavra Corporation
Balance Sheet
December 31, 20x8

Stockholders' Equity

Contributed capital			
Preferred stock, $100 par value, 8 percent convertible, 10,000 shares authorized, 3,000 shares issued and outstanding			$ 300,000
Common stock, $10 par value, 100,000 shares authorized, 41,800 shares issued, 41,300 shares outstanding		$418,000	
Additional paid-in capital		722,000	1,140,000
Total contributed capital			$1,440,000
Retained earnings			608,400
Total contributed capital and retained earnings			$2,048,400
Less: Treasury stock, common (500 shares, at cost)		$ 24,000	
Foreign currency translation adjustment		10,000	34,000
Total stockholders' equity			$2,014,400

Retained Earnings

The Retained Earnings column in Exhibit 5 has the same components as the statement of retained earnings. As we explained earlier in the text, **retained earnings** represent stockholders' claims to assets that arise from the earnings of the business. Retained earnings equal a company's profits since its inception, minus any losses, dividends to stockholders, or transfers to contributed capital.

It is important to remember that retained earnings are not the assets themselves. The existence of retained earnings means that assets generated by profitable operations have been kept in the company to help it grow or meet other business needs. A credit balance in Retained Earnings is *not* directly associated with a specific amount of cash or designated assets. Rather, it means that assets as a whole have increased.

Retained Earnings can have a debit balance. Generally, this happens when a company's dividends and subsequent losses are greater than its accumulated profits from operations. In this case, the company is said to have a **deficit** (debit balance) in Retained Earnings. A deficit is shown in the stockholders' equity section of the balance sheet as a deduction from contributed capital.

> ⌐⊃ Study Note
>
> A *deficit* is a negative (debit) balance in Retained Earnings. It is not the same as a net loss, which reflects a firm's performance in just one accounting period.

STOP • REVIEW • APPLY

5-1. What is comprehensive income? How does comprehensive income differ from net income?

5-2. How do the statement of stockholders' equity and the stockholders' equity section of the balance sheet differ?

5-3. When does a company have a deficit in retained earnings?

Stock Dividends and Stock Splits

Two transactions that commonly modify the content of stockholders' equity are stock dividends and stock splits. In the discussion that follows, we describe how to account for both kinds of transactions.

Stock Dividends

A **stock dividend** is a proportional distribution of shares among a corporation's stockholders. Unlike a cash dividend, a stock dividend involves no distribution of assets, and so it has no effect on a firm's assets or liabilities. A board of directors may declare a stock dividend for the following reasons:

1. It may want to give stockholders some evidence of the company's success without affecting working capital, which would be the case if it paid a cash dividend.

2. It may want to reduce the stock's market price by increasing the number of shares outstanding. (This goal is, however, more often met by a stock split.)

3. It may want to make a nontaxable distribution to stockholders. Stock dividends that meet certain conditions are not considered income and are therefore not taxed.

4. It may want to increase the company's permanent capital by transferring an amount from retained earnings to contributed capital.

Study Note

The declaration of a stock dividend results in a reshuffling of stockholders' equity—that is, a portion of retained earnings is converted to contributed capital (by closing the Stock Dividends account). Total stockholders' equity is not affected.

A stock dividend does not affect total stockholders' equity. Basically, it transfers a dollar amount from retained earnings to contributed capital. The amount transferred is the fair market value (usually, the market price) of the additional shares that the company issues. The laws of most states specify the minimum value of each share transferred, which is normally the minimum legal capital (par or stated value). When stock distributions are small—less than 20 to 25 percent of a company's outstanding common stock—generally accepted accounting principles hold that market value reflects their economic effect better than par or stated value. For this reason, market price should be used to account for small stock dividends.[16]

To illustrate how to account for a stock dividend, suppose that stockholders' equity in Geminix Corporation is as follows:

Contributed capital	
Common stock, $5 par value, 100,000 shares authorized, 30,000 shares issued and outstanding	$ 150,000
Additional paid-in capital	30,000
Total contributed capital	$ 180,000
Retained earnings	900,000
Total stockholders' equity	$1,080,000

Now suppose that on February 24, the market price of Geminix's stock is $20 per share, and on that date, its board of directors declares a 10 percent stock dividend to be distributed on March 31 to stockholders of record on March 15. No entry is needed for the date of record (March 15). The entries for the declaration and distribution of the stock dividend are as follows:

Declaration Date

A = L + OE			
−60,000	Feb. 24	Stock Dividends	60,000	
+15,000		Common Stock Distributable		15,000
+45,000		Additional Paid-in Capital		45,000

Declared a 10 percent stock dividend on common stock, distributable on March 31 to stockholders of record on March 15:
30,000 shares × .10 = 3,000 shares
3,000 shares × $20/share = $60,000
3,000 shares × $5/share = $15,000

Date of Distribution

A = L + OE			
−15,000	Mar. 31	Common Stock Distributable	15,000	
+15,000		Common Stock		15,000

Distributed a stock dividend of 3,000 shares

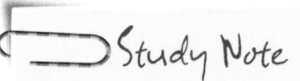

Study Note

For a small stock dividend, the portion of retained earnings transferred is determined by multiplying the number of shares to be distributed by the stock's market price on the declaration date.

Study Note

Common Stock Distributable is a contributed capital (stockholders' equity) account, not a liability account. When the shares are issued, Common Stock Distributable is converted to the Common Stock account.

This stock dividend permanently transfers the market value of the stock, $60,000, from retained earnings to contributed capital and increases the number of shares outstanding by 3,000. The Stock Dividends account is used to record the total amount of the stock dividend. When the Stock Dividends account is closed to Retained Earnings at the end of the accounting period, Retained Earnings is reduced by the amount of the stock dividend. Common Stock Distributable is credited for the par value of the stock to be distributed (3,000 × $5 = $15,000).

In addition, when the market value is greater than the par value of the stock, the Additional Paid-in Capital account must be credited for the amount by which the market value exceeds the par value. In our example, the total market value of the stock dividend ($60,000) exceeds the total par value ($15,000) by $45,000. On the date of distribution, Common Stock Distributable is debited and Common Stock is credited for the par value of the stock ($15,000).

Common Stock Distributable is not a liability account because there is no obligation to distribute cash or other assets. The obligation is to distribute additional shares of capital stock. If financial statements are prepared between the declaration date and the date of distribution, Common Stock Distributable should be reported as part of contributed capital:

Contributed capital	
Common stock, $5 par value, 100,000 shares	
authorized, 30,000 shares issued and outstanding	$ 150,000
Common stock distributable, 3,000 shares	15,000
Additional paid-in capital	75,000
Total contributed capital	$ 240,000
Retained earnings	840,000
Total stockholders' equity	$1,080,000

This example demonstrates the following points:

1. Total stockholders' equity is the same before and after the stock dividend.

2. The assets of the corporation are not reduced, as they would be by a cash dividend.

3. The proportionate ownership in the corporation of any individual stock-holder is the same before and after the stock dividend.

To illustrate these points, suppose a stockholder owns 1,000 shares before the stock dividend. After the 10 percent stock dividend is distributed, this stockholder would own 1,100 shares, as shown below:

	Stockholders' Equity	
	Before Dividend	After Dividend
Common stock	$ 150,000	$ 165,000
Additional paid-in capital	30,000	75,000
Total contributed capital	$ 180,000	$ 240,000
Retained earnings	900,000	840,000
Total stockholders' equity	$1,080,000	$1,080,000
Shares outstanding	30,000	33,000
Stockholders' equity per share	$ 36.00	$ 32.73

	Stockholders' Investment	
Shares owned	1,000	1,100
Shares outstanding	30,000	33,000
Percentage of ownership	3⅓%	3⅓%
Proportionate investment ($1,080,000 × 3⅓%)	$36,000	$36,000

Both before and after the stock dividend, stockholders' equity totals $1,080,000, and the stockholder owns 3⅓ percent of the company. The proportionate investment (stockholders' equity times percentage of ownership) remains at $36,000.

All stock dividends have an effect on the market price of a company's stock. But some stock dividends are so large that they have a material effect. For example, a 50 percent stock dividend would cause the market price of the stock to drop about 33 percent because the increase is now one-third of shares outstanding. The AICPA has decided that large stock dividends—those greater than 20 to 25 percent—should be accounted for by transferring the par or stated value of the stock on the declaration date from retained earnings to contributed capital.[17]

Study Note

When a stock dividend greater than 20 to 25 percent is declared, the transfer from retained earnings is based on the stock's par or stated value, not on its market value.

Study Note

Stock splits and stock dividends reduce earnings per share because they increase the number of shares issued and outstanding. Cash dividends have no effect on earnings per share.

Stock Splits

A **stock split** occurs when a corporation increases the number of shares of stock issued and outstanding and reduces the par or stated value proportionally. A company may plan a stock split when it wants to lower its stock's market value per share and increase the demand for the stock at this lower price. It may do so if the market price has become so high that it hinders the trading of the stock or if it wants to signal to the market its success in achieving its operating goals.

The Gillette Company achieved these strategic objectives in a recent year by declaring a 2-for-1 stock split and raising its cash dividend.[18] The market viewed these actions positively, pushing Gillette's share price from $77 to $106.

After the stock split, the number of the company's outstanding shares doubled, thereby cutting the share price in half and also reducing the dividend per share. Most important, the stock split left each stockholder's total wealth unchanged.

To illustrate a stock split, suppose that Calderon Corporation has 30,000 shares of $5.00 par value stock outstanding and the market value is $70.00 per share. The corporation plans a 2-for-1 split. This split will lower the par value to $2.50 and increase the number of shares outstanding to 60,000. A stockholder who previously owned 400 shares of the $5.00 par value stock would own 800 shares of the $2.50 par value stock after the split. When a stock split occurs, the market value tends to fall in proportion to the increase in outstanding shares of stock. For example, Calderon's 2-for-1 stock split would cause the price of its stock to drop by approximately 50 percent, to about $35.00. It would also halve earnings per share and cash dividends per share (unless the board increased the dividend). The lower price and increase in shares tend to promote the buying and selling of shares.

A stock split does not increase the number of shares authorized, nor does it change the balances in the stockholders' equity section of the balance sheet. It simply changes the par value and number of shares issued, both shares outstanding and treasury stock. Thus, an entry is unnecessary. However, it is appropriate to document the change with a memorandum entry in the general journal. For example:

July 15   The 30,000 shares of $5 par value common stock issued and outstanding were split 2 for 1, resulting in 60,000 shares of $2.50 par value common stock issued and outstanding.

The change for Calderon Corporation is as follows:

Before Stock Split

Contributed capital	
Common stock, $5 par value, 100,000 shares authorized; 30,000 shares issued and outstanding	$ 150,000
Additional paid-in capital	30,000
Total contributed capital	$ 180,000
Retained earnings	900,000
Total stockholders' equity	$1,080,000

Would a stock split make a difference to this Alcoa employee? Alcoa had five stock splits between 1974 and 2000. Except for the one in 1974, which was 3-for-2, all were 2-for-1. A stock split increases the number of shares of stock outstanding and reduces the stated value proportionately, but each stockholder's proportionate interest in the company remains the same.

> **Study Note**
>
> A stock split affects only the calculation of common stock. In this case, there are twice as many shares after the split, but par value is half of what it was.

After Stock Split

Contributed capital	
Common stock, $2.50 par value, 100,000 shares authorized, 60,000 shares issued and outstanding	$ 150,000
Additional paid-in capital	30,000
Total contributed capital	$ 180,000
Retained earnings	900,000
Total stockholders' equity	$1,080,000

Although the per share amount of stockholders' equity is half as much after the split, each stockholder's proportionate interest in the company remains the same.

If the number of split shares will exceed the number of authorized shares, the corporation's board of directors must secure state and stockholders' approval before it can issue the additional shares.

STOP • REVIEW • APPLY

6-1. How does the accounting treatment of stock dividends differ from that of cash dividends?

6-2. What is the difference between a stock dividend and a stock split?

6-3. What is the effect of a stock dividend and a stock split on a corporation's capital structure?

≡ Book Value

LO7 Calculate book value per share.

The word *value* is associated with shares of stock in several ways. Par value or stated value is set when the stock is authorized, and it establishes a company's legal capital. Neither par value nor stated value has any relationship to a stock's book value or market value. The **book value** of stock represents a company's total assets less its liabilities. It is simply the stockholders' equity in a company or, to put it another way, it represents a company's net assets. The **book value per share** is therefore the equity of the owner of one share of stock in the net assets of a company. That value, of course, generally does not equal the amount a stockholder receives if the company is sold or liquidated because in most cases, assets are recorded at historical cost, not at their current market value.

If a company has only common stock outstanding, book value per share is calculated by dividing stockholders' equity by the number of common shares outstanding. Common stock distributable is included in the number of shares outstanding, but treasury stock is not. For example, if a firm has total stockholders' equity of $1,030,000 and 29,000 shares outstanding, the book value per share of its common stock would be $35.52 ($1,030,000 ÷ 29,000 shares).

If a company has both preferred and common stock, determining the book value per share is not so simple. Generally, the preferred stock's call value (or par value, if a call value is not specified) and any dividends in arrears are subtracted from stockholders' equity to determine the equity pertaining to common stock. As an illustration, refer to the stockholders' equity section of Kavra Corporation's balance sheet in Exhibit 6. If Kavra has no dividends in arrears and its preferred stock is callable at $105, the equity pertaining to its common stock would be calculated as follows:

Total stockholders' equity	$2,014,400
Less equity allocated to preferred stockholders	
(3,000 shares × $105)	315,000
Equity pertaining to common stockholders	$1,699,400

As indicated in Exhibit 6, Kavra has 41,300 shares of common stock outstanding (41,800 shares issued less 500 shares of treasury stock). Its book values per share are computed as follows:

Preferred stock: $315,000 ÷ 3,000 Shares = $105 per Share
Common stock: $1,699,400 ÷ 41,300 Shares = $41.15 per Share

If we assume the same facts except that Kavra's preferred stock is 8 percent cumulative and that one year of dividends is in arrears, the stockholders' equity would be allocated as follows:

Total stockholders' equity		$2,014,400
Less call value of outstanding preferred shares	$315,000	
Dividends in arrears ($300,000 × .08)	24,000	
Equity allocated to preferred stockholders		339,000
Equity pertaining to common stockholders		$1,675,400

The book values per share would then be as follows:

Preferred stock: $339,000 ÷ 3,000 Shares = $113 per Share
Common stock: $1,675,400 ÷ 41,300 Shares = $40.57 per Share

S T O P • R E V I E W • A P P L Y

7-1. What is the formula for computing book value per share when a corporation has no preferred stock?

7-2. Would you expect a corporation's book value per share to equal its market value per share? Why or why not?

A LOOK BACK AT

MOTOROLA, INC.

In this chapter's Decision Point, we observed that in evaluating a company's performance, it is important to look beyond "bottom line" earnings and other common indicators of performance. We pointed out that to gain a proper perspective on a company's performance, one must examine the components of its income statement. Users of Motorola's income statement should ask questions like the following:

- **What items other than normal operating activities contributed to Motorola's performance?**
- **What does the company's income statement indicate about its quality of earnings?**
- **How does one put the various measures of performance (some of which are shown in Motorola's financial highlights) in perspective?**

The astute user of Motorola's income statement, shown in Exhibit 2, will take the following into account:

- Other charges (income) appear in the operating section of Motorola's income statement in all three years. They had an important effect on the company's performance in 2005, increasing operating earnings by $458 million. Reorganization costs were small and unimportant in 2003 and 2004.

- Gains on sales of investments and businesses were large in all three years, especially in 2005. Although such gains increase income, they lower the quality of earnings because they are one-time events, and the income they produce will not be sustained in the future. The analyst should therefore ignore them.

- Motorola had losses from discontinued operations in all three years. Losses from discontinued operations decrease earnings and often reflect poor decisions in the past. However, eliminating unprofitable operations should have a positive effect on Motorola's future operations.

To put Motorola's performance in perspective, the company had increased operating earnings and net earnings in each of the last two years. A careful reader of Motorola's income statement would realize that although the company's performance was better in 2005, it benefited significantly from other income and gains on sales of investments and businesses. Motorola's strong cash flows, which we discussed earlier in the chapter, are another indication that its performance is improving.

CHAPTER REVIEW

REVIEW of Learning Objectives

LO1 Define *quality of earnings,* and identify the components of a corporate income statement.

The quality of earnings refers to the substance of earnings and their sustainability into future accounting periods. The quality of a company's earnings may be affected by the accounting methods and estimates it uses and by the gains and losses, write-downs and restructurings, and nonoperating items that it reports on its income statement.

When a company has both continuing and discontinued operations, the operating income section of its income statement is called income from continuing operations. Income from continuing operations before income taxes is affected by choices of accounting methods and estimates and may contain gains and losses on the sale of assets, write-downs, and restructurings. The income taxes expense section of the statement is subject to special accounting rules. The lower part of the statement may contain such nonoperating items as discontinued operations, extraordinary gains and losses, and effects of accounting changes. Earnings per share information appears at the bottom of the statement.

The reason for considering quality of earnings issues is to assess their effect on cash flows and performance measures. Except for possible income tax effects, gains and losses, asset write-downs, restructurings, and nonoperating items generally have no effect on cash flows. However, quality of earnings issues can affect key performance ratios like profit margin, return on assets, and return on equity.

LO2 Show the relationships among income taxes expense, deferred income taxes, and net of taxes.

Income taxes expense is the tax applicable to income from operations on an accrual basis. Income tax allocation is necessary when there is a material difference between accrual-based accounting income and taxable income—that is, between the income taxes expense reported on the income statement and actual income tax liability. The difference between income taxes expense and income taxes payable is debited or credited to an account called Deferred Income Taxes. The phrase *net of taxes* indicates that taxes have been taken into account in reporting an item in the financial statements.

LO3 Describe the disclosure on the income statement of discontinued operations and extraordinary items.

Because of their unusual nature, gains or losses on discontinued operations and on extraordinary items must be disclosed on the income statement separately from continuing operations and net of income taxes.

LO4 Compute earnings per share.

Readers of financial statements use earnings per share to evaluate a company's performance and to compare it with the performance of other companies. Earnings per share of common stock are presented on the face of the income statement. The amounts are computed by dividing the income applicable to common stock by the number of common shares outstanding for the year. If the number of shares outstanding varied during the year, the weighted-average number of common shares outstanding is used in the computation. A company that has a complex capital structure must disclose both basic and diluted earnings per share on the face of its income statement.

LO5 Define *comprehensive income,* and describe the statement of stockholders' equity.

Comprehensive income includes all items from sources other than stockholders that account for changes in stockholders' equity during an accounting period. The statement of stockholders' equity summarizes changes over the period in each component of the stockholders' equity section of the balance sheet. This statement reveals much more than the statement of retained earnings does about the transactions that affect stockholders' equity.

LO6 Account for stock dividends and stock splits.

A stock dividend is a proportional distribution of shares among a corporation's stockholders. The following is a summary of the key dates and accounting treatments of stock dividends:

Key Date	Stock Dividend
Declaration date	Debit Stock Dividends for the market value of the stock to be distributed (if the stock dividend is small), and credit Common Stock Distributable for the stock's par value and Additional Paid-in Capital for the excess of the market value over the stock's par value.
Record date	No entry is needed.
Date of distribution	Debit Common Stock Distributable and credit Common Stock for the par value of the stock.

A company usually declares a stock split to reduce the market value of its stock and thereby improve the demand for the stock. Because the par value of the stock normally decreases in proportion to the number of additional shares issued, a stock split has no effect on the dollar amount in stockholders' equity. A stock split does not require a journal entry, but a memorandum entry in the general journal is appropriate.

LO7 Calculate book value per share.

Book value per share is stockholders' equity per share. It is calculated by dividing stockholders' equity by the number of common shares outstanding. When a company has both preferred and common stock, the call or par value of the preferred stock and any dividends in arrears are deducted from stockholders' equity before dividing by the common shares outstanding.

REVIEW of Concepts and Terminology

The following concepts and terms were introduced in this chapter:

Book value: A company's total assets less its liabilities; stockholders' equity or net assets. **(LO7)**

Complex capital structure: A capital structure that includes preferred stocks, bonds, and stock options that can be converted to common stock. **(LO4)**

Comprehensive income: Items from sources other than owners that account for the change in stockholders' equity during an accounting period. **(LO5)**

Deferred Income Taxes: The account used to record the difference between income taxes expense and income taxes payable. **(LO2)**

Deficit: A debit balance in the Retained Earnings account. **(LO5)**

Discontinued operations: Segments that are no longer part of a company's operations. **(LO3)**

Extraordinary items: Events or transactions that are both unusual in nature and infrequent in occurrence. **(LO3)**

Income from continuing operations: The operating income section of the income statement when a company has both continuing and discontinued operations. **(LO1)**

Income tax allocation: The accounting method used to accrue income taxes expense on the basis of accounting income when accounting income and taxable income differ. **(LO2)**

Net of taxes: A phrase indicating that taxes have been taken into account in reporting an item in the financial statements. **(LO2)**

Quality of earnings: The substance of earnings and their sustainability into the future. **(LO1)**

Restructuring: The estimated cost of a change in a company's operations, usually involving the closing of facilities and the laying off of personnel. **(LO1)**

Retained earnings: Stockholders' claims to assets arising from the earnings of the business; the accumulated earnings of a corporation since its inception, minus any losses, dividends, or transfers to contributed capital. **(LO5)**

Segments: Distinct parts of a company's operations. **(LO3)**

Simple capital structure: A capital structure in which there are no stocks, bonds, or stock options that can be converted to common stock. **(LO4)**

Statement of stockholders' equity: A financial statement that summarizes changes in the components of the stockholders' equity section of the balance sheet. Also called the *statement of changes in stockholders' equity.* **(LO5)**

Stock dividend: A proportional distribution of shares among a corporation's stockholders. **(LO6)**

Stock split: An increase in the number of outstanding shares of stock accompanied by a proportionate reduction in the par or stated value. **(LO6)**

Write-down: A reduction in the value of an asset below its carrying value on the balance sheet. Also called a *write-off.* **(LO1)**

Key Ratios

Basic earnings per share: The net income applicable to common stock divided by the weighted-average number of common shares outstanding. **(LO4)**

Book value per share: The equity of the owner of one share of stock in a corporation's net assets. **(LO7)**

Diluted earnings per share: The net income applicable to common stock divided by the sum of the weighted-average number of common shares outstanding and potentially dilutive securities. **(LO4)**

REVIEW Problem

LO5, LO6, LO7   **Comprehensive Stockholders' Equity Transactions**

The stockholders' equity of Skowski Company on June 30, 20x7, was as follows:

Contributed capital	
Common stock, no par value, $6 stated value,	
1,000,000 shares authorized, 250,000 shares	
issued and outstanding	$1,500,000
Additional paid-in capital	820,000
Total contributed capital	$2,320,000
Retained earnings	970,000
Total stockholders' equity	$3,290,000

Stockholders' equity transactions in the next fiscal year were as follows:

a. The board of directors declared a 2-for-1 stock split.
b. The board of directors obtained authorization to issue 50,000 shares of $100 par value, 6 percent noncumulative preferred stock, callable at $104.
c. Issued 12,000 shares of common stock for a building appraised at $96,000.
d. Purchased 8,000 shares of the company's common stock for $64,000.
e. Issued 20,000 shares of preferred stock for $100 per share.
f. Sold 5,000 shares of treasury stock for $35,000.
g. Declared cash dividends of $6 per share on preferred stock and $.20 per share on common stock.
h. Declared a 10 percent stock dividend on common stock to be distributed after the end of the fiscal year. The market value was $10 per share.
i. Closed net income for the year, $340,000.
j. Closed the Dividends and Stock Dividends accounts to Retained Earnings.

Required:

1. Record the stockholders' equity components of the preceding transactions in T accounts. Indicate when there is no entry.
2. Prepare the stockholders' equity section of the company's balance sheet on June 30, 20x8.
3. Compute the book values per share of common stock on June 30, 20x7 and 20x8, and of preferred stock on June 30, 20x8, using the end-of-year shares outstanding.

Answer to Review Problem

1. Entries in T accounts:

   a. No entry (memorandum in journal)

   b. No entry (memorandum in journal)

	A	B	C	D	E	F	G	H	I
1		Preferred Stock					Common Stock		
2			e.	2,000,000				Beg. Bal.	1,500,000
3								c.	36,000
4								End. Bal.	1,536,000
5									
6		Common Stock Distributable					Additional Paid-in Capital		
7			h.	152,700				Beg. Bal.	820,000
8								c.	60,000
9								h.	356,300
10								End. Bal.	1,236,000
11									
12		Retained Earnings					Treasury Stock		
13	f.		5,000	Beg. Bal.	970,000	d.	64,000	f.	40,000
14	j.		730,800	i.	340,000	End. Bal.	24,000		
15			End. Bal.	574,200					
16									
17		Dividends					Stock Dividends		
18	g.	221,800*	j.	221,800	h.	509,000**	j.	509,000
19									
20	* 20,000 × $6 = $120,000					**509,000 shares × .10 × $10 = $509,000			
21	509,000 × $.20 = $101,800								
22	Total = $221,800								

2. Stockholders' equity section of the balance sheet:

	A	B	C
1	**Skowski Company**		
2	**Balance Sheet**		
3	**June 30, 20x8**		
4			
5	**Stockholders' Equity**		
6	Contributed capital		
7	Preferred stock, $100 par value, 6 percent		
8	noncumulative, 50,000 shares authorized,		
9	20,000 shares issued and outstanding		$2,000,000
10	Common stock, no par value, $3 stated value,		
11	1,000,000 shares authorized, 512,000 shares		
12	issued, 509,000 shares outstanding	$1,536,000	
13	Common stock distributable, 50,900 shares	152,700	
14	Additional paid-in capital	1,236,300	2,925,000
15	Total contributed capital		$4,925,000
16	Retained earnings		574,200
17	Total contributed capital and retained earnings		$5,499,200
18	Less treasury stock (3,000 shares, at cost)		24,000
19	Total stockholders' equity		$5,475,200

3. Book values:
   June 30, 20x7
      Common Stock: $3,290,000 ÷ 250,000 shares = $13.16 per share
   June 30, 20x8
      Preferred Stock: Call price of $104 per share equals book value per share
      Common Stock:
         ($5,475,200 − $2,080,000) ÷ (509,000 shares + 50,900 shares)
         $3,395,200 ÷ 559,900 shares = $6.06* per share

   ─────────
   * Rounded.

CHAPTER ASSIGNMENTS

BUILDING Your Basic Knowledge and Skills

Short Exercises

LO1   Quality of Earnings

SE 1. Each of the items listed below is a quality of earnings issue. Indicate whether the item is (a) an accounting method, (b) an accounting estimate, or (c) a nonoperating item. For any item for which the answer is (a) or (b), indicate which alternative is usually the more conservative choice.

1. LIFO versus FIFO
2. Extraordinary loss
3. 10-year useful life versus 15-year useful life
4. Straight-line versus accelerated method
5. Discontinued operations
6. Immediate write-off versus amortization
7. Increase versus decrease in percentage of uncollectible accounts

LO1   Corporate Income Statement

SE 2. Assume that Jefferson Company's chief financial officer gave you the following information: net sales, $360,000; cost of goods sold, $175,000; loss from discontinued operations (net of income tax benefit of $35,000), $100,000; loss on disposal of discontinued operations (net of income tax benefit of $8,000), $25,000; operating expenses, $65,000; income taxes expense on continuing operations, $50,000. From this information, prepare the company's income statement for the year ended June 30, 20xx. (Ignore earnings per share information.)

LO2   Corporate Income Tax Rate Schedule

SE 3. Using the corporate tax rate schedule in Table 1, compute the income tax liability for taxable income of (1) $800,000 and (2) $40,000,000.

LO4   Earnings per Share

SE 4. During 20x7, Wells Corporation reported a net income of $1,338,400. On January 1, Wells had 720,000 shares of common stock outstanding. The company issued an additional 480,000 shares of common stock on August 1. In 20x7, the company had a simple capital structure. During 20x8, there were no transactions involving common stock, and the company reported net income of $1,740,000. Determine the weighted-average number of common shares outstanding for 20x7 and 20x8. Also compute earnings per share for 20x7 and 20x8.

LO5 **Statement of Stockholders' Equity**

SE 5. Refer to the statement of stockholders' equity for Kavra Corporation in Exhibit 5 to answer the following questions: (1) At what price per share were the 5,000 shares of common stock sold? (2) What was the conversion price per share of the common stock? (3) At what price was the common stock selling on the date of the stock dividend? (4) At what price per share was the treasury stock purchased?

LO5, LO6 **Effects of Stockholders' Equity Actions**

SE 6. Tell whether each of the following actions will increase, decrease, or have no effect on total assets, total liabilities, and total stockholders' equity:

1. Declaration of a stock dividend
2. Declaration of a cash dividend
3. Stock split
4. Purchase of treasury stock

LO6 **Stock Dividends**

SE 7. On February 15, Asher Corporation's board of directors declared a 2 percent stock dividend applicable to the outstanding shares of its $10 par value common stock, of which 400,000 shares are authorized, 260,000 are issued, and 40,000 are held in the treasury. The stock dividend was distributed on March 15 to stockholders of record on March 1. On February 15, the market value of the common stock was $15 per share. On March 30, the board of directors declared a $.50 per share cash dividend. No other stock transactions have occurred. Record, as necessary, the transactions of February 15, March 1, March 15, and March 30.

LO6 **Stock Split**

SE 8. On August 10, the board of directors of Perlman International declared a 3-for-1 stock split of its $9 par value common stock, of which 400,000 shares were authorized and 125,000 were issued and outstanding. The market value on that date was $60 per share. On the same date, the balance of additional paid-in capital was $3,000,000, and the balance of retained earnings was $3,250,000. Prepare the stockholders' equity section of the company's balance sheet after the stock split. What journal entry, if any, is needed to record the stock split?

LO7 **Book Value for Preferred and Common Stock**

SE 9. Using data from the stockholders' equity section of Soong Corporation's balance sheet shown below, compute the book value per share for both the preferred and the common stock.

Contributed capital	
Preferred stock, $100 par value, 8 percent cumulative, 20,000 shares authorized, 1,000 shares issued and outstanding*	$ 100,000
Common stock, $10 par value, 200,000 shares authorized, 80,000 shares issued and outstanding	800,000
Additional paid-in capital	1,032,000
Total contributed capital	$1,932,000
Retained earnings	550,000
Total stockholders' equity	$2,482,000

*The preferred stock is callable at $108 per share, and one year's dividends are in arrears.

Exercises

Discussion Questions

E 1. Develop brief answers to each of the following questions:

1. In what way is selling an investment for a gain potentially a negative in evaluating quality of earnings?
2. Is it unethical for new management to take an extra large write-off (a "big bath") in order to reduce future costs? Why or why not?
3. What is an argument against the recording of deferred income taxes?
4. Why is it useful to disclose discontinued operations separately on the income statement?

Discussion Questions

E 2. Develop brief answers to each of the following questions:

1. What is one way a company can improve its earnings per share without improving its earnings or net income?
2. Why is comprehensive income a part of stockholders' equity?
3. Upon receiving shares of stock from a stock dividend, why should the stockholder not consider the value of the stock as income?
4. What is the effect of a stock dividend or a stock split on book value per share?

Effect of Alternative Accounting Methods

E 3. At the end of its first year of operations, a company calculated its ending merchandise inventory according to three different accounting methods, as follows: FIFO, $47,500; average-cost, $45,000; LIFO, $43,000. If the company used the average-cost method, its net income for the year would be $17,000.

1. Determine net income if the company used the FIFO method.
2. Determine net income if the company used the LIFO method.
3. Which method is more conservative?
4. Will the consistency convention be violated if the company chooses to use the LIFO method? Why or why not?
5. Does the full-disclosure convention require disclosure of the inventory method used in the financial statements?

Corporate Income Statement

E 4. Assume that the St. Cloud Furniture Company's chief financial officer gave you the following information: net sales, $3,800,000; cost of goods sold, $2,100,000; extraordinary gain (net of income taxes of $7,000), $25,000; loss from discontinued operations (net of income tax benefit of $60,000), $100,000; loss on disposal of discontinued operations (net of income tax benefit of $26,000), $70,000; selling expenses, $100,000; administrative expenses, $80,000; income taxes expense on continuing operations, $600,000. From this information, prepare the company's income statement for the year ended June 30, 20xx. (Ignore earnings per share information.)

Corporate Income Statement

E 5. The items at the top of the opposite page are components of Munsey Company's income statement for the year ended December 31, 20xx. Recast the income statement in proper multistep form, including allocating income taxes to appropriate items (assume a 30 percent income tax rate) and showing earnings per share figures (200,000 shares outstanding).

Sales	$1,110,000
Cost of goods sold	(550,000)
Operating expenses	(225,000)
Restructuring	(110,000)
Total income taxes expense for period	(179,100)
Income from operations of a discontinued segment	160,000
Gain on disposal of segment	140,000
Extraordinary gain	72,000
Net income	$ 417,900
Earnings per share	$ 2.09

LO2 Corporate Income Tax Rate Schedule

E 6. Using the corporate tax rate schedule in Table 1, compute the income tax liability for the following situations:

Situation	Taxable Income
A	$ 70,000
B	85,000
C	320,000

LO2 Income Tax Allocation

E 7. The Danner Corporation reported the following accounting income before income taxes, income taxes expense, and net income for 20x8 and 20x9:

	20x8	20x9
Income before income taxes	$140,000	$140,000
Income taxes expense	44,150	44,150
Net income	$ 95,850	$ 95,850

On the balance sheet, deferred income taxes liability increased by $19,200 in 20x8 and decreased by $9,400 in 20x9.

1. How much did Danner actually pay in income taxes for 20x8 and 20x9?
2. Prepare entries in journal form to record income taxes expense for 20x8 and 20x9.

LO4 Earnings per Share

E 8. During 20x8, Chester Corporation reported a net income of $1,529,500. On January 1, Chester had 1,400,000 shares of common stock outstanding. The company issued an additional 840,000 shares of common stock on October 1. In 20x8, the company had a simple capital structure. During 20x9, there were no transactions involving common stock, and the company reported net income of $2,016,000.

1. Determine the weighted-average number of common shares outstanding each year.
2. Compute earnings per share for each year.

LO5 Statement of Stockholders' Equity

E 9. The stockholders' equity section of Ruff Corporation's balance sheet on December 31, 20x7, follows.

Contributed capital	
Common stock, $2 par value, 250,000 shares	
authorized, 200,000 shares issued and outstanding	$ 400,000
Additional paid-in capital	600,000
Total contributed capital	$1,000,000
Retained earnings	2,100,000
Total stockholders' equity	$3,100,000

Prepare a statement of stockholders' equity for the year ended December 31, 20x8, assuming these transactions occurred in sequence in 20x8:

a. Issued 5,000 shares of $100 par value, 9 percent cumulative preferred stock at par after obtaining authorization from the state.

b. Issued 20,000 shares of common stock in connection with the conversion of bonds having a carrying value of $300,000.

c. Declared and issued a 2 percent common stock dividend. The market value on the date of declaration was $14 per share.

d. Purchased 5,000 shares of common stock for the treasury at a cost of $16 per share.

e. Earned net income of $230,000.

f. Declared and paid the full year's dividend on preferred stock and a dividend of $.40 per share on common stock outstanding at the end of the year.

g. Had foreign currency translation adjustment of minus $50,000.

LO6   **Journal Entries: Stock Dividends**

E 10. Tung Company has 60,000 shares of its $1 par value common stock outstanding. Record in journal form the following transactions as they relate to the company's common stock:

July   17   Declared a 10 percent stock dividend on common stock to be distributed on August 10 to stockholders of record on July 31. Market value of the stock was $5 per share on this date.

       31   Date of record.

Aug.   10   Distributed the stock dividend declared on July 17.

Sept.   1   Declared a $.50 per share cash dividend on common stock to be paid on September 16 to stockholders of record on September 10.

LO6   **Stock Split**

E 11. Mendoza Company currently has 250,000 shares of $1 par value common stock authorized with 100,000 shares outstanding. The board of directors declared a 2-for-1 split on May 15, when the market value of the common stock was $2.50 per share. The retained earnings balance on May 15 was $350,000. Additional paid-in capital on this date was $10,000. Prepare the stockholders' equity section of the company's balance sheet before and after the stock split. What entry, if any, would be necessary to record the stock split?

LO6   **Stock Split**

E 12. On January 15, the board of directors of Picado International declared a 3-for-1 stock split of its $12 par value common stock, of which 1,600,000 shares were authorized and 400,000 were issued and outstanding. The market value on that date was $45 per share. On the same date, the balance of additional paid-in capital was $8,000,000, and the balance of retained earnings was $16,000,000. Prepare the stockholders' equity section of the company's balance sheet before and after the stock split. What entry, if any, is needed to record the stock split?

LO7 **Book Value for Preferred and Common Stock**

E 13. Below is the stockholders' equity section of Jobs Corporation's balance sheet. Determine the book value per share for both the preferred and the common stock.

Contributed capital	
Preferred stock, $100 per share, 6 percent cumulative, 5,000 shares authorized, 100 shares issued and outstanding*	$10,000
Common stock, $5 par value, 50,000 shares authorized, 5,000 shares issued, 4,500 shares outstanding	25,000
Additional paid-in capital	14,000
Total contributed capital	$49,000
Retained earnings	47,500
Total contributed capital and retained earnings	$96,500
Less treasury stock, common (500 shares at cost)	7,500
Total stockholders' equity	$89,000

*The preferred stock is callable at $105 per share, and one year's dividends are in arrears.

Problems

LO1 **Effect of Alternative Accounting Methods**

P 1. Zeigler Company began operations in 20xx. At the beginning of the year, the company purchased plant assets of $900,000, with an estimated useful life of ten years and no residual value. During the year, the company had net sales of $1,300,000, salaries expense of $200,000, and other expenses of $80,000, excluding depreciation. In addition, Zeigler Company purchased inventory as follows:

Jan. 15	400 units at $400	$160,000
Mar. 20	200 units at $408	81,600
June 15	800 units at $416	332,800
Sept. 18	600 units at $412	247,200
Dec. 9	300 units at $420	126,000
Total	2,300 units	$947,600

At the end of the year, a physical inventory disclosed 500 units still on hand. The managers of Zeigler Company know they have a choice of accounting methods, but they are unsure how those methods will affect net income. They have heard of the FIFO and LIFO inventory methods and the straight-line and double-declining-balance depreciation methods.

Required

1. Prepare two income statements for Zeigler Company, one using the FIFO and straight-line methods and the other using the LIFO and double-declining-balance methods. Ignore income taxes.
2. Prepare a schedule accounting for the difference in the two net income figures obtained in requirement 1.

3. **User Insight:** What effect does the choice of accounting method have on Zeigler's inventory turnover? What conclusions can you draw? Use the year-end balance to compute the ratio.

4. **User Insight:** How does the choice of accounting methods affect Zeigler's return on assets? Assume the company's only assets are cash of $80,000, inventory, and plant assets. Use year-end balances to compute the ratios. Is your evaluation of Zeigler's profitability affected by the choice of accounting methods?

LO1, LO2, LO3, LO4 **Corporate Income Statement**

P 2. Income statement information for Sim Corporation in 20x8 is as follows:

a. Administrative expenses, $220,000
b. Cost of goods sold, $880,000
c. Extraordinary loss from a storm (net of taxes, $20,000), $40,000
d. Income taxes expense, continuing operations, $84,000
e. Net sales, $1,780,000
f. Selling expenses, $380,000

Required

1. Prepare Sim Corporation's income statement for 20x8, including earnings per share, assuming a weighted average of 200,000 shares of common stock outstanding for 20x8.

2. **User Insight:** Which item in Sim Corporation's income statement affects the company's quality of earnings? Why does it have this effect?

LO1, LO2, LO3, LO4 **Corporate Income Statement and Evaluation of Business Operations**

P 3. During 20x9, Dasbol Corporation engaged in two complex transactions to improve the business—selling off a division and retiring bonds. The company has always issued a simple single-step income statement, and the accountant has accordingly prepared the December 31 year-end income statements for 20x8 and 20x9, as shown below.

Dasbol Corporation
Income Statements
For the Years Ended December 31, 20x9 and 20x8

	20x9	20x8
Net sales	$1,000,000	$1,200,000
Cost of goods sold	(550,000)	(600,000)
Operating expenses	(225,000)	(150,000)
Income taxes expense	(179,100)	(135,000)
Income from operations of a discontinued segment	160,000	
Gain on disposal of discontinued segment	140,000	
Extraordinary gain on retirement of bonds	72,000	
Net income	$ 417,900	$ 315,000
Earnings per share	$ 2.09	$ 1.58

Joseph Dasbol, the president of Dasbol Corporation, is pleased to see that both net income and earnings per share increased by almost 33 percent from 20x8 to 20x9 and intends to announce to the company's stockholders that the plan to improve the business has been successful.

Required

1. Recast the 20x9 and 20x8 income statements in proper multistep form, including allocating income taxes to appropriate items (assume a 30 percent income tax rate) and showing earnings per share figures (200,000 shares outstanding).
2. **User Insight:** What is your assessment of Dasbol Corporation's plan and business operations in 20x9?

LO5, LO6 **Dividends, Stock Splits, and Stockholders' Equity**

P 4. The stockholders' equity section of the balance sheet of Pittman Corporation as of December 31, 20x7, was as follows:

Contributed capital	
Common stock, $4 par value, 500,000 shares authorized,	
200,000 shares issued and outstanding	$ 800,000
Additional paid-in capital	1,000,000
Total contributed capital	$1,800,000
Retained earnings	1,200,000
Total stockholders' equity	$3,000,000

Pittman Corporation had the following transactions in 20x8:

Feb. 28   The board of directors declared a 10 percent stock dividend to stockholders of record on March 25 to be distributed on April 5. The market value on this date is $16.

Mar. 25   Date of record for stock dividend.

Apr. 5   Issued stock dividend.

Aug. 3   Declared a 2-for-1 stock split.

Nov. 20   Purchased 18,000 shares of the company's common stock at $8 per share for the treasury.

Dec. 31   Declared a 5 percent stock dividend to stockholders of record on January 25 to be distributed on February 5. The market value per share was $9.

Required

1. Record the stockholders' equity components of the transactions for Pittman Corporation in T accounts.
2. Prepare the stockholders' equity section of the company's balance sheet as of December 31, 20x8. Assume net income for 20x8 is $108,000.
3. **User Insight:** If you owned 1,000 shares of Pittman stock on February 1, 20x8, how many shares would you own February 5, 20x9? Would your proportionate share of the ownership of the company be different on the latter date than it was on the former date? Explain your answer.

LO5, LO6 **Dividends and Stock Split Transactions and Stockholders' Equity**

P 5. The stockholders' equity section of Rigby Moving and Storage Company's balance sheet as of December 31, 20x7, appears at the top of the next page. The company engaged in the following stockholders' equity transactions during 20x8:

Mar. 5   Declared a $.40 per share cash dividend to be paid on April 6 to stockholders of record on March 20.

5   20   Date of record.

Contributed capital	
Common stock, $2 par value, 3,000,000 shares authorized, 500,000 shares issued and outstanding	$1,000,000
Additional paid-in capital	400,000
Total contributed capital	$1,400,000
Retained earnings	1,080,000
Total stockholders' equity	$2,480,000

Apr.	6	Paid the cash dividend.
June	17	Declared a 10 percent stock dividend to be distributed August 17 to stockholders of record on August 5. The market value of the stock was $14 per share.
Aug.	5	Date of record.
	17	Distributed the stock dividend.
Oct.	2	Split its stock 2 for 1.
Dec.	27	Declared a cash dividend of $.20 payable January 27, 20x9, to stockholders of record on January 14, 20x9.

Required

1. Record the 20x8 transactions in journal form.
2. Prepare the stockholders' equity section of the company's balance sheet as of December 31, 20x8. Assume net income for the year is $400,000.
3. **User Insight:** If you owned some shares of Rigby, would you expect the total value of your shares to go up or down as a result of the stock dividends and stock split? What intangibles might affect the stock value?

LO5, LO6, LO7

Comprehensive Stockholders' Equity Transactions

P 6. On December 31, 20x7, the stockholders' equity section of Tsang Company's balance sheet appeared as follows:

Contributed capital	
Common stock, $8 par value, 200,000 shares authorized, 60,000 shares issued and outstanding	$ 480,000
Additional paid-in capital	1,280,000
Total contributed capital	$1,760,000
Retained earnings	824,000
Total stockholders' equity	$2,584,000

The following are selected transactions involving stockholders' equity in 20x8: On January 4, the board of directors obtained authorization for 20,000 shares of $40 par value noncumulative preferred stock that carried an indicated dividend rate of $4 per share and was callable at $42 per share. On January 14, the company sold 12,000 shares of the preferred stock at $40 per share and issued another 2,000 in exchange for a building valued at $80,000. On March 8, the board of directors declared a 2-for-1 stock split on the common stock. On April 20, after the stock split, the company purchased 3,000 shares of common stock for the treasury at an average price of $12 per share; 1,000 of these shares subsequently were sold on May 4 at an average price of $16 per share. On July 15, the board of directors declared a cash dividend of $4 per share on the preferred stock and $.40 per share on the common stock. The date of record was July 25. The dividends were paid on August 15. The board of directors declared a 15 percent stock dividend on November 28, when the common stock was selling for $20. The date of record for the stock dividend was December 15, and the dividend was to be distributed on January 5.

Required

1. Record the above transactions in journal form.
2. Prepare the stockholders' equity section of the company's balance sheet as of December 31, 20x8. Net loss for 20x8 was $218,000. (**Hint:** Use T accounts to keep track of transactions.)
3. User Insight: Compute the book value per share for preferred and common stock (including common stock distributable) on December 31, 20x7 and 20x8, using end-of-year shares outstanding. What effect would you expect the change in book value to have on the market price per share of the company's stock?

Alternate Problems

LO1, LO2, LO3, LO4 **Corporate Income Statement**

P 7. Information concerning operations of Norris Weather Gear Corporation during 20xx is as follows:

a. Administrative expenses, $180,000
b. Cost of goods sold, $840,000
c. Extraordinary loss from an earthquake (net of taxes, $72,000), $120,000
d. Sales (net), $1,800,000
e. Selling expenses, $160,000
f. Income taxes expense applicable to continuing operations, $210,000

Required

1. Prepare the corporation's income statement for the year ended December 31, 20xx, including earnings per share information. Assume a weighted average of 100,000 common shares outstanding during the year.
2. User Insight: Which item in Norris Weather Gear Corporation's income statement affects the company's quality of earnings? Why does it have an effect on quality of earnings?

LO5, LO6 **Dividends, Stock Splits, and Stockholders' Equity**

P 8. The stockholders' equity section of Waterbury Linen Mills, Inc., as of December 31, 20x7, was as follows:

Contributed capital	
Common stock, $3 par value, 500,000 shares	
authorized, 40,000 shares issued and outstanding	$120,000
Additional paid-in capital	37,500
Total contributed capital	$157,500
Retained earnings	120,000
Total stockholders' equity	$277,500

A review of the stockholders' equity records of Waterbury Linen Mills, Inc., disclosed the following transactions during 20x8:

Mar. 25 The board of directors declared a 5 percent stock dividend to stockholders of record on April 20 to be distributed on May 1. The market value of the common stock was $21 per share.

Apr.   20   Date of record for stock dividend.
May   1   Issued stock dividend.
Sept. 10   Declared a 3-for-1 stock split.
Dec.   15   Declared a 10 percent stock dividend to stockholders of record on January 15 to be distributed on February 15. The market price on this date is $9 per share.

Required

1. Record the stockholders' equity components of the transactions for Waterbury Linen Mills, Inc., in T accounts.
2. Prepare the stockholders' equity section of the company's balance sheet as of December 31, 20x8. Assume net income for 20x8 is $247,000.
3. **User Insight:** If you owned 1,000 shares of Waterbury Linen Mills stock on May 1, 20x8, how many shares would you own on February 15, 20x9? Would your proportionate share of the ownership of the company be different on the latter date than it was on the former date? Explain your answer.

ENHANCING Your Knowledge, Skills, and Critical Thinking

Conceptual Understanding Cases

LO6   **Stock Split**

C 1. When **Yahoo! Inc.** reported in early 2004 that its first quarter earnings had doubled from the previous year, its stock price jumped 10 percent to $53 per share. At the same time, the company announced a 2-for-1 stock split.[20] What is a stock split and what effect does it have on the company's stockholders' equity? What effect will it likely have on the market value of the company's stock? In light of your answers, do you think the stock split is positive for the company and for its stockholders?

LO1, LO3   **Classic Quality of Earnings Case**

C 2. On Tuesday, January 19, 1988, **IBM** reported greatly increased earnings for the fourth quarter of 1987. Despite this reported gain in earnings, the price of IBM's stock on the New York Stock Exchange declined by $6 per share to $111.75. In sympathy with this move, most other technology stocks also declined.[21]

IBM's fourth-quarter net earnings rose from $1.39 billion, or $2.28 a share, to $2.08 billion, or $3.47 a share, an increase of 49.6 percent and 52.2 percent over the same period a year earlier. Management declared that these results demonstrated the effectiveness of IBM's efforts to become more competitive and that, despite the economic uncertainties of 1988, the company was planning for growth.

The apparent cause of the stock price decline was that the huge increase in income could be traced to nonrecurring gains. Investment analysts pointed out that IBM's high earnings stemmed primarily from such factors as a lower tax rate. Despite most analysts' expectations of a tax rate between 40 and 42 percent, IBM's was a low 36.4 percent, down from the previous year's 45.3 percent. Analysts were also disappointed in IBM's revenue growth. Revenues within the United States were down, and much of the company's growth in revenues came through favorable currency translations, increases that might not be repeated. In fact, some estimates of IBM's fourth-quarter earnings attributed $.50 per share to currency translations and another $.25 to tax-rate changes.

Other factors contributing to IBM's rise in earnings were one-time transactions, such as the sale of Intel Corporation stock and bond redemptions, along with a corporate stock buyback program that reduced the amount of stock outstanding in the fourth quarter by 7.4 million shares.

The analysts were concerned about the quality of IBM's earnings. Identify four quality of earnings issues reported in the case and the analysts' concern about each. In percentage terms, what is the impact of the currency changes on fourth-quarter earnings? Comment on management's assessment of IBM's performance. Do you agree with management? (Optional question: What has IBM's subsequent performance been?) Be prepared to discuss your answers in class.

Interpreting Financial Reports

LO1, LO5 **Interpretation of Statement of Stockholders' Equity**

C 3. The consolidated statement of stockholders' equity for Jackson Electronics, Inc., a manufacturer of a broad line of electrical components, is presented below.

Jackson Electronics, Inc.
Consolidated Statement of Stockholders' Equity
For the Year Ended September 30, 20x8
(In thousands)

	Preferred Stock	Common Stock	Paid-in Capital in Excess of Par Value, Common	Retained Earnings	Treasury Stock, Common	Accumulated Other Comprehensive Income	Total
Balance at September 30, 20x7	$2,756	$3,902	$14,149	$119,312	($ 942)		$139,177
Net income	—	—	—	18,753	—		18,753
Unrealized gain on available for sale securities						$12,000	12,000
Redemption and retirement of preferred stock (27,560 shares)	(2,756)	—	—	—	—		(2,756)
Stock options exercised (89,000 shares)	—	89	847	—	—		936
Purchases of common stock for treasury (501,412 shares)	—	—	—	—	(12,552)		(12,552)
Issuance of common stock (148,000 shares) in exchange for convertible subordinated debentures	—	148	3,635	—	—		3,783
Issuance of common stock (715,000 shares) for cash	—	715	24,535	—	—		25,250
Issuance of 500,000 shares of common stock in exchange for investment in Electrix Company shares	—	500	17,263	—	—		17,763
Cash dividends—common stock ($.80 per share)	—	—	—	(3,086)	—		(3,086)
Balance at September 30, 20x8	$ —	$5,354	$60,429	$134,979	($13,494)	$12,000	$199,268

This statement of stockholders' equity has nine summary transactions. Show that you understand it by preparing an entry in journal form with an explanation for each transaction. In each case, if applicable, determine the average price per common share. At times, you will have to make assumptions about an offsetting part of the entry. For example, assume debentures (long-term bonds) are recorded at face value and that employees pay cash for stock purchased under company incentive plans. Also, define comprehensive income and determine the amount for Jackson Electronics.

LO2   **Analysis of Income Taxes from Annual Report**

C 4. In its 2005 annual report, **Nike, Inc.**, the athletic sportswear company, provided the following data about its current and deferred income tax provisions (in millions):

	2005
Current income taxes due	$622.8
Deferred income taxes	25.4
Total provision for income taxes	$648.2

1. What were the 2005 income taxes on the income statement? Record in journal form the overall income tax liability for 2005, using income tax allocation procedures.
2. Nike's balance sheet contains both deferred income tax assets and deferred tax liabilities. How do such deferred income tax assets arise? How do such deferred income tax liabilities arise? Given the definition of assets and liabilities, do you see a potential problem with the company's classifying deferred income taxes as a liability? Why or why not?

Decision Analysis Using Excel

LO5, LO6, LO7   **Analyzing Effects of Stockholders' Equity Transactions**

C 5. Metzger Steel Corporation (MSC) is a small specialty steel manufacturer located in northern Alabama. The Metzger family has owned the company for several generations. Arnold Metzger is a major shareholder in MSC by virtue of his having inherited 200,000 shares of common stock in the company. Metzger has not shown much interest in the business because of his enthusiasm for archaeology, which takes him to far parts of the world. However, when he received the minutes of the last board of directors meeting, he questioned a number of transactions involving stockholders' equity. He asks you as a person with knowledge of accounting to help him interpret the effect of these transactions on his interest in MSC.

You begin by examining the stockholders' equity section of MSC's December 31, 20x7, balance sheet, which appears at the top of the opposite page. Then you read these relevant parts of the minutes of the board of directors meeting on December 15, 20x8:

Item A   The president reported the following transactions involving the company's stock during the last quarter:

October 15. Sold 500,000 shares of authorized common stock through the investment banking firm of T.R. Kendall at a net price of $50 per share.

November 1. Purchased 100,000 shares for the corporate treasury from Lucy Metzger at a price of $55 per share.

Metzger Steel Corporation
Balance Sheet
December 31, 20x7

Stockholders' Equity

Contributed capital	
Common stock, $10 par value, 5,000,000 shares	
authorized, 1,000,000 shares issued and outstanding	$10,000,000
Additional paid-in capital	25,000,000
Total contributed capital	$35,000,000
Retained earnings	20,000,000
Total stockholders' equity	$55,000,000

Item B   The board declared a 2-for-1 stock split (accomplished by halving the par value and doubling each stockholder's shares), followed by a 10 percent stock dividend. The board then declared a cash dividend of $2 per share on the resulting shares. Cash dividends are declared on outstanding shares and shares distributable. All these transactions are applicable to stockholders of record on December 20 and are payable on January 10. The market value of MSC stock on the board meeting date after the stock split was estimated to be $30.

Item C   The chief financial officer stated that he expected the company to report net income for the year of $4,000,000.

1. Prepare a stockholders' equity section of MSC's balance sheet as of December 31, 20x8 that reflects the above transactions. (**Hint:** Use T accounts to analyze the transactions. Also use a T account to keep track of the shares of common stock outstanding.)
2. Write a memorandum to Arnold Metzger that shows the book value per share and Metzger's percentage of ownership at the beginning and end of the year. Explain the difference and state whether Metzger's position has improved during the year. Tell why or why not and state how Metzger may be able to maintain his percentage of ownership.

Annual Report Case: CVS Corporation

LO1, LO3, LO5   **Corporate Income Statement and Statement of Stockholders' Equity**

C 6. Refer to **CVS Corporation's** annual report in the Supplement to Chapter 5 to answer the following questions:

1. Does CVS have discontinued operations or extraordinary items? Are there any items that would lead you to question the quality of CVS's earnings? Would you say the income statement for CVS is relatively simple or relatively complex? Why?
2. What transactions most often affect the stockholders' equity section of the CVS balance sheet? (**Hint:** Examine the statements of stockholders' equity.)

Comparison Case: CVS Versus Southwest

LO7   **Book Value and Market Value**

C 7. Refer to the annual report for **CVS Corporation** and the financial statements for **Southwest Airlines Co.** in the Supplement to Chapter 5. Compute the 2005 and 2004 book value per share for both companies and compare the results to the average stock price of each in the fourth quarter of 2005 as shown in the notes to the financial statements. Southwest's average price per share was $15.09 in 2004 and $15.75 in 2005. How do you explain the differences in book value per share, and how do you interpret their relationship to market prices?

Ethical Dilemma Case

LO6 **Ethics and Stock Dividends**

C 8. For 20 years, Bass Products Corporation, a public corporation that has promoted itself to investors as a stable, reliable company, has paid a cash dividend every quarter. Recent competition from Asian companies has negatively affected the company's earnings and cash flows. As a result, Sandra Bass, president of the company, is proposing that the board of directors declare a stock dividend of 5 percent this year instead of a cash dividend. She stated: "This will maintain our consecutive dividend record and will not require any cash outflow." What is the difference between a cash dividend and a stock dividend? Why does a corporation usually distribute either kind of dividend, and how does each affect the financial statements? Is the action that Sandra Bass proposed ethical? Why or why not?

Internet Case

LO1, LO4, LO5 **Comparison of Comprehensive Income Disclosures**

 C 9. When the FASB ruled that public companies should report comprehensive income, it did not issue specific guidelines for how this amount and its components should be disclosed. Choose two companies in the same industry. Go to the annual reports on the websites of the two companies you have selected. In the latest annual report, look at the financial statements. How have your two companies reported comprehensive income—as part of the income statement, as part of stockholders' equity, or as a separate statement? What items create a difference between net income and comprehensive income? Is comprehensive income greater or less than net income? Is comprehensive income more volatile than net income? Which measure of income is used to compute basic earnings per share?

Group Activity Case

LO1, LO3, LO4, LO5, LO6, LO7 **C 10.** Divide into groups of three or four students each. Each group should choose a company in the technology industry, such as **Yahoo!**, **ebay**, **Apple**, or **Microsoft**. Obtain the company's annual report or SEC Form 10-K from the Internet. Find the corporate income statement and summary of significant accounting policies (usually the first note to the financial statements).

1. As a team, prepare a one-page executive summary that highlights the quality of earnings, the relationship of book value and market value, and the existence or absence of stock splits or dividends, including reference to management's assessment. Include a table with your report and answers to the following questions:

   a. Did the company report any discontinued operations or extraordinary items?

   b. What percentage of impact did these items have on earnings per share? (Summarize in your table the methods and estimates the company uses.)

    c. How would you evaluate the quality of earnings for the company?

    d. Did the company provide a statement of stockholders' equity or summarize changes in stockholders' equity in the notes only?

    e. Did the company declare any stock dividends or stock splits? Calculate book value per common share.

2. Find in the financial section of your local paper the current market prices of the company's common stock. Discuss the difference between market price per share and book value per share.

3. Find and read references to earnings per share in management's discussion and analysis in the company's annual report. Be prepared to share your report with the reports of other teams in class.

Business Communication Case

C 11. In a recent year, analysts expected **IBM** to earn $1.32 per share. The company actually earned $1.33. **Microsoft** was expected to earn $.43 per share, but it earned only $.41. The corporate income statements of these companies show that Microsoft had a special charge (with corresponding liability) of $660 million, or $.06 per share, based on settlement of a class-action lawsuit filed on behalf of consumers, whereas IBM had no such charge.[22]

    Assume you work for an investment manager who has asked you to write a memorandum in one page or less that assesses these results. Specifically, who did better, Microsoft or IBM? Use quality of earnings to support your answer and comment on the effect of Microsoft's special charge on current and future cash flows.

15

The Statement of Cash Flows

Cash flows are the lifeblood of a business. They enable a company to pay expenses, debts, employees' wages, and taxes, and to invest in the assets it needs for its operations. Without sufficient cash flows, a company cannot grow and prosper. Because of the importance of cash flows, one must be alert to the possibility that items may be incorrectly classified in a statement of cash flows and that the statement may not fully disclose all pertinent information. This chapter identifies the classifications used in a statement of cash flows and explains how to analyze the statement.

LEARNING OBJECTIVES

Making a Statement

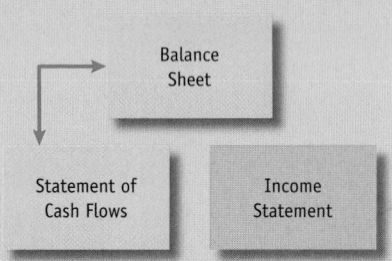

The statement of cash flows explains the changes in cash on the balance sheet.

LO1 Describe the principal purposes and uses of the statement of cash flows, and identify its components.

LO2 Analyze the statement of cash flows.

LO3 Use the indirect method to determine cash flows from operating activities.

LO4 Determine cash flows from investing activities.

LO5 Determine cash flows from financing activities.

MARRIOTT INTERNATIONAL, INC.

- Are operations generating sufficient operating cash flows?

- Is the company growing by investing in long-term assets?

- Has the company had to borrow money or issue stock to finance its growth?

Marriott International is a world leader in lodging and hospitality services. The company believes that maintaining strong cash flows is very important to its future. Its emphasis on cash flows is reflected in its compensation plan for top executives, which gives the greatest weight to cash flows. Why does Marriott place such emphasis on cash flows?

Strong cash flows are critical to achieving and maintaining liquidity. If cash flows exceed the amount a company needs for operations and expansion, it will not have to borrow additional funds. It can use its excess cash to reduce debt, thereby lowering its debt to equity ratio and improving its financial position. That, in turn, can increase the market value of its stock, which will increase shareholders' value.

The statement of cash flows provides information essential to evaluating a company's liquidity. The Financial Highlights below summarize key components of Marriott's statement of cash flows.[1]

MARRIOTT'S FINANCIAL HIGHLIGHTS:
Consolidated Statement of Cash Flows
(In millions)

	2005	2004	2003
Net cash provided by operating activities	$ 837	$891	$403
Net cash provided by investing activities	(130)	287	311
Net cash used in financing activities	(1,274)	(637)	(683)
Increase (decrease) in cash and equivlalents	($ 567)	$541	$ 31

Overview of the Statement of Cash Flows

> **LO1** Describe the principal purposes and uses of the statement of cash flows, and identify its components.

The **statement of cash flows** shows how a company's operating, investing, and financing activities have affected cash during an accounting period. It explains the net increase (or decrease) in cash during the period. For purposes of preparing this statement, **cash** is defined as including both cash and cash equivalents. **Cash equivalents** are investments that can be quickly converted to cash; they have a maturity of 90 days or less when they are purchased. They include money market accounts, commercial paper, and U.S. Treasury bills. A company invests in cash equivalents to earn interest on cash that would otherwise be temporarily idle.

Suppose, for example, that a company has $1,000,000 that it will not need for 30 days. To earn a return on this amount, the company could place the cash in an account that earns interest (such as a money market account), lend the cash to another corporation by purchasing that corporation's short-term notes (commercial paper), or purchase a short-term obligation of the U.S. government (a Treasury bill).

Because cash includes cash equivalents, transfers between the Cash account and cash equivalents are not treated as cash receipts or cash payments. On the statement of cash flows, cash equivalents are combined with the Cash account. Cash equivalents should not be confused with short-term investments, or marketable securities. These items are not combined with the Cash account on the statement of cash flows; rather, purchases of marketable securities are treated as cash outflows, and sales of marketable securities are treated as cash inflows.

Purposes of the Statement of Cash Flows

The primary purpose of the statement of cash flows is to provide information about a company's cash receipts and cash payments during an accounting period. A secondary purpose is to provide information about a company's operating, investing, and financing activities during the accounting period. Some information about those activities may be inferred from other financial statements, but the statement of cash flows summarizes *all* transactions that affect cash.

Uses of the Statement of Cash Flows

The statement of cash flows is useful to management, as well as to investors and creditors.

▶ Management uses the statement of cash flows to assess liquidity, to determine dividend policy, and to evaluate the effects of major policy decisions involving investments and financing. Examples include determining if short-term financing is needed to pay current liabilities, deciding whether to raise or lower dividends, and planning for investing and financing needs.

▶ Investors and creditors use the statement to assess a company's ability to manage cash flows, to generate positive future cash flows, to pay its liabilities, to pay dividends and interest, and to anticipate its need for additional financing.

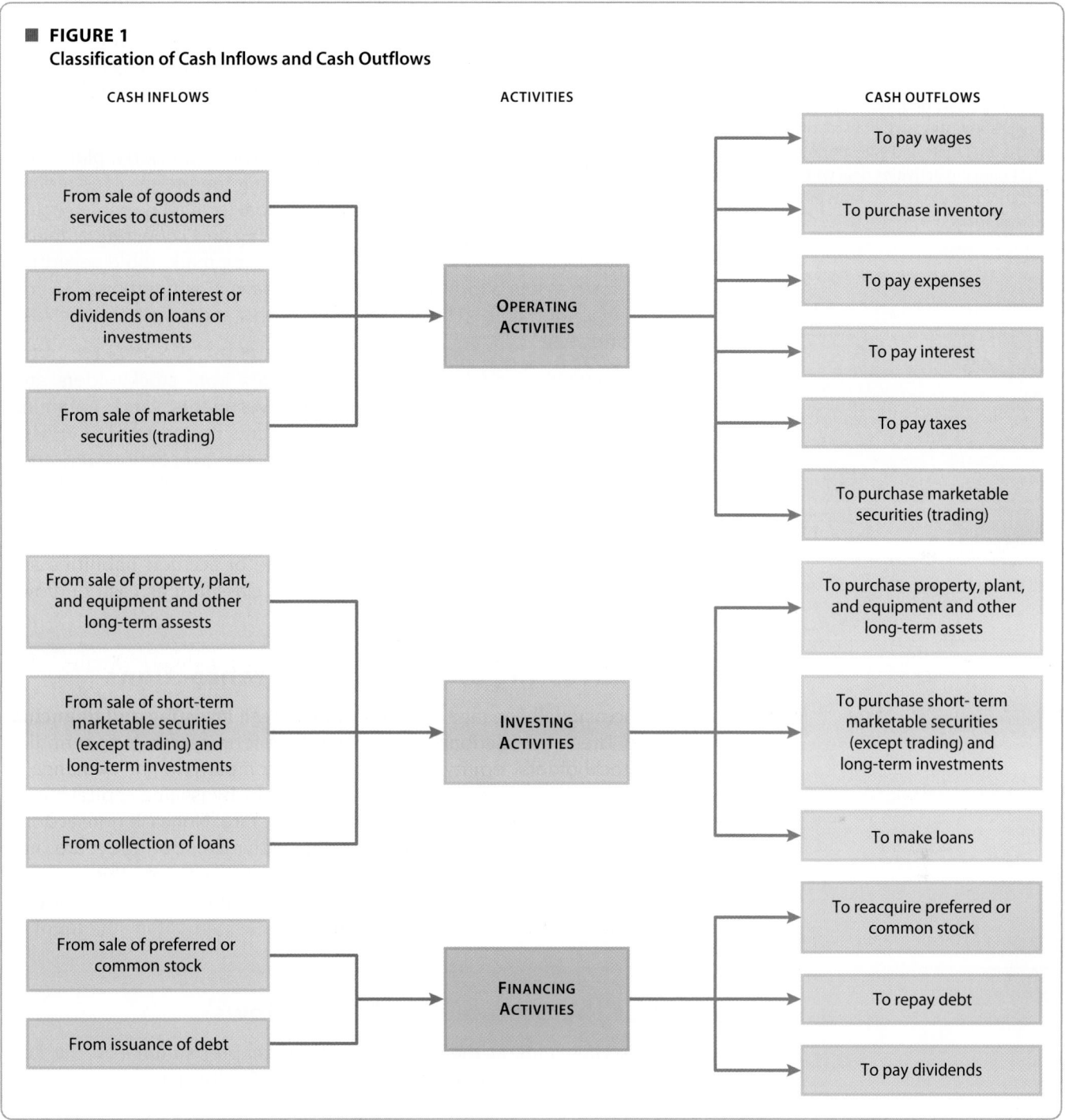

■ **FIGURE 1**
Classification of Cash Inflows and Cash Outflows

Classification of Cash Flows

The statement of cash flows has three major classifications: operating, investing, and financing activities. The components of these activities are illustrated in Figure 1 and summarized below.

1. **Operating activities** involve the cash inflows and outflows from activities that enter into the determination of net income. Cash inflows in this category include cash receipts from the sale of goods and services and from the sale of *trading securities*. Trading securities are a type of marketable security that a company buys and sells for the purpose of making a profit in the

Study Note

Operating activities involve the day-to-day sale of goods and services, investing activities involve long-term assets and investments, and financing activities deal with stockholders' equity accounts and debt (borrowing).

near term. Cash inflows also include interest and dividends received on loans and investments. Cash outflows include cash payments for wages, inventory, expenses, interest, taxes, and the purchase of trading securities. In effect, accrual-based income from the income statement is changed to reflect cash flows.

2. **Investing activities** involve the acquisition and sale of property, plant, and equipment and other long-term assets, including long-term investments. They also involve the acquisition and sale of short-term marketable securities, other than trading securities, and the making and collecting of loans. Cash inflows include the cash received from selling marketable securities and long-term assets and from collecting on loans. Cash outflows include the cash expended on purchasing these securities and assets and the cash lent to borrowers.

3. **Financing activities** involve obtaining resources from stockholders and providing them with a return on their investments, and obtaining resources from creditors and repaying the amounts borrowed or otherwise settling the obligations. Cash inflows include the proceeds from stock issues and from short- and long-term borrowing. Cash outflows include the repayments of loans (excluding interest) and payments to owners, including cash dividends. Treasury stock transactions are also considered financing activities. Repayments of accounts payable or accrued liabilities are not considered repayments of loans; they are classified as cash outflows under operating activities.

Noncash Investing and Financing Transactions

Companies occasionally engage in significant **noncash investing and financing transactions**. These transactions involve only long-term assets, long-term liabilities, or stockholders' equity. For instance, a company might exchange a long-term asset for a long-term liability, settle a debt by issuing capital stock, or take out a long-term mortgage to purchase real estate. Noncash transactions represent significant investing and financing activities, but they are not reflected on the statement of cash flows because they do not affect current cash inflows or outflows. They will, however, affect future cash flows. For this reason, they are disclosed in a separate schedule or as part of the statement of cash flows.

Format of the Statement of Cash Flows

The Financial Highlights at the beginning of the chapter summarize the key components of **Marriott's** statement of cash flows. Exhibit 1 presents the full statement.

▸ The first section of the statement of cash flows is cash flows from operating activities. When the indirect method is used to prepare this section, it begins with net income and ends with cash flows from operating activities. This is the method most commonly used; we discuss it in detail later in the chapter.

▸ The second section, cash flows from investing activities, shows cash transactions involving capital expenditures (for property and equipment) and loans. Cash outflows for capital expenditures are usually shown separately from cash inflows from their disposal, as they are in Marriott's statement. However, when the inflows are not material, some companies combine these two lines to show the net amount of outflow.

EXHIBIT 1 ▶ **Consolidated Statement of Cash Flows**

Marriott International, Inc., and Subsidiaries
Consolidated Statement of Cash Flows

(In millions)	For the Years Ended		
	2005	2004	2003
OPERATING ACTIVITIES			
Income from continuing operations	$ 668	$ 594	$ 476
Adjustments to reconcile cash provided by operating activities:			
Income from discontinued operations	1	2	7
Discontinued operations—gain on sale/exit	—	—	19
Depreciation and amortization	184	166	160
Minority interest in results of synthetic fuel operation	(47)	(40)	55
Income taxes	(86)	(63)	(171)
Timeshare activity, net	(6)	113	(111)
Other	160	(77)	(73)
Working capital changes:			
Accounts receivable	(128)	(6)	(81)
Other current assets	(22)	(16)	11
Accounts payable and accruals	113	218	111
Net cash provided by operating activities	$ 837	$ 891	$ 403
INVESTING ACTIVITIES			
Capital expenditures	$ (780)	$(181)	$(210)
Dispositions	298	402	494
Loan advances	(56)	(129)	(241)
Loan collections and sales	706	276	280
Other	(298)	(81)	(12)
Net cash (used in) provided by investing activities	$ (130)	$ 287	$ 311
FINANCING ACTIVITIES			
Commercial paper, net	$ 499	$ —	$(102)
Issuance of long-term debt	356	20	14
Repayment of long-term debt	(523)	(99)	(273)
Redemption of convertible debt	—	(62)	—
Debt exchange consideration, net	(29)	—	—
Issuance of Class A common stock	125	206	102
Dividends paid	(84)	(73)	(68)
Purchase of treasury stock	(1,644)	(664)	(373)
Earn-outs received, net	26	35	17
Net cash used in financing activities	$(1,274)	$(637)	$(683)
(DECREASE) INCREASE IN CASH AND EQUIVALENTS	$ (567)	$ 541	$ 31
CASH AND EQUIVALENTS, beginning of year	770	229	198
CASH AND EQUIVALENTS, end of year	$ 203	$ 770	$ 229

Source: Marriott International, Inc., *Annual Report,* 2005.

FOCUS ON BUSINESS PRACTICE
How Universal Is the Statement of Cash Flows?

Despite the importance of the statement of cash flows in assessing the liquidity of companies in the United States, there has been considerable variation in its use and format in other countries. For example, in many countries, the statement shows the change in working capital rather than the change in cash and cash equivalents. Although the European Union's principal directives for financial reporting do not address the statement of cash flows, international accounting standards require it, and international financial markets expect it to be presented. As a result, most multinational companies include the statement in their financial reports. Most European countries will adopt the statement of cash flows by 2006, when the European Union will require the use of international accounting standards.

▶ The third section, cash flows from financing activities, shows debt and common stock transactions, as well as payments for dividends and treasury stock.

▶ A reconciliation of the beginning and ending balances of cash appears at the bottom of the statement. These cash balances will tie into the cash balances of the balance sheets.

Ethical Considerations and the Statement of Cash Flows

Although cash inflows and outflows are not as subject to manipulation as earnings are, managers are acutely aware of users' emphasis on cash flows from operations as an important measure of performance. Thus, an incentive exists to overstate these cash flows.

In earlier chapters, we cited an egregious example of earnings management. As you may recall, by treating operating expenses of about $10 billion over several years as purchases of equipment, **WorldCom** reduced reported expenses and improved reported earnings. In addition, by classifying payments of operating expenses as investments on the statement of cash flows, it was able to show an improvement in cash flows from operations. The inclusion of the expenditures in the investing activities section did not draw special attention because the company normally had large capital expenditures.

Another way a company can show an apparent improvement in its performance is through lack of transparency, or lack of full disclosure, in its financial statements. For instance, securitization—the sale of batches of accounts receivable—is clearly a means of financing, and the proceeds from it should be shown in the financing section of the statement of cash flows. However, because the accounting standards are somewhat vague about where these proceeds should go, some companies net the proceeds against the accounts receivable in the operating section of the statement and bury the explanation in the notes to the financial statements. By doing so, they make collections of receivables in the operating activities section look better than they actually were. It is not illegal to do this, but from an ethical standpoint, it obscures the company's true performance.

S T O P • R E V I E W • A P P L Y

1-1. In the statement of cash flows, what does cash include?

1-2. What are the purposes of the statement of cash flows?

1-3. What are the three classifications of cash flows? Give two examples of each.

1-4. Why is it important to disclose certain noncash transactions? How should they be disclosed?

1-5. Why would a company want to classify an item that belongs in the operating activities section of the statement of cash flows in the investing or financing sections?

Suggested answers to all Stop, Review, and Apply questions are available at http://college.hmco.com/accounting/needles/poa/10e/student_home.html.

Analyzing Cash Flows

LO2 Analyze the statement of cash flows.

Like the analysis of other financial statements, an analysis of the statement of cash flows can reveal significant relationships. Two areas on which analysts focus when examining a company's statement of cash flows are cash-generating efficiency and free cash flow.

Cash-Generating Efficiency

Managers accustomed to evaluating income statements usually focus on the bottom-line result. While the level of cash at the bottom of the statement of cash flows is certainly an important consideration, such information can be obtained from the balance sheet. The focal point of cash flow analysis is on cash inflows and outflows from operating activities. These cash flows are used in ratios that measure **cash-generating efficiency**, which is a company's ability to generate cash from its current or continuing operations. The ratios that analysts use to compute cash-generating efficiency are cash flow yield, cash flows to sales, and cash flows to assets. In this section, we compute these ratios for **Marriott** in 2005 using data from Exhibit 1 and the following information from Marriott's 2005 annual report. (All dollar amounts are in millions.)

	2005	**2004**	**2003**
Net sales	$11,550	$10,099	$9,014
Total assets	8,530	8,668	8,177
Net income	669	596	502

Cash flow yield is the ratio of net cash flows from operating activities to net income:

$$\text{Cash Flow Yield} = \frac{\text{Net Cash Flows from Operating Activities}}{\text{Net Income}}$$

$$= \frac{\$837}{\$669}$$

$$= 1.3 \text{ times}$$

Marriott's cash flow yield of 1.3 times in 2005 means that its operating activities were generating about 30 percent more cash flow than net income. At a minimum, cash-flow yield should be 1.0, which is the level typical for a service enterprise. However, a firm with significant depreciable assets should have a cash flow yield greater than 1.0 because depreciation expense is added back to net income to arrive at cash flows from operating activities. If special items, such as discontinued operations, appear on the income statement and are material, income from continuing operations should be used as the denominator.

Cash flows to sales is the ratio of net cash flows from operating activities to sales:

%⁄ℝ

$$\text{Cash Flows to Sales} = \frac{\text{Net Cash Flows from Operating Activities}}{\text{Sales}}$$

$$= \frac{\$837}{\$11,550}$$

$$= 7.2\%$$

Thus, Marriott generated positive cash flows to sales of 7.2 percent in 2005.

Cash flows to assets is the ratio of net cash flows from operating activities to average total assets:

%⁄ℝ

$$\text{Cash Flows to Assets} = \frac{\text{Net Cash Flows from Operating Activities}}{\text{Average Total Assets}}$$

$$= \frac{\$837}{(\$8,530 + \$8,668) \div 2}$$

$$= 9.7\%$$

Marriott's cash flows to assets ratio is higher than its cash flows to sales ratio because of its good asset turnover ratio (sales ÷ average total assets) of 1.3 times (9.7% ÷ 7.2%). Cash flows to sales and cash flows to assets are closely related to the profitability measures of profit margin and return on assets. They exceed those measures by the amount of the cash flow yield ratio because cash flow yield is the ratio of net cash flows from operating activities to net income.

Free Cash Flow

As we noted in an earlier chapter, **free cash flow** is the amount of cash that remains after deducting the funds a company must commit to continue operating at its planned level. If free cash flow is positive, it means that the company has met all of its planned cash commitments and has cash available to reduce debt or to expand. A negative free cash flow means that the company will have to sell investments, borrow money, or issue stock in the short term to continue at its planned level; if a company's free cash flow remains negative for several years, it may not be able to raise cash by issuing stocks or bonds. On the statement of cash flows, cash commitments for current and continuing

FOCUS ON BUSINESS PRACTICE

Cash Flows Tell All.

In early 2001, the telecommunications industry began one of the biggest market crashes in history. Could it have been predicted? The capital expenditures that telecommunications firms must make for equipment, such as cable lines and computers, are sizable. When the capital expenditures (a negative component of free cash flow) of 41 telecommunications companies are compared with their cash flows from sales over the six years preceding the crash, an interesting pattern emerges. In the first three years, both capital expenditures and cash flows from sales were about 20 percent of sales. In other words, free cash flows were neutral, with operations generating enough cash flows to cover capital expenditures. In the next three years, cash flows from sales stayed at about 20 percent of sales, but the companies' capital expenditure increased dramatically, to 35 percent of sales. Thus, free cash flows turned very negative, and almost half of capital expenditures had to be financed by debt instead of operations, making these companies more vulnerable to the downturn in the economy that occurred in 2001.[2]

FOCUS ON BUSINESS PRACTICE
What Do You Mean, "Free Cash Flow"?

Because the statement of cash flows has been around for less than 20 years, no generally accepted analyses have yet been developed. For example, the term *free cash flow* is commonly used in the business press, but there is no agreement on its definition. An article in *Forbes* defines *free cash flow* as "cash available after paying out capital expenditures and dividends, but *before taxes and interest*"[3] [emphasis added]. An article in *The Wall Street Journal*

defines it as "operating income less maintenance-level capital expenditures."[4] The definition with which we are most in agreement is the one used in *BusinessWeek:* free cash flow is net cash flows from operating activities less net capital expenditures and dividends. This "measures truly discretionary funds—company money that an owner could pocket without harming the business."[5]

Study Note

The computation for free cash flow sometimes uses *net capital expenditures* in place of *(purchases of plant assets − sales of plant assets)*.

operations, interest, and income taxes are incorporated in cash flows from current operations.

Free cash flow for **Marriott** in 2005 is computed as follows (in millions):

$$\text{Free Cash Flow} = \text{Net Cash Flows from Operating Activities} - \text{Dividends} - (\text{Purchases of Plant Assets} - \text{Sales of Plant Assets})$$
$$= \$837 - \$84 - (\$780 - \$298)$$
$$= \$271$$

Purchases of plant assets (capital expenditures) and sales (dispositions) of plant assets appear in the investing activities section of the statement of cash flows. When sales of plant assets are small or immaterial, companies can subtract the sales amount from the purchases of plant assets and refer to the result as "net capital expenditures." Dividends appear in the financing activities section. Marriott's positive free cash flow of $271 million was due primarily to its strong operating cash flow of $837 million and the $298 million cash it received from the disposition of assets. Cash was used in financing activities in all three years primarily because of debt repayments and the purchase of treasury stock. The company relied mainly on the increased cash provided by operations to make up for these cash outflows.

Telecommunications firms must make large capital expenditures for plant assets, such as the radio tower shown here. These expenditures are a negative component of free cash flow, which is the amount of cash that remains after deducting the funds a company needs to operate at its planned level. Between 1998 and 2000, negative free cash flows forced a number of telecommunications firms to rely heavily on debt to finance their capital expenditures, thus increasing their vulnerability to the economic downturn of 2001.

Because cash flows can vary from year to year, analysts should look at trends in cash flow measures over several years. Marriott's management sums up its approach to managing cash flows as follows:

Cash from Operations

We consider [our borrowing] resources, together with cash we expect to generate from operations, adequate to meet short-term and long-term liquidity requirements, finance our long-term growth plans, meet debt service and fulfill other cash requirements.[6]

STOP • REVIEW • APPLY

2-1. What is cash-generating efficiency?

2-2. What are three ratios that measure cash-generating efficiency?

2-3. What is free cash flow?

2-4. What do *positive* and *negative free cash flows* mean?

Operating Activities

LO3 Use the indirect method to determine cash flows from operating activities.

To demonstrate the preparation of the statement of cash flows, we will work through an example step by step. The data for this example are presented in Exhibit 2, which shows Amir Corporation's income statement for 20x8, and in Exhibit 3, which shows Amir's balance sheets for December 31, 20x8 and 20x7. Exhibit 3 shows the balance sheet accounts that we use for analysis and whether the change in each account is an increase or a decrease.

EXHIBIT 2 ▶ **Income Statement**

Amir Corporation
Income Statement
For the Year Ended December 31, 20x8

Sales		$349,000
Cost of goods sold		260,000
Gross margin		$ 89,000
Operating expenses (including depreciation expense of $18,500)		73,500
Operating income		$ 15,500
Other income (expenses)		
Interest expense	($11,500)	
Interest income	3,000	
Gain on sale of investments	6,000	
Loss on sale of plant assets	(1,500)	(4,000)
Income before income taxes		$ 11,500
Income taxes expense		3,500
Net income		$ 8,000

▼ **EXHIBIT 3**

Comparative Balance Sheets Showing Changes in Accounts

Amir Corporation
Comparative Balance Sheets
December 31, 20x8 and 20x7

	20x8	20x7	Change	Increase or Decrease
Assets				
Current assets				
Cash	$ 23,000	$ 7,500	$ 15,500	Increase
Accounts receivable (net)	23,500	27,500	(4,000)	Decrease
Inventory	72,000	55,000	17,000	Increase
Prepaid expenses	500	2,500	(2,000)	Decrease
Total current assets	$119,000	$ 92,500	$ 26,500	
Investments	$ 57,500	$ 63,500	($ 6,000)	Decrease
Plant assets	$357,500	$252,500	$105,000	Increase
Less accumulated depreciation	(51,500)	(34,000)	(17,500)	Increase
Total plant assets	$306,000	$218,500	$ 87,500	
Total assets	$482,500	$374,500	$108,000	
Liabilities				
Current liabilities				
Accounts payable	$ 25,000	$ 21,500	$ 3,500	Increase
Accrued liabilities	6,000	4,500	1,500	Increase
Income taxes payable	1,500	2,500	(1,000)	Decrease
Total current liabilities	$ 32,500	$ 28,500	$ 4,000	
Long-term liabilities				
Bonds payable	147,500	122,500	25,000	Increase
Total liabilities				
	$180,000	$151,000	$ 29,000	
Stockholders' Equity				
Common stock, $5 par value	$138,000	$100,000	$ 38,000	Increase
Additional paid-in capital	107,000	57,500	49,500	Increase
Retained earnings	70,000	66,000	4,000	Increase
Treasury stock	(12,500)	0	(12,500)	Increase
Total stockholders' equity	$302,500	$223,500	$ 79,000	
Total liabilities and stockholders' equity	$482,500	$374,500	$108,000	

The first step in preparing the statement of cash flows is to determine cash flows from operating activities. The income statement indicates how successful a company has been in earning an income from its operating activities, but because that statement is prepared on an accrual basis, it does not reflect the inflow and outflow of cash related to operating activities. Revenues are recorded even though the company may not yet have received the cash, and expenses are recorded even though the company may not yet have expended

■ **FIGURE 2**
Indirect Method of Determining Net Cash Flows from Operating Activities

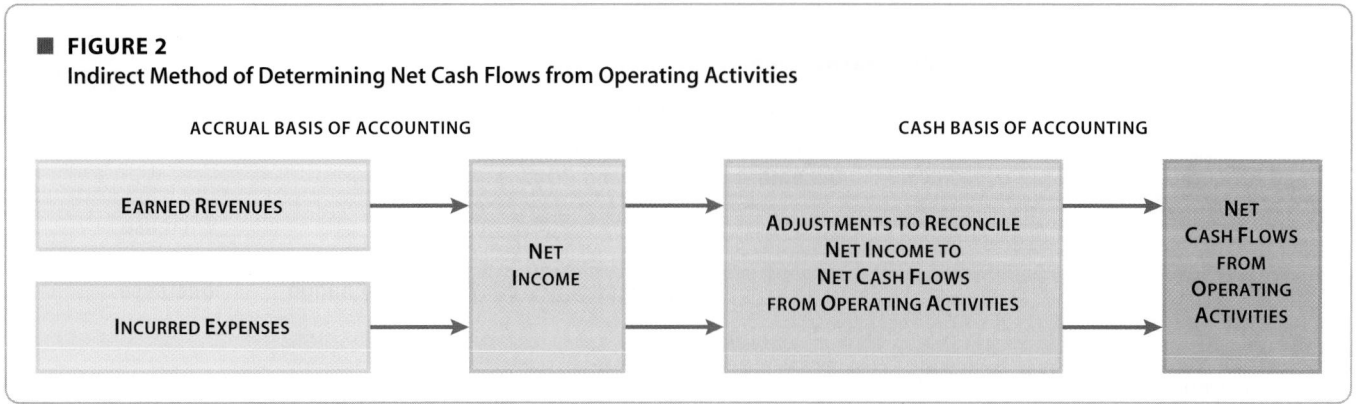

the cash. Thus, to ascertain cash flows from operations, the figures on the income statement must be converted from an accrual basis to a cash basis.

There are two methods of accomplishing this:

▶ The **direct method** adjusts each item on the income statement from the accrual basis to the cash basis. The result is a statement that begins with cash receipts from sales and interest and deducts cash payments for purchases, operating expenses, interest payments, and income taxes to arrive at net cash flows from operating activities.

▶ The **indirect method** does not require the adjustment of each item on the income statement. It lists only the adjustments necessary to convert net income to cash flows from operations.

The direct and indirect methods always produce the same net figure. The average person finds the direct method easier to understand because its presentation of operating cash flows is more straightforward than that of the indirect method. However, the indirect method is the overwhelming choice of most companies and accountants. A survey of large companies shows that 99 percent use this method.[7] From an analyst's perspective, the indirect method is superior to the direct method because it begins with net income and derives cash flows from operations; the analyst can readily identify the factors that cause cash flows from operations. From a company's standpoint, the indirect method is easier and less expensive to prepare. For these reasons, we use the indirect method in our example.

As Figure 2 shows, the indirect method focuses on adjusting items on the income statement to reconcile net income to net cash flows from operating activities. These items include depreciation, amortization, and depletion; gains and losses; and changes in the balances of current asset and current liability accounts. The schedule in Exhibit 4 shows the reconciliation of Amir Corporation's net income to net cash flows from operating activities. We discuss each adjustment in the sections that follow.

Depreciation

The investing activities section of the statement of cash flows shows the cash payments that the company made for plant assets, intangible assets, and natural resources during the accounting period. Depreciation expense, amortization expense, and depletion expense for these assets appear on the income statement as allocations of the costs of the original purchases to the current accounting period. The amount of these expenses can usually be found in the income statement or in a note to the financial statements. As you can see

Study Note

The direct and indirect methods relate only to the operating activities section of the statement of cash flows. They are both acceptable for financial reporting purposes.

EXHIBIT 4 ▶ | **Schedule of Cash Flows from Operating Activities: Indirect Method**

Amir Corporation
Schedule of Cash Flows from Operating Activities
For the Year Ended December 31, 20x8

Cash flows from operating activities		
Net income		$ 8,000
Adjustments to reconcile net income to net cash flows from operating activities		
Depreciation	$18,500	
Gain on sale of investments	(6,000)	
Loss on sale of plant assets	1,500	
Changes in current assets and current liabilities		
Decrease in accounts receivable	4,000	
Increase in inventory	(17,000)	
Decrease in prepaid expenses	2,000	
Increase in accounts payable	3,500	
Increase in accrued liabilities	1,500	
Decrease in income taxes payable	(1,000)	7,000
Net cash flows from operating activities		$15,000

in Exhibit 2, Amir Corporation's income statement discloses depreciation expense of $18,500, which would have been recorded as follows:

A = L + OE
−18,500   −18,500

Depreciation Expense	18,500	
Accumulated Depreciation		18,500
To record annual depreciation on plant assets		

⊃ Study Note

Operating expenses on the income statement include depreciation expense, which does not require a cash outlay.

Even though depreciation expense appears on the income statement, it involves no outlay of cash and so does not affect cash flows in the current period. Thus, to arrive at cash flows from operations on the statement of cash flows, an adjustment is needed to increase net income by the amount of depreciation expense shown on the income statement.

Gains and Losses

⊃ Study Note

Gains and losses by themselves do not represent cash flows; they are merely bookkeeping adjustments. For example, when a long-term asset is sold, it is the *proceeds* (cash received), not the gain or loss, that constitute cash flow.

Like depreciation expense, gains and losses that appear on the income statement do not affect cash flows from operating activities and need to be removed from this section of the statement of cash flows. The cash receipts generated by the disposal of the assets that resulted in the gains or losses are included in the investing activities section of the statement of cash flows. Thus, to reconcile net income to cash flows from operating activities (and prevent double counting), gains and losses must be removed from net income.

For example, on its income statement, Amir Corporation shows a $6,000 gain on the sale of investments. This amount is subtracted from net income to reconcile net income to net cash flows from operating activities. The reason for doing this is that the $6,000 is included in the investing activities section of the statement of cash flows as part of the cash from the sale of the investment. Because the gain has already been included in the calculation of net income, the $6,000 gain must be subtracted to prevent double counting.

Amir's income statement also shows a $1,500 loss on the sale of plant assets. This loss is already reflected in the sale of plant assets in the investing activities section of the statement of cash flows. Thus, the $1,500 is added to net income to reconcile net income to net cash flows from operating activities.

Changes in Current Assets

Decreases in current assets other than cash have positive effects on cash flows, and increases in current assets have negative effects on cash flows. A decrease in a current asset frees up invested cash, thereby increasing cash flow. An increase in a current asset consumes cash, thereby decreasing cash flow. For example, look at Amir Corporation's income statement and balance sheets in Exhibits 2 and 3. Note that net sales in 20x8 were $349,000 and that Accounts Receivable decreased by $4,000. Thus, collections were $4,000 more than sales recorded for the year, and the total cash received from sales was $353,000 ($349,000 + $4,000 = $353,000). The effect on accounts receivable can be illustrated as follows:

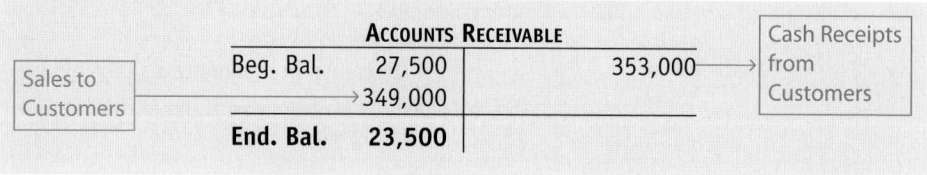

To reconcile net income to net cash flows from operating activities, the $4,000 decrease in Accounts Receivable is added to net income.

Inventory can be analyzed in the same way. For example, Exhibit 3 shows that Amir's Inventory account increased by $17,000 between 20x7 and 20x8. This means that Amir expended $17,000 more in cash for purchases than it included in cost of goods sold on its income statement. Because of this expenditure, net income is higher than net cash flows from operating activities, so $17,000 must be deducted from net income. By the same logic, the decrease of $2,000 in Prepaid Expenses shown on the balance sheets must be added to net income to reconcile net income to net cash flows from operations.

Changes in Current Liabilities

The effect that changes in current liabilities have on cash flows is the opposite of the effect of changes in current assets. An increase in a current liability represents a postponement of a cash payment, which frees up cash and increases cash flow in the current period. A decrease in a current liability consumes cash, which decreases cash flow. To reconcile net income to net cash flows from operating activities, increases in current liabilities are added to net income, and decreases are deducted. For example, Exhibit 3 shows that from 20x7 to 20x8, Amir's accounts payable increased by $3,500. This means that Amir paid $3,500 less to creditors than the amount indicated in the cost of goods sold on its income statement. The following T account illustrates this relationship:

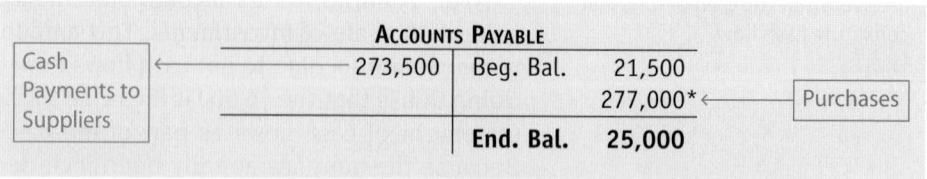

---

*Purchases = Cost of Goods Sold ($260,000) + Increase in Inventory ($17,000)

Thus, $3,500 must be added to net income to reconcile net income to net cash flows from operating activities. By the same logic, the increase of $1,500 in accrued liabilities shown on the balance sheets must be added to net income, and the decrease of $1,000 in income taxes payable must be deducted from net income.

Schedule of Cash Flows from Operating Activities

In summary, Exhibit 4 shows that by using the indirect method, net income of $8,000 has been adjusted by reconciling items totaling $7,000 to arrive at net cash flows from operating activities of $15,000. This means that although Amir's net income was $8,000, the company actually had net cash flows of $15,000 available from operating activities to use for purchasing assets, reducing debts, and paying dividends.

The treatment of income statement items that do not affect cash flows can be summarized as follows:

	Add to or Deduct from Net Income
Depreciation expense	Add
Amortization expense	Add
Depletion expense	Add
Losses	Add
Gains	Deduct

The following summarizes the adjustments for increases and decreases in current assets and current liabilities:

	Add to Net Income	Deduct from Net Income
Current assets		
Accounts receivable (net)	Decrease	Increase
Inventory	Decrease	Increase
Prepaid expenses	Decrease	Increase
Current liabilities		
Accounts payable	Increase	Decrease
Accrued liabilities	Increase	Decrease
Income taxes payable	Increase	Decrease

S T O P • R E V I E W • A P P L Y

3-1. What is the basic difference between the direct method and the indirect method of determining cash flows from operations?

3-2. What conditions might cause a corporation that had a net loss of $12,000 to have a positive cash flow from operations of $9,000?

3-3. Why is depreciation added to net income in arriving at cash flows from operating activities?

3-4. Why is a gain subtracted from net income in arriving at cash flows from operating activities?

3-5. Why do changes in current assets and current liabilities appear in the operating section of the statement of cash flows?

3-6. When the indirect method is used to determine net cash flows from operating activities, should (a) an increase in accounts receivable, (b) a decrease in inventory, (c) an increase in accounts payable, (d) a decrease in wages payable, (e) depreciation expense, and (f) amortization of patents be added to or subtracted from net income?

Cash Flows from Operating Activities: Indirect Method   For the year ended June 30, 20xx, Cirta Corporation's net income was $3,700. Its depreciation expense was $1,000. During the year, its Accounts Receivable increased by $2,200, Inventories increased by $3,500, Prepaid Rent decreased by $700, Accounts Payable increased by $7,000, Salaries Payable increased by $500, and Income Taxes Payable decreased by $300. The company also had a gain on the sale of investments of $900. Use the indirect method to prepare a schedule of cash flows from operating activities.

SOLUTION

Cirta Corporation
Schedule of Cash Flows from Operating Activities
For the Year Ended June 30, 20xx

Cash flows from operating activities		
Net income		$3,700
Adjustments to reconcile net income to net cash flows from operating activities		
Depreciation	$1,000	
Gain on sale of investments	(900)	
Changes in current assets and current liabilities		
Increase in accounts receivable	(2,200)	
Increase in inventories	(3,500)	
Decrease in prepaid rent	700	
Increase in accounts payable	7,000	
Increase in salaries payable	500	
Decrease in income taxes payable	(300)	2,300
Net cash flows from operating activities		$6,000

Investing Activities

> **LO4**   Determine cash flows from investing activities.

To determine cash flows from investing activities, accounts involving cash receipts and cash payments from investing activities are examined individually. The objective is to explain the change in each account balance from one year to the next.

Although investing activities center on the long-term assets shown on the balance sheet, they also include any short-term investments shown under current assets on the balance sheet and any investment gains and losses on the income statement. The balance sheets in Exhibit 3 show that Amir had no short-term investments and that its long-term assets consisted of investments and plant assets. The income statement in Exhibit 2 shows that Amir had a gain on the sale of investments and a loss on the sale of plant assets.

The following transactions pertain to Amir's investing activities in 20x8:

1. Purchased investments in the amount of $39,000.

2. Sold investments that cost $45,000 for $51,000.

3. Purchased plant assets in the amount of $60,000.

4. Sold plant assets that cost $5,000 and that had accumulated depreciation of $1,000 for $2,500.

5. Issued $50,000 of bonds at face value in a noncash exchange for plant assets.

In the following sections, we analyze the accounts related to investing activities to determine their effects on Amir's cash flows.

Study Note

Investing activities involve long-term assets and short- and long-term investments. Inflows and outflows of cash are shown in the investing activities section of the statement of cash flows.

Investments

Our objective in this section is to explain Amir Corporation's $6,000 decrease in investments. We do this by analyzing the increases and decreases in Amir's Investments account to determine their effects on the Cash account.

Item **1** in the list of Amir's transactions states that its purchases of investments totaled $39,000 during 20x8. This transaction, which caused a $39,000 decrease in cash flows, is recorded as follows:

A = L + OE		
+39,000	Investments	39,000	
−39,000	Cash		39,000
	Purchase of investments		

Item **2** states that Amir sold investments that cost $45,000 for $51,000. This transaction resulted in a gain of $6,000. It is recorded as follows:

A = L + OE		
+51,000 +6,000	Cash	51,000	
−45,000	Investments		45,000
	Gain on Sale of Investments		6,000
	Sale of investments for a gain		

The effect of this transaction is a $51,000 increase in cash flows. Note that the gain on the sale is included in the $51,000. This is the reason we excluded it in

Study Note

The $51,000 price obtained, not the $6,000 gained, constitutes the cash flow.

computing cash flows from operations. If it had been included in that section, it would have been counted twice.

We have now explained the $6,000 decrease in the Investments account during 20x8, as illustrated in the following T account:

	INVESTMENTS		
Beg. Bal.	63,500	Sales	45,000
Purchases	39,000		
End. Bal.	**57,500**		

The cash flow effects of these transactions are shown in the investing activities section of the statement of cash flows as follows:

Purchase of investments	($39,000)
Sale of investments	51,000

Notice that purchases and sales are listed separately as cash outflows and inflows to give readers of the statement a complete view of investing activity. However, some companies prefer to list them as a single net amount.

If Amir Corporation had short-term investments or marketable securities, the analysis of cash flows would be the same.

Plant Assets

For plant assets, we have to explain changes in both the Plant Assets account and the related Accumulated Depreciation account. Exhibit 3 shows that from 20x7 to 20x8, Amir Corporation's plant assets increased by $105,000 and that accumulated depreciation increased by $17,500.

Item **3** in the list of Amir's transactions in 20x8 states that the company purchased plant assets totaling $60,000. The following entry records this cash outflow:

A	= L + OE		
+60,000			
−60,000			

Plant Assets	60,000	
Cash		60,000
Purchase of plant assets		

Item **4** states that Amir Corporation sold plant assets that cost $5,000 and that had accumulated depreciation of $1,000 for $2,500. Thus, this transaction resulted in a loss of $1,500. The entry to record it is as follows:

A	= L +	OE	
+2,500		−1,500	
+1,000			
−5,000			

Cash	2,500	
Accumulated Depreciation	1,000	
Loss on Sale of Plant Assets	1,500	
Plant Assets		5,000
Sale of plant assets at a loss		

Note that in this transaction, the positive cash flow is equal to the amount of cash received, $2,500. The loss on the sale of plant assets is included in the investing activities section of the statement of cash flows and excluded from the operating activities section by adjusting net income for the amount of the loss. The amount of a loss or gain on the sale of an asset is determined by the amount of cash received and does not represent a cash outflow or inflow.

Study Note

Even though Amir had a loss on the sale of plant assets, it realized a positive cash flow of $2,500, which will be reported in the investing activities section of its statement of cash flows. When the indirect method is used, the loss is eliminated with an "add-back" to net income.

A	=	L	+ OE
+50,000		+50,000	

The investing activities section of Amir's statement of cash flows reports the firm's purchase and sale of plant assets as follows:

Purchase of plant assets	($60,000)
Sale of plant assets	2,500

Cash outflows and cash inflows are listed separately here, but companies sometimes combine them into a single net amount, as they do the purchase and sale of investments.

Item **5** in the list of Amir's transactions is a noncash exchange that affects two long-term accounts, Plant Assets and Bonds Payable. It is recorded as follows:

Plant Assets	50,000	
Bonds Payable		50,000
Issued bonds at face value for plant assets		

Although this transaction does not involve an inflow or outflow of cash, it is a significant transaction involving both an investing activity (the purchase of plant assets) and a financing activity (the issue of bonds payable). Because one purpose of the statement of cash flows is to show important investing and financing activities, the transaction is listed at the bottom of the statement of cash flows or in a separate schedule, as follows:

Schedule of Noncash Investing and Financing Transactions

Issue of bonds payable for plant assets $50,000

We have now accounted for all the changes related to Amir's plant asset accounts. The following T accounts summarize these changes:

PLANT ASSETS

Beg. Bal.	252,500	Sale	5,000
Cash Purchase	60,000		
Noncash Purchase	50,000		
End. Bal.	**357,500**		

ACCUMULATED DEPRECIATION

Sale	1,000	Beg. Bal.	34,000
		Dep. Exp.	18,500
		End. Bal.	**51,500**

Had the balance sheet included specific plant asset accounts (e.g., Equipment and the related accumulated depreciation account) or other long-term asset accounts (e.g., Intangibles), the analysis would have been the same.

STOP • REVIEW • APPLY

4-1. What are the two major categories of assets that relate to the investing activities section of the statement of cash flows?

4-2. What is the proper treatment on the statement of cash flows of a transaction in which a company had a loss of $5,000 when it sold a building that it had bought for $50,000 and that had accumulated depreciation of $32,000?

4-3. What is the proper treatment on the statement of cash flows of a transaction in which a company purchased buildings and land by taking out a mortgage for $234,000?

Cash Flows from Investing Activities: Plant Assets   The following T accounts show Chou Company's plant assets and accumulated depreciation at the end of 20xx:

PLANT ASSETS					ACCUMULATED DEPRECIATION		
Beg. Bal.	32,500	Disposals	11,500	Disposals 7,350	Beg. Bal.		17,250
Purchases	16,800				Depreciation		5,100
End. Bal.	**37,800**				**End. Bal.**		**15,000**

Chou's income statement shows a gain on the sale of plant assets of $2,200.

Compute the amounts that should be shown as cash flows from investing activities, and show how they should appear on Chou's 20xx statement of cash flows.

> **SOLUTION**
> Cash flows from investing activities:
>
> | Purchase of plant assets | ($16,800) |
> |---|---|
> | Sale of plant assets | $6,350 |
>
> The T accounts show total purchases of plant assets of $16,800, which is an outflow of cash, and disposal of plant assets that cost $11,500 and that had accumulated depreciation of $7,350. The income statement shows a $2,200 gain on the sale of the plant assets. The cash inflow from the disposal was as follows:
>
> | Plant assets | $11,500 |
> |---|---|
> | Less accumulated depreciation | 7,350 |
> | Book value | $ 4,150 |
> | Add gain on sale | 2,200 |
> | Cash inflow from sale of plant assets | $ 6,350 |
>
> Because the gain on the sale is included in the $6,350 in the investing activities section of the statement of cash flows, it should be deducted from net income in the operating activities section.

Financing Activities

LO5   Determine cash flows from financing activities.

Determining cash flows from financing activities is very similar to determining cash flows from investing activities, but the accounts analyzed relate to short-term borrowings, long-term liabilities, and stockholders' equity. Because Amir Corporation does not have short-term borrowings, we deal only with long-term liabilities and stockholders' equity accounts.

The following transactions pertain to Amir's financing activities in 20x8:

1. Issued $50,000 of bonds at face value in a noncash exchange for plant assets.

2. Repaid $25,000 of bonds at face value at maturity.

3. Issued 7,600 shares of $5 par value common stock for $87,500.

4. Paid cash dividends in the amount of $4,000.

5. Purchased treasury stock for $12,500.

Bonds Payable

Exhibit 3 shows that Amir's Bonds Payable account increased by $25,000 in 20x8. Both items **1** and **2** in the list above affect this account. We analyzed item **1** in connection with plant assets, but it also pertains to the Bonds Payable account. As we noted, this transaction is reported on the schedule of noncash investing and financing transactions. Item **2** results in a cash outflow, which is recorded as follows:

A	=	L	+ OE			
−25,000		−25,000		Bonds Payable	25,000	
				Cash		25,000
				Repayment of bonds at face value at maturity		

This appears in the financing activities section of the statement of cash flows as

Repayment of bonds   ($25,000)

The following T account explains the change in Bonds Payable:

BONDS PAYABLE			
Repayment 25,000	Beg. Bal.	122,500	
	Noncash Issue	50,000	
	End. Bal.	**147,500**	

If Amir Corporation had any notes payable, the analysis would be the same.

Common Stock

Like the Plant Asset account and its related accounts, accounts related to stockholders' equity should be analyzed together. For example, the Additional Paid-in Capital account should be examined along with the Common Stock account. In 20x8, Amir's Common Stock account increased by $38,000, and its Additional Paid-in Capital account increased by $49,500. Item **3** in the list of Amir's transactions, which states that the company issued 7,600 shares of $5 par value common stock for $87,500, explains these increases. The entry to record the cash inflow is as follows:

A	= L +	OE			
+87,500		+38,000	Cash	87,500	
		+49,500	Common Stock		38,000
			Additional Paid-in Capital		49,500
			Issued 7,600 shares of $5 par value common stock		

This appears in the financing activities section of the statement of cash flows as

Issue of common stock $87,000

FOCUS ON BUSINESS PRACTICE

How Much Cash Does a Company Need?

Some kinds of industries are more vulnerable to downturns in the economy than others. Historically, because of the amount of debt they carry and their large interest and loan payments, companies in the airline and automotive industries have been hard hit by economic downturns. But research has shown that high-tech companies with large amounts of intangible assets are also hard hit. Biotechnology, pharmaceutical, and computer hardware and software companies can lose up to 80 percent of their value in times of financial stress. In contrast, companies with large amounts of tangible assets, such as oil companies and railroads, can lose as little as 10 percent. To survive during economic downturns, it is very important for high-tech companies to use their cash-generating efficiency to build cash reserves. It makes sense for these companies to hoard cash and not pay dividends to the extent that companies in other industries do.[9]

The following analysis of this transaction is all that is needed to explain the changes in the two accounts during 20x8:

COMMON STOCK			ADDITIONAL PAID-IN CAPTIAL		
	Beg. Bal.	100,000		Beg. Bal.	57,500
	Issue	38,000		Issue	49,500
	End. Bal.	**138,000**		**End. Bal.**	**107,000**

Retained Earnings

At this point, we have dealt with several items that affect retained earnings. The only item affecting Amir's retained earnings that we have not considered is the payment of $4,000 in cash dividends (item **4** in the list of Amir's transactions). At the time it declared the dividend, Amir would have debited its Dividends account. After paying the dividend, it would have closed the Dividends account to Retained Earnings and recorded the closing with the following entry:

A = L + OE
         −4,000
         +4,000

Retained Earnings	4,000	
Dividends		4,000
To close the Dividends account		

Study Note

It is dividends paid, not dividends declared, that appear on the statement of cash flows.

Cash dividends would be displayed in the financing activities section of Amir's statement of cash flows as follows:

Payment of dividends   ($4,000)

The following T account shows the change in the Retained Earnings account:

RETAINED EARNINGS			
Dividends	4,000	Beg. Bal.	66,000
		Net Income	8,000
		End. Bal.	**70,000**

High-tech companies with large amounts of intangible assets, such as PharmaMar, a pharmaceutical firm based in Madrid, can lose up to 80 percent of their value in times of financial stress. As a hedge against economic downturns, these companies need to build cash reserves, and they may therefore choose to hoard cash rather than pay dividends.

Treasury Stock

As we noted in the chapter on contributed capital, many companies buy back their own stock on the open market. These buybacks use cash, as this entry shows:

$$
\begin{array}{ccc}
A & = L + & OE \\
-12{,}500 & & -12{,}500
\end{array}
$$

Treasury Stock	12,500	
Cash		12,500

This use of cash is classified in the statement of cash flows as a financing activity:

Purchase of treasury stock   ($12,500)

The T account for this transaction is as follows:

TREASURY STOCK	
Purchase 12,500	

> **Study Note**
>
> The purchase of treasury stock qualifies as a financing activity, but it is also a cash outflow.

We have now analyzed all Amir Corporation's income statement items, explained all balance sheet changes, and taken all additional information into account. Exhibit 5 shows how our data are assembled in Amir's statement of cash flows.

EXHIBIT 5 ▶ | **Statement of Cash Flows: Indirect Method**

Amir Corporation
Statement of Cash Flows
For the Year Ended December 31, 20x8

Cash flows from operating activities		
Net income		$ 8,000
Adjustments to reconcile net income to net cash		
flows from operating activities		
Depreciation	$18,500	
Gain on sale of investments	(6,000)	
Loss on sale of plant assets	1,500	
Changes in current assets and current liabilities		
Decrease in accounts receivable	4,000	
Increase in inventory	(17,000)	
Decrease in prepaid expenses	2,000	
Increase in accounts payable	3,500	
Increase in accrued liabilities	1,500	
Decrease in income taxes payable	(1,000)	7,000
Net cash flows from operating activities		$15,000
Cash flows from investing activities		
Purchase of investments	($39,000)	
Sale of investments	51,000	
Purchase of plant assets	(60,000)	
Sale of plant assets	2,500	
Net cash flows from investing activities		(45,500)
Cash flows from financing activities		
Repayment of bonds	($25,000)	
Issue of common stock	87,500	
Payment of dividends	(4,000)	
Purchase of treasury stock	(12,500)	
Net cash flows from financing activities		46,000
Net increase (decrease) in cash		$15,500
Cash at beginning of year		7,500
Cash at end of year		$23,000

Schedule of Noncash Investing and Financing Transactions

Issue of bonds payable for plant assets	$50,000

S T O P • R E V I E W • A P P L Y

5-1. What major categories of liabilities and stockholders' equity relate to the financing activities section of the statement of cash flows?

5-2. What is the proper treatment on the statement of cash flows of a transaction in which $50,000 of bonds payable are converted to 2,500 shares of $6 par value common stock?

MARRIOTT INTERNATIONAL, INC.

As we pointed out in this chapter's Decision Point, strong cash flows are a basic ingredient in **Marriott's** plans for the future. Strong cash flows enable a company to achieve and maintain liquidity, to expand, and to increase the value of its shareholders' investments. A company's statement of cash flows provides information essential to evaluating the strength of its cash flows and its liquidity. A user of Marriott's statement of cash flows would want to ask the following questions:

- **Are operations generating sufficient operating cash flows?**
- **Is the company growing by investing in long-term assets?**
- **Has the company had to borrow money or issue stock to finance its growth?**

Using data from Exhibit 1, which presents Marriott's statements of cash flows, we can answer these questions. We can gauge Marriott's ability to generate cash flows from operations by calculating its cash flow yields in 2004 and 2005:

	Cash Flow Yield		**2005**	**2004**
%/	$\dfrac{\text{Net Cash Flows from Operating Activities}}{\text{Net Income}}$	=	$\dfrac{\$837}{\$669}$	$\dfrac{\$891}{\$596}$
		=	1.3 times	1.5 times

As you can see, Marriott's cash flow yield declined slightly over the two years. The 1.3 cash yield in 2005 surpassed the 1.0 level normally considered the minimum acceptable level of cash flows from operations. Because of the increase in cash provided by operations, Marriott's cash flows to sales and assets would also show improvement over the two-year period.

Free cash flow measures the sufficiency of cash flows in a different way. The following computations show that in 2005, Marriott's free cash flow was $768 million less than in 2004:

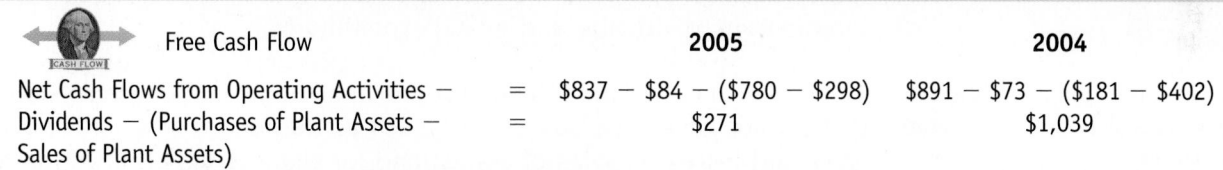

Free Cash Flow		**2005**	**2004**
Net Cash Flows from Operating Activities − Dividends − (Purchases of Plant Assets − Sales of Plant Assets)	=	$837 − $84 − ($780 − $298)	$891 − $73 − ($181 − $402)
	=	$271	$1,039

Marriott's statement of cash flows shows that the company was investing in long-term assets ($181 million in 2004 and $780 million in 2005) but that its sales of assets contributed to its free cash flow. The company did not have to rely on borrowing money or issuing stock to finance its growth. In fact, it repaid more long-term debt than it borrowed and purchased more than 13 times as much treasury stock as it issued in common stock. Financing activities used $637 million in 2004 and $1,274 million in 2005; the sum of these expenditures exceeds the sum of Marriott's free cash flows in the two years. As a result, Marriott's cash balance declined by $567 million in 2005.

CHAPTER REVIEW

REVIEW of Learning Objectives

LO1 Describe the principal purposes and uses of the statement of cash flows, and identify its components.

The statement of cash flows shows how a company's operating, investing, and financing activities have affected cash during an accounting period. For the statement of cash flows, *cash* is defined as including both cash and cash equivalents. The primary purpose of the statement is to provide information about a firm's cash receipts and cash payments during an accounting period. A secondary purpose is to provide information about a firm's operating, investing, and financing activities. Management uses the statement to assess liquidity, determine dividend policy, and plan investing and financing activities. Investors and creditors use it to assess the company's cash-generating ability.

The statement of cash flows has three major classifications: (1) operating activities, which involve the cash effects of transactions and other events that enter into the determination of net income; (2) investing activities, which involve the acquisition and sale of marketable securities and long-term assets and the making and collecting of loans; and (3) financing activities, which involve obtaining resources from stockholders and creditors and providing the former with a return on their investments and the latter with repayment. Non-cash investing and financing transactions are also important because they affect future cash flows; these exchanges of long-term assets or liabilities are of interest to potential investors and creditors.

LO2 Analyze the statement of cash flows.

In examining a firm's statement of cash flows, analysts tend to focus on cash-generating efficiency and free cash flow. Cash-generating efficiency is a firm's ability to generate cash from its current or continuing operations. The ratios used to measure cash-generating efficiency are cash flow yield, cash flows to sales, and cash flows to assets. Free cash flow is the cash that remains after deducting the funds a firm must commit to continue operating at its planned level. These commitments include current and continuing operations, interest, income taxes, dividends, and capital expenditures.

LO3 Use the indirect method to determine cash flows from operating activities.

The indirect method adjusts net income for all items in the income statement that do not have cash flow effects (such as depreciation, amortization, and gains and losses on sales of assets) and for changes in liabilities that affect operating cash flows. Generally, increases in current assets have a negative effect on cash flows, and decreases have a positive effect. Conversely, increases in current liabilities have a positive effect on cash flows, and decreases have a negative effect.

LO4 Determine cash flows from investing activities.

Investing activities involve the acquisition and sale of property, plant, and equipment and other long-term assets, including long-term investments. They also involve the acquisition and sale of short-term marketable securities, other than trading securities, and the making and collecting of loans. Cash flows from investing activities are determined by analyzing the cash flow effects of changes in each account related to investing activities. The effects of gains and losses reported on the income statement must also be considered.

LO5 Determine cash flows from financing activities.

Determining cash flows from financing activities is almost identical to determining cash flows from investing activities. The difference is that the accounts analyzed relate to short-term borrowings, long-term liabilities, and stockholders' equity. After the changes in the balance sheet accounts from one accounting period to the next have been explained, all the cash flow effects should have been identified.

REVIEW of Concepts and Terminology

The following concepts and terms were introduced in this chapter:

Cash: For purposes of the statement of cash flows, both cash and cash equivalents. **(LO1)**

Cash equivalents: Short-term (90 days or less), highly liquid investments, including money market accounts, commercial paper, and U.S. Treasury bills. **(LO1)**

Cash-generating efficiency: A company's ability to generate cash from its current or continuing operations. **(LO2)**

Direct method: The procedure for converting the income statement from an accrual basis to a cash basis by adjusting each item on the income statement. **(LO3)**

Financing activities: Business activities that involve obtaining resources from stockholders and creditors and providing the former with a return on their investments and the latter with repayment. **(LO1)**

Free cash flow: The amount of cash that remains after deducting the funds a company must commit to continue operating at its planned level; Net Cash Flows from Operating Activities − Dividends − (Purchases of Plant Assets − Sales of Plant Assets). **(LO2)**

Indirect method: The procedure for converting the income statement from an accrual basis to a cash basis by adjusting net income for items that do not affect cash flows, including depreciation, amortiza-

tion, depletion, gains, losses, and changes in current assets and current liabilities. **(LO3)**

Investing activities: Business activities that involve the acquisition and sale of marketable securities and long-term assets and the making and collecting of loans. **(LO1)**

Noncash investing and financing transactions: Significant investing and financing transactions involving only long-term assets, long-term liabilities, or stockholders' equity that do not affect current cash inflows or outflows. **(LO1)**

Operating activities: Business activities that involve the cash effects of transactions and other events that enter into the determination of net income. **(LO1)**

Statement of cash flows: A financial statement that shows how a company's operating, investing, and financing activities have affected cash during an accounting period. **(LO1)**

Key Ratios

Cash flows to assets: Net Cash Flows from Operating Activities ÷ Average Total Assets. **(LO2)**

Cash flows to sales: Net Cash Flows from Operating Activities ÷ Sales. **(LO2)**

Cash flow yield: Net Cash Flows from Operating Activities ÷ Net Income. **(LO2)**

REVIEW Problem

LO2, LO3, LO4, LO5   **The Statement of Cash Flows**

Northwest Corporation's income statement for 20x8 and its comparative balance sheets for 20x8 and 20x7 are presented on the following pages. The company's records for 20x8 provide this additional information:

a. Sold long-term investments that cost $70,000 for a gain of $12,500; made other long-term investments in the amount of $20,000.

b. Purchased five acres of land to build a parking lot for $25,000.

c. Sold equipment that cost $37,500 and that had accumulated depreciation of $25,300 at a loss of $2,300; purchased new equipment for $30,000.

d. Repaid notes payable in the amount of $100,000; borrowed $30,000 by signing new notes payable.

e. Converted $100,000 of bonds payable into 6,000 shares of common stock.

f. Reduced the Mortgage Payable account by $20,000.
g. Declared and paid cash dividends of $50,000.
h. Purchased treasury stock for $10,000.

	A	B	C
1	Northwest Corporation		
2	Income Statement		
3	For the Year Ended December 31, 20x8		
4			
5	Net sales		$1,650,000
6	Cost of goods sold		920,000
7	Gross margin		$ 730,000
8	Operating expenses (including depreciation		
9	expense of $12,000 on buildings and		
10	$23,100 on equipment and amortization		
11	expense of $4,800)		470,000
12	Operating income		$ 260,000
13	Other income		
14	Interest expense	$ (55,000)	
15	Dividend income	3,400	
16	Gain on sale of investments	12,500	
17	Loss on disposal of equipment	(2,300)	(41,400)
18	Income before income taxes		$ 218,600
19	Income taxes		52,200
20	Net income		$ 166,400

	A	B	C	D	E
1	Northwest Corporation				
2	Comparative Balance Sheets				
3	December 31, 20x8 and 20x7				
4					
5		20x8	20x7	Change	Increase or Decrease
6	Assets				
7	Cash	$ 105,850	$ 121,850	$ (16,000)	Decrease
8	Accounts receivable (net)	296,000	314,500	(18,500)	Decrease
9	Inventory	322,000	301,000	21,000	Increase
10	Prepaid expenses	7,800	5,800	2,000	Increase
11	Long-term investments	36,000	86,000	(50,000)	Decrease
12	Land	150,000	125,000	25,000	Increase
13	Buildings	462,000	462,000	—	—
14	Accumulated depreciation, buildings	(91,000)	(79,000)	(12,000)	Increase
15	Equipment	159,730	167,230	(7,500)	Decrease
16	Accumulated depreciation, equipment	(43,400)	(45,600)	2,200	Decrease
17	Intangible assets	19,200	24,000	(4,800)	Decrease
18	Total assets	$1,424,180	$1,482,780	$ (58,600)	

(*Continued*)

	A	B	C	D	E
19		20x8	20x7	Change	Increase or Decrease
20	**Liabilities and Stockholders' Equity**				
21	Accounts payable	$ 133,750	$ 233,750	$ (100,000)	Decrease
22	Notes payable (current)	75,700	145,700	(70,000)	Decrease
23	Accrued liabilities	5,000	—	5,000	Increase
24	Income taxes payable	20,000	—	20,000	Increase
25	Bonds payable	210,000	310,000	(100,000)	Decrease
26	Mortgage payable	330,000	350,000	(20,000)	Decrease
27	Common stock, $10 par value	400,000	340,000	60,000	Increase
28	Additional paid-in capital	90,000	50,000	40,000	Increase
29	Retained earnings	209,730	93,330	116,400	Increase
30	Treasury stock	(50,000)	(40,000)	(10,000)	Increase
31	Total liabilities and stockholders' equity	$1,424,180	$1,482,780	$ (58,600)	

Required

1. Prepare a statement of cash flows using the indirect method.
2. Compute cash flow yield, cash flows to sales, cash flows to assets, and free cash flow for 20x8.

Answer to Review Problem

1. Statement of cash flows using the indirect method:

	A	B	C
1	**Northwest Corporation**		
2	**Statement of Cash Flows**		
3	**For the Year Ended December 31, 20x8**		
4			
5	**Cash flows from operating activities**		
6	Net income		$166,400
7	Adjustments to reconcile net income to net cash flows from operating activities		
8	Depreciation expense, buildings	$ 12,000	
9	Depreciation expense, equipment	23,100	
10	Amortization expense, intangible assets	4,800	
11	Gain on sale of investments	(12,500)	
12	Loss on disposal of equipment	2,300	
13	Changes in current assets and current liabilities		
14	Decrease in accounts receivable	18,500	
15	Increase in inventory	(21,000)	
16	Increase in prepaid expenses	(2,000)	
17	Decrease in accounts payable	(100,000)	
18	Increase in accrued liabilities	5,000	
19	Increase in income taxes payable	20,000	(49,800)
20	Net cash flows from operating activities		$116,600

(*Continued*)

	A	B	C
21	**Cash flows from investing activities**		
22	Sale of long-term investments	$ 82,500 **a**	
23	Purchase of long-term investments	(20,000)	
24	Purchase of land	(25,000)	
25	Sale of equipment	9,900 **b**	
26	Purchase of equipment	(30,000)	
27	Net cash flows from investing activities		17,400
28			
29	**Cash flows from financing activities**		
30	Repayment of notes payable	$ (100,000)	
31	Issuance of notes payable	30,000	
32	Reduction in mortgage	(20,000)	
33	Dividends paid	(50,000)	
34	Purchase of treasury stock	(10,000)	
35	Net cash flows from investing activities		(150,000)
36			
37	Net increase (decrease) in cash		$ (16,000)
38	Cash at beginning of year		121,850
39	Cash at end of year		$ 105,850
40			
41	**Schedule of Noncash Investing and Financing Transactions**		
42	Conversion of bonds payable into common stock		$ 100,000
43			
44	**a** $70,000 + $12,500 (gain) = $82,500		
45	**b** $37,500 - $25,300 = $12,200 (book value) - $2,300 (loss) = $9,900		

2. Cash flow yield, cash flows to sales, cash flows to assets, and free cash flow for 20x8:

$$\text{Cash Flow Yield} = \frac{\$116,600}{\$166,400} = .7 \text{ times}$$

$$\text{Cash Flows to Sales} = \frac{\$116,600}{\$1,650,000} = 7.1\%$$

$$\text{Cash Flows to Assets} = \frac{\$116,600}{(\$1,424,180 + \$1,482,780) \div 2} = 8.0\%$$

$$\text{Free Cash Flow} = \$116,600 - \$50,000 - (\$25,000 + \$30,000 - \$9,900) = \$21,500$$

CHAPTER ASSIGNMENTS

BUILDING Your Basic Knowledge and Skills

Short Exercises

LO1 **Classification of Cash Flow Transactions**

SE 1. The list that follows itemizes Furlong Corporation's transactions. Identify each as (a) an operating activity, (b) an investing activity, (c) a financing activity, (d) a noncash transaction, or (e) none of the above.

1. Sold land.
2. Declared and paid a cash dividend.
3. Paid interest.
4. Issued common stock for plant assets.
5. Issued preferred stock.
6. Borrowed cash on a bank loan.

LO2 Cash-Generating Efficiency Ratios and Free Cash Flow

SE 2. In 20x9, Krall Corporation had year-end assets of $1,100,000, sales of $1,580,000, net income of $180,000, net cash flows from operating activities of $360,000, purchases of plant assets of $240,000, and sales of plant assets of $40,000, and it paid dividends of $80,000. In 20x8, year-end assets were $1,000,000. Calculate the cash-generating efficiency ratios of cash flow yield, cash flows to sales, and cash flows to assets. Also calculate free cash flow.

LO2 Cash-Generating Efficiency Ratios and Free Cash Flow

SE 3. Examine the cash flow measures in requirement **2** of the review problem in this chapter. Discuss the meaning of these ratios.

LO3 Computing Cash Flows from Operating Activities: Indirect Method

SE 4. Inter-Finance Corporation had a net income of $16,500 during 20x7. During the year, the company had depreciation expense of $7,000. Accounts Receivable increased by $5,500, and Accounts Payable increased by $2,500. Those were the company's only current assets and current liabilities. Use the indirect method to determine net cash flows from operating activities.

LO3 Computing Cash Flows from Operating Activities: Indirect Method

SE 5. During 20x7, Minh Corporation had a net income of $144,000. Included on its income statement were depreciation expense of $16,000 and amortization expense of $1,800. During the year, Accounts Receivable decreased by $8,200, Inventories increased by $5,400, Prepaid Expenses decreased by $1,000, Accounts Payable decreased by $14,000, and Accrued Liabilities decreased by $1,700. Use the indirect method to determine net cash flows from operating activities.

LO4 Cash Flows from Investing Activities and Noncash Transactions

SE 6. During 20x7, Howard Company purchased land for $375,000. It paid $125,000 in cash and signed a $250,000 mortgage for the rest. The company also sold a building that originally cost $90,000, on which it had $70,000 of accumulated depreciation, for $95,000 cash, making a gain of $75,000. Prepare the cash flows from investing activities section and the schedule of noncash investing and financing transactions of the statement of cash flows.

LO5 Cash Flows from Financing Activities

SE 7. During 20x7, Arizona Company issued $500,000 in long-term bonds at 96, repaid $75,000 of bonds at face value, paid interest of $40,000, and paid dividends of $25,000. Prepare the cash flows from the financing activities section of the statement of cash flows.

LO1, LO3, LO4, LO5 Identifying Components of the Statement of Cash Flows

SE 8. Assuming the indirect method is used to prepare the statement of cash flows, tell whether each of the following items would appear (a) in cash flows from operating activities, (b) in cash flows from investing activities,

(c) in cash flows from financing activities, (d) in the schedule of noncash investing and financing transactions, or (e) not on the statement of cash flows at all:

1. Dividends paid
2. Cash receipts from sales
3. Decrease in accounts receivable
4. Sale of plant assets
5. Gain on sale of investments
6. Issue of stock for plant assets
7. Issue of common stock
8. Net income

Exercises

LO1, LO2   Discussion Questions

E 1. Develop brief answers to each of the following questions:

1. Which statement is more useful—the income statement or the statement of cash flows?
2. How would you respond to someone who says that the most important item on the statement of cash flows is the change in the cash balance for the year?
3. If a company's cash flow yield is less than 1.0, would its cash flows to sales and cash flows to assets be greater or less than profit margin and return on assets, respectively?

LO3, LO4, LO5   Discussion Questions

E 2. Develop brief answers to each of the following questions:

1. If a company has positive earnings, can cash flows from operating activities ever be negative?
2. Which adjustments to net income in the operating activities section of the statement of cash flows are directly related to cash flows in other sections?
3. In computing free cash flow, what is an argument for treating the purchases of treasury stock like dividend payments?

LO1   Classification of Cash Flow Transactions

E 3. Minnow Corporation engaged in the transactions listed below. Identify each transaction as (a) an operating activity, (b) an investing activity, (c) a financing activity, (d) a noncash transaction, or (e) not on the statement of cash flows. (Assume the indirect method is used.)

1. Declared and paid a cash dividend.
2. Purchased a long-term investment.
3. Increased accounts receivable.
4. Paid interest.
5. Sold equipment at a loss.
6. Issued long-term bonds for plant assets.
7. Increased dividends receivable on securities held.
8. Issued common stock.
9. Declared and issued a stock dividend.
10. Repaid notes payable.
11. Decreased wages payable.
12. Purchased a 60-day Treasury bill.
13. Purchased land.

LO2 Cash-Generating Efficiency Ratios and Free Cash Flow

E 4. In 20x8, Maus Corporation had year-end assets of $2,400,000, sales of $3,300,000, net income of $280,000, net cash flows from operating activities of $390,000, dividends of $120,000, purchases of plant assets of $500,000, and sales of plant assets of $90,000. In 20x7, year-end assets were $2,100,000. Calculate free cash flow and the cash-generating efficiency ratios of cash flow yield, cash flows to sales, and cash flows to assets.

LO3 Cash Flows from Operating Activities: Indirect Method

E 5. The condensed single-step income statement for the year ended December 31, 20x9, of Sunderland Chemical Company, a distributor of farm fertilizers and herbicides, appears as follows:

Sales		$13,000,000
Less: Cost of goods sold	$7,600,000	
Operating expenses (including depreciation of $820,000)	3,800,000	
Income taxes expense	400,000	11,800,000
Net income		$ 1,200,000

Selected accounts from Sunderland Chemical Company's balance sheets for 20x9 and 20x8 are as follows:

	20x9	20x8
Accounts receivable	$2,400,000	$1,700,000
Inventory	840,000	1,020,000
Prepaid expenses	260,000	180,000
Accounts payable	960,000	720,000
Accrued liabilities	60,000	100,000
Income taxes payable	140,000	120,000

Present in good form a schedule of cash flows from operating activities using the indirect method.

LO3 Computing Cash Flows from Operating Activities: Indirect Method

E 6. During 20x7, Linz Corporation had net income of $82,000. Included on its income statement were depreciation expense of $4,600 and amortization expense of $600. During the year, Accounts Receivable increased by $6,800, Inventories decreased by $3,800, Prepaid Expenses decreased by $400, Accounts Payable increased by $10,000, and Accrued Liabilities decreased by $900. Determine net cash flows from operating activities using the indirect method.

LO3 Preparing a Schedule of Cash Flows from Operating Activities: Indirect Method

E 7. For the year ended June 30, 20xx, net income for Freed Corporation was $14,800. Depreciation expense was $4,000. During the year, Accounts Receivable increased by $8,800, Inventories increased by $14,000, Prepaid Rent decreased by $2,800, Accounts Payable increased by $28,000, Salaries Payable increased by $2,000, and Income Taxes Payable decreased by $1,200. Use the indirect method to prepare a schedule of cash flows from operating activities.

LO4 **Computing Cash Flows from Investing Activities: Investments**

E 8. LMN Company's T account for long-term available-for-sale investments at the end of 20x7 is as follows:

INVESTMENTS			
Beg. Bal.	76,000	Sales	78,000
Purchases	116,000		
End. Bal.	114,000		

In addition, LMN Company's income statement shows a loss on the sale of investments of $13,000. Compute the amounts to be shown as cash flows from investing activities and show how they are to appear in the statement of cash flows.

LO4 **Computing Cash Flows from Investing Activities: Plant Assets**

E 9. The T accounts for plant assets and accumulated depreciation for LMN Company at the end of 20x7 are as follows:

PLANT ASSETS				ACCUMULATED DEPRECIATION			
Beg. Bal.	130,000	Disposals	46,000	Disposals	29,400	Beg. Bal.	69,000
Purchases	67,200					Depreciation	20,400
End. Bal.	151,200					End. Bal.	60,000

In addition, LMN Company's income statement shows a gain on sale of plant assets of $8,800. Compute the amounts to be shown as cash flows from investing activities and show how they are to appear on the statement of cash flows.

LO5 **Determining Cash Flows from Financing Activities: Notes Payable**

E 10. All transactions involving Notes Payable and related accounts of Gaynor Company during 20x7 are as follows:

Cash	36,000	
Notes Payable		36,000
Bank loan		
Patent	60,000	
Notes Payable		60,000
Purchase of patent by issuing note payable		
Notes Payable	10,000	
Interest Expense	1,000	
Cash		11,000
Repayment of note payable at maturity		

Determine the amounts of the transactions affecting financing activities and show how they are to appear on the statement of cash flows for 20x7.

LO3, LO4, LO5 **Preparing the Statement of Cash Flows: Indirect Method**

E 11. Marisol Corporation's income statement for the year ended June 30, 20x9 and its comparative balance sheets for June 30, 20x9 and 20x8 appear on the opposite page.

Marisol Corporation
Income Statement
For the Year Ended June 30, 20x9

Sales	$234,000
Cost of goods sold	156,000
Gross margin	$ 78,000
Operating expenses	45,000
Operating income	$ 33,000
Interest expense	2,800
Income before income taxes	$ 30,200
Income taxes expense	12,300
Net income	$ 17,900

Marisol Corporation
Comparative Balance Sheets
June 30, 20x9 and 20x8

	20x9	20x8
Assets		
Cash	$ 69,900	$ 12,500
Accounts receivable (net)	21,000	26,000
Inventory	43,400	48,400
Prepaid expenses	3,200	2,600
Furniture	55,000	60,000
Accumulated depreciation, furniture	(9,000)	(5,000)
Total assets	$183,500	$144,500
Liabilities and Stockholders' Equity		
Accounts payable	$ 13,000	$ 14,000
Income taxes payable	1,200	1,800
Notes payable (long-term)	37,000	35,000
Common stock, $10 par value	115,000	90,000
Retained earnings	17,300	3,700
Total liabilities and stockholders' equity	$183,500	$144,500

Marisol issued a $22,000 note payable for purchase of furniture; sold furniture that cost $27,000 with accumulated depreciation of $15,300 at carrying value; recorded depreciation on the furniture for the year, $19,300; repaid a note in the amount of $20,000; issued $25,000 of common stock at par value; and paid dividends of $4,300. Prepare Marisol's statement of cash flows for the year 20x9 using the indirect method.

Problems

LO1 Classification of Cash Flow Transactions

P 1. Analyze each transaction listed in the table that follows and place X's in the appropriate columns to indicate the transaction's classification and its effect on cash flows using the indirect method.

Transaction	Cash Flow Classification				Effect on Cash Flows		
	Operating Activity	Investing Activity	Financing Activity	Noncash Trans-action	Increase	Decrease	No Effect
1. Increased accounts payable.							
2. Decreased inventory.							
3. Increased prepaid insurance.							
4. Earned a net income.							
5. Declared and paid a cash dividend.							
6. Issued stock for cash.							
7. Retired long-term debt by issuing stock.							
8. Purchased a long-term investment with cash.							
9. Sold trading securities at a gain.							
10. Sold a machine at a loss.							
11. Retired fully depreciated equipment.							
12. Decreased interest payable.							
13. Purchased available-for-sale securities (long-term).							
14. Decreased dividends receivable.							
15. Decreased accounts receivable.							
16. Converted bonds to common stock.							
17. Purchased 90-day Treasury bill.							

LO2, LO3, LO4, LO5

Statement of Cash Flows: Indirect Method

P 2. The comparative balance sheets for Sharma Fabrics, Inc., for December 31, 20x8 and 20x7 appear on the oposite page.

Additional information about Sharma Fabrics's operations during 20x8 is as follows: (a) net income, $56,000; (b) building and equipment depreciation expense amounts, $30,000 and $6,000, respectively; (c) equipment that cost $27,000 with accumulated depreciation of $25,000 sold at a gain of $10,600; (d) equipment purchases, $25,000; (e) patent amortization, $6,000; purchase of patent, $2,000; (f) funds borrowed by issuing notes payable, $50,000; notes payable repaid, $30,000; (g) land and building purchased for $324,000 by signing a mortgage for the total cost; (h) 3,000 shares of $20 par value common stock issued for a total of $100,000; and (i) paid cash dividend, $18,000.

Required

1. Using the indirect method, prepare a statement of cash flows for Sharma Fabrics, Inc.

2. **User Insight:** Why did Sharma Fabrics have an increase in cash of $134,400 when it recorded net income of only $56,000? Discuss and interpret.

3. **User Insight:** Compute and assess cash flow yield and free cash flow for 20x8. What is your assessment of Sharma's cash-generating ability?

Sharma Fabrics, Inc.
Comparative Balance Sheets
December 31, 20x8 and 20x7

	20x8	20x7
Assets		
Cash	$189,120	$ 54,720
Accounts receivable (net)	204,860	150,860
Inventory	225,780	275,780
Prepaid expenses	—	40,000
Land	50,000	—
Building	274,000	—
Accumulated depreciation, building	(30,000)	—
Equipment	66,000	68,000
Accumulated depreciation, equipment	(29,000)	(48,000)
Patents	8,000	12,000
Total assets	$958,760	$553,360
Liabilities and Stockholders' Equity		
Accounts payable	$ 21,500	$ 73,500
Notes payable (current)	20,000	—
Accrued liabilities	—	24,600
Mortgage payable	324,000	—
Common stock, $10 par value	360,000	300,000
Additional paid-in capital	114,400	74,400
Retained earnings	118,860	80,860
Total liabilities and stockholders' equity	$958,760	$553,360

LO2, LO3, LO4, LO5

Statement of Cash Flows: Indirect Method

P 3. The comparative balance sheets for Karidis Ceramics, Inc., for December 31, 20x9 and 20x8 are presented on the next page. During 20x9, the company had net income of $96,000 and building and equipment depreciation expenses of $80,000 and $60,000, respectively. It amortized intangible assets in the amount of $20,000; purchased investments for $116,000; sold investments for $150,000, on which it recorded a gain of $34,000; issued $240,000 of long-term bonds at face value; purchased land and a warehouse through a $320,000 mortgage; paid $40,000 to reduce the mortgage; borrowed $60,000 by issuing notes payable; repaid notes payable in the amount of $180,000; declared and paid cash dividends in the amount of $36,000; and purchased treasury stock in the amount of $20,000.

Required

1. Using the indirect method, prepare a statement of cash flows for Karidis Ceramics, Inc.
2. **User Insight:** Why did Karidis Ceramics experience a decrease in cash in a year in which it had a net income of $96,000? Discuss and interpret.
3. **User Insight:** Compute and assess cash flow yield and free cash flow for 20x9. Why is each of these measures important in assessing cash-generating ability?

Karidis Ceramics, Inc.
Comparative Balance Sheets
December 31, 20x9 and 20x8

	20x9	20x8
Assets		
Cash	$ 257,600	$ 305,600
Accounts receivable (net)	738,800	758,800
Inventory	960,000	800,000
Prepaid expenses	14,800	26,800
Long-term investments	440,000	440,000
Land	361,200	321,200
Building	1,200,000	920,000
Accumulated depreciation, building	(240,000)	(160,000)
Equipment	480,000	480,000
Accumulated depreciation, equipment	(116,000)	(56,000)
Intangible assets	20,000	40,000
Total assets	$4,116,400	$3,876,400
Liabilities and Stockholders' Equity		
Accounts payable	$ 470,800	$ 660,800
Notes payable (current)	40,000	160,000
Accrued liabilities	10,800	20,800
Mortgage payable	1,080,000	800,000
Bonds payable	1,000,000	760,000
Common stock	1,300,000	1,300,000
Additional paid-in capital	80,000	80,000
Retained earnings	254,800	194,800
Treasury stock	(120,000)	(100,000)
Total liabilities and stockholders' equity	$4,116,400	$3,876,400

LO2, LO3, LO4, LO5 **Statement of Cash Flows: Indirect Method**

P 4. Flanders Corporation's income statement for the year ended June 30, 20x8 and its comparative balance sheets as of June 30, 20x8 and 20x7 appear on the opposite page. During 20x8, the corporation sold equipment that cost $48,000, on which it had accumulated depreciation of $34,000, at a loss of $8,000. It also purchased land and a building for $200,000 through an increase of $200,000 in Mortgage Payable; made a $40,000 payment on the mortgage; repaid notes but borrowed an additional $60,000 through the issuance of a new note payable; and declared and paid a $120,000 cash dividend.

Required

1. Using the indirect method, prepare a statement of cash flows. Include a supporting schedule of noncash investing and financing transactions.
2. User Insight: What are the primary reasons for Flanders Corporation's large increase in cash from 20x7 to 20x8?
3. User Insight: Compute and assess cash flow yield and free cash flow for 20x8. How would you assess the corporation's cash-generating ability?

Flanders Corporation
Income Statement
For the Year Ended June 30, 20x8

Sales		$8,081,800
Cost of goods sold		7,312,600
Gross margin		$ 769,200
Operating expenses (including depreciation expense of $120,000)		378,400
Income from operations		$ 390,800
Other income (expenses)		
Loss on sale of equipment	($ 8,000)	
Interest expense	(75,200)	(83,200)
Income before income taxes		$ 307,600
Income taxes expense		68,400
Net income		$ 239,200

Flanders Corporation
Comparative Balance Sheets
June 30, 20x8 and 20x7

	20x8	20x7
Assets		
Cash	$ 334,000	$ 40,000
Accounts receivable (net)	200,000	240,000
Inventory	360,000	440,000
Prepaid expenses	1,200	2,000
Property, plant, and equipment	1,256,000	1,104,000
Accumulated depreciation, property, plant, and equipment	(366,000)	(280,000)
Total assets	$1,785,200	$1,546,000
Liabilities and Stockholders' Equity		
Accounts payable	$ 128,000	$ 84,000
Notes payable (due in 90 days)	60,000	160,000
Income taxes payable	52,000	36,000
Mortgage payable	720,000	560,000
Common stock, $5 par value	400,000	400,000
Retained earnings	425,200	306,000
Total liabilities and stockholders' equity	$1,785,200	$1,546,000

Alternate Problems

LO1 **Classification of Cash Flow Transactions**

P 5. Analyze each transaction listed in the table that follows and place X's in the appropriate columns to indicate the transaction's classification and its effect on cash flows using the indirect method.

	Cash Flow Classification				Effect on Cash Flows		
Transaction	Operating Activity	Investing Activity	Financing Activity	Noncash Trans-action	Increase	Decrease	No Effect
1. Paid a cash dividend.							
2. Decreased accounts receivable.							
3. Increased inventory.							
4. Incurred a net loss.							
5. Declared and issued a stock dividend.							
6. Retired long-term debt with cash.							
7. Sold available-for-sale securities at a loss.							
8. Issued stock for equipment.							
9. Decreased prepaid insurance.							
10. Purchased treasury stock with cash.							
11. Retired a fully depreciated truck (no gain or loss).							
12. Increased interest payable.							
13. Decreased dividends receivable on investment.							
14. Sold treasury stock.							
15. Increased income taxes payable.							
16. Transferred cash to money market account.							
17. Purchased land and building with a mortgage.							

LO2, LO3, LO4, LO5

Statement of Cash Flows: Indirect Method

P 6. O'Brien Corporation's comparative balance sheets as of December 31, 20x8 and 20x7 and its income statement for the year ended December 31, 20x8 are presented on the opposite page.

During 20x8, O'Brien Corporation engaged in these transactions:

a. Sold furniture and fixtures that cost $17,800, on which it had accumulated depreciation of $14,400, at a gain of $3,500.
b. Purchased furniture and fixtures in the amount of $19,800.
c. Paid a $10,000 note payable and borrowed $20,000 on a new note.
d. Converted bonds payable in the amount of $50,000 into 2,000 shares of common stock.
e. Declared and paid $3,000 in cash dividends.

Required

1. Using the indirect method, prepare a statement of cash flows for O'Brien Corporation. Include a supporting schedule of noncash investing transactions and financing transactions.
2. **User Insight:** What are the primary reasons for O'Brien Corporation's large increase in cash from 20x7 to 20x8, despite its low net income?

3. **User Insight:** Compute and assess cash flow yield and free cash flow for 20x8. Compare and contrast what these two performance measures tell you about O'Brien's cash-generating ability.

O'Brien Corporation
Comparative Balance Sheets
December 31, 20x8 and 20x7

	20x8	20x7
Assets		
Cash	$ 82,400	$ 25,000
Accounts receivable (net)	82,600	100,000
Merchandise inventory	175,000	225,000
Prepaid rent	1,000	1,500
Furniture and fixtures	74,000	72,000
Accumulated depreciation, furniture and fixtures	(21,000)	(12,000)
Total assets	$394,000	$411,500
Liabilities and Stockholders' Equity		
Accounts payable	$ 71,700	$100,200
Income taxes payable	700	2,200
Notes payable (long-term)	20,000	10,000
Bonds payable	50,000	100,000
Common stock, $20 par value	120,000	100,000
Additional paid-in capital	90,720	60,720
Retained earnings	40,880	38,380
Total liabilities and stockholders' equity	$394,000	$411,500

O'Brien Corporation
Income Statement
For the Year Ended December 31, 20x8

Sales		$804,500
Cost of goods sold		563,900
Gross margin		$240,600
Operating expenses (including depreciation expense of $23,400)		224,700
Income from operations		$ 15,900
Other income (expenses)		
Gain on sale of furniture and fixtures	$ 3,500	
Interest expense	(11,600)	(8,100)
Income before income taxes		$ 7,800
Income taxes expense		2,300
Net income		$ 5,500

ENHANCING Your Knowledge, Skills, and Critical Thinking

Conceptual Understanding Case

LO1, LO3 **EBITDA and the Statement of Cash Flows**

C 1. When **Fleetwood Enterprises, Inc.**, a large producer of recreational vehicles and manufactured housing, warned that it might not be able to generate enough cash to satisfy debt requirements and could be in default of a loan agreement, its cash flow, defined in the financial press as "EBITDA" (earnings before interest, taxes, depreciation, and amortization), was a negative $2.7 million. The company would have had to generate $17.7 million in the next accounting period to comply with the loan terms.[10] To what section of the statement of cash flows does EBITDA most closely relate? Is EBITDA a good approximation for this section of the statement of cash flows? Explain your answer, which should include an identification of the major differences between EBITDA and the section of the statement of cash flows you chose.

Interpreting Financial Reports

LO2 **Anatomy of a Disaster**

C 2. On October 16, 2001, Kenneth Lay, chairman and CEO of **Enron Corporation**, announced the company's earnings for the first nine months of 2001 as follows:

> Our 26 percent increase in recurring earnings per diluted share shows the very strong results of our core wholesale and retail energy businesses and our natural gas pipelines. The continued excellent prospects in these businesses and Enron's leading market position make us very confident in our strong earnings outlook.[11]

Less than six months later, the company filed for the biggest bankruptcy in U.S. history. Its stock dropped to less than $1 per share, and a major financial scandal was underway. Presented on the opposite page is Enron's statement of cash flows for the first nine months of 2001 and 2000 (restated to correct the previous accounting errors). Assume you report to an investment analyst who has asked you to analyze this statement for clues as to why the company went under.

1. For the two time periods shown, compute the cash-generating efficiency ratios of cash flow yield, cash flows to sales (Enron's revenues were $133,762 million in 2001 and $55,494 million in 2000), and cash flows to assets (use total assets of $61,783 million for 2001 and $64,926 million for 2000). Also compute free cash flows for the two years.
2. Prepare a memorandum to the investment analyst that assesses Enron's cash-generating efficiency in light of the chairman's remarks and that evaluates its available free cash flow, taking into account its financing activities. Identify significant changes in Enron's operating items and any special operating items that should be considered. Include your computations as an attachment.

LO2 **Cash-Generating Efficiency Ratios and Free Cash Flow**

C 3. The data that appear on page 728 pertain to two of Japan's best-known and most successful companies, **Sony Corporation** and **Canon, Inc.**[12] (Numbers are in billions of yen.)

Enron Corporation
Statement of Cash Flows
For the Nine Months Ended September 30, 2001 and 2000

(In millions)	2001	2000
Cash Flows from Operating Activities		
Reconciliation of net income to net cash provided by operating activities		
Net income	$ 225	$ 797
Cumulative effect of accounting changes, net of tax	(19)	0
Depreciation, depletion and amortization	746	617
Deferred income taxes	(134)	8
Gains on sales of non-trading assets	(49)	(135)
Investment losses	768	0
Changes in components of working capital		
Receivables	987	(3,363)
Inventories	1	339
Payables	(1,764)	2,899
Other	464	(455)
Trading investments		
Net margin deposit activity	(2,349)	541
Other trading activities	173	(555)
Other, net	198	(566)
Net Cash Provided by (Used in) Operating Activities	$ (753)	$ 127
Cash Flows from Investing Activities		
Capital expenditures	$(1,584)	$(1,539)
Equity investments	(1,172)	(858)
Proceeds from sales of non-trading investments	1,711	222
Acquisition of subsidiary stock	0	(485)
Business acquisitions, net of cash acquired	(82)	(773)
Other investing activities	(239)	(147)
Net Cash Used in Investing Activities	$(1,366)	$(3,580)
Cash Flows from Financing Activities		
Issuance of long-term debt	$ 4,060	$ 2,725
Repayment of long-term debt	(3,903)	(579)
Net increase in short-term borrowings	2,365	1,694
Issuance of common stock	199	182
Net redemption of company-obligated preferred securities of subsidiaries	0	(95)
Dividends paid	(394)	(396)
Net (acquisition) disposition of treasury stock	(398)	354
Other financing activities	(49)	(12)
Net Cash Provided by Financing Activities	$ 1,880	$ 3,873
Increase (Decrease) in Cash and Cash Equivalents	$ (239)	$ 420
Cash and Cash Equivalents, Beginning of Period	1,240	333
Cash and Cash Equivalents, End of Period	$ 1,001	$ 753

Source: Adapted from Enron Corporation, SEC filings, 2001.

	Sony Corporation		Canon, Inc.	
	2005	**2004**	**2005**	**2004**
Sales	¥6,565	¥6,883	¥3,754	¥3,468
Net income	164	89	384	343
Average total assets	9,295	8,731	3,815	3,385
Net cash flows from operating activities	647	633	606	562
Dividends paid	23	23	64	53
Net capital expenditures	419	378	380	249

Calculate the ratios of cash flow yield, cash flows to sales, and cash flows to assets, as well as free cash flow, for the two years, for both Sony Corporation and Canon, Inc. Which company is most efficient in generating cash flow? Which company has the best year-to-year trend? Which company do you think will most probably need external financing?

Decision Analysis Using Excel

LO2, LO3, LO4, LO5   **Analysis of Cash Flow Difficulty**

C 4. Lou Klein, certified public accountant, has just given his employer May Hashimi, the president of Hashimi Print Gallery, Inc., the following income statement:

Hashimi Print Gallery, Inc.
Income Statement
For the Year Ended December 31, 20x8

Sales	$884,000
Cost of goods sold	508,000
Gross margin	$376,000
Operating expenses (including depreciation expense of $20,000)	204,000
Operating income	$172,000
Interest expense	24,000
Income before income taxes	$148,000
Income taxes expense	28,000
Net income	$120,000

After examining the statement, Hashimi said to Klein, "Lou, the statement seems to be well done, but what I need to know is why I don't have enough cash to pay my bills this month. You show that I earned $120,000 in 20x8, but I have only $24,000 in the bank. I know I bought a building on a mortgage and paid a cash dividend of $48,000, but what else is going on?" Klein replied, "To answer your question, we have to look at comparative balance sheets and prepare another type of statement. Take a look at these balance sheets." The statement handed to Hashimi is on the opposite page.

1. To what other statement is Klein referring? From the information given, prepare the additional statement using the indirect method.
2. Hashimi Print Gallery, Inc., has a cash problem despite profitable operations. Why is this the case?

Hashimi Print Gallery, Inc.
Comparative Balance Sheets
December 31, 20x8 and 20x7

	20x8	20x7
Assets		
Cash	$ 24,000	$ 40,000
Accounts receivable (net)	178,000	146,000
Inventory	240,000	180,000
Prepaid expenses	10,000	14,000
Building	400,000	—
Accumulated depreciation	(20,000)	—
Total assets	$832,000	$380,000
Liabilities and Stockholders' Equity		
Accounts payable	$ 74,000	$ 96,000
Income taxes payable	6,000	4,000
Mortgage payable	400,000	—
Common stock	200,000	200,000
Retained earnings	152,000	80,000
Total liabilities and stockholders' equity	$832,000	$380,000

Annual Report Case: CVS Corporation

Analysis of the Statement of Cash Flows

C 5. Refer to the statement of cash flows in the **CVS Corporation** annual report in the Supplement to Chapter 5 to answer the following questions:

1. Does CVS use the indirect method of reporting cash flows from operating activities? Other than net earnings, what are the most important factors affecting the company's cash flows from operating activities? Explain the trend of each of these factors.
2. Based on the cash flows from investing activities, would you say that CVS is a contracting or an expanding company? Explain.
3. Has CVS used external financing? If so, where did it come from?

Comparison Case: CVS Versus Southwest

LO1, LO2, LO3, LO4, LO5   Cash Flows Analysis

C 6. Refer to the annual report of **CVS Corporation** and the financial statements of **Southwest Airlines Co.** in the Supplement to Chapter 5. Calculate for two years each company's cash flow yield, cash flows to sales, cash flows to assets, and free cash flow. At the end of 2003, Southwest's total assets were $9,878 million and CVS's total assets were $10,543.1 million. Discuss and compare the trends of the cash-generating ability of CVS and Southwest. Comment on each company's change in cash and cash equivalents over the two-year period.

Ethical Dilemma Case

LO2 **Ethics and Cash Flow Classifications**

C 7. Chemical Waste Treatment, Inc., a fast-growing company that disposes of chemical wastes, has an $800,000 line of credit at its bank. One section in the credit agreement says that the ratio of cash flows from operations to interest expense must exceed 3.0. If this ratio falls below 3.0, the company must reduce the balance outstanding on its line of credit to one-half the total line if the funds borrowed against the line of credit exceed one-half of the total line.

After the end of the fiscal year, the company's controller informs the president: "We will not meet the ratio requirements on our line of credit in 20x7 because interest expense was $1.2 million and cash flows from operations were $3.2 million. Also, we have borrowed 100 percent of our line of credit. We do not have the cash to reduce the credit line by $400,000." The president says, "This is a serious situation. To pay our ongoing bills, we need our bank to increase our line of credit, not decrease it. What can we do?" "Do you recall the $500,000 two-year note payable for equipment?" replied the controller. "It is now classified as 'Proceeds from Notes Payable' in cash flows provided from financing activities in the statement of cash flows. If we move it to cash flows from operations and call it 'Increase in Payables,' it would increase cash flows from operations to $3.7 million and put us over the limit." "Well, do it," ordered the president. "It surely doesn't make any difference where it is on the statement. It is an increase in both places. It would be much worse for our company in the long term if we failed to meet this ratio requirement."

What is your opinion of the controller and president's reasoning? Is the president's order ethical? Who benefits and who is harmed if the controller follows the president's order? What are management's alternatives? What would you do?

Internet Case

LO2 **Follow-up Analysis of Cash Flows**

C 8. Go to **CVS Corporation's** website and find the statement of cash flows in its latest annual report. Compare it with the 2005 statement in the Supplement to Chapter 5 by (1) identifying major changes in operating, investing, and financing activities; (2) reading management's financial review of cash flows; and (3) calculating the cash flow ratios (cash flow yield, cash flows to sales, cash flows to assets) and free cash flow for the most recent year. How does CVS's cash flow performance differ between these two years? Be prepared to discuss your conclusions in class.

Group Activity Case

LO1 **Cash Flow Versus Net Income**

C 9. The excerpt that follows is from a recent article on the financial reporting of **Amazon.com**, the famous Internet seller.

> From the beginning, Bezos [Amazon.com's Chairman and CEO] told shareholders that his goal was to build a company, not an artificial bottom line. "When forced to choose between optimizing the appearance of our GAAP accounting and maximizing the present value of future cash flows, we'll take the cash flows." . . . Amazon has since become famous for emphasizing its so-called pro-forma results, which exclude certain costs and highlight Bezo's beloved cash flow. Cash flow—is indeed a critical indicator of

whether Amazon will avoid being crushed by its debt. But ultimately Bezos will have to show that Amazon can make honest-to-God net profits under old-school accounting.[13]

Divide into class groups in order to develop a position in support of or against Bezo's reasoning. Then participate in a debate, defending your group's position. The basic question to address is, Which is more important for a young growing company—cash flows from operating activities or net income under GAAP?

Business Communication Case

LO1, LO2 ### Alternative Uses of Cash

C 10. Perhaps because of hard times in their start-up years, companies in the high-tech sector of American industry seem more prone than those in other sectors to building up cash reserves. For example, companies like **Cisco Systems**, **Intel**, **Dell**, and **Oracle** have amassed large cash balances.[14]

Assume you work for a company in the high-tech industry that has built up a substantial amount of cash. The company is still growing through development of new products, has some debt, and has never paid a dividend or bought treasury stock. The price of the company's stock is lagging. Write a one-page memo to the CEO that outlines at least four strategies for using the company's cash to improve the company's financial outlook.

CHAPTER

16

Investments

Many companies invest in the stock or debt securities of other firms. They may do so for several reasons. A company may temporarily have excess funds on which it can earn a return, or investments may be an integral part of its business, as in the case of a bank. A company may also invest in other firms for the purpose of partnering with or controlling them. This chapter presents an overview of both short-term and long-term investments, including the importance of avoiding unethical trading in securities.

LEARNING OBJECTIVES

Making a Statement

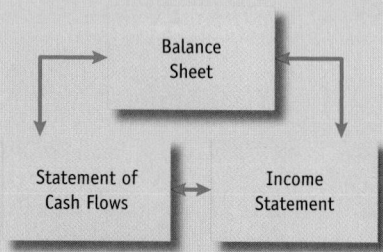

Investment activity affects all financial statements.

LO1 Identify and explain the management issues related to investments.

LO2 Explain the financial reporting implications of short-term investments.

LO3 Explain the financial reporting implications of long-term investments in stock and the cost-adjusted-to-market and equity methods used to account for them.

LO4 Explain the financial reporting implications of consolidated financial statements.

LO5 Explain the financial reporting implications of debt investments.

732

- What are the effects of eBay's investments on its financial performance?
- How does eBay's acquisition of other companies affect its financial performance?

eBay, the world's largest online trading company, enables a global community of buyers and sellers to interact and trade with one another. Since the company went public in 1998, it has grown very rapidly. In addition to having expanded its core business, it has grown by investing in and acquiring other companies. It has also invested cash in the debt securities of other companies. As you can see in eBay's Financial Highlights, these investments and the related accounts are important components of its financial statements.[1]

eBAY'S FINANCIAL HIGHLIGHTS
(In millions)

	2005	2004
Balance sheet		
Short-term investments	$ 775	$ 682
Long-term investments	826	1,268
Goodwill	6,120	2,710
Total assets	11,789	7,991
Income Statement		
Interest and other income, net	$ 111	$ 78
Income from operations	1,442	1,059
Statement of Cash Flows		
Cash flows from investing activities		
Purchases of investments	($1,324)	($1,755)
Sales of investments	1,929	1,080
Acquisitions, net of cash required	(2,732)	(1,036)

Management Issues Related to Investments

I n making investments, **eBay's** management, like the management of any company, must understand issues related to the recognition, valuation, classification, disclosure, and ethics of investments.

Recognition

Recognition of investments as assets follows the general rule for recording transactions that we described earlier in the text. Purchases of investments are recorded on the date on which they are made, and sales of investments are reported on the date of sale. At the time of the transaction, there is either a transfer of funds or a definite obligation to pay. Income from investments is reported as other income on the income statement. Any gains or losses on investments are also reported on the income statement. Gains and losses appear as adjustments in the operating activities section of the statement of cash flows. The cash amounts of purchases and sales of investments appear in the investing activities section of the statement of cash flows.

Valuation

Like other purchase transactions, investments are valued according to the *cost principle*—that is, they are valued in terms of their cost at the time they are purchased. The cost, or purchase price, includes any commissions or fees. However, after the purchase, the value of investments on the balance sheet is adjusted to reflect subsequent conditions. These conditions may reflect changes in the market value or fair value of the investments, changes caused by the passage of time (as in amortization), or changes in the operations of the investee companies. Long-term investments must be evaluated annually for any impairment or decline in value that is more than temporary. If such an impairment exists, a loss on the investment must be recorded.

Classification

Investments in debt and equity securities are classified as either short-term or long-term. **Short-term investments**, also called **marketable securities**, have a maturity of more than 90 days but are intended to be held only until cash is needed for current operations. (As we pointed out in an earlier chapter, investments with a maturity of *less* than 90 days are classified as cash equivalents.) *Long-term investments* are intended to be held for more than one year. Long-term investments are reported in the investments section of the balance sheet, not in the current assets section. Although long-term investments may be just as marketable as short-term assets, management intends to hold them for an indefinite time.

Short-term and long-term investments must be further classified as trading securities, available-for-sale securities, or held-to-maturity securities.[2]

◗ **Trading securities** are debt or equity securities bought and held principally for the purpose of being sold in the near term.

◗ **Available-for-sale securities** are debt or equity securities that do not meet the criteria for either trading or held-to-maturity securities. They may be short-term or long-term depending on what management intends to do with them.

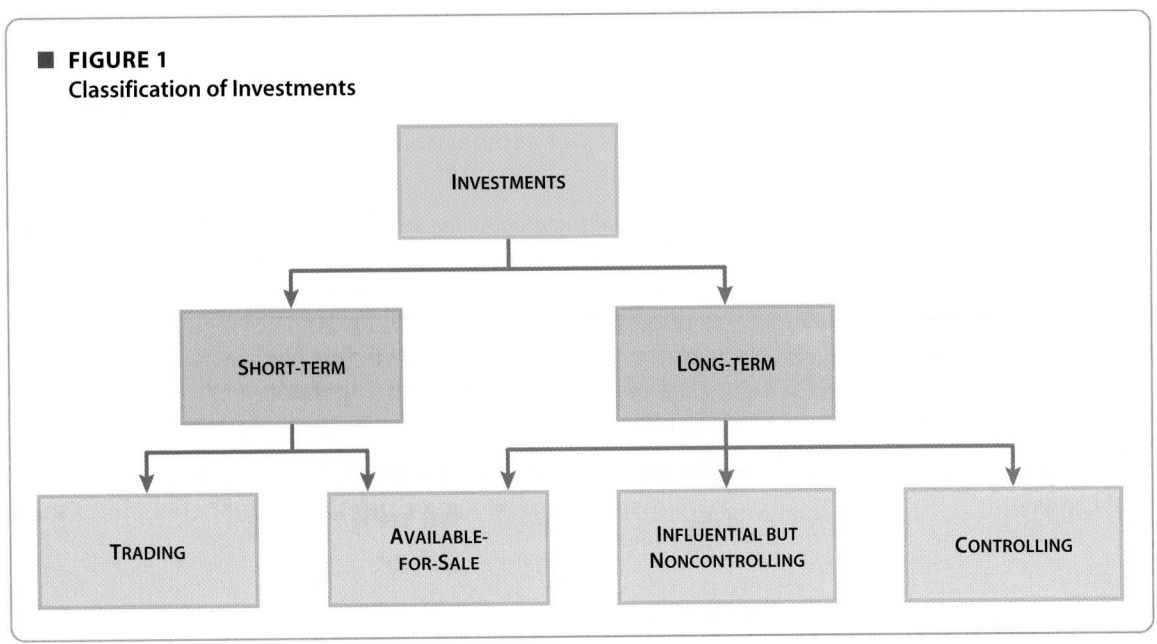

■ **FIGURE 1**
Classification of Investments

▶ **Held-to-maturity securities** are debt securities that management intends to hold until their maturity date.

Figure 1 illustrates the classification of short-term and long-term investments. Table 1 shows the relationship between the percentage of ownership in a company's stock and the investing company's level of control, as well as the classifications and accounting treatments of these stock investments. These classifications are important because each one requires a different accounting treatment. We discuss the accounting treatments later in this chapter.

TABLE 1. Accounting for Equity Investments			
Level of Control	Percentage of Ownership	Classification	Accounting Treatment
Noninfluential and noncontrolling	Less than 20%	Short-term investments—trading securities	Recorded at cost initially; cost adjusted after purchase for changes in market value; unrealized gains and losses reported on income statement
		Short-term or long-term investments—available-for-sale securities	Recorded at cost initially; cost adjusted for changes in market value with unrealized gains and losses to stockholders' equity
Influential but noncontrolling	Between 20% and 50%	Long-term investments	Equity method: recorded at cost initially; cost subsequently adjusted for investor's share of net income or loss and for dividends received
Controlling	More than 50%	Long-term investments	Financial statements consolidated

In general, the percentage of ownership in another company's stock has the following effects:

- *Noninfluential and noncontrolling investment*: A firm that owns less than 20 percent of the stock of another company has no influence on the other company's operations.

- *Influential but noncontrolling investment*: A firm that owns between 20 to 50 percent of another company's stock can exercise **significant influence** over that company's operating and financial policies, even though it holds 50 percent or less of the voting stock. Indications of significant influence include representation on the board of directors, participation in policymaking, exchange of managerial personnel, and technological dependency between the two companies.

- *Controlling investment*: A firm that owns more than 50 percent of another company's stock can exercise **control** over that company's operating and financial policies.

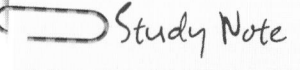

Study Note

Influence and control are related specifically to equity holdings, not debt holdings.

Disclosure

Companies provide detailed information about their investments and the manner in which they account for them in the notes to their financial statements. For instance, in a note summarizing its significant accounting policies, **eBay** makes the following disclosure:

> Short and long-term investments, which include marketable securities, government and corporate bonds, are classified as available for sale and reported at fair value.[3]

eBay's notes also provide detailed information about eight acquisitions the company made in 2005. Such disclosures help users assess the impact of the investments.

Ethics of Investing

When a company engages in investment transactions, there is always the possibility that its employees may use their knowledge about the transactions for personal gain. In the United States, **insider trading**, or making use of inside information for personal gain, is unethical and illegal. Before a publicly held company releases significant information about an investment to its stockhold-

FOCUS ON BUSINESS PRACTICE

What Are Special-Purpose Entities?

When **Enron** imploded in 2001 and its use of special purpose entities (SPEs) was widely reported, many accountants were unaware of the intricacies of accounting for these entities. SPEs are firms with limited lives that are created to achieve a specific objective (or objectives) of the parent company. They may take the form of a partnership, corporation, trust, or joint venture. SPEs have been around since the 1970s and have been used primarily by banks and other financial institutions as a way of raising funds by bundling together receivables and other loans into packages that can be sold to investors or used to borrow funds.

Enron turned this use of SPEs on its head. It used its SPEs to transfer assets and any related debt off its balance sheet, conceal its losses and borrow money, and generally make its financial statements look far better than they actually were. By setting up the SPEs as partnerships and using the arcane accounting rules for SPEs, Enron was able to avoid consolidating these entities even though it kept a 97 percent ownership in them. The FASB has since clarified the accounting rules for SPEs, which it calls Variable Interest Entities (VIEs).[4]

A bear and a bull guard the Frankfurt Stock Exchange in Germany. In 1995, Germany outlawed insider trading, eliminating what had been considered a management perk. It also required companies to warn investors of potential bad news. "In the U.S., the [SEC] has always been pretty ruthless with companies that didn't come clean, and it will be interesting to see what happens here," says Marco Becht, co-author of *The Control of Corporate Europe.*

ers and the general public, its officers and employees are not allowed to buy or sell stock in the company or in the firm whose shares the company is buying. Only after the information is released to the public can insiders engage in such trading. The Securities and Exchange Commission vigorously prosecutes any individual, whether employed by the company in question or not, who buys or sells shares of a publicly held company based on information not yet available to the public.

Not all countries prohibit insider trading. Until recently, insider trading was legal in Germany, but with the goal of expanding its securities markets, that country reformed its securities laws. It established the Federal Authority for Securities Trading (FAST), in part to oversee insider trading. However, only seven FAST staff members handle investigations of insider trading, as compared with the more than fifty staff members who handle the SEC's investigations.[5] Other countries continue to permit insider trading.

STOP • REVIEW • APPLY

1-1. In general, how are investments recognized and valued at date of purchase?

1-2. What is the difference between trading securities, available-for-sale securities, and held-to-maturity securities?

1-3. Why are the level and percentage of ownership important in accounting for equity investments?

1-4. Why is disclosure of investments important?

1-5. What is insider trading?

Suggested answers to all Stop, Review, and Apply questions are available at http://college.hmco.com/accounting/needles/poa/10e/student_home.html.

Investment Accounting Terminology   Indicate whether each phrase listed below is most closely related to (a) trading securities, (b) available-for-sale securities, (c) held-to-maturity securities, (d) noninfluential and noncontrolling ownership, (e) influential but noncontrolling ownership, or (f) controlling ownership:

1. No significant influence over investee
2. Securities bought and sold for short-term profit
3. Ability to make decisions for investee
4. Significant influence over investee
5. Securities that may be sold at any time
6. Debt securities that will be held until they are repaid

> **SOLUTIONS**
> 1. d   4. e
> 2. a   5. b
> 3. f   6. c

Short-Term Investments in Equity Securities

LO2   Explain the financial reporting implications of short-term investments.

As we pointed out earlier, all trading securities are short-term investments, while available-for-sale securities may be either short-term or long-term.

Trading Securities

Trading securities are frequently bought and sold to generate profits on short-term changes in their prices. They are classified as current assets on the balance sheet and are valued at fair value, which is usually the same as market value. An increase or decrease in the fair value of a company's total trading portfolio (the group of securities it holds for trading purposes) is included in net income in the accounting period in which the increase or decrease occurs.

For example, suppose Jackson Company buys 10,000 shares of **IBM** for $900,000 ($90 per share) and 10,000 shares of **Microsoft** for $300,000 ($30 per share) on October 25, 20x7. The purchase is made for trading purposes—that is, Jackson's management intends to realize a gain by holding the shares for only a short period. The entry to record the investment at cost is as follows:

Purchase

A	= L + OE			
+1,200,000		20x7		
−1,200,000		Oct. 25	Short-Term Investments	1,200,000
			Cash		1,200,000
			Investment in stocks for trading	
			($900,000 + $300,000 = $1,200,000)	

Assume that at year end, IBM's stock price has decreased to $80 per share and Microsoft's has risen to $32 per share. The trading portfolio is now valued at $1,120,000:

Security	Market Value	Cost	Gain (Loss)
IBM (10,000 shares)	$ 800,000	$ 900,000	
Microsoft (10,000 shares)	320,000	300,000	
Totals	$1,120,000	$1,200,000	($80,000)

Because the current fair value of the portfolio is $80,000 less than the original cost of $1,200,000, the following adjusting entry is needed:

Year-End Adjustment

A = L + OE
−80,000   −80,000

20x7			
Dec. 31	Unrealized Loss on Investments	80,000	
	Allowance to Adjust Short-Term		
	Investments to Market		80,000
	Recognition of unrealized loss		
	on trading portfolio		

The unrealized loss will appear on the income statement as a reduction in income. The loss is unrealized because the securities have not been sold; if unrealized gains occur, they are treated the same way. The Allowance to Adjust Short-Term Investments to Market account appears on the balance sheet as a contra-asset, as follows:

Study Note

The Allowance to Adjust Short-Term Investments to Market account is never changed when securities are sold. It changes only when an adjusting entry is made at year end.

Short-term investments (at cost)	$1,200,000
Less allowance to adjust short-term investments to market	80,000
Short-term investments (at market)	$1,120,000

or, more simply,

Short-term investments (at market value, cost is $1,200,000)	$1,120,000

If Jackson sells its 10,000 shares of Microsoft for $35 per share on March 2, 20x8, a realized gain on trading securities is recorded as follows:

Sale

A = L + OE
+350,000   +50,000
−300,000

20x8			
Mar. 2	Cash	350,000	
	Short-Term Investments		300,000
	Realized Gain on Investments		50,000
	Sale of 10,000 shares of Microsoft for		
	$35 per share; cost was $30 per share		

FOCUS ON BUSINESS PRACTICE
How Can Even a Big Company Make an Accounting Mistake?

Like many companies, **General Electric**, one of America's largest corporations, protects itself against future increases in interest rates on debt by hedging its debt transactions with *derivatives,* which are agreements to buy or sell stocks, bonds, or other securities in the future. A derivative can be set up in such a way that it has no value and therefore entails no gain or loss. But when a derivative has value, it is considered a trading security and a money-making (or money-losing) tool rather than a true hedge; in this case, any gain or loss that results from valuing the derivative at fair value must be reported on the income statement. General Electric thought it had no gains or losses on its derivatives, but when it recalculated their value over a two-year period, it found that it had gains amounting to about $.02 per share in each year. When the company issued a press release reporting the error, its CFO stated that "there are no exceptions to hedge accounting.... At the end of the day, the standard is the standard."[6]

The realized gain will appear on the income statement. Note that the realized gain is unaffected by the adjustment for the unrealized loss at the end of 20x7. The two transactions are treated independently. If the stock had been sold for less than cost, a realized loss on investments would have been recorded. Realized losses also appear on the income statement.

Now let's assume that during 20x8, Jackson buys 4,000 shares of **Apple Computer** at $32 per share and has no transactions involving its shares of IBM. Also assume that by December 31, 20x8, the price of IBM's stock has risen to $95 per share, or $5 per share more than the original cost, and that Apple's stock price has fallen to $29, or $3 less than the original cost. We can now analyze Jackson's trading portfolio as follows:

Security	Market Value	Cost	Gain (Loss)
IBM (10,000 shares)	$ 950,000	$ 900,000	
Apple (4,000 shares)	116,000	128,000	
Totals	$1,066,000	$1,028,000	$38,000

The market value of Jackson's trading portfolio now exceeds the cost by $38,000 ($1,066,000 − $1,028,000). This amount represents the targeted ending balance for the Allowance to Adjust Short-Term Investments to Market account. Recall that at the end of 20x7, that account had a credit balance of $80,000, meaning that the market value of the trading portfolio was less than the cost. Because no entries are made to the account during 20x8, it retains its balance until adjusting entries are made at the end of the year. The adjustment for 20x8 must be $118,000—enough to result in a debit balance of $38,000 in the allowance account:

Year-End Adjustment

A	= L +	OE
+118,000		+118,000

20x8			
Dec. 31	Allowance to Adjust Short-Term Investments to Market	118,000	
	Unrealized Gain on Investments		118,000
	Recognition of unrealized gain on trading portfolio		
	($80,000 + $38,000 = $118,000)		

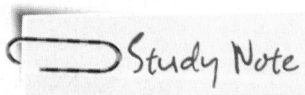

Study Note

The entry in the Allowance to Adjust Short-Term Investments to Market account is equal to the change in the market value. Compute the new allowance, and then compute the amount needed to change the account. The unrealized loss or gain is the other half of the entry.

The 20x8 ending balance of Jackson's allowance account can be determined as follows:

ALLOWANCE TO ADJUST SHORT-TERM INVESTMENTS TO MARKET

Dec. 31, 20x8 Adj.	118,000	Dec. 31, 20x7 Bal.	80,000
Dec. 31, 20x8 Bal.	38,000		

The balance sheet presentation of short-term investments is as follows:

Short-term investments (at cost)	$1,028,000
Plus allowance to adjust short-term investments to market	38,000
Short-term investments (at market)	$1,066,000

or, more simply,

Short-term investments (at market value, cost is $1,028,000)	$1,066,000

If the company also has held-to-maturity securities that will mature within one year, they are included in short-term investments at cost adjusted for the effects of interest.

Available-for-Sale Securities

Short-term available-for-sale securities are accounted for in the same way as trading securities with two exceptions: (1) an unrealized gain or loss is reported as a special item in the stockholders' equity section of the balance sheet, not as a gain or loss on the income statement; (2) if a decline in the value of a security is considered permanent, it is charged as a loss on the income statement.

For example, **eBay's** summary of significant accounting policies contains the following statement: "Unrealized gains and losses [on available-for-sale securities] are excluded from earnings and reported as a component of other comprehensive income (loss)." The company's statement of comprehensive income shows unrealized losses on investments of $8.7 million in 2004 and unrealized gains of $1.9 million in 2005. In addition, eBay's statement of cash flows shows impairment charges of $1.2 million in 2003, which resulted from a nontemporary decline in the value of some of eBay's investments in other companies. The company reported no impairment charges in 2004 or 2005.[7]

S T O P • R E V I E W • A P P L Y

2-1. How are trading securities valued at the balance sheet date?

2-2. What are unrealized gains and losses on trading securities? On what statement are they reported?

2-3. How does accounting for available-for-sale securities differ from accounting for trading securities?

Long-Term Investments in Equity Securities

LO3 Explain the financial reporting implications of long-term investments in stock and the cost-adjusted-to-market and equity methods used to account for them.

As indicated in Table 1, the accounting treatment of long-term investments in equity securities, such as common stock, depends on the extent to which the investing company can exercise control over the other company.

Noninfluential and Noncontrolling Investment

As noted earlier, available-for-sale securities are debt or equity securities that cannot be classified as trading or held-to-maturity securities. When long-term equity securities are involved, a further criterion for classifying them as available for sale is that they be noninfluential and noncontrolling investments of less than 20 percent of the voting stock. Accounting for long-term available-for-sale securities requires using the **cost-adjusted-to-market method**. With this method, the securities are initially recorded at cost and are thereafter adjusted periodically for changes in market value by using an allowance account.[8]

Available-for-sale securities are classified as long term if management intends to hold them for more than one year. When accounting for long-term available-for-sale securities, the unrealized gain or loss resulting from the adjustment is not reported on the income statement. Instead, the gain or loss is reported as a special item in the stockholders' equity section of the balance sheet and in the disclosure of comprehensive income.

At the end of each accounting period, the total cost and the total market value of these long-term stock investments must be determined. If the total market value is less than the total cost, the difference must be credited to a contra-asset account called Allowance to Adjust Long-Term Investments to Market. Because of the long-term nature of the investment, the debit part of the entry, which represents a decrease in value below cost, is treated as a temporary decrease and does not appear as a loss on the income statement. It is shown in a contra-stockholders' equity account called Unrealized Loss on Long-Term Investments.* Thus, both of these accounts are balance sheet accounts. If the market value exceeds the cost, the allowance account is added to Long-Term Investments, and the unrealized gain appears as an addition to stockholders' equity.

When a company sells its long-term investments in stock, the difference between the sale price and the cost of the stock is recorded and reported as a realized gain or loss on the income statement. Dividend income from such investments is recorded by a debit to Cash and a credit to Dividend Income. For example, assume the following facts about the long-term stock investments of Nardini Corporation:

June 1, 20x7	Paid cash for the following long-term investments: 10,000 shares of Herald Corporation common stock (representing 2 percent of outstanding stock) at $25 per share; 5,000 shares of Taza Corporation common stock (representing 3 percent of outstanding stock) at $15 per share.
Dec. 31, 20x7	Quoted market prices at year end: Herald common stock, $21; Taza common stock, $17
Apr. 1, 20x8	Change in policy required the sale of 2,000 shares of Herald common stock at $23.
July 1, 20x8	Received cash dividend from Taza equal to $.20 per share.
Dec. 31, 20x8	Quoted market prices at year end: Herald common stock, $24; Taza common stock, $13.

> **Study Note**
>
> Nardini's sale of stock on April 1, 20x8, was the result of a *change in policy*. This illustrates that intent is often the only difference between long-term investments and short-term investments.

Entries to record these transactions are as follows:

Investment

A = L + OE	20x7		
+325,000	June 1 Long-Term Investments	325,000	
−325,000	Cash		325,000
	Investments in Herald common stock (10,000 shares × $25 = $250,000) and Taza common stock (5,000 shares × $15 = $75,000)		

---

*If the decrease in market value of a long-term investment is deemed permanent or if the investment is deemed impaired, the decline or impairment is recorded by debiting a loss account on the income statement instead of the Unrealized Loss account.

Year-End Adjustment

A	= L +	OE
−30,000		−30,000

20x7				
Dec. 31	Unrealized Loss on Long-Term Investments		30,000	
	Allowance to Adjust Long-Term			
	Investments to Market			30,000
	To record reduction of long-term			
	investment to market			

This adjustment involves the following computations:

Company	Shares	Market Price	Total Market	Total Cost
Herald	10,000	$21	$210,000	$250,000
Taza	5,000	17	85,000	75,000
			$295,000	$325,000

Total Cost − Total Market Value = $325,000 − $295,000 = $30,000

Other entries are as follows:

Sale

A	= L +	OE
+46,000		−4,000
−50,000		

20x8				
Apr. 1	Cash		46,000	
	Loss on Sale of Investments		4,000	
	Long-Term Investments			50,000
	Sale of 2,000 shares of Herald			
	common stock			
	2,000 × $23 = $46,000			
	2,000 × $25 = 50,000			
	Loss $ 4,000			

Dividend Received

A	= L +	OE
+1,000		+1,000

20x8				
July 1	Cash		1,000	
	Dividend Income			1,000
	Receipt of cash dividend from Taza stock			
	5,000 × $.20 = $1,000			

Year-End Adjustment

A	= L +	OE
+12,000		+12,000

20x8				
Dec. 31	Allowance to Adjust Long-Term			
	Investments to Market		12,000	
	Unrealized Loss on Long-Term			
	Investments			12,000
	To record the adjustment in long-			
	term investment so it is reported			
	at market			

The adjustment equals the previous balance ($30,000 from the December 31, 20x7, entry) minus the new balance ($18,000), or $12,000. The new balance of $18,000 is the difference at the present time between the total market value and the total cost of all investments. It is figured as follows:

Company	Shares	Market Price	Total Market	Total Cost
Herald	8,000	$24	$192,000	$200,000
Taza	5,000	13	65,000	75,000
			$257,000	$275,000

Total Cost − Total Market Value = $275,000 − $257,000 = $18,000

The Allowance to Adjust Long-Term Investments to Market and the Unrealized Loss on Long-Term Investments are reciprocal contra accounts, each with the same dollar balance, as shown by the effects of these transactions on the T accounts:

CONTRA-ASSET ACCOUNT		CONTRA-STOCKHOLDERS' EQUITY ACCOUNT	
ALLOWANCE TO ADJUST LONG-TERM INVESTMENTS TO MARKET		UNREALIZED LOSS ON LONG-TERM INVESTMENT	
Dec. 31, 20x8 Adj. 12,000	Dec. 31, 20x7 Bal. 30,000	Dec. 31, 20x7 Bal. 30,000	Dec. 31, 20x8 Adj. 12,000
	Dec. 31, 20x8 Bal. 18,000	Dec. 31, 20x8 Bal. 18,000	

The Allowance account reduces long-term investments by the amount by which the cost of the investments exceeds market; the Unrealized Loss account reduces stockholders' equity by a similar amount. The opposite effects will exist if market value exceeds cost, resulting in an unrealized gain.

Influential but Noncontrolling Investment

As we have noted, ownership of 20 percent or more of a company's voting stock is considered sufficient to influence the company's operations. When that is the case, the **equity method** should be used to account for the stock investment. The equity method presumes that an investment of 20 percent or more is not a passive investment and that the investor should therefore share proportionately in the success or failure of the company. The three main features of this method are as follows:

1. The investor records the original purchase of the stock at cost.

2. The investor records its share of the company's periodic net income as an increase in the Investment account, with a corresponding credit to an income account. Similarly, it records its share of a periodic loss as a decrease in the Investment account, with a corresponding debit to a loss account.

3. When the investor receives a cash dividend, the asset account Cash is increased, and the Investment account is decreased.

eBay owns a minority interest of approximately 25 percent in **craigslist.inc.**, an online community featuring classified ad forums. Because the investment is more than 20 percent, eBay is presumed to have significant influence over craigslist's operations. Thus, eBay accounts for this investment and similar ones using the equity method of accounting."[9]

To illustrate the equity method, suppose that on January 1 of the current year, ITO Corporation acquired 40 percent of Quay Corporation's voting common stock for $180,000. With this share of ownership, ITO can exert significant influence over Quay's operations. During the year, Quay reported net income of $80,000 and paid cash dividends of $20,000. ITO recorded these transactions as follows:

Investment

A = L + OE	Investment in Quay Corporation	180,000	
+180,000	Cash		180,000
−180,000	Investment in Quay Corporation common stock		

Recognition of Income

A = L + OE	Investment in Quay Corporation	32,000	
+32,000 +32,000	Income, Quay Corporation Investment		32,000
	Recognition of 40% of income reported		
	by Quay Corporation		
	40% × $80,000 = $32,000		

Receipt of Cash Dividend

A = L + OE	Cash	8,000	
+8,000	Investment in Quay Corporation		8,000
−8,000	Cash dividend from Quay Corporation		
	40% × $20,000 = $8,000		

The balance of the Investment in Quay Corporation account after these transactions is $204,000, as shown here:

INVESTMENT IN QUAY CORPORATION			
Investment	180,000	Dividend Received	8,000
Share of Income	32,000		
Bal.	204,000		

 Study Note

Under the equity method, dividends received represent a return of investment and decrease the Investment account with a credit entry.

The share of income is reported as a separate line item on the income statement as a part of income from operations. The dividends received affect cash flows from operating activities on the statement of cash flows. The reported income exceeds the cash received by $24,000 ($32,000 − $8,000).

FOCUS ON BUSINESS PRACTICE

Accounting for International Joint Ventures

When U.S. companies make investments abroad, they often find it wise or necessary to partner with a local company or with the government of the country. Some countries require that their citizens own a minimum percentage of each business. In other countries—among them, Brazil, China, India, and the former United Soviet Socialist Republics—the government has traditionally had a share of ownership. Such business arrangements are usually called *joint ventures*. Because the resulting enterprise is jointly owned, it is appropriate to treat the U.S. company's status as "influential but noncontrolling." Thus, the most appropriate accounting method for these arrangements is the equity method.

Controlling Investment   Some investing firms that own less than 50 percent of a company's voting stock exercise such powerful influence that for all practical purposes, they control the policies of the other company. Nevertheless, ownership of more than 50 percent of the voting stock is required for accounting recognition of control. When a firm has a controlling interest in another company, a parent-subsidiary relationship is said to exist. The investing company is the **parent company**; the other company is a **subsidiary**.

Because a parent company and its subsidiaries are separate legal entities, each prepares separate financial statements. However, because of their special relationship, they are viewed for external financial reporting purposes as a single economic entity. For this reason, the FASB requires that they combine their financial statements into a single set of statements called **consolidated financial statements**.[10] For example, in its summary of significant accounting policies, **eBay** states that "the accompanying financial statements are consolidated and include the financial statements of eBay and our majority-owned subsidiaries. All significant intercompany balances and transactions have been eliminated in consolidation."[11]

Study Note

Parents and subsidiaries are separate legal entities even though they combine their financial reports at year end.

S T O P • R E V I E W • A P P L Y

3-1. What percentage of ownership applies to each of the following: (a) noninfluential and noncontrolling investment, (b) influential but noncontrolling investment, and (c) controlling investment? What is the appropriate accounting treatment for each of these investments?

3-2. What is a parent-subsidiary relationship?

3-3. American Home Products Corporation has many subsidiaries. Would its stockholders be more interested in its consolidated financial statements or in the individual statements of its subsidiaries? Explain your answer.

3-4. Merchant Corporation's summary of significant accounting policies contained this statement: "Investments in companies in which Merchant has significant influence in management are on the equity basis." What is the equity method of accounting for investments, and why did Merchant use it in this case?

Consolidated Financial Statements

LO4   Explain the financial reporting implications of consolidated financial statements.

Most major corporations find it convenient for economic, legal, tax, or other reasons to operate in parent-subsidiary relationships. When we speak of a large company, such as **PepsiCo** or **IBM**, we generally think of the parent company, not of its many subsidiaries. Potential investors, however, want a clear financial picture of the total economic entity. The main purpose of consolidated financial statements is to give such a view of the parent and subsidiary firms by treating them as if they were one company. On a consolidated balance sheet, the Inventory account includes the inventory held by the parent and all its subsidiaries. Similarly, on the consolidated income statement, the Sales account is the total revenue from sales by the parent and all its subsidiaries. This overview helps management, stockholders, and creditors of the parent company judge the company's progress in meeting its goals.

Consolidated Balance Sheet

The **purchase method** of preparing consolidated financial statements combines similar accounts from the separate statements of the parent and the subsidiaries. Some accounts result from transactions between the parent and the subsidiary—for example, sales and purchases between the two entities, and debt owed by one of the entities to the other. It is not appropriate to include these accounts in the consolidated financial statements; the sales and purchases are only transfers between different parts of the business, and the payables and receivables do not represent amounts due to or receivable from outside parties. For this reason, it is important that certain **eliminations** be made. These eliminations avoid the duplication of accounts and reflect the financial position and operations from the standpoint of a single entity. Eliminations appear only on the work sheets used in preparing consolidated financial statements. They are never shown in the accounting records of either the parent or the subsidiary.

Another good example of accounts that result from transactions between a parent and its subsidiary is the Investment in Subsidiary account on the parent's balance sheet and the stockholders' equity accounts of the subsidiary. When the balance sheets of the two companies are combined, these accounts must be eliminated to avoid duplicating them in the consolidated financial statements.

To illustrate the preparation of a consolidated balance sheet under the purchase method, we use the following balance sheet data for Parent Company and Subsidiary Company:

Accounts	Parent Company	Subsidiary Company
Cash	$100,000	$25,000
Other assets	760,000	60,000
Total assets	$860,000	$85,000
Liabilities	$ 60,000	$10,000
Common stock	600,000	55,000
Retained earnings	200,000	20,000
Total liabilities and stockholders' equity	$860,000	$85,000

100 Percent Purchase at Book Value Suppose that Parent Company purchases 100 percent of the stock of Subsidiary Company for an amount exactly equal to Subsidiary's book value. The book value of Subsidiary Company is $75,000 ($85,000 − $10,000). Parent Company would record the purchase as follows:

Investment in Subsidiary Company	75,000	
Cash		75,000
Purchase of 100 percent of Subsidiary Company at book value		

A = L + OE
+75,000
−75,000

It is helpful to use a work sheet like the one shown in Exhibit 1 in preparing consolidated financial statements. Note that the balance of Parent Company's

Study Note

As separate entities, the parent and subsidiary maintain individual accounting records. Work sheet eliminations remove only duplications that occur in consolidation and the effects of intercompany transactions.

▼ **EXHIBIT 1**

Work Sheet for Preparing a Consolidated Balance Sheet

Parent and Subsidiary Companies
Work Sheet for Consolidated Balance Sheet
As of Acquisition Date

Accounts	Balance Sheet, Parent Company	Balance Sheet, Subsidiary Company	Eliminations Debit	Eliminations Credit	Consolidated Balance Sheet
Cash	25,000	25,000			50,000
Investment in subsidiary company	75,000			(1) 75,000	—
Other assets	760,000	60,000			820,000
Total assets	860,000	85,000			870,000
Liabilities	60,000	10,000			70,000
Common stock	600,000	55,000	(1) 55,000		600,000
Retained earnings	200,000	20,000	(1) 20,000		200,000
Total liabilities and stockholders' equity	860,000	85,000	75,000	75,000	870,000

(1) Elimination of intercompany investment

Cash account is now $25,000 and that Investment in Subsidiary Company is shown as an asset in Parent Company's balance sheet, reflecting the purchase of the subsidiary. To prepare a consolidated balance sheet, it is necessary to eliminate the investment in the subsidiary, as shown in elimination entry 1 in Exhibit 1. This entry accomplishes two things. First, it eliminates the double counting that would take place when the net assets of the two companies are combined. Second, it eliminates the stockholders' equity section of Subsidiary Company.

As we have pointed out, the theory underlying consolidated financial statements is that parent and subsidiary are a single entity. Thus, the stockholders' equity section of the consolidated balance sheet is the same for Parent Company and Subsidiary Company. So, after eliminating the Investment in Subsidiary Company account and the stockholders' equity accounts of the subsidiary, we can take the information from the Consolidated Balance Sheet column in Exhibit 1 and present it in the following form:

Parent and Subsidiary Companies
Consolidated Balance Sheet
As of Acquisition Date

Cash	$ 50,000	Liabilities	$ 70,000
Other assets	820,000	Common stock	600,000
		Retained earnings	200,000
		Total liabilities and	
Total assets	$870,000	stockholders' equity	$870,000

▼ **EXHIBIT 2**

Work Sheet Showing Elimination When Purchase Is for Less than 100 Percent Ownership

Parent and Subsidiary Companies
Work Sheet for Consolidated Balance Sheet
As of Acquisition Date

Accounts	Balance Sheet, Parent Company	Balance Sheet, Subsidiary Company	Eliminations Debit	Eliminations Credit	Consolidated Balance Sheet
Cash	32,500	25,000			57,500
Investment in subsidiary company	67,500			(1) 67,500	—
Other assets	760,000	60,000			820,000
Total assets	860,000	85,000			877,500
Liabilities	60,000	10,000			70,000
Common stock	600,000	55,000	(1) 55,000		600,000
Retained earnings	200,000	20,000	(1) 20,000		200,000
Minority interest	—	—		(1) 7,500	7,500
Total liabilities and stockholders' equity	860,000	85,000	75,000	75,000	877,500

(1) Elimination of intercompany investment. Minority interest equals 10 percent of subsidiary's total stockholders' equity.

Study Note

When the elimination entry is made, all of the subsidiary's stockholders' equity accounts are eliminated. The percentage not owned by the parent company is assigned to minority interest.

Less Than 100 Percent Purchase at Book Value   When a parent company purchases less than 100 percent but more than 50 percent of a subsidiary's voting stock, it will have control over the subsidiary, and it must prepare consolidated financial statements. It must also account for the interests of the subsidiary's stockholders who own less than 50 percent of the voting stock. These are the minority stockholders, and their **minority interest** must appear on the consolidated balance sheet as an amount equal to their percentage of ownership times the subsidiary's net assets. eBay, for instance, has $4 million of minority interest on the liability side of its balance sheet, which stems mainly from its less than 100 percent ownership of Internet Auction.

Suppose that Parent Company buys 90 percent of Subsidiary Company's voting stock for $67,500. In this case, the portion of the company purchased has a book value of $67,500 (90% × $75,000). The work sheet used to prepare the consolidated balance sheet appears in Exhibit 2. The elimination is made just as in Exhibit 1, except that the minority interest must be accounted for. All of the Investment in Subsidiary Company account ($67,500) is eliminated against all of Subsidiary Company's stockholders' equity accounts (totaling $75,000). The difference ($7,500, or 10% × $75,000) is set as minority interest.

There are two ways to classify minority interest on a consolidated balance sheet. One is to place it between long-term liabilities and stockholders' equity. The other is to consider the stockholders' equity section as consisting of minority interest and the parent company's stockholders' equity, as shown here:

Minority interest	$ 7,500
Common stock	600,000
Retained earnings	200,000
Total stockholders' equity	$807,500

Purchase at More or Less than Book Value

The purchase price of a business depends on many factors, such as the current market price, the relative strength of the buyer's and seller's bargaining positions, and the prospects for future earnings. Thus, it is only by chance that the purchase price of a subsidiary equals the book value of its equity. Usually, it does not.

For example, a parent company may pay more than the subsidiary's book value for a controlling interest if the subsidiary's assets are understated. This happens when the historical cost less depreciation of the subsidiary's assets does not reflect current market values. The parent may also pay more than book value if the subsidiary has something the parent wants, such as an important technical process, a new and different product, or a new market. On the other hand, the parent may pay less than book value if the subsidiary's assets are not worth their depreciated cost. It may also pay less than book value if heavy losses suffered by the subsidiary have caused its stock price to drop.

The Accounting Principles Board has provided the following guidelines for consolidating a purchased subsidiary and its parent when the parent pays more than book value for its investment in the subsidiary:

> First, all identifiable assets acquired . . . and liabilities assumed in a business combination . . . should be assigned a portion of the cost of the acquired company, normally equal to their fair values at date of acquisition.
>
> Second, the excess of the cost of the acquired company over the sum of the amounts assigned to identifiable assets acquired less liabilities assumed should be recorded as goodwill.[12]

As explained in the chapter on long-term assets, goodwill is carried on the balance sheet at cost and is subject to an annual impairment test. **eBay** describes its treatment of goodwill as follows:

> Goodwill represents the excess of the purchase price over the fair value of the net tangible and identifiable intangible assets acquired in a business combination. We evaluate goodwill, at a minimum, on an annual basis and whenever events and changes in circumstances suggest that the carrying value may not be recoverable. . . . Our annual impairment test was carried out as of August 31, 2005 and we determined that there was no impairment.[13]

To illustrate the application of these principles, suppose that Parent Company purchases 100 percent of Subsidiary Company's voting stock for $92,500, or $17,500 more than book value. Parent Company considers $10,000 of the $17,500 to be due to the increased value of Subsidiary's other assets and $7,500 of the $17,500 to be due to the overall strength that Subsidiary Company would add to Parent Company's organization. The work sheet used to prepare the consolidated balance sheet appears in Exhibit 3. All of the Investment in Subsidiary Company ($92,500) has been eliminated against all of Subsidiary Company's stockholders' equity ($75,000). The excess of cost over book value ($17,500) has been debited in the amounts of $10,000 to Other Assets and $7,500 to a new account called **Goodwill**, or *Goodwill from Consolidation.*
The amount of goodwill is determined as follows:

Cost of investment in subsidiary	$92,500
Book value of subsidiary	75,000
Excess of cost over book value	$17,500
Portion of excess attributable to undervalued other assets of subsidiary	10,000
Portion of excess attributable to goodwill	$ 7,500

▼ **EXHIBIT 3**

Work Sheet Showing Elimination When Purchase Cost Is Greater than Book Value

Parent and Subsidiary Companies
Work Sheet for Consolidated Balance Sheet
As of Acquisition Date

Accounts	Balance Sheet, Parent Company	Balance Sheet, Subsidiary Company	Eliminations Debit	Eliminations Credit	Consolidated Balance Sheet
Cash	7,500	25,000			32,500
Investment in subsidiary company	92,500			(1) 92,500	—
Other assets	760,000	60,000	(1) 10,000		830,000
Goodwill	—	—	(1) 7,500		7,500
Total assets	860,000	85,000			870,000
Liabilities	60,000	10,000			70,000
Common stock	600,000	55,000	(1) 55,000		600,000
Retained earnings	200,000	20,000	(1) 20,000		200,000
Total liabilities and stockholders' equity	860,000	85,000	92,500	92,500	870,000

(1) Elimination of intercompany investment. Excess of cost over book value ($92,500 − $75,000 = $17,500) is allocated to Other Assets ($10,000) and Goodwill ($7,500).

Study Note

In this example, neither company has goodwill on its balance sheet. Goodwill is "created" when consolidated statements are prepared.

On the consolidated balance sheet, goodwill appears as an asset representing the portion of the excess of the cost of the investment over book value that cannot be allocated to any specific asset. Other assets appears on the consolidated balance sheet at the combined total of $830,000 ($760,000 + $60,000 + $10,000).

When the parent company pays less than book value for its investment in the subsidiary, *Opinion No.* 16 of the Accounting Principles Board requires that the excess of book value over cost of the investment be used to lower the carrying value of the subsidiary's long-term assets. The reasoning behind this is that market values of long-lived assets (other than marketable securities) are among the least reliable of estimates, since a ready market does not usually exist for such assets. In other words, the Accounting Principles Board advises against using negative goodwill, except in very special cases.

Intercompany Receivables and Payables If a subsidiary owes money to the parent company, there will be a receivable on the parent company's individual balance sheet and a payable on the subsidiary company's individual balance sheet. Conversely, if a parent owes money to a subsidiary, there will be a receivable on the subsidiary's balance sheet and a payable on the parent's balance sheet. When a consolidated balance sheet is prepared, both the receivable and the payable should be eliminated because from the viewpoint of the consolidated entity, neither the asset nor the liability exists. In other words, it does not make sense for a company to owe money to itself. The eliminating entry is made on the work sheet by debiting the payable and crediting the receivable for the amount of the intercompany loan.

Consolidated Income Statement

A consolidated income statement is prepared by combining the revenues and expenses of the parent and subsidiary companies. The procedure is the same as the one used to prepare a consolidated balance sheet—that is, intercompany transactions are eliminated to prevent double counting of revenues and expenses. The following intercompany transactions affect the consolidated income statement:

1. Sales and purchases of goods and services between parent and subsidiary

2. Income and expenses related to loans, receivables, or bond indebtedness between parent and subsidiary

3. Other income and expenses from intercompany transactions.

To illustrate the eliminating entries, suppose that Parent Company sold $120,000 of goods to Subsidiary Company, which in turn sold all the goods to others. Subsidiary Company paid Parent Company $2,000 interest on a loan.

The work sheet in Exhibit 4 shows how to prepare a consolidated income statement. Because the purpose of the eliminating entries is to treat the two companies as a single entity, it is important to include in Sales only sales made to outsiders and to include in Cost of Goods Sold only purchases made from outsiders. This goal is met with the first eliminating entry, which eliminates the $120,000 of intercompany sales and purchases by a debit of that amount to Sales and a credit of that amount to Cost of Goods Sold. As a result, only sales to outsiders ($510,000) and purchases from outsiders ($240,000) are included in the Consolidated Income Statement column. The intercompany interest income and expense are eliminated by a debit to Other Revenues and a credit to Other Expenses.

Study Note

Intercompany sales or purchases are not revenues or expenses to the consolidated entity. True revenues and expenses occur only when transactions are with parties outside the firm.

▼ **EXHIBIT 4**

Work Sheet for Preparing a Consolidated Income Statement

Parent and Subsidiary Companies
Work Sheet for Consolidated Income Statement
For the Year Ended December 31, 20xx

Accounts	Income Statement, Parent Company	Income Statement, Subsidiary Company	Eliminations Debit	Eliminations Credit	Consolidated Income Statement
Sales	430,000	200,000	(1) 120,000		510,000
Other revenues	60,000	10,000	(2) 2,000		68,000
Total revenues	490,000	210,000			578,000
Cost of goods sold	210,000	150,000		(1) 120,000	240,000
Other expenses	140,000	50,000		(2) 2,000	188,000
Total costs and expenses	350,000	200,000			428,000
Net income	140,000	10,000	122,000	122,000	150,000

(1) Elimination of intercompany sales and purchases
(2) Elimination of intercompany interest income and interest expense

An art installation of euro currency in Ludwigsburg, Germany, preceded the adoption of the Euro on January 1, 2002, as the only form of legal tender in twelve European countries. When a U.S. company owns more than 50 percent of a foreign company, it must prepare consolidated financial statements. The statements of the foreign subsidiary must be restated in dollars—not euros or other foreign currencies—before consolidation can take place.

Public corporations also prepare consolidated statements of stockholders' equity and consolidated statements of cash flows. For examples of these statements, see the **CVS** annual report in the Supplement to Chapter 5.

Restatement of Foreign Subsidiary Financial Statements

Companies often expand by establishing or buying foreign subsidiaries. Such companies are often referred to as **multinational or transnational corporations**. If a company owns more than 50 percent of a foreign subsidiary and thus exercises control, the foreign subsidiary should be included in the consolidated financial statements. The consolidation procedure is the same as the one we described for domestic subsidiaries, except that the statements of the foreign subsidiary must be restated in the reporting currency before consolidation takes place. The **reporting currency** is the currency in which the consolidated financial statements are presented, which for U.S. companies is usually the U.S. dollar. For example, **eBay** purchased a German company and an Indian company in 2004. Clearly, it makes no sense to combine the assets of German and Indian subsidiaries stated in euros and rupees with the assets of the U.S. parent company stated in dollars. Thus, **restatement** of the subsidiaries' statements into the currency of the parent company is necessary. After restatement, the parent's and subsidiaries' statements can be consolidated in the usual way.

S T O P • R E V I E W • A P P L Y

4-1. What are eliminating entries, and where do they appear?

4-2. What is the value of consolidated financial statements?

4-3. Merchant Corporation's summary of significant accounting policies contained the following statement: "Principles Applied in Consolidation: Majority-owned subsidiaries are consolidated, except for leasing and finance companies and those subsidiaries not considered to be material." What accounting rule does this practice violate, and why?

4-4. The following item appeared on Merchant's consolidated balance sheet: "Minority Interest—$50,000." How did this item arise, and where would you expect to find it on the consolidated balance sheet?

4-5. The following item also appeared on Merchant's consolidated balance sheet: "Goodwill from Consolidation—$70,000." How would this item arise, and where would you expect to find it on the consolidated balance sheet?

4-6. Why should intercompany receivables, payables, sales, and purchases be eliminated in consolidated financial statements?

4-7. Subsidiary Corporation, a wholly owned subsidiary, has total sales of $500,000, $100,000 of which were made to Parent Corporation. Parent Corporation has total sales of $1,000,000. What is the amount of sales on the consolidated income statement?

4-8. What step is necessary before consolidating the financial statements of foreign subsidiaries and their parent company?

Consolidation Calculations S Company has total stockholders' equity of $100,000. Fill in the dollar amounts for each of the following investments by P Company in S's common stock:

	Goodwill	Minority Interest
1. P pays $100,000 for 100% of S's common stock, and S's net assets are fairly valued at $100,000.	_____	_____
2. P pays $120,000 for 100% of S's common stock, and S's net assets are fairly valued at $100,000.	_____	_____
3. P pays $120,000 for 100% of S's common stock, and S's net assets are fairly valued at $120,000.	_____	_____
4. P pays $80,000 for 80% of S's common stock, and S's net assets are fairly valued at $100,000.	_____	_____
5. P pays $100,000 for 80% of S's common stock, and S's net assets are fairly valued at $125,000.	_____	_____

SOLUTION

	Goodwill	Minority Interest
1.	0	0
2.	$20,000	0
3.	0	0
4.	0	$20,000
5.	0	$25,000

Investments in Debt Securities

LO5 Explain the financial reporting implications of debt investments.

As noted in previous chapters, debt securities are considered financial instruments because they are claims that will be paid in cash. When a company purchases debt securities, it records them at cost plus any

commissions and fees. Like investments in equity securities, short-term investments in debt securities are valued at fair value at the end of the accounting period and are accounted for as trading securities or available-for-sale securities. However, the accounting treatment is different if they qualify as held-to-maturity securities.

Held-to-Maturity Securities

As we noted earlier, held-to-maturity securities are debt securities that management intends to hold to their maturity date. Such securities are recorded at cost and are valued on the balance sheet at cost adjusted for the effects of interest. For example, suppose that on December 1, 20x7, Webber Company pays $97,000 for U.S. Treasury bills, which are short-term debt of the federal government. The bills will mature in 120 days at $100,000. Webber would make the following entry:

A	= L + OE				
+97,000		20x7			
−97,000		Dec. 1	Short-Term Investments	97,000	
			Cash		97,000
			Purchase of U.S. Treasury bills that mature in 120 days		

At Webber's year end on December 31, the entry to accrue the interest income earned to date would be as follows:

A	= L + OE				
+750	+750	20x7			
		Dec. 31	Short-Term Investments	750	
			Interest Income		750
			Accrual of interest on U.S. Treasury bills $3,000 \times 30/120 = \$750$		

On December 31, the U.S. Treasury bills would be shown on the balance sheet as a short-term investment at their amortized cost of $97,750 ($97,000 + $750). When Webber receives the maturity value on March 31, 20x8, the entry is as follows:

A	= L + OE				
+100,000	+2,250	20x8			
−97,750		Mar. 31	Cash	100,000	
			Short-Term Investments		97,750
			Interest Income		2,250
			Receipt of cash at maturity of U.S. Treasury bills and recognition of related income		

Long-Term Investments in Bonds

Like all investments, investments in bonds are recorded at cost, which, in this case, is the price of the bonds plus the broker's commission. When bonds are purchased between interest payment dates, the purchaser must also pay an amount equal to the interest that has accrued on the bonds since the last interest payment date. Then, on the next interest payment date, the purchaser receives an interest payment for the whole period. The payment for accrued interest should be recorded as a debit to Interest Income, which will be offset by a credit to Interest Income when the semiannual interest is received.

Subsequent accounting for a corporation's long-term bond investments depends on the classification of the bonds. If the company plans to hold the bonds until they are paid off on their maturity date, they are considered held-to-maturity securities. Except in industries like insurance and banking, it is unusual for companies to buy the bonds of other companies with the express purpose of holding them until they mature, which can be in 10 to 30 years. Thus, most long-term bond investments are classified as available-for-sale securities, meaning that the company plans to sell them at some point before their maturity date. Such bonds are accounted for at fair value, much as equity or stock investments are; fair value is usually the market value. When bonds are intended to be held to maturity, they are accounted for not at fair value but at cost, adjusted for the amortization of their discount or premium. The procedure is similar to accounting for long-term bond liabilities, except that separate accounts for discounts and premiums are not used.

Study Note

The fair value of bonds is closely related to interest rates. An increase in interest rates lowers the fair value of bonds, and vice versa.

S T O P • R E V I E W • A P P L Y

5-1. What are held-to-maturity securities, and at what value are they shown on the balance sheet?

5-2. Are most long-term investments in bonds classified as held-to-maturity securities or as available-for-sale securities? Explain your answer.

A LOOK BACK AT

eBAY, INC.

As shown in the Financial Highlights at the beginning of the chapter, short- and long-term investments and goodwill from acquisitions constitute a large portion of the total assets on **eBay's** balance sheet. The company's investments also have important effects on its income statement and statement of cash flows. To fully evaluate eBay's performance, users of its financial statements must address the following questions:

● **What are the effects of eBay's investments on its financial performance?**

● **How does eBay's acquisition of other companies affect its financial performance?**

As we pointed out in this chapter, eBay classifies both short- and long-term investments as available-for-sale securities and reports them at fair value on its balance sheet. It reports the difference between unrealized gains and losses in other comprehensive income (a component of stockholders' equity) and subjects its equity investments to an impairment test, which can result in an income statement charge if a decline in an investment's value is deemed permanent. The company had unrealized gains in 2005 of $1.9 million and no impairments. Because more than 90 percent of eBay's investments are debt securities, interest income is a significant component—almost 8 percent—of the company's income from operations. The investing section of its statement of cash flows reveals that in 2005, eBay spent about $1.3 billion on investments while selling investments for about $1.9 billion.

In 2005, eBay made eight acquisitions totaling more than $2.7 billion. It uses the equity method to account for investments over 20 percent and the purchase method to account for acquisitions. For instance, its purchases of Rent.com and VeriSign resulted in both minority interest and goodwill.[14] In total, goodwill from all eBay's acquisitions represents over one-half of its assets.

In short, it is not possible to fully understand or evaluate eBay's performance without understanding the effect that investments and acquisitions have on that performance.

CHAPTER REVIEW

REVIEW of Learning Objectives

LO1 Identify and explain the management issues related to investments.

Investments are recorded on the date on which the transaction occurs, at which time there is either a transfer of funds or a definite obligation to pay. Investments are recorded at cost, or purchase price, including any commissions or fees. After the purchase, the balance sheet value of investments is adjusted to reflect subsequent conditions.

Investments are classified as short term or long term; as trading, available-for-sale, or held-to-maturity securities; and as noninfluential and noncontrolling, influential but noncontrolling, or controlling investments. These classifications play an important role in accounting for investments. Noninfluential and noncontrolling investments represent less than 20 percent ownership of a company; influential but noncontrolling investments represent 20 percent to 50 percent ownership; and controlling investments represent more than 50 percent ownership.

A company should disclose its accounting policies for investments and related details in the notes to its financial statements.

Managers and other employees must avoid using their knowledge of their company's planned investment transactions for personal gain.

LO2 Explain the financial reporting implications of short-term investments.

Short-term investments in stocks are classified as trading securities or available-for-sale securities. Trading securities are debt or equity securities that are bought and held principally for the purpose of being sold in the near term. They are classified as current assets on the balance sheet and are valued at fair value. Unrealized gains or losses on trading securities appear on the income statement.

Available-for-sale securities are debt or equity securities that do not meet the criteria for either trading or held-to-maturity securities. They are accounted for in the same way as trading securities with two exceptions: (1) an unrealized gain or loss is reported as a special item in the stockholders' equity section of the balance sheet; (2) if a decline in the value of a security is considered permanent, it is charged as a loss on the income statement.

LO3 Explain the financial reporting implications of long-term investments in stock and the cost-adjusted-to-market and equity methods used to account for them.

The cost-adjusted-to-market method is used to account for noninfluential and noncontrolling investments in stock. With this method, investments are initially recorded at cost and are then adjusted to market value by using an allowance account. The equity method is used to account for influential but noncontrolling investments. With this method, the investment is initially recorded at cost and is then adjusted for the investor's share of the company's net income or loss and subsequent dividends.

Consolidated financial statements are required when an investing company has legal and effective control over another company. Control exists when the parent company owns more than 50 percent of the voting stock of the subsidiary company.

LO4 Explain the financial reporting implications of consolidated financial statements.

Consolidated financial statements are useful to investors and others because they treat the parent company and its subsidiaries as an integrated economic unit. When a consolidated balance sheet is prepared at the date of acquisition, a work sheet entry is made to eliminate the investment from the parent company's financial statements and the stockholders' equity section of the subsidiary's financial statements. The assets and liabilities of the two companies are combined. If the parent owns less than 100 percent of the subsidiary, minority interest equal to the percentage of the subsidiary owned by minority stockholders multiplied by the subsidiary's net assets appears on the consolidated balance sheet. If the cost of the parent's investment in the subsidiary is greater than the subsidiary's book value, an amount equal to the excess of cost over book value is allocated to undervalued subsidiary assets and to goodwill. If the cost of the parent's investment in the subsidiary is less than book value, the excess of book value over cost should be used to reduce the book value of the subsidiary's long-term assets (other than long-term marketable securities).

When consolidated income statements are prepared, intercompany sales, purchases, interest income, interest expense, and other income and expenses from intercompany transactions must be eliminated to avoid double counting of these items.

The financial statements of foreign subsidiaries must be restated in terms of the parent company's reporting currency before consolidated financial statements can be prepared.

LO5 Explain the financial reporting implications of debt investments.

Held-to-maturity securities are debt securities that management intends to hold to their maturity date; they are valued on the balance sheet at cost adjusted for the effects of interest. Long-term investments in bonds fall into two categories: available-for-sale securities, which are recorded at cost and subsequently accounted for at fair value, and held-to-maturity securities.

REVIEW of Concepts and Terminology

The following concepts and terms were introduced in this chapter:

Available-for-sale securities: Debt or equity securities that do not meet the criteria for trading or held-to-maturity securities. **(LO1)**

Consolidated financial statements: Financial statements that reflect the combined operations of a parent company and its subsidiaries. **(LO3)**

Control: An investing company's ability to decide the operating and financial policies of another firm because it owns more than 50 percent of that firm's voting stock. **(LO1)**

Cost-adjusted-to-market method: A method of accounting for available-for-sale securities at cost adjusted for changes in the securities' market value. **(LO3)**

Eliminations: Entries made on consolidation work sheets to eliminate transactions between parent and subsidiary companies. **(LO4)**

Equity method: A method of accounting for influential but noncontrolling long-term investments in which the investment is initially recorded at cost and is then adjusted for the investor's share of the company's net income or loss and for dividends. **(LO3)**

Goodwill: The excess of the purchase price of a business over the fair market value of its net assets. Also called *goodwill from consolidation*. **(LO4)**

Held-to-maturity securities: Debt securities that management intends to hold until their maturity date. **(LO1)**

Insider trading: Making use of inside information for personal gain. **(LO1)**

Marketable securities: Investments with a maturity of more than 90 days but that are intended to be held only until cash is needed to pay current obligations. Also called *short-term investments*. **(LO1)**

Minority interest: An amount recorded on a consolidated balance sheet that represents the holdings of owners of less than 50 percent of a subsidiary's voting stock. **(LO4)**

Multinational or transnational corporations: Companies that expand by establishing or buying foreign subsidiaries. **(LO4)**

Parent company: A company that has a controlling interest in another firm. **(LO3)**

Purchase method: A method of accounting for controlling investments in which similar accounts from the parent's and subsidiaries' statements are combined. **(LO4)**

Reporting currency: The currency in which consolidated financial statements are presented. **(LO4)**

Restatement: The stating of one currency in terms of another. **(LO4)**

Short-term investments: Investments that have a maturity of more than 90 days but that management intends to hold only until cash is needed to pay current obligations. Also called *marketable securities*. **(LO1)**

Significant influence: An investing company's ability to affect the operating and financial policies of the firm in which it has invested, even though it holds 50 percent or less of the voting stock. **(LO1)**

Subsidiary: A firm in which another company owns a controlling interest. **(LO3)**

Trading securities: Debt or equity securities bought and held principally for the purpose of being sold in the near term. **(LO1)**

REVIEW Problem

LO4 **Consolidated Balance Sheet: Less than 100 Percent Ownership**

In a cash transaction on June 30, 20xx, Kohl Company purchased 90 percent of the outstanding stock of Shannon Company for $763,200. Directly after the acquisition, the balance sheets of the two companies were as follows:

	A	B	C
		Kohl Company	Shannon Company
1			
2			
3	**Assets**		
4	Cash	$ 400,000	$ 48,000
5	Accounts receivable	650,000	240,000
6	Inventory	1,000,000	520,000
7	Investment in Shannon Company	763,200	—
8	Plant and equipment (net)	1,500,000	880,000
9	Other assets	50,000	160,000
10	Total assets	$4,363,200	$1,848,000
11			
12	**Liabilities and Stockholders' Equity**		
13	Accounts payable	$ 800,000	$ 400,000
14	Long-term debt	1,000,000	600,000
15	Common stock	2,000,000	800,000
16	Retained earnings	563,200	48,000
17	Total liabilities and stockholders' equity	$4,363,200	$1,848,000

The following information is also available:

1. Shannon Company's other assets represent a long-term investment in Kohl Company's long-term debt. Shannon purchased the debt for an amount equal to Kohl's carrying value of the debt.
2. Kohl Company owes Shannon Company $100,000 for services rendered.

Required

Prepare a work sheet for a consolidated balance sheet as of the acquisition date.

Answer to Review Problem

	A	B	C	D	E	F
1			Kohl and Shannon Companies			
2			Work Sheet for Consolidated Balance Sheet			
3			June 30, 20xx			
4						
5					Eliminations	
6	Accounts	Balance Sheet, Kohl Company	Balance Sheet, Shannon Company	Debit	Credit	Consolidated Balance Sheet
7						
8	Cash	400,000	48,000			448,000
9	Accounts receivable	650,000	240,000		(3) 100,000	790,000
10	Inventory	1,000,000	520,000			1,520,000
11	Investment in					
12	Shannon Company	763,200	—		(1) 763,200	
13	Plant and equipment (net)	1,500,000	880,000			2,380,000
14	Other assets	50,000	160,000		(2) 160,000	50,000
15	Total assets	4,363,200	1,848,000			5,188,000
16						
17	Accounts payable	800,000	400,000	(3) 100,000		1,100,000
18	Long-term debt	1,000,000	600,000	(2) 160,000		1,440,000
19	Common stock	2,000,000	800,000	(1) 800,000		2,000,000
20	Retained earnings	563,200	48,000	(1) 48,000		563,200
21	Minority interest	—	—		(1) 84,800	84,800
22	Total liabilities and					
23	stockholders' equity	4,363,200	1,848,000	1,108,000	1,108,000	5,188,000

(1) Elimination of intercompany investment. Minority interest equals 10 percent of Shannon Company's stockholders' equity [10% × ($800,000 + $48,000) = $84,800].

(2) Elimination of intercompany long-term debt.

(3) Elimination of intercompany receivables and payables.

CHAPTER ASSIGNMENTS

BUILDING Your Basic Knowledge and Skills

Short Exercises

LO2 **Trading Securities**

SE 1. Murray Corporation began investing in trading securities in 20x8. At the end of 20x8, it had the following trading portfolio:

Security	Cost	Market Value
Sara Lee (10,000 shares)	$220,000	$330,000
Skyline (5,000 shares)	100,000	75,000
Totals	$320,000	$405,000

Prepare the necessary year-end adjusting entry on December 31 and the entry for the sale of all the Skyline shares on the following March 23 for $95,000.

LO3 **Cost-Adjusted-to-Market Method**

SE 2. On December 31, 20x8, the market value of Rapid Tech Company's portfolio of long-term available-for-sale securities was $640,000. The cost of these securities was $570,000. Prepare the entry to adjust the portfolio to market at year end, assuming that the company did not have any long-term investments prior to 20x8.

LO3 **Cost-Adjusted-to-Market Method**

SE 3. Refer to your answer to **SE 2**. Assume that on December 31, 20x9, the cost of Rapid Tech Company's portfolio of long-term available-for-sale securities was $1,280,000 and that its market value was $1,200,000. Prepare the entry to record the 20x9 year-end adjustment.

LO3 **Equity Method**

SE 4. Blanco Company owns 30 percent of Heaton Company. In 20x8, Heaton Company earned $60,000 and paid $40,000 in dividends. Prepare entries in journal form for Blanco Company's records on December 31 to reflect this information. Assume that the dividends are received on December 31.

LO3 **Methods of Accounting for Long-Term Investments**

SE 5. For each of the investments listed below, tell which of the following methods should be used for external financial reporting: (a) cost-adjusted-to-market method, (b) equity method, (c) consolidation of parent and subsidiary financial statements.

1. 49 percent investment in Irono Corporation
2. 51 percent investment in Barker Corporation
3. 5 percent investment in Hymir Corporation

LO4 **Purchase of 100 Percent at Book Value**

SE 6. Sutton Hills Corporation buys 100 percent ownership of Winter Treats Corporation for $100,000. At the time of the purchase, Winter Treats' stockholders' equity consisted of $20,000 in common stock and $80,000 in retained earnings. Sutton Hills' stockholders' equity consisted of $200,000 in common stock and $400,000 in retained earnings. After the purchase, what would be the amount, if any, of the following accounts on the consolidated balance sheet: goodwill, minority interest, common stock, and retained earnings?

LO4 **Purchase of Less than 100 Percent at Book Value**

SE 7. Assume the same facts as in **SE 6** except that Sutton Hills purchased 80 percent of Winter Treats Corporation for $80,000. After the purchase, what would be the amount, if any, of the following accounts on the consolidated balance sheet: goodwill, minority interest, common stock, and retained earnings?

LO4 **Purchase of 100 Percent at More than Book Value**

SE 8. Assume the same facts as in **SE 6** except that the purchase of 100 percent of Winter Treats Corporation was for $120,000. After the purchase, what would be the amount, if any, of the following accounts on the consolidated balance sheet: goodwill, minority interest, common stock, and retained earnings? Assume that the fair value of Winter Treats' net assets equals their book value.

LO4 Intercompany Transactions

SE 9. T Company owns 100 percent of C Company. The following are accounts from the balance sheets and income statements of both companies:

	T Company	C Company
Accounts receivable	$ 460,000	$ 300,000
Accounts payable	360,000	180,000
Sales	2,400,000	1,780,000
Cost of goods sold	1,420,000	1,080,000

What would be the combined amount of each of the above accounts on the consolidated financial statements assuming the following additional information? (1) C Company sold to T Company merchandise at cost in the amount of $540,000; (2) T Company sold all the merchandise it bought from C Company to customers, but it still owes C Company $120,000 for the merchandise.

LO5 Held-to-Maturity Securities

SE 10. On May 31, Fournier Company invested $98,000 in U.S. Treasury bills. The bills mature in 120 days at $100,000. Prepare entries to record the purchase on May 31; the adjustment to accrue interest on June 30, which is the end of the fiscal year; and the receipt of cash at the maturity date of September 28.

Exercises

LO1, LO2, LO3 Discussion Questions

E 1. Develop brief answers to each of the following questions:

1. Where in the financial statements are investment transactions reported?
2. What would cause an Allowance to Adjust Short-Term Investments to Market account that has a negative (credit) balance at the beginning of the year to have a positive (debit) balance at the end of the year?
3. When a company uses the equity method to record its proportionate share of the income and dividends of a company in which it has invested, what are the cash flow effects?

LO4, LO5 Discussion Questions

E 2. Develop brief answers to each of the following questions:

1. Under what conditions would a company have both minority interest and goodwill in a consolidation?
2. Why must the financial statements of foreign subsidiaries be restated?
3. What is the logic behind treating held-to-maturity securities different from any other investment?

LO2 Trading Securities

E 3. Omar Corporation, which has begun investing in trading securities, engaged in the following transactions:

Jan. 6 Purchased 7,000 shares of Quaker Oats stock, $30 per share.
Feb. 15 Purchased 9,000 shares of EG&G, $22 per share.

At year end on June 30, Quaker Oats was trading at $40 per share, and EG&G was trading at $18 per share.

Record the entries for the purchases. Then record the necessary year-end adjusting entry. (Include a schedule of the trading portfolio cost and market in the explanation.) Also record the entry for the sale of all the EG&G shares on August 20 for $16 per share. Is the last entry affected by the June 30 adjustment?

LO3 Long-Term Investments

E 4. Fulco Corporation has the following portfolio of long-term available-for-sale securities at year end, December 31, 20x8:

Company	Percentage of Voting Stock Held	Cost	Year-End Market Value
A Corporation	4	$ 80,000	$ 95,000
B Corporation	12	375,000	275,000
C Corporation	5	30,000	55,000
Total		$485,000	$425,000

Both the Unrealized Loss on Long-Term Investments account and the Allowance to Adjust Long-Term Investments to Market account currently have a balance of $40,000 from the last accounting period. Prepare T accounts with a beginning balance for each of these accounts. Record the effects of the above information on the accounts and determine the ending balances.

LO3 Long-Term Investments: Cost-Adjusted-to-Market and Equity Methods

E 5. On January 1, Rourke Corporation purchased, as long-term investments, 8 percent of the voting stock of Taglia Corporation for $250,000 and 45 percent of the voting stock of Curry Corporation for $2 million. During the year, Taglia Corporation had earnings of $100,000 and paid dividends of $40,000. Curry Corporation had earnings of $300,000 and paid dividends of $200,000. The market value did not change for either investment during the year. Which of these investments should be accounted for using the cost-adjusted-to-market method? Which should be accounted for using the equity method? At what amount should each investment be carried on the balance sheet at year end? Give a reason for each choice.

LO3 Long-Term Investments: Equity Method

E 6. On January 1, 20xx, Orchid Corporation acquired 40 percent of the voting stock of Vose Corporation, an amount sufficient to exercise significant influence over Vose Corporation's activities, for $4,800,000 in cash. On December 31, Orchid determined that Vose paid dividends of $800,000 but incurred a net loss of $400,000 for 20xx. Prepare entries in T account form to reflect this information.

LO3 Methods of Accounting for Long-Term Investments

E 7. Teague Corporation has the following long-term investments:

1. 60 percent of the common stock of Ariel Corporation
2. 13 percent of the common stock of Copper, Inc.
3. 50 percent of the nonvoting preferred stock of Staffordshire Corporation
4. 100 percent of the common stock of its financing subsidiary, EQ, Inc.
5. 35 percent of the common stock of the French company Rue de le Brasseur
6. 70 percent of the common stock of the Canadian company Nova Scotia Cannery

For each of these investments, tell which of the following methods should be used for external financial reporting, and why:

a. Cost-adjusted-to-market method
b. Equity method
c. Consolidation of parent and subsidiary financial statements

LO4 Elimination Entry for a Purchase at Book Value

E 8. Edson Manufacturing Company purchased 100 percent of the common stock of Liverpool Manufacturing Company for $600,000. Liverpool's stockholders' equity included common stock of $400,000 and retained earnings of $200,000. Prepare the eliminating entry in journal form that would appear on the work sheet for consolidating the balance sheets of these two entities as of the acquisition date.

LO4 Elimination Entry and Minority Interest

E 9. The stockholders' equity section of Caritas Corporation's balance sheet appeared as follows on December 31:

Common stock, $10 par value, 80,000 shares authorized and issued	$800,000
Retained earnings	96,000
Total stockholders' equity	$896,000

Swanson Manufacturing Company owns 80 percent of Caritas's voting stock and paid $11.20 per share. In journal form, prepare the entry (including minority interest) to eliminate Swanson's investment and Caritas's stockholders' equity that would appear on the work sheet used in preparing the consolidated balance sheet for the two firms.

LO4 Consolidated Balance Sheet with Goodwill

E 10. On September 1, 20x8, A Company purchased 100 percent of the voting stock of B Company for $480,000 in cash. The separate condensed balance sheets immediately after the purchase were as follows:

	A Company	B Company
Other assets	$1,103,000	$544,500
Investment in B Company	480,000	—
Total assets	$1,583,000	$544,500
Liabilities	$ 435,500	$ 94,500
Common stock	500,000	150,000
Retained earnings	647,500	300,000
Total liabilities and stockholders' equity	$1,583,000	$544,500

Prepare a work sheet for preparing the consolidated balance sheet immediately after A Company acquired control of B Company. Assume that any excess cost of A Company's investment in the subsidiary over book value is attributable to goodwill from consolidation.

LO4 Preparation of Consolidated Income Statement

E 11. Arnold Company has owned 100 percent of Van Rossum Company since 20x7. The income statements of these two companies for the year ended December 31, 20x8, follow.

	Arnold Company	Van Rossum Company
Net sales	$6,000,000	$2,400,000
Cost of goods sold	3,000,000	1,600,000
Gross margin	$3,000,000	$ 800,000
Less: Selling expenses	$1,000,000	$ 200,000
General and administrative expenses	1,200,000	400,000
Total operating expenses	$2,200,000	$ 600,000
Income from operations	$ 800,000	$ 200,000
Other income	240,000	—
Net income	$1,040,000	$ 200,000

The following is additional information: (1) Van Rossum Company purchased $1,120,000 of inventory from Arnold Company, which it had sold to Van Rossum customers by the end of the year. (2) Van Rossum Company leased its building from Arnold Company for $240,000 per year. Prepare a consolidated income statement work sheet for the two companies for the year ended December 31, 20x8. Ignore income taxes.

LO5 **Held-to-Maturity Securities**

E 12. Dale Company experiences heavy sales in the summer and early fall, after which time it has excess cash to invest until the next spring. On November 1, 20x8, the company invested $194,000 in U.S. Treasury bills. The bills mature in 180 days at $200,000. Prepare entries to record the purchase on November 1; the adjustment to accrue interest on December 31, which is the end of the fiscal year; and the receipt of cash at the maturity date of April 30.

Problems

LO1, LO2 **Accounting for Investments**

P 1. Gulf Coast Corporation is a successful oil and gas exploration business in the southwestern United States. At the beginning of 20xx, the company made investments in three companies that perform services in the oil and gas industry. The details of each of these investments follow.

Gulf Coast purchased 100,000 shares of Marsh Service Corporation at a cost of $16 per share. Marsh has 1.5 million shares outstanding and during 20xx paid dividends of $.80 per share on earnings of $1.60 per share. At the end of the year, Marsh's shares were selling for $24 per share.

Gulf Coast also purchased 2 million shares of Crescent Drilling Company at $8 per share. Crescent has 10 million shares outstanding. In 20xx, Crescent paid a dividend of $.40 per share on earnings of $.80 per share. During the year, the president of Gulf Coast was appointed to Crescent's board of directors. At the end of the year, Crescent's stock was selling for $12 per share.

In another action, Gulf Coast purchased 1 million shares of Logan Oil Field Supplies Company's 5 million outstanding shares at $12 per share. The president of Gulf Coast sought membership on Logan's board of directors but was rebuffed when a majority of shareholders stated they did not want to be associated with Gulf Coast. Logan paid a dividend of $.80 per share and reported a net income of only $.40 per share for the year. By the end of the year, its stock price had dropped to $4 per share.

Required

1. For each investment, make entries in journal form for (a) initial investment, (b) receipt of cash dividend, and (c) recognition of income (if appropriate).
2. What adjusting entry (if any) is required at the end of the year?
3. Assuming that Gulf Coast sells its investment in Logan after the first of the year for $6 per share, what journal entry would be made?
4. Assuming no other transactions occur and that the market value of Gulf Coast's investment in Marsh exceeds cost by $2,400,000 at the end of the second year, what adjusting entry (if any) would be required?
5. **User Insight:** What principal factors were considered in determining how to account for Gulf Coast's investments? Should they be shown on the balance sheet as short-term or long-term investments? What factors affect this decision?

LO3 **Long-Term Investments: Equity Method**

P 2. Rylander Corporation owns 35 percent of the voting stock of Waters Corporation. The Investment account on Rylander's books as of January 1, 20xx, was $720,000. During 20xx, Waters reported the following quarterly earnings and dividends:

Quarter	Earnings	Dividends Paid
1	$160,000	$100,000
2	240,000	100,000
3	120,000	100,000
4	(80,000)	100,000
	$440,000	$400,000

Because of the percentage of voting shares Rylander owns, it can exercise significant influence over the operations of Waters Corporation. Therefore, Rylander Corporation must account for the investment using the equity method.

Required

1. Prepare a T account for Rylander Corporation's investment in Waters, and enter the beginning balance, the relevant entries for the year in total, and the ending balance.
2. **User Insight:** What is the effect and placement of the entries in requirement 1 on Rylander Corporation's earnings as reported on the income statement?
3. **User Insight:** What is the effect and placement of the entries in requirement 1 on the statement of cash flows?
4. **User Insight:** How would the effects on the statements differ if Rylander's ownership represented only a 15 percent share of Waters?

LO4 **Consolidated Balance Sheet: Cost Exceeding Book Value**

P 3. The balance sheets of Saba and Joseph Companies as of December 31, 20xx, appear on the next page.

Assume that Saba Company purchased 100 percent of Joseph's common stock for $700,000 immediately prior to December 31, 20xx. Also assume that $160,000 of the excess of cost over book value is attributable to the increased value of Joseph Company's property, plant, and equipment. The rest of the excess is considered by Saba Company to be goodwill.

	Saba Company	Joseph Company
Assets		
Cash	$ 120,000	$ 80,000
Accounts receivable	200,000	60,000
Investment in Joseph Company	700,000	—
Property, plant, and equipment (net)	200,000	360,000
Total assets	$1,220,000	$500,000
Liabilities and Stockholders' Equity		
Accounts payable	$ 220,000	$ 60,000
Common stock, $20 par value	800,000	400,000
Retained earnings	200,000	40,000
Total liabilities and stockholders' equity	$1,220,000	$500,000

Required

1. Prepare a work sheet for preparing a consolidated balance sheet as of the acquisition date.

2. **User Insight:** If you were reading Saba's consolidated balance sheet, what account would indicate that Saba paid more than book value for Joseph and where would you find it on the balance sheet? Also, would you expect the amount of this account to change from year-to-year? What would cause it to change?

LO4 **Consolidated Balance Sheet: Less than 100 Percent Ownership**

P 4. In a cash transaction, Geis Company purchased 70 percent of the outstanding stock of Vogel Company for $593,600 cash on June 30, 20xx. Immediately after the acquisition, the separate balance sheets of the companies appeared as shown below.

	Geis Company	Vogel Company
Assets		
Cash	$ 320,000	$ 48,000
Accounts receivable	520,000	240,000
Inventory	800,000	520,000
Investment in Vogel Company	593,600	—
Property, plant, and equipment (net)	1,200,000	880,000
Other assets	40,000	160,000
Total assets	$3,473,600	$1,848,000
Liabilities and Stockholders' Equity		
Accounts payable	$ 640,000	$ 400,000
Long-term debt	800,000	600,000
Common stock, $10 par value	1,600,000	800,000
Retained earnings	433,600	48,000
Total liabilities and stockholders' equity	$3,473,600	$1,848,000

Additional information: (a) Vogel Company's other assets represent a long-term investment in Geis Company's long-term debt. The debt was purchased for an amount equal to Geis's carrying value of the debt. (b) Geis Company owes Vogel Company $80,000 for services rendered.

Required

1. Prepare a work sheet for preparing a consolidated balance sheet as of the acquisition date.
2. User Insight: If you were reading Geis's consolidated balance sheet, what account would indicate that Geis owned less than 100 percent of Vogel and where would you find it on the balance sheet?

Alternate Problems

LO3 Long-Term Investment Transactions

P 5. On January 2, 20x7, the Healey Company made several long-term investments in the voting stock of various companies. It purchased 10,000 shares of Zima at $4.00 a share, 15,000 shares of Kane at $6.00 a share, and 6,000 shares of Rodriguez at $9.00 a share. Each investment represents less than 20 percent of the voting stock of the company. The remaining securities transactions of Healey during 20x7 were as follows:

May   5   Purchased with cash 6,000 shares of Drennan stock for $6.00 per share. This investment represents less than 20 percent of the Drennan voting stock.

July   16   Sold the 10,000 shares of Zima stock for $3.60 per share.

Sept. 30   Purchased with cash 5,000 additional shares of Kane for $6.40 per share. This investment still represents less than 20 percent of the voting stock.

Dec. 31   The market values per share of the stock in the Long-Term Investments account were as follows: Kane, $6.50; Rodriguez, $8.00; and Drennan, $4.00.

Healey's transactions in securities during 20x8 were as follows:

Feb.   1   Received a cash dividend from Kane of $.20 per share.

July   15   Sold the 6,000 Rodriguez shares for $8.00 per share.

Aug.   1   Received a cash dividend from Kane of $.20 per share.

Sept. 10   Purchased 3,000 shares of Parmet Company for $14.00 per share. This investment represents less than 20 percent of the voting stock of the company.

Dec. 31   The market values per share of the stock in the Long-Term Investments account were as follows: Kane, $6.50; Drennan, $5.00; and Parmet, $13.00.

Required

1. Prepare entries in journal form to record all of Healey Company's transactions in long-term investments during 20x7 and 20x8.
2. User Insight: Assume that Healey increased its ownership in Kane to 25 percent and its ownership in Parmet to 60 percent in 20x9. How would these actions affect the methods used to account for the investments?

LO3 Long-Term Investments: Equity Method

P 6. Bon Company owns 40 percent of the voting stock of Macree Company. The investment account for this company on Bon's balance sheet had a balance of $300,000 on January 1, 20xx. During 20xx, the Macree Company reported the following quarterly earnings and dividends paid:

Quarter	Earnings	Dividends Paid
1	$ 40,000	$20,000
2	30,000	20,000
3	80,000	20,000
4	(20,000)	20,000
	$130,000	$80,000

Bon Company exercises a significant influence over Macree's operations and therefore uses the equity method to account for its investment.

Required

1. Prepare a T account for Bon's investment in Macree. Enter the beginning balance, the relevant entries for the year in total, and the ending balance.
2. **User Insight:** What is the effect and placement of the entries in requirement 1 on Bon Company's earnings as reported on the income statement?
3. **User Insight:** What is the effect and placement of the entries in requirement 1 on the statement of cash flows?
4. **User Insight:** How would the effects on the statements differ if Bon's ownership represented only a 10 percent share of Macree?

LO4 **Consolidated Balance Sheet: Cost Exceeding Book Value**

P 7. The balance sheets of Cheever and Ham Companies as of December 31, 20xx, are as follows.

	Cheever Company	Ham Company
Assets		
Cash	$ 400,000	$ 120,000
Accounts receivable	550,000	1,200,000
Investment in Ham Company	1,400,000	—
Property, plant, and equipment (net)	1,370,000	900,000
Total assets	$3,720,000	$2,220,000
Liabilities and Stockholders' Equity		
Accounts payable	$ 950,000	$1,070,000
Common stock, $20 par value	1,850,000	1,000,000
Retained earnings	920,000	150,000
Total liabilities and stockholders' equity	$3,720,000	$2,220,000

Assume that Cheever Company purchased 100 percent of Ham's common stock for $1,400,000 immediately prior to December 31, 20xx. Also assume that $100,000 of the excess of cost over book value is attributable to the increased value of Ham Company's property, plant, and equipment. Cheever considers the rest of the excess to be goodwill.

Required

1. Prepare a work sheet for preparing a consolidated balance sheet as of the acquisition date.
2. **User Insight:** If you were reading Cheever's consolidated balance sheet, what account would indicate that Cheever paid more than book value for Ham and where would you find it on the balance sheet? Also, would you expect the amount of this account to change from year-to-year? What would cause it to change?

LO2, LO5   **Held-to-Maturity and Trading Securities**

P 8. During certain periods, Yang Company invests its excess cash until it is needed. During 20x8 and 20x9, Yang engaged in these transactions:

20x8

Jan. 16   Invested $146,000 in 120-day U.S. Treasury bills that had a maturity value of $150,000.

Apr. 15   Purchased 10,000 shares of King Tools common stock at $40 per share and 5,000 shares of Mellon Gas common stock at $30 per share as trading securities.

May 16   Received maturity value of U.S. Treasury bills in cash.

June 2   Received dividends of $2.00 per share from King Tools and $1.50 per share from Mellon Gas.

June 30   Made year-end adjusting entry for trading securities. Market price per share for King Tools is $32; for Mellon Gas, it is $35.

Nov. 14   Sold all the shares of King Tools for $42 per share.

20x9

Feb. 15   Purchased 9,000 shares of MKD Communications for $50 per share.

Apr. 1   Invested $195,500 in 120-day U.S. Treasury bills that had a maturity value of $200,000.

June 1   Received dividends of $2.20 per share from Mellon Gas.

       30   Made year-end adjusting entry for held-to-maturity securities.

       30   Made year-end adjusting entry for trading securities. Market price of Mellon Gas shares is $33 per share and of MKD Communications shares is $60 per share.

Required

1. Prepare entries in journal form to record the preceding transactions, assuming that Yang Company's fiscal year ends on June 30.

2. Show the balance sheet presentation of short-term investments on June 30, 20x9.

3. User Insight: Explain the following statement: "Held to maturity and trading securities are opposites in terms of investment strategy and thus require opposite accounting treatments."

ENHANCING Your Knowledge, Skills, and Critical Thinking

Conceptual Understanding Cases

LO2, LO3   **Understanding Investment Accounting**

C 1. Dell Computer Corporation has significant investment activities. The following items are from Dell's fiscal year 2006 financial statements (in millions):[15]

Short-term investments	$ 2,016
Long-term investments	2,691
Investment income	227
Purchase of investments	7,562
Sales of investments	12,168
Change in unrealized gains (losses) on long-term investments, net	(24)

Dell states that all debt and equities securities are classified as available-for-sale and are subject to an annual impairment test.

1. Where would you find each of the above items in Dell Computer's financial statements?
2. What value (cost or fair value) would you expect the first two items on Dell's balance sheet to represent?
3. What are impairments, and how do they differ from unrealized losses on long-term investments?

LO4 Goodwill and Minority Interest

C 2. DreamWorks Animation makes well-known animated films like *Shrek* 2. Two items on the company's 2005 balance sheet are as follows:[16]

Goodwill	$34,216
Minority interest	2,941

1. What is the difference between goodwill and minority interest and where do these items appear on the balance sheet?
2. The amount of goodwill did not change from 2004 to 2005. Assuming no new acquisitions or sales, what would cause the amount of goodwill to change from year to year? Would it increase or decrease?

Interpreting Financial Reports

LO4 Effects of Consolidating Finance Subsidiaries

C 3. National Stores Corporation is one of the largest owners of discount appliance stores in the United States. It owns Bi-Lo Superstores and several other discount chains. It has a wholly owned finance subsidiary handle its accounts receivable. Condensed balance sheets for National Stores and its finance subsidiary are shown below (in millions). The fiscal year ends January 31, 20x8.

	National Stores Corporation	Finance Subsidiary
Assets		
Current assets (except accounts receivable)	$ 866	$ 1
Accounts receivable (net)	293	869
Property, equipment, and other assets	933	—
Investment in finance subsidiary	143	—
Total assets	$2,235	$870
Liabilities and Stockholders' Equity		
Current liabilities	$ 717	$ 10
Long-term liabilities	859	717
Stockholders' equity	659	143
Total liabilities and stockholders' equity	$2,235	$870

Total sales to customers were $4 billion. The FASB requires all majority-owned subsidiaries to be consolidated in the parent company's financial statements. National Stores' management believes it is misleading to consolidate the finance subsidiary because it distorts the real operations of the company.

1. Prepare a consolidated balance sheet for National Stores Corporation and its finance subsidiary.
2. Demonstrate the effects of consolidating by computing the following ratios for National Stores before and after the consolidation in **1**: receivable turnover, days' sales uncollected, and debt to equity ratio (use year-end balances).
3. What are some of the other ratios that will be affected by consolidating the financial statements? Does consolidation assist investors and creditors in assessing the risk of investing in National Stores' securities or lending the company money? Relate your answer to your calculations in **2**.
4. What do you think of management's view that it is misleading to consolidate the finance subsidiary?

Decision Analysis Using Excel

LO2 **Accounting for Short-Term Investments**

C 4. Jackson Christmas Tree Company's business—the growing and selling of Christmas trees—is seasonal. By January 1, after its heavy selling season, the company has cash on hand that will not be needed for several months. It has minimal expenses from January to October and heavy expenses during the harvest and shipping months of November and December. The company's management follows the practice of investing the idle cash in marketable securities, which can be sold when funds are needed for operations. The company's fiscal year ends on June 30.

On January 10 of the current year, Jackson has cash of $597,300 on hand. It keeps $20,000 on hand for operating expenses and invests the rest as follows:

$100,000 three-month Treasury bills	$ 97,800
5,000 shares of Ford Motor Co. ($10 per share)	50,000
5,000 shares of McDonald's ($25 per share)	125,000
4,350 shares of IBM ($70 per share)	304,500
Total short-term investments	$577,300

On February 10 and May 10, Jackson receives quarterly cash dividends from each company in which it has invested: $.10 per share from Ford Motor Co., $.14 per share from McDonald's, and $.20 per share from IBM. The Treasury bills are redeemed at face value on April 10. On June 1, management sells 1,000 shares of McDonald's at $28 per share.

On June 30, the market values of the investments are as follows:

Ford Motor Co.	$11 per share
McDonald's	$23 per share
IBM	$65 per share

Jackson receives another quarterly dividend from each company on August 10. It sells all its remaining shares on November 1 at the following prices:

Ford Motor Co.	$ 9 per share
McDonald's	$22 per share
IBM	$80 per share

1. Record the investment transactions that occurred on January 10, February 10, April 10, May 10, and June 1. The Treasury bills are accounted for as held-to-maturity securities, and the stocks are trading securities. Prepare the required adjusting entry on June 30 and record the investment transactions on August 10 and November 1.
2. Explain how the short-term investments would be shown on the balance sheet on June 30.

3. After November 1, what is the balance of Allowance to Adjust Short-Term Investments to Market, and what will happen to this account next June?
4. What is your assessment of Jackson Christmas Tree Company's strategy with regard to idle cash?

Annual Report Case: CVS Corporation

LO4 **Planned Acquisition**

C 5. Refer to Note 2 of **CVS Corporation's** annual report in the Supplement to Chapter 5. The company gives a final report on its acquisition of Eckerd Drugstores from J. C. Penney in July 2004. What was the purchase price of Eckerd? Did CVS pay more than the fair value for the net assets of Eckerd? If so, how much more did it pay and what does the excess represent?

Comparison Case: CVS Versus Southwest

LO2 **Investments in Derivatives**

C 6. Refer to the annual report of **CVS Corporation** and the financial statements of **Southwest Airlines Co**. in the Supplement to Chapter 5. Refer to comprehensive income (loss) in each company's statement of shareholders' equity. Which item for each company refers to derivatives (a type of investment involving future contracts)? What causes either an unrealized gain or loss to occur? In the case of Southwest, find the accounting policy with regard to financial derivatives instruments in Note 1 to the financial statements. What problem does Southwest's management face in determining the fair market value of its derivatives? How does management solve the problem?

Ethical Dilemma Case

LO1 **Insider Trading**

C 7. Refer to the discussion about insider trading in this chapter to answer the following questions:

1. What does *insider trading* mean?
2. Why do you think insider trading is illegal in the United States and in Germany?
3. Why do you think insider trading is permissible in some other countries?
4. Can you think of any reasons why insider trading should be permitted in the United States?

Internet Case

LO3, LO4 **Comparison of Two Recent Acquisitions**

C 8. Mergers and acquisitions are in the news almost every day. Go to the website for **MSNBC** and scan recent headlines to locate two articles related to one company purchasing or making an offer to purchase another company. Read the articles and summarize the nature of the actual or proposed acquisition. What are the companies' names? What industry are they in? What is the dollar amount of the acquisition? How will the acquisition be paid for—in cash, stock, or a combination of cash and stock? In what ways are the acquisitions similar? How do they differ? Be prepared to present your findings in class.

Group Activity Case

LO1, LO2, LO3 **Identification of Investments and Resulting Gains and Losses**

C 9. Microsoft, one of the most successful businesses in the history of commerce, has accumulated a large investment portfolio, which in a recent year consisted of the following (in millions):[17]

Cash and cash equivalents	$15,982
Short-term investments-available-for-sale	44,610
Corporate notes and bonds-held-to-maturity	1,481
Long-term investments—equity securities	10,729
Total investments	$72,802

In addition, during the year Microsoft had net realized gains on investments of $1.640 million, $82 million of impairments, and unrealized losses of $293 million.

Divide into at least seven groups to discuss each of the four types of investments and the three types of gains or losses. Each group should discuss the nature of each gain or loss and the nature of the investment that gave rise to it. Discuss where each investment and gain or loss would appear in the financial statements. Be prepared to present your group's findings in class.

Business Communication Case

LO1 **Presentation on Investment Classification and Valuation**

C 10. The classification and valuation of investments can be confusing for someone not familiar with classifying investments. Suppose you have been asked to make a short (five-minute) presentation that explains this classification scheme. Develop a one-page outline with talking points that explains the three types of short-term and long-term investments and how they are valued at year end. Then briefly cover how accounting for long-term investments depends on the level and percentage of ownership. Be prepared to give your presentation in class or to a small group.

Financial Performance Measurement

The ultimate purpose of financial reporting is to enable managers, creditors, investors, and other interested parties to evaluate a company's financial performance. In earlier chapters, we discussed the various measures used in assessing a company's financial performance; here, we provide a comprehensive summary of those measures. Because these measures play a key role in executive compensation, there is always the risk that they will be manipulated. Users of financial statements therefore need to be familiar with the analytical tools and techniques used in performance measurement and the assumptions that underlie them.

LEARNING OBJECTIVES

Making a Statement

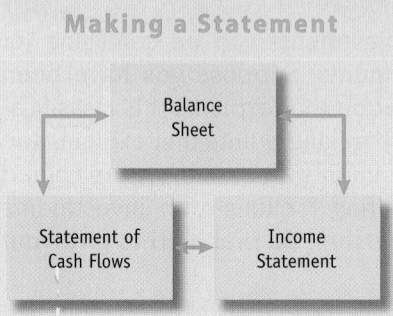

Comparisons within and across financial statements help the users of financial statements assess financial performance.

LO1 Describe the objectives, standards of comparison, sources of information, and compensation issues in measuring financial performance.

LO2 Apply horizontal analysis, trend analysis, vertical analysis, and ratio analysis to financial statements.

LO3 Apply ratio analysis to financial statements in a comprehensive evaluation of a company's financial performance.

STARBUCKS CORPORATION

- What standards should be used to evaluate Starbucks' performance?

- What analytical tools are available to measure performance?

- How successful has the company been in creating value for shareholders?

Formed in 1985, Starbucks is today a well-known specialty retailer. The company purchases and roasts whole coffee beans and sells them, along with a variety of freshly brewed coffees and other beverages and food items, in its retail shops. It also produces and sells bottled coffee drinks and a line of premium ice creams.

Like many other companies, Starbucks uses financial performance measures, primarily earnings per share, in determining compensation for top management. Earnings per share and some of the measures that drive earnings per share appear in the company's Financial Highlights below.[1] By linking compensation to financial performance, Starbucks provides its executives with incentive to improve the company's performance. Compensation and financial performance are thus linked to increasing shareholders' value.

STARBUCKS' FINANCIAL HIGHLIGHTS
(In thousands, except profit margin and earnings per share)

	2005	2004	2003
Net revenues	$6,369,300	$5,294,247	$4,075,522
Net earnings	494,467	388,973	265,355
Profit margin	7.8%	7.3%	6.5%
Earnings per share—basic	0.63	0.49	0.34

Foundations of Financial Performance Measurement

LO1 Describe the objectives, standards of comparison, sources of information, and compensation issues in measuring financial performance.

inancial performance measurement, also called *financial statement analysis*, uses all the techniques available to show how important items in a company's financial statements relate to the company's financial objectives. Persons with a strong interest in measuring a company's financial performance fall into two groups:

1. A company's top managers, who set and strive to achieve financial performance objectives; middle-level managers of business processes; and lower-level employees who own stock in the company

2. Creditors and investors, as well as customers who have cooperative agreements with the company

Financial Performance Measurement: Management's Objectives

All the strategic and operating plans that management formulates to achieve a company's goals must eventually be stated in terms of financial objectives. A primary objective is to increase the wealth of the company's stockholders, but this objective must be divided into categories. A complete financial plan should have financial objectives and related performance objectives in all the following categories:

Financial Objective	Performance Objective
Liquidity	The company must be able to pay bills when due and meet unexpected needs for cash.
Profitability	It must earn a satisfactory net income.
Long-term solvency	It must be able to survive for many years.
Cash flow adequacy	It must generate sufficient cash through operating, investing, and financing activities.
Market strength	It must be able to increase stockholders' wealth.

Management's main responsibility is to carry out its plan to achieve the company's financial objectives. This requires constant monitoring of key financial performance measures for each objective listed above, determining the cause of any deviations from the measures, and proposing ways of correcting the deviations. Management compares actual performance with the key performance measures in monthly, quarterly, and annual reports. The information in management's annual reports provides data for long-term trend analyses.

Financial Performance Measurement: Creditors' and Investors' Objectives

Creditors and investors use financial performance evaluation to judge a company's past performance and present position. They also use it to assess a company's future potential and the risk connected with acting on that potential. An investor focuses on a company's potential earnings ability because that ability will affect the market price of the company's stock and the amount of dividends the company will pay. A creditor focuses on the company's potential debt-paying ability.

Past performance is often a good indicator of future performance. To evaluate a company's past performance, creditors and investors look at trends in past sales, expenses, net income, cash flow, and return on investment. To evaluate its current position, they look at its assets, liabilities, cash position, debt in relation to equity, and levels of inventories and receivables. Knowing a company's past performance and current position can be important in judging its future potential and the related risk.

The risk involved in making an investment or loan depends on how easy it is to predict future profitability or liquidity. If an investor can predict with confidence that a company's earnings per share will be between $2.50 and $2.60 in the next year, the investment is less risky than if the earnings per share are expected to fall between $2.00 and $3.00. For example, the potential of an investment in an established electric utility company is relatively easy to predict on the basis of the company's past performance and current position. In contrast, the potential of an investment in a new Internet firm that has not yet established a record of earnings is very hard to predict. Investing in the Internet firm is therefore riskier than investing in the electric utility company.

In return for taking a greater risk, investors often look for a higher expected return (an increase in market price plus dividends). Creditors who take a greater risk by advancing funds to a company like the new Internet firm mentioned above may demand a higher interest rate and more assurance of repayment (a secured loan, for instance). The higher interest rate reimburses them for assuming the higher risk.

Standards of Comparison

When analyzing financial statements, decision makers must judge whether the relationships they find in the statements are favorable or unfavorable. Three standards of comparison that they commonly use are rule-of-thumb measures, a company's past performance, and industry norms.

Rule-of-Thumb Measures
Many financial analysts, investors, and lenders apply general standards, or rule-of-thumb measures, to key financial ratios. For example, most analysts today agree that a current ratio (current assets divided by current liabilities) of 2:1 is acceptable.

In its *Industry Norms and Key Business Ratios*, the credit-rating firm of Dun & Bradstreet offers such rules of thumb as the following:

> *Current debt to tangible net worth*: A business is usually in trouble when this relationship exceeds 80 percent.

> *Inventory to net working capital*: Ordinarily, this relationship should not exceed 80 percent.

Although rule-of thumb measures may suggest areas that need further investigation, there is no proof that the levels they specify apply to all companies. A company with a current ratio higher than 2:1 may have a poor credit policy (causing accounts receivable to be too large), too much inventory, or poor cash management. Another company may have a ratio lower than 2:1 but still have excellent management in all three of those areas. Thus, rule-of-thumb measures must be used with caution.

⌐⎯⎯) Study Note

Rules of thumb evolve and change as the business environment changes. Not long ago, an acceptable current ratio was higher than today's 2:1.

FOCUS ON BUSINESS PRACTICE

Take the Numbers with a Grain of Salt.

Traditionally, pro forma statements presented financial statements as they would appear after the occurrence of certain agreed-upon transactions, such as mergers or acquisitions. However, in recent years, companies have increasingly used pro forma statements as a way of presenting a better picture of their operations than would be the case in reports prepared under GAAP. According to a survey by the National Investor Relations Institute, 57 percent of companies across a range of industries use pro forma reporting.[2] In one quarter, Amazon.com reported a "pro forma operating" loss of $49 million and a "pro forma net" loss of $76 million; under GAAP, its net loss was $234 million. Pro forma statements, which are unaudited, have come to mean whatever a company's management wants them to mean. As a result, the SEC has issued new rules that prohibit companies from giving more prominence to non-GAAP measures and from using terms that are similar to GAAP measures. Although this helps, analysts should rely exclusively on financial statements that are prepared using GAAP and that are audited by an independent CPA.[3]

Past Performance   Comparing financial measures or ratios of the same company over time is an improvement over using rule-of-thumb measures. Such a comparison gives the analyst some basis for judging whether the measure or ratio is getting better or worse. Thus, it may be helpful in showing future trends. However, trends reverse at times, so such projections must be made with care.

Another problem with trend analysis is that past performance may not be enough to meet a company's present needs. For example, even though a company improves its return on investment from 3 percent in one year to 4 percent the next year, the 4 percent return may not be adequate for the company's current needs. In addition, using a company's past performance as a standard of comparison is not helpful in judging its performance relative to that of other companies.

Industry Norms   Using industry norms as a standard of comparison overcomes some of the limitations of comparing a company's measures or ratios over time. Industry norms show how a company compares with other companies in the same industry. For example, if companies in a particular industry have an average rate of return on investment of 8 percent, a 3 or 4 percent rate of return is probably not adequate. Industry norms can also be used to judge trends. Suppose that because of a downturn in the economy, a company's profit margin dropped from 12 percent to 10 percent, while the average drop in profit margin of other companies in the same industry was from 12 to 4 percent. By this standard, the company would have done relatively well. Sometimes, instead of industry averages, data for the industry leader or a specific competitor are used for analysis.

Using industry norms as standards has three limitations:

1. Companies in the same industry may not be strictly comparable. Consider two companies in the oil industry. One purchases oil products and markets them through service stations. The other, an international company, discovers, produces, refines, and markets its own oil products. Because of the disparity in their operations, these two companies cannot be directly compared.

2. Many large companies have multiple segments and operate in more than one industry. Some of these **diversified companies**, or *conglomerates*, oper-

EXHIBIT 1 ►

Selected Segment Information for Goodyear Tire & Rubber Company			
(In millions)	**2005**	**2004**	**2003**
Sales			
North American Tire	$ 9,091	$ 8,569	$ 7,279
European Union Tire	4,676	4,476	3,922
Eastern Europe, Africa, and Middle East Tire	1,437	1,279	1,073
Latin American Tire	1,466	1,245	1,041
Asia Tire	1,423	1,312	582
Total Tires	**18,093**	**16,881**	**13,897**
Engineered Products	1,630	1,472	1,205
Total Segment Sales	**19,723**	**18,353**	**15,102**
Income			
North American Tire	$ 167	$ 74	($ 103)
European Union Tire	317	253	130
Eastern Europe, Africa, and Middle East Tire	198	194	147
Latin American Tire	295	251	149
Asia Tire	84	60	49
Total Tires	**1,061**	**832**	**372**
Engineered Products	103	114	47
Total Segment Income	**1,164**	**946**	**419**
Assets*			
North American Tire	$ 5,438	$ 5,504	$ 5,494
European Union Tire	3,690	4,056	4,207
Eastern Europe, Africa, and Middle East Tire	1,227	1,315	1,103
Latin American Tire	900	846	710
Asia Tire	1,126	1,154	669
Total Tires	**12,381**	**12,875**	**12,183**
Engineered Products	799	764	681
Total Segment Assets	**13,180**	**13,639**	**12,864**

*2003 assets estimated.
Source: Goodyear Tire & Rubber Company, *Annual Report*, 2005.

> **Study Note**
>
> Each segment of a diversified company represents an investment that the home office or parent company evaluates and reviews frequently.

ate in many unrelated industries. The individual segments of a diversified company generally have different rates of profitability and different degrees of risk. In analyzing a diversified company's consolidated financial statements, it is often impossible to use industry norms as a standard because there simply are no comparable companies.

The FASB provides a partial solution to this problem. It requires diversified companies to report profit or loss, certain revenue and expense items, and assets for each of their segments. Segment information may be reported for operations in different industries or different geographical areas, or for major customers.[4] Exhibit 1 shows how **Goodyear Tire & Rubber Company** reports data on sales, income, and assets for its engineered

Shown here is Goodyear Tire & Rubber Company's polymer plant in Beaumont, Texas. The Beaumont plant is a major supplier of tire polymers and is part of Goodyear's North American Tire segment. The FASB requires diversified companies to report financial information for each of their segments. Goodyear has six segments in all.

products segment. These data allow the analyst to compute important profitability performance measures, such as profit margin, asset turnover, and return on assets, for each segment and to compare them with the appropriate industry norms.

3. Another limitation of industry norms is that even when companies in the same industry have similar operations, they may use different acceptable accounting procedures. For example, they may use different methods of valuing inventories and different methods of depreciating assets.

Despite these limitations, if little information about a company's past performance is available, industry norms probably offer the best available standards for judging current performance—as long as they are used with care.

Sources of Information

The major sources of information about public corporations are reports published by the corporations themselves, reports filed with the SEC, business periodicals, and credit and investment advisory services.

Reports Published by the Corporation   A public corporation's annual report is an important source of financial information. From a financial analyst's perspective, the main parts of an annual report are management's analysis of the past year's operations; the financial statements; the notes to the financial statements, which include a summary of significant accounting policies; the auditors' report; and financial highlights for a five- or ten-year period.

Most public corporations also publish **interim financial statements** each quarter and sometimes each month. These reports, which present limited information in the form of condensed financial statements, are not subject to a full audit by an independent auditor. The financial community watches interim statements closely for early signs of change in a company's earnings trend.

Reports Filed with the SEC Public corporations in the United States must file annual reports, quarterly reports, and current reports with the Securities and Exchange Commission (SEC). If they have more than $10 million in assets and more than 500 shareholders, they must file these reports electronically at www.sec.gov/edgar.shtml, where anyone can access them free of charge.

The SEC requires companies to file their annual reports on a standard form, called Form 10-K. Form 10-K contains more information than a company's annual report and is therefore a valuable source of information.

Companies file their quarterly reports with the SEC on Form 10-Q. This report presents important facts about interim financial performance.

The current report, filed on Form 8-K, must be submitted to the SEC within a few days of the date of certain significant events, such as the sale or purchase of a division or a change in auditors. The current report is often the first indicator of significant changes that will affect a company's financial performance in the future.

Business Periodicals and Credit and Investment Advisory Services Financial analysts must keep up with current events in the financial world. A leading source of financial news is *The Wall Street Journal*. It is the most complete financial newspaper in the United States and is published every business day. Useful periodicals that are published every week or every two weeks include *Forbes*, *Barron's*, *Fortune*, and the *Financial Times*.

Credit and investment advisory services also provide useful information. The publications of Moody's Investors Service and Standard & Poor's provide details about a company's financial history. Data on industry norms, average ratios, and credit ratings are available from agencies like Dun & Bradstreet. Dun & Bradstreet's *Industry Norms and Key Business Ratios* offers an annual analysis of 14 ratios for each of 125 industry groups, classified as retailing, wholesaling, manufacturing, and construction. *Annual Statement Studies*, published by Risk Management Association (formerly Robert Morris Associates), presents many facts and ratios for 223 different industries. The publications of a number of other agencies are also available for a yearly fee.

An example of specialized financial reporting readily available to the public is Mergent's *Handbook of Dividend Achievers*. It profiles companies that have increased their dividends consistently over the past ten years. A listing from that publication—for **PepsiCo Inc.**—is shown in Exhibit 2. As you can see, a wealth of information about the company, including the market action of its stock, its business operations, recent developments and prospects, and earnings and dividend data, is summarized on one page. We use the kind of data contained in Mergent's summaries in many of the analyses and ratios that we present later in this chapter.

Executive Compensation

As we noted earlier in the text, one intent of the Sarbanes-Oxley Act of 2002 was to strengthen the corporate governance of public corporations. Under this act, a public corporation's board of directors must establish a **compensation committee** made up of independent directors to determine how the company's top executives will be compensated. The company must disclose the components of compensation and the criteria it uses to remunerate top executives in

EXHIBIT 2 ▶ | **Listing from Mergent's Handbook of Dividend Achievers**

PEPSICO INC.

Exchange	Symbol	Price	52Wk Range	Yield	P/E
NYS	PEP	$58.24 (4/28/2006)	60.49-52.58	2.06	24.17

*7 Year Price Score 95.97   *NYSE Composite Index=100   *12 Month Price Score 95.25

Interim Earnings (Per Share)

Qtr.	Mar	Jun	Aug	Dec
2003	0.45	0.58	0.62	0.41
2004	0.46	0.61	0.79	0.58
2005	0.53	0.70	0.51	0.65
2006	0.60	...	...	...

Interim Dividends (Per Share)

Amt	Decl	Ex	Rec	Pay
0.26Q	7/22/2005	9/7/2005	9/9/2005	9/30/2005
0.26Q	11/18/2005	12/7/2005	12/9/2005	1/3/2006
0.26Q	2/3/2006	3/8/2006	3/10/2006	3/31/2006
0.30Q	5/3/2006	6/7/2006	6/9/2006	6/30/2006

Indicated Div: $1.20 (Div. Reinv. Plan)

Valuation Analysis

Forecast P/E   16.95 (5/31/2006)

Market Cap	$96.4 Billion	Book Value	14.8 Billion
Price/Book	6.51	Price/Sales	2.96

Dividend Achiever Status

Total Years of Dividend Growth   34

Business Summary: Food (MIC: 4.1 SIC: 2086 NAIC: 312111)

PepsiCo is a global snack and beverage company. Co. manufactures, markets and sells a variety of salty, convenient, sweet and grain-based snacks, carbonated and non-carbonated beverages and foods. Co.'s Frito-Lay North America division's brands include Lay's potato chips, Fritos corn chips, Quaker Chewy granola bars and Rold Gold pretzels. PepsiCo Beverages North America brands include Pepsi, Mountain Dew, Sierra Mist, Mug, SoBe, Gatorade, Tropicana Pure Premium and Propel. PepsiCo International brands include Sabritas in Mexico, Walkers in the UK, and Smith's in Australia. Quaker Foods North America's products include Quaker oatmeal and Cap'n Crunch and Life ready-to-eat cereals.

Recent Developments: For the twelve weeks ended Mar 25 2006, net income increased 11.7% to $1.02 billion compared with $912.0 million in the corresponding year-earlier period. Revenues were $7.21 billion, up 9.4% from $6.59 billion the year before. Operating income was $1.35 billion versus $1.25 billion in the prior-year quarter, an increase of 8.1%. Direct operating expenses rose 10.8% to $3.18 billion from $2.87 billion in the comparable period the year before. Indirect operating expenses increased 8.5% to $2.68 billion from $2.47 billion in the equivalent prior-year period.

Prospects: Co. continues to see strong revenue momentum across all its businesses, which is being driven by product innovation and strong marketplace execution. For instance, Co.'s net revenue in its Pepsico Beverages North America division is reflecting volume growth, a positive mix effect from the strong performance of its non-carbonated beverage portfolio, increased pricing, and the timing of concentrate shipments to bottlers. In addition, Co. is benefiting from solid profit performance despite continued pressure from inflation in some of its key input costs. Looking ahead to full-year 2006, Co. expects earnings of at least $2.93 per share.

Financial Data

(US$ in Thousands)	3 Mos	12/31/2005	12/25/2004	12/27/2003	12/28/2002	12/29/2001	12/30/2000	12/25/1999
Earnings Per Share	2.41	2.39	2.44	2.05	1.85	1.47	1.48	1.37
Cash Flow Per Share	3.16	3.45	2.99	2.53	2.65	2.39	2.66	2.07
Tang Book Value Per Share	5.50	5.20	4.84	3.82	4.93	2.17	1.91	1.47
Dividends Per Share	1.040	1.010	0.850	0.630	0.595	0.575	0.555	0.535
Dividend Payout %	43.15	42.26	34.84	30.73	32.16	39.12	37.50	39.05
Income Statement								
Total Revenue	7,205,000	32,562,000	29,261,000	26,971,000	25,112,000	26,935,000	20,438,000	20,367,000
EBITDA	1,718,000	7,732,000	6,848,000	6,269,000	6,077,000	5,189,000	4,209,000	4,843,000
Depn & Amortn	286,000	1,253,000	1,209,000	1,165,000	1,067,000	1,008,000	854,000	942,000
Income Before Taxes	1,415,000	6,382,000	5,546,000	4,992,000	4,868,000	4,029,000	3,210,000	3,656,000
Income Taxes	396,000	2,304,000	1,372,000	1,424,000	1,555,000	1,367,000	1,027,000	1,606,000
Net Income	1,019,000	4,078,000	4,212,000	3,568,000	3,313,000	2,662,000	2,183,000	2,050,000
Average Shares	1,695,000	1,706,000	1,729,000	1,739,000	1,789,000	1,807,000	1,475,000	1,496,000
Balance Sheet								
Current Assets	9,502,000	10,454,000	8,639,000	6,930,000	6,413,000	5,853,000	4,604,000	4,173,000
Total Assets	30,994,000	31,727,000	27,987,000	25,327,000	23,474,000	21,695,000	18,339,000	17,551,000
Current Liabilities	8,160,000	9,406,000	6,752,000	6,415,000	6,052,000	4,998,000	3,935,000	3,788,000
Long-Term Obligations	2,288,000	2,313,000	2,397,000	1,702,000	2,187,000	2,651,000	2,346,000	2,812,000
Total Liabilities	16,253,000	17,476,000	14,464,000	13,453,000	14,183,000	13,021,000	11,090,000	10,670,000
Stockholders' Equity	14,812,000	14,320,000	13,572,000	11,896,000	9,298,000	8,648,000	7,249,000	6,881,000
Shares Outstanding	1,656,000	1,656,000	1,679,000	1,705,000	1,722,000	1,756,000	1,446,000	1,455,000
Statistical Record								
Return on Assets %	13.74	13.44	15.84	14.66	14.71	13.34	11.97	10.22
Return on Equity %	28.49	28.77	33.17	33.76	37.02	33.58	30.40	30.95
EBITDA Margin %	23.84	23.75	23.40	23.24	24.20	19.26	20.59	23.78
Net Margin %	14.14	12.52	14.39	13.23	13.19	9.88	10.68	10.07
Asset Turnover	1.09	1.07	1.10	1.11	1.11	1.35	1.12	1.02
Current Ratio	1.16	1.11	1.28	1.08	1.06	1.17	1.17	1.10
Debt to Equity	0.15	0.16	0.18	0.14	0.24	0.31	0.32	0.41
Price Range	60.49-52.29	59.90-51.57	55.55-45.39	48.71-37.30	53.12-35.50	50.28-41.26	49.75-30.50	41.81-30.50
P/E Ratio	25.10-21.70	25.06-21.58	22.77-18.60	23.76-18.20	28.71-19.19	34.20-28.07	33.61-20.61	30.52-22.26
Average Yield %	1.83	1.82	1.66	1.43	1.29	1.25	1.36	1.46

Address: 700 Anderson Hill Road, Purchase, NY 10577-1444 **Telephone:** 914-253-2000 **Web Site:** www.pepsico.com	**Officers:** Steven S. Reinemund - Chmn., C.E.O. Indra K. Nooyi - Pres., C.F.O. **Transfer Agents:** The Bank of New York	**Investor Contact:** 914-253-3035 **No of Institutions:** 1209 **Shares:** 1,093,426,688 **% Held:** 66.17

Source: Listing from *Handbook of Dividend Achievers*, 2005. Reprinted by permission of Mergent.

documents that it files with the SEC. The components of **Starbucks'** compensation of executive officers are typical of those used by many companies:

- Annual base salary
- Incentive bonuses
- Stock option awards[5]

Incentive bonuses are based on performance measures that the compensation committee identifies as important to the company's long-term success. Many companies tie incentive bonuses to such measures as growth in revenues and return on assets, or return on equity. Starbucks bases 80 percent of its incentive bonus on an "earnings per share target approved by the compensation committee" and 20 percent on the executive's "specific individual performance." The Financial Highlights at the beginning of the chapter show the growth in the Starbucks' earnings per share.

Stock option awards are usually based on how well the company is achieving its long-term strategic goals. In 2005, a very good year for Starbucks, the company's CEO received a base salary of $1,190,000, an incentive bonus of an equal amount, and a stock option award of 200,000 shares of common stock.[6]

From one vantage point, earnings per share is a "bottom-line" number that encompasses all the other performance measures. However, using a single performance measure as the basis for determining compensation has the potential of leading to practices that are not in the best interests of the company or its stockholders. For instance, management could boost earnings per share by reducing the number of shares outstanding (the denominator in the earnings per share equation) while not improving earnings. It could accomplish this by using cash to repurchase shares of the company's stock (treasury stock), rather than investing the cash in more profitable operations. An understanding of the performance measures used in determining executive compensation and the factors that underlie them is critical in evaluating their fairness.

S T O P • R E V I E W • A P P L Y

1-1. How are the objectives of investors and creditors in using financial performance evaluation similar? How do they differ?

1-2. What role does risk play in making loans and investments?

1-3. What standards of comparison are commonly used to evaluate financial statements, and what are their relative merits?

1-4. Why would a financial analyst compare the ratios of Steelco, a steel company, with the ratios of other companies in the steel industry? What factors might invalidate such a comparison?

1-5. Where can investors find information about public corporations in which they are thinking of investing?

1-6. What is the role of a corporation's compensation committee, and what are three common components of executive compensation?

Suggested answers to all Stop, Review, and Apply questions are available at http://college.hmco.com/accounting/needles/poa/10e/student_home.html.

Performance Measurement Components Identify each of the following as (a) an objective of financial statement analysis, (b) a standard for financial statement analysis, (c) a source of information for financial statement analysis, or (d) an executive compensation issue:

1. A company's past performance
2. Investment advisory services
3. Assessment of a company's future potential
4. Incentive bonuses
5. Industry norms
6. Annual report
7. Creating shareholder value
8. Form 10-K

SOLUTION

1. b		5. b	
2. c		6. c	
3. a		7. d	
4. d		8. c	

Tools and Techniques of Financial Analysis

LO2 Apply horizontal analysis, trend analysis, vertical analysis, and ratio analysis to financial statements.

To gain insight into a company's financial performance, one must look beyond the individual numbers to the relationship between the numbers and their change from one period to another. The tools of financial analysis—horizontal analysis, trend analysis, vertical analysis, and ratio analysis—are intended to show these relationships and changes. To illustrate how these tools are used, we devote the rest of this chapter to a comprehensive financial analysis of **Starbucks Corporation**.

Horizontal Analysis

Study Note

It is important to ascertain the base amount used when a percentage describes an item. For example, inventory may be 50 percent of *total current assets* but only 10 percent of *total assets*.

Comparative financial statements provide financial information for the current year and the previous year. To gain insight into year-to-year changes, analysts use **horizontal analysis**, in which changes from the previous year to the current year are computed in both dollar amounts and percentages. The percentage change relates the size of the change to the size of the dollar amounts involved.

Exhibits 3 and 4 present **Starbuck Corporation's** comparative balance sheets and income statements and show both the dollar and percentage changes. The percentage change is computed as follows:

$$\text{Percentage Change} = 100 \times \left(\frac{\text{Amount of Change}}{\text{Base Year Amount}} \right)$$

The **base year** is always the first year to be considered in any set of data. For example, when comparing data for 2004 and 2005, 2004 is the base year. As the balance sheets in Exhibit 3 show, between 2004 and 2005, Starbucks' total current assets decreased by $141,561 thousand, from $1,350,895 thousand to $1,209,334 thousand, or by 10.5 percent. This is computed as follows:

$$\text{Percentage Change} = 100 \times \left(\frac{\$141,561 \text{ thousand}}{\$1,350,895 \text{ thousand}} \right) = 10.5\%$$

▼ **EXHIBIT 3**

Comparative Balance Sheets with Horizontal Analysis

Starbucks Corporation
Consolidated Balance Sheets
October 2, 2005 and October 3, 2004

(Dollar amounts in thousands)	2005	2004	Increase (Decrease) Amount	Percentage
Assets				
Current assets:				
Cash and cash equivalents	$ 173,809	$ 145,053	$ 28,756	19.8
Short-term investments	133,227	507,956	(374,729)	(73.8)
Accounts receivable, net of allowances of $3,079 and $2,231, respectively	190,762	140,226	50,536	36.0
Inventories	546,299	422,663	123,636	29.3
Prepaid expenses and other current assets	94,429	71,347	23,082	32.4
Deferred income taxes, net	70,808	63,650	7,158	11.2
Total current assets	$1,209,334	$1,350,895	$(141,561)	(10.5)
Long-term investments	261,936	302,919	(40,983)	(13.5)
Property, plant, and equipment, net	1,842,019	1,551,416	290,603	18.7
Other assets	72,893	85,561	(12,668)	(14.8)
Other intangible assets	35,409	26,800	8,609	32.1
Goodwill	92,474	68,950	23,524	34.1
Total assets	$3,514,065	$3,386,541	$127,524	3.8
Liabilities and Shareholders' Equity				
Current liabilities:				
Accounts payable	$ 220,975	$ 199,346	$ 21,629	10.8
Accrued compensation and related costs	232,354	208,927	23,427	11.2
Accrued occupancy costs	44,496	29,231	15,265	52.2
Accrued taxes	78,293	62,959	15,334	24.4
Short-term borrowings	277,000	—	277,000	N/A
Other accrued expenses	198,082	123,684	74,398	60.2
Deferred revenue	175,048	121,377	53,671	44.2
Current portion of long-term debt	748	735	13	1.8
Total current liabilities	$1,226,996	$ 746,259	$480,737	64.4
Deferred income taxes, net	—	21,770	(21,770)	(100.0)
Long-term debt	2,870	3,618	(748)	(20.7)
Other long-term liabilities	193,565	144,683	48,882	33.8
Shareholders' equity	2,090,634	2,470,211	(379,577)	(15.4)
Total liabilities and shareholders' equity	$3,514,065	$3,386,541	$127,524	3.8

Source: Data from Starbucks Corporation, 10K, 2005.

▼ **EXHIBIT 4**

Comparative Income Statements with Horizontal Analysis

Starbucks Corporation
Consolidated Income Statements
For the Years Ended October 2, 2005, and October 3, 2004

(Dollar amounts in thousands, except per share amounts)	2005	2004	Increase (Decrease) Amount	Percentage
Net revenues	$6,369,300	$5,294,247	$1,075,053	20.3
Cost of sales, including occupancy costs	2,605,212	2,191,440	413,772	18.9
Gross margin	$3,764,088	$3,102,807	$ 661,281	21.3
Operating expenses				
Store operating expenses	$2,165,911	$1,790,168	$ 375,743	21.0
Other operating expenses	197,024	171,648	25,376	14.8
Depreciation and amortization expenses	340,169	289,182	50,987	17.6
General and administrative expenses	357,114	304,293	52,821	17.4
Total operating expenses	$3,060,218	$2,555,291	$ 504,927	19.8
Operating income	$ 703,870	$ 547,516	$ 156,354	28.6
Other income, net	92,574	73,211	19,363	26.4
Earnings before income taxes	$ 796,444	$ 620,727	$ 175,717	28.3
Income taxes	301,977	231,754	70,223	30.3
Net earnings	$ 494,467	$ 388,973	$ 105,494	27.1
Net earnings per common share—basic	$ 0.63	$ 0.49	$ 0.14	28.6
Net earnings per common share—diluted	$ 0.61	$ 0.47	$ 0.14	29.8
Shares used in calculation of net earnings per common share—basic	789,570	794,347	(4,777)	(0.6)
Shares used in calculation of net earnings per common share—diluted	815,417	822,930	(7,513)	(0.9)

Source: Data from Starbucks Corporation, 10K, 2005.

When examining such changes, it is important to consider the dollar amount of the change as well as the percentage change in each component. For example, the percentage increase in prepaid expenses and other current assets (32.4 percent) is slightly greater than the increase in inventories (29.3 percent). However, the dollar increase in inventories is more than five times the dollar increase in prepaid expenses and other current assets ($123,636 thousand versus $23,082 thousand). Thus, even though the percentage changes differ by only 3.1 percent, inventories require much more investment.

Starbucks' balance sheets for this period, illustrated in Exhibit 3, also show an increase in total assets of $127,524 thousand, or 3.8 percent. This reflects an increase of property, plant, and equipment, net, of $290,603 thousand, or 18.7 percent, while short-term investments decreased by $374,729 thousand, or 73.8 percent. Starbucks is redeploying its assets for growth. In addition, shareholders' equity decreased by $379,577 thousand, or 15.4 percent. Starbucks' equity declined despite an increase in retained earnings because the company repurchased its common stock during the period.

Starbucks' income statements in Exhibit 4 show that net revenues increased by $1,075,053 thousand, or 20.3 percent, while gross margin increased by $661,281 thousand, or 21.3 percent. This indicates that cost of sales did not grow faster than net revenues. In fact, cost of sales increased only 18.9 percent compared with the 20.3 percent increase in net revenues.

Starbucks' total operating expenses increased by $504,927 thousand, or 19.8 percent, also not as fast as the 20.3 percent increase in net revenues. As a result, operating income increased by $156,354 thousand, or 28.6 percent, and net income increased by $105,494 thousand, or 27.1 percent. The primary reason for the increases in operating income and net income is that total cost of sales and operating expenses increased at a slower rate (18.9 and 19.8 percent, respectively) than net revenues (20.3 percent).

Trend Analysis

Trend analysis is a variation of horizontal analysis. With this tool, the analyst calculates percentage changes for several successive years instead of for just two years. Because of its long-term view, trend analysis can highlight basic changes in the nature of a business.

Many companies present a summary of key data for five or more years in their annual reports. Exhibit 5 shows a trend analysis of **Starbucks'** five-year summary of net revenues and operating income.

Trend analysis uses an **index number** to show changes in related items over time. For an index number, the base year is set at 100 percent. Other years are measured in relation to that amount. For example, the 2005 index for Starbucks' net revenues is figured as follows (dollar amounts are in thousands):

$$\text{Index} = 100 \times \left(\frac{\text{Index Year Amount}}{\text{Base Year Amount}}\right)$$

$$= 100 \times \left(\frac{\$6,369,300}{\$2,648,980}\right) = 240.4\%$$

The trend analysis in Exhibit 5 shows that Starbucks' net revenues increased over the five-year period, as did operating income. Overall, revenue grew 240.4 percent, while operating income grew 278.8 percent. The percentage changes reveal that Starbucks' management has the ability to control its costs while growing the revenue, resulting in faster growth in operating income. Figure 1 illustrates these trends.

> **Study Note**
>
> To reflect the general five-year economic cycle of the U.S. economy, trend analysis usually covers a five-year period. Cycles of other lengths exist and are tracked by the National Bureau of Economic Research. Trend analysis needs to be of sufficient length to show a company's performance in both up and down markets.

EXHIBIT 5 ▶

Trend Analysis

Starbucks Corporation
Net Revenues and Operating Income
Trend Analysis

	2005	2004	2003	2002	2001
Dollar values (In thousands)					
Net revenues	$6,369,300	$5,294,247	$4,075,522	$3,288,908	$2,648,980
Operating income*	703,870	547,516	383,947	282,893	252,479
Trend analysis (In percentages)					
Net revenues	240.4	199.9	153.9	124.2	100.0
Operating income*	278.8	216.9	152.1	112.0	100.0

*Excludes income from equity investees.
Source: Data from Starbucks Corporation, 10K, 2005.

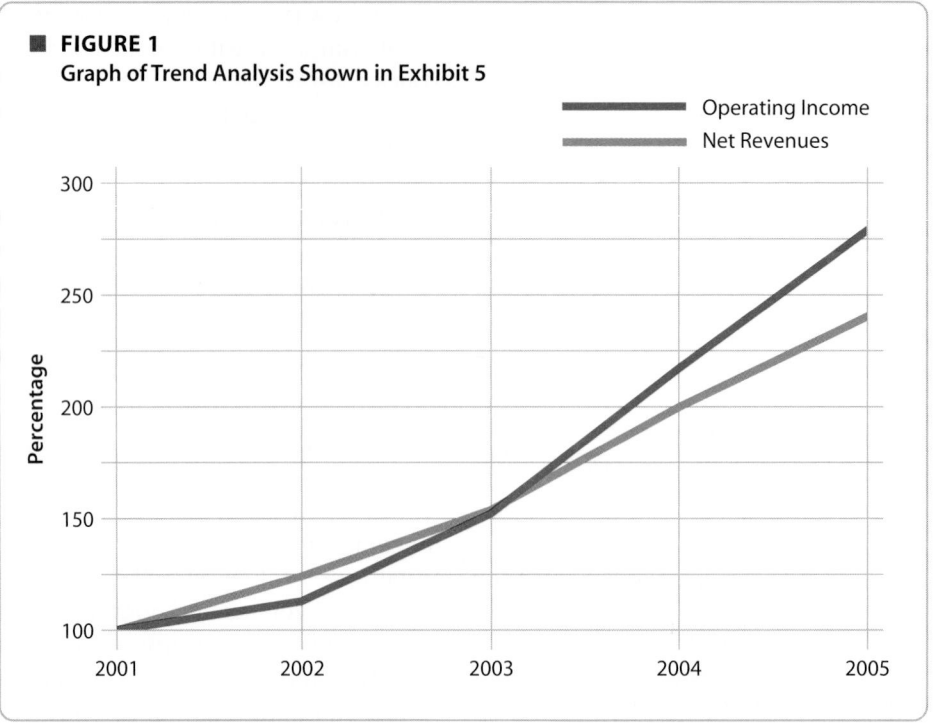

■ **FIGURE 1**
Graph of Trend Analysis Shown in Exhibit 5

Vertical Analysis

Vertical analysis shows how the different components of a financial statement relate to a total figure in the statement. The analyst sets the total figure at 100 percent and computes each component's percentage of that total. (On the balance sheet, the figure would be total assets or total liabilities and stockholders' equity, and on the income statement, it would be net revenues or net sales.) The resulting financial statement, which is expressed entirely in percentages, is called a **common-size statement**. Common-size balance sheets and common-size income statements for **Starbucks Corporation** are shown in pie-chart form in Figures 2 and 3 and in financial statement form in Exhibits 6 and 7.

Vertical analysis and common-size statements are useful in comparing the importance of specific components in the operation of a business and in identifying important changes in the components from one year to the next. The main conclusions to be drawn from our analysis of Starbucks are that the company's assets consist largely of current assets and property, plant, and equipment; that the company finances assets primarily through equity and current liabilities; and that it has few long-term liabilities.

Looking at the pie charts in Figure 2 and the common-size balance sheets in Exhibit 6, you can see that the composition of Starbucks' assets shifted from property, plant, and equipment to current assets. You can also see that the relationship of liabilities and equity shifted slightly from stockholders' equity to current liabilities.

The common-size income statements in Exhibit 7, illustrated in Figure 3, show that Starbucks reduced its operating expenses from 2004 to 2005 by 0.3 percent of revenues (48.3% − 48.0%). In other words, operating expenses did not grow as fast as revenues.

Common-size statements are often used to make comparisons between companies. They allow an analyst to compare the operating and financing characteristics of two companies of different size in the same industry. For example, the analyst might want to compare Starbucks with other specialty

■ **FIGURE 2**
Common-Size Balance Sheets Presented Graphically

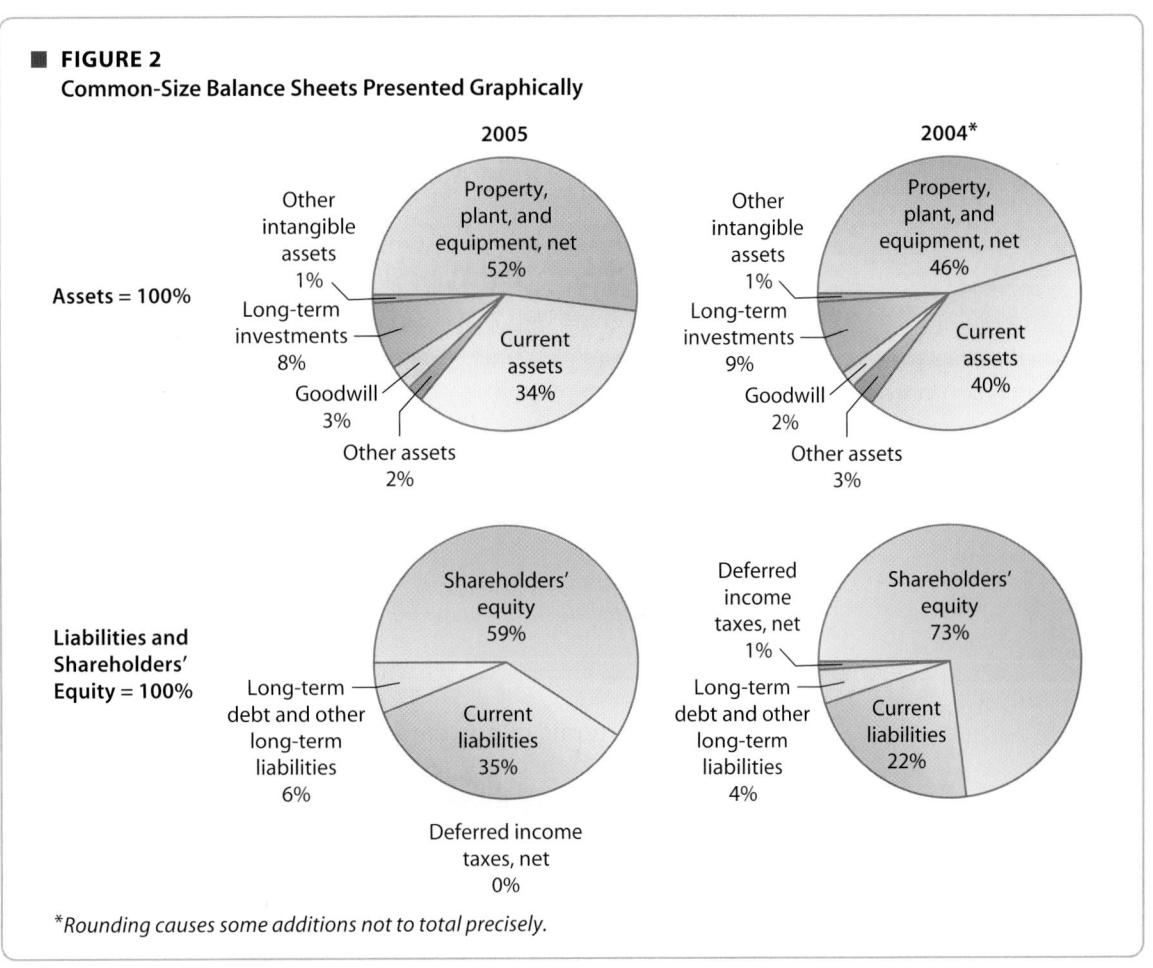

Rounding causes some additions not to total precisely.

EXHIBIT 6 ▶

Common-Size Balance Sheets

Starbucks Corporation
Common-Size Balance Sheets
October 2, 2005, and October 3, 2004

	2005	2004
Assets		
Current assets	34.4%	39.9%
Property, plant, and equipment, net	52.4	45.8
Long-term investments	7.5	8.9
Other assets	2.1	2.5
Goodwill	2.6	2.0
Other intangible assets	1.0	0.8
Total assets	100.0%	100.0%
Liabilities and Shareholders' Equity		
Current liabilities	34.9%	22.0%
Deferred income taxes, net	—	0.6
Long-term debt and other long-term liabilities	5.6	4.4
Shareholders' equity	59.5	72.9
Total liabilities and shareholders' equity	100.0%	100.0%

Source: Data from Starbucks Corporation, 10K, 2005.

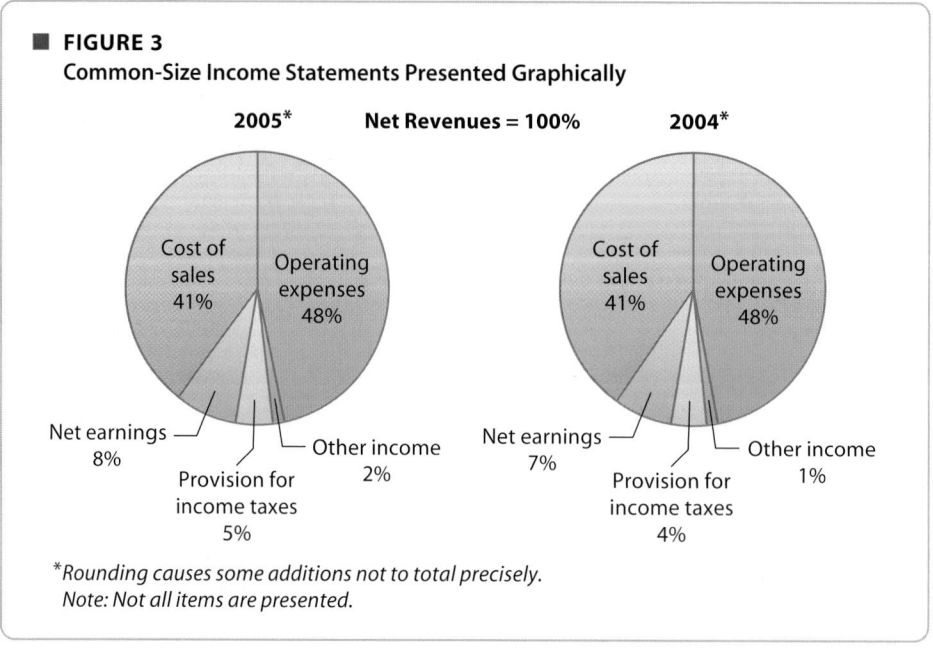

■ **FIGURE 3**
Common-Size Income Statements Presented Graphically

*Rounding causes some additions not to total precisely.
Note: Not all items are presented.*

retailers in terms of percentage of total assets financed by debt or in terms of operating expenses as a percentage of net revenues. Common-size statements would show those and other relationships. These statements can also be used to compare the characteristics of companies that report in different currencies.

EXHIBIT 7 ▶

Common-Size Income Statements

**Starbucks Corporation
Common-Size Income Statements
For the Years Ended October 2, 2005, and October 3, 2004**

	2005	2004
Net revenues	100.0%	100.0%
Cost of sales, including occupancy costs	40.9	41.4
Gross margin	59.1%	58.6%
Operating expenses		
Store operating expenses	34.0%	33.8%
Other operating expenses	3.1	3.2
Depreciation and amortization expenses	5.3	5.5
General and administrative expenses	5.6	5.7
Total operating expenses	48.0%	48.3%
Operating income	11.1%	10.3%
Other income, net	1.5	1.4
Earnings before income taxes	12.5%	11.7%
Income taxes	4.7	4.4
Net earnings	7.8%	7.3%

Note: Amounts do not precisely total 100 percent in all cases due to rounding.
Source: Data from Starbucks Corporation, 10K, 2005.

Ratio Analysis

Ratio analysis is an evaluation technique that identifies key relationships between the components of the financial statements. Ratios are useful tools for evaluating a company's financial position and operations and may reveal areas that need further investigation. To interpret ratios correctly, the analyst must have a general understanding of the company and its environment, financial data for several years or for several companies, and an understanding of the data underlying the numerator and denominator.

Ratios can be expressed in several ways. For example, a ratio of net income of $100,000 to sales of $1,000,000 can be stated as follows:

1. Net income is 1/10, or 10 percent, of sales.

2. The ratio of sales to net income is 10 to 1 (10:1), or sales are 10 times net income.

3. For every dollar of sales, the company has an average net income of 10 cents.

STOP • REVIEW • APPLY

2-1. Why would an investor want to see both horizontal and trend analyses of a company's financial statements?

2-2. What does this sentence mean: "Based on a 1990 index equaling 100, net income increased from 240 in 2000 to 260 in 2001"?

2-3. What is the difference between horizontal and vertical analysis?

2-4. What is the purpose of ratio analysis?

Comprehensive Illustration of Ratio Analysis

LO3   Apply ratio analysis to financial statements in a comprehensive evaluation of a company's financial performance.

In this section, to illustrate how analysts use ratio analysis in evaluating a company's financial performance, we perform a comprehensive ratio analysis of **Starbucks'** performance in 2004 and 2005. The following excerpt from the discussion and analysis section of Starbucks' 2005 annual report provides the context for our evaluation of the company's liquidity, profitability, long-term solvency, cash flow adequacy, and market strength:

> During the fiscal year ended October 2, 2005, all areas of Starbucks business, from U.S. and International Company-operated retail operations to the Company's specialty businesses, delivered strong financial performance. Starbucks believes the Company's ability to achieve the balance between growing the core business and building the foundation for future growth is the key to increasing long-term shareholder value. Starbucks fiscal 2005 performance reflects the Company's continuing commitment to achieving this balance.

Evaluating Liquidity

%/R

As you know, liquidity is a company's ability to pay bills when they are due and to meet unexpected needs for cash. Because debts are paid out of working capital, all liquidity ratios involve working capital or some part of it. (Cash flow ratios are also closely related to liquidity.)

Exhibit 8 presents **Starbucks'** liquidity ratios in 2004 and 2005. The **current ratio** and the **quick ratio** are measures of short-term debt-paying ability. The principal difference between the two ratios is that the numerator of the current ratio includes inventories and prepaid expenses. Inventories take longer to convert to cash than the current assets included in the numerator of the quick ratio. Starbucks' quick ratio was 1.1 times in 2004 and decreased to 0.4 times in 2005, primarily because of the more than $374 million decrease in short-term investments (marketable securities). Its current ratio was 1.8 times in 2004 and 1.0 in 2005. From 2004 to 2005, its current assets decreased $141,561 thousand due to the decline in short-term investments. At the same time, current liabilities increased, primarily because of new, short-term borrowing of $277,000 thousand.

Starbucks' management of receivables and inventories worsened from 2004 to 2005. The **receivable turnover**, which measures the relative size of accounts receivable and the effectiveness of credit policies, fell from 41.6 times in 2004 to 38.5 times in 2005. The related ratio of **days' sales uncollected** increased by almost one day, from 8.8 days in 2004 to 9.5 days in 2005. The number of days is quite low because the majority of Starbucks' revenues are from cash sales. The **inventory turnover**, which measures the relative size of inventories, decreased from 5.7 times in 2004 to 5.4 times in 2005. This resulted in almost a four-day increase in **days' inventory on hand**, from 64.0 days in 2004 to 67.6 days in 2005.

Starbucks' **operating cycle**, or the time it takes to sell products and collect for them, increased from 72.8 days in 2004 (8.8 days + 64.0 days, or the days' sales uncollected plus the days' inventory on hand) to 77.1 days in 2005 (9.5 days + 67.6 days). Related to the operating cycle is the number of days a company takes to pay its accounts payable. Starbucks' **payables turnover** increased from 12.3 times in 2004 to 13.0 times in 2005. This resulted in **days' payable** of 29.7 days in 2004 and 28.1 days in 2005. If the days' payable is subtracted from the operating cycle, Starbucks' financing period—the number of days of financing required—was 43.1 days in 2004 and 49.0 days in 2005 (see Figure 4). Overall, Starbucks' liquidity declined.

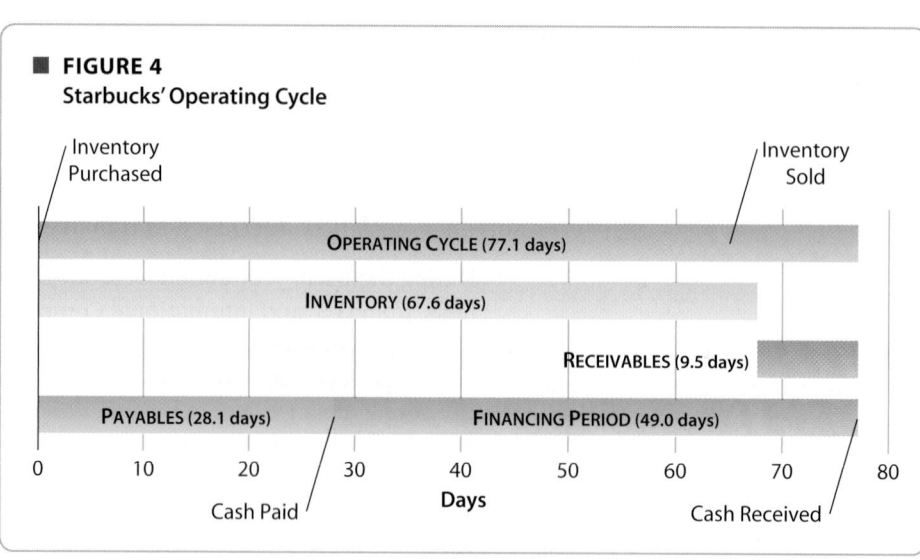

■ **FIGURE 4**
Starbucks' Operating Cycle

▼ **EXHIBIT 8**

Liquidity Ratios of Starbucks Corporation

(Dollar amounts in thousands)	2005	2004

Current ratio: Measure of short-term debt-paying ability

$$\frac{\text{Current Assets}}{\text{Current Liabilities}} \qquad \frac{\$1,209,334}{\$1,226,996} = 1.0 \text{ times} \qquad \frac{\$1,350,895}{\$746,259} = 1.8 \text{ times}$$

Quick ratio: Measure of short-term debt-paying ability

$$\frac{\text{Cash + Short-Term Investments + Receivables}}{\text{Current Liabilities}} \qquad \frac{\$173,809 + \$133,227 + \$190,762}{\$1,226,996} \qquad \frac{\$145,053 + \$507,956 + \$140,226}{\$746,259}$$

$$= \frac{\$497,798}{\$1,226,996} = 0.4 \text{ times} \qquad = \frac{\$793,235}{\$746,259} = 1.1 \text{ times}$$

Receivable turnover: Measure of relative size of accounts receivable and effectiveness of credit policies

$$\frac{\text{Net Revenue}}{\text{Average Accounts Receivable}} \qquad \frac{\$6,369,300}{(\$190,762 + \$140,226) \div 2} \qquad \frac{\$5,294,247}{(\$140,226 + \$114,448^*) \div 2}$$

$$= \frac{\$6,369,300}{\$165,494} = 38.5 \text{ times} \qquad = \frac{\$5,294,247}{\$127,337} = 41.6 \text{ times}$$

Days' sales uncollected: Measure of average days taken to collect receivables

$$\frac{\text{Days in Year}}{\text{Receivable Turnover}} \qquad \frac{365 \text{ days}}{38.5 \text{ times}} = 9.5 \text{ days} \qquad \frac{365 \text{ days}}{41.6 \text{ times}} = 8.8 \text{ days}$$

Inventory turnover: Measure of relative size of inventory

$$\frac{\text{Costs of Sales}}{\text{Average Inventory}} \qquad \frac{\$2,605,212}{(\$546,299 + \$422,663) \div 2} \qquad \frac{\$2,191,440}{(\$422,663 + \$342,944^*) \div 2}$$

$$= \frac{\$2,605,212}{\$484,481} = 5.4 \text{ times} \qquad = \frac{\$2,191,440}{\$382,804} = 5.7 \text{ times}$$

Days' inventory on hand: Measure of average days taken to sell inventory

$$\frac{\text{Days in Year}}{\text{Inventory Turnover}} \qquad \frac{365 \text{ days}}{5.4 \text{ times}} = 67.6 \text{ days} \qquad \frac{365 \text{ days}}{5.7 \text{ times}} = 64.0 \text{ days}$$

Payables turnover: Measure of relative size of accounts payable

$$\frac{\text{Costs of Sales +/- Change in Inventory}}{\text{Average Accounts Payable}} \qquad \frac{\$2,605,212 + \$123,636}{(\$220,975 + \$199,346) \div 2} \qquad \frac{\$2,191,440 + \$79,719^*}{(\$199,346 + \$168,984^*) \div 2}$$

$$= \frac{\$2,728,848}{\$210,161} = 13.0 \text{ times} \qquad = \frac{\$2,271,159}{\$184,165} = 12.3 \text{ times}$$

Days' payable: Measure of average days taken to pay accounts payable

$$\frac{\text{Days in Year}}{\text{Payables Turnover}} \qquad \frac{365 \text{ days}}{13.0 \text{ times}} = 28.1 \text{ days} \qquad \frac{365 \text{ days}}{12.3 \text{ times}} = 29.7 \text{ days}$$

*Figures for 2003 are from the balance sheet in Starbucks' 10K of 2004.
Source: Data from Starbucks Corporation, 10K, 2005; 10K, 2004.

Efforts to link management compensation to performance measures and the creation of shareholder wealth are increasing. **Starbucks** uses earnings per share (EPS) for this purpose. Some other companies, including **Target Corporation**, use a concept called economic value added (EVA).[7] This measure, which many analysts feel is superior to EPS, compares the company's return on assets with its cost of debt and equity capital. If the return on assets exceeds the cost of financing the assets with debt and equity, then management is indeed creating value for the

Evaluating Profitability

Investors and creditors are interested in evaluating not only a company's liquidity, but also its profitability—that is, its ability to earn a satisfactory income. Profitability is closely linked to liquidity because earnings ultimately produce the cash flow needed for liquidity. Exhibit 9 shows **Starbucks'** profitability ratios in 2004 and 2005.

Profit margin measures how well a company manages its costs per dollar of sales. Starbucks' profit margin increased from 7.3 to 7.8 percent between 2004 and 2005. Its **asset turnover**, which measures how efficiently assets are used to produce sales (or net revenues), increased from 1.7 to 1.8 times. The result is an increase in the company's earning power, or **return on assets**, from 12.6 percent in 2004 to 14.3 percent in 2005. These computations show the relationships (the small difference in the two sets of return on assets figures results from the rounding of the ratios):

Profit Margin		*Asset Turnover*		*Return on Assets*
$\dfrac{\text{Net Income}}{\text{Net Sales}}$	$\times$	$\dfrac{\text{Net Sales}}{\text{Average Total Assets}}$	$=$	$\dfrac{\text{Net Income}}{\text{Average Total Assets}}$
2004 7.3%	$\times$	1.7	$=$	12.4%
2005 7.8%	$\times$	1.8	$=$	14.0%

> **Study Note**
>
> In accounting literature, *profit* is expressed in different ways—for example, as income before income taxes, income after income taxes, or operating income. To draw appropriate conclusions from profitability ratios, analysts must be aware of the content of net income data.

In addition to using EVA (economic value added) to determine executive compensation, Target uses it to guide capital investment decisions. The company uses a benchmark of 9 percent for the estimated after-tax cost of capital invested in retail operations and a benchmark of 5 percent for capital invested in credit card operations. Target believes that a focus on EVA fosters its objective of increasing average annual earnings per share by 15 percent or more over time.

▼ EXHIBIT 9

Profitability Ratios of Starbucks Corporation

(Dollar amounts in thousands)	2005	2004

Profit margin: Measure of net income produced by each dollar of sales

$$\frac{\text{Net Income}}{\text{Net Sales}} \qquad \frac{\$494,467}{\$6,369,300} = 7.8\% \qquad \frac{\$388,973}{\$5,294,247} = 7.3\%$$

Asset turnover: Measure of how efficiently assets are used to produce sales

$$\frac{\text{Net Sales}}{\text{Average Total Assets}} \qquad \frac{\$6,369,300}{(\$3,514,065 + \$3,386,541) \div 2} \qquad \frac{\$5,294,247}{(\$3,386,541 + \$2,776,112^*) \div 2}$$

$$= \frac{\$6,369,300}{\$3,450,303} = 1.8 \text{ times} \qquad = \frac{\$5,294,247}{\$3,081,327} = 1.7 \text{ times}$$

Return on assets: Measure of overall earning power or profitability

$$\frac{\text{Net Income}}{\text{Average Total Assets}} \qquad \frac{\$494,467}{\$3,450,303} = 14.3\% \qquad \frac{\$388,973}{\$3,081,327} = 12.6\%$$

Return on equity: Measure of the profitability of stockholders' investments

$$\frac{\text{Net Income}}{\text{Average Stockholders' Equity}} \qquad \frac{\$494,467}{(\$2,090,634 + \$2,470,211) \div 2} \qquad \frac{\$388,973}{(\$2,470,211 + \$2,068,689^*) \div 2}$$

$$= \frac{\$494,467}{\$2,280,423} = 21.7\% \qquad = \frac{\$388,973}{\$2,269,450} = 17.1\%$$

*Figures for 2003 are from the five-year selected financial data in Starbucks' 10K of 2004.
Source: Data from Starbucks Corporation, 10K, 2005; 10K, 2004.

Study Note

The analysis of both asset turnover and return on assets is improved if only productive assets are used in the calculations. For example, when investments in unfinished new plant construction or in plants that are now obsolete or nonoperating are removed from the asset base, the result is a better picture of the productivity of assets.

Starbucks' **return on equity** also improved, from 17.1 percent in 2004 to 21.7 percent in 2005 due to stock repurchases during 2005.

Although we have used net income in computing profitability ratios for Starbucks, net income is not always a good indicator of a company's sustainable earnings. For instance, if a company has discontinued operations, income from continuing operations may be a better measure of sustainable earnings. For a company that has one-time items on its income statement—such as restructurings, gains, or losses—income from operations before these items may be a better measure. Some analysts like to use earnings before interest and taxes, or EBIT, for the earnings measure because it excludes the effects of the company's borrowings and the tax rates from the analysis. Whatever figure one uses for earnings, it is important to try to determine the effects of various components on future operations.

Evaluating Long-term Solvency

Long-term solvency has to do with a company's ability to survive for many years. The aim of evaluating long-term solvency is to detect early signs that a company is headed for financial difficulty. Increasing amounts of debt in a company's capital structure mean that the company is becoming more heavily leveraged. This condition has a negative effect on long-term solvency because it represents increasing legal obligations to pay interest periodically and the principal at maturity. Failure to make those payments can result in bankruptcy.

Declining profitability and liquidity ratios are key indicators of possible failure. Two other ratios that analysts consider when assessing long-term solvency are debt to equity and interest coverage, which are shown in Exhibit 10.

▼ **EXHIBIT 10**

Long-term Solvency Ratios of Starbucks Corporation		
(Dollar amounts in thousands)	**2005**	**2004**

Debt to equity ratio: Measure of capital structure and leverage

$$\frac{\text{Total Liabilities}}{\text{Stockholders' Equity}} \qquad \frac{\$1,423,431}{\$2,090,634} = .7 \text{ times} \qquad \frac{\$916,330}{\$2,470,211} = .4 \text{ times}$$

Interest coverage ratio: Measure of creditors' protection from default on interest payments

$$\frac{\text{Income Before Income Taxes } + \text{ Interest Expense}}{\text{Interest Expense}} \qquad \text{[Starbucks does not report interest expense]}$$

Source: Data from Starbucks Corporation, *Annual Report,* 2005.

 **Study Note**

Liquidity is a firm's ability to meet its current obligations; solvency is its ability to meet maturing obligations as they come due without losing the ability to continue operations.

 **Study Note**

Because of innovative financing plans and other means of acquiring assets, lease payments and similar types of fixed obligations should be considered when evaluating long-term solvency.

The **debt to equity ratio** measures capital structure and leverage by showing the amount of a company's assets provided by creditors in relation to the amount provided by stockholders. **Starbucks'** debt to equity ratio was at .4 times in 2004 and .7 times in 2005. Recall from Exhibit 3 that the company increased most of its liabilites from 2004 to 2005, while equity decreased. Although moving toward higher financial risk in absolute terms, Starbucks' long-term solvency is still strong.

If debt is risky, why have any? The answer is that the level of debt is a matter of balance. Despite its riskiness, debt is a flexible means of financing certain business operations. The interest paid on debt is tax-deductible, whereas dividends on stock are not. Because debt usually carries a fixed interest charge, the cost of financing can be limited, and leverage can be used to advantage. If a company can earn a return on assets greater than the cost of interest, it makes an overall profit. In addition, being a debtor in periods of inflation has advantages because the debt, which is a fixed dollar amount, can be repaid with cheaper dollars. However, the company runs the risk of not earning a return on assets equal to the cost of financing the assets, thereby incurring a loss.

The **interest coverage ratio** measures the degree of protection creditors have from default on interest payments. The amount of interest that Starbucks expensed is quite small. In such cases, the resulting interest coverage ratio is not meaningful. However, given Starbucks' improving profitability, its interest-paying ability is very strong.

Evaluating the Adequacy of Cash Flows

 ©/®

Because cash flows are needed to pay debts when they are due, cash flow measures are closely related to liquidity and long-term solvency. Exhibit 11 presents **Starbucks'** cash flow adequacy ratios in 2004 and 2005.

Cash flow yield shows the cash-generating ability of a company's operations; it is measured by dividing cash flows from operating activities by net income. Starbucks' net cash flows from operating activities increased from $858,537 thousand in 2004 to $923,608 thousand in 2005. Its cash flow yield actually decreased from 2.2 to 1.9 times, revealing that net income increased faster than net cash provided by operating activities. The primary reasons for this result are the increase in inventories consuming cash of $121,618 in 2005 compared with $77,662 in 2004 and the increase in accounts receivables of $49,311 in 2005 (representing revenue recorded but cash not yet received) compared with $24,977 in 2004.

▼ **EXHIBIT 11**

Cash Flow Adequacy Ratios of Starbucks Corporation		
(Dollar amounts in thousands)	**2005**	**2004**

Cash flow yield: Measure of the ability to generate operating cash flows in relation to net income

$$\frac{\text{Net Cash Flows from Operating Activities}}{\text{Net Income}} \quad \frac{\$923,608^*}{\$494,467} = 1.9 \text{ times} \quad \frac{\$858,537^*}{\$388,973} = 2.2 \text{ times}$$

Cash flows to sales: Measure of the ability of sales to generate operating cash flows

$$\frac{\text{Net Cash Flows from Operating Activities}}{\text{Net Sales}} \quad \frac{\$923,608}{\$6,369,300} = 14.5\% \quad \frac{\$858,537}{\$5,294,247} = 16.2\%$$

Cash flows to assets: Measure of the ability of assets to generate operating cash flows

$$\frac{\text{Net Cash Flows from Operating Activities}}{\text{Average Total Assets}} \quad \frac{\$923,608}{(\$3,514,065 + \$3,386,541) \div 2} \quad \frac{\$858,537}{(\$3,386,541 + \$2,776,112^\dagger) \div 2}$$

$$= \frac{\$923,608}{\$3,450,303} = 26.8\% \quad = \frac{\$858,537}{\$3,081,327} = 27.9\%$$

Free cash flow: Measure of cash remaining after providing for commitments

Net Cash Flows from Operating Activities − Dividends − Net Capital Expenditures

$$\$923,608 - \$0 - \$643,989^* \qquad \$858,537^* - \$0 - \$412,537^*$$
$$= \$279,619 \qquad\qquad = \$446,000$$

*These figures are from the statement of cash flows in Starbucks' 10K of 2005.
†The 2003 figure is from the five-year selected financial data in Starbucks' 10K of 2004.
Source: Data from Starbucks Corporation, 10K, 2005; 10K, 2004.

 Study Note

When the computation for free cash flow uses "net capital expenditures" in place of "purchases of plant assets minus sales of plant assets," it means that the company's sales of plant assets were too small or immaterial to be broken out.

Starbucks' ratios for cash flows to sales and cash flows to assets also declined. While the company's net sales and average total assets increased, the cash flows provided by its operations did not increase as fast. **Cash flows to sales**, or the cash-generating ability of sales, decreased from 16.2 to 14.5 percent. **Cash flows to assets**, or the ability of assets to generate operating cash flows, decreased from 27.9 to 26.8 percent.

Starbucks' **free cash flow**, the cash remaining after providing for commitments, also decreased. While the company's net capital expenditures increased by over $231 million, the net cash provided by its operating activities increased by only $65 million. Another factor in Starbucks' free cash flows is that the company pays no dividends. Management's comment with regard to cash flows in the future is as follows:

The Company manages its cash, cash equivalents and liquid investments in order to internally fund operating needs. The $421 million decline in total cash and cash equivalents and liquid investments from October 3, 2004 to October 2, 2005, was nearly all due to the sale of securities to fund common stock repurchases. The Company intends to use its available cash resources, including any borrowings under its revolving credit facility described below, to invest in its core businesses and other new business opportunities related to its core businesses. The Company may use its available cash resources to make proportionate capital contributions to its equity method and cost method investees, as well as purchase larger ownership interests in selected equity method investees, particularly in

▼ EXHIBIT 12

Market Strength Ratios of Starbucks Corporation

	2005	2004

Price/earnings (P/E) ratio: Measure of investors' confidence in a company

$$\frac{\text{Market Price per Share}}{\text{Earnings per Share}} \qquad \frac{\$24.72^*}{\$0.63} = 39.2 \text{ times} \qquad \frac{\$22.62^*}{\$0.49} = 46.2 \text{ times}$$

Dividends yield: Measure of a stock's current return to an investor

$$\frac{\text{Dividends per Share}}{\text{Market Price per Share}} \qquad \text{Starbucks does not pay a dividend.}$$

*Market price is the average for the fourth quarter reported in Starbucks' annual report.
Source: Data from Starbucks Corporation, 10K, 2005.

international markets. Depending on market conditions, Starbucks may repurchase shares of its common stock under its authorized share repurchase program. Management believes that strong cash flow generated from operations, existing cash and investments, as well as borrowing capacity under the revolving credit facility, should be sufficient to finance capital requirements for its core businesses.[8]

Evaluating Market Strength

 Market price is the price at which a company's stock is bought and sold. It indicates how investors view the potential return and risk connected with owning the stock. Market price by itself is not very informative, however, because companies have different numbers of shares outstanding, different earnings, and different dividend policies. Thus, market price must be related to earnings by considering the price/earnings (P/E) ratio and the dividends yield. Those ratios for **Starbucks** appear in Exhibit 12. We computed them by using the average market prices of Starbucks' stock during the fourth quarter of 2004 and 2005.

The **price/earnings (P/E) ratio**, which measures investors' confidence in a company, is the ratio of the market price per share to earnings per share. The P/E ratio is useful in comparing the earnings of different companies and the value of a company's shares in relation to values in the overall market. With a higher P/E ratio, the investor obtains less underlying earnings per dollar invested. Starbucks' P/E ratio decreased from 46.2 times in 2004 to 39.2 times in 2005, which signals that investors expect less growth in the future.

The **dividends yield** measures a stock's current return to an investor in the form of dividends. Because Starbucks pays no dividends, its stockholders must expect their return to come from increases in the stock's market value. ●

S T O P • R E V I E W • A P P L Y

3-1. Company A and Company B both have net incomes of $1,000,000. Is it possible to conclude from this information that these companies are equally successful? Why or why not?

3-2. Circo Company has a return on assets of 12 percent and a debt to equity ratio of .5. Would you expect return on equity to be more or less than 12 percent?

3-3. Consider the following statement: "Supermarket executives are beginning to look back with some nostalgia on the days when the standard profit margin was 1 percent of sales. Last year the industry overall margin came to a thin .72 percent." How could a supermarket earn a satisfactory return on assets with such a small profit margin?

3-4. What amount is common to all cash flow adequacy ratios? To what other groups of ratios are the cash flow adequacy ratios most closely related?

3-5. Which ratios are most relevant to determining the financing period?

3-6. Company J's stock and Company Q's stock have the same market price. How might you determine whether investors are equally confident about the future of these companies?

Effects of Transactions on Ratios Sasah's, a retail firm, engaged in the transactions listed below. Opposite each transaction is a ratio and space to mark the transaction's effect on the ratio.

Transaction	Ratio	Increase	Decrease	None
		Effect		
a. Accrued salaries.	Current ratio			
b. Purchased inventory.	Quick ratio			
c. Increased allowance for uncollectible accounts.	Receivable turnover			
d. Purchased inventory on credit.	Payables turnover			
e. Sold treasury stock.	Profit margin			
f. Borrowed cash by issuing bond payable.	Asset turnover			
g. Paid wages expense.	Return on assets			
h. Repaid bond payable.	Debt to equity			
i. Accrued interest expense.	Interest coverage			
k. Sold merchandise on account.	Return on equity			
l. Recorded depreciation expense.	Cash flow yield			
m. Sold equipment.	Free cash flow			

Show that you understand the effect of business activities on performance measures by placing an X in the appropriate column to show whether the transaction increased, decreased, or had no effect on the ratio.

SOLUTION

Transaction	Ratio	Increase	Decrease	None
		Effect		
a. Accrued salaries.	Current ratio		X	
b. Purchased inventory.	Quick ratio		X	
c. Increased allowance for uncollectible accounts.	Receivable turnover	X		
d. Purchased inventory on credit.	Payables turnover		X	
e. Sold treasury stock.	Profit margin			X
f. Borrowed cash by issuing bond payable.	Asset turnover		X	
g. Paid wages expense.	Return on assets		X	
h. Repaid bond payable.	Debt to equity	X		
i. Accrued interest expense.	Interest coverage		X	
k. Sold merchandise on account.	Return on equity	X		
l. Recorded depreciation expense	Cash flow yield	X		
m. Sold equipment.	Free cash flow	X		

A LOOK BACK AT

STARBUCKS CORPORATION

To assess a company's financial performance, managers, stockholders, creditors, and other interested parties use measures that are linked to creating shareholder value. The Financial Highlights at the beginning of the chapter show steady increases in **Starbucks'** revenues, earnings, profit margin, and earnings per share—all good signs, but for a comprehensive view of the company's performance, users of its financial statements must consider the following questions:

- **What standards should be used to evaluate Starbucks' performance?**
- **What analytical tools are available to measure performance?**
- **How successful has the company been in creating value for shareholders?**

Starbucks' performance should be compared with the performance of other companies in the same industry—the specialty retail business. In addition, Starbucks' performance in the current year should be compared with its performance in past years. To make this comparison, users of Starbucks' financial statements employ such techniques as horizontal or trend analysis, vertical analysis, and ratio analysis.

Our comprehensive ratio analysis of Starbucks clearly shows that the company's financial condition improved from 2004 to 2005, as measured by its liquidity, profitability, long-term solvency, and cash flow adequacy ratios. This performance resulted in an increase in earnings per share from $.49 to $.63 and an increase in shareholders' value, as represented by an increase in the market price per share from $22.60 to $24.70.

CHAPTER REVIEW

REVIEW of Learning Objectives

LO1 Describe the objectives, standards of comparison, sources of information, and compensation issues in measuring financial performance.

A primary objective in management's use of financial performance measurement is to increase the wealth of the company's stockholders. Creditors and investors use financial performance measurement to judge a company's past performance and current position, as well as its future potential and the risk associated with it. Creditors use the information gained from their analyses to make reliable loans that will be repaid with interest. Investors use the information to make investments that will provide a return that is worth the risk.

Three standards of comparison commonly used in evaluating financial performance are rule-of-thumb measures, a company's past performance, and industry norms. Rule-of-thumb measures are weak because of a lack of evidence that they can be widely applied. A company's past performance can offer a guideline for measuring improvement, but it is not helpful in judging performance relative to the performance of other companies. Although the use of industry norms overcomes this last problem, its disadvantage is that firms are not always comparable, even in the same industry.

The main sources of information about public corporations are reports that the corporations publish themselves, such as annual reports and interim financial statements; reports filed with the SEC; business periodicals; and credit and investment advisory services.

In public corporations, a committee made up of independent directors appointed by the board of directors determines the compensation of top executives. Although earnings per share can be regarded as a "bottom-line" number that encompasses all the other performance measures, using it as the sole basis for determining executive compensation may lead to management practices that are not in the best interests of the company or its stockholders.

LO2 Apply horizontal analysis, trend analysis, vertical analysis, and ratio analysis to financial statements.

Horizontal analysis involves the computation of changes in both dollar amounts and percentages from year to year.

Trend analysis is an extension of horizontal analysis in that it calculates percentage changes for several years. The analyst computes the changes by setting a base year equal to 100 and calculating the results for subsequent years as percentages of the base year.

Vertical analysis uses percentages to show the relationship of the component parts of a financial statement to a total figure in the statement. The resulting financial statements, which are expressed entirely in percentages, are called common-size statements.

Ratio analysis is a technique of financial performance evaluation that identifies key relationships between the components of the financial statements. To interpret ratios correctly, the analyst must have a general understanding of the company and its environment, financial data for several years or for several companies, and an understanding of the data underlying the numerators and denominators.

LO3 Apply ratio analysis to financial statements in a comprehensive evaluation of a company's financial performance.

A comprehensive ratio analysis includes the evaluation of a company's liquidity, profitability, long-term solvency, cash flow adequacy, and market strength. The ratios for measuring these characteristics are illustrated in Exhibits 8 through 12.

REVIEW of Concepts and Terminology

The following concepts and terms were introduced in this chapter:

Base year: In financial analysis, the first year to be considered in any set of data. **(LO2)**

Common-size statement: A financial statement in which the components are expressed as percentages of a total figure in the statement. **(LO2)**

Compensation committee: A committee of independent directors appointed by a public corporation's board of directors to determine how top executives will be compensated. **(LO1)**

Diversified companies: Companies that operate in more than one industry. Also called *conglomerates*. **(LO1)**

Financial performance measurement: An evaluation method that uses all the techniques available to show how important items in financial statements relate to a company's financial objectives. Also called *financial statement analysis*. **(LO1)**

Free cash flow: A measure of cash remaining after providing for commitments; Net Cash Flows from Operating Activities − Dividends − (Purchases of Plant Assets − Sales of Plant Assets). **(LO3)**

Horizontal analysis: A technique for analyzing financial statements in which changes from the previous year to the current year are computed in both dollar amounts and percentages. **(LO2)**

Index number: In trend analysis, a number that shows changes in related items over time and that is calculated by setting the base year equal to 100 percent. **(LO2)**

Interim financial statements: Financial statements issued for a period of less than one year, usually a quarter or a month. **(LO1)**

Operating cycle: The time it takes to sell products and collect for them; days' inventory on hand plus days' sales uncollected. **(LO3)**

Ratio analysis: A technique of financial performance evaluation that identifies key relationships between components of the financial statements. **(LO2)**

Trend analysis: A variation of horizontal analysis in which percentage changes are calculated for several successive years instead of for two years. **(LO2)**

Vertical analysis: A technique for analyzing financial statements that uses percentages to show how the different components of a statement relate to a total figure in the statement. **(LO2)**

Key Ratios

Asset turnover: A measure of how efficiently assets are used to produce sales; Net Sales ÷ Average Total Assets. **(LO3)**

Cash flows to assets: A measure of the ability of assets to generate operating cash flows; Net Cash Flows from Operating Activities ÷ Average Total Assets. **(LO3)**

Cash flows to sales: A measure of the ability of sales to generate operating cash flows; Net Cash Flows from Operating Activities ÷ Net Sales. **(LO3)**

Cash flow yield: A measure of a company's ability to generate operating cash flows in relation to net income; Net Cash Flows from Operating Activities ÷ Net Income. **(LO3)**

Current ratio: A measure of short-term debt-paying ability; Current Assets ÷ Current Liabilities. **(LO3)**

Days' inventory on hand: A measure that shows the average number of days taken to sell inventory; Days in Year ÷ Inventory Turnover. **(LO3)**

Days' payable: A measure that shows the average number of days taken to pay accounts payable; Days in Year ÷ Payables Turnover. **(LO3)**

Days' sales uncollected: A measure that shows the number of days, on average, that a company must wait to receive payment for credit sales; Days in Year ÷ Receivable Turnover. **(LO3)**

Debt to equity ratio: A measure that shows the relationship of debt financing to equity financing, or the extent to which a company is leveraged; Total Liabilities ÷ Stockholders' Equity. **(LO3)**

Dividends yield: A measure of a stock's current return to an investor; Dividends per Share ÷ Market Price per Share. **(LO3)**

Interest coverage ratio: A measure of the degree of protection creditors have from default on interest payments; (Income Before Income Taxes + Interest Expense) ÷ Interest Expense. **(LO3)**

Inventory turnover: A measure of the relative size of inventory; Cost of Goods Sold ÷ Average Inventory. **(LO3)**

Payables turnover: A measure of the relative size of accounts payable; (Cost of Goods Sold +/− Change in Inventory) ÷ Average Accounts Payable. **(LO3)**

Price/earnings (P/E) ratio: A measure of investors' confidence in a company and a means of comparing stock values; Market Price per Share ÷ Earnings per Share. **(LO3)**

Profit margin: A measure that shows the percentage of each revenue dollar that contributes to net income; Net Income ÷ Net Sales. **(LO3)**

Quick ratio: A measure of short-term debt-paying ability; (Cash + Marketable Securities + Receivables) ÷ Current Liabilities. **(LO3)**

Receivable turnover: A measure of the relative size of accounts receivable and the effectiveness of credit policies; Net Sales ÷ Average Accounts Receivable. **(LO3)**

Return on assets: A measure of overall earning power, or profitability, that shows the amount earned on each dollar of assets invested; Net Income ÷ Average Total Assets. **(LO3)**

Return on equity: A measure of how much income was earned on each dollar invested by stockholders; Net Income ÷ Average Stockholders' Equity. **(LO3)**

REVIEW Problem

LO3 Comparative Analysis of Two Companies

Maggie Washington is considering investing in a fast-food restaurant chain because she believes the trend toward eating out more often will continue. She has narrowed her choice to Quik Burger or Big Steak. The balance sheets of Quik Burger and Big Steak appear below. Their income statements are presented on the next page.

A	B	C
Balance Sheets		
December 31, 20xx		
(In thousands)		
	Quik Burger	**Big Steak**
Assets		
Cash	$ 2,000	$ 4,500
Accounts receivable (net)	2,000	6,500
Inventory	2,000	5,000
Property, plant, and equipment (net)	20,000	35,000
Other assets	4,000	5,000
Total assets	$30,000	$56,000
Liabilities and Stockholders' Equity		
Accounts payable	$ 2,500	$ 3,000
Notes payable	1,500	4,000
Bonds payable	10,000	30,000
Common stock, $1 par value	1,000	3,000
Additional paid-in capital	9,000	9,000
Retained earnings	6,000	7,000
Total liabilities and stockholders' equity	$30,000	$56,000

	A	B	C
1	**Income Statements**		
2	**For the Year Ended December 31, 20xx**		
3	(In thousands, except per share amounts)		
4			
5		**Quik Burger**	**Big Steak**
6	Net sales	$53,000	$86,000
7	Costs and expenses		
8	Cost of goods sold	$37,000	$61,000
9	Selling expenses	7,000	10,000
10	Administrative expenses	4,000	5,000
11	Total costs and expenses	$48,000	$76,000
12	Income from operations	$ 5,000	$10,000
13	Interest expense	1,400	3,200
14	Income before income taxes	$ 3,600	$ 6,800
15	Income taxes	1,800	3,400
16	Net income	$ 1,800	$ 3,400
17	Earnings per share	$ 1.80	$ 1.13

Quik Burger's statement of cash flows shows that it had net cash flows from operations of $2,200,000. Big Steak's statement of cash flows show that its net cash flows from operations were $3,000,000. Net capital expenditures were $2,100,000 for Quik Burger and $1,800,000 for Big Steak. Quik Burger paid dividends of $500,000, and Big Steak paid dividends of $600,000. The market prices of the stocks of Quik Burger and Big Steak were $30 and $20, respectively. Financial information pertaining to prior years is not readily available to Maggie Washington. Assume that all notes payable of these two companies are current liabilities and that all their bonds payable are long-term liabilities.

Required

Perform a comprehensive ratio analysis of both Quik Burger and Big Steak following the steps outlined below. Show dollar amounts in thousands, use end-of-year balances for averages, assume no change in inventory, and round all ratios and percentages to one decimal place.

1. Prepare an analysis of liquidity.
2. Prepare an analysis of profitability.
3. Prepare an analysis of long-term solvency.
4. Prepare an analysis of cash flow adequacy.
5. Prepare an analysis of market strength.
6. In each analysis, indicate the company that apparently had the more favorable ratio. (Consider differences of .1 or less to be neutral.)
7. In what ways would having access to prior years' information aid this analysis?

Answer to Review Problem

	Ratio Name		Quik Burger				Big Steak				6. Company with More Favorable Ratio
1											
2											
3	**1.** **Liquidity analysis**										
4											
5	a. Current ratio		$2,000 + $2,000 + $2,000				$4,500 + $6,500 + $5,000				
6			$2,500 + $1,500				$3,000 + $4,000				
7											
8			$6,000	=	1.5 times		$16,000	=	2.3 times		Big Steak
9			$4,000				$7,000				
10											
11	b. Quick ratio		$2,000 + $2,000				$4,500 + $6,500				
12			$2,500 + $1,500				$3,000 + $4,000				
13											
14			$4,000	=	1.0 times		$11,000	=	1.6 times		Big Steak
15			$4,000				$7,000				
16											
17	c. Receivable turnover		$53,000	=	26.5 times		$86,000	=	13.2 times		Quik Burger
18			$2,000				$6,500				
19											
20	d. Days' sales uncollected		365	=	13.8 days		365	=	27.7 days		Quik Burger
21			26.5				13.2				
22											
23	e. Inventory turnover		$37,000	=	18.5 times		$61,000	=	12.2 times		Quik Burger
24			$2,000				$5,000				
25											
26	f. Days' inventory on hand		365	=	19.7 days		365	=	29.9 days		Quik Burger
27			18.5				12.2				
28											
29	g. Payables turnover		$37,000	=	14.8 times		$61,000	=	20.3 times		Big Steak
30			$2,500				$3,000				
31											
32	h. Days' payable		365	=	24.7 days		365	=	18.0 days		Big Steak
33			14.8				20.3				
34											
35	* This analysis indicates the company with the apparently more favorable ratio. Class discussion may focus on conditions under which different conclusions may be drawn.										

(*Continued*)

	A	B	C	D	E	F	G	H	I	J	K	L
1		Ratio Name			Quik Burger				Big Steak			6. Company with More Favorable Ratio
2												
3	2.	Profitability analysis										
4												
5	a.	Profit margin		$\frac{\$1,800}{\$53,000}$	=	3.4%		$\frac{\$3,400}{\$86,000}$	=	4.0%		Big Steak
6												
7												
8	b.	Asset turnover		$\frac{\$53,000}{\$30,000}$	=	1.8 times		$\frac{\$86,000}{\$56,000}$	=	1.5 times		Quik Burger
9												
10												
11	c.	Return on assets		$\frac{\$1,800}{\$30,000}$	=	6.0%		$\frac{\$3,400}{\$56,000}$	=	6.1%		Neutral
12												
13												
14	d.	Return on equity			$\$1,800$				$\$3,400$			
15					$\$1,000 + \$9,000 + \$6,000$				$\$3,000 + \$9,000 + \$7,000$			
16												
17				$\frac{\$1,800}{\$16,000}$	=	11.3%		$\frac{\$3,400}{\$19,000}$	=	17.9%		Big Steak
18												

	A	B	C	D	E	F	G	H	I	J	K	L
1		Ratio Name			Quik Burger				Big Steak			6. Company with More Favorable Ratio
2												
3	3.	Long-term solvency analysis										
4												
5	a.	Debt to equity ratio			$\$2,500 + \$1,500 + \$10,000$				$\$3,000 + \$4,000 + \$30,000$			
6					$\$1,000 + \$9,000 + \$6,000$				$\$3,000 + \$9,000 + \$7,000$			
7												
8				$\frac{\$14,000}{\$16,000}$	=	.9 times		$\frac{\$37,000}{\$19,000}$	=	1.9 times		Quik Burger
9												
10												
11	b.	Interest coverage ratio			$\$3,600 + \$1,400$				$\$6,800 + \$3,200$			
12					$\$1,400$				$\$3,200$			
13												
14				$\frac{\$5,000}{\$1,400}$	=	3.6 times		$\frac{\$10,000}{\$3,200}$	=	3.1 times		Quik Burger
15												

	A	B	C	D	E	F	G	H	I	J	K	L
1		Ratio Name			Quik Burger				Big Steak			6. Company with More Favorable Ratio
2												
3	4.	Cash flow adequacy analysis										
4												
5	a.	Cash flow yield		$\frac{\$2,200}{\$1,800}$	=	1.2 times		$\frac{\$3,000}{\$3,400}$	=	.9 times		Quik Burger
6												
7												

	A	B	C	D	E	F	G	H	I	J	K	L
8		Ratio Name		Quik Burger				Big Steak				6. Company with More Favorable Ratio
9												
10	b.	Cash flows to sales		$\dfrac{\$2,200}{\$53,000}$	=	4.2%		$\dfrac{\$3,000}{\$86,000}$	=	3.5%		Quik Burger
11												
12												
13	c.	Cash flows to assets		$\dfrac{\$2,200}{\$30,000}$	=	7.3%		$\dfrac{\$3,000}{\$56,000}$	=	5.4%		Quik Burger
14												
15												
16	d.	Free cash flow		$2,200 - $500 - $2,100				$3,000 - $600 - $1,800				Big Steak
17				= ($400)				= $600				

	A	B	C	D	E	F	G	H	I	J	K	L
1		Ratio Name		Quik Burger				Big Steak				6. Company with More Favorable Ratio
2												
3	5.	**Market strength analysis**										
4												
5	a.	Price/earnings ratio		$\dfrac{\$30}{\$1.80}$	=	16.7 times		$\dfrac{\$20}{\$1.13}$	=	17.7 times		Big Steak
6												
7												
8	b.	Dividends yield		$\dfrac{\$500,000/1,000,000}{\$30}$	=	1.7%		$\dfrac{\$600,000/3,000,000}{\$20}$	=	1.0%		Quik Burger
9												

7. Prior years' information would be helpful in two ways. First, turnover, return, and cash flows to assets ratios could be based on average amounts. Second, a trend analysis could be performed for each company.

CHAPTER ASSIGNMENTS

BUILDING Your Basic Knowledge and Skills

Short Exercises

LO1 Objectives and Standards of Financial Performance Evaluation

SE 1. Indicate whether each of the following items is (a) an objective or (b) a standard of comparison of financial statement analysis:

1. Industry norms
2. Assessment of a company's past performance
3. The company's past performance
4. Assessment of future potential and related risk
5. Rule-of-thumb measures

LO1 Sources of Information

SE 2. For each piece of information in the list that follows, indicate whether the best source would be (a) reports published by the company, (b) SEC reports, (c) business periodicals, or (d) credit and investment advisory services.

1. Current market value of a company's stock
2. Management's analysis of the past year's operations
3. Objective assessment of a company's financial performance
4. Most complete body of financial disclosures
5. Current events affecting the company

LO2 Trend Analysis

SE 3. Using 20x7 as the base year, prepare a trend analysis for the following data, and tell whether the results suggest a favorable or unfavorable trend. (Round your answers to one decimal place.)

	20x9	20x8	20x7
Net sales	$316,000	$272,000	$224,000
Accounts receivable (net)	86,000	64,000	42,000

LO2 Horizontal Analysis

SE 4. The comparative income statements and balance sheets of Obras, Inc., appear on the opposite page. Compute the amount and percentage changes for the income statements, and comment on the changes from 20x8 to 20x9. (Round the percentage changes to one decimal place.)

LO2 Vertical Analysis

SE 5. Express the comparative balance sheets of Obras, Inc., as common-size statements, and comment on the changes from 20x8 to 20x9. (Round computations to one decimal place.)

LO3 Liquidity Analysis

%/R **SE 6.** Using the information for Obras, Inc., in **SE 4** and **SE 5**, compute the current ratio, quick ratio, receivable turnover, days' sales uncollected, inventory turnover, days' inventory on hand, payables turnover, and days' payable for 20x8 and 20x9. Inventories were $8,000 in 20x7, $10,000 in 20x8, and $14,000 in 20x9. Accounts receivable were $12,000 in 20x7, $16,000 in 20x8, and $20,000 in 20x9. Accounts payable were $18,000 in 20x7, $20,000 in 20x8, and $24,000 in 20x9. The company had no marketable securities or prepaid assets. Comment on the results. (Round computations to one decimal place.)

LO3 Profitability Analysis

%/R **SE 7.** Using the information for Obras, Inc., in **SE 4** and **SE 5**, compute the profit margin, asset turnover, return on assets, and return on equity for 20x8 and 20x9. In 2007, total assets were $200,000 and total stockholders' equity was $60,000. Comment on the results. (Round computations to one decimal place.)

LO3 Long-term Solvency Analysis

%/R **SE 8.** Using the information for Obras, Inc., in **SE 4** and **SE 5**, compute the debt to equity ratio and the interest coverage ratio for 20x8 and 20x9. Comment on the results. (Round computations to one decimal place.)

Obras, Inc.
Comparative Income Statements
For the Years Ended December 31, 20x9 and 20x8

	20x9	20x8
Net sales	$360,000	$290,000
Cost of goods sold	224,000	176,000
Gross margin	$136,000	$114,000
Operating expenses	80,000	60,000
Operating income	$ 56,000	$ 54,000
Interest expense	14,000	10,000
Income before income taxes	$ 42,000	$ 44,000
Income taxes expense	14,000	16,000
Net income	$ 28,000	$ 28,000
Earnings per share	$ 2.80	$ 2.80

Obras, Inc.
Comparative Balance Sheets
December 31, 20x9 and 20x8

	20x9	20x8
Assets		
Current assets	$ 48,000	$ 40,000
Property, plant, and equipment (net)	260,000	200,000
Total assets	$308,000	$240,000
Liabilities and Stockholders' Equity		
Current liabilities	$ 36,000	$ 44,000
Long-term liabilities	180,000	120,000
Stockholders' equity	92,000	76,000
Total liabilities and stockholders' equity	$308,000	$240,000

LO3 Cash Flow Adequacy Analysis

SE 9. Using the information for Obras, Inc., in **SE 4**, **SE 5**, and **SE 7**, compute the cash flow yield, cash flows to sales, cash flows to assets, and free cash flow for 20x8 and 20x9. Net cash flows from operating activities were $42,000 in 20x8 and $32,000 in 20x9. Net capital expenditures were $60,000 in 20x8 and $80,000 in 20x9. Cash dividends were $12,000 in both years. Comment on the results. (Round computations to one decimal place.)

LO3 Market Strength Analysis

SE 10. Using the information for Obras, Inc., in **SE 4**, **SE 5**, and **SE 9**, compute the price/earnings (P/E) ratio and dividends yield for 20x8 and 20x9. The company had 10,000 shares of common stock outstanding in both years. The price of Obras' common stock was $60 in 20x8 and $40 in 20x9. Comment on the results. (Round computations to one decimal place.)

Exercises

LO1, LO2 **Discussion Questions**

E 1. Develop brief answers to each of the following questions:

1. Why is it essential that management compensation, including bonuses, be linked to financial goals and strategies that achieve shareholder value?
2. How are past performance and industry norms useful in evaluating a company's performance? What are their limitations?
3. In a five-year trend analysis, why do the dollar values remain the same for their respective years while the percentages usually change when a new five-year period is chosen?

LO3 **Discussion Questions**

E 2. Develop brief answers to each of the following questions:

1. Why does a decrease in receivable turnover create the need for cash from operating activities?
2. Why would ratios that include one balance sheet account and one income statement account, such as receivable turnover or return on assets, be questionable if they came from quarterly or other interim financial reports?
3. Can you suggest a limitation of free cash flow in comparing one company to another?

LO1 **Issues in Financial Performance Evaluation: Objectives, Standards, Sources of Information, and Executive Compensation**

E 3. Identify each of the following as (a) an objective of financial statement analysis, (b) a standard for financial statement analysis, (c) a source of information for financial statement analysis, or (d) an executive compensation issue:

1. Average ratios of other companies in the same industry
2. Assessment of the future potential of an investment
3. Interim financial statements
4. Past ratios of the company
5. SEC Form 10-K
6. Assessment of risk
7. A company's annual report
8. Linking performance to shareholder value

LO2 **Trend Analysis**

E 4. Using 20x5 as the base year, prepare a trend analysis of the following data, and tell whether the situation shown by the trends is favorable or unfavorable. (Round your answers to one decimal place.)

	20x9	20x8	20x7	20x6	20x5
Net sales	$51,040	$47,960	$48,400	$45,760	$44,000
Cost of goods sold	34,440	30,800	31,080	29,400	28,000
General and administrative expenses	10,560	10,368	10,176	9,792	9,600
Operating income	6,040	6,792	7,144	6,568	6,400

LO2 **Horizontal Analysis**

E 5. Compute the amount and percentage changes for the following balance sheets, and comment on the changes from 20x8 to 20x9. (Round the percentage changes to one decimal place.)

Davis Company
Comparative Balance Sheets
December 31, 20x9 and 20x8

	20x9	20x8
Assets		
Current assets	$ 18,600	$ 12,800
Property, plant, and equipment (net)	109,464	97,200
Total assets	$128,064	$110,000
Liabilities and Stockholders' Equity		
Current liabilities	$ 11,200	$ 3,200
Long-term liabilities	35,000	40,000
Stockholders' equity	81,864	66,800
Total liabilities and stockholders' equity	$128,064	$110,000

LO2 Vertical Analysis

E 6. Express the partial comparative income statements that follow as common-size statements, and comment on the changes from 20x7 to 20x8. (Round computations to one decimal place.)

Davis Company
Partial Comparative Income Statements
For the Years Ended December 31, 20x8 and 20x7

	20x8	20x7
Net sales	$212,000	$184,000
Cost of goods sold	127,200	119,600
Gross margin	$ 84,800	$ 64,400
Selling expenses	$ 53,000	$ 36,800
General expenses	25,440	18,400
Total operating expenses	$ 78,440	$ 55,200
Operating income	$ 6,360	$ 9,200

LO3 Liquidity Analysis

E 7. Partial comparative balance sheet and income statement information for Allen Company is as follows:

	20x9	20x8
Cash	$ 13,600	$ 10,400
Marketable securities	7,200	17,200
Accounts receivable (net)	44,800	35,600
Inventory	54,400	49,600
Total current assets	$120,000	$112,800
Accounts payable	$ 40,000	$ 28,200
Net sales	$322,560	$220,720
Cost of goods sold	217,600	203,360
Gross margin	$104,960	$ 17,360

In 20x7, the year-end balances for Accounts Receivable and Inventory were $32,400 and $51,200, respectively. Accounts Payable was $30,600 in 20x7 and is the only current liability. Compute the current ratio, quick ratio, receivable turnover, days' sales uncollected, inventory turnover, days' inventory on hand, payables turnover, and days' payable for each year. (Round computations to one decimal place.) Comment on the change in the company's liquidity position, including its operating cycle and required days of financing from 20x8 to 20x9.

LO3 Turnover Analysis

E 8. Diamond Tuxedo Rental has been in business for four years. Because the company has recently had a cash flow problem, management wonders whether there is a problem with receivables or inventories. Here are selected figures from the company's financial statements (in thousands):

	20x9	20x8	20x7	20x6
Net sales	$144.0	$112.0	$96.0	$80.0
Cost of goods sold	90.0	72.0	60.0	48.0
Accounts receivable (net)	24.0	20.0	16.0	12.0
Merchandise inventory	28.0	22.0	16.0	10.0
Accounts payable	13.0	10.0	8.0	5.0

Compute the receivable turnover, inventory turnover, and payables turnover for each of the four years, and comment on the results relative to the cash flow problem that the firm has been experiencing. Merchandise inventory was $11,000, accounts receivable were $11,000, and accounts payable were $4,000 in 20x5. (Round computations to one decimal place.)

LO3 Profitability Analysis

E 9. Barr Company had total assets of $320,000 in 20x7, $340,000 in 20x8, and $380,000 in 20x9. Its debt to equity ratio was .67 times in all three years. In 20x8, Barr had net income of $38,556 on revenues of $612,000. In 20x9, it had net income of $49,476 on revenues of $798,000. Compute the profit margin, asset turnover, return on assets, and return on equity for 20x8 and 20x9. Comment on the apparent cause of the increase or decrease in profitability. (Round the percentages and other ratios to one decimal place.)

LO3 Long-term Solvency and Market Strength Ratios

E 10. An investor is considering investing in the long-term bonds and common stock of Companies M and N. Both firms operate in the same industry. Both also pay a dividend per share of $8 and have a yield of 10 percent on their long-term bonds. Other data for the two firms are as follows:

	Company M	Company N
Total assets	$4,800,000	$2,160,000
Total liabilities	2,160,000	1,188,000
Income before income taxes	576,000	259,200
Interest expense	194,400	106,920
Earnings per share	6.40	10.00
Market price of common stock	80	95

Compute the debt to equity, interest coverage, and price/earnings (P/E) ratios, as well as the dividends yield, and comment on the results. (Round computations to one decimal place.)

LO3   Cash Flow Adequacy Analysis

E 11. Using the data below from the financial statements of Braugh, Inc., compute the company's cash flow yield, cash flows to sales, cash flows to assets, and free cash flow. (Round computations to one decimal place.)

Net sales	$3,200,000
Net income	352,000
Net cash flows from operating activities	456,000
Total assets, beginning of year	2,890,000
Total assets, end of year	3,120,000
Cash dividends	120,000
Net capital expenditures	298,000

Problems

LO2   Horizontal and Vertical Analysis

P 1. Sanborn Corporation's condensed comparative income statements for 20x8 and 20x7 appear below. The corporation's condensed comparative balance sheets for 20x8 and 20x7 appear on the next page.

Sanborn Corporation Comparative Income Statements For the Years Ended December 31, 20x8 and 20x7		
	20x8	**20x7**
Net sales	$3,276,800	$3,146,400
Cost of goods sold	2,088,800	2,008,400
Gross margin	$1,188,000	$1,138,000
Operating expenses		
Selling expenses	$ 476,800	$ 518,000
Administrative expenses	447,200	423,200
Total operating expenses	$ 924,000	$ 941,200
Income from operations	$ 264,000	$ 196,800
Interest expense	65,600	39,200
Income before income taxes	$ 198,400	$ 157,600
Income taxes expense	62,400	56,800
Net income	$ 136,000	$ 100,800
Earnings per share	$ 3.40	$ 2.52

Required

1. Prepare schedules showing the amount and percentage changes from 20x7 to 20x8 for the comparative income statements and the balance sheets.
2. Prepare common-size income statements and balance sheets for 20x7 and 20x8.

Sanborn Corporation
Comparative Balance Sheets
December 31, 20x8 and 20x7

	20x8	20x7
Assets		
Cash	$ 81,200	$ 40,800
Accounts receivable (net)	235,600	229,200
Inventory	574,800	594,800
Property, plant, and equipment (net)	750,000	720,000
Total assets	$1,641,600	$1,584,800
Liabilities and Stockholders' Equity		
Accounts payable	$ 267,600	$ 477,200
Notes payable	200,000	400,000
Bonds payable	400,000	—
Common stock, $10 par value	400,000	400,000
Retained earnings	374,000	307,600
Total liabilities and stockholders' equity	$1,641,600	$1,584,800

3. **User Insight:** Comment on the results in requirements **1** and **2** by identifying favorable and unfavorable changes in the components and composition of the statements.

LO3 **Effects of Transactions on Ratios**

 P 2. Koz Corporation engaged in the transactions listed in the first column of the following table. Opposite each transaction is a ratio and space to indicate the effect of each transaction on the ratio.

Transaction	Ratio	Effect		
		Increase	**Decrease**	**None**
a. Sold merchandise on account.	Current ratio			
b. Sold merchandise on account.	Inventory turnover			
c. Collected on accounts receivable.	Quick ratio			
d. Wrote off an uncollectible account.	Receivable turnover			
e. Paid on accounts payable.	Current ratio			
f. Declared cash dividend.	Return on equity			
g. Incurred advertising expense.	Profit margin			
h. Issued stock dividend.	Debt to equity ratio			
i. Issued bonds payable.	Asset turnover			
j. Accrued interest expense.	Current ratio			
k. Paid previously declared cash dividend.	Dividends yield			
l. Purchased treasury stock.	Return on assets			
m. Recorded depreciation expense.	Cash flow yield			

Required

User Insight: Show that you understand the effect of business activities on performance measures by placing an X in the appropriate column to show whether the transaction increased, decreased, or had no effect on the indicated ratio.

LO3 Comprehensive Ratio Analysis

P 3. Data for Sanborn Corporation in 20x8 and 20x7 follow. These data should be used in conjunction with the data in **P 1**.

	20x8	20x7
Net cash flows from operating activities	($196,000)	$144,000
Net capital expenditures	$40,000	$65,000
Dividends paid	$44,000	$34,400
Number of common shares	40,000,000	40,000,000
Market price per share	$18	$30

Selected balances at the end of 20x6 were accounts receivable (net), $206,800; inventory, $547,200; total assets, $1,465,600; accounts payable, $386,600; and stockholders' equity, $641,200. All Sanborn's notes payable were current liabilities; all its bonds payable were long-term liabilities.

Required

Perform a comprehensive ratio analysis following the steps outlined below. Round all answers to one decimal place.

1. Prepare a liquidity analysis by calculating for each year the (a) current ratio, (b) quick ratio, (c) receivable turnover, (d) days' sales uncollected, (e) inventory turnover, (f) days' inventory on hand, (g) payables turnover, and (h) days' payable.
2. Prepare a profitability analysis by calculating for each year the (a) profit margin, (b) asset turnover, (c) return on assets, and (d) return on equity.
3. Prepare a long-term solvency analysis by calculating for each year the (a) debt to equity ratio and (b) interest coverage ratio.
4. Prepare a cash flow adequacy analysis by calculating for each year the (a) cash flow yield, (b) cash flows to sales, (c) cash flows to assets, and (d) free cash flow.
5. Prepare a market strength analysis by calculating for each year the (a) price/earnings (P/E) ratio and (b) dividends yield.
6. **User Insight:** After making the calculations, indicate whether each ratio improved or deteriorated from 20x7 to 20x8 (use F for favorable and U for unfavorable and consider changes of .1 or less to be neutral).

LO3 Comprehensive Ratio Analysis of Two Companies

P 4. Ginger Adair is considering an investment in the common stock of a chain of retail department stores. She has narrowed her choice to two retail companies, Lewis Corporation and Ramsey Corporation, whose income statements and balance sheets are presented on the next page.

During the year, Lewis Corporation paid a total of $100,000 in dividends. The market price per share of its stock is currently $60. In comparison, Ramsey Corporation paid a total of $228,000 in dividends, and the current market price of its stock is $76 per share. Lewis Corporation had net cash flows from operations of $543,000 and net capital expenditures of $1,250,000. Ramsey Corporation had net cash flows from operations of $985,000 and net capital expenditures of $2,100,000. Information for prior years is not readily available. Assume that all notes payable are current liabilities and all bonds payable are long-term liabilities and that there is no change in inventory.

Income Statements

	Lewis	Ramsey
Net sales	$25,120,000	$50,420,000
Costs and expenses		
Cost of goods sold	$12,284,000	$29,668,000
Selling expenses	9,645,200	14,216,400
Administrative expenses	1,972,000	4,868,000
Total costs and expenses	$23,901,200	$48,752,400
Income from operations	$ 1,218,800	$ 1,667,600
Interest expense	388,000	456,000
Income before income taxes	$ 830,800	$ 1,211,600
Income taxes expense	400,000	600,000
Net income	$ 430,800	$ 611,600
Earnings per share	$ 4.31	$ 10.19

Balance Sheets

	Lewis	Ramsey
Assets		
Cash	$ 160,000	$ 384,800
Marketable securities (at cost)	406,800	169,200
Accounts receivable (net)	1,105,600	1,970,800
Inventory	1,259,600	2,506,800
Prepaid expenses	108,800	228,000
Property, plant, and equipment (net)	5,827,200	13,104,000
Intangibles and other assets	1,106,400	289,600
Total assets	$9,974,400	$18,653,200
Liabilities and Stockholders' Equity		
Accounts payable	$ 688,000	$ 1,145,200
Notes payable	300,000	800,000
Income taxes payable	100,400	146,800
Bonds payable	4,000,000	4,000,000
Common stock, $20 par value	2,000,000	1,200,000
Additional paid-in capital	1,219,600	7,137,200
Retained earnings	1,666,400	4,224,000
Total liabilities and stockholders' equity	$9,974,400	$18,653,200

Required

Conduct a comprehensive ratio analysis for each company, using the available information. Compare the results. Round percentages and ratios to one decimal place, and consider changes of .1 or less to be indeterminate.

1. Prepare a liquidity analysis by calculating for each company the (a) current ratio, (b) quick ratio, (c) receivable turnover, (d) days' sales uncollected,

(e) inventory turnover, (f) days' inventory on hand, (g) payables turnover, and (h) days' payable.

2. Prepare a profitability analysis by calculating for each company the (a) profit margin, (b) asset turnover, (c) return on assets, and (d) return on equity.

3. Prepare a long-term solvency analysis by calculating for each company the (a) debt to equity ratio and (b) interest coverage ratio.

4. Prepare a cash flow adequacy analysis by calculating for each company the (a) cash flow yield, (b) cash flows to sales, (c) cash flows to assets, and (d) free cash flow.

5. Prepare an analysis of market strength by calculating for each company the (a) price/earnings (P/E) ratio and (b) dividends yield.

6. **User Insight:** Compare the two companies by inserting the ratio calculations from 1 through 5 in a table with the following column headings: Ratio, Name, Lewis, Ramsey, and Company with More Favorable Ratio. Indicate in the last column which company had the more favorable ratio in each case.

7. **User Insight:** How could the analysis be improved if information about these companies' prior years were available?

Alternate Problems

LO3 Effects of Transactions on Ratios

 P 5. Benson Corporation, a clothing retailer, engaged in the transactions listed in the first column of the table below. Opposite each transaction is a ratio and space to mark the effect of each transaction on the ratio.

		Effect		
Transaction	**Ratio**	**Increase**	**Decrease**	**None**
a. Issued common stock for cash.	Asset turnover			
b. Declared cash dividend.	Current ratio			
c. Sold treasury stock.	Return on equity			
d. Borrowed cash by issuing note payable.	Debt to equity ratio			
e. Paid salaries expense.	Inventory turnover			
f. Purchased merchandise for cash.	Current ratio			
g. Sold equipment for cash.	Receivable turnover			
h. Sold merchandise on account.	Quick ratio			
i. Paid current portion of long-term debt.	Return on assets			
j. Gave sales discount.	Profit margin			
k. Purchased marketable securities for cash.	Quick ratio			
l. Declared 5% stock dividend.	Current ratio			
m. Purchased a building.	Free cash flow			

Required

User Insight: Show that you understand the effect of business activities on performance measures by placing an X in the appropriate column to show whether the transaction increased, decreased, or had no effect on the indicated ratio.

LO3 Comprehensive Ratio Analysis

 **P 6.** The condensed comparative income statements and balance sheets of Basie Corporation appear on the next page. All figures are given in thousands of dollars, except earnings per share.

Basie Corporation
Comparative Income Statements
For the Years Ended December 31, 20x8 and 20x7

	20x8	20x7
Net sales	$800,400	$742,600
Cost of goods sold	454,100	396,200
Gross margin	$346,300	$346,400
Operating expenses		
Selling expenses	$130,100	$104,600
Administrative expenses	140,300	115,500
Total operating expenses	$270,400	$220,100
Income from operations	$ 75,900	$126,300
Interest expense	25,000	20,000
Income before income taxes	$ 50,900	$106,300
Income taxes expense	14,000	35,000
Net income	$ 36,900	$ 71,300
Earnings per share	$ 1.23	$ 2.38

Basie Corporation
Comparative Balance Sheets
December 31, 20x8 and 20x7

	20x8	20x7
Assets		
Cash	$ 31,100	$ 27,200
Accounts receivable (net)	72,500	42,700
Inventory	122,600	107,800
Property, plant, and equipment (net)	577,700	507,500
Total assets	$803,900	$685,200
Liabilities and Stockholders' Equity		
Accounts payable	$104,700	$ 72,300
Notes payable	50,000	50,000
Bonds payable	200,000	110,000
Common stock, $10 par value	300,000	300,000
Retained earnings	149,200	152,900
Total liabilities and stockholders' equity	$803,900	$685,200

Additional data for Basie Corporation in 20x8 and 20x7 follow.

	20x8	20x7
Net cash flows from operating activities	$64,000	$99,000
Net capital expenditures	$119,000	$38,000
Dividends paid	$31,400	$35,000
Number of common shares	30,000	30,000
Market price per share	$40	$60

Balances of selected accounts at the end of 20x6 were accounts receivable (net), $52,700; inventory, $99,400; accounts payable, $64,800; total assets, $647,800; and stockholder's equity, $376,600. All of the bonds payable were long-term liabilities.

Required

Perform the following analyses. Round percentages and ratios to one decimal place.

1. Prepare a liquidity analysis by calculating for each year the (a) current ratio, (b) quick ratio, (c) receivable turnover, (d) days' sales uncollected, (e) inventory turnover, (f) days' inventory on hand, (g) payables turnover, and (h) days' payable.
2. Prepare a profitability analysis by calculating for each year the (a) profit margin, (b) asset turnover, (c) return on assets, and (d) return on equity.
3. Prepare a long-term solvency analysis by calculating for each year the (a) debt to equity ratio and (b) interest coverage ratio.
4. Prepare a cash flow adequacy analysis by calculating for each year the (a) cash flow yield, (b) cash flows to sales, (c) cash flows to assets, and (d) free cash flow.
5. Prepare an analysis of market strength by calculating for each year the (a) price/earnings (P/E) ratio and (b) dividends yield.
6. **User Insight:** After making the calculations, indicate whether each ratio improved or deteriorated from 20x7 to 20x8 (use F for favorable and U for unfavorable and consider changes of .1 or less to be neutral).

ENHANCING Your Knowledge, Skills, and Critical Thinking

Conceptual Understanding Cases

LO1, LO3   **Standards for Financial Performance Evaluation**

C 1. In a dramatic move, **Standard & Poor's Ratings Group**, the large financial company that evaluates the riskiness of companies' debt, downgraded its rating of **General Motors** and **Ford Motor Co**. debt to "junk" bond status because of concerns about the companies' profitability and cash flows. Despite aggressive cost cutting, both companies still face substantial future liabilities for health-care and pension obligations. They are losing money or barely breaking even on auto operations that concentrate on slow-selling SUVs. High gas prices and competition force them to sell the cars at a discount. The companies are counting on SUVs to make a comeback.[9] What standards do you think Standard & Poor's would use to evaluate Ford's progress? What performance measures would Standard & Poor's most likely use in making its evaluation?

LO1   **Using Segment Information**

C 2. Refer to Exhibit 1, which shows the segment information of **Goodyear Tire & Rubber Company**. In what business segments does Goodyear operate? What is the relative size of its business segments in terms of sales and income in the most recent year shown? Which segment is most profitable in terms of return on assets? In which region of the world is the tires segment largest, and which tire segment is most profitable in terms of return on assets?

LO1   **Using Investors' Services**

C 3. Refer to Exhibit 2, which contains the **PepsiCo Inc**. listing from Mergent's *Handbook of Dividend Achievers*. Assume that an investor has asked you to assess

PepsiCo's recent history and prospects. Write a memorandum to the investor that addresses the following points:

1. PepsiCo's earnings history. What has been the general relationship between PepsiCo's return on assets and its return on equity over the last seven years? What does this tell you about the way the company is financed? What figures back up your conclusion?
2. The trend of PepsiCo's stock price and price/earnings (P/E) ratio for the seven years shown.
3. PepsiCo's prospects, including developments likely to affect the company's future.

Interpreting Financial Reports

LO2 Trend Analysis

C 4. H. J. Heinz Company is a global company engaged in several lines of business, including food service, infant foods, condiments, pet foods, and weight-control food products. Below is a five-year summary of operations and other related data for Heinz.[10] (Amounts are expressed in thousands.)

H. J. Heinz Company and Subsidiaries
Five-Year Summary of Operations and Other Related Data

	2006	2005	2004	2003	2002
Summary of operations					
Sales	$8,643,438	$8,103,456	$7,625,831	$7,566,800	$7,040,934
Cost of products sold	5,550,364	5,069,926	4,733,314	4,825,462	4,441,194
Interest expense	316,296	232,088	211,382	222,729	230,027
Provision for income taxes	250,700	299,511	352,117	283,541	363,465
Net income (before special items)	442,761	688,004	715,451	478,303	593,042
Other related data					
Dividends paid: common	408,137	398,854	379,910	521,592	562,547
Total assets	9,737,767	10,577,718	9,877,189	9,224,751	10,278,354
Total debt	4,411,982	4,695,253	4,974,430	4,930,929	5,345,613
Shareholders' equity	2,048,823	2,602,573	1,894,189	1,199,157	1,718,616

Prepare a trend analysis for Heinz with 2002 as the base year and discuss the results. Identify important trends and state whether the trends are favorable or unfavorable. Discuss significant relationships among the trends.

Decision Analysis Using Excel

LO2, LO3 Effect of a One-Time Item on a Loan Decision

C 5. Apple a Day, Inc., and Unforgettable Edibles, Inc. are food catering businesses that operate in the same metropolitan area. Their customers include Fortune 500 companies, regional firms, and individuals. The two firms reported similar profit margins for the current year, and both base bonuses for managers on the achievement of a target profit margin and return on equity. Each firm has submitted a loan request to you, a loan officer for City National Bank. They have provided you with the following information:

	Apple a Day	Unforgettable Edibles
Net sales	$625,348	$717,900
Cost of goods sold	225,125	287,080
Gross margin	$400,223	$430,820
Operating expenses	281,300	371,565
Operating income	$118,923	$ 59,255
Gain on sale of real estate	—	81,923
Interest expense	(9,333)	(15,338)
Income before income taxes	$109,590	$125,840
Income taxes expense	25,990	29,525
Net income	$ 83,600	$ 96,315
Average stockholders' equity	$312,700	$390,560

1. Perform a vertical analysis and prepare a common-size income statement for each firm. Compute profit margin and return on equity.
2. Discuss these results, the bonus plan for management, and loan considerations. Identify the company that is the better loan risk.

Annual Report Case: CVS Corporation

LO3 **Comprehensive Ratio Analysis**

C 6. Using data from the **CVS Corporation** annual report in the Supplement to Chapter 5, conduct a comprehensive ratio analysis that compares the company's performance in 2005 and 2004. If you have computed ratios for CVS in previous chapters, you may prepare a table that summarizes the ratios and show calculations only for the ratios not previously calculated. If this is the first ratio analysis you have done for CVS, show all your computations. In either case, after each group of ratios, comment on the performance of CVS. Round your calculations to one decimal place. Prepare and comment on the following categories of ratios:

Liquidity analysis: current ratio, quick ratio, receivable turnover, days' sales uncollected, inventory turnover, days' inventory on hand, payables turnover, and days' payable. (Accounts Receivable, Inventories, and Accounts Payable were [in millions] $1,349.6, $4,016.5, and $1,666.4, respectively, in 2003.)

Profitability analysis: profit margin, asset turnover, return on assets, and return on equity. (Total assets and total shareholders' equity were [in millions] $10,543.1 and $6,021.8, respectively, in 2003.)

Long-term solvency analysis: debt to equity ratio and interest coverage ratio.

Cash flow adequacy analysis: cash flow yield, cash flows to sales, cash flows to assets, and free cash flow.

Market strength analysis: price/earnings (P/E) ratio and dividends yield.

Comparison Case: CVS Versus Southwest

LO3 **Comparison of Key Financial Performance Measures**

C 7. Refer to the annual report of **CVS Corporation** and the financial statements of **Southwest Airlines Co.** in the Supplement to Chapter 5. Prepare a table for the following key financial performance measures for the two most recent years for both companies. Use your computations in **C6** or perform those analyses if you have not done so. Total assets for Southwest in 2003 were $9,878 million.

Profitability:	profit margin
	asset turnover
	return on assets
Long-term solvency:	debt to equity ratio
Cash flow adequacy:	cash flow yield
	free cash flow

Evaluate and comment on the relative performance of the two companies with respect to each of the above categories.

Ethical Dilemma Case

LO1   **Executive Compensation**

C 8. Executive compensation is often based on meeting certain targets for revenue growth, earnings, earnings per share, return on assets, or other performance measures. But what if performance is not living up to expectations? Some companies are simply changing the targets. For instance, **Sun Microsystems'** proxy as quoted in The Wall Street Journal states that "due to economic challenges experienced during the last fiscal year, our earnings per share and revenues are significantly below plan. As such, the Bonus Plan was amended to reduce the target bonus to 50% of the original plan and base the target bonus solely on the third and fourth quarters."[11] Sun Microsystems was not alone. Other companies, such as **AT&T Wireless**, **Estee Lauder**, and **UST**, also lowered targets for executive bonuses. Do you think it is acceptable to change the bonus targets for executives during the year if the year turns out to be not as successful as planned? What if an unexpected negative event like 9/11 happens? What are three standards of comparison? Which of these might justify changing the bonus targets during the year?

Internet Case

LO1   **Using Investors' Services**

C 9. Go to the website for **Moody's Investors Service**. Click on "ratings," which will show revisions of debt ratings issued by Moody's in the past few days. Choose a rating that has been upgraded or downgraded and read the short press announcement related to it. What reasons does Moody's give for the change in rating? What is Moody's assessment of the future of the company or institution? What financial performance measures are mentioned in the article? Summarize your findings and be prepared to share them in class.

Group Activity Case

LO3   **Analyzing the Airline Industry**

C 10. Divide into groups. Assume your group is analyzing the fate of the larger airlines, such as **United** and **American**. You have the following information:

a. Between 1999 and now, the long-term debt, including lease obligations, of the largest airlines more than doubled.
b. The price of fuel has increased by one-third.
c. Passenger loads are only now getting back to pre-9/11 levels.
d. Severe price competition from discount airlines exists.

Identify the ratios that you consider most important to consider in assessing the future of the large airlines and discuss the effect of each of the above factors on the ratios. Be prepared to present all or part of your findings in class.

Business Communication Case

LO3 **Comparison of International Companies' Operating Cycles**

C 11. Ratio analysis enables one to compare the performance of companies whose financial statements are presented in different currencies. Selected data from 2005 for two large pharmaceutical companies—one American, **Pfizer, Inc.**, and one Swiss, **Roche**—are presented below (in millions).[12]

	Pfizer, Inc. (U.S.)	Roche (Swiss)
Net sales	$51,298	SF35,511
Cost of goods sold	8,525	9,304
Accounts receivable	9,765	7,698
Inventories	6,039	5,041
Accounts payable	2,226	2,373

For each company, calculate the receivable turnover, days' sales uncollected, inventory turnover, days' inventory on hand, payables turnover, and days' payable. Then determine the operating cycle and days of financing required for each company. (Accounts receivable in 2004 were $9,367 for Pfizer and SF7,014 for Roche. Inventories in 2004 were $6,660 for Pfizer and SF4,614 for Roche. Accounts payable in 2004 were $2,672 for Pfizer and SF1,844 for Roche.) Prepare a memo containing your analysis of the operating cycles of these companies.

The Changing Business Environment: A Manager's Perspective

Management is expected to ensure that the organization uses its resources wisely, operates profitably, pays its debts, and abides by laws and regulations. To fulfill these expectations, managers establish the goals, objectives, and strategic plans that guide and control the organization's operating, investing, and financing activities. In this chapter, we describe the approaches that managers have developed to meet the challenges of today's changing business environment and the role that management accounting plays in meeting those challenges in an ethical manner.

LEARNING OBJECTIVES

LO1 Distinguish management accounting from financial accounting and explain how management accounting supports the management process.

LO2 Describe the value chain and its usefulness in analyzing a business.

LO3 Identify the management tools used for continuous improvement.

LO4 Explain the balanced scorecard and its relationship to performance measures.

LO5 Prepare an analysis of nonfinancial data.

LO6 Identify the standards of ethical conduct for management accountants.

WAL-MART STORES, INC.

- What is Wal-Mart's strategic plan?

- What management accounting tools does Wal-Mart use to stay ahead of its competitors?

- What role does management accounting play in Wal-Mart's endeavors?

If organizations are to prosper, they must identify the factors that are critical to their success. Key success factors include satisfying customer needs, developing efficient operating processes, fostering career paths for employees, and being an innovative leader in marketing products and services. Wal-Mart had all these factors in mind when it entered the grocery business in 1988 (it is now the largest grocer in the United States) and when it began marketing toys (it now has 28 percent of that market). What drives Wal-Mart's success? Wal-Mart's CEO, Lee Scott, sums up his company's strategy this way: "What we look at is, when you end the year, did you produce the record results you wanted and are you positioned to do that again next year?"[1]

The Role of Management Accounting

LO1 Distinguish management accounting from financial accounting and explain how management accounting supports the management process.

To plan and control an organization's operations, to measure its performance, and to make decisions about pricing products or services and many other matters, managers need accurate and timely accounting information. To do their jobs efficiently, employees who handle daily operations, such as managing the flow of materials into a production system, also rely on accurate and timely accounting information. The role of management accounting is to provide an information system that enables persons throughout an organization to make informed decisions, to be more effective at their jobs, and to improve the organization's performance.

The need for management accounting information exists regardless of the type of organization—manufacturing, retail, service, or governmental—or its size. Although multidivisional corporations need more information and more complex accounting systems than small ones, even small businesses need certain types of management accounting information to ensure efficient operating conditions. The precise type of information needed depends on an organization's goals and the nature of its operations.

In 1982, the Institute of Management Accountants (IMA) defined **management accounting** as

> the process of identification, measurement, accumulation, analysis, preparation, interpretation, and communication of financial information used by management to plan, evaluate, and control within the organization and to assure appropriate use of and accountability for its resources.[2]

Since this definition was written, the importance of nonfinancial information has increased significantly. Today, management accounting information includes such nonfinancial data as the time needed to complete one cycle of the production process or to rework production errors, as well as nonfinancial data pertaining to customer satisfaction.

Management Accounting and Financial Accounting: A Comparison

Both management accounting and financial accounting assist decision makers by identifying, measuring, and processing relevant information and communicating this information through reports. Both provide managers with key measures of a company's performance and with cost information for valuing inventories on the balance sheet. Despite the overlap in their functions, management accounting and financial accounting differ in a number of ways. Table 1 summarizes these differences.

Management accounting provides managers and employees with the information they need to make informed decisions, to perform their jobs effectively, and to achieve their organization's goals. Thus, the primary users of management accounting information are people inside the organization. Financial accounting takes the actual results of management decisions about operating, investing, and financing activities and prepares financial statements for parties outside the organization—owners or stockholders, lenders, customers, and governmental agencies. Although these reports are prepared

Study Note

Management accounting is *not* a subordinate activity to financial accounting. Rather, it is a process that includes financial accounting, tax accounting, information analysis, and other accounting activities.

TABLE 1. Comparison of Management and Financial Accounting

Areas of Comparison	Management Accounting	Financial Accounting
Primary users	Managers, employees, supply chain partners	Owners or stockholders, lenders, customers, governmental agencies
Report format	Flexible, driven by user's needs	Based on generally accepted accounting principles
Purpose of reports	Provide information for planning, control, performance measurement, and decision making	Report on past performance
Nature of information	Objective and verifiable for decision making; more subjective for planning (relies on estimates)	Objective and verifiable
Units of measure	Monetary at historical or current market or projected values; physical measures of time or number of objects	Monetary at historical and current market values
Frequency of reports	Prepared as needed; may or may not be on a periodic basis	Prepared on a periodic basis

primarily for external use, managers also rely on them in evaluating an organization's performance.

Because management accounting reports are for internal use, their format can be flexible, driven by the user's needs. They may report either historical or future-oriented information without any formal guidelines or restrictions. In contrast, financial accounting reports, which focus on past performance, must follow standards and procedures specified by generally accepted accounting principles.

The information in management accounting reports may be objective and verifiable, expressed in monetary terms or in physical measures of time or objects; if needed for planning purposes, the information may be based on estimates, and in such cases, it will be more subjective. In contrast, the statements that financial accounting provides must be based on objective and verifiable information, which is generally historical in nature and measured in monetary terms. Management accounting reports are prepared as often as needed—annually, quarterly, monthly, or even daily. Financial statements, on the other hand, are prepared and distributed periodically, usually on a quarterly and annual basis.

Management Accounting and the Management Process

As we noted at the beginning of the chapter, management is expected to ensure that the organization uses its resources wisely, operates profitably, pays its debts, and abides by laws and regulations. To fulfill these expectations, managers establish the goals, objectives, and strategic plans that guide and control the organization's operating, investing, and financing activities.

Study Note

Financial accounting must adhere to the conventions of consistency and comparability to ensure the usefulness of information to parties outside the firm. Management accounting, on the other hand, can use innovative analyses and presentation techniques to enhance the usefulness of information to people within the firm.

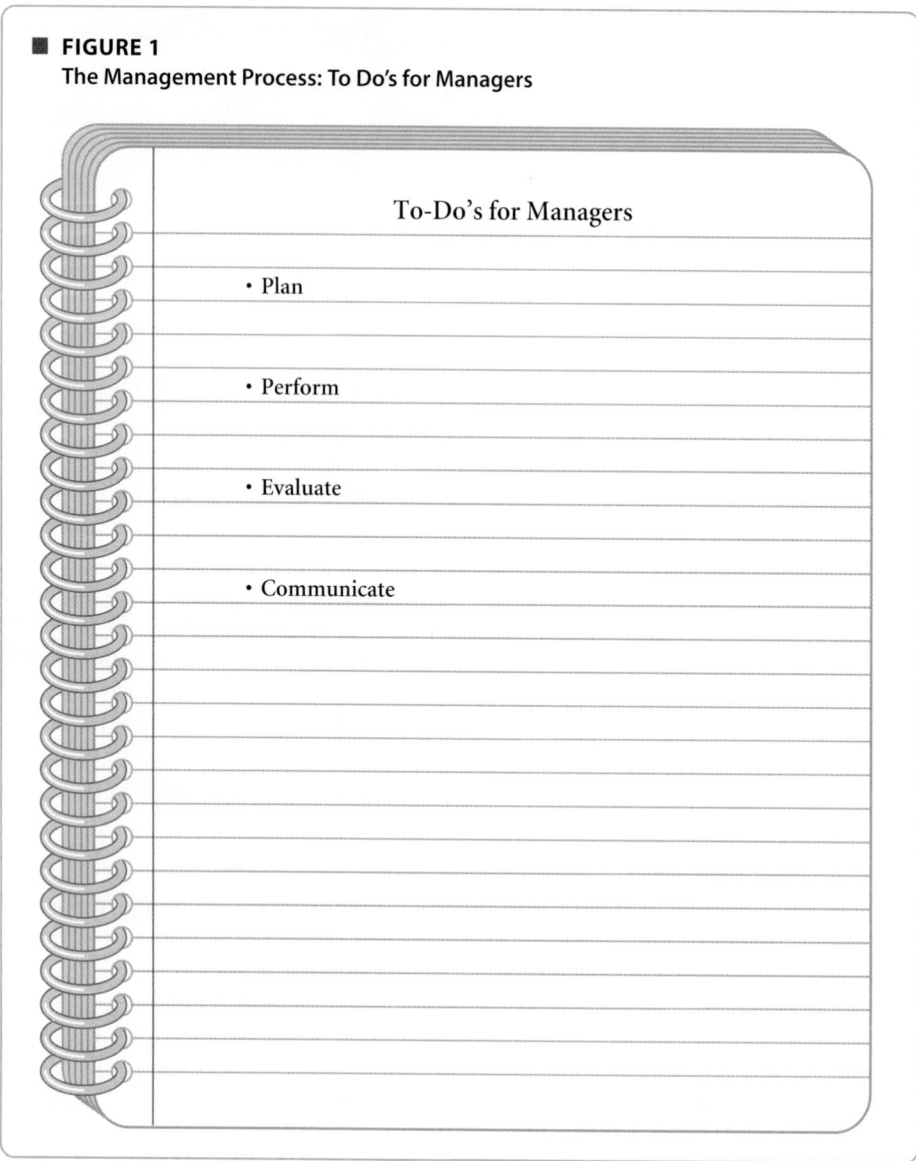

■ **FIGURE 1**
The Management Process: To Do's for Managers

To-Do's for Managers

• Plan

• Perform

• Evaluate

• Communicate

Although management actions differ from organization to organization, they generally follow a four-stage management process. As illustrated in Figure 1, the four stages of this process are planning, performing, evaluating, and communicating. Management accounting supports each stage of the process.

Planning Figure 2 shows the overall framework in which planning takes place. The overriding goal of a business is to increase the value of the stakeholders' interest in the business. It specifies the business's end point, or ideal state. For example, **Wal-Mart's** end point is "to become the worldwide leader in retailing."

A company's **mission statement** describes the fundamental way in which the company will achieve its goal of increasing stakeholders' value. It also expresses the company's identity and unique character; for instance, in its mission statement, Wal-Mart says that it wants "to give ordinary folk the chance to buy the same things as rich people." The mission statement is essential to the planning process, which must consider how to add value through strategic objectives, tactical objectives, and operating objectives.

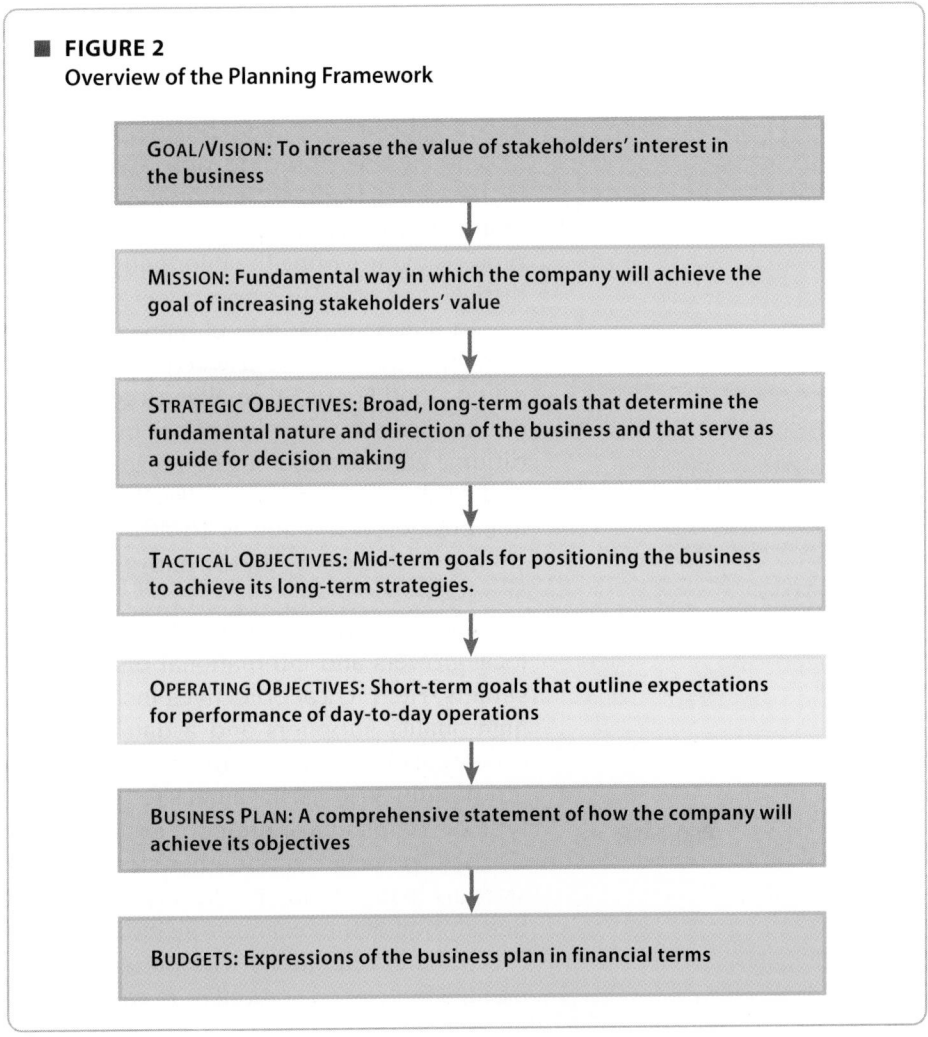

■ FIGURE 2
Overview of the Planning Framework

GOAL/VISION: To increase the value of stakeholders' interest in the business

↓

MISSION: Fundamental way in which the company will achieve the goal of increasing stakeholders' value

↓

STRATEGIC OBJECTIVES: Broad, long-term goals that determine the fundamental nature and direction of the business and that serve as a guide for decision making

↓

TACTICAL OBJECTIVES: Mid-term goals for positioning the business to achieve its long-term strategies.

↓

OPERATING OBJECTIVES: Short-term goals that outline expectations for performance of day-to-day operations

↓

BUSINESS PLAN: A comprehensive statement of how the company will achieve its objectives

↓

BUDGETS: Expressions of the business plan in financial terms

◗ **Strategic objectives** are broad, long-term goals that determine the fundamental nature and direction of a business and that serve as a guide for decision making. Strategic objectives involve such basic issues as what a company's main products or services will be, who its primary customers will be, and where it will operate. They stake out the strategic position that a company will occupy in the market—whether it will be a cost leader, quality leader, or niche satisfier. For example, Wal-Mart's strategic objective in entering the grocery and toy markets in the late 1980s was to become the low-cost leader in those markets. In 2006, Wal-Mart was considering entering the banking field—a strategy that its management believed would give customers a better deal.[3]

◗ **Tactical objectives** are mid-term goals that position an organization to achieve its long-term strategies. These objectives, which usually cover a three- to five-year period, lay the groundwork for attaining the company's strategic objectives. For example, to implement its banking strategy, Wal-Mart applied for federal deposit insurance, a requirement for any bank.

◗ **Operating objectives** are short-term goals that outline expectations for the performance of day-to-day operations. Operating objectives link to performance targets and specify how success will be measured. Wal-Mart's operating objectives focus on increasing sales, earnings per share, and real profit dollars everyday—as evidenced by the daily posting of the company's stock price in every store.

To develop strategic, tactical, and operating objectives, managers must formulate a business plan. A **business plan** is a comprehensive statement of how a company will achieve its objectives. It is usually expressed in financial terms in the form of budgets, and it often includes performance goals for individuals, teams, products, or services. Management accounting supports the planning process by providing the information that managers need to develop strategic, tactical, and operating objectives and the comprehensive business plan.

To illustrate the role of management accounting in the planning process, let's suppose that Anna Wang is about to open her own retail grocery store called Good Foods Store. Wang's goal is to obtain an income from the business and to increase the value of her investment in it. After reading about how traditional grocers are being squeezed out by low-cost competitors like Wal-Mart and quality-focused stores like **Whole Foods Market**, Wang has decided that her business's mission is to attract upscale customers and retain them by selling high-quality foods and providing excellent service in a pleasant atmosphere.

Wang's strategic objectives call for buying high-quality fresh foods from local growers and international distributors and reselling these items to consumers. Her tactical objectives include implementing a stable supply chain of high-quality suppliers and a database to track customers' preferences. Her operating objectives call for courteous and efficient customer service. To measure performance in this area, she decides to keep a record of the number and type of complaints about poor customer service.

Before Wang can open her store, she needs to apply to a local bank for a start-up loan. To do so, she must have a business plan that provides a full description of the business, including a complete operating budget for the first two years of operations. The budget must include a forecasted income statement, a forecasted statement of cash flows, and a forecasted balance sheet for both years.

Because Wang does not have a financial background, she consults a local accounting firm for help in developing her business plan. To provide relevant input for the plan, she has to determine the types of products she wants to sell; the volume of sales she anticipates; the selling price for each product; the monthly costs of leasing or purchasing facilities, employing personnel, and maintaining the facilities; and the number of display counters, storage units, and cash registers that she will need.

FOCUS ON BUSINESS PRACTICE
What's Going On in the Grocery Business?

Over the last five years, sales at large supermarket chains, such as **Kroger**, **Safeway**, and **Albertson's**, have been flat and profits weak because both ends of their customer market are being squeezed. Large-scale retailers like **Wal-Mart** and **Costco** are attracting cost-conscious grocery shoppers, and upscale grocery customers are being lured to specialty grocers like **Trader Joe's** and **Whole Foods Market**. Albertson's strategy to combat its flat sales and profits was to sell itself to other retailers, like **Supervalu** and **CVS**, to form larger businesses. Other grocery chains are using the planning framework to reconsider their company's mission and strategic options. Some are adding new products and services, such as walk-in medical clinics; others are closing stores and downsizing; still others are entering new geographic markets.[4]

Performing Planning alone does not guarantee satisfactory operating results. Management must implement the business plan in ways that make optimal use of available resources. Smooth operations require one or more of the following:

- Hiring and training personnel

- Matching human and technical resources to the work that must be done

- Purchasing or leasing facilities

- Maintaining an inventory of products for sale

- Identifying operating activities, or tasks, that minimize waste and improve the quality of products or services

Managers execute the business plan by overseeing the company's daily operations. In small companies like Anna Wang's, managers generally have frequent direct contact with their employees. They supervise them and interact with them to help them learn a task or improve their performance. In larger, more complex organizations, there is usually less direct contact between managers and employees. Instead of directly observing employees, managers in large companies like Wal-Mart monitor their employees' performance by measuring the time taken to complete an activity (such as how long it takes to process customer sales) or the frequency of an activity (such as the number of customers served per hour).

To illustrate how management accounting provides information to support the performance of managers, let's assume that Good Foods Store is now open for business. The budget prepared for the store's first two years of operation provides the link between the business plan and the execution of the plan. Items that relate to the business plan appear in the budget and become authorizations for expenditures. They include such matters as spending on store fixtures, hiring employees, developing advertising campaigns, and pricing items for special sales.

Critical to managing any retail business is the supply chain. As Figure 3 shows, the **supply chain** (also called the *supply network*) is the path that leads from the suppliers of the materials from which a product is made to the final consumer. In the supply chain for grocery stores, produce and other items flow from growers and suppliers to manufacturers or distributors to retailers to consumers. Wang must coordinate deliveries from local growers and international distributors so that she meets the demands of her customers without having too much inventory on hand, which would tie up cash, or being out of stock

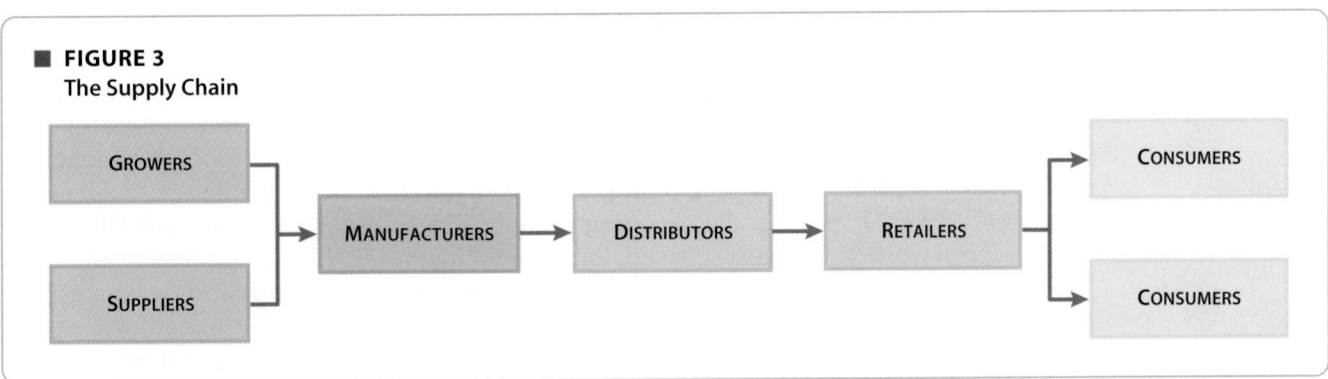

■ **FIGURE 3**
The Supply Chain

The supply chain is the path that leads from suppliers to the final consumer. In the supply chain for grocery stores, produce flows from growers and suppliers to manufacturers or distributors to retailers to consumers. The supply chain for this farmer's market is much shorter: grower to consumer.

when a customer asks for a certain product. Management accounting information about deliveries and sales will help her manage the supply chain.

Evaluating   When managers evaluate operating results, they compare the organization's actual performance with the performance levels they established in the planning stage. They earmark any significant variations for further analysis so that they can correct the problems. If the problems are the result of a change in the organization's operating environment, the managers may revise the original objectives. Ideally, the adjustments made in the evaluation stage will improve the company's performance.

To evaluate how well Good Foods Store is doing, Anna Wang will compare the amounts estimated in the budget with actual results. If any differences appear, she will analyze why they have occurred. The reasons for these differences may lead Wang to change parts of her original business plan. In addition to reviewing employees' performance with regard to financial goals, such as avoiding waste, Wang will want to review how well her employees served customers. As noted earlier, she decided to monitor service quality by keeping a record of the number and type of complaints about poor customer service. Her review of this record may help her develop new and better strategies.

Communicating   Whether accounting reports are prepared for internal or external use, they must provide accurate information and clearly communicate this information to the reader. Internal reports that provide inaccurate information or present information in such a way that it is unclear to the employee or the manager can have a negative effect on a company's operations and ultimately on its profitability. Full disclosure and transparency in financial statements issued to external parties is a basic concept of generally accepted accounting principles, and violation of this principle can result in stiff penalties. After the reporting violations by **Enron**, **WorldCom**, and other companies, Congress passed legislation that requires the top management of companies that file financial statements with the Securities and Exchange Commission to certify that these statements are accurate. The penalty for issuing false public reports can be loss of compensation, fines, and jail time.

The key to producing a management accounting report that communicates accurate and useful information whose meaning is transparent to the reader is to apply the four *w*'s: why, who, what, and when.

- ◆ W*hy*? Know the purpose of the report. Focus on it as you write.

- ◆ W*ho*? Identify the audience for your report. Communicate at a level that matches your readers' understanding of the issue and their familiarity with accounting information. A detailed, informal report may be appropriate for your manager, but a more concise summary may be necessary for other audiences, such as the president or board of directors of your organization.

- ◆ W*hat*? What information is needed, and what method of presentation is best? Select relevant information from reliable sources. You may draw information from pertinent documents or from interviews with knowledgeable managers and employees. The information should be not only relevant, but also easy to read and understand. You may need to include visual aids, such as bar charts or graphs, to present the information clearly.

- ◆ W*hen*? Know the due date for the report. Strive to prepare an accurate report on a timely basis. If the report is urgently needed, you may have to sacrifice some accuracy in the interest of timeliness.

The four *w*'s are also applicable to financial accounting reports. Assume that Anna Wang has hired Sal Chavez to be her company's accountant. In the financial statements that he prepares, the purpose—or *why*—is to report on the financial health of Good Foods Store. In this case, Wang, her bank and other creditors, and potential investors are the *who*. The *what* consists of disclosures about assets, liabilities, product costs, and sales. The required reporting deadline for the accounting period answers the question of *when*.

Wang will also want periodic internal reports on various aspects of her store's operations. For example, a monthly report may summarize the costs of ordering products from international distributors and the related shipping charges. If the costs in the monthly reports appear to be too high, she may ask Sal Chavez to conduct a special study. The results of such a study might result in a memorandum report like the one shown in Exhibit 1.

EXHIBIT 1 ▶

A Management Accounting Report

Memorandum

When: Today's Date

Who: To: A. Wang, Good Foods Store

        From: Sal Chavez, Accountant

Why: Re: International Distributors Ordering and Shipping Costs—Analysis and Recommendations

What: As you requested, I have analyzed the ordering and shipping costs incurred when buying from international distributors. I found that during the past year, these costs were 9 percent of sales, or $36,000.

        On average, we are placing about two orders per week, or eight orders per month. Placing each order requires about two and one-half hours of an employee's time. Further, the international distributors charge a service fee for each order, and shippers charge high rates for orders as small as ours.

        My recommendations are (1) to reduce orders to four per month (the products' freshness will not be affected if we order at least once a week) and (2) to begin placing orders through the international distributors' websites (our international distributors do not charge a service fee for online orders). If we follow these recommendations, I project that the costs of receiving products will be reduced to 4 percent of sales, or $16,000, annually—a savings of $20,000.

In summary, management accounting can provide a constant stream of relevant information. Compare Wang's activities and information needs with the steps of the management process shown in Figure 1. She started with a business plan, implemented the plan, and evaluated the results. Accounting information helped her develop her business plan, communicate that plan to her bank and employees, evaluate the performance of her employees, and report the results of operations. As you can see, accounting plays a critical role in managing the operations of any organization.

S T O P • R E V I E W • A P P L Y

1-1. What is management accounting, and how is it similar to financial accounting?

1-2. What is the supply chain?

1-3. What are the four *w*'s of report preparation? Explain the importance of each.

1-4. A financial report often contains estimates and projections. How does the writer of such a report make sure that the reader understands the uncertainties involved?

Suggested answers to all Stop, Review, and Apply questions are available at http://college.hmco.com/accounting/needles/poa/10e/student_home.html.

Value Chain Analysis

LO2 Describe the value chain and its usefulness in analyzing a business.

Each step in the manufacture of a product or the delivery of a service can be thought of as a link in a chain that adds value to the product or service. This concept of how a business fulfills its mission and objectives is known as the **value chain**. As shown in Figure 4, the steps that add value to a product or service—which range from research and development to customer service—are known as **primary processes**. The value chain also includes **support services**, such as legal services and management accounting. These services facilitate the primary processes but do not add value to the final product or service. Their roles are critical, however, to making the primary processes as efficient and effective as possible.

Primary Processes and Support Services

Let's assume that Good Foods Store has had some success, and Anna Wang now wants to determine the feasibility of making and selling her own brand of candy. The primary processes that will add value to the new candy are as follows:

Research and development: developing new and better products or services. Wang plans to add value by developing a candy that has less sugar content than similar confections.

Design: creating improved and distinctive shapes, labels, or packages for products. For example, a package that is attractive and that describes the desirable features of Wang's new candy will add value to the product.

■ **FIGURE 4**
The Value Chain

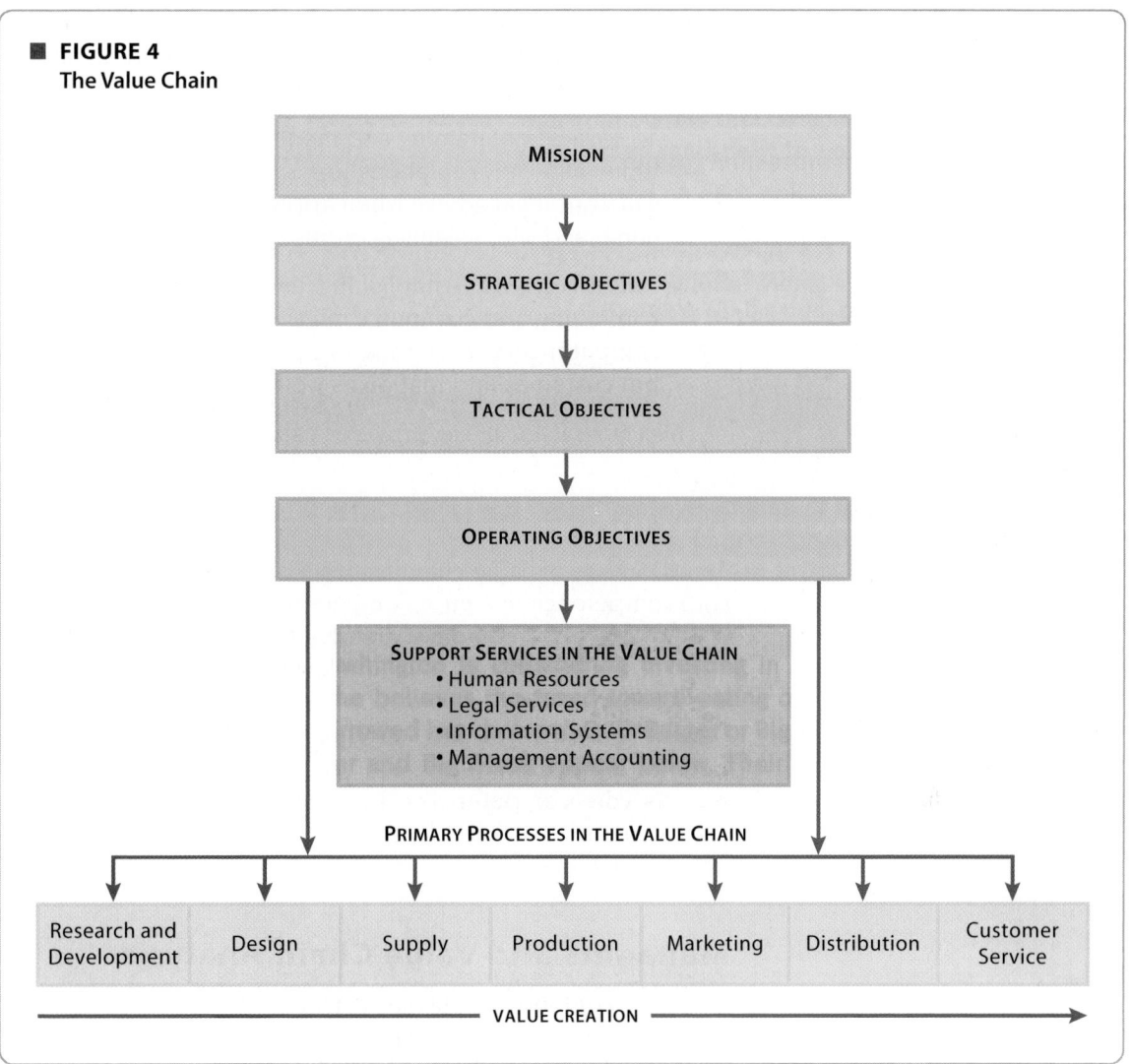

Supply: purchasing materials for products or services. Wang will want to purchase high-quality sugar, chocolate, and other ingredients for the candy, as well as high-quality packaging.

Production: manufacturing the product or service. To add value to the new candy, Wang will want to implement efficient manufacturing and packaging processes.

Marketing: communicating information about the products or services and selling them. Attractive advertisements will facilitate sale of the new candy to customers.

Distribution: delivering the product or service to the customer. Courteous and efficient service for in-store customers will add value to the product. Wang may also want to accommodate Internet customers by providing shipping.

Customer service: following up with service after sales or providing warranty service. For example, Wang may offer free replacement of any candy that does not satisfy the customer. She could also use questionnaires to measure customer satisfaction.

The services that support the primary processes are as follows:

Human resources: hiring and training employees to carry out all the functions of the business. Wang will need to hire and train personnel to make the new candy.

Legal services: maintaining and monitoring all contracts, agreements, obligations, and other relationships with outside parties. For example, Wang will want legal advice when applying for a trademark for the new candy's name and when signing contracts with suppliers.

Information systems: establishing and maintaining technological means of controlling and communicating within the organization. Wang will want a computerized accounting system that keeps not only financial records, but customer information as well.

Management accounting: provides essential information in any business.

Advantages of Value Chain Analysis

Study Note

A company cannot succeed by trying to do everything at the highest level. It has to focus on its core competencies to give customers the best value.

An advantage of value chain analysis is that it allows a company to focus on its core competencies. A **core competency** is the thing that a company does best. It is what gives a company an advantage over its competitors. For example, **Wal-Mart** is known for having the lowest prices; that is its core competency.

A common result of value chain analysis is outsourcing, which can also be of benefit to a business. **Outsourcing** is the engagement of other companies to perform a process or service in the value chain that is not among an organization's core competencies. For instance, Wal-Mart outsources its inventory management to its vendors, who monitor and stock Wal-Mart's stores and warehouses.

Managers and Value Chain Analysis

In today's competitive business environment, analysis of the value chain is critical to most companies' survival. Managers at Wal-Mart and other organizations must provide the highest value to customers at the lowest cost, and low cost often equates with the speed at which the primary processes of the value chain are executed. Time to market is very important.

Managers must also make the services that support the primary processes as efficient as possible. These services are essential and cannot be eliminated, but because they do not add value to the final product, they must be implemented as economically as possible. Businesses have been making progress in this area. For example, over the past ten years, the cost of the accounting function in many companies as a percentage of total revenue has declined from 6 percent to 2 percent. Technology has played a big role in making this economy possible.

As a support service, management accounting must be efficient and provide value to managers by developing information that is useful for decision making. For example, to determine whether manufacturing and selling her own brand of candy will be profitable, Anna Wang will need accurate information about the cost of the candy. She knows that if her candy is to be competitive, she cannot sell it for more than $10 per pound. Further, she has an idea of how much candy she can sell in the first year. Based on this information, her accountant, Sal Chavez, analyzes the value chain and projects the initial costs per pound shown in Exhibit 2. The total cost of $8 per pound worries Wang because with a selling price of $10, it leaves only $2, or 20 percent of revenue, to cover all the support services and provide a profit. Wang believes that if the enterprise is to be successful, this percentage, called the *margin*, must be at

EXHIBIT 2 ▶   **Value Chain Analysis**

Good Foods Store
Projected Costs of New Candy
June 1, 20x9

Primary Process	Initial Costs per Pound	Revised Costs per Pound
Research and development	$ .25	$ .25
Design	.10	.10
Supply	1.10	.60
Production	4.50	3.50
Marketing	.50	.50
Distribution	.90	.90
Customer service	.65	.65
Total cost	$8.00	$6.50

least 35 percent. Since the selling price is constrained by the competition, she must find a way to reduce costs.

Chavez tells her that the company could achieve a lower total cost per pound by selling a higher volume of candy, but that is not realistic for the new product. He also points out that the largest projected costs in the store's value chain are for supply and production. Because Wang plans to order ingredients from a number of suppliers, her orders would not be large enough to qualify for quantity discounts and savings on shipping. Using a single supplier could reduce the supply cost by $.50 per unit. Another way of reducing the cost of production would be to outsource this process to a candy manufacturer, whose high volume of products would allow it to produce the candy at a much lower cost than could be done at Good Foods Store. Outsourcing would reduce the production cost to $3.50 per unit. Thus, the total unit cost would be reduced to $6.50, as shown in Exhibit 2. This per unit cost would enable the company to sell the candy at a competitive $10 per pound and make the targeted margin of 35 percent ($3.50 ÷ $10).

This value chain analysis illustrates two important points. First, Good Food Store's mission is as a retailer. The company has no experience in making candy. Manufacturing candy would require a change in the company's mission and major changes in the way it does business. Second, outsourcing portions of the value chain that are not part of a business's core competency is often the best business policy. Since Good Foods Store does not have a core competency in manufacturing candy, it would not be competitive in this field. Anna Wang would be better off having an experienced candy manufacturer produce the candy according to her specifications and then selling the candy under her store's label. As Wang's business grows, increased volume may allow her to reconsider undertaking the manufacture of candy. ●

S T O P • R E V I E W • A P P L Y

2-1. What is the value chain?

2-2. What are primary processes and support services? How do primary processes and support services differ?

2-3. Is it better for a company to have a primary process or a support service as a core competency?

The Total Cost per Unit of Primary Processes and Support Services The following unit costs were determined by dividing the total costs of each component by the number of products produced. From these unit costs, determine the total cost per unit of primary processes and the total cost per unit of support services.

Research and development	$ 1.25
Human resources	1.35
Design	.15
Supply	1.10
Legal services	.40
Production	4.00
Marketing	.80
Distribution	.90
Customer service	.65
Information systems	.75
Management accounting	.10
Total cost per unit	$11.45

SOLUTION

Primary processes:

Research and development	$1.25
Design	.15
Supply	1.10
Production	4.00
Marketing	.80
Distribution	.90
Customer service	.65
Total cost per unit	$8.85

Support services:

Human resources	$1.35
Legal services	.40
Information systems	.75
Management accounting	.10
Total cost per unit	$2.60

Continuous Improvement

LO3 Identify the management tools used for continuous improvement.

Today, managers in all parts of the world have ready access to international markets and to current information for informed decision making. As a result, global competition has increased significantly. One of the most valuable lessons gained from this increase in competition is that management cannot afford to become complacent. The concept of **continuous improvement** evolved to avoid such complacency. Organizations that adhere to continuous

FOCUS ON BUSINESS PRACTICE

Becoming a Leader: What Qualities, Skills, and Education Do CEOs Possess?

According to the consulting firm Leadership Worth Following, top business leaders have vision, good judgment, and excellent communication skills and are futurists who persevere and adapt. A profile of leading CEOs reveals the following:

• The average age is 52 for men and 47 for women.

• About 97 percent have an undergraduate degree, and 38 percent have an MBA.

• About 33 percent have international experience.

• Women occupy many leadership positions in health care, consumer products, and financial services, but very few women are leaders in the manufacturing, chemical, entertainment, and wholesale businesses.

• On average, women CEOs receive about 30 percent less in pay, bonuses, and options than male CEOs.[5]

improvement are never satisfied with what is; they constantly seek improved quality and lower cost through better methods, products, services, processes, or resources. In response to this concept, several important management tools have emerged. These tools help companies remain competitive by focusing on continuous improvement of business methods.

Management Tools for Continuous Improvement

Among the management tools that companies use are the just-in-time operating philosophy, total quality management, activity-based management, and the theory of constraints.

Just-in-Time Operating Philosophy

The **just-in-time (JIT) operating philosophy** requires that all resources—materials, personnel, and facilities—be acquired and used only when they are needed. Its objectives are to improve productivity and eliminate waste. In a JIT environment, production processes are consolidated, and workers are trained to be multiskilled so that they can operate several different machines. Materials and supplies are scheduled for delivery just at the time they are needed in the production process, which significantly reduces inventories of materials. Goods are produced continuously, so work in process inventories are very small. Production is usually started only when an order is received, and the ordered goods are shipped when completed, which reduces the inventories of finished goods.

Adopting the JIT operating philosophy reduces production time and costs, investment in materials inventory, and materials waste, and it results in higher-quality goods. Funds that are no longer invested in inventory can be redirected according to the goals of the company's business plan. Management accounting responds to a JIT operating environment by providing an information system that is sensitive to changes in production processes. JIT methods help retailers like **Wal-Mart** and manufacturers like **Harley-Davidson** assign more accurate costs to their products and identify the costs of waste and inefficient operation. Wal-Mart, for example, requires vendors to restock inventory

The JIT operating philosophy requires that all resources be acquired and used only when needed. After implementing JIT and other reforms in 1981, Harley-Davidson's breakeven point dropped from 53,000 bikes to 35,000 bikes. For JIT to work, Harley-Davidson must trust suppliers to deliver the materials it needs at 100 percent quality.

often and pays them only when the goods sell. This minimizes the funds invested in inventory and allows the retailer to focus on offering high-demand merchandise at attractive prices.

Total Quality Management

Total quality management (TQM) requires that all parts of a business work together to build quality into the business's product or service. Improved quality of both the product or service and the work environment is TQM's goal. Workers act as team members and are empowered to make operating decisions that improve quality in both areas.

TQM has many of the same characteristics as the JIT operating philosophy. It focuses on improving product or service quality by identifying and reducing or eliminating the causes of waste. The emphasis is on examining current operations to spot possible causes of poor quality and on using resources efficiently and effectively to improve quality and reduce the time needed to complete a task or provide a service. Like JIT, TQM results in reduced waste of materials, higher-quality goods, and lower production costs in manufacturing environments, such as those of Wal-Mart's vendors, and helps Wal-Mart realize time savings and provide higher-quality services.

To determine the impact of poor quality on profits, TQM managers use accounting information about the costs of quality. The **costs of quality** include both the costs of achieving quality (such as training costs and inspection costs) and the costs of poor quality (such as the costs of rework and of handling customer complaints). Managers use information about the costs of quality to relate their organization's business plan to its daily operating activities, to stimulate improvement by sharing this information with all employees, to identify opportunities for reducing costs and customer dissatisfaction, and to determine the costs of quality relative to net income. For retailers like Wal-Mart and Good Foods Store, TQM results in a quality customer experience before, during, and after the sale.

Activity-Based Management

Activity-based management (ABM) is an approach to managing an organization that identifies all major operating activities or tasks, determines the resources consumed by each of those activities and the cause of the resource usage, and categorizes the activities as either adding value to a product or service or not adding value. ABM includes a management accounting practice called activity-based costing. **Activity-based costing (ABC)** identifies all of an organization's major operating activities (both production and nonproduction), traces costs to those activities or cost pools, and then assigns costs to the products or services that use the resources supplied by those activities.

Activities that add value to a product or service, as perceived by the customer, are known as **value-adding activities**. All other activities are called **nonvalue-adding activities**; they add cost to a product or service but do not increase its market value. ABM eliminates nonvalue-adding activities that do not support the organization; those that do support the organization are focal points for cost reduction. ABM results in reduced costs, reduced waste of resources, increased efficiency, and increased customer satisfaction. In addition, ABC produces more accurate costs than traditional cost allocation methods, which leads to improved decision making.

Theory of Constraints

According to the **theory of constraints (TOC)**, limiting factors, or bottlenecks, occur during the production of any product or service, but once managers identify such a constraint, they can focus their attention and resources on it and achieve significant improvements. TOC thus

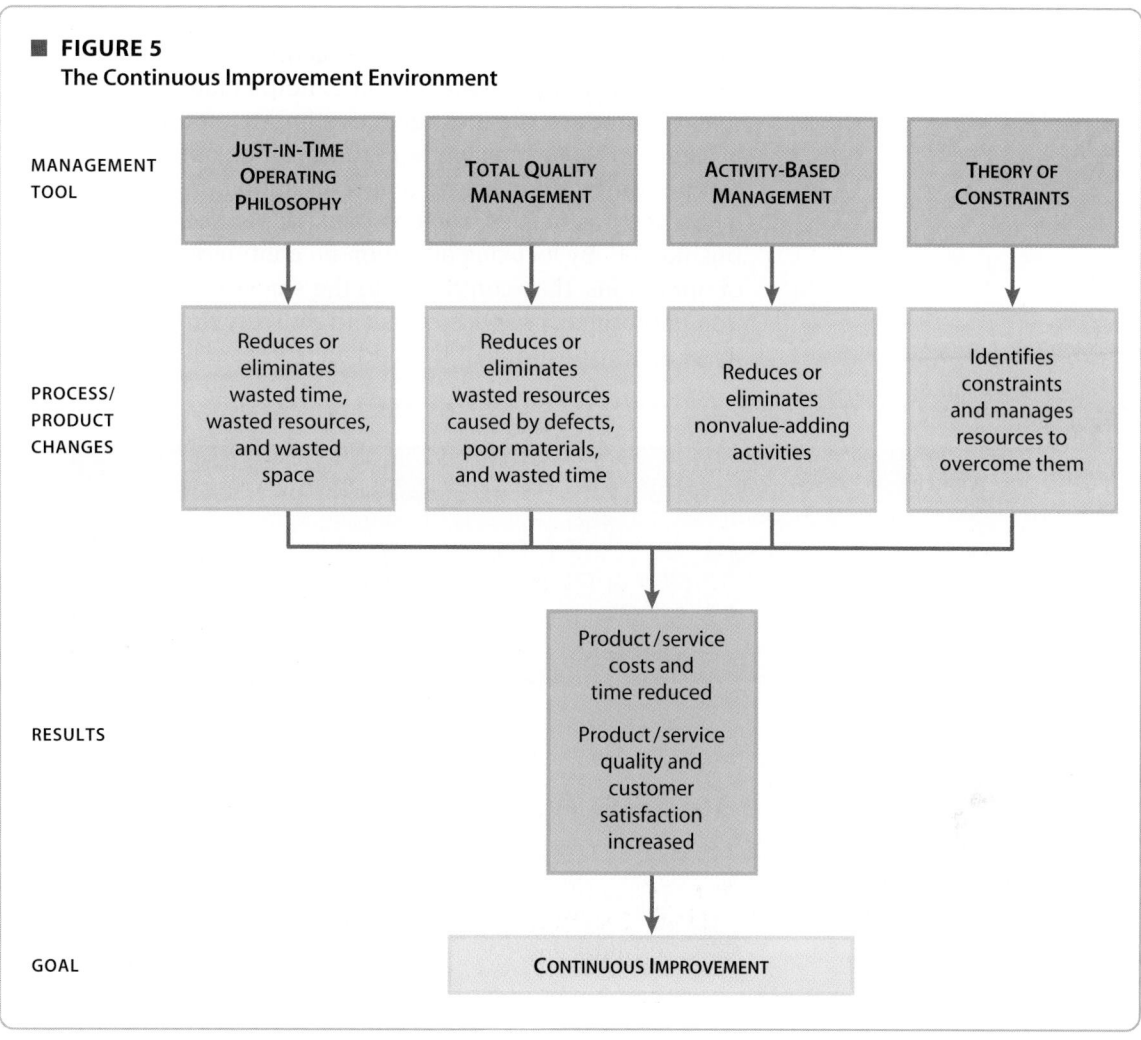

■ **FIGURE 5**
The Continuous Improvement Environment

helps managers set priorities for how they spend their time and resources. In identifying constraints, managers rely on the information that management accounting provides.

To illustrate TOC, suppose Anna Wang wants to increase sales of store-roasted coffees. After reviewing management accounting reports, she concludes that the limited production capacity of her equipment—a roaster that can roast only 100 pounds of coffee beans per hour—limits the sales of the store's coffee. To overcome this constraint, she can rent or purchase a second roaster. The increase in production will enable her to increase coffee sales.

TOC complements JIT, TQM, and ABM by focusing resources on efforts that will yield the most effective improvements.

Achieving Continuous Improvement

JIT, TQM, ABM, and TOC all make a contribution to continuous improvement, as shown in Figure 5. In the just-in-time operating environment, management wages war on wasted time, wasted resources, and wasted space. All employees are encouraged to look for ways of improving processes and saving time. Total quality management focuses on improving the quality of the product or service and the work environment. It pursues continuous improvement by reducing the number of defective products and the time needed to complete a task or provide a service. Activity-based management seeks continuous improvement by emphasizing the ongoing reduction or elimination of nonvalue-adding activities. The theory of constraints helps managers focus resources on efforts that will produce the most effective improvements.

Each of these management tools can be used individually, or parts of them can be combined to create a new operating environment. They are applicable in service businesses, such as banking, as well as in manufacturing and retail businesses. By focusing attention on continuous improvement and fine-tuning of operations, they contribute to the same results in any organization: a reduction in product or service costs and delivery time, an improvement in the quality of the product or service, and an increase in customer satisfaction.

S T O P • R E V I E W • A P P L Y

3-1. How does a company know whether the quality of its products or services is improving?

3-2. What is the goal of all the management approaches described in this chapter?

Performance Measures: A Key to Achieving Organizational Objectives

LO4 Explain the balanced scorecard and its relationship to performance measures.

erformance measures are quantitative tools that gauge an organization's performance in relation to a specific goal or an expected outcome. Performance measures may be financial or nonfinancial. Financial performance measures include return on investment, net income as a percentage of sales, and the costs of poor quality as a percentage of sales. Such measures use monetary information to gauge the performance of a profit-generating organization or its segments—its divisions, departments, product lines, sales territories, or operating activities.

Nonfinancial performance measures include the number of times an activity occurs or the time taken to perform a task. Examples are number of customer complaints, number of orders shipped the same day, and the time taken to fill an order. Such performance measures are useful in reducing or eliminating waste and inefficiencies in operating activities.

Using Performance Measures in the Management Process

Managers use performance measures in all stages of the management process. In the planning stage, they establish performance measures that will support the organization's mission and the objectives of its business plan, such as reducing costs and increasing quality, efficiency, timeliness, and customer satisfaction. As you will recall from earlier in the chapter, Anna Wang selected the number of customer complaints as a performance measure to monitor the quality of service at Good Foods Store.

As managers perform their duties, they use the performance measures they established in the planning stage to guide and motivate employees and to assign costs to products, departments, and operating activities. Anna Wang will record the number of customer complaints during the year. She can group the information by type of complaint or by the employee involved in the service.

When evaluating performance, managers use the information that performance measures have provided to analyze significant differences between actual and planned performance and to identify ways of improving performance. By comparing the actual and planned number of customer complaints, Wang can identify problem areas and develop solutions.

When communicating with stakeholders, managers use information derived from performance measurement to report results and develop new budgets. If Wang needed formal reports, she could prepare performance evaluations based on this information.

The Balanced Scorecard

If an organization is to achieve its mission and objectives, it must identify the areas in which it needs to excel and establish measures of performance in these critical areas. As we have indicated, effective performance measurement requires an approach that uses both financial and nonfinancial measures that are tied to a company's mission and objectives. One such approach that has gained wide acceptance is the balanced scorecard.

The **balanced scorecard** is a framework that links the perspectives of an organization's four stakeholder groups to the organization's mission, objectives, resources, and performance measures. The four stakeholder groups are as follows:

Study Note

The balanced scorecard focuses all perspectives of a business on accomplishing the business's mission.

- Stakeholders with a financial perspective (owners, investors, and creditors) value improvements in financial measures, such as net income and return on investment.

- Stakeholders with a learning and growth perspective (employees) value high wages, job satisfaction, and opportunities to fulfill their potential.

- Stakeholders who focus on the business's internal processes value the safe and cost-effective production of high-quality products.

- Stakeholders with a customer perspective value high-quality products that are low in cost.

Although their perspectives differ, these stakeholder groups may be interested in the same measurable performance goals. For example, holders of

FOCUS ON BUSINESS PRACTICE
How Does the Balanced Scorecard Measure Success at Futura Industries?

Futura Industries is not a famous company, but it is one of the best. Based in Utah, it is rated as that state's top privately owned employer and serves a high-end niche in such diverse markets as floor coverings, electronics, transportation, and shower doors. In achieving its success, Futura uses the balanced scorecard. Futura has developed the following performance measures:

- Employee turnover is a measure of learning and growth.

- Percentage of sales from new products and total production cost per standard hour are measures of the company's internal processes.

- Number of customers' complaints and percentage of materials returned are the measures of customer satisfaction.

- Income and gross margin are among the measures of financial performance.[6]

■ **FIGURE 6**
The Balanced Scorecard for Good Foods Store

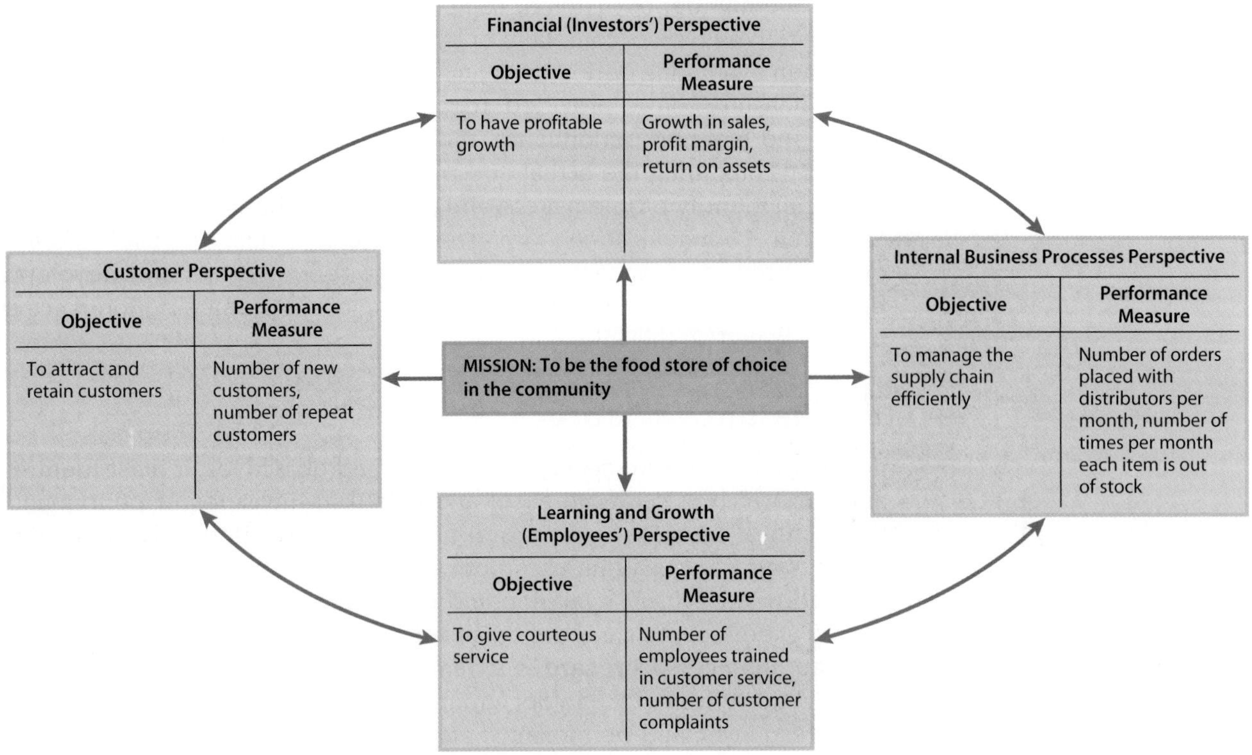

Financial (Investors') Perspective

Objective	Performance Measure
To have profitable growth	Growth in sales, profit margin, return on assets

Customer Perspective

Objective	Performance Measure
To attract and retain customers	Number of new customers, number of repeat customers

MISSION: To be the food store of choice in the community

Internal Business Processes Perspective

Objective	Performance Measure
To manage the supply chain efficiently	Number of orders placed with distributors per month, number of times per month each item is out of stock

Learning and Growth (Employees') Perspective

Objective	Performance Measure
To give courteous service	Number of employees trained in customer service, number of customer complaints

Source: Adapted from Robert S. Kaplan and David P. Norton, "The Balanced Scorecard: Measures That Drive Performance," *Harvard Business Review,* July-August 2005.

both the customer and internal business processes perspectives are interested in performance that results in high-quality products.

Figure 6 applies the balanced scorecard to Good Foods Store. The company's mission is to be the food store of choice in the community. This mission is at the center of the company's balanced scorecard. Surrounding it are the four interrelated perspectives.

At the base of the scorecard is the learning and growth perspective. Here, part of the objective, or performance goal, is to provide courteous service. Because training employees in customer service should result in courteous service, performance related to this objective can be measured in terms of how many employees have received training. The number of customer complaints is another measure of courteous service.

From the perspective of internal business processes, the objective is to help achieve the company's mission by managing the supply chain efficiently, which should contribute to customer satisfaction. Efficiency in the ordering process can be measured by recording the number of orders placed with distributors each month and the number of times per month that customers ask for items that are not in stock.

If the objectives of the learning and growth and internal business processes perspectives are met, this should result in attracting customers and retaining them, which is the objective of the customer perspective. Performance related to this objective is measured by tracking the number of new customers and the number of repeat customers. Satisfied customers should

Study Note

The balanced scorecard provides a way of linking the management of employees, internal business processes, and customer needs to external financial results. In other words, if managers can foster excellent performance for three of the stakeholder groups, good financial results will occur for the investor stakeholder group.

help achieve the objective of the financial perspective, which is profitable growth. Profitable growth is measured by growth in sales, profit margin, and return on assets.

Benchmarking

The balanced scorecard enables a company to determine whether it is making continuous improvement in its operations. But to ensure its success, a company must also compare its performance with that of similar companies in the same industry. **Benchmarking** is a technique for determining a company's competitive advantage by comparing its performance with that of its closest competitors. **Benchmarks** are measures of the best practices in an industry. To obtain information about benchmarks in the retail grocery industry, Anna Wang might join a trade association for small retail shops or food stores. Information about these benchmarks would be useful to her in setting targets for the performance measures in Good Foods Store's balanced scorecard.

S T O P • R E V I E W • A P P L Y

4-1. In what sense is the balanced scorecard "balanced"?

4-2. What are performance measures? Give examples of both financial and nonfinancial performance measures.

4-3. How does the balanced scorecard help managers evaluate performance?

Analysis of Nonfinancial Data in a Retail Organization

LO5 Prepare an analysis of nonfinancial data.

As we have noted throughout this chapter, managers use many kinds of nonfinancial measures to determine whether performance targets for internal business processes and customer satisfaction are being met. The following example illustrates how Good Foods Store can use nonfinancial data to analyze changes in performance at its checkout registers.

Lucy Bass supervises checkout procedures at Good Foods Store. The store has three registers to record customer sales. In the past, each register served an average of 30 customers per hour. However, on November 1, 20x9, Bass implemented a new scanning procedure that has reduced the number of customers served per hour.

Data on the number of customers served for the three-month period ended December 31, 20x9, are shown in Part A of Exhibit 3. Each register operated an average of 170 hours per month. Register 1 is always the busiest. Registers 2 and 3 receive progressively less business. Bass is preparing a report for Anna Wang on the effects of the new procedure.

Part B of Exhibit 3 shows Bass's analysis of the number of customers served at each register over the three months. She computed the number of customers served per hour by dividing the number of customers served by the register's monthly average operating hours (170). By averaging the customer service rates for the three registers, she got 28.43 customers per hour per register for November and 28.83 customers for December. As you can see, the service rate decreased in November. But December's average is higher than November's, which means that the register clerks, as a group, are becoming more accustomed to the new procedure. Part C of Exhibit 3 is a graphic comparison of the number of customers served per hour.

EXHIBIT 3 ▶

Analysis of Nonfinancial Data

Good Foods Store
Summary of Number of Customers Served
For the Quarter Ended December 31, 20x9

Part A: Number of Customers Served

Register	October	November	December	Quarter Totals
1	5,428	5,186	5,162	15,776
2	5,280	4,820	4,960	15,060
3	4,593	4,494	4,580	13,667
Totals	15,301	14,500	14,702	44,503

Part B: Number of Customers Served per Hour

Register	October	November	December	Quarter Averages
1	31.93	30.51	30.36	30.93
2	31.06	28.35	29.18	29.53
3	27.02	26.44	26.94	26.80
Totals	90.01	85.30	86.48	87.26
Average per hour per register	30.00	28.43	28.83	26.09

Part C: Graphic Comparison of the Number of Customers Served per Hour

Register 1   Register 2   Register 3   Average

S T O P • R E V I E W • A P P L Y

5-1. Which is more important in managing a company: financial data or non-financial data?

5-2. Postal Services Inc. is having a problem with its three fully automated postal processing machines. The time for each operation has been increasing at an erratic rate. Management has asked that the time intervals be analyzed to see if the cause of the problem can be determined. The number of letters processed (in thousands) per shift during the previous week is as follows:

	Machine Number	Monday	Tuesday	Wednesday	Thursday	Friday
First shift:						
K	1	640	630	620	610	600
A	2	730	730	730	720	730
G	3	740	720	710	690	680
Second shift:						
D	1	420	410	410	400	398
B	2	650	650	660	660	670
F	3	520	520	510	504	502

From this information, assess the operations of the three machines.

Standards of Ethical Conduct

LO6 Identify the standards of ethical conduct for management accountants.

Managers are responsible to external parties (e.g., owners, creditors, governmental agencies, and the local community) for the proper use of organizational resources and the financial reporting of their actions. Conflicts may arise that require managers to balance the interests of all external parties, and management accountants have a responsibility to help them balance those interests. For example, the community wants a safe living environment, while owners seek to maximize profits. If management decides to

FOCUS ON BUSINESS PRACTICE
What Is Management's Responsibility for the Financial Statements?

Top-level managers have not only an ethical responsibility to ensure that the financial statements issued by their companies adhere to the principles of full disclosure and transparency; today, they have a legal responsibility as well. The Securities and Exchange Commission (SEC) requires the chief executive officers and chief financial officers of companies filing reports with the SEC to certify that those reports contain no untrue statements and include all facts needed to ensure that the reports are not misleading. In addition, the SEC requires managers to ensure that the information in reports filed with the SEC "is recorded, processed, summarized and reported on a timely basis."[7]

▼ **EXHIBIT 4**

Statement of Ethical Professional Practice

Members of IMA shall behave ethically. A commitment to ethical professional practice includes: overarching principles that express our values, and standards that guide our conduct.

PRINCIPLES

IMA's overarching ethical principles include: Honesty, Fairness, Objectivity, and Responsibility. Members shall act in accordance with these principles and shall encourage others within their organizations to adhere to them.

STANDARDS

A member's failure to comply with the following standards may result in disciplinary action.

I. COMPETENCE

Each member has a responsibility to:

1. Maintain an appropriate level of professional expertise by continually developing knowledge and skills.
2. Perform professional duties in accordance with relevant laws, regulations, and technical standards.
3. Provide decision support information and recommendations that are accurate, clear, concise, and timely.
4. Recognize and communicate professional limitations or other constraints that would preclude responsible judgment or successful performance of an activity.

II. CONFIDENTIALITY

Each member has a responsibility to:

1. Keep information confidential except when disclosure is authorized or legally required.
2. Inform all relevant parties regarding appropriate use of confidential information. Monitor subordinates' activities to ensure compliance.
3. Refrain from using confidential information for unethical or illegal advantage.

III. INTEGRITY

Each member has a responsibility to:

1. Mitigate actual conflicts of interest. Regularly communicate with business associates to avoid apparent conflicts of interest. Advise all parties of any potential conflicts.
2. Refrain from engaging in any conduct that would prejudice carrying out duties ethically.
3. Abstain from engaging in or supporting any activity that might discredit the profession.

IV. CREDIBILITY

Each member has a responsibility to:

1. Communicate information fairly and objectively.
2. Disclose all relevant information that could reasonably be expected to influence an intended user's understanding of the reports, analyses, or recommendations.
3. Disclose delays or deficiencies in information, timeliness, processing, or internal controls in conformance with organization policy and/or applicable law.

RESOLUTION OF ETHICAL CONFLICT

In applying the Standards of Ethical Professional Practice, you may encounter problems identifying unethical behavior or resolving an ethical conflict. When faced with ethical issues, you should follow your organization's established policies on the resolution of such conflict. If these policies do not resolve the ethical conflict, you should consider the following courses of action:

Discuss the issue with your immediate supervisor except when it appears that the supervisor is involved. In that case, present the issue to the next level. If you cannot achieve a satisfactory resolution, submit the issue to the next management level. If your immediate superior is the chief executive officer or equivalent, the acceptable reviewing authority may be a group such as the audit committee, executive committee, board of directors, board of trustees, or owners. Contact with levels above the immediate superior should be initiated only with your superior's knowledge, assuming he or she is not involved. Communication of such problems to authorities or individuals not employed or engaged by the organization is not considered appropriate, unless you believe there is a clear violation of the law.

Clarify relevant ethical issues by initiating a confidential discussion with an IMA Ethics Counselor or other impartial advisor to obtain a better understanding of possible courses of action.

Consult your own attorney as to legal obligations and rights concerning the ethical conflict.

Source: IMA Statement of Ethical Professional Practice, Institute of Management Accountants, www.imanet.org. Reprinted by permission.

FOCUS ON BUSINESS PRACTICE
How to Blow the Whistle on Fraud

Fraud is on the rise, according to PricewaterhouseCoopers's 2005 biennial survey of more than 3,000 corporate officers in 34 countries. Of those interviewed, 43 percent admitted to having been involved in at least one unethical workplace act in the previous year, and 75 percent observed such an act and did nothing about it. Employees reported their silence comes from fear of retaliation, retribution, or being ostracized. What is the best defense against employee silence about fraud? A confidential anonymous hotline operated by a third party. The Association of Certified Fraud Examiners reported in 2002 that organizations with hotlines can cut their losses by approximately 50 percent per scheme.[8]

purchase an expensive device to extract pollutants from the production process, it will protect the community, but profits will decline. The benefit will be greater for the community than for the owners. On the other hand, management could achieve higher profits for the owners by purchasing a less expensive, less effective antipollution device that would not protect the community as well. Such conflicts between external parties can create ethical dilemmas for management and for accountants.

To be viewed credibly by the various parties who rely on the information they provide, management accountants must adhere to the highest standards of performance. To provide guidance, the Institute of Management Accountants has issued standards of ethical conduct for practitioners of management accounting and financial management. Those standards, presented in Exhibit 4, emphasize that management accountants have responsibilities in the areas of competence, confidentiality, integrity, and credibility.

STOP • REVIEW • APPLY

6-1. If you encounter financial irregularities in your company, what should your first step be? What is your last recourse?

6-2. Why is it so important for management accountants to maintain their integrity?

A LOOK BACK AT

WAL-MART STORES, INC.

The Decision Point at the beginning of this chapter focused on **Wal-Mart,** a company whose mission is to give ordinary folk the chance to buy the same things as rich people around the world. It posed these questions:

• **What is Wal-Mart's strategic plan?**

• **What management accounting tools does Wal-Mart use to stay ahead of its competitors?**

• **What role does management accounting play in Wal-Mart's endeavors?**

Wal-Mart's strategic plan focuses on achieving the company's objective of being the low-cost leader in the markets that it enters. This strategy drives the way Wal-Mart' managers address stakeholder perspectives, as well as how they formulate tactical and operating plans. To stay agile, flexible, and ahead of its competitors, Wal-Mart uses management tools like supply and value chains to standardize requirements and procedures and keep the costs of doing business low. These cost containment measures demonstrate Wal-Mart's resolve to remain an industry leader. But what role does management accounting play in this endeavor?

Management accounting provides the information necessary for effective decision making. Wal-Mart's managers use management accounting information in making decisions about everything from entering new markets like banking and religious books, to selecting vendors and products, to developing and implementing new supply chain processes, to pricing, marketing, and distributing goods.

Management accounting also provides Wal-Mart's managers with objective data that they can use to measure the company's performance in terms of its key success factor—cost. Among the management accounting tools used are budgets, which set daily operating goals for stores and provide targets for evaluating a store's performance. As Wal-Mart strives to improve its sales, earnings per share, and profitability by maintaining its record of successes, it will continue to rely on the information that management accounting provides.

CHAPTER REVIEW

REVIEW of Learning Objectives

LO1 Distinguish management accounting from financial accounting and explain how management accounting supports the management process.

Management accounting is the process of identifying, measuring, accumulating, analyzing, preparing, interpreting, and communicating information that management uses to plan, evaluate, and control an organization and to ensure that its resources are used and accounted for appropriately. Management accounting reports provide information for planning, control, performance measurement, and decision making to managers and employees when they need such information. These reports have a flexible format; they can present either historical or future-oriented information expressed in dollar amounts or physical measures. In contrast, financial accounting reports provide information about an organization's past performance to owners, lenders, customers, and governmental agencies on a periodic basis. Financial accounting reports follow strict guidelines defined by generally accepted accounting principles.

Management accounting supports each stage of the management process. When managers plan, they use management accounting information to establish strategic, tactical, and operating objectives that reflect their company's mission and to formulate a comprehensive business plan for achieving those objectives. The plan is usually expressed in financial terms in the form of budgets. When managers implement the plan, they use the information provided in the budgets. In evaluating performance, managers compare actual performance with planned performance and take steps to correct any problems. Reports reflect the results of planning, executing, and evaluating operations and may be prepared for external or internal use.

LO2 Describe the value chain and its usefulness in analyzing a business.

The value chain conceives of each step in the production of a product or the delivery of a service as a link in a chain that adds value to the product or service. These value-adding steps—research and development, design, supply, production, marketing, distribution, and customer service—are known as primary processes. The value chain also includes support services—human resources, legal services, information services, and management accounting. Support services facilitate the primary processes but do not add value to the final product. Value chain analysis enables a company to focus on its core competencies. Parts of the value chain that are not core competencies are frequently outsourced.

LO3 Identify the management tools used for continuous improvement.

Management tools for continuous improvement include the just-in-time (JIT) operating philosophy, total quality management (TQM), activity-based management (ABM), and the theory of constraints (TOC). These tools are designed to help businesses meet the demands of global competition by reducing resource waste and costs and by improving product or service quality, thereby increasing customer satisfaction.

Management accounting responds to a just-in-time operating environment by providing an information system that is sensitive to changes in production processes. In a total quality management environment, management accounting provides information about the costs of quality. Activity-based management's assignment of overhead costs to products or services relies on the accounting practice known as activity-based costing (ABC). In businesses that use the theory of constraints, management accounting identifies process or product constraints.

LO4 Explain the balanced score-card and its relationship to performance measures.	The balanced scorecard links the perspectives of an organization's stakeholder groups—financial (investors and owners), learning and growth (employees), internal business processes, and customers—to the organization's mission, objectives, resources, and performance measures. Performance measures are used to assess whether the objectives of each of the four perspectives are being met. Benchmarking is a technique for determining a company's competitive advantage by comparing its performance with that of its industry peers.
LO5 Prepare an analysis of nonfinancial data.	Using management tools like TQM and ABM and comprehensive frameworks like the balanced scorecard requires analysis of both financial and nonfinancial data. In analyzing nonfinancial data, it is important to compare performance measures with the objectives that are to be achieved.
LO6 Identify the standards of ethical conduct for management accountants.	Standards of ethical conduct for management accountants emphasize practitioners' responsibilities in the areas of competence, confidentiality, integrity, and credibility. These standards of conduct help management accountants recognize and avoid situations that could compromise their ability to supply management with accurate and relevant information.

REVIEW of Concepts and Terminology

The following concepts and terms were introduced in this chapter:

Activity-based costing (ABC): A management accounting practice that identifies all of an organization's major operating activities (both production and nonproduction), traces costs to those activities, and then assigns costs to the products or services that use the resources and services supplied by the activities. **(LO3)**

Activity-based management (ABM): An approach to managing an organization that identifies all major operating activities, determines the resources consumed by each of those activities and the cause of the resource usage, categorizes the activities as either adding value to a product or service or not adding value, and seeks to eliminate or reduce nonvalue-adding activities. **(LO3)**

Balanced scorecard: A framework that links the perspectives of an organization's stakeholder groups to the organization's mission, objectives, resources, and performance measures. **(LO4)**

Benchmarking: A technique for determining a company's competitive advantage by comparing its performance with that of its best competitors. **(LO4)**

Benchmarks: Measures of the best practices in an industry. **(LO4)**

Business plan: A comprehensive statement of how a company will achieve its objectives. **(LO1)**

Continuous improvement: The management concept that one should never be satisfied with what is, but should instead constantly seek improved efficiency and lower cost through better methods, products, services, processes, or resources. **(LO3)**

Core competency: The thing a company does best and that gives it an advantage over its competitors. **(LO2)**

Costs of quality: Both the costs of achieving quality and the costs of poor quality in the manufacture of a product or the delivery of a service. **(LO3)**

Just-in-time (JIT) operating philosophy: A management tool aimed at improving productivity and eliminating waste by requiring that all resources—materials, personnel, and facilities—be acquired and used only as needed. **(LO3)**

Management accounting: The process of identifying, measuring, accumulating, analyzing, preparing, interpreting, and communicating information that management uses to plan, evaluate, and control an organization and to ensure that its resources are used and accounted for appropriately. **(LO1)**

Mission statement: A description of the fundamental way in which a business will achieve its goal of increasing the value of the owners' interest in the business. **(LO1)**

Nonvalue-adding activities: Activities that add cost to a product or service but do not increase its market value. **(LO3)**

Operating objectives: Short-term goals that outline expectations for the performance of day-to-day operations. **(LO1)**

Outsourcing: The engagement of other companies to perform a process or service in the value chain that is not among an organization's core competencies. **(LO2)**

Performance measures: Quantitative tools that gauge an organization's performance in relation to a specific goal or expected outcome. **(LO4)**

Primary processes: Components of the value chain that add value to a product or service. **(LO2)**

Strategic objectives: Broad, long-term goals that determine the fundamental nature and direction of a business and that serve as a guide for decision making. **(LO1)**

Supply chain: The path that leads from the suppliers of the materials from which a product is made to the final consumer. Also called the *supply network*. **(LO1)**

Support services: Components of the value chain that facilitate the primary processes but do not add value to a product or service. **(LO2)**

Tactical objectives: Interim goals that position a business to achieve its long-term strategies. **(LO1)**

Theory of constraints (TOC): A management theory that contends that limiting factors, or bottlenecks, occur during the production of any product or service, but that once managers identify such a constraint, they can focus their attention and resources on it and achieve significant improvements. **(LO3)**

Total quality management (TQM): A management tool that requires that all parts of a business work together to build quality into the business's product or service. **(LO3)**

Value-adding activities: Activities that add value to a product or service as perceived by the customer. **(LO3)**

Value chain: A way of defining a business as a set of primary processes and support services that link together to add value to a business's products or services, thus fulfilling the business's mission and objectives. **(LO2)**

REVIEW Problem

LO5 **Analysis of Nonfinancial Data**

Good Foods Store employs chefs who specialize in gourmet baked goods and bistro foods. Anna Wang prepared the following table estimating the number of hours that the chefs would work during June:

	A	B	C	D	E	F
1	Estimated Hours to Be Worked					
2		Week 1	Week 2	Week 3	Week 4	Totals
3	Baked goods	80	80	80	80	320
4	Bistro goods	120	120	120	120	480
5						

On July 2, Anna Wang assembled the following data on the actual number of hours worked:

	A	B	C	D	E	F
1	Actual Hours Worked					
2		Week 1	Week 2	Week 3	Week 4	Totals
3	Baked goods	96	108	116	116	436
4	Bistro goods	104	108	116	108	436
5						

Anna Wang is concerned about the excess hours worked during June.

Required

1. For each group of chefs (Baked goods and Bistro goods), prepare an analysis that shows the estimated hours, the actual hours worked, and the number of hours under or over the estimates for each week and in total.

2. Using the same information, prepare a line graph for a each group of chefs. Place the weeks on the *x* axis and the number of hours on the *y* axis.
3. Using the information from 1 and 2, identify the group of chefs who worked more hours than Anna Wang had planned and offer several reasons for the additional hours.

Answer to Review Problem

1.

Baked Goods Chefs

	A	B	C	D
	Week	Estimated Hours	Actual Hours	Hours Under or (Over) Estimate
1	80	96	(16)
2	80	108	(28)
3	80	116	(36)
4	80	116	(36)
Total	320	436	(116)

Bistro Goods Chefs

	A	B	C	D
	Week	Estimated Hours	Actual Hours	Hours Under or (Over) Estimate
1	120	104	16
2	120	108	12
3	120	116	4
4	120	108	12
Total	480	436	44

2.

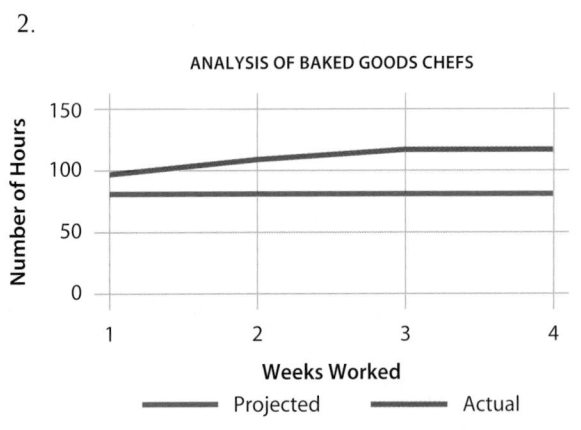

ANALYSIS OF BAKED GOODS CHEFS

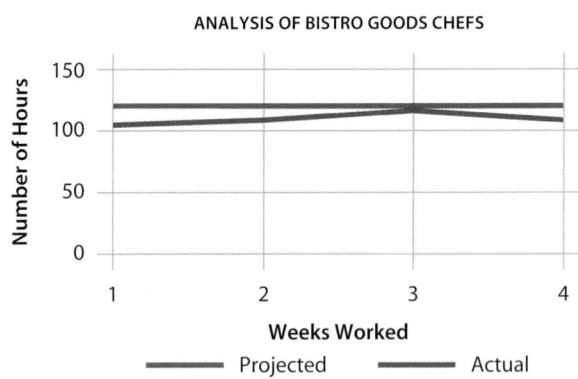

ANALYSIS OF BISTRO GOODS CHEFS

3. The baked goods chefs worked more hours than Wang had planned. The following are possible reasons for the additional hours:
   a. The quality of the materials may have been poor, which would have required extra work by the chefs.
   b. One of the chefs may have been recently hired and inexperienced. He would therefore have worked more slowly than anticipated, and the other chefs may have taken extra time to train him.

c. The equipment may have broken, in which case the chefs would have had to wait until it was repaired.
d. Wang may have underestimated the time required for baked goods.

CHAPTER ASSIGNMENTS

BUILDING Your Basic Knowledge and Skills

Short Exercises

LO1 Management Accounting Versus Financial Accounting

SE 1. Management accounting differs from financial accounting in a number of ways. Indicate whether each of the following characteristics relates to management accounting (MA) or financial accounting (FA):

1. Focuses on various segments of the business entity
2. Demands objectivity
3. Relies on the criterion of usefulness rather than formal guidelines in reporting information
4. Measures units in historical dollars
5. Reports information on a regular basis
6. Uses only monetary measures for reports
7. Adheres to generally accepted accounting principles
8. Prepares reports whenever needed

LO1 Strategic Positioning

SE 2. Organizations stake out different strategic positions to add value and achieve success. Some strive to be low-cost leaders like **Wal-Mart**, while others become the high-end quality leaders like **Whole Foods Market**. Identify which of the following organizations are low-cost leaders (C) and which are quality leaders (Q):

1. Nordstrom's
2. Harvard University
3. Local community college
4. Lexus
5. Kia
6. Rent-a-Wreck
7. Hertz Rental Cars
8. Coca-Cola
9. Store-brand soda

LO1 The Management Process

SE 3. Indicate whether each of the following management activities in a department store is part of planning (PL), performing (PE), evaluating (E), or communicating (C):

1. Completing a balance sheet and income statement at the end of the year
2. Training a clerk to complete a cash sale
3. Meeting with department managers to develop performance measures for sales personnel
4. Renting a local warehouse to store excess inventory of clothing
5. Evaluating the performance of the shoe department by examining the significant differences between its actual and planned expenses for the month
6. Preparing an annual budget of anticipated sales for each department and the entire store

LO1   Report Preparation

SE 4. Melissa Mertz, president of Mertz Industries, asked controller Rick Caputo to prepare a report on the use of electricity by each of the organization's five divisions. Increases in electricity costs in the divisions ranged from 20 to 35 percent over the past year. What questions should Rick ask before he begins his analysis?

LO1, LO2   The Supply Chain and the Value Chain

SE 5. Indicate whether each of the following is part of the supply chain (SC), a primary process (PP) in the value chain, or a support service (SS) in the value chain:

1. Human resources
2. Research and development
3. Supplier
4. Management accounting
5. Customer service
6. Retailer

LO2   The Value Chain

SE 6. The following unit costs were determined by dividing the total costs of each component by the number of products produced. From these unit costs, determine the total cost per unit of primary processes and the total cost per unit of support services.

Research and development	$ 1.40
Human resources	1.45
Design	0.15
Supply	1.10
Legal services	0.50
Production	4.00
Marketing	0.80
Distribution	0.90
Customer service	0.65
Information systems	0.85
Management accounting	0.20
Total cost per unit	$12.00

LO3   JIT and Continuous Improvement

SE 7. The just-in-time operating environment focuses on reducing or eliminating the waste of resources. Resources include physical assets such as machinery and buildings, labor time, and materials and parts used in the production process. Choose one of those resources and describe how it could be wasted. How can an organization prevent the waste of that resource? How can the concept of continuous improvement be implemented to reduce the waste of that resource?

LO4   The Balanced Scorecard: Stakeholder Values

SE 8. In the balanced scorecard approach, stakeholder groups with different perspectives value different performance goals. Sometimes, however, they may be interested in the same goal. Indicate which stakeholder groups—financial (F), learning and growth (L), internal business processes (P), and customers (C)—value the following performance goals:

1. High wages
2. Safe products
3. Low-priced products
4. Improved return on investment

5. Job security
6. Cost-effective production processes

LO5   **Analysis of Nonfinancial Data**

SE 9. Precision Technologies has been having a problem with the computerized welding operation in its extractor assembly line. The extractors are used to separate metal shavings into piles of individual metals for recycling and scrap sales. The time for each welding operation has been increasing at an erratic rate. Management has asked that the time intervals be analyzed to see if the cause of the problem can be determined. The number of parts welded per shift during the previous week is as follows:

	Machine Number	Monday	Tuesday	Wednesday	Thursday	Friday
First shift:						
Kovacs	1	642	636	625	617	602
Abington	2	732	736	735	729	738
Geisler	3	745	726	717	694	686
Second shift:						
Deragon	1	426	416	410	404	398
Berwager	2	654	656	661	664	670
Grass	3	526	524	510	504	502

What can you deduce from this information that may help management solve the welding operation problem?

LO6   **Ethical Conduct**

SE 10. Tyler Jones, a management accountant for Pegstone Cosmetics Company, has lunch every day with his friend Joe Blaik, who is a management accountant for Shepherd Cosmetics, Inc., a competitor of Pegstone Cosmetics. Last week, Jones couldn't decide how to treat some information in a report he was preparing, so he discussed it with Blaik. Is Jones adhering to the ethical standards of management accountants? Defend your answer.

Exercises

LO1   **Management Accounting Versus Financial Accounting**

E 1. Explain this statement: "It is impossible to distinguish the point at which financial accounting ends and management accounting begins."

LO1   **The Management Process**

E 2. Indicate whether each of the following management activities in a community hospital is part of planning (PL), performing (PE), evaluating (E), or communicating (C):

1. Leasing five ambulances for the current year
2. Comparing the actual number with the planned number of patient days in the hospital for the year
3. Developing a strategic plan for a new pediatric wing
4. Preparing a report showing the past performance of the emergency room
5. Developing standards, or expectations, for performance in the hospital admittance area for next year
6. Preparing the hospital's balance sheet and income statement and distributing them to the board of directors
7. Maintaining an inventory of bed linens and bath towels

8. Formulating a corporate policy for the treatment and final disposition of hazardous waste materials
9. Preparing a report on the types and amounts of hazardous waste materials removed from the hospital in the last three months
10. Recording the time taken to deliver food trays to patients

LO1   Report Preparation

E 3. Jeff Johnson is the sales manager for Sunny Days Greeting Cards, Inc. At the beginning of the year, the organization introduced a new line of humorous birthday cards to the U.S. market. Management held a strategic planning meeting on August 31 to discuss next year's operating activities. One item on the agenda was to review the success of the new line of cards and decide if there was a need to change the selling price or to stimulate sales volume in the five sales territories. Johnson was asked to prepare a report addressing those issues and to present it at the meeting. His report was to include the profits generated in each sales territory by the new card line only.

On August 31, Johnson arrived at the meeting late and immediately distributed his report to the strategic planning team. The report consisted of comments made by seven of Johnson's leading sales representatives. The comments were broad in scope and touched only lightly on the success of the new card line. Johnson was pleased that he had met the deadline for distributing the report, but the other team members were disappointed in the information he provided.

Using the four w's for report presentation, comment on Johnson's effectiveness in preparing his report.

LO1   The Planning Framework

E 4. Edward Ortez has just opened a company that imports fine ceramic gifts from Mexico and sells them over the Internet. In planning his business, Ortez did the following:

1. Listed his expected expenses and revenues for the first six months of operations
2. Decided that he wanted the company to provide him with income for a good lifestyle and funds for retirement
3. Determined that he would keep his expenses low and generate enough revenues during the first two months of operations so that he would have a positive cash flow by the third month
4. Decided to focus his business on providing customers with the finest Mexican ceramics at a favorable price
5. Developed a complete list of goals, objectives, procedures, and policies relating to how he would find, buy, store, sell, and ship goods and collect payment
6. Decided not to have a retail operation but to rely solely on the Internet to market the products
7. Decided to expand his website to include ceramics from other Central American countries over the next five years

Match each of Ortez's actions to the components of the planning framework: goal, mission, strategic objectives, tactical objectives, operating objectives, business plan, and budget.

LO1   The Supply Chain

E 5. In recent years, **United Parcel Service (UPS)** has been positioning itself as a solver of supply chain issues. Visit its website and read one of the case studies related to its supply chain solutions. Explain how UPS helped improve the supply chain of the business featured in the case.

LO2   **The Value Chain**

E 6. As mentioned in **E4**, Edward Ortez recently opened his own company. He has been thinking of ways to improve the business. Here is a list of the actions that he will be undertaking:

1. Engaging an accountant to help analyze progress in meeting the objectives of the company
2. Hiring a company to handle payroll records and employee benefits
3. Developing a logo for labeling and packaging the ceramics
4. Making gift packages by placing gourmet food products in ceramic pots and wrapping them in plastic
5. Engaging an attorney to write contracts
6. Traveling to Mexico himself to arrange for the purchase of products and their shipment back to the company
7. Arranging new ways of taking orders over the Internet and shipping the products
8. Keeping track of the characteristics of customers and the number and types of products they buy
9. Following up with customers to see if they received the products and if they are happy with them
10. Arranging for an outside firm to keep the accounting records
11. Distributing brochures that display the ceramics and refer to the website

Classify each of Ortez's actions as one of the value chain's primary processes—research and development, design, supply, production, marketing, distribution, or customer service—or as a support service—human resources, legal services, information systems, or management accounting. Of the 11 actions, which are the most likely candidates for outsourcing? Why?

LO3   **Management Tools**

E 7. Recently, you were dining with four chief financial officers (CFOs) who were attending a seminar on management tools and approaches to improving operations. During dinner, the CFOs shared information about their organizations' current operating environments. Excerpts from the dinner conversation appear below. Indicate whether each excerpt describes activity-based management (ABM), the just-in-time (JIT) operating philosophy, total quality management (TQM), or the theory of constraints (TOC).

> **CFO 1:** We think quality can be achieved through carefully designed production processes. We focus on minimizing the time needed to move, store, queue, and inspect our materials and products. We've reduced inventories by purchasing and using materials only when they're needed.

> **CFO 2:** Your approach is good. But we're more concerned with our total operating environment, so we have a strategy that asks all employees to contribute to the quality of both our products and our work environment. We focus on eliminating poor product quality by reducing waste and inefficiencies in our current operating methods.

> **CFO 3:** Our organization has adopted a strategy for producing high-quality products that incorporates many of your approaches. We also want to manage our resources effectively, and we do it by monitoring

operating activities. We analyze all activities to eliminate or reduce the ones that don't add value to products.

CFO 4: All of your approaches are good, but how do you set priorities for your management efforts? We find that we achieve the greatest improvements by focusing our time and resources on the bottlenecks in our production processes.

LO3   TQM and Value

E 8. De Silva Dry Cleaners recently adopted total quality management. Jorge De Silva, the owner, has hired you as a consultant. Classify each of the following activities as either value-adding (V) or nonvalue-adding (NV):

1. Providing same-day service
2. Closing the store on weekends
3. Providing free delivery service
4. Having a seamstress on site
5. Making customers pay for parking

LO4   The Balanced Scorecard

E 9. Connie's Takeout caters to young professionals who want a good meal at home but do not have time to prepare it. Connie's has developed the following business objectives:

1. To provide fast, courteous service
2. To manage the inventory of food carefully
3. To have repeat customers
4. To be profitable and grow

Connie's has also developed the following performance measures:

5. Growth in revenues per quarter and net income
6. Average unsold food at the end of the business day as a percentage of the total food purchased that day
7. Average customer time at the counter before being waited on
8. Percentage of customers who have shopped in the store before

Match each of these objectives and performance measures with the four perspectives of the balanced scorecard: financial perspective, learning and growth perspective, internal business processes perspective, and customer perspective.

LO5   Nonfinancial Data Analysis

E 10. Bluegrass Landscaping specializes in lawn installations requiring California bluegrass sod. The sod comes in 1-yard squares. To evaluate performance in laying sod, Bluegrass Landscaping uses the guideline of 500 square yards per person per hour. The company collected the following data about its operations during the first week of March:

Employee	Hours Worked	Square Yards of Sod Planted
S. Elway	38	18,240
R. Mahoney	45	22,500
N. Fenton	40	19,800
O. Pfister	42	17,640
B. Onski	44	22,880
J. Mantero	45	21,500

Evaluate the performance of the six employees.

LO5 Nonfinancial Data Analysis

E 11. Mother's Cookie Company recently adopted total quality management. According to a quality performance measure set by Elián Gomez, the vice president in charge of production, no more than ten cookies should be rejected per day. Data gathered for a recent week showed that the actual number of rejected cookies per day was as follows.

Day	Actual Number of Rejected Cookies
Monday	5
Tuesday	6
Wednesday	7
Thursday	4
Friday	8
Total	30

Analyze the activity for the week by preparing a table showing each day's maximum number of rejected cookies allowed, actual number of rejected cookies, and variance from the maximum number allowed. Compute the daily average for each column. Based on the information in your table, how successful was Gomez in increasing the quality of the company's cookies?

LO5 Nonfinancial Data Analysis

E 12. Sara Fowler, who is in charge of information technology at Cergo Corporation, must decide whether to purchase additional memory for her department's three computers or to buy additional new computers to increase her department's productivity. Six weeks ago, Fowler installed additional memory on Computer CM. She is impressed with the processing improvement, but she has yet to decide between the two courses of action. Information on the number of bytes processed per nanosecond by each computer for the past ten weeks is as follows:

Computer	One	Two	Three	Four	Five	Six	Seven	Eight	Nine	Ten
					Week					
CM	51	52	53	50	80	82	84	87	88	89
CN	52	51	52	52	54	54	53	54	54	54
CP	50	49	50	48	50	52	51	50	52	50

Fowler has asked you to analyze the two courses of action based on the assumption that two memory upgrades can be purchased for the price of one new computer. Your analysis is to include the computation of the average weekly output per nanosecond for Computers CN and CP, a comparison of that average with the output of Computer CM, and the computation of the weekly difference between the average output and the output of Computer CM. What course of action do you recommend?

LO6 Ethical Conduct

E 13. Katrina Kim went to work for Billings Industries five years ago. She was recently promoted to cost accounting manager and now has a new boss, Vic Howard, the corporate controller. Last week, Kim and Howard went to a two-day professional development program on accounting changes in the manufacturing environment. During the first hour of the first day's program, Howard disappeared, and Kim didn't see him again until the cocktail hour. The same thing happened on the second day. During the trip home, Kim asked Howard if he had enjoyed the conference. He replied:

> Katrina, the golf course was excellent. You play golf. Why don't you join me during the next conference? I haven't sat in on one of those sessions in ten years. This is my R&R time. Those sessions are for the new people. My experience is enough to keep me current. Plus, I have excellent people to help me as we adjust our accounting system to the changes being implemented on the production floor.

Does Katrina Kim have an ethical dilemma? If so, what is it? What are her options? How would you solve her problem? Be prepared to defend your answer.

LO6 **Ethical Responsibility**

E 14. Rank in order of importance the management accountant's four areas of responsibility: competence, confidentiality, integrity, and credibility. Explain the reasons for your ranking.

LO6 **Corporate Ethics**

E 15. To answer the following questions, conduct a search of several companies' websites: (1) Does the company have an ethics statement? (2) Does it express a commitment to environmental or social issues? (3) In your opinion, is the company ethically responsible? Select one of the companies you researched and write a brief description of your findings.

Problems

LO1 **Report Preparation**

P 1. Classic Industries, Inc., is deciding whether to expand its line of women's clothing called Pants by Olene. Sales in units of this product were 22,500, 28,900, and 36,200 in 20x7, 20x8, and 20x9, respectively. The product has been very profitable, averaging 35 percent profit (above cost) over the three-year period. The company has ten sales representatives covering seven states in the Northeast. Production capacity at present is about 40,000 pants per year. There is adequate plant space for additional equipment, and the labor needed can be easily hired and trained.

The organization's management is made up of four vice presidents: the vice president of marketing, the vice president of production, the vice president of finance, and the vice president of management information systems. Each vice president is directly responsible to the president, Teresa Jefferson.

Required

1. What types of information will Jefferson need before she can decide whether to expand the Pants by Olene line?
2. Assume that one report needed to support Jefferson's decision is an analysis of sales, broken down by sales representative, over the past three years. How would each of the four *w*'s pertain to this report?
3. Design a format for the report described in **2**.

LO2 **The Value Chain**

P 2. Zeigler Electronics is a manufacturer of cell phones, a highly competitive business. Zeigler's phones carry a price of $99, but competition forces the company to offer significant discounts and rebates. As a result, the average price of Zeigler's cell phones has dropped to around $50, and the company is losing money. Management is applying value chain analysis to the company's operations in an effort to reduce costs and improve product quality. A study by the company's management accountant has determined the following per unit costs for primary processes:

Primary Process	Cost per Unit
Research and development	$ 2.50
Design	3.50
Supply	4.50
Production	6.70
Marketing	8.00
Distribution	1.90
Customer service	.50
Total cost	$27.60

To generate a gross margin large enough for the company to cover its overhead costs and earn a profit, Zeigler must lower its total cost per unit for primary processes to no more than $20. After analyzing operations, management reached the following conclusions about primary processes:

- Research and development and design are critical functions because the market and competition require constant development of new features with "cool" designs at lower cost. Nevertheless, management feels that the cost per unit of these processes must be reduced by 10 percent.
- Six different suppliers currently provide the components for the cell phones. Ordering these components from just two suppliers and negotiating lower prices could result in a savings of 15 percent.
- The cell phones are currently manufactured in Mexico. By shifting production to China, the unit cost of production can be lowered by 20 percent.
- Most cell phones are sold through wireless communication companies that are trying to attract new customers with low-priced cell phones. Management believes that these companies should bear more of the marketing costs and that it is feasible to renegotiate its marketing arrangements with them so that they will bear 35 percent of the current marketing costs.
- Distribution costs are already very low, but management will set a target of reducing the cost per unit by 10 percent.
- Customer service is a weakness of the company and has resulted in lost sales. Management therefore proposes increasing the cost per unit of customer service by 50 percent.

Required

1. Prepare a table showing the current cost per unit of primary processes and the projected cost per unit based on management's proposals for cost reduction.
2. **Manager Insight:** Will management's proposals for cost reduction achieve the targeted total cost per unit? What further steps should management take to reduce costs? Which steps that management is proposing do you believe will be the most difficult to accomplish?
3. **Manager Insight:** What are the company's support services? What role should these services play in the value chain analysis?

LO4 **The Balanced Scorecard and Benchmarking**

P 3. Bychowski Associates is an independent insurance agency that sells business, automobile, home, and life insurance. Myra Bychowski, senior partner of the agency, recently attended a workshop at the local university in which the balanced scorecard was presented as a way of focusing all of a company's functions on its mission. After the workshop, she met with her managers in a weekend brainstorming session. The group determined that Bychowski Associates' mission was to provide high-quality, innovative risk-protection services to individuals and businesses. To ensure that the agency would fulfill this mission, the group established the following objectives:

- To provide a sufficient return on investment by increasing sales and maintaining the liquidity needed to support operations
- To add value to the agency's services by training employees to be knowledgeable and competent
- To retain customers and attract new customers
- To operate an efficient and cost-effective office support system for customer agents

To determine the agency's progress in meeting these objectives, the group established the following performance measures:

- Number of new ideas for customer insurance
- Percentage of customers who rate services as excellent
- Average time for processing insurance applications
- Number of dollars spent on training
- Growth in revenues for each type of insurance
- Average time for processing claims
- Percentage of employees who complete 40 hours of training during the year
- Percentage of new customer leads that result in sales
- Cash flow
- Number of customer complaints
- Return on assets
- Percentage of customers who renew policies
- Percentage of revenue devoted to office support system (information systems, accounting, orders, and claims processing)

Required

1. Prepare a balanced scorecard for Bychowski Associates by stating the agency's mission and matching its four objectives to the four stakeholder perspectives: the financial, learning and growth, internal business processes, and customer perspectives. Indicate which of the agency's performance measures would be appropriate for each objective.
2. **Manager Insight:** Bychowski Associates is a member of an association of independent insurance agents that provides industry statistics about many aspects of operating an insurance agency. What is benchmarking, and in what ways would the industry statistics assist Bychowski Associates in further developing its balanced scorecard?

LO5 **Nonfinancial Data Analysis**

P 4. Action Skateboards, Inc., manufactures state-of-the-art skateboards and related equipment. The production process involves the following departments and tasks: the Molding Department, where the board's base is molded; the Sanding Department, where the base is sanded after being taken out of the mold; the Fiber-Ap Department, where a fiberglass coating is applied; and the Assembling Department, where the wheels are attached and the board is inspected. After the board is molded, all processes are performed by hand.

Linda Raymond, the manager of the firm's California branch, is concerned about the number of hours her employees are working.

The California plant has a two-shift labor force. The actual hours worked for the past four weeks are as follows:

Actual Hours Worked—First Shift

Department	Week 1	Week 2	Week 3	Week 4	Totals
Molding	420	432	476	494	1,822
Sanding	60	81	70	91	302
Fiber-Ap	504	540	588	572	2,204
Assembling	768	891	952	832	3,443

Actual Hours Worked—Second Shift

Department	Week 1	Week 2	Week 3	Week 4	Totals
Molding	360	357	437	462	1,616
Sanding	60	84	69	99	312
Fiber-Ap	440	462	529	506	1,937
Assembling	670	714	782	726	2,892

Expected labor hours per product for each operation are Molding, 3.4 hours; Sanding, 0.5 hour; Fiber-Ap, 4.0 hours; and Assembling, 6.5 hours. Actual units completed are as follows:

Week	First Shift	Second Shift
1	120	100
2	135	105
3	140	115
4	130	110

Required

1. Prepare an analysis of each week to determine the average actual labor hours worked per board for each phase of the production process and for each shift. Carry your solution to two decimal places.
2. Using the information from 1 and the expected labor hours per board for each department, prepare an analysis showing the differences in each phase for each shift. Identify possible reasons for the differences.

LO5   Nonfinancial Data Analysis

P 5. The flow of passenger traffic is an important factor in an airport's success, and over the past year, heightened security measures at Winnebago County Airport in Rockford, Illinois, have slowed passenger flow significantly. The airport uses eight metal detectors to screen passengers for weapons. The facility is open from 6:00 A.M. to 10:00 P.M. daily, and the present machinery allows a maximum of 45,000 passengers to be checked each day.

The security team has selected four of the metal detectors for special analysis to determine if additional equipment is needed or if funding an additional homeland security officer could solve the problem. The additional homeland security officer would be responsible for guiding people to different machines and instructing them on the detection process. Because this solution would be less expensive than acquiring new machines, the team decides to fund a position for this function on a trial basis. The team hopes that this procedure will speed up the flow of passenger traffic by at least 10 percent. Manufacturers of the machinery have stated that each machine can handle an average of 400 passengers per hour. Data on passenger traffic through the four machines for the past 10 days are as follows:

Passengers Checked by Metal Detectors

Date	Machine 1	Machine 2	Machine 3	Machine 4	Totals
March 6	5,620	5,490	5,436	5,268	21,814
March 7	5,524	5,534	5,442	5,290	21,790
March 8	5,490	5,548	5,489	5,348	21,875
March 9	5,436	5,592	5,536	5,410	21,974
March 10	5,404	5,631	5,568	5,456	22,059
March 11	5,386	5,667	5,594	5,496	22,143
March 12	5,364	5,690	5,638	5,542	22,234
March 13	5,678	6,248	6,180	6,090	24,196
March 14	5,720	6,272	6,232	6,212	24,436
March 15	5,736	6,324	6,372	6,278	24,710

In the past, passenger flow has favored Machine 1 because of its location. Overflow traffic goes to Machine 2, Machine 3, and Machine 4, in that order. The new homeland security officer, Lynn Hedlund, began her duties on March 13. If her work results in at least a 10 percent increase in the number of passengers handled, the security team plans to fund another homeland security officer for the other four machines rather than purchasing additional metal detectors.

Required

1. Calculate the average daily traffic flow for the period March 6–12 and then calculate management's traffic flow goal.
2. **Manager Insight:** Calculate the average traffic flow for the period March 13–15. Did the additional homeland security officer's work result in the minimum increase in flow set by the security team, or should airport officials purchase additional metal detectors?
3. **Manager Insight:** Is there anything unusual in the analysis of passenger traffic flow that the security team should look into? Explain your answer.

Alternate Problems

LO1 **Report Preparation**

P 6. Sam Ratha recently purchased Yard & More, Inc., a wholesale distributor of equipment and supplies for lawn and garden care. The organization, which is headquartered in Baltimore, has four distribution centers that service 14 eastern states. The centers are located in Boston, Massachusetts; Rye, New York; Reston, Virginia; and Lawrenceville, New Jersey. The company's profits for 20x7, 20x8, and 20x9 were $225,400, $337,980, and $467,200, respectively.

Shortly after purchasing the organization, Ratha appointed people to the following positions: vice president, marketing; vice president, distribution; corporate controller; and vice president, research and development. Ratha has called a meeting of his management group. He wants to create a deluxe retail lawn and garden center that would include a large, fully landscaped plant and tree nursery. The purposes of the retail center would be (1) to test equipment and supplies before selecting them for sales and distribution and (2) to showcase the effects of using the company's products. The retail center must also make a profit on sales.

Required

1. What types of information will Ratha need before deciding whether to create the retail lawn and garden center?
2. To support his decision, Ratha will need a report from the vice president of research and development analyzing all possible plants and trees that could be planted and their ability to grow in the places where the new retail center might be located. How would each of the four *w*'s pertain to this report?
3. Design a format for the report in **2**.

LO5 Nonfinancial Data Analysis

P 7. Holiday Candy Company, which recently developed a strategic plan based on total quality management, wants its candy canes to have the highest quality of color, texture, shape, and taste possible. To ensure that quality standards are met, management has chosen many quality performance measures, including the number of rejected candy canes. Working with Luisa Ortes, the production supervisor, management has decided that no more than 50 candy canes should be rejected each day.

Using data on rejections in Week 1, Luisa Ortes prepared the following summary and graph:

Week 1	Maximum Number of Rejected Candy Canes Allowed	Actual Number of Rejected Candy Canes	Variance Under (Over) Allowed Maximum
Monday	50	60	(10)
Tuesday	50	63	(13)
Wednesday	50	58	(8)
Thursday	50	59	(9)
Friday	50	62	(12)
Total for the week	250	302	(52)
Daily average	50	60.4	

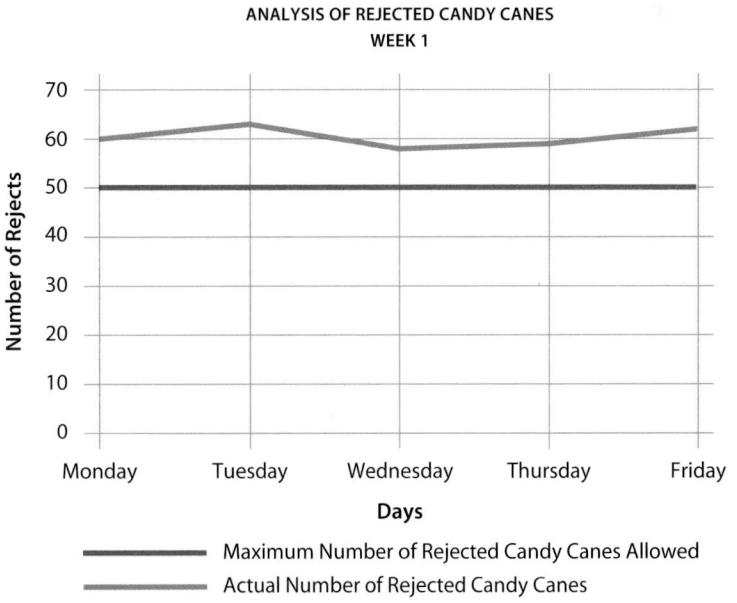

ANALYSIS OF REJECTED CANDY CANES
WEEK 1

—— Maximum Number of Rejected Candy Canes Allowed
—— Actual Number of Rejected Candy Canes

Because the variance was 20.8 percent ($52 \div 250$), Ortes decided to analyze the data further. She found that the rejected candy canes contained too little sugar (ingredients), were not circular (shaping), or were under-cooked (cooking time). The number of rejects in each category appears below.

Week 1	Reasons for Rejects
Ingredients	40
Shaping	195
Cooking time	67
Total	302

The following week, Ortes reviewed the recipe with the cooks. She trained them to measure ingredients more precisely, to shape the candy more carefully, and to time the cooking process more accurately. Then, in Week 3, she gathered the following information on the actual number of rejected candy canes and reasons for the rejects:

Week 3	Actual Number of Rejects	Week 3	Reasons for Rejects
Monday	20	Ingredients	7
Tuesday	21	Shaping	63
Wednesday	22	Cooking time	30
Thursday	19	Total	100
Friday	18		
Total	100		

Required

1. Analyze the activity in Week 3 by preparing a table showing each day's maximum number of rejected candy canes allowed, actual number of rejected candy canes, and variance under (over) the maximum number allowed. In addition, prepare a graph comparing the maximum and actual numbers for each day of Week 3.
2. Analyze how the reasons for rejecting candy canes changed from Week 1 to Week 3 by preparing a table showing the number of times each reason occurred each week. In addition, prepare a graph comparing the reasons for rejects each week.
3. **Manager Insight:** How successful was Ortes in increasing the quality of Holiday's candy canes? What recommendations, if any, would you make about monitoring candy cane production in the future?

LO5 **Nonfinancial Data Analysis**

P 8. Texas State Bank was founded in 1869. It has had a record of slow, steady growth since its inception. Management has always kept the processing of information as current as technology allows. Leslie Oistins, manager of the Brazas branch, is upgrading the check-sorting equipment in her office. There are ten check-sorting machines in operation. Information on the number of checks sorted by machine during the past eight weeks is at the top of the following page.

The Brazas branch has increased its checking business significantly over the past two years. Oistins must decide whether to purchase additional check-sorting machines or attachments for the existing machines to increase productivity. Five weeks ago the Colonnade Company convinced her to experiment with one such attachment, and it was placed on Machine BD. Oistins is impressed with the attachment but has yet to

| | | | | Week | | | | |
Machine	One	Two	Three	Four	Five	Six	Seven	Eight
AA	89,260	89,439	89,394	90,288	90,739	90,658	90,676	90,630
AB	91,420	91,237	91,602	91,969	91,950	92,502	92,446	92,816
AC	94,830	95,020	94,972	95,922	96,401	96,315	96,334	96,286
AD	91,970	91,786	92,153	92,522	92,503	93,058	93,002	93,375
AE	87,270	87,445	87,401	88,275	88,716	88,636	88,654	88,610
BA	92,450	92,265	92,634	93,005	92,986	93,544	93,488	93,862
BB	91,910	92,094	92,048	92,968	93,433	93,349	93,368	93,321
BC	90,040	89,860	90,219	90,580	90,562	91,105	91,051	91,415
BD	87,110	87,190	87,210	130,815	132,320	133,560	134,290	135,770
BE	94,330	94,519	94,471	95,416	95,893	95,807	95,826	95,778

decide between the two courses of action. Labor costs are not a factor in her decision.

Required

1. Compute the average weekly output of all machines except BD.
2. Compare the weekly output of Machine BD with the average weekly output of the nine machines without the attachment. Compute the weekly difference in the number of checks and the percentage change (difference divided by the average weekly output of the nine machines).
3. Manager Insight: Assume that Colonnade's attachment costs about the same as a new check-sorting machine. Which alternative would you recommend that Oistins choose?
4. Manager Insight: Would you change your recommendation if two attachments could be purchased for the price of one check-sorting machine? Does this decision require more data?
5. Manager Insight: If three attachments could be purchased for the price of one check-sorting machine, what action would you recommend?

ENHANCING Your Knowledge, Skills, and Critical Thinking

Conceptual Understanding Cases

LO2 **The Value Chain and Core Competency**

C 1. Medical Products Company (MPC) is known for developing innovative and high-quality products for use in hospitals and medical and dental offices. Its latest product is a nonporous, tough, and very thin disposable glove that will not leak or split and molds tightly to the hand, making it ideal for use in medical and dental procedures. MPC buys the material it uses in making the gloves from another company, which manufactures it according to MPC's exact specifications and quality standards. MPC makes two models of the glove—one white and one transparent—in its own plant and sells them through independent agents who represent various manufacturers. When an agent informs MPC of a sale, MPC ships the order directly to the buyer. MPC advertises the gloves in professional journals and gives free samples to physicians and dentists. It provides a product warranty and periodically surveys users about the product's quality.

Briefly explain how MPC accomplishes each of the primary processes in the value chain. What is a core competency? Which one of the primary processes would you say is MPC's core competency? Explain your choice.

LO4 **Performance Measures and the Balanced Scorecard**

C 2. In 2005, **General Motors Corporation (GM)** sold 9.2 million vehicles worldwide, the second-largest volume in the company's history. The good news was that sales increased in three of GM's four business regions, and all-time sales records were set for the Asia Pacific, Latin America, and Africa and Middle East regions. The bad news was that unit sales were down 3.1 percent in North America. As a result, GM's share of the global automotive market was 14.2 percent in 2005, down from 14.4 percent in 2004. The company is therefore revamping the way it does business. For example, it is investing $545 million in five core Michigan plants, pursuing hybrid technologies and alternative fuels, and seeking sensible labor contracts with its unions. Before answering the following questions, do a quick Internet search to determine what else GM is doing to revitalize itself.

1. What financial and other performance measures mentioned in the chapter would have prompted GM to revitalize itself?
2. The balanced scorecard uses performance measures that are linked to the perspectives of all stakeholder groups. Who are GM's stakeholders, and what performance measures do they value?
3. In your opinion, what options does GM have for revitalization?

Interpreting Management Reports

LO1 **Management Information**

C 3. Obtain a copy of a recent annual report of a publicly held organization in which you have a particular interest. (Copies of annual reports are available at your campus library, at a local public library, on the Internet, or by direct request to an organization.) Assume that you have just been appointed to a middle-management position in a division of the organization you have chosen. You are interested in obtaining information that will help you better manage the activities of your division, and you have decided to study the contents of the annual report in an attempt to learn as much as possible.

You particularly want to know about the following: (1) size of inventory maintained; (2) ability to earn income; (3) reliance on debt financing; (4) types, volume, and prices of products or services sold; (5) type of production process used; (6) management's long-range strategies; (7) success (profitability) of the division's various product lines; (8) efficiency of operations; and (9) operating details of your division.

1. Write a brief description of the organization and its products or services and activities.
2. Based on a review of the financial statements and the accompanying disclosure notes, prepare a written summary of information pertaining to items 1 through 9 above.
3. Can you find any of the information in which you are interested in other sections of the annual report? If so, which information, and in which sections of the report is it?
4. The annual report also includes other types of information that you may find helpful in your new position. In outline form, summarize this additional information.

LO1 **Management Information Needs**

C 4. In **C 3**, you examined your new employer's annual report and found some useful information. However, you are interested in knowing whether your division's products or services are competitive, and you were unable to find the necessary information in the annual report.

1. What kinds of information about your competition do you want to find?
2. Why is this information relevant? (Link your response to a particular decision about your organization's products or services. For example, you might seek information to help you determine a new selling price.)
3. From what sources could you obtain the information you need?
4. When would you want to obtain this information?
5. Create a report that will communicate your findings to your superior.

Decision Analysis Using Excel

Nonfinancial Data Analysis

LO5

C 5. Aviation Products Company is a subcontractor that specializes in producing housings for landing gears on jet airplanes. Its production process begins with Machine 1, which bends metal into cylinder-shaped housings and trims off the rough edges. Machine 2 welds the seam of the cylinder and pushes the entire piece into a large die to mold the housing into its final shape.

Joe Mee, the production supervisor, believes that the current process creates too much scrap (i.e., wasted metal). To verify this, James Kincaid, the company's accountant, began comparing the amounts of scrap generated in the last four weeks with the amounts of scrap the company anticipated for that period. Kincaid could not complete his analysis; his incomplete report appears below. Mee asks you to complete the report and submit a recommendation to him.

Aviation Products Company
Comparison of Actual Scrap and Expected Scrap
Four-Week Period

	Scrap in Pounds		Difference Under (Over)	
	Actual	Expected	Pounds	Percentage
Machine 1				
Week 1	36,720	36,720		
Week 2	54,288	36,288		
Week 3	71,856	35,856		
Week 4	82,440	35,640		
Machine 2				
Week 1	43,200	18,180		
Week 2	39,600	18,054		
Week 3	7,200	18,162		
Week 4	18,000	18,108		

1. Present the information in two ways:
   a. Prepare a table that shows the difference between the actual and expected scrap in pounds per machine per week. Calculate the difference in pounds and as a percentage (divide the difference in pounds by the expected pounds of scrap for each week). If the actual poundage of scrap is less than the expected poundage, record the difference as a negative. (This means there is less scrap than expected.)
   b. Prepare a line graph for each machine showing the weeks on the x axis and the pounds of scrap on the y axis.

2. Examine the differences for the four weeks for each machine, and determine which machine operation is creating excessive scrap.
3. What could be causing this problem?
4. What could Mee do to encourage early identification of the specific cause of such problems?

LO5   Nonfinancial Data Analysis

C 6. Refer to assignment **P 4** in this chapter. Linda Raymond needs to analyze the work performed by each shift in each department during Weeks 1 through 4.

1. For each department, calculate the average labor hours worked per board for each shift during Weeks 1 through 4. Carry your solution to two decimal places. (Note: Hours worked per board = hours worked each week ÷ boards produced each week.)
2. Using Excel's ChartWizard and the information from **1**, prepare a line graph for each department that compares the hours per board worked by the first and second shifts and the estimate for that department during Weeks 1 through 4. The following is the suggested format to use for the information table needed to complete the line graph for the Molding Department:

Molding Department

	Week 1	Week 2	Week 3	Week 4
First shift	3.50	3.20	3.40	3.80
Second shift	3.60	3.40	3.80	4.20
Estimated	3.40	3.40	3.40	3.40

3. Examine the four graphs that you prepared in **2**. Which shift is more efficient in all four departments? List some reasons for the differences between the shifts.

Ethical Dilemma Case

LO6   Professional Ethics

C 7. Mark Taylor is the controller for Krohm Corporation. He has been with the company for 17 years and is being considered for the job of chief financial officer. His boss, who is the current chief financial officer and former company controller, will be Krohm Corporation's new president. Taylor has just discussed the year-end closing with his boss, who made the following statement during their conversation:

> Mark, why are you being so inflexible? I'm only asking you to postpone the $2,500,000 write-off of obsolete inventory for ten days so that it won't appear on this year's financial statements. Ten days! Do it. Your promotion is coming up, you know. Make sure you keep all the possible outcomes in mind as you complete your year-end work. Oh, and keep this conversation confidential—just between you and me. Okay?

Identify the ethical issue or issues involved, and state the appropriate solution to the problem. Be prepared to defend your answer.

Internet Case

LO4   Comparison of Performance Measures

C 8. Honda Motor Company makes a green car called the Insight. Toyota Motor Company also makes a green car, which it calls the Prius. Search the websites of both these companies for data concerning the success of their green cars. (**Hint:** Review annual reports and press releases, or use the company's search engine.)

1. List the financial and nonfinancial performance measures that Toyota uses. List the measures used by Honda.
2. Use the data you found to prepare a brief comparison of the two cars. Do the two companies use comparable performance measures? If so, use these measures to evaluate the performance of the Prius and the Insight. If the measures are not comparable, how do they differ?

Group Activity Case

LO5 **Management Information Needs**

C 9. McDonald's is a leading competitor in the fast-food restaurant business. One component of McDonald's marketing strategy is to increase sales by expanding its foreign markets. At present, more than 40 percent of McDonald's restaurants are located outside the United States. In making decisions about opening restaurants in foreign markets, the company uses quantitative and qualitative financial and nonfinancial information. The following types of information would be important to such a decision: the cost of a new building (quantitative financial information), the estimated number of hamburgers to be sold in the first year (quantitative nonfinancial information), and site desirability (qualitative information).

You are a member of a management team that must decide whether to open a new restaurant in England. Identify at least two examples each of the (a) quantitative financial, (b) quantitative nonfinancial, and (c) qualitative information that you will need before you can make a decision.

Your instructor will divide the class into groups to discuss this case. Summarize your group's discussion and select someone from the group to present the group's findings to the rest of the class.

Business Communication Case

LO1 **Report Preparation**

C 10. The registrar's office of Polk Community College is responsible for maintaining a record of each student's grades and credits for use by students, instructors, and administrators.

1. Assume that you are a manager in the registrar's office and that you recently joined a team of managers to review the grade-reporting process. Explain how you would prepare a report of grades for students' use and the same report for instructors' use by answering the following questions:
   a. Who will read the grade report?
   b. Why is the grade report necessary?
   c. What information should the grade report contain?
   d. When is the grade report due?
2. Why does the information in a grade report for students' use and in a grade report for instructors' use differ?
3. Visit the registrar's office of your school in person or through your school's website. Obtain a copy of your grade report and a copy of the form that the registrar's office uses to report grades to instructors. Compare the information that these reports supply with the information you listed in 1. Explain any differences.
4. What can the registrar's office do to make sure that its grade reports are effective in communicating all necessary information to readers?

Cost Concepts and Cost Allocation

One of a company's primary goals is to be profitable. Because a company's owners expect to earn profits, managers have a responsibility to use the company's resources ethically and wisely so that they generate revenues that exceed the costs of the company's operating, investing, and financing activities. In this chapter, we describe how managers use information about costs, classify costs, compile product unit costs, and allocate overhead costs using the traditional method and the activity-based approach.

LEARNING OBJECTIVES

LO1 Describe how managers use information about costs.

LO2 Explain how managers classify costs and how they use these cost classifications.

LO3 Compare how service, retail, and manufacturing organizations report costs on their financial statements and how they account for inventories.

LO4 Describe the flow of costs through a manufacturer's inventory accounts.

LO5 Define *product unit cost* and compute the unit cost of a product or service.

LO6 Define *cost allocation* and explain how cost objects, cost pools, and cost drivers are used to assign overhead costs.

LO7 Using the traditional method of allocating overhead costs, calculate product or service unit cost.

LO8 Using activity-based costing to assign overhead costs, calculate product or service unit cost.

SOUTHWEST AIRLINES

- How do managers at Southwest Airlines determine the cost of selling tickets or of operating a flight?

- How do they use cost information?

With more than 3,000 flights a day, an average trip length of 793 miles, an average of 69.5 percent of its flights full, and an average one-way fare of $92.63, Southwest Airlines is the nation's leading high-frequency, short-haul, low-fare carrier. It is also the only large domestic airline to have remained profitable for more than 31 years. For nine years running, *Fortune* magazine has recognized Southwest as the most admired airline in the world, and for the past five years, *Business Ethics* magazine has included Southwest in its "100 Best Corporate Citizens" list.

To have achieved such a status and to maintain it, managers at Southwest must know the costs that the airline is incurring, including the cost of selling tickets and the cost of operating a flight. Online ticket sales generate approximately 65 percent of Southwest's passenger revenues, so classifying and analyzing the costs of these sales is very important to the company's profitability.[1]

Cost Information

One of a company's primary goals is to be profitable. Because a company's owners expect to earn profits, managers have a responsibility to use the company's resources wisely and to generate revenues that will exceed the costs of the company's operating, investing, and financing activities. In this chapter, we focus on costs related to the operating activities of manufacturing, retail, and service organizations. We begin by looking at how managers in these different organizations use information about costs.

Managers' Use of Cost Information

Managers use information about operating costs to plan, perform, evaluate, and communicate the results of operating activities. Figure I provides an overview of how managers use operating costs.

Planning   When they plan, managers in service organizations, such as **Southwest Airlines**, **Federal Express** and **USAA**, use the estimated costs of rendering services to develop budgets, estimate revenues, and manage the organization's work force. In retail companies, such as **Wal-Mart** and **Target**, managers work with estimates of the cost of merchandise purchases to develop budgets for purchases and net income, as well as to determine the selling prices or sales units required to cover all costs. Managers of manufacturing companies, such as **Apple**, **Motorola**, and **Honda**, use estimates of product costs to develop budgets for production, materials, labor, and overhead, as well as to determine the selling price or sales level required to cover all costs.

Performing   Managers in service organizations find the estimated cost of services helpful in monitoring profitability and making decisions about such matters as bidding on future business, lowering or negotiating their fees, or dropping one of their services.

Colleen Barrett, president of Southwest Airlines, is shown here with some of the company's pilots. She believes that a stable work environment encourages learning and personal growth and helps fulfill Southwest's mission of providing the highest quality of customer service. Like managers in other service organizations, Barrett and her management team use cost information to plan work force levels, estimate the cost of labor, and evaluate performance.

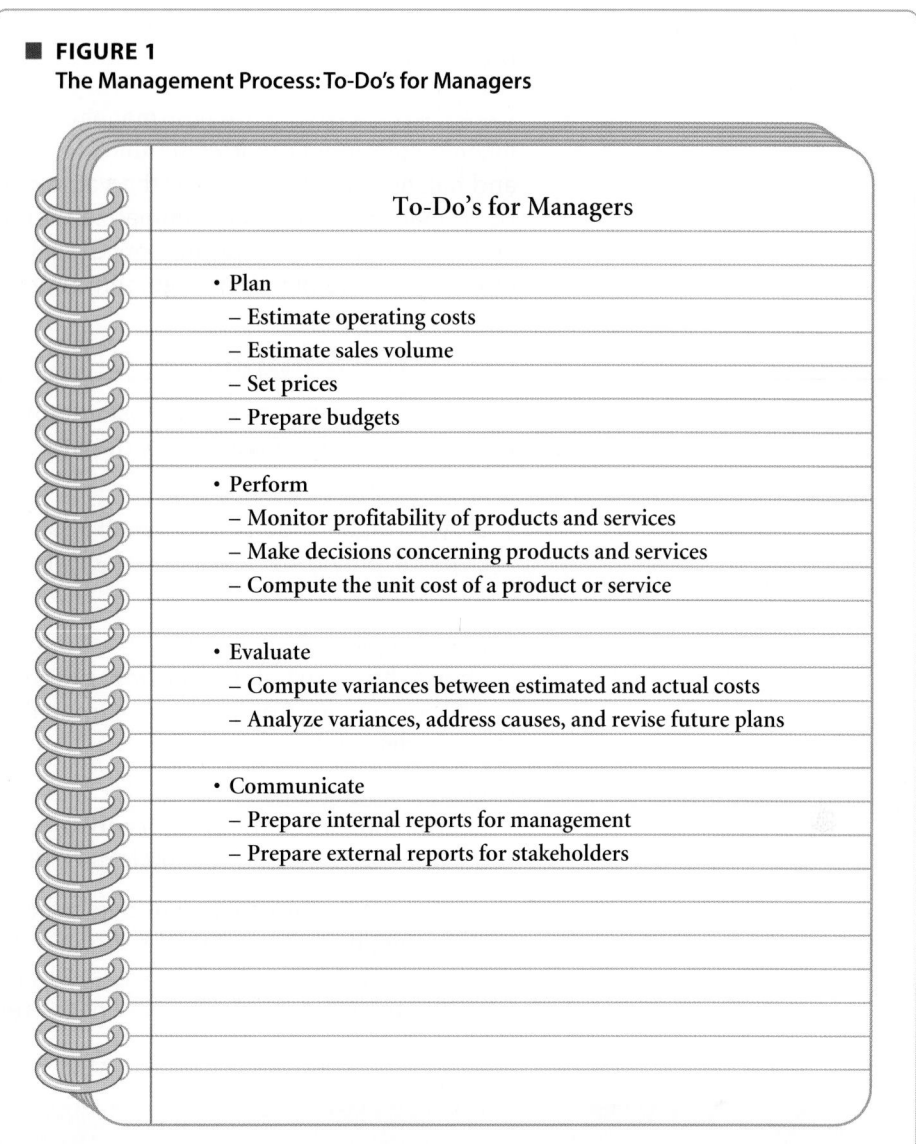

■ FIGURE 1
The Management Process: To-Do's for Managers

To-Do's for Managers

- Plan
  - Estimate operating costs
  - Estimate sales volume
  - Set prices
  - Prepare budgets

- Perform
  - Monitor profitability of products and services
  - Make decisions concerning products and services
  - Compute the unit cost of a product or service

- Evaluate
  - Compute variances between estimated and actual costs
  - Analyze variances, address causes, and revise future plans

- Communicate
  - Prepare internal reports for management
  - Prepare external reports for stakeholders

In retail organizations, such as Good Foods Store, which we used as an example in the last chapter, managers work with the estimated cost of merchandise purchases to predict gross margin, operating income, and value of merchandise sold. They also use this information to make decisions about matters like reducing selling prices for clearance sales, lowering selling prices for bulk sales, or dropping a product line.

Managers of manufacturing companies use estimated product costs to predict the gross margin and operating income on sales and to make decisions about such matters as dropping a product line, outsourcing the manufacture of a part to another company, bidding on a special order, or negotiating a selling price. In this chapter, we will use The Choice Candy Company, a hypothetical manufacturer of gourmet chocolate candy bars, to illustrate how managers of manufacturing companies use cost information.

Evaluating When managers evaluate performance, they want to know about significant differences between the estimated costs and actual costs of their products, merchandise purchases, or services. The identification of variances between estimated and actual costs helps them determine the causes of cost overruns, which may enable them to make decisions that will avoid such problems in the future.

Communicating When managers look at external reports, they expect income statements that communicate the actual costs of operating activities and balance sheets that show the value of inventory. They also expect internal performance reports that summarize their plans, their performance outcomes, and their evaluation of performance, such as the variance analyses done in the evaluating stage of the management process.

Cost Information and Organizations

Although all organizations use cost information to determine profits and selling prices and to value inventories, different types of organizations have different types of costs.

- Service organizations like **Southwest Airlines** need information about the costs of providing services, which include the costs of labor and related overhead.

- Retail organizations like **Wal-Mart** and Good Foods Store need information about the costs of purchasing products for resale. These costs include adjustments for freight-in costs, purchase returns and allowances, and purchase discounts.

- Manufacturing organizations like **Coca-Cola** and the Choice Candy Company need information about the costs of manufacturing products. Product costs include the costs of direct materials, direct labor, and overhead.

Among the other costs that organizations incur are the costs of marketing, distributing, installing, and repairing a product or the costs of marketing and supporting the delivery of services. Ultimately, a company is profitable only when its revenues from sales or services rendered exceed all its costs.

S T O P • R E V I E W • A P P L Y

1-1. How do managers use information about costs?

1-2. Do managers in all organizations need the same type of cost information?

Suggested answers to all Stop, Review, and Apply questions are available at http://college.hmco.com/accounting/needles/poa/10e/student_home.html.

Cost Classifications and Their Uses

LO2 Explain how managers classify costs and how they use these cost classifications.

A single cost can be classified and used in several ways, depending on the purpose of the analysis. Figure 2 provides an overview of commonly used cost classifications. These classifications enable managers to do the following:

1. Control costs by determining which are traceable to a particular cost object, such as a service or product

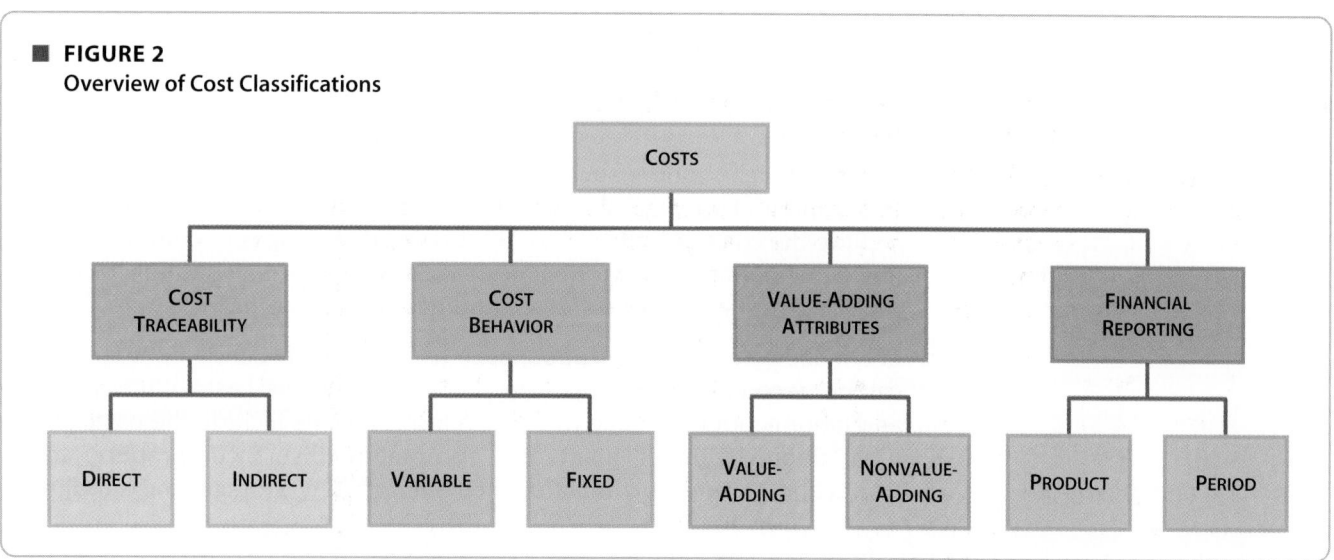

■ FIGURE 2
Overview of Cost Classifications

2. Calculate the number of units that must be sold to achieve a certain level of profit (cost behavior)

3. Identify the costs of activities that do and do not add value to a product or service

4. Classify costs for the preparation of financial statements

Cost classifications are important in all types of organizations. They help managers select and use relevant information to improve the efficiency of operations, provide quality products or services, and satisfy customer needs.

Cost Traceability

Managers trace costs to cost objects, such as products or services, sales territories, departments, or operating activities, to develop a fairly accurate measurement of costs. They use both direct and indirect measures of costs to support pricing decisions or decisions to reallocate resources to other cost objects. **Direct costs** are costs that can be conveniently and economically traced to a cost object. For example, the wages of a **Southwest Airlines** flight crew can be conveniently traced to a flight because the time worked and the hourly wages are shown on time cards and payroll records. Similarly, jet fuel (1.2 billion gallons consumed in 2004) costs for a flight can be easily traced.

In some cases, even though a material becomes part of a finished product or service, the expense of tracing its cost is too great. Some examples include the nails used in furniture, the salt used in candy, and the rivets used in airplanes. Such costs are considered indirect costs of the product or service. **Indirect costs** are costs that cannot be conveniently and economically traced to a cost object. For the sake of accuracy, however, indirect costs must be included in the cost of a product or service. Because they are difficult to trace, management uses a formula to assign them. For example, Southwest Airlines' insurance costs cannot be conveniently traced to individual flights; management solves the problem by assigning a portion of the insurance costs to each flight flown.

The following examples illustrate cost objects and their direct and indirect costs in service, retail, and manufacturing organizations:

◗ In a service organization, such as an accounting firm, costs can be traced to a specific service, such as preparation of tax returns. Direct costs for such a service include the costs of government reporting forms, computer usage, and the accountant's labor. Indirect costs include the costs of supplies, office rental, utilities, secretarial labor, telephone usage, and depreciation of office furniture.

◗ In a retail organization, such as Good Foods Store, costs can be traced to a department. For example, the direct costs of the produce department include the costs of fruits and vegetables and the wages of employees working in that department. Indirect costs include the costs of utilities to cool the produce displays and the storage and handling of the produce.

◗ In a manufacturing organization, such as The Choice Candy Company, costs can be traced to the product. Direct costs include the costs of the materials and labor needed to make the candy. Indirect costs include the costs of utilities, depreciation of plant and equipment, insurance, property taxes, inspection, supervision, maintenance of machinery, storage, and handling.

Cost Behavior

Managers are also interested in the way costs respond to changes in volume or activity. By analyzing those patterns of behavior, they gain information about how changes in selling prices or operating costs affect the company's net income, and they can then make adjustments so that the company obtains a certain level of profit.

Costs can be separated into variable costs and fixed costs. A **variable cost** is a cost that changes in direct proportion to a change in productive output (or some other measure of volume). A **fixed cost** is a cost that remains constant within a defined range of activity or time period.

All types of organizations have variable and fixed costs. The following are a few examples:

◗ Because the number of passengers drives the consumption of food and beverages on a flight, the cost of peanuts and beverages is a variable cost for Southwest Airlines. Fixed costs include the depreciation on the plane and the salaries and benefits of the flight and ground crews.

◗ The variable costs of Good Foods Store include the cost of groceries sold and any sales commissions. Fixed costs include the costs of building and lot rental, depreciation on store equipment, and the manager's salary.

◗ The variable costs of The Choice Candy Company include the costs of direct materials (e.g., sugar, cocoa), direct labor, indirect materials (e.g., salt), and indirect labor (e.g., inspection and maintenance labor). Fixed costs include the costs of supervisors' salaries and depreciation on buildings.

As a grocery store sells more products or as a candy manufacturer increases its output of products, its variable costs will increase proportionately. But its

FOCUS ON BUSINESS PRACTICE
How Does an Airline Manage Its Fixed Costs?

One of **Southwest Airlines'** nonfinancial performance measures is a 20-minute turnaround time on the ground. This standard helps Southwest efficiently manage the many fixed costs of running an airline. If additional security measures or other circumstances forced Southwest to add even 10 minutes to its ground turnaround time, it would result in higher fixed costs because the company would need additional planes to keep to its daily flight schedule. For an airline to be profitable, it needs to maximize its fleet's time in the air and minimize its time on the ground.[2]

A fixed cost is a cost that remains constant within a defined range of activity or time period. For Southwest Airlines, fixed costs include the salaries and benefits of ground crews. By keeping turnaround time on the ground to 20 minutes, Southwest minimizes the number of planes it needs to keep to daily schedules, thus avoiding some higher fixed costs.

fixed costs will remain the same for a specified period. Its rent, for example, will not change over the term of the lease, and its property taxes will remain the same until the next assessment.

Value-Adding Versus Nonvalue-Adding Costs

A **value-adding cost** is the cost of an activity that increases the market value of a product or service. A **nonvalue-adding cost** is the cost of an activity that adds cost to a product or service but does not increase its market value. Costs incurred to improve the quality of a product are value-adding costs if the customer is willing to pay more for the higher-quality product; otherwise, they are nonvalue-adding costs because they do not increase the product's market value.

Managers examine the value-adding attributes of their company's operating activities and, wherever possible, reduce or eliminate activities that do not directly add value to the company's products or services. For example, the costs of administrative activities, such as accounting and human resource management, are nonvalue-adding costs; they are necessary for the operation of the business, but they do not add value to the products or services produced, so they are monitored closely. Information about value-adding and nonvalue-adding costs influences the design of future products or services.

Cost Classifications for Financial Reporting

For purposes of preparing financial statements, managers classify costs as product costs or period costs. **Product costs**, or *inventoriable* costs, are costs assigned to inventory; they include direct materials, direct labor, and overhead. Product costs appear on the income statement as cost of goods sold and on the balance sheet as inventory. **Period costs**, or *noninventoriable* costs, are costs of resources used during the accounting period that are not assigned to products. They appear as operating expenses on the income statement. For example, among the period costs listed on the income statement are selling, administrative, and general expenses.

> **Study Note**
>
> Product costs and period costs can be explained by using the matching rule. Product costs must be charged to the period in which the product generates revenue, and period costs are charged against the revenue of the current period.

TABLE 1. Examples of Cost Classifications for a Candy Manufacturer

Cost Examples	Traceability to Product	Cost Behavior	Value Attribute	Financial Reporting
Sugar for candy	Direct	Variable	Value-adding	Product (direct materials)
Labor for mixing	Direct	Variable	Value-adding	Product (direct labor)
Labor for supervision	Indirect	Fixed	Nonvalue-adding	Product (overhead)
Depreciation on mixing machine	Indirect	Fixed	Value-adding	Product (overhead)
Sales commission	—*	Variable	Value-adding†	Period
Accountant's salary	—*	Fixed	Nonvalue-adding	Period

*Sales commissions and accountants' salaries cannot be directly or indirectly traced to a cost object; they are not product costs.

†Sales commissions can be value-adding because customers' perceptions of the salesperson and the selling experience can strongly affect their perceptions of the product's market value.

Table 1 shows how some costs of a candy manufacturer can be classified in terms of traceability, behavior, value attribute, and financial reporting.

STOP • REVIEW • APPLY

2-1. Why do managers use different classifications of costs?

2-2. Are the costs of a product always traceable as direct or indirect costs?

2-3. What is the difference between a value-adding cost and a nonvalue-adding cost?

2-4. What are product costs and period costs?

Financial Statements and the Reporting of Costs

LO3 Compare how service, retail, and manufacturing organizations report costs on their financial statements and how they account for inventories.

Managers prepare financial statements at least once a year to communicate the results of their management activities for the period. The key to preparing an income statement or a balance sheet in any kind of organization is to determine its cost of goods or services sold and the value of its inventories, if any.

Cost Reporting and Accounting for Inventories

Because the operations of service and retail organizations differ from those of manufacturers, the accounts presented in their financial statements differ as well. For example, because service organizations like **Southwest Airlines** and **United Parcel Service (UPS)** sell services and not products, they maintain no inventories for sale or resale. As a result, unlike manufacturing and retail organizations, they have no inventory accounts on their balance sheets. When preparing income statements, they calculate the cost of sales rather than the cost of goods sold, using the following equation:

$$\text{Cost of Sales} = \text{Net Cost of Services Sold}$$

For instance, suppose that Good Foods Store, the retail shop that we used as an example in the last chapter, employs UPS to deliver its products. The cost of sales for UPS would include the wages and salaries of personnel plus the expense of the trucks, planes, supplies, and anything else that UPS uses to deliver packages for Good Foods Store.

Retail organizations, such as **Wal-Mart** and Good Foods Store, which purchase products ready for resale, maintain just one inventory account on the balance sheet. Called the Merchandise Inventory account, it reflects the costs of goods held for resale. Retail organizations include the cost of purchases in the calculation of cost of goods sold, as follows:

$$\text{Cost of Goods Sold} = \begin{matrix} \text{Beginning} \\ \text{Merchandise} \\ \text{Inventory} \end{matrix} + \begin{matrix} \text{Net Cost of} \\ \text{Purchases} \end{matrix} - \begin{matrix} \text{Ending} \\ \text{Merchandise} \\ \text{Inventory} \end{matrix}$$

Suppose that Good Foods Store had a balance of $3,000 in its Merchandise Inventory account on December 31, 20x8. During the next year, its purchases of food products totaled $23,000 (adjusted for purchase discounts, returns and allowances, and freight-in). On December 31, 20x9, its Merchandise Inventory balance was $4,500. The cost of goods sold for 20x9 is thus $21,500:

$$\text{Cost of Goods Sold} = \$3{,}000 + \$23{,}000 - \$4{,}500 = \$21{,}500$$

Manufacturing organizations like The Choice Candy Company, which make products for sale, maintain three inventory accounts on the balance sheet: the Materials Inventory, Work in Process Inventory, and Finished Goods Inventory accounts. The Materials Inventory account shows the cost of materials that have been purchased but not used in the production process. During the production process, the costs of manufacturing the product are accumulated in the Work in Process Inventory account; the balance of this account represents the costs of the unfinished product. Once the product is complete and ready for sale, its cost is transferred to the Finished Goods Inventory account; the balance in this account is the cost of the unsold completed product. When the product is sold, the manufacturing organization uses the following equation to calculate the cost of goods sold:

$$\text{Cost of Goods Sold} = \begin{matrix} \text{Beginning} \\ \text{Finished Goods} \\ \text{Inventory} \end{matrix} + \begin{matrix} \text{Cost of} \\ \text{Goods} \\ \text{Manufactured} \end{matrix} - \begin{matrix} \text{Ending} \\ \text{Finished Goods} \\ \text{Inventory} \end{matrix}$$

For example, suppose that The Choice Candy Company had a balance of $52,000 in its Finished Goods Inventory account on December 31, 20x8. During the next year, the cost of the products that the company manufactured totaled $144,000. On December 31, 20x9, its Finished Goods Inventory balance was $78,000. The cost of goods sold for 20x9 is thus $118,000:

$$\text{Cost of Goods Sold} = \$52{,}000 + \$144{,}000 - \$78{,}000 = \$118{,}000$$

Remember that all organizations—service, retail, and manufacturing—use the following income statement format:

$$\text{Sales} - \begin{matrix} \text{Cost of Sales} \\ \text{or} \\ \text{Cost of Goods Sold} \end{matrix} = \begin{matrix} \text{Gross} \\ \text{Margin} \end{matrix} - \begin{matrix} \text{Operating} \\ \text{Expenses} \end{matrix} = \text{Operating Income}$$

FIGURE 3
Financial Statements of Service, Retail, and Manufacturing Organizations

	Service Company	Retail Company	Manufacturing Company
Income Statement	Sales – Cost of sales Gross margin – Operating expenses Operating income	Sales – Cost of goods sold* Gross margin – Operating expenses Operating income *Cost of goods sold: Beginning merchandise inventory + Net cost of purchases Cost of goods available for sale – Ending merchandise inventory Cost of goods sold	Sales – Cost of goods sold† Gross margin – Operating expenses Operating income †Cost of goods sold: Beginning finished goods inventory + Cost of goods manufactured Cost of goods available for sale – Ending finished goods inventory Cost of goods sold

Balance Sheet (current assets section)	No inventory accounts	One inventory account:
		  Merchandise Inventory
		  (finished product ready for sale)
			Three inventory accounts:
			  Materials Inventory
			  (unused materials)
			  Work in Process Inventory
			  (unfinished product)
			  Finished Goods Inventory
			  (finished product ready for sale)

Example with numbers		Income Statement: Beg. merchandise inventory $ 3,000 + Net cost of purchases 23,000 Cost of goods available for sale $26,000 – End. merchandise inventory 4,500 Cost of goods sold $21,500 Balance Sheet: Merchandise inventory, ending $ 4,500	Income Statement: Beg. finished goods inventory $ 52,000 + Cost of goods manufactured 144,000 Cost of goods available for sale $196,000 – End. finished goods inventory 78,000 Cost of goods sold $118,000 Balance Sheet: Finished goods inventory, ending $ 78,000

Figure 3 compares the financial statements of service, retail, and manufacturing organizations. Note in particular the differences in inventory accounts and cost of goods sold. As pointed out earlier, product costs, or inventoriable costs, appear as inventory on the balance sheet and as cost of goods sold on the income statement. Period costs, also called *noninventoriable costs* or *selling, administrative, and general expenses*, are reflected in the operating expenses on the income statement.

Statement of Cost of Goods Manufactured

The key to preparing an income statement for a manufacturing organization is computing its cost of goods sold, which means that you must first determine the cost of goods manufactured. This dollar amount is calculated on the **statement of cost of goods manufactured**, a special report based on an analysis of the Work in Process Inventory account. At the end of an accounting period, the flow of all manufacturing costs incurred during the period is sum-

EXHIBIT 1 ▶   **Statement of Cost of Goods Manufactured and Partial Income Statement for a Manufacturing Organization**

The Choice Candy Company
Statement of Cost of Goods Manufactured
For the Year Ended December 31, 20x9

Direct materials used		
Materials inventory, December 31, 20x8	$100,000	
Direct materials purchased	200,000	
Cost of direct materials available for use	$300,000	
Less materials inventory, December 31, 20x9	50,000	
Step 1: Cost of direct materials used		$250,000
Direct labor		120,000
Overhead		60,000
Step 2: Total manufacturing costs		$430,000
Add work in process inventory, December 31, 20x8		20,000
Total cost of work in process during the year		$450,000
Less work in process inventory, December 31, 20x9		150,000
Step 3: Cost of goods manufactured		$300,000

The Choice Candy Company
Income Statement
For the Year Ended December 31, 20x9

Sales		$500,000
Cost of goods sold		
Finished goods inventory, December 31, 20x8	$ 78,000	
Cost of goods manufactured	300,000 ←	
Cost of finished goods available for sale	$378,000	
Less finished goods inventory, December 31, 20x9	138,000	
Cost of goods sold		240,000
Gross margin		$260,000
Selling and administrative expenses		160,000
Operating income		$100,000

marized in this statement. Exhibit 1 shows The Choice Candy Company's statement of cost of goods manufactured for the year ended December 31, 20x9. It is helpful to think of the statement of cost of goods manufactured as being developed in three steps, as described below.

Step 1   *Compute the cost of direct materials used during the accounting period.* To do this, add the beginning balance in the Materials Inventory account to the direct materials purchased ($100,000 + $200,000). The subtotal ($300,000) represents the cost of direct materials available for use during the accounting period. Next, subtract the ending balance of the Materials Inventory account from the cost of direct materials available for use. The difference is the cost of direct materials used during the period ($300,000 − $50,000 = $250,000).

Step 2 *Calculate total manufacturing costs for the period.* As shown in Exhibit 1, the costs of direct materials used ($250,000) and direct labor ($120,000) are added to total overhead costs incurred during the period ($60,000) to arrive at total manufacturing costs ($430,000).

Step 3 *Determine total cost of goods manufactured for the period.* To do so, add the beginning balance in the Work in Process Inventory account to total manufacturing costs to arrive at the total cost of work in process during the period. From this amount, subtract the ending balance in the Work in Process Inventory account to arrive at the cost of goods manufactured ($450,000 − $150,000 = $300,000).

Do not confuse total manufacturing costs with the cost of goods manufactured. To understand the difference between these two amounts, look again at the computations in Exhibit 1. Total manufacturing costs of $430,000 incurred during the period are added to the $20,000 beginning balance in the Work in Process Inventory account to arrive at the total cost of work in process for the period ($430,000 + $20,000 = $450,000). The costs of products still in process at the end of the period ($150,000) are then subtracted from the total cost of work in process during the year. The remainder, $300,000, is the cost of goods manufactured (completed) during the current year. Note that the costs attached to the ending balance of Work in Process Inventory come from the current period's total manufacturing costs; they will not become part of the cost of goods manufactured until the next period, when the products are completed.

Study Note

An alternative to the cost of goods manufactured calculation uses the cost flow concept that is discussed in LO 4.

Study Note

It is important not to confuse the cost of goods manufactured with the cost of goods sold.

Cost of Goods Sold and a Manufacturer's Income Statement

Exhibit 1 shows the relationship between The Choice Candy Company's income statement and its statement of cost of goods manufactured. The total amount of the cost of goods manufactured during the period is carried over to the income statement, where it is used to compute the cost of goods sold. The beginning balance of the Finished Goods Inventory account is added to the cost of goods manufactured to arrive at the total cost of finished goods available for sale during the period ($78,000 + $300,000 = $378,000). The cost of goods sold is then computed by subtracting the ending balance in Finished Goods Inventory (the cost of goods completed but not sold) from the total cost of finished goods available for sale ($378,000 − $138,000 = $240,000). The cost of goods sold is considered an expense in the period in which the goods are sold.

S T O P • R E V I E W • A P P L Y

3-1. How do service, retail, and manufacturing organizations differ, and how do these differences affect accounting for inventories?

3-2. What inventory accounts accumulate the cost information used in the statement of cost of goods manufactured?

3-3. How is the cost of goods manufactured used in computing the cost of goods sold?

Income Statement for a Manufacturing Organization Incomplete inventory and income statement data for Sample Manufacturing Corporation follow. Determine the missing amounts.

Cost of Goods Sold	Beginning Finished Goods Inventory	Cost of Goods Manufactured	Ending Finished Goods Inventory
$2,000	$1,000	$5,000	?

SOLUTION:

Cost of Goods Sold		Beginning Finished Goods Inventory		Cost of Goods Manufactured		Ending Finished Goods Inventory
$2,000	=	$1,000	+	$5,000	−	$4,000

Inventory Accounts in Manufacturing Organizations

LO4   Describe the flow of costs through a manufacturer's inventory accounts.

Transforming materials into finished products ready for sale requires a number of production and production-related activities, including purchasing, receiving, inspecting, storing, and moving materials; converting them into finished products using labor, equipment, and other resources; and moving, storing, and shipping the finished products. A manufacturing organization's accounting system tracks these activities as product costs flowing through the Materials Inventory, Work in Process Inventory, and Finished Goods Inventory accounts. The **Materials Inventory account** shows the balance of the cost of unused materials, the **Work in Process Inventory account** shows the manufacturing costs that have been incurred and assigned to partially completed units of product, and the **Finished Goods Inventory account** shows the costs assigned to all completed products that have not been sold.

Document Flows and Cost Flows Through the Inventory Accounts

In many companies, managers accumulate and report manufacturing costs based on documents pertaining to production and production-related activities. Although paper documents are still used for this purpose, electronic documents have become increasingly common. Looking at how the documents for the three elements of product cost relate to the flow of costs through the three inventory accounts provides insight into when an activity must be recorded in the accounting records. Figure 4 summarizes the relationships among the production activities, the documents for each of the three cost elements, and the inventory accounts affected by the activities.

To illustrate document flow and changes in inventory balances for production activities, we continue with our example of The Choice Candy Company.

Purchase of Materials   The same process is used for purchasing both direct and indirect materials. The purchasing process starts with a *purchase request* for specific quantities of materials needed in the manufacturing process but not currently available in the materials storeroom. A qualified manager approves the request. Based on the information in the purchase request, the

■ **FIGURE 4**
Activities, Documents, and Cost Flows Through the Inventory Accounts of a Manufacturing Organization

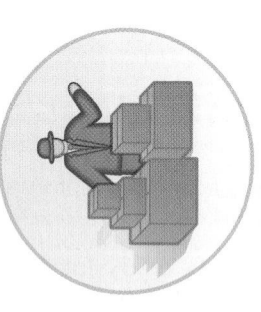
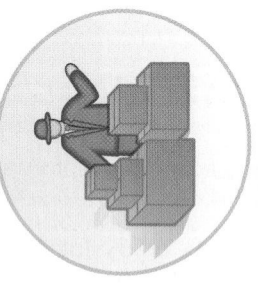
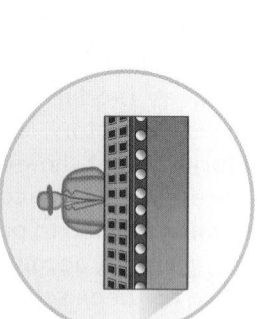

	PURCHASE OF MATERIALS	**PRODUCTION OF GOODS**	**PRODUCT COMPLETION**	**PRODUCT SALE**
ACTIVITIES	1. Purchase, receive, inspect and store materials. 2. Confirm receipt of materials. 3. Match documents.	1. Move materials to production area. 2. Convert materials into finished product using direct labor and overhead.	1. Move completed products to finished goods storage area and store until sold. 2. Move sold units to shipping.	1. Ship products sold to customer.
DOCUMENTS	• Purchase request • Purchase order • Receiving report • Vendor's invoice	• Materials request form • Time card • Job order cost card	• Job order cost card	• Sales invoice • Shipping document • Job order cost card
INVENTORY ACCOUNTS (RELATED DOCUMENTS)	**MATERIALS INVENTORY**	**WORK IN PROCESS INVENTORY**	**FINISHED GOODS INVENTORY**	**COST OF GOODS SOLD**
	Cost of materials purchased (vendor's invoice) Cost of materials used in production (materials request form)	Cost of materials used in production (materials request form) Cost of direct labor (time card) Cost of overhead Cost of completed products (job order cost card)	Cost of completed products (job order cost card) Cost of sold units (job order cost card)	Cost of sold units (job order cost card)

Purchasing Department sends a *purchase order* to a supplier. When the materials arrive, an employee on the receiving dock counts and examines them and prepares a *receiving report*. Later, an accounting clerk matches the information on the receiving report with the descriptions and quantities listed on the purchase order. A materials handler moves the newly arrived materials from the receiving area to the materials storeroom. Soon, The Choice Candy Company receives a *vendor's invoice* from the supplier requesting payment for the purchased materials. The cost of those materials increases the balance of the Materials Inventory account.

Production of Goods   When candy bars are scheduled for production, the storeroom clerk receives a *materials request form*. The materials request form is essential for controlling materials. In addition to showing the supervisor's signature of approval, it describes the types and quantities of materials that the storeroom clerk is to send to the production area, and it authorizes the release of those materials from the materials inventory into production. If the appropriate manager has approved the materials request form, the storeroom clerk has the materials handler move the materials to the production floor. The cost of the direct materials transferred will increase the balance of the Work in Process Inventory account and decrease the balance of the Materials Inventory account. The cost of the indirect materials transferred will increase the balance of the Overhead account and decrease the balance of the Materials Inventory account. (We discuss overhead in more detail later in this chapter.)

Each of the production employees who make the candy bars prepares a *time card* to record the number of hours he or she has worked on this and other orders each day. The costs of the direct labor and overhead used to manufacture the candy bars increase the balance of the Work in Process Inventory account. A *job order cost card* can be used to record all costs incurred as the products move through production.

Product Completion and Sale   Employees place completed candy bars in cartons and then move the cartons to the finished goods storeroom, where they are kept until they are shipped to customers. The cost of the completed candy bars increases the balance of the Finished Goods Inventory account and decreases the balance of the Work in Process Inventory account.

When candy bars are sold, a clerk prepares a *sales invoice*, and another employee fills the order by removing the candy bars from the storeroom, packaging them, and shipping them to the customer. A *shipping document* shows the quantity of the products that are shipped and gives a description of them. The cost of the candy bars sold increases the Cost of Goods Sold account and decreases the balance of the Finished Goods Inventory account.

The Manufacturing Cost Flow

Manufacturing cost flow is the flow of manufacturing costs (direct materials, direct labor, and overhead) through the Materials Inventory, Work in Process Inventory, and Finished Goods Inventory accounts into the Cost of Goods Sold account. A defined, structured manufacturing cost flow is the foundation for product costing, inventory valuation, and financial reporting. It supplies all the information necessary to prepare the statement of cost of goods manufactured and compute the cost of goods sold, as shown in Exhibit 1.

Figure 5 summarizes the manufacturing cost flow as it relates to the inventory accounts and production activity of The Choice Candy Company for the year ended December 31, 20x9. To show the basic flows in this example, we

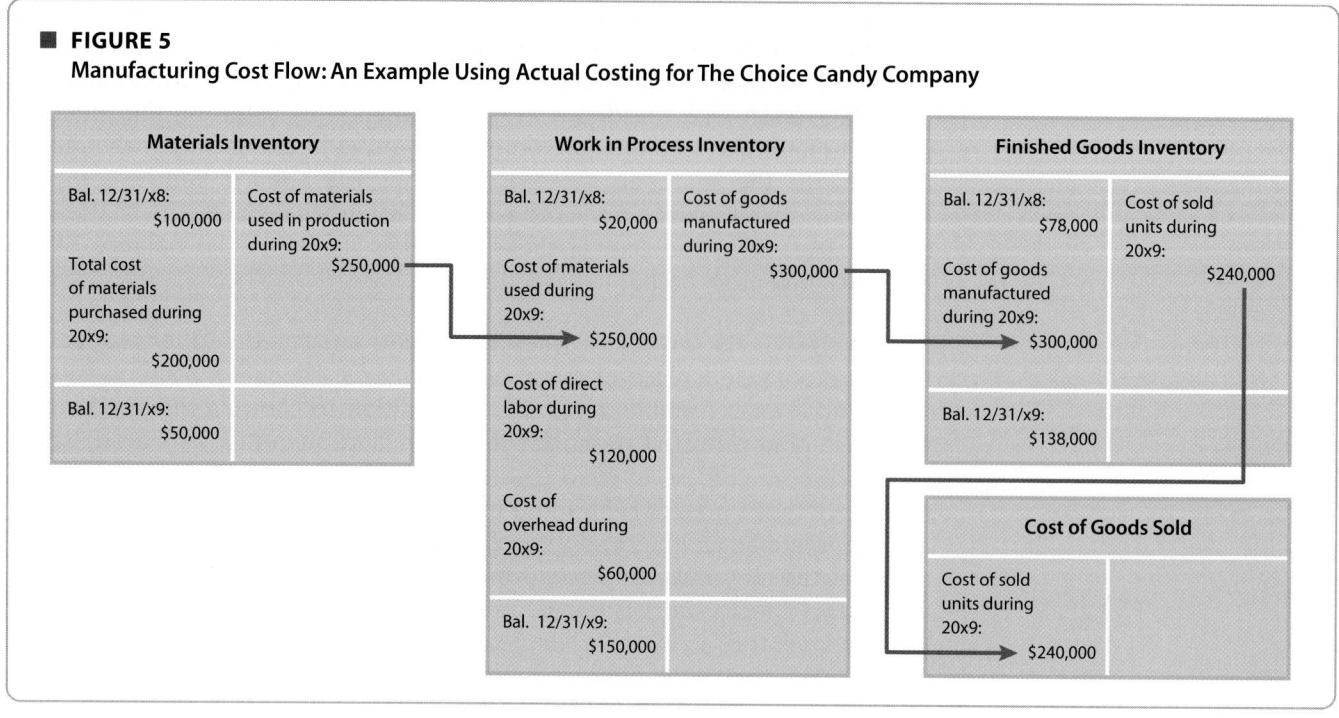

■ **FIGURE 5**
Manufacturing Cost Flow: An Example Using Actual Costing for The Choice Candy Company

assume that all materials can be traced directly to the candy bars. This means that there are no indirect materials in the Materials Inventory account. We also work with the actual amount of overhead, rather than an estimated amount.

Materials Inventory Because there are no indirect materials in this case, the Materials Inventory account shows the balance of unused direct materials. The cost of direct materials purchased increases the balance of the Materials Inventory account, and the cost of direct materials used by the Production Department decreases it.

Figure 5 shows the flows of material purchased and used through the Materials Inventory T account. Alternatively, the following formula may be used to summarize the activity of The Choice Candy Company's Materials Inventory account during the year:

Materials Inventory, Ending Balance	=	Materials Inventory, Beginning Balance	+	Cost of Materials Purchased	−	Cost of Materials Used
$50,000	=	$100,000	+	$200,000	−	$250,000

Work in Process Inventory The Work in Process Inventory account records the balance of partially completed units of the product. As direct materials and direct labor enter the production process, their costs are added to the Work in Process Inventory account. The cost of overhead for the current period is also added. The total costs of direct materials, direct labor, and overhead incurred and transferred to work in process inventory during an accounting period are called **total manufacturing costs** (also called *current manufacturing costs*). These costs increase the balance of the Work in Process Inventory account.

The cost of all units completed and moved to finished goods inventory during an accounting period is the **cost of goods manufactured**. The cost of goods manufactured for the period decreases the balance of the Work in Process Inventory account.

Study Note

When costs are transferred from one inventory account to another in a manufacturing company, they remain assets. They are inventoriable product costs and are not expensed until the finished goods are sold.

Figure 5 recaps the inflows of direct materials, direct labor, and overhead into the Work in Process T account and the resulting outflow of completed product costs. The following formulas can also be used to recap the same activity in The Choice Candy Company's Work in Process Inventory account:

Total Manufacturing Costs	=	Cost of Direct Materials Used	+	Direct Labor Costs	+	Overhead Costs
$430,000	=	$250,000	+	$120,000	+	$60,000

Work in Process Inventory, Ending Balance	=	Work in Process Inventory, Beginning Balance	+	Total Manufacturing Costs	−	Cost of Goods Manufactured
$150,000	=	$20,000	+	$430,000	−	$300,000

Finished Goods Inventory The Finished Goods Inventory account holds the balance of costs assigned to all completed products that a manufacturing company has not yet sold. The cost of goods manufactured increases the balance, and the cost of goods sold decreases the balance.

Figure 5 shows the inflow of cost of goods manufactured and the outflow of cost of goods sold to the Finished Goods inventory T account. The following formula may also be used to recap the activity in The Choice Candy Company's Finished Goods Inventory account during the year:

Finished Goods Inventory, Ending Balance	=	Finished Goods Inventory, Beginning Balance	+	Cost of Goods Manufactured	−	Cost of Goods Sold
$138,000	=	$78,000	+	$300,000	−	$240,000

Study Note

Materials Inventory and Work in Process Inventory support the production process, while Finished Goods Inventory supports the sales and distribution functions.

STOP • REVIEW • APPLY

4-1. Identify and describe the inventory accounts of a manufacturing company.

4-2. What does the term *manufacturing cost flow* mean?

4-3. How do total manufacturing costs differ from the cost of goods manufactured?

Cost Flows in a Manufacturing Organization Given the following information, compute the ending balances of the Materials Inventory, Work in Process Inventory, and Finished Goods Inventory accounts:

Materials Inventory, beginning balance	$ 230
Work in Process Inventory, beginning balance	250
Finished Goods Inventory, beginning balance	380
Direct materials purchased	850
Direct materials placed into production	740
Direct labor costs	970
Overhead costs	350
Cost of goods completed	1,230
Cost of goods sold	935

SOLUTION

Materials Inventory, ending balance:

Materials Inventory, beginning balance	$ 230
Direct materials purchased	850
Direct materials placed into production	(740) ←
Materials Inventory, ending balance	$ 340

Work in Process Inventory, ending balance:

Work in Process Inventory, beginning balance	$ 250
Direct materials placed into production	740 ←
Direct labor costs	970
Overhead costs	350
Cost of goods completed	(1,230) ←
Work in Process Inventory, ending balance	$1,080

Finished Goods Inventory, ending balance:

Finished Goods Inventory, beginning balance	$ 380
Cost of goods completed	1,230 ←
Cost of goods sold	(935)
Finished Goods Inventory, ending balance	$ 675

Elements of Product Costs

LO5   Define *product unit cost* and compute the unit cost of a product or service.

As noted above, product costs include all costs related to the manufacturing process. The three elements of product cost are direct materials costs, direct labor costs, and overhead costs, which are indirect costs.

Direct materials costs are the costs of materials used in making a product that can be conveniently and economically traced to specific units of the product. Some examples of direct materials are the iron ore used in making steel, the sheet metal used in making automobiles, and the sugar used in making candy. Direct materials may also include parts that a company purchases from another manufacturer.

Direct labor costs are the costs of the labor needed to make a product that can be conveniently and economically traced to specific units of the product. For example, the wages of production-line workers are direct labor costs.

Overhead costs (also called *service overhead, factory overhead, factory burden, manufacturing overhead,* or *indirect manufacturing costs*) are production-related costs that cannot be practically or conveniently traced directly to an end product. They include **indirect materials costs**, such as the costs of nails, rivets, lubricants, and small tools, and **indirect labor costs**, such as the costs of labor for machinery and tool maintenance, inspection, engineering design, supervision, and materials handling. Other indirect manufacturing costs include the costs of building maintenance, property taxes, property insurance, depreciation on plant and equipment, rent, and utilities. As indirect costs, overhead costs are allocated to a product's cost using traditional or activity-based costing methods, which we discuss later in the chapter.

To illustrate product costs and the manufacturing process, we'll refer again to The Choice Candy Company. Maggie Evans, the company's founder and

Has Technology Shifted the Elements of Product Costs?

New technology and manufacturing processes have created new patterns of product costs. The three elements of product costs are still direct materials, direct labor, and overhead, but the percentage that each contributes to the total cost of a product has changed. From the 1950s through the 1970s, direct labor was the dominant element, making up over 40 percent of total product cost, while direct materials contributed 35 percent and overhead, around 25 percent. Thus, direct costs, traceable to the product, accounted for 75 percent of total product cost. Improved production technology caused a dramatic shift in the three product cost elements. Machines replaced people, significantly reducing direct labor costs. Today, only 50 percent of the cost of a product is directly traceable to the product; the other 50 percent is overhead, an indirect cost.

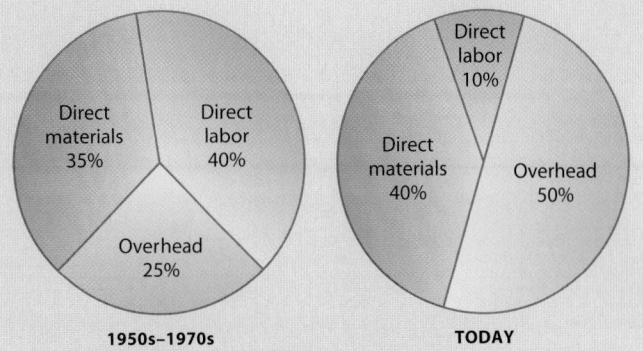

president, has identified the following elements of the product cost of one candy bar:

▶ *Direct materials costs*: costs of sugar, chocolate, and wrapper

▶ *Direct labor costs*: costs of labor used in making the candy bar

▶ *Overhead costs*: indirect materials costs, including the costs of salt and flavorings; indirect labor costs, including the costs of labor to move materials to the production area and to inspect the candy bars during production; other indirect overhead costs, including depreciation on the building and equipment, utilities, property taxes, and insurance

Prime Costs and Conversion Costs

The three elements of manufacturing costs can be grouped into prime costs and conversion costs. **Prime costs** are the primary costs of production; they are the sum of the direct materials costs and direct labor costs. **Conversion costs** are the costs of converting direct materials into a finished product; they are the sum of direct labor costs and overhead costs. These classifications are important for understanding the costing methods discussed in later chapters. Figure 6 summarizes the relationships among the product cost classifications presented so far.

Computing Product Unit Cost

Product unit cost is the cost of manufacturing a single unit of a product. It is made up of the costs of direct materials, direct labor, and overhead. These three cost elements are accumulated as a batch or production run of products is being produced. When the batch or run has been completed, the product unit cost is computed either by dividing the total cost of direct materials, direct labor, and overhead by the total number of units produced, or by determining the cost per unit for each element of the product cost and summing those per-unit costs.

Unit cost information helps managers price products and calculate gross margin and net income. Managers and accountants can calculate product unit

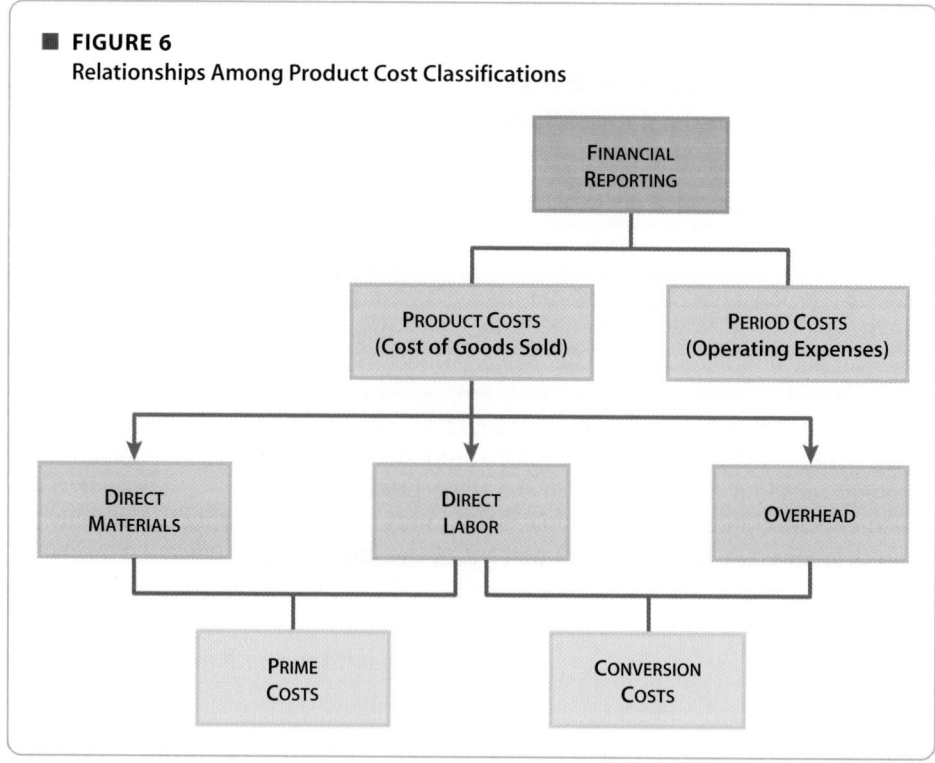

■ **FIGURE 6**
Relationships Among Product Cost Classifications

cost by using the actual costing, the normal costing, or the standard costing method. Table 2 summarizes how these three cost-measurement methods use actual and estimated costs.

Actual Costing Method   The **actual costing** method uses the costs of direct materials, direct labor, and overhead at the end of an accounting period or when actual costs become known to calculate the product unit cost. The actual product unit cost is assigned to the finished goods inventory on the balance sheet and to the cost of goods sold on the income statement. For example, assume that The Choice Candy Company produced 3,000 candy bars on December 28 for Good Foods Store. Sara Kearney, the company's accountant, calculated that the actual costs for the order were direct materials, $540; direct labor, $420; and overhead, $240. The actual product unit cost for the order was $.40, calculated as follows:

Direct materials ($540 ÷ 3,000 candy bars)	$.18
Direct labor ($420 ÷ 3,000 candy bars)	.14
Overhead ($240 ÷ 3,000 candy bars)	.08
Product cost per candy bar ($1,200 ÷ 3,000 candy bars)	$.40

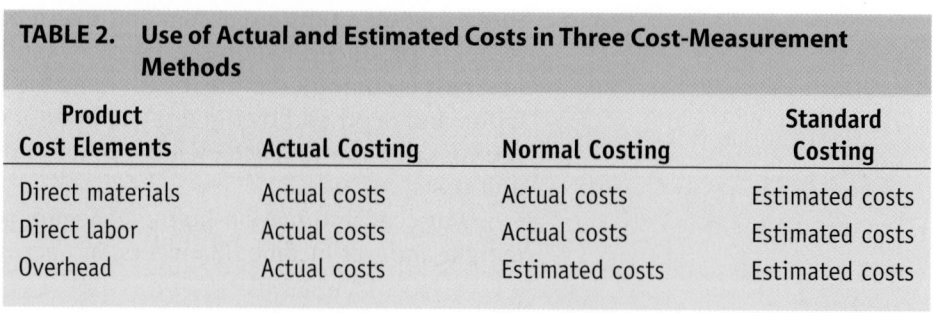

TABLE 2.   Use of Actual and Estimated Costs in Three Cost-Measurement Methods

Product Cost Elements	Actual Costing	Normal Costing	Standard Costing
Direct materials	Actual costs	Actual costs	Estimated costs
Direct labor	Actual costs	Actual costs	Estimated costs
Overhead	Actual costs	Estimated costs	Estimated costs

In this case, the product unit cost was computed after the job was completed and all cost information was known. Sometimes, however, a manufacturer needs to know product unit cost during production, when the actual direct materials costs and direct labor costs are known, but the actual overhead costs are uncertain. In that case, the computation of product unit cost will include an estimate of the overhead, and the normal costing method will be helpful. The use of normal costing is widespread, since many overhead bills, such as utilities, are not received until after products or services are produced and sold.

Normal Costing Method

The **normal costing** method combines the actual direct costs of materials and labor with estimated overhead costs to determine a product unit cost. The normal costing method is simple and allows a smoother, more even assignment of overhead costs to production during an accounting period than is possible with the actual costing method. It also contributes to better pricing decisions and profitability estimates. However, at the end of the accounting period, any difference between the estimated and actual costs must be identified and removed so that the financial statements show only the actual product costs.

Assume that Sara Kearney used normal costing to price the Good Foods Store order for 3,000 candy bars and that overhead was applied to the product's cost using an estimated rate of 60 percent of direct labor costs. In this case, the costs for the order would include the actual direct materials cost of $540, the actual direct labor cost of $420, and an estimated overhead cost of $252 ($420 × 60%). The product unit cost would be $.40:

Direct materials ($540 ÷ 3,000 candy bars)	$.18
Direct labor ($420 ÷ 3,000 candy bars)	.14
Overhead ($252 ÷ 3,000 candy bars)	.08
Product cost per candy bar	
($1,212 ÷ 3,000 candy bars)	$.40

Standard Costing Method

Managers sometimes need product cost information before the accounting period begins so that they can control the cost of operating activities or price a proposed product for a customer. In such situations, product unit costs must be estimated, and the **standard costing** method can be helpful. This method uses estimated or standard costs of direct materials, direct labor, and overhead to calculate the product unit cost.

Assume that The Choice Candy Company is placing a bid to manufacture 2,000 candy bars for a new customer. From standard cost information developed at the beginning of the period, Kearney estimates the following costs: $.20 per unit for direct materials, $.15 per unit for direct labor, and $.09 per unit for overhead (assuming a standard overhead rate of 60 percent of direct labor cost). The standard cost per unit would be $.44:

Direct materials	$.20
Direct labor	.15
Overhead ($.15 × 60%)	.09
Product cost per candy bar	$.44

The $.44 product unit cost is useful in determining the cost of the bid, $880 ($.44 × 2,000 candy bars), estimating the gross margin for the job, and deciding the price to bid for the business. We cover standard costing in more detail in another chapter.

Computing Service Unit Cost

Delivering products, representing people in courts of law, selling insurance policies, and computing people's income taxes are typical of the services performed in many service organizations. Like other services, these are labor-intensive processes supported by indirect materials, indirect labor, and other overhead costs.

Because no products are manufactured in the course of providing services, service organizations have no direct materials costs. As noted, however, they do have both labor and overhead costs, which must be included in the cost of providing a service. The most important cost in a service organization is the direct cost of labor, and the usual standard is applicable; that is, the direct labor cost must be traceable to the service rendered. The indirect costs incurred in performing a service are similar to those incurred in manufacturing a product. They are classified as overhead and, along with direct labor costs, are considered service costs rather than period costs. Just as product costs appear on manufacturers' income statements as cost of goods sold, service costs appear on service organizations' income statements as cost of sales.

To illustrate how to compute service unit cost, assume that Fresh Express, a grocery delivery service in New York City, wants to determine the total cost and unit cost of a typical home grocery delivery. Its policy for the past five years has been to charge a $15 fee per home delivery, but this may now be too low, because operating costs have soared in the past five years. Fresh Express has asked you to compute the actual cost of a home delivery and has given you the following information about its delivery operations:

Study Note

Any material costs in a service organization would be for supplies used in providing services. Because these are indirect materials costs, they are included in overhead.

Direct labor

Monthly salaries:

4 people at $2,500 each	$10,000

Indirect monthly overhead costs:

Supervisor's salary	$ 4,500
Telephone	750
Depreciation	5,000
Delivery supplies	2,460
Customer relations	640
Credit check function	980
Utilities	1,690
Clerical personnel	3,080
Miscellaneous	900
Total overhead costs	$20,000

Home deliveries usually total 1,000 each month. The Delivery Department has other functions in addition to deliveries to homes and offices. After determining how many of the deliveries were home deliveries, you conclude that only 25 percent of the overhead costs of the Delivery Department were applicable to home deliveries. The cost of one home delivery can be computed as:

Direct professional labor cost:	
$10,000 ÷ 1,000	$10.00
Overhead cost:	
$20,000 × 25% ÷ 1,000	5.00
Service cost per home delivery	$15.00

From the service unit cost, you conclude that the present fee of $15.00 just covers the current costs of a home delivery. To allow for a profit margin, the home delivery fee should be raised to $20 or $25. Further analysis using normal or standard costing could also be done for future planning and decisions.

S T O P • R E V I E W • A P P L Y

5-1. What three kinds of costs are included in a product's cost?

5-2. What characteristics identify a cost as part of overhead?

5-3. How do the costing methods used to compute a product's cost per unit affect the three elements of product cost? What is the difference between actual costing and normal costing?

Unit Costs in a Service Business   Fickle Picking Services provides inexpensive, high-quality labor for farmers growing vegetable and fruit crops. In September, Fickle Picking Services paid laborers $4,000 to harvest 500 acres of apples. The company incurred overhead costs of $2,400 for apple-picking services in September. This amount included the costs of transporting the laborers to the orchards; of providing facilities, food, and beverages for the laborers; and of scheduling, billing, and collecting from the farmers. Of this amount, 50 percent was related to picking apples. Compute the cost per acre to pick apples.

SOLUTION

Total cost to pick apples: $4,000 + (0.50 \times \$2,400) = \$5,200$

Cost per acre to pick apples: $\$5,200 \div 500 \text{ acres} = \$10.40 \text{ per acre}$

Cost Allocation

LO6   Define *cost allocation* and explain how cost objects, cost pools, and cost drivers are used to assign overhead costs.

As noted earlier, the costs of direct materials and direct labor can be easily traced to a product or service, but overhead costs are indirect costs that must be collected and allocated in some manner. **Cost allocation** is the process of assigning a collection of indirect costs to a specific **cost object**, such as a product or service, a department, or an operating activity, using an allocation base known as a **cost driver**. A cost driver might be direct labor hours, direct labor costs, units produced, or another activity base that has a cause-and-effect relationship with the cost. As the cost driver increases in volume, it causes the **cost pool**—the collection of indirect costs assigned to a cost object—to increase in amount.

For example, suppose The Choice Candy Company has a candy machine-maintenance cost pool. The cost pool consists of overhead costs for the supplies and labor needed to maintain the candy machines, the cost object is the candy product, and the cost driver is machine hours. As more machine hours are used, the amount of the cost pool increases, thus increasing the costs assigned to the candy product.

For purposes of product or service costing, cost allocation is defined as the assignment of overhead costs to the product or service (cost object) during an accounting period. It requires (1) the pooling of overhead costs that are affected by a common activity (e.g., machine maintenance) and (2) the selection of a cost driver whose activity level causes a change in the cost pool (e.g., machine hours).

Allocating the Costs of Overhead

Allocating overhead costs to products or services is a four-step process that corresponds to the four stages of the management process:

1. *Planning.* In the first step, managers estimate overhead costs and calculate a rate at which they will assign those costs to products or services.

2. *Performing.* In the second step, this rate is applied to products or services as overhead costs are incurred and recorded during production.

3. *Evaluating.* In the third step, actual overhead costs are recorded as they are incurred, and managers calculate the difference between the estimated (or applied) and actual costs.

4. *Communicating.* In the fourth step, managers report on this difference.

Figure 7 summarizes these four steps in terms of their timing, the procedures involved, and the journal entries they require. It also shows how the cost flows in the various steps affect the accounting records.

Planning the Overhead Rate Before an accounting period begins, managers determine cost pools and cost drivers and calculate a **predetermined overhead rate** by dividing the cost pool of total estimated overhead costs by the total estimated cost driver level. Grouping all estimated overhead costs into one cost pool and using direct labor hours or machine hours as the cost driver results in a single, plantwide overhead rate. By applying this predetermined rate to all units of production during the period in the same way, managers can better estimate product costs. This step requires no journal entry because no business activity has occurred.

Applying the Overhead Rate As units of the product or service are produced during the accounting period, the estimated overhead costs are assigned to the product or service using the predetermined overhead rate. The overhead rate for each cost pool is multiplied by that pool's actual cost driver level (e.g., the actual number of direct labor hours used to complete the product). The purpose of this calculation is to assign a consistent overhead cost to each unit produced during the accounting period. A journal entry records the allocation of overhead. For example, the entry to apply overhead to a product is recorded as a debit or increase to the Work in Process Inventory account and a credit or decrease to the Overhead account.

Recording Actual Overhead Costs The actual overhead costs are recorded as they are incurred during the accounting period. These costs, which include the actual costs of indirect materials, indirect labor, depreciation, property taxes, and other production costs, will be part of the actual product cost. The journal entry made for the actual overhead costs records a debit in the Overhead account and a credit in the asset, contra-asset, or liability accounts affected.

■ **FIGURE 7**
Allocating Overhead Costs: A Four-Step Process

Year 20x8 ├──────────────────────────┼──────────── Year 20x9 ──────────────────────→
                              January 1   December 31

	Step 1: Planning the Overhead Rate	Step 2: Applying the Overhead Rate	Step 3: Recording Actual Overhead Costs	Step 4: Reconciling Applied and Actual Overhead Costs
Timing and Procedure	Before the accounting period begins, determine cost pools and cost drivers. Calculate the overhead rate by dividing the cost pool of total estimated overhead costs by the total estimated cost driver level.	During the accounting period, as units are produced, apply overhead costs to products by multiplying the predetermined overhead rate for each cost pool by the actual cost driver level for that pool. Record costs.	Record actual overhead costs as they are incurred during the accounting period.	At the end of the accounting period, calculate and reconcile the difference between applied and actual overhead costs.
Journal Entry	None	Increase Work in Process Inventory account and decrease Overhead account: Dr. Work in Process XX Cr. Overhead XX	Increase Overhead account and decrease asset accounts or increase contra-asset or liability accounts: Dr. Overhead XX Cr. Various Accounts XX	Entry will vary depending on how costs have been applied. If overapplied, increase Overhead and decrease Cost of Goods Sold. If underapplied, increase Cost of Goods Sold and decrease Overhead.
Cost Flow Through the Accounts		*(see T-accounts below)*	*(see T-accounts below)*	*(see T-accounts below)*

Step 2 — T-accounts:

Overhead
	Overhead applied using predetermined rate

Work in Process Inventory
Overhead applied using predetermined rate	

Step 3 — T-accounts:

Overhead
Actual overhead costs recorded	

Various Asset and Liability Accounts
	Actual costs recorded

Step 4 — T-accounts:

Overapplied:
Overhead
Actual overhead costs recorded	Overhead applied using predetermined rate
	Overapplied
Bal. $0	

Cost of Goods Sold
Bal.	
	Overapplied
Actual bal.	

Underapplied:
Overhead
Actual overhead costs recorded	Overhead applied using predetermined rate
	Underapplied
Bal. $0	

Cost of Goods Sold
Bal.	
Underapplied	
Actual bal.	

Reconciling the Applied and Actual Overhead Amounts At the end of the accounting period, the difference between the applied and actual overhead costs is calculated and reconciled.

Overapplied Overhead If the overhead costs applied to production during the period are greater than the actual overhead costs, the difference in the amounts represents **overapplied overhead costs**. If this difference is immaterial, the Overhead account is debited or increased and the Cost of Goods Sold or Cost of Sales account is credited or decreased by the difference. If the difference is material for the products produced, adjustments are made to the accounts affected—that is, the Work in Process Inventory, Finished Goods Inventory, and Cost of Goods Sold accounts.

Underapplied Overhead If the overhead costs applied to production during the period are less than the actual overhead costs, the difference represents **underapplied overhead costs**. The Cost of Goods Sold or Cost of Sales account is debited or increased and the Overhead account is credited or decreased by this difference, assuming that the difference is not material.

Actual Cost of Goods Sold or Cost of Sales The adjustment for overapplied or underapplied overhead costs, whether they are immaterial or material, is necessary to reflect the actual overhead costs on the income statement.

The Importance of Good Estimates

A predetermined, or estimated, overhead rate has two main uses. First, it enables managers to make decisions about pricing products or services and controlling costs before some of the actual costs are known. The product or service cost calculated at the end of a period, when all costs are known, is, of course, more accurate. But when the overhead portion of product or service cost is estimated in advance, managers can compare actual and estimated costs throughout the year and more quickly correct any problems that may be causing the under- or overallocation of overhead costs.

Second, an advance estimate allows managers to apply overhead costs to each unit produced in an equitable and timely manner. Actual overhead costs fluctuate from month to month as a result of the timing of the costs and the variability of the amounts. For example, some overhead costs (such as supervisors' salaries and depreciation on equipment) may be expensed monthly. Others (like payroll taxes) may be paid quarterly, and still others (like property taxes and insurance) may be paid annually. In addition, indirect hourly labor costs (such as the costs of machine maintenance and materials handling) fluctuate with changes in output levels.

The successful allocation of overhead costs depends on two factors. One is a careful estimate of the total overhead costs. The other is a good forecast of the cost driver level.

An accurate estimate of total overhead costs is crucial. If the estimate is wrong, the overhead rate will be wrong. This will cause an overstatement or understatement of the product or service unit cost. If an organization relies on information that overstates its unit cost, it may fail to bid on profitable projects because the costs appear too high. If it relies on information that understates its unit cost, the projects that it accepts may not be as profitable as expected. So, to have reliable product or service unit costs, managers must be careful to include all overhead items and to forecast the costs of those items accurately.

The budgeting process usually includes estimating overhead costs. Managers who use production-related resources will provide cost estimates for direct and indirect production activities. For example, the managers for materials handling and inspection at The Choice Candy Company estimate the costs related to their departments' activities, and Sara Kearney, the accountant, includes their cost estimates in developing total overhead costs.

Managers also need to provide accurate estimates of cost driver levels. An understated cost driver level will cause an overstatement of the predetermined overhead rate (the cost is spread over a lesser level), and an overstated cost driver level will cause an understatement of the predetermined overhead rate (the cost is spread over a greater level).

In the following sections, we present two approaches to allocating overhead. We use the first two steps of the four-step overhead allocation process to demonstrate these approaches.

S T O P • R E V I E W • A P P L Y

6-1. Explain the relationship among cost objects, cost pools, and cost drivers. Give an example of each.

6-2. What are the two main uses of a predetermined overhead rate?

6-3. List the four steps involved in allocating overhead costs. Briefly explain each step.

Allocating Overhead: The Traditional Approach

LO7 Using the traditional method of allocating overhead costs, calculate product or service unit cost.

The traditional approach to applying overhead costs to a product or service is to use a single predetermined overhead rate. This approach is especially useful when companies manufacture only one product or a few very similar products that require the same production processes and production-related activities, such as setup, inspection, and materials handling. The total overhead costs constitute one cost pool, and a traditional activity base—such as direct labor hours, direct labor costs, machine hours, or units of production—is the cost driver.

As we continue with our example of The Choice Candy Company, let's assume that the company will be selling two product lines in the coming year—plain candy bars and candy bars with nuts—and that Sara Kearney chooses direct labor hours as the cost driver. Kearney estimates that total overhead costs for the next year will be $20,000 and that total direct labor hours (DLH) worked will be 400,000 hours.

Table 3 summarizes the first two steps in the traditional approach to allocating overhead costs. In the first step, Kearney uses the following formula to compute the rate at which overhead costs will be applied:

$$\text{Predetermined Overhead Rate} = \frac{\$20{,}000}{400{,}000 \text{ DLH}} = \$.05 \text{ per DLH}$$

TABLE 3.   Allocating Overhead Costs and Calculating Product Unit Cost: Traditional Approach

Step 1. Calculate overhead rate for cost pool:

$$\frac{\text{Estimated Total Overhead Costs}}{\text{Estimated Total Cost Driver Level}} = \frac{\$20,000}{400,000 \text{ (DLH)}} = \$.05 \text{ per DLH}$$

Step 2. Apply predetermined overhead rate to products:

	Plain Candy Bars	Candy Bars with Nuts
	Predetermined Overhead Rate × Actual Cost Driver Level = Cost Applied to Production	Predetermined Overhead Rate × Actual Cost Driver Level = Cost Applied to Production
Overhead applied: $.05 per DLH	$.05 × 250,000 DLH = $12,500	$.05 × 150,000 DLH = $7,500
Overhead cost per unit: Cost Applied ÷ Number of Units	$12,500 ÷ 100,000 = $.13	$7,500 ÷ 50,000 = $.15

Product unit cost using normal costing:

	Plain Candy Bars	Candy Bars with Nuts
Product costs per unit:		
Direct materials	$.18	$.21
Direct labor	.14	.16
Applied overhead	.13	.15
Product unit cost	$.45	$.52

In the second step, Kearney applies the predetermined overhead rate to the products. During the year, The Choice Candy Company actually uses 250,000 direct labor hours to produce 100,000 plain candy bars and 150,000 direct labor hours to produce 50,000 candy bars with nuts. When Kearney applies the predetermined overhead rate during the year, the portion of the overhead cost applied to the plain candy bars totals $12,500 ($.05 × 250,000 DLH), or $.13 per unit ($12,500 ÷ 100,000 units), and the portion applied to the candy bars with nuts totals $7,500 ($.05 × 150,000 DLH), or $.15 per unit ($7,500 ÷ 50,000 units).

Kearney also wanted to calculate the product unit cost for the accounting period using normal costing. She gathered the following data for the two product lines:

	Plain Candy Bars	Candy Bars with Nuts
Actual direct materials cost per unit	$.18	$.21
Actual direct labor cost per unit	.14	.16
Prime cost per unit	$.32	$.37

Study Note

Don't make the mistake of thinking that because a cost is not traced directly to a product, it is not a product cost. All manufacturing costs, both direct and indirect, are product costs.

At the bottom of Table 3 is Kearney's calculation of the normal product unit cost for each product line. The product unit cost of the candy bar with nuts ($.52) is higher than the plain candy bar's cost ($.45) because producing the candy bar with nuts required more expensive materials and more labor time.

S T O P • R E V I E W • A P P L Y

7-1. How many overhead cost pools are used in the traditional approach to cost allocation?

7-2. What are three examples of activity bases that are often used in the traditional approach to allocating overhead?

Computation of Overhead Rate Compute the overhead rate per service request for the Sample Service Company if estimated overhead costs are $15,000 and the number of estimated service requests is 5,000.

> **SOLUTION**
>
> $$\frac{\text{Predetermined Overhead}}{\text{Rate per Service Request}} = \frac{\text{Total Estimated Overhead Costs}}{\text{Total Estimated Service Requests}}$$
>
> $$= \frac{\$15,000}{5,000}$$
>
> $$= \underline{\underline{\$3.00}}$$

Application of Overhead Rate Calculate the amount of overhead costs applied if the predetermined overhead rate is $3 per direct labor hour and 1,000 direct labor hours were worked.

> **SOLUTION**
>
> Overhead Costs Applied = $3 per Direct Labor Hour
>
> $$\times\ 1,000$$
>
> $$= \underline{\underline{\$3,000}}$$

Allocating Overhead: The ABC Approach

LO8 Using activity-based costing to assign overhead costs, calculate product or service unit cost.

Activity-based costing (ABC) is a more accurate method of assigning overhead costs to products or services than the traditional approach. It categorizes all indirect costs by activity, traces the indirect costs to those activities, and assigns activity costs to products or services using a cost driver related to the cause of the cost. A company that uses ABC identifies production-related activities and the events and circumstances that cause, or drive, those activities, such as number of inspections or maintenance hours. As a result, many smaller activity pools are created from the single overhead cost pool used in the traditional method. This means that managers will calculate an overhead rate, or activity cost rate, for each activity pool and then use that rate and a cost driver amount to determine the portion of overhead costs to assign to a product or service produced. Managers must select an appropriate number of activity pools for overhead, and a system must be designed to capture

the actual cost driver amounts. Because each activity pool requires a cost driver, the benefit of grouping overhead costs into several smaller pools to obtain more accurate estimates of products or services is offset by the additional costs of measuring many different cost drivers.

ABC will improve the accuracy of product or service cost estimates for organizations that sell many different types of products or services (product diversity) or that use varying, significant amounts of different production-related activities to complete the products or services (process complexity). More careful cost allocation means that managers will have better information for decision making, especially when it comes to making decisions about pricing, outsourcing processes to other organizations, or choosing to keep a product or service item or drop it from the product line.

For other organizations, some products or services are more complicated to manufacture, store, move, package, or ship than others (process complexity). For example, a distributor of dairy products and eggs receives, stores, selects, moves, consolidates, packs, and ships items to various stores like **Wal-Mart** or Good Foods Store or to production facilities like The Choice Candy Company's factory. The distributor's greatest costs are overhead costs, which under the traditional method are assigned based on what it costs to purchase an item for resale. With the traditional method, more expensive items like whipping cream receive a greater allocation of overhead costs than do less expensive items like eggs. However, because some items, like the eggs, are more delicate than others, it may cost the distributor more to move, store, pack, and ship them. If ABC were used, the cost of the more delicate items like the eggs would increase to reflect a fairer allocation of the distributor's overhead costs. Thus, by assigning overhead costs based on the relative use of overhead resources, ABC would provide managers with better information for making decisions, such as pricing, choosing to discontinue selling certain items, or reducing the amount of storage space.

Planning Overhead Rates

As discussed earlier, Sara Kearney, the accountant for The Choice Candy Company, calculated product unit cost by computing one overhead rate for one cost pool and applying that rate to the direct labor hours used to manufacture plain candy bars and candy bars with nuts. As we continue with our example, we find that Maggie Evans, president of The Choice Candy Company, is concerned about the product cost for each type of candy bar. Evans believes that the difference in cost between the plain and nut candy bars should be more than $.07 ($.52 − $.45). She has asked Kearney to review her estimate. Kearney

TABLE 4. Allocating Overhead Costs and Calculating Product Unit Cost: ABC Approach

Step 1. Calculate activity cost rate for cost pool:

$$\frac{\text{Estimated Total Activity Costs}}{\text{Estimated Total Cost Driver Level}} = \text{Activity Cost Rate for Cost Pool}$$

Activity	Estimated Total Activity Costs	Estimated Total Cost Driver Level	Activity Cost Rate for Cost Pool
Setup	$ 7,000	700 setups	$7,000 ÷ 700 = $10 per setup
Inspection	6,000	500 inspections	$6,000 ÷ 500 = $12 per inspection
Packaging	5,000	2,000 packaging hours	$5,000 ÷ 2,000 = $2.50 per packaging hour
Building	2,000	10,000 machine hours	$2,000 ÷ 10,000 = $.20 per machine hour
	$20,000		

Step 2. Apply predetermined activity cost rates to products:

Activity Pool	Plain Candy Bars — Predetermined Overhead Rate × Actual Cost Driver Level = Cost Applied to Production	Candy Bars with Nuts — Predetermined Overhead Rate × Actual Cost Driver Level = Cost Applied to Production
Setup	$10 × 300 = $3,000	$10 × 400 = $ 4,000
Inspection	$12 × 150 = 1,800	$12 × 350 = 4,200
Packaging	$2.50 × 600 = 1,500	$2.50 × 1,400 = 3,500
Building	$.20 × 4,000 = 800	$.20 × 6,000 = 1,200
Total overhead applied	$7,100	$12,900

Applied overhead cost per unit:

Cost Applied ÷ Number of Units	$7,100 ÷ 100,000 = $.07	$12,900 ÷ 50,000 = $.26

Product unit cost using normal costing:

Product costs per unit:	Plain Candy Bars	Candy Bars with Nuts
Direct materials	$.18	$.21
Direct labor	.14	.16
Applied overhead	.07	.26
Product unit cost	$.39	$.63

found no errors when she rechecked the calculation of direct materials costs and direct labor costs. However, she believes that the traditional approach to assigning overhead cost could be misleading, so she wants to use activity-based costing to obtain a more accurate estimate of product cost. Table 4 illustrates the use of ABC to assign overhead costs to two product lines.

Kearney analyzed the production-related activities and decided that the estimated $20,000 in overhead cost could be grouped into four activity pools. The first activity, setup, includes estimated total costs of $7,000 for indirect labor and indirect materials used in preparing machines for each batch of products. The second activity, inspection, includes $6,000 for salaries and indirect materials costs, indirect labor, and depreciation on testing equipment. The third activity, packaging, includes estimated total costs of $5,000 for indirect materials, indirect labor, and equipment depreciation. The last activity, building operations, includes estimated total overhead costs of $2,000 for building depreciation, maintenance, janitorial wages, property taxes, insurance, security, and all other costs not related to the first three activities.

After identifying the four activity pools, Kearney selected a cost driver and estimated the cost driver level for each activity pool. The following schedule shows those amounts by product line and in total:

Estimated Cost Driver Level

Cost Driver	Plain	Nut	Total
Number of setups	300	400	700
Number of inspections	150	350	500
Packaging hours	600	1,400	2,000
Machine hours	4,000	6,000	10,000

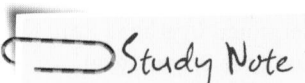

Study Note

Under ABC, activity pools are allocated to cost objects using multiple cost drivers.

After identifying activity pools, estimated activity pool amounts, cost drivers, and estimated cost driver levels, Kearney performed Step 1 of the overhead allocation process by calculating the activity cost rate for each activity pool. The activity cost rate is the estimated activity pool amount divided by the estimated cost driver level. Step 1 of Table 4 shows that the activity cost rates are $10 per setup, $12 per inspection, $2.50 per packaging hour, and $.20 per machine hour.

Applying the Overhead Rates

In Step 2, Kearney applied overhead to the two product lines using the cost driver level for each cost driver multiplied by the activity cost rate shown in the preceding schedule. Step 2 of Table 4 shows those calculations. For example, Kearney applied $3,000 in setup costs ($10 × 300 setups) to the plain candy bar line and $4,000 ($10 × 400 setups) to the nut candy bar line. After applying the overhead costs from the four activity pools to the product lines, Kearney estimated that total overhead costs of $7,100, or $.07 per bar ($7,100 ÷ 100,000 units), should be applied to the plain candy bar line and that $12,900, or $.26 per bar ($12,900 ÷ 50,000 units), should be applied to the nut candy bar line.

Kearney also wanted to calculate the unit cost for each product line using normal costing. Her calculations appear at the bottom of Table 4. The product unit cost is $.39 for the plain line and $.63 for the nut line.

Kearney presented the following information to Maggie Evans:

	Plain	Nut
Product unit cost: Traditional approach with one overhead cost pool	$.45	$.52
Product unit cost: ABC with four activity pools	.39	.63
Difference: Decrease (increase)	$.06	($.11)

Because ABC assigned more costs to the product line that used more resources, it provided a more accurate estimate of product unit cost. The increased information about the production requirements for the nut candy bar line that went into the ABC calculation of product unit cost also provided valuable insights. Evans found that the candy bars with nuts cost more to manufacture because the different ingredients require more setups and machine hours and because more inspections are needed to test the candy quality. Because the nut candy bar line requires more production and production-related activities, its product unit cost is higher. Based on this analysis, Evans may want to reconsider some of her decisions about the manufacture and sale of these two product lines.

S T O P • R E V I E W • A P P L Y

8-1. How does traditional overhead allocation differ from ABC overhead allocation?

8-2. How many overhead cost pools are used in the ABC approach to cost allocation?

8-3. What allocation measure does ABC use to relate an activity pool to a cost object? Explain your answer.

A LOOK BACK AT

SOUTHWEST AIRLINES

In this chapter's Decision Point, we posed these questions:

- **How do managers at Southwest Airlines determine the cost of selling tickets or of operating a flight?**
- **How do they use cost information?**

To determine the cost of selling tickets online or the cost of operating a flight, managers at Southwest Airlines must conduct complex analyses of many costs. When determining the cost of online ticket sales, Southwest's managers analyze the costs of direct labor and materials, as well as the costs of activities needed to support these sales, such as supervision, equipment maintenance, depreciation, and utilities. When determining the cost of operating a flight, they analyze the costs of the materials (e.g., peanuts, drinks, and jet fuel) and labor used (e.g., flight attendants and pilot), as well as overhead costs, such as aircraft maintenance and depreciation. Southwest's managers also consider any other relevant selling, administrative, or general operating costs that the flight incurs.

Classifying and analyzing costs helps managers make decisions that will sustain Southwest's profitability. All costs must be analyzed in terms of their traceability and behavior and in terms of whether they add value and how they affect the financial statements. Because many costs cannot be directly traced to specific flights, activities, or departments, managers must use a method of allocation to assign them. Possibilities include traditional allocation methods and the activity-based costing method, both of which we introduced in this chapter.

CHAPTER REVIEW

REVIEW of Learning Objectives

LO1 Describe how managers use information about costs.

Managers in manufacturing, retail, and service organizations use information about operating costs and product or service costs to prepare budgets, make pricing and other decisions, calculate variances between estimated and actual costs, and communicate results.

LO2 Explain how managers classify costs and how they use these cost classifications.

A single cost can be classified as a direct or an indirect cost, a variable or a fixed cost, a value-adding or a nonvalue-adding cost, and a product or a period cost. These cost classifications enable managers to control costs by tracing them to cost objects, to calculate the number of units that must be sold to obtain a certain level of profit, to identify the costs of activities that do and do not add value to a product or service, and to prepare financial statements for parties outside the organization.

LO3 Compare how service, retail, and manufacturing organizations report costs on their financial statements and how they account for inventories.

Because the operations of service, retail, and manufacturing organizations differ, their financial statements differ as well. A service organization maintains no inventory accounts on its balance sheet. The cost of sales on its income statement reflects the net cost of the services sold. A retail organization, which purchases products ready for resale, maintains only a Merchandise Inventory account, which is used to record and account for items in inventory. The cost of goods sold is simply the difference between the cost of goods available for sale and the ending merchandise inventory. A manufacturing organization, because it creates a product, maintains three inventory accounts: Materials Inventory, Work in Process Inventory, and Finished Goods Inventory. Manufacturing costs flow through all three inventory accounts. During the accounting period, the cost of completed products is transferred to the Finished Goods Inventory account, and the cost of units that have been manufactured and sold is transferred to the Cost of Goods Sold account.

LO4 Describe the flow of costs through a manufacturer's inventory accounts.

The flow of costs through the inventory accounts begins when costs for direct materials, direct labor, and overhead are incurred. Materials costs flow first into the Materials Inventory account, which is used to record the costs of materials when they are received and again when they are issued for use in a production process. All manufacturing-related costs—direct materials, direct labor, and overhead—are recorded in the Work in Process Inventory account as the production process begins. When products are completed, their costs are transferred from the Work in Process Inventory account to the Finished Goods Inventory account. Costs remain in the Finished Goods Inventory account until the products are sold, at which time they are transferred to the Cost of Goods Sold account.

LO5 Define *product unit cost* and compute the unit cost of a product or service.

Direct materials costs are the costs of materials used in making a product that can be conveniently and economically traced to specific product units. Direct labor costs include all labor costs needed to make a product or service that can be conveniently and economically traced to specific product units. All other production-related costs are classified and accounted for as overhead costs. Such costs cannot be conveniently or economically traced to end products or services, so a cost allocation method is used to assign them to products or services.

When a batch of products has been completed, the product unit cost is computed by dividing the total cost of direct materials, direct labor, and overhead by the total number of units produced. The product unit cost can be calculated using the actual, normal, or standard costing method. Under normal costing, the actual costs of direct materials and direct labor are combined with the estimated cost of overhead to determine the product unit cost. Under standard costing, the estimated costs of direct materials, direct labor, and overhead are used to calculate the product unit cost. The components of product cost may be classified as prime costs or conversion costs. Prime costs are the primary costs of production; they are the sum of direct materials costs and direct labor costs. Conversion costs are the costs of converting direct materials into finished product; they are the sum of direct labor costs and overhead costs.

Because no products are manufactured in the course of providing services, service organizations have no materials costs. They do, however, have both direct labor costs and overhead costs, which are similar to those in manufacturing organizations. To determine the cost of performing a service, professional labor and service-related overhead costs are included in the analysis.

LO6 Define *cost allocation* and explain how cost objects, cost pools, and cost drivers are used to assign overhead costs.

Cost allocation is the process of assigning collected indirect costs to a specific cost object using an allocation base known as a cost driver. The allocation of overhead costs requires the pooling of overhead costs that are affected by a common activity and the selection of a cost driver whose activity level causes a change in the cost pool. A cost pool is the collection of overhead costs assigned to a cost object. A cost driver is an activity base that causes the cost pool to increase in amount as the cost driver increases.

Allocating overhead is a four-step process that involves planning a rate at which overhead costs will be assigned to products or services, assigning overhead costs at this predetermined rate to products or services during production, recording actual overhead costs as they are incurred, and reconciling the difference between the actual and applied overhead costs. The Cost of Goods Sold or Cost of Sales account is corrected for an amount of over- or underapplied overhead costs assigned to the products or services. In manufacturing companies, if the difference is material, adjustments are made to the Work in Process Inventory, Finished Goods Inventory, and Cost of Goods Sold accounts.

LO7 Using the traditional method of allocating overhead costs, calculate product or service unit cost.

The traditional method applies overhead costs to a product or service by estimating one predetermined overhead rate and multiplying that rate by the actual cost driver level. The product or service unit cost is computed either by dividing the total product or service cost (the sum of the total applied overhead cost and the actual costs of direct materials and direct labor) by the total number of units produced or by determining the cost per unit for each element of the product's or service's cost and summing those per-unit costs.

LO8 Using activity-based costing to assign overhead costs, calculate product or service unit cost.

When ABC is used, overhead costs are grouped into a number of cost pools related to specific activities. For each activity pool, cost drivers are identified, and cost driver levels are estimated. Each activity cost rate is calculated by dividing the estimated activity pool amount by the estimated cost driver level. Overhead, which is divided into the activity pools, is applied to the product or service by multiplying the various activity cost rates by their actual cost driver levels. The product or service unit cost is computed by dividing the total product or service cost (the sum of the total applied cost pools and the actual costs of direct materials and direct labor) by the total number of units produced.

REVIEW of Concepts and Terminology

The following concepts and terms were introduced in this chapter:

Activity-based costing (ABC): A method of assigning overhead costs that categorizes all indirect costs by activity, traces the indirect costs to those activities, and assigns activity costs to products using a cost driver related to the cause of the cost. **(LO8)**

Actual costing: A method of cost measurement that uses the actual costs of direct materials, direct labor, and overhead to calculate a product or service unit cost. **(LO5)**

Conversion costs: The costs of converting direct materials into a finished product; the sum of direct labor costs and overhead costs. **(LO5)**

Cost allocation: The process of assigning a collection of indirect costs to a specific cost object using an allocation base known as a cost driver. **(LO6)**

Cost driver: An activity base that causes a cost pool to increase in amount as the cost driver increases in volume. **(LO6)**

Cost object: The destination of an assigned, or allocated, cost. **(LO6)**

Cost of goods manufactured: The cost of all units completed and moved to finished goods storage during an accounting period. **(LO4)**

Cost pool: The collection of overhead costs assigned to a cost object. **(LO6)**

Direct costs: Costs that can be conveniently and economically traced to a cost object. **(LO2)**

Direct labor costs: The costs of the labor needed to make a product or perform a service that can be conveniently and economically traced to specific units of the product or service. **(LO5)**

Direct materials costs: The costs of the materials used in making a product that can be conveniently and economically traced to specific units of the product. **(LO5)**

Finished Goods Inventory account: An inventory account that shows the costs assigned to all completed products that have not been sold. **(LO4)**

Fixed cost: A cost that remains constant within a defined range of activity or time period. **(LO2)**

Indirect costs: Costs that cannot be conveniently or economically traced to a cost object. **(LO2)**

Indirect labor costs: The costs of labor for production-related activities that cannot be conveniently or economically traced to a unit of the product or service. **(LO5)**

Indirect materials costs: The costs of materials that cannot be conveniently and economically traced to a unit of the product or service. **(LO5)**

Manufacturing cost flow: The flow of manufacturing costs (direct materials, direct labor, and overhead) through the Materials Inventory, Work in Process Inventory, and Finished Goods Inventory accounts into the Cost of Goods Sold account. **(LO4)**

Materials Inventory account: An inventory account that shows the balance of the cost of unused materials. **(LO4)**

Nonvalue-adding cost: The cost of an activity that adds cost to a product or service but does not increase its market value. **(LO2)**

Normal costing: A method of cost measurement that combines the actual direct costs of materials and labor with estimated overhead costs to determine a product or service unit cost. **(LO5)**

Overapplied overhead costs: The amount by which overhead costs applied using the predetermined overhead rate exceed the actual overhead costs for the accounting period. **(LO6)**

Overhead costs: Production-related costs that cannot be practically or conveniently traced to an end product or service. Also called *factory overhead, factory burden, manufacturing overhead, service overhead,* or *indirect manufacturing costs.* **(LO5)**

Period costs: The costs of resources used during an accounting period that are not assigned to products or services. Also called *noninventoriable costs* or *selling, administrative, and general expenses.* **(LO2)**

Predetermined overhead rate: The rate calculated before an accounting period begins by dividing the cost pool of total estimated overhead costs by the total estimated cost driver for that pool. **(LO6)**

Prime costs: The primary costs of production; the sum of direct materials costs and direct labor costs. **(LO5)**

Product costs: The costs assigned to inventory, which include the costs of direct materials, direct labor, and overhead. Also called *inventoriable costs.* **(LO2)**

Product unit cost: The cost of manufacturing a single unit of a product, computed either by dividing the total cost of direct materials, direct labor, and overhead by the total number of units produced, or by determining the cost per unit for each element of the product cost and summing those per-unit costs. **(LO5)**

Standard costing: A method of cost measurement that uses the estimated costs of direct materials, direct labor, and overhead to calculate a product unit cost. **(LO5)**

Statement of cost of goods manufactured: A formal statement summarizing the flow of all manufacturing costs incurred during an accounting period. **(LO3)**

Total manufacturing costs: The total costs of direct materials, direct labor, and overhead incurred and transferred to Work in Process Inventory during an accounting period. Also called *current manufacturing costs.* **(LO4)**

Underapplied overhead costs: The amount by which actual overhead costs exceed the overhead costs

applied using the predetermined overhead rate for the accounting period. **(LO6)**

Value-adding cost: The cost of an activity that increases the market value of a product or service. **(LO2)**

Variable cost: A cost that changes in direct proportion to a change in productive output (or some other measure of volume). **(LO2)**

Work in Process Inventory account: An inventory account used to record the manufacturing costs incurred and assigned to partially completed units of product. **(LO4)**

REVIEW Problem

LO3, LO4, LO5   **Calculating Cost of Goods Manufactured: Three Fundamental Steps**

Sample Company requires its controller to prepare not only a year-end balance sheet and income statement, but also a statement of cost of goods manufactured. During the year, the company purchased $361,920 of direct materials. The company's direct labor costs for the year were $99,085 (10,430 hours at $9.50 per hour); its indirect labor costs totaled $126,750 (20,280 hours at $6.25 per hour). Account balances for the year were as follows:

Account	Balance
Plant Supervision	$ 42,500
Factory Insurance	8,100
Utilities, Factory	29,220
Depreciation–Factory Building	46,200
Depreciation–Factory Equipment	62,800
Factory Security	9,460
Factory Repair and Maintenance	14,980
Selling and Administrative Expenses	76,480
Materials Inventory, beginning	26,490
Work in Process Inventory, beginning	101,640
Finished Goods Inventory, beginning	148,290
Materials Inventory, ending	24,910
Work in Process Inventory, ending	100,400
Finished Goods Inventory, ending	141,100

Required

1. Compute the cost of materials used during the year.
2. Given the cost of materials used, compute the total manufacturing costs for the year.
3. Given the total manufacturing costs for the year, compute the cost of goods manufactured during the year.
4. If 13,397 units were manufactured during the year, what was the actual product unit cost? (Round your answer to two decimal places.)

Answer to Review Problem

1. Cost of materials used:

Materials inventory, beginning	$ 26,490
Direct materials purchased	361,920
Cost of materials available for use	$388,410
Less materials inventory, ending	24,910
Cost of materials used	$363,500

2. Total manufacturing costs:

Cost of materials used		$363,500
Direct labor costs		99,085
Overhead costs		
Indirect labor	$126,750	
Plant supervision	42,500	
Factory insurance	8,100	
Utilities, factory	29,220	
Depreciation, factory building	46,200	
Depreciation, factory equipment	62,800	
Factory security	9,460	
Factory repair and maintenance	14,980	
Total overhead costs		340,010
Total manufacturing costs		$802,595

3. Cost of goods manufactured:

Total manufacturing costs	$802,595
Add work in process inventory, beginning	101,640
Total cost of work in process during the year	$904,235
Less work in process inventory, ending	100,400
Cost of goods manufactured	$803,835

4. Actual product unit cost:

$$\frac{\text{Cost of Goods Manufactured}}{\text{Number of Units Manufactured}} = \frac{\$803,835}{13,397} = \$60.00^*$$

*Rounded.

CHAPTER ASSIGNMENTS

BUILDING Your Basic Knowledge and Skills

Short Exercises

LO2 **Cost Classifications**

SE 1. Indicate whether each of the following is a direct cost (D), an indirect cost (ID), or neither (N) and a variable (V) or a fixed (F) cost. Also indicate whether each adds value (VA) or does not add value (NVA) to the product and whether each is a product cost (PD) or a period cost (PER).

1. Production supervisor's salary
2. Sales commission
3. Wages of a production-line worker

LO3 **Income Statement for a Manufacturing Organization**

SE 2. Using the following information from Hakim Company, prepare an income statement through operating income for the year:

Sales	$900,000
Finished goods inventory, beginning	45,000
Cost of goods manufactured	585,000
Finished goods inventory, ending	60,000
Operating expenses	275,000

LO4 **Cost Flow in a Manufacturing Organization**

SE 3. Given the following information, compute the ending balances of the Materials Inventory, Work in Process Inventory, and Finished Goods Inventory accounts:

Materials Inventory, beginning balance	$ 23,000
Work in Process Inventory, beginning balance	25,750
Finished Goods Inventory, beginning balance	38,000
Direct materials purchased	85,000
Direct materials placed into production	74,000
Direct labor costs	97,000
Overhead costs	35,000
Cost of goods manufactured	123,000
Cost of goods sold	93,375

LO4 **Document Flows in a Manufacturing Organization**

SE 4. Identify the document needed to support each of the following activities in a manufacturing organization:

1. Placing an order for direct materials with a supplier
2. Recording direct labor time at the beginning and end of each work shift
3. Receiving direct materials at the shipping dock
4. Recording the costs of a specific job requiring direct materials, direct labor, and overhead
5. Issuing direct materials into production
6. Billing the customer for a completed order
7. Fulfilling a request from the Production Scheduling Department for the purchase of direct materials

LO5 **Elements of Manufacturing Costs**

SE 5. Daisy Luna, the bookkeeper at Candlelight, Inc., must group the costs of manufacturing candles. Indicate whether each of the following items should be classified as direct materials (DM), direct labor (DL), overhead (O), or none of these (N). Also indicate whether each is a prime cost (PC), a conversion cost (CC), or neither (N).

1. Depreciation of the cost of vats to hold melted wax
2. Cost of wax
3. Rent on the factory where candles are made
4. Cost of George's time to dip the wicks into the wax
5. Cost of coloring for candles
6. Cost of Ray's time to design candles for Halloween
7. Sam's commission to sell candles to Candles Plus

LO5 **Computation of Product Unit Cost**

SE 6. What is the product unit cost for Job 14, which consists of 300 units and has total manufacturing costs of direct materials, $4,500; direct labor,

$7,500; and overhead, $3,600? What are the prime costs and conversion costs per unit?

LO6 **Calculation of Underapplied or Overapplied Overhead**

SE 7. At year end, records show that actual overhead costs incurred were $25,870 and the amount of overhead costs applied to production was $27,000. Identify the amount of under- or overapplied overhead, and indicate whether the Cost of Goods Sold account should be increased or decreased to reflect actual overhead costs.

LO6, LO7 **Computation of Overhead Rate**

SE 8. Compute the overhead rate per service request for the Maintenance Department if estimated overhead costs are $18,290 and the number of estimated service requests is 3,100.

LO6, LO7 **Allocation of Overhead to Production**

SE 9. Calculate the amount of overhead costs applied to production if the predetermined overhead rate is $4 per direct labor hour and 1,200 direct labor hours were worked.

LO8 **Activity-Based Costing and Cost Drivers**

SE 10. Mazzola Clothiers Company relies on the information from its activity-based costing system when setting prices for its products. Compute ABC rates from the following estimated data for each of the activity centers:

Estimated Activity	Pool Amount	Cost Driver Level
Cutting/Stitching	$5,220,000	145,000 machine hours
Trimming/Packing	998,400	41,600 operator hours
Designing	1,187,500	62,500 designer hours

Exercises

LO1 **The Management Process and Operating Costs**

E 1. Indicate whether each of the following activities takes place during the planning (PL), performing (PE), evaluating (E), or communicating (C) stage of the management process:

1. Changing regular price to clearance price
2. Reporting results to appropriate personnel
3. Preparing budgets of operating costs
4. Comparing estimated and actual costs to determine variances

LO2 **Cost Classifications**

E 2. Indicate whether each of the following costs for a bicycle manufacturer is a product or a period cost, a variable or a fixed cost, a value-adding or a nonvalue-adding cost, and, if it is a product cost, a direct or an indirect cost of the bicycle:

	Cost Classification			
Example	Product or Period	Variable or Fixed	Value-adding or Nonvalue-adding	Direct or Indirect
Bicycle tire	Product	Variable	Value-adding	Direct

1. Depreciation on office computer
2. Labor to assemble bicycle
3. Labor to inspect bicycle
4. Internal auditor's salary
5. Lubricant for wheels

LO3   **Comparison of Income Statement Formats**

E 3. Indicate whether each of these equations applies to a service organization (SER), a retail organization (RET), or a manufacturing organization (MANF):

1. Cost of Goods Sold = Beginning Merchandise Inventory + Net Cost of Purchases − Ending Merchandise Inventory
2. Cost of Sales = Net Cost of Services Sold
3. Cost of Goods Sold = Beginning Finished Goods Inventory + Cost of Goods Manufactured − Ending Finished Goods Inventory

LO3   **Statement of Cost of Goods Manufactured**

E 4. During August, Rao Company's purchases of direct materials totaled $139,000; direct labor for the month was 3,400 hours at $8.75 per hour. Rao also incurred the following overhead costs: utilities, $5,870; supervision, $16,600; indirect materials, $6,750; depreciation, $6,200; insurance, $1,830; and miscellaneous, $1,100.

Beginning inventory accounts were as follows: Materials Inventory, $48,600; Work in Process Inventory, $54,250; and Finished Goods Inventory, $38,500. Ending inventory accounts were as follows: Materials Inventory, $50,100; Work in Process Inventory, $48,400; and Finished Goods Inventory, $37,450.

From the information given, prepare a statement of cost of goods manufactured.

LO3   **Statement of Cost of Goods Manufactured and Cost of Goods Sold**

E 5. Treetec Corp. makes irrigation sprinkler systems for tree nurseries. Rama Shih, Treetec's new controller, can find only the following partial information for the past year:

	Oak Division	Loblolly Division	Maple Division	Spruce Division
Direct materials used	$3	$ 7	$ g	$ 8
Total manufacturing costs	6	d	h	14
Overhead	1	3	2	j
Direct labor	a	6	4	4
Ending work in process inventory	b	3	2	5
Cost of goods manufactured	7	20	12	l
Beginning work in process inventory	2	e	3	k
Ending finished goods inventory	2	6	i	9
Beginning finished goods inventory	3	f	5	7
Cost of goods sold	c	18	13	9

Using the information given, compute the unknown values. List the accounts in the proper order, and show subtotals and totals as appropriate.

LO3   **Characteristics of Organizations**

E 6. Indicate whether each of the following is typical of a service organization (SER), a retail organization (RET), or a manufacturing organization (MANF):

1. Maintains only one balance sheet inventory account
2. Maintains no balance sheet inventory accounts
3. Maintains three balance sheet inventory accounts
4. Purchases products ready for resale
5. Designs and makes products for sale
6. Sells services
7. Determines the net cost of services sold

8. Includes the cost of goods manufactured in calculating cost of goods sold
9. Includes the cost of purchases in calculating cost of goods sold

LO3 **Missing Amounts—Manufacturing**

E 7. Presented below are incomplete inventory and income statement data for Trevor Corporation. Determine the missing amounts.

	Cost of Goods Sold	Cost of Goods Manufactured	Beginning Finished Goods Inventory	Ending Finished Goods Inventory
1.	$ 10,000	$12,000	$ 1,000	?
2.	$140,000	?	$45,000	$60,000
3.	?	$89,000	$23,000	$20,000

LO3 **Inventories, Cost of Goods Sold, and Net Income**

E 8. The data presented below are for a retail organization and a manufacturing organization.

1. Fill in the missing data for the retail organization:

	First Quarter	Second Quarter	Third Quarter	Fourth Quarter
Sales	$9	$e	$15	$k
Gross margin	a	4	5	l
Ending merchandise inventory	5	f	5	m
Beginning merchandise inventory	4	g	h	5
Net cost of purchases	b	7	9	n
Operating income	3	2	i	2
Operating expenses	c	2	2	4
Cost of goods sold	5	6	j	11
Cost of goods available for sale	d	12	15	15

2. Fill in the missing data for the manufacturing organization:

	First Quarter	Second Quarter	Third Quarter	Fourth Quarter
Ending finished goods inventory	$a	$3	$h	$6
Cost of goods sold	6	3	5	l
Operating income	1	3	1	m
Cost of finished goods available for sale	8	d	10	13
Cost of goods manufactured	5	e	i	8
Gross margin	4	f	j	7
Operating expenses	3	g	5	6
Beginning finished goods inventory	b	2	3	n
Sales	c	10	k	14

LO4 **Documentation**

E 9. Lisette Company manufactures music boxes. Seventy percent of its products are standard items produced in long production runs. The other 30 percent are special orders with specific requests for tunes. The latter cost from three to six times as much as the standard product because they require additional materials and labor.

Reza Seca, the controller, recently received a complaint memorandum from Iggy Paulo, the production supervisor, about the new network of source documents that has been added to the existing cost accounting system. The new documents include a purchase request, a purchase order, a receiving report, and a materials request. Paulo claims that the forms create extra work and interrupt the normal flow of production.

Prepare a written memorandum from Reza Seca to Iggy Paulo that fully explains the purpose of each type of document.

LO4   Cost Flows and Inventory Accounts

E 10. For each of the following activities, identify the inventory account (Materials Inventory, Work in Process Inventory, or Finished Goods Inventory), if any, that is affected. If an inventory account is affected, indicate whether the account balance will increase or decrease. (*Example*: Moved completed units to finished goods inventory. *Answer*: Increase Finished Goods Inventory; decrease Work in Process Inventory.) If no inventory account is affected, use "None of these" as your answer.

1. Moved materials requested by production
2. Sold units of product
3. Purchased and received direct materials for production
4. Used direct labor and overhead in the production process
5. Received payment from customer
6. Purchased office supplies and paid cash
7. Paid monthly office rent

LO5   Unit Cost Determination

E 11. The Pattia Winery is one of the finest wineries in the country. One of its famous products is a red wine called Old Vines. Recently, management has become concerned about the increasing cost of making Old Vines and needs to determine if the current selling price of $10 per bottle is adequate. The winery wants to achieve a 25 percent gross profit on the sale of each bottle. The following information is given to you for analysis:

Batch size	10,550 bottles
Costs	
Direct materials	
Olen Millot grapes	$22,155
Chancellor grapes	9,495
Bottles	5,275
Total direct materials costs	$36,925
Direct labor	
Pickers/loaders	$ 2,110
Crusher	422
Processors	8,440
Bottler	13,293
Total direct labor costs	$24,265
Overhead	
Depreciation, equipment	$2,743
Depreciation, building	5,275
Utilities	1,055
Indirect labor	6,330
Supervision	7,385
Supplies	9,917
Repairs	1,477
Miscellaneous	633
Total overhead costs	$34,815
Total production costs	$96,005

1. Compute the unit cost per bottle for materials, labor, and overhead.
2. How would you advise management regarding the price per bottle of wine?
3. Compute the prime costs per unit and the conversion costs per unit.

Unit Costs in a Service Business

LO6, LO7, LO8

E 12. Walden Green provides custom farming services to owners of five-acre wheat fields. In July, he earned $2,400 by cutting, turning, and baling 3,000 bales. In the same month, he incurred the following costs: gas, $150; tractor maintenance, $115; and labor, $600. His annual tractor depreciation is $1,500. What was Green's cost per bale? What was his revenue per bale? Should he increase the amount he charges for his services?

Computation of Overhead Rate

E 13. The overhead costs that Lucca Industries, Inc., used to compute its overhead rate for the past year are as follows:

Indirect materials and supplies	$ 79,200
Repairs and maintenance	14,900
Outside service contracts	17,300
Indirect labor	79,100
Factory supervision	42,900
Depreciation, machinery	85,000
Factory insurance	8,200
Property taxes	6,500
Heat, light, and power	7,700
Miscellaneous overhead	5,760
Total overhead costs	$346,560

The allocation base for the past year was 45,600 total machine hours. For the next year, all overhead costs except depreciation, property taxes, and miscellaneous overhead are expected to increase by 10 percent. Depreciation should increase by 12 percent, and property taxes and miscellaneous overhead are expected to increase by 20 percent. Plant capacity in terms of machine hours used will increase by 4,400 hours.

1. Compute the past year's overhead rate. (Carry your answer to three decimal places.)
2. Compute the overhead rate for next year. (Carry your answer to three decimal places.)

Computation and Application of Overhead Rate

E 14. Compumatics specializes in the analysis and reporting of complex inventory costing projects. Materials costs are minimal, consisting entirely of operating supplies (DVDs, inventory sheets, and other recording tools). Labor is the highest single expense, totaling $693,000 for 75,000 hours of work in 20x8. Overhead costs for 20x8 were $916,000 and were applied to specific jobs on the basis of labor hours worked. In 20x9, the company anticipates a 25 percent increase in overhead costs. Labor costs will increase by $130,000, and the number of hours worked is expected to increase by 20 percent.

1. Determine the total amount of overhead anticipated in 20x9.
2. Compute the overhead rate for 20x9. (Round your answer to the nearest cent.)

3. During April 20x9, 11,980 labor hours were worked. Calculate the overhead amount assigned to April production.

LO6, LO7 **Disposition of Overapplied Overhead**

E 15. At the end of 20x9, Compumatics had compiled a total of 89,920 labor hours worked. The actual overhead incurred was $1,143,400.

1. Using the overhead rate computed in **E 14**, determine the total amount of overhead applied to operations during 20x9.
2. Compute the amount of overapplied overhead for the year.
3. Will the Cost of Goods Sold account be increased or decreased to correct the over-application of overhead?

LO7, LO8 **Activities and Activity-Based Costing**

E 16. Zone Enterprises produces wireless components used in telecommunications equipment. One of the most important features of the company's new just-in-time production process is quality control. Initially, a traditional allocation method was used to assign the costs of quality control to products; all these costs were included in the plant's overhead cost pool and allocated to products based on direct labor dollars. Recently, the firm has implemented an activity-based costing system. The activities, cost drivers, and rates for the quality control function are summarized below, along with cost allocation information from the traditional method. Also shown is information related to one order, Order HL14. Compute the quality control cost that would be assigned to the order under both the traditional method and the activity-based costing method.

Traditional costing method:
Quality control costs were assigned at a rate of 12 percent of direct labor dollars. Order HL14 was charged with $9,350 of direct labor costs.

Activity-based costing method:

Activity	Activity Cost Driver	Activity Usage for Cost Rate	Order HL14
Incoming materials inspection	Types of materials used	$17.50 per type of material used	17 types of materials
In-process inspection	Number of products	$.06 per product	2,400 products
Tool and gauge control	Number of processes per cell	$26.50 per process per cell	11 processes
Product certification	Per order	$94.00 per order	1 order

Problems

LO3 **Statement of Cost of Goods Manufactured**

P 1. Dillo Vineyards, a large winery in Texas, produces a full line of varietal wines. The company, whose fiscal year begins on November 1, has just completed a record-breaking year. Its inventory account balances on October 31 of this year were Materials Inventory, $1,803,800; Work in Process Inventory, $2,764,500; and Finished Goods Inventory, $1,883,200. At the beginning of the year, the inventory account balances were Materials Inventory, $2,156,200; Work in Process Inventory, $3,371,000; and Finished Goods Inventory, $1,596,400.

During the fiscal year, the company's purchases of direct materials totaled $6,750,000. Direct labor hours totaled 142,500, and the average labor rate was $8.20 per hour. The following overhead costs were incurred during the year: depreciation, plant and equipment, $685,600; indirect labor, $207,300; property tax, plant and equipment, $94,200; plant maintenance, $83,700; small tools, $42,400; utilities, $96,500; and employee benefits, $76,100.

Required

Prepare a statement of cost of goods manufactured for the fiscal year ended October 31.

LO3 **A Manufacturing Organization's Balance Sheet**

P 2. The following information is from the balance sheet of Mills Manufacturing Company:

	Debit	Credit
Cash	$ 34,000	
Accounts receivable	27,000	
Materials inventory, ending	31,000	
Work in process inventory, ending	47,900	
Finished goods inventory, ending	54,800	
Production supplies	5,700	
Small tools	9,330	
Land	160,000	
Factory building	575,000	
Accumulated depreciation, factory building		$ 199,000
Factory equipment	310,000	
Accumulated depreciation, factory equipment		137,000
Patents	33,500	
Accounts payable		26,900
Insurance premiums payable		6,700
Income taxes payable		41,500
Mortgage payable		343,000
Common stock		200,000
Retained earnings		334,130
	$1,288,230	$1,288,230

Required

1. Manufacturing organizations use asset accounts that are not needed by retail organizations.
   a. List the titles of the asset accounts that are specifically related to manufacturing organizations.
   b. List the titles of the asset, liability, and equity accounts that you would see on the balance sheets of both manufacturing and retail organizations.
2. Assuming that the following information reflects the results of operations for the year, calculate the (a) gross margin, (b) cost of goods sold, (c) cost of goods available for sale, and (d) cost of goods manufactured:

Operating income	$138,130
Operating expenses	53,670
Sales	500,000
Finished goods inventory, beginning	50,900

3. **Manager Insight:** Does Mills Manufacturing use the periodic or perpetual inventory system?

LO5 **Computation of Unit Cost**

P 3. Carola Industries, Inc., manufactures discs for several of the leading recording studios in the United States and Europe. Department 60 is responsible for the electronic circuitry within each disc. Department 61 applies the plastic-like surface to the discs and packages them for shipment. Carola recently produced 4,000 discs for the Milo Company. In fulfilling this order, the departments incurred the following costs:

	Department	
	60	**61**
Direct materials used	$29,440	$3,920
Direct labor	6,800	2,560
Overhead	7,360	4,800

1. Compute the unit cost for each department.
2. Compute the total unit cost for the Milo Company order.
3. **Manager Insight:** The selling price for this order was $14 per unit. Was the selling price adequate? List the assumptions and/or computations upon which you based your answer. What suggestions would you make to Carola Industries' management about the pricing of future orders?
4. Compute the prime costs and conversion costs per unit for each department.

LO6, L07 **Allocation of Overhead**

P 4. Natural Cosmetics Company applies overhead costs on the basis of machine hours. The overhead rate is computed by analyzing data from the previous year to determine the percentage change in costs. Thus, the 20x9 overhead rate will be based on the percentage change multiplied by the 20x8 costs. The controller prepared the overhead rate analysis for 20x9 using the following information:

	20x7	**20x8**
Machine hours	47,800	57,360
Overhead costs		
Indirect labor	$ 18,100	$ 23,530
Employee benefits	22,000	28,600
Manufacturing supervision	16,800	18,480
Utilities	10,350	14,490
Factory insurance	6,500	7,800
Janitorial services	11,000	12,100
Depreciation, factory and machinery	17,750	21,300
Miscellaneous overhead	5,750	7,475
Total overhead	$108,250	$133,775

In 20x9, the cost of utilities is expected to increase by 40 percent over the previous year; the cost of indirect labor, employee benefits, and miscellaneous overhead is expected to increase by 30 percent over the previous year; the cost of insurance and depreciation is expected to increase by 20 percent over the previous year; and the cost of supervision and janitorial services is expected to increase by 10 percent over the previous year. Machine hours are expected to total 68,832.

Required

1. Compute the projected costs and the overhead rate for 20x9, using the information about expected cost increases. (Carry your answer to three decimal places.)

2. Jobs completed during 20x9 and the machine hours used were as follows:

Job No.	Machine Hours
2214	12,300
2215	14,200
2216	9,800
2217	13,600
2218	11,300
2219	8,100

Determine the amount of overhead to be applied to each job and to total production during 20x9. (Round answers to whole dollars.)

3. Actual overhead costs for 20x9 were $165,845. Was overhead underapplied or overapplied? By how much? Should the Cost of Goods Sold account be increased or decreased to reflect actual overhead costs?

LO8 Activities and Activity-Based Costing

P 5. Byte Computer Company, a manufacturing organization, has just completed an order that Grater, Ltd., placed for 80 computers. Byte recently shifted from a traditional system of allocating costs to an activity-based costing system. Simone Faure, Byte's controller, wants to know the impact that the ABC system had on the Grater order. Direct materials, purchased parts, and direct labor costs for the Grater order are as follows:

Cost of direct materials	$36,750.00	Direct labor hours	220
Cost of purchased parts	$21,300.00	Average direct labor pay rate	$15.25

Other operating costs are as follows:

Traditional costing data:
Overhead costs were applied at a single, plantwide overhead rate of 270 percent of direct labor dollars.

Activity-based costing data:

Activity	Cost Driver	Activity Cost Rate	Activity Usage for Grater Order
Electrical engineering design	Engineering hours	$19.50 per engineering hour	32 engineering hours
Setup	Number of setups	$29.40 per setup	11 setups
Parts production	Machine hours	$26.30 per machine hour	134 machine hours
Product testing	Product testing hours	$32.80 per product testing hour	52 product testing hours
Packaging	Packaging hours	$17.50 per packaging hour	22 packaging hours
Building occupancy	Machine hours	$9.80 per machine hour	134 machine hours

Required

1. Using the traditional costing method, compute the total cost of the Grater order.

2. Using the activity-based costing method, compute the total cost of the Grater order.

3. Manager Insight: What difference in the amount of cost assigned to the Grater order resulted from the shift to activity-based costing? Was Byte's shift to activity-based costing a good management decision?

Alternate Problems

LO6, LO7 Allocation of Overhead

P 6. Lund Products, Inc., uses a predetermined overhead rate in its production, assembly, and testing departments. One rate is used for the entire company; it is based on machine hours. The rate is determined by analyzing data from the previous year to determine the percentage change in costs. Thus the 20x9 overhead rate will be based on the percentage change multiplied by the 20x8 costs. Lise Jensen is about to compute the rate for 20x9 using the following data:

	20x7	20x8
Machine hours	38,000	41,800
Overhead costs		
Indirect materials	$ 44,500	$ 57,850
Indirect labor	21,200	25,440
Supervision	37,800	41,580
Utilities	9,400	11,280
Labor-related costs	8,200	9,020
Depreciation, factory	9,800	10,780
Depreciation, machinery	22,700	27,240
Property taxes	2,400	2,880
Insurance	1,600	1,920
Miscellaneous overhead	4,400	4,840
Total overhead	$162,000	$192,830

In 20x9, the cost of indirect materials is expected to increase by 30 percent over the previous year. The cost of indirect labor, utilities, machinery depreciation, property taxes, and insurance is expected to increase by 20 percent over the previous year. All other expenses are expected to increase by 10 percent over the previous year. Machine hours for 20x9 are estimated at 45,980.

Required

1. Compute the projected costs and the overhead rate for 20x9 using the information about expected cost increases. (Round your answer to three decimal places.)

2. During 20x9, Lund Products completed the following jobs using the machine hours shown:

Job No.	Machine Hours	Job No.	Machine Hours
H–142	7,840	H–201	10,680
H–164	5,260	H–218	12,310
H–175	8,100	H–304	2,460

Determine the amount of overhead applied to each job. What was the total overhead applied during 20x9? (Round answers to the nearest dollar.)

3. Actual overhead costs for 20x9 were $234,485. Was overhead underapplied or overapplied in 20x9? By how much? Should the Cost of Goods Sold account be increased or decreased to reflect actual overhead costs?

4. At what point during 20x9 was the overhead rate computed? When was it applied? Finally, when was underapplied or overapplied overhead determined and the Cost of Goods Sold account adjusted to reflect actual costs?

LO8 **Activities and Activity-Based Costing**

P 7. Fraser Products, Inc., which produces copy machines for wholesale distributors in the Pacific Northwest, has just completed packaging an order from Kent Company for 150 Model 14 machines. Fraser recently switched from a traditional system of allocating costs to an activity-based costing system. Before the Kent order is shipped, the controller wants a unit cost analysis comparing the amounts computed under the traditional costing system with those computed under the ABC system. Direct materials, purchased parts, and direct labor costs for the Kent order are as follows:

Cost of direct materials	$17,450.00
Cost of purchased parts	$14,800.00
Direct labor hours	140
Average direct labor pay rate	$16.50

Other operating costs are as follows:

Traditional costing data:
Overhead costs were applied at a single, plantwide overhead rate of 240 percent of direct labor dollars.

Activity-based costing data:

Activity	Cost Driver	Activity Cost Rate	Activity Usage for Kent Order
Engineering systems design	Engineering hours	$28.00 per engineering hour	18 engineering hours
Setup	Number of setups	$42.00 per setup	8 setups
Parts production	Machine hours	$37.50 per machine hour	84 machine hours
Assembly	Assembly hours	$44.00 per assembly hour	36 assembly hours
Packaging	Packaging hours	$28.50 per packaging hour	28 packaging hours
Building occupancy	Machine hours	$10.40 per machine hour	84 machine hours

Required

1. Using the traditional costing approach, compute the total cost of the Kent order.
2. Using the activity-based costing approach, compute the total cost of the Kent order.
3. Manager Insight: What difference in the amount of cost assigned to the Kent order resulted from the shift to activity-based costing? Does the use of activity-based costing guarantee cost reduction for every product?

LO6, LO7, LO8   **Allocation of Overhead: Traditional and Activity-Based Costing Methods**

P 8. Sea Scout, Inc., manufactures two types of underwater vehicles. Oil companies use the vehicle called Rigger II to examine offshore oil rigs, and marine biology research foundations use the BioScout to study coastlines. The company's San Diego factory is not fully automated and requires some direct labor. Using estimated overhead costs of $220,000 and an estimated 16,000 hours of direct labor, Oz Parson, the company's controller, calculated a traditional overhead rate of $13.75 per direct labor hour. He used normal costing to calculate the product unit cost for both product lines, as shown in the following summary:

	Rigger II	BioScout
Product costs per unit		
Direct materials	$10,000.00	$12,000.00
Direct labor	1,450.00	1,600.00
Applied overhead	412.50*	550.00†
Product unit cost	$11,862.50	$14,150.00
Units of production	400	100
Direct labor hours	12,000	4,000

*$13.75 per Direct Labor Hour × 30 Direct Labor Hours per Unit = $412.50
†$13.75 per Direct Labor Hour × 40 Direct Labor Hours per Unit = $550

Parson believes that the product unit cost for the BioScout is too low. After carefully observing the production process, he has concluded that the BioScout requires much more attention than the Rigger II. Because of the BioScout's more intricate design, it requires more production activities, and fewer subassemblies can be produced by suppliers. He has therefore created four overhead activity pools, estimated the overhead costs of the activity pools, selected a cost driver for each pool, and estimated the cost driver levels for each product line, as shown in the following summary:

Activity Pool	Estimated Overhead Cost
Setup	$ 70,000
Inspection	20,000
Engineering	50,000
Assembly	80,0000
Total	$220,000

Cost Driver	Rigger II Driver Level	BioScout Driver Level	Total Driver Level
Number of setups	250	450	700
Number of inspections	150	350	500
Engineering hours	600	1,400	2,000
Machine hours	5,000	5,000	10,000

Required

1. Use activity-based costing to do the following:
    a. Calculate the activity cost rate for each activity pool.
    b. Compute the overhead costs applied to each product line by activity pool and in total.
    c. Calculate the product unit cost for each product line.
2. **Manager Insight:** What differences in the costs assigned to the two product lines resulted from the shift to activity-based costing?

ENHANCING Your Knowledge, Skills, and Critical Thinking

Conceptual Understanding Cases

LO1, LO2   **Comparison of Costs in Different Types of Businesses**

C 1. **H & R Block** is a service company that prepares tax returns; **Borders** is a retail company that sells books and CDs; **Indian Motorcycle Corporation** is a manufacturing company that makes motorcycles. Show that you understand how these companies differ by giving for each one an example of a direct and an indirect cost, a variable and a fixed cost, a value-adding and a nonvalue-adding cost, and a product and a period cost. Discuss the use of cost classifications in these three types of organizations.

LO6, LO7, LO8   **Comparison of Approaches to Developing Overhead Rates**

C 2. Both Matos Company and Stubee Corporation use predetermined overhead rates for product costing, inventory valuation, and sales quotations. The two businesses are about the same size, and they compete in the corrugated box industry. Because the overhead rate is an estimated measure, Matos Company's management believes that the controller's department should spend little effort in developing it. The company computes the rate annually based on an analysis of the previous year's costs. No one monitors its accuracy during the year. Stubee Corporation takes a different approach. One person in the controller's office is responsible for developing overhead rates on a monthly basis. All cost estimates are checked carefully to make sure they are realistic. Accuracy checks are done routinely at the end of each month, and forecasts of changes in business activity are taken into account.

Assume that Cooke Corporation, an East Coast manufacturer of corrugated boxes, has hired you as a consultant. Asimina Hiona, Cooke's controller, wants you to recommend the best method of developing overhead rates. Based on your knowledge of Matos's and Stubee's practices, write a memo to Hiona that answers the following questions:

1. What are the advantages and disadvantages of Matos's and Stubee's approaches to developing overhead rates?
2. Which company has taken the more cost-effective approach to developing overhead rates? Defend your answer.
3. Is an accurate overhead rate most important for product costing, inventory valuation, or sales quotations? Why?
4. What is activity-based costing (ABC)? Would it be better than the two approaches discussed above? Explain.

LO5 **Unit Costs in a Service Business**

C 3. Municipal Hospital relies heavily on cost data to keep its pricing structures in line with those of its competitors. The hospital provides a wide range of services, including intensive care, intermediate care, and a neonatal nursery. Joo Young, the hospital's controller, is concerned about the profits generated by the 30-bed intensive care unit (ICU), so she is reviewing current billing procedures for that unit. The focus of her analysis is the hospital's billing per ICU patient day. This billing equals the per diem cost of intensive care plus a 40 percent markup to cover other operating costs and generate a profit. ICU patient costs include the following:

Doctors' care	2 hours per day @ $360 per hour (actual)
Special nursing care	4 hours per day @ $85 per hour (actual)
Regular nursing care	24 hours per day @ $28 per hour (average)
Medications	$237 per day (average)
Medical supplies	$134 per day (average)
Room rental	$350 per day (average)
Food and services	$140 per day (average)

One other significant ICU cost is equipment, which is about $185,000 per room. Young has determined that the cost per patient day for the equipment is $179.

Wiley Dix, the hospital director, has asked Young to compare the current billing procedure with another that uses industry averages to determine the billing per patient day.

1. Compute the cost per patient per day.
2. Compute the billing per patient day using the hospital's existing markup rate. (Round answers to whole dollars.)
3. Industry averages for markup rates are as follows:

Equipment	30%	Medications	50%
Doctors' care	50	Medical supplies	50
Special nursing care	40	Room rental	30
Regular nursing care	50	Food and services	25

Using these rates, compute the billing per patient day. (Round answers to the nearest whole dollars.)

4. Based on your findings in **2** and **3**, which billing procedure would you recommend? Why? Be prepared to discuss your response.

Interpreting Management Reports

LO3 **Financial Performance Measures**

C 4. Tarbox Manufacturing Company makes sheet metal products for heating and air conditioning installations. For the past several years, the company's income has been declining. Its statements of cost of goods manufactured and income statements for 20x9 and 20x8 follow. You have been asked to comment on why the ratios for Tarbox's profitability have deteriorated.

1. In preparing your comments, compute the following ratios for each year:
   a. Ratios of cost of direct materials used to total manufacturing costs, direct labor to total manufacturing costs, and total overhead to total manufacturing costs. (Round to one decimal place.)
   b. Ratios of sales salaries and commission expense, advertising expense, other selling expenses, administrative expenses, and total selling and administrative expenses to sales. (Round to one decimal place.)

Tarbox Manufacturing Company
Statements of Cost of Goods Manufactured
For the Years Ended December 31, 20x9 and 20x8

	20x9		20x8	
Direct materials used				
Materials inventory, beginning	$ 91,240		$ 93,560	
Direct materials purchased (net)	987,640		959,940	
Cost of direct materials available for use	$1,078,80		$1,053,500	
Less materials inventory, ending	95,020		91,240	
Cost of direct materials used		$ 983,860		$ 962,260
Direct labor		571,410		579,720
Overhead				
Indirect labor	$ 182,660		$ 171,980	
Power	34,990		32,550	
Insurance	22,430		18,530	
Supervision	125,330		120,050	
Depreciation	75,730		72,720	
Other overhead costs	41,740		36,820	
Total overhead		482,880		452,110
Total manufacturing costs		$2,038,150		$1,994,090
Add work in process inventory, beginning		148,875		152,275
Total cost of work in process during the period		$2,187,025		$2,146,365
Less work in process inventory, ending		146,750		148,875
Cost of goods manufactured		$2,040,275		$1,997,490

Tarbox Manufacturing Company
Income Statements
For the Years Ended December 31, 20x9 and 20x8

	20x9	20x8
Sales	$2,942,960	$3,096,220
Cost of goods sold		
Finished goods inventory, beginning	$ 142,640	$ 184,820
Cost of goods manufactured	2,040,275	1,997,490
Cost of finished goods available for sale	$2,182,915	$2,182,310
Less finished goods inventory, ending	186,630	142,640
Total cost of goods sold	1,996,285	2,039,670
Gross margin	$ 946,675	$1,056,550
Selling and administrative expenses		
Sales salaries and commission expense	$ 394,840	$ 329,480
Advertising expense	116,110	194,290
Other selling expenses	82,680	72,930
Administrative expenses	242,600	195,530
Total selling and administrative expenses	836,230	792,230
Income from operations	$ 110,445	$ 264,320
Other revenues and expenses		
Interest expense	54,160	56,815
Income before income taxes	$ 56,285	$ 207,505
Income taxes expense	19,137	87,586
Net income	$ 37,148	$ 119,919

   c. Ratios of gross margin to sales and net income to sales. (Round to one decimal place.)

2. From your evaluation of the ratios computed in 1, state the probable causes of the decline in net income.

3. What other factors or ratios do you believe should be considered in determining the cause of the company's decreased income?

Decision Analysis Using Excel

LO6, LO7, LO8   **Allocation of Overhead: Traditional and Activity-Based Costing Methods**

C 5. Refer to **P 8** in this chapter. Assume that Oz Parson, the controller of Sea Scout, Inc., has received some additional information from the production manager, Parvin Hrinda. Hrinda reported that robotic equipment has been installed on the factory floor to increase productivity. As a result, direct labor hours per unit will decrease by 20 percent. Depreciation and other machine costs for the robots will increase total overhead from $220,000 to $320,000 for the year, which will increase the assembly activity cost pool from $80,000 to $180,000. The cost driver level for the assembly cost pool will change from 5,000 machine hours to 2,000 machine hours for the Rigger II and from 5,000 machine hours to 8,000 machine hours for the BioScout. The cost driver levels and cost pool amounts for setup, inspection, and engineering activities will remain the same.

1. Use the traditional method of applying overhead costs to
   a. Calculate the overhead rate.
   b. Compute the amount of the total overhead costs applied to each product line.
   c. Calculate the product unit cost for each product line.
2. Use the activity-based costing method to
   a. Calculate the overhead activity cost rate for each activity pool.
   b. Compute the overhead costs applied to each product line by activity pool and in total.
   c. Calculate the product unit cost for each product line.
3. Complete the following table and discuss the differences in the costs assigned to the two product lines resulting from the additional information in this assignment:

Product unit cost	Rigger II	BioScout
Traditional		
Activity-based costing		
Difference: decrease (increase)		

Ethical Dilemma Case

LO5   **Preventing Pollution and the Costs of Waste Disposal**

C 6. Lake Weir Power Plant provides power to a metropolitan area of 4 million people. Sundeep Guliani, the plant's controller, has just returned from a conference on the Environmental Protection Agency's regulations concerning pollution prevention. She is meeting with Alton Guy, the president of the company, to discuss the impact of the EPA's regulations on the plant.

"Alton, I'm really concerned. We haven't been monitoring the disposal of the radioactive material we send to the Willis Disposal Plant. If Willis is disposing of our waste material improperly, we could be sued," said Guliani. "We also haven't been recording the costs of the waste as part of our product cost. Ignoring those costs will have a negative impact on our decision about the next rate hike."

"Sundeep, don't worry. I don't think we need to concern ourselves with the waste we send to Willis. We pay the company to dispose of it. The company takes it off our hands, and it's their responsibility to manage its disposal. As for the cost of waste disposal, I think we would have a hard time justifying a rate increase based on a requirement to record the full cost of waste as a cost of producing power. Let's just forget about waste and its disposal as a component of our power cost. We can get our rate increase without mentioning waste disposal," replied Guy.

What responsibility for monitoring the waste disposal practices at the Willis Disposal Plant does Lake Weir Power Plant have? Should Guliani take Guy's advice to ignore waste disposal costs in calculating the cost of power? Be prepared to discuss your response.

Internet Case

Identification of a Manufacturing Company's Costs

C 7. **Gateway, Inc.,** and **Dell Computer Corporation** assemble computers and sell them over the telephone or the Internet. Access the website of either of these companies. Become familiar with the products of the company you have chosen. For one of these products, such as a desktop or laptop computer, give examples of a direct and an indirect cost, a variable and a fixed cost, a value-adding and a nonvalue-adding cost, and a product and a period cost. Also give examples of the three elements of product cost: direct materials, direct labor, and overhead.

Group Activity Case

Management Information Needs

C 8. The H&W Pharmaceuticals Corporation manufactures most of its three pharmaceutical products in Indonesia. Inventory balances for March and April are as follows:

	March 31	April 30
Materials Inventory	$258,400	$228,100
Work in Process Inventory	138,800	127,200
Finished Goods Inventory	111,700	114,100

During April, purchases of direct materials, which include natural materials, basic organic compounds, catalysts, and suspension agents, totaled $612,600. Direct labor costs were $160,000, and actual overhead costs were $303,500. Sales of the company's three products for April totaled $2,188,400. General and administrative expenses were $362,000.

1. Prepare a statement of cost of goods manufactured and an income statement through operating income for the month ended April 30.
2. Why is it that the total manufacturing costs do not equal the cost of goods manufactured?
3. What additional information would you need to determine the profitability of each of the three product lines?
4. Indicate whether each of the following is a product cost or a period cost:
   a. Import duties for suspension agent materials
   b. Shipping expenses to deliver manufactured products to the United States
   c. Rent for manufacturing facilities in Jakarta
   d. Salary of the American production-line manager working at the Indonesian manufacturing facilities
   e. Training costs for an Indonesian accountant

Your instructor will divide the class into groups to work through the case. One student from each group should present the group's finding to the class.

Business Communication Cases

Management Decision About a Supporting Service Function

C 9. As the manager of grounds maintenance for Latchey, a large insurance company in Missouri, you are responsible for maintaining the grounds surrounding the company's three buildings, the six entrances to the property, and the recreational facilities, which include a golf course, a soccer field, jogging and bike paths, and tennis, basketball, and volleyball courts. Maintenance includes gardening (watering, planting, mowing, trimming, removing debris, and so on) and land improvements (e.g., repairing or replacing damaged or worn concrete and gravel areas).

Early in January, you receive a memo from the president of Latchey requesting information about the cost of operating your department for the last 12 months. She has received a bid from Xeriscape Landscapes, Inc., to perform the gardening activities you now perform. You are to prepare a cost report that will help her decide whether to keep gardening activities within the company or to outsource the work.

1. Before preparing your report, answer the following questions:
   a. What kinds of information do you need about your department?
   b. Why is this information relevant?
   c. Where would you go to obtain this information (sources)?
   d. When would you want to obtain this information?
2. Draft a report showing only headings and line items that best communicate the costs of your department. How would you change your report if the president asked you to reduce the costs of operating your department?
3. One of your department's cost accounts is the Maintenance Expense–Garden Equipment account.
   a. Is this a direct or an indirect cost?
   b. Is it a product or a period cost?
   c. Is it a variable or a fixed cost?
   d. Does the activity add value to Latchey's provision of insurance services?
   e. Is it a budgeted or an actual cost in your report?

Cost Classifications

C 10. Visit a local fast-food restaurant. Observe all aspects of the operation and take notes on the entire process. Describe the procedures used to take, process, and fill an order and deliver the food to the customer. Based on your observations, make a list of the costs incurred by the restaurant. Then create a table similar to Table 1 in the text, in which you classify the costs you have identified by their traceability (direct or indirect), cost behavior (variable or fixed), value attribute (value-adding or nonvalue-adding), and implications for financial reporting (product or period costs). Bring your notes and your table to class and be prepared to discuss your findings.

20

Costing Systems: Job Order and Process Costing

A product costing system is expected to provide information about unit costs, to supply cost data for management decisions, and to furnish ending values for the Materials, Work in Process, and Finished Goods Inventory accounts. The appropriateness of a product costing system depends on the nature of the production process. Because the manufacture of custom orders and the manufacture of large quantities of similar products involve different processes, they generally require different costing systems. In this chapter, we describe the two basic types of product costing systems: job order costing and process costing.

LEARNING OBJECTIVES

LO1 Discuss the role that information about costs plays in the management process, and explain why unit cost is important.

LO2 Distinguish between the two basic types of product costing systems, and identify the information each provides.

LO3 Explain cost flow in a job order costing system, prepare a job order cost card, and compute product unit cost.

LO4 Explain product flow and cost flow in a process costing system.

LO5 Define *equivalent production,* and compute equivalent units.

LO6 Prepare a process cost report using the FIFO costing method.

LO7 Evaluate operating performance using information about product cost.

- Is the product costing system that is used for custom-made items appropriate for mass-produced items?

- What performance measures would be most useful in evaluating the results of each type of product?

However you like your ice cream, **Cold Stone Creamery** can create it for you. The personalized process begins on a frozen granite stone countertop with high-quality ice cream, which is freshly made every day, and your choice of mix-ins—chocolate, candy, nuts, fruit, and even homemade cake batter. Once the customer selects the mix-in, the server "spades" the ingredients together into one of three sizes: Like It, Love It, or Gotta Have It.

When the company was founded in Tempe, Arizona, in 1999, its management team set a tactical goal of opening 1,000 profitable stores by 2006. The team met its goal, and Cold Stone Creamery is now among the country's fastest-growing privately owned companies.[1] So what is next for Cold Stone Creamery? The company has no immediate plans to create a product for sale in grocery stores or other retail establishments. But, as you will see in this chapter, if it did create such a product, it would need to adjust its product costing system, as well as its performance measures.

Product Cost Information and the Management Process

Managers depend on relevant and reliable information about costs to manage their organizations. Although they vary in their approaches to gathering, analyzing, and reporting information about costs, managers share the same basic concerns as they move through the management process. Figure 1 summarizes the management process and what managers have to address with relevant and timely information about costs.

Planning

When managers plan, they use information about costs to set performance expectations and estimate unit costs. In manufacturing companies, such as **Cold Stone Creamery, Toyota,** and **Levi Strauss & Co.,** managers use cost information to develop budgets, establish product prices, and plan production volumes. In service organizations, such as **Century 21, H&R Block,** and **Orkin Exterminating Company,** managers use cost information to develop budgets, establish prices, set sales goals, and determine human resource needs. During the planning process, knowledge of unit costs helps managers of both manufacturing and service companies set reasonable selling prices and estimate the cost of their products or services.

Performing

Managers make decisions every day about controlling costs, managing the company's activity volume, ensuring quality, and negotiating prices. They use timely cost and volume information and actual unit costs to support their decisions. In manufacturing companies, managers use information about costs to decide whether to drop a product line, add a production shift, outsource the manufacture of a subassembly to another company, bid on a special order, or negotiate a selling price. In service organizations, managers use cost information to make decisions about bidding on jobs, dropping a service, outsourcing a task to an independent contractor, adding staff, or negotiating a price. All these decisions can have far-reaching effects, including possible changes in unit cost or quality. When making such decisions, managers will want to consider whether they add value to all stakeholders and whether the decisions are ethical.

FOCUS ON BUSINESS PRACTICE
How Hard Is It to Detect Fraud?

Managers are finding fraud to be an increasingly common business problem. Fortunately, some types of fraud, including scams that involve product costs and expenses, are relatively easy to detect. In a study in which fraud examiners were asked to rate their difficulty in detecting fraud on a scale of 1 (most difficult to detect) to 7 (easiest to detect), the results showed that the most difficult scams to detect were extortion (2.5) and illegal gratuities (2.86). Cash larceny (5.04), check tampering (4.40), illegal disbursements (4.35), expense scams (4.34), financial statement irregularities (4.28), skimming (4.24), and payroll schemes (4.20) were much easier to uncover.[2]

■ **FIGURE 1**
The Management Process: To-Do's for Managers

To-Do's for Managers

- Plan
  - Set performance expectations by developing budgets
  - Establish prices, plan sales and production volumes, and determine resource needs
  - Estimate unit costs of products or services

- Perform
  - Make decisions about controlling costs, managing the company's activity volume, ensuring quality, and negotiating contracts
  - Use timely cost, volume, and actual unit cost data

- Evaluate
  - Compare actual and targeted total and unit costs
  - Monitor relevant price and volume information
  - Analyze information to evaluate performance
  - Adjust plans and decision-making strategies

- Communicate
  - Prepare external reports, such as financial statements
  - Prepare internal performance evaluation reports comparing actual and targeted costs, analyzing nonfinancial measures of performance, and presenting data on whether goals for products or services are being achieved

Evaluating

When managers evaluate results, they watch for changes in cost and quality. They compare actual and targeted total and unit costs and monitor relevant price and volume information. They analyze the information to evaluate their performance, and on the basis of this evaluation, they adjust their planning and decision-making strategies. For example, if a product's quality is suffering, managers may study the design, materials purchasing, and manufacturing processes to determine the source of the problem so that they can make changes that will ensure the product's quality. If operating costs in a service business have risen too high, managers may break a unit cost of service down into its many components to analyze where costs can be cut or how the service can be performed more efficiently.

Communicating

When managers report to stakeholders, they prepare financial statements. In manufacturing companies, managers use product unit costs to determine inventory balances for the organization's balance sheet and the cost of goods sold for its income statement. In service organizations, managers use unit costs of services to determine cost of sales for the income statement. Managers also prepare performance evaluation reports for internal use. These reports compare actual unit costs and targeted costs, as well as actual and targeted nonfinancial measures of performance. Managers in both manufacturing and service organizations analyze the data in the performance evaluation reports to determine whether they are achieving cost goals for their products or services.

STOP • REVIEW • APPLY

1-1. When they plan, how do managers in manufacturing and service organizations use cost information?

1-2. When managers use cost information to support their decision making, what kinds of decisions do they make?

1-3. How do managers use cost information to evaluate results?

Suggested answers to all Stop, Review, and Apply questions are available at http://college.hmco.com/accounting/needles/poa/10e/student_home.html.

Job Order Versus Process Costing

LO2 Distinguish between the two basic types of product costing systems, and identify the information each provides.

For an organization to succeed, its managers must sell its products or services at prices that exceed the costs of creating and delivering them, thus ensuring a profit. To do so, managers need extensive information about such product-related costs as setup, production, and distribution. To meet managers' needs for cost information, it is necessary to have a highly reliable product costing system specifically designed to record and report the organization's operations.

A **product costing system** is a set of procedures used to account for an organization's product costs and to provide timely and accurate unit cost information for pricing, cost planning and control, inventory valuation, and financial statement preparation. The product costing system enables managers to track costs throughout the management process. It provides a structure for recording the revenue earned from sales and the costs incurred for direct materials, direct labor, and overhead.

Two basic types of product costing systems have been developed: job order costing and process costing systems. A **job order costing system** is used by companies that make unique, or special-order products, such as customized publications, specially built cabinets, made-to-order draperies, or personalized ice cream desserts. Such a system uses a single Work in Process Inventory account to record the costs of all job orders. It traces the costs of direct materials, direct labor, and overhead to a specific batch of products or a specific **job order** (i.e., a customer order for a specific number of specially designed, made-to-order products) by using a subsidiary ledger of job order cost cards. A **job order cost card** is the document on which all costs incurred in

Study Note

The product cost arrived at by both job order and process costing systems is an average cost. Process costing usually averages cost over a greater volume of product.

TABLE 1. Characteristics of Job Order Costing and Process Costing Systems

Job Order Costing System	Process Costing System
Traces manufacturing costs to a specific job order	Traces manufacturing costs to processes, departments, or work cells and then assigns the costs to products manufactured
Measures the cost of each completed unit	Measures costs in terms of units completed during a specific period
Uses a single Work in Process Inventory account to summarize the cost of all job orders	Uses several Work in Process Inventory accounts: one for each process, department, or work cell
Typically used by companies that make unique or special-order products, such as customized publications, built-in cabinets, or made-to-order draperies	Typically used by companies that make large amounts of similar products or liquid products or that have long, continuous production runs of identical products, such as makers of paint, soft drinks, bricks, and paper

Study Note

In job order costing, costs are assigned to jobs; in process costing, costs are assigned to production processes.

the production of a particular job order are recorded. The costs that a job order costing system gathers are used to measure the cost of each completed unit.

Companies that produce large amounts of similar products or liquid products or that have long, continuous production runs of identical products use a **process costing system**. Makers of paint, soft drinks, candy, bricks, paper, and gallon containers of ice cream would use such a system. A process costing system first traces the costs of direct materials, direct labor, and overhead to processes, departments, or work cells and then assigns the costs to the products manufactured by those processes, departments, or work cells during a specific period. A process costing system uses several Work in Process Inventory accounts—one for each process, department, or work cell. Table 1 summarizes the characteristics of job order costing and process costing systems.

In reality, few production processes are a perfect match for either a job order costing system or a process costing system. The typical product costing system therefore combines parts of job order costing and process costing to create a hybrid system designed specifically for an organization's production process. For example, an automobile maker like **Toyota** or **General Motors** may use process costing to track the costs of manufacturing a standard car and job order costing to track the costs of customized features, such as a convertible top or a stick shift. Managers who know the terms and procedures related

FOCUS ON BUSINESS PRACTICE

Why Does Toyota Use a Hybrid Product Costing System?

Thanks to its virtual production line, **Toyota** can now manufacture custom vehicles in five days. Computer software allows Toyota to calculate the exact number of parts needed at each precise point on its production line for a certain mix of cars. The mix can be modified up to five days in advance of actual production, allowing Toyota to modify a production run to include custom orders. When Toyota announced its hybrid approach, **General Motors** was taking 17 to 18 days to assemble a custom vehicle, and **DaimlerChrysler** needed an average of 10 to 12 days. Because most vehicles are mass-produced either in batches or on continuous flow assembly lines, manufacturers' process costing systems have not handled custom orders well. With its virtual production line and a hybrid product costing system, Toyota has gained a competitive advantage.[3]

to both job order and process costing can help design product costing systems that fit their information needs in any operating environment.

In recent years, global competition, technology, and the shifting mix of materials, labor, and overhead in the manufacturing process have changed the way companies approach product costing. The use of multidisciplinary teams of managers has fostered the development of new management accounting practices to improve product costing. These new practices emphasize the elimination of waste, the importance of quality, value-added processing, and increased customer satisfaction. We discuss some of the new practices, including the value chain, process value analysis, activity-based management, and the just-in-time operating environment elsewhere in the text.

S T O P • R E V I E W • A P P L Y

2-1. What is a product costing system?

2-2. What are the main similarities and differences between a job order costing system and a process costing system? (Focus on the characteristics of each type of system.)

2-3. What kind of product costing system do most companies use?

THE JOB ORDER COSTING SYSTEM

LO3 Explain cost flow in a job order costing system, prepare a job order cost card, and compute product unit cost.

> **Study Note**
>
> In a job order costing system, the specific job or batch of product, *not* a department or work center, is the focus of cost accumulation.

A job order costing system traces the costs of a specific order or batch of products to provide timely, accurate cost information and to facilitate the smooth and continuous flow of that information. Because such a system emphasizes cost flow, it is important to understand how costs are incurred, recorded, and transferred within the system. A basic part of a job order costing system is the set of procedures, documents, and accounts that a company uses when it incurs costs for materials, labor, and overhead. Job order cost cards and subsidiary ledgers for materials and finished goods inventories form the core of a job order costing system.

Cost Flow in a Job Order Costing System for a Manufacturing Company

To study the cost flows in a job order costing system, let's look at how Joann Lytton, the owner of Augusta, Inc., operates her business. For the past few years, Lytton has been building both customized and general-purpose golf carts. The direct materials costs for a golf cart include the costs of a cart frame, wheels, upholstered seats, a windshield, a motor, and a rechargeable battery. Direct labor costs include the wages of the two production workers who assemble the golf carts. Overhead includes indirect materials costs for upholstery zippers, cloth straps to hold equipment in place, wheel lubricants, screws and fasteners, and silicon to attach the windshield. It also includes indirect labor

Businesses that make special-order items, such as the kitchen cabinets shown here, use a job order costing system. With such a system, the costs of direct materials (e.g., the wood used in framing the cabinets), labor, and overhead (e.g., insurance and depreciation on tools and vehicles) are traced to a specific batch of products or job order. All costs are recorded on a job order cost card.

costs for moving materials to the production area and inspecting a golf cart during its construction; depreciation on the manufacturing plant and equipment used to make the golf carts; and utilities, insurance, and property taxes related to the manufacturing plant. Exhibit 1 shows the flow of each of these costs. Notice that all three inventory accounts have subsidiary ledgers backing up their totals. The beginning balance in the Materials Inventory account means there are already direct and indirect materials in the materials storeroom. (The materials ledger contains cost information about individual materials.) The beginning balance in Work in Process Inventory means Job CC is in production (with specifics given in the job order cost cards). The zero beginning balance in Finished Goods Inventory means all previously completed golf carts have been shipped.

Materials   When Augusta receives or expects to receive a sales order, the purchasing process begins with a request for specific quantities of direct and indirect materials needed for the order but not currently available in the materials storeroom. When the new materials arrive at Augusta, the Accounting Department records the materials purchased by making an entry that debits or increases the balance of the Materials Inventory account and credits either the Cash or Accounts Payable account (depending on if the purchase was for cash or credit):

Materials Inventory	XX	
Accounts Payable or Cash		XX

During the month, Augusta made two purchases on credit. In transaction **1**, the company purchased cart frames costing $572 and wheels costing $340 from one of its vendors. As shown in Exhibit 1, these purchases increase the debit balances in the Materials Inventory account and the corresponding accounts in the materials ledger. In transaction **2**, the company purchased indirect materials costing $82 from another vendor. This purchase also increases the debit

▼ **EXHIBIT 1**

The Job Order Costing System—Augusta, Inc.

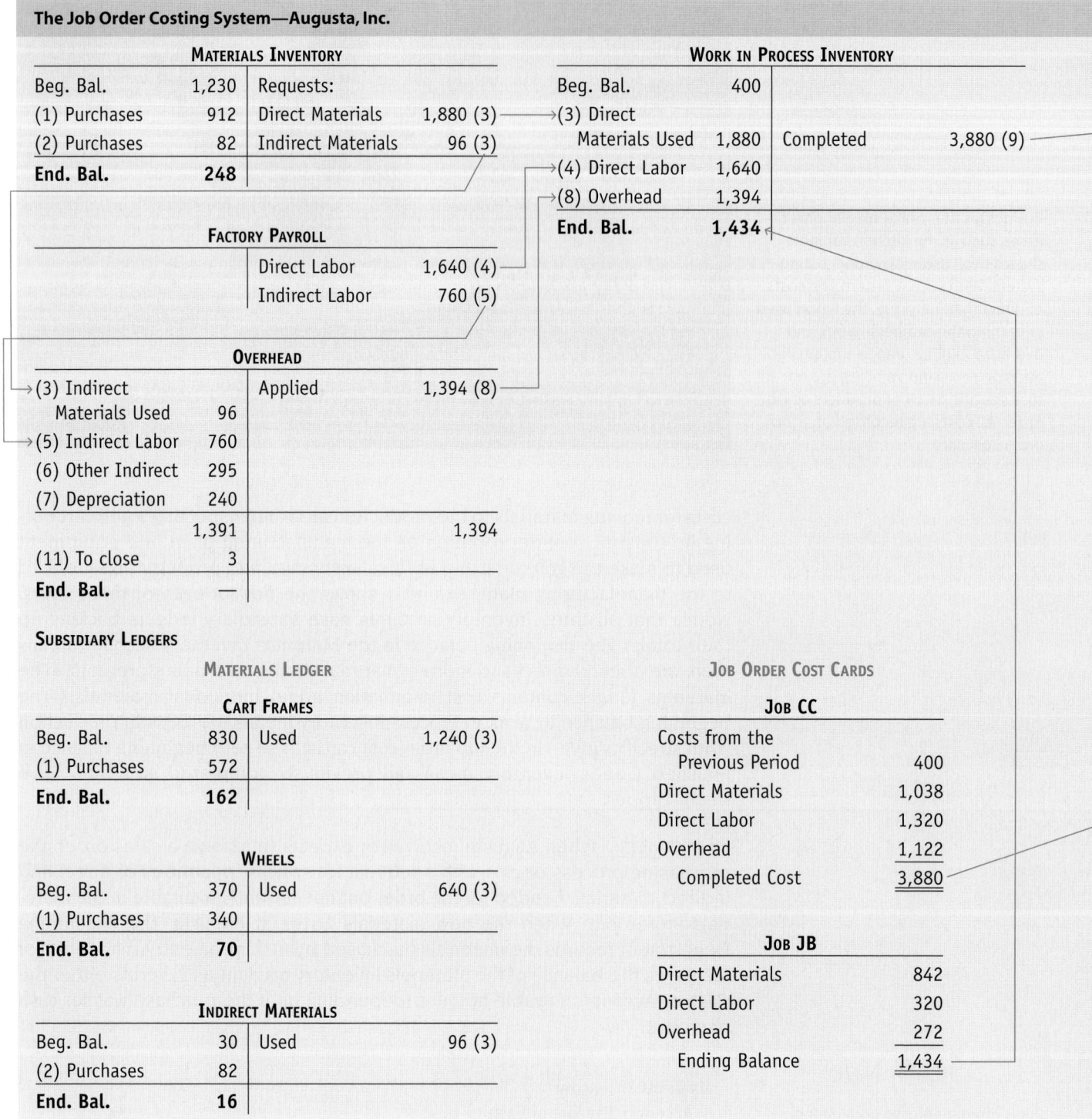

MATERIALS INVENTORY			
Beg. Bal.	1,230	Requests:	
(1) Purchases	912	Direct Materials	1,880 (3)
(2) Purchases	82	Indirect Materials	96 (3)
End. Bal.	248		

WORK IN PROCESS INVENTORY			
Beg. Bal.	400		
(3) Direct Materials Used	1,880	Completed	3,880 (9)
(4) Direct Labor	1,640		
(8) Overhead	1,394		
End. Bal.	1,434		

FACTORY PAYROLL			
		Direct Labor	1,640 (4)
		Indirect Labor	760 (5)

OVERHEAD			
(3) Indirect Materials Used	96	Applied	1,394 (8)
(5) Indirect Labor	760		
(6) Other Indirect	295		
(7) Depreciation	240		
	1,391		1,394
(11) To close	3		
End. Bal.	—		

SUBSIDIARY LEDGERS

MATERIALS LEDGER

CART FRAMES			
Beg. Bal.	830	Used	1,240 (3)
(1) Purchases	572		
End. Bal.	162		

WHEELS			
Beg. Bal.	370	Used	640 (3)
(1) Purchases	340		
End. Bal.	70		

INDIRECT MATERIALS			
Beg. Bal.	30	Used	96 (3)
(2) Purchases	82		
End. Bal.	16		

JOB ORDER COST CARDS

JOB CC	
Costs from the Previous Period	400
Direct Materials	1,038
Direct Labor	1,320
Overhead	1,122
Completed Cost	3,880

JOB JB	
Direct Materials	842
Direct Labor	320
Overhead	272
Ending Balance	1,434

balance in the Materials Inventory account, as well as the debit balance in the Indirect Materials account in the materials ledger. Not shown in Exhibit 1 are the two credit entries to the Accounts Payable account.

When golf carts are scheduled for production, requested materials are sent to the production area. The entry to record the flow of direct materials requested from the Materials Inventory account into the Work in Process Inventory account is as follows:

FINISHED GOODS INVENTORY			
Beg. Bal.	—		
(9) Completed During Period	3,880	Sold	1,940 (10)
End. Bal.	**1,940**		

COST OF GOODS SOLD			
(10) Sold During Period	1,940	Adjustment	3 (11)
End. Bal.	**1,937**		

FINISHED GOODS LEDGER

JOB CC			
Beg. Bal.	—	Sold	1,940 (10)
(9) Completed	3,880		
End. Bal.	**1,940**		

Work in Process Inventory	XX	
Materials Inventory		XX

The entry to record the flow of indirect materials requested from the Materials Inventory account into the Overhead account follows.

Overhead	XX	
Materials Inventory		XX

Transaction **3** shows the request for materials for the production of two jobs. Of the $1,880 of direct materials requested, the materials ledger shows that $1,240 was for cart frames and $640 was for wheels. Job CC, a batch of two general-purpose golf carts already in production, required $1,038 of the additional direct materials. Job JB, a customized golf cart made to the specifications of an individual customer, required $842 of the direct materials. Notice that the $1,880 of direct materials requested appears as a debit in the Work in Process Inventory account because that account records the costs of partially completed units of product and as a credit in the Materials Inventory account. The cost of direct materials requested is also recorded on the corresponding job order cost cards.

In addition, transaction **3** accounts for the $96 of indirect materials requested for production as a $96 debit to Overhead and a $96 credit to Materials Inventory. As you will see in our discussion of overhead, because the $96 was for indirect materials rather than direct materials, it flows into the Overhead account instead of to a specific Work in Process job.

Labor   Every pay period, the payroll costs are recorded. In general, the payroll costs include salaries and wages for direct and indirect production labor as well as for non-production-related employees. As noted earlier, Augusta's two production employees assemble the golf carts. Several other employees support production by moving materials and inspecting the products. The following entry records the payroll:

Work in Process Inventory (direct labor costs)	XX	
Overhead (indirect labor costs)	XX	
Selling and Administrative Expenses (nonproduction-related	XX	
salary and wage costs)		
Factory Payroll		XX

Transaction **4** and **5** show the total production-related wages earned by these employees during the period. Job CC required direct labor of $1,320, and Job JB required $320. The total direct labor cost of $1,640 ($1,320 + $320) is shown as a debit to the Work in Process Inventory account. The indirect labor cost of $760, shown in transaction **5**, flows to the Overhead account instead of to a particular job. The corresponding credit is made to Augusta's Factory Payroll account.

Overhead   Thus far, indirect materials and indirect labor have been the only costs debited to the Overhead account. Other indirect production costs, such as utilities, property taxes, insurance, and depreciation, are also charged to the Overhead account as they are incurred during the period. In general, the entry appears as:

Overhead	XX	
Accounts Payable or Cash		XX
Accumulated Depreciation		XX

Transaction **6** shows that other indirect costs amounting to $295 were paid. Transaction **7** records the $240 of factory-related depreciation. The corresponding credits, not shown here, are to Augusta's Cash account for $295 and to the Accumulated Depreciation account for $240.

During the period, to recognize all product-related costs for a job, an overhead cost estimate is applied using a predetermined rate. Based on its budget and past experience, Augusta currently uses a predetermined overhead rate of 85 percent of direct labor costs. The entry to apply overhead using a predetermined rate is:

Work in Process Inventory	XX	
Overhead		XX

In transaction **8**, total overhead of $1,394 is applied, with $1,122 going to Job CC (85 percent of $1,320) and $272 to Job JB (85 percent of $320). Notice that the Work in Process Inventory account is debited for $1,394 (85% of $1,640—see transaction **4**), and the Overhead account is credited for the applied overhead of $1,394.

Completed Units   When a custom job or a batch of general-purpose golf carts is completed and ready for sale, the products are moved from the manufacturing area to the finished goods storeroom. To record the cost flow of completed products from the Work in Process Inventory account into the Finished Goods Inventory account, the entry is:

Finished Goods Inventory	XX	
Work in Process Inventory		XX

As shown in transaction **9,** when Job CC is completed and moved to the finished goods storeroom, its cost of $3,880 is transferred from the Work in Process Inventory account to the Finished Goods Inventory account by debiting Finished Goods Inventory $3,880 and crediting Work in Process Inventory $3,880. Its job order cost card is also completed and transferred to the finished goods file.

Figure 2 shows the job order cost card for Job CC. Notice that the product unit cost for each of the two golf carts in the job is computed.

Sold Units   When a company uses a perpetual inventory system, as Augusta does, two accounting entries are made when products are sold. One is prompted by the sales invoice and records the quantity and selling price of the

Study Note

This example shows the company using a perpetual inventory system. In a periodic inventory system, the cost of goods sold is calculated at the end of the period.

■ **FIGURE 2**
Job Order Cost Card—Manufacturing Company

Job Order: __CC__

JOB ORDER COST CARD
Augusta, Inc.
Spring Hill, Florida

Customer: __Stock__   Batch: __X__   Custom: _____
Specifications: __Two general-purpose golf carts__
Date of Order: __2/26/xx__
Date of Completion: __3/6/xx__

Costs Charged to Job	Previous Months	Current Month	Cost Summary
Direct Materials	$165	$1,038	$1,203
Direct Labor	127	1,320	1,447
Overhead (85% of direct labor cost)	108	1,122	1,230
Totals	$400	$3,480	$3,880
Units Completed			2
Product Unit Cost			$1,940

products sold. The other entry, prompted by the delivery of products to a customer, records the quantity and cost of the products shipped. These entries are as follows:

Accounts Receivable or Cash (Sales price × Units sold)	XX	
Sales (Sales price × Units sold)		XX

Cost of Goods Sold (Unit cost × Units sold)	XX	
Finished Goods Inventory (Unit cost × Units sold)		XX

In transaction **10**, the $1,940 cost of the one general-purpose golf cart that was sold during the period is transferred from the Finished Goods Inventory account to the Cost of Goods Sold account. The sales entry for this golf cart is not shown in Exhibit 1. The Finished Goods Inventory account has an ending balance of $1,940 for the remaining one unsold cart.

Reconciliation of Overhead Costs   To prepare financial statements at the end of the accounting period, the Cost of Goods Sold account must reflect actual product costs, including actual overhead. Thus, the Overhead account must be reconciled every period. As you learned in a previous chapter,

if at the end of the accounting period the actual overhead debit balance exceeds the applied overhead credit balance, then the Overhead account is said to be underapplied, and the debit balance must be closed to the Cost of Goods Sold account. Here is the entry:

Cost of Goods Sold	XX	
Overhead		XX

Or, as is shown in transaction 11, if the actual overhead cost for the period ($1,391) is less than the estimated overhead that was applied during the period ($1,394), then the Overhead account is overapplied and the $3 credit balance must be closed to the Cost of Goods Sold account. Here is the entry:

Overhead	3	
Cost of Goods Sold		3

Because the applied overhead exceeded the actual overhead by $3, Cost of Goods Sold must be reduced by the amount of the overcharge. It will then reflect the actual overhead costs incurred. Given that the amount is minor, the company prefers to subtract it from the cost of the cart that was sold rather than tracing it back to the individual units worked on during the period. Thus, $3 is deducted from the Cost of Goods Sold account, making the ending balance of that account $1,937.

The Job Order Cost Card and Computation of Product Unit Costs

As is evident from the preceding discussion, job order cost cards play a key role in a job order costing system. Because all manufacturing costs are accumulated in one Work in Process Inventory account, a separate accounting procedure is needed to trace those costs to specific jobs. The solution is the subsidiary ledger made up of job order cost cards. Each job being worked on has a job order cost card. As costs are incurred, they are classified by job and recorded on the appropriate card.

As you can see in Figure 2, a manufacturer's job order cost card has space for direct materials, direct labor, and overhead costs. It also includes the job order number, product specifications, the name of the customer, the date of the order, the projected completion date, and a cost summary. As a job incurs direct materials and direct labor costs, its job order cost card is updated. Overhead is also posted to the job order cost card at the predetermined rate. Job order cost cards for incomplete jobs make up the subsidiary ledger for the Work in Process Inventory account. To ensure correctness, the ending balance in the Work in Process Inventory account is compared with the total of the costs shown on the job order cost cards.

A job order costing system simplifies the calculation of product unit costs. When a job is finished, the costs of direct materials, direct labor, and overhead that have been recorded on its job order cost card are totaled. The product unit cost is computed by dividing the total costs for the job by the number of good (i.e., salable) units produced. The product unit cost is entered on the job order cost card and will be used to value items in inventory. The job order cost card in Figure 2 shows the costs for completed Job CC. Two golf carts were produced at a total cost of $3,880, so the product unit cost was $1,940.

Job Order Costing in a Service Organization

Many service organizations use a job order costing system to compute the cost of rendering services. As pointed out elsewhere in the text, the costs of service organizations are different from those of a manufacturing organization in that they are not associated with a physical product that can be assembled, stored, and valued as inventory. Because these organizations sell services rather than

 Study Note

Job order cost cards for service businesses may record costs by activities done for the job. Notice that the activity cost includes supplies, labor, and overhead.

■ **FIGURE 3**
Job Order Cost Card—Service Organization

JOB ORDER COST CARD
Gartner Landscaping Services

Customer:	Rico Corporation
Job Order Number:	
Contract Type:	Cost-Plus
Type of Service:	Landscape Corporate Headquarters
Date Completed:	May 31, 20xx

Costs Charged to Job	Previous Months	Current Month	Total Cost
Landscape Design			
Supplies	$ 100	$ —	$ 100
Design Labor	850	—	850
Service Overhead (40% of design labor)	340	—	340
Totals	$1,290	$ —	$1,290
Landscape Installation			
Planting Materials	$ 970	$1,200	$2,170
Installation Labor	400	620	1,020
Service Overhead (50% of installation labor)	200	310	510
Totals	$1,570	$2,130	$3,700
Job-Site Cleanup			
Janitorial Service Cost	$ 90	$ 320	$ 410
Totals	$2,950	$2,450	$5,400

Cost Summary to Date	Total Cost
Landscape Design	$ 1,290
Landscape Installation	3,700
Job-Site Cleanup	410
Totals	$ 5,400
Profit Margin (15%)	810
Contract Revenue	$ 6,210

making products for sale, the costs that they incur for materials are usually negligible. Their most important cost is labor, which is carefully accounted for through the use of time cards.

The cost flow of services is similar to the cost flow of manufactured products. Job order cost cards are used to keep track of the costs incurred for each job. Job costs include labor, materials and supplies, and service overhead. To cover these costs and earn a profit, many service organizations base jobs on **cost-plus contracts**. Such contracts require the customer to pay all costs incurred in performing the job plus a predetermined amount of profit, which is based on the amount of costs incurred. When the job is complete, the costs on the completed job order cost card become the cost of services. The cost of services is adjusted at the end of the accounting period for the difference between the applied service overhead costs and the actual service overhead costs.

To illustrate how a service organization uses a job order costing system, let's assume that a company called Gartner Landscaping Services employs 15 people and serves the San Francisco Bay area. The company earns its revenue by designing and installing landscapes for homes and offices. Figure 3 shows Gartner's job order cost card for the landscaping of Rico Corporation's corporate headquarters. Costs have been categorized into three separate activities: landscape design, landscape installation, and job-site cleanup.

Costs have been tracked to the Rico Corporation job throughout its duration, and now that the job is finished, it is time to complete the job order cost card. The service overhead cost for landscape design is 40 percent of design labor cost, and the service overhead cost for landscape installation is 50 percent of installation labor cost. Total costs incurred for this job were $5,400. Gartner's cost-plus contract with Rico has a 15 percent profit guarantee; therefore, $810 of profit margin is added to the total cost to arrive at the total contract revenue of $6,210, which is the amount billed to Rico.

STOP • REVIEW • APPLY

3-1. What is the purpose of the Work in Process Inventory account?

3-2. Why is the Overhead account reconciled at the end of an accounting period?

3-3. How do the costs of a service organization and a manufacturing organization differ? How do these differences affect the job order costing system of a service organization?

T Account Analysis with Unknowns   Partial operating data for Sample Company—accounts and transactions—for the month of October are presented below. Sample Company's management has set the predetermined overhead rate for the current year at 60 percent of direct labor costs.

Beginning Materials Inventory	$ 4,000
Beginning Work in Process Inventory	6,000
Beginning Finished Goods Inventory	2,000
Direct materials used	16,000
Direct materials purchased	**a**
Direct labor costs	24,000

Overhead applied	**b**
Cost of units completed	**c**
Cost of goods sold	50,000
Ending Materials Inventory	3,000
Ending Work in Process Inventory	10,000
Ending Finished Goods Inventory	**d**

Using T accounts and the data provided, compute the unknown values. Show all your computations.

SOLUTION

MATERIALS INVENTORY

	Beg. Bal.	4,000		
(a)	Purchases	15,000	Used	16,000
	End. Bal.	*3,000*		

WORK IN PROCESS INVENTORY

	Beg. Bal.	6,000		
	Direct Materials Used	16,000		
	Direct Labor	24,000	(c) Completed During	
(b)	Overhead Applied	14,400*	Period	50,400
	End. Bal.	*10,000*		

FINISHED GOODS INVENTORY

	Beg. Bal.	2,000		
(c)	Completed During Period	50,400	Cost of Goods Sold	50,000
(d)	*End. Bal.*	*2,400*		

*$24,000 × 60% = $14,400

Computation of Product Unit Cost Complete the following job order cost card for five custom-built cabinets:

Job Order 16

JOB ORDER COST CARD
Unique Cupboards, LLP
Sample City, Oregon

Customer:	Brian Tofer	Batch: ___	Custom: _X_
Specifications:	5 Custom cabinets		
Date of Order:	5/4/xx	Date of Completion:	6/8/xx

Costs Charged to Job	Previous Months	Current Month	Cost Summary
Direct materials	$3,500	$2,800	$?
Direct labor	2,300	1,600	?
Overhead applied	1,150	800	?
Totals	$?	$?	$?
Units completed			?
Product unit cost			$?

SOLUTION

Job Order 16

JOB ORDER COST CARD
Unique Cupboards, LLP
Sample City, Oregon

Customer:	Brian Tofer	Batch: ___	Custom: __X__
Specifications:	5 Custom cabinets		
Date of Order:	5/4/xx	Date of Completion:	6/8/xx

Costs Charged to Job	Previous Months	Current Month	Cost Summary
Direct materials	$3,500	$2,800	$ 6,300
Direct labor	2,300	1,600	3,900
Overhead applied	1,150	800	1,950
Totals	$6,950	$5,200	$12,150
Units completed			÷ 5
Product unit cost			$ 2,430

The Process Costing System

LO4 Explain product flow and cost flow in a process costing system.

As discussed earlier, a process costing system is used by businesses that produce large amounts of similar products or liquid products or that have long, continuous production runs of identical products. Companies that produce paint, beverages, bricks, canned foods, milk, and paper are typical users of a process costing system. Tracking costs to individual products in a continuous flow environment would be too difficult and too expensive and would not reveal significantly different product costs. One gallon of green paint

Companies like Coca-Cola that produce large amounts of identical items in a continuous flow use a process costing system. With such a system, the manufacturing costs are traced to processes, departments, or work cells and are then assigned to the products manufactured during a specific period.

■ **FIGURE 4**
Production Flows for Process Costing

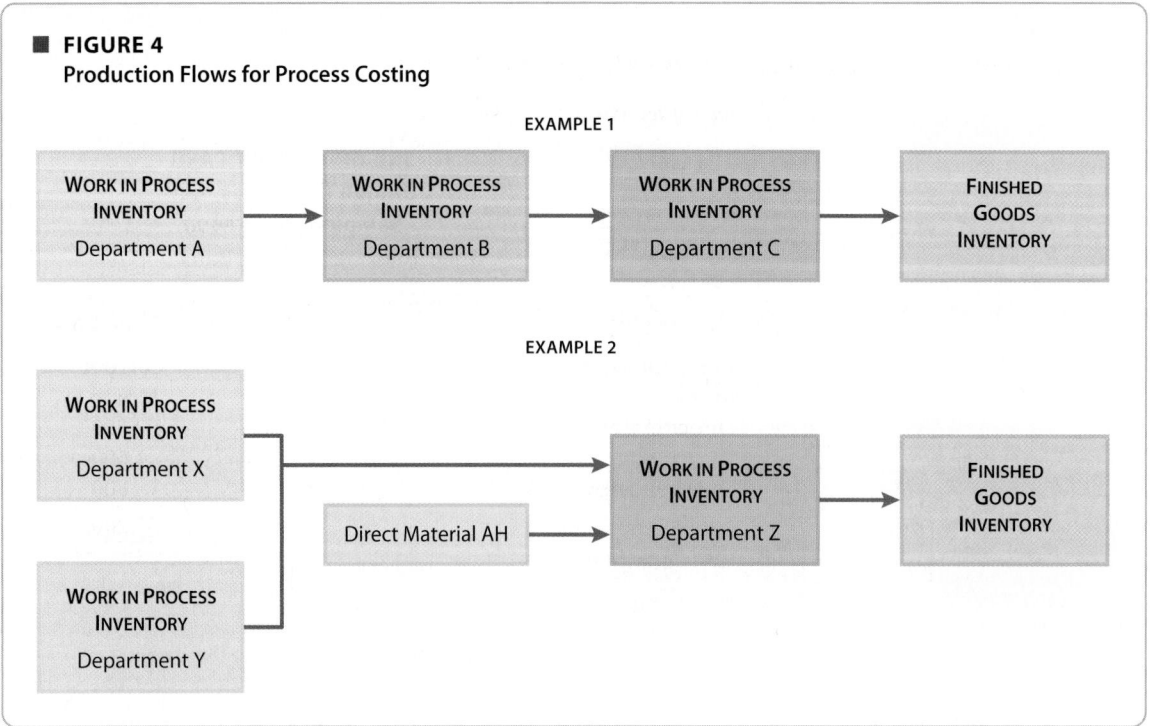

is identical to the next gallon of green paint; one brick looks just like the next brick. Because the products are alike, they should cost the same amount to produce. A process costing system accumulates the costs of direct materials, direct labor, and overhead for each process, department, or work cell and assigns those costs to the products as they are produced during a particular period.

Patterns of Product Flows and Cost Flows

During production in a process costing environment, products flow in a first-in, first-out (FIFO) fashion through several processes, departments, or work cells. Along the way, they may undergo many different combinations of operations. Figure 4 illustrates two basic production flows. Example 1 shows a series of three processing steps, or departments. The completed product from one department becomes the direct materials for the next department. The product unit cost is the sum of the cost elements in all departments.

Example 2 in Figure 4 shows a different kind of production flow. Again there are three departments, but the product does not flow through all the departments in a simple 1–2–3 order. Instead, two separate products are developed: one in Department X and the other in Department Y. Both products then go to Department Z, where they are joined with a third direct material, Material AH. The unit cost that is transferred to the Finished Goods Inventory account when the products are completed includes cost elements from Departments X, Y, and Z.

Product flow in a process costing environment almost always follows a linear pattern. Because a linear approach illustrates all the concepts that would be applied in both simple and complex environments, we present only that approach in this chapter. To further illustrate this linear pattern of production flow, let's consider an example from the computer chip–making industry. The steps that follow, which describe the production flow during the manufacture of computer chips, are shown in Figure 5.

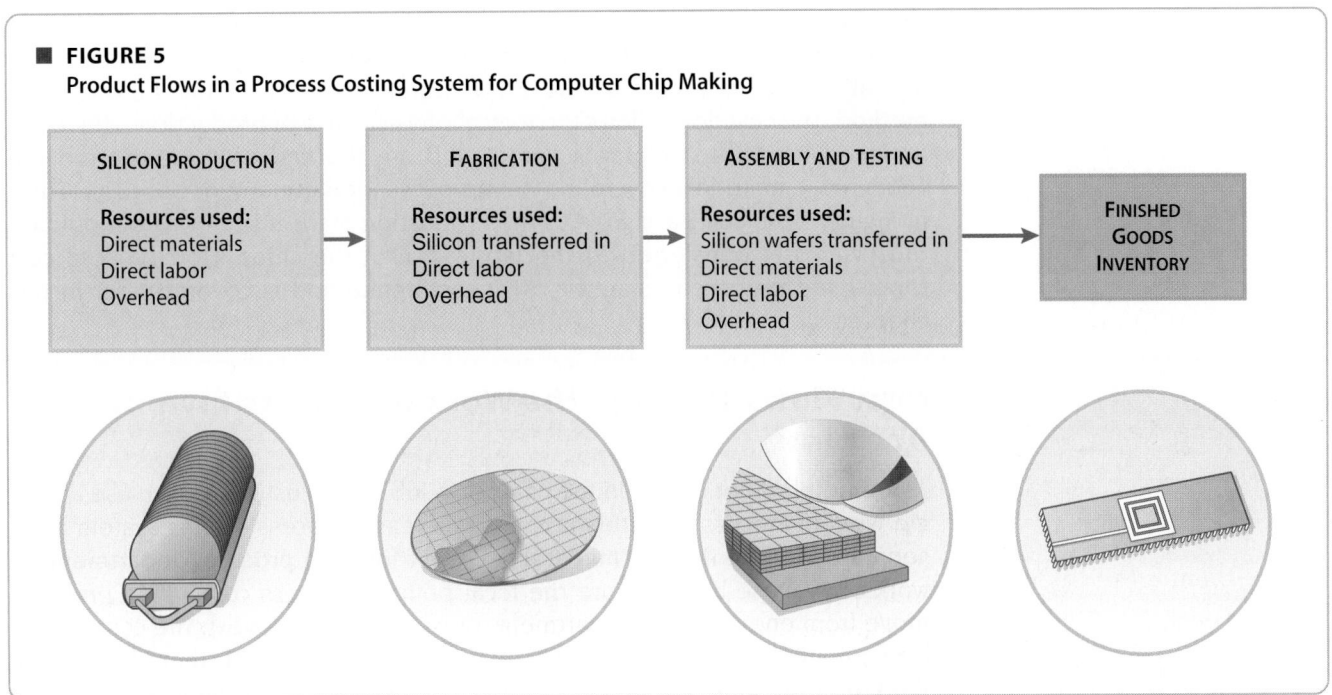

■ **FIGURE 5**
Product Flows in a Process Costing System for Computer Chip Making

1. *Producing the silicon wafer* Silicon, which is extracted from sand and then purified, is the direct material from which computer chips are made. Through a process of crystallization, the refined, molten silicon is converted to a cylindrical ingot. The ingot is then sliced into wafers, and the wafers are polished to meet flatness and thickness specifications. The workers involved in these steps provide direct labor. Overhead includes the costs of the equipment the workers use and the resources necessary to operate and maintain the equipment.

2. *Fabricating the chips* Fabrication includes photolithography, etching, ion implantation, and all the other steps needed to create the electronic circuits that make up each chip on a wafer. Additional direct labor and overhead costs are incurred during fabrication.

3. *Final testing, assembly, and packaging of the chips* Although the wafers are tested at each step in the fabrication process, each chip on a wafer is tested again when fabrication is complete. Those that pass this test are cut from the wafer, placed in metal or plastic packages, tested once again, and transferred to finished goods inventory in the warehouse. These steps incur additional direct labor, direct materials, and overhead costs.

Process costing environments can be considerably more or less complex than the one we have just described, but even in simple process costing environments, production generally involves a number of separate manufacturing processes, departments, or works cells. For example, the separate processes involved in manufacturing sofas include making the frames and cushions, upholstering the frames, and assembling the frames and cushions into finished products.

As products pass through each manufacturing process, department, or work cell, the process costing system accumulates their costs and passes them on to the next process, department, or work cell. At the end of every accounting period, the system generates a report that assigns the costs that have accumulated during the period to the units that have transferred out of the process, department, or work cell and to the units that are still work in process. Managers use this report, called a **process cost report**, to assign costs using a cost allocation method, such as the FIFO costing method. In the **FIFO costing method**, the cost flow follows the logical physical flow of production—the costs assigned to the first materials processed are the first costs transferred out when those materials flow to the next process, department, or work cell. Thus, in Figure 5, the costs assigned to the production of the silicon wafers would be the first costs transferred to the fabrication of the chips. How process cost reports are prepared using the FIFO costing method is covered later in this chapter.

Cost Flows Through the Work in Process Inventory Accounts

As we pointed out earlier in the chapter, a job order costing system uses a single Work in Process Inventory account, whereas a process costing system has a separate Work in Process Inventory account for each process, department, or work cell. These accounts are the focal point of process costing. As products move from one process, department, or work cell to the next, the costs of the direct materials, direct labor, and overhead associated with them flow to the Work in Process Inventory account of that process, department, or work cell. The entry to transfer product costs from one process, department, or work cell to another is:

Work in Process Inventory (next department)	XX	
Work in Process Inventory (this department)		XX

Once the products are completed, packaged, and ready for sale, their costs are transferred to the Finished Goods Inventory account. The journal entry to transfer the completed product costs out of Work in Process Inventory into Finished Goods Inventory is:

Finished Goods Inventory	XX	
Work in Process Inventory		XX

As you will learn later in this chapter, the costs associated with these entries are the result of completing a process cost report for the process, department, or work cell.

To illustrate how costs flow through the Work in Process Inventory accounts in a process costing system, let's consider a company like **Nabisco**, which makes large quantities of identical cookies in a continuous flow. Such a company would have mixing, baking, and packaging departments. After its Mixing Department has prepared the cookie dough, the costs incurred for direct materials, direct labor, and overhead are transferred from that department's Work in Process Inventory account to the Work in Process Inventory account of the Baking Department. When the cookies are baked, the costs of the cookie dough and the baking costs are transferred from the Baking Department's Work in Process Inventory account to the Work in Process Inventory account of the Packaging Department. After the cookies are packaged and ready for sale, all their costs—for dough, baking, and packaging—transfer to the Finished Goods Inventory account. When the packages of cookies are sold, their costs transfer from the Finished Goods Inventory account to the Cost of Goods Sold account.

Because the production of homogeneous products like packaged cookies, paint, or computer chips is continuous, it would be impractical to try to assign their costs to a specific batch of products, as is done with a job order costing system. Instead, as we have noted, in a process costing system, the process cost report prepared at the end of every accounting period assigns the costs that have accumulated in each Work in Process Inventory account to the units transferred out and to the units still in process. Managers use the process cost report to compute the unit cost of all products worked on during the period. Thus, the product unit cost includes all costs from all processes, departments, or work cells.

To compute the unit cost, the total cost of direct materials, direct labor, and overhead is divided by the total number of units worked on during the period. Thus, a critical question is exactly how many units were worked on during the period? Do we count only units started and completed during the period? Or should we include partially completed units in the beginning work in process inventory? And what about incomplete products in the ending work in process inventory? The answers to these questions relate to the concept of equivalent production, which we discuss next.

S T O P ● R E V I E W ● A P P L Y

4-1. Why would a business use a process costing system rather than a job order costing system?

4-2. Why does process costing require multiple Work in Process Inventory accounts?

Process Costing Versus Job Order Costing   Indicate whether the manufacturer of each of the following products should use a job order costing system or a process costing system to accumulate product costs:

1.   Plastics
2.   Cereal
3.   Ocean cruise ships
4.   Medical drugs for veterinary practices

> **SOLUTION**
> 1.   Process
> 2.   Process
> 3.   Job Order
> 4.   Process

Computing Eqivalent Production

LO5   Define *equivalent production*, and compute equivalent units.

A process costing system, because it makes no attempt to associate costs with particular job orders, assigns the costs incurred in a process, department, or work cell to the units worked on during an accounting period by computing an average cost per unit. **Equivalent production** (also called *equivalent units*) is a measure that applies a percentage-of-completion factor to partially completed units to calculate the equivalent number of whole units produced in an accounting period for each type of input (i.e., direct materials, direct labor, and overhead). The number of equivalent units produced is

■ **FIGURE 6**
Computation of Equivalent Production

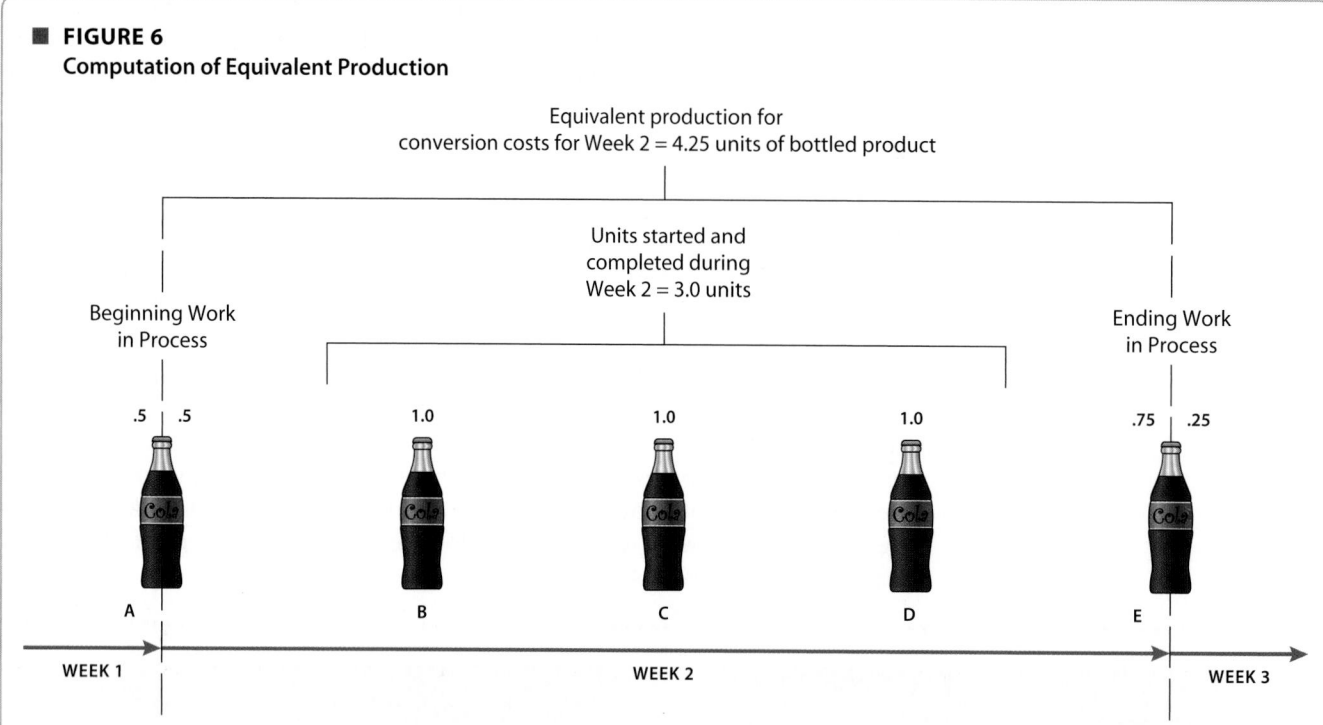

Note: Conversion costs (the cost of direct labor and overhead) are incurred uniformly as each physical unit of drink moves through production. Equivalent production for Week 2 is 4.25 units for conversion costs. But direct materials costs are all added to production at the beginning of the process. Because four physical units of drinks entered production in Week 2, equivalent production for the week is 4.0 units of effort for direct materials costs.

> **Study Note**
>
> The number of units started and completed is not the same as the total number of units completed during the period. Total units completed includes two categories: units in beginning work in process inventory that were completed and units started and completed.

the sum of (1) total units started and completed during the period and (2) an amount representing the work done on partially completed products in both the beginning and the ending work in process inventories.

Equivalent production must be computed separately for each type of input because of differences in the ways the costs are incurred. Direct materials are usually added to production at the beginning of the process. The costs of direct labor and overhead are often incurred uniformly throughout the production process. Thus, it is convenient to combine direct labor and overhead when calculating equivalent units. These combined costs are called **conversion costs** or **processing costs**.

We will explain the computation of equivalent production by using a simplified example. Soda Products Company makes bottled soft drinks. As illustrated in Figure 6, the company started Week 2 with one half-completed drink in process. During Week 2, it started and completed three drinks, and at the end of Week 2, it had one drink that was three-quarters completed.

Equivalent Production for Direct Materials

> **Study Note**
>
> Don't make the mistake of thinking that direct materials always go into production at the beginning of the process. In reality, direct materials are often added at different stages of production (e.g., for chocolate chip cookies, chips are added at the end of the mixing process).

At Soda Products, all direct materials, including the liquids and the bottles, are added at the beginning of production. Thus, the drink that was half-completed at the beginning of Week 2 had had all its direct materials added during the previous week. For this reason, no direct materials costs for this drink are included in the computation of Week 2's equivalent units since no direct materials efforts occurred during the week for the beginning inventory units.

During Week 2, Soda Products began work on four new drinks—the three drinks that were completed and the drink that was three-quarters completed at the end of the week. Because all direct materials are added at the beginning of the production process, all four drinks were 100 percent complete in regard to direct materials at the end of Week 2. Thus, for Week 2, the equivalent production for direct materials was 4.0 units. This figure includes direct materials for both the 3.0 units that were started and completed and the 1.0 unit that was three-quarters completed.

Equivalent Production for Conversion Costs

Because conversion costs at Soda Products are incurred uniformly throughout the production process, the equivalent production for conversion costs during Week 2 consists of three components: the cost to finish the half-completed unit in beginning work in process inventory (0.5), the cost to begin and finish three completed units (3.0), and the cost to begin work on the three-quarters completed unit in ending work in process inventory (0.75). For Week 2, the total equivalent production for conversion costs was 4.25 (0.5 + 3.0 + 0.75) units.

In reality, Soda Products would make many more drinks during an accounting period and would have many more partially completed drinks in its beginning and ending work in process inventories. The number of partially completed drinks would be so great that it would be impractical to take a physical count of them. So, instead of taking a physical count, Soda Products would estimate an average percentage of completion for all drinks in process.

Summary of Equivalent Production

The following is a recap of the current equivalent production for material and conversion costs for the period:

	Physical Units	Equivalent Units			
		Direct Materials		**Conversion Costs**	
Beginning inventory	1.00				
Units started this period	4.00				
Units to be accounted for	5.00				
Beginning inventory	1.00	—	0%	0.50	50%
Units started and completed	3.00	3.00	100%	3.00	100%
Ending inventory	1.00	1.00	100%	0.75	75%
Units accounted for	5.00	4.00		4.25	

S T O P • R E V I E W • A P P L Y

5-1. What is *equivalent production* (also called *equivalent units*)?

5-2. Why must actual unit data be changed to equivalent unit data to cost products in a process costing system?

5-3. Why does a process costing system compute conversion costs?

Equivalent Production Sample Company adds direct materials at the beginning of its production process and adds conversion costs uniformly throughout the process. The information that follows is from Sample Company's records for July. Using this information, compute the current period's equivalent units of production.

Units in beginning inventory 2,000

Units started during the period 13,000

Units partially completed 500

Percentage of completion of beginning inventory: 100% for direct materials; 40% for conversion costs

Percentage of completion of ending work in process inventory: 100% for direct materials; 70% for conversion costs

SOLUTION

Sample Company
For the Month Ended July 31

	Physical Units				
Beginning inventory	2,000		**Equivalent Units**		
Units started this period	13,000		**Direct**		**Conversion**
Units to be accounted for	15,000		**Materials**		**Costs**
Beginning inventory	2,000	—	0%	1,200	60%
Units started and completed	12,500	12,500	100%	12,500	100%
Ending inventory	500	500	100%	350	70%
Units accounted for	15,000	13,000		14,050	

Preparing a Process Cost Report Using the FIFO Costing Method

LO6 Prepare a process cost report using the FIFO costing method.

As mentioned earlier, a process cost report is a report that managers use to track and analyze costs for a process, department, or work cell in a process costing system. In a process cost report that uses the FIFO costing method, the cost flow follows the logical physical flow of production—the costs assigned to the first products processed are the first costs transferred out when those products flow to the next process, department, or work cell.

As illustrated in Exhibit 2, the preparation of a process cost report has five steps. The first two steps account for the units of product being processed. The next two steps account for the costs of the direct material, direct labor, and overhead that are being incurred. The final step assigns costs to products transferring out of the area and to those remaining behind in ending work in process inventory.

Accounting for Units

Managers must account for the physical flow of products through their areas (Step 1) before they can compute equivalent production for the accounting period (Step 2). To continue with the Soda Products example, assume the following facts for the accounting period of February:

▸ The beginning work in process inventory consists of 6,200 partially completed units (60 percent processed in the previous period).

▼ **EXHIBIT 2**

Process Cost Report: FIFO Costing Method

Step 1:
Account for physical units.

Beginning inventory (units started last period)	6,200
Units started this period	57,500
Units to be accounted for	→ 63,700

Step 2:
Account for equivalent units.

	Physical Units	Direct Materials	% Incurred During Period	Conversion Costs	% Incurred During Period
Beginning inventory (units completed this period)	6,200	0	0%	2,480	40%
Units started and completed this period	52,500	52,500	100%	52,500	100%
Ending inventory (units started but not completed this period)	5,000	5,000	100%	2,250	45%
Units accounted for	→ 63,700	57,500		57,230	

Step 3:
Account for costs.

	Total Costs				
Beginning inventory	→ $ 41,540	=	$ 20,150	+	$ 21,390
Current costs	510,238	=	189,750	+	320,488
Total costs	→ $551,778				

Step 4:
Compute cost per equivalent unit.

Current Costs / Equivalent Units			$189,750 / 57,500		$320,488 / 57,230
Cost per equivalent unit	$8.90	=	$3.30	+	$5.60

Step 5:
Assign costs to cost of goods manufactured and ending inventory.

Cost of goods manufactured and transferred out:				
From beginning inventory	→ $ 41,540			
Current costs to complete	13,888	=	$0	+ (2,480 × $5.60)
Units started and completed this period	467,250	=	(52,500 × $3.30) +	(52,500 × $5.60)
Cost of goods manufactured	$522,678	(No rounding necessary)		
Ending inventory	29,100	=	(5,000 × $3.30) +	(2,250 × $5.60)
Total costs	→ $551,778			

WORK IN PROCESS INVENTORY ACCOUNT: COST RECAP

Beg. Bal.	41,540	522,678 (Cost of goods manufactured and transferred out)
Direct materials	189,750	
Conversion costs	320,488	
End. Bal.	**29,100**	

WORK IN PROCESS INVENTORY ACCOUNT: UNIT RECAP

Beg. Bal.	6,200	58,700 (FIFO units transferred out from the 6,200 in beginning inventory plus the 52,500 started and completed)
Units started	57,500	
End. Bal.	**5,000**	

◆ During the period, the 6,200 units in beginning inventory were completed, and 57,500 units were started into production.

◆ Of the 57,500 units started during the period, 52,500 units were completed. The other 5,000 units remain in ending work in process inventory and are 45 percent complete.

In Step 1 of Exhibit 2, the manager computes the total units to be accounted for by adding the 6,200 units in beginning inventory to the 57,500 units started into production in this period. These 63,700 units are the actual physical units that the manager is responsible for during the period. Step 2 continues accounting for physical units. As shown in the Physical Units column of Exhibit 2, the 6,200 units in beginning inventory that were completed during the period, the 52,500 units that were started and finished in the period, and the 5,000 units remaining in the department at the end of the period are summed, and the total is listed as "units accounted for." (Notice that the "units accounted for" in Step 2 must equal the "units to be accounted for" in Step 1.) These amounts are used to compute equivalent production for the department's direct materials and conversion costs for the month, as described below.

Beginning Inventory

Because all direct materials are added at the beginning of the production process, the 6,200 partially completed units that began February as work in process were already 100 percent complete in regard to direct materials. They were 60 percent complete in regard to conversion costs on February 1. The remaining 40 percent of their conversion costs were incurred as they were completed during the month. Thus, as shown in the far right column of Exhibit 2, the equivalent production for their conversion costs is 2,480 units (40% × 6,200).

Units Started and Completed During the Period

All the costs of the 52,500 units started and completed during February were incurred during this accounting period. Thus, the full amount of 52,500 is entered as the equivalent units for both direct materials and conversion costs.

Ending Inventory

Because the materials for the 5,000 drinks still in process at the end of February were added when the drinks went into production during the month, the full amount of 5,000 is entered as the equivalent units for their direct materials cost. However, these drinks are only 45 percent complete in terms of conversion costs. Thus, as shown in the far right column of Exhibit 2, the equivalent production for their conversion costs is 2,250 units (45% × 5,000).

Totals

Step 2 is completed by summing all the physical units to be accounted for, all equivalent units for direct materials, and all equivalent units for conversion costs. Exhibit 2 shows that for February, Soda Products accounted for 63,700 units. Equivalent units for direct materials totaled 57,500, and equivalent units for conversion costs totaled 57,230. Once Soda Products knows February's equivalent unit amounts, it can complete the remaining three steps in the preparation of a process cost report.

Accounting for Costs

Thus far, we have focused on accounting for units of productive output—in our example, bottled soft drinks. We now turn our focus to cost information. Step 3 in preparing a process cost report accumulates and analyzes all costs charged to the Work in Process Inventory account of each production process, department,

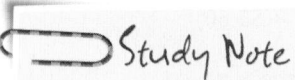
Study Note

The percentage of completion for beginning work in process inventory is the amount of work completed in the prior period. Under FIFO, the amount of effort required to *complete* beginning work in process inventory is the relevant percentage.

Study Note

Units in beginning work in process inventory represent work accomplished in the previous accounting period that has already been assigned a certain portion of its total cost. Those units must be completed in the current period, incurring additional costs.

or work cell. Step 4 computes the cost per equivalent unit for direct materials and conversion costs.

The following information about Soda Products' manufacture of soft drinks during February enables us to complete Steps 3 and 4:

WORK IN PROCESS INVENTORY		
Costs from beginning inventory:		
Direct materials costs	20,150	
Conversion costs	21,390	
Current period costs:		
Direct materials costs	189,750	
Conversion costs	320,488	

As shown in Step 3 of Exhibit 2, all costs for the period are accumulated in the Total Costs column. Beginning inventory's direct material costs of $20,150 are added to the conversion costs of $21,390 to determine the total cost of beginning inventory ($41,540). Current period costs for direct materials ($189,750) are added to conversion costs ($320,488) to determine the total current manufacturing costs ($510,238). The grand total of $551,778 is the sum of beginning inventory costs ($41,540) and current period costs ($510,238). Notice that only the Total Costs column is totaled. Since only the current period costs for direct materials and conversion costs are used in Step 4, there is no need to find the total costs of the direct materials and conversion costs columns in Step 3.

In Step 4, the direct materials and conversion costs for the current period are divided by their respective units of equivalent production to arrive at the cost per equivalent unit. Prior period costs attached to units in beginning inventory are not included in these computations because the FIFO costing method uses separate costing analyses for each accounting period. (The FIFO method treats the costs of beginning inventory separately, in Step 5.) Exhibit 2 shows that the total current cost of $8.90 per equivalent unit consists of $3.30 per equivalent unit for direct materials ($189,750 ÷ 57,500 equivalent units) plus $5.60 per equivalent unit for conversion costs ($320,488 ÷ 57,230 equivalent units). (The equivalent units are taken from Step 2 of Exhibit 2.)

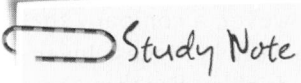

Study Note

The cost per equivalent unit using the FIFO method measures the current cost divided by current effort. Notice that the cost of beginning work in process inventory is omitted.

Study Note

The process cost report is developed for the purpose of assigning a value to one transaction: the transfer of goods from one department to another or to finished goods inventory. The ending balance in the Work in Process Inventory account represents the costs that remain after this transfer.

Assigning Costs

Step 5 in the preparation of a process costing report uses information from Steps 2 and 4 to assign costs, as shown in Exhibit 2. This final step determines the costs that are transferred out either to the next production process, department, or work cell or to the Finished Goods Inventory account (i.e., the cost of goods manufactured), as well as the costs that remain in the ending balance in the Work in Process Inventory account. The total costs assigned to units completed and transferred out and to ending inventory must equal the total costs in Step 3.

Cost of Goods Manufactured and Transferred Out
Step 5 of Exhibit 2 shows that the costs transferred to the Finished Goods Inventory account include the $41,540 in direct materials and conversion costs for completing the 6,200 units in beginning inventory. Step 2 in the exhibit shows that 2,480 equivalent units of conversion costs were required to complete these 6,200 units. Because the equivalent unit conversion cost for February is $5.60, the cost to complete the units carried over from January is $13,888 (2,480 units × $5.60).

Each of the 52,500 units started and completed in February cost $8.90 to produce. Their combined cost of $467,250 is added to the $41,540 and $13,888 of costs required to produce the 6,200 units from beginning inventory to arrive at the total of $522,678 that is transferred to the Finished Goods Inventory account. The entry resulting from doing the process cost report for February is:

Finished Goods Inventory	522,678	
Work in Process Inventory		522,678

Ending Inventory   All costs remaining in Soda Products' Work in Process Inventory account after the cost of goods manufactured have been transferred out represent the costs of the drinks still in production at the end of February. As shown in Step 5 of Exhibit 2, the balance of $29,100 in the ending Work in Process Inventory is made up of $16,500 of direct materials costs (5,000 units $\times$ $3.30 per unit) and $12,600 of conversion costs [(5,000 $\times$ 45%) $\times$ $5.60 per unit].

Rounding Differences   As you perform Step 5 in any process cost report, remember that the total costs in Steps 3 and 5 must always be the same number. In Exhibit 2, for example, they are both $551,778. If the numbers are not the same, first check for omission of any costs and for calculation errors. If that does not solve the problem, check to see if any rounding was necessary in computing the costs per equivalent unit in Step 4. If rounding was done in Step 4, rounding differences will occur when assigning costs in Step 5. Adjust the total costs transferred out for any rounding difference so that the total costs in Step 5 equal the total costs in Step 3.

Recap of Work in Process Inventory Account   When the process cost report is complete, an account recap may be prepared to show the effects of the report on the Work in Process Inventory account for the period. Two recaps of Soda Products' Work in Process Inventory account for February—one for costs and one for units—appear at the end of Exhibit 2.

Process Costing for Two or More Production Departments

Because Soda Products Company has only one production department, it needs only one Work in Process Inventory account. However, a company that has more than one production department must have a Work in Process Inventory account for each department. For instance, a soft drink maker that has a production department for formulation, another for bottling, and another for packaging needs three Work in Process Inventory accounts. When products flow from the Formulation Department to the Bottling Department, their costs flow from the Formulation Department's Work in Process Inventory account to the Bottling Department's Work in Process Inventory account. The costs transferred into the Bottling Department's Work in Process Inventory account are treated in the same way as the cost of direct materials added at the beginning of the production process. When production flows to the Packaging Department, the accumulated costs (incurred in the two previous departments) are transferred to that department's Work in Process Inventory account. At the end of the accounting period, a separate process cost report is prepared for each department.

S T O P • R E V I E W • A P P L Y

6-1. What five steps does a process cost report entail?

6-2. What are the purposes of accounting for costs in a process cost report?

6-3. What two important dollar amounts come from the assignment of costs in Step 5 of a process cost report? How do they relate to the year-end financial statements?

6-4. How many process cost reports are prepared each period?

Using Information About Product Cost to Evaluate Performance

LO7 Evaluate operating performance using information about product cost.

A product costing system—whether it's a job order or a process costing system—provides managers with valuable information. As we have noted, managers use the information that such a system provides in determining a product's price and in computing the balances in the Materials Inventory, Work in Process Inventory, and Finished Goods Inventory accounts on the balance sheet and the Cost of Goods Sold account on the income statement. Managers also use product costing information to evaluate operating performance. Such an analysis may include consideration of the following:

▶ Cost trends of a product or product line

▶ Units produced per time period

▶ Materials usage per unit produced

▶ Labor cost per unit produced

▶ Special needs of customers

▶ Cost-effectiveness of changing to a more advanced production process

Cost trends can be developed from product cost data over several time periods. Such trends help managers identify areas of rising costs or areas in which cost-effectiveness has improved. Tracking units produced per time period, a figure easily pulled from a product cost analysis, can help managers evaluate operating efficiency.

Direct materials and labor costs are significant parts of a product's cost and should be monitored constantly. Trends in direct materials usage and labor costs per unit produced can help managers determine optimal resource usage.

Anticipating customers' needs is very important to managers. By tracking the size, cost, and type of products ordered by customers, managers can see which customers are increasing or reducing their orders and take action to improve customer relations.

Finally, decisions to purchase new machinery and equipment are often based on the savings that the change is expected to produce. Information from

Study Note

Performance measures are quantitative tools that help managers assess the performance of a specific process or expected outcome.

a product costing system helps managers make such decisions in that it enables them to estimate unit costs for the new equipment and to compare them with cost trends for the existing equipment.

S T O P • R E V I E W • A P P L Y

7-1. How can information about product cost help managers evaluate operating performance?

7-2. What type of operating performance can be evaluated with the information that a product costing system provides about (a) units produced per time period, (b) labor cost per unit produced, and (c) special needs of customers?

A LOOK BACK AT

COLD STONE CREAMERY, INC.

The Decision Point at the beginning of this chapter focused on **Cold Stone Creamery**, a company known for its method of making and serving ice cream. It posed these questions:

- Is the product costing system that is used for custom-made items appropriate for mass-produced items?

- What performance measures would be most useful in evaluating the results of each type of product?

Whether a product costing system is appropriate depends on the nature of the production process. Because the production of personalized creations and the manufacture of large quantities of retail products involve different processes, they generally require different costing systems. When a product is custom-made, it is possible to collect the costs of each order. When a product is mass-produced, the costs of a specific unit cannot be collected because there is a continuous flow of similar products; in this case, costs are collected by process, department, or work cell. Thus, if Cold Stone Creamery introduced a product for sale in grocery stores or other retail establishments, it would have to adjust its costing system to determine the product cost of a unit.

Performance measures would also differ if Cold Stone Creamery were to create a retail product line. Its management can now measure the profitability of each personalized order by comparing the order's cost and price. If a retail product were introduced, management would measure performance by comparing the budgeted and actual costs for a process, department, or work cell.

CHAPTER REVIEW

REVIEW of Learning Objectives

LO1 Discuss the role that information about costs plays in the management process, and explain why unit cost is important.

When managers plan, they use information about costs to develop budgets, establish prices, set sales goals, plan production volumes, estimate product or service unit costs, and determine human resource needs. Daily, managers use cost information to make decisions about controlling costs, managing the company's volume of activity, ensuring quality, and negotiating prices. When managers evaluate results, they analyze actual and targeted information to evaluate performance and make any necessary adjustments to their planning and decision-making strategies. When managers communicate with stakeholders, they use unit costs to determine inventory balances and the cost of goods or services sold for the financial statements. They also analyze internal reports that compare the organization's measures of actual and targeted performance to determine whether cost goals for products or services are being achieved.

LO2 Distinguish between the two basic types of product costing systems, and identify the information each provides.

A job order costing system is a product costing system used by companies that make unique or special-order products. Such a system traces the costs of direct materials, direct labor, and overhead to a specific batch of products or a specific job order. A job order costing system measures the cost of each complete unit and summarizes the cost of all jobs in a single Work in Process Inventory account that is supported by job order cost cards.

A process costing system is a product costing system used by companies that produce large amounts of similar products or liquid products or that have long, continuous production runs of identical products. Such a system first traces the costs of direct materials, direct labor, and overhead to processes, departments, or work cells and then assigns the costs to the products manufactured by those processes, departments, or work cells. A process costing system uses several Work in Process Inventory accounts: one for each department, process, or work cell.

LO3 Explain cost flow in a job order costing system, prepare a job order cost card, and compute product unit cost.

In a manufacturer's job order costing system, the costs of materials are first charged to the Materials Inventory account and to the respective materials accounts in the subsidiary ledger. The various actual overhead costs are charged to the Overhead account. As products are manufactured, the costs of direct materials and direct labor are debited to the Work in Process Inventory account and are recorded on the job's job order cost card. Overhead costs are applied and debited to the Work in Process Inventory account and credited to the Overhead account using a predetermined overhead rate. They too are recorded on the job order cost card. When products and jobs are completed, the costs assigned to them are transferred to the Finished Goods Inventory account. Then, when the products are sold and shipped, their costs are transferred to the Cost of Goods Sold account.

All costs of direct materials, direct labor, and overhead for a particular job are accumulated on a job order cost card. When the job has been completed, those costs are totaled. The total is then divided by the number of good units produced to find the product unit cost for that order. The product unit cost is entered on the job order cost card and will be used to value items in inventory.

Job order costing in a service organization differs in that the costs are not associated with a physical product but rather with services, for which the most important cost is labor. Job order cost cards are kept and include the costs for labor, materials and supplies, and service overhead.

LO4 Explain product flow and cost flow in a process costing system.

Process costing is used by companies that produce large amounts of similar products or liquids or that have a continuous production flow. A process costing system accumulates the costs of direct materials, direct labor, and overhead for each process, department, or work cell and assigns those costs to the products as they are produced during a particular period. The cost flow follows the logical physical flow of production using the FIFO costing method—that is, the costs assigned to the first products processed are the first costs transferred out when those products flow to the next process, department, or work cell.

LO5 Define *equivalent production,* and compute equivalent units.

Equivalent production is a measure that applies a percentage-of-completion factor to partially completed units to compute the equivalent number of whole units produced in an accounting period for each type of input. Equivalent units are computed from (1) units in the beginning work in process inventory and their percentage of completion, (2) units started and completed during the period, and (3) units in the ending work in process inventory and their percentage of completion.

LO6 Prepare a process cost report using the FIFO costing method.

In a process cost report that uses the FIFO costing method, the cost flow follows the logical physical flow of production—that is, the costs assigned to the first products processed are the first costs transferred out when those products flow to the next process, department, or work cell. Preparation of a process cost report involves five steps. Steps 1 and 2 account for the physical flow of products and compute the equivalent units of production. Once equivalent production has been determined, the focus of the report shifts to accounting for costs. In Step 3, all direct materials and conversion costs for the current period are added to arrive at total costs. In Step 4, the cost per equivalent unit for both direct materials and conversion costs is found by dividing those current period costs by their respective equivalent units. In Step 5, costs are assigned to the units completed and transferred out during the period, as well as to the ending work in process inventory. The costs assigned to units completed and transferred out include the costs incurred in the preceding period and the conversion costs needed to complete those units during the current period. That amount is added to the total cost of producing all units started and completed during the period. The result is the total cost transferred out for the units completed during the period. Step 5 also assigns costs to units still in process at the end of the period by multiplying their direct materials and conversion costs by their respective equivalent units. The total equals the balance in the Work in Process Inventory account at the end of the period.

LO7 Evaluate operating performance using information about product cost.

Both the job order and the process costing systems supply information that managers can use to evaluate operating performance. Such an analysis may include consideration of the following: cost trends of a product or product line, units produced per time period, materials usage per unit produced, labor cost per unit produced, special needs of customers, and the cost-effectiveness of changing to a more advanced production process.

REVIEW of Concepts and Terminology

The following concepts and terms were introduced in this chapter:

Conversion costs: The combined total costs of direct labor and overhead. Also called *processing costs.* **(LO5)**

Cost-plus contracts: Job contracts that require the customer to pay all costs incurred in performing the job plus a predetermined amount of profit. **(LO3)**

Equivalent production: A measure that applies a percentage-of-completion factor to partially completed units to compute the equivalent number of whole units produced in an accounting period for each type of input. Also called *equivalent units.* **(LO5)**

FIFO costing method: A process costing method in which the cost flow follows the actual flow of production, so that the costs assigned to the first products processed are the first costs transferred out when those products flow to the next process, department, or work cell. **(LO4)**

Job order: A customer order for a specific number of specially designed, made-to-order products. **(LO2)**

Job order cost card: A document on which all costs incurred in the production of a particular job order are recorded; part of the subsidiary ledger for the Work in Process Inventory account. **(LO2)**

Job order costing system: A product costing system that traces the costs of direct materials, direct labor, and overhead to a specific batch of products or a specific job order; used by companies that make unique or special-order products. **(LO2)**

Process costing system: A product costing system that traces the costs of direct materials, direct labor, and overhead to processes, departments, or work cells and then assigns the costs to the products manufactured by those processes, departments, or work cells; used by companies that produce large amounts of similar products or liquid products or that have long, continuous production runs of identical products. **(LO2)**

Process cost report: A report that managers use to track and analyze costs in a process costing system. **(LO4)**

Processing costs: The combined total costs of direct labor and overhead. Also called *conversion costs.* **(LO5)**

Product costing system: A set of procedures used to account for an organization's product costs and to provide timely and accurate unit cost information for pricing, cost planning and control, inventory valuation, and financial statement preparation. **(LO2)**

Review Problem

LO5, LO6   **Process Costing Using the FIFO Costing Method**

Pop Chewing Gum Company produces several flavors of bubble gum. Two basic direct materials, gum base and flavored sweetener, are blended at the beginning of the manufacturing process. No materials are lost in the process, so 1 kilogram of materials input produces 1 kilogram of bubble gum. Direct labor and overhead costs are incurred uniformly throughout the blending process. On June 30, 16,000 units were in process. All direct materials had been added, but the units were only 70 percent complete in regard to conversion costs. Direct materials costs of $8,100 and conversion costs of $11,800 were attached to the beginning inventory. During the month of July, 405,000 kilograms of materials were used at a cost of $202,500. Direct labor charges were $299,200, and overhead costs applied during July were $284,000. The ending work in process inventory was 21,600 kilograms. All direct materials have been added to those units, and 25 percent of the conversion costs have been assigned. Output from the Blending Department is transferred to the Packaging Department.

Required

1. Prepare a process cost report using the FIFO costing method for the Blending Department for July. (Remember to adjust the total costs transferred out for any rounding difference so that the total costs in Step 5 equal the total costs in Step 3.)
2. Identify the amount that should be transferred out of the Work in Process Inventory account, and state where those dollars should be transferred. What is the journal entry?

Answer to Review Problem

1. Process cost report using the FIFO costing method:

Pop Chewing Gum Company
Blending Department
Process Cost Report: FIFO Method
For the Month Ended July 31

Step 1:
Account for physical units.

Beginning inventory	
(units started last period)	16,000
Units started this period	405,000
Units to be accounted for	421,000

Step 2:
Account for equivalent units.

	Physical Units	Direct Materials	% Incurred During Period	Conversion Costs	% Incurred During Period
Beginning inventory (units completed this period)	16,000	0	0%	4,800	30%
Units started and completed this period	383,400	383,400	100%	383,400	100%
Ending inventory (units started but not completed this period)	21,600	21,600	100%	5,400	25%
Units accounted for	421,000	405,000		393,600	

Step 3:
Account for costs.

	Total Costs		Direct Costs		
Beginning inventory	$ 19,900	=	$ 8,100	+	$ 11,800
Current costs	785,700	=	202,500	+	583,200
Total costs	$805,600				

Step 4:
Compute cost per equivalent unit.

$\dfrac{\text{Current Costs}}{\text{Equivalent Units}}$			$\dfrac{\$202,500}{405,000}$		$\dfrac{\$583,200}{393,600}$
Cost per equivalent unit	$1.98	=	$.50	+	$1.48*

*Rounded to nearest cent

Step 5:
Assign costs to cost of goods manufactured and ending inventory.

Cost of goods manufactured and transferred out:					
From beginning inventory	$ 19,900				
Current costs to complete	7,104	=	$0	+	(4,800 × $1.48)
Units started and completed this period	759,132	=	(383,400 × $.50) +		(383,400 × $1.48)
Cost of goods manufactured	$786,808	(Add rounding, $672)			
Ending inventory	18,792	=	(21,600 × $.50) +		(5,400 × $1.48)
Total costs	$805,600				

WORK IN PROCESS INVENTORY ACCOUNT: COST RECAP

Beg. Bal.	19,900	786,808 (Cost of goods
Direct materials	202,500	manufactured and
Conversion costs	583,200	transferred out)
End. Bal.	**18,792**	

WORK IN PROCESS INVENTORY ACCOUNT: UNIT RECAP

Beg. Bal.	16,000	399,400 (FIFO units transferred
Units started	405,000	out from the 16,000 in
		beginning inventory plus the
		383,400 started and completed)
End. Bal.	**21,600**	

2. The amount of $786,808 should be transferred to the Work in Process Inventory account of the Packaging Department. The journal entry is:

Work in Process Inventory, Packaging Department	786,808	
Work in Process Inventory, Blending Department		786,808

CHAPTER ASSIGNMENTS

BUILDING Your Basic Knowledge and Skills

Short Exercises

LO1   **Uses of Product Costing Information**

SE 1. Shelley's Kennel provides boarding for dogs and cats. Shelley, the owner of the kennel, must make several business decisions soon. Write *yes* or *no* to indicate whether knowing the cost to board one animal per day (i.e., the product unit cost) can help Shelley answer the following questions:

1. Is the boarding fee high enough to cover the kennel's costs?
2. How much profit will the kennel make if it boards an average of 10 dogs per day for 50 weeks?
3. What costs can be reduced to make the kennel's boarding fee competitive with that of its competitor?

LO2   **Job Order Versus Process Costing Systems**

SE 2. State whether a job order costing system or a process costing system would typically be used to account for the costs of the following:

1. Manufacturing cat collars
2. Manufacturing custom-designed fencing for outdoor breeding kennels
3. Providing pet grooming
4. Manufacturing one-gallon aquariums
5. Manufacturing dog food
6. Providing veterinary services

LO3   **Transactions in a Manufacturer's Job Order Costing System**

SE 3. For each of the following transactions, state which account(s) would be debited and credited in a job order costing system:

1. Purchased materials on account, $12,890
2. Charged direct labor to production, $3,790
3. Requested direct materials for production, $6,800
4. Applied overhead to jobs in process, $3,570

LO3   **Transactions in a Manufacturer's Job Order Costing System**

SE 4. Enter the following transactions into T accounts:

1. Incurred $34,000 of direct labor and $18,000 of indirect labor
2. Applied overhead based on 12,680 labor hours @ $6.50 per labor hour

LO3   **Accounts for Job Order Costing**

SE 5. Dom's Furniture, a custom manufacturer of oak tables and chairs, engaged in the transactions that follow. For each transaction, identify the accounts that would be debited and credited.

1. Issued oak materials into production for Job ABC
2. Recorded direct labor time for the first week in February for Job ABC
3. Purchased indirect materials from a vendor on account
4. Received a production-related electricity bill
5. Applied overhead to Job ABC
6. Completed but did not yet sell Job ABC

LO3 **Computation of Product Unit Cost**

SE 6. Complete the following job order cost card:

Job Order **168**

JOB ORDER COST CARD
Keeper, 3000
Apache City, North Dakota

Customer: Brian Patcher   Batch: _____   Custom: __X__

Specifications: 6 Custom computer systems

Date of Order: 4/4/xx   Date of Completion: 6/8/xx

Costs Charged to Job	Previous Months	Current Month	Cost Summary
Direct materials	$3,540	$2,820	$ _____
Direct labor	2,340	1,620	_____
Overhead applied	2,880	2,550	_____
Totals	$ _____	$ _____	$ _____
Units completed			_____
Product unit cost			$ _____

LO5, LO6 **Equivalent Production: FIFO Costing Method**

SE 7. Blue Blaze adds direct materials at the beginning of its production process and adds conversion costs uniformly throughout the process. Given the following information from Blue Blaze's records for July and using Steps 1 and 2 of the FIFO costing method, compute the equivalent units of production:

Units in beginning inventory	3,000
Units started during the period	17,000
Units partially completed	2,500
Percentage of completion of ending work in process inventory	70%
Percentage of completion of beginning inventory	100% for direct materials; 40% for conversion costs

LO6 **Determining Unit Cost: FIFO Costing Method**

SE 8. Using the information from **SE 7** and the following data, compute the total cost per equivalent unit.

	Costs for the Period	Beginning Work in Process
Direct materials costs	$20,400	$7,600
Conversion costs	32,490	2,545

LO6 **Assigning Costs: FIFO Costing Method**

SE 9. Using the data in **SE 7** and **SE 8**, assign costs to the units transferred out and to the units in ending inventory for July.

LO7 **Measuring Performance with Product Costing Data**

SE 10. The following table presents the weekly average of direct materials costs per unit for two products. How could the manager of the department that makes these products use this information?

Week	Product A	Product B
1	$45.20	$23.90
2	46.10	23.80
3	48.30	23.80
4	49.60	23.60

Exercises

LO2 **Product Costing**

E 1. Anniversary Printing Company specializes in wedding invitations. Anniversary needs information to budget next year's activities. Write *yes* or *no* to indicate whether each of the following costs is likely to be available in the company's product costing system:

1. Cost of paper and envelopes
2. Printing machine setup costs
3. Depreciation of printing machinery
4. Advertising costs
5. Repair costs for printing machinery
6. Costs to deliver stationery to customers
7. Office supplies costs
8. Costs to design a wedding invitation
9. Cost of ink
10. Sales commissions

LO2 **Costing Systems: Industry Linkage**

E 2. Which of the following products would typically be accounted for using a job order costing system? Which would be accounted for using a process costing system? (a) Paint, (b) jelly beans, (c) jet aircraft, (d) bricks, (e) tailor-made suit, (f) liquid detergent, (g) aluminum compressed-gas cylinders of standard size and capacity, and (h) aluminum compressed-gas cylinders with a special fiberglass wrap for a Mount Everest expedition.

LO3 **Work in Process Inventory: T Account Analysis**

E 3. On June 30, the beginning balances of Specialty Company's Work in Process Inventory account and Materials Inventory account were $29,400 and $240,000, respectively. Production activity in July was as follows: Direct materials costing $238,820 were requested for production; total manufacturing payroll was $140,690, of which $52,490 was used to pay for indirect labor; indirect materials costing $28,400 were purchased and used; and overhead was applied at a rate of 150 percent of direct labor costs.

1. Record Specialty's materials, labor, and overhead costs for July in T accounts.
2. Compute the ending balance in the Work in Process Inventory account. During the period, $461,400 transferred to the Finished Goods Inventory account.

LO3 **T Account Analysis with Unknowns**

E 4. Partial operating data for Starke Company follow. Starke Company's management has set the predetermined overhead rate for the current year at 80 percent of direct labor costs. Using T accounts and the data provided, compute the unknown values. Show all your computations.

Account/Transaction	December
Beginning Materials Inventory	$42,000
Beginning Work in Process Inventory	66,000
Beginning Finished Goods Inventory	29,000
Direct materials used	168,000
Direct materials purchased	**a**
Direct labor costs	382,000
Overhead applied	**b**
Cost of units completed	**c**
Cost of goods sold	808,000
Ending Materials Inventory	38,000
Ending Work in Process Inventory	138,600
Ending Finished Goods Inventory	**d**

LO3 **Job Order Cost Card and Computation of Product Unit Cost**

E 5. During January, the Cabinet Company worked on six different job orders for specialty kitchen cabinets. It began Job A-62 for Thomas Cabinets, Inc., on January 10 and completed the job on January 24. Partial data for Job A-62 are as follows:

	Costs	Machine Hours Used
Direct materials		
Cedar	$7,900	
Pine	6,320	
Hardware	2,930	
Assembly supplies	988	
Direct labor		
Sawing	$2,840	120
Shaping	2,200	220
Finishing	2,250	180
Assembly	2,890	50

The Cabinet Company produced a total of 34 cabinets for Job A-62. Its current predetermined overhead rate is $21.60 per machine hour. From the information given, prepare a job order cost card and compute the job order's product unit cost. (Round to whole dollars.)

LO3 **Computation of Product Unit Cost**

E 6. Style Corporation manufactures specialty lines of women's apparel. During February, the company worked on three special orders: A-25, A-27, and B-14. Cost and production data for each order are as follows:

	Job A-25	Job A-27	Job B-14
Direct materials			
Fabric Q	$10,840	$12,980	$17,660
Fabric Z	11,400	12,200	13,440
Fabric YB	5,260	6,920	10,900
Direct labor			
Garment maker	8,900	10,400	16,200
Layout	6,450	7,425	9,210
Packaging	3,950	4,875	6,090
Overhead			
(120% of direct labor costs)	?	?	?
Number of units produced	700	775	1,482

1. Compute the total cost associated with each job. Show the subtotals for each cost category.
2. Compute the product unit cost for each job. (Round your computations to the nearest cent.)

LO3   **Job Order Costing in a Service Organization**

E 7. A job order cost card for Personal Trainers, Inc., appears below. Compute the missing information.

Job Order **H.W.**

JOB ORDER COST CARD
Personal Trainers, Inc.

Customer: Hillary White   Batch: _____   Custom: ___X___
Specifications: Marathon Training
Date of Order: 4/2/xx   Date of Completion: 7/24/xx

Costs Charged to Job	Previous Months	Current Month	Total
In-person consultation			
Training logbook	$ 20.00	$ 0	$20.00
Labor ($10 per hour)	20.00	?	50.00
Overhead (10% of in-person labor costs)	?	3.00	5.00
Total	$?	$?	$?
Training			
Bike rental	$ 30.00	$?	$60.00
Labor ($5 per hour)	150.00	300.00	?
Overhead (25% of labor costs)	37.50	?	?
Total	$?	$?	$?
Telephone consultations			
Cell phone calls ($1 per call)	$ 30.00	$ 10.00	?
Labor ($10 per hour)	10.00	10.00	?
Overhead (50% of telephone labor costs)	?	?	?
Total	$?	$?	$?
Total cost			$?

Job Revenue and Profit

Logbook and bike rental	$?
Service fee: 97 hours × $30	$?
Job revenue	$2,990.00
Less total cost	?
Profit	$2,222,50

LO3   **Computation of Product Unit Cost**

E 8. Wild Things, Inc., manufactures custom-made stuffed animals. Last month, the company produced 4,540 stuffed bears with stethoscopes for the local children's hospital to sell at a fundraising event. Using job order costing, determine the product unit cost of a stuffed bear based on the following costs that were incurred during the month: manufacturing utilities, $500;

depreciation on manufacturing equipment, $450; indirect materials, $300; direct materials, $1,300; indirect labor, $800; direct labor, $2,400; sales commissions, $3,000; president's salary, $4,000; insurance on manufacturing plant, $600; advertising expense, $500; rent on manufacturing plant, $5,000; rent on sales office, $4,000; and legal expense, $250. Carry your answer to two decimal places.

LO4 **Use of Process Costing Information**

E 9. Tom's Bakery makes a variety of cakes, cookies, and pies for distribution to five major chains of grocery stores in the Quad-City area. The company uses a standard manufacturing process for all items except special-order cakes. It currently uses a process costing system. Tom, the owner of the company, has some urgent questions, which are listed below. Which of these questions can be answered using information from a process costing system? Which can be best answered using information from a job order costing system? Explain your answers.

1. How much does it cost to make one chocolate cheesecake?
2. Did the cost of making special-order cakes exceed the cost budgeted for this month?
3. What is the value of the pie inventory at the end of June?
4. What were the costs of the cookies sold during June?
5. At what price should Tom's Bakery sell its famous brownies to the grocery store chains?
6. Were the planned production costs of $3,000 for making pies in June exceeded?

LO5, LO6 **Equivalent Production: FIFO Costing Method**

E 10. Olivares Enterprises makes Rainberry Shampoo for beauty salons. On July 31, it had 5,200 liters of shampoo in process, which were 80 percent complete in regard to conversion costs and 100 percent complete in regard to direct materials costs. During August, it put 212,500 liters of direct materials into production. Data for work in process inventory on August 31 were as follows: shampoo, 4,500 liters; stage of completion, 60 percent for conversion costs and 100 percent for direct materials. Using these data and the FIFO costing method, compute the equivalent units of production for direct materials and conversion costs for the month.

LO5, LO6 **Equivalent Production: FIFO Costing Method**

E 11. Cunningham Paper Corporation produces wood pulp that is used in making paper. The following data pertain to the company's production of pulp during September:

	Tons	Percentage Complete Direct Materials	Conversion Costs
Work in process, Aug. 31	40,000	100%	60%
Placed into production	250,000	—	—
Work in process, Sept. 30	80,000	100%	40%

Compute the equivalent units of production for direct materials and conversion costs for September using the FIFO costing method.

LO6 **Work in Process Inventory Accounts: Total Unit Cost**

E 12. Scientists at Anschultz Laboratories, Inc., have just perfected Dentalite, a liquid substance that dissolves tooth decay. The substance, which is generated by a complex process involving five departments, is very expensive. Cost and equivalent unit data for the latest week are as follows (units are in ounces):

	Direct Materials		Conversion Costs	
Dept.	Dollars	Equivalent Units	Dollars	Equivalent Units
A	$12,000	1,000	$33,825	2,050
B	21,835	1,985	13,065	1,005
C	23,896	1,030	20,972	2,140
D	—	—	22,086	2,045
E	—	—	15,171	1,945

From these data, compute the unit cost for each department and the total unit cost of producing one ounce of Dentalite.

LO6 **Determining Unit Cost: FIFO Costing Method**

E 13. Turner's Pots, Inc., manufactures sets of heavy-duty cookware. It has just completed production for August. At the beginning of August, its Work in Process Inventory account showed direct materials costs of $31,700 and conversion costs of $29,400. The cost of direct materials used in August was $275,373; conversion costs were $175,068. During the month, the company started and completed 15,190 sets. For August, a total of 16,450 equivalent sets for direct materials and 16,210 equivalent sets for conversion costs have been computed.

From this information, determine the cost per equivalent unit for August. Use the FIFO costing method.

LO6 **Assigning Costs: FIFO Costing Method**

E 14. The Beach Bakery produces Healthnut coffee bread. It uses a process costing system. In March, its beginning inventory was 450 units, which were 100 percent complete for direct materials costs and 10 percent complete for conversion costs. The cost of beginning inventory was $655. Units started and completed during the month totaled 14,200. Ending inventory was 410 units, which were 100 percent complete for direct materials and 70 percent complete for conversion costs. Costs per equivalent unit for March were $1.40 for direct materials and $0.80 for conversion costs.

From this information, compute the cost of goods transferred to the Finished Goods Inventory account, the cost remaining in the Work in Process Inventory account, and the total costs accounted for. Use the FIFO costing method.

LO7 **Measuring Performance with Nonfinancial Product Data**

E 15. During December, Carola Products Company conducted a study of the productivity of its metal-trimming operation, which requires the use of three machines. The data were condensed into product units per hour so that managers could analyze the productivity of the three workers who operate the machines. The target output established for the year was 125 units per hour. From the following data, analyze the productivity of Carola Products' three machine operators:

Week	Operator 1	Operator 2	Operator 3
1	119 per hour	129 per hour	124 per hour
2	120 per hour	127 per hour	124 per hour
3	122 per hour	125 per hour	123 per hour
4	124 per hour	122 per hour	124 per hour

Problems

LO3 **T Account Analysis with Unknowns**

P 1. Flagstaff Enterprises makes peripheral equipment for computers. Dana Dona, Flagstaff's new controller, can find only the following partial information for the past two months:

Account/Transaction	May	June
Materials Inventory, Beginning	$ 36,240	e
Work in Process Inventory, Beginning	56,480	f
Finished Goods Inventory, Beginning	44,260	g
Materials purchased	a	$ 96,120
Direct materials requested	82,320	h
Direct labor costs	b	72,250
Overhead applied	53,200	i
Cost of units completed	c	221,400
Cost of units sold	209,050	j
Materials Inventory, Ending	38,910	41,950
Work in Process Inventory, Ending	d	k
Finished Goods Inventory, Ending	47,940	51,180

The current year's predetermined overhead rate is 80 percent of direct labor costs.

Required

Using the data provided and T accounts, compute the unknown values.

LO3 **Job Order Costing: T Account Analysis**

P 2. Par Carts, Inc., produces electric golf carts. The carts are special-order items, so the company uses a job order costing system. Overhead is applied at the rate of 90 percent of direct labor cost. The following is a list of transactions for January:

Jan. 1 Purchased direct materials on account, $215,400.
2 Purchased indirect materials on account, $49,500.
4 Requested direct materials costing $193,200 (all used on Job X) and indirect materials costing $38,100 for production.
10 Paid the following overhead costs: utilities, $4,400; manufacturing rent, $3,800; and maintenance charges, $3,900.
15 Recorded the following gross wages and salaries for employees: direct labor, $120,000 (all for Job X) and indirect labor, $60,620.
15 Applied overhead to production.
19 Purchased indirect materials costing $27,550 and direct materials costing $190,450 on account.
21 Requested direct materials costing $214,750 (Job X, $178,170; Job Y, $18,170; Job Z, $18,410) and indirect materials costing $31,400 for production.
31 Recorded the following gross wages and salaries for employees: direct labor, $132,000 (Job X, $118,500; Job Y, $7,000; Job Z, $6,500) and indirect labor, $62,240.
31 Applied overhead to production.
31 Completed and transferred Job X (375 carts) and Job Y (10 carts) to finished goods inventory; total cost was $855,990.
31 Shipped Job X to the customer; total production cost was $824,520 and sales invoice totaled $996,800.

Jan. 31 Recorded these overhead costs (adjusting entries): prepaid insurance expired, $3,700; property taxes (payable at year end), $3,400; and depreciation, machinery, $15,500.

Required

1. Record the entries for all transactions in January using T accounts for the following: Materials Inventory, Work in Process Inventory, Finished Goods Inventory, Overhead, Cash, Accounts Receivable, Prepaid Insurance, Accumulated Depreciation–Machinery, Accounts Payable, Factory Payroll, Property Taxes Payable, Sales, and Cost of Goods Sold. Use job order cost cards for Job X, Job Y, and Job Z. Determine the partial account balances. Assume no beginning inventory balances.
2. Compute the amount of underapplied or overapplied overhead as of January 31, and transfer it to the Cost of Goods Sold account.
3. **Manager Insight:** Why should the Overhead account's underapplied or overapplied overhead be transferred to the Cost of Goods Sold account?

LO3 Job Order Cost Flow

P 3. On May 31, the inventory balances of Abbey Designs, a manufacturer of high-quality children's clothing, were as follows: Materials Inventory, $21,360; Work in Process Inventory, $15,112; and Finished Goods Inventory, $17,120. Job order cost cards for jobs in process as of June 30 had these totals:

Job No.	Direct Materials	Direct Labor	Overhead
24-A	$1,596	$1,290	$1,677
24-B	1,492	1,380	1,794
24-C	1,984	1,760	2,288
24-D	1,608	1,540	2,002

The predetermined overhead rate is 130 percent of direct labor costs. Materials purchased and received in June were as follows:

June 4 $33,120
June 16   28,600
June 22   31,920

Direct labor costs for June were as follows:

June 15 payroll $23,680
June 29 payroll   25,960

Direct materials requested by production during June were as follows:

June 6 $37,240
June 23   38,960

On June 30, Abbey Designs sold on account finished goods with a 75 percent markup over cost for $320,000.

Required

1. Using T accounts for Materials Inventory, Work in Process Inventory, Finished Goods Inventory, Overhead, Accounts Receivable, Factory Payroll, Sales, and Cost of Goods Sold, reconstruct the transactions in June.
2. Compute the cost of units completed during the month.
3. What was the total cost of units sold during June?
4. Determine the ending inventory balances.
5. Jobs 24-A and 24-C were completed during the first week of July. No additional materials costs were incurred, but Job 24-A required $960 more of

direct labor, and Job 24-C needed an additional $1,610 of direct labor. Job 24-A was composed of 1,200 pairs of trousers; Job 24-C, of 950 shirts. Compute the product unit cost for each job. (Round your answers to two decimal places.)

LO5, LO6 **Process Costing: FIFO Costing Method**

P 4. Lightning Industries, located in northern New England, specializes in making Flash, a low-alkaline wax that is used to protect and preserve skis. The company began producing a new, improved brand of Flash on January 1. Materials are introduced at the beginning of the production process. During January, 15,300 pounds were used at a cost of $46,665. Direct labor of $17,136 and overhead costs of $25,704 were incurred uniformly throughout the month.

By January 31, 13,600 pounds of Flash had been completed and transferred to the finished goods inventory (one pound of input equals one pound of output). Because no spoilage occurred, the leftover materials remained in production and were 40 percent complete on average.

Required

1. Using the FIFO costing method, prepare a process cost report for the month of January.
2. From the information in the process cost report, identify the amount that should be transferred out of the Work in Process Inventory account, and state where those dollars should be transferred.

LO5, LO6 **Process Costing: FIFO Costing Method**

P 5. Liquid Extracts Company produces a line of fruit extracts for home use in making wine, jams and jellies, pies, and meat sauces. Fruits enter the production process in pounds; the product emerges in quarts (one pound of input equals one quart of output). On May 31, 4,250 units were in process. All direct materials had been added, and the units were 70 percent complete for conversion costs. Direct materials costs of $4,607 and conversion costs of $3,535 were attached to the units in beginning work in process inventory. During June, 61,300 pounds of fruit were added at a cost of $71,108. Direct labor for the month totaled $19,760, and overhead costs applied were $31,375.

On June 30, 3,400 units remained in process. All direct materials for these units had been added, and 50 percent of conversion costs had been incurred.

Required

1. Using the FIFO costing method, prepare a process cost report for the month of June.
2. From the information in the process cost report, identify the amount that should be transferred out of the Work in Process Inventory account, and state where those dollars should be transferred.

Alternate Problems

LO3 **Job Order Cost Flow**

P 6. Dori Hatami is the chief financial officer of Gotham Industries, a company that makes special-order sound systems for home theaters. Her records for February revealed the following information:

Beginning inventory balances

Materials Inventory	$27,450
Work in Process Inventory	22,900
Finished Goods Inventory	19,200

Direct materials purchased and received

February 6	$ 7,200
February 12	8,110
February 24	5,890

Direct labor costs

February 14	$13,750
February 28	13,230

Direct materials requested for production

February 4	$ 9,080
February 13	5,940
February 25	7,600

Job order cost cards for jobs in process on February 28 had the following totals:

Job No.	Direct Materials	Direct Labor	Overhead
AJ-10	$3,220	$1,810	$2,534
AJ-14	3,880	2,110	2,954
AJ-15	2,980	1,640	2,296
AJ-16	4,690	2,370	3,318

The predetermined overhead rate for the month was 140 percent of direct labor costs. Sales for February totaled $152,400, which represented a 70 percent markup over the cost of production.

Required

1. Using T accounts for Materials Inventory, Work in Process Inventory, Finished Goods Inventory, Overhead, Accounts Receivable, Factory Payroll, Sales, and Cost of Goods Sold, reconstruct the February transactions.
2. Compute the cost of units completed during the month.
3. What was the total cost of units sold during February?
4. Determine the ending balances in the inventory accounts.
5. During the first week of March, Jobs AJ-10 and AJ-14 were completed. No additional direct materials costs were incurred, but Job AJ-10 needed $720 more of direct labor, and Job AJ-14 needed an additional $1,140 of direct labor. Job AJ-10 was 40 units; Job AJ-14, 55 units. Compute the product unit cost for each completed job (round to two decimal places).

LO3

Job Order Costing in a Service Organization

P 7. Peruga Engineering Company specializes in designing automated characters and displays for theme parks. It uses cost-plus profit contracts, and its profit factor is 30 percent of total cost. A job order costing system is used to track the costs of developing each job.

Costs are accumulated for three primary activities: bid and proposal, design, and prototype development. Current service overhead rates based on engineering hours are as follows: bid and proposal, $18 per hour; design, $22 per hour; and prototype development, $20 per hour. Supplies are treated as direct materials, traceable to each job. Peruga worked on jobs P-12, P-15, and P-19 during January. The table that follows shows the costs for those jobs.

	P-12	P-15	P-19
Beginning Balances			
Bid and proposal	$2,460	$2,290	$ 940
Design	1,910	460	—
Prototype development	2,410	1,680	—
Costs During January			
Bid and proposal			
Supplies	$ —	$ 280	$2,300
Labor: hours	12	20	68
Dollars	$ 192	$ 320	$1,088
Design			
Supplies	$ 400	$ 460	$ 290
Labor: hours	64	42	26
Dollars	$1,280	$ 840	$ 520
Prototype development			
Supplies	$6,744	$7,216	$2,400
Labor: hours	120	130	25
Dollars	$2,880	$3,120	$ 600

Required

1. Using the format shown in Figure 3 in this chapter, create the job order cost card for each of the three jobs.

2. Peruga completed Jobs P-12 and P-15, and the customers approved of the prototype products. Customer A plans to produce 12 special characters using the design and specifications created by Job P-12. Customer B plans to make 18 displays from the design developed by Job P-15. What dollar amount will each customer use as the cost of design for each of those products (i.e., what is the product unit cost for Jobs P-12 and P-15)? Round to the nearest dollar.

3. What is the January ending balance of Peruga's Contract in Process account?

4. **Manager Insight:** Rank the jobs in order of most costly to least costly based on each job's total cost. From the rankings of cost, what observations can you make?

5. **Manager Insight:** Speculate on the price Peruga should charge for such jobs.

LO5, LO6 **Process Costing: FIFO Costing Method**

P 8. Canned fruits and vegetables are the main products made by Good Foods, Inc. All direct materials are added at the beginning of the Mixing Department's process. When the ingredients have been mixed, they go to the Cooking Department. There the mixture is heated to 100° Celsius and simmered for 20 minutes. When cooled, the mixture goes to the Canning Department for final processing. Throughout the operations, direct labor and overhead costs are incurred uniformly. No direct materials are added in the Cooking Department.

Cost data and other information for the Mixing Department for the month of January appear at the top of the opposite page. The company experienced no spoilage or evaporation loss during January.

Required

1. Using the FIFO costing method, prepare a process cost report for the Mixing Department for January.

Production Cost Data	Direct Materials	Conversion Costs
Mixing Department		
Beginning inventory	$ 28,560	$ 5,230
Current period costs	$450,000	$181,200
Work in process inventory		
Beginning inventory		
Mixing Department (40% complete)	5,000 liters	
Ending inventory		
Mixing Department (60% complete)	6,000 liters	
Unit production data		
Units started during January	90,000 liters	
Units transferred out during January	89,000 liters	

2. **Manager Insight:** Explain how the analysis for the Cooking Department will differ from the analysis for the Mixing Department.

ENHANCING Your Knowledge, Skills, and Critical Thinking

Conceptual Understanding Cases

LO1 **Business Plans**

C 1. Fortune 500 companies continue to eliminate jobs, and yet the U.S. economy keeps growing. New businesses have created most of the new employment. A key step in starting a new business is a realistic analysis of the people, opportunities, context, risks, and rewards of the venture and the formulation of a business plan. Note the similarities in the questions managers answer in the management process and the nine questions every great business plan should answer:[4]

1. Who is the new company's customer?
2. How does the customer make decisions about buying this product or service?
3. To what degree is the product or service a compelling purchase for the customer?
4. How will the product or service be priced?
5. How will the company reach all the identified customer segments?
6. How much does it cost (in time and resources) to acquire a customer?
7. How much does it cost to produce and deliver the product or service?
8. How much does it cost to support a customer?
9. How easy is it to retain a customer?

Assume a new business has hired you as a consultant because of your knowledge of the management process. Write a memo that discusses how the nine questions fit into the management process.

LO4 **Concept of Process Costing Systems**

C 2. For more than 60 years, **Dow Chemical Company** has made and sold a tasteless, odorless, and calorie-free substance called Methocel. When heated, this liquid plastic (methyl cellulose) has the unusual characteristic of becoming a gel that resembles cooked egg whites. It is used in over 400 food products, including gravies, soups, and puddings. It was also used as wampa drool in *The Empire Strikes Back* and dinosaur sneeze in *Jurassic Park*. What kind of costing system is most appropriate for the manufacture of Methocel? Why is that system most appropriate? Describe the system; include in the description a general explanation of how costs are determined.

LO1, LO4 **Process Costing and Work in Process Inventory Accounts**

C 3. SvenskStål, AB, is a steel-producing company located in Solentuna, Sweden. The company originally produced only specialty steel products that were made to order for customers. A job order costing system is used for the made-to-order products. This year, after purchasing three continuous processing work cells, the company created a new division that produces three types of sheet steel in continuous rolls. Ingrid Bjorn, the company controller, has redesigned the management accounting system to accommodate these changes and has installed a process costing system for the new division.

At a recent meeting of the company's executive committee, Bjorn explained that the new product costing system uses three new Work in Process Inventory accounts, one for each of the three work cells. Lars Karlsson, the production supervisor, questioned the need to change product costing approaches and also asked why so many new Work in Process Inventory accounts were necessary.

Why did Bjorn install a process costing system in the new division? Was a new division necessary, or could the three new work cells have been merged with the specialty production facilities? Why were three new Work in Process Inventory accounts required? Could the single Work in Process Inventory account used for the specialty orders have tracked and accumulated the costs incurred in the three new work cells?

Interpreting Managerial Reports

LO5, LO6, LO7 **Analysis of Product Cost**

C 4. Ready Tire Corporation makes several lines of automobile and truck tires. The company operates in a competitive marketplace, so it relies heavily on cost data from its FIFO-based process costing system. It uses that information to set prices for its most competitive tires. The company's radial line has lost some of its market share during each of the past four years. Management believes that price breaks allowed by the company's three biggest competitors are the main reason for the decline in sales.

The company controller, Sara Birdsong, has been asked to review the product costing information that supports price decisions on the radial line. In preparing her report, she collected the following data for the most recent full year of operations:

		Units	Dollars
Equivalent units:	Direct materials	84,200	
	Conversion costs	82,800	
Manufacturing costs:	Direct materials		$1,978,700
	Direct labor		800,400
	Overhead		1,600,800
Unit cost data:	Direct materials		23.50
	Conversion costs		29.00
Work in process inventory:	Beginning (70% complete)	4,200	
	Ending (30% complete)	3,800	

Units started and completed during the year totaled 80,400. Attached to the beginning Work in Process Inventory account were direct materials of $123,660 and conversion costs of $57,010. Birdsong found that little spoilage had occurred. The proper cost allowance for spoilage was included in the predetermined overhead rate of $2 per direct labor dollar. The review of direct labor costs revealed, however, that $90,500 had been charged twice to the production account, the second time in error. This resulted in overly high overhead costs being charged to the production account.

So far this year, the radial has sold for $92 per tire. This price was based on the most recent operations unit data plus a 75 percent markup to cover operating costs and profit. During the year, Ready Tire's three main competitors have charged about $87 for a tire of comparable quality. The company's process costing system adds all direct materials at the beginning of the process, and conversion costs are incurred uniformly throughout the process.

1. Identify what inaccuracies in costs, inventories, and selling prices result from the company's cost-charging error.
2. Prepare a revised process cost report for the most recent full year of operations. Round unit costs to two decimal places. Round total costs to whole dollars.
3. What should have been the minimum selling price per tire this year?
4. Suggest ways of preventing such errors in the future.

Decision Analysis Using Excel

LO3 **Job Order Costing in a Service Organization**

C 5. Refer to **P 7** in this chapter. Peruga Engineering Company needs to analyze its jobs in process during the month of January.

1. Using Excel's Chart Wizard and the job order cost cards that you created for Jobs P-12, P-15, and P-19, prepare a bar chart that compares the bid and proposal costs, design costs, and prototype development costs of the jobs. Below is the suggested format to use for the information table necessary to complete the bar chart.

	A	B	C	D	E
1	1		P-12	P-15	P-19
2	2	Bid and proposal			
3	3	Design			
4	4	Prototype development			
5	5	Total job cost			
6					

2. List some reasons for the differences between the costs of the various jobs.

Ethical Dilemma Case

LO3 **Costing Procedures and Ethics**

C 6. Jennifer Martin, the production manager of Fabricated Products Company, entered the office of controller Joe Barnes and asked, "Joe, what gives here? I was charged for 330 direct labor hours on Job AD22, and my records show that we spent only 290 hours on that job. That 40-hour difference caused the total cost of direct labor and overhead for the job to increase by over $5,500. Are my records wrong, or was there an error in the direct labor assigned to the job?"

Barnes replied, "Don't worry about it, Jennifer. This job won't be used in your quarterly performance evaluation. Job AD22 was a federal government job, a cost-plus contract, so the more costs we assign to it, the more profit we make. We decided to add a few hours to the job in case there is some follow-up work to do. You know how fussy the feds are."

What should Martin do? Discuss Barnes's costing procedure.

Internet Case

LO4 **Comparison of Companies That Use Process Costing Systems**

C 7. Process costing is appropriate for companies in many types of industries. The following list provides some examples:

Industry	Company
Aluminum	Alcoa, Inc.
Beverages	Coors
Building materials	Owens Corning
Chemicals	Engelhard Corporation
Computers	Apple Computer
Containers	Crown Cork & Seal
Electrical equipment	Emerson Electric
Foods	Kellogg Company
Machinery	Caterpillar Inc.
Manufacturing	Minnesota Mining & Manufacturing
Oil and gas	Exxon
Paper products	Boise Cascade
Photography	Eastman Kodak
Plastic products	Tupperware
Soft drinks	Coca-Cola

Access the websites of at least two of these companies. Find as much information as you can about the products the companies make and how they make them, including the manufacturing processes involved. For which products would process costing be most appropriate? For which products would it be inappropriate? Identify differences in the nature of the business conducted by the companies you chose. Do those differences have any bearing on the type of product costing system the company uses? Explain your answer. Do the companies make any products that might require a costing system other than process costing? Be prepared to present the results of your research in class.

Group Activity Case

LO3 **Job Order Costing**

C 8. Many businesses accumulate costs for each job performed. Examples of businesses that use a job order costing system include print shops, car repair shops, health clinics, and kennels.

Visit a local business that uses job order costing, and interview the owner, manager, or accountant about the job order process and the documents the business uses to accumulate product costs. Write a paper that summarizes the information you obtained. Include the following in your summary:

1. The name of the business and the type of operations performed
2. The name and position of the individual you interviewed
3. A description of the process of starting and completing a job
4. A description of the accounting process and documents used to track a job
5. Your responses to these questions:
   a. Did the person you interviewed know the actual amount of materials, labor, and overhead charged to a particular job? If the job includes some estimated costs, how are the estimates calculated? Do the costs affect the determination of the selling price of the product or service?
   b. Compare the documents discussed in this chapter with the documents used by the company you visited. How are they similar, and how are they different?

c. In your opinion, does the business record and accumulate its product costs effectively? Explain your answer.

Your instructor will divide the class into groups according to the type of businesses to discuss this case. Summarize your group's discussion and select someone from the group to present the group's findings to the rest of the class.

Business Communications Case

LO4, LO5, LO6, LO7

Using the Process Costing System

C 9. You are the production manager for Great Grain Corporation, a manufacturer of four cereal products. The company's best-selling product is Smackaroos, a sugar-coated puffed rice cereal. Yesterday, Clark Winslow, the controller, reported that the production cost for each box of Smackaroos has increased approximately 22 percent in the past four months. Because the company is unable to increase the selling price for a box of Smackaroos, the increased production costs will reduce profits significantly.

Today, you received a memo from Gilbert Rom, the company president, asking you to review your production process to identify inefficiencies or waste that can be eliminated. Once you have completed your analysis, you are to write a memo presenting your findings and suggesting ways to reduce or eliminate the problems. The president will use your information during a meeting with the top management team in ten days.

You are aware of previous problems in the Baking Department and the Packaging Department. At your request, Winslow has provided you with process cost reports for the two departments. He has also given you the following detailed summary of the cost per equivalent unit for a box of Smackaroos cereal:

	April	May	June	July
Baking Department				
Direct materials	$1.25	$1.26	$1.24	$1.25
Direct labor	0.50	.61	.85	.90
Overhead	0.25	.31	.34	.40
Department totals	$2.00	$2.18	$2.43	$2.55
Packaging Department				
Direct materials	$ .35	$ .34	$ .33	$ .33
Direct labor	.05	.05	.04	.06
Overhead	.10	.16	.15	.12
Department totals	$ .50	$ .55	$ .52	$ .51
Total cost per equivalent unit	$2.50	$2.73	$2.95	$3.06

1. In preparation for writing your memo, answer the following questions:
   a. For whom are you preparing the memo? Does this affect the length of the memo? Explain.
   b. Why are you preparing the memo?
   c. What actions should you take to gather information for the memo? What information is needed? Is the information that Winslow provided sufficient for analysis and reporting?
   d. When is the memo due? What can be done to provide accurate, reliable, and timely information?
2. Based on your analysis of the information that Winslow provided, where is the main problem in the production process?
3. Prepare an outline of the sections you would want in your memo.

21

Activity-Based Systems: ABM and JIT

To remain competitive in today's changing business environment, companies have had to rethink their organizational processes and basic operating methods. Managers focus on creating value for their customers. They design their internal value chain and external supply chain to provide customer-related, activity-based information; to track costs; and to eliminate waste and inefficiencies. In this chapter, we describe two systems that help managers improve operating processes and make better decisions: activity-based management and the just-in-time operating philosophy.

LEARNING OBJECTIVES

LO1 Explain the role of managers in activity-based systems.

LO2 Define *activity-based management (ABM)* and discuss its relationship to the supply chain and the value chain.

LO3 Distinguish between value-adding and nonvalue-adding activities, and describe process value analysis.

LO4 Define *activity-based costing* and explain how a cost hierarchy and a bill of activities are used.

LO5 Define the *just-in-time (JIT) operating philosophy* and identify the elements of a JIT operating environment.

LO6 Identify the changes in product costing that result when a firm adopts a JIT operating environment.

LO7 Define and apply *backflush costing*, and compare the cost flows in traditional and backflush costing.

LO8 Compare ABM and JIT as activity-based systems.

- How have ABM and JIT helped La-Z-Boy improve its production processes and reduce delivery time?

- How do the managers of La-Z-Boy plan to remain the industry's leading marketer and manufacturer of upholstered products?

A critical factor in the success of **La-Z-Boy, Inc.,** is the speed of its value chain. La-Z-Boy makes about 11,000 built-to-order sofas and chairs each week in its Tennessee plant, and it generally delivers them less than three weeks after customers have placed their orders with a retailer. This is quite a feat, especially since the company offers 85 styles of sofas and a choice of 550 fabrics. It also gives La-Z-Boy a competitive advantage.[1]

Activity-Based Systems and Management

Many companies, including **La-Z-Boy, Inc.**, operate in volatile business environments that are strongly influenced by customer demands. Managers know that customers buy value, usually in the form of quality products or services that are delivered on a timely basis for a reasonable price. Companies generate revenue when customers see value and buy their products or services. Thus, companies measure value as revenue (customer value = revenue generated).

Value exists when some characteristic of a product or service satisfies customers' wants or needs. For example, customers who appreciate comfort are an important market segment for La-Z-Boy. In response to their needs, La-Z-Boy creates value and increases revenue by selling recliners and customized sofas that include the patented La-Z-Boy mechanism, the strongest frame, the most reclining positions, a secure locking footrest, and total body and lumbar support.

Creating value by satisfying customers' needs for quality, reasonable price, and timely delivery requires that managers do the following:

- Work with suppliers and customers.

- View the organization as a collection of value-adding activities.

- Use resources for value-adding activities.

- Reduce or eliminate nonvalue-adding activities.

- Know the total cost of creating value for a customer.

If an organization's business plan focuses on providing products or services that customers esteem, then managers will work with suppliers and customers to find ways of improving quality, reducing costs, and shortening delivery time. Managers will also focus their attention internally to find the best ways of using resources to create and maintain the value of their products or services. This requires matching resources to the operating activities that add value to a product or service. Managers will examine all business activities, including research and development, purchasing, production, storing, selling, shipping, and customer service, so that they can allocate resources effectively.

In addition, managers need to know the **full product cost**, which includes not only the costs of direct materials and direct labor, but also the costs of all production and nonproduction activities required to satisfy the customer. For example, the full product cost of a La-Z-Boy recliner or sofa includes the cost of the frame and upholstery, as well as the costs of taking the sales order, processing the order, packaging and shipping the furniture, and providing subsequent customer service for warranty work. If the activities are executed well and in agreement with the business plan, and if costs are assigned fairly, the company can improve its product pricing and quality, increase productivity, and generate revenues (value) and profits.

Activity-Based Systems

Organizations that focus on their customers design their accounting information systems to provide customer-related, activity-based information.

Activity-based systems are information systems that provide quantitative information about an organization's activities. They create opportunities to improve the cost information supplied to managers. They also help managers view their organization as a collection of activities. Activity-based cost information helps managers improve operating processes and make better pricing decisions.

Activity-based systems developed because traditional accounting systems failed to produce the types of information that today's managers need for decision making. Traditional systems focused primarily on the measurements needed for financial reporting and auditing, such as the measurement of cost of goods sold and the valuation of inventory. Because they were not designed to capture data on activities or to trace the full cost of a product, these systems could not isolate the cost of unnecessary activities, penalize for overproduction, or quantify measures that improved quality or reduced throughput time.

In this chapter, we explore two types of activity-based systems—activity-based management (ABM) and the just-in-time (JIT) operating environment—and consider how they affect product costing. Both systems help organizations manage activities, not costs, but by managing activities, organizations can reduce or eliminate many nonvalue-adding activities, which leads to reduced costs and hence to increased income.

Study Note

ABM and JIT focus on value-adding activities—not costs—to increase income.

Using Activity-Based Cost Information

In this section, we look at the ways in which managers use activity-based cost information. Figure 1 summarizes these uses.

Planning When managers plan, they want answers to questions like "Which activities add value to a product or service?" "What resources are needed to perform those activities?" and "How much should the product or service cost?" By examining their company's value-adding activities and the related costs, managers can ensure that the company is offering quality products or services at the lowest cost. With budgeted costs prepared for each activity, they can not only better allocate resources to cost objects (such as product or service lines, customer groups, or sales territories) and estimate product or service unit cost more accurately, but also measure operating performance. If managers assume that resource-consuming activities cause costs and that products and services incur costs through the activities that they require, the estimated unit cost will be more accurate.

Performing During the period in which managers are performing their duties, they want an answer to the question "What is the actual cost of making our product or providing our service?" They want to know what activities are being performed, how well they are being performed, and what resources they are consuming. Although managers focus on the activities that create the most value for customers, they also monitor some nonvalue-adding activities that have been reduced but not completely eliminated. An activity-based accounting information system measures actual quantities of activity (a quantitative nonfinancial measure) and accumulates related activity costs (a quantitative financial measure). Gathering quantitative information at the activity level gives managers the flexibility to create cost pools for different types of cost objects. For example, the costs of the selling activity can be assigned to a customer, a sales territory, or a product or service line.

■ **FIGURE 1**
The Management Process: To-Do's for Managers

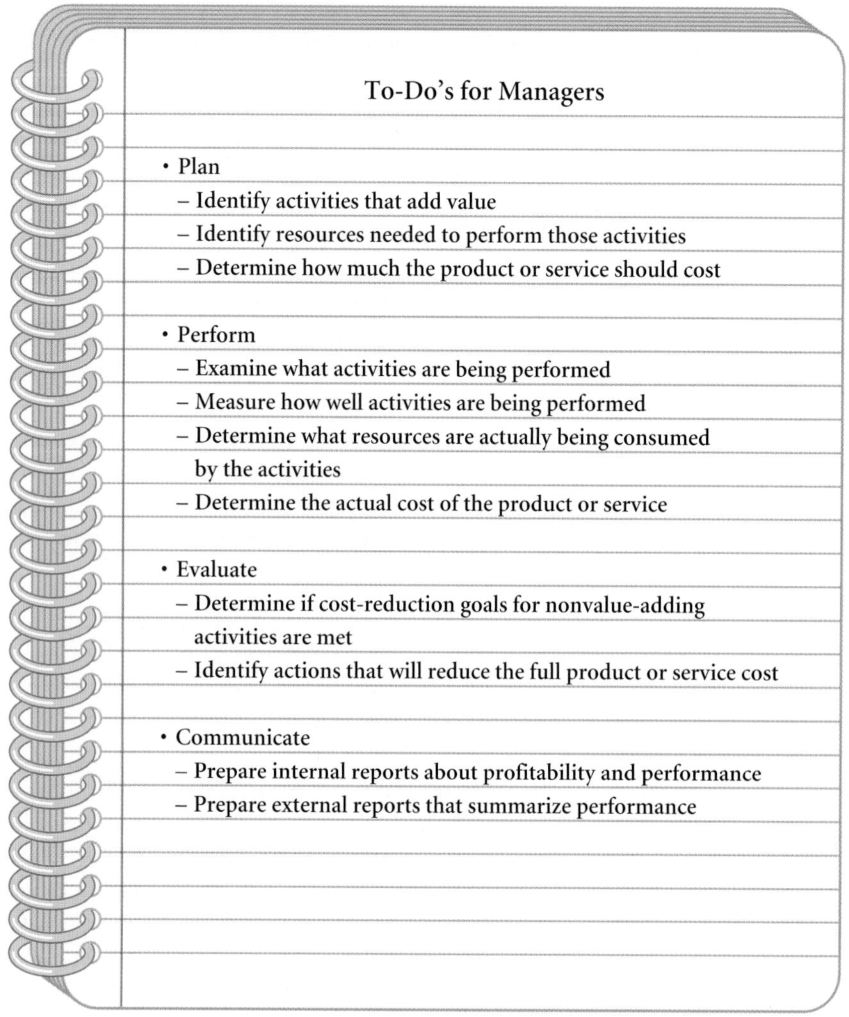

To-Do's for Managers

• Plan
– Identify activities that add value
– Identify resources needed to perform those activities
– Determine how much the product or service should cost

• Perform
– Examine what activities are being performed
– Measure how well activities are being performed
– Determine what resources are actually being consumed
by the activities
– Determine the actual cost of the product or service

• Evaluate
– Determine if cost-reduction goals for nonvalue-adding
activities are met
– Identify actions that will reduce the full product or service cost

• Communicate
– Prepare internal reports about profitability and performance
– Prepare external reports that summarize performance

Evaluating   When managers evaluate performance, they want answers to the questions "What actions will reduce the full product and service cost?" and "Did we meet our cost-reduction goals for nonvalue-adding activities?" Managers measure an activity's performance by reviewing the difference between its actual and budgeted costs. With this information, they can analyze the variances in activity levels, identify waste and inefficiencies, and take action to improve processes and activities. They can also continue to monitor the costs of nonvalue-adding activities to see if the company met its goals of reducing or eliminating those costs. Careful review and analysis will increase value for the customer by improving product quality and reducing costs and cycle time.

Communicating   Managers communicate plans and performance results when they prepare reports about the company's performance for internal and external use. Internal reports show the application of the costs of activities to cost objects, which results in a better measurement of profitability, as we discuss later in the chapter. External reports summarize past performance and answer such questions as "Did the company earn a profit?" and "Were company resources utilized efficiently and effectively?"

S T O P • R E V I E W • A P P L Y

1-1. How do companies measure customer value? What do managers do to create value and satisfy customers' needs?

1-2. What is the main focus of an activity-based system?

1-3. What is the value of gathering quantitative information at the activity level?

Suggested answers to all Stop, Review, and Apply questions are available at http://college.hmco.com/accounting/needles/poa/10e/student_home.html.

Activity-Based Management

LO2 Define *activity-based management (ABM)* and discuss its relationship to the supply chain and the value chain.

As you may recall from an earlier chapter, **activity-based management (ABM)** is an approach to managing an organization that identifies all major operating activities, determines the resources consumed by each activity and the cause of the resource usage, and categorizes the activities as either adding value to a product or service or not adding value. ABM focuses on reducing or eliminating nonvalue-adding activities. Because it provides financial and performance information at the activity level, ABM is useful both for strategic planning and for making operational decisions about business segments, such as product lines, market segments, and customer groups. It also helps managers eliminate waste and inefficiencies and redirect resources to activities that add value to the product or service. Activity-based costing (ABC) is the tool used in an ABM environment to assign activity costs to cost objects. ABC helps managers make better pricing decisions, inventory valuations, and profitability decisions.

Value Chains and Supply Chains

As we noted earlier in the text, a **value chain** is a sequence of activities inside the organization, also known as *primary processes*, that add value to a company's product or service; the value chain also includes support services, such as management accounting, that facilitate the primary processes. ABM enables managers to see their organization's internal value chain as part of a larger system that includes the value chains of suppliers and customers. This larger

FOCUS ON BUSINESS PRACTICE

How Can a Changing Economy Cause Strategy Shifts in a Company's Value Chain?

When the economy took a downturn a few years ago, high-tech companies like Oracle and SAP experienced over-capacity. They therefore shifted the emphasis of their value chains from marketing to customer service. Measures that had been used to gauge the performance of an aggressive sales force, such as sales volume, were now irrelevant and were replaced by measures of customer satisfaction and retention.[2]

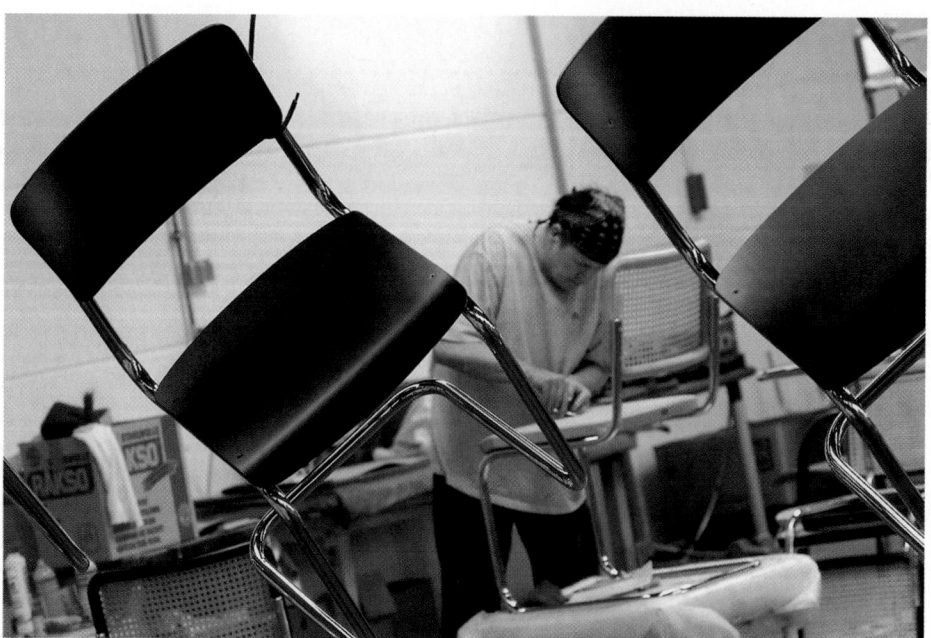

Each company in a supply chain is a customer of an earlier supplier. The furniture maker shown here would be a customer of a metal manufacturer, a caning supplier, a supplier of high-quality wood, and perhaps a leather manufacturer. His customer might be a furniture wholesaler or retail store. The retail store, which sells the furniture to customers, is the final link in the supply chain.

system is the **supply chain**—the path that leads from the suppliers of the materials from which a product is made to the final customer. The supply chain (also called the *supply network*) includes both suppliers and suppliers' suppliers, and customers and customers' customers. It links businesses together in a relationship chain of business to business to business.

As Figure 2 shows, in the supply chain for a furniture company like **La-Z-Boy**, a metal manufacturer supplies metal to the recliner mechanism manufacturer, which supplies recliner mechanisms to the furniture manufacturer. The furniture manufacturer supplies furniture to furniture stores, which in turn supply furniture to the final customers. Each organization in this supply chain is a customer of an earlier supplier, and each has its own value chain. The sequence of primary processes in the value chain varies from company to company depending on a number of factors, including the size of the company and the types of products or services that it sells. Figure 2 also shows the primary processes that add value for a furniture manufacturer—marketing, research and development, purchasing, production, sales, shipping, and customer service.

Understanding value chains and supply chains gives managers a better grasp of their company's internal and external operations. Managers who understand the supply chain and how their company's value-adding activities fit into their suppliers' and customers' value chains can see their company's role in the overall process of creating and delivering products or services. Such an understanding can also make a company more profitable. By working with suppliers and customers across the entire supply chain, managers may be able to reduce the total cost of making a product, even though costs for a particular activity may increase.

For example, La-Z-Boy places computers for online order entry in its licensed furniture galleries. The computers streamline the processing of orders and make the orders more accurate. In this case, even though La-Z-Boy incurs the cost of the computers, the total cost of making and delivering furniture decreases because the cost of order processing decreases. When organizations work cooperatively with others in their supply chain, they can develop new processes that reduce the total costs of their products or services.

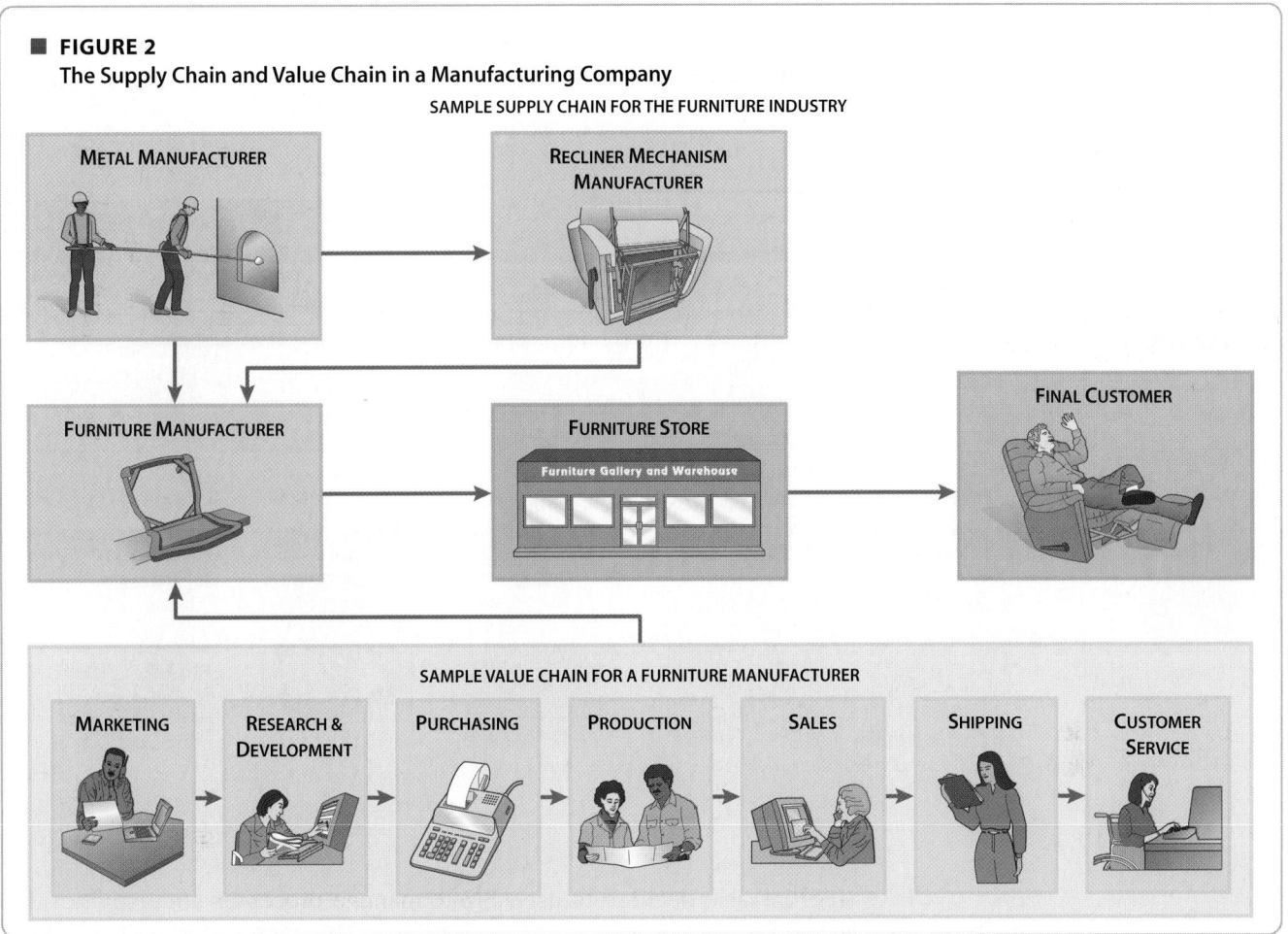

■ FIGURE 2
The Supply Chain and Value Chain in a Manufacturing Company

SAMPLE SUPPLY CHAIN FOR THE FURNITURE INDUSTRY

METAL MANUFACTURER

RECLINER MECHANISM MANUFACTURER

FURNITURE MANUFACTURER

FURNITURE STORE

Furniture Gallery and Warehouse

FINAL CUSTOMER

SAMPLE VALUE CHAIN FOR A FURNITURE MANUFACTURER

MARKETING | RESEARCH & DEVELOPMENT | PURCHASING | PRODUCTION | SALES | SHIPPING | CUSTOMER SERVICE

ABM in a Service Organization

To illustrate how a service organization can use ABM, let's assume that a firm called Direct Ads, Inc. (DAI), offers database marketing strategies to help companies like La-Z-Boy increase their sales. DAI's basic package of services includes the design of a mailing piece (either a Direct Mailer or a Store Mailer), creation and maintenance of marketing databases containing information about the client's target group, and a production process that prints a promotional piece and prepares it for mailing. In its marketing strategies, DAI targets working women ages 25 to 54 who are married with children and who have an annual household income in excess of $50,000.

In preparing DAI's business plan, Fran Teerlink, the owner and manager of DAI, reviewed the company's supply chain. As Figure 3 shows, this supply chain includes suppliers, DAI as a service provider, one customer group (licensed furniture galleries), and the customer group's customers. DAI has a number of suppliers, including office supply companies, printers, and computer stores. Teerlink chose licensed furniture galleries as the supply chain's primary customer group because they represent a sizable percentage of revenues. The customers of the furniture galleries are included in the supply chain because they receive the mailing pieces that DAI prepares. Based on his review of the supply chain, Teerlink concluded that DAI's strategy to work with suppliers and the licensed furniture galleries to improve DAI's services was sound.

■ **FIGURE 3**
The Supply Chain and Value Chain in a Service Organization

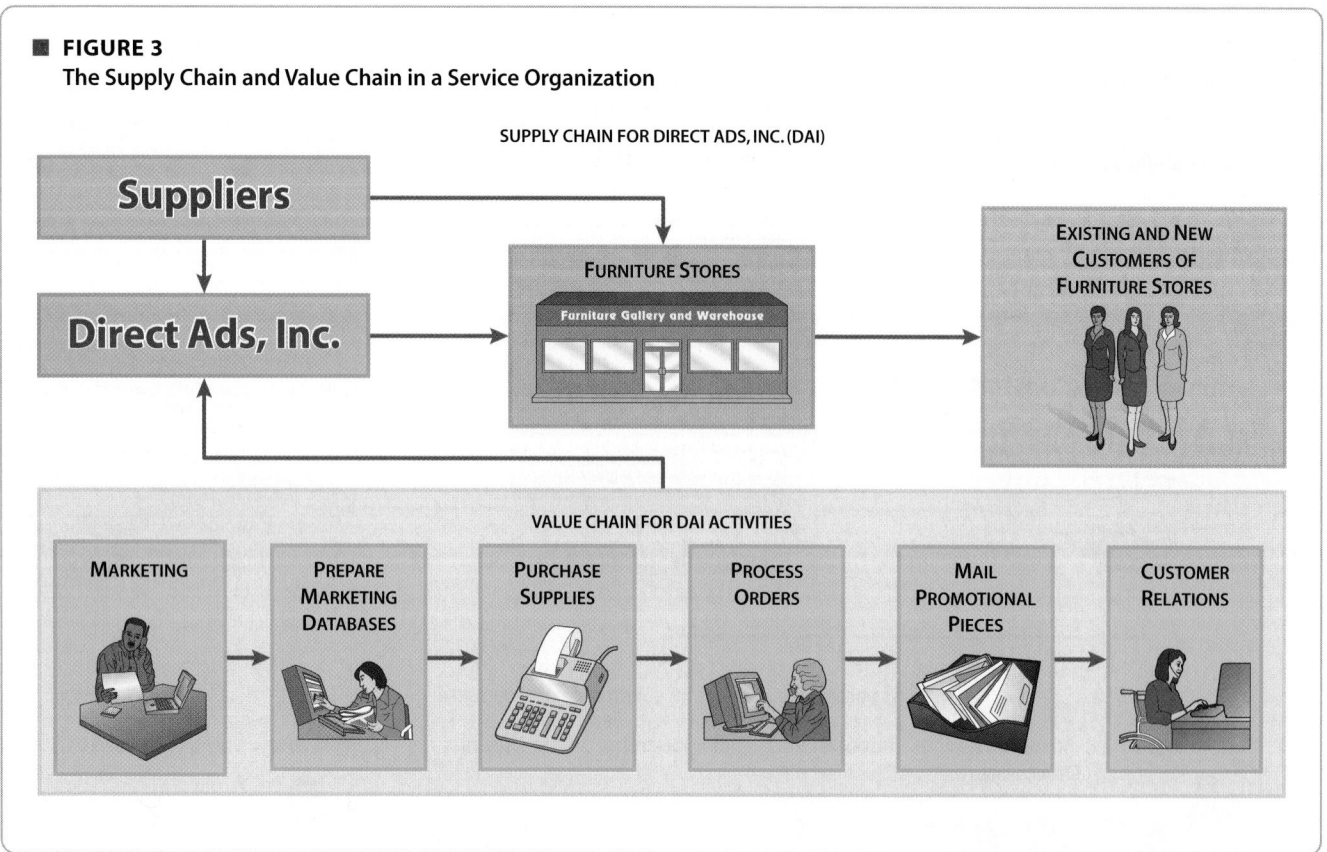

Teerlink also decided to use ABM to manage processes and activities. He developed a value chain of activities for DAI so that he could identify all major operating activities, the resources each activity consumes, and the cause of the resource usage. As shown in Figure 3, the activities that add value to DAI's services are marketing, preparing marketing databases, purchasing supplies, processing orders, mailing promotional pieces, and customer relations.

S T O P • R E V I E W • A P P L Y

2-1. What is activity-based management (ABM)? How is ABM useful for strategic planning and operational decision making?

2-2. How does the focus of a supply chain differ from that of a value chain?

Value-Adding and Nonvalue-Adding Activities and Process Value Analysis

LO3 Distinguish between value-adding and nonvalue-adding activities, and describe process value analysis.

An important element of activity-based management is the identification of value-adding and nonvalue-adding activities. A **value-adding activity** is one that adds value to a product or service as perceived by the customer. Examples include designing the components of a new recliner, assem-

bling the recliner, and upholstering it. A **nonvalue-adding activity** is one that adds cost to a product or service but does not increase its market value. ABM focuses on eliminating nonvalue-adding activities that are not essential to an organization and on reducing the costs of those that are essential, such as legal services, management accounting, machine repair, materials handling, and building maintenance. The costs of both value-adding and nonvalue-adding activities are accumulated to measure performance and to determine whether the goal of reducing the cost of nonvalue-adding activities has been achieved.

To minimize costs, managers continuously seek to improve processes and activities. To manage the cost of an activity, they can reduce the activity's frequency or eliminate it entirely. For example, inspection costs can be reduced if an inspector samples one of every three reclining mechanisms received from a supplier rather than inspecting every mechanism. If the supplier is a reliable source of high-quality mechanisms, such a reduction in inspection activity is appropriate. Another way to reduce costs is to outsource an activity—that is, to have it done by another company that is more competent at the work and can perform it at a lower cost. Many companies outsource purchasing, accounting, and the maintenance of their information systems.

Some activities can be eliminated completely if business processes are changed. For example, when a company adopts a just-in-time operating philosophy, it can eliminate some recordkeeping activities. Because it purchases materials just in time for production and manufactures products just in time for customer delivery, it no longer needs to accumulate costs as the product is made.

Value-Adding and Nonvalue-Adding Activities in a Service Organization

To illustrate how service organizations deal with value-adding and nonvalue-adding activities, let's suppose that Fran Teerlink, the owner and manager of DAI, has examined the activities related to the design, processing, and mailing of his company's Direct Mailers and has drawn up the list of value-adding activities shown in Table 1. When Teerlink's customers ask for database marketing

TABLE 1. Value-Adding Activities for a Service Organization

Direct Ads, Inc.
Value-Adding Activities for the Direct Mailers

Value-Adding Activities	How the Activity Adds Value
Designing the mailer	Enhances the effectiveness of the communication
Creating a database of customers' names and addresses sorted in ZIP code order	Increases the probability that the client will efficiently and effectively reach the targeted customer group
Verifying the conformity of mailings with USPS requirements	Ensures that the client's mailing will receive the best postal rate
Processing the job: A computer prints a personalized mailer A machine folds the mailer, inserts it and other information into an envelope, prints the address on the envelope, and seals and meters the envelope	Creates the client mailing
Delivering the mailers to the post office	Begins the delivery process

services, these are the activities they pay for. Teerlink has also identified the following nonvalue-adding activities:

- Preparing a job order form and scheduling the job
- Ordering, receiving, inspecting, and storing paper, envelopes, and other supplies
- Setting up machines to process a specific letter size
- Logging the total number of items processed in a batch
- Billing the client and recording and depositing payments from the client

After reviewing the list of nonvalue-adding activities, Teerlink arranged with his suppliers to have paper, envelopes, and other supplies delivered the day a job is performed. This helped reduce DAI's storage costs. Teerlink was also able to reduce the costs of some value-adding activities. For example, he reduced the cost of the labor involved in verifying the conformity of mailings with United States Postal Service (USPS) requirements by purchasing computer software that verifies addresses, determines postage, and automatically sorts the letters.

Process Value Analysis

Process value analysis (PVA) is a technique that managers use to identify and link all the activities involved in the value chain. It analyzes business processes by relating activities to the events that prompt those activities and to the resources that the activities consume. PVA forces managers to look critically at all phases of their operations. Managers who use ABM find it an effective way of reducing nonvalue-adding activities and their costs. PVA improves cost traceability and results in significantly more accurate product costs, which in turn improves management decisions and increases profitability.

By using PVA to identify nonvalue-adding activities, companies can reduce their costs and redirect their resources to value-adding activities. For example, PVA has enabled companies like **Westinghouse Electric**, **Pepsi-Cola North America**, and **Land O'Lakes** to reduce the processing costs of purchasing and accounts payable. After identifying the nonvalue-adding activities involved in small-dollar purchases (e.g., recording and paying small bills, setting up accounts, and establishing credit with seldom-used suppliers) and their costs, managers of these companies decided to stop performing such activities internally. Instead, they chose the less expensive alternative of using a special credit card known as a procurement (or purchasing) card from Visa, Master-Card, or American Express to handle large volumes of small-dollar purchases.

FOCUS ON BUSINESS PRACTICE

What Is VBM?

Value-based management (VBM) is a long-term strategy that many businesses use to reward managers who create and sustain shareholder wealth and value. In other words, VBM encourages managers to think like business owners. Three elements are essential for a successful VBM program. First, VBM must have the full support of top management. Second, performance and compensation must be linked, because "what gets measured and rewarded gets done." Finally, everyone involved must understand the what, why, and how of the program. Since a variety of VBM approaches exist, each company can tailor its VBM performance metrics and implementation strategy to meet its particular needs.[3]

S T O P • R E V I E W • A P P L Y

3-1. Are customers willing to pay for nonvalue-adding activities?

3-2. Define process value analysis.

Activity-Based Costing

LO4 Define *activity-based costing* and explain how a cost hierarchy and a bill of activities are used.

A s access to value chain data has improved, managers have refined the issue of how to assign costs fairly to products or services to determine unit costs. You may recall from an earlier chapter that traditional methods of allocating overhead costs to products use such cost drivers as direct labor hours, direct labor costs, or machine hours. In the mid-1980s, organizations began realizing that these methods did not assign overhead costs to their product lines accurately and that the resulting inaccuracy in product unit costs was causing poor pricing decisions. In their search for more accurate product costing, many organizations embraced activity-based costing.

Activity-based costing (ABC) is a method of assigning costs that calculates a more accurate product cost than traditional methods. It does so by categorizing all indirect costs by activity, tracing the indirect costs to those activities, and assigning those costs to products using a cost driver related to the cause of the cost.

Activity-based costing is an important tool of activity-based management because it improves the allocation of activity-driven costs to cost objects. To implement activity-based costing, managers

1. Identify and classify each activity.

2. Estimate the cost of resources for each activity.

3. Identify a cost driver for each activity and estimate the quantity of each cost driver.

4. Calculate an activity cost rate for each activity.

5. Assign costs to cost objects based on the level of activity required to make the product or provide the service.

Study Note

With ABC, indirect costs like overhead are assigned to cost objects using an appropriate allocation scheme.

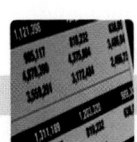

FOCUS ON BUSINESS PRACTICE

A Simpler and More Time-Focused ABC

Full-scale implementation of ABC has historically been difficult, since much of the data were gathered by employee surveys. In a revised ABC model called Time-Driven Activity-Based Costing, managers can estimate how much it costs per time unit of capacity to supply resources to an activity, and how long it takes to carry out one unit of each activity. Time-Driven ABC is easier to adopt and use because it requires only two measures and time equations to reflect the complexity of what is done for specific orders or customers.[4]

The Cost Hierarchy and the Bill of Activities

Two tools used in implementing ABC are a cost hierarchy and a bill of activities.

Cost Hierarchy   A **cost hierarchy** is a framework for classifying activities according to the level at which their costs are incurred. Many companies use this framework to allocate activity-based costs to products or services. In a manufacturing company, the cost hierarchy typically has four levels: the unit level, the batch level, the product level, and the facility level.

▶ **Unit-level activities** are performed each time a unit is produced and are generally considered variable costs. For example, when a furniture manufacturer like **La-Z-Boy** installs a recliner mechanism in a chair, unit-level activities include the direct cost of the recliner mechanism and connecting the mechanism to the chair frame. Because each chair contains only one mechanism, these activities have a direct correlation to the number of chairs produced.

▶ **Batch-level activities** are performed each time a batch or production run of goods is produced. Examples of batch-level activities include setup, inspection, scheduling, and materials handling for the production run of a certain style of recliner. These activities vary with the number of batches prepared or production runs completed.

▶ **Product-level activities** are performed to support a particular product line. Examples of product-level activities include implementing engineering or marketing changes for a particular brand of product and redesigning the installation process for that product line.

▶ **Facility-level activities** are performed to support a facility's general manufacturing process and are generally fixed costs. Examples for a furniture manufacturer include maintaining, lighting, securing, and insuring the factory.

Note that the frequency of activities varies across levels and that the cost hierarchy includes both value-adding and nonvalue-adding activities. Service organizations can also use a cost hierarchy to group their activities; the four levels typically are the unit level, the batch level, the service level, and the operations level. Table 2 lists examples of activities in the cost hierarchies of a manufacturing company and a service organization.

TABLE 2.   Sample Activities in Cost Hierarchies

Activity Level	Furniture Manufacturer: Recliner Mechanism Installation	Direct Mail Service: Preparing a Mailing to Store Customers
Unit level	Install mechanism Test mechanism	Print and fold letter Insert letter and other information into envelope
Batch level	Set up installation process Move mechanisms Inspect mechanisms	Retool machines Verify correct postage Bill client
Product or service level	Redesign installation process	Train employees Develop and maintain computer systems and databases
Facility or operations level	Provide facility maintenance, lighting, and security	Provide facility maintenance, lighting, and security

▼ **EXHIBIT 1**

Bill of Activities for a Service Organization

Direct Ads, Inc.
Bill of Activities for Direct Mailers and Store Mailers
For the Month Ended May 31, 20x9

Activity	Activity Cost Rate	Direct Mailers (110,000 mailers)		Store Mailers (48,000 mailers)	
		Cost Driver Level	Activity Cost	Cost Driver Level	Activity Cost
Unit level					
Process mailers	$20 per machine hour	300 machine hours	$ 6,000	90 machine hours	$ 1,800
Batch level					
Prepare databases	$85 per 1,000 names	50,000 names	4,250	20,000 names	1,700
Set up machines	$10 per direct labor hour	220 direct labor hours	2,200	100 direct labor hours	1,000
Inspect for USPS compliance	$12 per inspection hour	100 inspection hours	1,200	80 inspection hours	960
Service level					
Develop databases	$25 per design hour	118 design hours	2,950	81 design hours	2,025
Solicit new customers	$3 per solicitation	300 solicitations	900	95 solicitations	285
Operations level					
Provide utilities and space	$15 per machine hour	300 machine hours	$ 4,500	90 machine hours	1,350
Total activity costs assigned to services			$22,000		$ 9,120
Total volume			÷110,000		÷48,000
Activity costs per unit (total activity costs ÷ total volume)			$ 0.20		$ 0.19
Cost summary					
Direct materials cost			$ 7,700		$ 5,280
Postage costs			17,600		7,680
Activity costs (includes labor and overhead)			22,000		$ 9,120
Total costs for month			$47,300		$22,080
Product unit cost (total costs for month ÷ total volume)			$ 0.43		$ 0.46

Bill of Activities Once managers have created the cost hierarchy, they group the activities into the specified levels and prepare a summary of the activity costs assigned to the selected cost objects. A **bill of activities** is a list of activities and related costs that is used to compute the costs assigned to activities and the product unit cost. More complex bills of activities group activities into activity pools and include activity cost rates and the cost driver levels used to assign costs to cost objects. A bill of activities may be used as the primary document or as a supporting schedule to calculate the product unit cost in both job order and process costing systems and in both manufacturing and service businesses. Exhibit 1 shows a bill of activities for DAI.

Fran Teerlink uses the bill of activities to see how activity costs contribute to unit costs. As Exhibit 1 shows, DAI produces two types of mailing pieces, the Direct Mailer and the Store Mailer.

▶ Preparing the Direct Mailer involves printing, folding, and collating letters and other materials, inserting them into a printed, addressed envelope, and then metering and sealing the envelope. The cost of the Direct Mailer includes the costs of direct materials (envelopes, letters, and other materials), postage, and service overhead.

▶ The Store Mailer is a one-page solicitation that can be refolded and returned to the store's address. Its cost includes the costs of direct materials (a single piece of paper for each mailer), postage, and service overhead.

The volume of mailings for a customer like **La-Z-Boy** can vary from 150 to 20,000 addresses in a single mailing. The sizes of the databases that are prepared and the number of machine setups and inspection hours also vary from job to job. The service overhead costs for the activities identified in the cost hierarchy are assigned using ABC. The activity costs are calculated for the service overhead related to each type of mailing piece. These are then added to the costs of direct materials and postage to calculate a unit cost.

Teerlink grouped activities by unit, batch, service, and operations levels:

▶ At the unit level, Teerlink included the costs of all activities needed to process each Direct Mailer and Store Mailer. He used machine hours as the cost driver.

▶ At the batch level, for each job, he included the costs of all activities required to prepare the database of names and addresses for mailing, to set up the machines, and to inspect the letters for compliance with postal regulations. He used the number of names in the database, direct labor hours, and inspection hours as the cost drivers.

▶ At the service level, he included the costs of all activities required to develop databases for new clients and to solicit new business for DAI. He used design hours and number of solicitations as the cost drivers.

▶ At the operations level, he included the costs of all activities related to providing utilities and space. He used machine hours as the cost driver.

Teerlink prepared a bill of activities for one month ending May 31, 20x9. He supported each activity's cost with information about the activity cost rate and the cost driver level. He also calculated the total activity costs and the activity cost per unit for each type of mailing piece. At the bottom of the bill of activities for the month, he prepared a summary of the total costs of the mailings and calculated the unit cost for each type (the total costs divided by the number of units mailed).

The cost information gathered in the bill of activities helped Teerlink estimate the company's profits by allowing him to compare costs with revenues. To be competitive, he is currently offering the Direct Mailer for $.50 per letter and the Store Mailer for $.45 per mailer. The Direct Mailer is generating a positive gross margin of $.07 ($.50 − $.43) per letter, but the Store Mailer shows a negative gross margin of $.01 ($.45 − $.46) per mailer. Teerlink must find ways to increase fee revenue, reduce costs, or increase volume for the Store Mailer. ABC can help him reduce costs because the activity costs, including labor and overhead, are categorized by activities and grouped into activity levels. Teerlink can examine those activities to identify and reduce or eliminate some of the company's nonvalue-adding activities.

Activity-Based Costing for Selling and Administrative Activities

Activity-based costing can also be used to assign the costs of selling and administrative activities. The costs of these activities include salaries, benefits, depreciation on buildings and equipment, sales commissions, and utilities. ABC groups such costs into activity pools and assigns them to cost objects using cost drivers like the number of sales calls, sales orders, invoices, or billings. The cost objects might be products, services, customers, or sales territories. Because it is difficult to assign costs to individual customers, many companies treat similar customers, such as distributors or retailers, as a single group.

Because customer groups and sales territories differ in their complexity and diversity, each should support its related costs. For example, some customers place larger or more frequent orders than others, and a larger portion of the costs of selling and administrative activities can therefore be traced to them. Sales territories differ in size and in the number of customers served; thus, some sales territories may require more support services than others.

Exhibit 2 presents a customer-related income statement for DAI. A similar format can be used to create an income statement for any cost object. Service organizations typically group clients according to significant characteristics, such as the length of time required to perform the service or the frequency of the service. In our example, Fran Teerlink can use the ABC information to review the profitability of each customer or customer group. He can also use it to compare selling and administrative costs across customer groups and as a basis for making changes in selling and administrative activities that will increase his company's profitability.

EXHIBIT 2 ▶

Income Statement for a Cost Object

Direct Ads, Inc.
Customer-Related Income Statement
Muncie Furniture Gallery
For the Month Ended May 31, 20x9

Fee revenue ($.50 × 12,000 Direct Mailers)	$6,000
Cost of processing order ($.43 × 12,000 Direct Mailers)	5,160
Gross margin	$ 840
Less: Selling and administrative activity costs	726 ←
Operating income contributed by Muncie Furniture Gallery	$ 114

Activity	Activity Cost Rate	Cost Driver Level	Activity Cost
Make sales calls	$12 per sales call	10 sales calls	$120
Prepare sales orders	$6 per sales order	25 sales orders	150
Handle inquiries	$.50 per minute	120 minutes	60
Process credits	$20 per notice	1 notice	20
Process invoices	$10 per invoice	12 invoices	120
Follow-ups	$8 per follow-up	20 follow-ups	160
Process billings and collections	$4 per billing	24 billings	96
Total selling and administrative activity costs			$726

S T O P • R E V I E W • A P P L Y

4-1. Why have many organizations turned to activity-based costing?

4-2. What are the five steps involved in implementing activity-based costing?

4-3. List and define the four levels in the cost hierarchy for a company.

4-4. How does a bill of activities differ from a job order cost card?

The New Operating Environment and JIT Operations

LO5 Define the *just-in-time (JIT) operating philosophy* and identify the elements of a JIT operating environment.

To remain competitive in today's changing business environment, companies have had to rethink their organizational processes and basic operating methods. One of the operating philosophies that managers have devised for the new operating environment is JIT. The **just-in-time (JIT) operating philosophy** requires that all resources—materials, personnel, and facilities—be acquired and used only as needed. Its objectives are to enhance productivity, eliminate waste, reduce costs, and improve product quality.

Traditionally, a company operated with large amounts of inventory, including finished goods stored in anticipation of customers' orders; purchased materials infrequently but in large amounts; had long production runs with infrequent setups; manufactured large batches of products; and trained each member of its work force to perform a limited number of tasks. Managers determined that changes in this process were necessary because

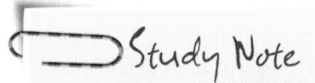

Study Note

Traditional environments emphasize *functional* departments that tend to group similar activities together (e.g., a typing pool).

▶ Large amounts of an organization's space and money were tied up in inventory.

▶ The source of poor-quality materials, products, or services was hard to pinpoint.

▶ The number of nonvalue-adding manufacturing activities was growing.

▶ Accounting for the manufacturing process was becoming ever more complex.

To achieve JIT's objectives, a company must redesign its operating systems, plant layout, and basic management methods to conform to several basic concepts:

▶ Simple is better.

▶ The quality of the product or service is critical.

▶ The work environment must emphasize continuous improvement.

▶ Maintaining large inventories wastes resources and may hide poor work.

▶ Activities or functions that do not add value to a product or service should be eliminated or reduced.

FOCUS ON BUSINESS PRACTICE

Just-in-Time Who's Who

- Eli Whitney perfected the concept of interchangeable parts in 1799, when he produced 10,000 muskets for the U.S. Army for the low price of $13.40 per musket.

- In the late 1890s, Frederick W. Taylor used his ideas of scientific management to standardize work through time studies.

- In the early twentieth century, Frank and Lillian Galbraith (parents of the authors of *Cheaper by the Dozen*) focused on eliminating waste by studying worker motivation and using motion studies and process charting.

- Starting in 1910, Henry Ford and Charles E. Sorensen arranged all the elements of manufacturing into a continuous system called the *production line.*

- After World War II, Taichii Ohno and Shigeo Shingo recognized the importance of inventory management, and they perfected the Toyota production system, also known as the *just-in-time system (JIT).*[5]

▶ Goods should be produced only when needed.

▶ Workers must be multiskilled and must participate in improving efficiency and product quality.

Application of these concepts creates a JIT operating environment. Here, we describe the elements used in a JIT operating environment to enhance productivity, eliminate waste, reduce costs, and improve product quality.

Minimum Inventory Levels

Maintaining minimum inventory levels is fundamental to the JIT operating philosophy. In the traditional manufacturing environment, parts, materials, and supplies are purchased far in advance and stored until the production department needs them. In contrast, in a JIT environment, materials and parts are

A basic rule in a JIT operating environment is to keep inventory at a minimum. Doing so has many advantages, including reducing the amount of storage space needed, the amount of materials handling, and the amount of capital tied up in inventory. Maintaining minimum inventory levels does, however, increase the risk of stock depletions, so employees must keep a careful eye on inventory. The employee shown here is checking inventory in an electronics warehouse.

purchased and received only when they are needed. The JIT system lowers costs by reducing the space needed for inventory storage, the amount of materials handling, and the amount of inventory obsolescence. It also reduces the need for inventory control facilities, personnel, and recordkeeping. In addition, it significantly decreases the amount of work in process inventory and the amount of working capital tied up in all inventories.

Maintaining minimum inventory levels does increase the risk of stock depletions and downtime, which can be costly and can result in late revenues. Before adopting the JIT operating philosophy, managers need to plan for such risks.

Pull-Through Production

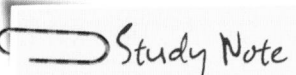

Study Note

Pull-through production represents a change in concept. Instead of producing goods in anticipation of customers' needs, customers' orders trigger the production process.

A JIT operating environment requires **pull-through production**, a system in which a customer's order triggers the purchase of materials and the scheduling of production for the products that have been ordered. In contrast, with the **push-through method** used in traditional manufacturing operations, products are manufactured in long production runs and stored in anticipation of customers' orders. With pull-through production, the size of a customer's order determines the size of a production run, and the company purchases materials and parts as needed. Inventory levels are kept low, but machines must be set up more frequently, resulting in more work stoppages.

Quick Setup and Flexible Work Cells

Study Note

In the JIT environment, normal operating activities—setup, production, and maintenance— still take place. But the timing of those activities is altered to promote smoother operations and to minimize downtime.

In the past, managers felt that it was more cost-effective to produce large batches of goods because producing small batches increases the number of machine setups. The success of JIT has disproved this. By placing machines in more efficient locations, setup time can be minimized. In addition, when workers perform frequent setups, they become more efficient at it.

In a traditional factory layout, similar machines are grouped together, forming functional departments. Products are routed through these departments in sequence, so that all necessary operations are completed in order. This process can take several days or weeks, depending on the size and complexity of the job. By changing the factory layout so that all the machines needed for sequential processing are placed together, the JIT operating environment may cut the manufacturing time of a product from days to hours, or from weeks to days. The new cluster of machinery forms a flexible **work cell**, an autonomous production line that can perform all required operations efficiently and continuously. The flexible work cell handles a "family of products"—that is, products of similar shape or size. Product families require minimal setup changes as workers move from one job to the next. The more flexible the work cell is, the greater its potential to minimize total production time.

A Multiskilled Work Force

In the flexible work cells of a JIT environment, one worker may be required to operate several types of machines simultaneously. The worker may have to set up and retool the machines and even perform routine maintenance on them. A JIT operating environment thus requires a multiskilled work force, and multiskilled workers have been very effective in contributing to high levels of productivity.

High Levels of Product Quality

JIT operations result in high-quality products since high-quality direct materials are used and because inspections are made throughout the production process. According to the JIT philosophy, inspection as a separate step does not add value to a product, so inspection is incorporated into ongoing operations. A JIT machine operator inspects the products as they pass through the manufacturing process. If the operator detects a flaw, he or she shuts down the work cell to prevent the production of similarly flawed products while the cause of the problem is being determined. The operator either fixes the problem or helps the engineer or quality control person find a way to correct it. This integrated inspection procedure, combined with high-quality materials, produces high-quality finished goods.

Effective Preventive Maintenance

When a company rearranges its machinery into flexible work cells, each machine becomes an integral part of its cell. If one machine breaks down, the entire work cell stops functioning, and the product cannot easily be routed to another machine while the malfunctioning machine is being repaired. Continuous JIT operations therefore require an effective system of preventive maintenance. Preventing machine breakdowns is considered more important and more cost-effective than keeping machines running continuously. Machine operators are trained to perform minor repairs when they detect problems. Machines are serviced regularly—much as an automobile is—to help guarantee continued operation. The machine operator conducts routine maintenance during periods of downtime between orders. (Remember that in a JIT setting, the work cell does not operate unless there is a customer order for the product. Machine operators take advantage of such downtime to perform routine maintenance.)

Continuous Improvement of the Work Environment

A JIT environment fosters loyalty among workers, who are likely to see themselves as part of a team because they are so deeply involved in the production process. Machine operators must have the skills to run several types of machines, detect defective products, suggest measures to correct problems, and maintain the machinery within their work cells. In addition, each worker is encouraged to suggest improvements to the production process. Companies with a JIT operating environment receive thousands of employee suggestions and implement a high percentage of them, and they reward workers for suggestions that improve the process. Such an environment fosters workers' initiative and benefits the company.

Study Note

That inspections are necessary is an admission that problems with quality do occur. Continuous inspection throughout production as opposed to inspection only at the end creates awareness of a problem at the point where it occurs.

Study Note

Although separate inspection costs are reduced in a JIT operating environment, some additional time is added to production because the machine operator is now performing the inspection function. The objectives are to reduce *total* costs and to increase quality.

Study Note

The JIT operating philosophy must be adopted by everyone in a company before its total benefits can be realized.

S T O P • R E V I E W • A P P L Y

5-1. What are the objectives of a JIT operating environment?

5-2. What is pull-through production, and how is it different from the push-through method?

5-3. How does the inspection function change in a JIT operating environment?

Accounting for Product Costs in the New Operating Environment

LO6   Identify the changes in product costing that result when a firm adopts a JIT operating environment.

When a firm shifts to the new operating environment, managers must take a new approach to evaluating costs and controlling operations. The changes in the operations will affect how costs are determined and what measures are used to monitor performance.

When a company adopts a JIT operating environment, the work cells and the goal of reducing or eliminating nonvalue-adding activities change the way costs are classified and assigned. In this section, we examine those changes.

Classifying Costs

The traditional production process can be divided into five time frames:

Processing time	The actual amount of time spent working on a product
Inspection time	The time spent looking for product flaws or reworking defective units
Moving time	The time spent moving a product from one operation or department to another
Queue time	The time a product spends waiting to be worked on once it arrives at the next operation or department
Storage time	The time a product spends in materials inventory, work in process inventory, or finished goods inventory

In product costing under JIT, costs associated with processing time are classified as either direct materials costs or conversion costs. **Conversion costs** are the sum of the direct labor costs and overhead costs incurred by a production department, work cell, or other work center. According to the JIT philosophy, costs associated with inspection, moving, queue, and storage time should be reduced or eliminated because they do not add value to the product.

Assigning Costs

In a JIT operating environment, managers focus on **throughput time**, the time it takes to move a product through the entire production process. Measures of product movement, such as machine time, are used to apply conversion costs to products.

Sophisticated computer monitoring of the work cells allows many costs to be traced directly to the cells in which products are manufactured. As Table 3 shows, several costs that in a traditional environment are treated as indirect costs and applied to products using an overhead rate are treated as the direct costs of a JIT work cell. Because the products that a work cell manufactures are similar in nature, direct materials and conversion costs should be nearly uniform for each product in a cell. The costs of repairs and maintenance, materials handling, operating supplies, utilities, and supervision can be traced directly to work cells as they are incurred. Depreciation charges are based on units of output, not on time, so depreciation can be charged directly to work cells based on the number of units produced. Building occupancy costs, insurance premiums, and ABM property taxes remain indirect costs and must be assigned to the work cells for inclusion in the conversion cost.

TABLE 3. Direct and Indirect Costs in Traditional and JIT Environments

	Costs in a Traditional Environment	Costs in a JIT Environment
Direct materials	Direct	Direct
Direct labor	Direct	Direct
Repairs and maintenance	Indirect	Direct to work cell
Materials handling	Indirect	Direct to work cell
Operating supplies	Indirect	Direct to work cell
Utilities costs	Indirect	Direct to work cell
Supervision	Indirect	Direct to work cell
Depreciation	Indirect	Direct to work cell
Supporting service functions	Indirect	Mostly direct to work cell
Building occupancy	Indirect	Indirect
Insurance and taxes	Indirect	Indirect

S T O P • R E V I E W • A P P L Y

6-1. Which time frame in the production process is value-adding?

6-2. How do JIT operations affect the classification of costs?

Backflush Costing

LO7 Define and apply *backflush costing,* and compare the cost flows in traditional and backflush costing.

Managers in a just-in-time operating environment are continuously seeking ways of reducing wasted resources and wasted time. So far, we have focused on how they can trim waste from operations, but they can reduce waste in other areas as well, including the accounting process. Because a JIT environment reduces labor costs, the accounting system can combine the costs of direct labor and overhead into the single category of conversion costs, and because materials arrive just in time to be used in the production process, there is little reason to maintain a separate Materials Inventory account. Thus, by simplifying cost flows through the accounting records, a JIT environment makes it possible to reduce the time it takes to record and account for the costs of the manufacturing process.

A JIT organization can also streamline its accounting process by using backflush costing. In **backflush costing**, all product costs are first accumulated in the Cost of Goods Sold account; at the end of the accounting period, they are "flushed back," or worked backward, into the appropriate inventory accounts. By having all product costs flow straight to a final destination and working back to determine the proper balances for the inventory accounts at the end of the period, this method saves recording time. As illustrated in Figure 4, it eliminates the need to record several transactions that must be recorded in traditional operating environments.

Study Note

Backflush costing eliminates the need to make journal entries during the period to track cost flows through the production process as the product is made.

■ **FIGURE 4**
Comparison of Cost Flows in Traditional and Backflush Costing

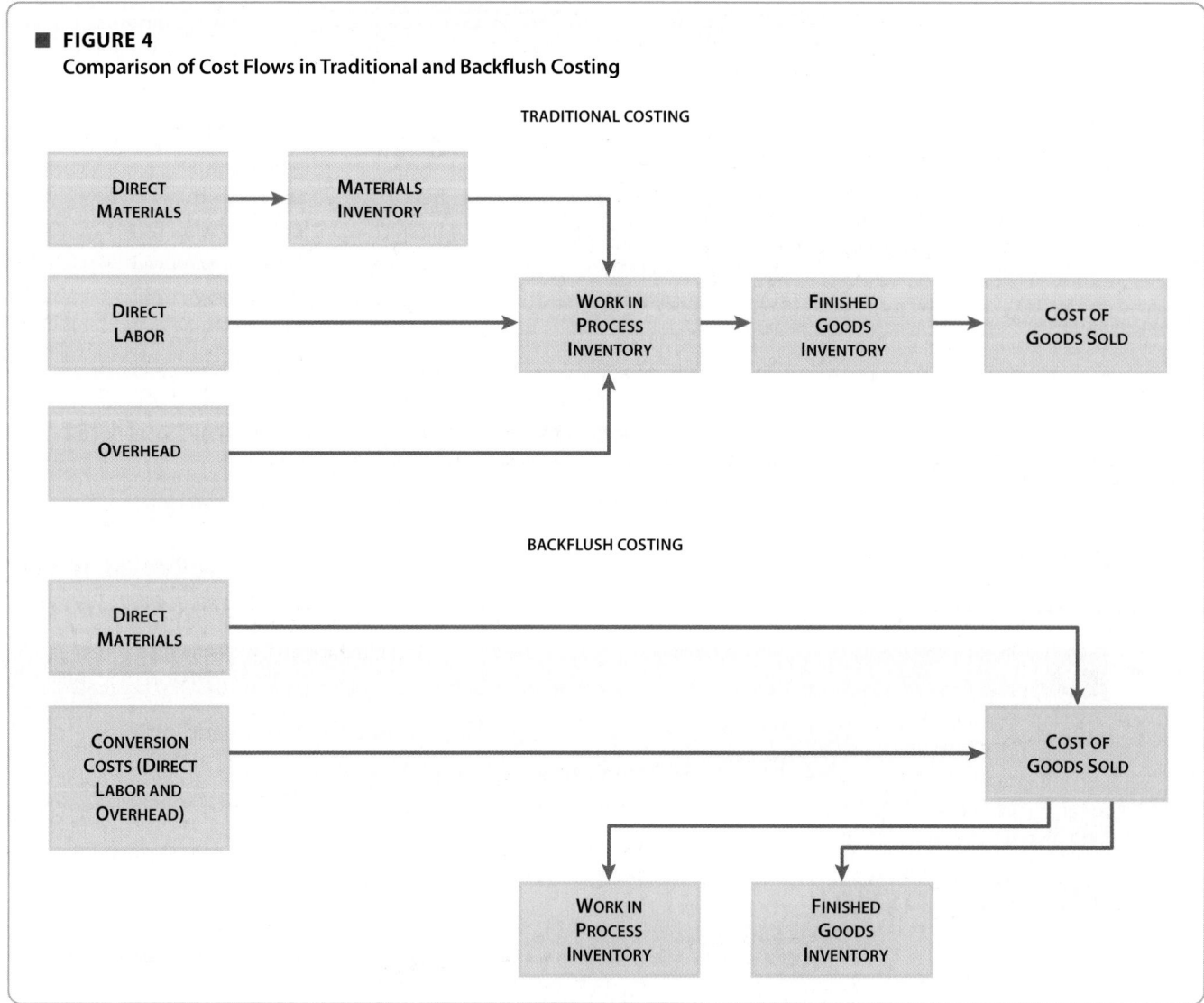

When direct materials arrive at a factory in which traditional costing methods are used, their costs flow into the Materials Inventory account. Then, when the direct materials are requisitioned into production, their costs flow into the Work in Process Inventory account. When direct labor is used, its costs are added to the Work in Process Inventory account. Overhead is applied to production using a base like direct labor hours, machine hours, or number of units produced and is added to the other costs in the Work in Process Inventory account. At the end of the manufacturing process, the costs of the finished units are transferred to the Finished Goods Inventory account, and when the units are sold, their costs are transferred to the Cost of Goods Sold account.

In a JIT setting, direct materials arrive just in time to be placed into production. As you can see in Figure 4, when backflush costing is used, the direct materials costs and the conversion costs (direct labor and overhead) are immediately charged to the Cost of Goods Sold account. At the end of the period, the costs of goods in work in process inventory and in finished goods inventory are determined, and those costs are flushed back to the Work in Process Inventory account and the Finished Goods Inventory account. Once those costs have been flushed back, the Cost of Goods Sold account contains only the costs of units completed and sold during the period.

Study Note

In backflush costing, entries to the Work in Process Inventory and Finished Goods Inventory accounts are made at the end of the period.

■ **FIGURE 5**
Cost Flows Through T Accounts in Traditional and Backflush Costing

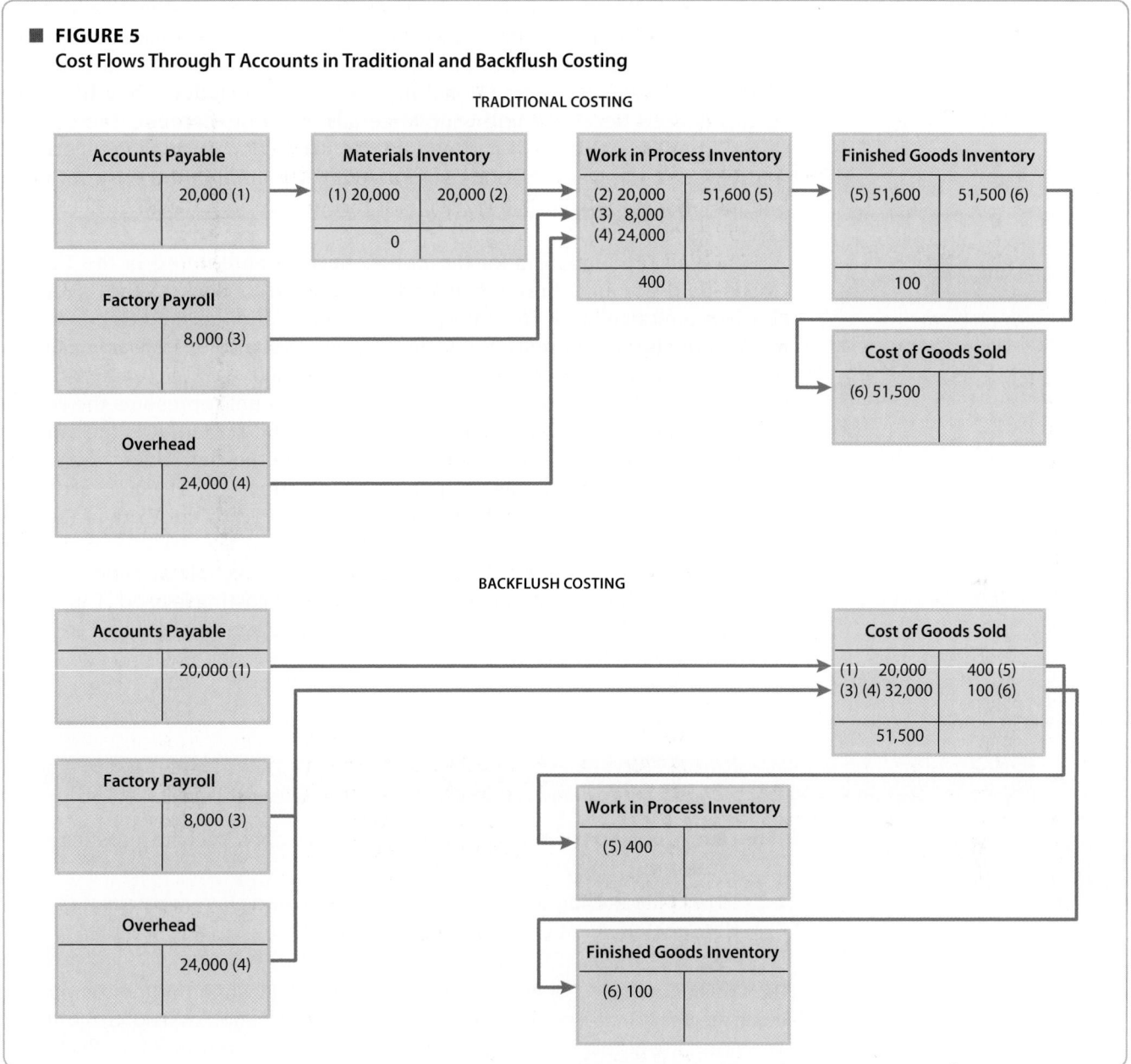

To illustrate, assume that the following transactions occurred at one of La-Z-Boy's factories last month:

1. Purchased $20,000 of direct materials on account.

2. Used all of the direct materials in production during the month.

3. Incurred direct labor costs of $8,000.

4. Applied $24,000 of overhead to production.

5. Completed units costing $51,600 during the month.

6. Sold units costing $51,500 during the month.

The top diagram in Figure 5 shows how these transactions would be entered in T accounts when traditional product costing is used. You can trace the flow of each cost by following its transaction number.

The bottom diagram in Figure 5 shows how backflush costing in a JIT environment would treat the same transactions. The cost of direct materials (Transaction 1) is charged directly to the Cost of Goods Sold account. Transaction 2, which is included in the traditional method, is not included when backflush costing is used because there is no Materials Inventory account. The costs of direct labor (Transaction 3) and overhead (Transaction 4) are combined and transferred to the Cost of Goods Sold account. The total in the Cost of Goods Sold account is then $52,000 ($20,000 for direct materials and $32,000 for conversion costs).

Once all product costs for the period have been entered in the Cost of Goods Sold account, the amounts to be transferred back to the inventory accounts are calculated. The amount transferred to the Finished Goods Inventory account is the difference between the cost of units sold (Transaction 6) and the cost of completed units (Transaction 5) ($51,600 − $51,500 = $100). The remaining difference in the Cost of Goods Sold account represents the cost of the work that is still in production at the end of the period. It is the amount charged to the Cost of Goods Sold account during the period less the actual cost of goods finished during the period (Transaction 5) [($20,000 + $8,000 + $24,000) − $51,600 = $400]; this amount is transferred to the Work in Process Inventory account.

Notice that the ending balance in the Cost of Goods Sold account, $51,500, is the same as the ending balance when traditional costing is used. The difference is that backflush costing enabled us to use fewer accounts and to avoid recording several transactions.

S T O P • R E V I E W • A P P L Y

7-1. Does JIT or ABM use backflush costing? How does backflush costing reduce the time spent on recordkeeping?

7-2. How is the ending balance in the Finished Goods Inventory account determined when backflush costing is used?

Backflush Costing For work done during August, Plush Furniture Company incurred direct materials costs of $123,450 and conversion costs of $265,200. The company employs a just-in-time operating philosophy and backflush costing.

At the end of August, it was determined that the Work in Process Inventory account had been assigned $980 of costs, and the ending balance of the Finished Goods Inventory account was $1,290. There were no beginning inventory balances. How much was charged to the Cost of Goods Sold account during August? What was the ending balance of the Cost of Goods Sold account?

SOLUTION

A total of $388,650 ($123,450 + $265,200) was charged to the Cost of Goods Sold account during August. The ending balance of Cost of Goods Sold was $386,380 ($388,650 − $980 − $1,290).

Comparison of ABM and JIT

 **Study Note**

ABM's primary goal is to calculate product or service cost accurately. JIT's primary goal is to simplify and standardize business processes.

ABM and JIT have several things in common. As activity-based systems, both analyze processes and identify value-adding and nonvalue-adding activities. Both seek to eliminate waste and reduce nonvalue-adding activities to improve product or service quality, reduce costs, and improve an organization's efficiency and productivity. Both improve the quality of the information that managers use to make decisions about bidding, pricing, product lines, and outsourcing. However, the two systems differ in their methods of costing and cost assignment.

ABM's tool, ABC, calculates product or service cost by using cost drivers to assign the indirect costs of production to cost objects. ABC affects only the assignment of overhead costs to products or services; the costs of direct materials and direct labor are traced directly to products or services and are unaffected by ABC. ABC is often a fairly complex accounting method used with job order and process costing systems. Note that the ABC method can also be used to examine nonproduction-related activities, such as marketing and shipping.

JIT reorganizes many activities so that they are performed within work cells. The costs of those activities become direct costs of the work cell and of the products made in that cell. The total production costs within the cell can then be assigned by using simple cost drivers, such as process hours or direct materials cost. Companies that have implemented JIT manufacturing may use backflush costing rather than job order costing or process costing. This approach focuses on the output at the end of the production process and simplifies the accounting system. Table 4 summarizes the characteristics of ABM and JIT.

TABLE 4.   Comparison of ABM and JIT Activity-Based Systems

	ABM	JIT
Primary purpose	To eliminate or reduce nonvalue-adding activities	To eliminate or reduce waste
Cost assignment	Uses ABC to assign overhead costs to the product cost by using appropriate cost drivers	Reorganizes activities so that they are performed within work cells; overhead costs incurred in the work cell become direct costs of the products made in that cell
Costing method	Integrates ABC with job order or process costing to calculate product costs	May use backflush costing to calculate product costs when the products are completed

A company can use both ABM and JIT. ABM and ABC will improve the accuracy of the company's product or service costing and help it to reduce or eliminate business activities that do not add value for its customers. It can apply the JIT operating philosophy to simplify processes, use resources effectively, and eliminate waste. To remain competitive in today's fast-changing business environment, many organizations rely on both of these activity-based systems.

S T O P • R E V I E W • A P P L Y

8-1. How do ABM and JIT differ in their approaches to product costing?

8-2. Can a business use both ABM and JIT?

A LOOK BACK AT

LA-Z-BOY, INC.

In this chapter's Decision Point, we asked the following questions:

- **How have ABM and JIT helped La-Z-Boy improve its production processes and reduce delivery time?**
- **How do the managers of La-Z-Boy plan to remain the industry's leading marketer and manufacturer of upholstered products?**

La-Z-Boy's managers use activity-based management (ABM) and a just-in-time (JIT) operating environment to identify and reduce or eliminate activities that do not add value to the company's products. These systems focus on minimizing waste, reducing costs, improving the allocation of resources, and ensuring that suppliers deliver materials just at the time the company needs them. They help managers make better decisions about costing and pricing products, adding or dropping product styles, changing production and delivery systems, and contracting with suppliers. The continuous flow of information that ABM and JIT provide has enabled La-Z-Boy's managers to improve the company's production processes and act in an ethical, responsible manner. They are able to adjust their labor needs each week to meet order requirements; to schedule timely deliveries from suppliers, thus maintaining appropriate inventory levels; and to keep track of the company's fleet of delivery trucks.

La-Z-Boy's disciplined monitoring of order, production, and delivery activities gives the company a competitive edge. By using ABM and JIT, La-Z-Boy has achieved higher productivity than other furniture manufacturers, is able to offer more than 40,000 product variations, and has cut its delivery time to its licensed furniture galleries by one-half to one-third.[6]

CHAPTER REVIEW

REVIEW of Learning Objectives

LO1 Explain the role of managers in activity-based systems.

Activity-based systems are information systems that provide quantitative information about an organization's activities. They help managers view the organization as a collection of related activities. Activity-based cost information enables managers to improve operating processes and make better pricing decisions. When managers plan, activity-based systems help them identify value-adding activities, determine the resources needed for those activities, and estimate product costs. As managers manage and evaluate operating performance, these systems help them determine the full product or service cost, identify actions that will reduce that cost, and establish whether cost-reduction goals for nonvalue-adding activities were reached. Activity-based systems also help managers communicate the cost of inventory and determine the degree to which product goals were achieved.

LO2 Define *activity-based management (ABM)* and discuss its relationship to the supply chain and the value chain.

Activity-based management (ABM) is an approach to managing an organization that identifies all major operating activities, determines the resources consumed by each activity and the cause of the resource usage, and categorizes the activities as either adding value to a product or service or not adding value. ABM enables managers to see their organization as a collection of value-creating activities (a value chain) that operates as part of a larger system that includes suppliers' and customers' value chains (a supply chain). This perspective helps managers work cooperatively both inside and outside their organizations to reduce costs by eliminating waste and inefficiencies and by redirecting resources toward value-adding activities.

LO3 Distinguish between value-adding and nonvalue-adding activities, and describe process value analysis.

A value-adding activity adds value to a product or service as perceived by the customer. Examples include designing the components of a new recliner, assembling the recliner frame, and upholstering it. A nonvalue-adding activity adds cost to a product or service but does not increase its market value. Examples include legal services, management accounting, machine repair, materials handling, and building maintenance. PVA is a technique that managers use to identify and link all the activities involved in the value chain. It analyzes business processes by relating activities to the events that prompt the activities and to the resources that the activities consume.

LO4 Define *activity-based costing* and explain how a cost hierarchy and a bill of activities are used.

Activity-based costing (ABC) is a method of assigning costs that calculates a more accurate product cost than traditional methods do. It does so by categorizing all indirect costs by activity, tracing the indirect costs to those activities, and assigning those costs to products using a cost driver related to the cause of the cost. To implement ABC, managers (1) identify and classify each activity, (2) estimate the cost of resources for each activity, (3) identify a cost driver for each activity and estimate the quantity of each cost driver, (4) calculate an activity cost rate for each activity, and (5) assign costs to cost objects based on the level of activity required to make the product or provide the service.

Two tools—a cost hierarchy and a bill of activities—help in the implementation of ABC. To create a cost hierarchy, managers classify activities into four levels. Unit-level activities are performed each time a unit is produced. Batch-level activities are performed each time a batch of goods is produced. Product-level activities are performed to support a particular product line or brand. Facility-level activities are performed to support a facility's general manufacturing process. A bill of activities is then used to compute the costs assigned to activities and the product or service unit cost.

LO5 Define the *just-in-time (JIT) operating philosophy* and identify the elements of a JIT operating environment.

The just-in-time (JIT) operating philosophy is a management philosophy that requires that all resources—materials, personnel, and facilities—be acquired and used only as needed. Its objectives are to enhance productivity, eliminate waste, reduce costs, and improve product quality. The elements in a JIT operating environment that are designed to achieve those objectives are minimum inventory levels, pull-through production, quick setup and flexible work cells, a multiskilled work force, high levels of product quality, effective preventive maintenance, and continuous improvement of the work environment.

LO6 Identify the changes in product costing that result when a firm adopts a JIT operating environment.

In product costing under JIT, processing costs are classified as either direct materials costs or conversion costs. The costs associated with inspection time, moving time, queue time, and storage time are reduced or eliminated. With computerized monitoring of the work cells, many costs that are treated as indirect or overhead costs in traditional manufacturing settings, such as the costs of utilities and operating supplies, can be traced directly to work cells. The only costs that remain indirect costs and must be assigned to the work cells for inclusion in the overhead cost are those associated with building occupancy, insurance, and property taxes.

LO7 Define and apply *backflush costing,* and compare the cost flows in traditional and backflush costing.

In backflush costing, all product costs are first accumulated in the Cost of Goods Sold account; at the end of the accounting period, they are "flushed back," or worked backward, into the appropriate inventory accounts. Backflush costing is commonly used to account for product costs in a JIT operating environment. It differs from the traditional costing approach, which records the costs of materials purchased in the Materials Inventory account and uses the Work in Process Inventory account to record the costs of direct materials, direct labor, and overhead during the production process. The objective of backflush costing is to save recording time, which cuts costs.

LO8 Compare ABM and JIT as activity-based systems.

As activity-based systems, both ABM and JIT seek to eliminate waste and reduce nonvalue-adding activities. However, they differ in their approaches to cost assignment and calculation of product cost. ABM uses ABC to assign indirect costs to products using cost drivers; JIT reorganizes activities so that they are performed within work cells, and the overhead costs incurred in a work cell become direct costs of the products made in that cell. ABM uses job order or process costing to calculate product costs, whereas JIT may use backflush costing.

REVIEW of Concepts and Terminology

The following concepts and terms were introduced in this chapter:

Activity-based costing: A method of assigning costs that calculates a more accurate product cost than traditional methods by categorizing all indirect costs by activity, tracing the indirect costs to those activities, and assigning those costs to products using a cost driver related to the cause of the cost. **(LO4)**

Activity-based management (ABM): An approach to managing an organization that identifies all major operating activities, determines the resources consumed by each activity and the cause of the resource usage, categorizes the activities as either adding value to a product or service or not adding value, and seeks to reduce or eliminate nonvalue-adding activities. **(LO2)**

Activity-based systems: Information systems that provide quantitative information about an organization's activities. **(LO1)**

Backflush costing: A product costing approach in which all product costs are first accumulated in the Cost of Goods Sold account and at the end of the period are "flushed back," or worked backward, into the appropriate inventory accounts. **(LO7)**

Batch-level activities: Activities performed each time a batch of goods is produced. **(LO4)**

Bill of activities: A list of activities and related costs that is used to compute the costs assigned to activities and the product unit cost. **(LO4)**

Conversion costs: The sum of the direct labor costs and overhead costs incurred by a production department, work cell, or other work center. **(LO6)**

Cost hierarchy: A framework for classifying activities according to the level at which their costs are incurred. **(LO4)**

Facility-level activities: Activities performed to support a facility's general manufacturing process. **(LO4)**

Full product cost: A cost that includes not only the costs of direct materials and direct labor, but also the costs of all production and nonproduction activities required to satisfy the customer. **(LO1)**

Inspection time: The time spent looking for product flaws or reworking defective units. **(LO6)**

Just-in-time (JIT) operating philosophy: An operating philosophy that requires that all resources—materials, personnel, and facilities—be acquired and used only as needed; it focuses on eliminating or reducing waste. **(LO5)**

Moving time: The time spent moving a product from one operation or department to another. **(LO6)**

Nonvalue-adding activity: An activity that adds cost to a product or service but does not increase its market value. **(LO3)**

Processing time: The actual amount of time spent working on a product. **(LO6)**

Process value analysis (PVA): A technique that analyzes business processes by relating activities to the events that prompt those activities and to the resources that the activities consume. **(LO3)**

Product-level activities: Activities performed to support a particular product line. **(LO4)**

Pull-through production: A production system in which a customer's order triggers the purchase of materials and the scheduling of production for the required products. **(LO5)**

Push-through method: A production system in which products are manufactured in long production runs and stored in anticipation of customers' orders. **(LO5)**

Queue time: The time a product spends waiting to be worked on once it enters a new operation or department. **(LO6)**

Storage time: The time a product spends in materials storage, work in process inventory, or finished goods inventory. **(LO6)**

Supply chain: The path that leads from the suppliers of the materials from which a product is made to the final customer. **(LO2)**

Throughput time: The time it takes to move a product through the entire production process. **(LO6)**

Unit-level activities: Activities performed each time a unit is produced. **(LO4)**

Value-adding activity: An activity that adds value to a product or service as perceived by the customer. **(LO3)**

Value chain: A sequence of activities, or primary processes, that add value to a product or service; also includes support services that facilitate these activities. **(LO2)**

Work cell: An autonomous production line that can perform all required operations efficiently and continuously. **(LO5)**

REVIEW Problem

LO4 **Activity-Based Costing**

Quality Sofas Corporation produces more than a dozen styles of sofas and upholstered furniture. The eight-piece modular seating group is the most difficult to produce and the most expensive. The reclining sofa, which is the company's leading seller, is the easiest to produce. The other styles increase in difficulty of production as the number of pieces increases. Stylemaker Stores recently ordered 175 of the six-piece modular seating group. Because Quality Sofas Corporation is considering a shift to activity-based costing, its controller, Sam Overstreet, is interested in using this order to compare ABC with traditional costing. Costs directly traceable to the Stylemaker Stores order are as follows:

Direct materials	$57,290
Purchased parts	$76,410
Direct labor hours	1,320
Average direct labor pay rate per hour	$ 14.00

With the traditional costing approach, Sam Overstreet applies overhead costs at a rate of 320 percent of direct labor costs.

For activity-based costing of the Stylemaker Stores order, Overstreet uses the following data:

Activity	Cost Driver	Activity Cost Rate	Activity Usage
Product design	Engineering hours	$62 per engineering hour	76 engineering hours
Work cell setup	Number of setups	$90 per setup	16 setups
Parts production	Machine hours	$38 per machine hour	380 machine hours
Assembly	Assembly labor hours	$40 per assembly labor hour	500 assembly labor hours
Product simulation	Testing hours	$90 per testing hour	28 testing hours
Packaging and shipping	Product units	$26 per unit	175 units
Building occupancy	Direct labor cost	125% of direct labor cost	$18,480 direct labor cost

Required

1. Use the traditional costing approach to compute the total cost and product unit cost of the Stylemaker Stores order.
2. Using the cost hierarchy for manufacturing companies, classify each activity of the Stylemaker Stores order according to the level at which it occurs.
3. Prepare a bill of activities for the operating costs.
4. Use ABC to compute the total cost and product unit cost.
5. What is the difference between the product unit cost you computed using the traditional approach and the one you computed using ABC? Does the use of ABC guarantee cost reduction for every order?

Answer to Review Problem

1. Traditional costing approach:

Direct materials	$ 57,290
Purchased parts	76,410
Direct labor	18,480
Overhead (320% of direct labor cost)	59,136
Total cost of order	$ 211,316
Product unit cost (total cost ÷ 175 units)	$1,207.52

2. Activities classified by level of the manufacturing cost hierarchy:

Unit level:	Parts production
	Assembly
	Packaging and shipping
Batch level:	Work cell setup
Product level:	Product design
	Product simulation
Facility level:	Building occupancy

3, 4. Bill of activities and total cost and product unit cost computed with ABC:

Quality Sofas Corporation
Bill of Activities
Stylemaker Stores Order

Activity	Activity Cost Rate	Cost Driver Level	Activity Cost
Unit level			
Parts production	$38 per machine hour	380 machine hours	$ 14,440
Assembly	$40 per assembly labor hour	500 assembly labor hours	20,000
Packaging and shipping	$26 per unit	175 units	4,550
Batch level			
Work cell setup	$90 per setup	16 setups	1,440
Product level			
Product design	$62 per engineering hour	76 engineering hours	4,712
Product simulation	$90 per testing hour	28 testing hours	2,520
Facility level			
Building occupancy	125% of direct labor cost	$18,480 direct labor cost	23,100
Total activity costs assigned to job			$ 70,762
Total job units			÷175
Activity costs per unit (total activity costs ÷ total units)			$ 404.35
Cost summary			
Direct materials			$ 57,290
Purchased parts			76,410
Activity costs (includes labor and overhead)			70,762
Total cost of order			$ 204,462
Product unit cost (total cost of order ÷ 175 units)			$1,168.35

5. Product unit cost using traditional costing approach: $1,207.52
   Product unit cost using activity-based costing approach: 1,168.35
   Difference: $ 39.17

   Although the product unit cost computed using ABC is lower than the one computed using the traditional costing approach, ABC does not guarantee cost reduction for every product. It does improve cost traceability, which often identifies products that are undercosted or overcosted by a traditional product costing system.

CHAPTER ASSIGNMENTS

BUILDING Your Basic Knowledge and Skills

Short Exercises

LO1   Activity-Based Systems

SE 1. Amber Lutz started a retail clothing business two years ago. Lutz's first year was very successful, but sales dropped 50 percent in the second year. A friend who is a business consultant analyzed Lutz's business and came up with two basic reasons for the decline in sales: (1) Lutz has been placing orders late in each season, and (2) shipments of clothing have been arriving late and in poor condition. What measures can Lutz take to improve her business and persuade customers to return?

LO2   The Value Chain

SE 2. Which of the following activities would be part of the value chain of a manufacturing company? Which activities do not add value?

1. Product inspection
2. Machine drilling
3. Materials storage
4. Product engineering
5. Product packing
6. Cost accounting
7. Moving work in process
8. Inventory control

LO2   The Supply Chain

SE 3. Thom DuBois is developing plans to open a restaurant called Ribs 'n Slaw. He has located a building and will lease all the furniture and equipment he needs for the restaurant. Food Servers, Inc., will supply all the restaurant's personnel. Identify the components of Ribs 'n Slaw's supply chain.

LO3   Value-Adding and Nonvalue-Adding Activities

SE 4. Indicate whether the following activities of a submarine sandwich shop are value-adding (V) or nonvalue-adding (NV):

1. Purchasing sandwich ingredients
2. Storing condiments
3. Making sandwiches
4. Cleaning up the shop
5. Making home deliveries
6. Accounting for sales and costs

LO4   The Cost Hierarchy

SE 5. Engineering design is an activity that is vital to the success of any motor vehicle manufacturer. Identify the level at which engineering design would be classified in the cost hierarchy used with ABC for each of the following:

1. A maker of unique editions of luxury automobiles
2. A maker of built-to-order city and county emergency vehicles (orders are usually placed for 10 to 12 identical vehicles)
3. A maker of a line of automobiles sold throughout the world

LO4   The Cost Hierarchy

SE 6. Match the four levels of the cost hierarchy to the following activities of a blue jeans manufacturer that uses activity-based management:

1. Routine maintenance of sewing machines
2. Designing a pattern for a new style

3. Sewing seams on a garment
4. Producing 100 jeans of a certain style in a certain size

LO5 **Elements of a JIT Operating Environment**

SE 7. Maintaining minimum inventory levels and using pull-through production are important elements of a just-in-time operating environment. How does pull-through production help minimize inventories?

LO6 **Product Costing Changes in a JIT Environment**

SE 8. Aromatherapy Products Company is in the process of adopting the just-in-time operating philosophy for its lotion-making operations. Indicate which of the following overhead costs are nonvalue-adding costs (NVA) and which can be traced directly to the new lotion-making work cell (D):

1. Storage containers for work in process inventory
2. Inspection labor
3. Machine electricity
4. Machine repairs
5. Depreciation of the storage container moving equipment
6. Machine setup labor

LO7 **Backflush Costing**

SE 9. For work done during August, Pansey Company incurred direct materials costs of $120,000 and conversion costs of $260,000. The company employs a just-in-time operating philosophy and backflush costing. At the end of August, it was determined that the Work in Process Inventory account had been assigned $900 of costs, and the ending balance of the Finished Goods Inventory account was $1,300. There were no beginning inventory balances. How much was charged to the Cost of Goods Sold account during August? What was the ending balance of that account?

LO8 **Comparison of ABM and JIT**

SE 10. Hwang Corp. recently installed three just-in-time work cells in its screen-making division. The work cells will make large quantities of products for major window and door manufacturers. Should Hwang use JIT and backflush costing or ABM and ABC to account for product costs? Defend your choice of activity-based system.

Exercises

LO1 **Management Reports**

E 1. The reports that follow are from a department in an insurance company. Which report would be used for financial purposes, and which would be used for activity-based decision making? Why?

Salaries	$ 1,400	Enter claims into system	$ 2,000
Equipment	1,200	Analyze claims	1,000
Travel expenses	8,000	Suspend claims	1,500
Supplies	300	Receive inquiries	1,500
Use and occupancy	3,000	Resolve problems	400
		Process batches	3,000
		Determine eligibility	4,000
		Make copies	200
		Write correspondence	100
		Attend training	200
Total	$13,900	Total	$13,900

LO2   **The Supply Chain and Value Chain**

E 2. Indicate which of the following persons and activities associated with a lawn and garden nursery are part of the supply chain (S) and which are part of the value chain (V):

1. Plant and tree vendor
2. Purchasing potted trees
3. Computer and software company
4. Creating marketing plans
5. Advertising company
6. Scheduling delivery trucks
7. Customer service

LO2   **The Supply Chain and Value Chain**

E 3. The items in the following list are associated with a hotel. Indicate which are part of the supply chain (S) and which are part of the value chain (V).

1. Travel agency
2. Housekeeping supplies
3. Special events and promotions
4. Customer service
5. Travel bureau website
6. Tour agencies

LO3   **Value Analysis**

E 4. Libbel Enterprises has been in business for 30 years. Last year, the company purchased Chemcraft Laboratory and entered the chemical processing business. Libbel's controller prepared a process value analysis of the new operation and identified the following activities:

New product research	Product sales	Product bottling process
Solicitation of vendor bids	Packaging process	Product warranty work
Materials storage	Materials inspection	Product engineering
Product curing process	New product marketing	Purchasing of direct materials
Product scheduling	Product inspection	Finished goods storage
Product spoilage	Product delivery	Cleanup of processing areas
Customer follow-up	Materials delivery	Product mixing process

Identify the value-adding activities in this list, and classify them into the activity areas of the value chain illustrated in Figure 2 in this chapter. Prepare a separate list of the nonvalue-adding activities.

LO3   **Value-Adding Activities**

E 5. When Courtney Tybee prepared a process value analysis for her company, she identified the following primary activities. Identify the value-adding activities.

1. Production scheduling
2. Customer follow-up
3. Materials moving
4. Product inspection
5. Engineering design
6. Product marketing
7. Product sales
8. Materials storage

LO4   **The Cost Hierarchy**

E 6. Copia Electronics makes speaker systems. Its customers range from new hotels and restaurants that need specifically designed sound systems to nationwide retail outlets that order large quantities of similar products. The following activities are part of the company's operating process:

New retail product design	Purchasing of materials	Assembly labor
Retail product marketing	Building repair	Assembly line setup

Unique system design   Retail sales commissions   Building security

Unique system   Bulk packing of orders   Facility supervision
packaging

Classify each activity as unit level (UL), batch level (BL), product level (PL), or facility level (FL).

LO4   **Bill of Activities**

E 7. Lake Corporation has received an order for handheld computers from Union, LLC. A partially complete bill of activities for that order appears below. Fill in the missing data.

Lake Corporation
Bill of Activities for Union, LLC
Order Form

Activity	Activity Cost Rate	Cost Driver Level	Activity Cost
Unit level			
Parts production	$50 per machine hour	200 machine hours	$?
Assembly	$20 per direct labor hour	100 direct labor hours	?
Packaging and shipping	$12.50 per unit	400 units	?
Batch level			
Work cell setup	$100 per setup	16 setups	?
Product level			
Product design	$60 per engineering hour	80 engineering hours	?
Product simulation	$80 per testing hour	30 testing hours	?
Facility level			
Building occupancy	200% of assembly labor cost	?	?
Total activity costs assigned to job			$?
Total job units			400
Activity costs per unit (total activity costs ÷ total units)			$?
Cost summary			
Direct materials			$60,000
Purchased parts			80,000
Activity costs			?
Total cost of order			$?
Product unit cost (total cost ÷ 400 units)			$?

LO4   **Activity Cost Rates**

E 8. Compute the activity cost rates for materials handling, assembly, and design based on these data:

Materials

Cloth	$26,000
Fasteners	4,000
Purchased parts	40,000

Materials handling

Labor	$8,000
Equipment depreciation	5,000
Electrical power	2,000
Maintenance	6,000

Assembly

Machine operators	5,000

Design

Labor	5,000
Electrical power	1,000
Overhead	8,000

Output totaled 40,000 units. Each unit requires three machine hours of effort. Materials handling costs are allocated to the products based on direct materials cost. Design costs are allocated based on units produced. Assembly costs are allocated based on 500 machine operator hours.

LO5   Elements of a JIT Operating Environment

E 9. The numbered items below are concepts that underlie activity-based systems, such as ABM and JIT. Match each concept to the related lettered element(s) of a JIT operating environment.

1. Business processes are simplified.
2. The quality of the product or service is critical.
3. Employees are cross-trained.
4. Large inventories waste resources and may hide bad work.
5. Goods should be produced only when needed.
6. Equipment downtime is minimized.

a. Minimum inventory levels
b. Pull-through production
c. Quick machine setups and flexible work cells
d. A multiskilled work force
e. High levels of product quality
f. Effective preventive maintenance

LO5   Comparison of Traditional Manufacturing Environments and JIT

E 10. Identify which of the following exist in a traditional manufacturing environment and which exist in a JIT environment:

1. Large amounts of inventory
2. Complex manufacturing processes
3. A multiskilled labor force
4. Flexible work cells
5. Push-through production methods
6. Materials purchased infrequently but in large lot sizes
7. Infrequent setups

LO6   Direct and Indirect Costs in JIT and Traditional Manufacturing Environments

E 11. The cost categories in this list are typical of many manufacturing operations:

Direct materials:	Direct labor	Depreciation, machinery
Sheet steel	Engineering labor	Supervisory salaries
Iron castings	Indirect labor	Electrical power
Assembly parts:	Operating supplies	Insurance and taxes, plant
Part 24RE6	Small tools	President's salary
Part 15RF8	Depreciation, plant	Employee benefits

Identify each cost as direct or indirect, assuming that it was incurred in (1) a traditional manufacturing setting and (2) a JIT environment. State the reasons for changes in classification.

LO7 **Backflush Costing**

E 12. Conda Products Company implemented a JIT work environment in its trowel division eight months ago, and the division has been operating at near capacity since then. At the beginning of May, Work in Process Inventory and Finished Goods Inventory had zero balances. The following transactions took place last week:

May 28 Ordered, received, and used handles and sheet metal costing $11,340.
29 Direct labor costs incurred, $5,400.
29 Overhead costs incurred, $8,100.
30 Completed trowels costing $24,800.
31 Sold trowels costing $24,000.

Using backflush costing, calculate the ending balance in the Work in Process Inventory and Finished Goods Inventory accounts.

LO7 **Backflush Costing**

E 13. Good Morning Enterprises produces digital alarm clocks. It has a just-in-time assembly process and uses backflush costing to record production costs. Overhead is assigned at a rate of $17 per assembly labor hour. There were no beginning inventories in March. During March, the following operating data were generated:

Cost of direct materials purchased and used	$53,200
Direct labor costs incurred	$27,300
Overhead costs assigned	?
Assembly hours worked	3,840 hours
Ending work in process inventory	$1,050
Ending finished goods inventory	$960

Using T accounts, show the flow of costs through the backflush costing system. What is the total cost of goods sold in March?

LO8 **Comparison of ABM and JIT**

E 14. Identify each of the following as a characteristic of ABM or JIT:

1. Backflush costing
2. ABC used to assign overhead costs to the product cost
3. ABC integrated with job order or process costing systems
4. Complexity reduced by using work cells, minimizing inventories, and reducing or eliminating nonvalue-adding activities
5. Activities reorganized so that they are performed within work cells

LO8 **Comparison of ABM and JIT**

E 15. The following are excerpts from a conversation between two managers about their companies' activity-based systems. Identify the manager who works for a company that emphasizes ABM and the one who works for a company that emphasizes a JIT system.

Manager 1: We try to manage our resources effectively by monitoring operating activities. We analyze all major operating activities, and we focus on reducing or eliminating the ones that don't add value to our products.

Manager 2: We're very concerned with eliminating waste. We've designed our operations to reduce the time it takes to move, store, queue, and inspect materials. We've also reduced our inventories by buying and using materials only when we need them.

Problems

LO2, LO3 **The Value Chain and Process Value Analysis**

P 1. Lindstrom Industries, Inc., produces chain saws, weed whackers, and lawn mowers for major retail chains. Lindstrom makes these products to order in large quantities for each customer. It has adopted activity-based management, and its controller is in the process of developing an ABC system. The controller has identified the following primary activities of the company:

Product delivery	Production—assembly
Customer follow-up	Engineering design
Materials and parts purchasing	Product inspection
Materials storage	Processing areas cleanup
Materials inspection	Product marketing
Production—drilling	Building maintenance
Product packaging	Product sales
New product testing	Product rework
Finished goods storage	Production—grinding
Production—machine setup	Personnel services
Materials moving	Production scheduling

Required

1. Identify the activities that do not add value to Lindstrom's products.
2. Assist the controller's analysis by grouping the value-adding activities into the activity areas of the value chain shown in Figure 2 of this chapter.
3. **Manager Insight:** State whether each nonvalue-adding activity is necessary or unnecessary. Suggest how each unnecessary activity could be reduced or eliminated.

LO4 **Activity-Based Costing**

P 2. Boulware Products, Inc., produces printers for wholesale distributors. It has just completed packaging an order from Shawl Company for 150 printers. Before the order is shipped, the controller wants to compare the unit costs computed under the company's new activity-based costing system with the unit costs computed under its traditional costing system. Boulware's traditional costing system assigned overhead costs at a rate of 240 percent of direct labor cost.

Data for the Shawl order are as follows: direct materials, $17,552; purchased parts, $14,856; direct labor hours, 140; and average direct labor pay rate per hour, $17.

Data for activity-based costing related to processing direct materials and purchased parts for the Shawl order are as follows:

Activity	Cost Driver	Activity Cost Rate	Activity Usage
Engineering systems design	Engineering hours	$28 per engineering hour	18 engineering hours
Setup	Number of setups	$36 per setup	12 setups
Parts production	Machine hours	$37 per machine hour	82 machine hours
Product assembly	Assembly hours	$42 per assembly hour	96 assembly hours
Packaging	Number of packages	$5.60 per package	150 packages
Building occupancy	Machine hours	$10 per machine hour	82 machine hours

Required

1. Use the traditional costing approach to compute the total cost and the product unit cost of the Shawl order.
2. Using the cost hierarchy, identify each activity as unit level, batch level, product level, or facility level.
3. Prepare a bill of activities for the activity costs.
4. Use ABC to compute the total cost and product unit cost of the Shawl order.
5. **Manager Insight:** What is the difference between the product unit cost you computed using the traditional approach and the one you computed using ABC? Does the use of ABC guarantee cost reduction for every order?

LO4 **Activity Cost Rates**

P 3. Noir Company produces four versions of its model J17-21 bicycle seat. The four versions have different shapes, but their processing operations and production costs are identical. During July, these costs were incurred:

Direct materials	
Leather	$25,430
Metal frame	39,180
Bolts	3,010
Materials handling	
Labor	8,232
Equipment depreciation	4,410
Electrical power	2,460
Maintenance	5,184
Assembly	
Direct labor	13,230
Engineering design	
Labor	4,116
Electrical power	1,176
Engineering overhead	7,644
Overhead	
Equipment depreciation	7,056
Indirect labor	30,870
Supervision	17,640
Operating supplies	4,410
Electrical power	10,584
Repairs and maintenance	21,168
Building occupancy overhead	52,920

July's output totaled 29,400 units. Each unit requires three machine hours of effort. Materials handling costs are allocated to the products based on direct materials cost, engineering design costs are allocated based on units produced, and overhead is allocated based on machine hours. Assembly costs are allocated based on direct labor hours, which are estimated at 882 for July.

During July, Noir Company completed 500 bicycle seats for Job 142. The activity usage for Job 142 was as follows: direct materials, $1,150; direct labor hours, 15.

Required

1. Compute the following activity cost rates: (a) materials handling cost rate; (b) assembly cost rate, (c) engineering design cost rate, and (d) overhead rate.

2. Prepare a bill of activities for Job 142.
3. Use activity-based costing to compute the job's total cost and product unit cost.

LO6 Direct and Indirect Costs in JIT and Traditional Manufacturing Environments

P 4. Funz Company, which produces wooden toys, is about to adopt a JIT operating environment. In anticipation of the change, Letty Hernando, Funz's controller, prepared the following list of costs for December:

Wood	$3,200	Insurance, plant	$ 324
Bolts	32	President's salary	4,000
Small tools	54	Engineering labor	2,700
Depreciation, plant	450	Utilities	1,250
Depreciation, machinery	275	Building occupancy	1,740
Direct labor	2,675	Supervision	2,686
Indirect labor	890	Operating supplies	254
Purchased parts	58	Repairs and maintenance	198
Materials handling	74	Employee benefits	2,654

Required

1. Identify each cost as direct or indirect, assuming that it was incurred in a traditional manufacturing setting.
2. Identify each cost as direct or indirect, assuming that it was incurred in a just-in-time (JIT) environment.
3. Assume that the costs incurred in the JIT environment are for a work cell that completed 1,250 toy cars in December. Compute the total direct cost and the direct cost per unit for the cars produced.

LO7 Backflush Costing

P 5. Automotive Parts Company produces 12 parts for car bodies and sells them to three automobile assembly companies in the United States. The company implemented just-in-time operating and costing procedures three years ago. Overhead is applied at a rate of $26 per work cell hour used. All direct materials and purchased parts are used as they are received.

One of the company's work cells produces automotive fenders that are completely detailed and ready to install when received by the customer. The cell is operated by four employees and involves a flexible manufacturing system with 14 workstations. Operating details for February for this cell are as follows:

Beginning work in process inventory	—
Beginning finished goods inventory	$420
Cost of direct materials purchased on account and used	$213,400
Cost of parts purchased on account and used	$111,250
Direct labor costs incurred	$26,450
Overhead costs assigned	?
Work cell hours used	8,260
Costs of goods completed during February	$564,650
Ending work in process inventory	$1,210
Ending finished goods inventory	$670

Required

1. Using T accounts, show the cost flows through a backflush costing system.

2. Using T accounts, show the cost flows through a traditional costing system.
3. What is the total cost of goods sold for the month?

Alternate Problems

LO4 **Activity-Based Costing**

P 6. Kaui Company produces cellular phones. It has just completed an order for 80 phones placed by Many Hands, Ltd. Kaui recently shifted to an activity-based costing system, and its controller is interested in the impact that the ABC system had on the Many Hands order. Data for that order are as follows: direct materials, $36,950; purchased parts, $21,100; direct labor hours, 220; average direct labor pay rate per hour, $15.

Under Kaui's traditional costing system, overhead costs were assigned at a rate of 270 percent of direct labor cost.

Data for activity-based costing for the Many Hands order are as follows:

Activity	Cost Driver	Activity Cost Rate	Activity Usage
Electrical engineering design	Engineering hours	$19 per engineering hour	32 engineering hours
Setup	Number of setups	$29 per setup	11 setups
Parts production	Machine hours	$26 per machine hour	134 machine hours
Product testing	Number of tests	$32 per test	52 tests
Packaging	Number of packages	$4.675 per package	80 packages
Building occupancy	Machine hours	$9.80 per machine hour	134 machine hours
Assembly	Direct labor hours	$15 per direct labor hour	220 direct labor hours

Required

1. Use the traditional costing approach to compute the total cost and the product unit cost of the Many Hands order.
2. Using the cost hierarchy, identify each activity as unit level, batch level, product level, or facility level.
3. Prepare a bill of activities for the activity costs.
4. Use ABC to compute the total cost and product unit cost of the Many Hands order.
5. Manager Insight: What is the difference between the product unit cost you computed using the traditional approach and the one you computed using ABC? Does the use of ABC guarantee cost reduction for every order?

LO4 **Activity Cost Rates**

P 7. Alligood Company produces three models of aluminum skateboards. The models have minor differences, but their processing operations and production costs are identical. During June, these costs were incurred:

Direct materials	
Aluminum frame	$162,524
Bolts	3,876
Purchased parts	
Wheels	74,934
Decals	5,066

Materials handling (assigned based on direct materials cost)

Labor	$17,068
Utilities	4,438
Maintenance	914
Depreciation	876

Assembly line (assigned based on labor hours)

Labor	46,080

Setup (assigned based on number of setups)

Labor	6,385
Supplies	762
Overhead	3,953

Product testing (assigned based on number of tests)

Labor	2,765
Supplies	435

Building occupancy (assigned based on machine hours)

Insurance	5,767
Depreciation	2,452
Repairs and maintenance	· 3,781

For June, output totaled 32,000 skateboards. Each board required 1.5 machine hours of effort. During June, Alligood's assembly line worked 2,304 hours, performed 370 setups and 64,000 product tests, and completed an order for 1,000 skateboards placed by Executive Toys Company. The job incurred costs of $5,200 for direct materials and $2,500 for purchased parts. It required 3 setups, 2,000 tests, and 72 assembly line hours.

Required

1. Compute the following activity cost rates:
   a. Materials handling cost rate
   b. Assembly line cost rate
   c. Setup cost rate
   d. Product testing cost rate
   e. Building occupancy cost rate
2. Prepare a bill of activities for the Executive Toys job.
3. Use activity-based costing to compute the job's total cost and product unit cost. (Round your answer to two decimal places.)

LO7   **Backflush Costing**

P 8. Reilly Corporation produces metal fasteners using six work cells, one for each of its product lines. It implemented just-in-time operations and costing methods two years ago. Overhead is assigned using a rate of $14 per machine hour for the Machine Snap Work Cell. There were no beginning inventories on April 1. All direct materials and purchased parts are used as they are received. Operating details for April for the Machine Snap Work Cell are as follows:

Cost of direct materials purchased on account and used	$104,500
Cost of parts purchased on account and used	$78,900
Direct labor costs incurred	$39,000
Overhead costs assigned	?
Machine hours used	12,220
Costs of goods completed during April	$392,540

Ending work in process inventory	$940
Ending finished goods inventory	$1,020

Required

1. Using T accounts, show the flow of costs through a backflush costing system.
2. Using T accounts, show the flow of costs through a traditional costing system.
3. What is the total cost of goods sold for April using a traditional costing system?

ENHANCING Your Knowledge, Skills, and Critical Thinking

Conceptual Understanding Cases

LO5   **JIT in a Service Business**

C 1. The initiation banquet for new members of your business club is being held at an excellent restaurant. You are sitting next to two college students who are majoring in marketing. In discussing the accounting course they are taking, they mention that they are having difficulty understanding the just-in-time philosophy. They have read that the elements of a company's JIT operating system support the concepts of simplicity, continuous improvement, waste reduction, timeliness, and efficiency. They realize that to understand JIT in a complex manufacturing environment, they must first understand JIT in a simpler context. They ask you to explain the philosophy and provide an example.

Briefly explain the JIT philosophy. Apply the elements of a JIT operating system to the restaurant where the banquet is being held. Do you believe the JIT philosophy applies in all restaurant operations? Explain your answer.

LO2, LO3   **Adding Value**

C 2. In a new business model called "zero time," time is the primary focus that drives everything else in an organization. According to this model, instantaneous, or "zero-time," Internet access to relevant information allows a company to add value for customers at every point along its value chain—marketing, research and development, purchasing, production, sales, shipping, and customer service.[7]

1. Identify and comment on the primary focus of traditional business models, such as job order or process costing.
2. Speculate on how focusing on time would add value for customers throughout an organization's value chain.

LO3, LO5, LO6   **Activities, Cost Drivers, and JIT**

C 3. Fifteen years ago, Bruce Sable, together with 10 financial supporters, founded Sable Corporation. Located in Atlanta, the company originally manufactured roller skates, but 12 years ago, on the advice of its marketing department, it switched to making skateboards. More than 4 million skateboards later, Sable Corporation finds itself an industry leader in both volume and quality. To retain market share, it has decided to automate its manufacturing process. It has ordered flexible manufacturing systems for wheel assembly and board shaping. Manual operations will be retained for board decorating because some hand painting is involved. All operations will be converted to a just-in-time environment.

Bruce Sable wants to know how the JIT approach will affect the company's product costing practices and has called you in as a consultant.

1. Summarize the elements of a JIT environment.
2. How will the automated systems change product costing?
3. What are some cost drivers that the company should employ? In what situations should it employ them?

Interpreting Management Reports

LO3, LO4   **ABC and Selling and Administrative Expenses**

C 4. Sandy Star, the owner of Star Bakery, wants to know the profitability of each of her bakery's customer groups. She is especially interested in the State Institutions customer group, which is one of the company's largest customer groups. Currently, the bakery is selling doughnuts and snack foods to ten state institutions in three states. The controller has prepared the following income statement for the State Institutions customer group:

Star Bakery
Income Statement for State Institutions Customer Group
For the Year Ended December 31, 20x8

Sales ($5 per case × 50,000 cases)	$250,000
Cost of goods sold ($3.50 per case × 50,000 cases)	175,000
Gross margin	$ 75,000
Less: Selling and administrative activity costs	94,750
Operating income (loss) contributed by State Institutions customer group	($19,750)

Activity	Activity Cost Rate	Actual Cost Driver Level	Activity Cost
Make sales calls	$60 per sales call	60 sales calls	$ 3,600
Prepare sales orders	$10 per sales order	900 sales orders	9,000
Handle inquiries	$5 per minute	1,000 minutes	5,000
Ship products	$1 per case sold	50,000 cases	50,000
Process invoices	$20 per invoice	950 invoices	19,000
Process credits	$20 per notice	40 notices	800
Process billings and collections	$7 per billing	1,050 billings	7,350
Total selling and administrative activity costs			94,750

The controller has also provided budgeted information about selling and administrative activities for the State Institutions customer group. For 20x8, the planned activity cost rates and the annual cost driver levels for each selling and administrative activity are as follows:

Activity	Activity Cost Rate	Planned Annual Cost Driver Level
Make sales calls	$60 per sales call	59 sales calls
Prepare sales orders	$10 per sales order	850 sales orders
Handle inquiries	$5.10 per minute	1,000 minutes
Ship products	$.60 per case sold	50,000 cases
Process invoices	$1 per invoice	500 invoices
Process credits	$10 per notice	5 notices
Process billings and collections	$4 per billing	600 billings

You have been called in as a consultant on the State Institutions customer group.

1. Calculate the planned activity cost for each activity.
2. Calculate the differences between the planned activity cost and the State Institutions customer group's activity costs for 20x8.
3. From your evaluation of the differences calculated in **2** and your review of the income statement, identify the nonvalue-adding activities and state which selling and administrative activities should be examined.
4. What actions might the company take to reduce the costs of nonvalue-adding selling and administrative activities?

Decision Analysis Using Excel

LO3, LO4 **ABC in Planning and Control**

C 5. Refer to the income statement in **C 4** for the State Institutions customer group for the year ended December 31, 20x8. Sandy Star, the owner of Star Bakery, is in the process of budgeting income for 20x9. She has asked the controller to prepare a budgeted income statement for the State Institutions customer group. She estimates that the selling price per case, the number of cases sold, the cost of goods sold per case, and the activity costs for making sales calls, preparing sales orders, and handling inquiries will remain the same for 20x9. She has contracted with a new freight company to ship the 50,000 cases at $.60 per case sold. She has also analyzed the procedures for invoicing, processing credits, billing, and collecting and has decided that it would be less expensive for a customer service agency to do the work. The agency will charge the bakery 1.5 percent of the total sales revenue.

1. Prepare a budgeted income statement for the State Institutions customer group for the year ended December 31, 20x9.
2. Refer to the information in **C 4**. Assuming that the planned activity cost rate and planned annual cost driver level for each selling and administrative activity remain the same in 20x9, calculate the planned activity cost for each activity.
3. Calculate the differences between the planned activity costs (determined in requirement **2**) and the State Institutions customer group's budgeted activity costs for 20x9 (determined in **1**).
4. Evaluate the results of changing freight companies and outsourcing the customer service activities.

Ethical Dilemma Case

LO5 **Ethics and JIT Implementation**

C 6. For almost a year, Traki Company has been changing its manufacturing process from a traditional to a JIT approach. Management has asked for employees' assistance in the transition and has offered bonuses for suggestions that cut time from the production operation. Deb Hinds and Jack Snow each identified a time-saving opportunity and turned in their suggestions to their manager, Randall Soder.

Soder sent the suggestions to the committee charged with reviewing employees' suggestions, which inadvertently identified them as being Soder's own. The committee decided that the two suggestions were worthy of reward and voted a large bonus for Soder. When notified of this, Soder could not bring himself to identify the true authors of the suggestions.

When Hinds and Snow heard about Soder's bonus, they confronted him with his fraudulent act and expressed their grievances. He told them that he needed the recognition to be eligible for an upcoming promotion and promised that if they kept quiet about the matter, he would make sure that they both received significant raises. Prepare written responses to the following questions so that you can discuss them in class:

1. Should Hinds and Snow keep quiet? What other options are open to them?
2. How should Soder have dealt with Hinds's and Snow's complaints?

Internet Case

LO3 **Value-Adding and Nonvalue-Adding Activities**

C7. **Levi Strauss & Co.** has been making jeans since 1853. Today, it manufactures different types of jeans for different market segments. For example, **Wal-Mart** sells Levi Strauss's Signature brand of jeans for about $15 less than department stores sell the company's Levi's brand.[8]

Visit the Levi Strauss website to learn more about the company's brands. What value-adding production and nonproduction activities do you think might account for the higher price of the Levi's brand? Which of these activities do you think Levi Strauss would eliminate for the less costly Signature brand? (By visiting the website, you can also discover what Levi Strauss called jeans when it first sold them 150 years ago, as well as the year in which the company officially changed the name to "jeans.")

Group Activity Case

LO4 **ABM and ABC in a Service Business**

C 8. Kendle and Watson, a CPA firm, has provided audit and tax services to businesses in the London area for over 50 years. Recently, the firm decided to use ABM and activity-based costing to assign its overhead costs to those service functions. Bellamy Kendle is interested in seeing how the change from the traditional to the activity-based costing approach affects the average cost per audit job. The following information has been provided to assist in the comparison:

Total direct labor costs	£400,000
Other direct costs	120,000
Total direct costs	£520,000

The traditional costing approach assigned overhead costs at a rate of 120 percent of direct labor costs.

Data for activity-based costing of the audit function are as follows:

Activity	Cost Driver	Activity Cost Rate	Activity Usage
Professional development	Number of employees	£2,000 per employee	50 employees
Administration	Number of jobs	£1,000 per job	50 jobs
Client development	Number of new clients	£5,000 per new client	29 new clients

1. Using direct labor cost as the cost driver, calculate the total costs for the audit function. What is the average cost per job?
2. Using activity-based costing to assign overhead, calculate the total costs for the audit function. What is the average cost per job?

3. Calculate the difference in total costs between the two approaches. Why would activity-based costing be the better approach for assigning overhead to the audit function?

4. Your instructor will divide the class into groups to work through the case. One student from each group should present the group's findings to the class.

Business Communication Cases

LO5 **JIT Production**

C 9. To compete for new domestic and foreign business, many large, multinational companies, as well as many smaller firms, have installed automated just-in-time production processes. Locate an article about a company that has recently installed a JIT system or an annual report from such a company. Conduct your search using an Internet search engine like Google and a business periodical like *The Wall Street Journal*.

Choose a source that describes the changes the company made to its plant to increase product quality and to compete as a world-class manufacturer. Prepare a one-page description of those changes. Include in your report the name of the company, its location, the name of the chief executive officer and/or president, and, if available, the dollar amount of the company's total sales for the most recent year. Be prepared to present your findings in class.

LO5 **Manufacturing Processes**

C 10. Classic Clubs, Inc., manufactures professional golf clubs in a continuous manufacturing process. Demand has been so great that the company has built a special plant that makes only custom-crafted clubs. The clubs are shaped by machines but vary according to the customer's sex, height, weight, and arm length. Ten basic sets of clubs are produced, five for females and five for males. Slight variations in machine setup produce the differences in the club weights and lengths.

In the past six months, several problems have developed. Even though a computer-controlled machine is used in the manufacturing process, the company's backlog is growing rapidly, and customers are complaining that delivery is too slow. Quality is declining because clubs are being pushed through production without proper inspection. Working capital is tied up in excessive amounts of inventory and storage space. Workers are complaining about the pressure to produce the backlogged orders. Machine breakdowns are increasing. Production control reports are not useful because they are not timely and contain irrelevant information. The company's profitability and cash flow are suffering.

Classic Clubs has hired you as a consultant to analyze its problems and suggest a solution. Denise Rodeburg, the president, asks that you complete your work within a month so that she can prepare a plan to present to the board of directors at the midyear board meeting.

1. In memo form, prepare a report for Rodeburg recommending specific changes in the manufacturing processes.
2. In preparing the report, answer the following questions:
   a. Why are you preparing the report? What is its purpose?
   b. Who is the audience for this report?
   c. What kinds of information do you need to prepare the report, and where will you find it (i.e., what sources will you use)?
   d. When do you need to obtain the information?

Cost Behavior Analysis

Knowing how costs will behave is essential knowledge for managers as they chart their organization's course and make ethical decisions on behalf of all the organization's stakeholders. Managers commonly analyze alternative courses of action using cost behavior information so they can select the course that will best generate income for an organization's owners, maintain liquidity for its creditors, and use the organization's resources responsibly. Thus, analysis of cost behavior is important not only in achieving profitability, but also in using resources wisely.

LEARNING OBJECTIVES

LO1 Define *cost behavior* and explain how managers use this concept.

LO2 Identify variable, fixed, and mixed costs, and separate mixed costs into their variable and fixed components.

LO3 Define *cost-volume-profit (C-V-P) analysis* and discuss how managers use it as a tool for planning and control.

LO4 Define *breakeven point* and use contribution margin to determine a company's breakeven point for multiple products.

LO5 Use C-V-P analysis to project the profitability of products and services.

- How does Kraft decide which products to offer?
- Why do Kraft's managers analyze cost behavior to project the profitability of the company's core sectors?

Kraft, Philadelphia, Maxwell House, Nabisco, Oscar Mayer, Jell-O, and Post are among the brands that **Kraft Foods** brings to households around the world. The company has five core sectors—snacks and cereals, beverages, cheese, grocery, and convenience meals—and locations in more than 155 countries around the globe. Kraft's 98,000 employees work to make food a simpler, easier, and more enjoyable part of life by adding innovative products and optimizing line and geographic extensions of current offerings.[1]

The types and numbers of products that Kraft makes and sells vary from year to year depending on shoppers' preferences. The challenge for Kraft's management is to offer a product mix that excites consumers and allows the company to charge higher prices at the supermarket.

Cost Behavior and Management

Cost behavior—the way costs respond to changes in volume or activity—is a factor in almost every decision managers make. Managers commonly use it to analyze alternative courses of action so they can select the course that will best generate income for an organization's owners and maintain liquidity for its creditors. Figure 1 shows how managers use cost behavior to plan, perform, evaluate, and communicate.

Planning

When managers plan, they use cost behavior to determine how many units of products or services must be sold to generate a targeted amount of profit and how changes in planned operating, investing, and financing activities will affect operating income. For example, when **Kraft's** managers launched a product

FIGURE 1
The Management Process: To-Do's for Managers

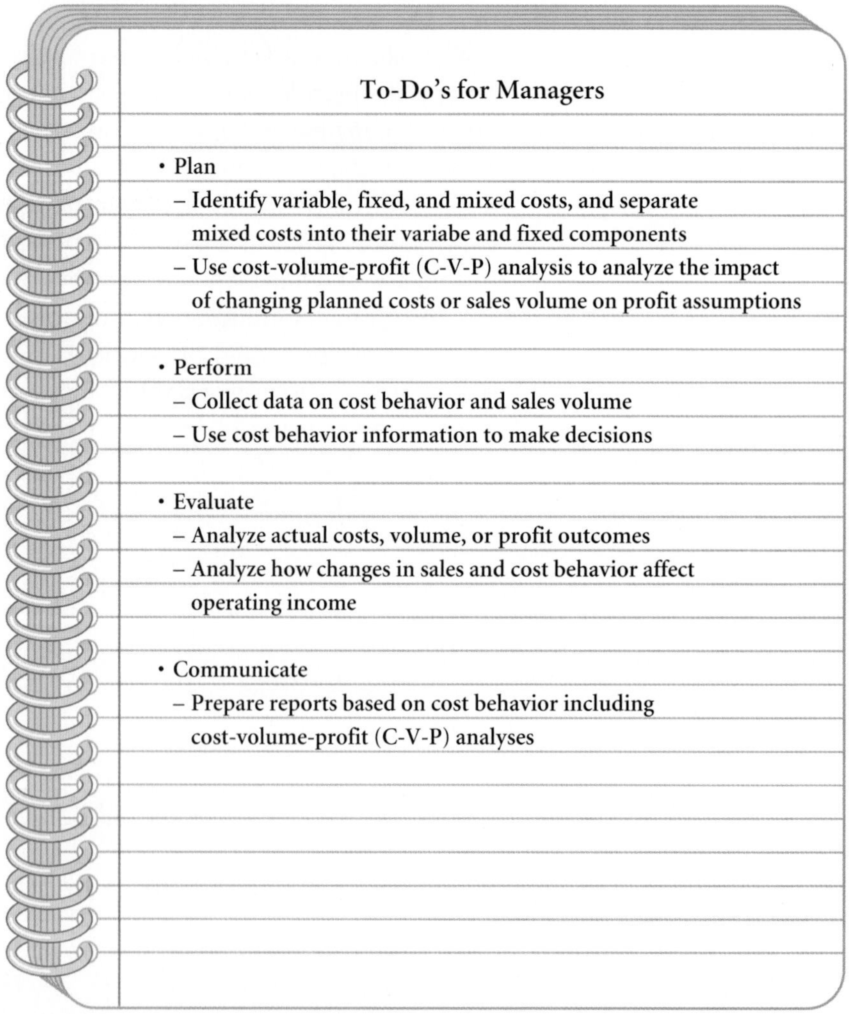

To-Do's for Managers

- Plan
  - Identify variable, fixed, and mixed costs, and separate mixed costs into their variabe and fixed components
  - Use cost-volume-profit (C-V-P) analysis to analyze the impact of changing planned costs or sales volume on profit assumptions

- Perform
  - Collect data on cost behavior and sales volume
  - Use cost behavior information to make decisions

- Evaluate
  - Analyze actual costs, volume, or profit outcomes
  - Analyze how changes in sales and cost behavior affect operating income

- Communicate
  - Prepare reports based on cost behavior including cost-volume-profit (C-V-P) analyses

called Boca, they used cost behavior to analyze how offering two flavors of this soy-based burger would contribute to the organization's operating income.

Service-based businesses like **Google** also find cost behavior analyses useful to determine the optimal mix of services to offer. For example, Google's managers analyze cost behavior of new products like Writely, a free Web-based word processor, or Gmail, an email program with upward of two to six gigabytes of storage space in their online Google Labs to gather user data and feedback before officially deciding to add a new feature.

Performing

As we have noted, managers use information about cost behavior in almost every decision they make. Throughout the year, managers at **Kraft** and at service businesses like **Google, Sprint,** and **Verizon** must understand and anticipate cost behavior to determine the impact of their actions on operating income. For example, Google's managers must understand the changes in income that can result from buying new, more productive servers or launching an online advertising product like AdWords or AdSense.

Evaluating and Communicating

When evaluating operations and preparing reports for various product or service lines or geographic regions, managers in all types of organizations, including businesses like **Kraft, Google, Federal Express,** and **UPS,** need to understand cost behavior. As you will learn later in the chapter, cost-volume-profit reports, such as a contribution margin income statement (sometimes referred

to as a variable costing income statement), are commonly used to analyze how changes in cost and sales affect the profitability of product lines, sales territories, customers, departments, and other segments. Other reports based on cost behavior are used when deciding whether to eliminate a product line, accept a special order, or outsource services.

S T O P • R E V I E W • A P P L Y

1-1. Define *cost behavior*.

1-2. Why is an understanding of cost behavior useful to managers?

Suggested answers to all Stop, Review, and Apply questions are available at http://college.hmco.com/accounting/needles/poa/10e/student_home.html.

The Behavior of Costs

> **LO2**   Identify variable, fixed, and mixed costs, and separate mixed costs into their variable and fixed components.

Although our focus in this chapter is on cost behavior as it relates to products and services, cost behavior can also be observed in selling, administrative, and general activities. For example, increases in the number of shipments affect shipping costs; the number of units sold or total sales revenue affects the cost of sales commissions; and the number of customers billed or the number of hours needed to bill affects total billing costs. If managers can predict how costs behave, then costs become manageable.

Some costs vary with volume or operating activity (variable costs). Others remain fixed as volume changes (fixed costs). Between those two extremes are costs that exhibit characteristics of each type (mixed costs).

Variable Costs

Study Note

Variable costs change in *direct proportion* to changes in activity; that is, they increase *in total* with an increase in volume and decrease *in total* with a decrease in volume, but they remain the same on a *per unit* basis.

Total costs that change in direct proportion to changes in productive output (or any other measure of volume) are called **variable costs**. To explore how variable costs work, consider the tire costs of Land Rover, a maker of off-road vehicles. Each new vehicle has four tires, and each tire costs $48. The total cost of tires, then, is $192 for one vehicle, $384 for two, $960 for five, $1,920 for ten, $19,200 for one hundred, and so on. In the production of off-road vehicles, the total cost of tires is a variable cost. On a per unit basis, however, a variable cost remains constant. In this case, the cost of tires per vehicle is $192 whether the automaker produces one vehicle or one hundred vehicles. True, the cost of tires will vary depending on the number purchased if discounts are available for purchases of large quantities. But once the purchase has been made, the cost per tire is established.

Figure 2 illustrates other examples of variable costs. All those costs—whether incurred by a manufacturer like **Kraft, La-Z-Boy,** or **Intel,** a service business like **Google,** or a merchandiser like **Wal-Mart**—are variable based on either productive output or total sales.

Operating Capacity   Because variable costs increase or decrease in direct proportion to volume or output, it is important to know an organization's operating capacity. **Operating capacity** is the upper limit of an organization's

■ **FIGURE 2**
Examples of Variable, Fixed, and Mixed Costs

Costs	Manufacturing Company—Tire Manufacturer	Merchandising Company—Department Store	Service Company—Bank
VARIABLE	Direct materials Direct labor (hourly) Indirect labor (hourly) Operating supplies Small tools	Merchandise to sell Sales commissions Shelf stockers (hourly)	Computer equipment leasing (based on usage) Computer operators (hourly) Operating supplies Data storage disks

FIXED	Depreciation, machinery
	  and building
	Insurance premiums
	Labor (salaried)
	Supervisory salaries
	Property taxes (on machinery
	  and building)
		Depreciation, building
		Insurance premiums
		Buyers (salaried)
		Supervisory salaries
		Property taxes (on equipment
		  and building)
			Depreciation, furniture and fixtures
			Insurance premiums
			Salaries:
			  Programmers
			  Systems designers
			  Bank administrators
			Rent, buildings

MIXED	Electrical power Telephone Heat	Electrical power Telephone Heat	Electrical power Telephone Heat

productive output capability, given its existing resources. It describes just what an organization can accomplish in a given period. Operating capacity can be expressed in several ways, including total labor hours, total machine hours, and total units of output. Any increase in volume or activity over operating capacity requires additional expenditures for buildings, machinery, personnel, and operations. When additional operating capacity is added, cost behavior patterns can change. In our discussion of those patterns, we assume that operating capacity is constant and that all activity occurs within the limits of current operating capacity.

There are three common measures, or types, of operating capacity: theoretical, or ideal, capacity; practical capacity; and normal capacity. **Theoretical (ideal) capacity** is the maximum productive output for a given period in which all machinery and equipment are operating at optimum speed, without interruption. In a just-in-time operating environment, the long-term goal is to approach theoretical capacity through continuous improvement; however, no company ever actually operates at such an ideal level. **Practical capacity** is theoretical capacity reduced by normal and expected work stoppages, such as machine breakdowns; downtime for retooling, repairs, and maintenance; and employees' breaks. Although theoretical capacity and practical capacity are

Study Note

In a just-in-time operating environment, theoretical (ideal) capacity is used as a benchmark, a relatively constant reference point against which to measure improvement.

useful when estimating maximum production levels, neither measure is realistic when planning operations. Practical capacity is sometimes called *engineering capacity*.

When planning operations, managers use **normal capacity**, which is the average annual level of operating capacity needed to meet expected sales demand. The sales demand figure is adjusted for seasonal changes and industry and economic cycles. Normal capacity is therefore a realistic measure of what an organization is *likely* to produce, not what it *can* produce. Each variable cost should be related to an appropriate measure of normal capacity, but often more than one measure of normal capacity applies. Operating costs can be related to machine hours used or total units produced. Sales commissions, on the other hand, usually vary in direct proportion to total sales dollars.

The basis for measuring the activity of variable costs should be carefully selected for two reasons. First, an appropriate activity base simplifies cost planning and control. Second, managers must combine (aggregate) many variable costs with the same activity base so that the costs can be analyzed in a reasonable way. Such aggregation also provides information that allows management to predict future costs.

The general guide for selecting an activity base is to relate costs to their most logical or causal factor. For example, machinery setup costs should be considered variable in relation to the number of setups needed for a particular job. This will allow machinery setup costs to be budgeted and controlled more effectively.

Linear Relationships and the Relevant Range The traditional definition of a variable cost assumes that costs go up or down as volume increases or decreases, as demonstrated by the linear relationship in the tire example we cited earlier. Figure 3 shows a similar straight-line relationship. There, each unit of output requires $2.50 of labor cost. Total labor costs grow in direct proportion to the increase in units of output. For two units, total labor costs are $5.00; for six units, the organization incurs $15.00 in labor costs.

Many costs, however, vary with operating activity in a nonlinear fashion. Graph A in Figure 4 shows the behavior of power costs as usage increases and the unit cost of power consumption falls. Graph B shows the behavior of rental

Study Note

An activity base is often called *denominator activity*; it is the activity for which relationships are established. The basic relationships should not change greatly if activity fluctuates around the level of denominator activity.

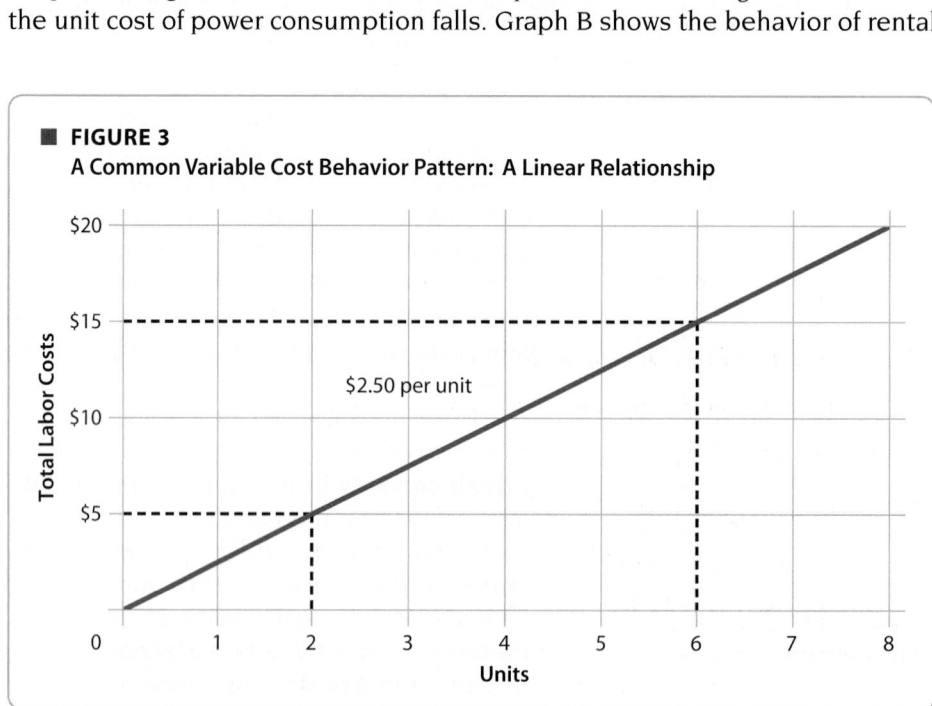

■ **FIGURE 3**
A Common Variable Cost Behavior Pattern: A Linear Relationship

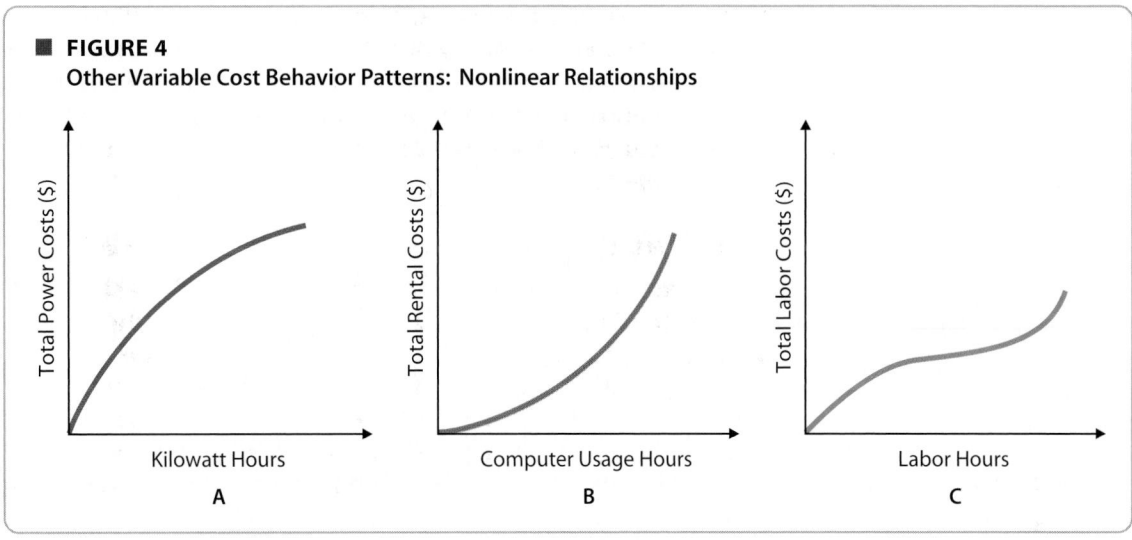

■ **FIGURE 4**
Other Variable Cost Behavior Patterns: Nonlinear Relationships

> Study Note
>
> Nonlinear costs can be roughly estimated by treating them as if they were linear (variable) costs within set limits of volume.

costs when each additional hour of computer usage costs more than the previous hour. Graph C shows how labor costs vary as efficiency increases and decreases. These three nonlinear cost patterns are variable in nature, but they differ from the linear variable cost pattern shown in Figure 3.

Variable costs with linear relationships to a volume measure are easy to analyze and project for cost planning and control. Nonlinear variable costs are not easy to use. But all costs must be included in an analysis if the results are to be useful to management. To simplify cost analysis procedures and make variable costs easier to use, accountants have developed a method of converting nonlinear variable costs into linear variable costs. Called *linear approximation*, this method relies on the concept of relevant range. **Relevant range** is the span of activity in which a company expects to operate. Within the relevant range, it is assumed that both total fixed costs and per unit variable costs are constant. Under that assumption, many nonlinear costs can be estimated using the linear approximation approach illustrated in Figure 5. Those estimated costs can then be treated as part of the other variable costs.

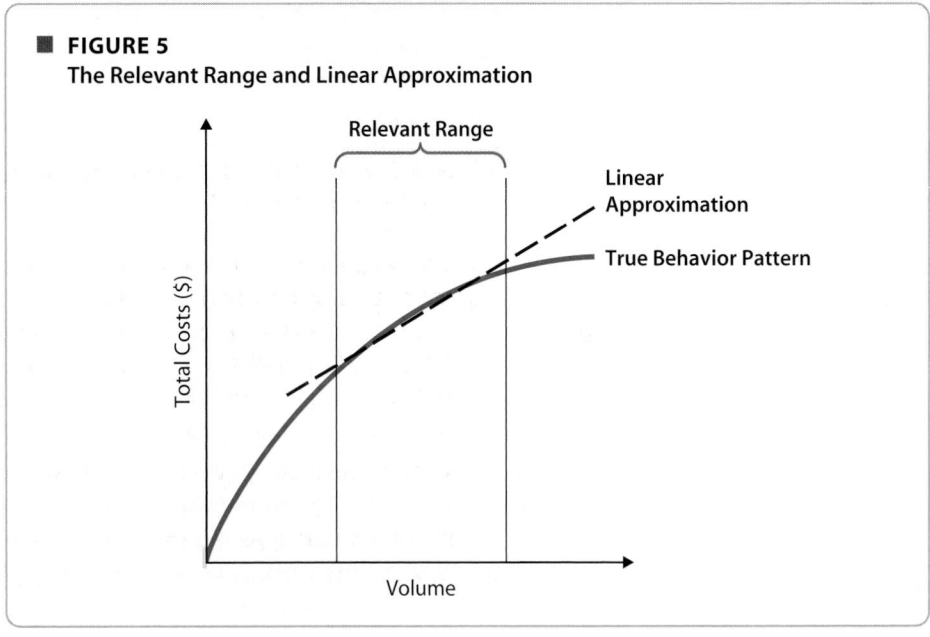

■ **FIGURE 5**
The Relevant Range and Linear Approximation

A linear approximation of a nonlinear variable cost is not a precise measure, but it allows the inclusion of nonlinear variable costs in cost behavior analysis, and the loss of accuracy is usually not significant. The goal is to help management estimate costs and prepare budgets, and linear approximation helps accomplish that goal.

Fixed Costs

Study Note

Because fixed costs are expected to hold relatively constant over the entire relevant range of activity, they can be described as the costs of providing capacity.

Study Note

Cost behavior is closely linked to the concept of cost control. In the short run, it is generally easier to control variable costs than fixed costs.

Fixed costs behave very differently from variable costs. **Fixed costs** are total costs that remain constant within a relevant range of volume or activity—that is, the range in which actual operations are likely to occur. Look back at Figure 2 for examples of fixed costs. The manufacturer, the department store, and the bank all incur depreciation costs and fixed annual insurance premiums. In addition, all salaried personnel have fixed earnings for a particular period. The manufacturer and the department store own their buildings and pay annual property taxes, and the bank pays an annual fixed rental charge for the use of its building.

According to economic theory, all costs tend to be variable in the long run; thus, as the examples in Figure 2 suggest, a cost is fixed only within a limited period. A change in plant capacity, machinery, labor needs, or other production factors causes fixed costs to increase or decrease. For planning, management usually considers a one-year period, and fixed costs are expected to be constant within that period.

Of course, fixed costs change when activity exceeds the relevant range. For example, assume that a manufacturer of aluminum cans needs one supervisor for an eight-hour work shift. Production can range from zero to 500,000 units (cans) per month per shift. The relevant range, then, is from zero to 500,000 units. The supervisor's salary is $4,000 per month. The cost behavior analysis is as follows:

Units of Output per Month	Total Supervisory Salaries per Month
0–500,000	$4,000
Over 500,000–1,000,000	$8,000

If a maximum of 500,000 units can be produced per month per shift, output over 500,000 units would require another shift and another supervisor. Like all fixed costs, the new fixed cost remains constant in total within the new relevant range.

What about unit costs? Fixed unit costs vary inversely with activity or volume. On a per unit basis, fixed costs go down as volume goes up, as long as a firm is operating within the relevant range of activity. Look at how supervisory costs per unit fall as the volume of activity increases within the relevant range:

Volume of Activity	Supervisory Cost per Unit
100,000 units	$4,000 ÷ 100,000 = $.0400
300,000 units	$4,000 ÷ 300,000 = $.0133
500,000 units	$4,000 ÷ 500,000 = $.0080
600,000 units	$8,000 ÷ 600,000 = $.0133

At 600,000 units, the activity level is above the relevant range, which means another shift must be added and another supervisor must be hired; thus, the per unit cost increases to $.0133.

Figure 6 shows this behavior pattern. The fixed supervisory costs for the first 500,000 units of production are $4,000. Those costs hold steady at $4,000

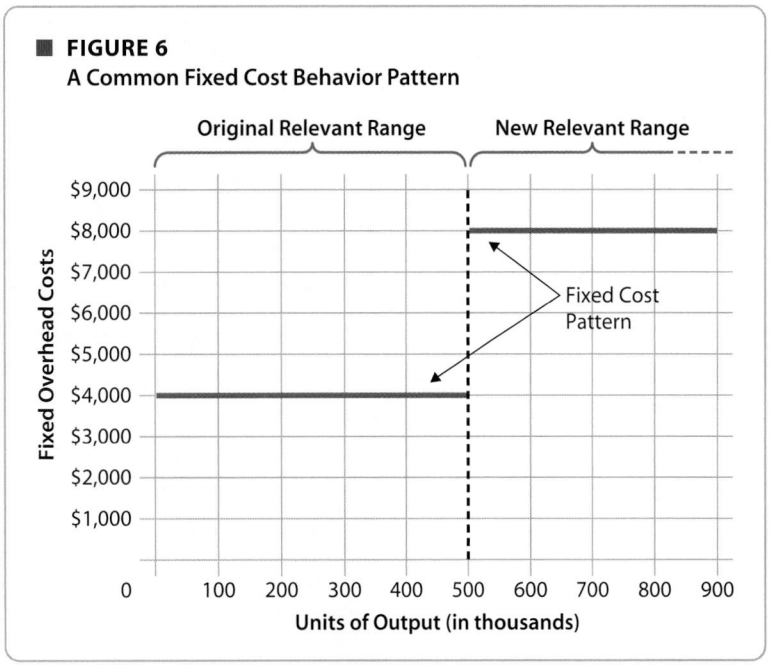

■ **FIGURE 6**
A Common Fixed Cost Behavior Pattern

for any level of output within the relevant range. But if output goes above 500,000 units, another supervisor must be hired, pushing fixed supervisory costs to $8,000.

Mixed Costs

Mixed costs have both variable and fixed cost components. Part of a mixed cost changes with volume or usage, and part is fixed over a particular period. Monthly electricity costs are an example. Such costs include charges per kilo-watt hour used plus a basic monthly service charge. The kilowatt-hour charges are variable because they depend on the amount of use; the monthly service charge is a fixed cost.

Graph A in Figure 7 depicts an organization's total electricity costs. The monthly bill begins with a fixed service charge and increases as kilowatt hours

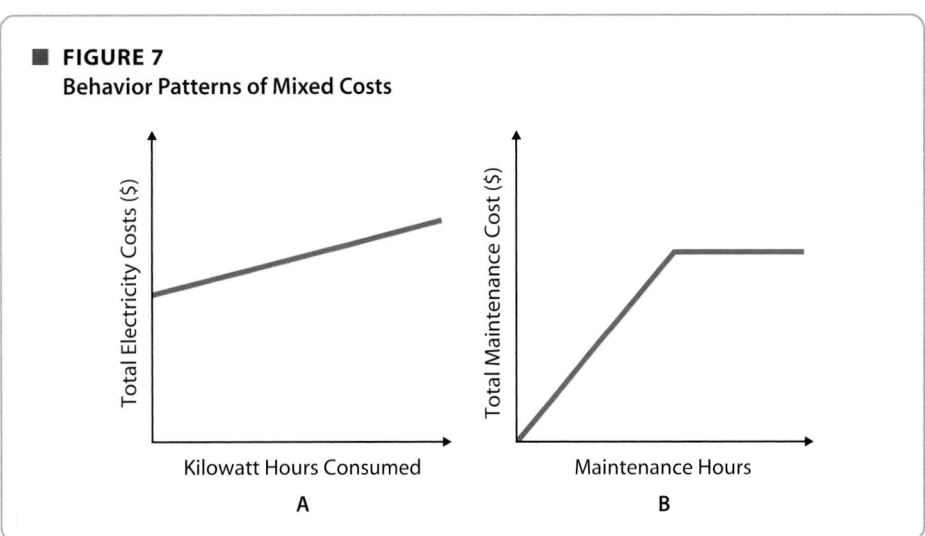

■ **FIGURE 7**
Behavior Patterns of Mixed Costs

Study Note

A business's cost accounts often fall into the mixed-cost category.

Like most businesses, the U.S. Postal Service is concerned about delivery time. To determine how many deliveries a postal worker should be able to make within a certain period, it conducts periodic audits using the engineering method (a type of analysis that is also known as a *time and motion study*). To speed delivery time, it has provided some of its workers with Segways, such as the one shown here.

are consumed. Graph B illustrates a special contractual arrangement. Here, the annual cost of equipment maintenance provided by an outside company increases for each maintenance hour worked, up to a maximum amount per period. After the maximum is reached, additional maintenance is done at no cost.

For cost planning and control purposes, mixed costs must be divided into their variable and fixed components. The separate components can then be grouped with other variable and fixed costs for analysis. Four methods are commonly used to separate costs into their variable and fixed components: the engineering, scatter diagram, high-low, and statistical methods. Because the results yielded by each of these methods are likely to differ, managers often use multiple approaches before determining the best possible estimate for a mixed cost.

The Engineering Method The **engineering method** of separating costs measures the work required by performing a step-by-step analysis of the tasks, costs, and processes involved. It is generally used to estimate the cost of activities and new products. For example, the U.S. Postal Service conducts periodic audits of how many letters a postal worker should be able to deliver on a particular mail route within a certain period. This type of analysis is sometimes called a *time and motion study*. The engineering method is expensive to use because it is so detailed. In addition, this method requires the expertise of engineers to determine the cost of a new product or activity for which no prior data exist.

The Scatter Diagram Method When there is doubt about the behavior pattern of a particular cost, especially a mixed cost, it helps to plot past costs and related measures of volume in a scatter diagram. A **scatter diagram** is a chart of plotted points that helps determine whether a linear relationship exists between a cost item and its related activity measure. It is a form of linear approximation. If the diagram suggests a linear relationship, a cost line can be imposed on the data by either visual means or statistical analysis.

Suppose, for example, that the Piedmont Corporation's Park Division incurred the following machine hours and electricity costs last year:

Month	Machine Hours	Electricity Costs
January	6,250	$ 24,000
February	6,300	24,200
March	6,350	24,350
April	6,400	24,600
May	6,300	24,400
June	6,200	24,300
July	6,100	23,900
August	6,050	23,600
September	6,150	23,950
October	6,250	24,100
November	6,350	24,400
December	6,450	24,700
Totals	$75,150	$290,500

Figure 8 shows a scatter diagram of these data. The diagram suggests a linear relationship between machine hours and the cost of electricity. If we were to add a line to the diagram to represent the linear relationship, the estimated fixed electricity cost would occur at the point at which the line intersects the vertical axis. The variable cost per unit can be estimated by determining the slope of the line, much as is done in Step 1 of the high-low method.

The High-Low Method   The **high-low method** is a common, three-step approach to determining the variable and fixed components of a mixed cost. It is based on the premise that only two data points are necessary to define a linear cost-volume relationship. It is a relatively crude method since it uses only the high and low data observations to predict cost behavior. The disadvantage of this method is that if one or both data points are not representative of the remaining data set, the estimate of variable and fixed costs may not be accurate. Its advantage is that it can be used when only limited data are available. The method involves three steps.

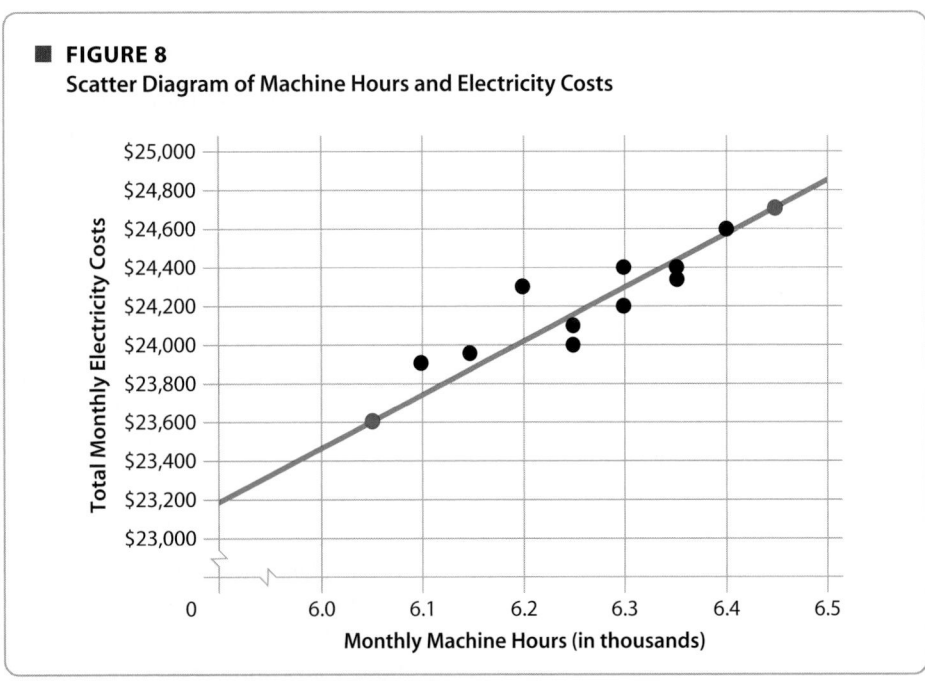

■ **FIGURE 8**
Scatter Diagram of Machine Hours and Electricity Costs

⌐⏋Study Note

A scatter diagram shows how closely volume and costs are correlated. A tight, closely associated group of data is better for linear approximation than a random or circular pattern of data points.

Step 1. *Calculate the variable cost per activity base.* Select the periods of highest and lowest activity within the accounting period. In our example, the Park Division experienced its highest machine-hour activity in December and its lowest machine-hour activity in August. Find the difference between the highest and lowest amounts for both the machine hours and their related electricity costs:

Volume	Month	Activity Level	Cost
Highest	December	6,450 machine hours	$24,700
Lowest	August	6,050 machine hours	23,600
Difference		400 machine hours	$ 1,100

To determine the variable cost per machine hour, divide the difference in cost by the difference in machine hours:

$$\text{Variable Cost per Machine Hour} = \$1,100 \div 400 \text{ Machine Hours}$$
$$= \$2.75 \text{ per Machine Hour}$$

Step 2. *Calculate the total fixed costs.* Compute total fixed costs for a month by selecting the information from the month with either the highest or the lowest volume. Here, we use the month with the highest volume:

$$\text{Total Fixed Costs} = \text{Total Costs} - \text{Total Variable Costs}$$
$$\text{Total Fixed Costs for December} = \$24,700.00 - (6,450 \times \$2.75) = \$6,962.50$$

You can check your answer by recalculating total fixed costs using the month with the lowest activity. Total fixed costs will be the same:

$$\text{Total Fixed Costs for August} = \$23,600.00 - (6,050 \times \$2.75) = \$6,962.50$$

Step 3. *Calculate the formula to estimate the total costs within the relevant range:*

$$\text{Total Costs per Month} = \$6,962.50 + \$2.75 \text{ per Machine Hour}$$

Remember that the cost formula will work only within the relevant range. In this example, the formula would work for amounts between 6,050 machine hours and 6,450 machine hours. To estimate the electricity costs for machine hours outside the relevant range (in this case, below 6,050 machine hours or above 6,450 machine hours), a new cost formula must be calculated.

Statistical Methods Statistical methods, such as **regression analysis**, mathematically describe the relationship between costs and activities. Because all data observations are used, the resulting linear equation is more representative of cost behavior than either the high-low or scatter diagram methods. Regression analysis can be performed using one or more activities to predict costs. For example, overhead costs can be predicted using only machine hours (a simple regression analysis), or they can be predicted using both machine hours and labor hours (a multiple regression analysis) because both activities affect overhead. We leave further description of regression analysis to statistics courses, which provide detailed coverage of this method. •

S T O P • R E V I E W • A P P L Y

2-1. What is normal capacity? Why is normal capacity considered more relevant and useful than either theoretical or practical capacity?

2-2. What does relevant range of activity mean?

2-3. "Fixed costs remain constant in total but decrease per unit as productive output increases." Explain this statement.

2-4. What is a mixed cost? Give an example.

The High-Low Method   Using the high-low method and the information below, compute the monthly variable cost per kilowatt hour and the monthly fixed electricity cost for GLE Corporation.

Month	Kilowatt Hours Used	Electricity Expenses
April	90	$450
May	80	430
June	70	420

SOLUTION

Volume	Month	Activity Level	Cost
High	April	90 hours	$450
Low	June	70 hours	420
Difference		20 hours	$ 30

$$\text{Variable cost per kilowatt hour} = \$30 \div 20 \text{ hours}$$
$$= \$1.50 \text{ per hour}$$

Fixed costs for April: $450 − (90 × $1.50) = $315

Fixed costs for June: $420 − (70 × $1.50) = $315

Cost-Volume-Profit Analysis

LO3   Define *cost-volume-profit (C-V-P) analysis* and discuss how managers use it as a tool for planning and control.

Like **Kraft Foods**, many companies produce and distribute a variety of products and services. For example, a division of **Sony Corporation,** Sony Records, makes compact disks (CDs). Producing these CDs is a complex process that requires hiring and organizing hundreds of people, including

To make and market its compact disks, Sony Records has to hire and organize hundreds of people, including singers like Joss Stone, who is shown here posing for photographs at the Sony Studios in New York. To determine how many CDs it must sell just to break even and what the profit will be if the CD is a hit, Sony uses cost-volume-profit analysis. C-V-P analysis is also an important tool in setting sales targets.

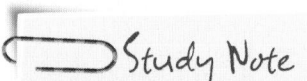

One of the important benefits of C-V-P analysis is that it allows managers to adjust different variables and to evaluate how these changes affect profit.

musicians, and maintaining studios and offices. The company hopes, of course, that all its CDs will be hits, but the reality is that only some will be. At the least, the company wants to break even—that is, not lose any money—on each CD. Cost-volume-profit analysis is an important tool that enables Sony's managers to determine how many CDs they must sell to avoid losing money and what their profit will be if they have a hit. It is also an important tool in setting sales targets.

Cost-volume-profit (C-V-P) analysis is an examination of the cost behavior patterns that underlie the relationships among cost, volume of output, and profit. C-V-P analysis usually applies to a single product, product line, or division of a company. For that reason, *profit*, which is only part of an entire company's operating income, is the term used in the C-V-P equation. The equation is expressed as

$$\text{Sales Revenue} - \text{Variable Costs} - \text{Fixed Costs} = \text{Profit}$$

or as

$$S - VC - FC = P$$

In cases involving the income statement of an entire company, the term *operating income* is more appropriate than *profit*. In the context of C-V-P analysis, however, *profit* and *operating income* mean the same thing.

C-V-P analysis is a tool for both planning and control. The techniques and the problem-solving procedures involved in the process express relationships among revenue, sales mix, cost, volume, and profit. Those relationships provide a general model of financial activity that managers can use for short-range planning and for evaluating performance and analyzing alternative courses of action.

For planning, managers can use C-V-P analysis to calculate net income when sales volume is known, or they can determine the level of sales needed to reach a targeted amount of net income. C-V-P analysis is used extensively in budgeting as well. C-V-P analysis is also a way of measuring how well an organization's departments are performing. At the end of a period, sales volume and related actual costs are analyzed to find actual net income. A department's performance is measured by comparing actual costs with expected costs—

costs that have been computed by applying C-V-P analysis to actual sales volume. The result is a performance report on which managers can base the control of operations.

In addition, managers use C-V-P analysis to measure the effects of alternative courses of action, such as changing variable or fixed costs, expanding or contracting sales volume, and increasing or decreasing selling prices. C-V-P analysis is useful in making decisions about product pricing, product mix (when an organization makes more than one product or offers more than one service), adding or dropping a product line, and accepting special orders.

C-V-P analysis has many applications, all of which managers use to plan and control operations effectively. However, it is useful only under certain conditions and only when certain assumptions hold true. Those conditions and assumptions are as follows:

1. The behavior of variable and fixed costs can be measured accurately.

2. Costs and revenues have a close linear approximation. For example, if costs rise, revenues rise proportionately.

3. Efficiency and productivity hold steady within the relevant range of activity.

4. Cost and price variables also hold steady during the period being planned.

5. The sales mix does not change during the period being planned.

6. Production and sales volume are roughly equal.

If one or more of these conditions and assumptions are absent, the C-V-P analysis may be misleading.

STOP • REVIEW • APPLY

3-1. Define cost-volume-profit analysis.

3-2. Identify two uses of C-V-P analysis and explain their significance to management.

3-3. What conditions must be met for C-V-P computations to be accurate?

Breakeven Analysis

LO4 Define *breakeven point* and use contribution margin to determine a company's breakeven point for multiple products.

Breakeven analysis uses the basic elements of cost-volume-profit relationships. The **breakeven point** is the point at which total revenues equal total costs. It is thus the point at which an organization can begin to earn a profit. When a new venture or product line is being planned, the likelihood of the project's success can be quickly measured by finding its breakeven point. If, for instance, the breakeven point is 24,000 units and the total market is only 25,000 units, the margin of safety would be very low, and the idea should be considered carefully. The **margin of safety** is the number of sales units or amount of sales dollars by which actual sales can fall below planned sales without resulting in a loss—in this example, 1,000 units.

Sales (S), variable costs (VC), and fixed costs (FC) are used to compute the breakeven point, which can be stated in terms of sales units or sales dollars. The general equation for finding the breakeven point is as follows:

$$S - VC - FC = \$0$$

Suppose, for example, that a company called Valley Metal Products, Inc., makes ornamental iron plant stands. Variable costs are $50 per unit, and fixed costs average $20,000 per year. Each plant stand sells for $90. Given this information, we can compute the breakeven point for this product in sales units (x equals sales units):

$$S - VC - FC = \$0$$
$$\$90x - \$50x - \$20,000 = \$0$$
$$\$40x = \$20,000$$
$$x = 500 \text{ Units}$$

We can also compute it in sales dollars:

$$\$90 \times 500 \text{ Units} = \$45,000$$

In addition, we can make a rough estimate of the breakeven point using a scatter graph. This method is less exact, but it does yield meaningful data. Figure 9 shows a breakeven graph for Valley Metal Products. As you can see there, the graph has five parts:

1. A horizontal axis for units of output

2. A vertical axis for dollars

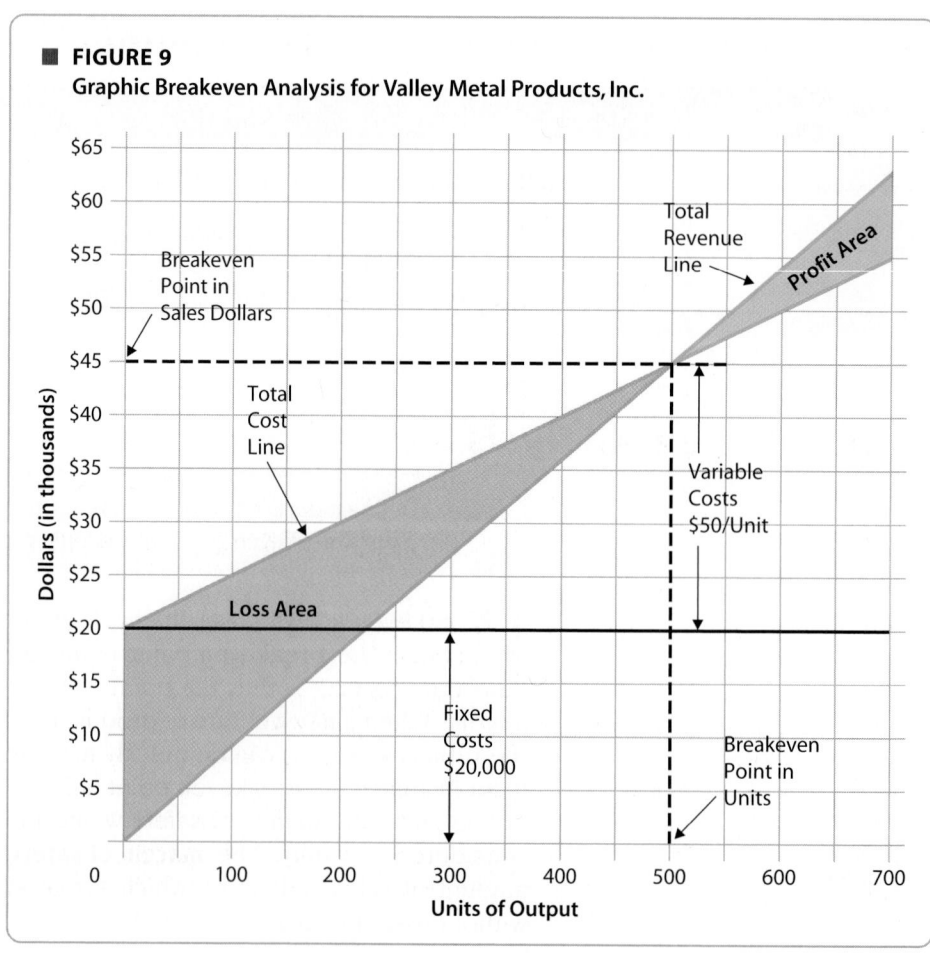

■ **FIGURE 9**
Graphic Breakeven Analysis for Valley Metal Products, Inc.

3. A line running horizontally from the vertical axis at the level of fixed costs

4. A total cost line that begins at the point where the fixed cost line crosses the vertical axis and slopes upward to the right (The slope of the line depends on the variable cost per unit.)

5. A total revenue line that begins at the origin of the vertical and horizontal axes and slopes upward to the right (The slope depends on the selling price per unit.)

At the point at which the total revenue line crosses the total cost line, revenues equal total costs. The breakeven point, stated in either sales units or dollars of sales, is found by extending broken lines from this point to the axes. As Figure 9 shows, Valley Metal Products will break even when it has sold 500 plant stands for $45,000.

Using Contribution Margin to Determine the Breakeven Point

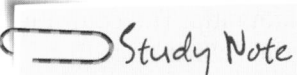

Study Note

Contribution margin equals sales minus variable costs, whereas gross margin equals sales minus the cost of goods sold.

Study Note

The maximum contribution a unit of product or service can make is its selling price. After paying for itself (variable costs), a product or service provides a contribution margin to help pay total fixed costs and then earn a profit.

A simpler method of determining the breakeven point uses contribution margin. **Contribution margin (CM)** is the amount that remains after all variable costs are subtracted from sales:

$$S - VC = CM$$

A product line's contribution margin represents its net contribution to paying off fixed costs and earning a profit. Profit (P) is what remains after fixed costs are paid and subtracted from the contribution margin:

$$CM - FC = P$$

The example that follows uses contribution margin to determine the profitability of Valley Metal Products.

Symbols		Units Produced and Sold 250	500	750
S	Sales revenue ($90 per unit)	$22,500	$45,000	$67,500
VC	Less variable costs ($50 per unit)	12,500	25,000	37,500
CM	Contribution margin ($40 per unit)	$10,000	$20,000	$30,000
FC	Less fixed costs	20,000	20,000	20,000
P	Profit (loss)	($10,000)	$ 0	$10,000

FOCUS ON BUSINESS PRACTICE
Supersizing Value Meals

Understanding their costs helps fast-food restaurants like McDonald's increase their profitability in at least two ways. One way is to encourage customers to buy "value meals"—combinations of three products, such as sandwich, drink, and fries—by offering them at a lower price than the three items purchased separately. Although the contribution margin of a value meal is lower than the combined contribution margins of the three products sold separately, fast-food restaurants know from experience that value meals lead to higher total sales.

Another way fast-food restaurants increase profitability is by offering "supersized" orders for only a few cents more than the price of a regular order. Supersizing increases the total contribution margin because the additional variable cost of the larger size is very small. Profitability is enhanced even though revenue increases by only a small amount. Selling larger sizes is so important to a fast-food restaurant's profitability that a common performance measure in the industry is the percentage of value meals that are supersized.

The breakeven point (BE) can be expressed as the point at which contribution margin minus total fixed costs equals zero (or the point at which contribution margin equals total fixed costs). In terms of units of product, the equation for the breakeven point looks like this:

$$(\text{CM per Unit} \times \text{BE Units}) - \text{FC} = \$0$$

It can also be expressed like this:

$$\text{BE Units} = \frac{\text{FC}}{\text{CM per unit}}$$

To show how the formula works, we use the data for Valley Metal Products:

$$\text{BE} = \frac{\text{FC}}{\text{CM per unit}} = \frac{\$20,000}{\$90 - \$50} = \frac{\$20,000}{\$40} = 500 \text{ Units}$$

The breakeven point in total sales dollars may be determined by multiplying the breakeven point in units by the selling price (SP) per unit:

$$\text{BE Dollars} = \text{SP} \times \text{BE Units} = \$90 \times 500 \text{ Units} = \$45,000$$

An alternative way of determining the breakeven point in total sales dollars is to divide the fixed costs by the contribution margin ratio. The contribution margin ratio is the contribution margin divided by the selling price:

$$\text{CM Ratio} = \frac{\text{CM}}{\text{SP}} = \frac{\$40}{\$90} = .444, \text{ or } 4/9$$

$$\text{BE Dollars} = \frac{\text{FC}}{\text{CM Ratio}} = \frac{\$20,000}{.444} = \$45,045^*$$

*Difference due to rounding up.

The Breakeven Point for Multiple Products

To satisfy the needs of different customers, many manufacturers sell a variety of products, which often have different variable and fixed costs and different selling prices. To calculate the breakeven point for each product, its unit contribution margin must be weighted by the sales mix. The **sales mix** is the proportion of each product's unit sales relative to the company's total unit sales.

Let's assume that Valley Metal Products sells two types of plant stands: a floor stand model and a smaller tabletop model. If the company sells 500 units, of which 300 units are floor stands and 200 are tabletops, the sales mix would be 3:2. For every three floor stands sold, two tabletops are sold. The sales mix can also be stated in percentages. Of the 500 units sold, 60 percent (300 ÷ 500) are floor stand sales, and 40 percent (200 ÷ 500) are tabletop sales (see Figure 10).

The breakeven point for multiple products can be computed in three steps. To illustrate, we will use Valley Metal Products' sales mix of 60 percent floor stands to 40 percent tabletops and total fixed costs of $32,000; the selling price, variable cost, and contribution margin per unit for each product line are shown in Step 1 below.

Step 1. *Compute the weighted-average contribution margin.* To do so, multiply the contribution margin for each product by its percentage of the sales mix, as follows:

	Selling Price		Variable Costs		Contribution Margin (CM)		Percentage of Sales Mix		Weighted-Average CM
Floor stand	$90	−	$50	=	$40	×	60%	=	$24
Tabletop	$40	−	$20	=	$20	×	40%	=	8
Weighted-average contribution margin									$32

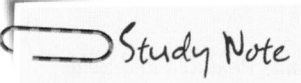

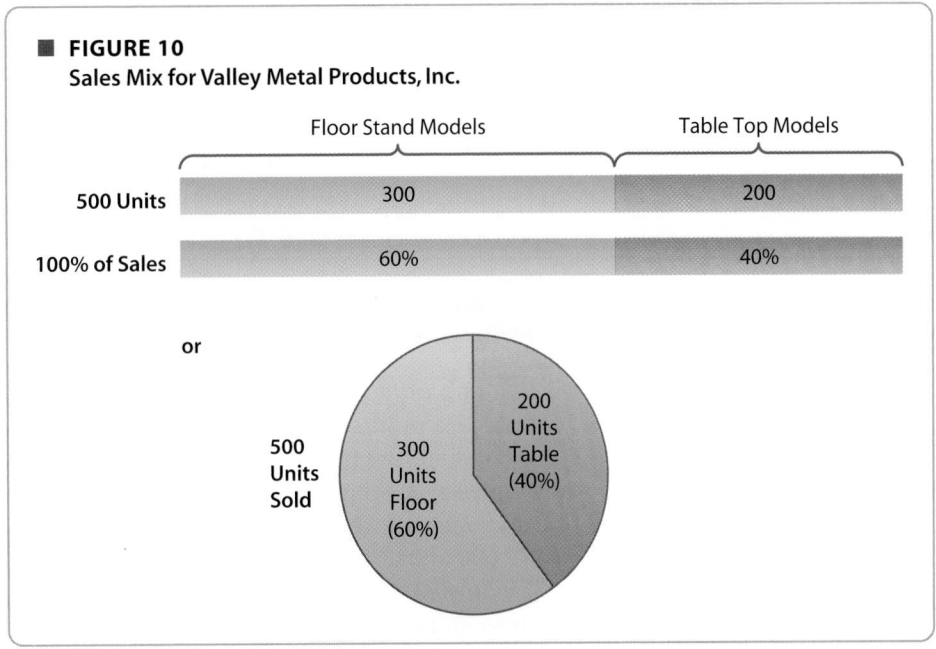

■ FIGURE 10
Sales Mix for Valley Metal Products, Inc.

Step 2. *Calculate the weighted-average breakeven point.* Divide total fixed costs by the weighted-average contribution margin:

Weighted-Average Breakeven Point = Total Fixed Costs ÷ Weighted-Average
Contribution Margin
= $32,000 ÷ $32
= 1,000 Units

Step 3. *Calculate the breakeven point for each product.* Multiply the weighted-average breakeven point by each product's percentage of the sales mix:

	Weighted-Average Breakeven Point		Sales Mix		Breakeven Point
Floor stand	1,000 units	×	60%	=	600 units
Tabletop	1,000 units	×	40%	=	400 units

To verify, determine the contribution margin of each product and subtract the total fixed costs:

Contribution margin

Floor stand	600 × $40 =	$24,000
Tabletop	400 × $20 =	8,000
Total contribution margin		$32,000
Less fixed costs		32,000
Profit		$ 0

STOP • REVIEW • APPLY

4-1. Define *breakeven point.* Why is information about the breakeven point important to managers?

4-2. Define *contribution margin,* and describe its use in breakeven analysis.

4-3. Why does the total revenue line in a breakeven graph start at the origin (zero units, zero dollars) while the total cost line usually starts higher on the vertical axis?

Using C-V-P Analysis to Plan Future Sales, Costs, and Profits

LO5 Use C-V-P analysis to project the profitability of products and services.

The primary goal of a business venture is not to break even; it is to generate profits. C-V-P analysis adjusted for targeted profit can be used to estimate the profitability of a venture. This approach is excellent for "what-if" analysis, in which managers select several scenarios and compute the profit that may be anticipated from each. For instance, what if sales increase by 17,000 units? What effect will the increase have on profit? What if sales increase by only 6,000 units? What if fixed costs are reduced by $14,500? What if the variable unit cost increases by $1.40? Each scenario generates a different amount of profit or loss.

Applying C-V-P to a Manufacturing Business

To illustrate how a manufacturing business can apply C-V-P analysis, assume that Van Bryce, the president of Valley Metal Products, Inc., has set $4,000 in profit as this year's goal for the plant stands. If all the data in our earlier example remain the same, how many plant stands must Valley Metal Products sell to reach the targeted profit? Again, x equals the number of units.

$$S = VC + FC + P$$
$$\$90x = \$50x + \$20,000 + \$4,000$$
$$\$40x = \$24,000$$
$$x = 600 \text{ Units}$$

To check the answer, insert all known data into the equation:

$$S - VC - FC = P$$
$$(600 \times \$90) - (600 \times \$50) - \$20,000 = \$4,000$$
$$\$54,000 - \$30,000 - \$20,000 = \$4,000$$

The contribution margin approach can also be used for profit planning. To do so, simply add the targeted profit to the numerator of the contribution margin breakeven equation:

$$\text{Targeted Sales Units} = \frac{FC + P}{CM \text{ per Unit}}$$

The number of sales units Valley Metal Products needs to generate $4,000 in profit is computed this way:

$$\text{Targeted Sales Units} = \frac{FC + P}{CM \text{ per Unit}} = \frac{\$20,000 + \$4,000}{\$40} = \frac{\$24,000}{\$40} = 600 \text{ Units}$$

Contribution income statements (sometimes referred to as *variable costing income statements*), which are prepared for internal use, are also useful to managers in planning and making decisions about their company's operations. As you can see in the contribution income statement for Valley Metal Products that appears below, the focus of such a statement is on cost behavior, *not* cost function. All variable costs related to production, selling, and administration are subtracted from sales to determine the total contribution margin. All fixed costs related to production, selling, and administration are subtracted from the total contribution margin to determine operating income. (As we noted earlier, in income statements involving an entire company, the term *operating income* is more appropriate than *profit*.)

Valley Metal Products, Inc.
Contribution Income Statement
For the Year Ended December 31

	Per Unit	Total for 600 Units
Sales revenue	$90	$54,000
Less variable costs	50	30,000
Contribution margin	$40	$24,000
Less fixed costs		20,000
Operating income		$ 4,000

Van Bryce wants Valley Metal Products' planning team to consider three alternatives to the original plan shown in the contribution income statement. In the following sections, we examine each of these alternatives and its impact on operating income. In the summary, we review our work and analyze the different breakeven points.

Alternative 1: Decrease Variable Costs, Increase Sales Volume

The planning team worked with production, purchasing, and sales employees to determine what operating income would be if the company purchased and used aluminum rather than iron to make the plant stands. If aluminum were used, the direct materials cost per unit would decrease by $3 to $47. If the company painted the aluminum to meet the needs of a new customer group, it would increase sales volume by 10 percent to 660 units. What is the estimated operating income for this alternative? How does this alternative affect operating income?

	Per Unit	Total for 660 units
Sales revenue	$90	$59,400
Less variable costs	47	31,020
Contribution margin	$43	$28,380
Less fixed costs		20,000
Operating income		$ 8,380
Increase in operating income ($8,380 − $4,000)		$ 4,380

A different way to determine the impact of changes in selling price, cost, or sales volume on operating income is to analyze only the data that change between the original plan and the proposed alternative. If Alternative 1 is used, variable costs will decrease by $3 (from $50 to $47), which will increase the contribution margin per unit by $3 (from $40 to $43). This will increase the total contribution margin and operating income by $1,800 ($3 × 600). In addition, a sales increase of 60 units (.10 × 600) will increase the total contribution margin and operating income by $2,580 ($43 × 60). The total increase in operating income due to the decrease in variable costs and the increase in sales volume will be $4,380.

Analysis of Changes Only

Increase in contribution margin from

Planned sales [($43 − $40) × 600 units]	$1,800
Additional sales ($43 × 60 units)	2,580
Increase in operating income	$4,380

Alternative 2: Increase Fixed Costs, Increase Sales Volume

Instead of changing the direct materials, the Marketing Department suggested that a $500 increase in advertising costs would increase sales volume by 5 percent. What is the estimated operating income for this alternative? How does this alternative affect operating income?

	Per Unit	Total for 630 Units
Sales revenue	$ 90	$56,700
Less variable costs	50	31,500
Contribution margin	$ 40	$25,200
Less fixed costs		20,500
Operating income		$ 4,700
Increase in operating income ($4,700 − $4,000)		$ 700

Additional advertising costs will affect both sales volume and fixed costs. The sales volume will increase by 30 plant stands, from 600 units to 630 units (600 × 1.05), which increases the total contribution margin and operating income by $1,200 (from $24,000 to $25,200). Fixed costs will increase from $20,000 to $20,500, which decreases operating income by $500. The increase in operating income will be $700 ($1,200 − $500).

Analysis of Changes Only

Increase in contribution margin from

additional units sold [($40 × (600 × .05)]	$1,200
Less increase in fixed costs	500
Increase in operating income	$ 700

Alternative 3: Increase Selling Price, Decrease Sales Volume

Van Bryce asked the planning team to evaluate the impact of a $10 increase in selling price on the company's operating income. If the selling price is increased, the team estimates that the sales volume will decrease by 15 percent to 510 units. What is the estimated operating income for this alternative? How does this alternative affect operating income?

	Per Unit	Total for 510 Units
Sales revenue	$ 100	$51,000
Less variable costs	50	25,500
Contribution margin	$ 50	$25,500
Less fixed costs		20,000
Operating income		$ 5,500
Increase in operating income ($5,500 − $4,000)		$ 1,500

Analysis of Changes Only

Increase in contribution margin from increase in selling price ($10 increase in selling price × 510 units sold)	$5,100
Decrease in contribution margin from decrease in sales volume ($40 contribution margin per unit × 90 sales units lost)	(3,600)
Increase in operating income	$1,500

Comparative Summary In preparation for a meeting with Van Bryce, the planning team at Valley Metal Products compiled the summary presented in Exhibit 1. It compares the three alternatives with the original plan and shows how changes in variable and fixed costs, selling price, and sales volume affect the breakeven point.

Note that the decrease in variable costs (direct materials) proposed in Alternative 1 increases the contribution margin per unit (from $40 to $43), which reduces the breakeven point. Because fewer sales dollars are required to cover variable costs, the breakeven point is reached sooner than in the original plan—at a sales volume of 466 units rather than at 500 units. In Alternative 2, the increase in fixed costs has no effect on the contribution margin per unit, but it does require the total contribution margin to cover more fixed costs before reaching the breakeven point. Thus, the breakeven point is higher than in the original plan—513 units as opposed to 500. The increase in selling price in Alternative 3 increases the contribution margin per unit, which reduces the breakeven point. Because more sales dollars are available to cover fixed costs,

EXHIBIT 1 ▶ | **Comparative Summary of Alternatives at Valley Metal Products, Inc.**

	Original Plan	Alternative 1	Alternative 2	Alternative 3
	Totals For 600 Units	Decrease Direct Materials Costs for 660 Units	Increase Advertising Costs for 630 Units	Increase Selling Price for 510 Units
Sales revenue	$54,000	$59,400	$56,700	$51,000
Less variable costs	30,000	31,020	31,500	25,500
Contribution margin	$24,000	$28,380	$25,200	$25,500
Less fixed costs	20,000	20,000	20,500	20,000
Operating income	$ 4,000	$ 8,380	$ 4,700	$ 5,500

Breakeven point in whole units (FC ÷ CM)

$20,000 ÷ $40 =	500			
$20,000 ÷ $43 =		466*		
$20,500 ÷ $40 =			513*	
$20,000 ÷ $50 =				400

*Rounded up to next whole unit.

the breakeven point of 400 units is lower than the breakeven point in the original plan.

Which plan should Bryce choose? If he wants the highest operating income, he will choose Alternative 1. If, however, he wants the company to begin generating operating income more quickly, he will choose the plan with the lowest breakeven point, Alternative 3. Remember that the breakeven point provides a rough estimate of the number of units that must be sold to cover the total costs.

Additional qualitative information may help Bryce make a better decision. Will customers perceive that the quality of the plant stands is lower if the company uses aluminum rather than iron, as proposed in Alternative 1? Will increased expenditures on advertising yield a 5 percent increase in sales volume, as Alternative 2 suggests? Will the increase in selling price suggested in Alternative 3 create more than a 15 percent decline in unit sales?

Quantitative information is essential for planning, but managers must also be sensitive to qualitative factors, such as product quality, reliability and quality of suppliers, and availability of human and technical resources.

Applying C-V-P Analysis to a Service Business

In this section, we look at how a service business can use C-V-P analysis in planning its operations. Assume that Glenda Haley, the manager of the Appraisal Department at Edmunds Mortgage Company, wants to plan the home appraisal activities that each mortgage loan application requires. She estimates that over the next year, her department will perform an average of 100 appraisals per month and service fee revenue will be $400 per appraisal. Other estimated data for the year are as follows:

Variable costs: direct professional labor, $160 per appraisal; county survey map fee, $99 per appraisal

Mixed costs (monthly service overhead):

Volume	Month	Activity Level	Cost
Highest	March	180 appraisals	$23,380
Lowest	February	98 appraisals	$20,018

Estimating Service Overhead Costs Haley wants to estimate the total service overhead cost of appraisals for next year. She uses the high-low method to do so:

Step 1. *Calculate the variable service overhead cost per appraisal.*

$$\text{Variable Service Overhead Cost per Appraisal} = \frac{(\text{Highest Cost} - \text{Lowest Cost}) \div}{(\text{Highest Volume} - \text{Lowest Volume})}$$
$$= (\$23,380 - \$20,018) \div (180 - 98)$$
$$= \$3,362 \div 82 \text{ Appraisals} = \$41$$

Step 2. *Calculate the total fixed service overhead costs.*

Total Fixed Service Overhead Costs = Total Service Overhead Costs − Total Variable Service Overhead Costs

Total Fixed Service Overhead Costs for March = $23,380 − ($41 × 180)
= $16,000

Step 3. *Calculate the total service overhead costs for one month.*

Total Service   = Total Fixed Service Overhead Costs +
Overhead Costs   (Variable Rate × Estimated Number of Appraisals)
                  = $16,000 + ($41 per Appraisal × Number of Appraisals)

Step 4. *Calculate the total service overhead costs for one month assuming that 100 appraisals will be made.*

Total Overhead Service Costs = $16,000 + ($41 × 100) = $20,100

Determining the Breakeven Point

Glenda Haley also wants to know how many appraisals her department must perform each month to cover the fixed and variable appraisal costs. She calculates the breakeven point as follows:

Let x = Number of Appraisals per Month at Breakeven Point
$$S - VC - FC = 0$$
$$\$400x - \$300x - \$16,000 = 0$$
$$\$100x = \$16,000$$
$$x = 160 \text{ Appraisals per Month}$$

The variable rate of $300 per appraisal includes the variable service overhead rate, the direct professional labor, and the county survey map fee ($41 + $160 + $99).

Determining the Effect of a Change in Operating Costs

Haley is worried because her department can perform an average of only 100 appraisals each month, but the estimated breakeven point is 160 appraisals per month. Because of strong competition, increasing the appraisal fee is not an option; to make the appraisals profitable, the mortgage company has asked Haley to find ways of reducing costs. In reviewing the situation, Haley has determined that improved scheduling of appraisals will reduce appraisers' travel time. Travel time is included in the current professional labor cost of $160 per appraisal (four hours of an appraiser's time at $40 per hour). By scheduling the jobs according to location, Haley can reduce the appraisers' travel time enough to reduce the total time required by 50 percent, thus cutting the professional labor cost to $80 per appraisal [(.50 × 4 hours) × $40 per hour]. The new scheduling process will increase fixed costs by $200 per month. Given these circumstances, what will the breakeven point be?

Let x = Number of Appraisals per Month at Breakeven Point
$$S - VC - FC = 0$$
$$\$400x - \$220x - \$16,200 = 0$$
$$\$180x = \$16,200$$
$$x = 90 \text{ Appraisals per Month}$$

Variable costs become $220 ($300 − $80) per appraisal due to the reduced labor costs. This change increases the contribution margin by $80 per appraisal. Fixed costs increase from $16,000 to $16,200. The increase in the contribution margin is greater than the increase in the fixed costs, so the breakeven point decreases from 160 appraisals per month to 90 appraisals per month.

Achieving a Targeted Profit

How many appraisals would Glenda Haley's department have to perform each month to achieve a targeted profit of $18,000 per month?

$$\text{Let } x = \text{Targeted Sales in Units}$$
$$S - VC - FC = P$$
$$\$400x - \$220x - \$16,200 = \$18,000$$
$$\$180x = \$34,200$$
$$x = 190 \text{ Appraisals per Month}$$

S T O P • R E V I E W • A P P L Y

5-1. State the equation that uses fixed costs, targeted profit, and contribution margin per unit to determine targeted sales units.

5-2. Give three examples of the ways in which a service business can use C-V-P analysis.

5-3. What are the differences and similarities in C-V-P analysis for manufacturing organizations and service organizations?

A LOOK BACK AT

KRAFT FOODS

The Decision Point at the beginning of this chapter focused on **Kraft Foods,** a company whose five key sectors produce brands sold around the world. It posed these questions:

● **How does Kraft decide which products to offer?**

● **Why do Kraft's managers analyze cost behavior to project the profitability of the company's core sectors?**

Kraft's managers must consider the variable and fixed costs of making products when determining the profitability of the company's sales mix and projecting the operating results of its core sectors. They use cost information to determine selling prices that cover both fixed and variable costs and that take into account the variability of demand for the company's brands. For example, the variable costs of the direct materials and direct labor the company uses to make each one-pound package of cheese are roughly the same, but the total cost of direct materials will vary according to the number of packages produced in any one year. Similarly, the fixed costs of operating the factories and of the manufacturing equipment used in making the cheese will not change significantly from year to year in relation to the number of pounds produced. However, the portion of those costs applied to each pound of product will vary depending on the number of pounds actually produced. In short, to project the profitability of a brand or one of its five key sectors for a particular year, Kraft's managers must take into account both the selling price and the estimated production and sales mix of products and the effects those estimates have on a brand's unit cost.

CHAPTER REVIEW

REVIEW of Learning Objectives

LO1 Define *cost behavior* and explain how managers use this concept.

Cost behavior is the way costs respond to changes in volume or activity. When managers plan, they use cost behavior to determine how many units of products or services must be sold to generate a targeted amount of profit and how changes in planned activities will affect operating income. During the period, managers must understand and anticipate cost behavior to determine the impact of their decisions on operating income. When managers evaluate performance and communicate results, they analyze how changes in cost and sales affect the profitability of product lines, sales territories, customers, departments, and other business segments by preparing reports using variable costing.

LO2 Identify variable, fixed, and mixed costs, and separate mixed costs into their variable and fixed components.

Some costs vary in relation to volume or operating activity; other costs remain fixed as volume changes. Cost behavior depends on whether the focus is total costs or cost per unit. Total costs that change in direct proportion to changes in productive output (or any other volume measure) are called *variable costs*. They include hourly wages, the cost of operating supplies, direct materials costs, and the cost of merchandise. Total *fixed costs* remain constant within a relevant range of volume or activity. They change only when volume or activity exceeds the relevant range—for example, when new equipment or new buildings must be purchased, higher insurance premiums and property taxes must be paid, or additional supervisory personnel must be hired to accommodate increased activity. A *mixed cost*, such as the cost of electricity, has both variable and fixed cost components. For cost planning and control, mixed costs must be separated into their variable and fixed components. To separate them, managers use a variety of methods, including the engineering, scatter diagram, high-low, and statistical methods.

LO3 Define *cost-volume-profit (C-V-P) analysis* and discuss how managers use it as a tool for planning and control.

Cost-volume-profit analysis is an examination of the cost behavior patterns that underlie the relationships among cost, volume of output, and profit. It is a tool for both planning and control. The techniques and problem-solving procedures involved in C-V-P analysis express relationships among revenue, sales mix, cost, volume, and profit. Those relationships provide a general model of financial activity that management can use for short-range planning and for evaluating performance and analyzing alternatives.

LO4 Define *breakeven point* and use contribution margin to determine a company's breakeven point for multiple products.

The *breakeven point* is the point at which total revenues equal total costs—in other words, the point at which net sales equal variable costs plus fixed costs. Once the number of units needed to break even is known, the number can be multiplied by the product's selling price to determine the breakeven point in sales dollars. *Contribution margin* is the amount that remains after all variable costs have been subtracted from sales. A product's contribution margin represents its net contribution to paying off fixed costs and earning a profit. The breakeven point in units can be computed by using the following formula:

$$\text{BE Units} = \frac{\text{FC}}{\text{CM per Unit}}$$

Sales mix is used to calculate the breakeven point for each product when a company sells more than one product.

LO5 Use C-V-P analysis to project the profitability of products and services.

The addition of targeted profit to the breakeven equation makes it possible to plan levels of operation that yield the targeted profit. The formula in terms of contribution margin is

$$\text{Targeted Sales Units} = \frac{\text{FC} + \text{P}}{\text{CM per Unit}}$$

C-V-P analysis, whether used by a manufacturing company or a service organization, enables managers to select several "what if" scenarios and evaluate the outcome of each to determine which will generate the desired amount of profit.

REVIEW of Concepts and Terminology

The following concepts and terms were introduced in this chapter:

Breakeven point: The point at which total revenues equal total costs. **(LO4)**

Contribution margin (CM): The amount that remains after all variable costs are subtracted from sales. **(LO4)**

Cost behavior: The way costs respond to changes in volume or activity. **(LO1)**

Cost-volume-profit (C-V-P) analysis: An examination of the cost behavior patterns that underlie the relationships among cost, volume of output, and profit. **(LO3)**

Engineering method: A method that separates costs into their fixed and variable components by performing a step-by-step analysis of the tasks, costs, and processes involved in completing an activity or product. **(LO2)**

Fixed costs: Total costs that remain constant within a relevant range of volume or activity. **(LO2)**

High-low method: A three-step approach to separating a mixed cost into its variable and fixed components. **(LO2)**

Margin of safety: The number of sales units or amount of sales dollars by which actual sales can fall below planned sales without resulting in a loss. **(LO4)**

Mixed costs: Costs that have both variable and fixed components. **(LO2)**

Normal capacity: The average annual level of operating capacity needed to meet expected sales demand. **(LO2)**

Operating capacity: The upper limit of an organization's productive output capability, given its existing resources. **(LO2)**

Practical capacity: Theoretical capacity reduced by normal and expected work stoppages. **(LO2)**

Regression analysis: A mathematical approach to separating a mixed cost into its variable and fixed components. **(LO2)**

Relevant range: The span of activity in which a company expects to operate. **(LO2)**

Sales mix: The proportion of each product's unit sales relative to the company's total unit sales. **(LO4)**

Scatter diagram: A chart of plotted points that helps determine whether a linear relationship exists between a cost item and its related activity measure. **(LO2)**

Theoretical (ideal) capacity: The maximum productive output for a given period in which all machinery and equipment are operating at optimum speed, without interruption. **(LO2)**

Variable costs: Total costs that change in direct proportion to changes in productive output or any other measure of volume. **(LO2)**

REVIEW Problem

LO4, LO5 **Breakeven Analysis and Profitability Planning**

Olympia, Inc., is a major producer of golf clubs. Its oversized putter has a large potential market. The following is a summary of data from the company's operations this year:

Selling price per unit: $95

Overhead	$195,000
Advertising	55,000
Administrative expense	68,000
Total fixed costs	$318,000

Direct materials	$23
Direct labor	8
Overhead	6
Selling expense	5
Variable costs per unit	$42

Required

1. Compute the breakeven point in units for the year.
2. Olympia sold 6,500 putters this year. How much profit did it realize?
3. To improve profitability next year, management is considering the four alternative courses of action indicated below. (In performing the required steps, use the figures from items **1** and **2** and treat each alternative independently.)

   a. Calculate the number of units Olympia must sell to generate a targeted profit of $95,400. Assume that costs and selling price remain constant.
   b. Calculate the operating income if the company increases the number of units sold by 20 percent and cuts the selling price by $5 per unit.
   c. Determine the number of units that must be sold to break even if advertising costs are increased by $47,700.
   d. Find the number of units that must be sold to generate a targeted profit of $120,000 if variable costs are cut by 10 percent.

Answer to Review Problem

1. Breakeven point in units for this year:

$$\text{Breakeven Units} = \frac{FC}{CM \text{ per Unit}} = \frac{\$318,000}{\$95 - \$42} = \frac{\$318,000}{\$53} = 6,000 \text{ Units}$$

2. Profit from sale of 6,500 units:

Units sold	6,500
Units required to break even	6,000
Units over breakeven	500

Profit = $53 per unit × 500 = $26,500

Contribution margin equals sales minus all variable costs. Contribution margin per unit equals the amount left to cover fixed costs and earn a profit after variable costs have been subtracted from sales dollars. If all fixed costs have been absorbed by the time breakeven is reached, the entire contribution margin of each unit sold in excess of breakeven represents profit.

3. a. Number of units that must be sold to generate a targeted profit of $95,400:

$$\text{Targeted Sales Units} = \frac{FC + P}{CM \text{ per Unit}}$$

$$\frac{\$318,000 + \$95,400}{\$53} = \frac{\$413,400}{\$53} = 7,800 \text{ Units}$$

b. Operating income if unit sales increase 20 percent and unit selling price decreases by $5:

Sales revenue [7,800 (6,500 × 1.20) units at $90 per unit]	$702,000
Less variable costs (7,800 units × $42)	327,600
Contribution margin	$374,400
Less fixed costs	318,000
Operating income	$ 56,400

c. Number of units needed to break even if advertising costs (fixed costs) increase by $47,700:

$$\text{BE Units} = \frac{FC}{\text{CM per Unit}}$$

$$\frac{\$318,000 + \$47,700}{\$53} = \frac{\$365,700}{\$53} = 6,900 \text{ Units}$$

d. Number of units that must be sold to generate a targeted profit of $120,000 if variable costs decrease by 10 percent:

$$\text{CM per Unit} = \$95.00 - (\$42.00 \times .90) = \$95.00 - \$37.80 = \$57.20$$

$$\text{Targeted Sales Units} = \frac{FC + P}{\text{CM per Unit}}$$

$$\frac{\$318,000 + \$120,000}{\$57.20} = \frac{\$438,000}{\$57.20} = 7,658 \text{ Units*}$$

_____

*Note that the answer is rounded up to the next whole unit.

CHAPTER ASSIGNMENTS

BUILDING Your Basic Knowledge and Skills

Short Exercises

LO1 Concept of Cost Behavior

SE 1. Dapper Hat Makers is in the business of designing and producing specialty hats. The material used for derbies costs $4.50 per unit, and Dapper pays each of its two full-time employees $250 per week. If Employee A makes 15 derbies in one week, what is the variable cost per derby, and what is this worker's fixed cost per derby? If Employee B makes only 12 derbies in one week, what are this worker's variable and fixed costs per derby? (Round to two decimal places where necessary.)

LO2 Identification of Variable, Fixed, and Mixed Costs

SE 2. Identify the following as (a) fixed costs, (b) variable costs, or (c) mixed costs:

1. Direct materials
2. Electricity
3. Operating supplies
4. Personnel manager's salary
5. Factory building rent

LO2 **Mixed Costs: High-Low Method**

SE 3. Using the high-low method and the information below, compute the monthly variable cost per telephone hour and total fixed costs for Sadiko Corporation.

Month	Telephone Hours Used	Telephone Costs
April	96	$4,350
May	93	4,230
June	105	4,710

LO3 **C-V-P Analysis**

SE 4. DeLuca, Inc., wants to make a profit of $20,000. It has variable costs of $80 per unit and fixed costs of $12,000. How much must it charge per unit if 4,000 units are sold?

LO4 **Breakeven Analysis**

SE 5. How many units must Braxton Company sell to break even if the selling price per unit is $8.50, variable costs are $4.30 per unit, and fixed costs are $3,780? What is the breakeven point in total dollars of sales?

LO4 **Contribution Margin**

SE 6. Using the contribution margin approach, find the breakeven point in units for Norcia Consumer Products if the selling price per unit is $11, the variable cost per unit is $6, and the fixed costs are $5,500.

LO4 **Contribution Margin Ratio**

SE 7. Using the information in **SE 6** and the contribution margin ratio, compute the breakeven point in total sales dollars.

LO4 **Breakeven Analysis for Multiple Products**

SE 8. Using the contribution margin approach, find the breakeven point in units for Sardinia Company's two products. Product A's selling price per unit is $10, and its variable cost per unit is $4. Product B's selling price per unit is $8, and its variable cost per unit is $5. Fixed costs are $15,000, and the sales mix of Product A to Product B is 2:1.

LO4, LO5 **Contribution Margin and Projected Profit**

SE 9. If Oui Watches sells 300 watches at $48 per watch and has variable costs of $18 per watch and fixed costs of $4,000, what is the projected profit?

LO5 **Cost Behavior in a Service Business**

SE 10. Guy Spy, a private investigation firm, has the following costs for December:

Direct labor: $190 per case

Service overhead

Salary for director of investigations	$ 4,800
Telephone	930
Depreciation	8,300
Legal advice	2,300
Supplies	590
Advertising	360
Utilities	1,560
Wages for clerical personnel	2,000
Total service overhead	$20,840

Service overhead for October was $21,150; for November, it was $21,350. The number of cases investigated during October, November, and December was 93, 97, and 91, respectively. Compute the variable and fixed cost components of service overhead. Then determine the variable and fixed costs per case for December. (Round to nearest dollar where necessary.)

Exercises

LO2 Identification of Variable and Fixed Costs

E 1. Indicate whether each of the following costs of productive output is usually (a) variable or (b) fixed:

1. Packing materials for stereo components
2. Real estate taxes
3. Gasoline for a delivery truck
4. Property insurance
5. Depreciation expense of buildings (calculated with the straight-line method)
6. Supplies
7. Indirect materials
8. Bottles used to package liquids
9. License fees for company cars
10. Wiring used in radios
11. Machine helper's wages
12. Wood used in bookcases
13. City operating license
14. Machine depreciation based on machine hours used
15. Machine operator's hourly wages
16. Cost of required outside inspection of each unit produced

LO2 Variable Cost Analysis

E 2. Zero Time Oil Change has been in business for six months. The company pays $0.50 per quart for the oil it uses in servicing cars. Each job requires an average of four quarts of oil. The company estimates that in the next three months, it will service 240, 288, and 360 cars.

1. Compute the cost of oil for each of the three months and the total cost for all three months.

Month	Cars to Be Serviced	Required Quarts/Car	Cost/Quart	Total Cost/Month
1	240	4	$0.50	_____
2	288	4	0.50	_____
3	360	4	0.50	_____
Three-month total	888			_____

2. Complete the following sentences by choosing the words that best describe the cost behavior at Zero Time Oil Change:
   a. Cost per unit (increased, decreased, remained constant).
   b. Total variable cost per month (increased, decreased) as the quantity of oil used (increased, decreased).

LO2 Mixed Costs: High-Low Method

E 3. Whitehouse Company manufactures major appliances. Because of growing interest in its products, it has just had its most successful year. In preparing the budget for next year, its controller compiled these data:

Month	Volume in Machine Hours	Electricity Cost
July	6,000	$ 60,000
August	5,000	53,000
September	4,500	49,500
October	4,000	46,000
November	3,500	42,500
December	3,000	39,000
Six month total	26,000	$290,000

Using the high-low method, determine (1) the variable electricity cost per machine hour, (2) the monthly fixed electricity cost, and (3) the total variable electricity costs and fixed electricity costs for the six-month period.

LO2 **Mixed Costs: High-Low Method**

E 4. When Jerome Company's monthly costs were $75,000, sales were $80,000; when its monthly costs were $60,000, sales were $50,000. Use the high-low method to develop a monthly cost formula for Jerome's coming year.

LO4 **Contribution Margin**

E 5. Senora Company manufactures a single product that sells for $110 per unit. The company projects sales of 500 units per month. Projected costs are as follows:

Type of Cost	Manufacturing	Nonmanufacturing
Variable	$10,000	$5,000
Nonvariable	$12,500	$7,500

1. What is the company's contribution margin per unit?
2. What is the contribution margin ratio?
3. What volume, in terms of units, must the company sell to break even?

LO4, LO5 **Breakeven Point and C-V-P Analysis**

E 6. Using the data in the contribution income statement for Sedona, Inc., that appears below, calculate (1) selling price per unit, (2) variable costs per unit, and (3) breakeven point in sales dollars.

Sedona, Inc.
Contribution Income Statement
For the Year Ended December 31

Sales (10,000 units)		$16,000,000
Less variable costs		
Cost of goods sold	$8,000,000	
Selling, administrative, and general	4,000,000	
Total variable costs		12,000,000
Contribution margin		$ 4,000,000
Less fixed costs		
Overhead	$1,200,000	
Selling, administrative, and general	800,000	
Total fixed costs		2,000,000
Operating income		$ 2,000,000

LO4 **Graphic Breakeven Analysis**

E 7. Identify the letter of the point, line segment, or area of the breakeven graph shown below that correctly completes each of the following statements:

1. The maximum possible operating loss is

   a. A.   c. B.
   b. D.   d. F.

2. The breakeven point in sales dollars is

   a. C.   c. A.
   b. D.   d. G.

3. At volume F, total contribution margin is

   a. C.   c. E.
   b. D.   d. G.

4. Net income is represented by area

   a. KDL.   c. BDC.
   b. KCJ.   d. GCJ.

5. At volume J, total fixed costs are represented by

   a. H.   c. I.
   b. G.   d. J.

6. If volume increases from F to J, the change in total costs is

   a. HI minus DE.   c. BC minus DF.
   b. DF minus HJ.   d. AB minus DE.

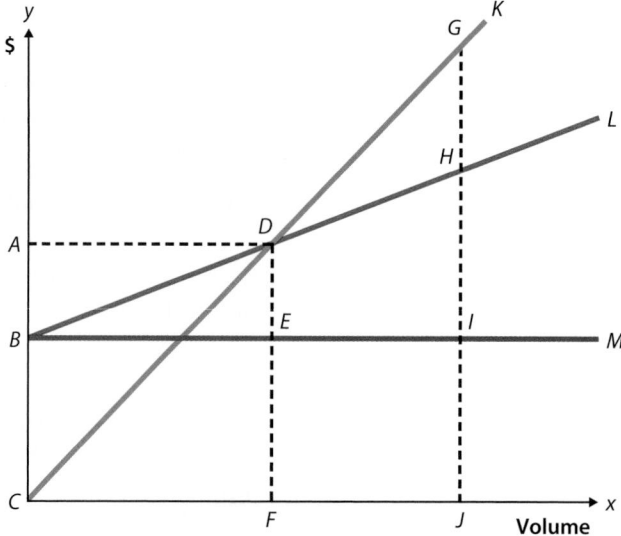

LO4 **Breakeven Analysis**

E 8. Techno Designs produces head covers for golf clubs. The company expects to generate a profit next year. It anticipates fixed manufacturing costs of $126,500 and fixed general and administrative expenses of $82,030 for the year. Variable manufacturing and selling costs per set of head covers will be $4.65 and $2.75, respectively. Each set will sell for $13.40.

1. Compute the breakeven point in sales units.
2. Compute the breakeven point in sales dollars.
3. If the selling price is increased to $14 per unit and fixed general and administrative expenses are cut by $33,465, what will the new breakeven point be in units?
4. Prepare a graph to illustrate the breakeven point computed in **2**.

LO4, LO5   Breakeven Analysis and Pricing

E 9. McLennon Company has a plant capacity of 100,000 units per year, but its budget for this year indicates that only 60,000 units will be produced and sold. The entire budget for this year is as follows:

Sales (60,000 units at $4)		$240,000
Less cost of goods produced (based on production of 60,000 units)		
Direct materials (variable)	$60,000	
Direct labor (variable)	30,000	
Variable overhead costs	45,000	
Fixed overhead costs	75,000	
Total cost of goods produced		210,000
Gross margin		$ 30,000
Less selling and administrative expenses		
Selling (fixed)	$24,000	
Administrative (fixed)	36,000	
Total selling and administrative expenses		60,000
Operating income (loss)		($ 30,000)

1. Given the budgeted selling price and cost data, how many units would McLennon have to sell to break even? (**Hint:** Be sure to consider selling and administrative expenses.)
2. Market research indicates that if McLennon were to drop its selling price to $3.80 per unit, it could sell 100,000 units. Would you recommend the drop in price? What would the new operating income or loss be?

LO4   Breakeven Point for Multiple Products

E 10. Saline Aquarium, Inc., manufactures and sells aquariums, water pumps, and air filters. The sales mix is 1:2:2 (i.e., for every one aquarium sold, two water pumps and two air filters are sold). Using the contribution margin approach, find the breakeven point in units for each product. The company's fixed costs are $26,000. Other information is as follows:

	Selling Price per Unit	Variable Costs per Unit
Aquariums	$60	$25
Water pumps	20	12
Air filters	10	3

LO4   Sales Mix Analysis

E 11. Ella Mae Simpson is the owner of a hairdressing salon in Palm Coast, Florida. Her salon provides three basic services: shampoo and set, permanents, and cut and blow dry. The following are its operating results from the past quarter:

Type of Service	Number of Customers	Total Sales	Contribution Margin Dollars
Shampoo and set	1,200	$24,000	$14,700
Permanents	420	21,000	15,120
Cut and blow dry	1,000	15,000	10,000
	2,620	$60,000	$39,820
Total fixed costs			30,000
Profit			$ 9,820

Compute the breakeven point in units based on the weighted-average contribution margin for the sales mix.

LO4, LO5   Contribution Margin and Profit Planning

E 12. Target Systems, Inc., makes heat-seeking missiles. It has recently been offered a government contract from which it may realize a profit. The contract purchase price is $130,000 per missile, but the number of units to be purchased has not yet been decided. The company's fixed costs are budgeted at $3,973,500, and variable costs are $68,500 per unit.

1. Compute the number of units the company should agree to make at the stated contract price to earn a profit of $1,500,000.
2. Using a lighter material, the variable unit cost can be reduced by $1,730, but total fixed overhead will increase by $27,500. How many units must be produced to make $1,500,000 in profit?
3. Given the figures in **2**, how many additional units must be produced to increase profit by $1,264,600?

LO5   Planning Future Sales

E 13. Short-term automobile rentals are the specialty of ASAP Auto Rentals, Inc. Average variable operating costs have been $12.50 per day per automobile. The company owns 60 cars. Fixed operating costs for the next year are expected to be $145,500. Average daily rental revenue per automobile is expected to be $34.50. Management would like to earn a profit of $47,000 during the year.

1. Calculate the total number of daily rentals the company must have during the year to earn the targeted profit.
2. On the basis of your answer to **1**, determine the average number of days each automobile must be rented.
3. Determine the total revenue needed to achieve the targeted profit of $47,000.
4. What would the total rental revenue be if fixed operating costs could be lowered by $5,180 and the targeted profit increased to $70,000?

LO5   Cost Behavior in a Service Business

E 14. Luke Ricci, CPA, is the owner of a firm that provides tax services. The firm charges $50 per return for the direct professional labor involved in preparing standard short-form tax returns. In January, the firm prepared 850 such returns; in February, 1,000; and in March, 700. Service overhead (telephone and utilities, depreciation on equipment and building, tax forms, office supplies, and wages of clerical personnel) for January was $18,500; for February, $20,000; and for March, $17,000.

1. Determine the variable and fixed cost components of the firm's Service Overhead account.
2. What would the estimated total cost per tax return be if the firm prepares 825 standard short-form tax returns in April?

LO5   C-V-P Analysis in a Service Business

E 15. Flossmoor Inspection Service specializes in inspecting cars that have been returned to automobile leasing companies at the end of their leases. Flossmoor's charge for each inspection is $50; its average cost per inspection is $15. Tony Lomangeno, Flossmoor's owner, wants to expand his business by hiring another employee and purchasing an automobile. The fixed costs of the new employee and automobile would be $3,000 per month. How many inspections per month would the new employee have to perform to earn Lomangeno a profit of $1,200?

Problems

LO2, LO5   **Cost Behavior and Projection**

P 1. Luster Auto, Inc., specializes in "detailing" automobile exteriors—that is, revitalizing them so the cars look as if they had just rolled off the showroom floor. The company charges $100 for a full exterior detailing. It has just completed its first year of business and has asked its accountants to analyze the operating results. Management wants costs divided into variable, fixed, and mixed components and would like them projected for the coming year. Anticipated volume for next year is 1,100 jobs. The process used to detail a car's exterior is as follows:

1. One $20-per-hour employee spends 20 minutes cleaning the car's exterior.
2. One can per car of Bugg-Off, a cleaning compound, is used on trouble spots.
3. A chemical compound called Buff Glow is used to remove oxidants from the paint surface and restore the natural oils to the paint.
4. Poly Wax is applied by hand, allowed to sit for 10 minutes, and then buffed off.
5. The final step is an inspection to see that all wax and debris have been removed.

On average, two hours are spent on each car, including cleaning time and drying time for the wax. Operating information for Luster Auto's first year is as follows:

Number of automobiles detailed	840
Labor per auto	2 hours at $20.00 per hour
Containers of Bugg-Off consumed	840 at $3.50 per can
Pounds of Buff Glow consumed	105 pounds at $32.00 per pound
Pounds of Poly Wax consumed	210 pounds at $8.00 per pound
Rent	$1,400.00 per month

During the year, utilities costs ranged from $800 for 40 jobs in March to $1,801 for 110 jobs in August.

Required

1. Classify the costs as variable, fixed, or mixed.
2. Using the high-low method, separate the mixed costs into their variable and fixed components. Use number of jobs as the basis.
3. Project the same costs for next year, assuming that the anticipated increase in activity will occur and that fixed costs will remain constant.
4. Compute the unit cost per job for next year.
5. **Manager Insight:** Given your answer to **4**, should the price remain at $100 per job?

LO4, LO5   **Breakeven Analysis**

P 2. Luce & Morgan, a law firm in downtown Jefferson City, is considering opening a legal clinic for middle- and low-income clients. The clinic would bill at a rate of $18 per hour. It would employ law students as paraprofessional help and pay them $9 per hour. Other variable costs are anticipated to be $5.40 per hour, and annual fixed costs are expected to total $27,000.

Required

1. Compute the breakeven point in billable hours.

2. Compute the breakeven point in total billings.
3. Find the new breakeven point in total billings if fixed costs should go up by $2,340.
4. Using the original figures, compute the breakeven point in total billings if the billing rate decreases by $1 per hour, variable costs decrease by $0.40 per hour, and fixed costs go down by $3,600.

LO4, LO5 **Planning Future Sales: Contribution Margin Approach**

P 3. Icon Industries is considering a new product for its Trophy Division. The product, which would feature an alligator, is expected to have global market appeal and to become the mascot for many high school and university athletic teams. Expected variable unit costs are as follows: direct materials, $18.50; direct labor, $4.25; production supplies, $1.10; selling costs, $2.80; and other, $1.95. Annual fixed costs are depreciation, building and equipment, $36,000; advertising, $45,000; and other, $11,400. Icon Industries plans to sell the product for $55.00.

Required

1. Using the contribution margin approach, compute the number of units the company must sell to (a) break even and (b) earn a profit of $70,224.
2. Using the same data, compute the number of units that must be sold to earn a profit of $139,520 if advertising costs rise by $40,000.
3. Using the original information and sales of 10,000 units, compute the selling price the company must use to make a profit of $131,600. (**Hint:** Calculate contribution margin per unit first.)
4. **Manager Insight:** According to the vice president of marketing, Albert Flora, the most optimistic annual sales estimate for the product would be 15,000 units, and the highest competitive selling price the company can charge is $52 per unit. How much more can be spent on fixed advertising costs if the selling price is $52, if the variable costs cannot be reduced, and if the targeted profit for 15,000 unit sales is $251,000?

LO4, LO5 **Breakeven Analysis and Planning Future Sales**

P 4. Write Company has a maximum capacity of 200,000 units per year. Variable manufacturing costs are $12 per unit. Fixed overhead is $600,000 per year. Variable selling and administrative costs are $5 per unit, and fixed selling and administrative costs are $300,000 per year. The current sales price is $23 per unit.

Required

1. What is the breakeven point in (a) sales units and (b) sales dollars?
2. How many units must Write Company sell to earn a profit of $240,000 per year?
3. A strike at one of the company's major suppliers has caused a shortage of materials, so the current year's production and sales are limited to 160,000 units. To partially offset the effect of the reduced sales on profit, management is planning to reduce fixed costs to $841,000. Variable cost per unit is the same as last year. The company has already sold 30,000 units at the regular selling price of $23 per unit.

   a. What amount of fixed costs was covered by the total contribution margin of the first 30,000 units sold?
   b. What contribution margin per unit will be needed on the remaining 130,000 units to cover the remaining fixed costs and to earn a profit of $210,000 this year?

LO2, LO5 **Cost Behavior and Projection for a Service Business**

P 5. Power Brite Painting Company specializes in refurbishing exterior painted surfaces that have been hard hit by humidity and insect debris. It uses a special technique, called pressure cleaning, before priming and painting the surface. The refurbishing process involves the following steps:

1. Unskilled laborers trim all trees and bushes within two feet of the structure.
2. Skilled laborers clean the building with a high-pressure cleaning machine, using about six gallons of chlorine per job.
3. Unskilled laborers apply a coat of primer.
4. Skilled laborers apply oil-based exterior paint to the entire surface.

On average, skilled laborers work 12 hours per job, and unskilled laborers work 8 hours. The refurbishing process generated the following operating results during the year on 628 jobs:

Skilled labor	$20 per hour
Unskilled labor	$8 per hour
Gallons of chlorine used	3,768 gallons at $5.50 per gallon
Paint primer	7,536 gallons at $15.50 per gallon
Paint	6,280 gallons at $16 per gallon
Depreciation of paint spraying equipment	$600 per month depreciation
Lease of two vans	$800 per month total
Rent on storage building	$450 per month

Data on utilities for the year are as follows:

Month	Number of Jobs	Cost	Hours Worked
January	42	$ 3,950	840
February	37	3,550	740
March	44	4,090	880
April	49	4,410	980
May	54	4,720	1,080
June	62	5,240	1,240
July	71	5,820	1,420
August	73	5,890	1,460
September	63	5,370	1,260
October	48	4,340	960
November	45	4,210	900
December	40	3,830	800
Totals	628	$55,420	12,560

Required

1. Classify the costs as variable, fixed, or mixed.
2. Using the high-low method, separate mixed costs into their variable and fixed components. Use total hours worked as the basis.
3. Compute the average cost per job for the year. (**Hint:** Divide the total of all costs for the year by the number of jobs completed.)
4. Project the average cost per job for next year if variable costs per job increase 20 percent.

Alternate Problems

LO4, LO5 **Breakeven Analysis**

P 6. At the beginning of each year, the Accounting Department at Moon Glow Lighting, Ltd., must find the point at which projected sales revenue will equal total budgeted variable and fixed costs. The company produces custom-made, low-voltage outdoor lighting systems. Each system sells for an average of $435. Variable costs per unit are $210. Total fixed costs for the year are estimated to be $166,500.

Required

1. Compute the breakeven point in sales units.
2. Compute the breakeven point in sales dollars.
3. Find the new breakeven point in sales units if the fixed costs go up by $10,125.
4. Using the original figures, compute the breakeven point in sales units if the selling price decreases to $425 per unit, fixed costs go up by $15,200, and variable costs decrease by $15 per unit.

Planning Future Sales: Contribution Margin Approach

P 7. Garden Marbles manufactures birdbaths, statues, and other decorative items, which it sells to florists and retail home and garden centers. Its Design Department has proposed a new product, a statue of a frog, that it believes will be popular with home gardeners. Expected variable unit costs are direct materials, $9.25; direct labor, $4.00; production supplies, $0.55; selling costs, $2.40; and other, $3.05. The following are fixed costs: depreciation, building and equipment, $33,000; advertising, $40,000; and other, $6,000. Management plans to sell the product for $29.25.

LO4, LO5   **Required**

1. Using the contribution margin approach, compute the number of statues the company must sell to (a) break even and (b) earn a profit of $50,000.
2. Using the same data, compute the number of statues that must be sold to earn a profit of $70,000 if advertising costs rise by $20,000.
3. Using the original data and sales of 15,000 units, compute the selling price the company must charge to make a profit of $100,000.
4. **Manager Insight:** According to the vice president of marketing, Yvonne Palmer, if the price of the statues is reduced and advertising is increased, the most optimistic annual sales estimate is 25,000 units. How much more can be spent on fixed advertising costs if the selling price is reduced to $28.00 per statue, if the variable costs cannot be reduced, and if the targeted profit for sales of 25,000 statues is $120,000?

Planning Future Sales for a Service Business

P 8. Lending Hand Financial Corporation is a subsidiary of Gracey Enterprises. Its main business is processing loan applications. Last year, Bettina Brent, the manager of the corporation's Loan Department, established a policy of charging a $250 fee for every loan application processed. Next year's variable costs have been projected as follows: loan consultant's wages, $15.50 per hour (a loan application takes five hours to process); supplies, $2.40 per application; and other variable costs, $5.60 per application. Annual fixed costs include depreciation of equipment, $8,500; building rental, $14,000; promotional costs, $12,500; and other fixed costs, $8,099.

LO5   **Required**

1. Using the contribution margin approach, compute the number of loan applications the company must process to (a) break even and (b) earn a profit of $14,476.
2. Using the same approach and assuming promotional costs increase by $5,662, compute the number of applications the company must process to earn a profit of $20,000.

3. Assuming the original information and the processing of 500 applications, compute the loan application fee the company must charge if the targeted profit is $41,651.

4. **Manager Insight:** Brent's staff can handle a maximum of 750 loan applications. How much more can be spent on promotional costs if the highest fee tolerable to the customer is $280, if variable costs cannot be reduced, and if the targeted profit for the loan applications is $50,000?

ENHANCING Your Knowledge, Skills, and Critical Thinking

Conceptual Understanding Cases

LO1, LO2 Concept of Cost Behavior

C 1. Gulf Coast Shrimp Company is a small company. It owns an icehouse and processing building, a refrigerated van, and three shrimp boats. Bob Jones inherited the company from his father three months ago. The company employs three boat crews of four people each and five processing workers. Trey Goodfellow of Bayou Accountants, a local accounting firm, has kept the company's financial records for many years. In his last analysis of operations, Goodfellow stated that the company's fixed cost base of $100,000 is satisfactory for its type and size of business. However, variable costs have averaged 70 percent of sales over the last two years, which is too high for the volume of business. Last year, only 30 percent of the sales revenue of $300,000 contributed to covering fixed costs. As a result, the company reported a $10,000 operating loss.

Jones wants to improve the company's net income, but he is confused by Goodfellow's explanation of the fixed and variable costs. Prepare a response to Jones from Goodfellow in which you explain the concept of cost behavior as it relates to Gulf Coast's operations. Include ideas for improving the company's net income based on changes in fixed and variable costs.

LO5 Comparison of Cost Behavior

C 2. **Allstate Insurance Co.** and **USAA** are two well-known insurers of motorists. Allstate has agents and offices all over the country. USAA sells only through the mail and over the telephone or Internet. In addition to offering collision and liability coverage for automobiles, each company offers life insurance and homeowners' insurance. When a motorist buys auto insurance from Allstate, the agent generally offers life insurance and homeowners' insurance as well—a strategy that helps increase Allstate's profitability. Although USAA usually sells its policies at lower prices than Allstate does, it is a very profitable company.

Identify and discuss the role that fixed costs, sales mix, and contribution margin can play in increasing profitability. Suggest a performance measure that could be used to evaluate agents who sell auto insurance. What is the role of variable costs? What is it about the relationship of USAA's fixed and variable costs that allows the company to sell policies at lower prices than Allstate and yet remain profitable?

LO2 Mixed Costs

C 3. Officials of the Hidden Hills Golf and Tennis Club are in the process of preparing a budget for the year ending December 31. Because Ramon Saud, the club treasurer, has had difficulty with two expense items, the process has been delayed by more than four weeks. The two items are mixed costs—expenses for electricity and for repairs and maintenance—and Saud has been having trouble breaking them down into their variable and fixed components.

An accountant friend has suggested that he use the high-low method to divide the costs into their variable and fixed parts. The spending patterns and activity measures related to each cost during the past year are as follows:

	Electricity Expense		Repairs and Maintenance	
Month	Amount	Kilowatt Hours	Amount	Labor Hours
January	$ 7,500	210,000	$ 7,578	220
February	8,255	240,200	7,852	230
March	8,165	236,600	7,304	210
April	8,960	268,400	7,030	200
May	7,520	210,800	7,852	230
June	7,025	191,000	8,126	240
July	6,970	188,800	8,400	250
August	6,990	189,600	8,674	260
September	7,055	192,200	8,948	270
October	7,135	195,400	8,674	260
November	8,560	252,400	8,126	240
December	8,415	246,600	7,852	230
Totals	$92,550	2,622,000	$96,416	2,840

1. Using the high-low method, compute the variable cost rates used last year for each expense. What was the monthly fixed cost for electricity and for repairs and maintenance?
2. Compute the total variable cost and total fixed cost for each expense category for last year.
3. Saud believes that in the coming year, the electricity rate will increase by $0.005 and the repairs rate, by $1.20. Usage of all items and their fixed cost amounts will remain constant. Compute the projected total cost for each category. How will the cost increases affect the club's profits and cash flow?

LO3 **C-V-P Analysis and Decision Making**

C 4. The Goslar Corporation cuts granite, marble, and sandstone for use in building and restoring cathedrals throughout Europe. The German-based company has operations in Italy and Switzerland. Gunder Shillar, the controller, recently determined that the breakeven point was €325,000 in sales. For a quarterly planning meeting, Shillar must provide information about the following six proposals, which the planning team will discuss individually:

a. Increase the selling price of marble slabs by 10 percent.
b. Change the sales mix to respond to an increased demand for marble slabs—that is, increase production and sales of marble slabs and decrease the production and sales of sandstone slabs, the least profitable product.
c. Increase fixed production costs by €40,000 annually to cover depreciation on new stone-cutting equipment.
d. Increase variable costs by 1 percent to cover higher export duties on foreign sales.
e. Decrease the sales volume of sandstone slabs because of a reduction in demand in Eastern Europe.
f. Decrease the number of days a customer can defer payment without being charged interest.

1. For each proposal, determine whether cost-volume-profit (C-V-P) analysis would provide useful financial information.
2. Indicate how each proposal that lends itself to C-V-P analysis would affect profit.

LO3, LO4   **C-V-P Analysis**

C 5. Based in Italy, Datura, Ltd., is an international importer-exporter of pottery with distribution centers in the United States, Europe, and Australia. The company was very successful in its early years, but its profitability has since declined. As a member of a management team selected to gather information for Datura's next strategic planning meeting, you have been asked to review its most recent contribution income statement, which appears below.

Datura, Ltd.
Contribution Income Statement
For the Year Ended December 31, 20x7

Sales revenue		€13,500,000
Less variable costs		
Purchases	€6,000,000	
Distribution	2,115,000	
Sales commissions	1,410,000	
Total variable costs		9,525,000
Contribution margin		€ 3,975,000
Less fixed costs		
Distribution	€ 985,000	
Selling	1,184,000	
General and administrative	871,875	
Total fixed costs		3,040,875
Operating income		€ 934,125

In 20x7, Datura sold 15,000 sets of pottery.

1. For each set of pottery sold in 20x7, calculate the (a) selling price, (b) variable purchases cost, (c) variable distribution cost, (d) variable sales commission, and (e) contribution margin.
2. Calculate the breakeven point in units and in sales euros.
3. Historically, Datura's variable costs have been about 60 percent of sales. What was the ratio of variable costs to sales in 20x7? List three actions Datura could take to correct the difference.
4. How would fixed costs have been affected if Datura had sold only 14,000 sets of pottery in 20x7?

Interpreting Management Reports

LO4, LO5   **Planning Future Sales and Costs**

C 6. In a recent annual report, read management's letter to the stockholders. This section of an annual report typically discusses initiatives or actions that the company implemented during the year as part of its strategic plan. Identify at least three such initiatives or actions that you believe affected the company's annual sales or costs. Also identify one initiative or action the company is planning for the coming year that you believe will affect revenue or expenses.

Decision Analysis Using Excel

LO5   **Planning Future Sales**

C 7. As noted in **C 5**, Datura, Ltd., sold 15,000 sets of pottery in 20x7. In 20x8, Datura's strategic planning team targeted sales of 15,000 sets of pottery, reduced the selling price to £890 per set, increased sales commissions to 12 percent of the selling price, and decreased fixed distribution costs by 10 percent and variable distribution costs by 4 percent. It was assumed that all other costs would stay the same.

Based on an analysis of these changes, Sophia Callas, Datura's president, is concerned that the proposed strategic plan will not meet her goal of increasing Datura's operating income by 10 percent over last year's income and that the operating income will be less than last year's income. She has come to you for spreadsheet analysis of the proposed strategic plan and for analysis of a special order she just received from an Australian distributor for 4,500 sets of pottery. The order's selling price, variable purchases cost per unit, sales commission, and total fixed costs will be the same as for the rest of the business, but the variable distribution costs will be €160 per unit.

Using an Excel spreadsheet, complete the following tasks:

1. Calculate the targeted operating income for 20x8 using just the proposed strategic plan.
2. Prepare a budgeted contribution income statement for 20x8 based on just the strategic plan. Do you agree with Datura's president that the company's projected operating income for 20x8 will be less than the operating income for 20x7? Explain your answer.
3. Calculate the total contribution margin from the Australian sales.
4. Prepare a revised budgeted contribution income statement for 20x8 that includes the Australian order. (**Hint:** Combine the information from **2** and **3** above.)
5. Does Datura need the Australian sales to achieve its targeted operating income for 20x8?

Ethical Dilemma Case

LO4 **Breaking Even and Ethics**

C 8. Lesley Chomski is the supervisor of the New Product Division of MCO Corporation. Her annual bonus is based on the success of new products and is computed on the number of sales that exceed each new product's projected breakeven point. In reviewing the computations supporting her most recent bonus, Chomski found that although an order for 7,500 units of a new product called R56 had been refused by a customer and returned to the company, the order had been included in the calculations. She later discovered that the company's accountant had labeled the return an overhead expense and had charged the entire cost of the returned order to the plantwide Overhead account. The result was that product R56 appeared to exceed breakeven by more than 5,000 units and Chomski's bonus from this product amounted to over $800. What actions should Chomski take? Be prepared to discuss your response in class.

Internet Case

LO4, LO5 **Planning Future Sales and Costs**

C 9. The video rental business is changing as more customers are downloading movies from the Internet rather than renting them through the mail from online sites like **Netflix** or from stores like **Blockbuster**. Go to Blockbuster's and Netflix's websites and review the initiatives or actions that these companies are implementing as part of their strategic plan to address the changing nature of their business (see Management's Discussion in their annual reports).

1. Identify at least two initiatives or actions that one of these companes is implementing that you believe will affect revenue or expenses.
2. Identify the variable costs and fixed costs of these companies.
3. Speculate on how the changes that these companies are making will affect their breakeven point in units (movie rentals).

Group Activity Case

LO2, LO4   **Cost Behavior and Contribution Margin**

C 10. Visit a local fast-food restaurant. Observe all aspects of the operation and take notes on the entire process. Describe the procedures used to take, process, and fill an order and deliver the order to the customer. Based on your observations, make a list of the costs incurred by the operation. Identify at least three variable costs and three fixed costs. Can you identify any potential mixed costs? Why is the restaurant willing to sell a large drink for only a few cents more than a medium drink? How is the restaurant able to offer a "value meal" (e.g., sandwich, drink, and fries) for considerably less than those items would cost if they were bought separately? Bring your notes to class and be prepared to discuss your findings.

Your instructor will divide the class into groups to discuss the case. Summarize your group's discussion and ask one member of the group to present the summary to the rest of the class.

Business Communication Case

LO5   **C-V-P Analysis Applied**

C 11. Refer to the information in **C 5**. In January 20x8, Sophia Callas, the president of Datura, Ltd., conducted a strategic planning meeting. During the meeting, Phillipe Mazzeo, vice president of distribution, noted that because of a new contract with an international shipping line, the company's fixed distribution costs for 20x8 would be reduced by 10 percent and its variable distribution costs by 4 percent. Gino Roma, vice president of sales, offered the following information:

> We plan to sell 15,000 sets of pottery again in 20x8, but based on review of the competition, we are going to lower the selling price to €890 per set. To encourage increased sales, we will raise sales commissions to 12 percent of the selling price.

Sophia Callas is concerned that the changes described by Roma and Mazzeo may not improve operating income sufficiently in 20x8. If operating income does not increase by at least 10 percent, she will want to find other ways to reduce the company's costs. She asks you to evaluate the situation in a written report. Because it is already January of 20x8 and changes need to be made quickly, she requests your report within five days.

1. Prepare a budgeted contribution income statement for 20x8. Your report should show the budgeted (estimated) operating income based on the information provided above and in **C 5**. Will the changes improve operating income sufficiently? Explain.
2. In preparation for writing your report, answer the following questions:
   a. Why are you preparing the report?
   b. Who needs the report?
   c. What sources of information will you use?
   d. When is the report due?

The Budgeting Process

Budgeting is not only an essential part of planning; it also helps managers control, evaluate, and report on operations. When managers develop budgets, they match their organizational goals with the resources necessary to accomplish those goals. During the budgeting process, they evaluate operational, tactical, value chain, and capacity issues; assess how resources for operating, investing, and financing activities are currently being used and how they can be efficiently used in the future; and develop contingency budgets as business conditions change. Managers also use budget information to control daily operations, measure and report on performance outcomes, and allocate resources wisely. In this chapter, we describe the budgeting process, identify the elements of a master budget, and demonstrate how managers prepare operating budgets and financial budgets.

LEARNING OBJECTIVES

LO1 Define *budgeting,* and explain management's role in the budgeting process.

LO2 Identify the elements of a master budget in different types of organizations and the guidelines for preparing budgets.

LO3 Prepare the operating budgets that support the financial budgets.

LO4 Prepare a budgeted income statement, a cash budget, and a budgeted balance sheet.

- How is Johnson & Johnson's budgeting process linked to the company's long-term goals and objectives?

- How does Johnson & Johnson's budgeting process work?

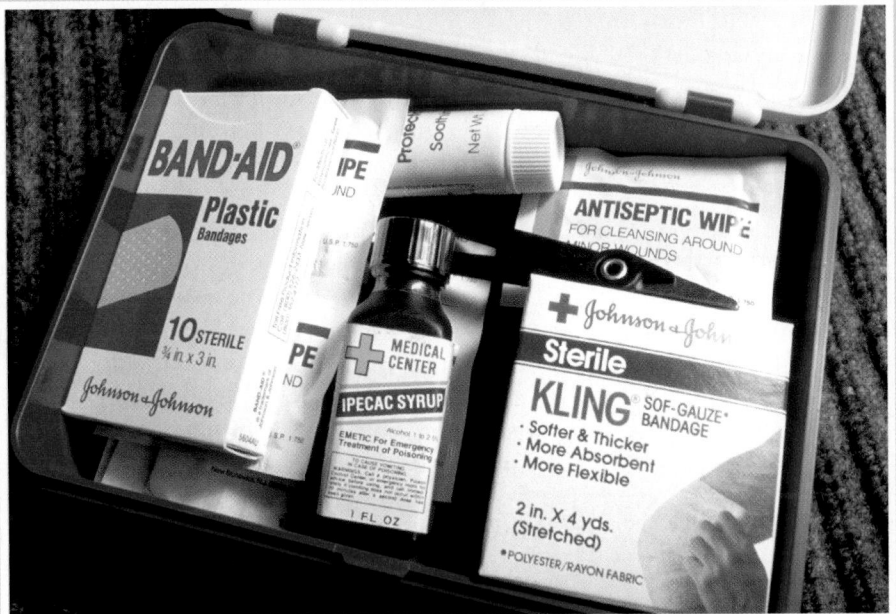

With products that range from baby powder, Band-Aids, Tylenol, and contact lenses to diagnostic and surgical devices, Johnson & Johnson is the largest and most diversified manufacturer of health care products in the world. It has had affiliated companies operating in Latin America, Europe, Africa, and Australia for more than fifty years. Today, it is a global family of over two hundred decentralized companies. Unifying the strategic planning of these companies' management teams are the common values and ethical principles expressed in Johnson & Johnson's credo, or mission statement. The strategic direction and major developments of the various companies are discussed at board meetings throughout the year and at meetings between management and board members. This ongoing dialogue provides managers with insight into the activities and direction of the company's businesses and is the basis for Johnson & Johnson's budgeting decisions.[1]

The Budgeting Process

LO1   Define *budgeting*, and explain management's role in the budgeting process.

Budgeting is the process of identifying, gathering, summarizing, and communicating financial and nonfinancial information about an organization's future activities. It is an essential part of the continuous planning that an organization must do to accomplish its long-term goals and intermediate objectives. The budgeting process provides managers of all types of organizations—including for-profit organizations, such as **Johnson & Johnson** and **Merck**, and not-for-profit organizations, such as the United Way and the United Nations—the opportunity to match their organizational goals with the resources necessary to accomplish those goals. As part of the ongoing budgeting process, managers evaluate operational, tactical, value chain, and capacity issues; assess how resources for operating, investing, and financing activities are currently being used and how they can be efficiently used in the future; and develop contingency budgets as business conditions change.

Budgets—plans of action based on forecasted transactions, activities, and events—are synonymous with managing an organization. They are essential to accomplishing the goals articulated in an organization's strategic plan. They are used to communicate information, coordinate activities and resource usage, motivate employees, and evaluate performance. For example, a board of directors may use budgets to determine managers' areas of responsibility and to measure managers' performance in those areas. Budgets are, of course, also used to manage and account for cash. Such budgets establish minimum or targeted levels of cash receipts and limits on the spending of cash for particular purposes.

Budgets come in many forms. For example, a cash budget focuses on financial information; it shows, among other things, how cash resources will be allotted to operating, investing, and financing activities over a future period. A production budget, on the other hand, focuses on nonfinancial information; it shows planned production in units and identifies the activities needed to meet certain requirements or standards established during the planning process.

To compete successfully in today's global market, an organization must ensure that its managers have continuously updated operating data against which to measure performance. Thus, an ongoing budgeting process is especially important in the current business environment.

Johnson & Johnson

Study Note

For-profit organizations often use the term *profit planning* rather than *budgeting*.

FOCUS ON BUSINESS PRACTICE

A Global Look at Leadership

The number of women in corporate leadership positions is increasing. For example, the president of **Southwest Airlines** is a woman, and before **Albertson's** was sold, the grocery chain's board of directors was predominantly female.

A survey of women serving on the corporate boards that govern the world's 200 largest companies reveals widely different participation rates among countries. Norway has the greatest number of women serving on corporate boards, with a 33.3 percent participation rate, followed by the United States, with 17.5 percent; the United Kingdom, with 12.5 percent; and Malaysia and Finland, with 12.5 percent each. The countries in which the smallest number of women serve on corporate boards are Japan, with 0.7 percent; Spain, with 1.8 percent; Italy, with 1.8 percent; and China, with 2.7 percent.[2]

Shown here at an opening bell ceremony of the New York Stock Exchange are some of the women whom *Fortune* magazine named as the 50 most powerful women in business. The number of women in corporate leadership positions varies widely among countries. Norway has the largest number of women serving on corporate boards—a 33 percent participation rate—and it will soon have even more. A Norwegian law requires that by 2008, women make up 40 percent of the board membership of the country's corporations.

Budgeting and Goals

Long-Term Goals

Strategic planning is the process by which management establishes an organization's long-term goals. These goals define the strategic direction that an organization will take over a five- to ten-year period and are the basis for making annual operating plans and preparing budgets. You may recall from an earlier chapter that long-term goals should take into consideration economic and industry forecasts, employee-management relations, the structure and role of management, value chain considerations, organizational capacity, and any other operational and tactical issues facing the organization, such as the expected quality of products or services, growth rates, and desired market share.

Long-term goals cannot be vague; they must set specific tactical targets and timetables and assign responsibility for achieving the goals to specific personnel. For example, a long-term goal for a company that currently holds only 4 percent of its product's market share might specify that the vice president of marketing is to develop strategies to ensure that the company controls 10 percent of the market in five years and 15 percent by the end of ten years. An organization's strategic plan should include a range of long-term goals and give direction to its efforts to achieve those goals. It should include profit projections and describe new products or services in general terms.

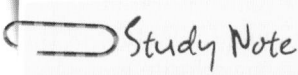

Study Note

As plans are formulated for time periods closer to the current date, they become more specific and quantified. The annual budget is a very specific plan of action.

Short-Term Goals

Annual operating plans involve every part of an enterprise and are much more detailed than long-term strategic plans. To formulate an annual operating plan, an organization must restate its long-term goals in terms of what it needs to accomplish during the next year. The process entails making decisions about sales and profit targets, human resource needs, and the introduction of new products or services. The short-term goals identified in an annual operating plan are the basis of an organization's operating budgets for the year.

Once management has established short-term goals, the organization's controller plays a central role in coordinating the budgeting process. This person designs a complete set of budget-development directions, including a timetable complete with deadlines for all parts of the year's operating plan,

and assigns clearly defined responsibilities for carrying out each part of the budget's development to specific individuals or management teams.

Depending on organizational practice, a budget may be reviewed and revised during the year. As pointed out in the focus box above, there is a growing trend toward more frequent budget revisions.

The Importance of Participation

Because an organization's main activities—such as production, sales, and employee training—take place at its lower levels, the information necessary for establishing a budget flows from the supervisors of those activities through middle managers to senior executives. Each person in this chain of communication thus plays a role in developing a budget, as well as in implementing it. If these individuals feel that they have a voice in setting the budget targets, they will be motivated to ensure that their departments attain those targets and stay within the budget. If they do not feel that they have a role in the budgeting process, motivation will suffer. The key to a successful budget is therefore **participative budgeting**, a process in which personnel at all levels of an organization actively engage in making decisions about the budget.

Because the controller is at the center of the budgeting process, collecting and distributing information and coordinating all budgeting activities, that person has considerable influence over the nature of the budgeting process. Participative budgeting depends on joint decision making, and to foster a climate in which that can take place, a controller must be able to communicate and negotiate effectively with people at all levels of an organization—from the senior executives who formulate the organization's long- and short-term goals to the middle managers and supervisors responsible for daily operations.

Senior executives also play a central role in determining the nature of the budgeting process. If they dictate targets instead of allowing middle managers and supervisors a voice in setting them, the budgeting process will be authoritative rather than participative. Without input from personnel at operational levels, the targets may be unrealistic and impossible to attain, which will further undermine the motivation of the managers and supervisors whose cooperation is essential for successful budget implementation. Problems may also arise if senior executives allow the controller to develop the budget without consulting other managers. In that case, managers may feel that budgeting is not a top priority and that budgets need not be taken seriously. Such difficulties can be avoided if senior executives recognize the importance of allowing personnel at all levels to play meaningful roles in the budgeting process.

Budget Implementation

As we have noted, an organization's controller plays a central role in designing and coordinating the budgeting process. The controller is part of a **budget committee** that has overall responsibility for budget implementation. This committee oversees each stage in the preparation of the organization's overall budget, mediates any departmental disputes that may arise in the process, and gives final approval to the budget. Other top managers who are part of the budget committee include the company's president and the vice presidents in charge of various functional areas, such as production, purchasing, marketing, and human resources. The make-up of the committee ensures that the budgeting process has a companywide perspective.

A budget may have to go through many revisions before it includes all planning decisions and has the approval of the budget committee. Once the committee approves the budget, periodic reports from department managers allow the committee to monitor the company's progress in attaining budget targets.

Successful budget implementation depends on two factors—clear communication and the support of top management. To ensure their cooperation in implementing the budget, all key persons involved must know what roles they are expected to play and must have specific directions on how to achieve their performance goals. Thus, the controller and other members of the budget committee must be very clear in communicating performance expectations and budget targets. Equally important, top management must show support for the budget and encourage its implementation. The process will succeed only if middle- and lower-level managers are confident that top management is truly interested in the outcome and is willing to reward personnel for meeting the budget targets. Today, many organizations have employee incentive plans that tie the achievement of budget targets to bonuses or other types of compensation.

Study Note

Because good communication can eliminate many of the problems that typically arise in the budgeting process, companywide dialogue is extremely important.

Managers and the Budgeting Process

As Figure 1 shows, budgeting helps managers do their jobs. To illustrate the relationship between budgeting and managers, we will refer to the budgeting activities of Framecraft Company, a manufacturer specializing in high-quality plastic picture frames. Framecraft's sole stockholder, Chase Vitt, believes that the future growth of his company depends on a good budgeting process.

Planning Budgets put managers' plans into operation. They reflect an organization's long- and short-term plans for achieving key success factors, such as high-quality products, reasonable costs, and timely delivery. Chase Vitt believes that by distributing workloads carefully and allotting resources to specific products, departments, and sales territories, budgets help his managers orchestrate short-term activities to accomplish long-term goals. Because

FOCUS ON BUSINESS PRACTICE

What Can Cause the Planning Process to Fail?

When chief financial officers were asked what caused their planning process to fail, these were the six factors they most commonly cited:[4]

- An inadequately defined strategy
- No clear link between strategy and the operational budget

- Lack of individual accountability for results
- Lack of meaningful performance measures
- Inadequate pay for performance
- Lack of appropriate data

■ **FIGURE 1**
The Management Process: To-Do's for Managers

To-Do's for Managers

- Plan
  - Review strategic, tactical, and operating objectives
  - Analyze and forecast sales
  - Analyze costs and determine cost formulas
  - Prepare operating budgets
  - Prepare financial budgets
  - Analyze effects of alternative scenarios on the budget
  - Finalize and approve budget

- Perform
  - Implement budget

- Evaluate
  - Compare actual results with budget, revise budget if needed

- Communicate
  - Prepare internal budget reports
  - Prepare comparative analyses of budget to actual results

Vitt recognizes the benefits of participative budgeting, he includes personnel from all levels of the company in the budgeting process. To motivate employees to achieve the targets set forth in the budget, Framecraft Company awards bonuses for good performance. As measures of performance, managers have selected profits, number of units sold, number of defective units, and cycle time (the time to obtain, manufacture, and ship an order).

Performing Managers use budget information to control daily operations, measure performance outcomes, and allocate resources. The managers of Framecraft Company use budget information daily, weekly, and monthly to communicate expectations about performance, to measure performance and motivate employees, and to coordinate activities and allot resources among various departments. For example, Geoff Kovic, the production manager, uses the units of production specified in the budget as an operating target for his workers and the number of defective units as a performance measure to motivate them to manufacture high-quality products. Chase Vitt uses standard product costs, generated in the planning process, to submit bids and estimate profits.

↰ Study Note

Budgeting is not only an essential part of planning; it also helps in controlling operations.

Evaluating When managers assess performance results, they look for variances between planned and actual performance and create solutions for the variances they detect. As we have already indicated, Framecraft Company's managers use the targets established in the planning stage as targets for actual performance. When Vitt and Kovic review Framecraft's results, they compare planned performance with actual performance. If they identify variances, they focus on finding solutions to the problems, which promotes continuous improvement of the company's products and processes. Framecraft Company's managers review their budgets on a regular basis because doing so helps them evaluate past performance and chart the course of future operations.

Communicating Because budgets are plans of action based on forecasts of transactions, activities, and events, they serve as a reference point for many kinds of reports. For example, performance reports that support bonuses and promotions are based on budget information. Other budget-based reports support operating decisions. To provide continuous feedback about an organization's operating, investing, and financing activities, managers prepare and distribute reports based on budget information throughout the year.

S T O P • R E V I E W • A P P L Y

1-1. What is a budget? What types of information does a budget include?

1-2. How do long-term strategic plans and annual operating plans differ?

1-3. Who are the people responsible for ensuring that budget implementation is successful? What are their responsibilities?

Suggested answers to all Stop, Review, and Apply questions are available at http://college.hmco.com/accounting/needles/poa/10e/student_home.html.

The Master Budget

LO2 Identify the elements of a master budget in different types of organizations and the guidelines for preparing budgets.

A **master budget** consists of a set of operating budgets and a set of financial budgets that detail an organization's financial plans for a specific accounting period, generally a year. When a master budget covers an entire year, some of the operating and financial budgets may show planned results by month or by quarter. As the term implies, **operating budgets** are plans used in daily operations. They are also the basis for preparing the **financial budgets**, which are projections of financial results for the accounting period. Financial budgets include a budgeted income statement, a capital expenditures budget, a cash budget, and a budgeted balance sheet.

The budgeted financial statements—that is, the budgeted income statement and budgeted balance sheet—are also called **pro forma statements**, meaning that they show projections rather than actual results. Pro forma statements are often used to communicate business plans to external parties. If, for example, you wanted to obtain a bank loan so that you could start a new business, you would have to present the bank with a pro forma, or budgeted,

Study Note

Budgeted financial statements are often referred to as *forecasted financial statements, pro forma statements,* or *forward-looking statements.*

■ **FIGURE 2**
Preparation of a Master Budget for a Manufacturing Organization

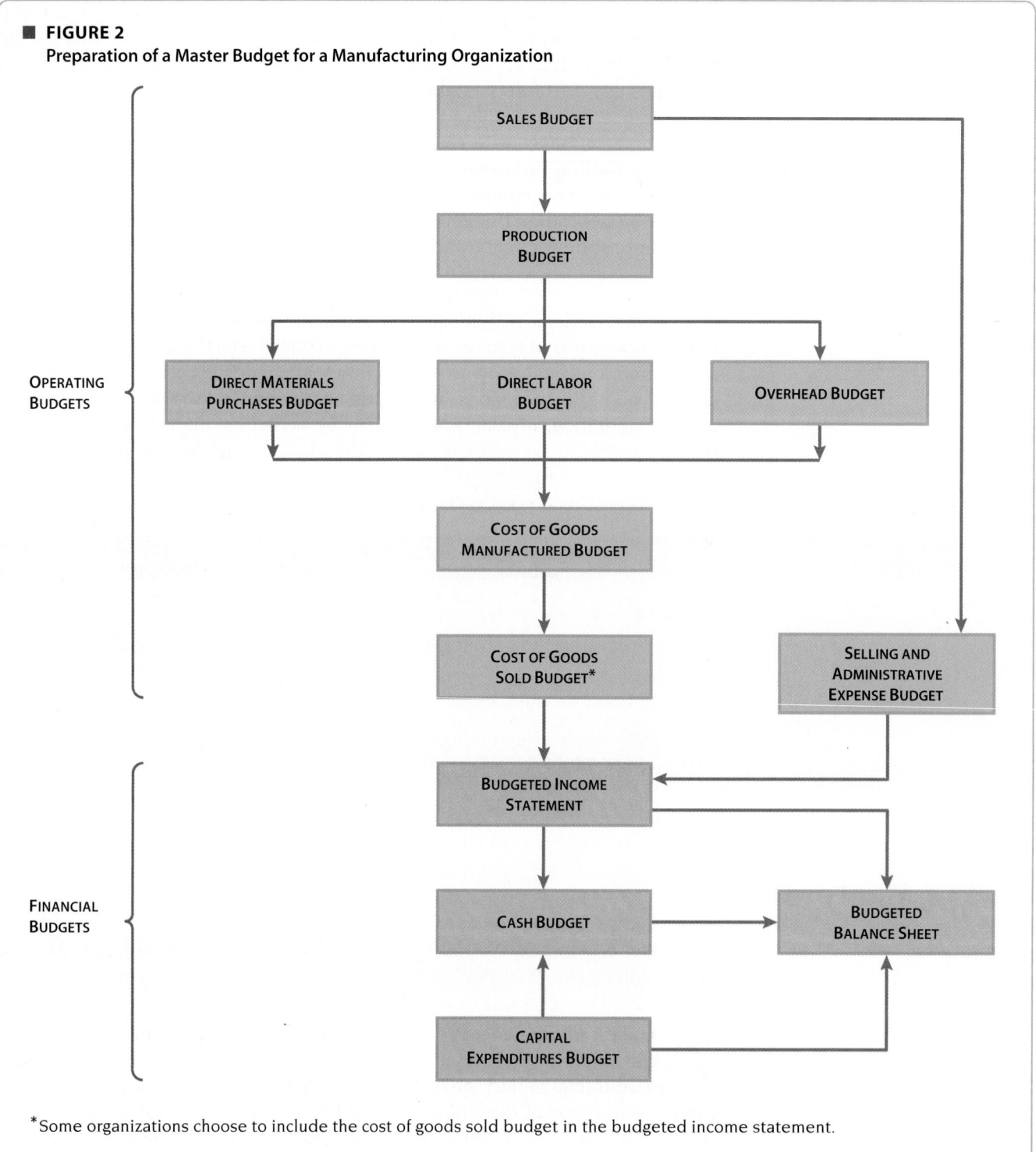

*Some organizations choose to include the cost of goods sold budget in the budgeted income statement.

income statement and balance sheet showing that you could repay the loan with cash generated by profitable operations.

Suppose you have started your own business. Whether it is a manufacturing, retail, or service organization, to manage it effectively, you would prepare a master budget each period. A master budget provides the information needed to match long-term goals to short-term activities and to plan the resources needed to ensure an organization's profitability and liquidity.

Figures 2, 3, and 4 display the elements of a master budget for a manufacturing organization, a retail organization, and a service organization, respec-

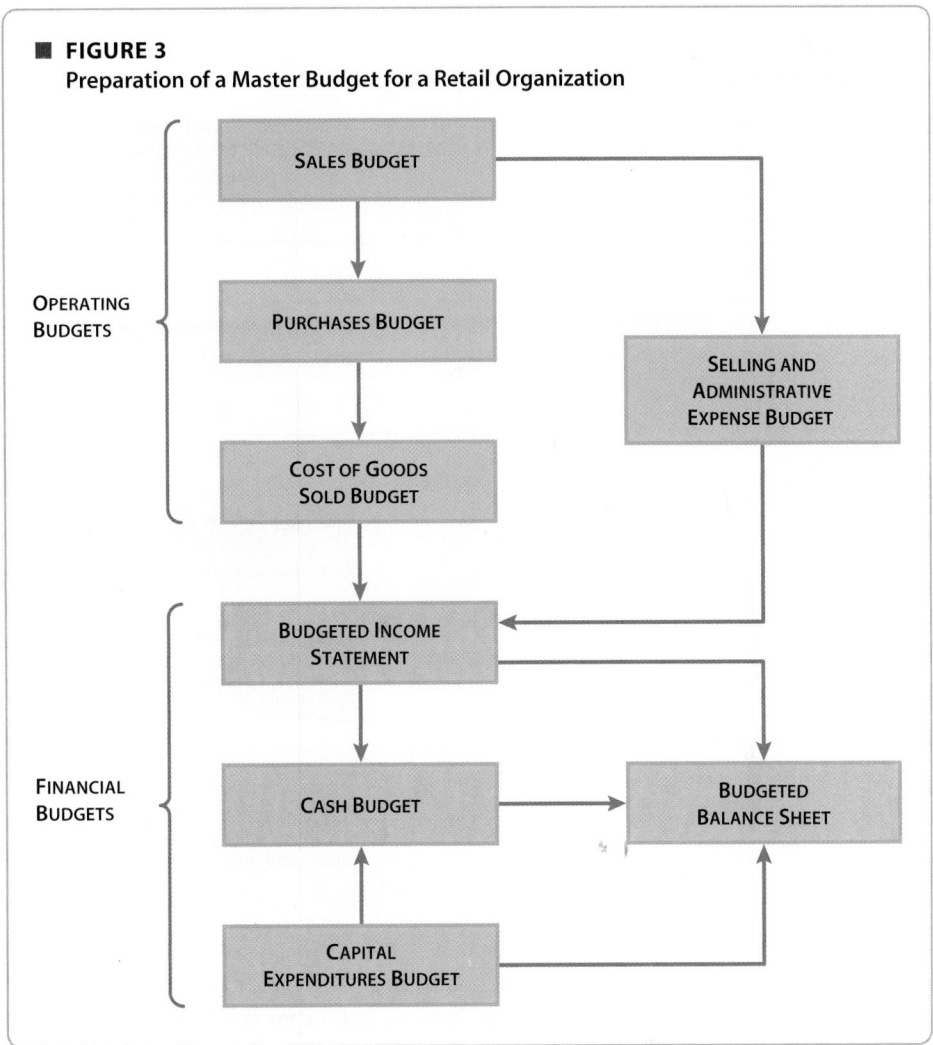

■ **FIGURE 3**
Preparation of a Master Budget for a Retail Organization

tively. As these illustrations indicate, the process of preparing a master budget is similar in all three types of organizations in that each prepares a set of operating budgets that serve as the basis for preparing the financial budgets. The process differs mainly in the kinds of operating budgets that each type of organization prepares.

The operating budgets of manufacturing organizations, such as **Johnson & Johnson, Intel,** and **John Deere,** include budgets for sales, production, direct materials, direct labor, overhead, selling and administrative expenses, and cost of goods manufactured. Retail organizations, such as **Nordstrom, Talbots,** and **Lowe's,** prepare a sales budget, a purchases budget, a selling and administrative expense budget, and a cost of goods sold budget. The operating budgets of service organizations, such as **Enterprise Rent-A-Car, UPS,** and **Amtrak,** include budgets for revenue (sales), labor, overhead, and selling and administrative expenses.

The sales budget (or, in service organizations, the service revenue budget) is prepared first because it is used to estimate sales volume and revenues. Once managers know the quantity of products or services to be sold and how many sales dollars to expect, they can develop other budgets that will enable them to manage their organization's resources so that they generate profits on those sales.

For example, in a retail organization, the purchases budget provides managers with information about the quantity of merchandise needed to meet the

■ **FIGURE 4**
Preparation of a Master Budget for a Service Organization

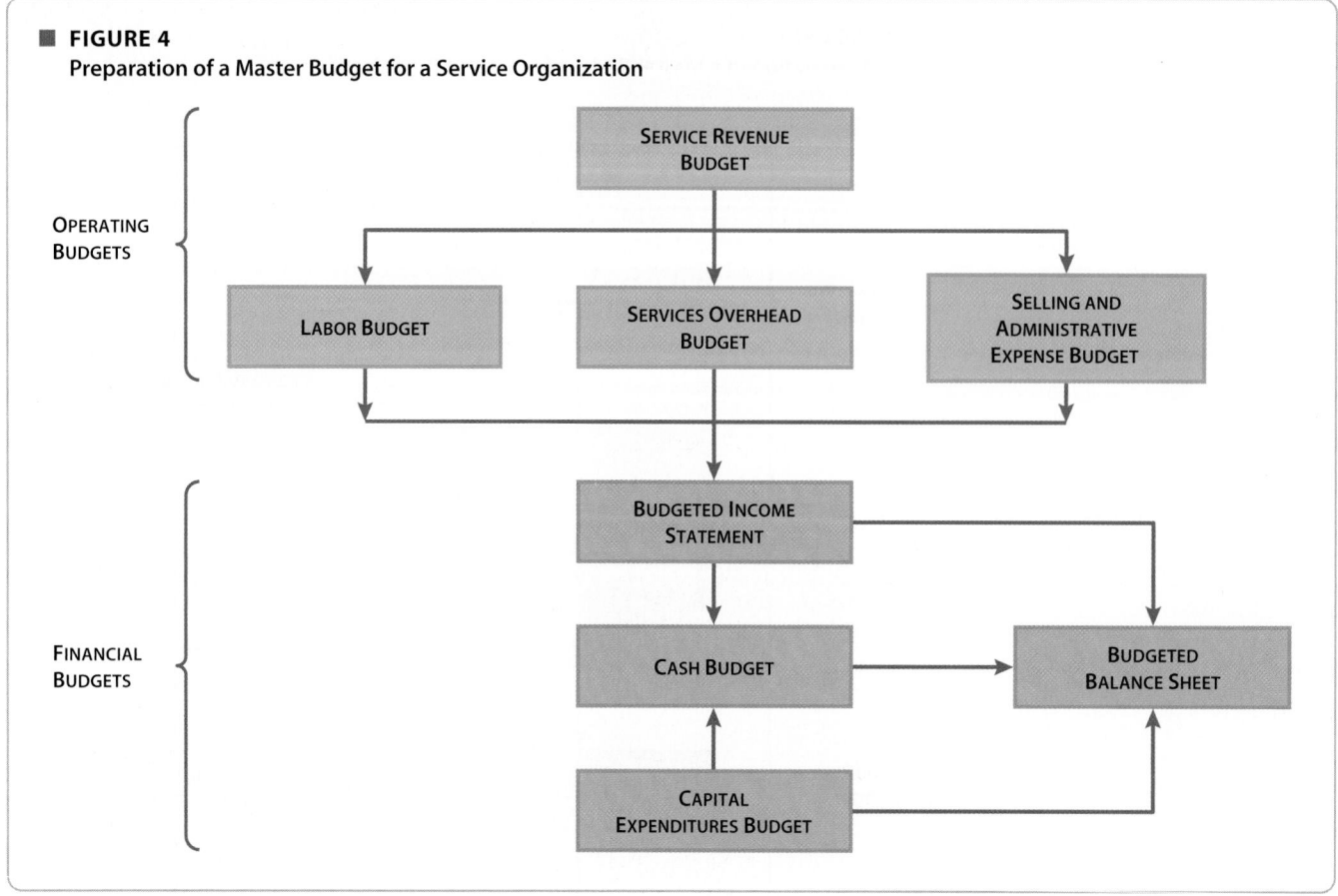

sales demand and yet maintain a minimum level of inventory. In a service organization, the labor budget provides information about the labor hours and labor rates needed to provide services and generate the revenues planned for each period; managers use this information in scheduling services and setting prices.

Because procedures for preparing budgets vary from organization to organization, there is no standard format for budget preparation. The only universal requirement is that budgets communicate the appropriate information to the reader in a clear and understandable manner. By keeping that in mind and using the following guidelines, managers can improve the quality of budgets in any type of organization:

1. Know the purpose of the budget.

2. Identify the user group and its information needs.

3. Identify sources of accurate, meaningful budget information. Such information may be gathered from documents or from interviews with employees, suppliers, or managers who work in the related areas.

4. Establish a clear format for the budget. A budget should begin with a clearly stated heading that includes the organization's name, the type of budget, and the accounting period under consideration. The budget's components should be clearly labeled, and the unit and financial data should be listed in an orderly manner.

5. Use appropriate formulas and calculations in deriving the quantitative information.

6. Revise the budget until it includes all planning decisions. Several revisions may be required before the final version is ready for distribution.

S T O P • R E V I E W • A P P L Y

2-1. What is a master budget? What is its purpose?

2-2. In what ways are the master budgets of manufacturing, retail, and service organizations similar?

2-3. List the guidelines for preparing a budget.

Operating Budgets

LO3 Prepare the operating budgets that support the financial budgets.

Although procedures for preparing operating budgets vary, the tools used in the process do not. They include cost behavior analysis, cost-volume-profit (C-V-P) analysis, and a product costing method. In this section, we use Framecraft Company to illustrate how a manufacturing organization prepares its operating budgets. Because Framecraft makes only one product—a plastic picture frame—it prepares only one of each type of operating budget. Organizations that manufacture a variety of products or provide many types of services may prepare either separate operating budgets or one comprehensive budget for each product or service.

The Sales Budget

Study Note

The sales budget is the only budget based on an estimate of customer demand. Other budgets for the period are prepared from it and are based on the numbers it provides.

As we indicated earlier, the first step in preparing a master budget is to prepare a sales budget. A **sales budget** is a detailed plan, expressed in both units and dollars, that identifies the sales expected during an accounting period. Sales managers use this information to plan sales- and marketing-related activities and to determine their human, physical, and technical resource needs. Accountants use the information to determine estimated cash receipts for the cash budget.

The following equation is used to determine the total budgeted sales:

$$\text{Total Budgeted Sales} = \text{Estimated Selling Price per Unit} \times \text{Estimated Sales in Units}$$

Although the calculation is easy, selecting the best estimates for the selling price per unit and the sales demand in units can be difficult. An estimated selling price below the current selling price may be needed if competitors are currently selling the same product or service at lower prices or if the organization wants to increase its share of the market. On the other hand, if the organization has improved the quality of its product or service by using more expensive materials or processes, the estimated selling price may have to be higher than the current price.

The estimated sales volume is very important because it will affect the level of operating activities and the amount of resources needed for operations. The resources needed for production, packing, shipping, accounting,

EXHIBIT 1 ▶ **Sales Budget**

Framecraft Company
Sales Budget
For the Year Ended December 31, 20x9

| | Quarter | | | | |
	1	2	3	4	Year
Sales in units	10,000	30,000	10,000	40,000	90,000
× Selling price per unit	× $5	× $5	× $5	× $5	× $5
Total sales	$50,000	$150,000	$50,000	$200,000	$450,000

purchasing, selling, and administrative activities will increase in varying degrees with increases in the estimated sales volume. To help estimate sales volume, managers often use a **sales forecast**, which is a projection of sales demand (the estimated sales in units) based on an analysis of external and internal factors. The external factors include

1. The state of the local and national economies
2. The state of the industry's economy
3. The nature of the competition and its sales volume and selling price

Internal factors taken into consideration in a sales forecast include

1. The number of units sold in prior periods
2. The organization's credit policies
3. The organization's collection policies
4. The organization's pricing policies
5. Any new products that the organization plans to introduce to the market
6. The capacity of the organization's manufacturing facilities

Exhibit 1 illustrates Framecraft Company's sales budget for the year 20x9. The budget shows the estimated number of unit sales and dollar revenue amounts for each quarter and for the entire year. Because a sales forecast indicated a highly competitive marketplace, Framecraft's managers have estimated a selling price of $5 per unit. The sales forecast also indicated highly seasonal sales activity; the estimated sales volume therefore varies from 10,000 to 40,000 per quarter.

The Production Budget

A **production budget** is a detailed plan showing the number of units that a company must produce to meet budgeted sales and inventory needs. Production managers use this information to plan for the materials and human resources that production-related activities will require. To prepare a production budget, managers must know the budgeted number of unit sales (which is specified in the sales budget) and the desired level of ending finished goods inventory for each period in the budget year. That level is often stated as a percentage of the next period's budgeted unit sales. For example, Framecraft

EXHIBIT 2 ▶   Production Budget

Framecraft Company
Production Budget
For the Year Ended December 31, 20x9

	Quarter				
	1	**2**	**3**	**4**	**Year**
Sales in units	10,000	30,000	10,000	40,000	90,000
Plus desired units of ending finished goods inventory	3,000	1,000	4,000	1,500	1,500
Desired total units	13,000	31,000	14,000	41,500	91,500
Less desired units of beginning finished goods inventory	1,000	3,000	1,000	4,000	1,000
Total production units	12,000	28,000	13,000	37,500	90,500

Company's desired level of ending finished goods inventory is 10 percent of the next quarter's budgeted unit sales. (Its desired level of beginning finished goods inventory is 10 percent of the current quarter's budgeted unit sales.)

The following formula identifies the production needs for each accounting period:

$$\text{Total Production Units} = \text{Budgeted Sales in Units} + \text{Desired Units of Ending Finished Goods Inventory} - \text{Desired Units of Beginning Finished Goods Inventory}$$

Exhibit 2 shows Framecraft Company's production budget for 20x9. Notice that each quarter's desired total units of ending finished goods inventory become the next quarter's desired total units of beginning finished goods inventory. Because unit sales of 15,000 are budgeted for the first quarter of 201x, the ending finished goods inventory for the fourth quarter of 20x9 is 1,500 units (.10 × 15,000 units), which is the same as the desired number of units of ending finished goods inventory for the entire year. Similarly, the number of desired units for the first quarter's beginning finished goods inventory—1,000—is the same as the desired number of units of beginning finished goods inventory for the entire year.

The Direct Materials Purchases Budget

A **direct materials purchases budget** is a detailed plan that identifies the quantity of purchases required to meet budgeted production and inventory needs and the costs associated with those purchases. A purchasing department uses this information to plan purchases of direct materials. Accountants use the same information to estimate cash payments to suppliers.

To prepare a direct materials purchases budget, managers must know what production needs will be in each accounting period in the budget; this information is provided by the production budget. They must also know the desired level of the direct materials inventory for each period and the per-unit cost of direct materials. The desired level of ending direct materials inventory is usually stated as a percentage of the next period's production needs. Framecraft's desired level of ending direct materials inventory is 20 percent of the

EXHIBIT 3 ▶

Direct Materials Purchases Budget

Framecraft Company
Direct Materials Purchases Budget
For the Year Ended December 31, 20x9

	Quarter				
	1	2	3	4	Year
Total production units	12,000	28,000	13,000	37,500	90,500
× 10 ounces per unit	× 10	× 10	× 10	× 10	× 10
Total production needs in ounces	120,000	280,000	130,000	375,000	905,000
Plus desired ounces of ending direct materials inventory	56,000	26,000	75,000	30,000	30,000
	176,000	306,000	205,000	405,000	935,000
Less desired ounces of beginning direct materials inventory	24,000	56,000	26,000	75,000	24,000
Total ounces of direct materials to be purchased	152,000	250,000	179,000	330,000	911,000
× Cost per ounce	× $.05	× $.05	× $.05	× $.05	× $.05
Total cost of direct materials purchases	$ 7,600	$ 12,500	$ 8,950	$ 16,500	$ 45,550

next quarter's budgeted production needs. (Its desired level of beginning direct materials inventory is 20 percent of the current quarter's budgeted production needs.)

The first step in preparing a direct materials purchases budget is to calculate each period's total production needs in units of direct materials. Plastic is the only direct material used in Framecraft Company's picture frames; each frame requires 10 ounces of plastic. Framecraft's managers therefore calculate units of production needs in ounces; they multiply the number of frames budgeted for production in a quarter by the 10 ounces of plastic that each frame requires.

In the second step, the following formula is used to determine the quantity of direct materials to be purchased during each accounting period in the budget:

$$\begin{matrix} \text{Total Units of} \\ \text{Direct} \\ \text{Materials to} \\ \text{Be Purchased} \end{matrix} = \begin{matrix} \text{Total Production} \\ \text{Needs in} \\ \text{Units of Direct} \\ \text{Materials} \end{matrix} + \begin{matrix} \text{Desired Units of} \\ \text{Ending Direct} \\ \text{Materials} \\ \text{Inventory} \end{matrix} - \begin{matrix} \text{Desired Units of} \\ \text{Beginning Direct} \\ \text{Materials} \\ \text{Inventory} \end{matrix}$$

The third step is to calculate the cost of the direct materials purchases by multiplying the total number of unit purchases by the direct materials cost. Framecraft's Purchasing Department has estimated the cost of the plastic used in the picture frames at $.05 per ounce.

Exhibit 3 shows Framecraft's direct materials purchases budget for 20x9. Notice that each quarter's desired units of ending direct materials inventory become the next quarter's desired units of beginning direct materials inventory. The company's budgeted number of units for the first quarter of 201x is 150,000 ounces; its ending direct materials inventory for the fourth quarter of 20x9 is therefore 30,000 ounces (.20 × 150,000 ounces), which is the same as the number of desired units of ending direct materials inventory for the entire year. Similarly, the number of desired units for the first quarter's beginning direct materials inventory—24,000 ounces—is the same as the beginning amount for the entire year.

The Direct Labor Budget

A **direct labor budget** is a detailed plan that estimates the direct labor hours needed during an accounting period and the associated costs. Production managers use estimated direct labor hours to plan how many employees will be required during the period and the hours that each will work, and accountants use estimated direct labor costs to plan for cash payments to the workers. Managers of human resources use the information in a direct labor budget in deciding whether to hire new employees or reduce the existing work force, and also as a guide in training employees and preparing schedules of employee fringe benefits.

The first step in preparing a direct labor budget is to estimate the total direct labor hours by multiplying the estimated direct labor hours per unit by the anticipated units of production (see Exhibit 2). The second step in preparing such a budget is to calculate the total budgeted direct labor cost by multiplying the estimated total direct labor hours by the estimated direct labor cost per hour. A company's human resources department provides an estimate of the hourly labor wage.

$$\text{Total Budgeted Direct Labor Costs} = \text{Estimated Total Direct Labor Hours} \times \text{Estimated Direct Labor Cost per Hour}$$

Exhibit 4 shows how Framecraft Company uses these formulas to estimate the total direct labor cost. Framecraft's Production Department needs an estimated one-tenth (.10) of a direct labor hour to complete one unit. Its Human Resources Department estimates a direct labor cost of $6 per hour.

EXHIBIT 4 ▶

Direct Labor Budget

Framecraft Company
Direct Labor Budget
For the Year Ended December 31, 20x9

| | Quarter | | | | |
	1	2	3	4	Year
Total production units	12,000	28,000	13,000	37,500	90,500
× Direct labor hours per unit	× .1	× .1	× .1	× .1	× .1
Total direct labor hours	1,200	2,800	1,300	3,750	9,050
× Direct labor cost per hour	× $6	× $6	× $6	× $6	× $6
Total direct labor cost	$ 7,200	$16,800	$ 7,800	$22,500	$54,300

EXHIBIT 5 ▶ **Overhead Budget**

Framecraft Company
Overhead Budget
For the Year Ended December 31, 20x9

	Quarter				
	1	2	3	4	Year
Variable overhead costs					
Factory supplies	$ 2,160	$ 5,040	$ 2,340	$ 6,750	$ 16,290
Employee benefits	2,880	6,720	3,120	9,000	21,720
Inspection	1,080	2,520	1,170	3,375	8,145
Maintenance and repair	1,920	4,480	2,080	6,000	14,480
Utilities	3,600	8,400	3,900	11,250	27,150
Total variable overhead costs	$11,640	$27,160	$12,610	$36,375	$ 87,785
Fixed overhead costs					
Depreciation, machinery	$ 2,810	$ 2,810	$ 2,810	$ 2,810	$ 11,240
Depreciation, building	3,225	3,225	3,225	3,225	12,900
Supervision	9,000	9,000	9,000	9,000	36,000
Maintenance and repair	2,150	2,150	2,150	2,150	8,600
Other overhead expenses	3,175	3,175	3,175	3,175	12,700
Total fixed overhead costs	$20,360	$20,360	$20,360	$20,360	$ 81,440
Total overhead costs	$32,000	$47,520	$32,970	$56,735	$169,225

The Overhead Budget

An **overhead budget** is a detailed plan of anticipated manufacturing costs, other than direct materials and direct labor costs, that must be incurred to meet budgeted production needs. It has two purposes: to integrate the overhead cost budgets developed by the managers of production and production-related departments, and to group information for the calculation of overhead rates for the next accounting period. The format for presenting information in an overhead budget is flexible. Grouping information by activities is useful for organizations that use activity-based costing. This approach makes it easier for accountants to determine the application rates for each cost pool.

As Exhibit 5 shows, Framecraft Company prefers to group information into variable and fixed costs to facilitate C-V-P analysis. The single overhead rate is the estimated total overhead costs divided by the estimated total direct labor hours. Framecraft's predetermined overhead rate for 20x9 is $18.70 per direct labor hour ($169,225 ÷ 9,050 direct labor hours), or $1.87 per unit produced ($18.70 per direct labor hour × .10 direct labor hour per unit). The variable portion of the overhead rate is $9.70 per direct labor hour ($87,785 ÷ 9,050 direct labor hours), which includes factory supplies, $1.80; employee benefits, $2.40; inspection, $.90; maintenance and repair, $1.60; and utilities, $3.00.

The Selling and Administrative Expense Budget

A **selling and administrative expense budget** is a detailed plan of operating expenses, other than those related to production, that are needed to support

EXHIBIT 6 ▶ | **Selling and Administrative Expense Budget**

Framecraft Company
Selling and Administrative Expense Budget
For the Year Ended December 31, 20x9

	Quarter				
	1	2	3	4	Year
Variable selling and administrative expenses					
Delivery expenses	$ 800	$ 2,400	$ 800	$ 3,200	$ 7,200
Sales commissions	1,000	3,000	1,000	4,000	9,000
Accounting	700	2,100	700	2,800	6,300
Other administrative expenses	400	1,200	400	1,600	3,600
Total variable selling and administrative expenses	$ 2,900	$ 8,700	$ 2,900	$11,600	$ 26,100
Fixed selling and administrative expenses					
Sales salaries	$ 4,500	$ 4,500	$ 4,500	$ 4,500	$ 18,000
Executive salaries	12,750	12,750	12,750	12,750	51,000
Depreciation–office equipment	925	925	925	925	3,700
Taxes and insurance	1,700	1,700	1,700	1,700	6,800
Total fixed selling and administrative expenses	$19,875	$19,875	$19,875	$19,875	$ 79,500
Total selling and administrative expenses	$22,775	$28,575	$22,775	$31,475	$105,600

Study Note

Remember that selling and administrative expenses are period costs, not product costs.

sales and overall operations during an accounting period. Accountants use this budget to estimate cash payments for products or services not used in production-related activities.

Framecraft Company's selling and administrative expense budget for 20x9 appears in Exhibit 6. The company groups its selling and administrative expenses into variable and fixed components for purposes of cost behavior analysis, C-V-P analysis, and profit planning. Framecraft Company's estimated variable selling and administrative expense rate for 20x9 is $.29 per unit sold, which includes delivery expenses, $.08; sales commissions, $.10; accounting, $.07; and other administrative expenses, $.04.

The Cost of Goods Manufactured Budget

A **cost of goods manufactured budget** is a detailed plan that summarizes the estimated costs of production during an accounting period. The sources of information for total manufacturing costs are the direct materials, direct labor, and overhead budgets. Most manufacturing organizations anticipate some work in process at the beginning or end of the period covered by a budget. However, Framecraft Company has a policy of no work in process on December 31 of any year. Exhibit 7 summarizes the company's estimated costs of

EXHIBIT 7 ▶

Cost of Goods Manufactured Budget			
Framecraft Company **Cost of Goods Manufactured Budget** **For the Year Ended December 31, 20x9**			**Sources of Data**
Direct materials used			
Direct materials inventory, December 31, 20x8	$ 1,200*		**Exhibit 3**
Purchases for 20x9	45,550		**Exhibit 3**
Cost of direct materials available for use	$46,750		
Less direct materials inventory, December 31, 20x9	1,500*		**Exhibit 3**
Cost of direct materials used		$45,250	
Direct labor costs		54,300	**Exhibit 4**
Overhead costs		169,225	**Exhibit 5**
Total manufacturing costs		$268,775	
Work in process inventory, December 31, 20x8		—†	
Less work in process inventory, December 31, 20x9		—†	
Cost of goods manufactured		$268,775	

* The desired direct materials inventory balance at December 31, 20x8, is $1,200 (24,000 ounces × $.05 per ounce); at December 31, 20x9, it is $1,500 (30,000 ounces × $.05 per ounce).
† It is the company's policy to have no units in process at the beginning or end of the year.

production in 20x9. (The right-hand column of the exhibit shows the sources of key data.) The budgeted, or standard, product unit cost for one picture frame is rounded to $2.97 ($268,775 ÷ 90,500 units).

STOP • REVIEW • APPLY

3-1. What is a sales forecast? What internal and external factors does a sales forecast take into consideration?

3-2. What are the three steps in preparing a direct materials purchases budget?

3-3. What are the two steps in preparing a direct labor budget?

3-4. Why does a selling and administrative expense budget use units sold rather than units produced?

Production Budget Sample Company is preparing a production budget for the year. The company's policy is to maintain a finished goods inventory equal to one-half of the next month's sales. Sales of 4,000 units are budgeted for April. Use the following monthly production budget for the first quarter to determine how many units should be produced in January, February, and March:

	January	February	March
Sales in units	3,000	2,400	6,000
Add desired units of ending finished goods inventory	___	___	___
Desired total units			
Less desired units of beginning finished goods inventory	___	___	___
Total production units	═══	═══	═══

SOLUTION

	January	February	March
Sales in units	3,000	2,400	6,000
Add desired units of ending finished goods inventory	1,200	3,000	2,000
Desired total units	4,200	5,400	8,000
Less desired units of beginning finished goods inventory	1,500	1,200	3,000
Total production units	2,700	4,200	5,000

Financial Budgets

LO4 Prepare a budgeted income statement, a cash budget, and a budgeted balance sheet.

With revenues and expenses itemized in the operating budgets, an organization's controller is able to prepare the financial budgets, which, as we noted earlier, are projections of financial results for the accounting period. Financial budgets include a budgeted income statement, a capital expenditures budget, a cash budget, and a budgeted balance sheet.

The Budgeted Income Statement

A **budgeted income statement** projects an organization's net income for an accounting period based on the revenues and expenses estimated for that period. Exhibit 8 shows Framecraft Company's budgeted income statement for 20x9. The company's expenses include 8 percent interest paid on a $70,000 note payable and income taxes paid at a rate of 30 percent.

Information about projected sales and costs comes from several operating budgets, as indicated by the right-hand column of Exhibit 8, which identifies the sources of key data and makes it possible to trace how Framecraft company's budgeted income statement was developed. At this point, you can review the overall preparation of the operating budgets and the budgeted income statement by comparing the preparation flow in Figure 2 with the budgets in Exhibits 1 through 8. You will notice that Framecraft Company has no budget for cost of goods sold; that information is included in its budgeted income statement.

The Capital Expenditures Budget

A **capital expenditures budget** is a detailed plan outlining the anticipated amount and timing of capital outlays for long-term assets during an accounting period. Managers rely on the information in a capital expenditures budget

EXHIBIT 8 ▶ | **Budgeted Income Statement**

Framecraft Company
Budgeted Income Statement
For the Year Ended December 31, 20x9

			Sources of Data
Sales		$450,000	**Exhibit 1**
Cost of goods sold			
Finished goods inventory, December 31, 20x8	$ 2,970		**Exhibit 2**
Cost of goods manufactured	268,775		**Exhibit 7**
Cost of finished goods available for sale	$271,745		
Less finished goods inventory, December 31, 20x9	4,455		**Exhibit 2**
Cost of goods sold		267,290	
Gross margin		$182,710	
Selling and administrative expenses		105,600	**Exhibit 6**
Income from operations		$ 77,110	
Interest expense (8% × $70,000)		5,600	
Income before income taxes		$ 71,510	
Income taxes expense (30%)		21,453	
Net income		$ 50,057	

Note: Finished goods inventory balances assume that product unit costs were the same in 20x8 and 20x9:

December 31, 20x8	December 31, 20x9
1,000 units (Exhibit 2)	1,500 units (Exhibit 2)
× $2.97*	× $2.97*
$2,970	$4,455

*$268,775 ÷ 90,500 units (Exhibits 7 and 2)

when making decisions about such matters as buying equipment, building a new plant, purchasing and installing a materials handling system, or acquiring another business. Framecraft Company's capital expenditures budget for 20x9 includes $30,000 for the purchase of a new extrusion machine. The company plans to pay $15,000 in the first quarter of 20x9, when the order is placed, and $15,000 in the second quarter of 20x9, when it receives the extrusion machine. This information is necessary for preparing the company's cash budget. We discuss capital expenditures in more detail in another chapter.

The Cash Budget

A **cash budget** is a projection of the cash that an organization will receive and the cash that it will pay out during an accounting period. It summarizes the cash flow prospects of all transactions considered in the master budget. The information that the cash budget provides enables managers to plan for short-term loans when the cash balance is low and for short-term investments when the cash balance is high. Table 1 shows how the elements of a cash budget relate to operating, investing, and financing activities.

A cash budget excludes planned noncash transactions, such as depreciation expense, amortization expense, issuance and receipt of stock dividends, uncollectible accounts expense, and gains and losses on sales of assets. Some

A worker oversees a newspaper being printed out on a large press. A printing press like this is a long-term asset and would be included in a company's capital expenditures budget. This budget is a detailed plan outlining the amount and timing of capital outlays for long-term assets during an accounting period.

organizations also exclude deferred taxes and accrued interest from the cash budget.

The following formula is useful in preparing a cash budget:

$$\begin{array}{c} \text{Estimated} \\ \text{Ending Cash} \\ \text{Balance} \end{array} = \begin{array}{c} \text{Total} \\ \text{Estimated} \\ \text{Cash Receipts} \end{array} - \begin{array}{c} \text{Total} \\ \text{Estimated} \\ \text{Cash Payments} \end{array} + \begin{array}{c} \text{Estimated} \\ \text{Beginning Cash} \\ \text{Balance} \end{array}$$

Estimates of cash receipts are based on information from several sources. Among these sources are the sales budget, the budgeted income statement, cash budgets from previous periods, cash collection records and analyses of collection trends, and records pertaining to notes, stocks, and bonds. Information used in estimating cash payments comes from the operating budgets, the

TABLE 1.	Elements of a Cash Budget	
Activities	**Cash Receipts From**	**Cash Payments For**
Operating	Cash sales	Purchases of direct materials
	Cash collections on credit sales	Purchases of indirect materials
	Interest income from investments	Direct labor
	Cash dividends from investments	Overhead expenses
		Selling expenses
		Administrative expenses
		Interest expense
		Income taxes
Investing	Sale of investments	Purchases of investments
	Sale of long-term assets	Purchases of long-term assets
Financing	Proceeds from loans	Loan repayments
	Proceeds from issue of stock	Cash dividends to stockholders
	Proceeds from issue of bonds	Purchases of treasury stock
		Retirement of bonds

Note: Classifications of cash receipts and cash payments correspond to those in a statement of cash flows.

EXHIBIT 9 ▶ | Schedule of Expected Cash Collections from Customers

Framecraft Company
Schedule of Expected Cash Collections from Customers
For the Year Ended December 31, 20x9

	Quarter				
	1	2	3	4	Year
Accounts receivable, Dec. 31, 20x8	$38,000	$ 10,000	$ —	$ —	$ 48,000
Cash sales	10,000	30,000	10,000	40,000	90,000
Collections of credit sales					
First quarter ($40,000)	24,000	12,000	4,000		40,000
Second quarter ($120,000)		72,000	36,000	12,000	120,000
Third quarter ($40,000)			24,000	12,000	36,000
Fourth quarter ($160,000)				96,000	96,000
Total cash to be collected from customers	$72,000	$124,000	$74,000	$160,000	$430,000

budgeted income statement, the capital expenditures budget, the previous year's financial statements, and loan records.

In estimating cash receipts and cash payments for the cash budget, many organizations prepare supporting schedules. For example, Framecraft Company's controller converts credit sales to cash inflows and purchases made on credit to cash outflows, and then discloses those conversions on schedules that support the cash budget. The schedule in Exhibit 9 shows the cash that Framecraft Company expects to collect from customers in 20x9. Cash sales represent 20 percent of the company's expected sales; the other 80 percent are credit sales. Experience has shown that Framecraft collects payments for 60 percent of all credit sales in the quarter of sale, 30 percent in the quarter following sale, and 10 percent in the second quarter following sale.

As you can see in Exhibit 9, Framecraft's balance of accounts receivable was $48,000 at December 31, 20x8. The company expects to collect $38,000 of that amount in the first quarter of 20x9 and the remaining $10,000 in the second quarter. At December 31, 20x9, the estimated ending balance of accounts receivable is $68,000—that is, $4,000 from the third quarter's credit sales [($50,000 × .80) × .10] plus $64,000 from the fourth quarter's sales [($200,000 × .80) × .40]. The expected cash collections for each quarter and for the year appear in the total cash receipts section of the cash budget.

Exhibit 10 shows Framecraft's schedule of expected cash payments for direct materials in 20x9. This information is summarized in the first line of the cash payments section of the company's cash budget. Framecraft pays 50 percent of the invoices it receives in the quarter of purchase and the other 50 percent in the following quarter. The beginning balance of accounts payable for the first quarter is $4,200. At December 31, 20x9, the estimated ending balance of accounts payable is $8,250 (50 percent of the $16,500 of direct materials purchases in the fourth quarter).

EXHIBIT 10 ▶   **Schedule of Expected Cash Payments for Direct Materials**

Framecraft Company
Schedule of Expected Cash Payments for Direct Materials
For the Year Ended December 31, 20x9

| | Quarter | | | | |
	1	2	3	4	Year
Accounts payable, Dec. 31, 20x8	$4,200	$ —	$ —	$ —	$ 4,200
First quarter ($7,600)	3,800	$ 3,800			7,600
Second quarter ($12,500)		6,250	$ 6,250		12,500
Third quarter ($8,950)			4,475	$ 4,475	8,950
Fourth quarter ($16,500)				8,250	8,250
Total cash payments for direct materials	$8,000	$10,050	$10,725	$12,725	$41,500

Framecraft's cash budget for 20x9 appears in Exhibit 11. It shows the esti-mated cash receipts and cash payments for the period, as well as the cash increase or decrease. The cash increase or decrease plus the period's begin-ning cash balance equals the ending cash balance anticipated for the period. As you can see in Exhibit 11, the beginning cash balance for the first quarter is $20,000. This amount is also the beginning cash balance for the year. Note that each quarter's budgeted ending cash balance becomes the next quarter's beginning cash balance. Also note that equal income tax payments are made quarterly. You can trace the development of this budget by referring to the data sources listed in the exhibit.

Many organizations maintain a minimum cash balance to provide a margin of safety against uncertainty. If the ending cash balance on the cash budget falls below the minimum level required, short-term borrowing may be neces-sary to cover planned cash payments during the year. If the ending cash bal-ance is significantly larger than the organization needs, it may invest the excess cash in short-term securities to generate additional income. For example, if Framecraft Company wants a minimum of $10,000 cash available at the end of each quarter, its balance of $7,222 at the end of the first quarter indicates that there is a problem. Framecraft's management has several options for handling this problem. It can borrow cash to cover the first quarter's cash needs, delay purchasing the new extrusion machine until the second quarter, or reduce some of the operating expenses. On the other hand, the balance at the end of the fourth quarter may be higher than the company wants, in which case man-agement might invest a portion of the idle cash in short-term securities.

FOCUS ON BUSINESS PRACTICE

Does Budgeting Lead to a Breakdown in Corporate Ethics?

When budgets are used to force performance results, as they were at **WorldCom**, breaches in corporate ethics can occur. One former WorldCom employee described the situ-ation at that company as follows: "You would have a budget, and he [WorldCom CEO Bernard Ebbers] would mandate that you had to be 2% under budget. Nothing else was acceptable."[5] This type of restrictive budget policy appears to have been a factor in many of the recent corpo-rate scandals.

▼ **EXHIBIT 11**

Cash Budget

Framecraft Company Cash Budget For the Year Ended December 31, 20x9						Sources of Data
	Quarter					
	1	**2**	**3**	**4**	**Year**	
Cash receipts						
Cash collections from customers	$ 72,000	$124,000	$74,000	$160,000	$430,000	Exhibit 9
Total cash receipts	$ 72,000	$124,000	$74,000	$160,000	$430,000	
Cash payments						
Direct materials	$ 8,000	$ 10,050	$10,725	$ 12,725	$ 41,500	Exhibit 10
Direct labor	7,200	16,800	7,800	22,500	54,300	Exhibit 4
Factory supplies	2,160	5,040	2,340	6,750	16,290	
Employee benefits	2,880	6,720	3,120	9,000	21,720	
Inspection	1,080	2,520	1,170	3,375	8,145	
Variable maintenance and repair	1,920	4,480	2,080	6,000	14,480	
Utilities	3,600	8,400	3,900	11,250	27,150	Exhibit 5
Supervision	9,000	9,000	9,000	9,000	36,000	
Fixed maintenance and repair	2,150	2,150	2,150	2,150	8,600	
Other overhead expenses	3,175	3,175	3,175	3,175	12,700	
Delivery expenses	800	2,400	800	3,200	7,200	
Sales commissions	1,000	3,000	1,000	4,000	9,000	
Accounting	700	2,100	700	2,800	6,300	
Other administrative expenses	400	1,200	400	1,600	3,600	Exhibit 6
Sales salaries	4,500	4,500	4,500	4,500	18,000	
Executive salaries	12,750	12,750	12,750	12,750	51,000	
Taxes and insurance	1,700	1,700	1,700	1,700	6,800	
Capital expenditures*	15,000	15,000			30,000	
Interest expense	1,400	1,400	1,400	1,400	5,600	Exhibit 8
Income taxes	5,363	5,363	5,363	5,364	21,453	
Total cash payments	$ 84,778	$117,748	$74,073	$123,239	$399,838	
Cash increase (decrease)	$(12,778)	$ 6,252	$ (73)	$ 36,761	$ 30,162	
Beginning cash balance	20,000	7,222	13,474	13,401	20,000	
Ending cash balance	$ 7,222	$ 13,474	$13,401	$ 50,162	$ 50,162	

*The company plans to purchase an extrusion machine costing $30,000 and to pay for it in two installments of $15,000 each in the first and second quarters of 20x9.

The Budgeted Balance Sheet

A **budgeted balance sheet** projects an organization's financial position at the end of an accounting period. It uses all estimated data compiled in the course of preparing a master budget and is the final step in that process. Exhibit 12 presents Framecraft Company's budgeted balance sheet at December 31, 20x9. Again, the data sources are listed in the exhibit. The beginning balances for Land, Notes Payable, Common Stock, and Retained Earnings were $50,000, $70,000, $150,000, and $50,810, respectively.

EXHIBIT 12 ▶

Budgeted Balance Sheet

Framecraft Company
Budgeted Balance Sheet
December 31, 20x9

Sources of Data

Assets

Current assets

Cash		$ 50,162	**Exhibit 11**
Accounts receivable		68,000ᵃ	**Exhibit 9**
Direct materials inventory		1,500	**Exhibit 7**
Work in process inventory		—	**Exhibit 7, Note**
Finished goods inventory		4,455	**Exhibit 8, Note**
Total current assets		$124,117	

Property, plant, and equipment

Land		$ 50,000	
Plant and equipmentᵇ	$200,000		
Less accumulated depreciationᶜ	45,000	155,000	
Total property, plant, and equipment		205,000	
Total assets		$329,117	

Liabilities

Current liabilities

Accounts payable		$ 8,250ᵈ	**Exhibit 10**
Total current liabilities		$ 8,250	

Long-term liabilities

Notes payable		70,000
Total liabilities		$ 78,250

Stockholders' Equity

Contributed capital

Common stock	$150,000	
Retained earningsᵉ	100,867	
Total stockholders' equity		250,867
Total liabilities and stockholders' equity		$329,117

ᵃThe accounts receivable balance at December 31, 20x9, is $68,000: $4,000 from the third quarter's sales [($50,000 × .80) × .10] plus $64,000 from the fourth quarter's sales [($200,000 × .80) × .40].
ᵇThe plant and equipment balance includes the $30,000 purchase of an extrusion machine.
ᶜThe accumulated depreciation balance includes depreciation expense of $27,840 for machinery, building, and office equipment ($11,240, $12,900, and $3,700, respectively).
ᵈAt December 31, 20x9, the estimated ending balance of accounts payable is $8,250 (50 percent of the $16,500 of direct materials purchases in the fourth quarter).
ᵉThe retained earnings balance at December 31 equals the beginning retained earnings balance plus the net income projected for 20x9 ($50,810 and $50,057, respectively).

S T O P • R E V I E W • A P P L Y

4-1. How is the cash budget related to the master budget? What are the purposes of preparing a cash budget?

4-2. What is the final step in developing a master budget?

4-3. Why must a cash budget be prepared before a budgeted balance sheet can be completed?

Computing Retained Earnings from Balance Sheet Information Sample Corporation's budgeted balance sheet for the coming year shows total assets of $5,000,000 and total liabilities of $2,000,000. Common stock and retained earnings make up the entire stockholders' equity section of the balance sheet. Common stock remains at its beginning balance of $1,500,000. The projected net income for the year is $350,000. The company pays no cash dividends. What is the balance of retained earnings at the beginning and end of the year?

SOLUTION

Using the accounting equation (A=L+OE) and the information given, the beginning balance sheet would show assets of $5,000,000 equaling liabilities of $2,000,000 plus common stock of $1,500,000 plus beginning retained earnings. Thus, the beginning balance of retained earnings is $1,500,000. To compute the ending retained earnings, add the beginning retained earnings of $1,500,000 and the net income for the year of $350,000. Because no dividends were paid, there is no subtraction. Thus, at the end of the year, retained earnings are $1,850,000.

A LOOK BACK AT

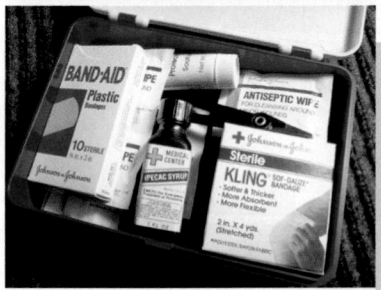

JOHNSON & JOHNSON

The budgeting process can be a highly effective way of linking strategic planning to operations, especially when it is coupled with ongoing discussions about a company's activities and direction. In this chapter's Decision Point, we pointed out that such discussions are the basis for **Johnson & Johnson's** budgeting decisions; we also asked these questions:

- **How is Johnson & Johnson's budgeting process linked to the company's long-term goals and objectives?**

- **How does Johnson & Johnson's budgeting process work?**

Like all corporate budgets, Johnson & Johnson's budget sets forth the company's goals and long-term objectives in concrete terms. It thus enables managers and employees to act in ways that will attain those objectives, and it also gives them a means of monitoring the results of their actions.

Johnson & Johnson's budgeting process is as follows:

- Sales and marketing teams from the decentralized companies develop sales budgets by product, geographic territory, and distribution channel. Senior management and staff then review the sales budgets to see that they meet the goals of Johnson & Johnson's strategic plan.

- Scheduling teams prepare production and shipping schedules to coordinate activities at the different manufacturing plants.

- Managers responsible for functional areas (such as research and development, production, marketing, distribution, and customer service) prepare cost and expense budgets.

- The accounting group reviews all budgets from the decentralized companies and analyzes their contents to determine whether they are in accordance with the overall strategic plan.

- The controller prepares a complete set of companywide budgeted financial statements and submits them to the budget committee and top corporate leaders for approval.

At Johnson & Johnson, the budgeting process and ongoing dialogue about strategy foster rapid improvements in productivity and customer service, as well as innovation in product and market development.

CHAPTER REVIEW

REVIEW of Learning Objectives

LO1 Define *budgeting*, and explain management's role in the budgeting process.

Budgeting is the process of identifying, gathering, summarizing, and communicating financial and nonfinancial information about an organization's future activities. When managers plan, budgeting helps them relate an organization's long-term and intermediate goals to short-term activities, plan the distribution of resources, and establish performance measures. When managers perform, they use budget information to communicate expectations, measure performance, motivate employees, coordinate activities, and allot resources. When managers evaluate performance results, they check for variances between planned and actual performance and create solutions to the problems that they detect. To provide continuous feedback about an organization's operating, investing, and financing activities, managers prepare and distribute reports based on budget information throughout the year.

Participative budgeting, a process in which personnel at all levels actively engage in making decisions about the budget, is key to a successful budget. The controller has considerable influence over the nature of the budgeting process, and to ensure that budgeting is participative, that person must be able to communicate and negotiate effectively with people at all levels of the organization. Senior executives also play a central role in determining whether budgeting is participative.

A budget committee made up of top management has overall responsibility for budget implementation. The committee oversees each stage in the preparation of the master budget, mediates any departmental disputes that may arise during the process, and gives final approval to the budget. After the committee approves the master budget, periodic reports from department managers enable it to monitor the progress the company is making in attaining budget targets. To ensure the cooperation of personnel in implementing the budget, top managers must clearly communicate performance expectations and budget targets. They must also show their support for the budget and encourage its implementation.

LO2 Identify the elements of a master budget in different types of organizations and the guidelines for preparing budgets.

A master budget consists of a set of operating budgets and a set of financial budgets that detail an organization's financial plans for a specific accounting period. The operating budgets serve as the basis for preparing the financial budgets, which include a budgeted income statement, a capital expenditures budget, a cash budget, and a budgeted balance sheet.

The operating budgets of a manufacturing organization include budgets for sales, production, direct materials purchases, direct labor, overhead, selling and administrative expenses, and cost of goods manufactured. The operating budgets of a retail organization include budgets for sales, purchases, selling and administrative expenses, and cost of goods sold. The operating budgets of a service organization include budgets for service revenue, labor, services overhead, and selling and administrative expenses.

The guidelines for preparing budgets include identifying the purpose of the budget, the user group and its information needs, and the sources of budget information; establishing a clear format for the budget; and using appropriate formulas and calculations to derive the quantitative information.

LO3 Prepare the operating budgets that support the financial budgets.

The initial step in preparing a master budget in any type of organization is to prepare a sales budget. Once sales have been estimated, the manager of a manufacturing organization's production department is able to prepare a budget that shows how many units of products must be manufactured to meet the projected sales volume. With that information in hand, other managers are able to prepare budgets for direct materials purchases, direct labor, overhead, selling and administrative expenses, and cost of goods manufactured. A cost of goods sold budget may be prepared separately, or it may be included in the cost of goods manufactured budget. The operating budgets supply the information needed to prepare the financial budgets.

LO4 Prepare a budgeted income statement, a cash budget, and a budgeted balance sheet.

With estimated revenues and expenses itemized in the operating budgets, a controller is able to prepare the financial budgets. A budgeted income statement projects an organization's net income for a specific accounting period. A capital expenditures budget estimates the amount and timing of the organization's capital outlays during the period. A cash budget projects its cash receipts and cash payments for the period. Estimates of cash receipts and payments are needed to prepare a cash budget. Information about cash receipts comes from several sources, including the sales budget, the budgeted income statement, and various financial records. Sources of information about cash payments include the operating budgets, the budgeted income statement, and the capital expenditures budget. The difference between the total estimated cash receipts and total estimated cash payments is the cash increase or decrease anticipated for the period. That total plus the period's beginning cash balance equals the ending cash balance. The final step in developing a master budget is to prepare a budgeted balance sheet, which projects the organization's financial position at the end of the accounting period. All budgeted data are used in preparing this statement.

REVIEW of Concepts and Terminology

The following concepts and terms were introduced in this chapter:

Budget committee: A committee made up of top management that has overall responsibility for budget implementation. **(LO1)**

Budgeted balance sheet: A statement that projects an organization's financial position at the end of an accounting period. **(LO4)**

Budgeted income statement: A projection of an organization's net income for an accounting period based on the revenues and expenses estimated for that accounting period. **(LO4)**

Budgeting: The process of identifying, gathering, summarizing, and communicating financial and nonfinancial information about an organization's future activities. **(LO1)**

Budgets: Plans of action based on forecasted transactions, activities, and events. **(LO1)**

Capital expenditures budget: A detailed plan outlining the anticipated amount and timing of capital outlays for long-term assets during an accounting period. **(LO4)**

Cash budget: A projection of the cash that an organization will receive and the cash that it will pay out during an accounting period. **(LO4)**

Cost of goods manufactured budget: A detailed plan that summarizes the estimated costs of production during an accounting period. **(LO3)**

Direct labor budget: A detailed plan that estimates the direct labor hours needed during an accounting period and the associated costs. **(LO3)**

Direct materials purchases budget: A detailed plan that identifies the quantity of purchases required to meet budgeted production and inventory needs and the costs associated with those purchases. **(LO3)**

Financial budgets: Budget projections of the financial results for an accounting period. **(LO2)**

Master budget: A set of operating budgets and a set of financial budgets that detail an organization's financial plans for a specific accounting period. **(LO2)**

Operating budgets: Budget plans used in daily operations. **(LO2)**

Overhead budget: A detailed plan of anticipated manufacturing costs, other than direct materials and direct labor costs, that must be incurred to meet budgeted production needs. **(LO3)**

Participative budgeting: A process in which personnel at all levels of an organization actively engage in making decisions about a budget. **(LO1)**

Production budget: A detailed plan showing the number of units that a company must produce to meet budgeted sales and inventory needs. **(LO3)**

Pro forma statements: Financial statements that show projections rather than actual results and that are often used to communicate business plans to external parties. **(LO2)**

Sales budget: A detailed plan, expressed in both units and dollars, that identifies the product (or

service) sales expected during an accounting period. **(LO3)**

Sales forecast: A projection of sales demand based on an analysis of external and internal factors. **(LO3)**

Selling and administrative expense budget: A detailed plan of operating expenses, other than those related to production, that are needed to support sales and overall operations during an accounting period. **(LO3)**

Strategic planning: The process by which management establishes an organization's long-term goals. **(LO1)**

REVIEW Problem

LO4

Preparing a Cash Budget

Info Processing Company provides database management services. It uses state-of-the-art equipment and employs five information specialists. Each specialist works an average of 160 hours a month. Info Processing's controller has compiled the following information:

	Actual Data for 20x8		Forecasted Data for 20x9		
	November	December	January	February	March
Client billings (sales)	$25,000	$35,000	$25,000	$20,000	$40,000
Selling and administrative expenses	12,000	13,000	12,000	11,000	12,500
Operating supplies	2,500	3,500	2,500	2,500	4,000
Processing overhead	3,200	3,500	3,000	2,500	3,500

Of the client billings, 60 percent are cash sales collected during the month of sale, 30 percent are collected in the first month following the sale, and 10 percent are collected in the second month following the sale. Operating supplies are paid for in the month of purchase. Selling and administrative expenses and processing overhead are paid in the month following the cost's incurrence.

The company has a bank loan of $12,000 at a 12 percent annual interest rate. Interest is paid monthly, and $2,000 of the loan principal is due on February 28, 20x9. Income taxes of $4,550 for calendar year 20x8 are due and payable on March 15, 20x9. The information specialists earn $8.50 an hour, and all payroll-related employee benefit costs are included in processing overhead. The company anticipates no capital expenditures for the first quarter of the coming year. It expects its cash balance on December 31, 20x8, to be $13,840.

Required

Prepare a monthly cash budget for Info Processing Company for the three-month period ended March 31, 20x9. Comment on whether the ending cash balances are adequate for Info Processing's cash needs.

Answer to Review Problem

	A	B	C	D	E
1	Info Processing Company				
2	Monthly Cash Budget				
3	For the Three-Month Period Ended March 31, 20x9				
4					
5		January	February	March	Totals
6	Cash receipts				
7	Client billings	$28,000	$23,000	$32,500	$83,500
8	Cash payments				
9	Operating supplies	$ 2,500	$ 2,500	$ 4,000	$ 9,000
10	Direct labor	6,800	6,800	6,800	20,400
11	Selling and administrative				
12	Expenses	13,000	12,000	11,000	36,000
13	Processing overhead	3,500	3,000	2,500	9,000
14	Interest expense	120	120	100	340
15	Loan payment	—	2,000	—	2,000
16	Income tax payment	—	—	4,550	4,550
17	Total cash payments	$25,920	$26,420	$28,950	$81,290
18	Cash increase (decrease)	$ 2,080	($ 3,420)	$ 3,550	$ 2,210
19	Beginning cash balance	13,840	15,920	12,500	13,840
20	Ending cash balance	$15,920	$12,500	$16,050	$16,050
21					

The details supporting the individual computations in this cash budget are as follows:

	January	February	March
Client billings			
November	$ 2,500	—	—
December	10,500	$ 3,500	—
January	15,000	7,500	$ 2,500
February	—	12,000	6,000
March	—	—	24,000
	$28,000	$23,000	$32,500
Operating supplies			
Paid for in the month purchased	$ 2,500	$ 2,500	$ 4,000
Direct labor			
5 employees × 160 hours a month × $8.50 an hour	6,800	6,800	6,800
Selling and administrative expenses			
Paid in the month following incurrence	13,000	12,000	11,000
Processing overhead			
Paid in the month following incurrence	3,500	3,000	2,500
Interest expense			
January and February = 1% of $12,000	120	120	—
March = 1% of $10,000	—	—	100
Loan payment	—	2,000	—
Income tax payment	—	—	4,550

The ending cash balances of $15,920, $12,500, and $16,050 for January, February, and March 20x9, respectively, appear to be comfortable but not too large for Info Processing Company.

CHAPTER ASSIGNMENTS

BUILDING Your Basic Knowledge and Skills

Short Exercises

LO1 Budgeting in a Retail Organization

SE 1. Sam Zubac is the manager of the shoe department in a discount department store. During a recent meeting, Zubac and his supervisor agreed that Zubac's goal for the next year would be to increase the number of pairs of shoes sold by 20 percent. The department sold 8,000 pairs of shoes last year. Two salespersons currently work for Zubac. What types of budgets should Zubac use to help him achieve his sales goal? What kinds of information should those budgets provide?

LO1 Budgetary Control

SE 2. Toby Andres owns a tree nursery. She analyzes her business's results by comparing actual operating results with figures budgeted at the beginning of the year. When the business generates large profits, she often overlooks the differences between actual and budgeted data. But when profits are low, she spends many hours analyzing the differences. If you owned Andres's business, would you use her approach to budgetary control? If not, what changes would you make?

LO2, LO3 Components of a Master Budget

SE 3. A master budget is a compilation of forecasts for the coming year or operating cycle made by various departments or functions within an organization. What is the most important forecast made in a master budget? List the reasons for your answer. Which budgets must managers prepare before they can prepare a direct materials purchases budget?

LO3 Production Budget

SE 4. Isobel Law, the controller for Aberdeen Lock Company, is preparing a production budget for the year. The company's policy is to maintain a finished goods inventory equal to one-half of the following month's sales. Sales of 7,000 locks are budgeted for April. Complete the monthly production budget for the first quarter:

	January	February	March
Sales in units	5,000	4,000	6,000
Add desired units of ending finished goods inventory	2,000	?	?
Desired total units	7,000		
Less desired units of beginning finished goods inventory	?	?	?
Total production units	4,500	?	?

LO3 Preparing an Operating Budget

SE 5. Quester Company expects to sell 50,000 units of its product in the coming year. Each unit sells for $45. Sales brochures and supplies for the year are expected to cost $7,000. Three sales representatives cover the southeast region. Each representative's base salary is $20,000, and each earns a sales commission of 5 percent of the selling price of the units he or she sells. The sales representatives supply their own transportation;

they are reimbursed for travel at a rate of $.40 per mile. The company estimates that the sales representatives will drive a total of 75,000 miles next year. From the information provided, calculate Quester Company's budgeted selling expenses for the coming year.

LO3, LO4   **Budgeted Gross Margin**

SE 6. Operating budgets for the DiPaolo Company reveal the following information: net sales, $450,000; beginning materials inventory, $23,000; materials purchased, $185,000; beginning work in process inventory, $64,700; beginning finished goods inventory, $21,600; direct labor costs, $34,000; overhead applied, $67,000; ending work in process inventory, $61,200; ending materials inventory, $18,700; and ending finished goods inventory, $16,300. Compute DiPaolo Company's budgeted gross margin.

LO4   **Estimating Cash Collections**

SE 7. KD Insurance Company specializes in term life insurance contracts. Cash collection experience shows that 20 percent of billed premiums are collected in the month before they are due, 60 percent are paid in the month in which they are due, and 16 percent are paid in the month following their due date. Four percent of the billed premiums are paid late (in the second month following their due date) and include a 10 percent penalty payment. Total billing notices in January were $58,000; in February, $62,000; in March, $66,000; in April, $65,000; in May, $60,000; and in June, $62,000. How much cash does the company expect to collect in May?

LO4   **Cash Budget**

SE 8. The projections of direct materials purchases that follow are for the Stromboli Corporation.

	Purchases on Account	Cash Purchases
December 20x8	$40,000	$20,000
January 20x9	60,000	30,000
February 20x9	50,000	25,000
March 20x9	70,000	35,000

The company pays for 60 percent of purchases on account in the month of purchase and 40 percent in the month following the purchase. Prepare a monthly schedule of expected cash payments for direct materials for the first quarter of 20x9.

LO4   **Cash Budget**

SE 9. Alberta Limited needs a cash budget for the month of November. The following information is available:

a. The cash balance on November 1 is $6,000.
b. Sales for October and November are $80,000 and $60,000, respectively. Cash collections on sales are 30 percent in the month of sale and 65 percent in the month after the sale; 5 percent of sales are uncollectible.
c. General expenses budgeted for November are $25,000 (depreciation represents $2,000 of this amount).
d. Inventory purchases will total $30,000 in October and $40,000 in November. The company pays for half of its inventory purchases in the month of purchase and for the other half the month after purchase.
e. The company will pay $4,000 in cash for office furniture in November. Sales commissions for November are budgeted at $12,000.

f. The company maintains a minimum ending cash balance of $4,000 and can borrow from the bank in multiples of $100. All loans are repaid after 60 days.

Prepare a cash budget for Alberta Limited for the month of November.

LO4 **Budgeted Balance Sheet**

SE 10. Wellman Corporation's budgeted balance sheet for the coming year shows total assets of $4,650,000 and total liabilities of $1,900,000. Common stock and retained earnings make up the entire stockholders' equity section of the balance sheet. Common stock remains at its beginning balance of $1,500,000. The projected net income for the year is $349,600. The company pays no cash dividends. What is the balance of retained earnings at the beginning of the budget period?

Exercises

LO1 **Characteristics of Budgets**

E 1. You recently attended a workshop on budgeting and overheard the following comments as you walked to the refreshment table:

1. "Budgets are the same regardless of the size of an organization or management's role in the budgeting process."
2. "Budgets can include financial or nonfinancial data. In our organization, we plan the number of hours to be worked and the number of customer contacts we want our salespeople to make."
3. "All budgets are complicated. You have to be an expert to prepare one."
4. "Budgets don't need to be highly accurate. No one in our company stays within a budget anyway."

Do you agree or disagree with each comment? Explain your answers.

LO1 **Budgeting and Goals**

E 2. Effective planning of long- and short-term goals has contributed to the success of Multitasker Calendars, Inc. Described below are the actions that the company's management team took during a recent planning meeting. Indicate whether the goals related to those actions are short-term or long-term.

1. In forecasting the next 10-year period, the management team considered economic and industry forecasts, employee-management relationships, and the structure and role of management.
2. Based on the 10-year forecast, the team made decisions about next year's sales and profit targets.

LO1 **Budgeting and Goals**

E 3. Assume that you work in the accounting department of a small wholesale warehousing company. Inspired by a recent seminar on budgeting, the company's president wants to develop a budgeting system and has asked you to direct it. Identify the points concerning the initial steps in the budgeting process that you should communicate to the president. Concentrate on principles related to long-term goals and short-term goals.

LO2, LO3, LO4 **Components of a Master Budget**

E 4. Identify the order in which the following budgets are prepared. Use the letter *a* to indicate the first budget to be prepared, *b* for the second, and so on.

1. Production budget
2. Direct labor budget
3. Direct materials purchases budget
4. Sales budget
5. Budgeted balance sheet
6. Cash budget
7. Budgeted income statement

LO3 **Sales Budget**

E 5. Quarterly and annual sales for 20x8 for Steen Manufacturing Company follow. Prepare a sales budget for 20x9 for the company. Show both quarterly and annual totals for each product class.

Steen Manufacturing Company
Actual Sales Revenue
For the Year Ended December 31, 20x8

Product Class	January–March	April–June	July–September	October–December	Annual Totals	Estimated 20x9 Percent Increases by Product Class
Marine products	$ 44,500	$ 45,500	$ 48,200	$ 47,900	$ 186,100	10%
Mountain products	36,900	32,600	34,100	37,200	140,800	5%
River products	29,800	29,700	29,100	27,500	116,100	30%
Hiking products	38,800	37,600	36,900	39,700	153,000	15%
Running products	47,700	48,200	49,400	49,900	195,200	25%
Biking products	65,400	65,900	66,600	67,300	265,200	20%
Totals	$263,100	$259,500	$264,300	$269,500	$1,056,400	

LO3 **Production Budget**

E 6. Santa Fe Corporation produces and sells a single product. Expected sales for September are 12,000 units; for October, 15,000 units; for November, 9,000 units; for December, 10,000 units; and for January, 14,000 units. The company's desired level of ending finished goods inventory at the end of a month is 10 percent of the following month's sales in units. At the end of August, 1,200 units were on hand. How many units need to be produced in the fourth quarter?

LO3 **Direct Materials Purchases Budget**

E 7. The U-Z Door Company manufactures garage door units. The units include hinges, door panels, and other hardware. Prepare a direct materials purchases budget for the first quarter of the year based on budgeted production of 16,000 garage door units. Sandee Morton, the controller, has provided the information that follows.

Hinges	4 sets per door	$11.00 per set
Door panels	4 panels per door	$27.00 per panel
Other hardware	1 lock per door	$31.00 per lock
	1 handle per door	$22.50 per handle
	2 roller tracks per door	$16.00 per set of 2 roller tracks
	8 rollers per door	$4.00 per roller

Assume no beginning or ending quantities of direct materials inventory.

LO3 **Direct Materials Purchases Budget**

E 8. Hard Corporation projects sales of $230,000 in May, $250,000 in June, $260,000 in July, and $240,000 in August. Since the dollar value of the company's cost of goods sold is generally 65 percent of total sales, cost of goods sold is $149,500 in May, $162,500 in June, $169,000 in July, and $156,000 in August. The dollar value of its desired ending inventory is 25 percent of the following month's cost of goods sold. Compute the total purchases in dollars budgeted for June and the total purchases in dollars budgeted for July.

LO3 **Direct Labor Budget**

E 9. Paige Metals Company has two departments—Cutting and Grinding—and manufactures three products. Budgeted unit production for the coming year is 21,000 of Product T, 36,000 of Product M, and 30,000 of Product B. The company is currently analyzing direct labor hour requirements for the coming year. Data for each department are as follows:

	Cutting	Grinding
Estimated hours per unit		
Product T	1.1	.5
Product M	.6	2.9
Product B	3.2	1.0
Hourly labor rate	$9	$7

Prepare a direct labor budget for the coming year that shows the budgeted direct labor costs for each department and for the company as a whole.

LO3 **Overhead Budget**

E 10. Carole Dahl is chief financial officer of the Phoenix Division of Dahl Corporation, a multinational company with three operating divisions. As part of the budgeting process, Dahl's staff is developing the overhead budget for next year. The division estimates that it will manufacture 50,000 units during the year. The budgeted cost information is as follows:

	Variable Rate per Unit	Total Fixed Costs
Indirect materials	$1.00	
Indirect labor	4.00	
Supplies	.40	
Repairs and maintenance	3.00	$ 40,000
Electricity	.10	20,000
Factory supervision		180,000
Insurance		25,000
Property taxes		35,000
Depreciation, machinery		82,000
Depreciation, building		72,000

Using these data, prepare the division's overhead budget for next year.

Cash Collections

E 11. Dacahr Bros., Inc., is an automobile maintenance and repair company with outlets throughout the western United States. Henley Turlington, the company controller, is starting to assemble the cash budget for the fourth quarter. Projected sales for the quarter are as follows:

	On Account	Cash
October	$452,000	$196,800
November	590,000	214,000
December	720,500	218,400

Cash collection records pertaining to sales on account indicate the following collection pattern:

Month of sale	40%
First month following sale	30%
Second month following sale	28%
Uncollectible	2%

Sales on account during August were $346,000. During September, sales on account were $395,000.

Compute the amount of cash to be collected from customers during each month of the fourth quarter.

Cash Collections

E 12. XYZ Company collects payment on 50 percent of credit sales in the month of sale, 40 percent in the month following sale, and 5 percent in the second month following the sale. Its sales budget is as follows:

Month	Cash Sales	Credit Sales
May	$20,000	$ 40,000
June	40,000	60,000
July	60,000	80,000
August	80,000	100,000

Compute XYZ Company's total cash collections in July and its total cash collections in August.

Cash Budget

E 13. SABA Enterprises needs a cash budget for the month of June. The following information is available:

a. The cash balance on June 1 is $4,000.

b. Sales for May and June are $50,000 and $40,000, respectively. Cash collections on sales are 40 percent in the month of sale and 50 percent in the month after the sale; 10 percent of sales are uncollectible.

c. General expenses budgeted for June are $20,000 (depreciation represents $1,000 of this amount).

d. Inventory purchases will total $40,000 in May and $30,000 in June. The company pays for half of its inventory purchases in the month of purchase and for the other half the month after purchase.

e. The company will pay $5,000 in cash for office furniture in June. Sales commissions for June are budgeted at $6,000.

f. The company maintains a minimum ending cash balance of $4,000 and can borrow from the bank in multiples of $100. All loans are repaid after 60 days.

Prepare a cash budget for SABA Enterprises for the month of June.

LO4 **Cash Budget**

E 14. Tex Kinkaid's dream was to develop the biggest produce operation with the widest selection of fresh fruits and vegetables in northern Texas. Within three years of opening Minigarden Produce, Inc., Kincaid accomplished his objective. Kinkaid has asked you to prepare monthly cash budgets for Minigarden Produce for the quarter ended September 30.

Credit sales to retailers in the area constitute 80 percent of Minigarden Produce's business; cash sales to customers at the company's retail outlet make up the other 20 percent. Collection records indicate that Minigarden Produce collects payment on 50 percent of all credit sales during the month of sale, 30 percent in the month after the sale, and 20 percent in the second month after the sale.

The company's total sales in May were $66,000; in June, they were $67,500. Anticipated sales in July are $69,500; in August, $76,250; and in September, $84,250. The company's purchases are expected to total $43,700 in July, $48,925 in August, and $55,725 in September. The company pays for all purchases in cash.

Projected monthly costs for the quarter include $1,040 for heat, light, and power; $375 for bank fees; $1,925 for rent; $1,120 for supplies; $1,705 for depreciation of equipment; $1,285 for equipment repairs; and $475 for miscellaneous expenses. Other projected costs for the quarter are salaries and wages of $18,370 in July, $19,200 in August, and $20,300 in September.

The company's cash balance at June 30 was $2,745. It has a policy of maintaining a minimum monthly cash balance of $1,500.

1. Prepare a monthly cash budget for Minigarden Produce, Inc., for the quarter ended September 30.
2. Should Minigarden Produce anticipate taking out a loan during the quarter? If so, how much should it borrow, and when?

LO4 **Budgeted Income Statement**

E 15. Delft House, Inc., a multinational company based in Amsterdam, organizes and coordinates art shows and auctions throughout the world. Its budgeted and actual costs for last year are as follows:

	Budgeted Cost	Actual Cost
Salaries expense, staging	€ 480,000	€ 512,800
Salaries expense, executive	380,000	447,200
Travel costs	640,000	652,020
Auctioneer services	540,000	449,820
Space rental costs	251,000	246,580
Printing costs	192,000	182,500
Advertising expense	169,000	183,280
Insurance, merchandise	84,800	77,300
Insurance, liability	64,000	67,100
Home office costs	209,200	219,880
Shipping costs	105,000	112,560
Miscellaneous	25,000	25,828
Total operating expenses	€3,140,000	€3,176,868
Net receipts	€6,200,000	€6,369,200

Delft House, Inc., has budgeted the following fixed costs for the coming year: executive salaries, €440,000; advertising expense, €190,000; merchandise insurance, €80,000; and liability insurance, €68,000. Additional information pertaining to the operations of Delft House, Inc., in the coming years is as follows:

a. Net receipts are estimated at €6,400,000.
b. Salaries expense for staging will increase 20 percent over the actual figures for the last year.
c. Travel costs are expected to be 11 percent of net receipts.
d. Auctioneer services will be billed at 9.5 percent of net receipts.
e. Space rental costs will be 20 percent higher than the amount budgeted in the last year.
f. Printing costs are expected to be €190,000.
g. Home office costs are budgeted for €230,000.
h. Shipping costs are expected to be 20 percent higher than the amount budgeted in the last year.
i. Miscellaneous expenses for the coming year will be budgeted at €28,000.

   Because the company sells only services, it has expenses only and no cost of sales. (Net receipts equal gross margin.)

1. Using a 34 percent income tax rate, prepare the company's budgeted income statement for the coming year.
2. Should the budget committee be worried about the trend in the company's operations? Explain your answer.

Problems

LO3 **Preparing Operating Budgets**

P 1. The principal product of Yangsoo Enterprises, Inc., is a multipurpose hammer that carries a lifetime guarantee. Listed below are cost and production data for the Yangsoo hammer.

   Direct materials
      Anodized steel: 2 kilograms per hammer at $1.60 per kilogram
      Leather strapping for the handle: .5 square meter per hammer at $4.40 per square meter

   Direct labor
      Forging operation: $12.50 per labor hour; 6 minutes per hammer
      Leather-wrapping operation: $12.00 per direct labor hour; 12 minutes per hammer

   Overhead
      Forging operation: rate equals 70 percent of department's direct labor dollars
      Leather-wrapping operation: rate equals 50 percent of department's direct labor dollars

In October, November, and December, Yangsoo Enterprises expects to produce 108,000, 104,000, and 100,000 hammers, respectively. The company has no beginning or ending balances of direct materials inventory or work in process inventory for the year.

Required

1. For the three-month period ending December 31, prepare monthly production cost information for the Yangsoo hammer. Classify the costs as direct materials, direct labor, or overhead and show your computations.

2. Prepare a cost of goods manufactured budget for the hammer. Show monthly cost data and combined totals for the quarter for each cost category.

LO3, LO4 **Preparing a Comprehensive Budget**

P 2. Bertha's Bathworks began manufacturing hair and bath products in 20x1. Its biggest customer is a national retail chain that specializes in such products. Bertha Jackson, the owner of Bertha's Bathworks, would like to have an estimate of the company's net income in 20x9.

Required

Calculate Bertha's Bathworks' net income in 20x9 by completing the operating budgets and budgeted income statement that follow.

1. Sales budget:

Bertha's Bathworks
Sales Budget
For the Year Ended December 31, 20x9

	Quarter				
	1	**2**	**3**	**4**	**Year**
Sales in units	4,000	3,000	5,000	5,000	17,000
× Selling price per unit	× $5	× ?	× ?	× ?	× ?
Total sales	$20,000	?	?	?	?

2. Production budget:

Bertha's Bathworks
Production Budget
For the Year Ended December 31, 20x9

	Quarter				
	1	**2**	**3**	**4**	**Year**
Sales in units	4,000	?	?	?	?
Plus desired units of ending finished goods inventory*	300	?	?	600	600
Desired total units	4,300				
Less desired units of beginning finished goods inventory†	400	?	?	?	400
Total production units	3,900	?	?	?	?

*Desired units of ending finished goods inventory = 10% of next quarter's budgeted sales.
†Desired units of beginning finished goods inventory = 10% of current quarter's budgeted sales.

3. Direct materials purchases budget:

Bertha's Bathworks
Direct Materials Purchases Budget
For the Year Ended December 31, 20x9

			Quarter		
	1	2	3	4	Year
Total production units	3,900	3,200	5,000	5,100	17,200
× 3 ounces per unit	× 3	× ?	× ?	× ?	× ?
Total production needs in ounces	11,700	?	?	?	?
Plus desired ounces of ending direct materials inventory*	1,920	?	?	3,600	3,600
	13,620	?	?	?	?
Less desired ounces of beginning direct materials inventory†	2,340	?	?	?	2,340
Total ounces of direct materials to be purchased	11,280	?	?	?	?
× Cost per ounce	× $.10	× ?	× ?	× ?	× ?
Total cost of direct materials purchases	$1,128	?	?	?	?

*Desired ounces of ending direct materials inventory = 20% of next quarter's budgeted production needs in ounces.
†Desired ounces of beginning direct materials inventory = 20% of current quarter's budgeted production needs in ounces.

4. Direct labor budget:

Bertha's Bathworks
Direct Labor Budget
For the Year Ended December 31, 20x9

			Quarter		
	1	2	3	4	Year
Total production units	3,900	?	?	?	?
× Direct labor hours per unit	× .1	× ?	× ?	× ?	× ?
Total direct labor hours	390	?	?	?	?
× Direct labor cost per hour	× $7	× ?	× ?	× ?	× ?
Total direct labor cost	$2,730	?	?	?	?

5. Overhead budget:

Bertha's Bathworks
Overhead Budget
For the Year Ended December 31, 20x9

	Quarter				
	1	2	3	4	Year
Variable overhead costs					
Factory supplies ($.05)	$ 195	?	?	?	?
Employee benefits ($.25)	975	?	?	?	?
Inspection ($.10)	390	?	?	?	?
Maintenance and repair ($.15)	585	?	?	?	?
Utilities ($.05)	195	?	?	?	?
Total variable overhead costs	$2,340	?	?	?	?
Fixed overhead costs					
Depreciation, machinery	$ 500	?	?	?	?
Depreciation, building	700	?	?	?	?
Supervision	1,800	?	?	?	?
Maintenance and repair	400	?	?	?	?
Other overhead expenses	600	?	?	?	?
Total fixed overhead costs	$4,000	?	?	?	?
Total overhead costs	$6,340	?	?	?	?

Note: The figures in parentheses are variable costs per unit.

6. Selling and administrative expense budget:

Bertha's Bathworks
Selling and Administrative Expense Budget
For the Year Ended December 31, 20x9

	Quarter				
	1	2	3	4	Year
Variable selling and administrative expenses					
Delivery expenses ($.10)	$ 400	?	?	?	?
Sales commissions ($.15)	600	?	?	?	?
Accounting ($.05)	200	?	?	?	?
Other administrative expenses ($.20)	800	?	?	?	?
Total variable selling and administrative expenses	$2,000	?	?	?	?
Fixed selling and administrative expenses					
Sales salaries	$5,000	?	?	?	?
Depreciation, office equipment	900	?	?	?	?
Taxes and insurance	1,700	?	?	?	?
Total fixed selling and administrative expenses	$7,600	?	?	?	?
Total selling and administrative expenses	$9,600	?	?	?	?

Note: The figures in parentheses are variable costs per unit.

7. Cost of goods manufactured budget:

> **Bertha's Bathworks**
> **Cost of Goods Manufactured Budget**
> **For the Year Ended December 31, 20x9**
>
> | | | |
> |---|---|---|
> | Direct materials used | | |
> | Direct materials inventory, December 31, 20x8 | ? | |
> | Purchases for 20x9 | ? | |
> | Cost of direct materials available for use | ? | |
> | Less direct materials inventory, December 31, 20x9 | ? | |
> | Cost of direct materials used | | ? |
> | Direct labor costs | | ? |
> | Overhead costs | | ? |
> | Total manufacturing costs | | ? |
> | Work in process inventory, December 31, 20x8* | | ? |
> | Less work in process inventory, December 31, 20x9* | | ? |
> | Cost of goods manufactured | | ? |
> | Manufactured Cost per Unit = Cost of Goods Manufactured ÷ Units Produced | | ? |

*It is the company's policy to have no units in process at the end of the year.

8. Budgeted income statement:

> **Bertha's Bathworks**
> **Budgeted Income Statement**
> **For the Year Ended December 31, 20x9**
>
> | | | |
> |---|---|---|
> | Sales | | ? |
> | Cost of goods sold | | |
> | Finished goods inventory, December 31, 20x8 | ? | |
> | Cost of goods manufactured | ? | |
> | Cost finished of goods available for sale | ? | |
> | Less finished goods inventory, December 31, 20x9 | ? | |
> | Cost of goods sold | | ? |
> | Gross margin | | ? |
> | Selling and administrative expenses | | ? |
> | Income from operations | | ? |
> | Income taxes expense (30%)* | | ? |
> | Net income | | ? |

*The figure in parentheses is the company's income tax rate.

LO4   **Basic Cash Budget**

P 3. Felasco Nurseries, Inc., has been in business for six years and has four divisions. Ethan Poulis, the corporation's controller, has been asked to prepare a cash budget for the Southern Division for the first quarter. Projected data supporting this budget follow.

Sales (60 percent on credit)		Purchases	
November	$160,000	December	$ 86,800
December	200,000	January	124,700
January	120,000	February	99,440
February	160,000	March	104,800
March	140,000		

Collection records of accounts receivable have shown that 30 percent of all credit sales are collected in the month of sale, 60 percent in the month following the sale, and 8 percent in the second month following the sale; 2 percent of the sales are uncollectible. All purchases are paid for in the month after the purchase. Salaries and wages are projected to be $25,200 in January, $33,200 in February, and $21,200 in March. Estimated monthly costs are utilities, $4,220; collection fees, $1,700; rent, $5,300; equipment depreciation, $5,440; supplies, $2,480; small tools, $3,140; and miscellaneous, $1,900.

Each of the corporation's divisions maintains a $6,000 minimum cash balance. As of December 31, the Southern Division had a cash balance of $9,600.

Required

1. Prepare a monthly cash budget for Felasco Nurseries' Southern Division for the first quarter.
2. **Manager Insight:** Should Felasco Nurseries anticipate taking out a loan for the Southern Division during the quarter? If so, how much should it borrow, and when?

LO4   **Cash Budget**

P 4. Security Services Company provides security monitoring services. It employs five security specialists. Each specialist works an average of 160 hours a month. The company's controller has compiled the following information:

	Actual Data for Last Year		Forecasted Data for Next Year		
	November	December	January	February	March
Security billings (sales)	$30,000	$35,000	$25,000	$20,000	$30,000
Selling and administrative expenses	10,000	11,000	9,000	8,000	10,500
Operating supplies	2,500	3,500	2,500	2,000	3,000
Service overhead	3,000	3,500	3,000	2,500	3,000

Sixty percent of the client billings are cash sales collected during the month of sale; 30 percent are collected in the first month following the sale; and 10 percent are collected in the second month following the sale. Operating supplies are paid for in the month of purchase. Selling and administrative expenses and service overhead are paid in the month following the cost's incurrence.

The company has a bank loan of $12,000 at a 12 percent annual interest rate. Interest is paid monthly, and $2,000 of the loan principal is due on February 28. Income taxes of $4,500 for last calendar year are due and payable on March 15. The five security specialists each earn $8.50 an hour, and all payroll-related employee benefit costs are included in service overhead. The company anticipates no capital expenditures for the first quarter of the coming year. It expects its cash balance on December 31 to be $13,000.

Required

Prepare a monthly cash budget for Security Services Company for the three-month period ended March 31.

LO4 **Budgeted Income Statement and Budgeted Balance Sheet**

P 5. Moontrust Bank has asked the president of Wishware Products, Inc., for a budgeted income statement and budgeted balance sheet for the quarter ended June 30. These pro forma statements are needed to support Wishware Products' request for a loan.

Wishware Products routinely prepares a quarterly master budget. The operating budgets prepared for the quarter ending June 30 have provided the following information: Projected sales for April are $220,400; for May, $164,220; and for June, $165,980. Direct materials purchases for the period are estimated at $96,840; direct materials usage, at $102,710; direct labor expenses, at $71,460; overhead, at $79,940; selling and administrative expenses, at $143,740; capital expenditures, at $125,000 (to be spent on June 29); cost of goods manufactured, at $252,880; and cost of goods sold, at $251,700.

Balance sheet account balances at March 31 were as follows: Accounts Receivable, $26,500; Materials Inventory, $23,910; Work in Process Inventory, $31,620; Finished Goods Inventory, $36,220; Prepaid Expenses, $7,200; Plant, Furniture, and Fixtures, $498,600; Accumulated Depreciation, Plant, Furniture, and Fixtures, $141,162; Patents, $90,600; Accounts Payable, $39,600; Notes Payable, $105,500; Common Stock, $250,000; and Retained Earnings, $207,158.

Projected monthly cash balances for the second quarter are as follows: April 30, $20,490; May 31, $35,610; and June 30, $45,400. During the quarter, accounts receivable are expected to increase by 30 percent, patents to go up by $6,500, prepaid expenses to remain constant, and accounts payable to go down by 10 percent (Wishware Products will make a $5,000 payment on a note payable, $4,100 of which is principal reduction). The federal income tax rate is 34 percent, and the second quarter's tax is paid in July. Depreciation for the quarter will be $6,420, which is included in the overhead budget. The company will pay no dividends.

Required

1. Prepare a budgeted income statement for the quarter ended June 30. Round answers to the nearest dollar.
2. Prepare a budgeted balance sheet as of June 30.

Alternate Problems

LO3, LO4 **Preparing a Comprehensive Budget**

P 6. The Bottled Water Company has been bottling and selling water since 1940. Ginnie Adams, the current owner of The Bottled Water Company, would like to know how a new product would affect the company's net income in the coming year.

Required

Calculate The Bottled Water Company's net income for the new product in the coming year by completing the operating budgets and budgeted income statement that follow.

1. Sales budget:

The Bottled Water Company
Sales Budget
For the Year Ended December 31

	Quarter				
	1	2	3	4	Year
Sales in units	40,000	30,000	50,000	55,000	175,000
× Selling price per unit	× $1	× ?	× ?	× ?	× ?
Total sales	$40,000	?	?	?	?

2. Production budget:

The Bottled Water Company
Production Budget
For the Year Ended December 31

	Quarter				
	1	2	3	4	Year
Sales in units	40,000	?	?	?	?
Plus desired units of ending finished goods inventory*	3,000	?	?	6,000	6,000
Desired total units	43,000				
Less desired units of beginning finished goods inventory†	4,000	?	?	?	4,000
Total production units	39,000	?	?	?	?

*Desired units of ending finished goods inventory = 10% of next quarter's budgeted sales.
†Desired units of beginning finished goods inventory = 10% of current quarter's budgeted sales.

3. Direct materials purchases budget:

The Bottled Water Company
Direct Materials Purchases Budget
For the Year Ended December 31

	Quarter				
	1	2	3	4	Year
Total production units	39,000	32,000	50,500	55,500	?
× 20 ounces per unit	× 20	× ?	× ?	× ?	× ?
Total production needs in ounces	780,000	?	?	?	?
Plus desired ounces of ending direct materials inventory*	128,000	?	?	240,000	240,000
	908,000	?	?	?	?
Less desired ounces of beginning direct materials inventory†	156,000	?	?	?	156,000
Total ounces of direct materials to be purchased	752,000	?	?	?	?
× Cost per ounce	× $.01	× ?	× ?	× ?	× ?
Total cost of direct materials purchases	$ 7,520	?	?	?	?

*Desired ounces of ending direct materials inventory = 20% of next quarter's budgeted production needs in ounces.
†Desired ounces of beginning direct materials inventory = 20% of current quarter's budgeted production needs in ounces.

4. Direct labor budget:

The Bottled Water Company
Direct Labor Budget
For the Year Ended December 31

	Quarter				
	1	2	3	4	Year
Total production units	39,000	?	?	?	?
× Direct labor hours per unit	× .001	× ?	× ?	× ?	× ?
Total direct labor hours	39	?	?	?	?
× Direct labor cost per hour	× $8	× ?	× ?	× ?	× ?
Total direct labor cost	$312	?	?	?	?

5. Overhead budget:

The Bottled Water Company
Overhead Budget
For the Year Ended December 31

	Quarter				
	1	2	3	4	Year
Variable overhead costs					
Factory supplies ($.01)	$ 390	?	?	?	?
Employee benefits ($.05)	1,950	?	?	?	?
Inspection ($.01)	390	?	?	?	?
Maintenance and repair ($.02)	780	?	?	?	?
Utilities ($.01)	390	?	?	?	?
Total variable overhead costs	$3,900	?	?	?	?
Total fixed overhead costs	1,500	?	?	?	?
Total overhead costs	$5,400	?	?	?	?

Note: The figures in parentheses are variable costs per unit.

6. Selling and administrative expense budget:

The Bottled Water Company
Selling and Administrative Expense Budget
For the Year Ended December 31

	Quarter				
	1	2	3	4	Year
Variable selling and administrative expenses					
Delivery expenses ($.01)	$ 400	?	?	?	?
Sales commissions ($.02)	800	?	?	?	?
Accounting ($.01)	400	?	?	?	?
Other administrative expenses ($.01)	400	?	?	?	?
Total variable selling and administrative expenses	$2,000	?	?	?	?
Total fixed selling and administrative expenses	5,000	?	?	?	?
Total selling and administrative expenses	$7,000	?	?	?	?

Note: The figures in parentheses are variable costs per unit.

7. Cost of goods manufactured budget:

The Bottled Water Company
Cost of Goods Manufactured Budget
For the Year Ended December 31

Direct materials used		
Direct materials inventory, beginning	?	
Purchases	?	
Cost of direct materials available for use	?	
Less direct materials inventory, ending		?
Cost of direct materials used		?
Direct labor costs		?
Overhead costs		?
Total manufacturing costs		?
Work in process inventory, beginning*		0
Less work in process inventory, ending*		0
Cost of goods manufactured		?
Manufactured Cost per Unit = Cost of Goods Manufactured ÷ Units Produced		?

*It is the company's policy to have no units in process at the end of the year.

8. Budgeted income statement:

The Bottled Water Company
Budgeted Income Statement
For the Year Ended December 31

Sales		?
Cost of goods sold		
Finished goods inventory, beginning	?	
Cost of goods manufactured	?	
Cost of finished goods available for sale	?	
Less finished goods inventory, ending	?	
Cost of goods sold		?
Gross margin		?
Selling and administrative expenses		?
Income from operations		?
Income taxes expense (30%)*		?
Net income		?

*The figure in parentheses is the company's income tax rate.

LO4 **Comprehensive Cash Budget**

P 7. Located in Telluride, Colorado, Wellness Centers, Inc., emphasizes the benefits of regular workouts and the importance of physical examinations. The corporation operates three fully equipped fitness centers, as well as a medical center that specializes in preventive medicine. The data that follow pertain to the corporation's first quarter.

Cash Receipts

Memberships: December, 870; January, 880; February, 910; March, 1,030

Membership dues: $90 per month, payable on the 10th of the month (80 percent collected on time; 20 percent collected one month late)

Medical examinations: January, $35,610; February, $41,840; March, $45,610

Special aerobics classes: January, $4,020; February, $5,130; March, $7,130

High-protein food sales: January, $4,890; February, $5,130; March, $6,280

Cash Payments

Salaries and wages:

   Corporate officers: 2 at $12,000 per month

   Physicians: 2 at $7,000 per month

   Nurses: 3 at $2,900 per month

   Clerical staff: 2 at $1,500 per month

   Aerobics instructors: 3 at $1,100 per month

   Clinic staff: 6 at $1,700 per month

   Maintenance staff: 3 at $900 per month

   Health-food servers: 3 at $750 per month

Purchases:

   Muscle-toning machines: January, $14,400; February, $13,800 (no purchases in March)

   Pool supplies: $520 per month

   Health food: January, $3,290; February, $3,460; March, $3,720

   Medical supplies: January, $10,400; February, $11,250; March, $12,640

   Medical uniforms and disposable garments: January, $7,410; February, $3,900; March, $3,450

   Medical equipment: January, $11,200; February, $3,400; March $5,900

   Advertising: January, $2,250; February, $1,190; March, $2,450

   Utilities expense: January, $5,450; February, $5,890; March, $6,090

Insurance:

   Fire: January, $3,470

   Liability: March, $3,980

Property taxes: $3,760 due in January

Federal income taxes: Last year's taxes of $21,000 due in March

Miscellaneous: January, $2,625; February, $2,800; March, $1,150

Wellness Centers' controller anticipates that the beginning cash balance on January 1 will be $9,840.

Required

Prepare a cash budget for Wellness Centers, Inc., for the first quarter of the year. Use **January, February, March,** and **Quarter** as the column headings.

LO4   Budgeted Income Statement and Budgeted Balance Sheet

P 8. Whatever Video Company, Inc., produces and markets two popular video games, "High Range" and "Star Boundary." The closing account balances on the company's balance sheet for last year are as follows: Cash, $18,735; Accounts Receivable, $19,900; Materials Inventory, $18,510; Work in Process Inventory, $24,680; Finished Goods Inventory, $21,940; Prepaid Expenses, $3,420; Plant and Equipment, $262,800; Accumulated Depreciation, Plant and Equipment, $55,845; Other Assets, $9,480; Accounts Payable, $52,640; Mortgage Payable, $70,000; Common Stock, $90,000; and Retained Earnings, $110,980.

Operating budgets for the first quarter of the coming year show the following estimated costs: direct materials purchases, $58,100; direct materials usage, $62,400; direct labor expense, $42,880; overhead, $51,910; selling expenses, $35,820; general and administrative expenses, $60,240; cost of goods manufactured, $163,990; and cost of goods sold, $165,440. Estimated ending cash balances are as follows: January, $34,610; February, $60,190; and March, $54,802. The company will have no capital expenditures during the quarter.

Sales are projected to be $125,200 in January, $105,100 in February, and $112,600 in March. Accounts receivable are expected to double during the quarter, and accounts payable are expected to decrease by 20 percent. Mortgage payments for the quarter will total $6,000, of which $2,000 will be interest expense. Prepaid expenses are expected to go up by $20,000, and other assets are projected to increase by 50 percent over the budget period. Depreciation for plant and equipment (already included in the overhead budget) averages 5 percent of total plant and equipment per year. Federal income taxes (34 percent of profits) are payable in April. The company pays no dividends.

Required

1. Prepare a budgeted income statement for the quarter ended March 31.
2. Prepare a budgeted balance sheet as of March 31.

ENHANCING Your Knowledge, Skills, and Critical Thinking

Conceptual Understanding Cases

LO4 **Budgeting for Cash Flows**

C 1. The nature of a company's business affects its need to budget for cash flows. **H&R Block** is a service company whose main business is preparing tax returns. Most tax returns are prepared after January 31 and before April 15. For a fee and interest, the company will advance cash to clients who are due refunds. The clients are expected to repay the cash advances when they receive their refunds. Although H&R Block has some revenues throughout the year, it devotes most of the nontax season to training potential employees in tax preparation procedures and to laying the groundwork for the next tax season.

Toys "R" Us is a toy retailer whose sales are concentrated in October, November, and December of one year and January of the next year. Sales continue at a steady but low level during the rest of the year. The company purchases most of its inventory between July and September.

Johnson & Johnson sells the many health care products that it manufactures to retailers, and the retailers sell them to the final customer. Johnson & Johnson offers retailers credit terms.

Discuss the nature of cash receipts and cash disbursements over a calendar year in the three companies we have just described. What are some key estimates that the management of these companies must make when preparing a cash budget?

LO4 **Goals and the Cash Budget**

C 2. The products of **Minnesota Mining and Manufacturing Company (3M)** range from office supplies, duct tape, and road reflectors to laser imagers for CAT scanners. One of the company's goals is to accelerate sales and product development. Toward that end, it spends over $1 billion a year on research and development (R&D) and related investment activities. It has also redesigned many of its products to satisfy the needs of its three international operations groups.[6] Suppose the manager of 3M's Asia-Pacific group is preparing the cash budget for next year's operations. Explain how R&D expenses would affect the cash receipts and cash payments in that cash budget.

LO1, LO2 **Policies for Budget Development**

C 3. Hector Corporation is a manufacturing company with annual sales of $25 million. Its budget committee has created the following policy that the company uses each year in developing its master budget for the following calendar year:

May	The company's controller and other members of the budget committee meet to discuss plans and objectives for next year. The controller conveys all relevant information from this meeting to division managers and department heads.
June	Division managers, department heads, and the controller meet to discuss the corporate plans and objectives for next year. They develop a timetable for developing next year's budget data.
July	Division managers and department heads develop budget data. The vice president of sales provides them with final sales estimates, and they complete monthly sales estimates for each product line.
August	Estimates of next year's monthly production activity and inventory levels are completed. Division managers and department heads communicate these estimates to the controller, who distributes them to other operating areas.
September	All operating areas submit their revised budget data. The controller integrates their labor requirements, direct materials requirements, unit cost estimates, cash requirements, and profit estimates into a preliminary master budget.
October	The budget committee meets to discuss the preliminary master budget and to make any necessary corrections, additions, or deletions. The controller incorporates all authorized changes into a final draft of the master budget.
November	The controller submits the final draft to the budget committee for approval. If the committee approves it, it is distributed to all corporate officers, division managers, and department heads.

1. Comment on this policy.
2. What changes would you recommend?

Interpreting Management Reports

LO1, LO4 **Budgeting Procedures**

C 4. Since Rood Enterprises inaugurated participative budgeting 10 years ago, everyone in the organization—from maintenance personnel to the president's staff—has had a voice in the budgeting process. Until recently, participative budgeting has worked in the best interests of the company as a whole. Now, however, it is becoming evident that some managers are using the practice solely to benefit their own divisions. The budget committee has therefore asked you, the company's controller, to analyze this year's divisional budgets carefully before incorporating them into the company's master budget.

The Motor Division was the first of the company's six divisions to submit its budget request for 20x9. The division's budgeted income statement follows.

Rood Enterprises
Motor Division
Budgeted Income Statement
For the Years Ended December 31, 20x8 and 20x9

	Budget 12/31/x8	Budget 12/31/x9	Increase (Decrease)
Net sales			
Radios	$ 850,000	$ 910,000	$ 60,000
Appliances	680,000	740,000	60,000
Telephones	270,000	305,000	35,000
Miscellaneous	84,400	90,000	5,600
Net sales	$1,884,400	$2,045,000	$160,600
Less cost of goods sold	750,960	717,500*	(33,460)
Gross margin	$1,133,440	$1,327,500	$194,060
Operating expenses			
Wages			
Warehouse	$ 94,500	$ 102,250	$ 7,750
Purchasing	77,800	84,000	6,200
Delivery/shipping	69,400	74,780	5,380
Maintenance	42,650	45,670	3,020
Salaries			
Supervisory	60,000	92,250	32,250
Executive	130,000	164,000	34,000
Purchases, supplies	17,400	20,500	3,100
Merchandise moving equipment			
Maintenance	72,400	82,000	9,600
Depreciation	62,000	74,750†	12,750
Building rent	96,000	102,500	6,500
Sales commissions	188,440	204,500	16,060
Insurance			
Fire	12,670	20,500	7,830
Liability	18,200	20,500	2,300
Utilities	14,100	15,375	1,275
Taxes			
Property	16,600	18,450	1,850
Payroll	26,520	41,000	14,480
Miscellaneous	4,610	10,250	5,640
Total operating expenses	$1,003,290	$1,173,275	$169,985
Income from operations	$ 130,150	$ 154,225	$ 24,075

*Less expensive merchandise will be purchased in 20x9 to boost profits.
†Depreciation is increased because additional equipment must be bought to handle increased sales.

1. Recast the Motor Division's budgeted income statement in the following format (round percentages to two places):

	Budget for 12/31/x8		Budget for 12/31/x9	
Account	Amount	Percentage of Net Sales	Amount	Percentage of Net Sales

2. Actual results for 20x8 revealed the following information about revenues and cost of goods sold:

	Amount	Percentage of Sales
Net sales		
Radios	$ 780,000	43.94
Appliances	640,000	36.06
Telephones	280,000	15.77
Miscellaneous	75,000	4.23
Net sales	$1,775,000	100.00
Less cost of goods sold	763,425	43.01
Gross margin	$1,011,575	56.99

On the basis of this information and your analysis in requirement 1, what do you think the budget committee should say to the managers of the Motor Division? Identify any specific areas of the budget that may need to be revised and explain why the revision is needed.

Decision Analysis Using Excel

LO3, LO4   **The Budgeting Process**

C 5. Refer to our development of Framecraft Company's master budget for 20x9 in this chapter. Suppose that because of a new customer in Canada, Chase Vitt has decided to increase budgeted sales in the first quarter of 20x9 by 5,000 units. The expenses for this sale will include direct materials, direct labor, variable overhead, and variable selling and administrative expenses. The delivery expense for the Canadian customer will be $.18 per unit rather than the regular $.08 per unit. The desired units of beginning finished goods inventory will remain at 1,000 units.

1. Using an Excel spreadsheet, revise Framecraft Company's budgeted income statement and the operating budgets that support it to reflect the changes described above. (Round manufactured cost per unit to three decimals.)
2. What was the change in income from operations? Would you recommend accepting the order from the Canadian customer? If so, why?

Ethical Dilemma Case

LO1, LO3   **Ethical Considerations in Budgeting**

C 6. Javier Gonzales is the manager of the Repairs and Maintenance Department of JG Industries. He is responsible for preparing his department's annual budget. Most managers in the company inflate their budget numbers by at least 10 percent because their bonuses depend upon how much below budget their departments operate. Gonzales turned in the following information for his department's 20x9 budget to the company's budget committee:

	Budget 20x8	Actual 20x8	Budget 20x9
Supplies	$ 20,000	$ 16,000	$ 24,000
Labor	80,000	82,000	96,000
Utilities	8,500	8,000	10,200
Tools	12,500	9,000	15,000
Hand-carried equipment	25,000	16,400	30,000
Cleaning materials	4,600	4,200	5,520
Miscellaneous	2,000	2,100	2,400
Totals	$152,600	$137,700	$183,120

Because the figures for 20x9 are 20 percent above those in the 20x8 budget, the budget committee questioned them. Gonzales defended them by saying that he expects a significant increase in activity in his department in 20x9.

What do you think are the real reasons for the increase in the budgeted amounts? What ethical considerations enter into this situation?

Internet Case

The Budgeting Process

LO1 **C 7.** Some corporate websites include areas specifically designed for student needs. Search the student area of Johnson & Johnson's website (www.jnj.com/student_resources/index.htm). What kinds of information does it provide? How does the information apply to the material discussed in this chapter?

Group Activity Case

The Budgeting Process

LO1, LO2 **C 8.** Many people believe that the budgeting process is wasteful and ineffective. They maintain that managers spend too much time focusing on the mechanics of budgeting and not enough time on strategic issues. They believe that this emphasis on the budgeting process causes managers to neglect more important matters, such as eliminating nonvalue-adding activities that waste resources. Critics of the budgeting process also maintain that the information and formats that managers use in budgets fail to communicate the short-term business activities needed to achieve long-term goals. Place yourself in the role of a company's controller and search the Internet for articles on budgeting. Based on your research, prepare a memorandum to your company's owner that (1) justifies the use of budgeting and (2) suggests ways of making the budgeting process, the budget information, and the budgets themselves efficient, effective, and meaningful.

After you complete this part of the assignment, your instructor will divide the class into groups. Group members will compare their memorandums and prepare a summary statement, which one member of the group will present to the rest of the class.

Business Communication Case

Financial Budgets

LO1, LO2, LO4 **C 9.** Suppose you have just signed a partnership agreement with your cousin Eddie to open a bookstore near your college. You believe that the store will be able to provide excellent service and undersell the local competition. To fund operations, you and Eddie have applied for a loan from the Small Business Administration. The loan application requires you to submit two financial budgets—a pro forma income statement and a pro forma balance sheet—within six weeks. Because of your expertise in accounting and business, Eddie has asked you to prepare the financial budgets.

1. How do the four *w*'s of preparing an accounting report apply in this situation—that is, *why* are you preparing these financial budgets, *who* needs them, *what* information do you need to prepare for them, and *when* are they due?
2. If you obtain the loan and open the bookstore, how can you and Eddie use the pro forma statements that you prepared?

Performance Management and Evaluation

If managers want satisfactory results, they must understand the cause and effect relationships between their actions and their organization's overall performance. By measuring and tracking the relationships that they are responsible for, managers can improve performance and thereby add value for all of their organization's stakeholders. In this chapter, we describe the role of the balanced scorecard, responsibility accounting, and economic value added as they relate to performance management and evaluation. We also point out how managers can use a wide range of financial and nonfinancial data to manage and evaluate performance more effectively.

LEARNING OBJECTIVES

LO1 Describe how the balanced scorecard aligns performance with organizational goals.

LO2 Discuss performance measurement, and identify the issues that affect management's ability to measure performance.

LO3 Define *responsibility accounting,* and describe the role that responsibility centers play in performance management and evaluation.

LO4 Prepare performance reports for cost centers using flexible budgets and for profit centers using variable costing.

LO5 Prepare performance reports for investment centers using the traditional measures of return on investment and residual income and the newer measure of economic value added.

LO6 Explain how properly linked performance incentives and measures add value for all stakeholders in performance management and evaluation.

- How do managers at Vail Resorts link performance measures and set performance targets to achieve performance objectives?

- How do they use the PEAKS system and its integrated database to improve performance management and evaluation?

Vail Resorts includes five Colorado vacation spots: Vail, Breckenridge, Keystone, Heavenly, and Beaver Creek. To help guests enjoy all the activities that these places offer, Vail Resorts instituted its PEAKS system. PEAKS is an all-in-one card that guests at the five resort areas can use to pay for lift tickets, skiing and snowboarding lessons, equipment rentals, dining, and more.

Guests like the PEAKS system's convenience and its program for earning points toward free or reduced-rate lift tickets, dining, and lodging. They enroll in the system by filling out a one-page form that asks for their name, home address, email address, phone number, date of birth, credit card number, and a signature to authorize charge privileges. Data for up to eight family members can be integrated in one membership account. All family members receive a bar-coded picture identification card that is scanned each time they ride the ski lifts, attend ski school, or charge purchases, meals, or lodging.[1]

Managers at Vail Resorts like the PEAKS system because it enables them to collect huge amounts of information—both financial and nonfinancial—in a simple way and because the data have so many uses. New data are entered in the system each time a guest's card is scanned. Those data then become part of an integrated management information system that managers use to measure and evaluate the performance of their resorts in many ways.

Organizational Goals and the Balanced Scorecard

LO1 Describe how the balanced scorecard aligns performance with organizational goals.

The **balanced scorecard**, developed by Robert S. Kaplan and David P. Norton, is a framework that links the perspectives of an organization's four basic stakeholder groups—financial (investors), learning and growth (employees), internal business processes, and customers—with the organization's mission and vision, performance measures, strategic and tactical plans, and resources. To succeed, an organization must add value for all groups in both the short and the long term. Thus, an organization will determine each group's objectives and translate them into performance measures that have specific, quantifiable performance targets. Ideally, managers should be able to see how their actions contribute to the achievement of organizational goals and understand how their compensation is related to their actions. The balanced scorecard assumes that an organization will get only what it measures.

VAIL RESORTS®

Just Another Day In Paradise™

The Balanced Scorecard and Management

To illustrate how managers use the balanced scorecard, we will refer to **Vail Resorts'** PEAKS system, which we described in the Decision Point.

Planning During the planning stage, the balanced scorecard provides a framework that enables managers to translate their organization's vision and strategy into operational terms. Managers evaluate the company's vision from the perspective of each stakeholder group and seek to answer one key question for each group:

- **Financial (investors):** To achieve our organization's vision, how should we appear to our shareholders?

- **Learning and growth (employees):** To achieve our organization's vision, how should we sustain our ability to improve and change?

- **Internal business processes:** To succeed, in which business processes must our organization excel?

- **Customers:** To achieve our organization's vision, how should we appeal to our customers?

These key questions align the organization's strategy from all perspectives. The answers to the questions result in performance objectives that are mutually beneficial to all stakeholders. Once the organization's objectives are set, managers can select performance measures and set performance targets to translate the objectives into an action plan.

FOCUS ON BUSINESS PRACTICE

Risky Business

The balanced scorecard provides a platform for managing business risk. It fits well with enterprise risk management systems (ERMs), which identify events that may affect a business and help manage them so that they are deemed ethical and provide reasonable assurance that the business will achieve its objectives. The linking of goals, measures, and targets from multiple perspectives is the key.[2]

For example, if Vail Resorts' collective vision and strategy is to please guests, its managers might establish the following overall objectives:

Perspective	Objective
Financial (investors)	Increase guests' spending at the resorts.
Learning and growth (employees)	Continually cross-train employees in each other's duties to sustain premium-quality service for guests.
Internal business processes	Leverage market position by introducing and improving innovative marketing and technology-driven advances that clearly benefit guests.
Customers	Create new premium-price experiences and facilities for vacations in all seasons.

These overall objectives are then translated into specific performance objectives and measures for managers. For example, a ski lift manager's performance objectives might be measured in terms of the following:

▶ **Financial (investors):** hourly lift cost, lift ticket sales in dollars and in units

▶ **Learning and growth (employees):** number of cross-trained tasks per employee, employee turnover

▶ **Internal business processes:** number of accident-free days, number and cost of mechanical breakdowns, average lift cycle time (that is, the time between getting in line to ride the ski lift and completing the ski run)

▶ **Customers:** average number of ski runs per daily lift ticket, number of repeat customers, number of PEAKS points redeemed

Figure 1 summarizes how Vail Resorts' managers might link their organization's vision and strategy to objectives, then link the objectives to logical performance measures, and, finally, set performance targets. As a result, a ski lift manager will have a variety of performance measures that balance the perspectives and needs of all stakeholders.

Performing   Managers use the mutually agreed-upon strategic and tactical objectives for the entire organization as the basis for decision making within their individual areas of responsibility. This practice ensures that they consider the needs of all stakeholder groups and shows how measuring and managing performance for some stakeholder groups can lead to improved performance for another stakeholder group. Specifically, improving the performance of leading indicators like internal business processes and learning and growth will create improvements for customers, which in turn will result in improved financial performance (a lagging indicator). For example, when making decisions about available ski lift capacity, the ski lift manager at Vail Resorts will balance such factors as lift ticket sales, snow conditions, equipment reliability, trained staff availability, and length of wait for ski lifts.

When managers understand the causal and linked relationship between their actions and their company's overall performance, they can see new ways to be more effective. For example, a ski lift manager may hypothesize that shorter waiting lines for the ski lifts would improve customer satisfaction and lead to more visits to the ski lift. The manager could test this possible cause-and-effect relationship by measuring and tracking the length of ski lift waiting lines and the number of visits to the ski lift. If a causal relationship exists, the

■ **FIGURE 1**
Sample Balanced Scorecard of Linked Objectives, Performance Measures, and Targets

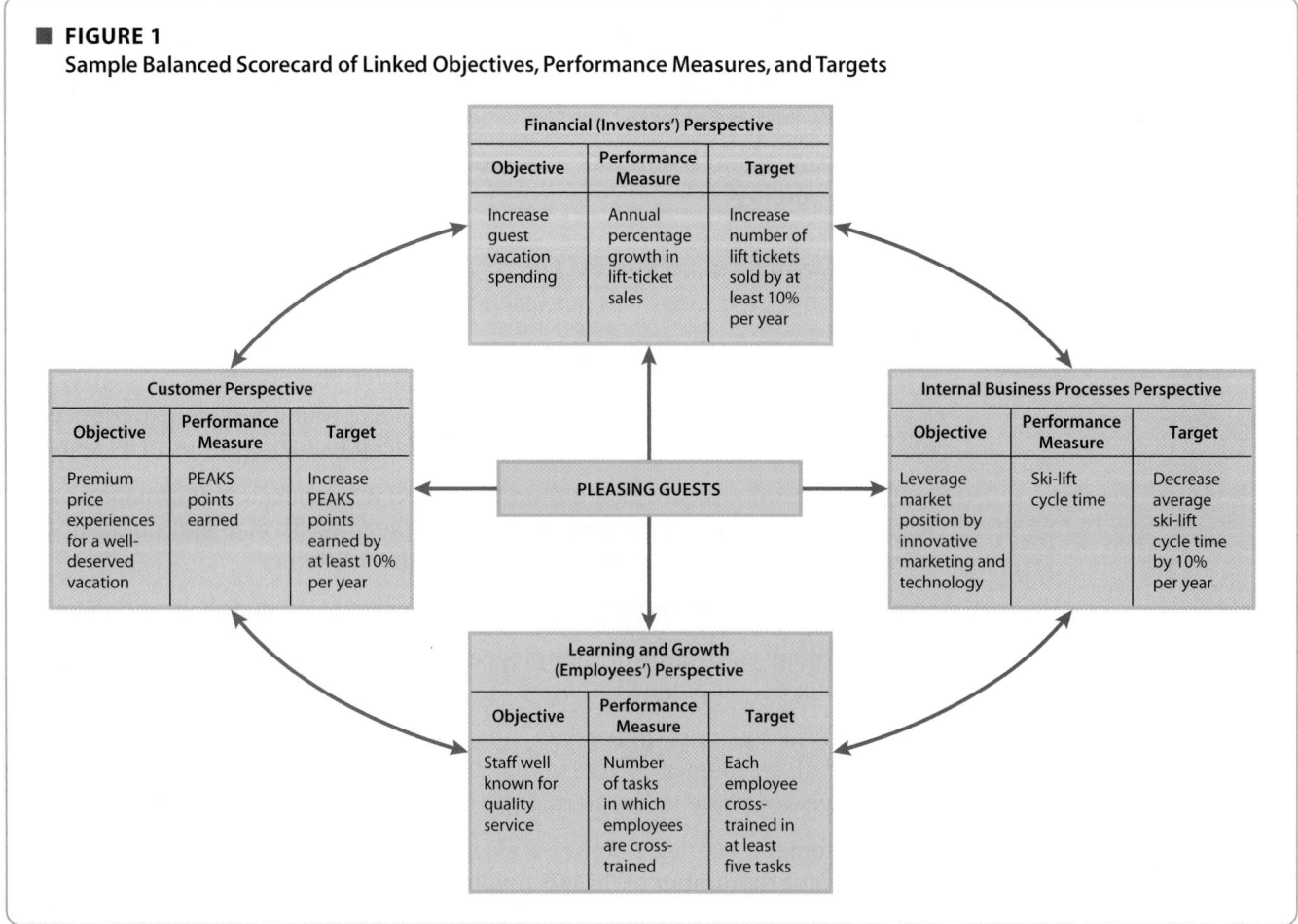

Source: Adapted from Robert S. Kaplan and David P. Norton, "Using the Balanced Scorecard as a Strategic Management System," *Harvard Business Review*, January–February 1996.

manager can improve the performance of the ski lift operation by doing everything possible to ensure that waiting lines are short because a quicker ride to the top will result in improved results for the operation and for other perspectives as well.

Evaluating   Managers review financial and nonfinancial results frequently during the year, at year end, and over longer periods to evaluate their strategies for meeting the objectives and performance targets set during the planning stage. They compare performance objectives and targets with actual results to determine if the targets were met, what measures need to be changed, and what strategies or objectives need revision. For example, the ski lift manager at Vail Resorts would analyze the reasons for performance gaps and make recommendations to improve the performance of the ski lift area.

Communicating   Finally, during the communication stage of the management process, a variety of reports are prepared. For example, the database makes it possible to prepare financial performance reports, customer PEAKS statements, internal business process reports for targeted performance measures and results, and performance appraisals of individual employees. Such reports enable managers to monitor and evaluate performance measures that add value for stakeholder groups.

■ FIGURE 2
The Management Process: To-Do's for Managers

To-Do's for Managers

- Plan
  - Translate organizational mission and vision into operational objectives from multiple stakeholders' perspectives
  - Select performance measures for objectives
  - Establish targets for each performance measure

- Perform
  - Balance needs of all stakeholders when making management decisions
  - Improve performance by tracking causal relationships between objectives, measures, and targets

- Evaluate
  - Compare financial and nonfinancial results with performance measurement targets
  - Analyze results and take corrective actions

- Communicate
  - Prepare reports of interest to stakeholder groups

As you can see in Figure 2, the balanced scorecard adds dimension to a manager's to do list. Managers plan, perform, evaluate, and communicate the organization's performance from multiple perspectives. By balancing the needs of all stakeholders, managers are more likely to achieve their objectives in both the short and the long term.

STOP • REVIEW • APPLY

1-1. What four basic stakeholder groups are included in the balanced scorecard?

1-2. On which perspective do most businesses focus?

1-3. Why is it important for managers to see the causal relationships between their actions and the company's overall performance?

Suggested answers to all Stop, Review, and Apply questions are available at http://college.hmco.com/accounting/needles/poa/10e/student_home.html.

Performance Measurement

> **LO2** Discuss performance measurement, and identify the issues that affect management's ability to measure performance.

As a company's management philosophy changes, so must the measures in its performance management and evaluation system. A **performance management and evaluation system** is a set of procedures that account for and report on both financial and nonfinancial performance, so that a company can identify how well it is doing, where it is going, and what improvements will make it more profitable.

What to Measure, How to Measure

Performance measurement is the use of quantitative tools to gauge an organization's performance in relation to a specific goal or an expected outcome. For performance measurement to succeed, managers must be able to distinguish between what is being measured and the actual measures used to monitor performance. For instance, product or service quality is *not* a performance measure. It is part of a management strategy: Management wants to produce the highest-quality product or service possible, given the resources available. Product or service quality thus is what management *wants* to measure. To measure product or service quality, managers must collaborate with other managers to develop a group of measures, such as the balanced scorecard, that will identify changes in product or service quality and help employees determine what needs to be done to improve quality.

Other Measurement Issues

Each organization must develop a set of performance measures that is appropriate to its situation. In addition to answering the basic questions of what to measure and how to measure, management must consider a variety of other issues, including the following:

◗ What performance measures can be used?

◗ How can managers monitor the level of product or service quality?

◗ How can managers monitor production and other business processes to identify areas that need improvement?

◗ How can managers measure customer satisfaction?

Study Note

What a manager is measuring—for example, quality—is not the same thing as the actual measures used to monitor performance—for example, the number of defective units per hour.

FOCUS ON BUSINESS PRACTICE

"Old" Doesn't Mean "Out-of-Date"

The *tableau de bord*, or "dashboard," was developed by French engineers around 1900 as a concise performance measurement system that helped managers understand the cause-and-effect relationships between their decisions and the resulting performance. The indicators, both financial and nonfinancial, allowed managers at all levels to monitor their progress in terms of the mission and objectives of their unit and of their company overall. Like a set of nested Russian dolls, each unit's key success factors and key performance indicators were integrated with those of other units. The dashboard continues to encourage a performance measurement system that focuses on and supports an organization's strategic plan.[3]

◗ How can managers monitor financial performance?

◗ Are there other stakeholders to whom a manager is accountable?

◗ What performance measures do government entities impose on the company?

◗ How can a manager measure the company's effect on the environment?

S T O P • R E V I E W • A P P L Y

2-1. What is a performance management and evaluation system?

2-2. When managers make changes in how work should be done, should performance measures be reviewed?

Responsibility Accounting

LO3 Define *responsibility accounting,* and describe the role that responsibility centers play in performance management and evaluation.

As part of their performance management systems, many organizations assign resources to specific areas of responsibility and track how the managers of those areas use those resources. For example, **Vail Resorts** assigns resources to its Lodging, Dining, Retail and Rental, Ski School, and Real Estate divisions and holds the managers of those divisions responsible for generating revenue and managing costs. In addition, the company may give the managers resources to invest in assets that will support the growth of their divisions. Within each division, other managers are assigned responsibility for such areas as Children and Adult Ski School, Snowboard School, or Private Lessons. All managers at all levels are then evaluated in terms of their ability to manage their areas of responsibility in keeping with the organization's goals.

To assist in performance management and evaluation, many organizations use responsibility accounting. **Responsibility accounting** is an information system that classifies data according to areas of responsibility and reports each area's activities by including only the revenue, cost, and resource categories that the assigned manager can control. A **responsibility center** is an organizational unit whose manager has been assigned the responsibility of managing a portion of the organization's resources. The activities of a responsibility center dictate the extent of a manager's responsibility.

Types of Responsibility Centers

There are five types of responsibility centers: (1) cost centers, (2) discretionary cost centers, (3) revenue centers, (4) profit centers, and (5) investment centers. The key characteristics of the five types of responsibility centers are summarized in Table 1.

Cost Centers
A responsibility center whose manager is accountable only for controllable costs that have well-defined relationships between the center's resources and certain products or services is called a **cost center**. Manufacturing companies like **Coach, Inc.**, **DaimlerChrysler**, **Apple Computer**, and **Kraft** use cost centers to manage assembly plants, where the relationship

TABLE 1. Types of Responsibility Centers

Responsibility Center	Manager Accountable For	How Performance Is Measured	Examples
Cost center	Only controllable costs, where there are well-defined links between the costs of resources and the resulting products or services	Compare actual costs with flexible and master budget costs Analyze resulting variances	Product: Manufacturing assembly plants Service: Food service for hospital patients
Discretionary cost center	Only controllable costs; the links between the costs of resources and the resulting products or services are *not* well defined	Compare actual noncost-based measures with targets Determine compliance with preapproved budgeted spending limits	Product or service: Administrative activities such as accounting, human resources, and research and development
Revenue center	Revenue generation	Compare actual revenue with budgeted revenue Analyze resulting variances	Product: Phone or ecommerce sales for pizza delivery Service: National car rental reservation center
Profit center	Operating income resulting from controllable revenues and costs	Compare actual variable costing income statement with the budgeted income statement	Product or service: Local store of a national chain
Investment center	Controllable revenues, costs, and the investment of resources to achieve organizational goals	Return on investment Residual income Economic value added	Product: A division of a multinational corporation Service: A national office of a multinational consulting firm

between the costs of resources (direct material, direct labor) and the resulting products is well defined.

Nonmanufacturing organizations use cost centers to manage activities in which resources are clearly linked with a service that is provided at no additional charge. For example, in nursing homes and hospitals, there is a clear relationship between the costs of food and direct labor and the number of inpatient meals served.

The performance of a cost center is usually evaluated by comparing an activity's actual cost with its budgeted cost and analyzing the resulting variances. You will learn more about this performance evaluation process in the chapter on standard costing.

Shown here at the Monsanto Research Centre in Bangalore, India, is a scientist engaged in mapping the rice genome. Research and development units are a type of discretionary cost center, in which a manager is accountable for costs only and the relationship between resources and products or services produced is not well defined. A common performance measure used to evaluate research and development activities is the number of patents obtained.

Discretionary Cost Centers

A responsibility center whose manager is accountable for costs only and in which the relationship between resources and the products or services produced is not well defined is called a **discretionary cost center**. Units that perform administrative activities, such as accounting, human resources, and legal services, are typical examples of discretionary cost centers. These centers, like cost centers, have approved budgets that set spending limits.

Because the spending and use of resources in discretionary cost centers are not clearly linked to the production of a product or service, cost-based measures usually cannot be used to evaluate performance (although such centers are penalized if they exceed their approved budgets). For example, among the performance measures used to evaluate the research and development activities at manufacturing companies such as **DaimlerChrysler**, **Monsanto**, and **Intel** are the number of patents obtained and the number of cost-saving innovations that are developed. At service organizations, such as the **United Way**, a common measure of administrative activities is how low their costs are as a percentage of total contributions.

Revenue Centers

A responsibility center whose manager is accountable primarily for revenue and whose success is based on its ability to generate revenue is called a **revenue center**. Examples of revenue centers are **Hertz**'s national car reservation center and the clothing retailer **Nordstrom**'s ecommerce order department. A revenue center's performance is usually evaluated by comparing its actual revenue with its budgeted revenue and analyzing the resulting variances. Performance measures at both manufacturing and service organizations may include sales dollars, number of customer sales, or sales revenue per minute.

Profit Centers

A responsibility center whose manager is accountable for both revenue and costs and for the resulting operating income is called a **profit center**. A good example is a local store of a national chain, such as **Wal-Mart**, **Coach, Inc.**, or **Jiffy Lube**. The performance of a profit center is usually evaluated by comparing the figures in its actual income statement with the figures in its master or flexible budget income statement.

Investment Centers   A responsibility center whose manager is accountable for profit generation and can also make significant decisions about the resources that the center uses is called an **investment center**. For example, the president of **DaimlerChrysler's** Jeep Division, the president of **Harley-Davidson's** Buell subsidiary, and the president of **Brinker International's** Chili's Grill and Bar can control revenues, costs, and the investment of assets to achieve organizational goals. The performance of these centers is evaluated using such measures as return on investment, residual income, and economic value added. These measures are used in all types of organizations, both manufacturing and nonmanufacturing, and are discussed later in this chapter.

Organizational Structure and Performance Management

Much can be learned about an organization by examining how its managers organize activities and resources. A company's organizational structure formalizes its lines of managerial authority and control. An **organization chart** is a visual representation of an organization's hierarchy of responsibility for the purposes of management control. Within an organization chart, the five types of responsibility centers are arranged by level of management authority and control.

A responsibility accounting system establishes a communications network within an organization that is ideal for gathering and reporting information about the operations of each area of responsibility. The system is used to prepare budgets by responsibility area and to report the actual results of each responsibility center. The report for a responsibility center should contain only the costs, revenues, and resources that the manager of that center can control. Such costs and revenues are called **controllable costs and revenues** because they are the result of a manager's actions, influence, or decisions. A responsibility accounting system ensures that managers will not be held responsible for items that they cannot change.

Shown here is the interior of a Chili's Grill and Bar. Each restaurant in the Chili's chain is a profit center for Brinker International. Typically, in a corporate division like Chili's, restaurant managers report to vice presidents, who report to the president of the restaurant division. The division president's office is an investment center because capital investment decisions are made at this level.

■ **FIGURE 3**
Partial Organization Chart of Café Cubano, a Restaurant Chain

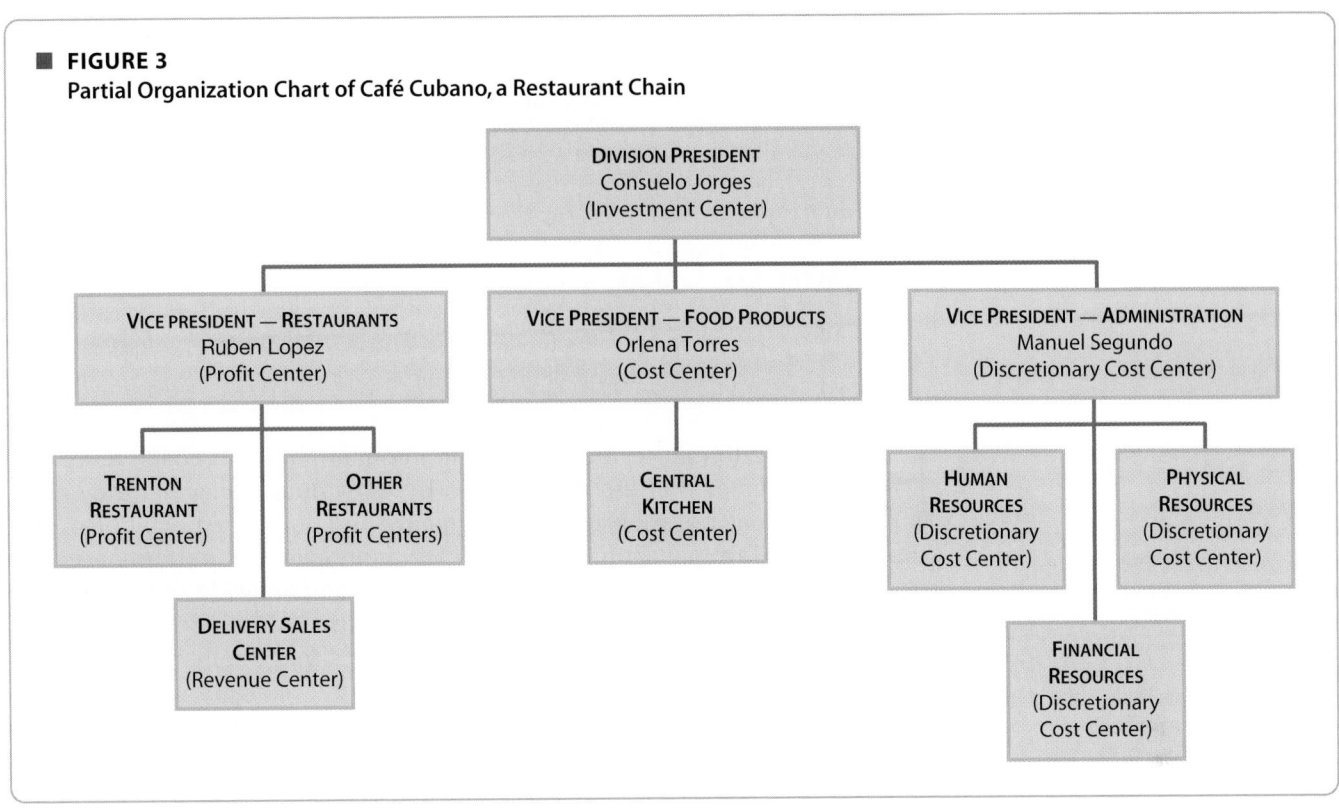

By examining a typical corporate organization chart, you can see how a responsibility accounting system works. Figure 3 shows part of the management structure for Café Cubano, a multiconcept restaurant chain like **Brinker International, Inc.,** and **Carlson Restaurants Worldwide Inc.** Typically, several vice presidents report to the president of a restaurant division like Chili's or T.G.I. Friday's U.S.A. Notice that the figure shows examples of all five types of responsibility centers. The office of Consuelo Jorges, the division president, is an investment center because capital investment decisions are made at the division level. The vice president–restaurants, Ruben Lopez, manages both profit and revenue centers. The vice president–administration, Manuel Segundo, supervises three discretionary cost centers, and the vice president–food products, Orlena Torres, is responsible for the operation of the central kitchen, a cost center.

In a responsibility accounting system, the performance reports for each level of management are tailored to each manager's individual needs for information. Because the system provides a report for every manager and lower-level managers report to higher-level managers, the same information may appear in varying formats in several different reports. When information about lower-level operations appears in upper-level managers' reports, it is usually condensed. Performance reporting by responsibility level enables an organization to trace the source of a cost, revenue, or resource to the manager who controls it and to evaluate that manager's performance accordingly.

S T O P • R E V I E W • A P P L Y

3-1. Define responsibility accounting.

3-2. Describe a responsibility center.

3-3. How should managers' performance be evaluated?

3-4. How does a company's organizational structure affect its responsibility accounting system?

Performance Evaluation of Cost Centers and Profit Centers

LO4 Prepare performance reports for cost centers using flexible budgets and for profit centers using variable costing.

Because performance reports contain information about costs, revenues, and resources that are controllable by individual managers, they allow comparisons between actual performance and budget expectations. Such comparisons allow management to evaluate an individual's performance with respect to responsibility center objectives and companywide objectives and to recommend changes. It is important to emphasize that performance reports should contain only costs, revenues, and resources that the manager can control. If a performance report includes items that the manager cannot control, the credibility of the entire responsibility accounting system can be called into question. It is up to management to structure and interpret the performance results fairly.

The content and format of a performance report depend on the nature of the responsibility center. Let us take a closer look at the performance reports for cost centers and profit centers.

> **Study Note**
>
> Only controllable items should be included on a manager's performance report.

Evaluating Cost Center Performance Using Flexible Budgeting

Orlena Torres, the vice president–food products at Café Cubano, is responsible for the central kitchen, where the food products that the restaurants sell are prepared. The central kitchen is a cost center because its costs have well-defined relationships with the resulting products. To ensure that the central kitchen is meeting its performance goals, Torres has decided to evaluate the performance of each food item produced. She will prepare a separate report for each product that compares its actual costs with the corresponding amounts from the budget. The performance report for Café Cubano's House Dressing, one of the chain's signature menu items, is presented in Exhibit 1.

The performance report in Exhibit 1 compares data from the master budget (prepared at the beginning of the period) with the actual results for the period. As you can see, actual costs exceeded budgeted costs. Most managers would consider such a cost overrun significant. But was there really a cost overrun? The amounts budgeted in the master budget are based on an output of 1,000 units of dressing; however, the actual output was 1,200 units of dressing. To judge the central kitchen's performance accurately, the company's managers must change the budgeted data in the master budget to reflect an output of 1,200 units. They can do this by using a flexible budget.

A **flexible budget** (also called a *variable budget*) is a summary of expected costs for a range of activity levels. Unlike a static budget, a flexible budget provides forecasted data that can be adjusted for changes in the level of output. A flexible budget is derived by multiplying actual unit output by predetermined unit costs for each cost item in the report. The flexible budget is used primarily

EXHIBIT 1 ▶

	Actual Results	Variance	Flexible Budget	Variance	Master Budget
Central Kitchen's Performance Report on Café Cubano's House Dressing					
Gallons produced	1,200	0	1,200	200 (F)	1,000
Center costs					
Direct materials ($.25 per gallon)	$312	$12 (U)	$300	$50 (U)	$250
Direct labor ($.05 per gallon)	72	12 (U)	60	10 (U)	50
Variable overhead ($.03 per gallon)	33	3 (F)	36	6 (U)	30
Fixed overhead	2	3 (F)	5	0	5
Total cost	$419	$18 (U)	$401	$66 (U)	$335
Performance measures					
Defect-free gallons to total produced	.98	.01 (U)	N/A	N/A	.99
Average throughput time per gallon	11 minutes	1 minute (F)	N/A	N/A	12 minutes

as a cost control tool in evaluating performance at the end of a period, as in Exhibit 1.

In another chapter, you will learn that favorable (positive, or F) and unfavorable (negative, or U) variances between actual costs and the flexible budget can be further examined by using standard costing to compute specific variances for direct materials, direct labor, and variable and fixed overhead. Also, you will use the flexible budget as a cost control tool to evaluate performance and derive a flexible budget by multiplying actual unit output by the standard unit costs. Refer to the chapter on standard costing for further information on performance evaluation using variances or the flexible budget.

Evaluating Profit Center Performance Using Variable Costing

Ruben Lopez, the vice president–restaurants, oversees many restaurants. Because the restaurants are profit centers, each is accountable for its own revenues and costs and for the resulting operating income. A profit center's performance is usually evaluated by comparing its actual income statement results to its budgeted income statement.

Variable costing is a method of preparing profit center performance reports that classifies a manager's controllable costs as either variable or fixed. Variable costing produces a variable costing income statement instead of a traditional income statement (also called a *full costing* or *absorption costing income statement*), which is used for external reporting purposes. A variable costing income statement is the same as a contribution income statement, the format of which you may recall from its use in cost-volume-profit analysis. Such an income statement is useful in performance management and evaluation because it focuses on cost variability and the profit center's contribution to operating income.

When variable costing is used to evaluate profit center performance, the variable cost of goods sold and the variable selling and administrative

EXHIBIT 2 ▶

Variable Costing Income Statement Versus Traditional Income Statement for Trenton Restaurant

Variable Costing Income Statement		Traditional Income Statement	
Sales	$2,500	Sales	$2,500
Variable cost of goods sold	1,575	Cost of goods sold	1,745
Variable selling expenses	325	($1,575 + $170 = $1,745)	
Contribution margin	$ 600	Gross margin	$ 755
Fixed manufacturing costs	170	Variable selling expenses	325
Fixed selling expenses	230	Fixed selling expenses	230
Profit center income	$ 200	Profit center income	$ 200

expenses are subtracted from sales to arrive at the contribution margin for the center. All the controllable fixed costs of a profit center, including those from manufacturing, selling, and administrative activities, are subtracted from the contribution margin to determine the operating income.

The variable costing income statement differs from the traditional income statement prepared for financial reporting, as shown by the two income statements in Exhibit 2 for Trenton Restaurant, part of the Café Cubano restaurant chain. In the traditional income statement, all manufacturing costs are assigned to cost of goods sold; in the variable costing income statement, only the variable manufacturing costs are included. Under variable costing, direct materials costs, direct labor costs, and variable overhead costs are the only cost elements used to compute variable cost of goods sold. Fixed manufacturing costs are considered costs of the current accounting period. Notice that fixed manufacturing costs are listed with fixed selling expenses after the contribution margin has been computed.

▼ **EXHIBIT 3**

Performance Report Based on Variable Costing and Flexible Budgeting for Trenton Restaurant

	Actual Results	Variance	Flexible Budget	Variance	Master Budget
Meals served	750	0	750	250 (U)	1,000
Sales (average meal $2.85)	$2,500.00	$362.50 (F)	$2,137.50	$712.50 (U)	$2,850.00
Controllable variable costs					
Variable cost of goods sold ($1.50)	1,575.00	450.00 (U)	1,125.00	375.00 (F)	1,500.00
Variable selling expenses ($.40)	325.00	25.00 (U)	300.00	100.00 (F)	400.00
Contribution margin	$ 600.00	$112.50 (U)	$ 712.50	$237.50 (U)	$ 950.00
Controllable fixed costs					
Fixed manufacturing expenses	170.00	30.00 (F)	200.00	0.00	200.00
Fixed selling expenses	230.00	20.00 (F)	250.00	0.00	250.00
Profit center income	$ 200.00	$ 62.50 (U)	$ 262.50	$237.50 (U)	$ 500.00
Other nonfinancial performance measures					
Number of orders processed	300	50 (F)	N/A	N/A	250
Average sales order	$8.34	$3.06 (U)	N/A	N/A	$11.40

The manager of a profit center may also want to measure and evaluate non-financial information. For example, Ruben Lopez of Café Cubano may want to track the number of food orders processed and the average amount of a sales order at Trenton Restaurant. The resulting report, based on variable costing and flexible budgeting, is shown in Exhibit 3.

Although performance reports vary in format depending on the type of responsibility center, they have some common themes. For example, all responsibility center reports compare actual results to budgeted figures and focus on the differences. Often, comparisons are made to a flexible budget as well as to the master budget. Only the items that the manager can control are included in the performance report. Nonfinancial measures are also examined to achieve a more balanced view of the manager's responsibilities.

S T O P • R E V I E W • A P P L Y

4-1. What types of information are in performance reports?

4-2. When is a flexible budget prepared?

4-3. What are some similarities among the performance reports for the various kinds of responsibility centers?

Performance Evaluation of Investment Centers

> **LO5** Prepare performance reports for investment centers using the traditional measures of return on investment and residual income and the newer measure of economic value added.

The evaluation of an investment center's performance requires more than a comparison of controllable revenues and costs with budgeted amounts. Because the managers of investment centers also control resources and invest in assets, other performance measures must be used to hold them accountable for revenues, costs, and the capital investments that they control. In this section, we focus on the traditional performance evaluation measures of return on investment and residual income and the relatively new performance measure of economic value added.

Return on Investment

Traditionally, the most common performance measure that takes into account both operating income and the assets invested to earn that income is **return on investment (ROI)**. Return on investment is computed as follows:

$$\text{Return on Investment (ROI)} = \frac{\text{Operating Income}}{\text{Assets Invested}}$$

In this formula, *assets invested* is the average of the beginning and ending asset balances for the period.

Properly measuring the income and the assets specifically controlled by a manager is critical to the quality of this performance measure. Using ROI, it is

EXHIBIT 4 ▶

	Actual Results	Variance	Master Budget
Performance Report Based on Return on Investment for the Café Cubano Restaurant Division			
Operating income	$610	$280 (U)	$ 890
Assets invested	$800	$200 (F)	$1,000
Performance measure			
ROI	76%	13% (U)	89%

ROI = Operating Income ÷ Assets Invested

$890 ÷ $1,000 = .89 = 89\%$

$610 ÷ $800 = .76 = 76\%$

possible to evaluate the manager of any investment center, whether it is an entire company or a unit within a company, such as a subsidiary, division, or other business segment. For example, assume that the Café Cubano Restaurant Division had actual operating income of $610 and that the average assets invested were $800. The master budget called for $890 in operating income and $1,000 in invested assets. As shown in Exhibit 4, the budgeted ROI for Consuelo Jorges, the president of the division, would be 89 percent, and the actual ROI would be 76 percent. The actual ROI was lower than the budgeted ROI because the division's actual operating income was lower than expected relative to the actual assets invested.

For investment centers, the ROI computation is really the aggregate measure of many interrelationships. The basic ROI equation, Operating Income ÷ Assets Invested, can be rewritten to show the many elements within the aggregate ROI number that a manager can influence. Two important indicators of performance are profit margin and asset turnover. **Profit margin** is the ratio of operating income to sales; it represents the percentage of each sales dollar that results in profit. **Asset turnover** is the ratio of sales to average assets invested; it indicates the productivity of assets, or the number of sales dollars generated by each dollar invested in assets. Return on investment is equal to profit margin multiplied by asset turnover:

$$\text{ROI} = \text{Profit Margin} \times \text{Asset Turnover}$$

$$\text{ROI} = \frac{\text{Operating Income}}{\text{Sales}} \times \frac{\text{Sales}}{\text{Assets Invested}} = \frac{\text{Operating Income}}{\text{Assets Invested}}$$

Profit margin and asset turnover help explain changes in return on investment for a single investment center or differences in return or investment among investment centers. Therefore, the formula ROI = Profit Margin × Asset Turnover is useful for analyzing and interpreting the elements that make up a business's overall return on investment.

Du Pont, one of the first organizations to recognize the many interrelationships that affect ROI, designed a formula similar to the one diagrammed in Figure 4. You can see that ROI is affected by a manager's decisions about pricing, product sales mix, capital budgeting for new facilities, product sales volume, and other financial matters. In essence, a single ROI number is a composite index of many cause-and-effect relationships and interdependent financial elements. A manager can improve ROI by increasing sales, decreasing costs, or decreasing assets.

Study Note

Profit margin focuses on the income statement, and asset turnover focuses on the balance sheet aspects of ROI.

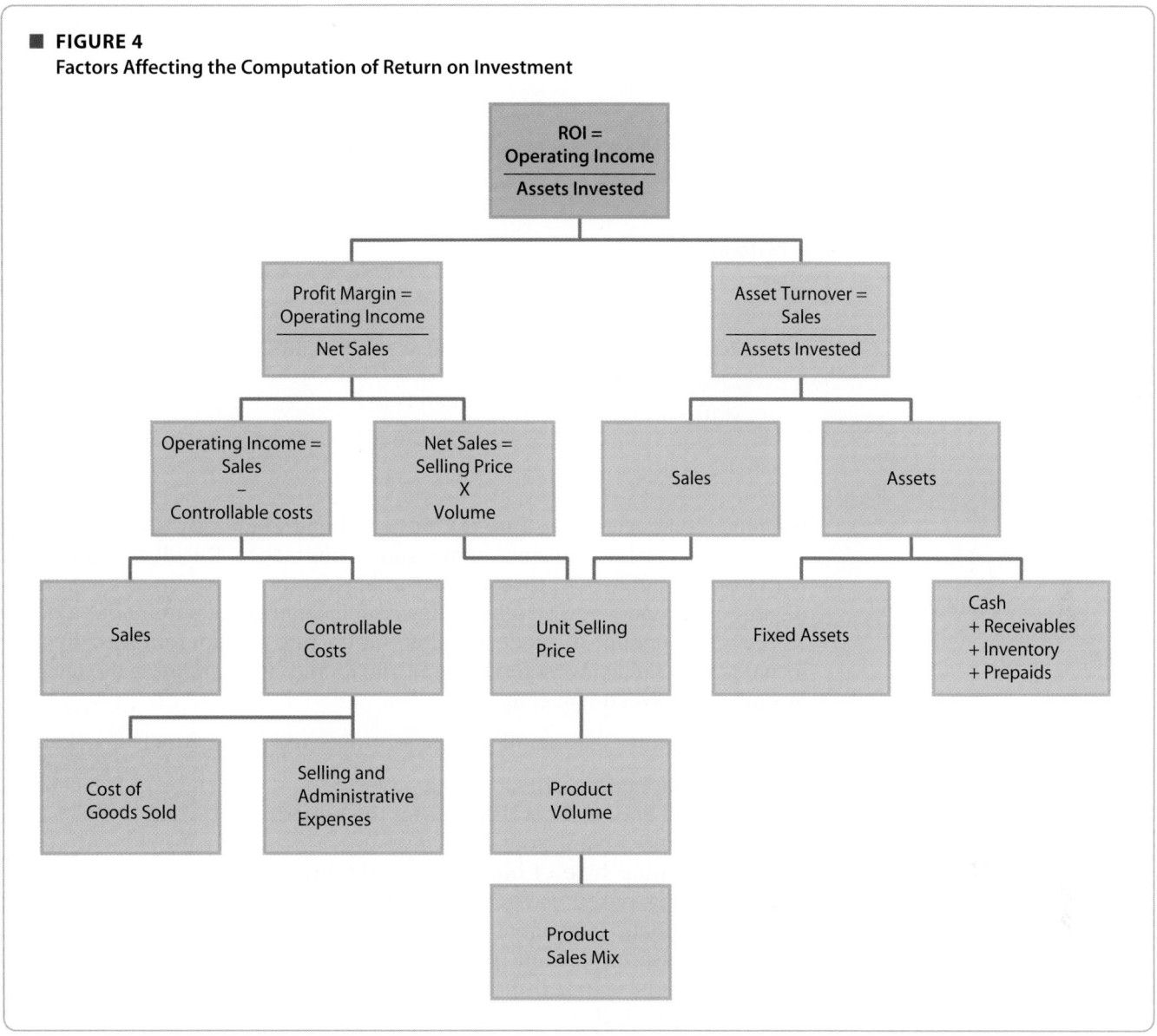

■ **FIGURE 4**
Factors Affecting the Computation of Return on Investment

Because of the many factors that affect ROI, management should use this measure cautiously in evaluating performance. If ROI is overemphasized, investment center managers may react by making business decisions that favor their personal ROI performance at the expense of companywide profits or the long-term success of other investment centers. To avoid such problems, other performance measures should always be used in conjunction with ROI—for example, comparisons of revenues, costs, and operating income with budget amounts or past trends; sales growth percentages; market share percentages; or other key variables in the organization's activity. ROI should also be compared with budgeted goals and with past ROI trends because changes in this ratio over time can be more revealing than any single number.

Residual Income

Because of the pitfalls of using return on investment as a performance measure, other approaches to evaluating investment centers have evolved. For

EXHIBIT 5 ▶

Performance Report Based on Residual Income for the Café Cubano Restaurant Division			
	Actual Results	Variance	Master Budget
Operating income	$610	$280 (U)	$ 890
Assets invested	$800	$200 (F)	$1,000
Desired ROI			20%
Performance measures			
ROI	76%	13% (U)	89%
Residual income	$450	$240 (U)	$ 690
Residual Income = Operating Income − (Desired ROI × Assets Invested)			
$890 − 20%($1,000) = $690			
$610 − 20%($800) = $450			

Study Note

ROI is expressed as a percentage, and residual income is expressed in dollars.

example, companies like **General Motors**, **General Electric**, **Coca-Cola**, and **UPS** now use residual income to measure performance. **Residual income (RI)** is the operating income that an investment center earns above a minimum desired return on invested assets. Residual income is not a ratio, but a dollar amount: the amount of profit left after subtracting a predetermined desired income target for an investment center. The formula for computing the residual income of an investment center is:

Residual Income = Operating Income − (Desired ROI × Assets Invested)

As in the computation of ROI, assets invested is the average of the center's beginning and ending asset balances for the period.

The desired RI will vary from investment center to investment center depending on the type of business and the level of risk assumed. The performance report based on residual income for Consuelo Jorges, the president of the Café Cubano Restaurant Division, is shown in Exhibit 5. Assume that the president's residual income performance target is to exceed a 20 percent return on assets invested in the division. Note that the division's residual income is $450, which was lower than the $690 that was projected in the master budget.

Comparisons with other residual income figures will strengthen the analysis. To add context to the analysis of the division and its manager, questions such as the following need to be answered: How did the division's residual income this year compare with its residual income in previous years? Did the actual residual income exceed the budgeted residual income? How did this division's residual income compare with the amounts generated by other investment centers of the company?

Caution is called for when using residual income to compare investment centers within a company. For their residual income figures to be comparable, all investment centers must have equal access to resources and similar asset investment bases. Some managers may be able to produce larger residual incomes simply because their investment centers are larger rather than because their performance is better. Like ROI, RI has some flaws.

Economic Value Added

More and more businesses are using the shareholder wealth created by an investment center, or the **economic value added (EVA)**, as an indicator of per-

EXHIBIT 6 ▶

Performance Report Based on Economic Value Added for the Café Cubano Restaurant Division

	Actual Results	Variance	Master Budget
Performance measures			
ROI	76%	13% (U)	89%
Residual income	$450	$240 (U)	$690
Economic value added	$334		

Economic Value Added = After-Tax Operating Income −
[Cost of Capital × (Total Assets − Current Liabilities)]
$400 − 12% ($800 − $250) = $334

formance. The calculation of EVA, a registered trademark of the consulting firm Stern Stewart & Company, can be quite complex because it makes various cost of capital and accounting principles adjustments. You will learn more about the cost of capital in the chapter that discusses capital investment decisions. However, for the purposes of computing EVA, the **cost of capital** is the minimum desired rate of return on an investment, such as the assets invested in an investment center.

Basically, the computation of EVA is similar to the computation of residual income, except that after-tax operating income is used instead of pretax operating income, and a cost of capital percentage is multiplied by the center's invested assets less current liabilities instead of a desired ROI percentage being multiplied by invested assets. Also, like residual income, the economic value added is expressed in dollars. The formula is:

$$EVA = \text{After-Tax Operating Income} - \text{Cost of Capital in Dollars}$$

$$EVA = \text{After-Tax Operating Income} - [\text{Cost of Capital} \times (\text{Total Assets} - \text{Current Liabilities})]$$

A very basic computation of economic value added for Consuelo Jorges, the president of the Café Cubano Restaurant Division, is shown in Exhibit 6. The report assumes that the division's after-tax operating income is $400, its cost of capital is 12 percent, its total assets are $800, and its current liabilities are $250.

The report shows that the division has added $334 to its economic value after taxes and cost of capital. In other words, the division produced after-tax profits of $334 in excess of the cost of capital required to generate those profits.

Because many factors affect the economic value of an investment center, management should be cautious when drawing conclusions about performance. The evaluation will be more meaningful if the current economic value added is compared to EVAs from previous periods, target EVAs, and EVAs from other investment centers.

The factors that affect the computation of economic value added are illustrated in Figure 5. An investment center's economic value is affected by managers' decisions on pricing, product sales volume, taxes, cost of capital, capital investments, and other financial matters. In essence, the EVA number is a composite index drawn from many cause-and-effect relationships and interdependent financial elements. A manager can improve the economic value of an investment center by increasing sales, decreasing costs, decreasing assets, or lowering the cost of capital.

■ **FIGURE 5**
Factors Affecting the Computation of Economic Value Added

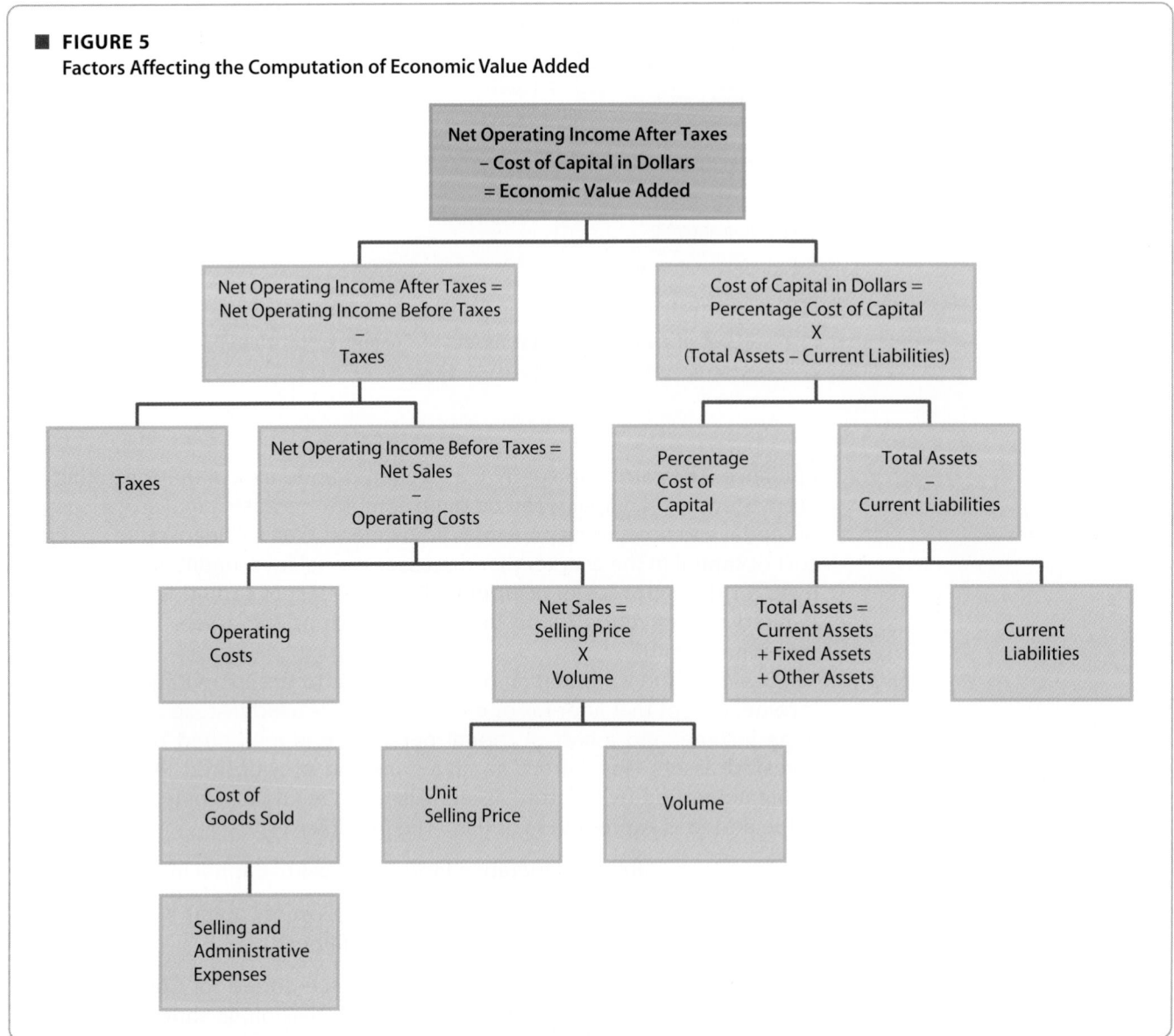

The Importance of Multiple Performance Measures

In summary, to be effective, a performance management system must consider both operating results and multiple performance measures, such as return on investment, residual income, and economic value added. Comparing actual results to budgeted figures adds meaning to the evaluation. Performance measures such as ROI, RI, and EVA indicate whether an investment center is effective in coordinating its own goals with companywide goals because these measures take into account both operating income and the assets used to produce that income. However, all three measures are limited by their focus on short-term financial performance. To obtain a fuller picture, management needs to break these three measures down into their components, analyze such information as responsibility center income over time, and compare current results to the targeted amounts in the flexible or master budget. In addition, the analysis of such nonfinancial performance indicators as average through-put time, employee turnover, and number of orders processed will ensure a more balanced view of a business's well-being and how to improve it.

S T O P • R E V I E W • A P P L Y

5-1. Why is return on investment more than a ratio of two numbers?

5-2. What are the similarities and differences between RI and EVA?

Performance Measures   Brew Mountain Company sells coffee and hot beverages. Its Coffee Cart Division sells to skiers as they come off the mountain. The balance sheet for the Coffee Cart Division showed that the company had invested assets of $30,000 at the beginning of the year and $50,000 at the end of the year. During the year, the division's operating income was $80,000 on sales of $120,000.

a. Compute the division's residual income if the desired ROI is 20 percent.

b. Compute the return on investment for the division.

c. Compute the economic value added for Brew Mountain Company if total corporate assets are $600,000, current liabilities are $80,000, after-tax operating income is $70,000, and the cost of capital is 12 percent.

SOLUTION
a. $80,000 − [20\% × (\$30,000 + \$50,000) ÷ 2] = \$72,000$
b. $80,000 ÷ [(\$30,000 + \$50,000) ÷ 2] = 200\%$
c. $70,000 − [12\% × (\$600,000 − \$80,000)] = \$7,600$

Performance Incentives and Goals

LO6   Explain how properly linked performance incentives and measures add value for all stakeholders in performance management and evaluation.

The effectiveness of a performance management and evaluation system depends on how well it coordinates the goals of responsibility centers, managers, and the entire company. Two factors are key to the successful coordination of goals: the logical linking of goals to measurable objectives and targets, and the tying of appropriate compensation incentives to the achievement of the targets, that is, performance-based pay.

Linking Goals, Performance Objectives, Measures, and Performance Targets

The causal links between an organization's goals, performance objectives, measures, and targets must be apparent. For example, if a company seeks to be an environmental steward, as **Vail Resorts** does, it may choose the following linked goal, objective, measure, and performance target:

Goal	Objective	Measure	Performance Target
To be an environmental steward	To reduce, reuse, and recycle	Number of tons recycled per year	To recycle at least one pound per guest

You may recall that the balanced scorecard also links objectives, measures, and targets, as shown in Figure 1 earlier in this chapter.

Performance-Based Pay

The tying of appropriate compensation incentives to performance targets increases the likelihood that the goals of responsibility centers, managers, and the entire organization will be well coordinated. Unfortunately, this linkage does not always happen. Responsibility center managers are more likely to achieve their performance targets if their compensation depends on it. **Performance-based pay** is the linking of employee compensation to the achievement of measurable business targets.

Cash bonuses, awards, profit-sharing plans, and stock programs are common types of incentive compensation. Cash bonuses are usually given to reward an individual's short-term performance. A bonus may be stated as a fixed dollar amount or as a percentage of a target figure, such as 5 percent of operating income or 10 percent of the dollar increase in operating income. An award may be a trip or some other form of recognition for desirable individual or group performance. For example, many companies sponsor a trip for all managers who have met their performance targets during a specified period. Other companies award incentive points that employees may redeem for goods or services. (Notice that awards can be used to encourage both short-term and long-term performance.) Profit-sharing plans reward employees with a share of the company's profits. Employees often receive company stock as recognition of their contribution to a profitable period. Using stock as a reward encourages employees to think and act as investors as well as employees and encourages a stable work force. In terms of the balanced scorecard, employees assume two stakeholder perspectives and take both a short- and a long-term viewpoint. Companies use stock to motivate employees to achieve financial targets that increase the company's stock price.

The Coordination of Goals

What performance incentives and measures should a company use to manage and evaluate performance? What actions and behaviors should an organization reward? Which incentive compensation plans work best? The answers to such questions depend on the facts and circumstances of each organization. Something that promotes the coordination of goals for one organization may not do so for another. To be effective, incentive plans must be developed with input from all employees. All must understand the causal links between goals, objectives, measures, and performance targets. To determine the right performance incentives for their organization, employees and managers must answer several questions:

FOCUS ON BUSINESS PRACTICE
Aligning Incentives Among Supply Chain Partners

A study of more than 50 supply networks found that misaligned performance incentives are often the cause of inventory buildups or shortages, misguided sales efforts, and poor customer relations. A supply chain works only if the partners work together effectively by adopting revenue-sharing contracts, using technology to track shared information, and/or working with intermediaries to build trust. Such incentives among supply chain partners must be reassessed periodically, as business conditions change.[5]

- When should the reward be given: now or sometime in the future?

- Whose performance should be rewarded: that of responsibility centers, individual managers, or the entire company?

- How should the reward be computed?

- On what should the reward be based?

- What performance criteria should be used?

- Does our performance incentive plan address the interests of all stakeholders?

The effectiveness of a performance management and evaluation system relies on the coordination of responsibility center, managerial, and company goals. Performance can be optimized by linking goals to measurable objectives and targets and by tying appropriate compensation incentives to the achievement of the targets. Common types of incentive compensation are cash bonuses, awards, profit-sharing plans, and stock programs. Each organization's unique circumstances will determine the correct mix of measures and compensation incentives for that organization. If management values the perspectives of all of its stakeholder groups, its performance management and evaluation system will balance and benefit all interests.

STOP • REVIEW • APPLY

6-1. Why do incentive plans use performance-based pay?

6-2. Which performance incentives work best?

A LOOK BACK AT

VAIL RESORTS

In this chapter's Decision Point, we asked these questions:

- **How do managers at Vail Resorts link performance measures and set performance targets to achieve performance objectives?**

- **How do they use the PEAKS system and its integrated database to improve performance management and evaluation?**

Managers at **Vail Resorts** link their organization's vision and strategy to their performance objectives; they then link the objectives to logical performance measures; and, finally, they set performance targets. A balanced scorecard approach enables them to consider the perspectives of all the organization's stakeholders: financial (investors), learning and growth (employees), internal business processes, and customers.

As we indicated in the Decision Point, Vail Resorts' managers like the PEAKS all-in-one-card system because it enables them to quickly and easily collect huge amounts of valuable and highly versatile information. Whenever a guest's card is scanned, new data enter the system and become part of an integrated management information system that allows managers to measure and control costs, quality, and performance in all resort areas. The system's ability to store both financial and nonfinancial data about all aspects of the resorts enables managers to learn about and balance the interests of all the organization's stakeholders: The managers can then use the information to answer traditional financial questions about such matters as the cost of sales and the value of inventory (e.g., food ingredients in the resorts' restaurants and the merchandise in their shops) and to obtain performance data about the resorts' activities, products, services, and customers. In addition, managers and employees receive timely feedback about their performance, and this encourages continuous improvement.

CHAPTER REVIEW

REVIEW of Learning Objectives

LO1 Describe how the balanced scorecard aligns performance with organizational goals.

The balanced scorecard is a framework that links the perspectives of an organization's four basic stakeholder groups—financial, learning and growth, internal business processes, and customers—with its mission and vision, performance measures, strategic and tactical plans, and resources. Ideally, managers should see how their actions help to achieve organizational goals and understand how their compensation is linked to their actions. The balanced scorecard assumes that an organization will get what it measures.

LO2 Discuss performance measurement, and identify the issues that affect management's ability to measure performance.

An effective performance measurement system accounts for and reports on both financial and nonfinancial performance so that an organization can ascertain how well it is doing, where it is going, and what improvements will make it more profitable. Each organization must develop a unique set of performance measures that are appropriate to its specific situation. Besides answering basic questions about what to measure and how to measure, management must consider a variety of other issues. Managers must collaborate to develop a group of measures, such as the balanced scorecard, that will help them determine how to improve performance.

LO3 Define *responsibility accounting,* and describe the role that responsibility centers play in performance management and evaluation.

Responsibility accounting classifies data according to areas of responsibility and reports each area's activities by including only the revenue, cost, and resource categories that the assigned manager can control. There are five types of responsibility centers: cost, discretionary cost, revenue, profit, and investment. Performance reporting by responsibility center allows the source of a cost, revenue, or resource to be traced to the manager who controls it and thus makes it easier to evaluate a manager's performance.

LO4 Prepare performance reports for cost centers using flexible budgets and for profit centers using variable costing.

Performance reports contain information about the costs, revenues, and resources that individual managers can control. The content and format of a performance report depend on the nature of the responsibility center.

The performance of a cost center can be evaluated by comparing its actual costs with the corresponding amounts in the flexible and master budgets. A flexible budget is a summary of anticipated costs for a range of activity levels. It provides forecasted cost data that can be adjusted for changes in the level of output. A flexible budget is derived by multiplying actual unit output by predetermined standard unit costs for each cost item in the report. As you will learn in another chapter, the resulting variances between actual costs and the flexible budget can be examined further by using standard costing to compute specific variances for direct materials, direct labor, and overhead.

The performance of a profit center is usually evaluated by comparing the profit center's actual income statement results with its budgeted income statement. When variable costing is used, the controllable costs of the profit center's manager are classified as variable or fixed. The resulting performance report takes the form of a contribution income statement instead of a traditional income statement. The variable costing income statement is useful because it focuses on cost variability and the profit center's contribution to operating income.

LO5 Prepare performance reports for investment centers using the traditional measures of return on investment and residual income and the newer measure of economic value added.

Traditionally, the most common performance measure has been return on investment (ROI). The basic formula is ROI = Operating Income ÷ Assets Invested. Return on investment can also be examined in terms of profit margin and asset turnover. In this case, ROI = Profit Margin × Asset Turnover, where Profit Margin = Operating Income ÷ Sales, and Asset Turnover = Sales ÷ Assets Invested. Residual income (RI) is the operating income that an investment center earns above a minimum desired return on invested assets. It is expressed as a dollar amount: Residual Income = Operating Income − (Desired ROI × Assets Invested). It is the amount of profit left after subtracting a predetermined desired income target for an investment. Today, businesses are increasingly using the shareholder wealth created by an investment center, or economic value added (EVA), as a performance measure. The calculation of economic value added can be quite complex because of the various adjustments it involves. Basically, it is similar to the calculation of residual income: EVA = After-Tax Operating Income − Cost of Capital in Dollars. A manager can improve the economic value of an investment center by increasing sales, decreasing costs, decreasing assets, or lowering the cost of capital.

LO6 Explain how properly linked performance incentives and measures add value for all stakeholders in performance management and evaluation.

The effectiveness of a performance management and evaluation system depends on how well it coordinates the goals of responsibility centers, managers, and the entire company. Performance can be optimized by linking goals to measurable objectives and targets and tying appropriate compensation incentives to the achievement of those targets. Common types of incentive compensation are cash bonuses, awards, profit-sharing plans, and stock programs. If management values the perspectives of all of its stakeholder groups, its performance management and evaluation system will balance and benefit all interests.

REVIEW of Concepts and Terminology

The following concepts and terms were introduced in this chapter:

Asset turnover: The productivity of assets, or the number of sales dollars generated by each dollar invested in assets; Sales ÷ Assets Invested. **(LO5)**

Balanced scorecard: A framework that links the perspectives of an organization's four basic stakeholder groups—financial (investors), learning and growth (employees), internal business processes, and customers—with the organization's mission and vision, performance measures, strategic plan, and resources. **(LO1)**

Controllable costs and revenues: Costs and revenues that are the result of a manager's actions, influence, or decisions. **(LO3)**

Cost center: A responsibility center whose manager is accountable only for controllable costs that have well-defined relationships between the center's resources and certain products or services. **(LO3)**

Cost of capital: The minimum desired rate of return on an investment, such as assets invested in an investment center. **(LO5)**

Discretionary cost center: A responsibility center whose manager is accountable for costs only and in which the relationship between resources and the products or services produced is not well defined. **(LO3)**

Economic value added (EVA): The shareholder wealth created by an investment center; Economic Value Added = After-Tax Operating Income − Cost of Capital in Dollars. **(LO5)**

Flexible budget: A summary of expected costs for a range of activity levels. Also called a *variable budget*. **(LO4)**

Investment center: A responsibility center whose manager is accountable for profit generation and can also make significant decisions about the resources the center uses. **(LO3)**

Organization chart: A visual representation of an organization's hierarchy of responsibility for the purposes of management control. **(LO3)**

Performance-based pay: The linking of employee compensation to the achievement of measurable business targets. **(LO6)**

Performance management and evaluation system:
A set of procedures that account for and report on both financial and nonfinancial performance, so that a company can identify how well it is doing, where it is going, and what improvements will make it more profitable. **(LO2)**

Performance measurement: The use of quantitative tools to gauge an organization's performance in relation to a specific goal or an expected outcome. **(LO2)**

Profit center: A responsibility center whose manager is accountable for both revenue and costs and for the resulting operating income. **(LO3)**

Profit margin: The percentage of each sales dollar that results in profit; Operating Income ÷ Sales. **(LO5)**

Residual income (RI): The operating income that an investment center earns above a minimum desired return on invested assets; Residual Income = Investment Center's Operating Income − (Desired ROI × Assets Invested). **(LO5)**

Responsibility accounting: An information system that classifies data according to areas of responsibility and reports each area's activities by including only the categories that the manager can control. **(LO3)**

Responsibility center: An organizational unit whose manager has been assigned the responsibility of managing a portion of the organization's resources. The five types of responsibility centers are a cost center, discretionary cost center, revenue center, profit center, and investment center. **(LO3)**

Return on investment (ROI): A traditional performance measure that takes into account both operating income and the assets invested to produce that income; ROI = Operating Income ÷ Assets Invested. ROI can also be expressed as Profit Margin × Asset Turnover. **(LO5)**

Revenue center: A responsibility center whose manager is accountable primarily for revenue and whose success is based on its ability to generate revenue. **(LO3)**

Variable costing: A method of preparing profit center performance reports that classifies a manager's controllable costs as either fixed or variable and produces a contribution income statement. **(LO4)**

REVIEW Problem

LO3, LO4, LO5   **Evaluating Profit Center and Investment Center Performance**

Winter Wonderland is a full-service resort and spa. Mary Fortenberry, the resort's general manager, is responsible for guest activities, administration, and food and lodging. In addition, she is solely responsible for the resort's capital investments. The organization chart below shows the resort's various activities and the levels of authority that Fortenberry has established:

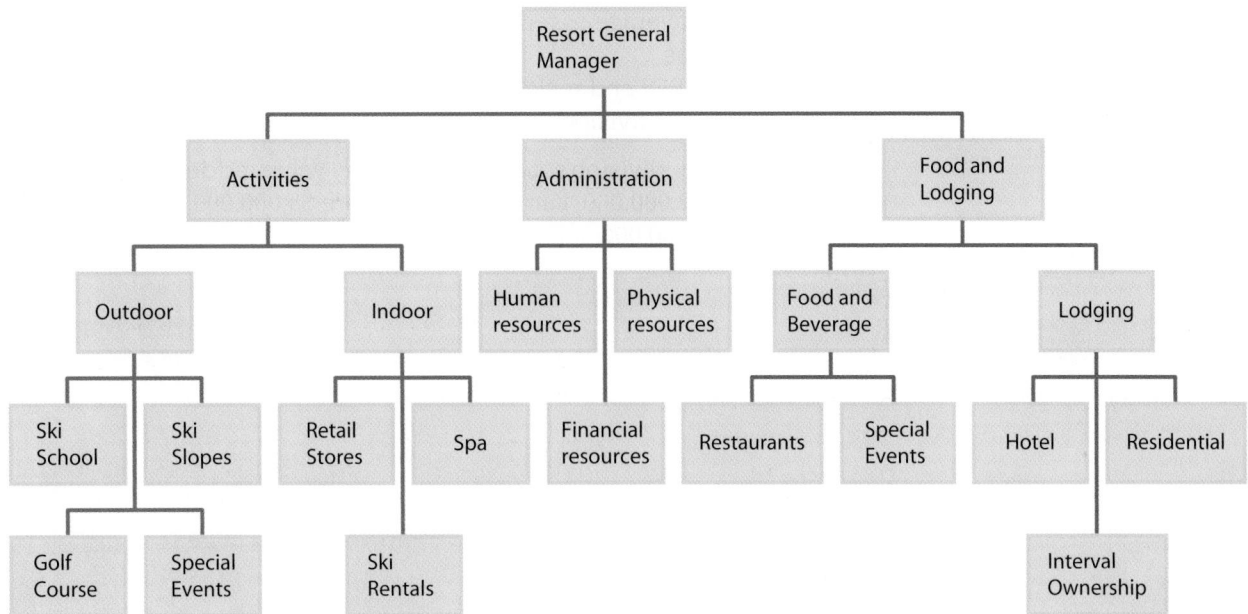

Three divisional managers receive compensation based on their division's performance and have the authority to make employee compensation decisions for their division. Alexandra Patel manages the Food and Lodging Division. The Food and Lodging Division's master budget and actual results for the year ended June 30 follow.

		Winter Wonderland		
		Food and Lodging Division		
		For the Year Ended June 30		
		(Dollar amounts in thousands)		
			Master	Actual
			Budget	Results
Guest days			4,000	4,100
Sales			$38,000	$40,000
Variable cost of sales			24,000	25,000
Variable selling and administrative expenses			4,000	4,250
Fixed cost of sales			2,000	1,800
Fixed selling and administrative expenses			2,500	2,500

Required

1. What types of responsibility centers are Administration, Food and Lodging, and Resort General Manager?

2. Assume that Food and Lodging is a profit center. Prepare a performance report using variable costing and flexible budgeting. Determine the variances between actual results and the corresponding figures in the flexible budget and the master budget.

3. Assume that the divisional managers have been assigned responsibility for capital expenditures and that their divisions are thus investment centers. Food and Lodging is expected to generate a desired ROI of at least 30 percent on average assets invested of $10,000,000.

   a. Compute the division's return on investment and residual income using the average assets invested in both the actual and the budget calculations.

   b. Using the ROI and residual income, evaluate Alexandra Patel's performance as divisional manager.

4. Compute the division's actual economic value added if the division's assets are $12,000,000, current liabilities are $3,000,000, after-tax operating income is $4,500,000, and the cost of capital is 20 percent.

Answer to Review Problem

1. Administration: discretionary cost center; Food and Lodging: profit center; Resort General Manager: investment center.
2. Performance report:

	Actual Results	Variance		Flexible Budget	Variance		Master Budget
Winter Wonderland							
Food and Lodging Division							
For the Year Ended June 30							
(Dollar amounts in thousands)							
Guest days	4,100	—		4,100	100	(F)	4,000
Sales	$40,000	$1,050	(F)	$38,950	$950	(F)	$38,000
Controllable variable costs							
Variable cost of sales	25,000	400	(U)	24,600	600	(U)	24,000
Variable selling and administrative expenses	4,250	150	(U)	4,100	100	(U)	4,000
Contribution margin	$10,750	$ 500	(F)	$10,250	$250	(F)	$10,000
Controllable fixed costs							
Fixed cost of sales	1,800	200	(F)	2,000	—		2,000
Fixed selling and administrative expenses	2,500	—		2,500	—		2,500
Division operating income	$ 6,450	$ 700	(F)	$ 5,750	$250	(F)	$ 5,500

3. a. **Return on investment**

Actual results: $6,450,000 ÷ $10,000,000 = 64.50%
Flexible budget: $5,750,000 ÷ $10,000,000 = 57.50%
Master budget: $5,500,000 ÷ $10,000,000 = 55.00%

Residual income

Actual results: $6,450,000 − 30%($10,000,000) = $3,450,000
Flexible budget: $5,750,000 − 30%($10,000,000) = $2,750,000
Master budget: $5,500,000 − 30%($10,000,000) = $2,500,000

b. Alexandra Patel's performance as the divisional manager of Food and Lodging exceeds company performance expectations. Actual ROI was 64.5 percent, whereas the company expected an ROI of 30 percent and the flexible budget and the master budget showed projections of 57.5 percent and 55.0 percent, respectively. Residual income also exceeded expectations. The Food and Lodging Division generated $3,450,000 in residual income when the flexible budget and master budget had projected RIs of $2,750,000 and $2,500,000, respectively. The performance report for the division shows 100 more guest days than had been anticipated and a favorable controllable fixed cost variance. As a manager, Patel will investigate the unfavorable variances associated with her controllable variable costs.

4. Economic value added:
$4,500,000 − 20%($12,000,000 − $3,000,000) = $2,700,000

CHAPTER ASSIGNMENTS

BUILDING Your Basic Knowledge and Skills

Short Exercises

LO1 Balanced Scorecard

SE 1. One of your college's overall goals is customer satisfaction. In light of that goal, match each of the following stakeholders' perspectives with the appropriate objective:

Perspective	Objective
1. Financial (investors)	a. Customer satisfaction means that the faculty engages in cutting-edge research.
2. Learning and growth (employees)	b. Customer satisfaction means that students receive their degrees in four years.
3. Internal business processes	c. Customer satisfaction means that the college has a winning athletics program.
4. Customers	d. Customer satisfaction means that fundraising campaigns are successful.

LO3 Responsibility Centers

SE 2. Identify each of the following as a cost center, a discretionary cost center, a revenue center, a profit center, or an investment center:

1. The manager of center A is responsible for generating cash inflows and incurring costs with the goal of making money for the company. The manager has no responsibility for assets.
2. Center B produces a product that is not sold to an external party.
3. The manager of center C is responsible for the telephone order operations of a large retailer.
4. Center D designs, produces, and sells products to external parties. The manager makes both long-term and short-term decisions.
5. Center E provides human resource support for the other centers in the company.

LO3 Controllable Costs

SE 3. Adana Kim is the manager of the Paper Cutting Department in the Northwest Division of Williams Paper Products. Identify each of the following costs as either controllable or not controllable by Kim:

1. Salaries of cutting machine workers
2. Cost of cutting machine parts
3. Cost of electricity for the Northwest Division
4. Lumber Department hauling costs
5. Vice president's salary

LO4 Cost Center Performance Report

SE 4. Complete the following performance report for cost center C for the month ended December 31:

	Actual Results	Variance	Flexible Budget	Variance	Master Budget
Units produced	80	0	?	(20) U	100
Center costs					
Direct materials	$ 84	$?	$ 80	$?	$100
Direct labor	150	?	?	40 (F)	200
Variable overhead	?	20 (U)	240	?	300
Fixed overhead	280	?	250	?	250
Total cost	$?	$44 (U)	$?	$120 (F)	$850
Performance measures					
Defect-free units to total produced	75%	?	N/A	N/A	90%
Average throughput time per unit	12 minutes	?	N/A	N/A	10 minutes

LO4 Profit Center Performance Report

SE 5. Complete the following performance report for profit center P for the month ended December 31:

	Actual Results	Variance	Master Budget
Sales	$?	$20 (F)	$120
Controllable variable costs			
Variable cost of goods sold	25	10 (U)	?
Variable selling and administrative expenses	15	?	5
Contribution margin	$100	$?	$100
Controllable fixed costs	?	$10 (F)	60
Profit center income	$ 50	$10 (F)	$?
Performance measures			
Number of orders processed	50	20 (F)	?
Average daily sales	$?	$.66 (F)	$4.00
Number of units sold	100	40 (F)	?

LO5 Return on Investment

SE 6. Complete the profit margin, asset turnover, and return on investment calculations for investment centers D and V:

	Subsidiary D	Subsidiary V
Total sales	$1,650	$2,840
Operating income	$ 180	$ 210
Average assets invested	$ 940	$1,250
Profit margin	?	7.39%
Asset turnover	1.76 times	?
ROI	?	?

LO5 Return on Investment

SE 7. Complete the average assets invested, profit margin, asset turnover, and return on investment calculations for investment centers J and K on the next page.

	Subsidiary J	Subsidiary K
Total sales	$2,000	$2,000
Operating income	$ 500	$ 800
Beginning assets invested	$4,000	$ 500
Ending assets invested	$6,000	$1,500
Average assets invested	$?	$?
Profit margin	25%	?
Asset turnover	?	2 times
ROI	?	?

LO5 Residual Income

SE 8. Complete the operating income, ending assets invested, average assets invested, and residual income calculations for investment centers H and F:

	Subsidiary H	Subsidiary F
Total sales	$20,000	$25,000
Operating income	$ 1,500	$?
Beginning assets invested	$ 4,000	$ 500
Ending assets invested	$ 6,000	$?
Average assets invested	$?	$ 1,000
Desired ROI	20%	20%
Residual income	$?	$ 600

LO5 Economic Value Added

SE 9. Complete the current liabilities, total assets − current liabilities, and economic value added calculations for investment centers M and N:

	Subsidiary M	Subsidiary N
Total sales	$15,000	$18,000
After-tax operating income	$ 1,000	$ 1,100
Total assets	$ 4,000	$ 5,000
Current liabilities	$ 1,000	$?
Total assets − current liabilities	$?	$ 3,500
Cost of capital	15%	15%
Economic value added	$?	$?

LO6 Coordination of Goals

SE 10. One of your college's goals is customer satisfaction. In view of that goal, identify each of the following as a linked objective, a measure, or a performance target:

1. To have successful fund-raising campaigns
2. Number of publications per year per tenure-track faculty
3. To increase the average donation by 10 percent
4. Average number of dollars raised per donor
5. To have faculty engage in cutting-edge research
6. To increase the number of publications per faculty member by at least one per year

Exercises

LO1 Balanced Scorecard

E 1. Biggs Industries is considering adopting the balanced scorecard and has compiled the following list of possible performance measures. Select the balanced scorecard perspective that best matches each performance measure.

Performance Measure	Balanced Scorecard Perspective
1. Residual income	a. Financial (investors)
2. Customer satisfaction rating	b. Learning and growth (employees)
3. Employee absentee rate	c. Internal business processes
4. Growth in profits	d. Customers
5. On-time deliveries	
6. Manufacturing process time	

LO1 **Balanced Scorecard**

E 2. Virtual Online Products is considering adopting the balanced scorecard and has compiled the following list of possible performance measures. Select the balanced scorecard perspective that best matches each performance measure.

Performance Measure	Balanced Scorecard Perspective
1. Economic value added	a. Financial (investors)
2. Employee turnover	b. Learning and growth (employees)
3. Average daily sales	c. Internal business processes
4. Defect-free units	d. Customers
5. Number of repeat customer visits	
6. Employee training hours	

LO2 **Performance Measures**

E 3. Eva Washington wants to measure her division's product quality. Link an appropriate performance measure with each balanced scorecard perspective:

Product Quality	Possible Performance Measures
1. Financial (investors)	a. Number of defective products returned
2. Learning and growth (employees)	b. Number of products failing inspection
3. Internal business processes	c. Increased market share
4. Customers	d. Savings from employee suggestions

LO2 **Performance Measures**

E 4. Monty Sams wants to measure customer satisfaction within his region. Link an appropriate performance measure with each balanced scorecard perspective:

Customer Satisfaction	Possible Performance Measures
1. Financial (investors)	a. Number of cross-trained staff
2. Learning and growth (employees)	b. Customer satisfaction rating
3. Internal business processes	c. Time lapse from order to delivery
4. Customers	d. Dollar sales to repeat customers

LO3 **Responsibility Centers**

E 5. Identify the most appropriate type of responsibility center for each of the following organizational units:

1. A pizza store in a pizza chain
2. The ticket sales center of a major airline
3. The South American division of a multinational company

4. A subsidiary of a business conglomerate
5. The information technology area of a company
6. A manufacturing department of a large corporation
7. An eye clinic in a community hospital
8. The food service function at a nursing home
9. The food preparation plant of a large restaurant chain
10. The catalog order department of a retailer

LO3   Controllable Costs

E 6. Angel Sweets produces pies. The company has the following three-tiered manufacturing structure:

Vice President–Production
↑
Plant Manager
↑
Production Supervisors

Identify the manager responsible for each of the following costs:

1. Repair and maintenance costs
2. Materials handling costs
3. Direct labor
4. Supervisors' salaries
5. Maintenance of plant grounds
6. Depreciation, equipment
7. Plant manager's salary
8. Cost of materials used
9. Storage of finished goods
10. Property taxes, plant
11. Depreciation, plant

LO3   Organization Chart

E 7. Hooper Industries wants to formalize its management structure by designing an organization chart. The company has a president, a board of directors, and two vice presidents. Four discretionary cost centers—Financial Resources, Human Resources, Information Resources, and Physical Resources—report to one of the vice presidents. The other vice president has one manufacturing plant with three subassembly areas reporting to her. Draw the company's organization chart.

LO4   Performance Reports

E 8. Jackie Jefferson, a new employee at Handown, Inc., is learning about the various types of performance reports. Describe the typical contents of a performance report for each type of responsibility center.

LO4   Variable Costing Income Statement

E 9. Vegan, LLC, owns a chain of gourmet vegetarian take-out markets. Last month, Store P generated the following information: sales, $890,000; direct materials, $220,000; direct labor, $97,000; variable overhead, $150,000; fixed overhead, $130,000; variable selling and administrative expenses, $44,500; and fixed selling expenses, $82,300. There were no beginning or ending inventories. Average daily sales (25 business days) were $35,600. Customer orders processed totaled 15,000. Vegan had budgeted monthly sales of $900,000; direct materials, $210,000; direct labor, $100,000; variable overhead, $140,000; fixed overhead, $140,000; variable selling and administrative expenses, $45,000; and fixed selling expenses, $85,000. Store P had been projected to do $36,000 in daily sales and process 16,000 customer orders. Using this information, prepare a performance report for Store P.

LO4   Variable Costing Income Statement

E 10. The income statement in the traditional reporting format for Green Products, Inc., for the year ended December 31, is as follows:

Green Products, Inc.
Income Statement
For the Year Ended December 31

Sales	$296,400
Cost of goods sold	112,750
Gross margin	$183,650
Operating expenses	
Selling expenses	
Variable	69,820
Fixed	36,980
Administrative expenses	27,410
Operating income	$ 49,440

Total fixed manufacturing costs for the year were $16,750. All administrative expenses are considered to be fixed.

Using this information, prepare an income statement for Green Products, Inc., for the year ended December 31, using the variable costing format.

LO4   Performance Report for a Cost Center

E 11. Archer, LLC, owns a blueberry processing plant. Last month, the plant generated the following information: blueberries processed, 50,000 pounds; direct materials, $50,000; direct labor, $10,000; variable overhead, $12,000; and fixed overhead, $13,000. There were no beginning or ending inventories. Average daily pounds processed (25 business days) were 2,000. Average rate of processing was 250 pounds per hour. At the beginning of the month, Archer had budgeted costs of blueberries, $45,000; direct labor, $10,000; variable overhead, $14,000; and fixed overhead, $14,000. The monthly master budget was based on producing 50,000 pounds of blueberries each month. This means that the plant had been projected to process 2,000 pounds daily at the rate of 240 pounds per hour.

Using this information, prepare a performance report for the month for the blueberry processing plant. Include a flexible budget and a computation of variances in your report. Indicate whether the variances are favorable (F) or unfavorable (U) to the performance of the plant.

LO5   Investment Center Performance

E 12. Momence Associates is evaluating the performance of three divisions: Maple, Oaks, and Juniper. Using the following data, compute the return on investment and residual income for each division, compare the divisions' performance, and comment on the factors that influenced performance:

	Maple	Oaks	Juniper
Sales	$100,000	$100,000	$100,000
Operating income	$ 10,000	$ 10,000	$ 20,000
Assets invested	$ 25,000	$ 12,500	$ 25,000
Desired ROI	40%	40%	40%

LO5   Economic Value Added

E 13. Leesburg, LLP, is evaluating the performance of three divisions: Lake, Sumter, and Poe. Using the data that appear on the next page, compute the economic value added by each division, and comment on each division's performance.

	Lake	Sumter	Poe
Sales	$100,000	$100,000	$100,000
After-tax operating income	$ 10,000	$ 10,000	$ 20,000
Total assets	$ 25,000	$ 12,500	$ 25,000
Current liabilities	$ 5,000	$ 5,000	$ 5,000
Cost of capital	15%	15%	15%

LO6 Performance Incentives

E 14. Dynamic Consulting is advising Solid Industries on the short-term and long-term effectiveness of cash bonuses, awards, profit sharing, and stock as performance incentives. Prepare a chart identifying the effectiveness of each incentive as either long-term or short-term or both.

LO6 Goal Congruence

E 15. Necessary Toys, Inc., has adopted the balanced scorecard to motivate its managers to work toward the companywide goal of leading its industry in innovation. Identify the four stakeholder perspectives that would link to the following objectives, measures, and targets:

Perspective	Objective	Measure	Target
	Profitable new products	New product ROI	New product ROI of at least 75 percent
	Work force with cutting-edge skills	Percentage of employees cross-trained on work-group tasks	100 percent of work group cross-trained on new tasks within 30 days
	Agile product design and production processes	Time to market (the time between a product idea and its first sales)	Time to market less than one year for 80 percent of introductions
	Successful product introductions	New product market share	Capture 80 percent of new product market within one year

Problems

LO3, LO4 Evaluating Cost Center Performance

P 1. Beverage Products, LLC, manufactures metal beverage containers. The division that manufactures soft drink beverage cans for the North American market has two plants that operate 24 hours a day, 365 days a year. The plants are evaluated as cost centers. Small tools and plant supplies are considered variable overhead. Depreciation and rent are considered fixed overhead. The master budget for a plant and the operating results of the two North American plants, East Coast and West Coast, are as follows:

	Master Budget	East Coast	West Coast
Center costs			
Rolled aluminum ($.01)	$4,000,000	$3,492,000	$5,040,000
Lids ($.005)	2,000,000	1,980,000	2,016,000
Direct labor ($.0025)	1,000,000	864,000	1,260,000
Small tools and supplies ($.0013)	520,000	432,000	588,000
Depreciation and rent	480,000	480,000	480,000
Total cost	$8,000,000	$7,248,000	$9,384,000

Performance measures

Cans processed per hour	45,662	41,096	47,945
Average daily pounds of scrap metal	5	6	7
Cans processed (in millions)	400	360	420

Required

1. Prepare a performance report for the East Coast plant. Include a flexible budget and variance analysis.
2. Prepare a performance report for the West Coast plant. Include a flexible budget and variance analysis.
3. Compare the two plants, and comment on their performance.
4. Manager Insight: Explain why a flexible budget should be prepared.

LO4   Traditional and Variable Costing Income Statements

P 2. Roofing tile is the major product of the Tops Corporation. The company had a particularly good year, as shown by its operating data. It sold 88,400 cases of tile. Variable cost of goods sold was $848,640; variable selling expenses were $132,600; fixed overhead was $166,680; fixed selling expenses were $152,048; and fixed administrative expenses were $96,450. Selling price was $18 per case. There were no partially completed jobs in process at the beginning or the end of the year. Finished goods inventory had been used up at the end of the previous year.

Required

1. Prepare the calendar year-end income statement for the Tops Corporation using the traditional reporting format.
2. Prepare the calendar year-end income statement for the Tops Corporation using the variable costing format.

LO3, LO4, LO5   Evaluating Profit and Investment Center Performance

P 3. Bobbie Howell, the managing partner of the law firm Howell, Bagan, and Clark, LLP, makes asset acquisition and disposal decisions for the firm. As managing partner, she supervises the partners in charge of the firm's three branch offices. Those partners have the authority to make employee compensation decisions. The partners' compensation depends on the profitability of their branch office. Victoria Smith manages the City Branch, which has the following master budget and actual results for the year:

	Master Budget	Actual Results
Billed hours	5,000	4,900
Revenue	$250,000	$254,800
Controllable variable costs		
Direct labor	120,000	137,200
Variable overhead	40,000	34,300
Contribution margin	$ 90,000	$ 83,300
Controllable fixed costs		
Rent	30,000	30,000
Other administrative expenses	45,000	42,000
Branch operating income	$ 15,000	$ 11,300

Required

1. Assume that the City Branch is a profit center. Prepare a performance report that includes a flexible budget. Determine the variances between actual results, the flexible budget, and the master budget.
2. Evaluate Victoria Smith's performance as manager of the City Branch.

3. Assume that the branch managers are assigned responsibility for capital expenditures and that the branches are thus investment centers. City Branch is expected to generate a desired ROI of at least 30 percent on average invested assets of $40,000.
   a. Compute the branch's return on investment and residual income.
   b. **Manager Insight:** Using the ROI and residual income, evaluate Victoria Smith's performance as branch manager.

LO5   **Return on Investment and Residual Income**

P 4. The financial results for the past two years for Ornamental Iron, a division of the Iron Foundry Company, follow.

Iron Foundry Company
Ornamental Iron Division
Balance Sheet
December 31, 20x8 and 20x7

	20x8	20x7
Assets		
Cash	$ 5,000	$ 3,000
Accounts receivable	10,000	8,000
Inventory	30,000	32,000
Other current assets	600	600
Plant assets	128,300	120,300
Total assets	$173,900	$163,900
Liabilities and Stockholders' Equity		
Current liabilities	$ 13,900	$ 10,000
Long-term liabilities	90,000	93,900
Stockholders' equity	70,000	60,0006
Total liabilities and stockholders' equity	$173,900	$163,900

Iron Foundry Company
Ornamental Iron Division
Income Statement
For the Years Ended December 31, 20x8 and 20x7

	20x8	20x7
Sales	$180,000	$160,000
Cost of goods sold	100,000	90,000
Selling and administrative expenses	27,500	26,500
Operating income	$ 52,500	$ 43,500
Income taxes	17,850	14,790
After-tax operating income	$ 34,650	$ 28,710

Required

1. Compute the division's profit margin, asset turnover, and return on investment for 20x8 and 20x7. Beginning total assets for 20x7 were $157,900. Round to two decimal places.

2. The desired return on investment for the division has been set at 12 percent. Compute Ornamental Iron's residual income for 20x8 and 20x7.
3. The cost of capital for the division is 8 percent. Compute the division's economic value added for 20x8 and 20x7.
4. **Manager Insight:** Before drawing conclusions about this division's performance, what additional information would you want?

LO5 **Return on Investment and Economic Value Added**

P 5. The balance sheet for the New Products Division of NuBone Corporation showed invested assets of $200,000 at the beginning of the year and $300,000 at the end of the year. During the year, the division's operating income was $12,500 on sales of $500,000.

Required

1. Compute the division's residual income if the desired ROI is 6 percent.
2. Compute the following performance measures for the division: (a) profit margin, (b) asset turnover, and (c) return on investment
3. Recompute the division's ROI under each of the following independent assumptions:
   a. Sales increase from $500,000 to $600,000, causing operating income to rise from $12,500 to $30,000.
   b. Invested assets at the beginning of the year are reduced from $200,000 to $100,000.
   c. Operating expenses are reduced, causing operating income to rise from $12,500 to $20,000.
4. Compute NuBone's EVA if total corporate assets are $500,000, current liabilities are $80,000, after-tax operating income is $50,000, and the cost of capital is 8 percent.

Alternate Problems

LO4 **Traditional and Variable Costing Income Statements**

P 6. Interior designers often use the deluxe carpet products of Lux Mills, Inc. The Maricopa blend is the company's top product line. In March, Lux produced and sold 174,900 square yards of Maricopa blend. Factory operating data for the month included variable cost of goods sold of $2,623,500 and fixed overhead of $346,875. Other expenses were variable selling expenses, $166,155; fixed selling expenses, $148,665; and fixed general and administrative expenses, $231,500. Total sales revenue equaled $3,935,250. All production took place in March, and there was no work in process at month end. Goods are usually shipped when completed.

Required

1. Prepare the March income statement for Lux Mills, Inc., using the traditional reporting format.
2. Prepare the March income statement for Lux Mills, Inc., using the variable costing format.

LO3, LO4, LO5 **Return on Investment and Residual Income**

P 7. Portia Carter is the president of a company that owns six multiplex movie theaters. Carter has delegated decision-making authority to the theater managers for all decisions except those relating to capital expenditures and film selection. The theater managers' compensation depends on the profitability of their theaters. Max Burgman, the manager of the Park Theater, had the following master budget and actual results for the month:

	Master Budget	Actual Results
Tickets sold	120,000	480,000
Revenue–tickets	$ 840,000	$ 880,000
Revenue–concessions	480,000	330,000
Total Revenue	$1,320,000	$1,210,000
Controllable variable costs		
Concessions	120,000	99,000
Direct labor	420,000	330,000
Variable overhead	540,000	550,000
Contribution margin	$ 240,000	$ 231,000
Controllable fixed costs		
Rent	55,000	55,000
Other administrative expenses	45,000	50,000
Theater operating income	$ 140,000	$ 126,000

Required

1. Assuming that the theaters are profit centers, prepare a performance report for the Park Theater. Include a flexible budget. Determine the variances between actual results, the flexible budget, and the master budget.
2. Evaluate Burgman's performance as manager of the Park Theater.
3. Assume that the managers are assigned responsibility for capital expenditures and that the theaters are thus investment centers. Park Theater is expected to generate a desired ROI of at least 6 percent on average invested assets of $2,000,000.
   a. Compute the theater's return on investment and residual income.
   b. **Manager Insight:** Using the ROI and residual income, evaluate Burgman's performance as manager.

LO5 Return on Investment and Economic Value Added

P 8. Micanopy Company makes replicas of Indian artifacts. The balance sheet for the Arrowhead Division showed that the company had invested assets of $300,000 at the beginning of the year and $500,000 at the end of the year. During the year, Arrowhead Division's operating income was $80,000 on sales of $1,200,000.

Required

1. Compute Arrowhead Division's residual income if the desired ROI is 20 percent.
2. Compute the following performance measures for the division: (a) profit margin, (b) asset turnover, and (c) return on investment.
3. Compute Micanopy Company's economic value added if total corporate assets are $6,000,000, current liabilities are $800,000, after-tax operating income is $750,000, and the cost of capital is 12 percent.

ENHANCING Your Knowledge, Skills, and Critical Thinking

LO3 Conceptual Understanding Cases

Comparison of Business Types Using Responsibility Accounting

C 1. The structure of an organization affects its responsibility accounting system. **Accenture**, a major management consulting firm, organizes its consultants by industry and location. **Target**, a retailer, has over 1,300 stores in 47 states, including more than 140 SuperTarget stores, as well as an online business. **Monsanto**, a manufacturer, structures its organization into two segments: Seeds and Genomics, and Agricultural Productivity (which includes Roundup and other herbicides).

What is a responsibility accounting system, what is it based on, and what is the criterion for including an item in a manager's operating report? Discuss the general effects that organizational structure has on the creation of a responsibility reporting system, and give an example of a cost center, a profit center, and an investment center at Accenture, Target, and Monsanto.

LO2, LO3, LO4, LO6   **Types of Responsibility Centers**

C 2. Yuma Foods acquired Aldo's Tortillas several years ago. Aldo's has continued to operate as an independent company, except that Yuma Foods has exclusive authority over capital investments, production quantity, and pricing decisions because Yuma has been Aldo's only customer since the acquisition. Yuma uses return on investment to evaluate the performance of Aldo's manager. The most recent performance report is as follows:

Yuma Foods
Performance Report for Aldo's Tortillas
For the Year Ended June 30

Sales	$6,000
Variable cost of goods sold	3,000
Variable administrative expenses	1,000
Variable corporate expenses (% of sales)	600
Contribution margin	$1,400
Fixed overhead (includes depreciation of $100)	400
Fixed administrative expenses	500
Operating income	$ 500
Average assets invested	$5,500
Return on investment	9.09%

1. Analyze the items listed in the performance report and identify the items that Aldo controls and those that Yuma controls. In your opinion, what type of responsibility center is Aldo's Tortillas? Explain your response.
2. Prepare a revised performance report for Aldo's Tortillas and an accompanying memo to the president of Yuma Foods that explains why it is important to change the content of the report. Cite some basic principles of responsibility accounting to support your recommendation.

LO2, LO5, LO6   **Economic Value Added and Performance**

C 3. Sevilla Consulting offers environmental consulting services worldwide. The managers of branch offices are rewarded for superior performance with bonuses based on the economic value that the office adds to the company. Last year's operating results for the entire company and for its three offices, expressed in millions of U.S. dollars, are as follows:

	Worldwide	Europe	Americas	Asia
Cost of capital	9%	10%	8%	12%
Total assets	$210	$70	$70	$70
Current liabilities	80	10	40	30
After-tax operating income	15	5	5	5

1. Compute the economic value added for each office worldwide. What factors affect each office's economic value added? How can an office improve its economic value added?
2. If managers' bonuses are based on economic value added to office performance, what specific actions will managers be motivated to take?
3. Is economic value added the only performance measure needed to evaluate investment centers adequately? Explain your response.

Interpreting Management Reports

LO1   **Balanced Scorecard Results**

C 4. IT, Inc., has adopted the balanced scorecard approach to motivate the managers of its product divisions to work toward the companywide goal of leading its industry in innovation. The corporation's selected performance measures and scorecard results are as follows:

Measure	Division A	Division B	Division C	Performance Target
New product ROI	80%	75%	70%	75%
Employees cross-trained in new tasks within 30 days	95	96	94	100
New product's time to market less than one year	85	90	86	80
New product's market share one year after introduction	50	100	80	80

Can you effectively compare the performance of the three divisions against the targets? What other measures mentioned in this chapter are needed to evaluate performance effectively?

LO2, LO3   **Responsibility Centers**

C 5. Wood4Fun makes wooden playground equipment for the institutional and consumer markets. The company strives for low-cost, high-quality production because it operates in a highly competitive market in which product price is set by the marketplace and is not based on production costs. The company is organized into responsibility centers. The vice president of manufacturing is responsible for three manufacturing plants. The vice president of sales is responsible for four sales regions. Recently, these two vice presidents began to disagree about whether the manufacturing plants are cost centers or profit centers. The vice president of manufacturing views the plants as cost centers because the managers of the plants control only product-related costs. The vice president of sales believes the plants are profit centers because product quality and product cost strongly affect company profits.

1. Identify the controllable performance that Wood4Fun values and wants to measure. Give at least three examples of performance measures that Wood4Fun could use to monitor such performance.
2. For the manufacturing plants, what type of responsibility center is most consistent with the controllable performance Wood4Fun wants to measure?
3. For the sales regions, what type of responsibility center is most appropriate?

Decision Analysis Using Excel

LO5   **Return on Investment and Residual Income**

C 6. Tina Patel, the manager of the Food and Lodging Division at Winter Wonderland, has hired you as a consultant to help her examine her division's performance under several different circumstances.

1. Type the data that follow into an Excel spreadsheet to compute the division's actual return on investment and residual income. (Data are from parts **3** and **4** of this chapter's Review Problem.) Match your data entries to the rows and columns shown below. (**Hint:** When entering a formula, begin with "= SUM," and enclose the formula in parentheses. The spreadsheet will then know to compute the answer. Remember to format each cell for the type of numbers it holds, such as percentage, currency, or general.)

	A	B	C	D
1				**Investment Center**
2				**Food and Lodging Division**
3				**Actual Results**
4	Sales			$40,000,000
5	Operating income			$ 6,450,000
6	Average assets invested			$10,000,000
7	Desired ROI			30%
8	Return on Investment			=SUM(D5/D6)
9	Profit Margin			=SUM(D5/D4)
10	Asset Turnover			=SUM(D4/D6)
11	Residual Income			=SUM(D5-(D7*D6))
12				

2. Patel would like to know how the figures would change if Food and Lodging had a desired ROI of 40 percent and average assets invested of $10,000,000. Revise your spreadsheet from requirement **1** to compute the division's return on investment and residual income under those conditions.

3. Patel also wants to know how the figures would change if Food and Lodging had a desired ROI of 30 percent and average assets invested of $12,000,000. Revise your spreadsheet from requirement **1** to compute the division's return on investment and residual income under those conditions.

4. Does the use of formatted spreadsheets simplify the computation of ROI and residual income? Do such spreadsheets make it easier to perform "what-if" analyses?

Ethical Dilemma Case

LO5 **Effects of Manager's Decisions on ROI**

C 7. Cooper Huntington is the manager of the upstate store of a large retailer of farm products. His company is a stable, consistently profitable member of the farming industry. The upstate store is doing fine despite severe drought conditions in the area. At the first of the year, corporate headquarters set a targeted return on investment for the store of 20 percent. The upstate store currently averages $140,000 in invested assets (beginning invested assets, $130,000; ending invested assets, $150,000) and is projected to have an operating income of $30,800. Huntington is considering whether to take one or both of the following actions before year end:

- Hold off recording and paying $5,000 in bills owed until the start of the next fiscal year.

- Write down $3,000 in store inventory (nonperishable emergency flood supplies) to zero value because Huntington was unable to sell the items all year.

Currently, Huntington's bonus is based on store profits. Next year, corporate headquarters is changing its performance incentive program so that bonuses will be based on a store's actual return on investment.

1. What effect would each of Huntington's possible actions have on the store's operating income this year? (**Hint:** Use Figure 4 in this chapter to trace the effects.) In your opinion, is either action unethical?

2. Independent of question 1, if corporate headquarters changes its performance incentive plan for store managers, how will the inventory write-down affect next year's income and return on investment if the items are sold for $4,000 next year? In your opinion, does Huntington have an ethical dilemma?

Internet Case

LO6 **Top Executive Compensation**

C 8. Are top executives paid too much? Do the companies run by the most highly paid executives perform better than other companies? Do U.S. executives make more money than their foreign counterparts? These are some of the questions asked routinely in articles and surveys about executive compensation. Moreover, the Securities and Exchange Commission is calling for better disclosure of pay packages for a company's top five executives.

Use the Internet to locate the top executive salary rankings compiled annually by business publications and other sources. Study the rankings and select several U.S. and foreign companies in the same industry for comparison. You can access this type of information on the Internet in several ways. One way is to do key word searches using terms like *executive compensation* or *executive salary survey*. Another way is to go to the website of a business publication, such as www.forbes.com, and do key word searches of articles. You can also access corporate websites and read their annual reports. Some corporate websites are searchable by key word; you might use a phrase like *compensation discussion and analysis*.

1. In your review of top executive compensation, what types of incentives did you find included in annual compensation?
2. Are the companies with the highest-paid executives the best performers in their industry?
3. Do U.S. executives receive higher pay than their foreign counterparts? If so, do the U.S. companies perform better than their foreign counterparts?

Group Activity Case

LO1, LO2 **Performance Measures and the Balanced Scorecard**

C 9. Working in a group of four to six students, select a local business. The group should become familiar with the background of the business by interviewing its manager or accountant. Each group member should identify several performance measures for the business and link each measure with a specific stakeholder's perspective from the balanced scorecard. (Select at least one performance measure for each perspective.) For each measure, ask yourself, "If you were the manager of the business, how would you set performance targets for each measure?" Then prepare an email stating the business's name, location, and activities and your linked performance measures and perspectives.

In class, members of the group should compare their individual emails and compile them into a group report by having each group member assume a different stakeholder perspective (add government and community if you want more than four perspectives). Each group should be ready to present all perspectives and the group's report in class.

Business Communication Case

LO2, LO4, LO6   **Earnings Management**

C 10. Many large multinational companies have recently taken a large one-time write-off (known as a "big bath") or used other downsizing accounting practices that have affected the measurement of the company's performance for only one year. Conduct a search for information about a company that has recently taken a sizable reduction in income for just one year. Do a key word search on the Internet, using terms like *big bath* or *earnings management*. Prepare a one-page description of your findings. Include the name of the company, the reason for the large decrease in income, and the probable effect on the company's ROI. Be prepared to present your findings in class.

Standard Costing and Variance Analysis

Standard costs are useful tools for management because they are based on realistic estimates of operating costs. Managers use them to develop budgets, to control costs, and to prepare reports. Because of their usefulness in comparing planned and actual costs, standard costs have usually been most closely associated with the performance evaluation of cost centers. In this chapter, we describe how standard costs are computed and how managers use the variances between standard and actual costs to evaluate performance and control costs.

LEARNING OBJECTIVES

LO1 Define *standard costs*, and describe how managers use these costs.

LO2 Explain how standard costs are developed, and compute a standard unit cost.

LO3 Prepare a flexible budget, and describe how managers use variance analysis to control costs.

LO4 Compute and analyze direct materials variances.

LO5 Compute and analyze direct labor variances.

LO6 Compute and analyze overhead variances.

LO7 Explain how variances are used to evaluate managers' performance.

- How does setting performance standards help managers control costs?

- How do Coach's managers use standard costs to control costs?

- How do they use standard costs to evaluate the performance of cost centers?

The durability of a well-crafted baseball glove was the inspiration for the high-quality leather goods that **Coach** began making more than 50 years ago. Now sold worldwide, the company's products include not only leather goods, such as handbags and luggage, but also fine accessories and gifts for men and women. Coach's managers value a by-the-numbers approach to business. They keep Coach highly profitable by using design specifications to set standard costs for the company's product lines.[1] Managers use these figures as performance targets and as benchmarks against which to measure actual spending trends and continuously monitor changes in business conditions.

Standard Costing

LO1   Define *standard costs,* and describe how managers use these costs.

S tandard costs are realistic estimates of costs based on analyses of both past and projected operating costs and conditions. They are usually stated in terms of cost per unit. They provide a standard, or predetermined, performance level for use in **standard costing**, a method of cost control that also includes a measure of actual performance and a measure of the difference, or **variance**, between standard and actual performance. This method of measuring and controlling costs differs from the actual and normal costing methods in that it uses estimated costs exclusively to compute all three elements of product cost—direct materials, direct labor, and overhead. Standard costing is especially effective for managing cost centers. You may recall that a cost center is a responsibility center in which there are well-defined links between the cost of the resources (direct materials, direct labor, and overhead) and the resulting products or services.

Using standard costing can be expensive because the estimated costs are based not just on past costs, but also on engineering estimates, forecasted demand, worker input, time and motion studies, and type and quality of direct materials. However, this method can be used in any type of business. Both manufacturers and service businesses can use standard costing in conjunction with a job order costing, process costing, or activity-based costing system.

Standard Costs and Managers

As shown in Figure 1, standard costs are useful tools for management. Managers use them to develop budgets, to control costs, and to prepare reports. Because of their usefulness in comparing planned and actual costs, standard costs have usually been most closely associated with the performance evaluation of cost centers.

Planning   After managers have projected sales and production targets for the next accounting period, standard costs can be used in developing budgets for direct materials, direct labor, and variable overhead. These estimated operating costs not only serve as targets for product costing, but are also useful in making decisions about product distribution and pricing.

Performing   As actual costs for direct materials, direct labor, and overhead are incurred and recorded, managers apply standard costs to the work in process. By using these standards as yardsticks for measuring expenditures, they can control product costs as those costs occur. For example, when the

Study Note

Standard costs are necessary for planning and control. Budgets are developed from standard costs, and performance is measured against them.

FOCUS ON BUSINESS PRACTICE

Why Go on a Factory Tour?

If you've had some manufacturing experience, you probably understand the importance of standard costing and variance analysis. If you haven't had any manufacturing experience, you can gain insight into the importance of cost planning and control by visiting a factory. Consult your local chamber of commerce for factory tours near you. You can also tour factories online. Check out the virtual production tour of jelly beans at www.jellybelly.com or see how chocolate is made at www.hersheys.com.[2]

■ FIGURE 1
The Management Process: To-Do's for Managers

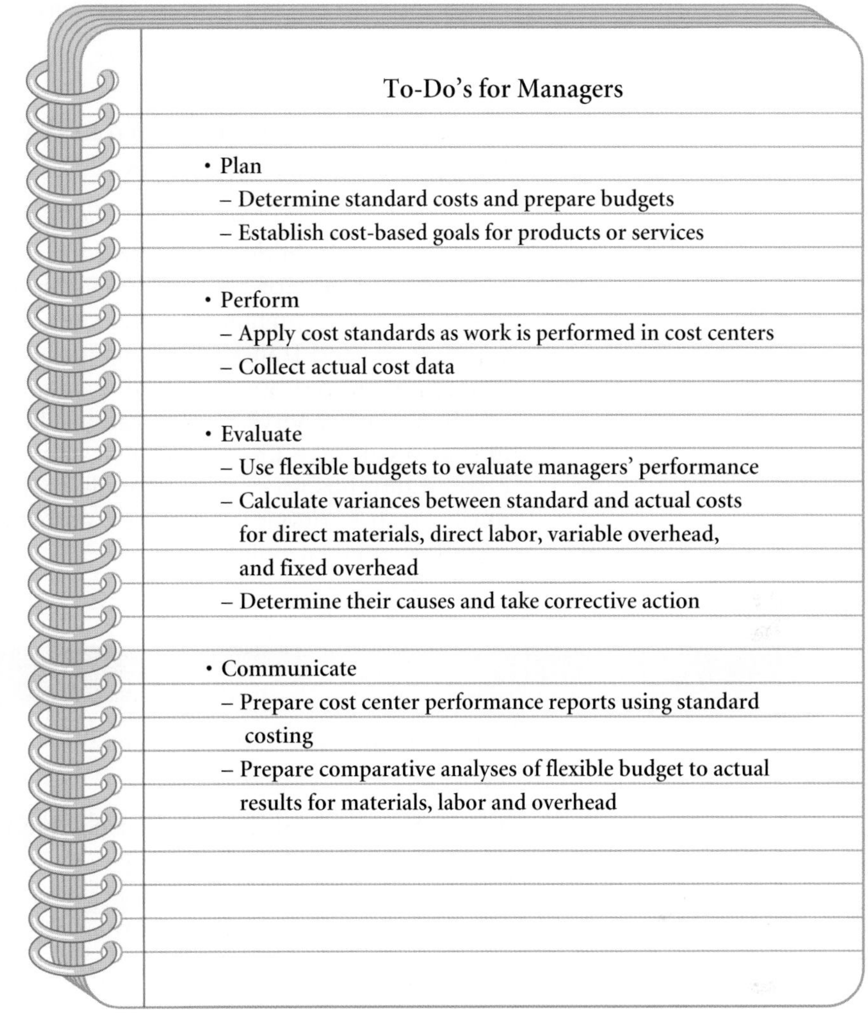

To-Do's for Managers

- Plan
  - Determine standard costs and prepare budgets
  - Establish cost-based goals for products or services

- Perform
  - Apply cost standards as work is performed in cost centers
  - Collect actual cost data

- Evaluate
  - Use flexible budgets to evaluate managers' performance
  - Calculate variances between standard and actual costs for direct materials, direct labor, variable overhead, and fixed overhead
  - Determine their causes and take corrective action

- Communicate
  - Prepare cost center performance reports using standard costing
  - Prepare comparative analyses of flexible budget to actual results for materials, labor and overhead

price that a vendor offers is higher than the standard cost, a manager may decide to take the company's business elsewhere.

Evaluating At the end of an accounting period—whether it is a day, a week, a month, or a quarter—managers compare the actual costs incurred for direct materials, direct labor, variable overhead, and fixed overhead with standard costs and compute the variances. Variances provide measures of performance that can be used to control costs. In evaluating a variance, managers compute its amount, and if the amount is significant, they analyze what is causing it. Their analysis of significant unfavorable variances may reveal operating problems of the cost center, such as inefficient functions within a department or work cell, which they can then act to correct. Managers also investigate significant favorable variances to determine why and how the positive performance occurred. Favorable variances may indicate desirable practices that should be implemented elsewhere or a need to revise the existing standards. Both favorable and unfavorable variances from standard costs can be used to evaluate a cost center and its individual manager's performance.

Communicating Managers use standard costs to report on cost center operations and managerial performance. A variance report tailored to a manager's specific responsibilities provides useful information about how well cost center operations are proceeding and how well the manager is controlling them.

The Relevance of Standard Costing in Today's Business Environment

In recent years, the increasing automation of manufacturing processes has caused a significant decrease in direct labor costs and a corresponding decline in the importance of labor-related standard costs and variances. As a result, **Coach** and other manufacturing companies, such as **Kraft Foods** and **Boeing**, which once used standard costing for all three elements of product cost, may now apply this method only to direct materials and overhead.

Today, many service organizations, including **Bank of America** and **Liberty Mutual Insurance Company**, also use standard costing. Although a service organization has no direct materials costs, labor and overhead costs are very much a part of providing services, and standard costing is an effective way of planning and controlling them.

S T O P • R E V I E W • A P P L Y

1-1. What are standard costs?

1-2. What is a variance?

1-3. Can a service organization use standard costing? Explain your answer.

Suggested answers to all Stop, Review, and Apply questions are available at http://college.hmco.com/accounting/needles/poa/10e/student_home.html.

Computing Standard Costs

LO2 Explain how standard costs are developed, and compute a standard unit cost.

A fully integrated standard costing system uses standard costs for all the elements of product cost: direct materials, direct labor, and overhead. Inventory accounts for materials, work in process, and finished goods, as well as the Cost of Goods Sold account, are maintained and reported in terms of standard costs, and standard unit costs are used to compute account balances. Actual costs are recorded separately so that managers can compare what should have been spent (the standard costs) with the actual costs incurred in the cost center.

A standard unit cost for a manufactured product has the following six elements: a price standard for direct materials, a quantity standard for direct materials, a standard for direct labor rate, a standard for direct labor time, a standard for variable overhead rate, and a standard for fixed overhead rate. To compute a standard unit cost, it is necessary to identify and analyze each of these elements. (A standard unit cost for a service includes only the elements that relate to direct labor and overhead.)

Standard Direct Materials Cost

The **standard direct materials cost** is found by multiplying the price standard for direct materials by the quantity standard for direct materials. If the price standard for a certain item is $2.75 and a specific job calls for a quantity standard of eight of the items, the standard direct materials cost for that job is computed as follows:

$$\text{Standard Direct Materials Cost} = \text{Direct Materials Price Standard} \times \text{Direct Materials Quantity Standard}$$
$$\$22.00 = \$2.75 \times 8$$

The **direct materials price standard** is a careful estimate of the cost of a specific direct material in the next accounting period. An organization's purchasing agent or its purchasing department is responsible for developing price standards for all direct materials and for making the actual purchases. When estimating a direct materials price standard, the purchasing agent or department must take into account all possible price increases, changes in available quantities, and new sources of supply.

The **direct materials quantity standard** is an estimate of the amount of direct materials, including scrap and waste, that will be used in an accounting period. It is influenced by product engineering specifications, the quality of direct materials, the age and productivity of machinery, and the quality and experience of the work force. Production managers or management accountants usually establish and monitor standards for direct materials quantity, but engineers, purchasing agents, and machine operators may also contribute to the development of these standards.

Standard Direct Labor Cost

The **standard direct labor cost** for a product, task, or job order is calculated by multiplying the standard wage for direct labor by the standard hours of direct labor. If the standard direct labor rate is $8.40 per hour and a product takes 1.5 standard direct labor hours to produce, the product's standard direct labor cost is computed as follows:

$$\text{Standard Direct Labor Cost} = \text{Direct Labor Rate Standard} \times \text{Direct Labor Time Standard}$$
$$\$12.60 = \$8.40 \times 1.5 \text{ hours}$$

The **direct labor rate standard** is the hourly direct labor rate that is expected to prevail during the next accounting period for each function or job classification. Although rate ranges are established for each type of worker and rates vary within those ranges according to each worker's experience and length of service, an average standard rate is developed for each task. Even if the person making the product is paid more or less than the standard rate, the standard rate is used to calculate the standard direct labor cost. Standard labor rates are fairly easy to develop because labor rates are either set by a labor union contract or defined by the company.

The **direct labor time standard** is the expected labor time required for each department, machine, or process to complete the production of one unit or one batch of output. In many cases, standard time per unit is a small fraction

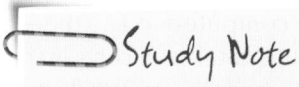
Study Note

Both the direct labor rate standard and the direct labor time standard are based on an average of the different levels of skilled workers, and both are related to the production of one unit or batch.

of an hour. Current time and motion studies of workers and machines, as well as records of their past performance, provide the data for developing this standard. The direct labor time standard should be revised whenever a machine is replaced or the quality of the labor force changes.

Standard Overhead Cost

The **standard overhead cost** is the sum of the estimates of variable and fixed overhead costs in the next accounting period. It is based on standard overhead rates that are computed in much the same way as the predetermined overhead rate that we discussed in an earlier chapter. Unlike that rate, however, the standard overhead rate has two parts, one for variable costs and one for fixed costs. The reason for computing the standard variable and fixed overhead rates separately is that their cost behavior differs.

The **standard variable overhead rate** is computed by dividing the total budgeted variable overhead costs by an expression of capacity, such as the number of standard machine hours or standard direct labor hours. (Other bases may be used if machine hours or direct labor hours are not good predictors, or drivers, of variable overhead costs.) Using standard machine hours as the base, the formula is as follows:

$$\frac{\text{Standard Variable}}{\text{Overhead Rate}} = \frac{\text{Total Budgeted Variable Overhead Costs}}{\text{Expected Number of Standard Machine Hours}}$$

The **standard fixed overhead rate** is computed by dividing the total budgeted fixed overhead costs by an expression of capacity, usually normal capacity in terms of standard hours or units. The denominator is expressed in the same terms as the variable overhead rate. Using normal capacity in terms of standard machine hours as the denominator, the formula is as follows:

$$\frac{\text{Standard Fixed}}{\text{Overhead Rate}} = \frac{\text{Total Budgeted Fixed Overhead Costs}}{\text{Normal Capacity in Terms of Standard Machine Hours}}$$

Recall that normal capacity is the level of operating capacity needed to meet expected sales demand. Using it as the application base ensures that all fixed overhead costs have been applied to units produced by the time normal capacity is reached.

Total Standard Unit Cost

Using standard costs eliminates the need to calculate unit costs from actual cost data every week or month or for each batch of goods produced. Once standard costs for direct materials, direct labor, and variable and fixed overhead have been developed, a total standard unit cost can be computed at any time.

To illustrate how standard costs are used to compute total unit cost, let's suppose that a company called Remember When, Inc., recently updated the standards for its line of watches. Direct materials price standards are now $9.20 per square foot for casing materials and $2.17 for each movement mechanism. Direct materials quantity standards are .025 square foot of casing materials per watch and one movement mechanism per watch. Direct labor time standards are .01 hour per watch for the Case Stamping Department and .05 hour per watch for the Watch Assembly Department. Direct labor rate standards are $8.00 per hour for the Case Stamping Department and $10.20 per hour for the Watch Assembly Department. Standard manufacturing overhead rates are $12.00 per direct labor hour for the standard variable overhead rate and $9.00 per direct labor hour for the standard fixed overhead rate. The standard cost of making one watch would be computed in the following manner:

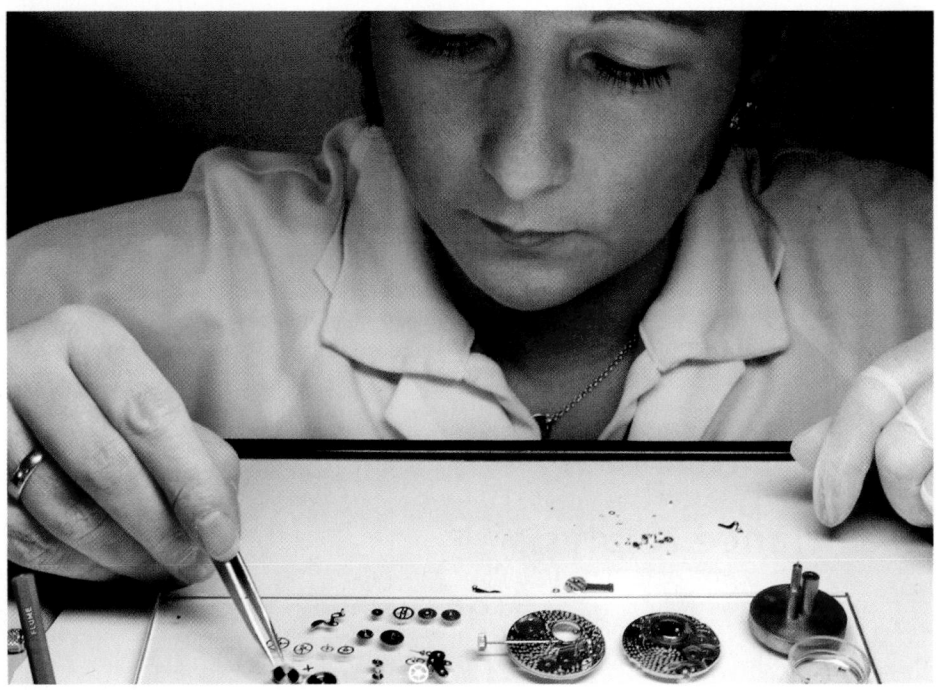

An employee at a German watch-making company works on a partially assembled watch. The total standard cost of producing a watch like this represents the desired production cost. It is based on the standards established for direct materials costs, direct labor costs, and variable and fixed overhead.

Direct materials costs:	
Casing ($9.20 per sq. ft. × .025 sq. ft.)	$ .23
One movement mechanism	2.17
Direct labor costs:	
Case Stamping Department ($8.00 per hour × .01 hour per watch)	.08
Watch Assembly Department ($10.20 per hour × .05 hour per watch)	.51
Variable overhead ($12.00 per hour × .06 hour per watch)	.72
Total standard variable cost of one watch	$3.71
Fixed overhead ($9.00 per hour × .06 hour per watch)	.54
Total standard cost of one watch	$4.25

Study Note

The total standard cost of $4.25 represents the *desired* cost of producing one watch.

S T O P • R E V I E W • A P P L Y

2-1. Explain the following statement: "Standard costing is a total unit cost concept in that standard unit costs are determined for direct materials, direct labor, and overhead."

2-2. What do a standard overhead rate and a predetermined overhead rate have in common? How do they differ?

2-3. Name the six elements used to compute a standard unit cost.

Computing a Standard Unit Cost Using the following information, compute the standard unit cost of a five-pound bag of sugar:

Direct materials quantity standard	5 pounds per unit
Direct materials price standard	$.05 per pound
Direct labor time standard	.01 hour per unit
Direct labor rate standard	$10.00 per hour
Variable overhead rate standard	$.15 per machine hour
Fixed overhead rate standard	$.10 per machine hour
Machine hour standard	.5 hour per unit

SOLUTION

Direct materials cost	
($0.05 × 5 pounds)	$0.25
Direct labor cost	
($10.00 × 0.01 hour)	0.10
Variable overhead	
($0.15 × 0.5 machine hour)	0.08
Fixed overhead	
($0.10 × 0.5 machine hour)	0.05
Total standard unit cost	$0.48

Variance Analysis

LO3   Prepare a flexible budget, and describe how managers use variance analysis to control costs.

Managers in all types of organizations constantly compare the costs of what was expected to happen with the costs of what actually did happen. By examining the differences, or variances, between standard and actual costs, they can gather much valuable information. **Variance analysis** is the process of computing the differences between standard costs and actual costs and identifying the causes of those differences. In this section, we look at how managers use flexible budgets to improve the accuracy of variance analysis and how they use variance analysis to control costs.

The Role of Flexible Budgets in Variance Analysis

The accuracy of variance analysis depends to a large extent on the type of budget that managers use when comparing variances. *Static*, or fixed, budgets forecast revenues and expenses for just one level of sales and just one level of output. The budgets that make up a master budget are usually based on a single level of output, but many things can happen over an accounting period that will cause actual output to differ from the estimated output. If a company produces more products than predicted, total production costs will almost always be greater than predicted. When that is the case, a comparison of actual production costs with fixed budgeted costs will inevitably show variances.

The performance report in Exhibit 1 compares data from Remember When's static master budget with the actual costs of its Watch Division for the

FOCUS ON BUSINESS PRACTICE

Why Complicate the Flexible Budget?

Because of the database capabilities of enterprise resource management (ERM) systems and the principles of resource consumption accounting (RCA), the flexible budget has become more complicated. This new and more complex version of a flexible budget is called *authorized reporting*. Authorized reporting is like a flexible budget in that it restates an accounting period's costs in terms of different levels of output, but it enhances cost restatement by taking into account all the factors that can influence a cost's behavior. With its sophisticated cost analyses, authorized reporting is a more relevant yardstick for cost comparison and control than the traditional flexible budget.[3]

EXHIBIT 1 ▶ **Performance Report Using Data from a Static Budget**

Remember When, Inc.
Performance Report—Watch Division
For the Year Ended December 31

Cost Category	Budgeted Costs*	Actual Costs†	Difference Under (Over) Budget
Direct materials	$42,000	$46,000	($4,000)
Direct labor	10,325	11,779	(1,454)
Variable overhead			
Indirect materials	3,500	3,600	(100)
Indirect labor	5,250	5,375	(125)
Utilities	1,750	1,810	(60)
Other	2,100	2,200	(100)
Fixed overhead			
Supervisory salaries	4,000	3,500	500
Depreciation	2,000	2,000	—
Utilities	450	450	—
Other	3,000	3,200	(200)
Totals	$74,375	$79,914	($5,539)

*Budgeted costs are based on an output of 17,500 units.
†Actual output was 19,100 units.

year ended December 31. As you can see, actual costs exceeded budgeted costs by $5,539, or 7.4 percent. On the face of it, most managers would consider such a cost overrun significant. But was there really a cost overrun? The budgeted amounts are based on an output of 17,500 units; however, the actual output was 19,100 units. To judge the division's performance accurately, the company's managers must change the budgeted data to reflect an output of 19,100 units. They can do this by using a flexible budget. A **flexible budget** (also called a *variable budget*) is a summary of expected costs for a range of activity levels. Unlike a static budget, a flexible budget provides forecasted data that can be adjusted for changes in the level of output. The flexible budget is used primarily as a cost control tool in evaluating performance at the end of a period.

A flexible budget for Remember When's Watch Division appears in Exhibit 2. It shows the estimated costs for 15,000, 17,500, and 20,000 units of output. The total cost of a variable cost item is found by multiplying the number of units produced by the item's per-unit cost. For example, if the Watch Division produces 15,000 units, direct materials will cost $36,000 (15,000 units × $2.40). An important element in this exhibit is the **flexible budget formula**, an equation that determines the expected, or budgeted, cost for any level of output. Its components include a per-unit amount for variable costs and a total amount for fixed costs. (In Exhibit 2, the $3.71 variable cost per unit is computed in the far right column, and the $9,450 is found in the section on fixed overhead costs.) Using the flexible budget formula, you can create a budget for the Watch Division for any level of output in the range of levels given.

The performance report in Exhibit 3 is based on data from the flexible budget shown in Exhibit 2. Variable unit costs have been multiplied by the 19,100 units actually produced to arrive at the total budgeted costs, and fixed

---

⌐◯ Study Note

Flexible budgets allow managers to compare budgeted and actual costs at the same level of output.

EXHIBIT 2 ▶ | **Flexible Budget for Evaluation of Overall Performance**

Remember When, Inc.
Flexible Budget—Watch Division
For the Year Ended December 31

Cost Category	Units Produced* 15,000	Units Produced* 17,500	Units Produced* 20,000	Variable Cost per Unit†
Direct materials	$36,000	$42,000	$48,000	$2.40
Direct labor	8,850	10,325	11,800	.59
Variable overhead				
Indirect materials	3,000	3,500	4,000	.20
Indirect labor	4,500	5,250	6,000	.30
Utilities	1,500	1,750	2,000	.10
Other	1,800	2,100	2,400	.12
Total variable costs	$55,650	$64,925	$74,200	$3.71
Fixed overhead				
Supervisory salaries	$ 4,000	$ 4,000	$ 4,000	
Depreciation	2,000	2,000	2,000	
Utilities	450	450	450	
Other	3,000	3,000	3,000	
Total fixed overhead costs	$ 9,450	$ 9,450	$ 9,450	
Total costs	$65,100	$74,375	$83,650	

Flexible budget formula:

Total Budgeted Costs = (Variable Cost per Unit × Number of Units Produced)
+ Budgeted Fixed Costs
= ($3.71 × Units Produced) + $9,450

*Flexible budgets are commonly used only for overhead costs; when they are, machine hours or direct labor hours are used in place of units produced.
†Computed by dividing the dollar amount in any column by the respective level of output.

overhead information has been carried over from Exhibit 2. In this report, actual costs are $397 less than the amount budgeted. In other words, when we use a flexible budget at the end of the period, we find that the performance of the Watch Division in this period actually exceeded budget targets by $397.

Using Variance Analysis to Control Costs

As Figure 2 shows, using variance analysis to control costs is a four-step process. First, managers compute the amount of the variance. If the amount is insignificant—meaning that actual operating results are close to those anticipated—no corrective action is needed. If the amount is significant, then managers analyze the variance to identify its cause. In identifying the cause, they are usually able to pinpoint the activities that need to be monitored. They then select performance measures that will enable them to track those activities, analyze the results, and determine the action needed to correct the problem. Their final step is to take the appropriate corrective action.

While computing the amount of a variance is important, it is also important to remember that this computation does nothing to prevent the variance from

EXHIBIT 3 ▶ | **Performance Report Using Data from a Flexible Budget**

Remember When, Inc.
Performance Report—Watch Division
For the Year Ended December 31

Cost Category (Variable Unit Cost)	Budgeted Costs*	Actual Costs	Difference Under (Over) Budget
Direct materials ($2.40)	$45,840	$46,000	($160)
Direct labor ($.59)	11,269	11,779	(510)
Variable overhead			
Indirect materials ($.20)	3,820	3,600	220
Indirect labor ($.30)	5,730	5,375	355
Utilities ($.10)	1,910	1,810	100
Other ($.12)	2,292	2,200	92
Fixed overhead			
Supervisory salaries	4,000	3,500	500
Depreciation	2,000	2,000	—
Utilities	450	450	—
Other	3,000	3,200	(200)
Totals	$80,311	$79,914	$397

*Budgeted costs are based on an output of 19,100 units.

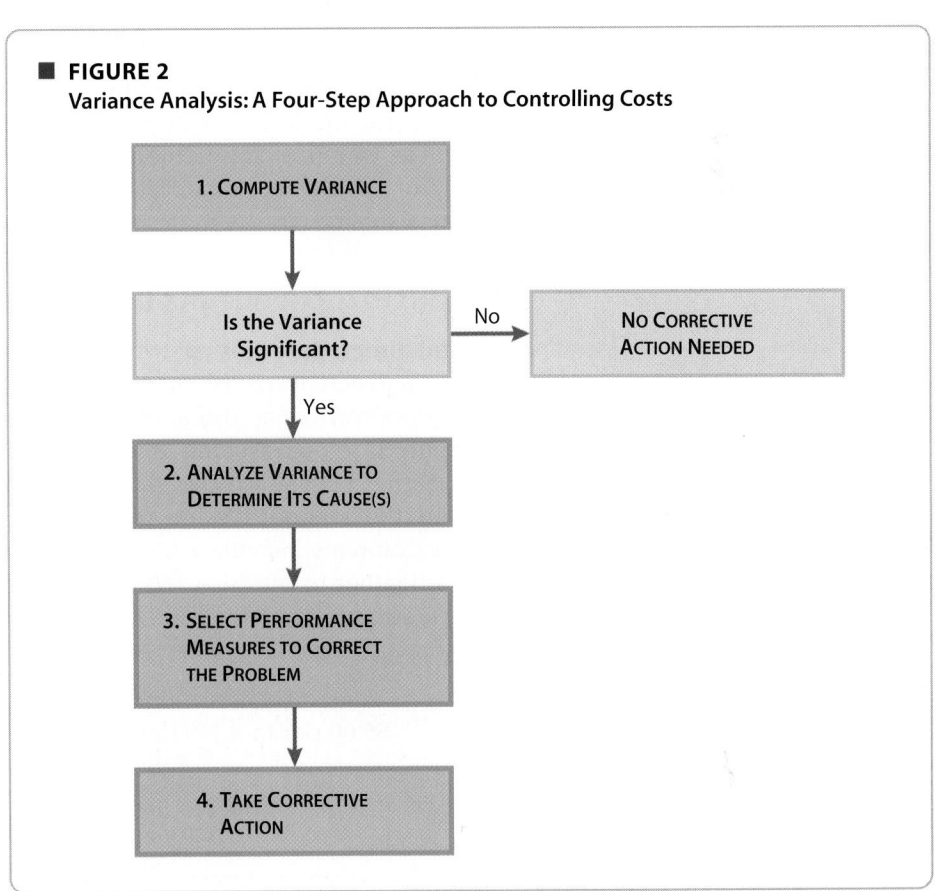

■ **FIGURE 2**
Variance Analysis: A Four-Step Approach to Controlling Costs

1. COMPUTE VARIANCE

Is the Variance Significant? — No → NO CORRECTIVE ACTION NEEDED

Yes

2. ANALYZE VARIANCE TO DETERMINE ITS CAUSE(S)

3. SELECT PERFORMANCE MEASURES TO CORRECT THE PROBLEM

4. TAKE CORRECTIVE ACTION

recurring. To control costs, managers must determine the cause of the variance and select performance measures that will help them track the problem and find the best solution for it.

As we focus on the computation and analysis of cost center variances in the next sections, we follow the steps outlined in Figure 2. We limit our analysis to eight variances, two for each of the cost categories of direct materials, direct labor, variable overhead, and fixed overhead. We give examples of operating problems that might cause each of these variances to occur. We also identify some financial and nonfinancial performance measures that can be used to track the cause of a variance and that can be helpful in correcting it.

S T O P • R E V I E W • A P P L Y

3-1. "Performance is evaluated by comparing what did happen with what should have happened." What does this statement mean? How does it relate to cost control?

3-2. What is a flexible budget? What is its purpose?

3-3. What are the components of the flexible budget formula? How are they related?

Computing and Analyzing Direct Materials Variances

> **LO4** Compute and analyze direct materials variances.

To control cost center operations, managers compute and analyze variances for whole cost categories, such as total direct materials costs, as well as variances for elements of those categories, such as the price and quantity of each direct material. The more detailed their analysis of direct materials variances is, the more effective they will be in controlling costs.

Computing Direct Materials Variances

The **total direct materials cost variance** is the difference between the standard cost and actual cost of direct materials used to produce the salable units; it is also referred to as the *good units produced*. To illustrate how this variance is computed, let us assume that a manufacturer called Cambria Company makes leather bags. Each bag should use four feet of leather (standard quantity), and the standard price of leather is $6.00 per foot. During August, Cambria Company purchased 760 feet of leather costing $5.90 per foot and used the leather to produce 180 bags. The total direct materials cost variance is calculated as follows:

Standard cost

$$\text{Standard price} \times \text{standard quantity} =$$
$$\$6.00 \text{ per foot} \times (180 \text{ bags} \times 4 \text{ feet per bag}) =$$
$$\$6.00 \text{ per foot} \times 720 \text{ feet} = \$4,320$$

Less actual cost

$$\text{Actual price} \times \text{actual quantity} =$$
$$\$5.90 \text{ per foot} \times 760 \text{ feet} = \underline{4,484}$$

Total direct materials cost variance $\underline{\$164 \text{ (U)}}$

A worker assembles a Louis Vuitton bag at the company's leather goods factory in Ducey, France. To control costs in a factory like this, managers compute and analyze variances for cost categories, such as the quantity of direct materials. For example, if more leather is used in the production of Louis Vuitton handbags than the standard quantity the company expected to use, the variance is said to be unfavorable, and the managers will take corrective action.

 Study Note

It is just as important to identify whether a variance is favorable or unfavorable as it is to compute the variance. This information is necessary for analyzing the variance and taking corrective action.

Study Note

The direct materials price variance measures the difference between the standard cost and the actual cost of purchased materials. It is not concerned with the quantity of materials used in the production process.

Here, actual cost exceeds standard cost. The situation is unfavorable, as indicated by the *U* in parentheses after the dollar amount. An *F* means a favorable situation.

To find the area or people responsible for the variance, the total direct materials cost variance must be broken down into two parts: the direct materials price variance and the direct materials quantity variance. The **direct materials price variance** (also called the *direct material spending* or *rate variance*) is the difference between the standard price and the actual price per unit multiplied by the actual quantity purchased. For Cambria Company, the direct materials price variance is computed as follows:

Standard price	$6.00
Less actual price	5.90
Difference per foot	$ .10 (F)

$$\text{Direct Materials Price Variance} = (\text{Standard Price} - \text{Actual Price}) \times \text{Actual Quantity}$$
$$= \$.10 \times 760 \text{ feet}$$
$$= \$76 \text{ (F)}$$

Because the price that the company paid for the direct materials was less than the standard price it expected to pay, the variance is favorable.

The **direct materials quantity variance** (also called the *direct material efficiency* or *usage variance*) is the difference between the standard quantity allowed and the actual quantity used multiplied by the standard price. It is computed as follows:

Standard quantity allowed (180 bags × 4 feet per bag)	720 feet
Less actual quantity	760 feet
Difference	40 feet (U)

$$\text{Direct Materials Quantity Variance} = \text{Standard Price} \times (\text{Standard Quantity Allowed} - \text{Actual Quantity})$$
$$= \$6 \times 40 \text{ feet}$$
$$= \$240 \text{ (U)}$$

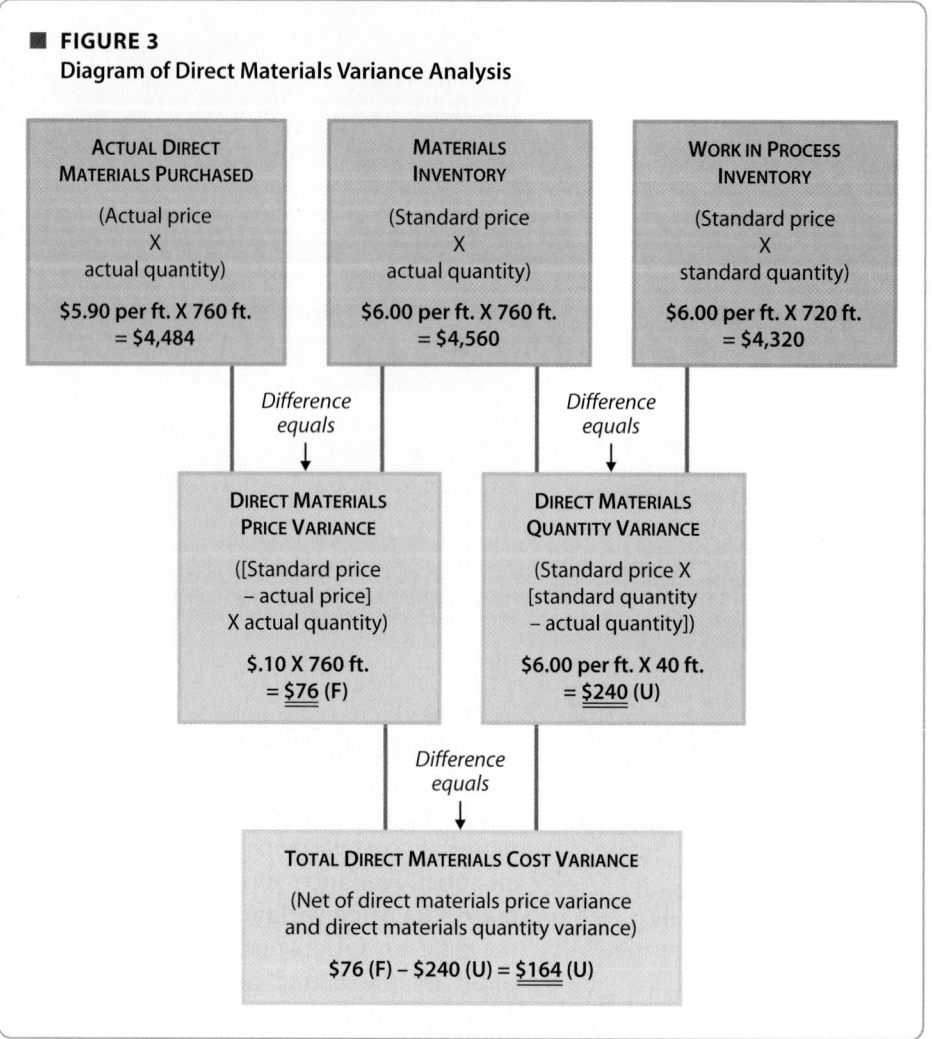

■ **FIGURE 3**
Diagram of Direct Materials Variance Analysis

Because more leather than the standard quantity was used in the production process, the direct materials quantity variance is unfavorable.

If the calculations are correct, the net of the direct materials price variance and the direct materials quantity variance should equal the total direct materials cost variance. The following check shows that the variances were computed correctly:

Direct materials price variance	$ 76 (F)
Direct materials quantity variance	240 (U)
Total direct materials cost variance	$164 (U)

Variance analyses are sometimes easier to interpret in diagram form. Figure 3 illustrates our analysis of Cambria Company's direct materials variances. Notice that although direct materials are purchased at actual cost, they are entered in the Materials Inventory account at standard price; thus, the direct materials price variance of $76 (F) is obvious when the costs are recorded. As Figure 3 shows, the standard price multiplied by the standard quantity is the amount entered in the Work in Process Inventory account.

Analyzing and Correcting Direct Materials Variances

Cambria Company's managers were concerned because the company had been experiencing direct materials price variances and quantity variances for some time; moreover, as our analysis shows, the price variances were always favorable, and the quantity variances were always unfavorable. By tracking the purchasing activity for three months, the managers discovered that the company's purchasing agent, without any authorization, had been purchasing a lower grade of leather at a reduced price. After careful analysis, the engineering manager determined that the substitute leather was not appropriate and that the company should resume purchasing the grade of leather originally specified. In addition, an analysis of scrap and rework revealed that the inferior quality of the substitute leather was causing the unfavorable quantity variance. By tracking the purchasing activity, Cambria's managers were able to solve the problems the company had been having with direct materials variances.

S T O P • R E V I E W • A P P L Y

4-1. How would you interpret an unfavorable direct materials price variance?

4-2. Can an unfavorable direct materials quantity variance be caused, at least in part, by a favorable direct materials price variance? Explain your answer.

Direct Materials Variances Using the following information, compare the actual and standard cost and usage data for the production of five-pound bags of sugar, and compute the direct materials price and direct materials quantity variances using formulas or diagram form:

Direct materials quantity standard	5 pounds per unit
Direct materials price standard	$.05 per pound
Direct materials purchased and used	55,100 pounds
Price paid for direct materials	$.04 per pound
Number of good units produced	11,000 units

SOLUTION

Direct Materials Price Variance
= (Standard Price − Actual Price) × Actual Quantity
= ($0.05 − $0.04) × 55,100 pounds
= $0.01 × 55,100 pounds = $551 (F)

Direct Materials Quantity Variance
= Standard Price × (Standard Quantity − Actual Quantity)
= $0.05 × [(11,000 × 5 pounds) − 55,100 pounds]
= $0.05 × (55,000 pounds − 55,100 pounds) = $5.00 (U)

Diagram Form:

	Actual Price × Actual Quantity		Standard Price × Actual Quantity		Standard Price × Standard Quantity
Direct Materials	$2,204[a]	Price Variance	$2,755[b]	Quantity Variance	$2.750[c]
		$551 (F)		$5 (U)	

[a] $0.04 × 55,100 = $2,204
[b] $0.05 × 55,100 = $2,755
[c] $0.05 × (11,000 × 5) = $2,750

Computing and Analyzing Direct Labor Variances

LO5 Compute and analyze direct labor variances.

The procedure for computing and analyzing direct labor cost variances parallels the procedure for finding direct materials variances. Again, the more detailed the analysis is, the more effective managers will be in controlling costs.

Computing Direct Labor Variances

The **total direct labor cost variance** is the difference between the standard direct labor cost for good units produced and actual direct labor costs. (*Good units* are the total units produced less units that are scrapped or need to be reworked—in other words, the salable units.) At Cambria Company, each leather bag requires 2.4 standard direct labor hours, and the standard direct labor rate is $8.50 per hour. During August, 450 direct labor hours were used to make 180 bags at an average pay rate of $9.20 per hour. The total direct labor cost variance is computed as follows:

Standard Cost

Standard rate × standard hours allowed	=
$8.50 × (180 bags × 2.4 hours per bag)	=
$8.50 × 432 hours	= $3,672

Less Actual Cost

Actual rate × actual hours = $9.20 × 450 hours =	4,140
Total direct labor cost variance	$ 468 (U)

Both the actual direct labor hours per bag and the actual direct labor rate varied from the standard. For effective performance evaluation, management must know how much of the total cost arose from different direct labor rates and how much from different numbers of direct labor hours. This information is found by computing the direct labor rate variance and the direct labor efficiency variance.

The **direct labor rate variance** (also called the *direct labor spending variance*) is the difference between the standard direct labor rate and the actual direct labor rate multiplied by the actual direct labor hours worked. It is computed as follows:

Standard rate	$8.50
Less actual rate	9.20
Difference per hour	$ .70 (U)

$$\text{Direct Labor Rate Variance} = (\text{Standard Rate} - \text{Actual Rate}) \times \text{Actual Hours}$$
$$= \$.70 \times 450 \text{ hours}$$
$$= \$315 \text{ (U)}$$

The **direct labor efficiency variance** (also called the *direct labor quantity* or *usage variance*) is the difference between the standard direct labor hours allowed for good units produced and the actual direct labor hours worked multiplied by the standard direct labor rate. It is computed this way:

Standard hours allowed (180 bags × 2.4 hours per bag)	432 hours
Less actual hours	450 hours
Difference	18 hours (U)

Study Note

The computation of the direct labor rate variance is very similar to the computation of the direct materials price variance. Computations of the direct labor efficiency variance and the direct materials quantity variance are also similar.

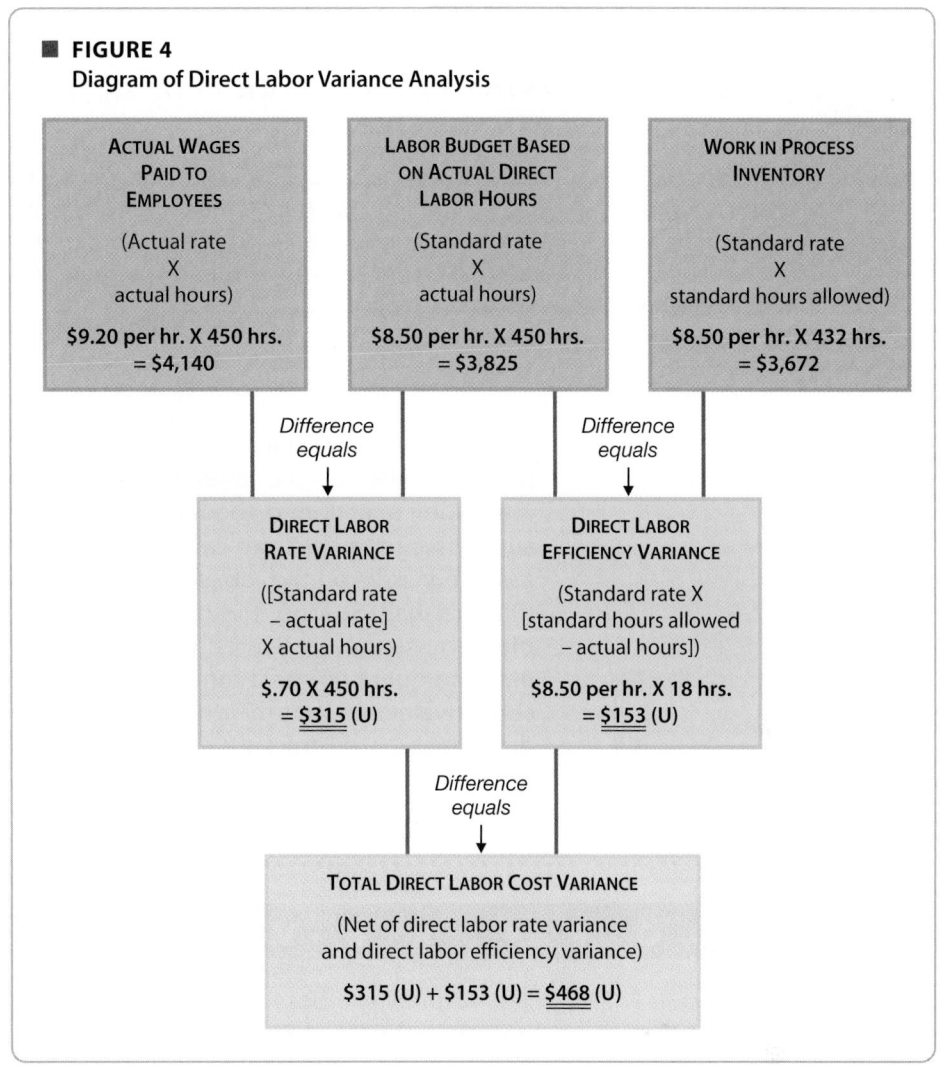

■ **FIGURE 4**
Diagram of Direct Labor Variance Analysis

$$\text{Direct Labor Efficiency Variance} = \text{Standard Rate} \times (\text{Standard Hours Allowed} - \text{Actual Hours})$$
$$= \$8.50 \times 18 \text{ hours}$$
$$= \underline{\$153} \text{ (U)}$$

If the calculations are correct, the net of the direct labor rate variance and the direct labor efficiency variance should equal the total direct labor cost variance. The following check shows that the variances were computed correctly:

Direct labor rate variance	$315 (U)
Direct labor efficiency variance	153 (U)
Total direct labor cost variance	$468 (U)

Figure 4 summarizes our analysis of Cambria Company's direct labor variances. Unlike direct materials variances, the direct labor rate and efficiency variances are usually computed and recorded at the same time.

Analyzing and Correcting Direct Labor Variances

Because Cambria Company's direct labor rate variance and direct labor efficiency variance were unfavorable, its managers investigated the causes of these variances. An analysis of employee time cards revealed that the Bag Assembly Department had replaced an assembly worker who was ill with a

machine operator from another department. The machine operator made $9.20 per hour, whereas the assembly worker earned the standard $8.50 per hour rate. When questioned about the unfavorable efficiency variance, the assembly supervisor identified two causes. First, the machine operator had had to learn assembly skills on the job, so his assembly time was longer than the standard time per bag. Second, the materials handling people were partially responsible because they delivered parts late on five different occasions. Because the machine operator was a temporary replacement, Cambria's managers took no corrective action, but they decided to keep a close eye on the materials handling function by tracking delivery times and number of delays for the next three months. Once they have collected and analyzed the new data, they will take whatever action is needed to correct the scheduling problem.

STOP • REVIEW • APPLY

5-1. Identify two possible causes of a direct labor rate variance, and describe the measures used to track performance in those areas. Then do the same for a direct labor efficiency variance.

5-2. If the direct labor rate variance is unfavorable, will the direct labor efficiency variance also be unfavorable?

Direct Labor Variances Using the following information, compare the standard cost and usage data for the production of five-pound bags of sugar, and compute the direct labor rate and direct labor efficiency variances using formulas or diagram form:

Direct labor time standard	.01 hour per unit
Direct labor rate standard	$10.00 per hour
Direct labor hours used	100 hours
Total cost of direct labor	$1,010
Number of good units produced	11,000 units

SOLUTION

Direct Labor Rate Variance = (Standard Rate − Actual Rate) × Actual Hours

= [$10.00 − ($1,010 ÷ 100 hours)] × 100 hours
= ($10.00 − $10.10) × 100 hours
= $0.10 × 100 hours = $10.00 (U)

Direct Labor
Efficiency = Standard Rate × (Standard Hours Allowed − Actual Hours)
Variance

= $10.00 × [(11,000 × 0.01 hour) − 100 hours]
= $10.00 × (110 hours − 100 hours)
= $10.00 × (10 hours) = ($100.00) (F)

Diagram Form:

	Actual Rate × Actual Hours		Standard Rate × Actual Hours		Standard Rate × Standard Hours
Direct Labor	$1,010[a]	Rate Variance	$1,000[b]	Efficiency Variance	$1,100[c]
		$10.00 (U)		($100.00) (F)	

[a] $10.10 × 100 = $1,010
[b] $10.00 × 100 = $1,000
[c] $10.00 × (11,000 × 0.01 hour) = $1,100

Computing and Analyzing Overhead Variances

LO6 Compute and analyze overhead variances.

Many types of variable and fixed overhead costs may contribute to variances from standard costs. Controlling these costs is more difficult than controlling direct materials and direct labor costs because the responsibility for overhead costs is hard to assign. Fixed overhead costs may be unavoidable past costs, such as depreciation and lease expenses; they are therefore not under the control of any department manager. If variable overhead costs can be related to departments or activities, however, some control is possible.

Using a Flexible Budget to Analyze Overhead Variances

Earlier in the chapter, we described the flexible budget that the managers of Remember When, Inc., use to evaluate overall performance. That budget, shown in Exhibit 2, is based on units of output. Cambria Company's managers also use a flexible budget, but to analyze overhead costs only. As you can see in Exhibit 4, Cambria's flexible budget uses direct labor hours as the expression of activity. Thus, variable costs vary with the number of direct labor hours worked. Total fixed overhead costs remain constant. The flexible budget formula in such cases is as follows:

Total Budgeted Overhead Costs = (Variable Costs per Direct Labor Hour
× Number of Direct Labor Hours)
+ Budgeted Fixed Overhead Costs

When applied to Cambria Company's data, the flexible budget formula is as follows:

Total Budgeted Overhead Costs = ($5.75 × Number of Direct
Labor Hours) + $1,300

EXHIBIT 4 ▶

Flexible Budget for Evaluation of Overhead Costs

Cambria Company
Flexible Budget—Overhead
Bag Assembly Department
For an Average One-Month Period

Cost Category	Direct Labor Hours (DLH) 400	432	500	Variable Cost per DLH
Budgeted variable overhead				
Indirect materials	$ 600	$ 648	$ 750	$1.50
Indirect labor	800	864	1,000	2.00
Supplies	300	324	375	.75
Utilities	400	432	500	1.00
Other	200	216	250	.50
Total budgeted variable overhead costs	$2,300	$2,484	$2,875	$5.75
Budgeted fixed overhead				
Supervisory salaries	$ 600	$ 600	$ 600	
Depreciation	400	400	400	
Other	300	300	300	
Total budgeted fixed overhead costs	$1,300	$1,300	$1,300	
Total budgeted overhead costs	$3,600	$3,784	$4,175	

Flexible budget formula (based on a normal capacity of 400 direct labor hours):

Total Budgeted Overhead Costs = (Variable Costs per Direct Labor Hour
× Number of DLH) + Budgeted Fixed Overhead
Costs

= ($5.75 × number of DLH) + $1,300

Cambria's flexible budget shows monthly overhead costs for 400, 432, and 500 direct labor hours. To find the total monthly flexible budgeted overhead costs for the 180 bags produced, you simply insert the direct labor hours allowed in the flexible budget formula—for example, ($5.75 × 432 direct labor hours) + $1,300 = $3,784.

Computing Overhead Variances

Analyses of overhead variances differ in degree of detail. The basic approach is to compute the **total overhead variance**, which is the difference between actual overhead costs and standard overhead costs applied. You may recall from a previous chapter how overhead was applied to production by using a standard overhead rate.

A standard overhead rate has two parts: a variable rate and a fixed rate. For Cambria Company, the standard variable rate is $5.75 per direct labor hour (from the flexible budget). The standard fixed overhead rate is found by dividing total budgeted fixed overhead ($1,300) by normal capacity set by the master budget at the beginning of the period. (Cambria's normal capacity is 400 direct labor hours.) The result is a fixed overhead rate of $3.25 per direct labor hour ($1,300 ÷ 400 hours). So, Cambria's total standard overhead rate is $9.00 per direct labor hour ($5.75 + $3.25).

Cambria Company's total overhead variance would be computed as follows:

Standard overhead costs applied to good units produced	
$9.00 per direct labor hour × (180 bags × 2.4 hr. per bag)	$3,888
Less actual overhead costs	4,100
Total overhead variance	$ 212 (U)

This amount can be divided into variable overhead variances and fixed overhead variances.

Variable Overhead Variances   The **total variable overhead variance** is the difference between actual variable overhead costs and the standard variable overhead costs that are applied to good units produced using the standard variable rate. The procedure for finding this variance is similar to the procedure for finding direct materials and labor variances.

Figure 5 shows an analysis of Cambria Company's variable overhead variances. At Cambria, each leather bag requires 2.4 standard direct labor hours,

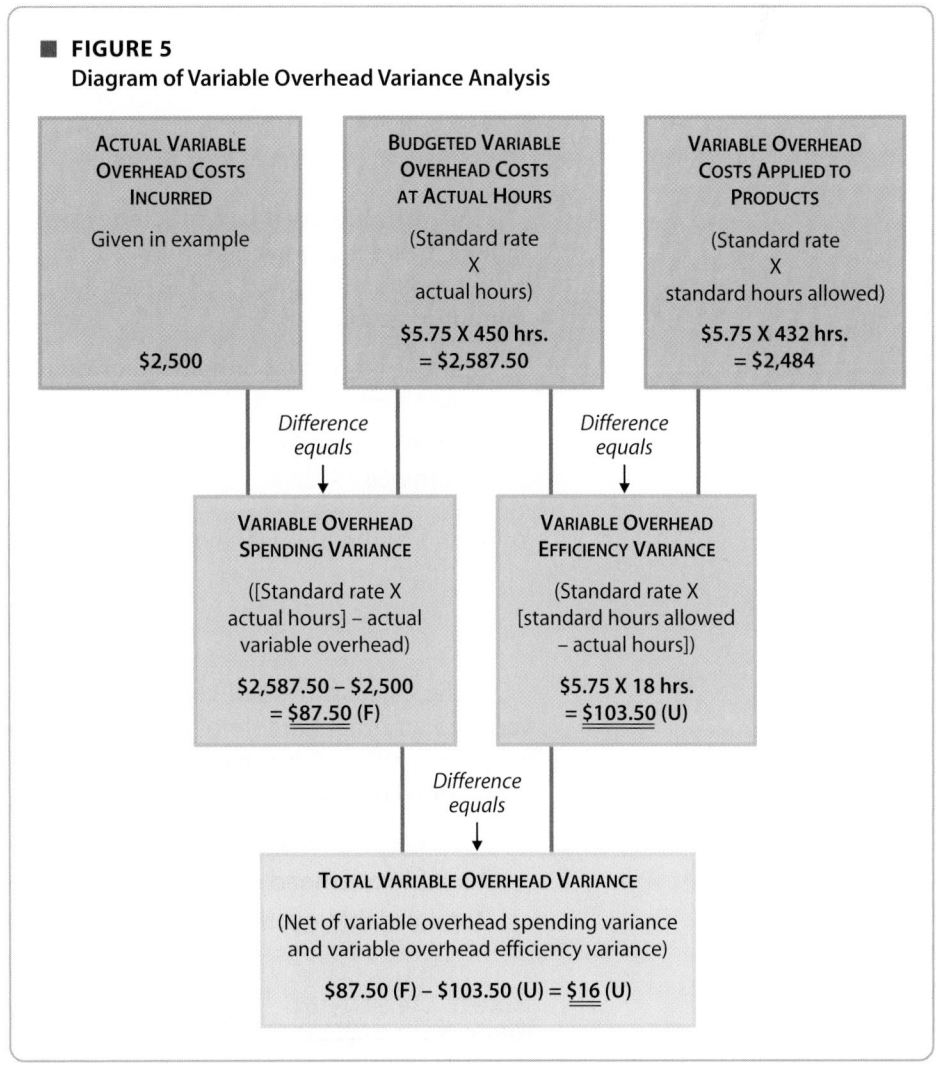

■ **FIGURE 5**
Diagram of Variable Overhead Variance Analysis

and the standard variable overhead rate is $5.75 per direct labor hour. During August, the company incurred $2,500 of variable overhead costs. The total variable overhead cost variance is computed as follows:

Overhead applied to good units produced
Standard variable rate × standard labor hours allowed =
$5.75 per hour × (180 bags × 2.4 hours per bag)   =
$5.75 × 432 hours   = $2,484
Less actual cost   2,500
Total variable overhead cost variance $ 16 (U)

Both the actual variable overhead and the direct labor hours per bag may vary from the standard. For effective performance evaluation, managers must know how much of the total cost arose from variable overhead spending deviations and how much from variable overhead application deviations (i.e., applied and actual direct labor hours). This information is found by computing the variable overhead spending variance and the variable overhead efficiency variance.

The **variable overhead spending variance** (also called the *variable overhead rate variance*) is computed by multiplying the actual hours worked by the difference between actual variable overhead costs and the standard variable overhead rate, as follows:

Variable Overhead Spending Variance = (Standard Variable Rate × Actual Hours Worked) − Actual Variable Overhead Cost
= ($5.75 × 450 hours) − $2,500
= $2,587.50 − $2,500
= $87.50 (F)

The **variable overhead efficiency variance** is the difference between the standard direct labor hours allowed for good units produced and the actual hours worked multiplied by the standard variable overhead rate per hour. It is computed as follows:

Standard direct labor hours allowed (180 bags × 2.4 hours per bag)   432 hours
Less actual hours   450 hours
Difference   18 hours (U)

Variable Overhead Efficiency Variance = Standard Variable Rate × (Standard Hours Allowed − Actual Hours)
= $5.75 × 18 hours
= $103.50 (U)

If the calculations are correct, the net of the variable overhead spending variance and the variable overhead efficiency variance should equal the total variable overhead variance. The following check shows that these variances have been computed correctly:

Variable overhead spending variance $ 87.50 (F)
Variable overhead efficiency variance   103.50 (U)
Total variable overhead cost variance $ 16.00 (U)

Fixed Overhead Variances   The **total fixed overhead variance** is the difference between actual fixed overhead costs and the standard fixed over-

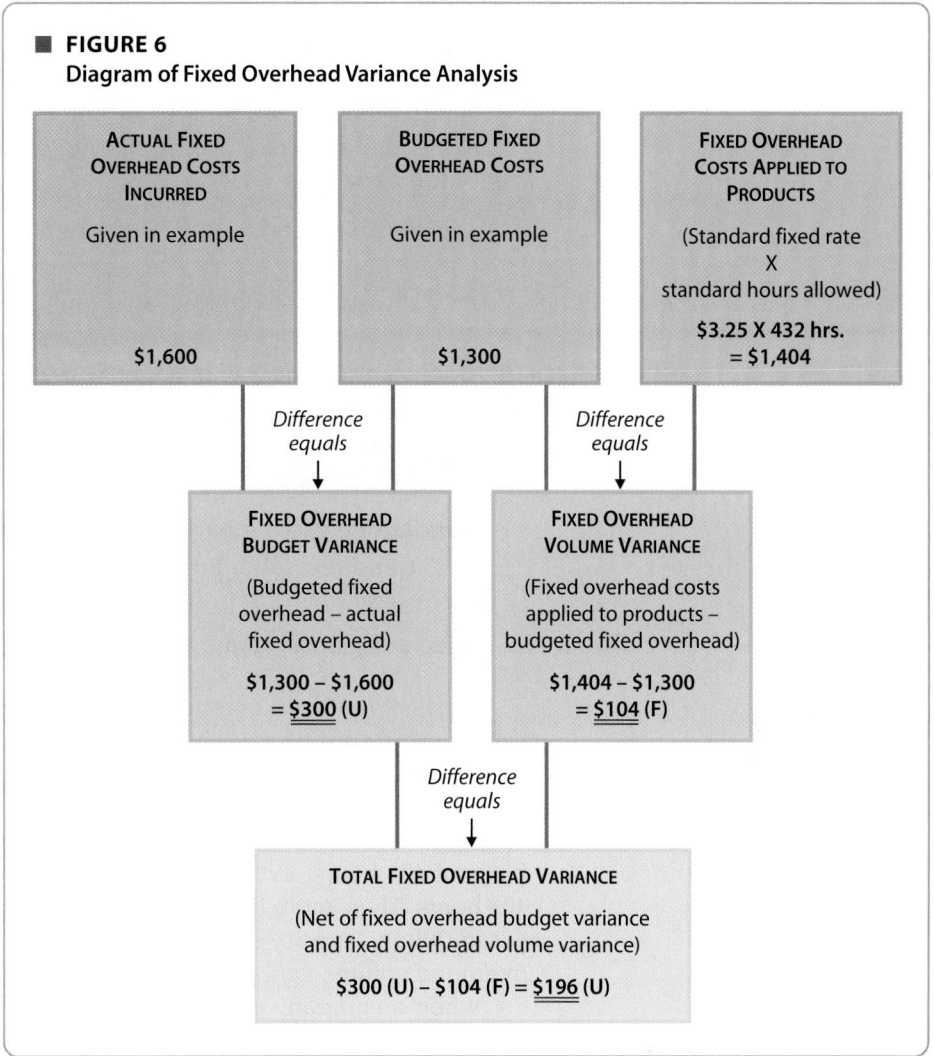

■ FIGURE 6
Diagram of Fixed Overhead Variance Analysis

head costs that are applied to good units produced using the standard fixed overhead rate. The procedure for finding this variance differs from the procedure used for finding direct materials, direct labor, and variable overhead variances.

Figure 6 shows an analysis of fixed overhead variances for Cambria Company. At Cambria, each bag requires 2.4 standard direct labor hours, and the standard fixed overhead rate is $3.25 per direct labor hour. As we noted earlier, the standard fixed overhead rate is found by dividing budgeted fixed overhead ($1,300) by normal capacity, which was set by the master budget at the beginning of the period. In this case, because normal capacity is 400 direct labor hours, the fixed overhead rate is $3.25 per direct labor hour ($1,300 ÷ 400 hours).

During August, Cambria incurred $1,600 of actual fixed overhead costs. The total fixed overhead variance is computed as follows:

Overhead applied to the good units produced
Standard fixed rate × standard direct labor hours allowed =
$3.25 × (180 bags × 2.4 hours per bag) =
$3.25 × 432 hours = $1,404

Less actual cost	1,600
Total fixed overhead cost variance	$ 196 (U)

For effective performance evaluation, managers break down the total fixed overhead variance into two additional variances: the fixed overhead budget variance and the fixed overhead volume variance.

The **fixed overhead budget variance** (also called the *budgeted fixed overhead variance*) is the difference between budgeted and actual fixed overhead costs, computed as follows:

$$
\begin{aligned}
\text{Fixed Overhead Budget Variance} &= \text{Budgeted Fixed Overhead} - \\
&\quad \text{Actual Fixed Overhead} \\
&= \$1,300 - \$1,600 \\
&= \$300 \text{ (U)}
\end{aligned}
$$

The **fixed overhead volume variance** is the difference between budgeted fixed overhead costs and the overhead costs that are applied to production using the standard fixed overhead rate. The fixed overhead volume variance is computed as follows:

Standard fixed overhead applied to good units produced	
$3.25 per direct labor hour × (180 bags × 2.4 hours per bag)	$1,404
Less total budgeted fixed overhead	1,300
Fixed overhead volume variance	$ 104 (F)

Because the fixed overhead volume variance measures the use of existing facilities and capacity, a volume variance will occur if more or less than normal capacity is used. At Cambria Company, 400 direct labor hours are considered normal use of facilities. Because fixed overhead costs are applied on the basis of standard hours allowed, Cambria Company's overhead was applied on the basis of 432 hours, even though the fixed overhead rate was computed using 400 hours. Thus, more fixed costs would be applied to products than were budgeted. When capacity exceeds the expected amount, the result is a favorable overhead volume variance because fixed overhead was overapplied.

When a company operates at a level below the normal capacity in units, the result is an unfavorable volume variance. Not all of the fixed overhead costs will be applied to units produced. In other words, fixed overhead is underapplied, and the cost of goods produced does not include the full budgeted cost of fixed overhead.

Summary of Overhead Variances

If our calculations of variable and fixed overhead variances are correct, the net of these variances should equal the total overhead variance. Checking the computations, we find that the variable and fixed overhead variances do equal the total overhead variance:

Variable overhead spending variance	$ 87.50 (F)
Variable overhead efficiency variance	103.50 (U)
Fixed overhead budget variance	300.00 (U)
Fixed overhead volume variance	104.00 (F)
Total overhead variance	$212.00 (U)

Figures 5 and 6 summarize our analysis of overhead variances. The total overhead variance is also the amount of overapplied or underapplied overhead. You may recall from an earlier chapter that actual variable and fixed overhead costs are recorded as they occur, that variable and fixed overhead are applied to products as they are produced, and that the overapplied or underapplied overhead is computed and reconciled at the end of each accounting period. By breaking down the total overhead variance into variable and fixed variances, managers can more accurately control costs and reconcile their causes. An analysis of these two overhead variances will help explain why the amount of overhead applied to units produced is different from the actual overhead costs incurred.

Analyzing and Correcting Overhead Variances

In analyzing the unfavorable total overhead variance of $212, the manager of Cambria Company's Bag Assembly Department found causes for the variances that contributed to it. Although the variable overhead spending variance was favorable ($87.50 less than expected because of savings on purchases), the inefficiency of the machine operator who substituted for an assembly worker created unfavorable variances for both direct labor efficiency and variable overhead efficiency. As a result, the manager is going to consider the feasibility of implementing a program for cross-training employees.

After reviewing the fixed overhead costs, the manager of the Bag Assembly Department concluded that higher than anticipated factory insurance premiums were the reason for the unfavorable fixed overhead budget variance and were the result of an increase in the number of insurance claims filed by employees. To obtain more specific information, the manager will study the insurance claims filed over a three-month period.

Finally, since the 432 standard hours were well above the normal capacity of 400 direct labor hours, fixed overhead was overapplied, and it resulted in a $104(F) volume variance. The overutilization of capacity was traced to high seasonal demand that pressed the company to use almost all its capacity. Management decided not to do anything about the fixed overhead volume variance because it fell within an anticipated seasonal range.

S T O P • R E V I E W • A P P L Y

6-1. Can the variable overhead efficiency variance have the same causes as the direct labor efficiency variance?

6-2. Distinguish between the fixed overhead budget variance and the fixed overhead volume variance.

6-3. If standard hours allowed exceed normal hours, will the period's fixed overhead volume variance be favorable or unfavorable? Explain your answer.

Using Cost Variances to Evaluate Managers' Performance

LO7 Explain how variances are used to evaluate managers' performance.

How effectively and fairly a manager's performance is evaluated depends on human factors—the people doing the evaluating—as well as on company policies. The evaluation process becomes more accurate when managerial performance reports include variances from standard costs.

To ensure that the evaluation of a manager's performance is effective and fair, a company's policies should be based on input from managers and

employees and should specify the procedures that managers are to use when doing the following:

- Preparing operational plans
- Assigning responsibility for carrying out the operational plans
- Communicating the operational plans to key personnel
- Evaluating performance in each area of responsibility
- Identifying the causes of significant variances from the operational plan
- Taking corrective action to eliminate problems

Because variance analysis provides detailed data about differences between standard and actual costs and thus helps identify the causes of those differences, it is usually more effective at pinpointing efficient and inefficient operating areas than are basic comparisons of budgeted and actual data. A managerial performance report based on standard costs and related variances should identify the causes of each significant variance, the personnel involved, and the corrective actions taken. It should be tailored to the cost center manager's specific areas of responsibility and explain clearly how the manager's department met or did not meet operating expectations. Managers should be held accountable only for the cost areas under their control.

Exhibit 5 shows a performance report for the manager of Cambria Company's Bag Assembly Department. The report summarizes all cost data and variances for direct materials, direct labor, and overhead. In addition, it identifies the causes of the variances and the corrective actions taken. Such a report would enable a supervisor to review a cost center manager's actions and evaluate his or her performance.

A point to remember is that the mere occurrence of a variance does not indicate that a manager of a cost center has performed poorly. However, if a variance occurs consistently, and no cause is identified and no corrective action is taken, it may well indicate poor managerial performance.

Exhibit 5 shows that the causes of the variances have been identified and corrective actions have been taken, indicating that the manager of the Cambria Company's Bag Assembly Department has the operation under control.

STOP • REVIEW • APPLY

7-1. Why should evaluations of the performance of cost center managers not follow a set pattern?

7-2. What should a managerial performance report based on standard costs and related variances include? How should it be prepared?

EXHIBIT 5 ▼

Managerial Performance Report Using Variance Analysis

Cambria Company
Managerial Performance Report
Bag Assembly Department
For the Month Ended August 31

Productivity Summary:

Normal capacity in units	167 bags
Normal capacity in direct labor hours (DLH)	400 DLH
Good units produced	180 bags
Performance level	
(standard hours allowed for good units produced)	432 DLH

Cost and Variance Analysis:

	Standard Costs	Actual Costs	Total Variance	Variance Breakdown Amount	Variance Breakdown Type
Direct materials	$ 4,320	$ 4,484	$164 (U)	$ 76.00 (F)	Direct materials price variance
				240.00 (U)	Direct materials quantity variance
Direct labor	3,672	4,140	468 (U)	315.00 (U)	Direct labor rate variance
				153.00 (U)	Direct labor efficiency variance
Variable overhead	2,484	2,500	16 (U)	87.50 (F)	Variable overhead spending variance
				103.50 (U)	Variable overhead efficiency variance
Fixed overhead	1,404	1,600	196 (U)	300.00 (U)	Fixed overhead budget variance
				104.00 (F)	Fixed overhead volume variance
Totals	$11,880	$12,724	$844 (U)	$844.00 (U)	

Causes of Variances	**Actions Taken**
Direct materials price variance:	
New direct materials purchased at reduced price	New direct materials deemed inappropriate; resumed purchasing materials originally specified
Direct materials quantity variance:	
Poor quality of new direct materials	New direct materials deemed inappropriate; resumed using direct materials originally specified
Direct labor rate variance:	
Machine operator who had to learn assembly skills	Temporary replacement; no action taken on the job
Direct labor efficiency variance:	
Machine operator who had to learn assembly skills	Temporary replacement; no action taken on the job
Late delivery of parts to assembly floor	Material delivery times and number of delays being tracked
Variable overhead spending variance:	
Cost savings on purchases	No action necessary
Variable overhead efficiency variance:	
Machine operator who had to learn assembly skills on the job	A cross-training program for employees now under consideration
Fixed overhead budget variance:	
Large number of factory insurance claims	Study of insurance claims being conducted
Fixed overhead volume variance:	
High number of orders caused by seasonal demand	No action necessary

COACH, INC.

The Decision Point at the beginning of this chapter focused on Coach, Inc., a manufacturer of high-quality leather goods and fine gifts and accessories. It asked these questions:

- How does setting performance standards help managers control costs?
- How do Coach's managers use standard costs to control costs?
- How do they use standard costs to evaluate the performance of cost centers?

Managers at Coach base standard costs on realistic estimates of operating costs. They use these figures as performance targets and as benchmarks against which they measure actual spending trends. By analyzing variances between standard and actual costs, they gain insight into the causes of those differences. Once they have identified an operating problem that is causing a cost variance, they can devise a solution to the problem and better control costs.

When evaluating the performance of cost centers, managers use standard costs to prepare flexible budgets, which will improve the accuracy of their variance analysis. This comparison of actual costs and a budget based on actual output provides Coach's managers with objective data that they can use to assess the center's performance in terms of its key success factor—cost.

CHAPTER REVIEW

REVIEW of Learning Objectives

LO1 Define *standard costs,* and describe how managers use these costs.

Standard costs are realistic estimates of costs based on analyses of both past and projected operating costs and conditions. They provide a standard, or pre-determined, performance level for use in standard costing, a method of cost control that also includes a measure of actual performance and a measure of the variance between standard and actual performance. When managers plan, they use standard costs to develop budgets for direct materials, direct labor, and variable overhead. These estimated costs not only serve as targets for product costing, but are also useful in making decisions about product distribution and pricing. During an accounting period, as managers perform, they use standard costs to measure expenditures and to control costs as they occur. At the end of the period, managers evaluate performance by comparing actual costs with standard costs and computing the variances. The variances provide measures of performance that can be used to control costs. Managers also use standard cost reports to communicate about operations and managerial performance.

LO2 Explain how standard costs are developed, and compute a standard unit cost.

A standard unit cost has six elements. The direct materials price standard is based on a careful estimate of all possible price increases, changes in available quantities, and new sources of supply in the next accounting period. The direct materials quantity standard is based on product engineering specifications, the quality of direct materials, the age and productivity of the machines, and the quality and experience of the work force. Labor union contracts or company policies define the direct labor rate standard. Current time and motion studies of workers and machines and records of their past performance provide the data for developing the direct labor time standard. Standard variable and fixed overhead rates are found by dividing total budgeted variable and fixed overhead costs by an appropriate application base, such as normal capacity. A total standard unit cost is computed by adding the following costs: direct materials costs (direct materials price standard times direct materials quantity standard), direct labor costs (direct labor rate standard times direct labor time standard), and overhead costs (standard variable and standard fixed overhead rate times standard direct labor hours allowed per unit).

LO3 Prepare a flexible budget, and describe how managers use variance analysis to control costs.

A flexible budget is a summary of anticipated costs for a range of activity levels. It provides forecasted cost data that can be adjusted for changes in level of output. The variable cost per unit and total fixed costs presented in a flexible budget are components of the flexible budget formula, an equation that determines the budgeted cost for any level of output. A flexible budget improves the accuracy of variance analysis, which is a four-step approach to controlling costs. First, managers compute the amount of the variance. If the amount is insignificant, no corrective action is needed. If the amount is significant, managers then analyze the variance to identify its cause. In identifying the cause, they are usually able to pinpoint the activities that need to be monitored. They then select performance measures that will enable them to track those activities, analyze the results, and determine the action needed to correct the problem. Their final step is to take the appropriate corrective action.

LO4 Compute and analyze direct materials variances.

The direct materials price variance is computed by finding the difference between the standard price and the actual price per unit and multiplying it by the actual quantity purchased. The direct materials quantity variance is the difference between the standard quantity that should have been used and the actual quantity used, multiplied by the standard price. An analysis of these variances enables managers to identify what is causing them and to formulate plans for correcting related operating problems.

LO5 Compute and analyze direct labor variances.

The direct labor rate variance is computed by determining the difference between the standard direct labor rate and the actual rate and multiplying it by the actual direct labor hours worked. The direct labor efficiency variance is the difference between the standard hours allowed for the number of good units produced and the actual hours worked multiplied by the standard direct labor rate. Managers analyze these variances to find the causes of differences between standard direct labor costs and actual direct labor costs.

LO6 Compute and analyze overhead variances.

The total overhead variance is equal to the amount of under- or overapplied overhead costs for an accounting period. An analysis of the variable and fixed overhead variances will help explain why the amount of overhead applied to units produced differs from the actual overhead costs incurred. The total overhead variance can be broken down into a variable overhead spending variance, a variable overhead efficiency variance, a fixed overhead budget variance, and a fixed overhead volume variance.

LO7 Explain how variances are used to evaluate managers' performance.

How effectively and fairly a manager's performance is evaluated depends on human factors—the people doing the evaluating—as well as on company policies. To ensure that performance evaluation is effective and fair, a company's evaluation policies should be based on input from managers and employees and should be specific about the procedures that managers are to follow. The evaluation process becomes more accurate when managerial performance reports for cost centers include variances from standard costs. A managerial performance report based on standard costs and related variances should identify the causes of each significant variance, along with the personnel involved and the corrective actions taken. It should be tailored to the cost center manager's specific areas of responsibility.

REVIEW of Concepts and Terminology

The following concepts and terms were introduced in this chapter:

Direct labor efficiency variance: The difference between the standard direct labor hours allowed for good units produced and the actual direct labor hours worked multiplied by the standard direct labor rate. Also called *direct labor quantity* or *usage variance*. **(LO5)**

Direct labor rate standard: The hourly direct labor rate that is expected to prevail during the next accounting period for each function or job classification. **(LO2)**

Direct labor rate variance: The difference between the standard direct labor rate and the actual direct labor rate multiplied by the actual direct labor hours worked. Also called *direct labor spending variance*. **(LO5)**

Direct labor time standard: The expected labor time required for each department, machine, or process to complete the production of one unit or one batch of output. **(LO2)**

Direct materials price standard: A careful estimate of the cost of a specific direct material in the next accounting period. **(LO2)**

Direct materials price variance: The difference between the standard price and the actual price per unit multiplied by the actual quantity purchased. Also called *direct materials spending* or *rate variance*. **(LO4)**

Direct materials quantity standard: An estimate of the amount of direct materials, including scrap and waste, that will be used in an accounting period. **(LO2)**

Direct materials quantity variance: The difference between the standard quantity allowed and the actual quantity used multiplied by the standard price. Also called *direct materials efficiency* or *usage variance*. **(LO4)**

Fixed overhead budget variance: The difference between budgeted and actual fixed overhead costs. Also called *budgeted fixed overhead variance*. **(LO6)**

Fixed overhead volume variance: The difference between budgeted fixed overhead costs and the overhead costs that are applied to production using the standard fixed overhead rate. **(LO6)**

Flexible budget: A summary of expected costs for a range of activity levels. Also called *variable budget*. **(LO3)**

Flexible budget formula: An equation that determines the expected, or budgeted, cost for any level of output. **(LO3)**

Standard costing: A method of cost control with three components: a standard, or predetermined, performance level; a measure of actual performance; and a measure of the difference, or variance, between standard and actual performance. **(LO1)**

Standard costs: Realistic estimates of costs based on analyses of both past and projected operating costs and conditions. **(LO1)**

Standard direct labor cost: The standard wage for direct labor multiplied by the standard hours of direct labor. **(LO2)**

Standard direct materials cost: The standard price for direct materials multiplied by the standard quantity for direct materials. **(LO2)**

Standard fixed overhead rate: Total budgeted fixed overhead costs divided by an expression of capacity, usually normal capacity in terms of standard hours or units. **(LO2)**

Standard overhead cost: The sum of the estimates of variable and fixed overhead costs in the next accounting period. **(LO2)**

Standard variable overhead rate: Total budgeted variable overhead costs divided by an expression of capacity, such as the expected number of standard machine hours or standard direct labor hours. **(LO2)**

Total direct labor cost variance: The difference between the standard direct labor cost for good units produced and actual direct labor costs. **(LO5)**

Total direct materials cost variance: The difference between the standard cost and actual cost of direct materials. Also called *good units produced*. **(LO4)**

Total fixed overhead variance: The difference between actual fixed overhead costs and the standard fixed overhead costs that are applied to good units produced using the standard fixed overhead rate. **(LO6)**

Total overhead variance: The difference between actual overhead costs and standard overhead costs applied. **(LO6)**

Total variable overhead variance: The difference between actual variable overhead costs and the standard variable overhead costs that are applied to good units produced using the standard variable overhead rate. **(LO6)**

Variable overhead efficiency variance: The difference between the standard direct labor hours allowed for good units produced and the actual hours worked multiplied by the standard variable overhead rate per hour. **(LO6)**

Variable overhead spending variance: The difference between actual variable overhead costs and the standard variable overhead rate multiplied by the actual hours used. Also called the *variable overhead rate variance*. **(LO6)**

Variance: The difference between a standard cost and an actual cost. **(LO1)**

Variance analysis: The process of computing the differences between standard costs and actual costs and identifying the causes of those differences. **(LO3)**

REVIEW Problem

LO2, LO4, LO5, LO6   **Variance Analysis**

Leather Goods Company has a standard costing system and keeps all its cost standards up to date. The company's main product is a leather briefcase, which is made in a single cost center. The standard variable costs for one unit are as follows:

Direct materials (3 sq. meters @ $12.50 per sq. meter)	$37.50
Direct labor (1.2 hours @ $9.00 per hour)	10.80
Variable overhead (1.2 hours @ $5.00 per direct labor hour)	6.00
Standard variable cost per unit	$54.30

The company's master budget was based on its normal capacity of 15,000 direct labor hours. Its budgeted fixed overhead costs for the year were $54,000. During the year, it produced and sold 12,200 units, and it purchased and used 37,500 square meters of direct materials; the purchase cost was $12.40 per square meter. The average labor rate was $9.20 per hour, and 15,250 direct labor hours were worked. The company's actual variable overhead costs for the year were $73,200, and its fixed overhead costs were $55,000.

Required

Using the data given, compute the following using formulas or diagram form:

1. Standard hours allowed for good output
2. Standard fixed overhead rate
3. Direct materials cost variances:
   a. Direct materials price variance
   b. Direct materials quantity variance
   c. Total direct materials variance
4. Direct labor cost variances:
   a. Direct labor rate variance
   b. Direct labor efficiency variance
   c. Total direct labor variance
5. Variable overhead cost variances:
   a. Variable overhead spending variance
   b. Variable overhead efficiency variance
   c. Total variable overhead variance
6. Fixed overhead cost variances:
   a. Fixed overhead budget variance
   b. Fixed overhead volume variance
   c. Total fixed overhead variance

Answer to Review Problem

1. Standard Hours Allowed = Good Units Produced × Standard Direct Labor Hours per Unit
   = 12,200 Units × 1.2 Direct Labor Hours per Unit
   = 14,640 Hours

2. Standard Fixed Overhead Rate = $\dfrac{\text{Budgeted Fixed Overhead Cost}}{\text{Normal Capacity}}$
   = $\dfrac{\$54,000}{15,000 \text{ Direct Labor Hours}}$
   = $3.60 per Direct Labor Hour

3. Direct materials cost variances:
   a. Direct materials price variance

Price difference: Standard price	$12.50
Less actual price	12.40
Difference	$ .10 (F)

   Direct Materials Price Variance = (Standard Price − Actual Price) × Actual Quantity
   = $.10 × 37,500 Sq. Meters
   = $3,750 (F)

b. Direct materials quantity variance

Quantity difference: Standard quantity
(12,200 units × 3 sq. meters)	36,600 Sq. Meters
Less actual quantity	37,500 Sq. Meters
Difference	900 Sq. Meters (U)

Direct Materials Quantity Variance = Standard Price × (Standard
Quantity − Actual Quantity)
= $12.50 per Sq. Meter ×
900 Sq. Meters
= $11,250 (U)

c. Total direct materials cost variance:

Total Direct Materials Cost Variance = Net of Direct Materials Price
Variance and Direct Materials
Quantity Variance
= $3,750 (F) − $11,250 (U)
= $7,500 (U)

Diagram Form:

	Actual Price × Actual Quantity		Standard Price × Actual Quantity		Standard Price × Standard Quantity
Direct Materials	$12.40 × 37,500 = $465,000	**Price Variance**	$12.50 × 37,500 = $468,750	**Quantity Variance**	$12.50 × (12,200 × 3) = $457,500
		$3,750 (F)	**Total Direct Materials Cost Variance**	$11,250 (U)	
			$7,500 (U)		

4. Direct labor cost variances:
a. Direct labor rate variance:

Rate difference: Standard labor rate $9.00
Less actual labor rate   9.20
Difference $ .20 (U)

Direct Labor Rate Variance = (Standard Rate − Actual Rate) ×
Actual Hours
= $.20 × 15,250 hours
= $3,050 (U)

b. Direct labor efficiency variance:

Difference in hours: Standard hours allowed   14,640 hours*
Less actual hours   15,250 hours
Difference   610 hours (U)

Direct Labor Efficiency Variance = Standard Rate × (Standard Hours
Allowed − Actual Hours)
= $9.00 per hour × 610 hours (U)
= $5,490 (U)

*12,200 units produced × 1.2 hours per unit = 14,640 hours.

c. Total direct labor cost variance:

Total Direct Labor Cost Variance = Net of Direct Labor Rate Variance and Direct Labor Efficiency Variance

= $3,050 (U) + $5,490 (U)

= $8,540 (U)

Diagram Form:

	Actual Rate × Actual Hours		Standard Rate × Actual Hours		Standard Rate × Standard Hours
Direct Labor	$9.20 × 15,250 = $140,300	**Rate Variance**	$9.00 × 15,250 = $137,250	**Efficiency Variance**	$9.00 × (12,200 × 1.2) = $131,760
		$3,050 (U)	**Total Direct Labor Cost Variance**	$5,490 (U)	
			$8,540 (U)		

5. Variable overhead cost variances:

a. Variable overhead spending variance:

Standard variable rate × actual hours worked ($5.00 per hour × 15,250 labor hours)	$76,250
Less actual variable overhead costs incurred	73,200
Variable overhead spending variance	$ 3,050 (F)

b. Variable overhead efficiency variance:

Variable overhead applied to good units produced (14,640 hours* × $5.00 per hour)	$73,200
Less budgeted variable overhead for actual hours (15,250 hours × $5.00 per hour)	76,250
Variable overhead efficiency variance	$ 3,050 (U)

*12,200 units produced × 1.2 hours per unit = 14,640 hours.

c. Total variable overhead cost variance:

Total Variable Overhead Cost Variance = Net of Variable Overhead Spending Variance and Variable Overhead Efficiency Variance

= $3,050 (F) − $3,050 (U)

= $0

Diagram Form:

	Actual Variable Overhead Costs		Standard Rate × Actual Hours		Standard Rate × Standard Hours
Variable Overhead	$73,200	**Spending Variance**	$5.00 × 15,250 = $76,250	**Efficiency Variance**	$5.00 × (12,200 × 1.2) = $73,200
		$3,050 (F)	**Total Variable Overhead Cost Variance**	$3,050 (U)	
			$0		

6. Fixed overhead cost variances:
   a. Fixed overhead budget variance:

Budgeted fixed overhead	$54,000
Less actual fixed overhead	55,000
Fixed overhead budget variance	$ 1,000 (U)

   b. Fixed overhead volume variance:

Standard fixed overhead applied (14,640 labor hours × $3.60* per hour)	$52,704
Less total budgeted fixed overhead	54,000
Fixed overhead volume variance	$ 1,296 (U)

   c. Total fixed overhead cost variance:
   Total Fixed Overhead Cost Variance = Net of Fixed Overhead Budget Variance and Fixed Overhead Volume Variance
   = $1,000 (U) + $1,296 (U)
   = $2,296 (U)

   _____
   *From answer to Requirement 2.

Diagram Form:

	Actual Fixed Overhead Costs		Budgeted Fixed Overhead Costs		Standard Rate × Standard Hours
Fixed Overhead	$55,000	**Budget Variance**	$54,000	**Volume Variance**	$3.60 × (12,200 × 1.2) = $52,704
		$1,000 (U)	**Total Fixed Overhead Variance**	$1,296 (U)	
			$2,296 (U)		

CHAPTER ASSIGNMENTS

≡ BUILDING Your Basic Knowledge and Skills

Short Exercises

LO1 Uses of Standard Costs

SE 1. Lago Corporation is considering adopting the standard costing method. Dan Sarkis, the manager of the Ohio Division, attended a corporate meeting at which Leah Rohr, the controller, discussed the proposal. Sarkis asked, "Leah, how will this new method benefit me? How will I use it?" Prepare Rohr's response to Sarkis.

LO1 Purposes of Standard Costs

SE 2. Suppose you are a management consultant and a client asks you why companies include standard costs in their cost accounting systems. Prepare your response, listing several purposes for using standard costs.

LO2 Computing a Standard Unit Cost

SE 3. Using the information that follows, compute the standard unit cost of Product JLT.

Direct materials quantity standard	5 pounds per unit
Direct materials price standard	$10.20 per pound
Direct labor time standard	.4 hour per unit
Direct labor rate standard	$10.75 per hour
Variable overhead rate standard	$7.00 per machine hour
Fixed overhead rate standard	$11.00 per machine hour
Machine hour standard	2 hours per unit

LO3   **Analyzing Cost Variances**

SE 4. Garden Metal Works produces lawn sculptures. The company analyzes only variances that differ by more than 5 percent from the standard cost. The controller computed the following direct labor efficiency variances for March:

	Direct Labor Efficiency Variance	Standard Direct Labor Cost
Product 4	$1,240 (U)	$26,200
Product 6	3,290 (F)	41,700
Product 7	2,030 (U)	34,300
Product 9	1,620 (F)	32,560
Product 12	2,810 (U)	59,740

For each product, determine the variance as a percentage of the standard cost (round to one decimal place). Then identify the products whose variances should be analyzed and suggest possible causes for the variances.

LO3   **Preparing a Flexible Budget**

SE 5. Prepare a flexible budget for 10,000, 12,000, and 14,000 units of output, using the following information:

Variable costs	
Direct materials	$8.00 per unit
Direct labor	$2.50 per unit
Variable overhead	$6.00 per unit
Total budgeted fixed overhead	$81,200

LO4   **Direct Materials Variances**

SE 6. Using the standard costs in **SE 3** and the following actual cost and usage data, compute the direct materials price and direct materials quantity variances:

Direct materials purchased and used	55,000 pounds
Price paid for direct materials	$10.00 per pound
Number of good units produced	11,000 units

LO5   **Direct Labor Variances**

SE 7. Using the standard costs in **SE 3** and the following actual cost and usage data, compute the direct labor rate and direct labor efficiency variances:

Direct labor hours used	4,950 hours
Total cost of direct labor	$53,460
Number of good units produced	11,000 units

LO6   **Overhead Variances**

SE 8. Sutherland Products uses standard costing. The following information about overhead was generated during August:

Standard variable overhead rate	$2 per machine hour
Standard fixed overhead rate	$3 per machine hour
Actual variable overhead costs	$443,200

Actual fixed overhead costs	$698,800
Budgeted fixed overhead costs	$700,000
Standard machine hours per unit produced	12
Good units produced	18,940
Actual machine hours	228,400

Compute the variable overhead spending and efficiency variances and the fixed overhead budget and volume variances.

LO6   **Fixed Overhead Rate and Variances**

SE 9. To the Point Manufacturing Company uses the standard costing method. The company's main product is a fine-quality fountain pen that normally takes 2.5 hours to produce. Normal annual capacity is 30,000 direct labor hours, and budgeted fixed overhead costs for the year were $15,000. During the year, the company produced and sold 14,000 units. Actual fixed overhead costs were $19,000. Compute the fixed overhead rate per direct labor hour and determine the fixed overhead budget and volume variances.

LO7   **Evaluating Managerial Performance**

SE 10. Gina Rolando, the controller at WAWA Industries, gave Jason Ponds, the production manager, a report containing the following information:

	Actual Cost	Standard Cost	Variance
Direct materials	$38,200	$36,600	$1,600 (U)
Direct labor	19,450	19,000	450 (U)
Variable overhead	62,890	60,000	2,890 (U)

Rolando asked for a response. If you were Ponds, how would you respond? What additional information might you need to prepare your response?

Exercises

LO1   **Uses of Standard Costs**

E 1. Summer Diaz has just assumed the duties of controller for Market Research Company. She is concerned that the company's methods of cost planning and control do not accurately track the operations of the business. She plans to suggest to the company's president, Sydney Tyson, that the company start using standard costing for budgeting and cost control. The new method could be incorporated into the existing accounting system. The anticipated cost of adopting it and training managers is around $7,500. Prepare a memo from Summer Diaz to Sydney Tyson that defines standard costing and outlines its uses and benefits.

LO2   **Computing Standard Costs**

E 2. Normal Corporation uses standard costing and is in the process of updating its direct materials and direct labor standards for Product 20B. The following data have been accumulated:

Direct materials

In the previous period, 20,500 units were produced, and 32,800 square yards of direct materials at a cost of $122,344 were used to produce them.

Direct labor

During the previous period, 57,400 direct labor hours were worked— 34,850 hours on machine H and 22,550 hours on machine K. Machine H operators earned $9.40 per hour, and machine K operators earned $9.20

per hour last period. A new labor union contract calls for a 10 percent increase in labor rates for the coming period.

Using this information as the basis for the new standards, compute the direct materials quantity and price standards and the direct labor time and rate standards for each machine for the coming accounting period.

LO2 Computing a Standard Unit Cost

E 3. Weather Aerodynamics, Inc., makes electronically equipped weather-detecting balloons for university meteorology departments. Because of recent nationwide inflation, the company's management has ordered that standard costs be recomputed. New direct materials price standards are $600 per set for electronic components and $13.50 per square meter for heavy-duty canvas. Direct materials quantity standards include one set of electronic components and 100 square meters of heavy-duty canvas per balloon. Direct labor time standards are 26 hours per balloon for the Electronics Department and 19 hours per balloon for the Assembly Department. Direct labor rate standards are $11 per hour for the Electronics Department and $10 per hour for the Assembly Department. Standard overhead rates are $16 per direct labor hour for the standard variable overhead rate and $12 per direct labor hour for the standard fixed overhead rate. Using these production standards, compute the standard unit cost of one weather balloon.

LO3 Preparing a Flexible Budget

E 4. Keel Company's fixed overhead costs for the year are expected to be as follows: depreciation, $72,000; supervisory salaries, $92,000; property taxes and insurance, $26,000; and other fixed overhead, $14,500. Total fixed overhead is thus expected to be $204,500. Variable costs per unit are expected to be as follows: direct materials, $16.50; direct labor, $8.50; operating supplies, $2.60; indirect labor, $4.10; and other variable overhead costs, $3.20. Prepare a flexible budget for the following levels of production: 18,000 units, 20,000 units, and 22,000 units. What is the flexible budget formula for the year ended December 31?

LO4 Direct Materials Price and Quantity Variances

E 5. SITO Elevator Company manufactures small hydroelectric elevators with a maximum capacity of ten passengers. One of the direct materials used is heavy-duty carpeting for the floor of the elevator. The direct materials quantity standard for April was 8 square yards per elevator. During April, the purchasing agent purchased this carpeting at $11 per square yard; the standard price for the period was $12. Ninety elevators were completed and sold during the month; the Production Department used an average of 8.5 square yards of carpet per elevator. Calculate the company's direct materials price and quantity variances for carpeting for April.

LO4 Direct Materials Variances

E 6. Diekow Productions manufactured and sold 1,000 products at $11,000 each during the past year. At the beginning of the year, production had been set at 1,200 products; direct materials standards had been set at 100 pounds of direct materials at $2 per pound for each product produced. During the year, the company purchased and used 98,000 pounds of direct materials; the cost was $2.04 per pound. Calculate Diekow Production's direct materials price and quantity variances for the year.

LO5 **Direct Labor Variances**

E 7. At the beginning of last year, Diekow Productions set direct labor standards of 20 hours at $15 per hour for each product produced. During the year, 20,500 direct labor hours were actually worked at an average cost of $16 per hour. Using this information and the applicable information in **E 6**, calculate Diekow Production's direct labor rate and efficiency variances for the year.

LO5 **Direct Labor Rate and Efficiency Variances**

E 8. NEO Foundry, Inc., manufactures castings that other companies use in the production of machinery. For the past two years, NEO's best-selling product has been a casting for an eight-cylinder engine block. Standard direct labor hours per engine block are 1.8 hours. A labor union contract requires that the company pay all direct labor employees $14 per hour. During June, NEO produced 16,500 engine blocks. Actual direct labor hours and costs for the month were 29,900 hours and $433,550, respectively.

1. Compute the direct labor rate variance for eight-cylinder engine blocks during June.
2. Using the same data, compute the direct labor efficiency variance for eight-cylinder engine blocks during June. Check your answer, assuming that the total direct labor cost variance is $17,750 (U).

LO6 **Variable Overhead Variances**

E 9. At the beginning of last year, Diekow Productions set variable overhead standards of 10 machine hours at a rate of $10 per hour for each product produced. During the year, 10,800 machine hours were used at a cost of $10.20 per hour. Using this information and the applicable information in **E 6**, calculate Diekow Production's variable overhead spending and efficiency variances for the year.

Fixed Overhead Variances

LO6 **E 10.** At the beginning of last year, Diekow Productions set budgeted fixed overhead costs at $456,000. During the year, actual fixed overhead costs were $500,000. Using this information and the applicable information in **E 6**, calculate Diekow Production's fixed overhead budget and volume variances for the year. Assume that fixed overhead is applied based on units of product.

LO6 **Variable Overhead Variances for a Service Business**

E 11. Design Architects, LLP, billed clients for 6,000 hours of design work for the month. Actual variable overhead costs for the month were $315,000, and 6,250 hours were worked. At the beginning of the year, a variable overhead standard of $50 per design hour had been developed based on a budget of 5,000 design hours each month. Calculate Design Architects' variable overhead spending and efficiency variances for the month.

LO6 **Fixed Overhead Variances for a Service Business**

E 12. Engineering Associates billed clients for 11,000 hours of engineering work for the month. Actual fixed overhead costs for the month were $435,000, and 11,850 hours were worked. At the beginning of the year, a fixed overhead standard of $40 per engineering hour had been developed based on a budget of 10,000 engineering hours each month. Calculate Engineering Associates' fixed overhead budget and volume variances for the month.

LO6 **Overhead Variances**

E 13. Cedar Key Company produces handmade clamming buckets and sells them to distributors along the Gulf Coast of Florida. The company incurred $9,400 of actual overhead costs ($8,000 variable; $1,400 fixed) in May. Budgeted standard overhead costs for May were $4 of variable overhead costs per direct labor hour and $1,500 of fixed overhead costs. Normal capacity was set at 2,000 direct labor hours per month. In May, the company produced 10,100 clamming buckets by working 1,900 direct labor hours. The time standard is .2 direct labor hour per clamming bucket. Compute (1) the variable overhead spending and efficiency variances and (2) the fixed overhead budget and volume variances for May.

LO6 **Overhead Variances**

E 14. Suncoast Industries uses standard costing and a flexible budget for cost planning and control. Its monthly budget for overhead costs is $200,000 of fixed costs plus $5.20 per machine hour. Monthly normal capacity of 100,000 machine hours is used to compute the standard fixed overhead rate. During December, employees worked 105,000 machine hours. Only 98,500 standard machine hours were allowed for good units produced during the month. Actual overhead costs incurred during December totaled $441,000 of variable costs and $204,500 of fixed costs. Compute (1) the under- or overapplied overhead during December and (2) the variable overhead spending and efficiency variances and the fixed overhead budget and volume variances.

LO7 **Evaluating Managerial Performance**

E 15. Ron LaTulip oversees projects for ACE Construction Company. Recently, the company's controller sent him a performance report regarding the construction of the Campus Highlands Apartment Complex, a project that LaTulip supervised. Included in the report was an unfavorable direct labor efficiency variance of $1,900 for roof structures. What types of information does LaTulip need to analyze before he can respond to this report?

Problems

LO2 **Computing and Using Standard Costs**

P 1. Prefabricated houses are the specialty of Affordable Homes, Inc., of Corsicana, Texas. Although Affordable Homes produces many models, the company's best-selling model is the Welcome Home, a three-bedroom, 1,400-square-foot house with an impressive front entrance. Last year, the standard costs for the six basic direct materials used in manufacturing the entrance were as follows: wood framing materials, $2,140; deluxe front door, $480; door hardware, $260; exterior siding, $710; electrical materials, $580; and interior finishing materials, $1,520. Three types of direct labor are used to build the entrance: carpenter, 30 hours at $12 per hour; door specialist, 4 hours at $14 per hour; and electrician, 8 hours at $16 per hour. Last year, the company used an overhead rate of 40 percent of total direct materials cost.

This year, the cost of wood framing materials is expected to increase by 20 percent, and a deluxe front door will cost $496. The cost of the door hardware will increase by 10 percent, and the cost of electrical materials will increase by 20 percent. Exterior siding cost should decrease by $16 per unit. The cost of interior finishing materials is expected to remain the same. The carpenter's wages will increase by $1 per hour, and the door specialist's wages should remain the same. The electrician's wages will increase by $.50 per hour. Finally, the overhead rate will decrease to 25 percent of total direct materials cost.

Required

1. Compute the total standard cost of direct materials per entrance for last year.
2. Using your answer to item 1, compute the total standard unit cost per entrance for last year.
3. Compute the total standard unit cost per entrance for this year.

LO3 **Preparing a Flexible Budget and Evaluating Performance**

P 2. Home Products Company manufactures a complete line of kitchen glassware. The Beverage Division specializes in 12-ounce drinking glasses. Erin Fisher, the superintendent of the Beverage Division, asked the controller to prepare a report of her division's performance in April. The following report was handed to her a few days later:

Cost Category (Variable Unit Cost)	Budgeted Costs*	Actual Costs	Difference Under (Over) Budget
Direct materials ($.10)	$ 5,000	$ 4,975	$ 25
Direct labor ($.12)	6,000	5,850	150
Variable overhead			
Indirect labor ($.03)	1,500	1,290	210
Supplies ($.02)	1,000	960	40
Heat and power ($.03)	1,500	1,325	175
Other ($.05)	2,500	2,340	160
Fixed overhead			
Heat and power	3,500	3,500	—
Depreciation	4,200	4,200	—
Insurance and taxes	1,200	1,200	—
Other	1,600	1,600	—
Totals	$28,000	$27,240	$760

*Based on normal capacity of 50,000 units.

In discussing the report with the controller, Fisher stated, "Profits have been decreasing in recent months, but this report indicates that our production process is operating efficiently."

Required

1. Prepare a flexible budget for the Beverage Division using production levels of 45,000 units, 50,000 units, and 55,000 units.
2. What is the flexible budget formula?
3. Assume that the Beverage Division produced 46,560 units in April and that all fixed costs remained constant. Prepare a revised performance report similar to the one above, using actual production in units as a basis for the budget column.
4. Manager Insight: Which report is more meaningful for performance evaluation, the original one above or the revised one? Why?

LO4, LO5 **Direct Materials and Direct Labor Variances**

P 3. Winners Trophy Company produces a variety of athletic awards, most of them in the form of trophies. Its deluxe trophy stands three feet tall above the base. The company's direct materials standards for the deluxe trophy include one pound of metal and eight ounces of wood for the base. Standard prices for the year were $3.30 per pound of metal and $.45 per ounce of wood. Direct labor standards for the deluxe trophy specify .2 hour of direct labor in the Molding Department and .4 hour in the Trimming/Finishing Department. Standard direct labor rates are $10.75 per hour in the Molding Department and $12.00 per hour in the Trimming/Finishing Department.

During January, the company made 16,400 deluxe trophies. Actual production data are as follows:

Direct materials
  Metal   16,640 pounds @ $3.25 per pound
  Wood   131,400 ounces @ $.48 per ounce
Direct labor
  Molding   3,400 hours @ $10.60 per hour
  Trimming/Finishing   6,540 hours @ $12.10 per hour

Required

1. Compute the direct materials price and quantity variances for metal and wood.
2. Compute the direct labor rate and efficiency variances for the Molding and the Trimming/Finishing Departments.

LO4, LO5, LO6 Direct Materials, Direct Labor, and Overhead Variances

P 4. The Doormat Division of Clean Sweep Company produces all-vinyl mats. Each doormat calls for .4 meter of vinyl material; the material should cost $3.10 per meter. Standard direct labor hours and labor cost per doormat are .2 hour and $1.84 (.2 hour × $9.20 per hour), respectively. Currently, the division's standard variable overhead rate is $1.50 per direct labor hour, and its standard fixed overhead rate is $.80 per direct labor hour.

In August, the division manufactured and sold 60,000 doormats. During the month, it used 25,200 meters of vinyl material; the total cost of the material was $73,080. The total actual overhead costs for August were $28,200, of which $18,200 was variable. The total number of direct labor hours worked was 10,800, and the factory payroll for direct labor for the month was $95,040. Budgeted fixed overhead for August was $9,280. Normal monthly capacity for the year was set at 58,000 doormats.

Required

1. Compute for August the (a) direct materials price variance, (b) direct materials quantity variance, (c) direct labor rate variance, (d) direct labor efficiency variance, (e) variable overhead spending variance, (f) variable overhead efficiency variance, (g) fixed overhead budget variance, and (h) fixed overhead volume variance.
2. **Manager Insight:** Prepare a performance report based on your variance analysis and suggest possible causes for each variance.

LO6 Overhead Variances

P 5. Celine Corporation's accountant left for vacation before completing the monthly cost variance report. George Celine, the corporation's president, has asked you to complete the report. The following data are available to you (capacities are expressed in machine hours):

Actual machine hours   17,100
Standard machine hours allowed   17,500
Actual variable overhead   **a**

Standard variable overhead rate	$2.50
Variable overhead spending variance	$250 (F)
Variable overhead efficiency variance	**b**
Actual fixed overhead	**c**
Budgeted fixed overhead	$153,000
Fixed overhead budget variance	$1,300 (U)
Fixed overhead volume variance	$4,500 (F)
Normal capacity in machine hours	**d**
Standard fixed overhead rate	**e**
Fixed overhead applied	**f**

Required

Analyze the data and fill in the missing amounts. (**Hint:** Use the structure of Figures 5 and 6 in this chapter to guide your analysis.)

Alternate Problems

LO2 **Computing Standard Costs for Direct Materials**

P 6. TickTock, Ltd., assembles clock movements for grandfather clocks. Each movement has four components: the clock facing, the clock hands, the time movement, and the spring assembly. For the current year, the company used the following standard costs: clock facing, $15.90; clock hands, $12.70; time movement, $66.10; and spring assembly, $52.50.

Prices of materials are expected to change next year. TickTock will purchase 60 percent of the facings from Company A at $18.50 each and the other 40 percent from Company B at $18.80 each. The clock hands, which are produced for TickTock by Hardware, Inc., will cost $15.50 per set next year. TickTock will purchase 30 percent of the time movements from Company Q at $68.50 each, 20 percent from Company R at $69.50 each, and 50 percent from Company S at $71.90 each. The manufacturer that supplies TickTock with spring assemblies has announced that it will increase its prices by 20 percent.

Required

1. Determine the total standard direct materials cost per unit for next year.
2. Suppose that because TickTock has guaranteed Hardware, Inc., that it will purchase 2,500 sets of clock hands next year, the cost of a set of clock hands has been reduced by 20 percent. Find the standard direct materials cost per clock.
3. **Manager Insight:** Suppose that to avoid the increase in the cost of spring assemblies, TickTock purchased substandard ones from a different manufacturer at $50 each; 20 percent of them turned out to be unusable and could not be returned. Assuming that all other data remain the same, compute the standard direct materials unit cost. Spread the cost of the defective materials over the good units produced.

LO4, LO5 **Direct Materials and Direct Labor Variances**

P 7. Fruit Packaging Company makes plastic baskets for food wholesalers. Each basket requires .8 gram of liquid plastic and .6 gram of an additive that includes color and hardening agents. The standard prices are $.15 per gram of liquid plastic and $.09 per gram of additive. Two kinds of direct labor—molding and trimming/packing—are required to make the baskets. The direct labor time and rate standards for a batch of 100 baskets are as follows: molding, 1.0 hour per batch at an hourly rate of $12; and trimming/packing, 1.2 hours per batch at $10 per hour.

During the year, the company produced 48,000 baskets. It used 38,600 grams of liquid plastic at a total cost of $5,404 and 28,950 grams of additive at $2,895. Actual direct labor included 480 hours for molding at a total cost of $5,664 and 560 hours for trimming/packing at $5,656.

Required

1. Compute the direct materials price and quantity variances for both the liquid plastic and the additive.
2. Compute the direct labor rate and efficiency variances for the molding and trimming/packing processes.

LO4, LO5, LO6 **Computing Variances and Evaluating Performance**

P 8. Last year, Biomed Laboratories, Inc., researched and perfected a cure for the common cold. Called Cold-Gone, the product sells for $28.00 per package, each of which contains five tablets. Standard unit costs for this product were developed late last year for use this year. Per package, the standard unit costs were as follows: chemical ingredients, 6 ounces at $1.00 per ounce; packaging, $1.20; direct labor, .8 hour at $14.00 per hour; standard variable overhead, $4.00 per direct labor hour; and standard fixed overhead, $6.40 per direct labor hour. Normal capacity is 46,875 units per week.

In the first quarter of this year, demand for the new product rose well beyond the expectations of management. During those three months, the peak season for colds, the company produced and sold over 500,000 packages of Cold-Gone. During the first week in April, it produced 50,000 packages but used materials for 50,200 packages costing $60,240. It also used 305,000 ounces of chemical ingredients costing $292,800. The total cost of direct labor for the week was $579,600; direct labor hours totaled 40,250. Total variable overhead was $161,100, and total fixed overhead was $242,000. Budgeted fixed overhead for the week was $240,000.

Required

1. Compute for the first week of April (a) all direct materials price variances, (b) all direct materials quantity variances, (c) the direct labor rate variance, (d) the direct labor efficiency variance, (e) the variable overhead spending variance, (f) the variable overhead efficiency variance, (g) the fixed overhead budget variance, and (h) the fixed overhead volume variance.
2. **Manager Insight:** Prepare a performance report based on your variance analysis and suggest possible causes for each significant variance.

ENHANCING Your Knowledge, Skills, and Critical Thinking

Conceptual Understanding Cases

LO1, LO2 **Cost Standards for Service Companies: A Comparison**

C 1. Both **ChemLawn** and **United Parcel Service (UPS)** use truck drivers to deliver services to clients. ChemLawn's drivers use a hose connected to the tanks on their trucks to spray liquid fertilizers and weed killers on clients' lawns. Drivers of UPS trucks deliver packages to residences and businesses. If you were setting cost standards for ChemLawn and UPS, what standards would you set that apply to the drivers, and what cost components would you use? What measures would you use to evaluate the drivers' performance? How would cost standards for these two service companies be similar, and how would they differ? How do cost standards for service companies differ from those of manufacturing companies?

LO5, LO6 **Standard Costing in a Service Company**

C 2. Annuity Life Insurance Company (ALIC) markets several types of life insurance policies, but P20A—a permanent, 20-year life annuity policy—is its most popular. This policy sells in $10,000 increments and features variable percentages of whole life insurance and single-payment annuities, depending on the policyholder's needs and age. ALIC devotes an entire department to supporting and marketing the P20A policy. Because both the support staff and the salespersons contribute to each P20A policy, ALIC categorizes them as direct labor for purposes of variance analysis, cost control, and performance evaluation. For unit costing, each $10,000 increment is considered one unit; thus, a $90,000 policy is counted as nine units. Standard unit cost information for January is as follows:

Direct labor	
Policy support staff	
3 hours at $12.00 per hour	$ 36.00
Policy salesperson	
8.5 hours at $14.20 per hour	120.70
Operating overhead	
Variable operating overhead	
11.5 hours at $26.00 per hour	299.00
Fixed operating overhead	
11.5 hours at $18.00 per hour	207.00
Standard unit cost	$662.70

Actual costs incurred for the 265 units sold during January were as follows:

Direct labor	
Policy support staff	
848 hours at $12.50 per hour	$10,600
Policy salespersons	
2,252.5 hours at $14.00 per hour	31,535
Operating overhead	
Variable operating overhead	78,440
Fixed operating overhead	53,400

Normal monthly capacity is 260 units, and the budgeted fixed operating overhead for January was $53,820.

1. Compute the standard hours allowed in January for policy support staff and policy salespersons.
2. What should the total standard costs for January have been? What were the total actual costs that the company incurred in January? Compute the total cost variance for the month.
3. Compute the direct labor rate and efficiency variances for policy support staff and policy salespersons.
4. Compute the variable and fixed operating overhead variances for January.
5. Identify possible causes for each variance and suggest possible solutions.

LO3, LO4, LO5 **Variance Analysis**

C 3. Ying Zsoa recently became the controller of a joint venture in Hong Kong. He has been using standard costing to plan and control the company's activities. In a meeting with the budget team, which includes managers and employees from purchasing, engineering, and production, Zsoa asked the team members to share any operating problems that they had encountered during the last quarter. He explained that his staff would use this information in analyzing the causes of significant cost variances that had occurred in the quarter.

For each of the following situations, identify the direct materials and/or direct labor variance(s) that could be affected and indicate whether the variances are favorable or unfavorable:

1. The production department used highly skilled, higher-paid workers.
2. Machines were improperly adjusted.
3. Direct labor personnel worked more carefully to manufacture the product.
4. The product design engineer substituted a direct material that was less expensive and of lower quality.
5. The Purchasing Department bought higher-quality materials at a higher price.
6. A major supplier used a less-expensive mode of transportation to deliver the raw materials.
7. Work was halted for two hours because of a power disruption.

Interpreting Management Reports

LO3 Flexible Budgets and Performance Evaluation

C 4. Cassen Realtors, Inc., specializes in the sale of residential properties. It earns its revenue by charging a percentage of the sales price. Commissions for salespersons, listing agents, and listing companies are its main costs. Business has improved steadily over the last ten years. Bonnie Cassen, the managing partner of Cassen Realtors, receives a report summarizing the company's performance each year. The report for the most recent year appears below.

Cassen Realtors, Inc.
Performance Report
For the Year Ended December 31

	Budgeted*	Actual†	Difference Under (Over) Budget
Total selling fees	$2,052,000	$2,242,200	($190,200)
Variable costs			
Sales commissions	$1,102,950	$1,205,183	($102,233)
Automobile	36,000	39,560	(3,560)
Advertising	93,600	103,450	(9,850)
Home repairs	77,400	89,240	(11,840)
General overhead	656,100	716,970	(60,870)
	$1,966,050	$2,154,403	($188,353)
Fixed costs			
General overhead	60,000	62,300	(2,300)
Total costs	$2,026,050	$2,216,703	($190,635)
Operating income	$ 25,950	$ 25,497	$ 453

*Budgeted data are based on 180 units sold.
†Actual data for 200 units sold.

1. Analyze the performance report. What does it say about the company's performance? Is the performance report reliable? Explain your answer.
2. Calculate the budgeted selling fee and budgeted variable costs per home sale.
3. Prepare a performance report using a flexible budget based on the actual number of home sales.

4. Analyze the report you prepared in **3.** What does it say about the company's performance? Is the report reliable? Explain your answer.
5. What recommendations would you make to improve the company's performance next year?

Decision Analysis Using Excel

LO3, LO6 Developing a Flexible Budget and Analyzing Overhead Variances

C 5. Ezelda Marva is the controller at FH Industries. She has asked you, her new assistant, to analyze the following data related to projected and actual overhead costs for October:

	Standard Variable Costs per Machine Hour (MH)	Actual Variable Costs in October
Indirect materials and supplies	$1.10	$ 2,380
Indirect machine setup labor	2.50	5,090
Materials handling	1.40	3,950
Maintenance and repair	1.50	2,980
Utilities	.80	1,490
Miscellaneous	.10	200
Totals	$7.40	$16,090

	Budgeted Fixed Overhead	Actual Fixed Overhead in October
Supervisory salaries	$ 3,630	$ 3,630
Machine depreciation	8,360	8,580
Other	1,210	1,220
Totals	$13,200	$13,430

For October, the number of good units produced was used to compute the 2,100 standard machine hours allowed.

1. Prepare a monthly flexible budget for operating activity at 2,000 machine hours, 2,200 machine hours, and 2,500 machine hours.
2. Develop a flexible budget formula.
3. The company's normal operating capacity is 2,200 machine hours per month. Compute the fixed overhead rate at this level of activity. Then break the rate down into rates for each element of fixed overhead.
4. Prepare a detailed comparative cost analysis for October. Include all variable and fixed overhead costs. Format your analysis by using columns for the following five elements: cost category, cost per machine hour, costs applied, actual costs incurred, and variance.
5. Develop an overhead variance analysis for October that identifies the variable overhead spending and efficiency variances and the fixed overhead budget and volume variances.
6. Prepare an analysis of the variances. Could a manager control some of the fixed costs? Defend your answer.

Ethical Dilemma Case

LO1, LO2 An Ethical Question Involving Standard Costs

C 6. Taylor Industries, Inc., develops standard costs for all its direct materials, direct labor, and overhead costs. It uses these costs to price products, cost inventories, and evaluate the performance of purchasing and production managers. It updates the standard costs whenever costs, prices, or rates change by 3 percent or more. It also reviews and updates all standard costs each December; this practice provides current standards that are appropriate for use in valuing year-end inventories on the company's financial statements.

Jody Elgar is in charge of standard costing at Taylor Industries. On November 30, she received a memo from the chief financial officer informing her that Taylor Industries was considering purchasing another company and that she and her staff were to postpone adjusting standard costs until late February; they were instead to concentrate on analyzing the proposed purchase.

In the third week of November, prices on more than 20 of Taylor Industries' direct materials had been reduced by 10 percent or more, and a new labor union contract had reduced several categories of labor rates. A revision of standard costs in December would have resulted in lower valuations of inventories, higher cost of goods sold because of inventory write-downs, and lower net income for the year. Elgar believed that the company was facing an operating loss and that the assignment to evaluate the proposed purchase was designed primarily to keep her staff from revising and lowering standard costs. She questioned the chief financial officer about the assignment and reiterated the need for updating the standard costs, but she was again told to ignore the update and concentrate on the proposed purchase. Elgar and her staff were relieved of the evaluation assignment in early February. The purchase never materialized.

Assess Jody Elgar's actions in this situation. Did she follow all ethical paths to solving the problem? What are the consequences of failing to adjust the standard costs?

Internet Case

LO1   **Resources for Developing Cost Standards**

C 7. Suppose you have recently taken a job at a company that manufactures parts for automobiles. You have been assigned the task of developing manufacturing cost standards. You want to gather as much background information as you can about these standards. Using a standard search engine, such as Google, search the Internet for websites that provide information about cost standards, manufacturing, and automobile manufacturers. Visit the sites that look most interesting, and list the five sites you think are most useful. Bring your list to class and compare your findings with those of your classmates.

Group Activity Case

LO2, LO3   **Standard Costs and Variance Analysis**

C 8. **Domino's Pizza** is a major purveyor of home-delivered pizzas. Although customers can pick up their orders at the shops where Domino's makes its pizzas, employees deliver most orders to customers' homes, and they use their own cars to do it.

Specify what standard costing for a Domino's pizza shop would entail. Where would you obtain the information for determining the cost standards? In what ways would the standards help in managing a pizza shop? If necessary to gain a better understanding of the operation, visit a pizzeria. (It does not have to be a Domino's.)

Your instructor will divide the class into groups to discuss the case. Summarize your group's discussion, and select one person from your group to report the group's findings to the class.

Business Communication Cases

LO3   Using Variance Analysis to Control Costs

C 9. Holding down operating costs is an ongoing challenge for managers. The lower the costs that a company incurs, the higher its profit will be. But two factors can make a target profit difficult to achieve. First, human error and unexpected machine breakdowns may cause dozens of operating inefficiencies, and each inefficiency will cause costs to rise. Second, a company may control its costs so strictly that it will use cheaper materials or labor, which may cause a decline in the quality of its product or service and in its sales. To control costs and still produce high-quality goods or services, managers must continually assess operating activities by analyzing both financial and nonfinancial data.

Write a one-page paper on how variance analysis helps managers control costs. Focus on both the financial and the nonfinancial data used in standard costing.

LO3, LO5, LO6   Preparing Performance Reports

C 10. Troy Corrente, the president of Forest Valley Spa, is concerned about the spa's operating performance during March. He budgeted his costs carefully so that he could reduce the annual membership fees. He now needs to evaluate those costs to make sure that the spa's profits are at the level he expected.

He has asked you, the spa's controller, to prepare a performance report on labor and overhead costs for March. He also wants you to analyze the report and suggest possible causes for any problems that you find. He wants to attend to any problems quickly, so he has asked you to submit your report as soon as possible. The following information for the month is available to you:

	Budgeted Costs	Actual Costs
Variable costs		
Operating labor	$10,880	$12,150
Utilities	2,880	3,360
Repairs and maintenance	5,760	7,140
Fixed overhead costs		
Depreciation, equipment	2,600	2,680
Rent	3,280	3,280
Other	1,704	1,860
Totals	$27,104	$30,470

Corrente's budget allows for eight employees to work 160 hours each per month. During March, nine employees worked an average of 150 hours each.

1. Answer the following questions:
   a. Why are you preparing this performance report?
   b. Who will use the report?
   c. What information do you need to develop the report? How will you obtain that information?
   d. When are the performance report and the analysis needed?
2. With the limited information available to you, compute the labor rate variance, the labor efficiency variance, and the variable and fixed overhead variances.
3. Prepare a performance report for the spa for March. Analyze the report and suggest causes for any problems that you find.

Analysis for Decision Making

Managers analyze both financial and nonfinancial quantitative information to determine the effect of past and potential business actions on their organization's resources and profits. Although many short-term business problems are unique and cannot be solved by following strict rules, managers frequently take predictable actions when making short-run decisions. When considering long-term capital investment decisions, such as when and how much to spend on facilities and other expensive long-term projects, managers are likely to use capital investment analysis to ensure that their choices make the maximum contribution to future profits and that they use resources ethically. This chapter explains how managers make short-run decisions using incremental analysis and long-term capital investment decisions using the net present value method and other methods of capital investment analysis.

LEARNING OBJECTIVES

LO1 Explain how managers make short-run decisions.

LO2 Define *incremental analysis,* and describe how it applies to short-run decision analysis.

LO3 Apply incremental analysis to outsourcing decisions, special order decisions, segment profitability decisions, sales mix decisions involving constrained resources, and sell or process-further decisions.

LO4 Identify the types of projected costs and revenues used to evaluate alternatives for capital investment.

LO5 Apply the concept of the time value of money.

LO6 Use the net present value method to analyze capital investment proposals.

LO7 Use the payback period method and the accounting rate-of-return method to analyze capital investment proposals.

- How do managers at Bank of America decide on new ways to increase business and protect customers' interests?

- How can incremental and capital investment analyses help managers at Bank of America take advantage of the business opportunities that online banking offers?

Bank of America has customers in over 150 countries and more online customers than any other bank in the world. It has received numerous awards for online customer satisfaction and for its initiatives in preventing online fraud and identity theft. In 2006, it had more than 14.6 million online customers (34 percent of all online banking customers) and 7.2 million online bill payers (more than 58 percent of online bill payers in the United States).

Managers at Bank of America believe the trend to online commerce is good for business. As customers gain confidence in dealing with their finances online, the bank's managers plan to offer more products and services, such as portfolio management, online account statements and cancelled check images, and the ability to open a new account or apply for a loan over the Internet. In their quest to find safe and innovative ways to meet the needs of commercial, consumer, global corporate, and investment banking customers, managers at Bank of America make short-run and long-run decisions that affect the bank's profits, resources, and opportunities to increase online banking.[1]

Short-Run Decision Analysis

LO1 Explain how managers make short-run decisions.

Readers of financial reports are interested in knowing what happened to produce the results presented in these reports. The historical information that the reports contain helps answer that question. For planning and control purposes, however, managers want to know why things happen and how they might affect their organization. They use historical financial and non-financial quantitative information to analyze the impact of past and potential business actions on their organization's resources and profits. Such information should be relevant, timely, and presented in a format that is easy to use in decision making.

Short-run decision analysis is the systematic examination of any management decision whose effects will be felt over the course of the next year. Although many business problems are unique and cannot be solved by following strict rules, managers frequently take five predictable actions when deciding what to do. Four of these actions take place during the planning stage of the management process; the fifth action occurs during the evaluating stage.

Planning

As illustrated in Figure 1, managers who use short-run decision analysis typically take the following four planning actions:

1. Discover a problem or need.

2. Identify all reasonable courses of action that can solve the problem or meet the need.

3. Prepare a thorough analysis of each possible solution and identify its total costs, savings, other financial effects, and any qualitative factors.

4. Select the best course of action.

As a rule, managers of companies like **Bank of America** make decisions that support the company's strategic plan. For example, the managers of a bank may have to make a decision about keeping or eliminating one of the bank's branch locations. Both quantitative and qualitative factors will influence the decision. The quantitative information includes the costs of operating the branch locations and the fee revenues that the branch generates. Management may also want to know the number of customers serviced each year, the types of services offered, and the number and dollar amount of the branch's accounts.

As the managers perform decision analyses, the following qualitative factors will influence their decision to keep or eliminate the branch:

▶ Competition (Do our competitors have a branch office located here?)

▶ Economic conditions (Is the community growing?)

▶ Social issues (Will our offering of this branch location benefit the community we serve?)

▶ Product or service quality (Can we attract more business because of the service quality of this branch?)

▶ Timeliness (Does the branch promote customer service?)

■ **FIGURE 1**
The Management Process: To-Do's for Managers

To-Do's for Managers

- Plan
  - Discover a problem or need
  - Identify all reasonable courses of action that can solve the problem or meet the need
  - Prepare a thorough analysis of each possible solution, identifying its total costs, savings, other financial effects, and any qualitative effects (e.g., competition, economic conditions, social issues, product or service quality, timeliness)
  - Select the best course of action

- Perform
  - Make decisions that affect operations in the current operating period
  - Take advantage of opportunities that will improve organization's profitability and liquidity in the short run (e.g., accept a special order, examine the profitability of a segment, select the appropriate product mix given a resource constraint, contract with outside suppliers of goods and services, sell a product as is or process it further)

- Evaluate
  - Examine how each decision was carried out and how it affected the organization
  - Identify and prescribe corrective action

- Communicate
  - Prepare reports related to short-run decisions throughout the year

Managers must identify and assess the importance of all such qualitative and quantitative factors when they plan for short-run decisions.

Performing

Managers must adapt to changing environments and take advantage of opportunities that will improve their organization's profitability and liquidity in the short run. In the course of a year, managers may decide to accept a special order, examine the profitability of a segment, select the appropriate product mix given a resource constraint, contract with outside suppliers of goods and services, or sell a product as is or process it further. We describe all of these decisions in detail later in the chapter. Each decision affects operations in the current operating period.

For example, the bank's management might eliminate a branch if the costs of the branch exceed the revenues generated by it. However, management may choose to keep the branch because the community expects the organization to provide this service.

Evaluating

When managers evaluate performance, they take the fifth predictable action associated with short-run decision analysis—that is, they evaluate each decision to determine whether it produced the forecasted results. They examine how each decision was carried out and how it affected the organization. If results fell short, the managers identify and prescribe corrective action. This resulting post-decision audit supplies feedback about the results of the short-run decision. If the solution is not completely satisfactory or if the problem remains, the management process begins again.

For example, if the bank decided to keep the branch location, the managers would evaluate the results of their decision in many ways. They would probably consider how successful the branch has been, how many people have benefited from the branch, and how well the branch fits in with the other kinds of services the bank offers. They would be interested in knowing how much operating income the branch has produced and in what other ways the branch has benefited the bank and the people the bank serves. Depending on what they discover during their evaluation, they might consider ways of improving the branch, or they might decide to close the branch after all.

Communicating

Managers communicate with others regarding short-run decisions throughout the year. They prepare reports focusing on those decisions. They develop budgets that show the estimated costs and revenues related to alternative courses of action. They compile analyses of data that support their decisions. And they issue reports that measure the effect their decisions had on the organization, including its operating income. When deciding whether to continue the branch location, the bank managers would develop budgets showing the costs and revenues they expect the branch to generate. They would also prepare written analyses of the expected costs and revenues and of the qualitative factors mentioned earlier. If the managers decided to continue the branch location, they would evaluate its success by comparing actual financial and nonfinancial results to the results predicted in the budget and initial analyses. They would create reports showing how much operating income the branch has produced and how else the branch has benefited the bank and the people whom the bank serves.

S T O P • R E V I E W • A P P L Y

1-1. List some common types of short-run decisions.

1-2. Are qualitative factors important in short-run decision making?

Suggested answers to all Stop, Review, and Apply questions are available at http://college.hmco.com/accounting/needles/poa/10e/student_home.html.

Incremental Analysis for Short-Run Decisions

LO2 Define *incremental analysis,* and describe how it applies to short-run decision analysis.

Once managers have determined that a problem or need is worthy of consideration and they have identified alternative courses of action, they must evaluate the effect that each alternative will have on their organization. The method of comparing alternatives by focusing on the differences in their projected revenues and costs is called **incremental analysis**. Incremental analysis is also called *differential analysis* if it ignores revenues or costs that stay the same or do not differ among the alternatives.

Irrelevant Costs and Revenues

A cost that changes between alternatives is known as a **differential cost** (also referred to as an *incremental cost*). For example, assume that Home State Bank managers are deciding which of two ATM machines—C or W—to buy. The ATMs have the same purchase price, but they have different revenue and cost characteristics. The company currently owns ATM B, which it bought three years ago for $15,000 and which has accumulated depreciation of $9,000 and a book value of $6,000. ATM B is now obsolete as a result of advances in technology and cannot be sold or traded in.

The manager has prepared the following comparison of the annual revenue and operating cost estimates for the two new machines:

	ATM C	ATM W
Increase in revenue	$16,200	$19,800
Increase in annual operating costs		
Direct materials	4,800	4,800
Direct labor	2,200	4,100
Variable overhead	2,100	3,050
Fixed overhead (depreciation included)	5,000	5,000

The first step in the incremental analysis is to eliminate any irrelevant revenues and costs. Irrelevant revenues are those that will not differ between the alternatives. Irrelevant costs include sunk costs and costs that will not differ between the alternatives. A **sunk cost** is a cost that was incurred because of a previous decision and cannot be recovered through the current decision. An example of a sunk cost is the book value of ATM B. A manager might be tempted to say that the ATM should not be junked because the company still

FOCUS ON BUSINESS PRACTICE

How Much Does It Cost to Process a Check?

The banking industry has found that it has options for processing checks. It can outsource the processing of paper checks, use the quasi-paperless system of ATMs, or process transactions over the Internet. Bank managers have concluded that online banking substantially reduces the cost of processing transactions. According to a study conducted by an international consulting firm, the cost of processing a transaction is 1 cent if completed over the Internet, 27 cents using an ATM, and $1.07 if processed by a teller.[2]

EXHIBIT 1 ▶

Incremental Analysis			

Home State Bank
Incremental Analysis

	ATM C	ATM W	Difference in Favor of ATM W
Increase in revenue	$16,200	$19,800	$3,600
Increase in operating costs that differ between alternatives			
Direct labor	$ 2,200	$ 4,100	($1,900)
Variable overhead	2,100	3,050	(950)
Total relevant operating costs	$ 4,300	$ 7,150	($2,850)
Resulting change in operating income	$11,900	$12,650	$ 750

has $6,000 invested in it. However, the manager would be incorrect because the book value of the old ATM represents money that was spent in the past and so does not affect the decision about whether to replace the old ATM with a new one. The old ATM would be of interest only if it could be sold or traded in, and the amount received for it would be different, depending on which new ATM was chosen. In that case, the amount of the sale or trade-in value would be relevant to the decision because it would affect the future cash flows of the alternatives.

Another look at the financial data for ATMs C and W reveals two other irrelevant costs—the costs of direct materials and fixed overhead (depreciation included). These costs can also be eliminated from the analysis because they are the same under both alternatives.

Once the irrelevant revenues and costs have been identified, the incremental analysis may be prepared using only the differential revenues and costs that will change between the alternative ATMs, as shown in Exhibit 1. The analysis shows that ATM W would produce $750 more in operating income than ATM C. Because the costs of buying the two ATMs are the same, this report would favor the purchase of ATM W.

Opportunity Costs

Because incremental analysis focuses on only the quantitative differences among the alternatives, it simplifies management's evaluation of a decision and reduces the time needed to choose the best course of action. However, incremental analysis is only one input to the final decision. Management needs to consider other issues. For instance, the manufacturer of ATM C might have a reputation for better quality or service than the manufacturer of ATM W. **Opportunity costs** are the benefits that are forfeited or lost when one alternative is chosen over another.

Consider a plant nursery that has been in business for many years at the intersection of two highways. Suburbs have grown up around the nursery, and a bank has offered the nursery owner a high price for the land. The interest that could be earned from investing the proceeds of the land sale is an opportunity cost for the nursery owner. It is revenue that the nursery owner has chosen to forgo to continue operating the nursery in that location.

Opportunity costs often come into play when a company is operating at or near capacity and must choose what products or services to offer. For example,

> *Study Note*
>
> Opportunity costs arise when the choice of one course of action eliminates the possibility of another course of action.

assume that The Debit Card Company, which currently services 20,000 cards, has the option of offering 15,000 premium debit cards, a higher-priced product, but it cannot do both. The amount of income from the 20,000 debit cards is an opportunity cost of the premium debit cards.

S T O P • R E V I E W • A P P L Y

2-1. What is incremental analysis? What types of decision analyses depend on the incremental approach?

2-2. What is an opportunity cost? When might opportunity costs arise?

Application of Incremental Analysis to Short-Run Decisions

LO3　Apply incremental analysis to outsourcing decisions, special order decisions, segment profitability decisions, sales mix decisions involving constrained resources, and sell or process-further decisions.

In the course of day-to-day operations, managers are called upon to make many decisions that will have an immediate or short-run effect on current or near-term profitability. In this section, we show how incremental analysis can be applied to the following common situations: (1) outsourcing decisions, (2) special order decisions, (3) segment profitability decisions, (4) sales mix decisions involving constrained resources, and (5) sell or process-further decisions.

Incremental Analysis for Outsourcing Decisions

Outsourcing is the use of suppliers outside the organization to perform services or produce goods that could be performed or produced internally. **Make-or-buy decisions**, which are decisions about whether to make a part internally or buy it from an external supplier, may lead to outsourcing. Or a company may decide to outsource entire operating activities, such as warehousing and distribution, that it traditionally performed in-house.

To improve operating income and compete effectively in global markets, many companies are focusing their resources on their core competencies—the activities they perform best. One way to obtain the financial, physical, human, and technological resources needed to emphasize those competencies is to outsource expensive, nonvalue-adding activities. Strong candidates for outsourcing include payroll processing, training, managing fleets of vehicles, sales and marketing, custodial services, and information management. Many such areas involve either relatively low skill levels (such as payroll processing or custodial services) or highly specialized knowledge (such as information management) that could be better acquired from experts outside the company.

Outsourcing production or operating activities can reduce a company's investment in physical assets and human resources, which can improve cash flow. It can also help a company reduce operating costs and improve operating income. Many companies like **Bank of America** and **Amazon.com** benefit from outsourcing to increase their online capabilities. Companies such as Amazon.com can provide additional value-adding services, such as online reviews by customers, personalized recommendations, and discussions and

To focus resources on their core competencies, many companies are outsourcing activities that they used to perform internally. Commonly outsourced activities include payroll processing, training, sales and marketing, and information management. In this photo, an employee at a call center in Bangalore, India, provides service support to international customers. India is the leader of emerging markets to which developed economies are outsourcing high-tech jobs.

⌐◯ *Study Note*

When performing an incremental analysis for an outsourcing decision, do not incorporate irrelevant information, such as depreciation and other fixed costs. Include only costs that change between the alternatives.

interviews about current products. Banks are also outsourcing to increase their online capabilities, especially in the areas of financial management software and analysis.

In manufacturing companies, a common decision facing managers is whether to make or to buy some or all of the parts used in product assembly. The goal is to select the more profitable choice by identifying the costs of each alternative and their effects on revenues and existing costs. Managers need the following information for this analysis:

Information About Making	*Information About Outsourcing*
Need for additional machinery	Purchase price of item
Variable costs of making the item	Rent or net cash flow to be generated from vacated space in the factory
Incremental fixed costs	Salvage value of unused machinery

The case of Box Company illustrates an outsourcing decision. For the past five years, the firm has purchased packing cartons from an outside supplier at a cost of $1.25 per carton. The supplier has just informed Box Company that it is raising the price 20 percent, to $1.50 per carton, effective immediately. Box Company has idle machinery that could be adjusted to produce the cartons. Annual production and usage would be 20,000 cartons. The company estimates the cost of direct materials at $.84 per carton. Workers, who will be paid $8.00 per hour, can process 20 cartons per hour ($.40 per carton). The cost of variable overhead will be $4 per direct labor hour, and 1,000 direct labor hours will be required. Fixed overhead includes $4,000 of depreciation per year and $6,000 of other fixed costs. The company has space and machinery to produce the cartons; the machines are currently idle and will continue to be idle if the part is purchased. Should Box Company continue to outsource the cartons?

Exhibit 2 presents an incremental analysis of the two alternatives. All relevant costs are listed. Because the machinery has already been purchased and neither the machinery nor the required factory space has any other use, the depreciation costs and other fixed overhead costs are the same for both alternatives; therefore, they are not relevant to the decision. The cost of making the needed cartons is $28,800. The cost of buying 20,000 cartons at the increased

EXHIBIT 2 ▶

Incremental Analysis: Outsourcing Decision

**Box Company
Outsourcing Decision
Incremental Analysis**

	Make	Outsource	Difference in Favor of Make
Direct materials (20,000 × $.84)	$16,800		($16,800)
Direct labor (20,000 × $.40)	8,000		(8,000)
Variable overhead (1,000 hours × $4)	4,000		(4,000)
To purchase completed cartons (20,000 × $1.50)		$30,000	30,000
Totals	$28,800	$30,000	$ 1,200

purchase price will be $30,000. Since the company would save $1,200 by making the cartons, management will decide to make the cartons.

Incremental Analysis for Special Order Decisions

Study Note

Special order decisions assume that excess capacity exists to accept the order and that the order, if accepted, will not have an impact on regular sales orders.

Managers are often faced with **special order decisions**, which are decisions about whether to accept or reject special orders at prices below the normal market prices. Special orders usually involve large numbers of similar products that are sold in bulk. Before a firm accepts a special product order, it must be sure that excess capacity exists to complete the order and that the order will not reduce unit sales from its full-priced regular product line.

The objective of a special order decision is to determine whether a special order should be accepted. A special order should be accepted only if it maximizes operating income, supports the organization's strategic plan and tactical objectives, and covers the relevant costs of the special order. In many situations, sales commission expenses are excluded from a special order decision analysis because the customer approached the company directly. In addition, the fixed costs of existing facilities usually do not change if a company accepts a special order, and therefore they are usually irrelevant to the decision. If additional fixed costs must be incurred to fill the special order, they would be relevant to the decision. Examples of relevant fixed costs are the purchase of additional machinery, an increase in supervisory help, and an increase in insurance premiums required by a specific order.

One approach to a special order decision is to compare the special order price to the relevant costs to produce, package, and ship the order. The relevant costs include the variable costs, variable selling costs, if any, and other costs directly associated with the special order (for example, freight, insurance, packaging, and labeling the product). Another approach is to prepare a special order bid price by calculating a minimum selling price for the special order. The bid price equals the relevant costs plus an estimated profit.

For example, suppose Home State Bank has been approved to provide and service four ATMs at a special event. The event sponsors want the fee reduced to $.50 per ATM transaction. At past special events, ATM use has averaged 2,000 transactions per machine. Home State Bank has located four idle ATMs and determined the following additional information:

ATM *Cost Data for Annual Use of One Machine (400,000 Transactions)*

Direct materials	$ .10
Direct labor	.05
Variable overhead	.20
Fixed overhead ($100,000 ÷ 400,000)	.25
Advertising ($60,000 ÷ 400,000)	.15
Other fixed selling and administrative expenses ($120,000 ÷ 400,000)	.30
Cost per transaction	$1.05
Regular fee per transaction	$1.25

Should Home State Bank accept the special event offer?

Exhibit 3 contains an incremental analysis in the contribution margin reporting format. The report shows the contribution margin for Home State Bank operations both with and without the special order. Fixed costs are not included because the only costs affected by the order are direct materials, direct labor, and variable overhead. The net result of accepting the special order is a $1,200 increase in contribution margin (and, correspondingly, in operating income). The analysis in Exhibit 3 shows that Home State should accept the special order. The $1,200 increase is verified by the following incremental analysis:

Special order sales (2,000 transactions × 4) × $.50		$4,000
Less variable costs		
Direct materials (8,000 transactions × $.10)	$ 800	
Direct labor (8,000 transactions × $.05)	400	
Variable overhead (8,000 transactions × $.20)	1,600	
Total variable costs		2,800
Special order contribution margin		$1,200

EXHIBIT 3 ▶

Incremental Analysis: Special Order Decision

Home State Bank
Special Order Decision
Incremental Analysis

	Without Order	With Order	Difference in Favor of Accepting Order
Sales	$2,400,000	$2,404,000	$4,000
Less variable costs			
Direct materials	$ 160,000	$ 160,800	($ 800)
Direct labor	80,000	80,400	(400)
Variable overhead	320,000	321,600	(1,600)
Total variable costs	$ 560,000	$ 562,800	($2,800)
Contribution margin	$1,840,000	$1,841,200	$1,200

Now let us assume that the event sponsor asks Home State what the minimum special order price is. If the incremental costs for the special order are $2,800, the relevant cost per transaction is $.35 ($2,800 ÷ 8,000). The special order price should cover this cost and generate a profit. If Home State would like to earn $800 from the special order, the special order price should be $.45 ($.35 cost per transaction plus $.10 profit per transaction [$800 ÷ 8,000 transactions]).

Of course, the decision that Home State management makes is influenced by qualitative factors. Qualitative factors that might influence the decision are (1) the impact of the special order on regular customers, (2) the potential of the special order to lead into new sales areas, and (3) the customer's ability to maintain an ongoing relationship that includes good ordering and paying practices.

Incremental Analysis for Segment Profitability Decisions

Another type of operating decision that management must face is whether to keep or to drop unprofitable segments, such as product lines, services, sales territories, divisions, departments, stores, or outlets. Management must select the alternative that maximizes operating income, based on the organization's strategic plan and tactical objectives, the relevant revenues and costs, and qualitative factors. The objective of this analysis is to identify the segments that have a negative segment margin so that managers can drop them or take corrective action.

A **segment margin** is a segment's sales revenue minus its direct costs (direct variable costs and direct fixed costs traceable to the segment). Such costs are assumed to be **avoidable costs**. An avoidable cost could be eliminated if management were to drop the segment. If a segment has a positive segment margin—that is, if the segment's revenue is greater than its direct costs—management should keep the segment. The segment is able to cover its own direct costs and contribute a portion of its revenue to cover common costs and add to operating income. If a segment has a negative segment margin—that is, the segment's revenue is less than its direct costs—management should eliminate the segment. However, certain common costs will be incurred regardless of the decision. Those are unavoidable costs, and the remaining segments must have sufficient contribution margin to cover their own direct costs and the common costs.

An analysis of segment profitability includes the preparation of a segmented income statement using variable costing to identify variable and fixed

FOCUS ON BUSINESS PRACTICE
To Drop or Not to Drop a Segment?

When Steve Bennett took over as president and CEO of Intuit Corporation in January 2000, he knew the company should have been doing much better than was indicated by its $1 billion in annual revenues from such popular software products as Quicken, QuickBooks, and Turbo Tax. Building on the reliable demand for Intuit's tax and accounting software, Bennett guided the company in making acquisitions and in building one of the industry's leading online subscription services. At the same time, Bennett began examining parts of Intuit that either weren't producing an adequate return or did not fit well with Intuit's core competencies. Since Bennett's arrival, Intuit has sold its mortgage loan division and eliminated its online insurance business.[3]

EXHIBIT 4 ▶ Segmented Income Statement

Home State Bank
Segmented Income Statement
For the Year Ended December 31, 20xx

	Bank Operations	Safe Deposit	Total Company
Sales	$135,000	$15,000	$150,000
Less variable costs	52,500	7,500	60,000
Contribution margin	$ 82,500	$ 7,500	$ 90,000
Less direct fixed costs	55,500	16,500	72,000
Segment margin	$ 27,000	($ 9,000)	$ 18,000
Less common fixed costs			12,000
Operating income			$ 6,000

costs. The fixed costs that are traceable to the segments are called direct fixed costs. The remaining fixed costs are common costs and are not assigned to segments.

Assume that management at Home State Bank wants to determine if the bank should eliminate its Safe Deposit Division. The managers prepare a segmented income statement, separating variable and fixed costs to calculate the contribution margin. They separate the total fixed costs of $84,000 further by directly tracing $55,500 to Bank Operations and $16,500 to Safe Deposit. The remaining $12,000 are considered common fixed costs. The segmented income statement in Exhibit 4 shows the segment margins for Bank Operations and Safe Deposit and the operating income for the total company.

The analysis of Situation 1 in Exhibit 5 shows that dropping the Safe Deposit Division will increase operating income by $9,000. Unless the bank can increase Safe Deposit's segment margin by increasing sales revenue or by reducing direct costs, management should drop the segment. The incremental approach to analyzing this decision isolates the segment and focuses on its segment margin, as shown in the last column of the exhibit.

The decision to drop a segment also requires a careful review of the other segments to see if they will be affected. Let's extend the illustration by assuming that Bank Operation's sales volume and variable costs will decrease 20 percent if management eliminates the Safe Deposit Division. The reduction in sales volume stems from the loss of customers who purchase products from both divisions. The analysis of Situation 2 in Exhibit 5 shows that dropping Safe Deposit would reduce both the segment margin and the bank's operating income by $7,500. In this situation, Home State Bank would want to keep Safe Deposit.

FOCUS ON BUSINESS PRACTICE

Why Banks Prefer Ebanking

After performing segment analysis of online banking and face-to-face banking, bank managers worldwide are encouraging customers to do their banking over the Internet. Banks have found that linking worldwide Internet access with customer relationship management (CRM), customer-friendly financial software, and online bill payment in a secure banking environment will reduce costs, increase service and product availability, and boost earnings.[4]

EXHIBIT 5 ▶ | Incremental Analysis: Segment Profitability Decision

Home State Bank
Segment Profitability Decision
Incremental Analysis—Situation 1

	Keep Safe Deposit	Drop Safe Deposit	Difference in Favor of Dropping Safe Deposit
Sales	$150,000	$135,000	($15,000)
Less variable costs	60,000	52,500	7,500
Contribution margin	$ 90,000	$ 82,500	($ 7,500)
Less direct fixed costs	72,000	55,500	16,500
Segment margin	$ 18,000	$ 27,000	$ 9,000
Less common fixed costs	12,000	12,000	0
Operating income	$ 6,000	$ 15,000	$ 9,000

Home State Bank
Segment Profitability Decision
Incremental Analysis—Situation 2

	Keep Safe Deposit	Drop Safe Deposit	Difference in Favor of Not Dropping Safe Deposit
Sales	$150,000	$108,000	($42,000)
Less variable costs	60,000	42,000	18,000
Contribution margin	$ 90,000	$ 66,000	($24,000)
Less direct fixed costs	72,000	55,500	16,500
Segment margin	$ 18,000	$ 10,500	($ 7,500)
Less common fixed costs	12,000	12,000	0
Operating income	$ 6,000	($ 1,500)	($ 7,500)

Incremental Analysis for Sales Mix Decisions

A company may not be able to provide the full variety of products or services that customers demand in a given period because of limits on resources like machine time or labor. Resource constraints can also be associated with other activities, such as inspection and equipment setup. The question is, Which products or services contribute the most to company profitability in relation to the amount of capital assets or other constrained resources needed to offer those items? To satisfy customers' demands and maximize operating income, management will choose to offer the most profitable product or service first. To identify such products or services, the managers calculate the contribution margin per constrained resource (such as labor hours or machine hours) for each product or service.

The objective of a **sales mix decision** is to select the alternative that maximizes the contribution margin per constrained resource based on the organization's strategic plan and tactical objectives, the relevant revenues and costs, and qualitative factors. The decision analysis, which uses incremental analysis to identify the relevant costs and revenues, consists of two steps. First, calculate the contribution margin per unit for each product or service affected by the

Study Note

When resources such as direct materials, direct labor, or machine time are scarce, the goal is to maximize the contribution margin per unit of scarce resource.

constrained resource. The contribution margin per unit equals the selling price per unit less the variable costs per unit. Second, calculate the contribution margin per unit of the constrained resource. The contribution margin per unit of the constrained resource equals the contribution margin per unit divided by the quantity of the constrained resource required per unit.

Assume that Home State Bank offers three types of loans: commercial loans, auto loans and home loans. The product line data are as follows:

	Commercial Loans	Auto Loans	Home Loans
Current loan application demand	20,000	30,000	18,000
Processing hours per loan application	2	1	2.5
Loan origination fee	$24.00	$18.00	$32.00
Variable processing costs	$12.50	$10.00	$18.75
Variable selling costs	$ 6.50	$ 5.00	$ 6.25

The current loan application capacity is 100,000 processing hours.

EXHIBIT 6 ▶

Incremental Analysis: Sales Mix Decision Involving Constrained Resources

Home State Bank
Sales Mix Decision: Ranking the Order of Loans
Incremental Analysis

	Commercial Loans	Auto Loans	Home Loans
Loan origination fee per loan	$24.00	$18.00	$32.00
Less variable costs			
Processing	$12.50	$10.00	$18.75
Selling	6.50	5.00	6.25
Total variable costs	$19.00	$15.00	$25.00
Contribution margin per loan (A)	$ 5.00	$ 3.00	$ 7.00
Processing hours per loan (B)	÷ 2	÷ 1	÷ 2.5
Contribution margin per processing hour (A ÷ B)	$ 2.50	$ 3.00	$ 2.80

Home State Bank
Sales Mix Decision: Number of Units to Sell
Incremental Analysis

	Processing Hours
Total processing hours available	100,000
Less processing hours to sell auto loans (30,000 loans × 1 processing hour)	30,000
Balance of processing hours available	70,000
Less processing hours to sell home loans (18,000 loans × 2.5 processing hours per loan)	45,000
Balance of processing hours available	25,000
Less processing hours to sell commercial loans (12,500 loans × 2 processing hours per loan)	25,000
Balance of processing hours available	0

Question 1: *Which loan type should be advertised and promoted initially because it is the most profitable for the bank? Which should be second? Which last?*

The sales mix analysis is shown in Exhibit 6. It indicates that the auto loans should be sold first because they provide the highest contribution margin per processing hour. Home loans would be sold second, and commercial loans would be sold last.

Question 2: *How many of each type of loan should be sold to maximize the company's contribution margin based on the current loan application activity of 100,000 processing hours? What is the total contribution margin for that combination?*

To begin the analysis, compare the current loan application activity to the required loan activity to meet the current loan demand. The company needs 115,000 processing hours to meet the current loan demand: 40,000 processing hours for commercial loans (20,000 loans × 2 processing hours), 30,000 processing hours for auto loans (30,000 loans × 1 processing hour per loan), and 45,000 processing hours for home loans (18,000 loans × 2.5 processing hours per loan). Because that amount exceeds the current capacity of 100,000 processing hours, management must determine the sales mix that maximizes the company's contribution margin, which will also maximize its operating income. The calculations in the second part of Exhibit 6 show that the bank should sell 30,000 auto loans, 18,000 home loans, and 12,500 commercial loans. The total contribution margin is:

	Contribution Margin
Auto loans (30,000 loans × $3.00 per loan)	$ 90,000
Home loans (18,000 loans × $7.00 per loan)	126,000
Commercial loans (12,500 loans × $5.00 per loan)	62,500
Total contribution margin	$278,500

As noted earlier, management makes the final decision based on the company's strategic plan and tactical objectives, all relevant revenues and costs, and qualitative factors.

Incremental Analysis for Sell or Process-Further Decisions

Some companies offer products or services that can either be sold in a basic form or be processed further and sold as a more refined product or service to a different market. For example, a meatpacking company processes cattle into meat and meat-related products, such as bones and hides. The company may choose to sell sides of beef and pounds of bones and hides to other companies for further processing. Alternatively, it could choose to cut and package the meat for immediate sale in grocery stores, process bone into fertilizer for gardeners, or tan hides into refined leather for purses.

A **sell or process-further decision** is a decision about whether to sell a joint product at the split-off point or sell it after further processing. **Joint products** are two or more products, made from a common material or process that cannot be identified as separate products or services during some or all of the processing. Only at a specific point, called the **split-off point**, do joint products or services become separate and identifiable. At that point, a company may choose to sell the product or service as is or to process it into another form for sale to a different market.

The objective of a sell or process-further decision is to select the alternative that maximizes operating income, based on the organization's strategic

Study Note

Products are made by combining materials or by dividing materials, such as in oil refining or ore extraction.

EXHIBIT 7 ▶

Incremental Analysis: Sell or Process-Further Decision		
Home State Bank		
Sell or Process-Further Decision		
Incremental Analysis		
	Premier Checking	**Personal Banker**
Incremental revenue if processed further:		
Process further	$50	$250
Split off—Basic Checking	25	25
Incremental revenue	$25	$225
Less incremental costs	30	200
Operating income (loss) from processing further	($ 5)	$ 25

> **Study Note**
>
> The common costs shared by two or more products before they are split off are called *joint costs*. Joint costs are irrelevant in a sell or process-further decision.

plan and tactical objectives, the relevant revenues and costs, and qualitative factors. To complete the analysis, calculate the incremental revenue, which is the difference between the total revenue if the product or service is sold at the split-off point and the total revenue if the product or service is sold after further processing. Compare the incremental revenue to the incremental costs of processing further. Choose to process a product or service further if the incremental revenue is greater than the incremental costs of processing further. If the incremental costs are greater than the incremental revenue, choose to sell the product or service at the split-off point. Be sure to ignore joint costs (or common costs) in your analysis, because they are incurred *before* the split-off point and do not change if further processing occurs. Although accountants assign joint costs to products or services when valuing inventories and calculating cost of goods sold, joint costs are not relevant to a sell or process-further decision and are omitted from the decision analysis.

For example, as part of the company's strategic plan, Home State Bank's management is looking for new markets for banking services, and management is considering whether it would be profitable to bundle banking services. Home State Bank is considering adding two levels of service, Premier Checking and Personal Banker, beyond its current Basic Checking account services. The three levels have the following features:

▶ Basic Checking: online checking account, debit card, and online bill payment with a required minimum average balance of $500

▶ Premier Checking: paper and online checking, a debit card, a credit card, and a small life insurance policy equal to the maximum credit limit on the credit card for customers who maintain a minimum average balance of $1,000

▶ Personal Banker: all of the features of the Premier Checking plus a safe deposit box, $5,000 personal line of credit at the prime interest rate, financial investment advice, and a toaster on opening the account for customers who maintain a minimum average balance of $5,000

Assume the bank can earn sales revenue of 5 percent on its checking account balances and that the total cost of offering Basic Checking services is currently $50,000. The bank's accountant provided these data for each level of service:

Product	Sales Revenue	Additional Costs
Basic Checking	$ 25	$ 0
Premier Checking	50	30
Personal Banker	250	200

The decision analysis in Exhibit 7 indicates that the bank should offer personal banking services in addition to Basic Checking accounts. Notice that the $50,000 joint costs of Basic Checking were ignored because they are sunk costs that will not influence the decision.

As mentioned earlier, management makes the final decision based on the bank's strategic plan and tactical objectives, the relevant revenues and costs, and qualitative factors.

S T O P • R E V I E W • A P P L Y

3-1. Which business activities are likely to be outsourced? What makes them attractive for outsourcing?

3-2. Which data are relevant to a make-or-buy decision in a manufacturing operation?

3-3. What are two approaches to making a special order decision?

3-4. What are the two steps in the analysis for a sales mix decision?

3-5. What is the role of joint costs in sell or process-further decision analysis?

Capital Investment Decisions

LO4 Identify the types of projected costs and revenues used to evaluate alternatives for capital investment.

Among the most significant decisions facing management are **capital investment decisions**, which are decisions about when and how much to spend on capital facilities and other long-term projects. Capital facilities and projects may include machinery, systems, or processes; building additions, renovations, or new structures; entire new divisions or product lines; or distribution and software systems. For example, Bank of America will make decisions about installing new equipment, replacing old equipment, expanding services by buying or building a new facility, and acquiring another company. Capital facilities and projects are expensive. A new building could cost millions of dollars and require several years to complete. Managers must make capital investment decisions carefully to ensure that their choices make the maximum contribution to future profits and use resources ethically.

Capital Investment Analysis

Capital investment analysis, or *capital budgeting*, is the process of making decisions about capital investments. It consists of identifying the need for a capital investment, analyzing courses of action to meet that need, preparing reports for managers, choosing the best alternative, and allocating funds among competing needs.

Study Note

Capital investment analysis is a decision process for the purchase of capital facilities, such as buildings and equipment.

Every part of the organization participates in this process. Financial analysts supply a target cost of capital or desired rate of return and an estimate of how much money can be spent annually on capital facilities. Marketing specialists predict sales trends and new product demands, which help in determining which operations need expansion or new equipment. Managers at all levels help identify facility needs and often prepare preliminary cost estimates for the desired capital investment. Then they all work together to implement the project selected and to keep the results within revenue and cost estimates.

Measures Used in Capital Investment Analysis

When evaluating a proposed capital investment, managers must predict how the new asset will perform and how it will benefit the company. Various measures are used to estimate the benefits to be derived from a capital investment.

Net Income and Net Cash Inflows

Each capital investment analysis must include a measure of the expected benefit from the investment project. The measure of expected benefit depends on the method of analyzing capital investment alternatives. One possible measure is net income, calculated in the usual way. Managers determine increases in net income resulting from the capital investment for each alternative.

A more widely used measure of expected benefit is projected cash flows. **Net cash inflows** are the balance of increases in projected cash receipts over increases in projected cash payments resulting from a capital investment. In some cases, equipment replacement decisions involve alternatives when revenues are the same among alternatives. In such cases, **cost savings** measure the benefits, such as reduced costs, from proposed capital investments. Either net cash inflows or cost savings can be used as the basis for an evaluation, but one measure should not be confused with the other. If the analysis involves cash receipts, net cash inflows are used. If the analysis involves only cash outlays, cost savings are used. Managers must measure and evaluate all the investment alternatives consistently.

Equal Versus Unequal Cash Flows

Projected cash flows may be the same for each year of an asset's life, or they may vary from year to year. Unequal cash flows are common and must be analyzed for each year of an asset's life. Proposed projects with equal annual cash flows require less detailed analysis. Both a project with equal cash flows and one with unequal cash flows are illustrated and explained later in this chapter.

Carrying Value of Assets

Carrying value is the undepreciated portion of the original cost of a fixed asset—that is, the asset's cost less its accumulated depreciation. Carrying value is also referred to as *book value*. When a decision to replace an asset is being evaluated, the carrying value of the old asset is irrelevant because it is a past, or historical, cost, and it will therefore not be altered by the decision. Net proceeds from the asset's sale or disposal are relevant, however, because the proceeds affect cash flows and may be different for each alternative.

Depreciation Expense and Income Taxes

The techniques of capital investment analysis in this chapter compare the relative benefits of proposed capital investments by measuring the cash receipts and payments for a facility or project. Income taxes alter the amount and timing of cash flows of projects under consideration by for-profit companies. To assess the benefits of a capital project, a company must include the effects of income taxes in its cap-

Because capital investments affect business processes, factors like international trade logistics should be considered when making a capital investment decision. A case in point is Koss Corporation of Milwaukee, Wisconsin, a maker of high-fidelity headphones for personal stereos, speakerphones, and other audio equipment. Company managers moved much of the production to China, where costs are low. However, that caused a problem with making timely deliveries to customers.[5] The just-in-time inventory philosophy had to be abandoned, and inventories were tripled from $2 million to $6 million to avoid customer backorders and dissatisfaction. Finished products are now stacked in the Milwaukee factory as insurance against dockworker strikes and missed deliveries. Looking beyond the numbers is obviously an important consideration in capital investment decisions.

ital investment analyses. Depreciation expense is deductible when determining income taxes. (You may recall that the annual depreciation expense computation using the straight-line method is the asset's cost less its residual value, divided by the asset's useful life.) Thus, depreciation expense strongly influences the amount of income taxes a company pays and can lead to significant income tax savings.

Corporate income tax rates vary and can change yearly. To examine how income taxes affect capital investment analysis, assume that a company has a tax rate of 30 percent on taxable income. The company is considering a capital project that will make the following annual contribution to operating income:

Cash revenues	$400,000
Cash expenses	(200,000)
Depreciation	(100,000)
Operating income	$100,000
Income taxes at 30%	(30,000)
Operating income after income taxes	$ 70,000

The net cash inflows for this project can be determined in two ways:

1. Net cash inflows—receipts and disbursements

Revenues (cash inflows)	$400,000
Cash expenses (outflows)	(200,000)
Income taxes (outflows)	(30,000)
Net cash inflows	$170,000

2. Net cash inflows—income adjustment procedure

Operating income after income taxes	$ 70,000
Add back noncash expenses (depreciation)	100,000
Less noncash revenues	—
Net cash inflows	$170,000

In both computations, the net cash inflows are $170,000, and the total effect of income taxes is to lower the net cash inflows by $30,000. Another way of stating the net cash inflows–income adjustment procedure is as follows: operating income after income taxes ($70,000) plus noncash expenses (i.e., depreciation of $100,000) minus noncash revenues (none in our example) equals net cash inflows of $170,000.

Disposal or Residual Values   Proceeds from the sale of an old asset are current cash inflows and are relevant to evaluating a proposed capital investment. Projected disposal or residual values of replacement equipment are also relevant because they represent future cash inflows and usually differ among alternatives. Remember that the residual value, sometimes called the *disposal* or *salvage value*, of an asset will be received at the end of the asset's estimated life.

S T O P • R E V I E W • A P P L Y

4-1. What are capital investments? Give examples of capital investments.

4-2. Define *capital investment analysis.*

4-3. How is capital investment analysis part of both the long-term planning and annual budgeting processes?

4-4. Distinguish between cost savings and net cash inflows.

4-5. Why is it important to know whether a capital investment will produce equal cash flows or unequal cash flows?

4-6. "In capital investment analysis, the carrying value of an asset is irrelevant, whereas current and future residual values are relevant." Is this statement valid? Why or why not?

4-7. How does the relationship between depreciation and income taxes affect capital investment analysis? Why is depreciation of the old equipment ignored?

The Time Value of Money

LO5   Apply the concept of the time value of money.

An organization has many options for investing capital besides buying fixed assets. Consequently, management expects a fixed asset to yield a reasonable return during its useful life. A key question in capital investment analysis is how to measure the return on a fixed asset. One way is to look at the cash flows the asset will generate during its useful life. When an asset has a long useful life, management will usually analyze those cash flows in terms of the time value of money. The **time value of money** is the concept that cash flows of equal dollar amounts separated by an interval of time have different present values because of the effect of compound interest. The notions of interest, present value, future value, and present value of an ordinary annuity are all related to the time value of money.

Interest

Interest is the cost associated with the use of money for a specific period of time. Because interest is a cost associated with time and "time is money," interest is an important consideration in any business decision. **Simple interest** is the interest cost for one or more periods when the amount on which the interest is computed stays the same from period to period. **Compound interest** is the interest cost for two or more periods when the amount on which interest is computed changes in each period to include all interest paid in previous periods. In other words, compound interest is interest earned on a principal sum that is increased at the end of each period by the interest for that period.

Example: Simple Interest Jo Sanka accepts an 8 percent, $30,000 note due in 90 days. How much will she receive in total when the note comes due? When using the formula for calculating simple interest, remember that the annual interest rate is expressed as a percentage and that time in days is expressed as a fraction of a 365-day year. The formula is as follows:

$$\text{Interest Expense} = \text{Principal} \times \text{Rate} \times \text{Time}$$
$$= \$30{,}000 \times 8\% \times 90/365$$
$$= \$591.78$$

The total that Sanka will receive at maturity is computed as follows:

$$\text{Total Maturity Value} = \text{Principal} + \text{Interest}$$
$$= \$30{,}000 + \$591.78$$
$$= \$30{,}591.78$$

Example: Compound Interest Andy Clayburn makes a deposit of $5,000 in a savings account that pays 6 percent interest. He expects to leave the principal and accumulated interest in the account for three years. What will be his account total at the end of three years? Assume that the interest is paid at the end of the year, that the interest is added to the principal at that time, and that this total in turn earns interest. The amount at the end of three years is computed as follows:

(1) Year	(2) Principal Amount at Beginning of Year	(3) Annual Amount of Interest (col. 2 × .06)	(4) Accumulated Amount at End of Year (col. 2 + col. 3)
1	$5,000.00	$300.00	$5,300.00
2	5,300.00	318.00	5,618.00
3	5,618.00	337.08	5,955.08

At the end of three years, Clayburn will have $5,955.08 in his savings account. Note that the annual amount of interest increases each year by the interest rate times the interest of the previous year. For example, between year 1 and year 2, the interest increased by $18 ($318 − $300), which exactly equals 6 percent times $300.

Present Value

Suppose that you had the choice of receiving $100 either today or one year from today. Intuitively, you would choose to receive the $100 today. Why? You know that if you have the $100 today, you can put it in a savings account to earn interest, so that you will have more than $100 a year from today. Therefore, we can say that an amount to be received in the future (future value) is not worth as much today as the same amount to be received today (present value) because of the cost associated with the passage of time.

Future value and present value are closely related. **Future value** is the amount an investment will be worth at a future date if invested today at compound interest. **Present value** is the amount that must be invested today at a given rate of compound interest to produce a given future value.

For example, assume that Daschel Company needs $1,000 one year from now. How much should the company invest today to achieve that goal if the interest rate is 5 percent? The following equation may be used:

$$\text{Present Value} \times (1.0 + \text{Interest Rate}) = \text{Future Value}$$
$$\text{Present Value} \times 1.05 = \$1,000.00$$
$$\text{Present Value} = \$1,000.00 \div 1.05$$
$$\text{Present Value} = \$952.38$$

Thus, to achieve a future value of $1,000.00, a present value of $952.38 must be invested. Interest of 5 percent on $952.38 for one year equals $47.62, and the two amounts added together equal $1,000.00.

Present Value of a Single Sum Due in the Future

When more than one time period is involved, the calculation of present value is more complicated. For example, Reza Company wants to be sure of having $4,000 at the end of three years. How much must the company invest today in a 5 percent savings account to achieve that goal? By adapting the preceding equation, the present value of $4,000 at compound interest of 5 percent for three years in the future may be computed as follows:

Year	Amount at End of Year	Divide by		Present Value at Beginning of Year
3	$4,000.00	÷ 1.05	=	$3,809.52
2	3,809.52	÷ 1.05	=	3,628.11
1	3,628.11	÷ 1.05	=	3,455.34

Reza Company must invest a present value of $3,455.34 to achieve a future value of $4,000 in three years. This calculation is made much easier by using the appropriate table from the appendix on future value and present value tables. In Table 3, we look down the 5 percent column until we reach period 3. There we find the factor .864. This factor when multiplied by $1 gives the present value of $1 to be received three years from now at 5 percent interest. Thus, we solve the problem as follows:

Future Value	×	Present-Value Factor	=	Present Value
$4,000	×	.864	=	$3,456

Except for a rounding difference of $.66, this gives the same result as the previous calculation.

FOCUS ON BUSINESS PRACTICE
How Would You Decide Whether to Buy Rare Dinosaur Bones?

Not-for-profit organizations can also use the techniques of capital investment analysis. For example, the officers of the Field Museum in Chicago employed these techniques when deciding whether to bid at auction on the most complete skeleton ever found of a Tyrannosaurus rex. The museum bought the bones for $8.2 million and spent another $9 million to restore and install the dinosaur, named Sue. The museum projected that Sue would attract 1 million new visitors, who would produce $5 million in admissions and spend several more million dollars on food, gifts, and the like. After deducting operating costs, museum officials used discounted present values to calculate a return on investment of 10.5 percent. Given that the museum's cost of capital was 8.5 percent, Sue's purchase was considered a financial success. Sue has been extremely popular with the public and more than met the museum's attendance goals in the first year after installation.[6]

Present Value of an Ordinary Annuity

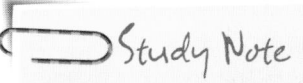

It is often necessary to compute the present value of a series of receipts or payments. When we calculate the present value of equal amounts equally spaced over a period of time, we are computing the present value of an ordinary annuity. An **ordinary annuity** is a series of equal payments or receipts that will begin one time period from the current date.

For example, assume that Fodor Company has sold a piece of property and is to receive $15,000 in three equal annual cash payments of $5,000, beginning one year from today. What is the present value of this sale, assuming a current interest rate of 5 percent?

We can determine this present value by calculating a separate present value for each of the three payments (using Table 3 in the appendix on future value and present value tables) and summing the results, as follows:

Future Cash Receipts (Annuity)				Present-Value Factor at 5 Percent (from Table 3)		Present Value
Year 1	Year 2	Year 3				
$5,000			×	.952	=	$ 4,760
	$5,000		×	.907	=	4,535
		$5,000	×	.864	=	4,320
Total Present Value						$13,615

The present value of this sale is $13,615. Thus, there is an implied interest cost (given the 5 percent rate) of $1,385 associated with the payment plan that allows the purchaser to pay in three installments.

We can calculate this present value more easily by using Table 4 in the appendix on future value and present value tables. We look down the 5 percent column until we reach period 3. There we find the factor 2.723. That factor, when multiplied by $1, gives the present value of a series of three $1 payments, spaced one year apart, at compound interest of 5 percent. Thus, we solve the problem as follows:

Periodic Payment	×	Present-Value Factor	=	Present Value
$5,000	×	2.723	=	$13,615

This result is the same as the one computed earlier. If Fodor Company is willing to accept a 5 percent rate of return, management will be equally satisfied to receive a single cash payment of $13,615 today or three equal annual cash payments of $5,000 spread over the next three years.

S T O P • R E V I E W • A P P L Y

5-1. Discuss this statement: "To treat all future income flows alike ignores the time value of money."

5-2. How are present value and future value different?

5-3. Which table in the appendix on future value and present value tables is used to determine the present value of a single sum to be received in the future? Which table in the appendix is used to determine the present value of a series of payments (ordinary annuity) to be received in the future?

Analyzing Capital Investment Proposals:
The Net Present Value Method

> **LO6**   Use the net present value method to analyze capital investment proposals.

When evaluating a proposed capital investment, managers must predict how the new asset will perform and how it will benefit the company. Various methods are used to estimate the benefits to be derived from a capital investment. The most important of these is the net present value method. The **net present value method** evaluates a capital investment by discounting its future cash flows to their present values and subtracting the amount of the initial investment from their sum. All proposed capital investments are evaluated in the same way, and the projects with the highest net present value—the amount that exceeds the initial investment—are selected for implementation.

Advantages of the Net Present Value Method

A significant advantage of the net present value method is that it incorporates the time value of money into the analysis of proposed capital investments. Future cash inflows and outflows are discounted by the company's minimum rate of return to determine their present values. The minimum rate of return should at least equal the company's average cost of capital. **Cost of capital** is the weighted-average rate of return a company must pay to its long-term creditors and shareholders for the use of their funds.

When dealing with the time value of money, use discounting to find the present value of an amount to be received in the future. To determine the present values of future amounts of money, use Tables 3 and 4 in the appendix on future value and present value tables.

Tables 3 and 4 are used to discount each future cash inflow and cash outflow over the life of the asset to the present. If the net present value is positive (the total of the discounted net cash inflows exceeds the cash investment at the beginning), the rate of return on the investment will exceed the company's minimum rate of return, or hurdle rate, and the project can be accepted. Assuming the project is accepted, investors will be pleased that the company earned a higher rate of return than they expected or required. Conversely, if the net present value is negative (the cash investment at the beginning exceeds the discounted net cash inflows), the return on the investment is less than the minimum rate of return, and the project should be rejected. If the net present value is zero (if discounted cash inflows equal discounted cash outflows), the project meets the minimum rate of return and can be accepted.

The Net Present Value Method Illustrated

Assume that Open Imaging Company is considering the purchase of an ultrasound machine that will improve efficiency in its Radiology Department. The management of Open Imaging Company must decide between two models of the machine, Model M and Model N:

▸ Model M costs $17,500 and will have an estimated residual value of $2,000 after five years. It is projected to produce cash inflows of $6,000, $5,500, $5,000, $4,500, and $4,000 during its five-year life.

Study Note

Remember that Table 3 deals with a single payment or amount, whereas Table 4 is used for a series of equal periodic amounts.

Study Note

If the net present value is zero, the investment will earn the minimum rate of return.

State lotteries use the net present value method to compute the lump-sum equivalent of the grand prize. In this photo, Mega Millions winners Margaret and James Jones hold a replica of their $77,744,832 check. Worth an annuity of $130 million, it was the second largest prize in Georgia's lottery history.

▶ Model N costs $21,000 and will have an estimated residual value of $2,000. It is projected to produce cash inflows of $6,000 per year for five years.

The company's minimum rate of return is 16 percent.

Because Model M is expected to produce unequal cash inflows, Table 3 in the appendix on future value and present value tables is used to determine the present value of each cash inflow from each year of the machine's life. The net present value of Model M is determined as follows:

Model M

Year	Net Cash Inflows	16% Factor	Present Value
1	$6,000	.862	$ 5,172.00
2	5,500	.743	4,086.50
3	5,000	.641	3,205.00
4	4,500	.552	2,484.00
5	4,000	.476	1,904.00
Residual value, year 5	2,000	.476	952.00
Total present value of cash inflows			$17,803.50
Less purchase price of Model M			17,500.00
Net present value			$ 303.50

All the factors for this analysis can be found in the column for 16 percent in Table 3. The factors discount the individual cash flows, including the expected residual value, to the present. The amount of the investment in Model M is deducted from the total present value of the cash inflows to arrive at the net present value of $303.50. Since the entire investment of $17,500 in Model M is a cash outflow at the beginning—that is, time zero—no discounting of the $17,500 purchase price is necessary. Because the net present value is positive, the proposed investment in Model M will achieve at least the minimum rate of return.

Because Model N is expected to produce equal cash receipts in each year of its useful life, Table 4 in the appendix on future value and present value tables is used to determine the combined present value of those future cash inflows. However, Table 3 is used to determine the present value of the machine's residual value because it represents a single payment, not an annuity. The net present value of Model N is calculated as follows:

Model N

Year	Net Cash Inflows	16% Factor	Present Value
1–5	$6,000	3.274	$19,644.00
Residual value, year 5	2,000	.476	952.00
Total present value of cash inflows			$20,596.00
Less purchase price of Model N			21,000.00
Net purchase value			($ 404.00)

Table 4 is used to determine the factor of 3.274, which is found in the column for 16 percent and the row for five periods. Because the residual value is a single inflow in the fifth year, the factor of .476 must be taken from Table 3 (the column for 16 percent and the row for five periods). The result is a net present value of ($404). Because the net present value is negative, the proposed investment in Model N will not achieve the minimum rate of return and should be rejected.

The two analyses show that Model M should be chosen because it has a positive net present value and would exceed the company's minimum rate of return. Model N should be rejected because it does not achieve the minimum rate of return.

STOP • REVIEW • APPLY

6-1. Why is the net present value method superior to other methods of capital investment analysis?

6-2. What is the role of the average cost of capital when the net present value method is used to evaluate capital investment proposals?

Time Value of Money Noway Jose Communications, Inc., is considering the purchase of a new piece of computerized data transmission equipment. Estimated annual net cash inflows for the new equipment are $575,000. The equipment costs $2 million, it has a five-year life, and it will have no residual value at the end of the five years. The company has a minimum rate of return of 12 percent. Compute the net present value of the piece of equipment. Should the company purchase it? (Use Table 4 in the appendix on future and present value tables.)

SOLUTION

$$
\begin{aligned}
\text{Net Present Value} &= \text{Present Value of Future Net Cash Inflow} - \\
&\quad \text{Cost of Equipment} \\
&= (\$575{,}000 \times 3.605) - \$2{,}000{,}000 \\
&= \$2{,}072{,}875 - \$2{,}000{,}000 \\
&= \$72{,}875
\end{aligned}
$$

The solution is positive, so the piece of equipment should be purchased. A positive answer means that the investment will yield more than the minimum 12 percent return that the company requires.

Other Methods of Capital Investment Analysis

LO7 Use the payback period method and the accounting rate-of-return method to analyze capital investment proposals.

The net present value method is the best method for capital investment analysis. However, two other commonly used methods provide rough guides to evaluating capital investment proposals. These methods are the payback period method and the accounting rate-of-return method.

The Payback Period Method

Study Note

The payback period method measures the estimated length of time necessary to recover in cash the cost of an investment.

Because cash is an essential measure of a business's health, many managers estimate the cash flow that the investment will generate. Their goal is to determine the minimum time it will take to recover the initial investment. If two investment alternatives are being studied, management should choose the investment that pays back its initial cost in the shorter time. That period of time is known as the payback period, and the method of evaluation is called the **payback period method**. The advantage of the payback period method is that it is simple to use. The payback period is computed as follows:

$$
\text{Payback Period} = \frac{\text{Cost of Investment}}{\text{Annual Net Cash Inflows}}
$$

To apply the payback period method, assume the Gordon Company is interested in buying a new bottling machine that costs $51,000 and has a residual value of $3,000. To evaluate the proposed capital investment of the Gordon Company, begin by determining the annual net cash inflows, which is the excess of annual cash revenues over cash expenses. First, find and eliminate the effects of all noncash revenue and expense items included in the analysis of net income. Assume that estimates for the proposal include revenue increases of $17,900 a year and operating cost increases of $11,696 a year (including depreciation and taxes). In this case, the only noncash expense or revenue is machine depreciation. To calculate this amount, you must know the asset's life and the depreciation method. Suppose the Gordon Company uses the straight-line method of depreciation, and the new bottling machine will have a ten-year service life. Using this information and the facts given earlier, compute the annual depreciation:

$$\text{Annual Depreciation} = \frac{\text{Cost} - \text{Residual Value}}{\text{Life of Asset}}$$

$$= \frac{\$51{,}000 - \$3{,}000}{10 \text{ years}} = \$4{,}800 \text{ per year}$$

After removing the noncash annual depreciation amount from the operating costs, the payback period is computed as follows:

$$\text{Payback period} = \frac{\text{Cost of Machine}}{\text{Cash Revenue} - \text{Cash Expenses}}$$

$$= \frac{\$51{,}000}{\$17{,}900 - (\$11{,}696 - \$4{,}800)}$$

$$= \frac{\$51{,}000}{\$11{,}004} = 4.6 \text{ years}$$

If the company's desired payback period is five years or less, this proposal would be approved.

If a proposed capital investment has unequal annual net cash inflows, the payback period is determined by subtracting each annual amount (in chronological order) from the cost of the capital investment. When a zero balance is reached, the payback period has been determined. This will often occur in the middle of a year.

The payback period method is widely used because it is easy to compute and understand. It is especially useful in areas in which technology changes rapidly, as in Internet companies, and when risk is high, such as when investing in emerging countries. However, the disadvantages of this approach far outweigh its advantages. First, the payback period method does not measure profitability. Second, it ignores differences in the present values of cash flows from different periods; thus, it does not adjust cash flows for the time value of money. Finally, the payback period method emphasizes the time it takes to recover the investment rather than the long-term return on the investment. It ignores all future cash flows after the payback period is reached.

The Accounting Rate-of-Return Method

The **accounting rate-of-return method** is an imprecise but easy way to measure the estimated performance of a capital investment since it uses financial statement information. This method does not use an investment's cash flows but considers the financial reporting effects of the investment instead. The accounting rate-of-return method measures expected performance using two variables: (1) estimated annual net income from the project and (2) average investment cost. The basic equation is:

$$\text{Accounting Rate of Return} = \frac{\text{Project's Average Annual Net Income}}{\text{Average Investment Cost}}$$

To compute average annual net income, use the cost and revenue data prepared for evaluating the project. Average investment in a proposed capital investment is calculated as follows:

$$\text{Average Investment Cost} = \left(\frac{\text{Total Investment} - \text{Residual Value}}{2}\right) + \text{Residual Value}$$

Study Note

Payback is expressed in time, net present value is expressed in money, and accounting rate of return is expressed as a percentage.

To see how this equation is used in evaluating a proposed capital investment, assume the same facts as before for the Gordon Company in its interest in purchasing a new bottling machine. Also assume the company's management will only consider projects that promise to yield more than a 16 percent return. To determine if the company should invest in the machine, compute the accounting rate of return as follows:

$$\text{Accounting Rate of Return} = \frac{\$17,900 - \$11,696}{\left(\frac{\$51,000 - \$3,000}{2}\right) + \$3,000}$$

$$= \frac{\$6,204}{\$27,000}$$

$$= 23\%$$

The projected rate of return is higher than the 16 percent minimum, so management should think seriously about making the investment.

Study Note

Both the payback period and accounting rate-of-return methods are appealing because they are easy to understand. They have flaws, however, such as the failure to consider the time value of money.

The accounting rate-of-return method has been widely used because it is easy to understand and apply. It does have several disadvantages, however. First, because net income is averaged over the life of the investment, it is not a reliable figure. Actual net income may vary considerably from the estimates. Second, the method is unreliable if estimated annual net incomes differ from year to year. Third, cash flows are ignored. Fourth, the time value of money is not considered in the analysis. Thus, future and present dollars are treated as equal.

STOP • REVIEW • APPLY

7-1. Why are the payback period method and the accounting rate-of-return method rough estimates?

7-2. Is the payback period method very accurate? Defend your answer.

Payback Period Method   Noway Jose Communications, Inc., is considering the purchase of a new piece of computerized data transmission equipment. Estimated annual net cash inflows for the new equipment are $575,000. The equipment costs $2 million, it has a five-year life, and it will have no residual value at the end of the five years. Compute the payback period of the piece of equipment. Does this method yield a positive or negative response to the proposal to buy the equipment, assuming the company set a maximum payback period of four years?

SOLUTION

$$\text{Payback Period} = \frac{\text{Cost of Investment}}{\text{Annual Net Cash Inflows}}$$

$$= \frac{\$2,000,000}{\$575,000}$$

$$= 3.5 \text{ Years}$$

The piece of equipment should be purchased because its payback period is less than the company's maximum payback period.

BANK OF AMERICA

In this chapter's Decision Point, we commented on the dominance of Bank of America in online banking. We asked the following questions:

- **How do managers at Bank of America decide on new ways to increase business and protect customers' interests?**

- **How can incremental and capital investment analyses help managers at Bank of America take advantage of the business opportunities that online banking offers?**

As managers at Bank of America pursue alternatives that will be good for business and that will protect online customers from fraud and identity theft, they ask a number of questions. For example: When should bank products and services like portfolio management or online customer support be outsourced? When should a special order for service be accepted? When is a bank segment profitable? What sales mix is best when resource constraints exist? When should bank products be sold as is or processed further into different products? Should the bank invest in the latest technology, and if so, how should bank managers evaluate the capital investment alternatives?

To answer such questions and determine what could happen under alternative courses of action, the bank's managers need pertinent information that they can get from incremental and capital investment analyses. On that basis, they can make sound, ethical decisions that will protect the bank's customers and increase both its traditional and online business.

CHAPTER REVIEW

REVIEW of Learning Objectives

LO1 Explain how managers make short-run decisions.

Both quantitative information and qualitative information are important for short-run decision analysis. Such information should be relevant, timely, and presented in a format that is easy to use in decision making. When managers plan, they discover a problem or need, identify alternative courses of action to solve the problem or meet the need, perform a complete analysis to determine the effects of each alternative on business operations, and choose the best alternative. Managers during the year accept or reject a special order, examine the profitability of a segment, select the appropriate product mix given a resource constraint, contract with outside suppliers of goods and services, or sell a product as is or process it further. When managers review actual performance, each decision is evaluated to determine if the forecasted results were obtained and if corrective actions are needed. Reporting occurs throughout the year to evaluate the information selected, the decision made, and the impact of that decision on the organization.

LO2 Define *incremental analysis,* and describe how it applies to short-run decision analysis.

Incremental analysis helps managers compare alternatives by focusing on the differences in their projected revenues and costs. Any data that relate to future costs, revenues, or uses of resources and that will differ among alternative courses of action are considered relevant decision information. Projected sales or estimated costs, such as direct materials or direct labor, which differ for each decision alternative, are examples of relevant information. The manager analyzes relevant information to determine which alternative contributes the most to profits or incurs the lowest costs. Only data that differ for each alternative appear in the report. Differential or incremental costs are costs that vary among alternatives and thus are relevant to the decision. Sunk costs are past costs that cannot be recovered; they are irrelevant to the decision process. Opportunity costs are revenue or income forgone as a result of choosing an alternative.

LO3 Apply incremental analysis to outsourcing decisions, special order decisions, segment profitability decisions, sales mix decisions involving constrained resources, and sell or process-further decisions.

Outsourcing (including make-or-buy) *decision analysis* helps managers decide whether to use suppliers from outside the organization to perform services or provide goods that could be performed or produced internally. An incremental analysis of the expected costs and revenues for each alternative is used to identify the best alternative. A *special order decision* is a decision about whether to accept or reject a special order at a price below the normal market price. One approach is to compare the special order price to the relevant costs to see if a profit can be generated. Another approach is to prepare a special order bid price by calculating a minimum selling price for the special order. Generally, fixed costs are irrelevant to a special order decision because such costs are covered by regular sales activity and do not differ among alternatives. *Segment profitability decisions* involve the review of segments of an organization, such as product lines, services, sales territories, divisions, or departments. Often managers must decide whether to add or drop a segment. A segment with a negative segment margin may be dropped. A segment margin is a segment's sales revenue minus its direct costs, which include variable costs and avoidable fixed costs. Avoidable costs are costs traceable to a specific segment. If the segment is eliminated, the avoidable costs will also be eliminated. *Sales mix decisions* require the selection of the most profitable combination of sales items when a company makes more than one product or service using a common constrained resource. The product or service generating the highest contribution margin per constrained resource is sold first. *Sell or process-further decisions* require managers to choose between selling a joint product at its split-off point or processing it into a more refined product. The managers compare the incremental revenues and costs of the two alternatives. Joint processing costs are irrelevant to the decision because they are identical for both alternatives. A product should be processed further only if the incremental revenues generated exceed the incremental costs incurred.

LO4 Identify the types of projected costs and revenues used to evaluate alternatives for capital investment.

When considering long-term decisions about when and how much to spend on capital facilities and other long-term projects that are expensive and require several years to complete, managers must make these capital investment decisions carefully using capital investment analysis. One method requires measures of net income. Other methods of evaluating capital investments evaluate net cash inflows or cost savings. The analysis process must take into consideration whether each period's cash flows will be equal or unequal. Unless the after-income-tax effects on cash flows are being considered, carrying values and depreciation expense of assets awaiting replacement are irrelevant. Net proceeds from the sale of an old asset and estimated residual value of a new facility represent future cash flows and must be part of the estimated benefit of a project. Depreciation expense on replacement equipment is relevant to evaluations based on after-tax cash flows.

LO5 Apply the concept of the time value of money.

Cash flows of equal dollar amounts at different times have different values because of the effect of compound interest. This phenomenon is known as the time value of money. Computing the time value of a single sum or multiple sums is made easier by using the appropriate table in the appendix on future value and present value tables. In this chapter, we used Table 3 (single sum) and Table 4 (ordinary annuity) to compute the present value of future receipts or payments.

LO6 Use the net present value method to analyze capital investment proposals.

The net present value method incorporates the time value of money into the analysis of a proposed capital investment. A minimum required rate of return, usually the average cost of capital, is used to discount an investment's expected future cash flows to their present values. The present values are added together, and the amount of the initial investment is subtracted from their total. If the resulting amount, called the net present value, is positive, the rate of return on the investment will exceed the required rate of return, and the investment should be accepted. If the net present value is negative, the return on the investment will be less than the minimum rate of return, and the investment should be rejected.

LO7 Use the payback period method and the accounting rate-of-return method to analyze capital investment proposals.

The payback period method of evaluating a capital investment focuses on the minimum length of time needed to get the amount of the initial investment back in cash. With the accounting rate-of-return method, managers evaluate two or more capital investment proposals and then select the alternative that yields the highest ratio of average annual net income to average cost of investment. Both methods are easy to use, but they are very rough measures that do not consider the time value of money. As a result, the net present value method is preferred.

REVIEW of Concepts and Terminology

The following concepts and terms were introduced in this chapter:

Accounting rate of return method: A method of evaluating capital investments that does not use an investment's cash flows but considers the financial reporting effects of the investment instead. **(LO7)**

Avoidable costs: Costs that can be eliminated by dropping a segment. **(LO3)**

Capital investment analysis: The process of making decisions about capital investments. Also called *capital budgeting*. **(LO4)**

Capital investment decisions: Management decisions about when and how much to spend on capital facilities and other long-term projects. **(LO4)**

Carrying value: The undepreciated portion of the original cost of a fixed asset. Also called *book value*. **(LO4)**

Compound interest: The interest cost for two or more periods when the amount on which interest is computed changes in each period to include all interest paid in previous periods. **(LO5)**

Cost of capital: The weighted-average rate of return a company must pay to its long-term creditors and shareholders for the use of their funds. **(LO6)**

Cost savings: Benefits, such as reduced costs, from a proposed capital investment. **(LO4)**

Differential cost: A cost that changes among alternatives. Also called *incremental cost*. **(LO2)**

Future value: The amount an investment will be worth at a future date if invested at compound interest. **(LO5)**

Incremental analysis: A technique used in decision analysis that compares alternatives by focusing on the differences in their projected revenues and costs. Also called *differential analysis*. **(LO2)**

Interest: The cost associated with the use of money for a specific period of time. **(LO5)**

Joint products: Two or more products made from a common material or process that cannot be identified as separate products during some or all of the production process. **(LO3)**

Make-or-buy decisions: Decisions about whether to make a part internally or buy it from an external supplier. **(LO3)**

Net cash inflows: The balance of increases in projected cash receipts over increases in projected cash payments resulting from a proposed capital investment. **(LO4)**

Net present value method: A method of evaluating capital investments in which all future cash flows for each proposed project are discounted to their present values, and the amount of the initial investment is subtracted from their sum. The projects with the highest positive net present value are selected for implementation. **(LO6)**

Opportunity costs: The benefits forfeited or lost when one alternative is chosen over another. **(LO2)**

Ordinary annuity: A series of equal payments or receipts that will begin one time period from the current date. **(LO5)**

Outsourcing: The use of suppliers outside the organization to perform services or produce goods that could be performed or produced internally. **(LO3)**

Payback period method: A method of evaluating capital investments that bases the decision to invest in a capital project on the minimum length of time it will take to get the amount of the initial investment back in cash. **(LO7)**

Present value: The amount that must be invested today at a given rate of compound interest to produce a given future value. **(LO5)**

Sales mix decision: A decision to select the alternative that maximizes the contribution margin per constrained resource. **(LO3)**

Segment margin: A segment's sales revenue minus its direct costs (direct variable costs and direct fixed costs traceable to the segment). **(LO3)**

Sell or process-further decision: A decision about whether to sell a joint product at the split-off point or sell it after further processing. **(LO3)**

Short-run decision analysis: The systematic examination of any decision whose effects will be most felt over the next year or less. **(LO1)**

Simple interest: The interest cost for one or more periods when the amount on which the interest is computed stays the same from period to period. **(LO5)**

Special order decisions: Decisions about whether to accept or reject a special order at a price below the normal market price. **(LO3)**

Split-off point: A specific point in the production process at which two or more joint products become separate and identifiable. At that point, a company may choose to sell the product as is or process it into another form for sale to a different market. **(LO3)**

Sunk cost: A cost that was incurred because of a previous decision and cannot be recovered through the current decision. **(LO2)**

Time value of money: The concept that cash flows of equal dollar amounts separated by an interval of time have different present values because of the effect of compound interest. **(LO5)**

REVIEW Problem

LO3   Analysis of a Short-Run Operating Decision

Home Services, Inc., specializes in repair and maintenance services. Recently, its profitability has declined, and Dale Bandy, the company's founder, wants to know which service lines are not meeting the company's profit targets. Once the services have been identified, he will either eliminate them or set higher prices. If higher prices are set, the price structure will cover all variable and fixed operating, selling, and general administrative costs. Four service lines are under serious review. The following data from the most recent year-end closing are available for analysis:

		Auto Repair	Boat Repair	Tile Floor Repair	Tree Trimming	Total Impact
	Home Services, Inc.					
	Segmented Income Statement					
	For the Year Ended December 31, 20xx					
8	Sales	$297,500	$114,300	$126,400	$97,600	$635,800
9	Less variable costs					
10	Direct labor	$119,000	$ 40,005	$ 44,240	$34,160	$237,405
11	Operating supplies	14,875	5,715	6,320	4,880	31,790
12	Small tools	11,900	4,572	5,056	7,808	29,336
13	Replacement parts	59,500	22,860	25,280	—	107,640
14	Truck costs	—	11,430	12,640	14,640	38,710
15	Selling costs	44,625	17,145	18,960	9,760	90,490
16	Other variable costs	5,950	2,286	2,528	1,952	12,716
17	Contribution margin	$ 41,650	$ 10,287	$ 11,376	$24,400	$ 87,713
18	Less direct fixed costs	35,800	16,300	24,100	5,200	81,400
19	Segment margin	$ 5,850	($ 6,013)	($ 12,724)	$19,200	$ 6,313
20	Less common fixed					
21	costs					32,100
22	Operating income					
23	(loss)					($ 25,787)

Required

1. Analyze the performance of the four service lines being reviewed. Should Dale Bandy eliminate any of the service lines? Explain your answer.
2. Why might Bandy want to continue providing unprofitable service lines?

3. Even though some of the unprofitable services can be eliminated, the company still has an operating loss. Identify some possible causes for poor performance by the services. What actions do you recommend?

Answer to Review Problem

1. When deciding whether to eliminate any of the four service lines, Dale Bandy should concentrate on the service lines that have a negative segment margin. If the revenues from a service line are less than the sum of its variable and direct fixed costs, then other service lines must cover some of the losing line's costs while carrying the burden of the common fixed costs.

   By looking at the segmented income statement, Dale Bandy can see that the company will improve its operating income by $18,737 ($6,013 + $12,724) if it eliminates the Boat Repair Service and the Tile Floor Repair Service, both of which have a negative segment margin. Bandy's decision can also be supported by the following analysis:

	A	B	C	D	E
1			Home Services, Inc.		
2			Segment Profitability Decision		
3					
4					Difference in
5					Favor of
6			Keep	Drop	Dropping
7			Boat Repair	Boat Repair	Boat Repair
8			and	and	and
9			Tile Floor Repair	Tile Floor Repair	Tile Floor Repair
10	Sales		$635,800	$395,100	($240,700)
11	Less variable costs		548,087	329,050	219,037
12	Contribution margin		$ 87,713	$ 66,050	($ 21,663)
13	Less direct fixed costs		81,400	41,000	40,400
14	Segment margin		$ 6,313	$ 25,050	$ 18,737
15	Less common fixed costs		32,100	32,100	—
16	Operating income (loss)		($ 25,787)	($ 7,050)	$ 18,737
17					

2. Bandy may want to continue offering the unprofitable service lines if their elimination would negatively affect the sale of auto repair or tree trimming services. Bandy may also want to diversify into new markets by offering new services. Bandy should be prepared to suffer some losses initially to enter the new markets.

3. Among the possible causes for poor performance by the company's four services are the following:

   a. Service fees set too low
   b. Inadequate advertising
   c. High direct labor costs
   d. Other variable costs too high
   e. Poor management of fixed costs
   f. Excessive supervision costs

   To improve profitability, the organization can eliminate nonvalue-adding costs, increase service fees, or increase the volume of services provided to customers.

CHAPTER ASSIGNMENTS

BUILDING Your Basic Knowledge and Skills

Short Exercises

LO1 **Qualitative and Quantitative Information in Short-Run Decision Analysis**

SE 1. The owner of Mimi's, a French restaurant, is deciding whether to take chicken à l'orange off the menu. Tell whether each of the following pieces of decision information is qualitative or quantitative. If the information is quantitative, specify whether it is financial or nonfinancial.

1. The time needed to prepare the chicken
2. The daily number of customers who order the chicken
3. Whether competing French restaurants have this entrée on the menu
4. The labor cost of the chef who prepares the chicken
5. The fact that the president of a nearby company, who brings ten guests with him each week, always orders chicken à l'orange.

LO2 **Using Incremental Analysis**

SE 2. Aries Corporation has assembled the following information related to the purchase of a new automated postage machine:

	Posen Machine	Valuet Machine
Increase in revenue	$43,200	$49,300
Increase in annual operating costs		
Direct materials	12,200	12,200
Direct labor	10,200	10,600
Variable overhead	24,500	26,900
Fixed overhead (including depreciation)	12,400	12,400

Using incremental analysis and only relevant information, compute the difference in favor of the Valuet machine.

LO3 **Outsourcing Decision**

SE 3. Marcus Company assembles products from a group of interconnecting parts. The company produces some of the parts and purchases other parts from outside vendors. The vendor for Part X has just increased its price by 35 percent, to $10 per unit for the first 5,000 units and $9 per additional unit ordered each year. The company uses 7,500 units of Part X each year. Unit costs if the company makes the part are:

Direct materials	$3.50
Direct labor	1.75
Variable overhead	4.25
Variable selling costs for the assembled product	3.75

Should the company continue to purchase the part, or should it begin making the part?

LO3 **Special Order Decision**

SE 4. Smith Accounting Services is considering a special order that it received from one of its corporate clients. The special order calls for Smith to prepare the individual tax returns of the corporation's four largest shareholders. The company has idle capacity that could be used to complete the special order. The following data have been gathered about the preparation of individual tax returns:

Materials cost per page	$ 1
Average hourly labor rate	$60
Standard hours per return	4
Standard pages per return	10
Variable overhead cost per page	$.50
Fixed overhead cost per page	$.50

Smith Accounting Services would be satisfied with a $40 gross profit per return. Compute the minimum bid price for the entire order.

LO3 Sales Mix Decision

SE 5. Snow, Inc., makes three kinds of snowboards, but it has a limited number of machine hours available to make them. Product line data are as follows:

	Wood	Plastic	Graphite
Machine hours per unit	1.25	1.0	1.5
Selling price per unit	$100	$120	$200
Variable cost per unit	45	50	100
Variable selling costs per unit	15	26	36

In what order should the snowboard product lines be produced?

LO4 Capital Investment Analysis and Revenue Measures

SE 6. Maize Corp. is analyzing a proposal to switch its factory over to a lights-out operation. To do so, it must acquire a fully automated machine. The machine will be able to produce an entire product line in a single operation. Projected annual net cash inflows from the machine are $180,000, and projected net income is $120,000. Why is projected net income $60,000 less than projected net cash inflows? Identify possible causes.

LO5 Time Value of Money

SE 7. Heidi Layne recently inherited a trust fund from a distant relative. On January 2, the bank managing the trust fund notified Layne that she has the option of receiving a lump-sum check for $175,500 or leaving the money in the trust fund and receiving an annual year-end check for $20,000 for each of the next 20 years. Layne likes to earn at least an 8 percent return on her investments. What should she do?

LO6 Capital Investment Decision: Net Present Value Method

SE 8. SCT is considering the purchase of a new security machine. The estimated life of the machine is 15 years, and the purchase price, including all setup charges, is $400,000. Residual value is estimated to be $40,000. The net addition to the company's cash inflows for the new machine is $70,000 a year. The company has a minimum rate of return of 14 percent. Compute the net present value of the machine. Should the company purchase it? Use Tables 3 and 4 in the appendix on future and present value tables.

LO7 Capital Investment Decision: Payback Period Method

SE 9. East-West Cable, Inc., is considering the purchase of new data transmission equipment. Estimated annual cash revenues for the new equipment are $1 million, and operating costs (including depreciation of $400,000) are $825,000. The equipment costs $2 million, it has a five-year life, and it will have no residual value at the end of the five years. Compute the payback period for the piece of equipment. Does this method yield a positive or a negative response to the proposal to buy the equipment, assuming the company sets a maximum payback period of four years?

LO7 **Capital Investment Decision: Accounting Rate-of-Return Method**

SE 10. Best Cleaners is considering whether to purchase a delivery truck that will cost $29,000, last six years, and have an estimated residual value of $5,000. Average annual net income from the delivery service is estimated to be $4,000. Best Cleaners' owners seek to earn an accounting rate of return of 20 percent. Compute the average investment cost and the accounting rate of return. Should the investment be made?

Exercises

LO2 **Incremental Analysis**

E 1. The managers of Lennox Company must decide which of two mill blade grinders—Y or Z—to buy. The grinders have the same purchase price but different revenues and cost characteristics. The company currently owns Grinder X, which it bought three years ago for $15,000 and which has accumulated depreciation of $9,000 and a carrying value of $6,000. Grinder X is now obsolete as a result of advances in technology and cannot be sold or traded in.

The accountant has collected the following annual revenue and operating cost estimates for the two new machines:

	Grinder Y	Grinder Z
Increase in revenue	$16,000	$20,000
Increase in annual operating costs		
Direct materials	4,800	4,800
Direct labor	3,000	4,100
Variable overhead	2,100	3,000
Fixed overhead		
(depreciation included)	5,000	5,000

1. Identify the relevant data in this problem.
2. Prepare an incremental analysis to aid the managers in their decision.
3. Should the company purchase Grinder Y or Z?

LO3 **Outsourcing Decision**

E 2. Sunny Hazel, the manager of Cyber Web Services, must decide whether to hire a new employee or to outsource some of the web design work to Ky To, a freelance graphic designer. If she hires a new employee, she will pay $32 per design hour for the employee to work 600 hours and incur service overhead costs of $2 per design hour. If she outsources the work to Ky To, she will pay $36 per design hour for 600 hours of work. She can also redirect the use of a computer and server to generate $4,000 in additional revenue from web page maintenance work. Should Cyber Web Services hire a new designer or outsource the work to Ky To?

LO3 **Special Order Decision**

E 3. Jens Sporting Goods, Inc., manufactures a complete line of sporting equipment. Leiden Enterprises operates a large chain of discount stores. Leiden has approached Jens with a special order for 30,000 deluxe baseballs. Instead of being packaged separately, the balls are to be bulk packed in boxes containing 500 baseballs each. Leiden is willing to pay $2.45 per baseball. Jens knows that annual expected production is 400,000 baseballs. It also knows that the current year's production is 410,000 baseballs and that the maximum production capacity is 450,000 baseballs. The following additional information is available:

Standard unit cost data for 400,000 baseballs

Direct materials	$ .90
Direct labor	.60
Variable overhead	.50
Fixed overhead ($100,000 ÷ 400,000)	.25
Packaging per unit	.30
Advertising ($60,000/400,000)	.15
Other fixed selling and administrative expenses ($120,000 ÷ 400,000)	.30
Product unit cost	$ 3.00
Unit selling price	$ 4.00
Total estimated bulk packaging costs for special order (30,000 baseballs: 500 per box)	$2,500

1. Should Jens Sporting Goods, Inc., accept Leiden's offer?
2. What would be the minimum order price per baseball if Jens would like to earn a profit of $3,000 from the special order?

LO3 **Elimination of Unprofitable Segment Decision**

E 4. Guld's Glass, Inc., has three divisions: Commercial, Nonprofit, and Residential. The segmented income statement for the current year revealed the following:

Guld's Glass, Inc.
Divisional Profit Summary and Decision Analysis

	Commercial Division	Nonprofit Division	Residential Division	Total Company
Sales	$290,000	$533,000	$837,000	$1,660,000
Less variable costs	147,000	435,000	472,000	1,054,000
Contribution margin	$143,000	$ 98,000	$365,000	$ 606,000
Less direct fixed costs	124,000	106,000	139,000	369,000
Segment margin	$ 19,000	($ 8,000)	$226,000	$ 237,000
Less common fixed costs				168,000
Operating income				$ 69,000

1. How will Guld's Glass, Inc., be affected if the Nonprofit Division is dropped?
2. If the Nonprofit Division is dropped, then the sales of the Residential Division will decrease by 10 percent. If this happens, how will Guld's Glass, Inc., be affected?

LO3 **Sales Mix Decision**

E 5. EZ, Inc., manufactures two products that require both machine processing and labor operations. Although there is unlimited demand for both products, EZ could devote all its capacities to a single product. Unit prices, cost data, and processing requirements are:

	Product E	Product Z
Unit selling price	$80	$220
Unit variable costs	$40	$ 90
Machine hours per unit	.4	1.4
Labor hours per unit	2	6

Next year the company will be limited to 160,000 machine hours and 120,000 labor hours. Fixed costs for the year are $1,000,000.

1. Compute the most profitable combination of products to be produced next year.
2. Prepare an income statement using the contribution margin format for the product volume computed in 1.

LO3 Sales Mix Decision

E 6. Grady Enterprises manufactures three computer games. They are called Rising Star, Ghost Master, and Road Warrior. The product line data are as follows:

	Rising Star	Ghost Master	Road Warrior
Current unit sales demand	20,000	30,000	18,000
Machine hours per unit	2	1	2.5
Selling price per unit	$24.00	$18.00	$32.00
Unit variable manufacturing costs	$12.50	$10.00	$18.75
Unit variable selling costs	$ 6.50	$ 5.00	$ 6.25

The current production capacity is 100,000 machine hours.

1. Which computer game should be manufactured first? Which should be manufactured second? Which last?
2. How many of each type of computer game should be manufactured and sold to maximize the company's contribution margin based on the current production activity of 100,000 machine hours? What is the total contribution margin for that combination?

LO3 Sell or Process-Further Decision

E 7. Six Star Pizza manufactures frozen pizzas and calzones and sells them for $4 each. Six Star is currently considering a proposal to manufacture and sell fully prepared products. Management has gathered the following relevant information:

Product	Sales Revenue with No Additional Processing	Sales Revenue if Processed Further	Additional Processing Product Costs
Pizza	$4	$ 8	$5
Calzone	$4	$10	$5

Use incremental analysis to determine which products Six Star Pizza should offer.

LO4 Income Taxes and Net Cash Flow

E 8. San Falesco Company has a tax rate of 25 percent on taxable income. It is considering a capital project that will make the following annual contribution to operating income:

Cash revenues	$500,000
Cash expenses	(300,000)
Depreciation	(150,000)
Operating income	$ 50,000
Income taxes at 25%	(12,500)
Operating income after income taxes	$ 37,500

1. Determine the net cash inflows for this project in two different ways. Are net cash flows the same under both approaches?
2. What is the impact of income taxes on net cash flows?

LO5 **Using the Present Value Tables**

E 9. For each of the following situations, identify the correct factor to use from Table 3 or 4 in the appendix on future value and present value tables. Also, compute the appropriate present value.

1. Annual net cash inflows of $22,500 for twelve years, discounted at 14%
2. The following five years of cash inflows, discounted at 10%:

Year 1	$35,000
Year 2	20,000
Year 3	30,000
Year 4	40,000
Year 5	50,000

3. The amount of $70,000 to be received at the beginning of year 7, discounted at 14%

LO6 **Capital Investment Decision: Net Present Value Method**

E 10. Qen and Associates wants to buy an automated coffee roaster/grinder/brewer. This piece of equipment would have a useful life of six years, would cost $219,500, and would increase annual net cash inflows by $57,000. Assume there is no residual value at the end of six years. The company's minimum rate of return is 14 percent.

Using the net present value method, prepare an analysis to determine whether the company should purchase the machine. Use Tables 3 and 4 in the appendix on future value and present value tables.

LO6 **Capital Investment Decision: Net Present Value Method**

E 11. H and Y Service Station is planning to invest in automatic car wash equipment valued at $250,000. The owner estimates that the equipment will increase annual net cash inflows by $46,000. The equipment is expected to have a ten-year useful life with an estimated residual value of $50,000. The company requires a 14 percent minimum rate of return. Using the net present value method, prepare an analysis to determine whether the company should purchase the equipment. How important is the estimate of residual value to this decision? Use Tables 3 and 4 in the appendix on future value and present value tables.

LO6 **Capital Investment Decision: Net Present Value Method**

E 12. Assume the same facts for H and Y Service Station as in **E11**, except that the company requires a 20 percent minimum rate of return. Using the net present value method, prepare an analysis to determine whether the company should purchase the equipment. Use Tables 3 and 4 in the appendix on future value and present value tables.

LO7 **Capital Investment Decision: Payback Period Method**

E 13. Soaking Wet, Inc., a manufacturer of gears for lawn sprinklers, is thinking about adding a new fully automated machine. This machine can produce gears the company currently produces on its third shift. The machine has an estimated useful life of 10 years and will cost $800,000. Gross cash revenue from the machine will be about $520,000 per year, and related operating expenses, including depreciation, should total $500,000. Depreciation is estimated to be $80,000 annually. The payback period should be five years or less.

Use the payback period method to determine whether the company should invest in the new machine. Show your computations to support your answer.

LO7   **Capital Investment Decision: Accounting Rate-of-Return Method**

E 14. Perfection Sound, Inc., a manufacturer of stereo speakers, is thinking about adding a new plastic injection molding machine. This machine can produce speaker parts that the company now buys from outsiders. The machine has an estimated useful life of 14 years and will cost $425,000. Residual value of the new machine is $42,500. Gross cash revenue from the machine will be about $400,000 per year, and related cash expenses should total $310,050. Depreciation is estimated to be $30,350 annually. Management has decided that only capital investments that yield at least a 20 percent return will be accepted.

Using the accounting rate-of-return method, decide whether the company should invest in the machine. Show all computations to support your decision.

Problems

LO3   **Sell or Process-Further Decision**

P 1. Bagels, Inc., produces and sells 20 types of bagels by the dozen. Bagels are priced at $6.00 per dozen (or $.50 each) and cost $.20 per unit to produce. The company is considering further processing the bagels into two products: bagels with cream cheese and bagel sandwiches. It would cost an additional $.50 per unit to produce bagels with cream cheese, and the new selling price would be $2.50 each. It would cost an additional $1.00 per sandwich to produce bagel sandwiches, and the new selling price would be $3.50 each.

Required

1. Identify the relevant per unit costs and revenues for the alternatives. Are there any sunk costs?
2. Based on the information in **1**, should Bagels, Inc., expand its product offerings?
3. **Manager Insight:** Suppose that Bagels, Inc., did expand its product line to include bagels with cream cheese and bagel sandwiches. Based on customer feedback, the company determined that it could further process those two products into bagels with fruit and cream cheese and bagel sandwiches with cheese. The company's accountant compiled the following information:

Product (per unit)	Sales Revenue if Sold with No Further Processing	Sales Revenue if Processed Further	Additional Processing Cost
Bagels with cream cheese	$2.50	$3.50	Fruit: $1.00
Bagel sandwiches	$3.50	$4.50	Cheese: $.50

Perform an incremental analysis to determine if Bagels, Inc., should process its products further. Explain your findings.

LO3   **Decision to Discontinue Segment**

P 2. Seven months ago, Naib Publishing Company published its first book (Book N). Since then, the company has added four more books to its product list (Books S, Q, X, and H). Management is considering proposals for three more new books, but editorial capacity limits the company to producing only seven books annually. Before deciding which of the proposed books to publish, management wants you to evaluate the performance of its existing book list. Recent revenue and cost data appear below.

Naib Publishing Company
Product Profit and Loss Summary
For the Year Ended December 31, 20x9

	Book N	Book S	Book Q	Book X	Book H	Company Totals
Sales	$813,800	$782,000	$634,200	$944,100	$707,000	$3,881,100
Less variable costs						
Materials and binding	$325,520	$312,800	$190,260	$283,230	$212,100	$1,323,910
Editorial services	71,380	88,200	73,420	57,205	80,700	370,905
Author royalties	130,208	125,120	101,472	151,056	113,120	620,976
Sales commissions	162,760	156,400	95,130	141,615	141,400	697,305
Other selling costs	50,682	44,740	21,708	18,334	60,700	196,164
Total variable costs	$740,550	$727,260	$481,990	$651,440	$608,020	$3,209,260
Contribution margin	$ 73,250	$ 54,740	$152,210	$292,660	$ 98,980	$ 671,840
Less total fixed costs	97,250	81,240	89,610	100,460	82,680	451,240
Operating income	($ 24,000)	($ 26,500)	$ 62,600	$192,200	$ 16,300	$ 220,600
Direct fixed costs included in total fixed costs above	$ 51,200	$ 65,100	$ 49,400	$ 69,100	$ 58,800	$ 293,600

Projected data for the proposed new books are Book P, sales, $450,000, contribution margin, $45,000; Book T, sales, $725,000, contribution margin, ($25,200); and Book R, sales, $913,200, contribution margin, $115,500. Projected direct fixed costs are: Book P, $5,000; Book T, $6,000; Book R, $40,000.

Required

1. Analyze the performance of the five books currently being published.
2. **Manager Insight:** Should the company eliminate any of its present products? If so, which one(s)?
3. **Manager Insight:** Identify the new books you would use to replace those eliminated. Justify your answer.

LO3 **Special Order Decision**

P 3. Keystone Resorts, Ltd., has approached Crystal Printers, Inc., with a special order to produce 300,000 two-page brochures. Most of Crystal's work consists of recurring short-run orders. Keystone Resorts is offering a one-time order, and Crystal has the capacity to handle the order over a two-month period.

Keystone's management has stated that the company would be unwilling to pay more than $48 per 1,000 brochures. Crystal's controller assembled the following cost data for this decision analysis: Direct materials (paper) would be $26.50 per 1,000 brochures. Direct labor costs would be $6.80 per 1,000 brochures. Direct materials (ink) would be $4.40 per 1,000 brochures. Variable production overhead would be $6.20 per 1,000 brochures. Machine maintenance (fixed cost) is $1.00 per direct labor dollar. Other fixed production overhead amounts to $2.40 per direct labor dollar. Variable packing costs would be $4.30 per 1,000 brochures. Also, the share of general and administrative expenses (fixed costs) to be allocated would be $5.25 per direct labor dollar.

Required

1. Prepare an analysis for Crystal management to use in deciding whether to accept or reject Keystone Resorts' offer. What decision should be made?
2. **Manager Insight:** What is the lowest possible price Crystal can charge per thousand and still make a $6,000 profit on the order?

LO5, LO6 **Net Present Value Method**

P 4. Sonja and Sons, Inc., owns and operates a group of apartment buildings. Management wants to sell one of its older four-family buildings and buy a new structure. The old building, which was purchased 25 years ago for $100,000, has a 40-year estimated life. The current market value is $80,000, and if it is sold, the cash inflow will be $67,675. Annual net cash inflows from the old building are expected to average $16,000 for the remainder of its estimated useful life.

The cost of the new building that the company wants to buy is $300,000. It has an estimated useful life of 25 years. Net cash inflows are expected to be $50,000 annually.

Assume that (1) all cash flows occur at year end, (2) the company uses straight-line depreciation, (3) the buildings will have a residual value equal to 10 percent of their purchase price, and (4) the minimum rate of return is 14 percent. Use Tables 3 and 4 in the appendix on future value and present value tables.

Required

1. Compute the net present value of future cash flows from the old building.
2. What will be the net present value of cash flows if the new building is purchased?
3. **Manager Insight:** Should the company keep the old building or purchase the new one?

LO7 **Accounting Rate-of-Return and Payback Period Methods**

P 5. The Raab Company is expanding its production facilities to include a new product line: a sporty automotive tire rim. Using new computerized machinery, tire rims can now be produced with little labor cost. The controller has advised management about two such machines. The details about each machine are as follows:

	XJS Machine	HZT Machine
Cost of machine	$500,000	$550,000
Residual value	50,000	55,000
Average annual net income	34,965	40,670
Annual net cash inflows	91,215	90,170

The minimum rate of return is 12 percent. The maximum payback period is six years. (Where necessary, round calculations to the nearest dollar.)

Required

1. For each machine, compute the projected accounting rate of return.
2. Compute the payback period for each machine.
3. **Manager Insight:** From the information generated in **1** and **2**, which machine should be purchased? Why?

Alternate Problems

LO3 **Outsourcing Decision**

P 6. The Stainless Refrigerator Company purchases and installs ice makers in its products. The ice makers cost $138 per case, and each case contains 12 ice makers. The supplier recently gave advance notice that the price will rise by 50 percent immediately. Stainless Refrigerator Company has idle equipment that, with only a few minor changes, could be used to produce similar ice makers.

Cost estimates have been prepared under the assumption that the company could make the product itself. Direct materials would cost $100.80 per 12 ice makers. Direct labor required would be 10 minutes per ice maker at a labor rate of $18.00 per hour. Variable overhead would be $4.60 per ice maker. Fixed overhead, which would be incurred under either decision alternative, would be $32,420 a year for depreciation and $234,000 a year for other costs. Production and usage are estimated at 75,000 ice makers a year. (Assume that any idle equipment cannot be used for any other purpose.)

Required

1. Prepare an incremental analysis to determine whether the ice makers should be made within the company or purchased from the outside supplier at the higher price.
2. Compute the unit cost to (1) make one ice maker and (2) buy one ice maker.
3. **Manager Insight:** What other factors might affect management's decision?

LO3 **Sales Mix Decision**

P 7. Dr. Massy, a physician specializing in internal medicine, wants to analyze his sales mix to find out how the time of his physician assistant, Consuela Ortiz, can be used to generate the highest operating income. Ortiz sees patients in the office, consults with patients over the telephone, and conducts one daily weight-loss support group attended by up to 50 patients. Statistics for the three daily services are:

	Office Visits	Phone Calls	Weight-Loss Support Group
Maximum number of patient billings per day	20	40	50
Hours per billing	.25	.10	1.0
Billing rate	$50	$25	$10
Variable costs	$25	$12	$ 5

Ortiz works seven hours a day.

Required

1. Determine the best sales mix. Rank the services offered in order of their profitability.
2. Based on the ranking in **1**, how much time should Ortiz spend on each service in a day? (**Hint:** Remember to consider the maximum number of patient billings per day.) What would be the daily total contribution margin generated by Ortiz?
3. Dr. Massy believes the ranking is incorrect. He knows that the daily 60-minute meeting of the weight-loss support group is attended by 50 patients and should continue to be offered. If the new ranking for the services is (1) weight-loss support group, (2) phone calls, and (3) office visits, how much time should Ortiz spend on each service in a day? What would be the total contribution margin generated by Ortiz, assuming the weight-loss support group has the maximum number of patient billings?
4. **Manager Insight:** Which ranking would you recommend? What additional amount of total contribution margin would be generated if your recommendation is accepted?

LO5, LO6, LO7 **Capital Investment Decision: Comprehensive**

P 8. The Arcadia Manufacturing Company, based in Arcadia, Florida, is one of the fastest growing companies in its industry. According to Ms. Prinze, the company's production vice president, keeping up-to-date with technological changes is what makes the company successful.

Prinze feels that a machine introduced recently would fill an important need. The machine has an estimated useful life of four years, a purchase price of $250,000, and a residual value of $25,000. The company controller has estimated average annual net income of $11,250 and the following cash flows for the new machine:

Year	Cash Inflows	Cash Outflows	Net Cash Inflows
1	$325,000	$250,000	$75,000
2	320,000	250,000	70,000
3	315,000	250,000	65,000
4	310,000	250,000	60,000

Prinze uses a 12 percent minimum rate of return and a three-year payback period for capital investment evaluation purposes.

Required

1. Analyze the data about the machine, and decide if the company should purchase it. Use the following methods in your analysis: (a) the net present value method, (b) the accounting rate-of-return method, and (c) the payback period method. Use Tables 3 and 4 in the appendix on future value and present value tables.
2. Summarize the information generated in **1**, and make a recommendation to Prinze.
3. **Manager Insight:** Why would a manager use different methods of capital investment analyses?

ENHANCING Your Knowledge, Skills, and Critical Thinking

Conceptual Understanding Cases

LO1 **Short-run Decision Process**

C 1. Two weeks ago your cousin Edna moved from New York City to Houston. She needs a car to drive to work and to run errands but has no experience in selecting a car, and has asked for your help.

1. Using the management process presented in this chapter, write her a letter explaining how she can approach making this decision.
2. How would your response change if the president of your company asked you to help make a decision about acquiring a fleet of cars for use by sales personnel?

LO4 **Factors in Capital Investment Decisions**

C 2. PPG Industries, founded in 1883, was the first commercially successful plate glass manufacturer in the United States. Today it is a global supplier of coatings, chemicals, and glass. Every year, its management approves capital spending for modernization and productivity improvements, expansion of existing businesses, and environmental control projects. Because PPG Industries' management receives many proposals for capital investment projects, it must set an appropriate acceptance-rejection standard.

1. What factors should management consider in setting this standard?

2. If more proposed projects meet the minimum standard than can be funded, what other factors should management consider, and what should management do?

LO2   **Defining and Identifying Relevant Information**

C 3. Gourmet Burgers is a competitor in the fast-food restaurant business. One component of the company's marketing strategy is to increase sales by expanding in foreign markets. The company uses both financial and nonfinancial quantitative and qualitative information when deciding whether to open restaurants in foreign markets.

Gourmet Burgers decided to open a restaurant in Prague (Czech Republic) five years ago. The following information helped the managers in making that decision.

Financial Quantitative Information
Operating information
  Estimated food, labor, and other operating costs (for example, taxes, insurance, utilities, and supplies)
  Estimated selling price for each food item
Capital investment information
  Cost of land, building, equipment, and furniture
  Financing options and amounts

Nonfinancial Quantitative Information
Estimated daily number of customers, hamburgers to be sold, employees to work
High-traffic time periods
Income of people living in the area
Ratio of population to number of restaurants in the market area
Traffic counts in front of similar restaurants in the area

Qualitative Information
Government regulations, taxes, duties, tariffs, political involvement in business operations
Property ownership restrictions
Site visibility
Accessibility of store location
Training process for local managers
Hiring process for employees
Local customs and practices

Gourmet Burgers has hired you as a consultant and has given you an income statement comparing the operating incomes of its five restaurants in Eastern Europe. You have noticed that the Prague location is operating at a loss (including unallocated fixed costs) and must decide whether to recommend closing that restaurant.

Review the information used in making the decision to open the restaurant. Identify the types of information that would also be relevant in deciding whether to close the restaurant. What period or periods of time should be reviewed in making your decision? What additional information would be relevant in making your decision?

Interpreting Management Reports

LO3   **Decision to Add a New Department**

C 4. Management at Transco Company is considering a proposal to install a third production department within its factory building. With the company's existing production setup, direct materials are processed through the Mixing Department to produce Materials A and B in equal proportions. Material A is then processed through the Shaping Department to yield Product C. Material B is sold as is at $20.25 per pound. Product C sells for $100 per pound.

There is a proposal to add a Baking Department to process Material B into Product D. It is expected that any quantity of Product D can be sold for $30 per pound. Costs per pound under this proposal are as follows:

	Mixing Department (Materials A and B)	Shaping Department (Product C)	Baking Department (Product D)
Cost from Mixing Department	—	$33.00	$13.20
Direct materials	$20.00	—	—
Direct labor	6.00	9.00	3.50
Variable overhead	4.00	8.00	4.00
Fixed overhead			
Traceable (direct, avoidable)	2.25	2.25	1.80
Allocated (common, unavoidable)	.75	.75	.75
	$33.00	$53.00	$23.25

1. If (a) sales and production levels are expected to remain constant in the foreseeable future and (b) there are no foreseeable alternative uses for the factory space, should Transco Company add a Baking Department and produce Product D, if 100,000 pounds of D can be sold? Show calculations of incremental revenues and costs to support your answer.
2. List at least two qualitative reasons that Transco Company may not want to install a Baking Department and produce Product D, even if it appears that this decision is profitable.
3. List at least two qualitative reasons why Transco Company may want to install a Baking Department and produce Product D, even if it appears that this decision is unprofitable.

LO5, LO6 **Capital Investment Analysis**

C 5. Automated teller machines (ATMs) have become common in the banking industry. San Angelo Federal Bank is planning to replace some old teller machines and has decided to use the York Machine. Nola Chavez, the controller, has prepared the analysis that appears on the facing page and has recommended the purchase of the machine based on the positive net present value shown in the analysis.

The York Machine has an estimated useful life of five years and an expected residual value of $35,000. Its purchase price is $385,000. Two existing ATMs, each having a carrying value of $25,000, can be sold to a neighboring bank for a total of $50,000. Annual operating cash inflows are expected to increase as follows:

Year 1	$79,900
Year 2	76,600
Year 3	79,900
Year 4	83,200
Year 5	86,500

The bank uses straight-line depreciation. The minimum rate of return is 12 percent.

1. What changes need to be made in Chavez's capital investment analysis?

San Angelo Federal Bank
Capital Investment Analysis
Net Present Value Method

Year	Net Cash Inflows	Present-Value Factors	Present Value
1	$ 85,000	.909	$ 77,265
2	80,000	.826	66,080
3	85,000	.751	63,835
4	90,000	.683	61,470
5	95,000	.621	58,995
5 (residual value)	35,000	.621	21,735
Total present value			$349,380
Initial investment	$385,000		
Less proceeds from the sale of existing ATMs	50,000		
Net capital investment			(335,000)
Net present value			$ 14,380

2. What would be your recommendation to bank management about the purchase of the York Machine?

Decision Analysis Using Excel

LO3 **Sell or Process-Further Decision**

C 6. Marketeers, Inc., has developed a promotional program for a large shopping center in Sunset Living, Arizona. After investing $360,000 in developing the original promotion campaign, the firm is ready to present its client with an add-on contract offer that includes the original promotion areas of (1) TV advertising campaign, (2) a series of brochures for mass mailing, and (3) a special rotating BIG SALE schedule for 10 of the 28 tenants in the shopping center. Following are the revenue terms from the original contract with the shopping center and the offer for an add-on contract, which extends the original contract terms.

	Contract Terms	
	Original Contract Terms	Extended Contract Including Add-On Terms
TV advertising campaign	$520,000	$ 580,000
Brochure series	210,000	230,000
Rotating BIG SALE schedule	170,000	190,000
Totals	$900,000	$1,000,000

Marketeers estimates that the following additional costs will be incurred by extending the contract:

	TV Campaign	Brochures	BIG SALE Schedule
Direct labor	$30,000	$ 9,000	$7,000
Variable overhead costs	22,000	14,000	6,000
Fixed overhead costs*	12,000	4,000	2,000

*80 percent are direct fixed costs applied to this contract.

1. Using an Excel spreadsheet, compute the costs that will be incurred for each part of the add-on portion of the contract.
2. Should Marketeers offer the add-on contract or ask for a final settlement check based on the original contract only? Defend your answer.
3. If management of the shopping center indicated the terms of the add-on contract were negotiable, how should Marketeers respond?

Ethical Dilemma Case

LO4, LO6　**Ethics, Capital Investment Decisions, and the Competitive Business Environment**

C 7. Marika Jonssen is the controller of Bramer Corporation, a globally competitive producer of standard and custom-designed window units for the housing industry. As part of the corporation's move to become automated, Jonssen was asked to prepare a capital investment analysis for a robot-guided aluminum extruding and stamping machine. This machine would automate the entire window-casing manufacturing line.

Jonssen had recently returned from an international seminar on the subject of qualitative inputs into the capital investment decision process, and she was eager to incorporate what she had learned into the analysis. In addition to the normal net present value analysis (which produced a significant negative result) Jonssen factored in figures for customer satisfaction, scrap reduction, reduced inventory needs, and reputation for quality. With the additional information included, the analysis produced a positive response to the decision question.

When the chief financial officer finished reviewing Jonssen's work, he threw the papers on the floor and said, "What kind of garbage is this! You know it's impossible to quantify such things as customer satisfaction and reputation for quality. How do you expect me to go to the board of directors and explain your work? I want you to redo the entire analysis and follow only the traditional approach to net present value. Get it back to me in two hours!"

What is Jonssen's dilemma? What ethical courses of action are available to her?

Internet Case

LO4　**Comparison of Capital Investment Disclosures by Two Large Companies**

C 8. Companies vary in the amount of information they disclose about their criteria for selecting capital investments. Access the websites of two companies—for example, **Coca-Cola** and **International Paper**. Find management's discussion and analysis (also called the financial review), which precedes the presentation of the financial statements. In that section, find the discussion of capital investments. Which company provides the more in-depth discussion? Does either disclose its criteria for making capital investment decisions? Also look at the investing activities listed in the statement of cash flows for each company. What is the extent of capital expenditures for each company? Compare each company's capital investments with the amount of total assets on the balance sheet. Which company is more of a growth company? Explain.

Group Activity Case

LO2　**Identifying Relevant Decision Information**

C 9. Assume you want to take a two-week vacation. Select two destinations for your vacation, and gather information about them from brochures, magazines, travel agents, the Internet, and people you know. Then list the relevant quantitative and qualitative information in its order of importance to your decision. Analyze the information, and select a destination. What factors were the most important to your decision? Why? What factors were the least important to your decision? Why? How would the process of identifying relevant decision information differ if you were asked by the president of your company to prepare a budget for the next training meeting, to be held at a location of your choice?

Your instructor will divide the class into groups, and ask each group to discuss this case. One student from each group will summarize his or her group's findings and debrief the entire class.

Business Communication Case

LO4, LO5, LO6, LO7   Evaluating a Capital Investment Proposal

C 10. Quality work and timely output are the distinguishing characteristics of Smile Photo, Inc. Smile Photo is a nationally franchised company with over 50 outlets located in the southern states. Part of the franchise agreement promises a centralized photo developing process with overnight delivery to the outlets.

Because of the tremendous increase in demand for its photo processing, Emma DuBarry, the corporation's president, is considering the purchase of a new, deluxe digital photo processing machine by the end of this month. DuBarry wants you to formulate a memo showing your evaluation of this purchase. Your memo will be presented at the board of directors' meeting next week.

According to your research, the new machine will cost $320,000. It will function for an estimated five years and should have a $32,000 residual value. All capital investments are expected to produce a 20 percent minimum rate of return, and the investment should be recovered in three years or less. All fixed assets are depreciated using the straight-line method. The forecast increases in operating results for the new machine are as follows:

Cash Flow Estimates

Year	Cash Inflows	Cash Outflows
1	$310,000	$210,000
2	325,000	220,000
3	340,000	230,000
4	300,000	210,000
5	260,000	180,000

1. In preparation for writing your memo, answer the following questions.
   a. What kinds of information do you need to prepare this memo?
   b. Why is the information relevant?
   c. Where would you find the information?
   d. When would you want to obtain the information?
2. Analyze the purchase of the machine, and decide if the company should purchase it. Use (a) the net present value method, (b) the accounting rate-of-return method, and (c) the payback period method.

Future Value and Present Value Tables

T able 1 provides the multipliers necessary to compute the future value of a *single* cash deposit made at the *beginning* of year 1. Three factors must be known before the future value can be computed: (1) the time period in years, (2) the stated annual rate of interest to be earned, and (3) the dollar amount invested or deposited.

Example—Table 1. Determine the future value of $5,000 deposited now that will earn 9 percent interest compounded annually for five years.

TABLE 1. Future Value of $1 After a Given Number of Time Periods

Periods	1%	2%	3%	4%	5%	6%	7%	8%	9%	10%	12%	14%	15%
1	1.010	1.020	1.030	1.040	1.050	1.060	1.070	1.080	1.090	1.100	1.120	1.140	1.150
2	1.020	1.040	1.061	1.082	1.103	1.124	1.145	1.166	1.188	1.210	1.254	1.300	1.323
3	1.030	1.061	1.093	1.125	1.158	1.191	1.225	1.260	1.295	1.331	1.405	1.482	1.521
4	1.041	1.082	1.126	1.170	1.216	1.262	1.311	1.360	1.412	1.464	1.574	1.689	1.749
5	1.051	1.104	1.159	1.217	1.276	1.338	1.403	1.469	1.539	1.611	1.762	1.925	2.011
6	1.062	1.126	1.194	1.265	1.340	1.419	1.501	1.587	1.677	1.772	1.974	2.195	2.313
7	1.072	1.149	1.230	1.316	1.407	1.504	1.606	1.714	1.828	1.949	2.211	2.502	2.660
8	1.083	1.172	1.267	1.369	1.477	1.594	1.718	1.851	1.993	2.144	2.476	2.853	3.059
9	1.094	1.195	1.305	1.423	1.551	1.689	1.838	1.999	2.172	2.358	2.773	3.252	3.518
10	1.105	1.219	1.344	1.480	1.629	1.791	1.967	2.159	2.367	2.594	3.106	3.707	4.046
11	1.116	1.243	1.384	1.539	1.710	1.898	2.105	2.332	2.580	2.853	3.479	4.226	4.652
12	1.127	1.268	1.426	1.601	1.796	2.012	2.252	2.518	2.813	3.138	3.896	4.818	5.350
13	1.138	1.294	1.469	1.665	1.886	2.133	2.410	2.720	3.066	3.452	4.363	5.492	6.153
14	1.149	1.319	1.513	1.732	1.980	2.261	2.579	2.937	3.342	3.798	4.887	6.261	7.076
15	1.161	1.346	1.558	1.801	2.079	2.397	2.759	3.172	3.642	4.177	5.474	7.138	8.137
16	1.173	1.373	1.605	1.873	2.183	2.540	2.952	3.426	3.970	4.595	6.130	8.137	9.358
17	1.184	1.400	1.653	1.948	2.292	2.693	3.159	3.700	4.328	5.054	6.866	9.276	10.760
18	1.196	1.428	1.702	2.026	2.407	2.854	3.380	3.996	4.717	5.560	7.690	10.580	12.380
19	1.208	1.457	1.754	2.107	2.527	3.026	3.617	4.316	5.142	6.116	8.613	12.060	14.230
20	1.220	1.486	1.806	2.191	2.653	3.207	3.870	4.661	5.604	6.728	9.646	13.740	16.370
21	1.232	1.516	1.860	2.279	2.786	3.400	4.141	5.034	6.109	7.400	10.800	15.670	18.820
22	1.245	1.546	1.916	2.370	2.925	3.604	4.430	5.437	6.659	8.140	12.100	17.860	21.640
23	1.257	1.577	1.974	2.465	3.072	3.820	4.741	5.871	7.258	8.954	13.550	20.360	24.890
24	1.270	1.608	2.033	2.563	3.225	4.049	5.072	6.341	7.911	9.850	15.180	23.210	28.630
25	1.282	1.641	2.094	2.666	3.386	4.292	5.427	6.848	8.623	10.830	17.000	26.460	32.920
26	1.295	1.673	2.157	2.772	3.556	4.549	5.807	7.396	9.399	11.920	19.040	30.170	37.860
27	1.308	1.707	2.221	2.883	3.733	4.822	6.214	7.988	10.250	13.110	21.320	34.390	43.540
28	1.321	1.741	2.288	2.999	3.920	5.112	6.649	8.627	11.170	14.420	23.880	39.200	50.070
29	1.335	1.776	2.357	3.119	4.116	5.418	7.114	9.317	12.170	15.860	26.750	44.690	57.580
30	1.348	1.811	2.427	3.243	4.322	5.743	7.612	10.060	13.270	17.450	29.960	50.950	66.210
40	1.489	2.208	3.262	4.801	7.040	10.290	14.970	21.720	31.410	45.260	93.050	188.900	267.900
50	1.645	2.692	4.384	7.107	11.470	18.420	29.460	46.900	74.360	117.400	289.000	700.200	1,084.000

From Table 1, the necessary multiplier for five years at 9 percent is 1.539, and the answer is $5,000 × 1.539 = $7,695.

Where r is the interest rate and n is the number of periods, the factor values for Table 1 are

$$\text{FV Factor} = (1 + r)^n$$

Situations requiring the use of Table 2 are similar to those requiring Table 1 except that Table 2 is used to compute the future value of a *series* of *equal* annual deposits at the end of each period.

Example—Table 2. What will be the future value at the end of 30 years if $1,000 is deposited each year on January 1, beginning in year 1, assuming 12 percent interest compounded annually? The required multiplier from Table 2 is 241.3, and the answer is $1,000 × 241.3 = $241,300.

The factor values for Table 2 are

$$\text{FVa Factor} = \frac{(1 + r)^n - 1}{r}$$

TABLE 2. Future Value of $1 Paid in Each Period for a Given Number of Time Periods

Periods	1%	2%	3%	4%	5%	6%	7%	8%	9%	10%	12%	14%	15%
1	1.000	1.000	1.000	1.000	1.000	1.000	1.000	1.000	1.000	1.000	1.000	1.000	1.000
2	2.010	2.020	2.030	2.040	2.050	2.060	2.070	2.080	2.090	2.100	2.120	2.140	2.150
3	3.030	3.060	3.091	3.122	3.153	3.184	3.215	3.246	3.278	3.310	3.374	3.440	3.473
4	4.060	4.122	4.184	4.246	4.310	4.375	4.440	4.506	4.573	4.641	4.779	4.921	4.993
5	5.101	5.204	5.309	5.416	5.526	5.637	5.751	5.867	5.985	6.105	6.353	6.610	6.742
6	6.152	6.308	6.468	6.633	6.802	6.975	7.153	7.336	7.523	7.716	8.115	8.536	8.754
7	7.214	7.434	7.662	7.898	8.142	8.394	8.654	8.923	9.200	9.487	10.090	10.730	11.070
8	8.286	8.583	8.892	9.214	9.549	9.897	10.260	10.640	11.030	11.440	12.300	13.230	13.730
9	9.369	9.755	10.160	10.580	11.030	11.490	11.980	12.490	13.020	13.580	14.780	16.090	16.790
10	10.460	10.950	11.460	12.010	12.580	13.180	13.820	14.490	15.190	15.940	17.550	19.340	20.300
11	11.570	12.170	12.810	13.490	14.210	14.970	15.780	16.650	17.560	18.530	20.650	23.040	24.350
12	12.680	13.410	14.190	15.030	15.920	16.870	17.890	18.980	20.140	21.380	24.130	27.270	29.000
13	13.810	14.680	15.620	16.630	17.710	18.880	20.140	21.500	22.950	24.520	28.030	32.090	34.350
14	14.950	15.970	17.090	18.290	19.600	21.020	22.550	24.210	26.020	27.980	32.390	37.580	40.500
15	16.100	17.290	18.600	20.020	21.580	23.280	25.130	27.150	29.360	31.770	37.280	43.840	47.580
16	17.260	18.640	20.160	21.820	23.660	25.670	27.890	30.320	33.000	35.950	42.750	50.980	55.720
17	18.430	20.010	21.760	23.700	25.840	28.210	30.840	33.750	36.970	40.540	48.880	59.120	65.080
18	19.610	21.410	23.410	25.650	28.130	30.910	34.000	37.450	41.300	45.600	55.750	68.390	75.840
19	20.810	22.840	25.120	27.670	30.540	33.760	37.380	41.450	46.020	51.160	63.440	78.970	88.210
20	22.020	24.300	26.870	29.780	33.070	36.790	41.000	45.760	51.160	57.280	72.050	91.020	102.400
21	23.240	25.780	28.680	31.970	35.720	39.990	44.870	50.420	56.760	64.000	81.700	104.800	118.800
22	24.470	27.300	30.540	34.250	38.510	43.390	49.010	55.460	62.870	71.400	92.500	120.400	137.600
23	25.720	28.850	32.450	36.620	41.430	47.000	53.440	60.890	69.530	79.540	104.600	138.300	159.300
24	26.970	30.420	34.430	39.080	44.500	50.820	58.180	66.760	76.790	88.500	118.200	158.700	184.200
25	28.240	32.030	36.460	41.650	47.730	54.860	63.250	73.110	84.700	98.350	133.300	181.900	212.800
26	29.530	33.670	38.550	44.310	51.110	59.160	68.680	79.950	93.320	109.200	150.300	208.300	245.700
27	30.820	35.340	40.710	47.080	54.670	63.710	74.480	87.350	102.700	121.100	169.400	238.500	283.600
28	32.130	37.050	42.930	49.970	58.400	68.530	80.700	95.340	113.000	134.200	190.700	272.900	327.100
29	33.450	38.790	45.220	52.970	62.320	73.640	87.350	104.000	124.100	148.600	214.600	312.100	377.200
30	34.780	40.570	47.580	56.080	66.440	79.060	94.460	113.300	136.300	164.500	241.300	356.800	434.700
40	48.890	60.400	75.400	95.030	120.800	154.800	199.600	259.100	337.900	442.600	767.100	1,342.000	1,779.000
50	64.460	84.580	112.800	152.700	209.300	290.300	406.500	573.800	815.100	1,164.000	2,400.000	4,995.000	7,218.000

TABLE 3. Present Value of $1 to Be Received at the End of a Given Number of Time Periods

Periods	1%	2%	3%	4%	5%	6%	7%	8%	9%	10%	12%
1	0.990	0.980	0.971	0.962	0.952	0.943	0.935	0.926	0.917	0.909	0.893
2	0.980	0.961	0.943	0.925	0.907	0.890	0.873	0.857	0.842	0.826	0.797
3	0.971	0.942	0.915	0.889	0.864	0.840	0.816	0.794	0.772	0.751	0.712
4	0.961	0.924	0.888	0.855	0.823	0.792	0.763	0.735	0.708	0.683	0.636
5	0.951	0.906	0.883	0.822	0.784	0.747	0.713	0.681	0.650	0.621	0.567
6	0.942	0.888	0.837	0.790	0.746	0.705	0.666	0.630	0.596	0.564	0.507
7	0.933	0.871	0.813	0.760	0.711	0.665	0.623	0.583	0.547	0.513	0.452
8	0.923	0.853	0.789	0.731	0.677	0.627	0.582	0.540	0.502	0.467	0.404
9	0.914	0.837	0.766	0.703	0.645	0.592	0.544	0.500	0.460	0.424	0.361
10	0.905	0.820	0.744	0.676	0.614	0.558	0.508	0.463	0.422	0.386	0.322
11	0.896	0.804	0.722	0.650	0.585	0.527	0.475	0.429	0.388	0.350	0.287
12	0.887	0.788	0.701	0.625	0.557	0.497	0.444	0.397	0.356	0.319	0.257
13	0.879	0.773	0.681	0.601	0.530	0.469	0.415	0.368	0.326	0.290	0.229
14	0.870	0.758	0.661	0.577	0.505	0.442	0.388	0.340	0.299	0.263	0.205
15	0.861	0.743	0.642	0.555	0.481	0.417	0.362	0.315	0.275	0.239	0.183
16	0.853	0.728	0.623	0.534	0.458	0.394	0.339	0.292	0.252	0.218	0.163
17	0.844	0.714	0.605	0.513	0.436	0.371	0.317	0.270	0.231	0.198	0.146
18	0.836	0.700	0.587	0.494	0.416	0.350	0.296	0.250	0.212	0.180	0.130
19	0.828	0.686	0.570	0.475	0.396	0.331	0.277	0.232	0.194	0.164	0.116
20	0.820	0.673	0.554	0.456	0.377	0.312	0.258	0.215	0.178	0.149	0.104
21	0.811	0.660	0.538	0.439	0.359	0.294	0.242	0.199	0.164	0.135	0.093
22	0.803	0.647	0.522	0.422	0.342	0.278	0.226	0.184	0.150	0.123	0.083
23	0.795	0.634	0.507	0.406	0.326	0.262	0.211	0.170	0.138	0.112	0.074
24	0.788	0.622	0.492	0.390	0.310	0.247	0.197	0.158	0.126	0.102	0.066
25	0.780	0.610	0.478	0.375	0.295	0.233	0.184	0.146	0.116	0.092	0.059
26	0.772	0.598	0.464	0.361	0.281	0.220	0.172	0.135	0.106	0.084	0.053
27	0.764	0.586	0.450	0.347	0.268	0.207	0.161	0.125	0.098	0.076	0.047
28	0.757	0.574	0.437	0.333	0.255	0.196	0.150	0.116	0.090	0.069	0.042
29	0.749	0.563	0.424	0.321	0.243	0.185	0.141	0.107	0.082	0.063	0.037
30	0.742	0.552	0.412	0.308	0.231	0.174	0.131	0.099	0.075	0.057	0.033
40	0.672	0.453	0.307	0.208	0.142	0.097	0.067	0.046	0.032	0.022	0.011
50	0.608	0.372	0.228	0.141	0.087	0.054	0.034	0.021	0.013	0.009	0.003

Table 3 is used to compute the value today of a single amount of cash to be received sometime in the future. To use Table 3, you must first know (1) the time period in years until funds will be received, (2) the stated annual rate of interest, and (3) the dollar amount to be received at the end of the time period.

Example—Table 3. What is the present value of $30,000 to be received 25 years from now, assuming a 14 percent interest rate? From Table 3, the required multiplier is .038, and the answer is $30,000 × .038 = $1,140.

14%	15%	16%	18%	20%	25%	30%	35%	40%	45%	50%	Periods
0.877	0.870	0.862	0.847	0.833	0.800	0.769	0.741	0.714	0.690	0.667	1
0.769	0.756	0.743	0.718	0.694	0.640	0.592	0.549	0.510	0.476	0.444	2
0.675	0.658	0.641	0.609	0.579	0.512	0.455	0.406	0.364	0.328	0.296	3
0.592	0.572	0.552	0.516	0.482	0.410	0.350	0.301	0.260	0.226	0.198	4
0.519	0.497	0.476	0.437	0.402	0.328	0.269	0.223	0.186	0.156	0.132	5
0.456	0.432	0.410	0.370	0.335	0.262	0.207	0.165	0.133	0.108	0.088	6
0.400	0.376	0.354	0.314	0.279	0.210	0.159	0.122	0.095	0.074	0.059	7
0.351	0.327	0.305	0.266	0.233	0.168	0.123	0.091	0.068	0.051	0.039	8
0.308	0.284	0.263	0.225	0.194	0.134	0.094	0.067	0.048	0.035	0.026	9
0.270	0.247	0.227	0.191	0.162	0.107	0.073	0.050	0.035	0.024	0.017	10
0.237	0.215	0.195	0.162	0.135	0.086	0.056	0.037	0.025	0.017	0.012	11
0.208	0.187	0.168	0.137	0.112	0.069	0.043	0.027	0.018	0.012	0.008	12
0.182	0.163	0.145	0.116	0.093	0.055	0.033	0.020	0.013	0.008	0.005	13
0.160	0.141	0.125	0.099	0.078	0.044	0.025	0.015	0.009	0.006	0.003	14
0.140	0.123	0.108	0.084	0.065	0.035	0.020	0.011	0.006	0.004	0.002	15
0.123	0.107	0.093	0.071	0.054	0.028	0.015	0.008	0.005	0.003	0.002	16
0.108	0.093	0.080	0.060	0.045	0.023	0.012	0.006	0.003	0.002	0.001	17
0.095	0.081	0.069	0.051	0.038	0.018	0.009	0.005	0.002	0.001	0.001	18
0.083	0.070	0.060	0.043	0.031	0.014	0.007	0.003	0.002	0.001		19
0.073	0.061	0.051	0.037	0.026	0.012	0.005	0.002	0.001	0.001		20
0.064	0.053	0.044	0.031	0.022	0.009	0.004	0.002	0.001			21
0.056	0.046	0.038	0.026	0.018	0.007	0.003	0.001	0.001			22
0.049	0.040	0.033	0.022	0.015	0.006	0.002	0.001				23
0.043	0.035	0.028	0.019	0.013	0.005	0.002	0.001				24
0.038	0.030	0.024	0.016	0.010	0.004	0.001	0.001				25
0.033	0.026	0.021	0.014	0.009	0.003	0.001					26
0.029	0.023	0.018	0.011	0.007	0.002	0.001					27
0.026	0.020	0.016	0.010	0.006	0.002	0.001					28
0.022	0.017	0.014	0.008	0.005	0.002						29
0.020	0.015	0.012	0.007	0.004	0.001						30
0.005	0.004	0.003	0.001	0.001							40
0.001	0.001	0.001									50

The factor values for Table 3 are

$$\text{PV Factor} = (1 + r)^{-n}$$

Table 3 is the reciprocal of Table 1.

TABLE 4. Present Value of $1 Received Each Period for a Given Number of Time Periods

Periods	1%	2%	3%	4%	5%	6%	7%	8%	9%	10%	12%
1	0.990	0.980	0.971	0.962	0.952	0.943	0.935	0.926	0.917	0.909	0.893
2	1.970	1.942	1.913	1.886	1.859	1.833	1.808	1.783	1.759	1.736	1.690
3	2.941	2.884	2.829	2.775	2.723	2.673	2.624	2.577	2.531	2.487	2.402
4	3.902	3.808	3.717	3.630	3.546	3.465	3.387	3.312	3.240	3.170	3.037
5	4.853	4.713	4.580	4.452	4.329	4.212	4.100	3.993	3.890	3.791	3.605
6	5.795	5.601	5.417	5.242	5.076	4.917	4.767	4.623	4.486	4.355	4.111
7	6.728	6.472	6.230	6.002	5.786	5.582	5.389	5.206	5.033	4.868	4.564
8	7.652	7.325	7.020	6.733	6.463	6.210	5.971	5.747	5.535	5.335	4.968
9	8.566	8.162	7.786	7.435	7.108	6.802	6.515	6.247	5.995	5.759	5.328
10	9.471	8.983	8.530	8.111	7.722	7.360	7.024	6.710	6.418	6.145	5.650
11	10.368	9.787	9.253	8.760	8.306	7.887	7.499	7.139	6.805	6.495	5.938
12	11.255	10.575	9.954	9.385	8.863	8.384	7.943	7.536	7.161	6.814	6.194
13	12.134	11.348	10.635	9.986	9.394	8.853	8.358	7.904	7.487	7.103	6.424
14	13.004	12.106	11.296	10.563	9.899	9.295	8.745	8.244	7.786	7.367	6.628
15	13.865	12.849	11.938	11.118	10.380	9.712	9.108	8.559	8.061	7.606	6.811
16	14.718	13.578	12.561	11.652	10.838	10.106	9.447	8.851	8.313	7.824	6.974
17	15.562	14.292	13.166	12.166	11.274	10.477	9.763	9.122	8.544	8.022	7.120
18	16.398	14.992	13.754	12.659	11.690	10.828	10.059	9.372	8.756	8.201	7.250
19	17.226	15.678	14.324	13.134	12.085	11.158	10.336	9.604	8.950	8.365	7.366
20	18.046	16.351	14.878	13.590	12.462	11.470	10.594	9.818	9.129	8.514	7.469
21	18.857	17.011	15.415	14.029	12.821	11.764	10.836	10.017	9.292	8.649	7.562
22	19.660	17.658	15.937	14.451	13.163	12.042	11.061	10.201	9.442	8.772	7.645
23	20.456	18.292	16.444	14.857	13.489	12.303	11.272	10.371	9.580	8.883	7.718
24	21.243	18.914	16.936	15.247	13.799	12.550	11.469	10.529	9.707	8.985	7.784
25	22.023	19.523	17.413	15.622	14.094	12.783	11.654	10.675	9.823	9.077	7.843
26	22.795	20.121	17.877	15.983	14.375	13.003	11.826	10.810	9.929	9.161	7.896
27	23.560	20.707	18.327	16.330	14.643	13.211	11.987	10.935	10.027	9.237	7.943
28	24.316	21.281	18.764	16.663	14.898	13.406	12.137	11.051	10.116	9.307	7.984
29	25.066	21.844	19.189	16.984	15.141	13.591	12.278	11.158	10.198	9.370	8.022
30	25.808	22.396	19.600	17.292	15.373	13.765	12.409	11.258	10.274	9.427	8.055
40	32.835	27.355	23.115	19.793	17.159	15.046	13.332	11.925	10.757	9.779	8.244
50	39.196	31.424	25.730	21.482	18.256	15.762	13.801	12.234	10.962	9.915	8.305

Table 4 is used to compute the present value of a *series* of *equal* annual cash flows.

Example—Table 4.   Arthur Howard won a contest on January 1, 20x7, in which the prize was $30,000, payable in 15 annual installments of $2,000 each December 31, beginning in 20x7. Assuming a 9 percent interest rate, what is the present value of Howard's prize on January 1, 20x7? From Table 4, the required multiplier is 8.061, and the answer is $2,000 × 8.061 = $16,122.

The factor values for Table 4 are

$$\text{PVa Factor} = 1 - \frac{(1 + r)^{-n}}{r}$$

Table 4 is the columnar sum of Table 3. Table 4 applies to *ordinary annuities*, in which the first cash flow occurs one time period beyond the date for which the present value is computed.

14%	15%	16%	18%	20%	25%	30%	35%	40%	45%	50%	Periods
0.877	0.870	0.862	0.847	0.833	0.800	0.769	0.741	0.714	0.690	0.667	1
1.647	1.626	1.605	1.566	1.528	1.440	1.361	1.289	1.224	1.165	1.111	2
2.322	2.283	2.246	2.174	2.106	1.952	1.816	1.696	1.589	1.493	1.407	3
2.914	2.855	2.798	2.690	2.589	2.362	2.166	1.997	1.849	1.720	1.605	4
3.433	3.352	3.274	3.127	2.991	2.689	2.436	2.220	2.035	1.876	1.737	5
3.889	3.784	3.685	3.498	3.326	2.951	2.643	2.385	2.168	1.983	1.824	6
4.288	4.160	4.039	3.812	3.605	3.161	2.802	2.508	2.263	2.057	1.883	7
4.639	4.487	4.344	4.078	3.837	3.329	2.925	2.598	2.331	2.109	1.922	8
4.946	4.772	4.607	4.303	4.031	3.463	3.019	2.665	2.379	2.144	1.948	9
5.216	5.019	4.833	4.494	4.192	3.571	3.092	2.715	2.414	2.168	1.965	10
5.453	5.234	5.029	4.656	4.327	3.656	3.147	2.752	2.438	2.185	1.977	11
5.660	5.421	5.197	4.793	4.439	3.725	3.190	2.779	2.456	2.197	1.985	12
5.842	5.583	5.342	4.910	4.533	3.780	3.223	2.799	2.469	2.204	1.990	13
6.002	5.724	5.468	5.008	4.611	3.824	3.249	2.814	2.478	2.210	1.993	14
6.142	5.847	5.575	5.092	4.675	3.859	3.268	2.825	2.484	2.214	1.995	15
6.265	5.954	5.669	5.162	4.730	3.887	3.283	2.834	2.489	2.216	1.997	16
6.373	6.047	5.749	5.222	4.775	3.910	3.295	2.840	2.492	2.218	1.998	17
6.467	6.128	5.818	5.273	4.812	3.928	3.304	2.844	2.494	2.219	1.999	18
6.550	6.198	5.877	5.316	4.844	3.942	3.311	2.848	2.496	2.220	1.999	19
6.623	6.259	5.929	5.353	4.870	3.954	3.316	2.850	2.497	2.221	1.999	20
6.687	6.312	5.973	5.384	4.891	3.963	3.320	2.852	2.498	2.221	2.000	21
6.743	6.359	6.011	5.410	4.909	3.970	3.323	2.853	2.498	2.222	2.000	22
6.792	6.399	6.044	5.432	4.925	3.976	3.325	2.854	2.499	2.222	2.000	23
6.835	6.434	6.073	5.451	4.973	3.981	3.327	2.855	2.499	2.222	2.000	24
6.873	6.464	6.097	5.467	4.948	3.985	3.329	2.856	2.499	2.222	2.000	25
6.906	6.491	6.118	5.480	4.956	3.988	3.330	2.856	2.500	2.222	2.000	26
6.935	6.514	6.136	5.492	4.964	3.990	3.331	2.856	2.500	2.222	2.000	27
6.961	6.534	6.152	5.502	4.970	3.992	3.331	2.857	2.500	2.222	2.000	28
6.983	6.551	6.166	5.510	4.975	3.994	3.332	2.857	2.500	2.222	2.000	29
7.003	6.566	6.177	5.517	4.979	3.995	3.332	2.857	2.500	2.222	2.000	30
7.105	6.642	6.234	5.548	4.997	3.999	3.333	2.857	2.500	2.222	2.000	40
7.133	6.661	6.246	5.554	4.999	4.000	3.333	2.857	2.500	2.222	2.000	50

An *annuity due* is a series of equal cash flows for N time periods, but the first payment occurs immediately. The present value of the first payment equals the face value of the cash flow; Table 4 then is used to measure the present value of N − 1 remaining cash flows.

Example—Table 4. Determine the present value on January 1, 20x7, of 20 lease payments; each payment of $10,000 is due on January 1, beginning in 20x7. Assume an interest rate of 8 percent.

Present Value = Immediate Payment + Present Value of
19 Subsequent Payments at 8%

= $10,000 + ($10,000 × 9.604) = $106,040

ENDNOTES

Chapter 1

1. *Statement of Financial Accounting Concepts* No. 1, "Objectives of Financial Reporting by Business Enterprises" (Norwalk, Conn.: Financial Accounting Standards Board, 1978), par. 9.
2. Ibid.
3. CVS Corporation, *Annual Report*, 2005.
4. Christopher D. Ittner, David F. Larcker, and Madhav V. Rajan, "The Choice of Performance Measures in Annual Bonus Contracts," *The Accounting Review*, April 1997.
5. National Commission on Fraudulent Financial Reporting, *Report of the National Commission on Fraudulent Financial Reporting* (Washington, D.C.: 1987), p. 2.
6. CVS Corporation, Form 10-K, March 16, 2006.
7. "Gallup Poll Shows the Public's Opinion of Accounting Profession Is Improving," www.picpa.org, August 24, 2004.
8. Robert Johnson, "The New CFO," *Crain's Chicago Business*, July 19, 2004.
9. *Accounting Principles Board Statement* No. 4, "Basic Concepts and Accounting Principles Underlying Financial Statements of Business Enterprises" (New York: AICPA, 1970), par. 138.
10. *Statement Number* 1C, "Standards of Ethical Conduct for Management Accountants" (Montvale, N.J.: Institute of Management Accountants, 1983; revised 1997).
11. Curtis C. Verschoor, "Corporate Performance Is Closely Tied to a Strong Ethical Commitment," *Journal of Business and Society*, Winter 1999; Verschoor, "Does Superior Governance Still Lead to Better Financial Performance?" *Strategic Finance*, October 2004.
12. CVS Corporation, *Annual Report*, 2005.
13. Costco Wholesale Corporation, *Annual Report*, 2003.
14. Southwest Airlines Co., *Annual Report*, 1996.
15. H&R Block, Inc., *Annual Report*, 2005.
16. Chad Terhune, "Recharging Coca-Cola," *The Wall Street Journal*, April 17, 2006.

Chapter 2

1. Jeremy Herron, "Boeing Stock Soars on China Order," *The Seattle Times*, April 12, 2006.
2. The Boeing Company, *Annual Report*, 2005.
3. Intel Corporation, *Annual Report*, 2003.
4. Gary McWilliams, "EDS Accounting Change Cuts Past Earnings by $2.24 Billion," *The Wall Street Journal*, October 28, 2003.
5. The Boeing Company, *Annual Report*, 2005.
6. Ibid.
7. Ibid.
8. Nike, Inc., *Annual Report*, 2004.
9. Mellon Financial Corporation, *Annual Report*, 2005.

Chapter 3

1. Yahoo! Inc., *Annual Report*, 2005.
2. Ibid.
3. "Microsoft Settles with SEC," CBSNews.com, June 5, 2002.
4. Securities and Exchange Commission, *Staff Accounting Bulletin* No. 10, 1999.
5. Yahoo! Inc., *Annual Report*, 2005.
6. Ibid.

7. Lyric Opera of Chicago, *Annual Report*, 2004.
8. The Walt Disney Company, *Annual Report*, 2005.

Chapter 4

1. Best Buy Co., Inc., *Annual Report*, 2005; revised figures for fiscal 2005 and 2004.
2. Adapted from Robert Half International, Inc., *Annual Report*, 2005.

Chapter 5

1. Dell Computer Corporation, *Annual Report*, 2005.
2. "Objectives of Financial Reporting by Business Enterprises," *Statement of Financial Accounting Concepts* No. 1 (Norwalk, Conn.: Financial Accounting Standards Board, 1978), pars. 32–54.
3. *Statement of Financial Accounting Concepts* No. 2, "Qualitative Characteristics of Accounting Information," (Norwalk, Conn.: Financial Accounting Standards Board, 1980), par. 20.
4. L. Todd Johnson, "Relevance and Reliability," *The FASB Report*, February 28, 2005.
5. Dell Computer Corporation, Form 10K for the Fiscal Year Ended February 3, 2006.
6. "Ex-Chief of WorldCom Is Found Guilty in $11 Billion Fraud," *The New York Times*, March 16, 2005.
7. *Accounting Principles Board, Opinion* No. 20, "Accounting Changes," (New York: AICPA, 1971), par. 17.
8. Scott Thurm and Kevin J. Delaney, "Yahoo, Google, and Internet Math," *The Wall Street Journal*, May 10, 2004.
9. Securities and Exchange Commission, *Staff Accounting Bulletin* No. 99, 1999.
10. Ray J. Groves, "Here's the Annual Report. Got a Few Hours?" *The Wall Street Journal Europe*, August 26–27, 1994.
11. Roger Lowenstein, "Investors Will Fish for Footnotes in 'Abbreviated' Annual Reports," *The Wall Street Journal*, September 14, 1995.
12. "Debt vs. Equity: Whose Call Counts," *BusinessWeek*, July 19, 1999.
13. Roger Lowenstein, "The '20% Club' Is No Longer Exclusive," *The Wall Street Journal*, May 4, 1995.
14. Dell Computer Corporation, *Annual Report*, 2005.
15. Albertson's Inc., *Annual Report*, 2004; Great Atlantic & Pacific Tea Company, *Annual Report*, 2004.

Chapter 6

1. Costco Wholesale Corporation, *Annual Report*, 2005.
2. Jathon Sapsford, "As Cash Fades, America Becomes a Plastic Nation," *The Wall Street Journal*, July 23, 2004.
3. Steve Stecklowe, Anita Raghavan, and Deborah Ball, "How a Quest for Rebates Sent Ahold on an Unusual Buying Spree," *The Wall Street Journal*, March 6, 2003.
4. Mylene Mangalindan, "Online Retail Sales Are Expected to Rise to $172 Billion This Year," *The Wall Street Journal*, May 24, 2005.
5. Joel Millman, "Here's What Happens to Many Lovely Gifts After Santa Rides Off," *The Wall Street Journal*, December 26, 2001.
6. Matthew Rose, "Magazine Revenue at Newsstands Falls in Worst Year Ever," *The Wall Street Journal*, May 15, 2001.

7. Costco Wholesale Corporation, *Annual Report*, 2005.

8. Sid R. Ewer, "A Roundtrip Ticket to Trouble," *Strategic Finance*, April 2004.

Chapter 7

1. Cisco Systems, Inc., *Annual Report*, 2005.

2. Ibid.

3. Gary McWilliams, "Whirlwind on the Web," *BusinessWeek*, April 7, 1997.

4. Karen Lundebaard, "Bumpy Ride," *The Wall Street Journal*, May 21, 2001.

5. American Institute of Certified Public Accountants, *Accounting Trends & Techniques* (New York: AICPA, 2005).

6. Cisco Systems, Inc., *Annual Report*, 2005.

7. "Cisco's Numbers Confound Some," *International Herald Tribune*, April 19, 2001.

8. "Kmart Posts $67 Million Loss Due to Markdowns," *The Wall Street Journal*, November 10, 2000.

9. Micah Frankel and Robert Trezevant, "The Year-End LIFO Inventory Purchasing Decision: An Empirical Test," *The Accounting Review*, April 1994.

10. American Institute of Certified Public Accountants, *Accounting Trends & Techniques* (New York: AICPA, 2005).

11. "SEC Case Judge Rules Crazy Eddie Principals Must Pay $72.7 Million," *The Wall Street Journal*, May 11, 2000.

12. American Institute of Certified Public Accountants, *Accounting Trends & Techniques* (New York: AICPA, 2005).

13. Exxon Mobil Corporation, *Annual Report*, 2003.

14. Ibid.

15. Yamaha Motor Company, Ltd., *Annual Report*, 2005; Pioneer Corporation, *Annual Report*, 2005.

Chapter 8

1. Nike, Inc., *Annual Report*, 2005.

2. Peter Coy and Michael Arndt, "Up a Creek with Lots of Cash," *BusinessWeek*, November 12, 2001.

3. "So Much for Detroit's Cash Cushion," *BusinessWeek*, November 5, 2001.

4. Geoffrey Smith, "The Bill Comes Due for Capital One," *BusinessWeek*, November 4, 2004.

5. Jesse Drucker, "Sprint Expects Loss of Subscribers," *The Wall Street Journal*, September 24, 2002.

6. Michael Selz, "Big Customers' Late Bills Choke Small Suppliers," *The Wall Street Journal*, June 22, 1994.

7. Circuit City Stores, Inc., *Annual Report*, 2004.

8. Heather Timmons, "Do Household's Numbers Add Up?" *BusinessWeek*, December 10, 2001.

9. Steve Daniels, "Bank One Reserves Feed Earnings," *Crain's Chicago Business*, December 15, 2003.

10. Jonathon Weil, "Accounting Scheme Was Straightforward but Hard to Detect," *The Wall Street Journal*, March 20, 2003.

11. Nike, Inc., *Annual Report*, 2005.

12. Ibid.

13. American Institute of Certified Public Accountants, *Accounting Trends & Techniques* (New York: AICPA, 2005).

14. Nilson Report as reported in *Santa Cruz Sentinel*, May 21, 2006.

15. "Bad Loans Rattle Telecom Vendors," *BusinessWeek*, February 19, 2001.

16. Scott Thurm, "Better Debt Bolsters Bottom Lines," *The Wall Street Journal*, August 18, 2003.

17. Information based on promotional brochures of Mitsubishi Corp.

18. Elizabeth McDonald, "Unhatched Chickens," *Forbes*, February 19, 2001.

19. Fosters Group Limited, *Annual Report*, 2005; Heineken N.V., *Annual Report*, 2005.

20. Rhonda L. Rundle and Paul Davies, "Hospitals Administer Antidote for Bad Debt," *The Wall Street Journal*, May 4, 2004.

Chapter 9

1. Amazon.com, Inc., *Annual Report*, 2005.

2. Pamela L. Moore, "How Xerox Ran Short of Black Ink," *BusinessWeek*, October 30, 2000.

3. Mark Heinzel, Deborah Solomon, and Joann S. Lublin, "Nortel Board Fires CEO and Others," *The Wall Street Journal*, April 29, 2004.

4. Hershey Foods Corporation, *Annual Report*, 2005.

5. Goodyear Tire & Rubber Company, *Annual Report*, 2005.

6. Andersen Enterprise Group, cited in *Crain's Chicago Business*, July 5, 1999.

7. Promomagazine.com, July 6, 2005.

8. Hershey Foods Corporation, *Annual Report*, 2005.

9. Scott McCartney, "Your Free Flight to Mars Is Hobbling the Airline Industry," *The Wall Street Journal*, February 4, 2004.

10. *Statement of Financial Accounting Standards* No. 5, "Accounting for Contingencies" (Norwalk, Conn.: Financial Accounting Standards Board, 1975).

11. American Institute of Certified Public Accountants, *Accounting Trends & Techniques* (New York: AICPA, 2005).

12. Ibid.

13. *Statement of Financial Accounting Concepts* No. 7, "Using Cash Flow Information and Present Value in Accounting Measurement" (Norwalk, Conn.: Financial Accounting Standards Board, 2000).

14. WorldCom (MCI), *Annual Report*, 2004.

15. Advertisement, *Chicago Tribune*, November 8, 2002.

16. Sun Microsystems Inc., *Annual Report*, 2005; Cisco Systems, Inc., *Annual Report*, 2005.

17. General Motors Corporation, Form 10-k, March 16, 2005.

18. Advertisement, *Chicago Tribune*, 2000.

Chapter 10

1. Home Depot, Inc., *Annual Report*, 2005.

2. Committee of Sponsoring Organizations of the Treadway Commission (COSO), *Internal Control—Integrated Framework*, 1985–2005.

3. Jonathan Weil, "Accounting Scheme Was Straightforward but Hard to Detect," *The Wall Street Journal*, July 23, 2004.

4. Home Depot, Inc., *Annual Report*, 2005.

5. Ibid.

6. *Professional Standards*, vol. 1, Sec. AU 325.16.

7. KPMG Peat Marwick, "1998 Fraud Survey," 1998.

8. Amy Merrick, "Starbucks Accuses Employee, Husband of Embezzling $3.7 Million from Firm," *The Wall Street Journal*, November 20, 2000.

Chapter 11

1. Apple Computer, Inc., *Annual Report*, 2005.

2. *Statement of Financial Accounting Standards* No. 144, "Accounting for the Impairment or Disposal of Long-Lived Assets" (Norwalk, Conn.: Financial Accounting Standards Board, 2001).

3. Sharon Young, "Large Telecom Firms, After WorldCom Moves, Consider Writedowns," *The Wall Street Journal*, March 18, 2003.

4. *Statement of Financial Accounting Standards* No. 34, "Capitalization of Interest Cost" (Norwalk, Conn.: Financial Accounting Standards Board, 1979), par. 9–11.

5. American Institute of Certified Public Accountants, *Accounting Trends & Techniques* (New York: AICPA, 2005).

6. Ibid.

7. *Statement of Financial Accounting Standards* No. 25, "Suspension of Certain Accounting Requirements for Oil and Gas Producing Companies" (Norwalk, Conn.: Financial Accounting Standards Board, 1979).

8. Jonathan Weil, "Oil Reserves Can Sure Be Slick," *The Wall Street Journal*, March 11, 2004.

9. *Statement of Financial Accounting Standards* No. 142, "Goodwill and Other Intangible Assets" (Norwalk, Conn.: Financial Accounting Standards Board, 2001), par. 11–17.

10. "The Top 100 Brands," *BusinessWeek*, August 5, 2002.

11. "What's in a Name?" *Time*, May 3, 1993.

12. General Motors Corporation, *Annual Report*, 2005.

13. Abbott Laboratories, *Annual Report*, 2005.

14. *Statement of Financial Accounting Standards* No. 2, "Accounting for Research and Development Costs" (Norwalk, Conn.: Financial Accounting Standards Board, 1974), par. 12.

15. *Statement of Financial Accounting Standards* No. 86, "Accounting for the Costs of Computer Software to Be Sold, Leased, or Otherwise Marketed" (Norwalk, Conn.: Financial Accounting Standards Board, 1985).

16. General Mills, Inc., *Annual Report*, 2004; H.J. Heinz Company, *Annual Report*, 2004; Tribune Company, *Annual Report*, 2004.

17. *Statement of Financial Accounting Standards* No. 142, "Goodwill and Other Intangible Assets" (Norwalk, Conn.: Financial Accounting Standards Board, 2001), par. 11–17.

18. Southwest Airlines Co., *Annual Report*, 2002.

19. Costco Wholesale Corporation, *Annual Report*, 2005.

20. IBM Corporation, *Annual Report*, 2005.

21. Hilton Hotels Corporation, *Annual Report*, 2005; Marriott International, Inc., *Annual Report*, 2005.

22. "Stock Gives Case the Funds He Needs to Buy New Technology," *BusinessWeek*, April 15, 1996.

23. Polaroid Corporation, *Annual Report*, 1997.

Chapter 12

1. Google, Inc., Form S-1 (Registration Statement), 2004; Form 10-Q, September 2004.

2. Securities Industry Asociation, "Sources of Capital Raised by Corporations in the United States," in *Securities Industry Yearbook* 2004–2005.

3. Microsoft Corporation, Form 10-K, 2005.

4. Deborah Solomon, "AT&T Slashes Dividends 83%, Cuts Forecasts," *The Wall Street Journal*, December 21, 2002.

5. Abbott Laboratories, *Annual Report*, 2005.

6. Google, Inc., Form S-1 (Registration Statement), 2005.

7. Robert A. Guth and Scott Thurm, "Microsoft to Dole Out Its Cash Hoard," *The Wall Street Journal*, July 21, 2004.

8. American Institute of Certified Public Accountants, *Accounting Trends & Techniques* (New York: AICPA, 2005).

9. *Statement of Accounting Standards* No. 123, "Stock-Based Payments" (Norwalk, Conn.: Financial Accounting Standards Board, 1995; amended 2004).

10. Jonathan Weil, "FASB Unveils Expensing Plan on Option Pay," *The Wall Street Journal*, April 1, 2004.

11. Joseph Weber, "One Share, Many Votes," *BusinessWeek*, March 29, 2004; Google, Inc., Form S-1 (Registration Statement), 2004.

12. Michael Rapoport and Jonathan Weil, "More Truth-in-Labeling for Accounting Carries Liabilities," *The Wall Street Journal*, August 23, 2003.

13. American Institute of Certified Public Accountants, *Accounting Trends & Techniques* (New York: AICPA, 2005).

14. Robert McGough, Suzanne McGee, and Cassell Bryan-Low, "Buyback Binge Now Creates Big Hangover," *The Wall Street Journal*, December 18, 2000.

15. "Avaya Prices Public Offering of Common Stock" and "Avaya Completes Sale of Approximately $200 Million Common Stock," *The Wall Street Journal Online*, March 22, 2002.

16. Tom Herman, "Preferreds' Rich Yields Blind Some Investors to Risks," *The Wall Street Journal*, March 24, 1992.

17. Stanley Ziemba, "USAir Defers Dividends on Preferred Stock," *Chicago Tribune*, September 30, 1994.

18. Susan Carey, "US Airways to Redeem Preferred Owned by Berkshire Hathaway," *The Wall Street Journal*, February 4, 1998.

Chapter 13

1. McDonald's Corporation, *Annual Report*, 2005.

2. Ibid.

3. Lee Hawkins Jr., "S&P Cuts Rating on GM and Ford to Junk Status," *The Wall Street Journal*, May 6, 2005.

4. David Reilly and Silvia Ascarelli, "History Is Made (Again) in Convertibles Boom," *The Wall Street Journal*, July 9, 2003.

5. *Statement of Financial Accounting Standards* No. 13, "Accounting for Leases" (Norwalk, Conn.: Financial Accounting Standards Board, 1976), par. 10.

6. *Statement of Financial Accounting Standards* No. 106, "Employers' Accounting for Postretirement Benefits Other than Pensions" (Norwalk, Conn.: Financial Accounting Standards Board, 1990).

7. Lee Hawkins Jr., "GM's Liabilities for Retiree Health Top $60 Billion," *The Wall Street Journal*, March 11, 2004.

8. Adapted from quotations in *The Wall Street Journal*, June 14, 2005.

9. Ken Brown and Scott Thurm, "Companies Find 'No-Nos' Are Hard to Resist," *The Wall Street Journal*, December 2, 2003.

10. Bill Barnhart, "Bond Bellwether," *Chicago Tribune*, December 4, 1996.

11. Accounting Principles Board, *Opinion* No. 21, "Interest on Receivables and Payables" (New York: AICPA, 1971), par. 15.

12. Elizabeth MacDonald, "False Front," *Forbes*, October 14, 2002.

13. Tom Sullivan and Sonia Ryst, "Kodak $1 Billion Issue Draws Crowds," *The Wall Street Journal*, October 8, 2003.

14. Safeway Inc., *Annual Report*, 2004.

15. "More Hotels Won't Be Able to Pay Debt from Operations, Study Says," *The Wall Street Journal*, October 20, 2001.

16. *The Wall Street Journal*, May 14, 2006.

17. Stanley Ziemba, "TWA, American Revise O'Hare Gate Agreement," *The Wall Street Journal*, May 13, 1992.

18. Ibid.

19. NEC Corporation, *Annual Report*, 2005; Sanyo Electric Co., *Annual Report*, 2005.

Chapter 14

1. Motorola, Inc., *Annual Report*, 2005.
2. Cited in *The Week in Review* (Deloitte Haskins & Sells), February 28, 1985.
3. "Up to the Minute, Down to the Wire," *Twentieth Century Mutual Funds Newsletter*, 1996.
4. David Carins International, *IAS Survey Update*, July 2001.
5. Elizabeth MacDonald, "Pro Forma Puff Jobs," *Forbes*, December 9, 2002.
6. Barbara A. Lougee and Carol A. Marquardt, "Earnings Informativeness and Strategic Disclosure: An Empirical Examination of 'Pro forma' Earnings," *The Accounting Review*, July 2004.
7. American Institute of Certified Public Accountants, *Accounting Trends & Techniques* (New York: AICPA, 2005).
8. Jesse Drucker, "Motorola's Profit: Special Again?" *The Wall Street Journal*, October 15, 2002.
9. *Statement of Financial Accounting Standards* No. 109, "Accounting for Income Taxes" (Norwalk, Conn.: Financial Accounting Standards Board, 1992).
10. American Institute of Certified Public Accountants, *Accounting Trends & Techniques* (New York: AICPA, 2005).
11. Accounting Principles Board, *Opinion* No. 30, "Reporting the Results of Operations" (New York: AICPA, 1973), par. 20.
12. Accounting Principles Board, *Opinion* No. 15, "Earnings per Share" (New York: AICPA, 1969), par. 12.
13. *Statement of Financial Accounting Standards* No. 128, "Earnings per Share and the Disclosure of Information About Capital Structure" (Norwalk, Conn.: Financial Accounting Standards Board, 1997).
14. *Statement of Financial Accounting Standards* No. 130, "Reporting Comprehensive Income" (Norwalk, Conn.: Financial Accounting Standards Board, 1997).
15. American Institute of Certified Public Accountants, *Accounting Trends & Techniques* (New York: AICPA, 2005).
16. American Institute of Certified Public Accountants, *Accounting Research Bulletin* No. 43 (New York: AICPA, 1953), chap. 7, sec. B, par. 10.
17. Ibid., par. 13.
18. The Gillette Company, *Annual Report*, 2003.
19. Robert O'Brien, "Tech's Chill Fails to Stem Stock Splits," *The Wall Street Journal*, June 8, 2000.
20. Mylene Mangalindan, "Yahoo's Not Sears; Stock Split Is Declared," *The Wall Street Journal*, April 8, 2004.
21. "Technology Firms Post Strong Earnings but Stock Prices Decline Sharply," *The Wall Street Journal*, January 21, 1988; Donald R. Seace, "Industrials Plunge 57.2 Points—Technology Stocks' Woes Cited," *The Wall Street Journal*, January 21, 1988.
22. Rebecca Buckman, "Microsoft Posts Hefty 18% Revenue Rise," *The Wall Street Journal*, January 18, 2002; William M. Bulkeley, "IBM Reports 13% Decline in Net Income," *The Wall Street Journal*, January 18, 2002.

Chapter 15

1. Marriott International, Inc., *Annual Report*, 2005.
2. "Deadweight on the Markets," *BusinessWeek*, February 19, 2001.
3. Gary Slutsker, "Look at the Birdie and Say: 'Cash Flow,'" *Forbes*, October 25, 1993.
4. Jonathan Clements, "Yacktman Fund Is Bloodied but Unbowed," *The Wall Street Journal*, November 8, 1993.

5. Jeffery Laderman, "Earnings, Schmearnings—Look at the Cash," *BusinessWeek*, July 24, 1989.
6. Marriott International, Inc., *Annual Report*, 2005.
7. American Institute of Certified Public Accountants, *Accounting Trends & Techniques* (New York: AICPA, 2005).
8. Martin Peers and Robin Sidel, "WorldCom Causes Analysts to Evaluate EBITDA's Role," *The Wall Street Journal*, July 15, 2002.
9. Richard Passov, "How Much Cash Does Your Company Need?" *Harvard Business Review*, November 2003.
10. "Cash Flow Shortfall in Quarter May Lead to Default on Loan," *The Wall Street Journal*, September 4, 2001.
11. Enron Corporation, *Press Release*, October 16, 2001.
12. Sony Corporation, *Annual Report*, 2005; Canon, Inc., *Annual Report*, 2005.
13. Chip Meyers, "The Last Laugh," *Business 2.0*, September 2002.
14. Dean Foust, "So Much Cash, So Few Dividends," *BusinessWeek*, January 20, 2003.

Chapter 16

1. eBay, Inc., *Annual Report*, 2005.
2. *Statement of Financial Accounting Standards* No. 115, "Accounting for Certain Investments in Debt and Equity Securities" (Norwalk, Conn.: Financial Accounting Standards Board, 1993).
3. eBay, Inc., *Annual Report*, 2005.
4. Jalal Soroosh and Jack T. Ciesielski, "Accounting for Special Purpose Entities Revised," FASB Interpretation (46R), *The CPA Journal*, July, 2004.
5. Greg Steinmetz and Cacilie Rohwedder, "SAP Insider Probe Points to Reforms Needed in Germany," *The Wall Street Journal*, May 8, 1997.
6. Kathryn Kranhold and Deborah Solomon, "GE Restates Several Years of Earnings," *The Wall Street Journal*, May 9, 2005.
7. eBay, Inc., *Annual Report*, 2005.
8. *Statement of Financial Accounting Standards* No. 115, "Accounting for Certain Investments in Debt and Equity Securities" (Norwalk, Conn.: Financial Accounting Standards Board, 1993).
9. eBay, Inc., *Annual Report*, 2005.
10. *Statement of Financial Accounting Standards* No. 94, "Consolidation of All Majority-Owned Subsidiaries" (Norwalk, Conn.: Financial Accounting Standards Board, 1987).
11. eBay, Inc., *Annual Report*, 2005.
12. Accounting Principles Board, *Opinion* No. 16, "Business Combinations" (New York: AICPA, 1970).
13. eBay, Inc., *Annual Report*, 2005.
14. Ibid.
15. Dell Computer Corporation, *Annual Report*, 2005.
16. Dreamworks Animation, SEC Form 10Q, 2004.
17. Microsoft Corporation, *Annual Report*, 2004.

Chapter 17

1. Starbucks Corporation, *Annual Report*, 2005.
2. David Henry, "The Numbers Game," *BusinessWeek*, May 14, 2001.
3. Jonathan Weil, "'Pro forma' in Earnings reports? . . . As If," *The Wall Street Journal*, April 24, 2003.
4. *Statement of Financial Accounting Standards* No.131, "Segment Disclosures" (Norwalk, Conn.: Financial Accounting Standards Board, 1997).

5. Starbucks Corporation, *Annual Report*, 2005.
6. Ibid.
7. Target Corporation, *Proxy Statement*, May 18, 2005.
8. Starbucks Corporation, *Annual Report*, 2005.
9. Lee Hawkins Jr., "S&P Cuts Rating on GM and Ford to Junk Status," *The Wall Street Journal*, May 6, 2005.
10. H.J. Heinz Company, *Annual Report*, 2005.
11. Jesse Drucker, "Performance Bonus Out of Reach? Move the Target," *The Wall Street Journal*, April 29, 2003.
12. Pfizer, Inc., *Annual Report*, 2005; Roche Group, *Annual Report*, 2005.

Chapter 18

1. "Wal-Mart CEO Pleased with Sales," *Fort Meyers News-Press*, January 5, 2006.
2. *Statement No. 1A* (New York: Institute of Management Accountants, 1982).
3. Andrew Ross Sorkin, "Albertsons Nears Deal, Yet Again, to Sell Itself," *New York Times*, January 23, 2006.
4. Kathleen Day, "Wal-Mart Rattles Bankers," *Gainesville Sun*, February 19, 2006.
5. "A Profile for Leadership," *Pink* magazine, December/January 2006, p. 104.
6. Andra Gumbus and Susan D. Johnson, "The Balanced Scorecard at Futura Industries," *Strategic Finance*, July 2003.
7. American Institute of Certified Public Accountants, "Summary of Sarbanes-Oxley Act of 2002," www.aicpa.org/info/sarbanes_oxley_summary.htm; Securities and Exchange Commission, "Final Rule: Certification of Disclosure in Companies' Quarterly and Annual Reports," August 28, 2002, www.sec.gov/rules/final/33-8124.htm.
8. "Combating Corporate Fraud," Accounting Web, January 13, 2006, www.accountingweb.com/cgi-bin/item.cgi?id=101663.

Chapter 19

1. Southwest Airlines, "Fact Sheet," www.southwest.com.
2. Melanie Trottman, "Vaunted Southwest Slips in On-Time Performance," *The Wall Street Journal*, September 25, 2002.
3. Robert Frank and Sarah Ellison, "Meltdown in Chocolatetown," *The Wall Street Journal*, September 19, 2002.
4. United Parcel Service, "About UPS," www.ups.com.
5. "A Global Look at Women on Boards," *Pink* magazine, June–July 2005, pp. 96–97, or www.globalwomen.com.

Chapter 20

1. Information from http://www.coldstonecreamery.com; Alycia de Mesa, "Cold Stone Creamery—The Scoop," June 21, 2004, http://www.brandchannel.com.
2. "Fraud Examiners Rate the Scams," *Journal of Accountancy*, June 2002.
3. Robert L. Simison, "Toyota Finds Way to Make Custom Car in 5 Days," *The Wall Street Journal*, August 6, 1999.
4. William A. Sahlman, "How to Write a Great Business Plan," *Harvard Business Review*, July–August 1997.

Chapter 21

1. Dan Morse, "Tennessee Producer Tries New Tactic in Sofas: Speed," *The Wall Street Journal*, November 19, 2002.
2. Mylene Mangalindan, "Oracle Puts Priority on Customer Service," *The Wall Street Journal*, January 21, 2003.

3. Lance Thompson, "Examining Methods of VBM," *Strategic Finance*, December 2002.
4. Robert Kaplan and Steven Anderson, "Time Driven Activity-Based Costing," *Harvard Business Review*, November 2004.
5. "Just In Time, Toyota Production System & Lean Manufacturing," http://www.strategosinc.com/just_in_time.htm.
6. Dan Morse, "Tennessee Producer Tries New Tactic in Sofas: Speed," *The Wall Street Journal*, November 19, 2002.
7. Gina Imperato, "Time for Zero Time," *Net Company*, Fall 1999.
8. Sally Beatty, "Levi's Strive to Keep a Hip Image," *The Wall Street Journal*, January 23, 2003.

Chapter 22

1. Kraft Foods, "Profile," www.kraft.com.
2. http://investor.google.com/conduct.html.
3. Kraft Foods, "Inside Kraft: A Company Overview," http://164.109.16.145/investors/overview.html.

Chapter 23

1. Johnson & Johnson, "Our Company," www.jnj.com.
2. "A Global Look at Women on Boards," *Pink* magazine, June–July 2005, pp. 96–97.
3. Richard Barrett, "From Fast Close to Fast Forward," *Strategic Finance*, January 2003.
4. Omar Aguilar, "How Strategic Performance Management Is Helping Companies Create Business Value," *Strategic Finance*, January 2003.
5. Jeremy Hope and Robin Frase, "Who Needs Budgets?" *Harvard Business Review*, February 2003.
6. Minnesota Mining and Manufacturing Company, "About 3M," www.3m.com.

Chapter 24

1. PEAKS Resorts, www.peakscard.com.
2. Mark Beasley, Al Chen, Karen Nunez, and Lorraine Wright, "Working Hand in Hand: Balanced Scorecards and Enterprise Risk Management," *Strategic Finance*, March 2006.
3. Marc J. Epstein and Jean-François Manzoni, "The Balanced Scorecard and Tableau de Bord: Translating Strategy into Action," *Management Accounting*, August 1997.
4. Kerry A. McDonald, "Meyners Does a Reality Check," *Journal of Accountancy*, February 2006.
5. V. G. Narayanan and Ananth Raman, "Aligning Incentives in Supply Chains," *Harvard Business Review*, November 2004.

Chapter 25

1. Erin White, "How Stodgy Turned Stylish," *The Wall Street Journal*, May 3, 2002.
2. Katy McLaughlin, "Factory Tours," *The Wall Street Journal*, October 29, 2002.
3. David E. Keys and Anton Van Der Merwe, "Gaining Effective Organizational Control with RCA," *Strategic Finance*, May 2002.
4. Gabriel Kahn, "Still Going for Gold," *The Wall Street Journal*, January 28, 2003.
5. www.coach.com/corporate/governance/integrityProgram.asp.

Chapter 26

1. Betty Riess, "Bank of America Expands Online Security Feature to the Northeast," Bank of America Newsroom Press Release, January 4, 2006.

2. Stephanie Miles, "What's a Check?" *The Wall Street Journal*, October 21, 2002, p. R5.
3. Michael Liedtke, "Keeping the Books," *The Gainesville Sun*, August 22, 2002.
4. Alan Fuhrman, "Your e-Banking Future," *Strategic Finance*, April 2002.
5. Paulette Thomas, "Case Study: Electronics Firm Ends Practice Just in Time," *The Wall Street Journal*, October 29, 2002.
6. From a speech by Jim Croft, vice president of finance and administration of the Field Museum, Chicago, November 14, 2000.
7. http://en.wikipedia.org/wiki/Total_cost_of_ownership.

Instructor Supplements

Course Management Systems

The Eduspace® (powered by Blackboard™) online learning tool pairs the widely recognized resources of Blackboard with quality, text-specific content from Houghton Mifflin. Using auto-graded homework, students can complete end-of-chapter assignments (short exercises, exercises, and problems) and receive immediate feedback on their work. Assignments are automatically graded and entered into a gradebook. Within the "Learn on Your Own" section, students can choose from a variety of resources aimed at helping them review, apply, and practice. Demonstration Videos, HMAccounting Tutor tutorials, audio (MP3) files of chapter summaries and quizzes, and links to SMARTHINKING online tutoring and the Online Study Center provide a wealth of review options. Algorithmic practice exercises let students work through exercises with different numbers every time. A **multimedia ebook** is available for quick access to text content and links to relevant tutorials and videos.

Included within Eduspace and new to this edition is **HM Assess**, an online diagnostic assessment and study tool. Working within HM Assess, students take Chapter Assessments and receive Individual Study Paths, with links to tutorials, video, practice, and online text content. Reporting and tracking are also available.

For instructors who use other course management systems (CMS), such as Blackboard and Web-CT, to manage their online courses, much of the text-specific content included in Eduspace is available in course cartridge form.

HMTesting with Algorithms

HMTesting—now powered by D*iploma*®—contains the computerized version of the printed test bank and is available on CD-ROM. With HMTesting, instructors can create, customize, and deliver multiple types of tests; import questions from the test bank; add their own questions; or edit existing questions, all within D*iploma's* powerful electronic platform. Online Testing and Gradebook functions allow instructors to administer tests via their local area network or the Internet, set up classes, record grades from tests or assignments, analyze grades, and compile class and individual statistics. HMTesting can be used on both PCs and Macintosh computers.

Online Teaching Center

The Online Teaching Center website provides instructors with password-protected course materials such as completely revised PowerPoint slides; Classroom Response System content; sample syllabi; Accounting Instructor's Report with teaching strategies for introductory accounting; and Electronic Solutions, which are fully functioning Excel spreadsheets for all exercises, problems, and cases.

PowerPoint Slides

Completely revised, the Premium Slides include video, photographs, line art, and additional Stop, Review, and Apply questions. Basic Slides provide a teaching outline of the text chapter. PowerPoint Slides are included on the Online Teaching Center website and within the Course Management Systems.

Instructor's Solutions Manual

This resource contains answers to all text exercises, problems, and cases. Also available as **Solutions Transparency Masters.**

Electronic Solutions

Contains all solutions from the Instructor's Solutions Manual in fully formatted Excel, with a new interface that makes it easy to find the solution you need. The electronic format allows instructors to manipulate the numbers in the classroom or distribute solutions via e-mail or the web. The solutions are available at the Online Teaching Center website and within Course Management Systems.

Printed Test Bank

The Test Bank provides more than 4,000 true/false, multiple-choice, short essay, and critical-thinking questions, as well as exercises and problems, all of which test students' ability to recall, comprehend, apply, and analyze information. Also included are two Achievement Tests per chapter.

Course Manual

Available on the Online Teaching Center website and through Course Management Systems, the Course Manual is filled with advice and teaching tips. It contains a planning matrix and time/difficulty chart, instructional materials, and quizzes.